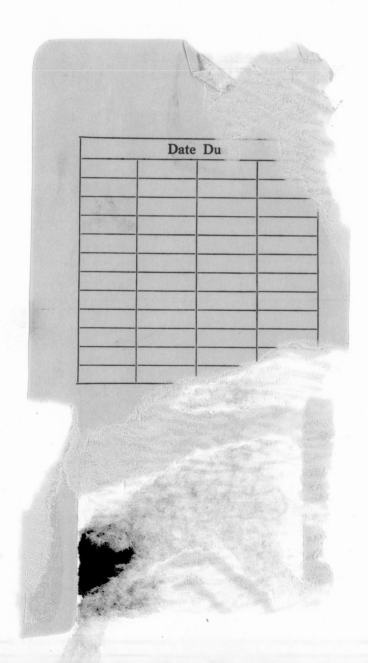

Date Du

TAKING
STATE
POWER

TAKING STATE POWER

the sources
and consequences
of political challenge

JOHN C. LEGGETT
Rutgers University

HARPER & ROW, PUBLISHERS
New York, Evanston, San Francisco, London

I dedicate this book to C. Wright Mills. With the Pentagon Papers
and Watergate disclosures, we now know that there is a power elite . . .
and that Mills was basically right.

Sponsoring Editor: Walter H. Lippincott, Jr.
Project Editor: William B. Monroe
Designer: Frances Torbert Tilley
Production Supervisor: Stefania J. Taflinska

TAKING STATE POWER: The Sources and Consequences of Political Challenge

Library of Congress Cataloging in Publication Data
Leggett, John C
  Taking state power.

  Bibliography: p.
  1. Revolutions. 2. Government, Resistance to.
I. Title.
JC491.L35   320.1   72-12006
ISBN 0-06-043943-2

Contents

Preface

Why and how do the oppressed and the exploited challenge those who dog it and hog it? Since man's invention of private property and the state, a small minority of persons have declared their commitment to coerce a majority and to justify minority use of force in the name of a common good. The evolutionary break was clear: a minority of persons had moved successfully to acquire the vast bulk of societal strategic resources—the land, the flora and the fauna, the minerals and the water—and to use them to insure a working relationship with a government that could generally and effectively claim a monopoly of violence within the territorial unit in question, be it a community or a society. The owners of private property and the state thereby developed relations that proved to be reciprocal for the few, as private property holders and state power wielders subordinated the many.

The flattened thereby suffered, and with few exceptions, they have, over the centuries, accepted their lot. To oppose their superiors would have meant both legal punishment and godly disapproval. In fact, since their inception 6000 or 7000 years ago, the vast bulk of the nonpropertied masses have never rebelled or revolutionized against their earthly lords. For the many who eked out miserable, diseased, humbled, and deluded lives of 25 or 30 years, at 1500 to 2000 calories a day, the thought of restoring an older, prized order, or creating a new utopian one, through collective insurgence—these defiant thoughts—seldom, if ever, ruminated in their skulls. For the subjugated had been educated by their families, their neighbors, and their churches to view life's perils and injustices as natural phenomena to be endured. If and when the thought of rebellion flickered, the poor generally dismissed the idea as absurd. To rebel was bad, even if the masses were grossly miserable and disadvantaged; hence, they should not do it. That value and that corresponding rule were clear. If the masses did rebel, they would certainly become subject to vicious punishment—here on earth and perhaps in an after-life as well. Thus have values, norms, and beliefs interlocked within man's cultures to be spread through institutions, as these ideas mentally maimed and thereby politically contained the vast bulk of those at the bottom.

But on occasion, despite the conservatizing power of institutions and culture, the subordinated have fought back, in many instances to the shock of oppressors who viewed the downtrodden as forever docile. Indeed, the history of the last 7000 years, especially the last 15 decades, has been one replete with insurgent social movements. People have gotten it together and, although history is a graveyard of social movements, many of them have rearranged historical landscapes. Think of China, Vietnam, Cambodia, Laos, and even our own country in just the last 40 years, and we can begin to fathom the degree of expressed collective discontent with those who rule.

One way to approach historical challenges from below is to observe peoples who have reacted over the last 150 years against the forces of incipient and full-blown capitalist imperialism. In this book, we will dwell on three types of people—pre-agrarian, agrarian, and industrial—as they challenged a small minority of persons who have mobilized land, labor, and capital to produce and sometimes export commodities at the expense of the overwhelming majority of the earth's inhabitants. From Cargo Cults among tribal peoples in Melanesia, through full-blown revolutions among the Chinese and the Vietnamese, to rebellion and revolution among industrialized peoples, the collective challenges have surfaced and moved unevenly toward the elimination of the fat-cats who have ripped-off people's bodies and minds to mine and export the gold of New Caledonia, to grow and trade East Bengal opium in exchange for Chinese tea and silver, and to deny modern industrial peoples, such as Ford and General Motors workers, much of what they as producers have created. Exploitation means taking the surplus created by the real producers and appropriating this surplus for members of the upper class. Humanity should never be mystified about this process; although some are, many have grasped this basic process.

In the course of human history, there have been those who have joined the long march against the accumulation of wealth by the few. A roll call would include a motley assemblage of horny-handed proletarians, angry peasants, discontented intellectuals, and many others. Their numbers have increased significantly in the last 70 years. Today their efforts have been made more difficult by the recent creation of the pentapolar détente among the states of Russia, China, Japan, the United States, and the western European countries. Yet we expect the peoples' struggles to continue, perhaps indefinitely.

Acknowledgments

To Irving Louis Horowitz I am indebted for his criticisms of various portions of this manuscript. His comments proved to be singularly helpful. Ruth and Bill Mathews carefully read and criticized the entire manuscript. Thanks. I'm also indebted to Luther Wilson, Robert Ginsberg, and William Monroe for their thoughtful and patient work.

Deborah De James, Leta Gandolfini, and Nancy Struhl worked diligently, as did Susan Olup, to proofread and to assemble the book's various sections. I am grateful for their self-discipline, energy, and ingenuity. Without their concern with detail, Luther Wilson, a forgiving editor, would still be waiting for this manuscript.

The manuscript typing was done by Jean Jordan and Victoria Bramson, with the help of Margaret Douglas, Mary Balfry, Iris Leggett, Lois McGarry, and Cindy Newell. I salute all of you.

Harriet Presser very carefully read the entire book. She helped to eliminate many of its inconsistencies. Because of her painstaking scrutiny, the book is a lot better than it would have been.

To the copyeditor Brenda Griffing I am especially indebted. She did a fine job helping to put together what is in fact a book with a complex organizational structure.

I offer my tardy but hardy bravo to the hundreds of poorly paid interviewers and unpaid as well as badly abused interviewees for their contributions. Without their presence, this effort would be altogether without empirical moorings.

Mordecai Briemberg, John Magney, Seymour Faber, Marlene Simon, Bob Yamada, Frances Moulder, Marty Glaberman, Wally Smith, Bernie Chodan, James Boggs, Grace Lee, Billy Simon, Werner Landecker, Gerhard Lenski, David Aberle, Lewis Killiam, Kathleen Gough, Guy Swanson, Marty Oppenheimer, Dan Katz, Ted Newcomb, Phillip Selznick, Dale Johnson, Eugene Litwak, David Matza, William Kornhauser, Hari Sharma, Ed Turner, Jerry Katz, Herbert Blumer, Hardy Frye, Chuck Irby, Seymour Lipset, Bill Livant, Ronald Freedman, Gerry Sperling, Celia Karch, Nathan Popkin, Sohan Sharma, Louie Feldhammer, Saghir Ahmad, Jim Cockcroft, Janet Roach, Richard Flacks, Tom Brose, David Street, Jack Roach, Morris Janowitz, and J. David Colfax—all in their own peculiar ways, have helped. Thanks.

To my students I am most indebted, for without their give-and-take stimulation, there would have been little motivation to write this book. Their ability to take advantage of the privilege of newness has hopefully extended my revolutionary potential.

John C. Leggett

Chapter 1 From the Bottom Up: An Evolutionary View of Underclass Challenge

Section One   *Challenge and Response*

Political sociology. The topic seems boundless. One book cannot hope to cover more than a portion of the field, and so what does get treated depends largely on the perspective of the political sociologist doing the writing. My own orientation is to determine who owns the strategic resources in society and to investigate the relationship between property owners or the propertyless and the state. These relationships take many forms, including those situations where the propertyless are unable to challenge the state.

In defining this subject, we can best express the ideas involved through terse propositional statements, but we should keep in mind that these assertions are tentative. First, however, we must specify the question to which I have chiefly addressed myself in writing this book: Under what conditions do underclasses challenge their social superiors, economic coordinators, and political regulators?

BASIC PROPOSITIONS

To answer this question, let me specify the basic propositions to be considered in the ensuing chapters:

1. *In order for political sociology to shed light on who will challenge the state, it is useful to take into account the law of evolutionary potential.*

Challenges take many forms. Included are left-electoral politics, rebellion, and revolution. We will have occasion to discuss all three forms from the vantage point of a political sociology that emphasizes the power of the state.

Political sociology. What is it—at least this book's working definition? The sociology of politics, or political sociology, dwells on how groups use force and symbols either to maintain or to alter the distribution of rewards. As indicated, we will focus on the challenge aspects of political sociology—how people mobilize against the state. The state, of course, is anything but a myth. Nor is it bequeathed by a god or a pantheon of lesser deified figures. Certainly the state is not present in all societies. It is absent from societies referred to in a nonpejorative sense as "primitive." The state is that organization that alone can claim a *monopoly of violence;* that is, it alone can claim the right to inflict bodily injury on persons found within its jurisdiction. In the United States, the government constitutes a state, although clearly some levels and areas of government—notably the federal and executive branches—are more important than others.

Lawrence Krader has expanded on the general qualities of the state:

> The state is the means of governing societies with large populations numbering many thousands of millions, and is found only in such societies. The state is found only in societies with numerous composite groups, social classes, and associations, bringing together under common rule many kinds of people; a society having a state form of government is not usually ethnically homogeneous. Such a society is divided into social classes and strata; it is unequal in the distribution of economic functions and of wealth. States bring together the different classes and communities under common rule. Authority in *any* form of state issues from one central office and is usually asserted impersonally and objectively, in the name of a god, or the majesty of the throne, or the people. Now there are means of conducting human affairs in formal offices and institutions of rule with specialized assignments of

roles to governors of provinces, judges, soldiers, kings, ministers, police, or by informal assignments of these roles. People on occasion act as judges, ministers, soldiers in simple societies. But differences in population size and complexity, and formality of office, make for radical differences in modes of government; the larger, more complex and formal governmental roles are usually found in states. The state is a complicating factor in the organization of society, a factor that works two ways: On the one hand, its presence is the mark that a complex form *has been achieved;* on the other, the process of forming the state is a means for achieving the transition to complex society. That is, a more complex society is established by the process of state formation. . . .

In the organization of the state, man concentrates his power over man in a single office. The monopoly of physical force by this office is absolute. It may channel its power by specifically delegating it; otherwise, unless the state is overthrown, the power remains at the disposal of the central authority. The force in the hands of the state takes various forms: banishment, death, imprisonment, enslavement, fines.[1]

In going about the activities specified by Krader, the state may also become legitimate, in the sense that the state is viewed as sacrosanct by the majority of people. Of course, not all states are legitimate, despite the gestures of many of their intellectuals. A society may contain numerous rebels and revolutionaries who call for the demise of the present state. Indeed, what is legitimate for some can well be illegitimate for others *within the same society.*

When a state organization is fortunate enough to obtain successful legitimation among most groups, this state finds itself in a better position to integrate persons into their daily work and other routines no matter how great the poverty of the multitude and the span of economic rewards might be. Writers such as Vilfredo Pareto and Gaetano Mosca have observed the restraining influence of political formulas and popular myths—"my country right or wrong," for example—among people both sorely deprived by the absolute standards

of caloric deprivation and recruited in disproportionate numbers for the armed forces of the state.[2] Not just the powerful and the wealthy may want to maintain the governmental status quo.

Having defined what we mean by the state, it is now necessary to specify the Law of Evolutionary Potential. Briefly put, it is as follows:

> The more specialized and adapted a form in a given evolutionary state, the smaller is its potential for passing to the next stage.
> Another way of putting it which is more succinct . . . is: Specific evolutionary progress is inversely related to general evolutionary potential.[3]

In the United States today, for example, one would not expect this highly differentiated state to initiate and bring about significant changes in its internal structure or external economy because of the high degree to which our state has differentiated itself to deal with internal and external problems. Not only has this state elaborated itself over the decades, but it has hardened its lines of authority and entrenched its bureaucracy so that it is difficult to change them and almost impossible to abolish them. This state, then, would not be expected to accept its own demise or its replacement by nonstate forms such as localized political syndicates established by labor bodies. However, were such a decentralized form to emerge, its presence would earn a designation as a specific evolutionary successor to the state. One would expect such a government to come into being in societies where revolutionary forces have recently eliminated their own state and where other organized states do not threaten the revolution. This allows the revolutionary leaders and the rank and file the luxury of experimenting with decentralized forms of power and, hence, an evolutionary leap in the exercise of political control.

2. *In order to grasp where people will participate in the challenge of revolution or for that matter, serious but reform demands, it is*

[1] Lawrence Krader, *Formation of the State* (Englewood Cliffs, N.J.: Prentice-Hall, 1968), pp. 3, 9–10, by permission of the publisher. Copyright 1968.

[2] James K. Meisel, *The Myth of the Ruling Class* (Ann Arbor: University of Michigan Press, 1961).
[3] Elman R. Service, "The Law of Evolutionary Potential," from Marshall D. Sahlins and Elman R. Service, ed., *Evolution and Culture* (Ann Arbor: .University of Michigan Press, 1960), p. 97.

necessary to consider the Phylogenetic Discontinuity of Progress and its geographical connotations for the law of evolutionary potential.

The Phylogenetic Discontinuity of Progress can be expressed quite simply: an advanced form seldom begets the next stage of advance—the next stage begins in a different line. Thus, for example, since upperclass protestants in the United States have become highly differentiated, specialized, and coordinated in their generally successful domination of other groups, one would not expect them to steer our government, our economy, and/or our race relations so as to bring about a major breakthrough in creating an economy without private property, and/or organizing the country along lines of racial equality. Such breakthroughs would require the elimination of this successful upper class protestant political adaptation. No force, as yet, exists that can remove the institutions and ways of thought that cement these upper classes in their control and ownership of most of this country's organizational and pecuniary resources.

Perhaps a geographical corollary to the law of evolutionary potential may be useful in making this point more precisely. Here we are referring to the Local Discontinuity of Progress. By this is meant that if successive stages of forms, whether in evolutionary or devolutionary sequence, are not likely to go from one species to its next descendant, then they are not likely to occur in the same locality or country.[4] Thus, one would not expect the upper classes in the United States to move to introduce major innovations on matters of state, economy, or race. However, the failure of our upper classes to act now does not preclude transformation in the event of a revolution to eliminate these political rigidities.

3. *The law of evolutionary potential has as its corollary the privilege of backwardness, a principal which strongly suggests which stratum will act forcefully in the political context.*

Leon Trotsky, in his *History of the Russian Revolution,* articulated the theory of the privilege of backwardness in his discussion of societies, and hence, implicitly, of the state as well:

[4] *Ibid.,* pp. 98–99.

Although compelled to follow after the advanced countries, a backward country does not take things in the same order. The privilege of historic backwardness—and such privilege exists—permits, or rather compels, the adoption of whatever is ready in advance of any specified date, skipping a whole series of intermediate stages.[5]

On close examination it would appear that Trotsky's theory of the privilege of backwardness refers to two quite different types of backwardness: first is the backwardness of a social unit (a class, a society, or a state) that is so highly differentiated and adapted as to make impossible any qualitative breakthrough unless and until a contending revolutionary social unit topples the structure and immediately erects in its place totally new forms—for example, the succession to the archaic czarist state of the Russian soviets. We may refer to this privilege as *the privilege of agedness and inflexibility*—the privilege of being toppled. Second is the backwardness of a social unit (a society or a state) that is largely *undifferentiated* and hence as yet not so highly adapted to either habitat or units around it as to make possible qualitative breakthroughs by the acceptance of internal inventions and/or external diffusions. For example, the existence and qualities of soviets that existed in Russia between the spring of 1917 and their destruction several years later. We may refer to this good fortune as *the privilege of newness.* Reflect for a moment and you can imagine how blacks, Puerto Ricans, and Chicanos living in the United States at the present time do in fact enjoy this privilege. You might also consider how their positions could conceivably compel them to press for change.

Trotsky deals with both forms of privilege when he comments on the development of Russian industry from rudimentary and relatively backward mechanical forms to a system containing the most advanced factories, mines, and units of transportation. Here he is contrasting the privilege of being succeeded, i.e., the privilege of agedness and inflexibility, with the privilege of newness—all within a larger formulation that notes the ways in which the two privileges

[5] Leon Trotsky, *History of the Russian Revolution* (Ann Arbor: University of Michigan Press, 1957), pp. 4–5.

and corresponding levels of ideology and organization can in fact be united within a combined development that leaps whole stages of industrialization:

> The law of combined development reveals itself most indubitably . . . in the history and character of Russian industry. Arising late, Russian industry did not repeat the development of the advanced countries, but inserted itself into this development, adapting their latest achievements to its own backwardness. Just as the economic evolution of Russia as a whole skipped over the epoch of craft-guilds and manufacture, so also the separate branches of industry made a series of special leaps over technical productive stages that had been measured in the West by decades. Thanks to this, Russian industry developed at certain periods with extraordinary speed.[6]

What applies to industries also applies to classes and status groups as well as to generations.

4. *In order to gauge where and when a class, status group, or generation will challenge the state, a sense of evolutionary potential, stage periodicity and a qualified view on the admitted importance of market economy and technology is needed.*

In the case of the U.S. working class for the last several decades, blue-collar blacks have maintained the highest potential in pressing for change because they have in many cases just entered the industrial community. They find themselves on the margins of market economy and learn that the managers and owners of technology use it largely—however, unintentionally—to worsen the relative economic condition of most black people. But before we develop this statement, as we will in later chapters, it might be useful to specify several key categories of analysis.

CLASS, STATUS, AND GENERATION AS DETERMINANTS OF BEHAVIOR

Briefly, a class consists of all those persons who share a common relationship to the means of production, whether as owners of tools or sellers of labor.[7] In agrarian—feudal societies,

for example, there are those who own, or benefit from royal lease, the society's strategic resources. In this sense, royal families own land whose land-use rights are realized locally by a panoply of titled but lesser families. The earnings of these local lords derive principally from the coordination of the energies and commodities emanating from those landless workers tied to arable land, fenced pastures, and wooded areas. Precisely because of privileged ownership and lease-right, there is by definition a fundamental and demarcated distinction between privileged property holders (or leasers) and those who do *not* own or lease these resources. At the top of the class structure is the royal family. Directly below the king but proximate to the top of this layered hierarchy are the nobles, the dukes, and the barons. In between is an array of service persons—priests, bards, and sheriffs, among others. At the base are the peasants. Industrial societies are similar in their propensity to be organized along class lines. Both in industrial settings and in our agrarian predecessor state, the fundamental distinction is between the property owners and the propertyless, except in advanced industrial societies with little private property. There, in Russia for example, the nearest equivalent to property ownership for the individual is to hold a decision-making position within the state.[8]

Unlike classes, status groups are *popularly* defined—differentiated by the people through consensus on matters of honor, as when whites agree that blacks are "at the bottom of society." Here the social scientist simply discovers already existing pecking orders, ranked groups quite visible to almost everyone, although many persons may wish to deny publicly what they know to be the case. In the United States, for example, black Americans constitute an ethnic group, one among many ethnics arranged hierarchically in a ranking system which pointedly includes Indians, Mexican-Americans, Jews, Italians, French-Canadians, Swedes, Irish, Germans, and English peoples. We live in tribes

---

[6] *Ibid.,* p. 9.

[7] For an extended discussion of my objective definition of class, see John C. Leggett, *Class, Race, and Labor* (New York: Oxford University Press, 1968), pp. 34–42.

[8] For a pathfinding analysis of Soviet managerial classes as equivalent to the upper classes in the West, see Milovan Djilas, *The New Class* (New York: Praeger, 1957).

ordered in terms of popular preference, although the rhetoric of equality would deny their pecking order and contradict the ranked consensus.[9]

Generations are a more nebulous category, but basically a generation is a wave (a cohort) of persons living in the same community or societal age group who have experienced during late adolescence an intensive and prolonged shock in the form of a social cataclysm such as an economic depression or a bloody war. Thus not everyone belongs to a generation. Crucial is presence within a cohort subject to a deep and abiding tragedy. These youthful experiences, as Karl Mannheim has observed, create indented attitudes which remain with this cohort throughout its life. The Great Depression young people of the 1930s, for example, are clearly a case in point, because after they had experienced the extreme deprivations of economic depression while they were growing up. They had acquired security-oriented political attitudes as they tried with varying degrees of failure to edge their way into the labor force. After all these jarring experiences, jobs and *job security* became and remained extremely important to them throughout their lives. Many of us have grandfathers who witnessed children eating potato peelings from garbage cans; should we wonder that they concern themselves with mundane matters of job and food? They had become and have remained a depression generation.[10]

MARKET ECONOMY AS DEHUMANIZING

Class, status, and generational positions differentiate people who in capitalist society share a common constant that they live in a society with a market economy, one where land, labor, and goods are to varying degrees exchanged on the basis of supply and demand considerations. This "backdrop" condition sets the tone for all other courses of human action: drinking, swearing, politicking, fighting, publishing, love-making—all fundamental processes. Pure capitalist societies, or more realistically, their close proximates such as midnineteenth-century England are generally organized with widespread consequences for all members of classes, status groups, and generations. Indeed to the degree that market relations on land, labor, and goods supersede, contravene, and replace the rules of natural economy, such as those of primitive peoples, intergroup struggle becomes more intense and prolonged. For example, the market economy has on occasion fostered the white policy of genocide against many primitive peoples. Consequently, most primitive people learn to loathe the practices of stealing land, buying labor, and selling goods, if only during the break-up period of their society's specific evolution. Preindustrial peoples reject these market relations. Their attachment to non-market practices leads them to struggle, if only momentarily, against the imperialist culture and state being imposed on them and against its immediate predecessor, entrepreneurial, capitalist colonialism.

With few and largely irrelevant exceptions, the market economy occurs within the context of private ownership of the means of production. There is a basic distinction between those who own society's strategic resources and those who do not own them. In effect, when a society has fences, locks, and keys, there is an upper class to build banks, to guard gates, and to position itself to use the state in order to market objects for profit. The propertied classes can interlock market, ownership, and technology, denounce the need for a state, its laws and personnel, yet rely heavily on state authority, state money, and state violence.

TECHNOLOGY AS ORGANIZATIONALLY INTEGRATED

Under the conditions stated above, technology stands alone only in theory, never in practice; it is never neutral. Profit-seekers and state officials use technology to mine land, process labor, and distribute goods as commodities. But this is not to say that technology always works to benefit its owners. Far from it. Those tools and techniques that work to maximize profit

[9] Max Weber is of course the classical theorist on status. See "Class Status, Party," in H. H. Gerth and C. Wright Mills, *From Max Weber: Essays in Sociology* (New York: Oxford University Press, 1946), pp. 180–195.

[10] Karl Mannheim is a very important contributor to our understanding of "The Problem of Generations." See his discussion on this matter in: *Essays on the Sociology of Knowledge* (London: Routledge & Kegan Paul, 1964), pp. 276-320.

simultaneously insure the very destruction of the natural resources necessary to create profit.

Today the investment of savings by business firms accelerates the propensity of large-scale business organizations to link technology to market economy in a way that despoils the environment by replacing nonpolluting resources with buildings, persons, and machines that create large amounts of waste. The investment of accumulated capital accelerates this wreckage. Getting profits from investment takes unquestioned precedence over the preservation of any technologically usable feature of the natural environment. Ironically, the interlocked force of market, property, technology, savings, and profit is creating unsolvable problems for those states organized primarily to aggrandize the interests of those few who derive their living almost exclusively from private investment. The pollution of land, lakes, air, and water continues more or less unabated because remedial cost would require a new and costly

technology that firms and states are unwilling to pay.

LEVELS AND DEVELOPMENT: A SCHEMATIC VIEW

Clearly then, certain categories of thought should prove useful in explaining and predicting how people act and think. But how does one begin to put these categories together to make sense of them? Perhaps the most useful device would be to view three types of societies as consisting of multiple layers, beginning with population and habitat and working up through technology and levels of organization to ideas, as indicated in Table 1.

Admittedly, this simplifying device takes us away from the complexities of society. Worse yet, it suggests that the causal arrows underlying man's behavior invariably run from the bottom to the top, from habitat and technology to man's ideas, that one consideration

TABLE 1   Levels of Society and Major Stages of Development

Layers of Society	Levels of Society	Stages of Development
Superstructure	*Justifications*: Ideologies as well as rules, including law	Industrial peoples
	Challenges: Utopias	↑
Intermediary facilitators	1. *Social organization*: Supportive social institutions—the family, the church, the media, the neighborhood, the school, among others *Status groups* *Generations*	Agrarian peoples
	2. *Political organization*: Government, the state, political social movements, and like forms focusing on ultimate authority and coercion	↑
Substructure	1. *Processes*: economic organization: production and distribution of goods *Structures*: classes, large-scale groups that create economic value	
	2. *Technology*: man's tools and their techniques of use	Primitive peoples
	3. *Population and habitat*	

TABLE 2   Forms of Social Evolution

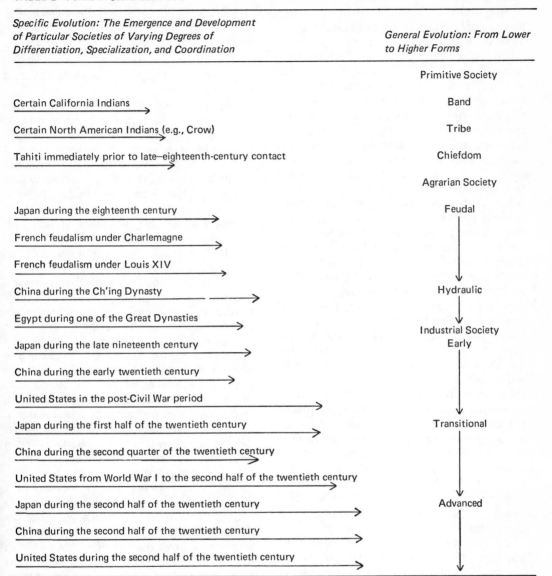

Specific Evolution: The Emergence and Development of Particular Societies of Varying Degrees of Differentiation, Specialization, and Coordination	General Evolution: From Lower to Higher Forms
	Primitive Society
Certain California Indians →	Band
Certain North American Indians (e.g., Crow) →	Tribe
Tahiti immediately prior to late–eighteenth-century contact →	Chiefdom
	Agrarian Society
Japan during the eighteenth century →	Feudal
French feudalism under Charlemagne →	
French feudalism under Louis XIV →	
China during the Ch'ing Dynasty →	Hydraulic
Egypt during one of the Great Dynasties →	
Japan during the late nineteenth century →	Industrial Society / Early
China during the early twentieth century →	
United States in the post-Civil War period →	
Japan during the first half of the twentieth century →	Transitional
China during the second quarter of the twentieth century →	
United States from World War I to the second half of the twentieth century →	
Japan during the second half of the twentieth century →	Advanced
China during the second half of the twentieth century →	
United States during the second half of the twentieth century →	

or a combination of considerations determines man's behavior. Actually, as we shall see, there are a variety of useful but too simple "mono-causal" or "single-variable" explanations of people's activities.

Again, the reader may oversimplify concrete complexity, examine this diagram, and falsely assume that all societies must evolve so as to recapitulate a master-plan of evolution—from primitive, through agrarian, to industrial. No such scheme is intended. However, following

Sahlins and Service,[11] we find it useful to distinguish societies in terms of the degree to which they are differentiated, specialized, and coordinated.

Sahlins has observed not only this distinction, but the general evolutionary hierarchy of primitive, agrarian, and industrial when classifying societies in terms of the degree to which

[11] Sahlins and Service, in *Evolution and Culture*, pp. 12–44, 93–122.

they approach the three-leveled, general evolutionary ladder. We have attempted to extrapolate some of his key ideas on this matter and to apply them accordingly (See Table 2).

Dealing with the dynamics of the interplay within specific societies as well as among general levels, Service has observed that the specific evolution of most societies does not recapitulate the general developmental scheme. Rather, specific societies often bypass whole general stages—sometimes simultaneously combining major elements of general stages—as they evolve. This conceptual effort does not imply that particular societies are simply classifiable artifacts to be found within an arbitrary scheme imposed by the social scientists. On the contrary, forces at work within specific societies can create new categories of thought as these societies evolve and create new and higher, hence general forms. But evolving societies do not create higher forms unless they have evolutionary potential. In this regard, Sahlins and Service have observed that the more differentiated, specialized, and coordinated a form within a given stage of general evolution, the less likely will it break with its adaptive niche and initiate as well as sustain a new and higher form. By contrast, we know that the privilege of backwardness holds that the very absence of full differentiation, specialization, and coordination allows for greater innovation—both through indigenous change and through the acceptance of diffused items. Hence, over and over again, the less developed forms within a stage create a specific form that sustains itself to become the general evolutionary successor of that particular stage.

By way of illustration, we observe that the young, not the aged generally make the qualitative break and forward thrust in the realm of invention. As Service observed in "The Law of Evolutionary Potential":

Young scientists tend to surpass their elders, when other things such as brains, of course, are equal. The well-established individuals ordinarily do not go on making successive important contributions because they become so committed, adapted, to a particular line of thought. The young are generalized and unstable, in a sense, and have the "privilege of backwardness" which enables them to appropriate only the more fruitful and

progressive of the older generation's accomplishments, disregarding or discarding as useless debris much of the work that went on before them.[12]

Thus, what can readily occur is the leaping of whole general stages, a process by no means suggested by Table 1.

Perhaps the weakest aspect of Table 1 is the way in which the reader and writer may be prone to define this diagram as reality itself, an ordered hierarchy of stale "cake slices," layered parts which together constitute a mutually complementary whole only grudgingly subject to change. Thus we sometimes find people ludicrously using the multilayered conception to portray real societies which are in fact both filled with serious structural conflicts and characterized by ongoing and uneven alterations of organizations and ideas.

From yet another perspective, a person might mistakenly ascribe the human characteristics of a healthy person to a layered abstraction called "society" and say "society" is temporarily and unfortunately doing bad things—like making young people smoke grass—without any idea who the concrete referents pushing the pot might be. We should have no such trouble with the category "state," a pusher of its own distinct and heady wares. Concretely, time and again we can observe its day-to-day referents ordering people to act in ways that are rational yet sometimes absurd. We can watch *governments* (not society) work to make people loyally accept work routines at the very time the state-favored corporations are publicly phasing out these people's occupations. Or during war, we can note governments successfully extol the virtues of "free will" as the basis for "the people choosing to fight the enemy" at the very time the government forcibly obtains most of its military personnel through a "draft," and seeks to punish its "draft dodgers" and "deserters." Sometimes these obvious contradictions become apparent to a sizable minority of persons who subsequently are moved by their circumstances to resolve these contradictions through political action.

---

[12] Elman R. Service, "The Law of Evolutionary Potential," *ibid.*, p. 104, by permission.

5. *As pertinent as a sense of evolutionary periodicity is an assessment of the conditions and processes associated with the full realization of high levels of revolutionary potential.*

In the first half of this book we spend considerable time spelling out the conditions and processes associated with the coming to power of revolutionaries, dwelling on both structural and ideological considerations. On the level of what is commonly thought of as ideology, we do make a distinction between ideology and utopia, between, in effect, obfuscation and hope.

IDEOLOGY AND UTOPIA

States depend on ideologies to foster legitimation, but political movements—especially the more militant variety—espouse utopias.

Ideologies refer to idea systems that purport to portray reality, although generally they obscure it. Ideologies may be specific or general. For example, rulers and their intellectual aides deliberately concoct specific ideas to falsify reality. They do so to make reality more palatable to the ordinary man, to the person who is generally dependent on rulers for acceptable information as well as plausible interpretations of current events. By contrast, ideologies express a general quality when their holders become the unconscious purveyors of ideas which grease the parts of the system. These ideas help to keep people moving from day-to-day slots located in the home—job—recreation routines. As Karl Mannheim[13] and Leslie White have observed, we find time and again that people "make choices" on the basis of general values about which they as carriers are unaware. They define situations without being fully aware of their own standards. In many instances, people become the unconscious users and conveyors of culture—whether in terms of values (dos and don'ts), beliefs (justifications), or norms (rules).

By contrast, utopian conceptions call for the conscious creation of a new society. Yet they portray destruction as well as creation, and therein lies their beauty, if only among those dedicated to revolutionary change.

Yet for all its symmetry and humanism, a utopian depiction of the good world is "unrealistic," for it clearly departs from tested reality. But in another sense, as Mannheim has made clear, utopia is realistic, for its contours stand diametrically opposed to ongoing odious circumstances. In this context utopian ideas have the potential for becoming part of the revolutionary aspirations of people no longer satisfied with a government that cannot meet the defined needs of those historically bereft of work, power, prestige, or purpose. In many cases, as we shall note time and again in this book, these ordinary people collectively create and espouse novel and sometimes messianic ideas that call for the cataclysmic ending of institutional domination and class—racial exploitation.

And when the oppressed have formulated their insurgent ideas, these aspirations often find full expression within utopian schemes—such as those of cargo cults among Melanesians, peyote cults among American Navajo Indians, and revolutionary movements among the Chinese.[14] In this regard, the bizarre behavior of the cargo cults of Melanesia is informative.

> In the eastern Highlands (of New Guinea), ANGAU (Australian) officers reported the existence of Cargo activity in areas near the Markham Valley as early as 1943. They found there large "wireless houses" in which bamboo cylinders were placed with "wires" running from these cylinders to a bamboo "insulator" in the roof and thence to a rope "aerial" outside stretched between two poles. The patrol suspected the presence of Japanese; they lay hidden till next morning, when they witnessed the villagers assemble outside the house to practice drill with canes instead of rifles. Two natives whom they seized explained that the cult had been started by Markham natives who had told them of the imminent Coming of Jesus. The wireless would give them advance notice of the Coming. Then rifles would be issued, and the ready-trained natives would expel the

[13] Karl Mannheim, *Ideology and Utopia* (New York: Harcourt, 1936).

[14] The followers of cargo cults believed that their dead ancestors would pilot a ship or plane filled with scarce commodities from their area of rest to the natives' place of residence. Furthermore, the arrival of the ancestors with cargo-items, such as knives and clothes, associated with intensive contact with Westerners would herald a revitalization of native culture. The arrival of cargo and the beginning of rejuvenation assumed utopian content. See Chapter 2 for a further discussion of cargo cults.

Whites. Several "wireless houses" were found and destroyed.

In the centre of the houses were poles with rungs to which Jesus was to come, or up which the natives would climb to Jesus; the natives were also equipped with cane "flashlights" with which to see Him. The officer who dealt with this movement informed the natives that Jesus would notify his coming to the "Governor" in the first instance . . . but it would be many years before such a thing happened; and if it ever did happen, the news of His coming would emanate from the "Governor" himself and only from him.

The repression of this cult seems only to have aggravated it, and to have provoked anti-White feeling. In the next outbreak, two years later, the people now believed that the Whites had been intercepting the Cargo coming from the ancestors. The affronted ancestors would now bring the goods direct and in person, out of a large mountain in the south; a "wireless" pointing to the mountain would receive the news, and a house was prepared for the ancestors. Graves were cleaned up, and native weapons and other goods destroyed; only enough food and goods for the interregnum period was preserved, the rest destroyed. Believers were anointed with coconut oil. . . . When the millennium arrived, black skins would be shed for white, and the White man's goods would go to the natives.

Deliberately breaking up the rules excluding women from the men's huts, all natives, male and female, lined up daily outside the huts, and then entered one by one saluting the leader as they entered. Inside they waited reverently while he communicated by "wireless" with the returning ancestors, and then sang songs. Planes engaged in aerial combat were said to be fighting battles between the ancestors and the Whites.[15]

Generally, however, the oppressed do not articulate and act on utopian schemes, millennial or otherwise; rather, they adapt to their circumstances. They do not organize for the coming of a Christ whose arrival will mark the immediate reorganization of the world. Nor do they struggle for secular utopias. Most frequently, they find a niche and they adapt.

[15] Peter M. Worsley, *The Trumpet Shall Sound* (London: McKee & Gibbon, 1968), pp. 199–200, by permission.

HARMLESS DISCHARGE: REPRESSIVE REDIRECTION

As Herbert Marcuse has implied, the upper classes facilitate adaptation by creating and using a number of processes, including "repressive redirection."[16] That is, through institutional channels which they control or tolerate, the upper classes direct energy, including the repressed sexual variety, into arenas where human activity results in the harmless release of pent-up feelings, frustrations, and anxieties that might otherwise find positive expression through revolt or revolution. The upper classes have not been averse to working through the state to join with missionaries, for example, to integrate natives into a new division of labor smacking of colonialism. However unconsciously, the rising British bourgeoisie of the early nineteenth century operated through the use of gunboats and missionaries to integrate Pacific islanders into the market economy, thereby setting in motion among the natives who were to be saved from their sins by evangelical Methodist fervor the psychic release of repressive redirection.[17]

Back of Great Britain's reluctance to extend sovereignty over islands in Oceania was a cultural condition prevailing in England at that time: "Victorianism," as it became known. . . . It began before Victoria ascended the throne and prevailed with unusual staying power for ten decades. An important component was the Evangelical revival, which comprised an entire system of religio-moral philosophy based upon a reaction against the Regency and "Popery" and upon a Protestant middle class standard of values. The typical Victorian has been characterized as a hard, commercial-minded tradesman who scrupulously went to church and vigorously supported good causes. At the government level Victorianism consisted of an economic-minded

[16] Herbert Marcuse, *Essays on Liberation* (Boston: Beacon, 1969).

[17] For the purpose of this book, *integration* has reference to a systemic operation in which (1) parts are introduced so as to act in concert, (2) the cultural components of values, norms and beliefs complement the workings of the parts, and (3) these three cultural components prove to be consistent with one another. Integration is always a matter of degree, for contradictions and inconsistencies prove omnipresent and disruptive.

bureaucracy which supported industrialism at home, bringing large profits for a few but creating stark misery for the English working class, while paradoxically backing the abolition of slavery abroad and supporting the formation of mission societies to wipe out heathenism.

Nowhere in English public life were these policies stronger than in the Colonial Office. With few exceptions Her Majesty's colonial ministers were supporters of the idea of foreign missions, many of them holding high offices in missionary societies. It has even been claimed that England's colonial policy was formulated out of resolutions coming from Essex Hall, the site of the annual meeting of mission societies. The effect of this on British colonial policy was to support missions, morally and with naval force if necessary, though rarely with money, but to stay clear of other kinds of colonial adventures, including annexation; the general argument was that colonies cost money and must be guarded, and that natives should be allowed to develop their own governments, aided by advice from missionaries. The only counters to this policy were the importunities of nonmissionary colonials and the threats of annexation from other powers, chiefly France.[18]

Today, as yesterday, the upper classes in the so-called home countries become purveyors of energy-releasing carnivals, current equivalents of the Methodist revival. Thus the North American and European upper classes frequently sponsor football extravaganzas, baseball games, bullfight theatricals, hockey smash-ups, and other sporting collisions. For the more highbrow, there are the daring plays, the critical films, and similar exhibitions. Some people have correctly observed that the white middle class use of marijuana, peyote, and the liberated film fails to alter the repressive social order, although group throngs may press people to question the sanctity of the state. However, under most circumstances the "cultural freakout" for the youth, or the Sunday afternoon TV game-of-the-week for the rotund, simply function as collective safety valves for the community and as mechanisms of catharsis for the

[18] Douglas Oliver, *Pacific Islanders* (Cambridge, Mass: Harvard University Press, 1961), pp. 98–99, by permission.

individual. In another sense, the freak-out protects the lone citizen from collisions with the state, as he and the alienated violate the lesser mores and laws—including those on proper use of nonchemical drugs. Over time, harmless releases become appended to the job, the week, the family, the community, the union, through such forms as the annual Christmas party, the Friday night drunk, the week-end "trip," the annual vacation, and the Labor Day weekend. Needless to say, these freak-outs are not enough to reorder society.

6. *The realization of both revolutionary and reformist changes requires a number of considerations, including the creation and maintenance of high levels of class and class racial consciousness.*

Revolution should not be confused with reform, especially in political sociology. Revolution has reference to the seizure of state power. Reform consists of the gradual modifications of the state and the society in question. In the case of reform of state power, the change agents do not attempt to throw out the old guard through the use of force. We spend considerable time on revolution as an alternative to reform, especially in Chapters 3 to 6.

7. *High levels of consciousness are required in part because persons can more readily acquire a critical political perspective on the role of the state—and this critical view should most frequently occur among groups in a position to take advantage of the privilege of newness.*

When dealing with the state, one often encounters two quite different conceptions of its character: the first bucolic, the second damning. The first conception fails to reflect society's crucial qualities. Hence, from a critical point of view, its presence and intellectual shortcomings require intensive public examination by a highly class-conscious group; this procedure will permit the false image to be brought into question and eliminated by revolutionaries. Here we are referring to the melodious conception of the state, popular not only in traditional bodies but in many new revolutionary groups found at the helms of certain states. In this perspective, the state is seen as a tranquilizer of conflicting groups, a neutral harmonizer of mutually antagonistic interests, a common guardian of the commonwealth, a mechanism organized to maintain equilibrium much as does the healthy brain in the normal human nervous system. When groups collide, the state arbitrates. When stray psychotic impulses threaten violence, the state restrains. When the public interests are at stake, the state defends. When the economy appears topsy-turvy, the state intervenes. This state is more an anthropomorphized entity—a projection of fond human wishes—than a bureaucracy. This image of the state exudes the qualities of a kindly relative without biased class attachments, status group prejudices, generational commitments, market mechanisms, or white people. The state is referee.

There is another perspective, however, one more angry and perhaps more adequate for our times; to wit:

It's the state that dehumanizes, threatens, and sometimes exploits. It's the state that drafts, kills, and maims. It's the state that atomizes the natives. For what, if not for profit and power? For whom, if not for those with wealth? With what consequences, if not the retention of inequalities—and the creation of high levels of consciousness among the oppressed—under certain conditions?

We might best understand the most significant qualities of the state by viewing it as quite capable of specific evolution: from repressive stabilizer during most relatively calm moments within a society to thorough-going, terrifying agent during the throes of revolution. From there to innovator, immediately after the revolutionaries have taken state power, to ruthless leader of the fight against domestic civil war and external reaction, and then on to repressor of grass roots groups such as soviets. Complementing the suppression of experimental and at times inefficient and ineffective local groups is state policy pressing for the revival of certain traditional practices and institutions. These include ordinary family activities and organized religion. Both help many people find an element of stability in a society replete with a recent history of chaos. From the point of view of state leaders, they must foster the revival and the return of couple-marriage, the nuclear family, church sermons, and marriage ceremony. Thus the revolutionary state leadership attempts to revive the very things whose legitimacy it had previously helped to disestablish. State leaders have done so in order to provide longevity for a wobbly, new regime. However, this restoration does not prevent future efforts to seize state power.

8. *If one applies the principle of the privilege of backwardness to an understanding of fascism, it becomes apparent that left-fascism (relative to the right and center varieties) has the greatest potential for creating grass-roots success by rallying manual blue-collar workers to effect dramatic changes in political, economic, and social arenas.*

In Chapter 7, we spend considerable time defining fascism, left, right, and center. Briefly however, left politics refers essentially to efforts to realize equality permanently. Equality here encompasses every area: wealth, politics, and honor, among others. Left politics also implies a willingness to use direct action, to mobilize the masses of disinherited—the poor, the wretched of the earth—to achieve equality.

On the other hand, the left-fascist leadership does *not* stress equality, and so in this sense left-fascism is not truly leftist. However, left-fascism does strive to achieve a major uplift for the lower classes. Left-fascism calls for the dramatic upgrading of society's shirtless ones, but not for the equalization of honor, whether in the class or political sphere. We can observe that all forms of fascism are committed to viewing society in terms of elite and mass. In the case of left-fascism, there is a distinction between those who lead the underdogs and those who are led. A paternal but revolutionary leadership posts itself in a position to take advantage of the revolutionary evolutionary potential of the laboring class.

In general, the right wing stands for the retention of tradition and property in their tried-and-tested forms. When the right opts for (a) the elimination, or nonintroduction, of parliamentary forms as well as (b) the rule of society through a self-appointed political elite defined as inherently superior to a mass, the right is fascist.

Admittedly, more is involved than these brief definitions indicate. Suffice it to say at this point that the political center traditionally stands for the politics of parliamentary governance within a framework of modified capitalism. Unlike the politics of the left, the center generally does not call for dramatic changes, i.e., an abrupt and widespread substitution of state ownership in place of private property. But there are moments of historical exception when center politics can include a fascist variant. The case of Nazi Germany constitutes an example, and the readings of Chapter 7 stress this historical episode as we consider the fascist alternative to communism.

9. *When we apply the privilege of backwardness principle to an understanding of communism, the left proves to be the one seemingly best able—during the preliminary moments of revolution—to attract subordinate strata having the greatest evolutionary potential.*

During the periods of revolutionary insurgence, left-communism speaks for the disinherited, most of whom are uncommitted to the retention of private property and state power. They are opposed, however passively, to racial inequalities, typical injustices of the regime, legalized tyrannies, and sexual inequalities. Left-communism calls for the creation of equality in perpetuity in all these spheres. Time and again, left-communism was found its greatest support among *workers* who have only recently entered work processes associated with capitalist industrialization, and *students* who have located themselves in status positions on the very margins of the labor force—both blue- and white-collar people. It is these and like groups which can and do make claim to a privilege of newness that allows them to generate the total demands of left-communism. This is partly because these groups have little invested, either in terms of personal commitment or private property, in the disintegrating economic order—be it under conditions of capitalism or communism. By the way, left-communism claims the support of many persons found among workers and students whenever this tendency attempts to revitalize left-governments and institutions. China's left-communists constituted a case in point during the Cultural Revolution of 1965–1970.

10. *If we apply the theory of backwardness to our understanding of democratic capitalist countries, we can observe that left-democrats* have the greatest potentiality for making reform capitalism attractive, since they do attempt to solve the problems of those groups having a high degree of reformist potential as well as revolutionary anger.*

In Chapters 9, 10 and 11, we comment at length on the potential and limits of democracy. Briefly, democracy exists when people have equal access to political decision-making within their own governments. We can observe within our own society that this left-democratic definition has considerable appeal among those groups which do, in fact, have great potential for bringing about political changes. Here we have in mind blue-collar racial minorities thrust into industrial settings containing militant unions and, of course, young intellectuals. Both the committed working-class minorities and the intellectuals find considerable support for their political perspectives, economic demands, and social hopes among left-democratic, often upper-class, persons and groups, e.g., the reform wing of the Democratic Party in the United States.

11. *Before a group can fully realize its potential and move against a seemingly intractable state, these groups must deal with a state fully capable of subverting their efforts by using the most advanced forms and the most advanced persons to repair the ongoing system as well as to destroy the mechanisms associated with either serious reform or revolutionary change.*

This insidious propensity is most successfully practiced among center-democrats found within professional bureaucratic organizations, as we shall see in Chapters 10 to 14. We will observe that although an Advanced Imperialist state may be unable to create a revolutionary breakthrough, it can check revolutionary forces through both (*a*) recruitment of personnel from the forces of serious reform and revolution, and (*b*) repression of persons unwilling to be co-opted.

12. *To counter the tendency of the state to suppress those seeking qualitative change, it is necessary to devise a grass-roots strategy on change that will bring together all the groups having the greatest evolutionary potential.*

Organizing from the bottom up proves to be a difficult and complex task. In Chapter 14 we attempt to specify some of the assumptions often involved in grass-roots efforts to go up against and to beat large-scale organizations in our own society. A crucial factor in these efforts to succeed is the active participation of minority, blue-collar women in the struggle. Their evolutionary potential remains great in part because of their relatively recent arrival on the political scene. Furthermore, we have learned that without their participation, broader-based grass roots groups seldom succeed.

In Chapter 15 we discuss the importance of women both in their own liberation movement and in the general struggle for change plus the relationship between one and the other.

TRANSITIONAL REMARKS

Aware of these propositions and categories, we will focus on class conflict in a multiplicity of settings, as upper classes attempt to resolve contradictory relations among themselves as well as with those with less prestige, power, and wealth. For us the problem will not be one of discovering whether an upper class governs. We assume that it does, except momentarily when successfully challenged by militant reformist and total revolutionary movements. That being the case, let us examine two questions. What do the propertied classes *do* with their power, especially when they act through the state? How and when do the oppressed fight back?

Historically, we can observe how some upper classes have involved themselves in preimperialist forms of capitalist colonialism. But before we turn to this page of political history, we must acquaint ourselves with at least one general argument on the origins of the state, in this case the pristine (primary) variety discussed by Morton Fried. Fried's general concern with the origins of the state becomes most relevant for our purposes when he discusses egalitarian and ranked forms of stratification among primitive peoples, for he makes clear that primitive societies are qualitatively different from our own. They are without private property, money, personal profit motive, and state organization. Fried is best in his discussions on reciprocity and redistribution, as well as the absence of private property.

Fried's article (Section Two) is pertinent, for

like the writings of Sahlins, it implies that many western anthropologists have misused the categories of capitalist political economy to characterize people who suffer from the misapplication and misuse of the very categories of classification. What better way to legitimate theft of land, minerals, water, timber, and animals than to attribute to native communities the properties of a capitalism unknown to the primitive world. Natives then lose their strategic resources through processes they presumably accept as part of their indigenous culture. The white westerner signs treaties, as it were, with native "kings" who have the power to dispose of "their property."

What is true of land also holds for native labor and its products. Some anthropologists have even imputed the conspicuous consumption propensities of the Gay Nineties robber barons to native leaders who *do in fact* engage in redistributive ceremonies associated with advanced primitive societies. Worse yet, items of prestige (e.g., wampum) have become capitalistic means of exchange when perceived by many anthropologists through the lenses of *laissez faire* economics. Not too surprisingly, most political sociologists have implicitly accepted this tinted analysis.

Imagine the following situation. After much bloodshed, a foreign army conquers the United States. Organized at home along the lines of community ownership of all resources, the conquerors enlist intellectual aid from their own social scientists who help to define all U.S. property as if it had always been collectively owned by the entire society. This property could then presumably be sold to conquering foreigners through representatives of the alleged collective, namely, the elected politicians. At gunpoint and with lucrative bribes to consider, these politicians sell the society's land as if the homes, factories, mines, and office buildings were not privately owned property subject to traditional and legal protections. Predictably, almost all the foreign social scientists then characterize the transactions, as well as the mores of the Americans, as being consistent with the overall parameters of an indigenous communism ripe for rip-off. All this would be done in the name of objective social science.

Despite the intellectual sham involved, this symbolic characterization would become insti-

tutionally accepted, even by many of the conquered. In textbooks, America would come to
stand for a people who have always welcomed
the wisdom of collective ownership of strategic
resources, yet have in general shared at one
time or another certain secondary characteristics associated with individualism. Mission
legitimation would stand accomplished.

Absurd? Hardly. The very categories of
thought used by social scientists can help to
embed its subjects within a colonial quagmire.

Section Two   *A Reading on Substructure, Superstructure, and State Formation*

On the Evolution of Social Stratification and the State

Morton H. Fried

*The evolutionists never discussed in detail—still less observed—what actually happened
when a society in Stage A changed into a society at Stage B; it was merely argued that
all Stage B societies must somehow have evolved out of the Stage A societies.*

E. R. Leach, 1954, p. 28

To some extent E. R. Leach's charge, which
relates to the evolution of political organization, is unfair. The climate in which pristine
systems of state organization took shape no
longer exists. The presence of numerous modern states and the efficiency of communications
have converted all movements toward state level organization into acculturation phenomena
of some degree. In fact, it seems likely that the
only truly pristine states—those whose origin
was *sui generis*, out of local conditions and not
in response to pressures emanating from an
already highly organized but separate political
entity—are those which arose in the great river
valleys of Asia and Africa and the one or two
comparable developments in the Western Hemisphere. Elsewhere the development of the state
seems to have been "secondary" and to have
depended upon pressures, direct or indirect,
from existing states. Where such pressures exist,
the process of development is accelerated, condensed, and often warped, so that a study of
contemporary state formation is a murky mir-

ror in which to discern the stages in the development of the pristine states.

Further, the conditions of emergence of
rank and stratification as pristine phenomena
are similarly obscured when the impetus to
change is the introduction of aspects of a market economy, money as a medium of exchange,
rationalization of production, and the transformation of labor into a commodity. It would be
extremely gratifying to actually observe societies in transition from a "Stage A" (egalitarian
organization) to a "Stage B" (rank society) and
from there to a "Stage C" (stratification society) and finally from that stage to a "Stage D"
(state society). Indeed, some of these observations have been made, though no one has yet
been able to follow a single society or even
selected exemplars from a group of genetically
related societies through all these stages. Instead a variety of unrelated societies are selected, each representing one or another of the
several possible transitions. Mr. Leach himself
has contributed one of the most valuable of the
accounts dealing with this matter in his analysis
of the movement from *gumlao* to *gumsa* organization among the Kachin of northern Burma.

Following leads supplied in the data of such

■ Reprinted from *Culture in History*, Stanley Diamond, ed. (New York: Columbia University Press,
1960), pp. 713-734. Reprinted by permission of the
publisher and the author.

accounts as that of Leach, just mentioned, of Douglas Oliver (1955), and others, it is our intention to discuss in detail the things which it seems to us must have occurred in order to make the previous transitions possible. Since the data are largely contemporary, the statements are to be viewed as hypotheses in their application to pristine situations beyond even archaeological recall.

Here then is what we seek to accomplish: (1) to suggest some specific institutional developments, the occurrences of which are normal and predictable in viable societies under certain conditions, and in the course of which the whole society perforce moves into a new level of socio-cultural organization; (2) to suggest some of the conditions under which these institutional developments occurred and came to florescence; (3) to indicate as a by-product, that the movement occurs without conscious human intervention, the alterations taking place slowly enough and with such inevitability that the society is revolutionized before the carriers of the culture are aware of major changes.

In approaching this task, it seems wise, if only to head off needless argument, to deny any intention or supplying a single master key to a lock that has defied the efforts of great talents from the time of the Classical civilizations to the present. It seems obvious that other sequences of events than those sketched here could, under proper circumstances, have had similar results. Indeed, the writer is eager to entertain other possibilities and hopes hereby to stimulate others to offer counter suggestions. It will also be obvious to the reader that substantial trains of thought herein stated are merely borrowed and not created by the writer. The recent strides in economic anthropology, and I refer primarily to the work of Polanyi, Arensberg, and Pearson (1957), the clarification of some basic concepts in the study of social organization, and the incentives provided by a seminal paper by Paul Kirchhoff (1935) have all been combined in the present effort.

THE NON-RANK, NON-STRATIFIED SOCIETY

Every human society differentiates among its members and assigns greater or less prestige to individuals according to certain of their attributes. The simplest and most universal criteria

of differential status are those two potent axes of the basic division of labor, age and sex. Beyond are a host of others which are used singly or in combination to distinguish among the members of a category otherwise undifferentiated as to sex or age group. Most important of the characteristics used in this regard are those which have a visible relation to the maintenance of subsistence, such as strength, endurance, agility, and other factors which make one a good provider in a hunting and gathering setting. These characteristics are ephemeral; moreover, the systems of enculturation prevalent at this level, with their emphasis upon the development of subsistence skills, make it certain that such skills are well distributed among the members of society of the proper sex and age groups.

The major deviation from this system of subsistence-oriented statuses is associated with age. However, it makes no difference to the argument of this paper whether the status of the old is high or low, since the basis of its ascription is universal. Anyone who is of the proper sex and manages to live long enough automatically enters into its benefits or disabilities.

Given the variation in individual endowment which makes a chimera of absolute equality, the primitive societies which we are considering are sufficiently undifferentiated in this respect to permit us to refer to them as "egalitarian societies." An egalitarian society can be defined more precisely: it is one in which there are as many positions of prestige in any given age-sex grade as there are persons capable of filling them. If within a certain kin group or territory there are four big men, strong, alert, keen hunters, then there will be four "strong men"; if there are six, or three, or one, so it is. Eskimo society fits this general picture. So do many others. Almost all of these societies are founded upon hunting and gathering and lack significant harvest periods when large reserves of food are stored.

There is one further point I wish to emphasize about egalitarian society. It accords quite remarkably with what Karl Polanyi has called a reciprocal economy.[1]

Production in egalitarian society is characteristically a household matter. There is no specialization; each family group repeats essentially similar tasks. There may be individuals who make certain things better than do others, and these individuals are often given recognition for their skills, but no favored economic role is established, no regular division of labor emerges at this point, and no political power can reside in the status (Leacock, 1958). Exchange in such a society takes place between individuals who belong to different small-scale kin groups; it tends to be casual and is not bound by systems of monetary value based upon scarcity. Such exchanges predominate between individuals who recognize each other as relatives or friends, and may be cemented by such procedures as the provision of hospitality and the granting of sexual access to wives.

Within the local group or band the economy is also reciprocal, but less obviously so. Unlike the exchanges between members of different local groups which, over the period of several years, tend to balance, the exchanges within a group may be quite asymmetrical over time. The skilled and lucky hunter may be continually supplying others with meat; while his family also receives shares from the catch of others, income never catches up with the amounts dispensed. However, the difference between the two quantities is made up in the form of prestige, though, as previously mentioned, it conveys no privileged economic or political role. There frequently is a feeling of transience as it is understood that the greatest hunter can lose his luck or his life, thereby making his family dependent on the largesse of others.

In all egalitarian economies, however, there is also a germ of redistribution. It receives its simplest expression in the family but can grow no more complex than the pooling and redisbursing of stored food for an extended family. In such an embryonic redistributive system the key role is frequently played by the oldest female in the active generation, since it is she who commonly coordinates the household and runs the kitchen.

THE RANK SOCIETY

Since a truly egalitarian human society does not exist, it is evident that we are using the word "rank" in a somewhat special sense. The crux of the matter, as far as we are concerned, is the structural way in which differential prestige is handled in the rank society as contrasted with the way in which egalitarian societies handle similar materials. If the latter have as many positions of valued status as they have individuals capable of handling them, the rank society places additional limitations on access to valued status. The limitations which are added have nothing to do with sex, age group, or personal attributes. Thus, the rank society is characterized by having fewer positions of valued status than individuals capable of handling them. Furthermore, most rank societies have a fixed number of such positions, neither expanding them nor diminishing them with fluctuations in the populations, save as totally new segmented units originate with fission or disappear as the result of catastrophe or sterility.

The simplest technique of limiting status, beyond those already discussed, is to make succession to status dependent upon birth order. This principle, which is found in kinship-organized societies, persists in many more complexly organized societies. At its simplest, it takes the form of primogeniture or ultimogeniture on the level of the family, extended family, or lineage. In more complex forms it may be projected through time so that only the first son of a first son of a first son enjoys the rights of succession, all others having been excluded by virtue of ultimate descent from a position-less ancestor. There are still other variants based on the theme: the accession to high status may be by election, but the candidates may come only from certain lineages which already represent selection by birth order.

The effects of rules of selection based on birth can be set aside by conscious action. Incompetence can be the basis for a decision to by-pass the customary heir, though it would seem more usual for the nominal office to remain vested in the proper heir while a more energetic person performed the functions of the status. A strategic murder could also accomplish the temporary voiding of the rule, but such a solution is much too dangerous and extreme to be practical on the level which we are considering. It is only in rather advanced cultures that the rewards associated with such statuses are sufficient to motivate patricide and fratricide.

Whether accomplished by a rule of succession or some other narrowing device, the rank society as a framework of statuses resembles a triangle, the point of which represents the leading status hierarchically exalted above the others. The hierarchy thus represented has very definite economic significance, going hand in hand with the emergence of a superfamilial redistributive network. The key status is that of the central collector of allotments who also tends to the redistribution of these supplies either in the form of feasts or as emergency seed and provender in time of need. Depending on the extent and maturity of the redistributive system, there will be greater or lesser develop-, ment of the hierarchy. Obviously, small-scale networks in which the members have a face-to-face relationship with the person in the central status will have less need of a bureaucracy.

In the typical ranked society there is neither exploitative economic power nor genuine political power. As a matter of fact, the central status closely resembles its counterpart in the embryonic redistributive network that may be found even in the simplest societies. This is not surprising, for the system in typical rank societies is actually based upon a physical expansion of the kin group and the continuation of previously known kinship rights and obligations. The kingpin of a redistributive network in an advanced hunting and gathering society or a simple agricultural one is as much the victim of his role as its manipulator. His special function is to collect, not to expropriate; to distribute, not to consume. In a conflict between personal accumulation and the demands of distribution it is the former which suffers. Anything else leads to accusations of hoarding and selfishness and undercuts the prestige of the central status; the whole network then stands in jeopardy, a situation which cannot be tolerated. This, by the way, helps to explain that "anomaly" that has so frequently puzzled students of societies of this grade: why are their "chiefs" so often poor, perhaps poorer than any of their neighbors? The preceding analysis makes such a question rhetorical.

It is a further characteristic of the persons filling these high status positions in typical rank societies that they must carry out their functions in the absence of political authority. Two kinds of authority they have: familial, in the extended sense, and sacred, as the redistributive feasts commonly are associated with the ritual life of the community. They do not, however, have access to the privileged use of force, and they can use only diffuse and supernatural sanctions to achieve their ends. Indeed, the two major methods by which they operate are by setting personal examples, as of industriousness, and by utilizing the principles of reciprocity to bolster the emergent redistributive economy.[2]

Despite strong egalitarian features in its economic and political sectors, the developing rank society has strong status differentials which are marked by sumptuary specialization and ceremonial function. While it is a fact that the literature abounds in references to "chiefs" who can issue no positive commands and "ruling classes" whose members are among the paupers of the realm, it must be stated in fairness that the central redistributive statuses *are* associated with fuss, feathers, and other trappings of office. These people sit on stools, have big houses, and are consulted by their neighbors. Their redistributive roles place them automatically to the fore in the religious life of the community, but they are also in that position because of their central kinship status as lineage, clan,[3] or kindred heads.

FROM EGALITARIAN TO RANK SOCIETY

The move from egalitarian to rank society is essentially the shift from an economy dominated by reciprocity to one having redistribution as a major device. That being the case, one must look for the causes of ranking (the limitation of statuses such that they are fewer than the persons capable of handling them) in the conditions which enable the redistributive economy to emerge from its position of latency in the universal household economy, to dominate a network of kin groups which extend beyond the boundaries of anything known on the reciprocal level.

Though we shall make a few suggestions relating to this problem, it should be noted that the focus of this paper does not necessitate immediate disposition of this highly complicated question. In view of the history of our topic, certain negative conclusions are quite significant. Most important of all is the deduction that the roots of ranking do not lie in features of human personality. The structural approach obviates, in this case, psychological explanations. To be precise, we need assume no universal human drive for power[4] in comprehending the evolution of ranking.

It is unthinkable that we should lead a reader this far without indicating certain avenues whereby the pursuit of the problem may be continued. We ask, therefore, what are the circumstances under which fissioning kin or local groups retain active economic interdigitation, the method of interaction being participation in the redistributive network?

In a broad sense, the problem may be seen as an ecological one. Given the tendency of a population to breed up to the limit of its resources and given the probably universal budding of kin and local groups which have reached cultural maxima of unit size, we look into different techno-geographical situations for clues as to whether more recently formed units will continue to interact significantly with their parent units, thereby extending the physical and institutional range of the economy. Such a situation clearly arises when the newer group moves into a somewhat different environment while remaining close enough to the parent group to permit relatively frequent interaction among the members of the two groups. Given such a condition, the maintenance of a redistributive network would have the effect of diversifying subsistence in both units and also providing insurance against food failures in one or the other. This is clearly something of a special case; one of its attractions is the amount of work that has been done upon it by another student of the problem (Sahlins, 1957, 1958).

It is possible to bring to bear upon this problem an argument similar to that employed by Tylor in the question of the incest taboo (Tylor, 1888, p. 267; White, 1948), to wit: the redistributive network might appear as a kind of random social mutation arising out of nonspecific factors difficult to generalize, such as a great personal dependence of the members of the offspring unit upon those they have left behind. Whatever the immediate reason for its appearance, it would quickly show a superiority over simple reciprocal systems in (*a*) productivity, (*b*) timeliness of distribution, (*c*) diversity of diet, and (*d*) coordination of mundane and ceremonial calendars (in a loose cyclical sense). It is not suggested that the success of the institution depends upon the rational cognition of these virtues by the culture carriers; rather the advantages of these institutions would have positive survival value over a long period of time.

We should not overlook one other possibility that seems less special than the first one given above. Wittfogel has drawn our attention on numerous occasions to the social effects of irrigation (see Wittfogel, 1957, for a summation of his latest thinking). The emergence of the superfamilial redistributive network and the rank society seem to go well with the developments he has discussed under the rubric "hydroagriculture," in which some supervision is needed in order to control simple irrigation and drainage projects yet these projects are not large enough to call into existence a truly professional bureaucracy.

It may be wondered that one of the prime explanations for the emergence of ranking, one much favored by notable sociologists of the past, has not appeared in this argument. Reference is to the effects of war upon a society. I would like in this article to take a deliberately extreme stand and assert that military considerations serve to institutionalize rank differences only when these are already implicit or manifest in the economy. I do not believe that pristine developments in the formalization of rank can be attributed to even grave military necessity.

THE STRATIFIED SOCIETY

The differences between rank society and stratified society are very great, yet it is rare that the two are distinguished in descriptive accounts or even in the theoretical literature. Briefly put, the essential difference is this: the rank society operates on the principle of differential status for members with similar abilities, but these statuses are devoid of privileged economic or political power, the former point being the essential one for the present analysis. Meanwhile, the stratified society is distinguished by the differential relationships between the members of the society and its subsistence means—some of the members of the society have unimpeded access to its strategic resources[5] while others have various impediments in their access to the same fundamental resources.

With the passage to stratified society man enters a completely new area of social life.

Whereas the related systems of redistribution and ranking rest upon embryonic institutions that are as universal as family organization (*any* family, elementary or extended, conjugal or consanguineal, will do equally well), the principles of stratification have no real foreshadowing on the lower level.

Furthermore, the movement to stratification precipitated many things which were destined to change society even further, and at an increasingly accelerated pace. Former systems of social control which rested heavily on enculturation, internalized sanctions, and ridicule now required formal statement of their legal principles, a machinery of adjudication, and a formally constituted police authority. The emergence of these and other control institutions were associated with the final shift of prime authority from kinship means to territorial means and describes the evolution of complex forms of government associated with the state. It was the passage to stratified society which laid the basis for the complex division of labor which underlies modern society. It also gave rise to various arrangements of socio-economic classes and led directly to both classical and modern forms of colonialism and imperialism.

THE TRANSITION TO STRATIFIED SOCIETY

The decisive significance of stratification is not that it sees differential amounts of wealth in different hands but that it sees two kinds of access to strategic resources. One of these is privileged and unimpeded; the other is impaired, depending on complexes of permission which frequently require the payment of dues, rents, or taxes in labor or in kind. The existence of such a distinction enables the growth of exploitation, whether of a relatively simple kind based upon drudge slavery or of a more complex type associated with involved divisions of labor and intricate class systems. The development of stratification also encourages the emergence of communities composed of kin parts and non-kin parts which, as wholes, operate on the basis of non-kin mechanisms.

So enormous is the significance of the shift to stratification that previous commentators have found it essential that the movement be associated with the most powerful people in the society. Landtman, for example, says: "It is in

conjunction with the dissimilarity of individual endowments that inequality of wealth has conduced to the rise of social differentiation. As a matter of course the difference as regards property in many cases goes hand in hand with difference in personal qualities. A skilful hunter or fisher, or a victorious warrior, has naturally a better prospect of acquiring a fortune than one who is inferior to him in these respects" (Landtman 1938, p. 68).

If our analysis is correct, however, such is definitely not the case. The statuses mentioned by Landtman are not those which stand to make great accumulations but rather stand to make great give-aways. Furthermore, the leap from distribution to power is unwarranted by the ethnographic evidence.

There are unquestionably a number of ways in which secondary conditions of stratification can emerge. That is, once the development of stratification proceeds from contact with and tutelage by cultures which are at the least already stratified and which may be the possessors of mature state organization, there are many specific ways in which simpler cultures can be transformed into stratified societies. The ways which come quickest to mind include the extension of the complex society's legal definitions of property to the simpler society, the introduction of all-purpose money and wage labor, and the creation of an administrative system for the operation of the simpler society on a basis which is acceptable to the superordinate state. Often the external provenance of these elements in obvious in their misfit appearance. A sharper look may reveal, indeed, that the stratified system is a mere facade operated for and often by persons who have no genuine local identities, while the local system continues to maintain informally, and sometimes in secrecy, the older organization of the society. Put more concretely, this means that "government" appointed chiefs are respected only in certain limited situations and that the main weight of social control continues to rest upon traditional authorities and institutions which may not even be recognized by the ruling power.

An excellent climate for the development of stratification in a simple society can be supplied in a relatively indirect way by a society of advanced organization. Let us take the situation in which a culture has no concept of nuclear family rights to land. The economy is based upon hunting, trapping, and fishing, with the streams and forests being associated in a general way with weakly organized bands which have a decided tendency to fragment and reconstitute, each time with potentially different membership. Subvert this setup with an external market for furs and a substantial basis for stratification has been laid. This system, like the direct intervention of a superordinate state, also seems to have certain limitations, for there is ample evidence that the development of private property in such a system as that just mentioned is confined to trapping lines and does not extend to general subsistence hunting and fishing in the area (see Leacock, 1958).

Another situation that bears study is one in which important trade routes linking two or more advanced societies traverse marginal areas in which simple societies are located. Certain geographical conditions make it possible for the relatively primitive folk to enhance their economies with fruits derived from the plunder of this trade or, in a more mature system, by extorting tribute from the merchants who must pass by. The remoteness of these areas, the difficulty of the terrain, and the extreme difficulties and costs of sending a punitive force to pacify the area often enables the simpler people to harass populations whose cultural means for organized violence far exceeds their own. Be this as it may, the combination of the examples of organization presented by the outposts of complexly organized societies and the availability of commodities which could not be produced in the simple culture may combine to lay the basis for an emergence of stratification. Precisely such conditions seem partially responsible for the political developments described for the Kachin (Leach, 1954, esp. pp. 235, 247 ff.).

None of this seems to apply to the pristine emergence of stratification. As a matter of fact, it is not even particularly suggestive. There is, however, one particular ecological condition that appears in highland Burma which also has been noted elsewhere, each time in association with rather basic shifts in social organization paralleling those already sketched in the previous section of this paper. We refer to the shift from rainfall to irrigation farming, particularly

to the construction of terraced fields. This is admittedly a restricted ethnographic phenomenon and as such it cannot bear the weight of any general theory. It is the suggestive character of these developments and the possibility of extrapolating from them to hypothetical pristine conditions that makes them so interesting.

In brief, the shift to irrigation and terracing is from swiddens or impermanent fields to plots which will remain in permanent cultivation for decades and generations. Whereas we have previously stressed the possible role of hydro-agriculture in the transition from egalitarian to rank society, we now note its possible role in the transition to stratification. This it could accomplish by creating conditions under which access to strategic resources, in this case land and water, would be made the specific prerogative of small-scale kin groups such as minimal lineages or even stem families. Through the emergence of hydro-agriculture a community which previously acknowledged no *permanent* association between particular component units and particular stretches of land now begins to recognize such permanent and exclusive rights. Incidentally, the evidence seems to indicate that the rank-forming tendencies of hydro-agriculture need not occur prior to the tendencies toward stratification: both can occur concomitantly. This in turn suggests that we must be cautious in constructing our theory not to make stratification emerge from ranking, though under particular circumstances this is certainly possible.

A point of considerable interest about hydro-agriculture is that it seems to present the possibility of an emergence of statification in the absence of a problem of overpopulation or resource limitation. We need a great deal of further thought on the matter. Studies of the last two decades, in which a considerably higher degree of agricultural expertise on the part of the fieldworkers has been manifested than was formerly the case, have increasingly tended to show that hydro-agriculture does not invariably out-produce slash and burn and that, other things being equal, a population does not automatically prefer hydro-agriculture as a more rationalized approach to agricultural subsistence. Here we can introduce a factor previously excluded. The hydro-agricultural system invariably has a higher degree of settlement concentration than swiddens. Accordingly, it would seem to have considerable value in the maintenance of systems of defense, given the presence of extensive warfare. Here then, is a point at which military considerations would seem to play an important if essentially reinforcing role in the broad evolutionary developments which we are considering.

The writer is intrigued with another possibility for the emergence of stratification. Once again, the conditions involved seem a little too specific to serve the purpose of a single unified theory. It requires the postulation of a society with a fixed rule of residence, preferably one of the simpler ones such as patrilocality/virilocality or matrilocality/uxorilocality[6] and a fixed rule of descent, preferably one parallel to the residence rule. It further postulates a condition of population expansion such that, given slash and burn agriculture, the society is very near the limits of the carrying capacity of the system. Such conditions are very likely to develop at varying speeds within an area of several hundred miles due to obvious imbalances in reproductive rates and to microecological variation. Now, as long as there is no notable pressure of people on the land, deviation in residence and even in descent will be expectable through quite unusual and lacking in motivation. As the situation grows grave in one area but remains relatively open in another, there may be a tendency for a slight readjustment in residence rules to occur. For example, in a normally virilocal society, the woman who brings her husband back to her natal group transgresses a few customary rules in doing so but presents her agnates with no basic problems in resource allocation since she, as a member of the agnatic group, has her own rights of access which may be shared by the spouse during her lifetime. The complication arises at her death when her husband and all of her children discover themselves to be in an anomalous position since they are not members of the kin community. Where local land problems are not severe and where such breaches of the residence pattern are yet uncommon, it is not unlikely that the aliens will be accepted as *de facto* members of the community with the expectation that future generations will revert to custom, the unorthodox switch of residence fading in memory with the passage of time. Here we have a crude

and informal *ambil-anak*. But as the local community enters worsening ecological circumstances and as the exceptional residence becomes more frequent, the residence and descent rules, particularly the latter, assume greater and greater importance. As the situation continues, the community is slowly altered, though the members of the community may be unable to state exactly what the changes are. The result, however, is clear. There are now two kinds of people in the village where formerly there was only one. Now there are kernel villagers, those who have unimpaired access to land, and those whose tenure rests upon other conditions, such as loyalty to a patron, or tribute, or even a precarious squatter's right.

THE STATE SOCIETY

The word should be abandoned entirely . . . after this chapter the word will be avoided scrupulously and no severe hardship in expression will result. In fact, clarity of expression demands this abstinence.

(Easton, 1953, p. 108)

The word was "state" and the writer, a political scientist, was reacting to some of the problems in his own field in making this judgment, but it does look as if he was pushed to drastic action by the work of some anthropologists in whose hands the concept of state lost all character and utility, finally ending as a cultural universal. E. Adamson Hoebel, one of the few United States anthropologists to make a serious specialization in the field of law and the state, formerly introduced students to this question by remarking that

where there is political organization there is a state. If political organization is universal, so then is the state. One is the group, the other an institutionalized complex of behavior.

(Hoebel, 1949, p. 376)

In a revision of the same book after a few years, Hoebel's treatment of the subject seems to indicate that he is in the process of rethinking the matter. His summary words, however, repeat the same conclusion:

Political organization is characteristic of every society. . . . That part of culture that is recognized as political organization is what constitutes the state.

(Hoebel, 1958, p. 506)

This is a far cry from the approach of evolutionists to the state as exemplified in Sumner and Keller (1927, I, 700):

> The term state is properly reserved for a somewhat highly developed regulative organization..... It is an organization with authority and discipline essential to large-scale achievements, as compared with the family, for example, which is an organization on the same lines but simpler and less potent.

Without making a special issue of the definition of the state (which would easily consume the entire space of this article, if not the volume) let me note one used by the jurist Léon Duguit which conveys the sense most useful to the point of view of this paper:

> En prenant le mot dans son sens le plus général, on peut dire qu'il y a un État toutes les fois qu'il existe dans une société donnée une différenciation politique, quelque rudimentaire ou quelque compliquée et developée qu'elle soit. Le mot État désigne soit les gouvernants où le pouvoir politique, soit la société elle-même, où existe cette différenciation entre gouvernants et gouvernés et où existe par là même une puissance politique.

(Duguit, 1921, p. 395)

The difference between Hoebel and Duguit seems to be in the clear statement of power. Reviewing our own paper in the light of this difference we note our previous emphasis on the absence of coercive economic or political power in the egalitarian and rank societies. It is only in the stratified society that such power emerges from embryonic and universal foreshadowings in familial organization.

The maturation of social stratification has manifold implications depending on the precise circumstances in which the developments take place. All subsequent courses, however, have a certain area of overlap; the new social order, with its differential allocation of access to strategic resources, must be maintained and strengthened. In a simple stratified society in which class differentials are more implicit than explicit the network of kin relations covers a sufficient portion of the total fabric of social relations so that areas not specifically governed by genuine kinship relations can be covered by their sociological extensions. The dynamic of stratification is such that this situation cannot endure. The stratified kin group emphasizes its exclusiveness: it erodes the corporative economic functions formerly associated with stipulated kinship and at every turn it amputates extensions of the demonstrated kin unit. The result of this pruning is that the network of kin relations fails more and more to coincide with the network of personal relations. Sooner or later the discrepancy is of such magnitude that, were non-kin sanctions and non-kin agencies absent or structured along customary lines only, the society would dissolve in uncomposable conflict.

The emergent state, then, is the organization of the power of the society on a supra-kin basis. Among its earliest tasks is the maintenance of general order, but scarcely discernible from this is its need to support the order of stratification. The defense of a complete system of individual statuses is impossible so the early state concentrates on a few key statuses (helping to explain the tendency to convert any crime into either sacrilege or *lèse majesté*) and on the basic principles of organization, e.g., the idea of hierarchy, property, and the power of the law.

The implementation of these primary functions of the state gives rise to a number of specific and characteristic secondary functions, each of which is associated with one or more particular institutions of its own. These secondary functions include population control in the most general sense (the fixing of boundaries and the definition of the unit; establishment of categories of membership; census). Also a secondary function is the disposal of trouble cases (civil and criminal laws moving toward the status of codes; regular legal procedure; regular officers of adjudication). The protection of sovereignty is also included (maintenance of military forces; police forces and power; eminent domain). Finally, all of the preceding require fiscal support, and this is achieved in the main through taxation and conscription.

In treating of this bare but essential list of state functions and institutions, the idea of the state as a universal aspect of culture dissolves as a fantasy. The institutions just itemized may be made to appear in ones or twos in certain primitive societies by exaggeration and by the neglect of known history. In no egalitarian society and in no rank society do a majority of the functions enumerated appear regardless of their guise. Furthermore there is no indication of their appearance as a unified functional response to basic sociocultural needs except in those stratified societies which are verging upon statehood.

THE TRANSITION TO STATE

Just as stratified society grew out of antecedent forms of society without the conscious awareness of the culture carriers, so it would seem that the state emerged from the stratified society in a similar, inexorable way. If this hypothesis is correct, then such an explanation as the so-called conquest theory can be accepted only as a special case of "secondary-state" formation. The conquests discussed by such a theorist as Franz Oppenheimer (1914) established not stratification but superstratification, either the conqueror or the conquered, or perhaps even both, already being internally stratified.

The problem of the transition to state is so huge and requires such painstaking application to the available archaeological and historical evidence that it would be foolish to pursue it seriously here. Let us conclude, therefore, by harking back to statements made at the outset of this paper, and noting again the distinction between pristine and secondary states. By the former term is meant a state that has developed *sui generis* out of purely local conditions. No previous state, with its acculturative pressures, can be discerned in the background of a pristine state. The secondary state, on the other hand, is pushed by one means or another toward a higher form of organization by an external power which has already been raised to statehood.

The number of pristine states is strictly limited; several centuries, possibly two millennia, have elapsed since the last one emerged in Meso-America, and there seems to be no possibility that any further states of the pristine type will evolve, though further research may bring to light some of the distant past of which we yet have no positive information. In all, there seems to have been some six centers at which pristine states emerged, four in the Old

World and two in the New: the Tigris-Euphrates area, the region of the lower Nile, the country drained by the Indus and the middle course of the Huang Ho where it is joined by the Han, Wei, and Fen. The separate areas of Peru-Bolivia and Meso-America complete the roster.

If there is utility in the concept of the pristine state and if history has been read correctly in limiting the designation to the six areas just enumerated, then we discover a remarkable correlation between areas demanding irrigation or flood control and the pristine state. Certainly this is no discovery of the author. It is one of the central ideas of Wittfogel's theory and has received extensive treatment from Julian Steward and others (see Steward, 1955, pp. 178-209; Steward et al., 1955). The implication of the "hydraulic theory" for this paper, however, is that the development of the state as an internal phenomenon is associated with major tasks of drainage and irrigation. The emergence of a control system to ensure the operation of the economy is closely tied to the appearance of a distinctive class system and certain constellations of power in the hands of a managerial bureaucracy which frequently operates below a ruler who commands theoretically unlimited power.

It is an interesting commentary on nineteenth-century political philosophy that the starting point of so many theories was, of necessity, the Classical world of Greece and Rome. According to the present hypothesis, however, both of these great political developments of antiquity were not pristine but secondary formations which built on cultural foundations laid two thousand years and more before the rise of Greece. Furthermore, it would seem that the active commercial and military influences of the truly ancient pristine states, mediated through the earliest of the secondary states to appear in Asia Minor and the eastern Mediterranean littoral, were catalysts in the events of the northern and western Mediterranean.

CONCLUSION

The close of a paper like this, which moves like a gadfly from time to time, place to place, and subject matter to subject matter, and which never pauses long enough to make a truly detailed inquiry or supply the needed documentation, the close of such a paper requires an apology perhaps more than a conclusion.

I have been led to write this paper by my ignorance of any modern attempt to link up the contributions which have been made in many subdisciplines into a single unified theory of the emergence of social stratification and the state. That the theory offered here is crude, often too special, and by no means documented seems less important than that it may be used as a sitting duck to attract the fire and better aim of others.

NOTES

1. The reader may object to crediting Polanyi with the concept of a reciprocal economy. While it is true that Thurnwald and Malinowski earlier expressed similar concepts, and Durkheim, with his distinction between segmental and organic societies, also foreshadows this development, it awaited Polanyi's analysis to place reciprocal economies into systematic harmony with other, more complex types of economy, such as the redistributive type discussed later on, and the market kind as well. For Polanyi's definitions of each of these types see Polanyi, Arensberg, and Pearson, 1957, pp. 250-56.

2. For an ethnographic illustration of this point see Oliver, 1955, pp. 422 ff.

3. These, of course, would be ranked lineages or ranked clans. Cf. Fried, 1957, pp. 23-26.

4. As does Leach, 1954, p. 10.

5. Strategic resources are those things which, given the technological base and environmental setting of the culture, maintain subsistence. See Fried, 1957, p. 24.

6. Our residence terms follow usage suggested by J. L. Fischer (1958).

REFERENCES

Duguit, Léon. 1921. Traité de droit constitutionnel. 2d ed. Vol. 1. Paris.

Easton, David. 1953. The Political System. New York.

Fischer, J. L. 1958. "The Classification of Residence in Censuses," *American Anthropologist*, 60:508-17.

Fried, Morton H. 1957. "The Classification of Corporate Unilineal Descent Groups," *Journal of the Royal Anthropological Institute*, 87:1-29.

Hoebel, E. Adamson. 1949. Man in the Primitive World. 1st ed. New York. ——— 1958. Man in the Primitive World. 2d ed. New York.

Kirchhoff, Paul. 1935. "The Principles of Clanship in Human Society." (Ms; cf. *Davidson Journal of Anthropology* 1 [1955]).

Landtman, Gunnar. 1938. The Origin of the Inequality of the Social Classes. London.

Leach, E. R. 1954. Political Systems of Highland Burma. Cambridge, Mass.

Leacock, Eleanor. 1958. "Status among the Montagnais-Naskapi of Labrador," *Ethnohistory*, 5:Part 3:200-209.

Oliver, Douglas. 1955. A Solomon Island Society. Cambridge, Mass.

Oppenheimer, Franz. 1914. The State: Its History and Development Viewed Sociologically. New York.

Polanyi, Karl, Conrad M. Arensberg, and Harry W. Pearson, eds. 1957. Trade and Market in the Early Empires. Glencoe, Ill.

Sahlins, Marshall. 1958. Social Stratification in Polynesia. Seattle.

——— 1957. "Differentiation by Adaptation in Polynesian Societies," *Journal of the Polynesian Society*, 66:291-300.

Steward, Julian H. 1955. Theory of Culture Change. Urbana, Ill.

Steward, Julian H., *et al.* 1955. Irrigation Civilizations: A Comparative Study. Social Science Monographs #1, Washington, D.C.

Sumner, W. G., and A. G. Keller. 1927. The Science of Society. New Haven, Conn.

Tylor, Edward B. 1888. "On a Method of Investigating the Development of Institutions; Applied to Laws of Marriage and Descent," *Journal of the Royal Anthropological Institute*, 18:245-69.

White, Leslie. 1948. "The Definition and Prohibition of Incest," *American Anthropologist*, 50:416-35.

Wittfogel, Karl A. 1957. Oriental Despotism. New Haven, Conn.

Chapter 2 Tribal Protest and Classical Imperialism

Section One   *Collision and Flux*

OBJECTS OF DISINTEGRATING DEPENDENCE

What are the conditions that move populations toward collective struggle? To reply to this question, we must understand the process and outcome of *exploitative dependence.* Briefly, we often rely on the very thing that we exploit but do not replenish. We do thereby create some of the preconditions of costly revolt against ourselves. There is no better example than the reliance of heartland capitalist countries such as the United States, England, France, and West Germany on preindustrial nations for food and raw materials while at the same time the heartland's corporations and military organizations are destroying the hinterland's pristine resources and indigenous customs for the exploiters' profit. Ironically, both are romanticized and cherished by colonial businessmen and intellectuals geared to the investment of available funds in emasculated hinterland countries rearranged for the marketing of land, labor, and goods. Few are more distraught than these businessmen when this allocation is questioned by the machete, for they had viewed their presence as benevolently progressive.

As the next three chapters hope to make clear, foreign imposition of market rules of commodity use took its toll among primitives and agrarians, many of whom later organized against the western intrusions of the eighteenth, nineteenth, and twentieth centuries. These retaliatory efforts proved to be fruitless in most cases, for preindustrial peoples were outgunned. Nonetheless, they did strike back. Why and how did they do so? More precisely, what are the sources of both successful and unsuccessful political protest among primitive peoples undergoing changes because of intensive Western contact?

To determine what moves an oppressed people to work together for their liberation, we will discuss the Melanesian peoples as a case in point. When observing the Melanesians and their struggles, we focus on cargo cults, as well as their successors as they went about making their collective replies to colonialism. The collective outrage expressed in their religious millenary outpourings tell of their dispossession by the colonial white man.

CONSERVATIVE VERSUS RADICAL EXPLANATIONS OF THE PROBLEM

If we examine the protests of primitive peoples who live at a low level of technology and without private property, we can discover *two* prominent and white explanations of the content and origins of these protests: the conservative and the radical definitions of the problem.

Suppose that a messianic Solomon Islander were to lead a group of native cane cutters to destroy a missionary hut, burn a South Pacific cane crop, and gather at the mini-landing strip of the local airport to await the arrival of American transport planes laden with candies, medical supplies, and sports equipment. The conservative academic buff would in all likelihood point to the source of the problem by singling out the native leader. From the point of view of the conservative analyst, it would be within the demagogue's crazed mind that one could observe the *demonic idea. It* had moved the black demagogue to rally duped natives about him as he strove to aggrandize his own status and power through a series of irrational acts designed to maximize his own ego satisfaction; for man, especially when insane, is an insatiable egotist. Furthermore, this mad black demagogue would destroy the society's "fabric" at the expense of a presumably just moral order.

In keeping with this perspective, colonial authorities in Melanesia have often placed messianic Melanesian political leaders in a prison for those judged to be insane. The prophet of utopia becomes the crazed resident of the mental wing of a state prison. The historian Vittorio Lanternarri has cited numerous and crass instances of this form of political incarceration.[1] The general ideology of the colonial white man was clear. The colonial society is without any significant imperfections and, hence, without structural contradictions that might move people to articulate disloyalty. Only inner and crazed impulse could produce such leadership.

The same psychological reductionism was reserved for a politicized successor to the cargo cults, most notably among the militant copra plantation workers employed around the Rabaul, New Guinea, during the period between World Wars I and II. As Worsley wrote:

> It was at Rabaul, capital of the Mandated Territory and the centre of the principal area of European plantations, that the most important strike of the inter-war period took place in 1929. Here, practically all the native labourers, including the "boss-boys" and the great majority of the police, suddenly left town and gathered at the Methodist and Catholic mission-stations nearby. The 3,000 strikers were apparently influenced by foreign seamen (variously described as "West Indians," "White," "Samoan," "Samarai" and "American Negroes") who jeered at them for accepting such low wages: 5/- per month for a labourer, with an average earning of 6/-. Led by the native master of a schooner and a Sergeant-Major of Police, and by the "boss-boys" and the police, the entire operation was conducted in complete secrecy and disciplined order. Partly through lack of food, but also because expectations of concessions of £1 per month were not forthcoming, the strike ended without violence, apart from some turbulence amongst the "Catholic" group.
>
> The rage of the Europeans knew no bounds. Demands for the removal of the Acting Government Secretary and the Inspector of Police were made, a "Citizens Association" was formed in opposition to the "pro-native" Government, and sanctions

against corporal punishment were temporarily suspended as employers thrashed their workers. Two hundred of the 217 police had struck; the leaders of the police were given two to three years' hard labour; the rest received lesser sentences. In the subsequent inquiry, carried out against a background of White rage, the board of inquiry poured scorn upon the idea that any "more deep seated and more involved" questions were involved *than the foolishness of sheep-like natives under bad leadership.* [Italics supplied.] The board urged the imposition of a *maximum* limit to wages, denied that there was any "general demand for higher wages," and suggested the removal of the labour lines farther out of Rabaul and the introduction of curfew passes.[a] Evidently, the European had learnt little from the strike; but the native had learnt a good deal, for in 1937 another strike occurred in which a doubling of existing wage-levels was demanded.[2]

Whatever the merits of accounting for conflict and struggle between brown cane cutters and white overseers by pointing to the ideas and the minds of foolish leadership, this interpretation fails to indicate whether in fact such psychological processes were at work. Here the conservative analyst might well confuse his interpretation of mental phenomena with the actual interneural activities of the natives.

Again, why would natives be predisposed to follow a leader—demonic or otherwise—in these violent episodes? Finally, why should such a protest leadership develop at all? After all, charismatic leaders are not always present.

A radical definition of conflict makes more sense. This perspective examines how thoroughly disrupted economies move people to struggle politically. Perhaps most pertinent in this regard, especially in the context of colonialism, are the writings of Rosa Luxemburg. Her seminal ideas on the upsetting effects of colonialism on peoples' lives serve to clarify the notion of exploitative dependency, especially with respect to the changing economic conditions which press people to fight.

[a]TNG, Ann. Rpt., 1928-1929, pp. 19–20, 107–109.

[2] Peter M. Worsley, *The Trumpet Shall Sound* (London: MacGibbon and Kee, 1968), pp. 47–48, by permission.

[1] See Vittorio Lanternari, *The Religions of the Oppressed* (New York: Alfred A. Knopf, 1963), p. 210.

ROSA LUXEMBURG AND NATURAL ECONOMY

Rosa Luxemburg observed how preimperial capitalism, in essence, the entrepreneurial and family-owned firms of the late eighteenth and early nineteenth centuries destroyed natural economy, only to replace it with a form to be subverted by capitalism.[3] She held that natural economy exists when the community produces for communal needs and not for personal sale. The preindustrial peoples in primitive societies did not create goods to be sold for coin in a market, since neither coin nor market existed. Moreover, Luxemburg observed how economic ties were embedded in family relations regulated by the cake of custom, both in the primitive community and the agrarian village. Economic activities were in fact family relations, although not all family ties were economic.

The family and village rules of primitive peoples determined how goods would be produced and distributed. Not by the axioms of supply and demand celebrated by Adam Smith, not by the unfettered flow of labor enunciated by nineteenth-century capitalism, and certainly not by the ready exploitation of fields, forests, and waters called for by the resourceful protestant missionaries during the eighteenth, nineteenth, and twentieth centuries; rather, by the custom of collective sharing, the age–sex division of labor, and the collective ownership of land and water did they conduct their economic relations. Nor would the native peoples budge from those time-honored commitments when Western capitalist man attempted to "liberate" them from "provincial" customs.

The ideology was clear. Western capitalism was prepared to act violently to liberate the natives from the fetters of traditionalism. Western business firms such as the Hudson's Bay Company and Lytton Industries had accumulated business savings and were ready to rework native lives for profit. Silly native rules would not be allowed to stand in the way.

In Rosa Luxemburg's analysis, and history has borne her out, Western business firms mounted a struggle against primitive people embedded in natural economy in order.

To gain immediate possession of important sources of productive forces such as land, game in primeval forests, minerals, precious stones and ores, products of exotic flora such as rubber, etc. . . .

To "liberate" labour power and to coerce it into service. . . .

To introduce a commodity economy. . . . [and]

To separate trade and agriculture.[4]

The gaining of possession of land, forests, minerals, and precious stones by preimperialist business firms complemented the North American and Western European market demands for such property. Indeed, during the middle and late nineteenth centuries as the Western capitalist family firm and the partnership gave way increasingly to the joint stock corporation, the growing mammoths in railroads, steel, rubber, and chemicals came to depend increasingly on these recently captured resources. The copper mines opened in the Belgian Congo, tungsten deposits extracted from Bengal, the copra plantations organized among Trobriand Islanders, the gold mines worked by the New Caledonians, and the rubber plantations planted and maintained by the Upper Amazonians. The list was long. Businessmen wanted the raw materials, and the upper classes sought as luxuries commodities such as the diamonds of British Guiana and the scented sandalwood of Polynesia. But from the point of view of natives, these trees, minerals, and stones were community possessions to which native peoples had always enjoyed a natural claim. They resented the depletion through intensive trade of the resources, especially since they were forced to labor to extract, accumulate, and load the foreign harvest.

Under these conditions, liberation of native labor from the customary work habits such as the woman gathering roots, herbs, and snails and the husband hunting for turtle, salmon, and boar, became a prerequisite for the successful launching of a sugar plantation, a cotton enterprise, or a gold mine. Native labor had to learn to work for a wage. Native labor had to adjust its work habits to accept the self-discipline associated with working ten to twelve hours a day for somebody else. Natives had to learn to

[3] Rosa Luxemburg, *The Accumulation of Capital* (New Haven: Yale University Press, 1951), especially chapters 27–32.

[4] *Ibid.,* p. 369.

accept the idea of keeping for themselves only a fraction of what they had produced, even though what they earned was often less than what they needed for their families.

Clearly, primitive peoples had departed from production for communal use and collective sufficiency to production for profitable exchange and foreign profit. Labor had become an exploited commodity. On another level, that of adjustment, natives had to accustom themselves to constructing docks and loading ships. They had to learn to accept the sight of friends being lashed in the name of labor discipline by German, Australian, or English overseers, angered by the accidental destruction of a tool or the illegal withdrawal of labor services. From the point of view of Western colonial man, labor had to be liberated from diversified economy unrelated to profit and put to work in monoagricultural settings specializing in one crop, one ore, one specialty of some kind, geared to overseas markets.

The owners of capital strove to introduce the use of wages to press natives to work and to purchase Western commodities such as shoes produced in Lowell, Massachusetts, trinkets glued together in London, cutlery manufactured in Sheffield, matches made in Stockholm, and rum distilled in Kingston, Jamaica. Following a period of bartering, these goods were to be exchanged for the natives' raw materials through the facilitating device of currency that was introduced, controlled, and used by the West. Induced coastal native demand for currency and what it could buy proved to be the primary source of trade. Later, under conditions of full-fledged imperialism, railroads were built, steamboats constructed, and the continental interiors reworked by natives now locked into a system that simultaneously paid them low wages and yet made them consumers. They had become dependent on the very wage and spending processes which subordinated them.

Finally, trade and agriculture had to be separated. At one time, ordinary household items such as shoes and pants were fashioned in the village by the family and were subject to customary village regulations on transfer. Rules of barter, not supply and demand, were paramount in deciding the flow. Elman Service has commented on the nature of exchange among primitive peoples prior to their reorganization by Western commerce and industry.

In this system, goods are distributed on the basis of reciprocity and/or redistribution. There are two types of reciprocity—general and specific. In the general case, person or group A gives certain items to person or group B with the understanding that at a later but unspecified time, group B will in turn give certain unspecified items to person or group A. By contrast, specific reciprocity itemizes time and item. In the case of redistribution, what is involved is a pyramidal flow of items during two succeeding time intervals. During the first time interval, the producers of items, such as breadfruit, pass this item up the status and power ladder to the paramount family within the society. At a second point in time, often during a festive occasion, the paramount chief or tribal leader passes these items back to their original producers. This is a nonexploitative exchange, for all can see that the dominant families keep only fine feathers and other esoterica for themselves. One more point: as one moves among primitive people from the bottom of the general evolutionary ladder to a higher rung, there is a decline of general reciprocity and an increase in redistribution.

Clearly, these customary regulations were a hindrance to trade in Western capitalist terms. They did not include the rules of sale for profit. Western traders became acutely aware of these values when they found them contradicting the rules of ongoing Western trade, for those indigenous rules were part of a native self-sufficiency. Being so organized, the natives saw little reason to forego reciprocity and redistribution in order to purchase items with foreign currency. The demands of market economy forced the businessmen to convince the natives through forceful, even violent means.

THE ATTEMPTED RESOLUTION OF CONTRADICTIONS THROUGH FORCE

Western business firms dealt abruptly with the contradiction between native organization and capitalist demand.[5] In the case of raw

[5] In this section I have relied heavily on Worsley's *The Trumpet Shall Sound, op. cit.,* and Douglas Oliver's *The Pacific Islands* (Garden City, N. Y.: Anchor Books, Doubleday, 1961).

materials, these settlers simply occupied the islands, peninsulas, valleys and mountains in question and redefined ownership to favor themselves. What had been communally owned became privately exploited. Land was taken by Western firms and settlers. The land was expropriated, generally with little if any compensation, sometimes with a kick in the rump for the recalcitrant native. Land was customarily seized, but sometimes it was taken and given to a leading native person or family living in the desired area. Sometimes the leading person would be the tax collector chosen by the white man, as in the case of the Zamindar in India, who took land in lieu of taxes during periods of calamity and the aftermaths. The coopted native leadership could in turn make the land available to the white man through sale or lease. The natives sometimes disagreed with the redefinition and new use of their land for a plantation, a mine, a mill, a military base, or a wharf; but after near-genocidal disaster in their camps, they discovered that they had no choice but to go along with the change or risk further onslaughts.

In the case of native labor, the white aliens imposed a state organization on the black harvestors, miners, and longshoremen. The alien state functioned to gather the necessary taxes and to encourage the otherwise recalcitrant laborer to do the job. Crucial in carrying out the twin tasks of exacting the necessary toil from the limbs and the energy from the soils were the head tax and corvée labor. The English government, for example, would levy a per annum tax on a native male. Not being in a money economy, he would be unable to pay this "head tax" in the specific currency, e.g., pounds or shillings. To obtain this money, he had to work on the docks loading copra, spend long work days in gold fields, or work with his machete throughout the cane-cutting season. Corvée labor was somewhat different in form, although identical in function. It simply required that each eligible native provide free services to the state in order to carry out a particular task such as the building of a road or a dam, for a certain period of time.

In this context, laborers were more valuable than monies from taxes; hence it was in the interest of exploitative governments to impose head taxes and so obtain more from natives than the nominal sums alone. Actually, imperial governments around the world used the head tax to compel strong native bodies to work on plantations, in mines, and for railroads.

Finally, and beyond wage and corvée labor, thousands of natives were simply seized, shanghaied aboard trains, ships, and other vehicles, and transported to work in diamond mines, on nitrate islands, and in houses of prostitution. Illustratively, natives were seized by whites on the western coast of Latin America (Peru was a favorite area, as was eastern Oceania) and forced to work under labor contracts to dig guano accumulations used by German manufacturers and agriculturalists. These laborers seldom returned to their homes from the guano pits. Again, hundreds if not thousands of lovely Marquesan Island women were captured by whites through guile as well as force and transported to Hong Kong and Singapore, where they soon died as diseased prostitutes. East Asian and Pacific Island peoples were slugged and dragged aboard ships bound for South African gold fields, a destination never reached by many of these terrorized people. On more than one occasion did the captain's reaction to the approach of a British patrol-cruiser lead to the watery demise of the ship's cargo. Chained Chinese were hauled from below decks to the gunwale and then shoved over the side before the English cruiser could arrest the captain engaged in the illegal but aptly named practice of "shanghai-ing." In this way untold numbers of men and women drowned in the Indian Ocean less than one hundred years ago.

Native labor thereby failed to enjoy capitalist liberation from native custom. Nor was this atrocity unique. Hobson told of thousands of Belgian Congolese losing both their hands and feet when they refused to perform compulsory-corvée labor, to pay the head tax, or to conform to another law designed to extract labor. Belgian magistrates administered on-the-spot retribution during the last two decades of the nineteenth century by using giant knives to lop off the appendages.

Fewer than 3,000 of the original 80,000 Marquesan people (a Polynesian group) survived the period of early hit-and-miss trade contact. As Oliver has indicated, most of them died of venereal disease, whooping cough, pneumonia, tuberculosis, measles, and murder.[6] As social

---

[6] Oliver, *op. cit.,* p. 208.

scientists we should divorce ourselves momentarily from analytical abstraction and listen to their screams. If we could relive their experiences, we might begin to comprehend the enormity of what happened throughout much of the Pacific, Asia, Africa, and Latin America as people were forced to participate in a new economic system geared to discipline and profit.

The West followed a similar pattern when it liberated trade from agriculture. Business firms simply sold their commodities to natives who used their scant wages to buy these cheap but relatively high-quality commodities. Given the successful foreign competition, the local families simply ceased to produce these items. The loss of labor and skill became especially noticeable during times of worldwide depression, for it was then that the people would go for years without wages necessary to purchase goods. They could not return to their old ways, for they had forgotten the necessary skills and lost the traditional consumers' values. The copra mill, the cane field, the jute mill, the rubber plantation, and the gold mine—all would close for years, sometimes forever. Thus were native populations introduced to the vicissitudes of the international business cycle.

PREPARATORY CONDITIONS

Rosa Luxemburg and others[7] have analyzed those forces which we may describe as "preparatory," generally economic considerations that have motivated people to participate in revolutionary change. These factors served both to jar native peoples from their habitat and to press them to accept new economic standards that could not be met consistently. Clearly, no native protest movement could occur without such a background. The preparatory considerations were necessary, but not sufficient, however; their mere presence was not enough to bring about revolutionary change. In addition there were facilitating, helping, and translating mechanisms at work whenever native peoples organized a successful political movement. We discuss these mechanisms at the end of this chapter.

[7] Two foremost writers in this regard are Lyford P. Edwards, *The Natural History of Revolution* (New York: Russell and Russell, 1965), and Crane Brinton, *The Anatomy of Revolution* (New York: Vintage Books, 1957).

REVOLUTIONARY SUCCESS AND EVOLUTIONARY POTENTIAL: A HYPOTHESIS

Whether a given group was in fact successful in initiating revolutionary change depended on its position in the general evolutionary scale. In the case of bands, members lacked the weapons, numbers, and organization to react successfully. Tribes were somewhat more successful, but their original cultural innocence prevented them from focusing clearly on their problems. It would take considerable travail and struggle before they could organize a protest such as the cargo cults. The colonial impact on chiefdoms generally resulted in the cooptative-recruitment of the indigenous leadership of a particular chiefdom. Allied with whites inside a government dominated by white foreigners, after a period of warfare among the chiefdoms, the coopted became paramount with the aid of the colonial power.

Thus, if we exclude the bands, we can observe how the "privilege of backwardness" may work to the benefit of tribes relative to chiefdoms. The tribes moved to the creation of countermovements, and from there to demands for political and economic independence. By contrast, the chiefdoms were more likely to bypass the stage of messianic protest and proceed through a period of power consolidation engineered by a dominant chiefdom allied with a white foreign power. The end result is a pacified political territory ruled essentially and indefinitely by whites.

Relative structural superiority (see Table 2) among native peoples may well lead to predictable cooptation and millenary preemption.

TRANSITIONAL REMARKS

These general propositions need to be fleshed out with historical materials and integrated into a general theory of insurgence. Let us begin with Elman R. Service's analysis of the Law of Evolutionary Potential, and then move to Peter M. Worsley's historical account of cargo cults in the southern portion of Oceania. Following these readings, we will continue our analysis of the conditions that prompt persons to move against the state through collective and violent means.

Section Two   *Readings on Cargo Cults and Potential*

The Law of Evolutionary Potential
Elman R. Service

The mid-century revival of interest in cultural evolutionism in anthropology seems to be a limited and one-sided one so far, concerned almost exclusively with problems of specific adaptation. Presumably, too, a large number of anthropologists remain uncommitted even to this. At any rate, evolutionism in its general as well as specific aspects needs further explication, especially in the context of its applications. A remark frequently made by anthropologists is that they want to be shown how evolutionary theory can be *used* before they pass judgment on it. This, we think, is a perfectly fair requirement. . . .

In order to test our ability to explain and predict the evolutionary progress of specific populations and cultures, we must first define the expectable results of the various evolutionary processes in their interaction. Once these relations have been discussed generally we shall attempt various interpretations with them. The illustrations will range diversely from some simple anthropological problems of the primitive world to the complex question of the modern and future world and America's place in it.

One of the virtues of the evolutionary view is that, more than any other perspective, it makes the concerns of cultural anthropology directly relevant to modern life and to the future. As Tylor once put it, it is the "knowledge of man's course of life, from the remote past to the present," the study of the *evolution* of culture, that will enable us to forecast the future. The modern social sciences, now that they are almost exclusively nontemporal, or functional, have not been able to help us to judge the future and thus guide our actions and deliberations in relation to modern political problems. The past-as-related-to-the-future has long since been left to dogmatic Marxists or to the more respectable but nevertheless equally

■ Taken from Marshall D. Sahlins and Elman R. Service, eds., *Evolution and Culture* (Ann Arbor: The University of Michigan Press, 1960), pp. 93–110, by permission.

nonscientific "universal" historians such as Brooks Adams, Spengler, Huntington, and Toynbee.

Let us briefly review those characteristics of evolution that we now want to consider as interrelated phenomena. First, it has been noted that evolution can be regarded as a double-faceted phenomenon. On the one hand any given system—a species, a culture, or an individual—improves its chances for survival, progresses in the efficiency of energy capture, by increasing its adaptive specialization. This is specific evolution. The obverse is directional advance or progress stage by stage, measured in absolute terms rather than by criteria relative to the degree of adaptation to particular environments. The systems also are assigned to stages irrespective of their phylogenetic relationship. A man is higher than an armadillo; yet they are each adapted differently and are contemporary species and members of different lines of descent. This is general evolution.

We have also seen that there is a limiting factor inherent in specific evolution. This has been called the Principle of Stabilization, and it occurs as an end product of adaptation. Specific evolution means increasing adaptation to an environment, which is to say that it ultimately becomes nonprogressive. Because adaptation is self-limiting at some point, if all the forms of life and culture were to become fully adapted, evolution, whether viewed specifically or generally, would halt.

The fact of the matter is, of course, that evolution continues precisely because new forms come into being which are *not* highly specialized. Some of these more generalized mutants have a potential for new kinds of environments. Thus we have the contradictory-sounding propositions: the evolution of species takes place *because* of adaptation; the evolution of the total system of life takes place *in spite of* adaptation.

Another factor, the dominance which a higher species may exert over lower species, tends to be the most effective inhibitor of any potential that may reside in an unspecialized species. Much of the struggle and warfare that is endemic in both the world of biology and of culture can be interpreted as the contest between the dominance factor and the potentiality factor. This also may be phrased in contradictory-sounding statements: specific evolution is a movement from homogeneity to heterogeneity, from few to more species; yet one of the frequent consequences of evolution is the movement from heterogeneity toward homogeneity, as a higher dominant form such as man spreads at the expense of the lower forms.

These ideas should not be unfamiliar to anyone conversant with recent literature on biological evolution. Julian Huxley, in particular, has pointed out that evolution is not a straight line of progress from one highly developed species to the next highest but that it proceeds in zigzag fashion as advances are countered by stabilization or dominance, that limitation is as likely as improvement. Most relevant to the present discussion is the recognition that what Simpson has called "opportunism" for evolutionary advance exists as a better possibility for a more generalized form than for the specialized, well-adapted and therefore stabilized one. As Huxley put it: ". . . the further a trend toward specialization has proceeded, the deeper will be the biological groove in which (the species) has thus entrenched itself."[1] Or again: ". . . there is no certain case on record of a line showing a high degree of specialization giving rise to a new type. All new types which themselves are capable of adaptive radiation seem to have been produced by relatively unspecialized lines."[2]

One of the main purposes of this [paper] is to show that this characteristic of biological evolution is expectable in the evolution of culture as well. Further, we wish to state the proposition in the form of a law—that is, to affirm its generality as explicitly as possible. It has been introduced in the context of biological evolution in order to argue for its acceptability as an idea; evolutionary ideas expressed in biological terms seem to find readier acceptance than they do in cultural terms. But this should not be taken to mean that the idea began in biology and that now it is simply being carried over into the cultural context. As we shall see,

there are evidences of its prior realization, incipiently at least, by students of cultural phenomena.

The law, which may be called The Law of Evolutionary Potential, is a simple one: The more specialized and adapted a form in a given evolutionary stage, the smaller is its potential for passing to the next stage. Another way of putting it which is more succinct and more in conformity with preceding chapters is: Specific evolutionary progress is inversely related to general evolutionary potential.

It is important to remember that because of the stabilization of specialized species and because new advances occur in less specialized species, over-all progress is characteristically irregular and discontinuous rather than a direct line from one advanced species to its next descendent. Instead of continuing the advance, related species diverge as they specialize and adapt. This discontinuity, which now seems obvious, has been usually overlooked as a significant feature of the evolutionary process. Evolution is usually diagrammed as a tree with the trunk representing the "main line" of progress, as though the advance is an important element in the understanding of some major problems. . . .

We are not sure where the lineal view of evolution came from, but it has been a mischievous one. The difficulty it has caused in anthropology has been discussed . . . , but here it may be well to remark that there has been a much more pervasive confusion than that. Hegel's "dialectical" conception of evolution is a special version of the lineal view, and when it was adopted by Marx and Engels and ultimately became part of a political dogma, the error was widespread as well as resistant to any arguments against it. According to Hegel, *everything*, including society and even human nature, is in a state of evolution; everything carries within itself the forces which change it. Never mind the famous "negations" that cause the revolutionary leaps; what is at issue now is Hegel's "flux," the idea that each and every system of things evolves as a self-contained unit. There is no phylogenetic discontinuity and no sound idea of variable potentiality in the Hegelian view. This fault is what led Marx, Engels, and others to presume that the revolution which would usher in the new stage of industrial socialism would occur in the most *advanced* industrial countries—that evolution proceeds from the most advanced form on to the next level. But when the Bolsheviks won in Russia, a most unlikely place from the Hegel–Marx point of view, the Marxists became confused. When expediency led Lenin and then Stalin to retain power in Russia no matter what the theory said, many others, "pure Marxists," rejected the Bolsheviks and formed the numerous splinter parties that exist to this day as opponents to Stalinism. What a lot of assassinations a mere theory can cause! Perhaps this is a sufficient answer to those who say that evolutionary laws are so general that they are meaningless.

In order to emphasize the nonlineal nature of progress, we shall state two new principles, obvious aspects of the law of potential. One could be called the Phylogenetic Discontinuity of Progress. It would mean only what was stated above, that an advanced form does not normally beget the next stage of advance; that the next stage begins in a different line.

Because species tend to occupy a given territory continuously, another obvious derivative principle suggests itself. This may be called the Local Discontinuity of Progress. It means merely that if successive stages of progress are not likely to go from one species to its next descendent, then they are not likely to occur in the same locality. As we shall see, this principle is especially appropriate for studies of cultural evolution because we so frequently name a culture after the territory in which it is found.

No one has completely or succinctly formulated any of these laws, but several writers have come close. Two in particular have discussed and used rather similar ideas in specific interpretations. They are Thorstein Veblen and Leon Trotsky.

Veblen's analysis of imperial Germany makes considerable use of two ideas reminiscent of the above discussion. One is that Germany became more efficient industrially than her predecessor, England, because of "merits of borrowing"; the other is that England, conversely, was finally less efficient than Germany because of "the penalty of taking the lead."[3] Later, Trotsky, in his *History of the Russian Revolution*, formulated the idea somewhat more aptly. He used one particularly luminous phrase: "the privilege of historic backward-

ness." In the context of his discussion this means that an "underdeveloped" civilization has certain evolutionary potentials that an advanced one lacks. He put it this way:

> Although compelled to follow after the advanced countries, a backward country does not take things in the same order. The privilege of historic backwardness—and such a privilege exists—permits, or rather compels, the adoption of whatever is ready in advance of any specified date, skipping a whole series of intermediate stages.[4]

Trotsky went on to develop his idea and to formulate it as the Law of Combined Development:

> The law of combined development reveals itself most indubitably . . . in the history and character of Russian industry. Arising late, Russian industry did not repeat the development of the advanced countries, but inserted itself into this development, adapting their latest achievements to its own backwardness. Just as the economic evolution of Russia as a whole skipped over the epoch of craft-guilds and manufacture, so also the separate branches of industry made a series of special leaps over technical productive stages that had been measured in the West by decades. Thanks to this, Russian industry developed at certain periods with extraordinary speed.[5]

Several writers prior to Veblen and Trotsky, including Lewis H. Morgan, had remarked on the tendency of backward societies to skip over whole stages of development by borrowing from the culture of advanced societies, but no one has been so explicit as Trotsky about the *potentiality* of backwardness, nor so daring as to propose it as a scientific law. The emphasis on diffusion in Trotsky's argument (as suggested in the phrase "combined development") and in Veblen's idea of the "merits of borrowing" calls attention to an important feature of the evolutionary process in culture which does not have its analogue in biological evolution. . . .

THE LAW ILLUSTRATED

The foregoing discussion of history shows that there has been for some time a nearly recognized utility for the law of evolutionary potential in the realm of civilizational phenomena, in these cases European history specifically. But if it is a *general* law of evolution it should be useful in any and all kinds of situations that involve the evolutionary process. It requires but a little reflection to accumulate numerous examples of the operation of the law and its corollaries.

The evolution of writing in the ancient Mediterranean provides one of the more simple and obvious instances. The Egyptian system of combining hieroglyphic and rebus writing was the most advanced and specialized example of that stage. Imbedded in it were a few suggestions of a new phase, certain symbols that stood for syllables, and some even for a few single phonetic sounds. But so fixed were they in the cumbersome Egyptian system, and so adjusted was the total system to the rest of Egyptian culture, that the potentiality of the phonetic elements could not be realized there. Instead, the much more effective and economical alphabetic system emerged elsewhere, among East Mediterranean peoples (some say the Phoenicians) who had *no writing at all* and who could, therefore, make a fresh start with only the most appropriate and efficient elements from the old composite system.

Science itself, because it is such a clear case of evolutionary progress, is full of examples of the Law of Evolutionary Potential. We see not only local (or national) discontinuity in the development of science, but also a sort of phylogenetic discontinuity—which may be more precisely described in this case as generational discontinuity. Young scientists tend to surpass their elders, when other things such as brains, of course, are equal. The well-established individuals ordinarily do not go on making successive important contributions because they become so committed, adapted, to a particular line of thought. The young are generalized and unstable, in a sense, and have the "privilege of backwardness" which enables them to appropriate only the more fruitful and progressive of the older generation's accomplishments, disregarding or discarding as useless debris much of the work that went on before them.

If the law of evolutionary potential is a good law, if it corresponds closely enough to what actually happens in nature so that predictions can be made from it, then we should find that the *faster* a science or civilization or whatever

kind of system is evolving the *more* discontinuous will be the character of the advance. Thus we see that physics, which has been progressing of late more rapidly than most other sciences, is also characterized by greater discontinuity. The generational discontinuity is particularly striking; very young people, however heavily bearded, seem to win most of the prizes. (In this connection, by the way, some practical advice may be adduced: When medical science is advancing rapidly, as it seems to be right now, go to a *young* doctor.)

The leapfrogging of age by youth can even characterize whole societies if the total culture is evolving fast enough. In the older stabilized cultures, youth is subordinated to age; the older the person, the wiser and more respected he becomes. But in rapid change, youth is served, and the experienced elders, adapted to the outmoded cultural forms, become merely old fogeys. In the past, our disrespect for age has been a most noticeable characteristic of the U.S.A. to European visitors. Lately we hear of the "cult of youth" in Russia and China, as might be expected. . . .

Now that the examples being used here have moved to the level of civilization, we may appropriately continue on to modern times. This is at some risk, it must be admitted, because we all tend to lose perspective and to become influenced by political dogmas when we deal with contemporary problems. But let us first discuss China, a prime example of a huge and complex civilization which, although contemporary, is nevertheless an "old" one, quite backward from the standpoint of modern industrial civilization.

Japan, once a poor cultural relative of China, moved into the modern industrial stage of coal and oil energy and became dominant in the Far East. Partly, this could occur because of the potentiality of its backwardness and "newness" as opposed to the great inertia of the ancient, highly adapted, and specialized agricultural civilization of China. Partly, too, Japan was free to advance because she was relatively independent of the dominance that Western civilization exerted over China. But now, perhaps paradoxically from the point of view of Japan, China has greater potential for moving into the new and radically different industrial stage to be based on the electronic storage and transmission of such new sources of power as atomic and direct solar energy. China is not nearly so adapted as Japan to the present and soon-to-be-outmoded industrial complex of coal and oil energy.

Mao Tse-tung has commented on this outlook in picturesque language:

> Apart from other characteristics, our people of over 600 million souls is characterized by poverty and by a vacuity which is like that of a sheet of blank paper. This may seem to be a bad thing, whereas in reality it is a good one.... Nothing is written on a sheet of paper which is still blank, but it lends itself admirably to receive the latest and most beautiful pictures. (Quoted by Bettelheim, 1959.)[6]

The potentiality of large nonindustrialized areas like China is great even in relatively small matters. As China borrows the alphabet she could make it a phonemic one. She could have simplified rules of spelling. She could institute a metric system of weights and measures. As she begins the manufacture of typewriters they could be built with a keyboard scientifically arranged for the spelling of the language rather than following our own illogical one, and so on. Improvements in all these matters and many others are already known to us, but our civilization seems unable to use them because of the prior commitment to earlier forms, whereas China should have less difficulty.

NOTES

1. Julian S. Huxley, *Evolution: The Modern Synthesis*, New York and London: Harper, 1943, p. 500.
2. *Ibid.*, p. 562.
3. Thorstein Veblen, *Imperial Germany and the Industrial Revolution*, New York: MacMillan, 1915, esp. Chapters II–IV.
4. Leon Trotsky, *The History of the Russian Revolution*, Ann Arbor: University of Michigan Press, n.d., pp. 4-5.
5. *Ibid.*, p. 9.
6. Quoted by Charles Bettelheim, "China's Economic Growth," *Monthly Review*, 1959, 10: 458.

Millenarism and Social Change

Peter M. Worsley

O stone-age child, why do you lie dreaming,
Of dreams and thoughts of your ancestor?
Why? Oh why do you continue clinging,
To way of life of your ancestor?

What sort of wealth did he possess for you,
And his knowledge of ability?
None but worthless heathen rubbish for sure,
Is now the cause of stupidity.

Leave all your heathen rubbish and behold,
An atomic-age and restless man,
Has come from land unknown just to unfold,
Way of life not as child but as man.

(Excerpt from the poem 'What Ancestral Wealth and Knowledge?' by A. P. Allan Natachee, a Mekeo of Papua, *Oceania*, Vol. XXII, 1951-2, p. 150.)

COPRA, GOLD AND RUBBER

In contrast to the more complex societies of Fiji, or of New Caledonia (where resistance to

■Taken from Peter M. Worsley, *The Trumpet Shall Sound* (London: MacGibbon & Kee, 1968), pp. 32–48, by permission.

European rule resulted in several secular revolts), most of the islands of Melanesia were occupied by people whose social organization and culture were of the simple types.... Whilst not minimizing the significant differences, there was considerable similarity between the social organization and culture of these peoples, and the impact of the Whites, too, generally took place in a limited number of ways.

The documentation necessary for a broad picture of the general effects of European rule on the whole of the Melanesian region is sadly deficient; it is least bad for Papua-New Guinea. We will therefore take this area, large enough in all conscience, as a representative area, before examining these social changes at the village level.

It must be observed initially that the problem of a large White minority, so important in many colonial territories, was not present in this region. Consequently, land alienation on the scale familiar, for example, in Kenya did not occur. In New Guinea, 59.3 million acres out of a total of 60 million remained unalienated by 1940: 158,000 of these were actually leased. But such crude figures, of course, obscure the fact that "much of the best economic land had passed out of native possession."[1] Many of the limited areas of good soil were alienated; the areas most suitable for copra production were particularly subject to alienation. And, as Mair notes, although much land remained unalienated, this was small consolation to natives in those areas where most land had been lost, and for whom there was in practice no land actually available locally.[2] In land purchases the protection of native interests before sale was often neglected on the grounds of "the wider interests of the territory."[3]

Developments in this region were largely determined by the nature of European enterprise. Of these, undoubtedly the most important—at least in the initial stages—was plantation agriculture of a few major crops, mainly of coconuts for export as copra. In 1923, the Director of Agriculture for the Mandated Territory referred to the territory as "labouring mentally under the desolating blight of an obsession of coconut planting."[4] The effort put into coconut-plantation economy brought the copra exports of the Territory up from 2,000 tons in 1883 (when there was a White population of only thirty) to over 70,000 tons in 1939. In 1925, copra exports produced over 95% of export values, but gold soon came to outstrip copra as the major export. The initial major discovery was made in 1926, but it was only after 1936 that intensive mining really began, raising the share of gold in export values from 66% of the total to 86% in 1941, while the share of copra declined from 30% to 8%.

A basically similar situation obtained in Papua. Here rubber was added to copra and gold as a third major export, gold remaining a fairly constant third of export values from 1936 to 1941, rubber increasing from 25% to 35%, and copra again declining from 28% to 12%.

THE VAGARIES OF THE EUROPEAN ECONOMY

Although copra production continued to rise fairly steadily right up to the outbreak of war, fluctuations of world economy reduced its value considerably. Indeed, this area would have been in a desperate situation had gold not come to the rescue. Thus economic and social changes were by no means determined by internal developments alone. Figure 1 shows the movements of world copra prices.

Belshaw writes of a wider period, "the price of copra . . . has fluctuated from £70/12/6 per ton to £2, and from £30 to £8 in a year."[5] Well over £100 per ton was being offered by Canadian buyers in 1951.[6] Besides these fluctuations, and similar fluctuations in the prices of

FIGURE 1 Average Price per Ton of New Guinea Copra, 1909 - 1938 (Australian Pounds)

(Figure from Reed, S. W. *The Making of Modern New Guinea.* (Memoirs of the American Philosophical Society. Vol. XVIII) Philadelphia, 1943, p. 194. Original source: R. E. P. Dwyer, "A Survey of the Coconut Industry in the Mandated Territory of New Guinea," *New Guinea Agricultural Gazette* Vol. 2, 1963, p. 2.

trade goods, the economy of this region was not strengthened by rising values of exports, since "heavy repatriations of profits lessened, and equipment imports narrowed, the spread of local benefits."[7] This meant that the continual favourable trade balances did not make for viability, since the profits transferred to external territories, particularly Australia, constantly drained the country of capital needed for development.[8]

The social implications of these dry figures are not far to seek. Constant changes in the price of trade goods, fluctuations in the price paid for primary products, the great copra slump of the early thirties with its ruination of the majority of small planters and their absorption by a few large enterprises, and the lack of visible return for the great values exported, made White society appear more mysterious and irrational to the islander than it had been even in periods of comparative economic stability. In the New Hebrides, natives considered that local merchants were responsible for these price variations.[9]

Many writers have drawn attention to important features of European society which must appear to be beyond rational explanation to the Melanesian with his limited knowledge. The processes of production of European goods, the nature of the tools used, the workers using those tools, and the relations between them and their employers, etc.—all these remain closed books to most islanders. Thus many visitors to colonial areas have found it difficult to persuade natives that the goods they see are made by White men, and it is even more difficult to persuade them that menial tasks are performed by Whites. The White men we see, the natives say, do not work thus. But these obvious gaps in knowledge are still matters which can be readily explained and appreciated. Not so readily explained and appreciated are the significance of boom and slump, the closing of plantations, experimental stations and other government and private enterprise which appears to be flourishing, the pressure on natives to produce cash crops which realize progressively less from year to year. And these violent swings affected not merely the small native producer, but also the vast numbers of migrant labourers. Hogbin notes, for the Solomons, how a minimum wage of £1 per month fell to 10/- in the depression year of 1934.[10]

This underlying irrationality of European society not only created great hardships; it undermined confidence in rational activity, it created frustrations, and it sapped morale more than mere ignorance of productive processes could do. For ignorance of these latter is a constant, not necessarily disturbing the social order. The vagaries of the economy are unpredictable, devastating and, for the most of the inter-war period, cumulatively worsening. They are also collective, and not merely individual, disasters. As Stanner, one of the few anthropologists who has pointed to this feature, remarks: "Two factors which, probably, have had much more to do with native disenchantment with European economy than is realized are the colonial terms of trade and the repatriation of savings and net profits by European enterprise. A simple calculation of New Guinea imports as a proportion of the value of exports shows a marked *downward* trend between 1920-40."[11]

There is evidently no close correlation between economic fluctuations and specific cult outbreaks. However, it is clear that the labelling of the cults as "irrational" begs the question. Indeed, a Melanesian might make out a good case for flinging the label of "madness" which has often been applied to these cults back at us, and asking whether his people, given the knowledge they possessed, have not made quite logical criticisms and interpretations of our own unpredictable and irrational society.

This instability and uncertainty strengthened such beliefs as the widely held notion that the Australian Government itself was merely a transient phenomenon: just as the Germans had gone, so would the Australians. As the years passed, this idea weakened, but it received a sudden lease of life as World War II loomed on the horizon. The belief, of course, was to prove correct. How far it was stimulated by pro-Nazi elements amongst German missionaries, who numbered over half the missionaries in the Mandated Territory, is now difficult to say.

THE DRIVE FOR LABOUR

The particular characteristic of this economy which was to make such great inroads upon indigenous social organization was its insatiable demand for ever-increasing supplies of unskilled labour, both for the plantations and the mines. Labour was for the most part obtained by indenture, and by 1938 nearly 42,000 indentured labourers were at work in the Mandated Territory, and some 10,000 in Papua. Mandated Territory labourers signed on for three years in the first instance, with a theoretical maximum of four years' continuous employment; in Papua the maximum was eighteen months' to three years' continuous service. But many served for much longer terms.

In addition to the pull of new wants, a powerful incentive to wage labour was the introduction of native taxation. In his report on "native affairs" in New Guinea for 1924, Col. Ainsworth stated that "the primary object of the head tax was not to collect revenue but to create among the natives a need for money, which would make labour for Europeans desirable and would force the natives to accept employment."[12] Since, in Papua, adult male natives in employment paid only 10/- instead of £1 tax, and in New Guinea the 10/- tax was not payable by indentured labourers, the pressure upon natives to "offer" for work was clear, especially since alternative sources of cash were rarely available.[13]

Natives went to great lengths to avoid paying their taxes. On Karkar Island a tax collector was met by a crowd of women dressed in mourning garb and wailing. All the men, they said, had died, and they led him to fresh graves which had been made in the bush. The sceptical official, however, insisted on one of the graves being opened for inspection: it proved to be empty.[14]

The indentured labourers were not necessarily men of mature age, for boys of twelve were recruited until 1935, when the minimum age was raised to fourteen, though the employment of boys of twelve was still permitted for domestic work; girls of ten were recruited before 1933, when the minimum age was raised to fourteen also.[15] However, the number of such young people recruited was not great. The natives were persuaded to sign on by professional recruiters; being under indenture, they were subject to penal sanctions if they infringed the conditions of their contract. In German times, these sanctions included floggings, administered by employers; this right was taken away only in August 1915, and "Field Punishment No. I" (hanging by the wrists) introduced by the British Military Administration in January 1920. Not until May 1919 was flogging for minor

offences and labour offences stopped; Field Punishment No. I and flogging were legally abolished in 1922. In Papua, fines and imprisonment had been the normal sanctions. As Mair remarks of the Mandated Territory: "It was in this period, during which most of the German employers were carrying on their normal business, that many of the Australians who later joined the public service or took up land in New Guinea acquired their first ideas on the treatment of native labour."[16]

Equally, one might observe, it was during this period that the natives of the Territory formed their opinions of the new régime. Desertions were common, because of "dissatisfaction with their employers or the conditions . . . [of] work" and brought sharp criticisms of the system from the Permanent Mandates Commission.[17] Offences against the labour code accounted for a very large proportion of all native convictions, which rose steadily "while convictions of Europeans and Asiatics fell in at least the same proportion. . . . [This] reinforces the impression . . . that social conditions among the indentured labourers were bad."[18] The indenture system and the great mobility of workers made for high turnover and instability of the labour force.

Unskilled New Guinea natives received 5/- per month; in Papua, 10/- was paid, wages which Decker described as "exceptionally low even for native labour in Pacific dependencies."

Without examining labour conditions in further detail, it can be seen that the experience of natives who signed on was likely to be highly unsettling under the conditions of barrack life, and destructive of confidence in the trustworthiness and honesty of the Whites. In New Guinea, in particular, a tradition of Black-White hostility and of the violent enforcement of European domination persisted into the Australian era.[19] Reed, in a detailed treatment of the question of Black-White relations characterized the situation as 'paternalistic peonage', whilst Stanner, who constantly stresses the practical difficulties facing the Whites, acknowledges that "it was simple for the critics to list fact after fact that, given even without comment, were an affront to the sense of compassion and social justice."

But the young native now signed on for work, not solely because he was driven by such spurs as the tax, though these were important, especially in the period of the creation of the labour force. Now he was caught up in a new web of social relations; he wished to acquire the White man's goods, to buy clothing, lamps, food, and a hundred and one objects for himself and his kin. To obtain these he needed cash and, to get cash, he had no choice but to seek employment with the Whites, except in those small areas where access to markets permitted the sale of cash crops. Once this new labour force had been brought into existence, all these new wants attracted an ever-growing army of recruits more effectively than any crude methods of compulsion. The native was now pulled both ways. Torn by his dislike of leaving home to work for the Whites, he was yet attracted by the hope of obtaining a portion of their riches, and by the fascination of many aspects of town, plantation, and mine life. Attracted by education and medical aid offered by Christian missions, the native nevertheless found a contradiction between mission teaching and the lives led by the White men he met. In a hundred and one ways, he found himself reacting strongly against White domination, but ever more strongly drawn—and often willingly—into closer and closer relations with the Whites.

Far from satisfying his new-found wants, he acquired yet further wants during his period of service. He also found himself in peculiar social surroundings, living in "barracks" where his companions were entirely male. The social stresses and strains arising from this situation, manifest in gambling, homosexuality, and prostitution, are well known.

Such experience ill qualified the returning labourer for the resumption of the comparatively dull routine of the village. The absence of the menfolk at work for years on end had serious effects not merely on the men themselves, but on the villages they left. In 1937 "over 22% of the enumerated adult male population in the Territory were indentured labourers, and, if allowance be made for cripples, the aged and others who would not be eligible for recruitment, the percentage . . . would be still higher."[20] Again, the incidence of recruiting did not fall evenly, since certain areas supplied the bulk of the labour. Thus the Sepik region supplied one quarter of indentured labour in the Mandated Territory in 1940. Even "uncontrolled" areas were recruited, and optimistic official estimates of the numbers which might be recruited without endangering community life in the villages were illegally exceeded.[21] In villages which had lost most of their adult males, the bulk of the horticultural work fell upon women, old men, and boys; there were less people to provide for the needs of the old, the sick, and the young; ritual activities were abandoned since insufficient numbers of participants were available. Returning migrants flouted the authority of their elders, since they knew that real political power now lay with the Whites. They were no longer content to play a subordinate role to old men who knew nothing of the "world," and many youths looked forward to migrant labour as an exciting liberation from parental and gerontocratic control. Then they would become economically and socially independent; if they remained in the villages, it might take years to advance to more senior status in the community through feast-giving, etc. And there was always the tax to be met.

It did not take many years before the first signs of strain in some of the village economies were reported. "In 1920 for the first time comes the significant comment that a dearth of native foodstuffs in the Baniara villages was due to the absence of many of the men as labourers."[22]

It seems not unlikely that much of the stress in cult movements upon the maintenance of fertility and good crops may relate to this growing concern with diminishing production, or, at the least, with the increased effort required to maintain existing levels. Such an hypothesis to be fully validated would require detailed production records which do not exist. . . . [T]he Taro cult, horticulture, the central economic activity of the people, acquires a special symbolic significance as epitomizing the maintenance of the well-being and viability of the society as a whole. In Melanesia, the major ritual performances of most societies thus centre upon the display and consumption of large quantities of staple foods—yams, taro, pigs, etc.

MISSION AND GOVERNMENT

Other important forces of change were Government and mission. Government in New Guinea has always been a direct form of administration. In Papua, "the principle of coercion ... covered almost every field of native development"[23] ; in the Mandated Territory, the German tradition set the tone of future administrative developments. In these territories, native officials appointed in the villages were "constitutionally mere mouthpieces of the Government"[24] as village elders are always telling the people. Since these individuals bore the brunt of official wrath during patrol officers' visits (estimated at two hours per year for most villages), and often had to receive "indignities and blows," it is not surprising that the real indigenous authorities frequently stayed in the background, thrusting forward some luckless individual to be government *luluai* or *tultul*.[25] This divorce between native "representatives" and the people resulted in the co-existence of two almost entirely separate authority-systems at village level, that recognized by the people, and that created by Government. Hogbin quotes these remarks of a Solomon Islander to a native official: "You think you're a leader just because the District Officer made you an Elder? ... Remember *he* chose you, *we* didn't. Who are you, anyway? Are you different from me? Of course you aren't. You never gave a feast in your life. If you want our respect you'd better start giving them quick."[26] And of the Native Courts another native remarked "The Court doesn't belong to us: we never had Courts before: it's a government affair." This does not mean that government officials were necessarily passive incumbents of office; Bumbu, *luluai* of Busama, for example, used his position to terrorize the people under his rule.[27] Amongst a few detribalized communities near Rabaul, Talasea, and Madang, native councils were set up just before World War II, but they had no powers of enforcing decisions and no money to expend.

Government was particularly active in enforcing regulations about village hygiene, the maintenance of roads, etc., but the Courts were largely occupied by cases arising from the control of labour contracts. Together with the Armed Constabulary, the Courts, the native officials and the District Officers represented the most obvious manifestations of "Government" to the people. Attempts at enforcing the regulations, however, were often met with passive resistance. The compulsory planting of specified plants (coconuts, rice, coffee, etc.), for example, seems to have been met with solid lack of enthusiasm even when penal sanctions for "failure to plant" were applied. Plantations owned jointly by Government and village were established in some areas: only two still exist. "Spontaneous" native production of cash crops remained at a low level, restricted by the loss of adult workers, the absence of local markets, and discouraged by price fluctuations and price discrimination against native growers.

The resources at the disposal of Government were so small as to make social improvement insignificant. It is not surprising that the Mandated Territory Government, whose financial resources were swallowed up by administrative salaries and "normal" departmental contingencies to the extent of between 73% and 85% of the budget in pre-war years, were only too glad to hand over responsibility for such services to other bodies. Education remained predominantly in the hands of missions, with government financial assistance, so much so that no ordinary government native schools existed in Papua before the war. New Guinea was criticized before the Permanent Mandates Commission as the Mandate in which education had shown least progress.

The role of the missions in education had profound social repercussions. Over 15% of the Europeans in the Mandated Territory were missionaries, and their activity had been considerable since the establishment of the first mission in 1875. By 1940, the eleven missionary societies in the Territory could report the existence of 2,500 schools of various kinds, 3,354 "native workers" and a nominal following of nearly half a million natives. All but a few of the schools were village schools; the remarks of one anthropologist about the character of some of these schools are a typical evaluation by a non-missionary: "The education given by the Mission is largely an adjunct of its primary aim to secure converts to the Christian faith ... the instruction received aims little higher than a sufficient literacy to increase the pupil's understanding of the Scriptures."[28]

As we shall see, Melanesians became so convinced that real education was being withheld from them that they placed special emphasis in their cult programmes upon obtaining the "Secret" which the White man was concealing. This Secret was sometimes declared to be the first page of the Bible which the Europeans had torn out of the Bibles they gave the islanders. Knowledge was inevitably seen as religious knowledge, for nearly all education was mission education.

The theoretical stress laid upon religion in mission education is paralleled, in native experience, by practical evidence of the worldly power and importance of the missions. Not only are the missionaries numerically strong, but they also possess mission stations, buildings, land, goods, money, and food. They are treated with respect by Government, given official assistance, are of the same ethnic stock as officials, and have been given hundreds of pieces of land for mission sites. In addition, they became large employers of labour and own coconut and other plantations "and in general followed the patterns of European exploitation."[29] This situation of combined spiritual and material power is perhaps best paralleled by the position of the Church in medieval Europe.

But there is one important difference from the medieval Church. There were eleven competing mission societies in the pre-war Mandate. "Spheres of influence" were gradually worked out (although not in other parts of Melanesia), but "native adherents" of rival sects in interstitial areas frequently became "engaged in acrimonious disputes as to which sect [had] the right to proselytize in new regions."[30]

In the very extreme, violence and the burning of rival adherents' huts occurred.

Such divergence between varieties of exposition of the Gospel have not merely introduced new, and often bitter, social divisions into native communities; they have introduced moral and religious uncertainty into an already unstable situation. This is exacerbated by the divergence natives note between Christian doctrines of equality and brotherly love, and actual practice. As one native of Tanna remarked: "Which way Missionary e no stop with em you long one table? Him e preach Jesus e say love one another, e preach, e no do it."[31]

On top of the peculiarity of the European economy, in addition to the instability of political régimes, and added to the new sectarian divisions, came an equivocal teaching. Said to be basically the same religion, it had numerous opposed representatives and sections. This moral difficulty was intensified by the open atheism and anti-mission sentiments and activities of many planters, traders, recruiters, and officials.

The stage was truly set, then, for the development of independent native movements, and for the casting of social and economic aspirations in religious form. The form of these movements in Melanesia, therefore, can in no way be attributed to any inherent mysticism or religiosity of the Melanesians themselves.

The hysterical phenomena found in most of the cults, equally, do not derive from any peculiar inherent psychological characteristics of Melanesians. They are the product of the ambivalent attitudes and feelings of men torn between hatred of the White people who had destroyed the old way of life and who now dominated them by force, and the desire to obtain for themselves the possessions of these very Whites.

Some writers have seen in the cults nothing more than an atavistic rejection of European culture. In fact, Melanesians by no means rejected European culture *in toto*: they wanted the White man's power and riches, but they did not want the perpetuation of his rule. The myth of a Cargo, rightly theirs, but usurped by the Whites, expressed their political mood neatly.

In the absence of knowledge of the material reality of European society, in the belief that Europeans apparently did no work for the goods they obtained, and under the influence of all-pervading mission education, the Melanesians concluded that secret magical power was the key to the wealth of the Europeans. This power they were determined to obtain.

Their desperation is mirrored in the powerful emotionality of the cults with their compulsive physical twitching, in the sudden rejection of ancient customs and the radical reordering of life. It was a desperation growing out of their ambivalent attitude toward European culture, their confusion at the queer fluctuations of the European-imposed order, and the frustration of their growing wants at a time when higher production and harder work often brought only diminishing returns.

As we shall see, millenarian movements spread over most of Melanesia within a very short time. Some areas were subject to repeated outbreaks, and the cults were found both in areas where European influence had been strong for generations and in areas only recently brought under control. Only the small urban areas were free from cult movements. Here movements of protest took more orthodox forms—strikes, independent native organizations, etc.—but they were few between the wars.

Many planters, recruiters, and commercial interests began to express uneasiness about the extent and continuity of the movements in the rural areas. Some of them blamed the missionaries, who exercised great influence over the rural population and whose teachings had provided much of the cult ideology. Public controversy between settler and missionary soon broke out.[32]

No very clear solution emerged from these altercations, for the answer did not lie in blaming any one section of the European community. The cults arose from the overall effects of the European impact on native society.

OTHER FORMS OF NATIVE ORGANIZATION

Social change did not take place at the same rate over the whole of Melanesia. It was very uneven, and the range of political and social variation was considerable: at one pole were the "uncontrolled" regions, and at the other, the urbanized native residents of Rabaul and Port Moresby. In between was a wide range of diversity: the native communities of the Highlands, only discovered in the thirties; areas long under government control, where migrant labour was long established; and areas such as that round Rabaul where European goods, native tradestores and other minor commercial enterprise, production for the market, and casual daylabouring were all to be found.

This variety of structure, and the varying degrees of dissolution of the traditional social relations under the impact of the new economy and Government, resulted in differential incidence of millenarian and other such movements. But the village economy, in which periodic migrant labour was as characteristic a feature as traditional hand horticulture, was typical of all but a very few spots. Millenarian movements appeared in such widely separated areas as New Ireland, the Rai Coast, the Gulf Division, and the Mekeo District, because the fundamental economic and political pattern in all these areas was basically similar.

But significant differences also existed, and they had significant social results. It would be distorting the picture of political developments in this part of the world if we isolated millenarian movements, and ignored other forms of social expression. The different historical experiences of peoples in different areas also resulted in varying attitudes towards the Whites and varying forms of native organization. In those remote areas where the Germans had never penetrated, or only slightly, the old régime was often idealized; those communities which had known German rule at first hand, as at Blanche Bay, Kavieng, Namatanai, and Madang, had quite different memories.[33] Of the non-millenarian forms of resistance, armed self-defence and attacks upon Whites, so characteristic of German times, now principally occurred in the semi-controlled and uncontrolled areas. But there were other non-millenarian forms of expression of native dissatisfaction in the controlled areas. Strikes, for example, showed a gradual increase over the years. Even the native police force was not free from disturbances, some of them violent. Three Europeans and a Chinese had been killed in a revolt of police at Astrolabe Bay as far back as 1900; with the advent of the Japanese, a rising of native constables was to take place at Madang, and, on the Sepik, an "amok" of police in which one Chinese and four Whites were killed.[34]

Although frequently expressed, unrest amongst indentured plantation labourers rarely led to any stable native organization because they were a migrant population, constantly changing and moving. It was therefore amongst the growing body of casual labourers that strike action was more common, though even here it was limited. At the outbreak of war some 9,000 indentured natives were employed in such capacities as stevedores, lorry-drivers, messengers, porters, etc., but an increasing number of natives near the townships worked at daily (and higher) rates of pay.

Some authorities stress that the urban areas were training-grounds for agitators who later returned to the villages. Secret night-time meetings were held near Rabaul, and three mysterious beings predicted the coming of a new epoch in which Whites would serve natives. . . .[35]

Later [after the strike at Rabaul, described in Section One], just before the Japanese arrival, the "Dog" movement was set up in the nearby Duke of York Islands and Kokopo, its objective being the purchase of land and the building of schools for native use. The name is said to reflect the native view of the way they were treated by Whites. As it began to reveal signs of becoming a strong organization with "seditious" tendencies, it was broken up by the arrest of the militants. Despite this unintelligent repression, the official who himself prosecuted these leaders recorded his sympathy with the aims of the movement.

The urban and adjoining areas of long settlement, then, on the whole found other forms of political expression than millenarism, and the casual labourers, peri-urban workers and small entrepreneurs had begun to develop orthodox political, economic, and social organizations before World War II. This divergence was to become more marked in the post-war period as social differentiation increased and as the differences in levels of development between urban and rival areas became more sharply emphasized....

NOTES

1. Stanner. W. E. H. *The South Seas in Transition.* London: Australasian Publishing Co., 1953, pp. 33.

2. Mair, L. P. *Australia in New Guinea.* London: Christophers; Mystic, Conn.: Verry, Lawrence, 1948, p. 97.

3. *Ibid.*, p. 95.

4. *Ibid.*, p. 98.

5. Belshaw, C. S. *Island Administration in the South West Pacific.* London: Royal Institute of International Affairs, 1950, pp. 40-41.

6. Stanner, *op. cit.*, p. 121.

7. *Ibid.*, p. 37.

8. *Loc. cit.*

9. Guiart, Jean. *Mythe, Evolution et Histoire, un siècle et demi de contacts culturels à Tanna*, 1957.

10. Hogbin, H. Ian. *Experiments in Civilization.* London: Routledge & Kegan Paul, 1939, p. 161.

11. Stanner, *op. cit.*, p. 73.

12. Decker, J. A. *Labour Problems in the Pacific Mandates.* (Institute of Pacific Relations.) London: Oxford University Press, 1941, p. 167. Mair, *op. cit.*, p. 63, gives a contrary opinion.

13. The cost of an indentured labourer was estimated at £26 8/- for an unskilled plantation labourer, £33 16/- for miners and other heavy workers, and in some areas up to £70.... Recruiters received from £3–£20 per head; "flagrant widespread illegalities" occurred during such periods as the gold-rushes. (Mair, *op. cit.*, p. 153).

14. Flierl, J. *Gottes Wort in den Urwalden von Neuguinea.* Neuendettelsau, 1929, p. 107.

15. Decker, *op. cit.*, p. 174.

16. Mair, *op. cit.*, p. 141.

17. Decker, *op. cit.*, p. 184.

18. Stanner, *op. cit.*, p. 27–28.

19. Relations between Germans and natives had often been very bitter. Fifty-five Whites were killed in the first twenty-five years of European rule; the White population was only 230 in 1910. For the killing of three Whites by Duke of York Islanders, for example, 750 troops were landed; villages were shelled for disciplinary reasons (Reed, S. W. *The Making of Modern New Guinea.* [Memoirs of the American Philosophical Society, Vol. XVIII.] Philadelphia, 1943, pp. 133-7). German punitive expeditions have been vividly described by Lajos Bíró, particularly his description of the shelling of Deslacs Island by a German battleship. After the bombardment, New Ireland natives armed with spears and European weapons were put ashore; no child under the age of ten was left alive. (Bodrogi, Tibor. "Colonization and Religious Movements in Melanesia," *Acta Etnografica Academiae Hungaricae,* II [1951], p. 284; cf. also Reed, p. 118.)

20. Decker, *op. cit.*, p. 169.

21. There seems much internal evidence to suggest that the aggressive, violent characteristics attributed to the Mundugumor of the Sepik region by Mead are largely a product of "over-rerecruiting" in an area only recently brought under administrative control. (Mead, Margaret. *Sex and Temperament in Three Primitive Societies.* London: Routledge & Kegan Paul, 1935; Gloucester, Mass.: Peter Smith, Part Two.)

22. Mair, *op. cit.*, p. 86.

23. *Ibid.*, p. 45.

24. *Ibid.*, p. 48.

25. The senior village official was called either *luluai* or *kukerai*; the *tultul* was supposed to assist with interpreting, and the third official, the "doctor boy," with medical problems. In fact, these duties were not clearly understood, nor were the individuals properly qualified: more often, they merely formed a village triumvirate of officials, not necessarily powerful.

26. Hogbin, H. Ian. "Native Councils and Native Courts in the Solomon Islands," *Oceania,* XIV, No. 4 (1944), p. 265. Cf. e.g. Blackwood, Beatrice. *Both Sides of Buka Passage.* Oxford: Clarendon Press, 1935, pp. 48-50, where hereditary aristocrats on Buka referred to the Government-appointed *kukerai* as "a nobody."

27. Hogbin, H. Ian. *Transformation Scene.* London: Routledge & Kegan Paul; New York: Humanities Press, 1951, pp. 151-163, etc.

28. Read, M. K. E. "Missionary Activities and Social Change in the Central Highlands of Papua and New Guinea," *South Pacific,* V, No. 11 (1952), p. 233.

29. Reed, *op. cit.*, p. 237.

30. *Ibid.*, p. 236.

31. "Why doesn't the missionary sit at the same table as us? He preaches that Jesus told us to love one

another. He preaches this, but he doesn't practise it."
(Guiart, *op. cit.*)

32. E.g., Thomas Gordon, "A Plea for Better Regulation of Mission Activities in New Guinea," PIM, 20th November 1935, pp. 25-26.

33. Reed, *op. cit.*, pp. 153-155.

34. PIM, November 1946.

35. See O'Reilly, P. "Les Chrétientés mélanésiennes et la guerre," *Neue Zeitschrift für Missionswissenschaft,* 3rd yr., No. 2 (1947), 106-117, and Eckert, G. "Prophetentum und Kulturwandel in Melanesien," *Bässler Archiv,* XXIII (1940), p. 33.

Section Three	*The Collective Is the Message*

Cargo Cults and Their Successors

John C. Leggett

CARGO CULTS DELIVER A MESSAGE

A group of Solomon Islanders quit work and thereby abandon the twelve-hour day. They disrobe, burn their clothes before startled missionaries, tear up their cash, grab their tools, perhaps kill a white overseer, and dash for the wharf. There they dance, sing, and await the arrival of a 10,000-ton Liberty Ship guided by a chalk-faced ancestor. Presumably, his return will initiate a millennium without plantation land, labor, and law, but with the traditional ways of harvesting and storing the yam, catching and preparing the fish, raising, dressing, and initiating the young, and relating to the spirit world and hence to the most pertinent ancestor. Paradoxically, all this would be accomplished in a world filled with western commodities earlier enjoyed by the natives and later withdrawn from them—with the closing of the gold mine, the sugar plantation, or the U.S. marine base.

Cargo cults deliver a message, sometimes consciously, sometimes unknowingly. Certain

■ In this essay I have relied heavily not only on the already cited works of Lanternari and Worsley, but Kenelm Burridge's *Mambu* (New York: Harper Torchbooks, 1970). I have also relied on the works of Elman R. Service, *The Hunters* (Englewood Cliffs, N. J.: Prentice-Hall, 1966); Marshall D. Sahlins, *Tribesmen* (Englewood Cliffs, N. J.: Prentice-Hall, 1968); Marshall D. Sahlins and Elman R. Service, *Evolution and Culture* (Ann Arbor: The University of Michigan Press, 1960).

Melanesian religious cults call for the return of dead ancestors who will trumpet the beginnings of a new millennium. Likewise, since their inception almost one hundred years ago, cargo cults have called for the elimination of white imperial control, the return of native traditional culture and social organization, but the acceptance of consumer goods associated with Western trade. These largely Melanesian movements have thereby rejected in their religious appeals the need for private property, the necessity for money, the discipline and hardships of plantation labor, the boom–bust economy of mono-agriculture, the presence of *corvée* labor, the discontinuance of an alien overlordship, and the elimination of the Christian religions of the oppressors.

Clearly, cargo cults have often expressed the antithesis of the exploitative reality. By the same token, because cargo cults have associated the return of the dead with the revitalization of their culture and social organization, their demands reflected as they magnified and reshaped the remnants of their traditional society. In this sense, cargo cults were irredentist. They called for the return of both the soils and the traditions to native ownership and control. But insofar as cargo cults moved toward the creation of trade unions, political parties, a native state, and a modern, noncolonial economy, as was the case in those areas commercialized and industrialized, cargo cults proved progressive, for they heralded native liberation.

CARGO CULT AND TRIBES GO TOGETHER

Where did these heralding religious forms emerge? And why? Under what conditions did they move step by step from elementary protest to sophisticated political expression?

Crucial in answering these questions is knowledge of where the cargo cults occurred. Apparently, they emerged almost exclusively among tribes, not in bands or chiefdoms.

The so-called band was never more than an uncoordinated assemblage of a small number of nuclear families; seldom did the older people live long enough to create the third-generational basis for an extended family. Leadership within the small community of perhaps 50 to 200 members was based largely on personal achievement, rather than inherited status. Leadership itself was also generally ephemeral, asserting itself only during the hunting seasons. In these situations, the middle-aged man of 18 or 20 could demonstrate exemplary hunting skills and thereby subsequently wield the greatest influence when the band hunted or fished. But once this sustenance activity had ended, there was no residue, no spillover of authoritative posture into other areas such as settling community disputes. Families returned to control relationships marked by both mutual dependence and loose decentralization.

Traditionally, leadership in the tribe has been both concentrated and centralized, hence the leader has had greater sanctioning power. Fewer persons have wielded power, and these few have acted in many areas where power was not exerted in the band. Not only during the hunt and other forages for sustenance, but on redistributive occasions, persons and families have played leading, sometimes inherited roles. As Sahlins has indicated:

> The tribal economic system is an extended family system, characterized throughout by kinship cooperation and mutual aid. The principal administrative operation in a tribal economy, therefore, is pooling and redistribution of goods by a central agent. Everywhere this central agent occupies a political, chiefly status, and his redistributive activities subsidize the division of labor and tribal enterprise.[1]

By contrast, the chiefdom exists when one tribal leader and his tribe become paramount in relation to other tribal chiefs and organizations sharing the same culture and territory. At this point, the ascendant tribe becomes by definition a paramount tribe. More precisely, in the case of the chiefdom, there exists a central body having decision-making authority; this body, moreover, takes the initiative on a regular basis rather than acting merely in crises. The dominant tribe exercises this initiative over two or more adjacent communities, although its authority is limited relative to state power, i.e., the coercive strength of a government to monopolize most acts of violence most of the time. Although the chiefdom has been capable of using force as an internal force or external sanction, it has not monopolized force. An example was Tahiti during the 1770s. A particular family became ascendant over other extended families to the degree that the first family did, in fact, conquer many other families and take over areas occupied by them. It wasn't until the successors to Captain Cook, whose intensive contact with the Tahitians occurred in the late 1770s, brought guns, gun powder, and political alliance to this dominant family that this coalition was able to subdue the other families, claim a monopoly of violence, exercise the right to exclusive control on bodily injury, and write a set of laws for a theocratic state (the Pomarean Code). Hawaii followed a similar specific evolutionary path.

According to the evolutionary criteria advanced by Sahlins and Service, tribes stand midway between the band and chiefdom, for tribes are more differentiated, specialized, and coordinated than bands, whereas relative to chiefdom, tribes display these characteristics to a lesser degree.

TRIBES, CARGO CULTS, AND THE LAW OF EVOLUTIONARY POTENTIAL

Why might cargo cults occur most frequently among tribes? In a historical sense, why did cargo cults occur hundreds of times among tribal peoples in Melanesia and seldom among chiefdoms such as those found on the volcanic islands of Polynesia? For example, nothing comparable to cargo cults emerged in Tahiti during 1780–1830, the years of first extensive than intensive European contact, the period of "contact colonialism." Nor was Tahiti atypical.

In Polynesian Hawaii, Samoa, and the Society Islands, cargo cults and their messianic equivalents failed to emerge. Only in Fiji were cargo-like cults of importance within Polynesia.

Crucial in our speculation on why cargo cults emerged at the tribal level is an understanding of the Law of Evolutionary Potential and the privilege of backwardness. Briefly, and to paraphrase while modifying Service's proposition on this law: The more advanced the specific evolutionary form within a "stage of development," such as primitive society, the less likely it will be to create within itself the next highest form in the general evolutionary sequence of mankind.

In primitive societies, as you will recall, the most advanced general form is the chiefdom, followed by the tribe and the band, in that order. The chiefdom as a form lends itself to amalgamation and loss of organizational identity through cooptation by a more powerful outsider of the so-called paramount tribe. This was a unit that wielded considerable peripheral control over nearby tribes sharing the same culture both immediately prior to, and during, the initial phases of contact colonialism. Such was the case, for example, in Tahiti during the last quarter of the eighteenth and the first quarter of the nineteenth centuries. In the case of this chiefdom, control by the paramount tribe was highly centralized and concentrated, although no state existed. Briefly, the Wesleyans worked with this tribe to concentrate authority within a theocratic state organized along strict Methodist principles.

Historically the dynamics of this Tahitian paramount form had pushed it to engage in nearly continuous struggles immediately prior to extensive trade contact with the West (the period of contact colonialism). During this period, the paramount tribe moved to create a pristine state, an instance of state formation based on struggle of indigenous and warring groups. However, by itself it had been unable to form a State. By contrast, when the white religious group took sides with the paramount tribe in order to stabilize domestic relations and thereby facilitate trade and industry, white agents became both agents and catalysts.

Because Westerners made the paramount tribe more efficient in the ways of warfare, it acquired sufficient military strength to ally successfully with whites to overcome the opposition of disordered and lesser tribes already decimated by immediate pre- and post-colonial contact. The death of tens of thousands of Tahitians occurred between 1770 and 1810, to the degree, that many tribes lacked even the manpower to resist the military onslaught of a paramount tribe armed with western guns.

After a coalition was accomplished, as in Tahiti, the defeated tribes found it difficult to fall back on their depleted resources, and they were no match for a ruling group often consisting of other peoples sharing the *same* culture. The subordinated and shattered tribes discovered many of their own people, representatives of the paramount tribe but sharers of the same values and beliefs, acting as rulers. It's as if the alien whites had knowingly played on the structural superiority of chiefdoms to take advantage of unconscious, incipient, state-formation tendencies. By locating intertribal conflicts and extending such struggles to include the fight for the creation of a paramount political body the white man would emerge as the strongest element in the partnership. The result was immobility and defeat of lesser tribes.

By contrast, a tribe in a nonchiefdom context is, by definition, uncoordinated by other tribes at times of extensive and later intensive colonial contact. Indeed, tribes are generally free of one another, although their propinquity and their common culture promote mutual dependence based on trade. The exception occurs when a "strong man" acts to coordinate several tribes on the basis of his personal charisma, a quality which, like his position, is not inherited. On the whole, each tribe is dependent on its own political, economic, and technological resources.

If and when white colonialism challenges a tribe, the colonial power must move alone to reorganize the tribes' political resources. The colonial groups cannot depend on a hitherto paramount tribe, as was the case in the chiefdom, to help repress and exploit a host of tribes simultaneously. In the context of the tribe, if colonial man is to be successful politically, he must pick off these tribes one by one. Although inter-tribal equality works against cooptation, the leader's retirement to the other side, that of colonialism, can occur. But the cooptation of one tribe is without authoritative consequence for the others. Under conditions that limit the utility and hence the incidence of multiple and simultaneous tribal political co-optation, there follows a relative lack of division among and within tribes sharing the same community and culture during the collective problem-solving period of contact colonialism.

Precisely because the tribe is backward relative to the chiefdom on matters of political coordination at time of contact, the tribe retains the *potential*, but *only* the potential, for creating the successor to a social system and culture admittedly damaged by colonialism. Potential for change should not be confused with protection from damage.

The "successor" is the cargo cult, a messianic social movement with the possibility of acting politically and economically to reorganize and to revitalize a people hammered over a period of decades, as has been the case in Southeast New Guinea. The privilege of backwardness, then, takes the form of relative evolutionary underdevelopment: the political potential for creating within itself a specific evolutionary form qualified to initiate a general evolutionary innovation with both socialist and irredentist elements.

POTENTIAL AND ITS REALIZATION

Certain conditions seem to be associated with moving a population toward revolutionary transformation. Fulfillment of the four conditions,[2] which are linked to one another, appears to be necessary before tribal peoples can take full advantage of the privilege of underdevelopment.

1. Preparatory
2. Facilitating
3. Abdicating
4. Translating

The first two conditions press a population toward the stage of cargo-cult formation. The last two move the population toward communal ownership and control of the means of production. The realization of socialism, however, depends on the presence of revolutionary movements with a disciplined, quasi-military party. In this context, perhaps unfortunately for Melanesians, this particular form of translat-

ing mechanism does not appear. The vanguard party is absent.

Preparatory conditions

Preparatory conditions refer to sharp changes in the economic substructure and mental framework associated with imperialism.

First, there are recurrent and steep inclines and subsequent declines in real wages among members of the subordinate group in question, in this case, Melanesian plantation and mining laborers. The decrease marks a sharp contrast with a gradual improvement experienced for several years, perhaps a decade, prior to the decline in the laborers' standard of living. Frequently, boom—bust economy takes the form of an endless roller coaster.

Second, there are indications of the formation and retention of progressively higher but unmet economic expectations. Both circumstances contribute to, but by no means completely account for, a minimal but growing degree of subordinate class—racial consciousness. Alienation from the foreign state is also observed. After cargo cults have existed in an area for approximately three or four generations, the level of consciousness becomes more sophisticated and the cult goals become clearer. In addition, the strategies find tighter intellectual connections with collective purposes as the cult itself passes from religious interpretations to hard, practical, and at times revolutionary demands.

You will recall Worsley's graphic depictions of economic unevenness on matters of world marketing and labor conditions. From boom to bust, from relative well-being to drastic penury, from hated but sustaining work to hunger, from field integration to massive lay-offs—all these conditions occurred over and over again among Melanesians. But then certain of these adverse circumstances occurred with some degree of breadth and intensity in Polynesia as well, where cargo cults seldom emerged. Hence, although preparatory circumstances are necessary to usher in cargo cults, they alone are an insufficient explanation, and they by no means exhaust the sources of expressed discontent. As previously indicated, the other three forces worthy of consideration are the phenomena of facilitation, abdication, and translation.

Facilitating circumstances

Facilitating considerations are ongoing, structural and local. Workplaces, neighborhoods, and peer groups are involved. These continuing factors prompt the formulation and retention of class–racial consciousness as well as alienation from the foreign-imposed government. Low levels of class–racial awareness initially take religious forms, from cognitive awareness of being both separate and exploited to collective action against a common oppressor. Action finds expression through the mechanisms afforded by messianic, millenary radicalism. The near-static quality of these facilitating mechanisms contrasts sharply with the fire of the vibrant movement itself. Yet their ongoing and continuing presence cannot be overlooked.

The *structural components* intensify collective problem-solving and hence consciousness and alienation. Two structural considerations would appear to be most pertinent: (1) the presence of impersonal sets of relations between class–racial groups which differ considerably from one another in terms of power, wealth, and racial prestige, and (2) the existence of a subordinate racial collectivity, whose class racial homogeneity facilitates the intensive interaction within a community that is isolated in terms of affectional but not pecuniary ties from class–racial masters, e.g., the white overseers, the authoritarian Jesuit or Methodist, or the colonial political administrator.

In Melanesia, these conditions were present, and whites treated Melanesians, at best, as paternal charges. Often the white taskmasters defined the islanders as heathen children who had no knowledge of the ways of decency, temperance, moderation, and like Victorian traits. The relationship to the native was essentially rational, economic, and impersonal, although the white might take a genuine and loving interest in several of the individuals in question.

When dealing with the new exigencies associated with participation in an international, capitalist division of labor, the Melanesians were able to fall back on a common language and a collective set of experiences, in short, a shared culture, as well as a common set of work experiences.

These "we–they" circumstances were absent from the *Polynesian* context, for some of the "we's" had lined up within the state as administrators and outright politicians. Hence, since a polarized circumstance failed to emerge, promoting a sense of solidarity among the Polynesians, one essential, indeed necessary, ingredient of a militant cargo cult was missing.

Abdicating circumstances

A governing group is inviting trouble when it fails to create a parliamentary form that might provide a legislative structure for policy suggestions formulated by lower class–racial groups. For when people cannot ameliorate their problems through parliamentary means, they will eventually put together a revolutionary movement. Clearly the Melanesians qualified in this regard.

When a governing group is unwilling to be conciliatory on peoples' grievances and hence to make concessions to the lower classes, the lower classes will in ever-increasing numbers move to define its rulers as without the unquestioned right to govern. The subordinate group will not only reject the rulers, but the rules of state and the sanctions it enjoys; in a word, the state will find itself popularly declared as illegitimate. Certainly one could observe this process among rebellious and at times revolutionary Melanesians, not only during the initial phases of cargo-cult formation but during the transitional periods when the oppressed, in most cases unknowingly, progressed from messianic protest to the creation of unions and political parties.

By contrast, there were strong elements of flexible paternalism in Polynesia, both under the French in Tahiti and under the Americans in Hawaii. Having realized control through violence and cooptation, white rulers magnanimously defined Polynesians as beautiful people, and not as "tribal head-hunters." In Polynesia, time and again, the white rulers made conciliatory gestures, although the slaughter of the Marquesans and the Tahitians reminds us that what is involved is an initial period characterized by slaughter of near-genocidal proportions. For example, the eventual white response to native dislike of plantation labor on such islands as Fiji, Tahiti, and Hawaii was to import Indian and Chinese laborers. Except in isolated instances, no such benevolence was extended to the New Guineans, the Solomon Islanders, or the natives of New Caledonia. Clearly the Melanesians were treated to malevolent brutality over an extended period of time.

By contrast, we might almost suppose that the foreign-controlled state and its predecessor, the paramount tribe had unknowingly facilitated the creation in Polynesia of a benign repression characterized both by conciliatory gestures and by significant concessions. This was evidenced especially on the matter of corvée labor *after* an initial period of extreme violence.

Translating mechanisms

Cargo cults could not have emerged without the presence of native intellectuals alienated from foreign authority and gifted enough to function as messianic leaders. Mind you, these leaders are not necessarily readers of books on revolutionary theory. But they do provide key slogans, religious references, and rebellious indictments of their oppressors and these leaders do command respect and awe. Indeed, at times their perspectives are accepted without question. These views are utopian, cataclysmic, and messianic. The prophets in question delineate the good society and explain how it will be immediately realized, associating its gestation with future social and natural upheavals that will be calamitous for white oppressors.

Defined as demagogues by white overseers, the messianic leaders sometimes find themselves as wards of the intruding state or as patients in mental hospitals, for conservative colonials work quickly to quarantine native laborers from the "madness" of a black-skinned messiah who damagingly depicts the exploitative nature of the white-owned plantation or mine. Although such a messiah is necessary for a successful revolution, the presence of such an individual alone cannot bring about revolution. Thus the white conservatives have been clever but mistaken. They have merely lopped off one head of the hydra. Despite the faulty analysis, the net result is the same—the hamstringing of a movement until other charismatic ones appear.

In most cases, however, the accoutrements of a revolutionary movement were lacking. In a word, Melanesians moving toward the creation of cargo cults were at that time unable to create a disciplined, revolutionary political organization, be it with a trade union or a formal political association. When Melanesians did go beyond the cargo cult, they formed militant trade unions and political associations, groups lacking the revolutionary potential of the vanguard party but organizationally apt nonetheless.

Without the quasimilitary association of a vanguard party, or an equivalent group similarly bent on the distribution of educational materials, Melanesian cargo cults were unable to articulate utopian ideas on the connection between the presence of consumer goods and the organic relation of such goods to modern tools and their techniques of use. The Melanesians lacked both a sophisticated political association (a group able to rely on the written, political knowledge of mankind) and the completeness of a concept of utopia incorporating the ideas of modern science. Thus they could not extend systematically their rebellious organizations and frames of reference to create and to embrace a confederation of hitherto disparate groups sharing common grievances as well as theories. Without this common counterculture throughout Melanesia, indeed, without a common revolutionary organization such as a miniature comintern,[3] the people have seldom been able to create anything more than recurrent rebellions that stand as isolated, limited, and violent protests. Exceptions have occurred in southeastern New Guinea, however, where intensive contact with Western commerce, force, and ideas has helped to produce a more advanced, although nonrevolutionary, response. Here, cargo cults to some degree paved the way for the subsequent creation of higher levels of class-racial consciousness and political sophistication. In some instances, cargo cults between the two World Wars aided the emergence of trade unions and political associations.

CONCLUSIONS

In our brief treatment of preagrarian peoples, focusing on subjugation and protest, we have developed generalizations on protest potential. However, at this point we would like to enter a disclaimer. At best these general formulations are propositional hopes, especially since they were put forth by a political sociologist and not a political anthropologist. Hopefully we are on less shaky grounds in the next chapter, when we consider people located at a higher level of general evolution. This moving up the ladder does *not* imply that primitive peoples are inferior to their general evolutionary successors. Indeed, the very absence of exploitation and state violence plus the presence of reciprocity and redistribution can only endear primitive peoples to those who suffer nowadays from a lack of these qualities.

NOTES

1. Marshall D. Sahlins, "Political Power and the Economy in Primitive Society," in *Essays in the Science of Culture*, eds. Gertrude E. Dole and Robert L. Carneiro, (New York: Crowell, 1960), p. 410.

2. These four conditions are discussed at much greater length in Chapter 4 when we examine the sources of revolutionary drive among peoples located at an agrarian–industrializing level of development. In a sense, cargo-cult formation has many of the qualities of a revolutionary movement; hence the use of these categories to understand cargo cults at the level of primitive social organization.

3. The Comintern was a worldwide revolutionary organization maintained between the two world wars by Communists directed ultimately by the leadership of the Russian Communist Party.

Chapter **3** **An Agrarian-Hydraulic Instance of Revolution: The Case of China**

Section One *Advanced Adaptation, Stifled Reform, and Subsequent Revolution*

HYDRAULIC SOCIETY:
THE STRUCTURE BEFORE TRANSFORMATION

Any analysis of revolutions in our time could benefit from a distinction between feudal and hydraulic society. Briefly, then, it is the difference between an agriculturally based society organized around private property but bounded by decentralized economy and polity, and a crop-rooted society that has constructed widespread and major flood and irrigation works, which are coordinated by a state characterized by considerable centralization of authority.

In our time, hydraulic societies have the greatest potential for total cultural revolutions—massive and recurrent uprisings which call for the remaking of an entire society. In sounding the trumpet for the qualitative transformation of everything, these communist revolutions take at least the first steps into the reworking of the base, i.e., all forms of habitat, technology, and economy, and social organization, as well as patterned ideas. Hydraulic societies today have this potential because yesterday they contained elements that successfully stifled reformist and revolutionary alterations. A hundred years ago, these societies were prevented from moving ahead rapidly by both imperialism and the hydraulic states' economic and technological commitment to massive irrigation and flood-control projects. Yet, their very inability to reform during one epoch became the partial basis for total revolution in the next.

In the last fifty years, great revolutionary movements have begun to unwind in those parts of the world associated with hydraulic society. The vast plains and deltaic areas locked into the Yellow and the Yangtze-Kiang rivers, as well as the Mekong, Brahmaputra, Ganges, Indus, and Nile rivers are examples.

What is hydraulic society? How does it facilitate revolution? Perhaps one way to respond would be to focus on one society. And in this regard, there could be no better illustration than China. By using the Chinese example, we can both (a) arrive at a clearer general distinction between hydraulic and feudal societies, and (b) set the stage for an understanding of revolutionary movements originating in the hydraulic as well as in the feudal context. In particular, we should be able to acquire a better understanding of the Chinese revolution—perhaps one of the two most important revolutions of this century.

IMPERIAL CHINA

Students of recent Chinese revolutionary movements should be acquainted with the impact of the West during the nineteenth century, for it was then that the melon was tapped. Several of the foremost observers of Chinese revolutionary movements have used yet another analogy to summarize the overall impact of Western trade, military, and industrial force:

The massive structure of traditional China was torn apart much as the earth's crust would be disrupted by a comet passing too near. In the end, the remnants of the Old China—its dress and manner, its classical written language and intricate system of imperial governments, its reliance upon the extended family, the Confucian ethic, and all the other institutional achievements and cultural ornaments of a glorious past—had to be thrown into the melting pot and refashioned. The old order was changed within the space of three generations.[1]

What was the old order and how was it unhinged? In answer to the first question, the same writers offer a terse summary:

It [Chinese society] was most unlike that of Western Europe and America; but how? Among several answers that could be given, one of the most illuminating [for those who seek to put societies in categories] is the concept of old China as an example of "Oriental Society." Even before Karl Marx used the term "Asiatic mode of production," Western scholars like J. S. Mill had noted certain general characteristics which seemed to make the ancient empires of the Near East and Asia quite different in kind from the society of Europe. Social historians today are developing this concept; while we can hardly try to summarize it here, we can note certain features. Traditional China, like other ancient empires, came to be organized under a centralized monolithic government in which the official bureaucracy dominated most aspects of large-scale activity—administrative, military, religious, economic, political. This agrarian bureaucratic state got its revenue largely from the agricultural production of the illiterate peasantry, who also provided the manpower for the conscript armies and for the corvée labor which was used to control the water supply through diking and ditching. Large-scale public works, like the Great Wall or the Grand Canal, comparable to roads and airfields of today, have been built by this mass-labor force, mobilized and superintended by the officials. The latter were of course drawn from the small literate element of the Chinese population, the literati who could transact public business using the intricate Chinese writing system. Since only the well-to-do could normally afford the years of study required for literacy in the classics, officials came more from the landlord-gentry class than from the peasant masses. Thus, the landlords produced scholars, and the scholars became officials, forming a complex upper stratum so closely interrelated and interdependent that the ideal

men of distinction were landlord-scholar-officials, rather than generals or merchants.[2]

Let us expand this compressed treatment of traditional China, a society whose structure was not altogether unique.

Traditional China as an instance of hydraulic society

Analyses of the kind advanced by Mill and Marx have suggested the utility of portraying China as corresponding to the generalized notion of a "hydraulic society."[3] In this setting, the bureaucratic apparatus of the state coordinates the large-scale irrigation and flood-prevention projects, which are operated in order to maintain an exploitative redistributive economy. Although the economy provides more benefits to the state bureaucrats than to the subordinate classes, nonetheless it smacks of paternalistic concern for the lower classes.

Now let us look at hydraulic society in another way, namely, through the prism of power defined in terms of the ability of a person or group to coerce others to act in ways that oppose the latter's objective interests. We can think of hydraulic society in terms of a network of functional relationships dependent to varying degrees on a large-scale irrigation system, which is administered by an absolutist bureaucratic organization responsible to an absolute autocrat. These structures plus corresponding values stress the importance of material sustenance and are devoted to the production, distribution, and control of material goods and manpower. This kind of bureaucratic organization can be considered to be absolute because its ruler is seldom checked in an effective manner by nongovernmental forces. The ruler of such an absolutist organization within this model becomes an autocrat when his decisions can no longer be vetoed by intragovernmental forces.

Before exploring the problem in greater detail, however, a few words should be added on the shifting levels of analysis used in this presentation. It must be kept in mind that "hy-

---

[1] Reprinted by permission of the publishers from Ssu-yü Teng and John K. Fairbank, *China's Response to the West: A Documentary Survey,* 1839–1923 (Cambridge: Harvard University Press, 1954), p. 1. Copyright 1954 by the President and Fellows of Harvard College.

[2] *Ibid.,* p. 4. Reprinted by permission of the publishers.

[3] In this analysis I have relied heavily on the works of Karl Wittfogel's *Oriental Despotism* (New Haven: Yale University Press, 1957).

draulic society" is an abstract construct, hence, the grammatical use of the present tense. On the other hand, in order to relieve what might otherwise develop into tedium, I sometimes shift to a concrete level and refer specifically to Imperial China. These historical references, however, could be refined and expressed as abstract categories. Although by first stating and then translating the abstract theory so as to make it meaningful to the Chinese scene, I would have maintained two distinct levels of analysis, the obvious duplication would have been excruciating for both reader and writer.

One more preliminary consideration. In dealing with hydraulic society, perhaps it might be useful to think in terms of tiered levels, beginning at its substructural base and working to a crest. The model, then, would be analogous to a layer cake. Starting with the lowest level, we could observe the importance of habitat and technology, then we could move to a consideration of economy, class structure, and political and social institutions; finally, we could examine several of the normative and valuative dimensions of this system. Let us begin with the base.

The geography and population

Although complex, substructures of the hydraulic society rest on a topography with patterned characteristics. Karl Wittfogel maintained that its historical counterparts have emerged in arid, semiarid, and humid geographical regions located within a particular kind of habitat. Earlier theorists on "Asiatic" (hydraulic) society took essentially the same position. They stressed the relevance of specific climatic and territorial conditions. Marx, for example, betrayed more than a trace of geographical determinism when he distinguished between "classical antiquity," "feudalism," and "Asia," and focused on the origins of the latter by observing that climatic and territorial conditions made both artificial irrigation and canal development the necessary basis for the formation and maintenance of this particular kind of agriculture. According to Marx, the system was characterized politically by the domination of a despot acting as the coordinator of labor for hydraulic and other communal works found in fluvial basins drained by a major river system such as the Nile or Yellow rivers.

The dense population of China at the turn of the nineteenth century was for the most part packed into three geographical areas. Each was split by, yet coordinated through, a particular riverine complex. The Pearl River system in the south, the Yangtze Valley–Szechuan Basin in central China, and the North China Plain all necessitated the kind of state coordination of agriculture posited by Marx if widespread and large-volume Chinese agriculture were to develop. Such a state emerged in approximately 221 B.C. It failed, however, to develop a viable transportation network between central and northern China, and for good reason. A high and rugged mountain chain followed by a gigantic swamp—marsh—lake complex divided peoples of the Yellow River from the Yangtze River population. These obstacles were judged to be surmountable as early as the Han Dynasty (about the time of Christ). A man-made waterway centered around a grand canal running north and south could simultaneously drain part of the swampy region and provide excellent transportation. During the Sui (late sixth century) and T'ang dynasties, the state, by utilizing the corvée, translated this possibility into a reality. Thus the rulers could take advantage of China's variegated habitat and regional crop specialization by uniting diverse regions within one territorial division of labor. The emergence of the state thereby made the "possible" first probable and then actual.

The population of traditional China was not only concentrated in riverine deltas and nearby plains but also distributed in one of two major climatic zones. Midway between the Yellow River and the Yangtze, and running west to east, the aforementioned mountain ranges and a series of large coastal lakes and rivers split north from South China. The north of the "Middle Kingdom," i.e., the historical center of Chinese civilization, contained soils inherently rich, although often parched. By contrast, the highly productive earth of the south was leached by heavy rainfall. Nevertheless certain areas, such as the Pearl Delta, produced as much as three successive crops per year. Rice was the most important item grown in the basins, deltas, and terraced river valleys of South China. In the dry northern plains, wheat, barley, kaoliang, and millet were the key staples. The combination of dependence on riverine cultivation accompanied by irregular rainfall presented many problems to the Chinese population.

China's various "sorrows"—the Pearl, Yangtze, and Yellow among them—had recurrently flooded inundating fields, devastating valleys, destroying crops, and in some cases, depopulating entire provinces. In the north, lack of rainfall also took its toll of animal and vegetable populations. Dust storms and grasshoppers periodically swept down out of Mongolia and Sinkiang to turn the population of North China into rootless, wandering, starving people. Flood control, of all things, also proved to be a problem, especially along the lower reaches of the Yellow River in Shantung. There, the silted river bottoms have over the centuries raised the water levels perilously close to the upper crests of the levies, which tower impressively over a countryside fearful of their river's power. Nevertheless, recurrent floods often turned communities into swarms of isolates roaming countryside and town in search of sustenance.

Under these circumstances, the state several millennia ago had begun to try to prevent these disasters, but its task was made difficult because so many mutually unintelligible languages have been spoken by the peoples of China. Communication between Chinese from different regions, or even neighboring counties (*hsien*) was diffifult in many cases for spoken languages were variegated in both morphology and syntax. Roughly two-thirds of the population spoke some variation of Mandarin—the official language being the Peking dialect of this most popular form. Mandarin was spoken in many parts of the Middle Kingdom, but particularly in northern, east-central, central, and southwest China. Non-Mandarin languages were common to populations located primarily in pockets found in eastern, southeastern, southwestern, western, northwestern and northeastern China. These languages included Hakkah, Cantonese, Lolo, Mongolian, and Manchu. Such linguistic differences hindered efforts by the government to coordinate Chinese society.

Technology, water use, and functional interdependence

In spite of these handicaps (none of which were unique to China), hydraulic societies have engineered a most impressive technology, especially compared with the meager counterparts of European feudal society. As Wittfogel indicated, the mechanical, material, physical, and chemical instruments of hydraulic society, i.e., its technology, included large-scale construction of river embankments, canals, water reservoirs, irrigation ditches, and roads.

Excellent examples could be found in pre-nineteenth century China, especially during the apex of the Ch'ing Dynasty. Very high embankments lined the lower reaches of the Yellow River, and the Grand Canal connected it with the Yangtze, thereby linking the two major river systems. The Canal itself was more than 500 miles long and proved to be an eminently good conveyor of grain to the capital and troops to the grain. The amount of grain available for taxation depended in part on the control of floods through the use of water reservoirs. These reservoirs consisted mainly of marginal agricultural areas which were allowed to flood during periods of heavy rain, especially during the monsoons.

Water-use practices exemplified by irrigation complemented flood control. Irrigation, although largely administered by local gentry at the village and market town levels, nonetheless was dependent on the efforts of governmental officials at the provincial, prefectural, and county levels to control flooding and to compute correct calendars.

The entire technological complex plus its organizational counterpart were shielded. A military wall several thousand miles long was partially constructed as early as the third century B.C., to cover the northern perimeter of China and to protect the hydraulic complex from the periodic invasions of pastoral peoples pressing out of Mongolia and Manchuria. In order to give his readers some idea of the technological wonders constructed by the Chinese, Wittfogel provided the following astounding illustrations:

> The relay system of the T'ang government (678–906 A.D.) operated through more than 1,500 stations, of which nearly 1,300 served as overland stations, 260 functioned as "water posts" and 86 as both. . . .
> The use of foot runners—as a supplement to the horse and boat-post—continued until the last imperial dynasty, Ch'ing (1616–1912). In 1825 the postal service operated an elaborate network of trunk and branch

roads with more than 2,000 express stations and almost 15,000 stations for foot messengers. For the former the administration budgeted 30,526 horses and 71,279 service men and for the latter, 47,435 foot messengers.[4]

As Wittfogel pointed out, these figures include only the technical personnel employed. This means that many more people were directly involved.

Clearly, this technological apparatus was quite unlike anything witnessed under European feudalism. For example, in China, there were roads hundreds of miles long. Some of them, amazingly enough, were perched atop a wall sufficiently wide to allow the simultaneous passage of two carriages. This kind of construction was common when much of feudal Europe was content with simple water transportation, dirt paths, and the remnants of Roman roads. While Chinese were capable of building a wall 40 feet high, 30 feet wide, and approximately 2000 miles long, medieval Europe settled for wooden stockades and stone walls at best several miles long. Immense irrigation systems directed by the government were unknown in European feudalism, as were large-scale flood-prevention projects.

Yet for all its technological grandeur, China remained highly vulnerable to invasions from without, partially because of the high degree of interdependence of parts within hydraulic society. The ideal hydraulic society is like a delicately calibrated watch, whose multiplicity and diversity of units and functions might go out of whack (with devastating consequences for the whole) if one unit failed to operate correctly. Perhaps useful in comprehending the consequences of the failure of one of the units is the distinction between functionally interdependent and independent societies. Societies characterized by functional interdependence exist when communities perform complementary, highly specialized tasks. In a functionally independent society at the other extreme, communities perform more general, less specialized activities, often in ways that result in the duplication of activities.

In functionally independent society, villages

and towns stress the maintenance of symbiotic and commensalistic ties within their respective communities, and deemphasize transportation and communication channels between towns and regions, although links within regions may occur. Such an arrangement, not unusual in a feudal setting, seldom occurs in the hydraulic situation. Functional interdependence more nearly typifies relations among communities found in hydraulic society. Here it is apparent that the population on the village level is dependent on other villages, market towns, and cities, and particularly the representatives of national government residing within them. If the state bureaucracy fails, members of the community frequently find themselves without crops, and the government loses part of its tax base. A lowered tax base could (*a*) further weaken the integrative power of the political center and (*b*) result in an acceleration of the drift toward the total collapse of agriculture.

By comparison, of course, the feudal community relies to a certain extent on trade, market outlets, and specialized production. But, there is considerably less interlacing of economic relations within and between regions highly dependent on a state organization. The relative lack of trade dependence under these circumstances is partly attributable to the greater cost of transportation of goods from rural areas to market towns (a problem less important in hydraulic society largely because of the extensive water networks available). Because trading in feudal society is relatively sparse, market towns seldom grow large enough to become important coordinators of regional economy.

Economic and political decentralization has yet another consequence: the confinement of most communication and transportation to nucleated enclaves, independent of a central government which might collapse. Consequently, when a feudal state (or kingdom) folded, operations of the feudal manor were not totally disrupted. In the case of hydraulic society, however, such a political collapse was often disastrous. Witness the recent (e.g., China) and sometimes lasting (e.g., Tigris–Euphrates valley of Mesopotamia, the northern plateau country of Iran, and the Tarim Basin of Sinkiang) decline of agricultural production which followed loss of coordinative ability on the part of the state.

---

[4] *Ibid.,* p. 58. Reprinted by permission of the publishers.

Economic organization and the state: a restricted economy

Crucial to understanding the development of revolutionary forces in China is the impact of Western economy and political power on the delicate balance of political relationships, especially those common to the coordinating mechanisms found at the center. A tenuous condition of equilibrium emerged approximately one hundred years after the establishment of the Ch'ing Dynasty (seventeenth century) and remained until the beginning of the nineteenth century, although apparently the dynasty had already begun to decline when struck by the partial thrust of Western imperialism during the first half of the century. A more or less stable set of economic, class, and political units had solidified during the middle of the eighteenth century, only to be weakened by internal attrition and dissolved by external force when the free market of technologically superior societies (England, in particular) came into continuous, intensive, and extensive contact with a nonfree market economy of a technologically inferior society (Imperial China). When this occurred, the commodity exchange system of China was drastically altered. These changes in turn accompanied irreversible alterations of many social relationships and philosophical ideas, thereby indicating that more was involved than dynastic decline.

But it makes little sense to state that "economy" was crucial in accounting for this qualitative change, unless we distinguish between generic definition and specific types. By economy is meant the relationships between groups in the spheres of production, distribution, and exchange of things to be used as capital or consumer goods. Following Polanyi,[5] we must not confuse this definition with the ideal conception of *free market economy.* The latter may exist as simplified concept and/or complex reality. The statement that a free market economy exists when commodity values and labor payments are determined almost exclusively by supply and demand mechanisms implies that neither a political authority nor any other social force will attempt to interfere with the flow of commodities or to fix the value of

[5] Karl Polanyi, *The Great Transformation* (Boston: Beacon, 1957).

labor. To repeat, the sole determinant of exchange and labor values is represented by supply and consumer considerations.

The role of political authority under these circumstances is to ensure the maintenance of these conditions, i.e., to prevent associations such as unions or guilds from interfering with the free functions of this market mechanism. A *quasi-free market economy* exists when (a) there is variability in price of commodities, (b) this variation corresponds somewhat to the relative scarcity or plentifulness of commodities, and (c) the interference of political authority in commodity exchange is minimal. Primary and secondary associations such as the family and craft guilds do to some extent restrict the flow of goods. A *nonfree market economy* is characterized by both state and nonstate regulatory efforts in commodity exchange. Needless to say, conditions never correspond precisely to these types. However, it would seem that circumstances in Britain during the 1840s closely resembled those features associated with a free market economy, whereas the economic structure of traditional China approached the other extreme—a nonfree market economy.

This regulative posture was based on the efforts of the Chinese state. Governmental officials in traditional China extended their control into economy where the state attempted consciously to maintain a prosperous society marked by relatively harmonious relations, however exploitive they might have been. In fact, the Chinese government placed itself at the center of a large redistributive network. It collected taxes through the gentry at the local level until the eighteenth century. After that, money payment was used, and after the government garnered its share, the remainder was divided among the lay tax collectors and local government officials, and thereby laid the basis for maintenance of an army capable of defending the northern borders from nomads and developing public works projects. The latter proved to be advantageous not only to the state organization but to the lesser classes, as well.

Limitations on the marketing of goods

The central government, with its paternalistic perspective and conscious concern for maintenance of the redistributive network, specified limitations on the sale of goods, labor, and land. Let us first consider restrictions on the flow of commodities. During the early years of the nineteenth century, the central government emphasized the conditions under which goods could be imported from abroad. In fact, at a time when British liberals found themselves enmeshed in the ideology of Manchester Economics, which called for unrestricted free trade, the Chinese central government maintained the following regulations on imports:

1. All trade was to be conducted through one Chinese port, Canton.

2. However, no vessels of war were to enter the Pearl River, the waterway which led to Canton.

3. The ships coming to trade at Canton were to anchor at Whampoa, thirteen miles below the city, where the loading and unloading were to be done.

4. No arms were to be brought to the European-run warehouses where the European and Chinese merchants carried on their business.

5. European businessmen in the Canton area were allowed to stay there for the trading season only (September to March) and were not allowed to bring their families with them.

6. All the pilots, boatmen, and agents working for the foreigners had to be licensed by the Chinese provincial government.

7. Not more than a fixed number of servants might be engaged by these foreigners.

8. Only certain forms of land transportation might be used.

9. Particular areas near the warehouses were clearly out of bounds for the merchants.

10. Foreigners could not mix with the public nor could they engage in public drunkeness.

11. No smuggling or credit was allowed.

12. Most important, all business carried on by the foreigners was to be conducted through a body of monopolist contractors known as Hong Merchants (a guild of merchants appointed by and responsible *directly* to the Emperor) who would also receive all complaints or petitions addressed to the local government authorities.[6]

[6] Maurice Collis, *Foreign Mud* (New York: Knopf, 1947), pp. 5–6. For a more detailed treatment of the problem, see John K. Fairbank, *Trade and Diplomacy on the China Coast* (Cambridge: Harvard University Press, 1953), pp. 23–74.

Such regulations on the exchange of goods with foreigners surprised even those Englishmen who had learned to smile contemptuously at the restrictions imposed by the mercantile system of Europe. British efforts to open China for trade during the latter part of the eighteenth century had reaped only condescension, epitomized by the Emperor's reply to the pleas of King George III:

AN IMPERIAL EDICT TO THE KING OF ENGLAND: You, O King, are so inclined toward our civilization that you have sent a special envoy across the seas to bring to our Court your memorial of congratulations on the occasion of my birthday and to present your native products as an expression of your thoughtfulness. On perusing your memorial, so simply worded and sincerely conceived, I am impressed by your genuine respectfulness and friendliness and greatly pleased.

As to the request made in your memorial, O King, to send one of your nationals to stay at the Celestial Court to take care of your country's trade with China, this is not in harmony with the state system of our dynasty and will definitely not be permitted. Traditionally people of the European nations who wished to render some service under the Celestial Court have been permitted to come to the capital. But after their arrival they are obliged to wear Chinese court costumes, are placed in a certain residence, and are never allowed to return to their own countries. This is the established rule of the Celestial Dynasty with which presumably you, O King, are familiar. Now you, O King, wish to send one of your nationals to live in the capital, but he is not like the Europeans, who come to Peking as Chinese employees, live there and never return home again, nor can he be allowed to go and come and maintain any correspondence. This is indeed a useless undertaking.

Moreover the territory under the control of the Celestial Court is very large and wide. There are well-established regulations governing tributary envoys from the outer states to Peking, giving them provisions of food and traveling expenses by our posthouses and limiting their going and coming. There has never been a precedent for letting them do whatever they like. Now if you, O King, wish to have a representative in Peking, his language will be unintelligible and his dress different from the regulations; there is no place to accommodate him. . . .

The Celestial Court has pacified and possessed the territory within the four seas. Its sole aim is to do its utmost to achieve good government and to manage political affairs, attaching no value to strange jewels and precious objects. The various articles presented by you, O King, this time are accepted by my special order to the office in charge of such functions in consideration of the offerings having come from a long distance with sincere good wishes. As a matter of fact, the virtue and prestige of the Celestial Dynasty having spread far and wide, the kings of the myriad nations come by land and sea with all sorts of precious things. Consequently there is nothing we lack, as your principal envoy and others have themselves observed. We have never set much store on strange or ingenious objects, nor do we need any more of your country's manufacturers. . . .[7]

After extensive exposure to this posture, a sense of unfairness undoubtedly grew among the English to feelings of consternation when they continually confronted regulations of trade *within* Chinese society as well. Foreign capitalist speculation with grain, for example, was highly unlikely, given the antiforeign stance of the government. Only state bureaucrats or domestic merchants whom the state tolerated could tap the melon. Outwardly, however, the government not only acted to discourage the speculation of foreigners but seemed to express genuine concern with stabilizing grain prices. The government was expected to play a dual role by both marketing and pricing grain. It should seek both to guarantee a supply and to stabilize price levels for the commodity. On the one hand, it was supposed to maintain granaries—storehouses of government-owned grain accumulated for distribution during famine. On the other hand, it was expected to stabilize grain prices by buying up the crop when prices were low.

These were the rules. It would seem that they were carried out in practice more often in the larger cities than in other areas, and more frequently during periods of prosperity than during periods of dynastic decline.

As might be imagined, within the traditional graft-ridden Chinese political system, bureaucratic deviations in grain distribution were not uncommon. For example, local government officials would act as independent speculators, buying up government grain for themselves and rigging its distribution to give maximal profit to the distributors. The net result was to make Mencius' ideal of "an ever-normal granary" just that, a seldom-realized ideal. The granary was emptied and purpose violated, as grain was distributed not on the basis of need but on ability to pay exorbitant prices. Nonetheless, however ineffectual the government might sometimes have been in the regulation of grain distribution, the presence and tone of its interference contrasted vividly with the experiences of early capitalist England, a system considerably more niggardly when it came to welfare services.

Circumscribed use of labor

In China, government regulations not only circumscribed the exchange of goods but specified the use of labor in ways quite unknown in early industrial Europe. Wages for labor contributed by peasants and artisans were not determined exclusively by supply and demand considerations. This being the case, how was labor used and reimbursed?

In the case of the corvée, the pecuniary value of labor employed by the state did not fluctuate according to supply and demand, since wages were not involved. One simply performed services stipulated by agents of the state for a length of time specified by state representatives. On the other hand, agricultural laborers often earned wages. But even under these circumstances, normative prescriptions limited the free play of the labor market. Traditional norms were important in the case of laborers, for if they sold their labor power to a landlord, the little evidence available suggests that the landlord was morally obligated to the peasant. He was supposed to provide the peasant with a living wage. Although these obligations were not always met, especially during periods of economic collapse, the exploitation involved was not of the order common to free market economies undergoing the early stages of industrialization. Witness the impact of supply-and-demand considerations on the wage structure of English workmen, especially during the early part of the nineteenth century. Workers frequently died at relatively young ages because of starvation wages despite the concerted efforts of England's aristocracy, which maintained a

[7] Teng and Fairbank, *op cit.,* p. 19. Reprinted by permission of the publishers.

paternalistic stance not too unlike the one common to the traditional Chinese countryside.

Much as was the case in feudal Europe, the pecuniary value of urban artisan labor also failed to fluctuate according to the principles expounded by Smith, Ricardo, and Bentham. Every artisan belonged to a guild corresponding to his craft. Silversmiths, tinsmiths, goldsmiths, ironmongers, and the like associated within guilds. Wages were fixed by them, often after close consultation with those occupying important positions in merchant guilds. Entrance into artisan guilds was restricted by the guild itself, thereby limiting the possibility of having an oversupply of skilled craftsmen. In other words, a monopoly was held by the guild in the areas of skills applied, products made, and prices charged. Clearly, the general wage conditions which underlay the labor of the Chinese urban artisan differed significantly from those of the wage workers of early industrial England. They were, however, in delicate accord with the expectations of other classes and political groups in Chinese society.

Restrictions on land use

The hydraulic state imposes its power most noticeably in the use and distribution of land. In traditional China, land could be exchanged, but only within limits, and some of these were imposed by the government. The state involved itself to varying degrees in five kinds of land control: government-managed land, government-regulated land, private-peasant land ownership, bureaucratic landlordism, and absentee landlordship.

Government-managed land referred to government-owned land, which in China did not include more than a small fraction of the total land area, most of it being concentrated (during the early Ch'ing Dynasty) in Manchuria. Perhaps less prevalent in China was the arrangement described as *government-regulated land,* in which the government assigned land to prospective landholders under set conditions. For example, land in certain border regions was given to ex-soldiers, who were to use it for the purpose of raising crops.

Private-peasant landownership existed when the proprietor had the right to hold his land

indefinitely and to sell it to a person outside his kinship group. Although no exact figures are available, this was undoubtedly the most common form of landownership in China, particularly in its northern parts during the 1800s.

Under *bureaucratic landlordism*, government officials engaged in the purchase of land for themselves and/or their families. They did so through salaries and power prerequisites inherent in their political positions. This form of landownership increased greatly during the nineteenth century, especially in South China, after the impact of the West had begun to bankrupt the peasants and to dissolve village relations.

Absentee landlordism, of course, existed where the land was owned by one who leased its use to tenant cultivators. This form became particularly visible and widespread during the course of the last century, especially in South China, where not a few government officials engaged in land speculation. Thus absentee and bureaucratic landlordism were not mutually exclusive.

The departure from the ideal of a free market economy was obvious. Government-managed and government-regulated lands did not qualify for free market exchange, since the land itself was not marketable except under extraordinary circumstances. Land in the other three instances, however, did qualify in this regard. Nonetheless, sale and accumulation of these landholdings were subject to control of informal mechanisms or state regulations. Limited and indirect evidence suggests that in the case of private-peasant landownership, land was not simply sold to the highest bidder. In many instances, members of the clan had first choice, which meant that those outside of the clan were bypassed, even if they offered a higher price. This was the rule. To the extent that the Chinese peasantry was somewhat prosperous, this arrangement was probably not unrealistic since relatives may have actually found themselves in a financial position to buy the property.

Other mechanisms, more pervasive in terms of numbers affected, operated to restrict land sale that occurred under normal conditions. During the apex of a dynasty, the central government prevented bureaucratic officials from accumulating large amounts of land. Certain officials were forced to resign when their land-holdings became too extensive. According to the rules, and they were most compellingly enforced at the height of the dynasty's economic splendor, the official was not allowed to settle in his home province, thereby limiting his ability to accumulate property around his family base. Furthermore, he moved periodically from one region to another as the state transferred him from post to post. Before moving, he had to sell whatever land he may have acquired. Nor was his land to be tax exempt.

However, bureaucrats did not always observe these regulations. In fact, there was a direct relationship between progression of dynasty and incidence of land-tax evasion among state bureaucrats. At the beginning of each dynastic cycle, the land-tax registers were complete, in the sense that all properties were listed. As the dynasty aged, the amount of land held by administrators of the state increased. And, contrary to the rules, land so claimed became tax exempt. This good fortune occurred partly because bureaucrats had access to tax registers, which they sometimes destroyed or falsified. Often these tactics were not used; rather, another alternative proved popular—keepers of the records were simply bribed.

Yet the bureaucratic gentry were in a position to exert legal authority on landowners when necessary. Ordinary landlords had to pay their taxes, although a bribe might reduce the amount. Also, merchants who were located in market towns and also involved in the accumulation of land sometimes felt the sting of the central government. Those who acquired much land and asserted themselves politically often lost their land and/or placed their lives in jeopardy. The seizure of land was more than a logical possibility, for expropriation was viewed by many as the traditional way in which the state could handle the overambitious.

An illustration comes to mind. Widespread ownership of land by the Buddhist Church during the height of the T'ang Dynasty had invited government expropriations of landholdings as well as other negative sanctions. Buddhism had played an economic role in the countryside not unlike that pursued by the Catholic Church in much of Eastern Europe until the industrial revolution. Before the breakup of its power began in A.D. 842, Buddhist organizations in China had owned 4,600 temples and 40,000 shrines and had claimed 260,000 monks and nuns. Between A.D. 842 and 845, the government destroyed almost all the temples and seized all images, except those made of stone, clay, or wood. When the temples and religious objects mentioned had been destroyed, all the monks and nuns were secularized (i.e., made to pay taxes). Not only were thousands of shrines wrecked and a sizable religious population reoriented, but millions of acres of land were seized. In addition, the state issued manumissions for 150,000 slaves who had been owned by the church. The role of the state on this matter of private accumulation of large amounts of land and other forms of property was altogether clear for generations to follow.[8]

Family inheritance also diminished the ready accumulation of land. It is interesting that the Chinese form of land inheritance, whatever its origins, complemented the perspective of the governmental bureaucracy. The system of land inheritance, by dividing the land more or less equally among the sons, helped to prevent the development of large landholdings like those common to Europe until the middle and latter part of the nineteenth century. In this sense, land inheritance assumed a form considerably unlike that in systems relying either on primogeniture or on ultimogeniture. When the land was not divided among the sons, but rather was passed on to the oldest or the youngest son, as the case might be, the accumulation of land was promoted.

Clearly then, some forms of land in China were nonsalable and others were subject to sale, although restrictions were involved. Yet, all land was theoretically subject to central government confiscation at any time. Expropriation, however, was seldom necessary because of the form of land inheritance. Parenthetically, use of certain other forms of "land," such as minerals, was also within the purview of the state. The extraction and sale of salt, for example, was a government monopoly, although the state contracted both the production and distribution functions to private merchants willing to pay the price for the rights involved.

[8]Wittfogel, *op. cit.,* p. 122. Also see Karl A. Wittfogel and Chia-sheng Feng, *History of Chinese Society, Liao,* American Philosophical Society, *Transactions,* Vol. XXXVI, p. 292 (Philadelphia).

The class structure:
political and economic levels

The traditional Chinese productive and distributive system was quite unlike the one associated with feudal European experience. For the purposes of analysis, class can be defined in terms of a category of roles which occupy a common relationship to the mode of production. In China, the basic distinction was between the state coordinators and the remaining producers and distributors. This definition, then, is not altogether political. Yet one set of roles proves to have a distinctly political flavor. Chinese government officials on various administrative levels helped to regulate not only the distribution of goods but the very productive processes that made possible the intensive use of land. The primary tasks of the officials in this regard were policy-making and enforcing and coordinating public works projects on the national, provincial, prefectural, and county levels.

The title "court official" was assigned to ranking Peking bureaucrats, whereas the class designation of those occupying principal provincial and prefectural positions was that of "middle-level official." Those who occupied positions on the county level, as well as government employees in "nonline" positions were called "lesser officials." Together they cooperated with the bureaucratic gentry in order to grapple not only with the mechanical problems of digging, dredging, and damming, but also organizational tasks. Determining the number of people needed for a project and the whereabouts of such people on the basis of a previously compiled register, and establishing criteria for the selection of corvée personnel were requirements. Transportation to work site, determination of operations to be performed (spading, carrying of mud and straw, etc.), provision of raw materials, food, and other necessities—all these demanded the consultative services of lesser officials.

On the periphery of the bureaucracy and fulfilling multiple roles linking government to peasant was the *bureaucratic gentry.*[9] It consisted of families which owned relatively large tracts of land and from whose ranks were recruited personnel for government posts. The bureaucratic gentry helped to implement government policies on public works projects by taking most of the responsibility for organizing corvée labor. During normal times, every commoner family within the village participated in construction teams. The gentry organized these teams annually in order to maintain and extend canals, roads, embankments, and the like. However, the bureaucratic gentry did not, by itself, make basic policy on these matters. As we have already noted, they very often worked with government officials in discussing mechanical problems and organizational tasks. In this regard, the gentry became most important in mobilizing corvée personnel at the work site and establishing a division of labor.

Clearly, the gentry helped to translate policy into accomplishment. For their efforts, they profited in a number of ways. One of the more lucrative rewards was the right to collect taxes, part of which they were expected to keep. This customary graft was sizable, and the dependence of the gentry on their cut of the taxes pressed them to develop and maintain informal relations with the peasantry in order to carry out the taxing operation efficiently.

The informal ties between landlord and peasant were calibrated in terms of amount of good will, or *kan-ching,* created and maintained between them. The good will rested on the performance of reciprocal tasks by the two parties, with the gentry performing protective services and the peasant responding through cooperation in payment of taxes and support of the corvée and military draft. The strength of the bond depended on the mutual performance of these and complementary activities. In some cases, the amount of *kan-shing* accumulated was minimal because of the failure of one or perhaps both of the parties to live up to expectations. In other instances, when the amount of *kan-ching* was quite great, the gentry were motivated in its efforts to protect the peasant from government officials and unscrupulous merchants. In any event, the clever member of the landed gentry had ample reason to cement ties with village peasants, as well as considerable basis for diagnosing his standing with peasant families.

[9] In my analysis of the gentry I have relied heavily upon Hsiao-tung Fei's "Peasantry and Gentry: An Interpretation of Chinese Social Structure and Its Changes," *American Journal of Sociology,* vol. 52 (1946): pp. 1–17.

When one of the gentry was successful as an official, he was in a fine position to engage in extensive purchases of land, although, as we have already noted, such accumulation of land was not without risk. The purchases would function in many cases as the original impetus for movement of himself or members of his family into, and up through, the governmental bureaucracy. With one foot at the periphery of governmental power and the other firmly planted in private economy, a member of the landed gentry occupied a most enviable position in dynastic China.

Next in order were the direct producers and exchangers of material values, the economic classes of hydraulic society: the artisans, peasants, and merchants. Briefly, an *artisan* was one who derived almost all his livelihood from the creation of goods through the skilled use of manual effort. The peasantry ranged from landless laborers to rich peasants. Farmers who owned their own land but did not labor for others for pay, and did not hire others to cultivate their fields, were *middle* peasants. Those who worked their own fields or leased lands and were periodically employed by others as cultivators were *poor* peasants. Farmers who worked their own fields and employed others to do so were *rich* peasants. The peasants who did not cultivate their own land but rather hired themselves out to carry on agrarian tasks for others were *agricultural laborers.* The third class, the *merchants,* not only exchanged goods but in some cases engaged others to produce them. Shops that produced goods were small in size and capital, partly because business enterprise in China never took a corporate form but remained family based.

It is interesting to note that these definitions, largely derived from Teng, Fairbank, Marx, and Wittfogel, failed to include the classical eighteenth- and nineteenth-century emphasis on economic criteria. Indeed, my approach would sound strange to Adam Smith, who was able to omit the relevance of political criteria from his definition of class position by viewing class simply as a correlate of private property. Wittfogel admitted that the classical conception of class, with its underlying stress on economy, was necessary for an understanding of societies in which private property as a powerful institution prevailed. He maintained, however, that it

did not make allowances for power as operating independent of private property ownership—a phenomenon altogether visible in hydraulic societies.

In the case of China, the political power of the state was often sufficiently important to decide where an individual would be located in the economic structure and whether he could attempt to accumulate capital. Members of such a class within the state might be thought of as a tiered political structure overlying economic strata found outside the perimeter of the government. Among those within this *political* class, the proximity of one's particular position to the upper echelons of the state (the emperor, his entourage, and the higher officials) specified his relative power. This determined, to a large extent, the probability of his achieving the more esteemed values in society, such as more power and wealth. Unlike feudal society, land ownership in itself was not *the* important consideration in the achievement and use of power since under normal conditions the bureaucratic apparatus of the state held ultimate control over everyone.

Very briefly, how does this system of political power compare with that of feudal society? Perhaps a general answer to this question might give us more perspective on the differences involved. The most important aspect of feudal society was its decentralization of power. Feudalism simply did not have a large-scale state organization. Feudal society generally consisted of loosely interconnected clusters of communities which included in each case a feudal lord and his serfs. The feudal lord was distinguished by his large landholdings, which were cultivated by nonlandowners, his vassals. Together, this class—economic unit operated independently of the meager state organization. At the very apex of the latter stood the king, his entourage, and the hierarchy of the Church. Although constituting an autonomous power, the Church maintained an organization reaching down to the village level, and more often than not it behaved to complement, but not dominate, the power position of the lord of the manor.

Of course, the Church itself in some instances combined the function of landholder and guardian of men's souls. When this unity occurred, the Church was indeed politically powerful, as the history of eastern Europe in the last one thousand years has indicated. Nonetheless, the successful use of power, whether held by Church or divided between it and a group of lords, depended a great deal on solidarity between the nobles and the king. Often these bonds were tenuous at best. Certainly the coalitions between Church, lord, and sovereign were not those connecting subordinates to absolute state; rather they were loose ties linking potential equals, especially when the particular lords or Church figures banded together with others of their own kind before confronting the sovereign. In fact, the king was typically dependent on his lords for what little economic and military power he might wish to mobilize.

In hydraulic society, on the other hand, the governmental organization during the apex of a dynasty did not have to tolerate powerful political combinations independent of the sovereign. In fact, all levels of the population were subordinate to a state apparatus which had its own military organization to deal with domestic dissidents or foreign invaders.

Power wielding and ethical principles: the amalgamation of formal and informal control structures

Let us now take up the total power of the state apparatus, so important in guiding hydraulic society. Wittfogel argued that the state could prevent all internal nongovernmental forces from exerting themselves against it. Of course, it was implied that this condition held true when the bureaucratic organization of a state was operative and not undermined by economic travail at the end of a dynastic cycle. Ordinarily, however, kin groups, representatives of religious organizations, independent and semiindependent leaders of military groups, and owners of various forms of property constituted potential sources of challenge. In order to deal with these possible threats from below, traditional Chinese governmental organization extended formally to the *hsien* and, informally, to the family levels. An amalgam of state and informal organization ordinarily prevented the mobilization of dissident groups, except when the state abused its power. A good illustration of brutal use of state power consists of the events surrounding the earlier efforts to construct the Grand Canal. During the Sui Dynasty (A.D.

590–618), the state drafted corvée labor, and 3.6 million laborers between the ages of 15 and 50 were forced into service. All who refused to participate were decapitated. Each cooperating family had to designate one additional person to help to perform the less demanding tasks, and in these cases, an old person or a child sufficed. A total of 5,430,000 people took direct part in the construction, not a few being flogged for dereliction in the performance of tasks. Parenthetically, discontent aroused by atrocities of this sort helped to precipitate a successful revolution and to pave the way for the establishment of the subsequent T'ang Dynasty.[10] Power, when wielded, was total. Under certain conditions, power abused led to the creation of successful revolutionaries.

Ordinarily, however, Chinese peasants could be readily mobilized for public work. The process involved provides an interesting example of thorough political control. The government on the local level attached itself to informal village organization through the bureaucratic gentry, as we have already observed. Information on signs of political unrest was quite frequently forwarded from peasants, thereby increasing their *kan-shing* to gentry, who in turn made the information available to government officials. The gentry were in fact politically responsible for the behavior of the local population. If the behavior of the latter displeased the central government, e.g., inability to pay taxes, the members of the gentry held responsible for lack of collection might very well lose favor with the government. Loss of favor frequently meant loss of the privilege to collect taxes. Partially because this possibility existed, the bureaucratic gentry enforced a localized system of political control. Family heads were held responsible for the political acts of their kin. When anyone stepped out of line, the gentry punished the parents. A Confucian ethic concerned with "the five relationships" mirrored, enforced, and extended these ties, and in so doing, linked the poorest agricultural laborer to the Emperor himself within an extended power relationship. Younger brothers were defined as subordinates in their relations to their older brothers, and all family members were expected to obey the male head of the household. Wives

[10] Wittfogel, *op. cit.*, p. 40.

were to obey their husbands. All villagers were to be loyal to their friends. Finally, all subjects were expected to obey the Emperor on all matters.

This system of social control was expressed locally through a mechanism of thought surveillance found at the village level—the *"pao-chia"* system. The heads of families were responsible to the gentry for any antistate remarks or behavior expressed by family members, whereas the heads of the villages (the gentry) were accountable to government officials for the actions of village members as a whole. The gentry were the most eminent and powerful people on the village level. Although they sometimes moved to nearby towns, they nonetheless maintained landowning privileges and political power in the villages from which they had just emigrated. In many cases they were able to remain preeminent by exerting various forms of power through relatives still living in the villages.

How did the system work? A *pao* consisted of ten contiguous households (i.e., *chia*) whose members aided one another in such activities as road clearing, transplanting rice, and carrying on religious ceremonies. Each *pao* contained a leader, approved by the gentry, whose principal tasks were to enforce law and uphold custom among his neighbors. The *pao* leader levied negative sanctions against household heads when individuals deviated from mores or law. Thus it was possible to police the community *without* the development of a local constabulary.

This inexpensive network probably had few counterparts in other types of societies. Did anything approaching this form of village control exist in feudal society? Wittfogel doubted it, and perhaps rightly. Feudal society lacked the state organization, the ethic, and the technology to enforce such controls, even if the nobles had desired them.

SUMMARY

During the apex of a dynasty, members of the state bureaucracy wielded considerable coercive power over the rest of the Chinese population, with the Emperor exercising ultimate sway through his bureaucratic organization and the landed gentry. Below these levels were the economic subordinates, the merchants, artisans, and peasants. The latter contributed taxes to a redistributive center which performed military and other services. Military power became not only the ultimate source for protecting as well as controlling peasants but also the principal means of maintaining a nonfree market economy whenever foreign or domestic threats appeared. The state regulated production and exchange. It maintained a monopoly of control over the production and distribution of key goods.

Nor were these the only economic activities of the state. It prevented the sale of some land on the open market, curtailed any free-wheeling accumulation of land or exploitation of labor by private enterprisers or religious organizations. In fact, it confiscated their wealth when they appeared to be too strong. Here the state differed from its counterparts in feudal and early capitalist Europe. From the point of view of those who espoused classical economic doctrine, the Chinese state restricted trade, monopolized control over production of certain goods, and threatened those who promoted the unfettered movement of goods and labor. Indeed, to the leaders of incipient industrial capitalism, barriers to trade and development stemmed from the noxious policies of a condescending imperial government. Undermining these policies would pave the way for destroying the nonfree market economy. Later, the principal task of Western economic imperialism was to abolish the nonfree market economy.

Unfortunately, our resorting to ideal typical forms may have somewhat exaggerated such matters as the traditional Chinese state's regulation of the domestic economy. Yet for comparative purposes, such a slight error in judgment may be useful if we remember that an analysis of traditional China on its own merits (i.e., the internal structure of traditional Chinese social organization) reveals many instances, areas, and time periods when state intervention on the local level was minimal. Also that foreign involvement in China during the early and middle nineteenth century may have only accelerated the pace of dynastic decline.

TRANSITIONAL REMARKS

Harold R. Isaacs's *The Tragedy of the Chinese Revolution* is a classic. Hence, an excerpt appears in Section Two. Almost forty years ago, Isaacs depicted many of the conditions that moved peasants and workers to play lead- ing revolutionary roles during the early decades of this century, a crucial period in the develop- ment of Chinese insurgence.

Section Two   *A Reading on China*

China's Crisis: The Class Pattern

Harold R. Isaacs

Social change came belatedly to China. That is why it is today a land of such deeply chiseled contrasts. It is forced by the pull of a whole world system to make the leap from wooden plow to tractor, from palanquin to airplane. Western imperialism forced the Celestial Empire to find its place in a terrestrial world that had already advanced materially beyond it. For China there was no chance of a gradual ascent nor the opportunity to pass through the stages of development that the dominant Western world had already left behind. Tardily forced to find a place in the main stream of world his- tory, China had to make a mighty leap forward. It had to try to make in decades the changes the West had accomplished in centuries. This wrench could not occur without the most pro- found convulsions. Hence the turmoil, the speed, the scope, the depth, the explosive char- acter of events in China during the last forty years.

To make the necessary changes, China had not only to break sharply with its past; it had to transform its present. Old and new fetters both had to be sundered. Imperialist penetration had introduced the most modern techniques in production, transport, communications, and finance, the tools of modern capitalism. Yet, by adapting to its own uses the merchants, land- lords, officials, and militarists, imperialism helped perpetuate the precapitalist forms of

■Taken from Harold R. Isaacs, *The Tragedy of the Chinese Revolution*, Second Revised Edition (Stan- ford, Calif.: Stanford University Press, ©, 1961 by the Board of Trustees of the Leland Stanford Junior Uni- versity, pp. 23–34 and notes pp. 352–353.

Chinese social organization. Foreign-built factories and railroads were used to extract profits out of the backwardness that survived in China as a whole. By occupying all the strategic positions in Chinese economy and drawing off tribute for the benefit of principals abroad, the imperialist system stifled the "nor- mal" or independent development of China's resources that might have raised the standard of living of the Chinese people and secured for China a less unequal competitive position in relation to the advanced West. The existence of the foreign "spheres of influence" prevented China from achieving any reasonable degree of internal coherence and unification. If the Chi- nese people were to raise themselves from intol- erable poverty, productive forces had to be freed to grow. To begin with, the farmer had to regain a stake in his land and his toil; industrial- ization had to begin to provide a new and more mutually fruitful relationship between town and country; and the foreign grip on Chinese economic and political life had to be broken. These were the inseparable elements of the cri- sis in modern Chinese society. These were, and amid all the changes still are, the problems of the Chinese revolution.

The heaving events of the last two decades, the world economic crisis, the Japanese inva- sion, the Pacific war, the collapse of Japan, the civil war in China, and the onset of ruinous inflation brought the crisis in China to the climax that ended with Communist conquest of power in 1949. These events altered the foreign relationship to China, both politically and eco- nomically. Extraterritoriality and the other special privileges acquired in the last century were finally yielded in treaties signed during the war. The foreign economic role in China was likewise transformed by the wartime dislocations and the subsequent political changes. But the root problem is still the same one that drove China into revolutionary upheaval two decades ago. China has suffered from being a vast, overpopulated, backward country in a world that has stubbornly refused it an opportunity to come abreast. The intense pressure of the swollen population in the crowded river valleys has been a product not merely of technical backwardness but of a whole encrusted system of social relations in which that backwardness was preserved. The events of 1925–1927, as well as all the more recent events, have their roots in the struggle of the Chinese peasant for survival.

As China entered upon its new period of revolutionary conflict after 1919, it was plain that any radical revision in Chinese life had to begin with restoring to the peasant his land and the product of his toil. Only in this way would the old landholding system be abolished. It was the indispensable first step in the eventual transformation of the whole rural economy and the increase of agricultural productivity in new forms and by new methods. More than three-quarters of China's population, or more than 300,000,000 people, depend upon the land for their livelihood. The problems of these millions are the problem of China. Their poverty is China's poverty. All of China's hopes for the future depend on releasing the productive energies of this great mass of people. Up to now they have been drained by a system which has taken away from them the fruits of their infinite toil as well as the land itself, and has given them nothing in return.

Chinese rural economy has been characterized by the following main features:

1. The increasingly swift concentration of land ownership in the hands of a constantly narrowing section of the population.

2. The passage of title in much of the land to absentee landlords, government officials, banks, and urban capitalists, who controlled the commercial capital penetrating to the remotest villages via the local merchants and usurers, and who were in turn dominated by foreign finance capital and the regime of the world market.

3. The dislocation and decline of agricultural production as a result of the uneconomic use of increasingly parcelized land, preservation of the most backward farming methods, the harsh impositions of the landlord, the usurer, and the state, exposure to the ravages of famine, flood, and drought, and civil wars fought by armies swollen by hordes of dispossessed peasants.

Scientific surveys made in recent years have destroyed the illusion, once so common, that China was a land of relatively comfortable small landholders. From sectional studies made under his direction, Professor Chen Han-seng estimated in 1936 that no less than 65 percent of the peasant population was either entirely landless or land-hungry, i.e., possessing land in parcels too small and too burdened by all the adverse conditions of the regime to provide a living even on the barest subsistence level.[1] Differences in land owned and tilled and in the labor applied or exploited on the land disclosed the deep cleavages within the peasant population.[2]

Conditions of land tenure provide the clearest mirror of class relations in agriculture. One official estimate made in 1927 held that 55 percent of the Chinese peasantry was entirely landless and 20 percent holders of inadequate land. It was calculated that 81 percent of the cultivable land was concentrated in the hands of 13 percent of the rural population.[3] These figures have been in the main substantiated by later investigators. In the north, where individual landholders predominated, study of a sample district showed that although only 5 percent of the farming population consisted of landless tenants, 70 percent of the total held less than 30 percent of the cultivated land in coverage plots of 10.9 mow, or less than two acres. In another district, it was found that 65.2 percent of the population held 25.9 percent of the land in parcels of less than seven mow, or a fraction above an acre. Landlords and rich peasants, together comprising 11.7 percent of the farming population, held 43 percent of the land, and middle peasants held the rest.

In the far more densely populated Yangtze Valley and in the south, where foreign influence had first been felt and where the commercialization of agriculture was more advanced, the disproportions were found to be much greater. In one district of Chekiang province, investigators found that 3 percent of the population owned 80 percent of the land. In Wusih, another district of Central China, 68.9 percent of the farming families owned only 14.2 percent of the land in individual average parcels of 1.4 mow, or less than a quarter of an acre. Landlords and rich peasants, 11.3 percent of the families, owned 65 percent of the land.[4] A separate survey made in the southern province of Kwantung[5] revealed that landowners in different sections of the province comprised 12 to 32 percent of the population, and tenants and agricultural laborers 68 to 88 percent. Of the poor peasants representing 64.3 percent of the population in one area, investigators found that 60.4 percent were landless. An average of all the districts studied showed that more than half the farming population owned no land. Of all the land tilled by the poor peasants, only 17.2 percent was owned and 82.8 was leased. The average area owned by a poor peasant family was found to be 0.87 mow and the average area cultivated, including leased land, 5.7 mow. The number of mow necessary to provide the barest subsistence for a peasant family was found, in different districts, to vary between six and ten, and twice that many for tenant farmers.

This extreme concentration of land came about partially through the gradual alienation of the once considerable state, temple, or community lands and the conversion of the large collective holdings of the rural clans into the virtual private property of small groups of powerful clan leaders. The steady decline in agricultural production and the increasing weight of the burden placed on the peasant's shoulders soon lost him what land he had left. His skill in coaxing growth out of his tiny plot of ground could not match the results of scientific advances made elsewhere in agriculture or enable him to halt the decrease in the productivity of his land. China's chief commercial crops, tea and silk, surrendered their positions in the world market because better products were more efficiently grown by more modern competitors.[6]

The invasion of the village by commercial capital and cheap manufactured commodities put an end to the peasant's old self-sufficiency. But because the country remained backward in communications and production techniques, the peasant could not adapt himself to the change. He was simply ruined by it. He had to produce for sale in order to exist, yet the smallness of his land and the primitive character of his farming made it difficult, if not impossible, for him to do this with much success. He not only could not produce enough to provide him with a surplus, but had to go into debt for fertilizer, for food to tide him over until harvesttime, for seed, for the rental and use of implements. For these he mortgaged away not only his crop but his land, at rates of interest never lower than 30 percent and more often 60, 70, 80 percent and even higher. The crushing burden of taxes and the rapacious extortions of the militarists who came to rule over him drove the peasant more deeply into debt each successive year and placed him and his land at the mercy of the usurer and the tax collector.[7] He was fleeced at will by the merchant because he could not ship his tiny crop to more distant markets and hope for a return. Crops were freely cornered and prices manipulated at the village level by the merchants. Invariably, new debts were all the peasant had to show at the end of a season's toil. They followed him into the next year and into the next generation. Losing his land, he became a tenant. To the landlord he had to surrender 40 to 70 percent of his crop and a substantial additional percentage, often in special dues, gifts, and obligations preserved from the dim feudal past, including the duty of free labor on special occasions fixed by ancient tradition. Famines, floods, and droughts, against which he was defenseless, often cost him his crop, his land if he had any, and frequently his life. Even in the best years, however, he and his family lived on the edge of starvation. He was little better than a bonded slave to the landlord, the tax collector, the merchant, and the usurer.

This process, in its manifold aspects, plunged the great mass of the peasantry into chronic, unrelieved pauperism. Millions driven off the land begged, starved, took to banditry, or swelled the armies of the war lords. From the south they had streamed abroad, to the Americas, to Malaya, and to the Indies. From the north, they emigrated to the undeveloped lands of Manchuria. Millions of them clogged the cities and towns on the rivers and on the sea board, an inexhaustible source of cheap man-power that the new infant industries could not absorb. Their labor was still cheaper than that of animals, and throughout the length and breadth of China men did the work of beasts of burden. More and more land was left untilled. China, one of the greatest agricultural coun-tries, was compelled to begin importing food-stuffs in steadily increasing measure.[8] The in-ternal and external markets entered upon a disastrous decline. The whole economic struc-ture rotted at its core.

Over the years these conditions erupted in violence that became chronic but remained lo-calized. Such was the banditry that became epidemic in China in the years following the 1911 revolution. It was obvious that the rise of any new revolutionary banner would bring the peasants to their feet and marshal them, almost at a word, in any new effort to revise the conditions of their life. It was also obvious that any new political force which undertook to lead the peasant masses toward a new dispensa-tion would have to undertake in the first place to relieve the peasants of their worst burdens and restore them to their land.

This did not mean that mere redivision and redistribution of the land was the final answer to peasant well-being. Parcelization of the land was already one of the basic ills of Chinese agrarian economy. Any revolutionary transfor-mation of Chinese society would have to in-clude a long-term and far-reaching program for increasing the efficiency of agricultural produc-tion in economically larger units making full use of modern farming methods and industrial organization. This is why in the most funda-mental sense a peasant economy, with all it contains of the narrow and limited outlook of the small and isolated producer, comes into conflict with the demands of a more rational-ized system of urban and rural production. This is why the process of change must necessarily be one of patient education, of experiment and example, and of gradual transformation based upon proved results. It is also the reason why, in the first instance, the conditions for such changes cannot be established until the peasant himself has overthrown the old system that keeps him in thrall. In a backward peasant society, it is impossible to think in terms of rational planning and modernization before the

peasant has been helped to free himself from all the older bonds of social subjection and igno-rance which hold him down. This is why, above all, these changes have to take place not in rural isolation but as part of a fundamental revision of the economy as a whole.

In China this meant, as we have stated, that the economy of the country as a whole had to be freed to develop in accordance with its own needs. Here it ran into the formidable barrier of foreign capital functioning not as fuel for the general welfare of the people but as a sluice for draining away the country's wealth. In the 1920's, foreign capital owned nearly half of the Chinese cotton industry, the largest industry in the country. It owned a third of the railways outright and held mortgages on the rest. It owned and operated more than half the ship-ping in Chinese waters and carried in its own bottoms nearly 80 percent of China's foreign and coastal trade. The drain of wealth was a steady one. China's adverse trade balance ac-cumulated between 1912 and 1924 to a total of $1,500,000,000[9] and to twice that sum in the next ten years. Between 1902 and 1914, for-eign investments in China doubled and in the next fifteen years doubled again, reaching an estimated total of $3,300,000,000 (U.S.). More than four-fifths of this sum was directly in-vested in transport and industrial enterprises and the rest in loans which converted the vari-ous Chinese governments into docile tools and preserved the foreign grip on internal and exter-nal revenues.[10]

To regain control of its own productive forces, then, China had to recapture this lost ground; it had to free itself from the political and economic control of the Western powers and Japan. It had to unify itself by cutting across the sectional rivalries perpetuated by ri-val militarist satrapies in the different foreign spheres of influence. Only in this way could internal peace be restored, the incubus of mili-tarism removed, and the internal market freed to develop by its own momentum. To gain the strength needed to do this, China needed a political leadership that would galvanize the peasantry by opening the way to release from its burdens. The Chinese revolution, in short, had to be an anti-imperialist movement that inscribed the slogans of the agrarian revolt on its banners.

How and by whom could this be done? The answer to this key question involves an estimate of the class forces and relationships as they existed at the time—and we speak now of the first years after the first World War—for each section of the population obviously stood in distinct and different relations to the land and to the foreign interests and each would enter the political arena with different objects in view. The peasantry itself, as history has abundantly proved, cannot function independently in the political arena. It is deeply cleft into layers with sharply conflicting economic interests. It is the most numerous, but also the most scattered and most backward section of the population. It is localized and limited, economically and psychologically. For these reasons the village has, in China as elsewhere, always been subject to the town. The peasantry has always been at the command of the urban class able to centralize, weld, control, whether in the economic process or in politics. Without the centripetal force of the city, around which rural economy must inevitably revolve, the peasant is helpless, especially the poorest peasant, the most exploited and the nearest to the soil. His own attempts to better his own lot, without the aid of or in defiance of the dominant city class, have almost invariably taken the form of isolated acts of violence without permanent issue.

This has been especially true in China, a land of impoverished millions, darkened by illiteracy and superstition, so divided sectionally that customs, habits, and the spoken language differ sharply from province to province, town to town, and even from village to village. China's great peasant wars, rising and falling at intervals through the centuries, had always ended in a restratification within the peasantry. The rebelling masses were usually taken in tow by a section of the ruling group which sought not a new society but a new dynasty. When the fighting was done, a new emperor sat on the Dragon Throne and the landlords rose anew. Only an urban ally capable of transforming all social relations could release the peasantry from this vicious historical circle, free it from its own exploiting minority in the countryside, and help it bridge the cultural gap separating town and country.

In Europe the bourgeois revolutions of two and three centuries before had played this historic role. The pattern had many variations, but in essence the rising capitalists of that time had to extend the rights of bourgeois property to the land and free labor from serfdom on the land in order to place it at the disposal of the newly rising industrial system. In France, England, and Holland, the most radical sections of the petty bourgeoisie came forward to help the peasantry break the bonds with which feudalism kept it chained to the soil and thus laid the foundations of the strong national bourgeois states. In twentieth-century China, however, a different social pattern in a different historic context imposed different solutions. The Chinese ruling class could not liberate the peasantry because, as a result of the peculiar conditions and belatedness of its growth, it was too organically tied to the exploitation of the peasantry. It has already been shown how this class rose, not as a distinctly urban grouping with a new economic stake, but out of the old ruling classes. Unlike the European burghers of the past, the urban men of property in China remained bound by a thousand links to the precapitalist or semifeudal system of exploitation on the land. The peasant was subject to the depredations of landlord, usurer, merchant, banker, war lord, tax collector, and local official. The interests of these groups fused and became the interlaced interests of the ruling class as a whole. Not uncommonly, the collector of rent, interest, feudal dues, and taxes, was one and the same person.

"Quite unlike the landlords in France *sous l'ancien régime*, the landlords in China are often quadrilateral beings," wrote Professor Chen Han-seng in a striking summary passage. "They are rent collectors, merchants, usurers, and administrative officers. Many landlord-usurers are becoming landlord-merchants; many landlord-merchants are turning themselves into landlord-merchant-politicians. At the same time many merchants and politicians become also landlords. Landlords often possess breweries, oil mills and grain magazines. On the other hand, the owners of warehouses and groceries are mortgagees of land, and eventually its lords. It is a well-known fact that pawnshops and business stores of the landlords are in one way or another affiliated with banks of military and civil authorities. ... While some big landlords practice usury as their chief profession, nearly all of them have something to do with it. Again, many landlords are military and civil officers."[11]

This was the real physiognomy of the Chinese ruling class and of the system through which it bore down upon the peasant. The fundamental relations that governed it were bourgeois in character. Feudalism in its classic form disappeared from China many centuries ago when land, the basic means of production, became alienable. The penetration of commercial capital into the village established there a predominantly capitalist economic structure which continued to bear many precapitalist features. Thus the landlord-merchant-banker-politician-tax collector derived his wealth from usury, market speculation, land mortgages, state taxes, industrial profits, and ground rent. At the same time, from the older sources of revenue imbedded in the social structure, he extracted tolls strongly feudal in character and origin: dues to the landlord in free labor and gifts, rent in kind, forced labor, military service, and "likin" or local customs taxes.

Under the molding pressure of imperialism, as we have seen, the most important section of the Chinese ruling class had also become brokers, once, twice, or thrice removed, for the operations of foreign or foreign-controlled capital, just as the war lords and their governments had been converted into pawns on the chessboard of interimperialist rivalries. Now aspiring Chinese industrialists looked forward, certainly, to developing their own wealth. They began to seek a loosening of the foreign grip on the country. But the fact was that they still leaned heavily on their foreign rivals and derived much of their revenue from them. The gulf which separated them from the great mass of the people was far wider and less bridgeable than the antagonism between them and the foreigners. From the foreigners they could and would try to exact concessions, to demand and secure a larger share of the spoils. But they could not hope to satisfy the masses of the people without undermining themselves. Land could not be restored to the peasants without upsetting all existing property relations and destroying the economic foundations of the ruling class itself in town and country alike. This fundamental and inescapable fact predetermined the limits

to which the propertied classes of China would go in the national-revolutionary movement that rose in the years following 1919.

But these were by no means the limits of the perspectives of the revolution in China. The same economic growth and circumstances which had stirred nationalist feeling among nascent Chinese industrialists after the first World War had also brought into being an urban working class which now also entered the political arena as a major participant. This section of the population was estimated in 1927 to consist of about 1,500,000 factory workers, about 1,750,000 other industrial workers (miners, seamen, railroad workers) still closely linked, socially and economically, to the mass of urban shopworkers and handicraftsmen, numbering more than 11,000,000.[12] This new urban class was still raw and young. The first modern labor unions, as distinct from the older craft guilds, appeared in China only in 1918. Yet, barely a year later, workers were already intervening in the political life of the country striking in support of nationalist students. Six years later, 1,000,000 Chinese workers participated in strikes, many of them directly political in character. Two years after that, Chinese unions counted 3,000,000 members and in Shanghai the workers carried out a victorious insurrection which placed political power within their grasp.

The existence of this class in Chinese society introduced a wholly new element and opened entirely new perspectives for the nationalist revolution. Unlike the city banker, industrialist, official, or money-lender, the Chinese worker had no stake in preserving the existing system of rural exploitation. On the contrary, he was a victim of that same system. In some ways, his close ties to the village represented a liability rather than an asset in a political sense. The typical Chinese worker was fresh from the ranks of the peasantry. His family was still possibly on the land somewhere, trying desperately to survive. He himself had come to the city because rural hardship had driven him there. The Chinese industrial worker had been physically severed from the land but he was psychologically still bound to it. His own dearest hope, usually, was to return to it. It was not impossible that the landlord who owned his family's land was his urban employer's father or uncle or cousin. But the Chinese worker, on the other hand, found himself able to come to grips with his problems in an entirely new way and with far greater power. Feeble as Chinese industry was, the specific gravity of the worker in it was still greater than that of the propertied class. The worker proved this by plunging swiftly and even decisively into political life. He became the newest and most significant among the political forces taking shape and getting into motion in the China of the early 1920's. He was not mature, either in the political or economic sense, but the situation into which he was thrust was maturely ripe for his intervention. The whole course of the oncoming revolution would be determined by the ability of the urban working class to assert its leadership over the mass of peasants in the countryside.

But this was not left to the interplay of Chinese social forces alone. The Chinese worker became the object—and ultimately the victim—of a whole new set of influences that had been set in motion far from China itself. In Russia a revolution had taken place only a few years before. Its leaders had proclaimed it to be a workers' revolution that marked the beginning of the end of world capitalism. The influence of that revolution moved eastward. The invasion of its ideas, its spokesmen, its representatives was the most fateful invasion of China since the arrival of Western merchants and warriors nearly a century before.

NOTES

1. Chen Han-seng, *Present Agrarian Problem in China;* also Buck, *Chinese Farm Economy;* Tawney, *Land and Labor in China.*

2. Professor Chen defined these categories as follows: [Note: This essay was first published in the 1930s, *J.C.L.*] When a peasant family is barely capable of self-support from the land, and in its agricultural labor is not directly exploited by, nor exploiting, others, we may say that such a family belongs to the class of *middle peasants.* The status of the middle peasants helps us to determine that of the other two classes of peasantry. When a peasant family hires one or more agricultural laborers by the day or by the season during busy times, to an extent exceeding in its total consumption of labor power that required by the average middle peasant family for self-support, or when the land which it cultivates surpasses in area the average of the land used by the middle peasant, we

shall then classify this family as that of a *rich peasant.* Where we see families cultivating twice as much land as the middle peasants in their village, we safely classify them as those of rich peasants without further considering the labor relations. The *poor peasants* are comparatively easy to recognize. All peasant families whose number of cultivated *mow* (one *mow* is one-sixth of an English acre) falls below that of the middle peasants and whose members, besides living on the fruits of their own cultivation have to rely upon a wage income or some income of an auxiliary nature, belong to the poor peasants in general. Those poor peasants who do not cultivate any land, either of their own or leased, but hire themselves out, or who cultivate a mere patch of land but have to support themselves chiefly by selling their labor power in agriculture, are called *hired agricultural laborers,* but still belong to the peasantry. *Agrarian Problems in Southernmost China* (Shanghai, 1936), p. 8.

3. "Report of the Land Committee of the Kuomintang," *Chinese Correspondence* (Hankow), May 8, 1927.

4. Chen Han-seng, *Present Agrarian Problem,* pp. 2-5.

5. Chen Han-seng, *Agrarian Problems in Southernmost China.*

6. Cf. Annexes 6 and 7, *Annexes to the Report of the Council of the League of Nations* (Nanking, April 1934); also briefer summary and bibliographical notes in Tawney, *op. cit.,* pp. 50-54.

7. Wong Yin-seng, *Requisitions and the Peasantry in North China;* Chen Han-seng, *Present Agrarian Problem,* pp. 15-18; Chen Han-seng, *Agrarian Problems in Southernmost China,* chap. v; "Kuomintang vs. Peasants," in H. R. Isaacs (ed.), *Five Years of Kuomintang Reaction.*

8. Cf. *Chinese Maritime Customs, Annual Report for 1932,* pp. 48 ff.; Chen Han-seng, "Economic Disintegration of China," *Pacific Affairs,* April-May 1933; Lowe, *Facing Labor Issues,* Table 1; Dr. Friedrich Otto, "Harvests and Imports of Cereals," *Chinese Economic Journal,* October 1934; Beale and Pelham, *Trade and Economic Conditions in China, 1931-33,* pp. 7 and 149 ff. Food imports were 5 percent of the total in 1918 and 20 percent in 1932. In the latter year it took 43 percent of the total exports to pay for imports of food alone.

9. Calculated in United States dollars at the then par rate, two to one.

10. Fong, "Cotton Industry and Trade," Table 2*b*; Remer, *Foreign Investments in China,* pp. 69, 86-91, 135; *China Year Book, 1926,* p. 822; Fang Fu-an, "Communications, the Extent of Foreign Control," *The Chinese Nation* (Shanghai), September 10, 1930; Tao and Lin, *Industry and Labor in China,* pp. 12, 16-17.

11. Chen Han-seng, *Present Agrarian Problem,* p. 18.

12. Lowe, *Facing Labor Issues,* pp. 54-55. For a summary of studies made of the industrial population, see Fang Fu-an, *Chinese Labour,* chap. ii.

Early Imperialism and Late Hydraulic China

China and the Impact of the West

John C. Leggett

INTRODUCTION

Background to revolution

We will now explore the relation between commodity exchange, class, and the power structure of Chinese society from 1800 to 1912. Violence and capital investments are treated as forces that complement a free market economy. When introduced into a significantly large sector of nonfree market economy, they seriously and subsequently alter commodity exchange relationships as well as the class and power formations of the entire society. Power and class are considered to stem from technology and economic organizations, yet to react on both as potential reinforcing agents.

Framework of analysis and important concepts

It would seem that every economy, over time, will give rise to class and power structures which in turn react on the economy and in so doing help to maintain it. It would also appear that when the free market economy of a technologically superior society comes into continuous and extensive relationship with the nonfree market economy of a technologically inferior society, the commodity exchange system of the inferior one will be drastically altered.

My third and fourth major hypotheses are that foreign classes and elites riding the crest of the free market economy hasten the dissolution of class, power, and commodity relationships of the subdominant society through capital investment and acts of violence. Foreign elites not only attempt to engage in selling land, labor, and goods under conditions closely approximating a free market economy, they also invest capital in transport and manufacturing. The consequence of these investments is the furthering of the development of new forms of commodity exchange. Both investment and exchange of commodities under new conditions are facilitated by use of violence on the part of the foreign elite.

■This essay was prepared especially for this volume.

A fifth tentative proposition is that drastic alterations of commodity exchange relationships are followed by the obsolescence of the very class and power structures that had been instrumental in maintaining the old basis of commodity exchange. (By structure is meant a more or less permanent arrangement of interrelated parts.) A common relationship to the mode of production is the basis for class position. The class dimension is not the only relevant one, however. Power must also be considered. When the behavior of group A is being ordered through the behavior of group B to conform to the legal, illegal, and extralegal demands of group B, political power is being wielded by group B. Those who get the most of what there is to get in the ordering of others are the elite; those ordered are the mass. The countermass consists of those who question the authority of the elite, although they have little or no state power. The counterelite are those who organize the countermass against the elite. The basis of elite power is rooted in the relation of the elite to the mode of production and the state.

THE IMPACT OF EUROPEAN FREE MARKET ECONOMY DURING THE NINETEENTH AND EARLY TWENTIETH CENTURIES

European market economy hit China in three successive yet overlapping waves:

1. It brought foreign *goods* into China and thereby plunged domestic goods into a free market competitive stance.
2. It altered the form of land sale in certain parts of China.
3. It helped to create the beginnings of a free labor market.

During these three stages, violence and investment were important complementary practices, with violence assuming roughly equal importance in all three cases. Investment of capital played its most important role in the creation of a free labor market in those sectors of the economy most affected by military control.

The movement of domestic goods into a free market economy was signaled by the heavy influx of foreign goods during the early part of the nineteenth century. Prior to this time, commodities produced overseas entered China under conditions stipulated by the domestic political elite. Moreover, goods entered only in relatively small quantities.

Soon after the turn of the century, the forerunners of a new form of large-scale trade began to emerge. Opium for the first time was smuggled in large quantities into the country. In 1821, 4,628 chests (each weighing around 160 pounds)[1] of opium were imported illegally into China. The market then soared—9,621 chests in 1825, 26,670 chests in 1830, 77,379 chests in 1854. In 1860, at gunpoint, the Chinese Emperor legalized opium imports. In 1873–1874 India produced 6.4 million *tons* of opium, of which 6.1 million tons went to China. By 1912 India still exported 4.8 million tons of opium, almost all of it going to China and the Malay Archipelago.[2] By then, however, China was growing its own crops.

Before Britain began to export opium to China, silver had been the primary export. However, as early as the 1820s textiles also became an important export, and by 1870 cotton goods accounted for 31 percent of China's imports.[3] In exchange for opium and textiles, China exported mainly tea, silk, and after the 1830s, silver.

The second phase might be characterized as government opposition to certain forms of trade. The top Chinese government officials in Peking opposed the import of opium. However, opium was nevertheless smuggled (until 1860) into China, with government officials from provincial viceroy on down taking bribes and in many cases opium as well. Even the top provincial officials were in many cases addicted.[4]

The third stage was initiated by the use of political power within a foreign elite group committed to cracking domestic elite constraint on trade of goods. In three wars (1840–1842, 1858–1860, 1898–1900), European land and naval forces extracted trade and other concessions from the Chinese government. The Chinese in every case were made to pay the military bill of both sides, and the costs were considerable. After the first fracas, the Chinese government was forced to allow trade at several large coastal seaports. Also, extraordinary political rights were granted foreigners, including immunity from the application of Chinese law. In addition, the Chinese had to grant land areas to the foreigners from which trade might be conducted. Restrictions on the import of goods were all but abolished, a mere 5-percent tariff being instituted.[5]

What were some of the consequences of goods being exchanged on an international basis? First, the Chinese merchants ceased to have a monopoly on the production and pricing of goods sold. Second, artisans, previously monopolizers of many items of production, were eliminated in many industries. They, like the rural handicraftsmen, could no longer create goods that were competitive on the open market. The quality of British goods and the "spirit" shown by the British in getting these goods to the peasants all but destroyed many rural handicraft industries—this trend began in the 1820s and continued right down to World War II. However, many rural handicraftsmen were driven to the wall at an early date. For example, the weavers produced 3,359,000 pieces of cloth for export in 1819, but they lost their livelihood when by 1833 their exports had dropped to almost zero.[6]

The bulk of southern Chinese farmers were also affected. Most of them were part-time handicraftsmen, and a large part of their income came from the production of articles such as tung oil, shoes, and cloth. For the most part, their goods were produced for the immediate local market.[7] British products simply overran the wares of the Chinese competitors.

A large part of the peasantry at this point began to skid from positions as middle and rich peasants to agricultural laborers. Their common poverty was at this time further complicated by their numerical increase. Under the Ch'ing Dynasty, by some estimates, the Chinese population almost doubled between 1644 and 1844. The introduction of new food crops and a century of peace (the eighteenth) saw a population increase which resulted in tremendous overcrowding on the land. This situation aggravated the economic position of the peasant at a time when many of them were losing a sizable part of their handicraft-based income.[8]

As for the government, it had become heavily involved in the opium trade and by 1875 had withdrawn altogether from grain price and supply maintenance activities.[9] Government officials in increasing numbers took on the additional and lucrative statuses of merchant, usurer, and landowner. Rather than ameliorating the peasants' misery, they waxed fat on it.

Moreover, in other respects government officials "went to pot." Irrigation and flood-prevention works were neglected. Government positions in increasing numbers were bought and used to make a rake-off on the illicit opium trade, rather than being earned through the (corrupt) examination system.[10] Large quantities of silver in exchange for opium left the country in the 1830s and 1840s, thereby giving rise to an inflation whose cost was borne by the peasants.[11] When a series of famines hit South China in the late 1840s, many peasants, already hard pressed by inflation and increased government taxation, lost their land. In many instances land passed out of the hands of the family into the control of the bureaucratic officials.[12]

The important point is that the central political elite by this time had lost much of its control over the distribution of goods within Chinese society. Second, Chinese goods now faced large-scale competition in the market place. Third, the placing of foreign goods in competition with domestically produced goods, under conditions now approaching a free market economy, had driven the peasantry in many cases into bankruptcy.

Finally, the central redistributive system began to break down, as the commodity exchange economy ceased to be an almost entirely national phenomenon and became instead part of an international network. The political center came to rely for its stability less on taxes and more on funds obtained through the purchase of political office and foreign loans. In addition, much of the currency in the form of silver left the country. Because of hydraulic mismanagement, less wealth was available for the political center.

By the end of the nineteenth century, not only had the government abandoned its roles as stabilizer of grain prices and emergency supplier of grain, it had failed in its irrigation-maintenance tasks as well. By 1900 the exploitative redistributive system had all but collapsed.

Once the question of goods import had been settled, Chinese restrictions on the exchange of land were considerably lessened.

As we noted, land had not been exchanged on a free market basis for a number of reasons, including the power wielded and land owned by the central government, and familial restrictions.

Beginning in the 1830s, and extending beyond the turn of the century, the import of foreign goods had the effect of depriving the Chinese peasant of a considerable part of his income. Again, as already noted, his taxes were being increased. As a participant in money economy,[13] the peasant was forced to turn to the usurer for funds for the purchase of tools and other commodities such as rice. Once this step was taken, a typical sequence of events generally followed. Funds were repeatedly borrowed on the land, and when the day of repayment came, no funds were available. Thus, the land passed into the hands of the usurer, a person who was often a member of the gentry as well. The one who had lost his land then became a landless laborer.

Especially in South China, where foreign trade had been greatest, millions of peasants were caught up in this process between 1840 and 1860. They formed the basis of a movement that under normal circumstances would have resulted in the end of a dynasty and the consequent redistribution of land.[14] The Taiping Rebellion, a 15-year affair that snuffed out the lives of an estimated 20 million people, might have been successful if it had not been for the military efforts of foreign powers.[15]

The government also lost much of its land to private individuals.[16] Land became increasingly concentrated in the hands of fewer and fewer people, especially government officials, while the central government stood by and watched.[17] This had not always been their role. In the past the central political authorities had often intervened in behalf of the peasant to break up high concentrations of landholdings and to redistribute the land among the peasants.[18] By World War I, land in some areas had become the plaything of urban speculators, who bought and sold it as a commodity on the Shanghai and Canton stock exchanges through intermediaries who rented it to tenants.[19] To sum up, in some areas land could be bought and sold under conditions approaching that of supply and demand, although in many areas the traditional forms still prevailed.

The altered character of goods and land exchange preceded and also helped to pave the way for change with respect to labor, the last commodity to be considered. Between 1840 and 1912 there occurred a gradual replacement by a free labor market—less so in the hinterland, more so in the more commercialized and industrial eastern sections of the country. Capital investment in transportation and industrial production facilitated the development of a free labor market.[20] And of course the omnipresent fleet of British cruisers was also important in accounting for this change, in that it gave assurance to prospective investors.

From the 1860s on, all foreign goods, hindered only by local tariffs,[21] flowed almost freely into China. Land and its subterranean resources of coal and iron became commodities sought by the foreigners. However, no modern transportation system was available to facilitate either the distribution of goods or the exploitation of land. At the same time, the investment of international capital in transportation and other facilities all over the world began to supply Europe with new markets and raw materials and areas of safe and highly profitable investment.[22] China was not to be excluded.

In China, the users of foreign capital took a special interest in railroad investment, and between the 1870s and the fall of the Manchus (1911), railroads were built in China to connect the major regions in the eastern half of the country. The pattern of investment took the following form. First, pressure for the establishment of a particular railroad line, say one connecting Peking and Nanking, would be put on Chinese government officials in Peking by Western businessmen and government officials. Negotiations for the right to build the railroad would ensue. A "Chinese" government corporation would be established which was in fact owned and run by the foreigners, more often than not the British. Foreign loans were made to the corporation. The head administrative and financial positions of the railroad were occupied by foreigners. When the corporation issued bonds, they were bought up almost exclusively by foreigners. Attempts by the Chinese merchant-gentry to buy up bonds and redeem the

foreign loans were unsuccessful. Some Chinese merchant-gentry even attempted to build the railroads by themselves, but they were blocked by the central government, which supported the foreign-built, financed, and owned type of railroad.[23]

Once investment savings were committed, labor was purchased to build and maintain the transportation facilities. Since minerals were to be hauled out of the country, labor was also purchased to carry on mining operations. Payments for labor were made on the basis of scarcity of skill. The only restrictions on working conditions stemmed from the activities of the secret societies, which imposed limitations on the sort of work that a laborer already performing a given task might in addition do. A man working as a stevedore, for example, would not shovel coal, even if engaged to do so by the firm.[24] The secret societies established these rules, and workers accepted them, as did employers. Informal pressures within the work group and informal ties with employers proved sufficient to maintain these work rules. Strikes were not used to enforce this noncontroversial understanding.

In the 1880s the cities began to develop light industries such as the manufacture of textiles and cigarettes. Factory organization was patterned after the European industrial model. Foreign capital was used, and the factories were usually managed by foreigners. Labor used in this setting was purchased as a commodity and put to work in the mill, much as had been the case in Manchester in the 1840s.[25]

To summarize, artisans began to be replaced by wage factory labor. Landless peasants in increasing numbers roamed the countryside or shuffled off to the cities with nothing but their labor power to sell. Even the peasants not directly involved in capitalist enterprises and still working under old conditions were affected, since they might at any time be pushed into the capitalist milieu by a land and goods market economy. In part, then, Chinese labor had been drawn into the vortex of early twentieth century capitalism. The trend was sharply accelerated during World War I.

SUMMARY

By 1911 the Ching Dynasty had ended. A government which had propped up if not closely regulated domestic commodity exchange activities in China had ceased to do so. Both consumers and capital goods poured into the country. Trade within the country was limited only by domestic tariffs on goods. The big merchant, quite often British, German, or French, or a Chinese controlled by these groups, could not be regulated in trade activities as had been the case in the past. In many areas, land was sold and accumulated under conditions closely approaching a free market economy. Increasingly, the value of labor fluctuated in terms of the relative scarcity of that commodity. When considering land and goods as well as labor, we can say that China had characteristics roughly corresponding to a quasi-free market economy.

The once-powerful central government had become a puppet, controlled by and indebted to foreign power and capital. Wealth went in increasing amounts to London, New York, and Paris, finding its way less and less to Peking. The Chinese government no longer performed many of its services.

The class structure also had been radically altered. The proportion of landless peasants had increased, and more and more artisans lost their positions because of the superiority of foreign power, goods, and capital. Merchants often passed from monopolists of a commodity to the role of go-betweens, acting as intermediaries between the foreigner and the Chinese consumer. At best, toward the very end of the Ch'ing Dynasty, merchants became involved in corrupt joint government—merchant investment schemes that usually resulted in economic failure.[26] An embryonic proletariat constituting but a fraction of 1 percent of the total population, yet concentrated in relatively few areas, had emerged in China. Political and economic power had come clearly to rest in the hands of the foreigners. No class or power group was available in 1912 to challenge this foreign power.

THE QUASI-FREE MARKET ECONOMY AND THE BEGINNINGS OF ITS DEMISE

The three-pronged forces of free market economy, capital investment, and state violence—"The Big Three"—set in motion within a subdominant society forces that guaranteed the destruction of the quasi-free market economy.

These forces can destroy the old and prevent the creation of a new stable class and power structure, if only momentarily, while at the same time wreaking havoc with the old forms of exchange and production.

Why should this be so? The foreign free market economy system, when accompanied by capital investment and state violence shatters almost simultaneously the old economic system and the class and power structures. What is most important, classes lose their basis for livelihood. A peasant can no longer survive as a peasant, simply on what he produces in the fields. Like it or not, he becomes involved in a money-market economy. When he is denied the sale of handicraft goods, he has in effect been told that he can no longer function as a peasant landholder. The artisan caught with equally useless skills is in the same position. When classes lose their occupational positions, i.e., when their occupations as such have been abolished, they often resort to violence to rectify the situation.

At that point, external legal constraint is often applied by those having domestic political power in order to prevent mass use of violence. But what if the division of class forces and shattered lines of power has made it impossible for native power groups to perform the necessary acts of suppression? The Big Three have then destroyed the old commodity exchange relationships, seriously impairing the power and class structures on which the former rested, and leaving the foreign elites with little more than an alien basis of control over the population.

At that time, those who have been permanently denied a subsistence base begin to challenge the given economic arrangement through scattered and often disconnected organizations. They develop goals that transcend reality yet nevertheless act to transform it. Social movements whose goals become articulate through the symbolic activities of the counterelite nevertheless reflect the conditions and grievances of the countermass. That is, the goals of the movements correspond to the economic conditions deleteriously affecting the masses.[27] The goals include a reorganization of the means of commodity exchange. The equality-oriented formulations of utopia then signal the beginning of the end of the quasi-free market economy whose corresponding political elite now face the privilege of being toppled.

CONCLUSIONS

Our analysis of revolution is preliminary. We have focused on a particular type of society—hydraulic—while dwelling on one instance—China. In so doing, we have kept in mind an even more general level of analysis appropriate for an understanding of revolutions. We now turn to that framework.

NOTES

1. According to Fairbank, "At the height of the opium trade in the 1880s, . . . Patna and Benares opium arrived in China in the form of round balls weighing about 4 pounds apiece and packed forty to a case. Each ball contained some three pounds of opium inside an inch-thick cover of many layers of poppy leaf . . .", John K. Fairbank, *Trade and Diplomacy on the China Coast* (Cambridge: Harvard University Press, 1953) pp. 64–65.

2. Rosa Luxemburg, *The Accumulation of Capital* (New Haven: Yale University Press, 1951), p. 387.

3. Harold R. Isaacs, *The Tragedy of the Chinese Revolution* (Stanford, Calif.: Stanford University Press, 1951), p. 4.

4. Maurice Collis, *Foreign Mud* (New York: Knopf, 1947), pp. 45–95.

5. For a discussion of wars and Western treaty exactions, see P. H. Clyde, *The Far East* (Englewood Cliffs, N.J.: Prentice-Hall, 1952), pp. 121–311.

6. Isaacs, *op. cit.,* p. 5.

7. Hsiao-tung Fei, *China's Gentry* (Chicago: University of Chicago Press, 1953), chap. VI, "Rural Livelihood: Agriculture and Handicraft," pp. 108–127.

8. John K. Fairbank, *The United States and China* (Cambridge: Harvard University Press, 1953), pp. 138–143.

9. Chi Yu Tang, *An Economic History of Chinese Agriculture* (Ithaca: Cornell University Press(?), 1924), p. 74.

10. Isaacs, *op. cit.,* p. 7.

11. *Ibid.,* p. 4: also see Fairbank, *Trade and Diplomacy on the China Coast, op. cit.,* pp. 75–78, 227, 286–287.

12. Isaacs, *op. cit.,* p. 6.

13. At the very end of the Ching Dynasty efforts were made by the Chinese central government to straighten out the currency problems and monetary policies of the Chinese state and economy. See Ssu-yü Teng and John K. Fairbank, *China's Response to the West* (Cambridge: Harvard University Press, 1954), pp. 212-216. Especially important is Sheng Hsuah-Huai's *Argument for Modern Banking* (1896).

14. Government-directed land redistribution and new land settlement often occurred simultaneously at the beginnings of many Chinese dynasties. See Mabel Ping-hua Lee, *The Economic History of China* (New York: Columbia University Press (?), 1921), pp. 30–44, 52, 61, 67, 73, 84, 85, 89, 93, 97, 113). Also see R. H. Tawney, *Land and Labor in China* (New York: Harcourt, 1932), p. 32. In addition, see Tang, *op. cit.,* pp. 57–65.

15. Isaacs, *op. cit.,* pp. 7–11.

16. *Ibid.,* p. 27.

17. *Ibid.,* p. 27.

18. Lee, *op. cit.,* pp. 25, 30, 32, 38.

19. Tawney, *op. cit.,* pp. 67–68. Tawney stated:

What appears to be occurring, in some regions at least, is the emergence, side by side with small landlords who live in their villages and are partners with their tenants in the business of farming, of a class of absentee owners whose connection with agriculture is purely financial.

This development naturally proceeds most rapidly in the neighborhood of great cities, in districts where the static conditions of rural life are broken up by the expansion of commerce and industry, and in regions like parts of Manchuria, which have recently been settled by an immigrant population. The symptoms accompanying it are land speculation, and the intrusion between landlord and tenant of a class of middlemen. In Kwangtung, it is stated, it is increasingly the practice for large blocks of land to be rented by well-to-do merchants, or even by companies especially formed for the purpose, and then to be sub-let piece-meal at a rack rent to peasant farmers. Elsewhere, a result of the growth of absentee ownership is the employment of agents, who relieve the landlord of the business of himself squeezing his tenants, browbeat the tenants by threats of eviction into paying more than they own, and make money out of both by cheating the former and intimidating the latter. In southern Kiangsu, it was recently reported, landlords combined to maintain an office which acts as an intermediary between them and their tenants, selecting the latter, seeing that rents are paid at the proper terms, setting in motion, when payments are in arrears, the machinery for eviction, and, with the connivance of the authorities, actually detaining defaulters in a private prison and inflicting physical punishment on them. Nor must it be forgotten that the landlord has often a double hold on the tenant, since the former is frequently the money-lender to whom the latter is in debt.

20. Isaacs, *op. cit.,* pp. 29–34; Tawney, *ibid.,* pp. 121–128.

21. That these internal "tariffs" were considerable is suggested by Fairbank, *Trade and Diplomacy on the China Coast,* pp. 299–310. Since these tariffs were imposed on goods traveling land routes, the British responded by making fuller use of river and sea routes. Internal tariffs survived until World War II, at least in North China, and possibly later. See Sidney D. Gamble, *Ting Hsien, A North China Rural Community* (New York: Institute of Pacific Relations, 1954), pp. 10, 167, 169, 193.

22. One of the acutest and earliest observers of this development was J. A. Hobson, *Imperialism* (London: Allen & Unwin, 1902, 1954 ed.). See especially pt. II, chap. IV, "Imperialism and the Lower Races," chap. V, "Imperialism in Asia," chap. VI, "Imperial Federation," and the prophetic chap. VII, "The Outcome." Also see Rosa Luxemburg, *The Accumulation of Capital, op. cit.,*chap. XXVII, "The Struggle Against Natural Economy," chap. XXVIII, "The Introduction of Commodity Economy," chap. XXIX, "The Struggle Against Peasant Economy," and chap. XXX, "International Loans."

23. E-tu Zen Sun, *Chinese Railways and British Interests, 1898–1911* (New York: King's Crown, 1954), pp. 27–142.

24. Rowland R. Gibson, *Forces Mining and Undermining China* (New York: Century, 1914), pp. 237–240.

25. For material on factory working conditions during World War I and the early 1920s, see William Ayers, *Shanghai Labor and the May 30th Movement* (Papers on China, Regional Studies Seminars, Harvard University, 1950), V 4-5. Also, William Ayers, *The Hong Kong Strikes*, 1920–1926 (Papers on China, Regional Studies Seminars, Harvard University, 1950), IV, 103. In addition, see Chen Ta, "Shipping Strikes in Hong Kong," *Monthly Labor Review*, May, 1922, p. 12. Also see, Chen Ta, "Rates of Wages in Principal Industries in Great Britain in February, 1922," *Monthly Labor Review*, June, 1922, p. 89. In 1938 Harold Isaacs [*op. cit.*, pp. 64–65)] had this to say about factory working conditions in China in the period immediately following World War I:

In foreign owned and Chinese factories in Canton, Shanghai, Hankow, Tientsin, and other cities, factory workers lived and toiled in conditions comparable only to the worst helotry of the early stages of the industrial revolution in England. Men, women and children worked, as low as eight cents a day, without the most elementary provisions for their safety or hygiene. An apprentice system provided small producers and shop keepers with an inexhaustible supply of child labor working daily up to 18 and 20 hours in return for a bowl of rice and a board to sleep on.

Also see Olga Lang, *Chinese Family and Society* (New Haven: Yale University Press, 1946), pp. 82–92.

26. See Ssu-yü Teng and John K. Fairbank, *China's Response to the West* (Cambridge: Harvard University Press, 1954), chap. XXI, "Problems of the Industrialization Effort," pp. 108–118.

27. *Ibid.*, chap. XXIX, "The Search for New Principles," chap. XXV, "Early Converts to Marxism," chap. XXVI, "Hu Hsih and Pragmatism in China," chap. XXVII, "Sun Yat-sen's Reorientation of the Revolution," pp. 231–264.

4 Agrarian Revolution: A General Formulation

AN OVERVIEW

Revolution. Its promises seem simple enough. Equality. Justice. Brotherhood. No more hierarchy, hypocrisy, or exploitation. Away with landlords, slumlords, employers, and other assorted rip-off artists. Let the people judge and rule. Let the oppressed stand up.

But the simplicity of the goals by no means suggests the sources and contours of revolutions. For both origins and trajectories remain complex.

The varieties of revolution occur in many times and places, but time and again we can observe their beginnings in an agrarian context. There, thoroughgoing revolutions most frequently originate. For when the feudal setting begins to unravel, it frequently reveals a number of antecedents associated with the classical democratic revolution. By contrast, the demise of the hydraulic-based society precedes, time and again, efforts to bring about even more sweeping revolutions, notably the total anticolonial struggles of this century.

Both kinds of revolutions have much in common. Both constitute total cultural revolutions—collective and potentially successful efforts of the underprivileged to eliminate all forms of inequities through the transformation of all levels of society. Nevertheless, there are areas where they do not overlap. Both the similarities and the differences will receive our attention as we focus on (*a*) two types of revolutions and (*b*) the necessary requisites of seizure

■This chapter is based largely on "Total Cultural Revolution, Class–Racial Consciousness and Current U.S. Insurrections: Revolution Abroad and Insurrections At Home," a paper presented at the 1967 American Sociological Meetings and written by J. C. Leggett, R. Apostle, A. Barons, and D. Driscoll. I am also indebted to earlier work done by John Magney.

of state power. We do not deal with all such efforts in this admittedly and heavily eclectic theory of change. Rather, we dwell on those revolutions which promise to sweep away all prior forms—total cultural revolutions. In so doing, we continue to focus on China.

TWO VIEWS ON AGRARIAN SOCIETY: THE CONTEXT OF REVOLUTION

There is an idyllic conception of agrarian society. Peasants live out their lives within a stable hierarchy of classes. These classes are joined in relations in which classes do not use one another to achieve selfish ends. These relations are essentially affectionate. Despite weather and the pitfalls of waves of disease and cold, the rural peasants and the urban poor learn to accept one another as well as their common fate within an organic community, one without the personal selfishness of capitalist individualism. The people endure the long winters and as costumed children of god, rejoice at springtime by consuming May wine, bock beer, and one another. Within this world there develops a sense of "we-ness," a mutual, common identity. What warms the heart is pure community. There is an absence of vulgar capitalism, with its emphasis on cut-throat competition, mutual sacrifice for profit, and grim rationalization of the division of labor. The latter proves to be particularly loathsome, for it carries with it a propensity to schedule *all* relationships and hence to disallow the deeply personal as well as the wholly orgiastic. Agrarian society promotes personal serenity through a social order marked by calendared festivals. Despite the presence of classes—peasants, artisans, merchants, nobles, and king—despite the obvious and wide span of pecuniary and honorific rewards—the world is essentially at peace with itself. In short, feudalism provides a milieu where the individual can accept himself and others.

Gerhard Lenski rightfully portrayed a different agrarian world, disabusing us of such romantic indulgence. The agrarian world is one in which the adventurers sought, seized, and used state power to aggrandize themselves at the expense of peasants. This exploitation became institutionalized on an intergenerational basis. Eventually, one-half to three-quarters of what the peasants were producing was taken from them by lords, tax collectors, religious personages, usurious loan merchants, and marauding armies. It's as if every person who failed to produce material value had leaped to the shoulders and backs of the peasants, there to ride the poor into near-starvation in order that 5 to 10 percent of the population might command most of that society's wealth:

It is difficult to determine accurately the real extent of the wealth of the rulers of agrarian states of the past, but scattered reports provide clear indication of the immensity of the resources they controlled. In the last decade of the twelfth century and the first decade of the thirteenth, the English Kings Richard I and John had incomes which averaged £24,000 a year [roughly $58,800—J.C.L.] (excluding two war years). This was thirty times the income of the wealthiest nobleman of the period, and, in fact, equalled three-fourths of the combined income of all 160 nobles. The King's income also equalled the combined annual incomes of about 24,000 field hands, who at that time were usually paid a penny a day. By the reign of Richard II, at the end of the fourteenth century, English kings averaged £135,000 a year (not counting the year 1380, when there were unusually heavy military expenses). This was almost forty times the income of the richest member of the nobility, and *was equal to 85 per cent of the combined incomes of the nearly 2,200 members of the nobility and squirearchy* as reported in the tax on income in 1436.

The incomes of these early English kings, as great as they were, were small in comparison with the incomes of rulers of greater states. Xerxes, the great Persian emperor of pre-Christian times, is reported to have had an annual income in gold which by current standards would be worth $35 million; Sulei-

man the Magnificent of Turkey, $421 million; Akbar the Great of India, $120 million; and his successor, Aurangzeb, $270 million. Of course, much of the income of these men was consumed in maintaining the government, suggesting that these figures constitute what a modern businessman would call "gross income" rather than "net income." On the other hand, all of these figures are based on the current cash value of bullion, and therefore, as scholars point out, may be too low as measures of actual purchasing power. Actually, what is important is the relation between the figures involved and others in the same society, not those in our society today. By this standard, the figures were in every case immense.

A few other examples will help to underline the enormity of the riches available to those in control of the machinery of state in agrarian societies. In sixteenth-century China, a eunuch, Liu Chin, managed to dominate a youthful and inexperienced emperor and turn the vast powers of the Chinese state to his own advantate for several years. In that short span of time he accumulated a fortune which, when recovered, included 240,000 bars of gold, 57,800 pieces of gold, 25,000,000 ounces of silver, three bushels of precious stones, 3,000 gold rings, and various other treasures. The value of this fortune exceeded the total annual budget of the government. History also tells of an eleventh-century emperor of China whose *personal budget* was nearly twice as great as the sum provided for the salaries of all the officials living in the national capital. In late fifteenth- or early sixteenth-century Spain, the king was reputed to enjoy one-third of all the revenues of the land, though the wording of the original statement suggests that what he actually received was one-third of the economic surplus. In eighteenth-century Prussia, the royal estates constituted "no less than one-third of the total arable area," a figure which was matched by the royal estates in neighboring Sweden. Even these figures were surpassed in midnineteenth-century Russia, where the crown owned almost half the European territories. Prior to the emancipation of the serfs, 27.4 million men and women were state peasants, whom the czars regarded as their property to dispose of as they wished. This explains how Catherine the Great and her son Paul were able to give away to various court favorites 1,400,000 serfs in the short period from

1762 to 1801 without seriously depleting the resources of the house of Romanov. In our own day the premier of Thailand, the late Marshal Sarit, accumulated an estate valued at $140,000,000 in only ten years, in an agrarian society with an annual per capita income of less than $100. . . .[1]

Lenski's analysis indicates the degree to which small propertied classes could take for themselves a great deal of what the majority had produced. And social science needs the kind of lucidity that Lenski brought to bear on the subject of ownership and exploitation. Still, his portrayal was incomplete. It missed one salient feature of agrarian societies: They have time and again provided contexts within which both embryonic capitalism and total cultural revolutions have flourished simultaneously. And in the case of those abiding and long-term revolutions which have occurred in older, more majestic civilizations, such as China, the more organized character of these irrigation-based civilizations has in the long haul inadvertently contributed to their subsequent reorganization.

THE SOURCES OF TOTAL CULTURAL REVOLUTIONS

This chapter focuses on two relevant questions. How can we analyze agrarian societies in order to understand their contribution to total cultural revolution?[2] Given the pertinence of

the known structures of agrarian societies, what are the sources of revolutions which herald total transformation? We direct this question to an understanding of revolutionary movements unwinding within the context of agrarian societies which are undergoing reorganization fostered largely by the forces of capitalism—those groups specialized to bring together and to use land, labor, and goods as commodities in the pursuit of private profit through the use of mechanical technology.

We pose the problem while recognizing the distinction between a feudal society and a hydraulic society. We are cognizant of the ways in which these two agrarian contexts help to shape alternative forms taken by total cultural revolutions. Very briefly, when total cultural revolutions originate in feudal settings with mercantile capitalist beginnings prior to the appearance of imperialism, these revolutions take a form different from total cultural revolutions that originate in the hydraulic context during the imperialist epoch. The difference, simply put, is that between the French and the Chinese revolutions. The French Revolution originated under conditions of feudalism in decline and capitalism on the upgrade. In a historical sense, the French Revolution is the prototype of the "classical revolution,"[3] one running the gamut of stages from the "prodromal period" to the "Thermidorean reaction" (discussed later in this chapter). By contrast, the revolution in China grew out of a hydraulic system in decline, one whose demise was hastened by imperialism but not by a nascent, indigenous capitalism. Unlike these total cultural revolutions originating in feudalism, the revolutionary trajectory is compressed. (See Figure 2.)

TWO PATHS TO REVOLUTION

We will try to deal with these two types of revolutions by focusing on their preliminary states. In order to indicate their content, we

---

[1] Gerhard Lenski, *Power and Privilege* (New York: McGraw-Hill, 1966) pp. 212–213. Used with permission of McGraw-Hill Book Company.

[2] By a "total cultural revolution" we mean those occasions of radical and violent change in which a mass movement rejects the legitimacy of the existing system and attempts to institute, by means of force, an entirely new system of values, organization, and technology. This, of course, is not an especially original definition. For example, in Herbert Blumer's well-known typology of social movements, the revolutionary movement is described as a movement which "challenges the existing mores and proposes a new scheme of moral values" and "seeks to reconstruct the entire social order." Herbert Blumer, "Collective Behavior," in *Principles of Sociology*, ed. A. M. Lee (New York: Barnes & Noble, 1951), p. 212. Essentially the same idea is expressed in Harold Lasswell's definition. For Lasswell, revolution is the most extreme and radical form of political change; as distinguished from all other forms of political change (succession, reform, *putsch*, etc.), a social revolution directly threatens the power (class) position of the

governing elite. A "total revolution" is Lasswell's designation for the social revolution which attempts to change the basic values of the culture as well as the power structure. See Harold Lasswell and Abraham Kaplan, *Power and Society* (New Haven: Yale University Press, 1950), pp. 268–274.

[3] For a discussion of the "classical" stages of total cultural revolution, see Crane Brinton, *The Anatomy of Revolution* (New York: Vintage, 1965), pp. 3–26.

FIGURE 2   Total Cultural Revolutions

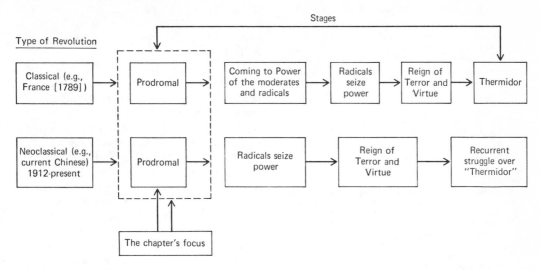

will schematically portray the "classical" (post-feudal) and "neoclassical" (posthydraulic) revolutions, beginning with the preliminary and ending with the Thermidorean stage. As we present our ideas on types and stages of revolution, we will cite examples derived from history.

THE SOURCES
AND DIRECTIONS OF REVOLUTION

The total cultural revolution

Our age is one of total cultural revolutions, efforts to use collective and violent techniques designed to destroy societal systems undergoing disintegration and to institute a new way of life. These commitments include a call to create a new system of technology, organization, and philosophy. From the point of view common to revolutionaries, tired tools, tired laws, and old traditions must end when revolutionary movements call for more than a changing of the political guard or the rotation of governmental forms. Lenin, Mao, and Trotsky would agree that the total cultural revolution is more than a palace coup or a political revolution, and they have dealt extensively with its importance.[4]

[4] V. I. Lenin, "The State and Revolution," in *Selected Works,* Vol. VII (New York: International Publishers, 1943).
V. I. Lenin, "Dual Power," in *The Soviet System,* eds. James H. Meisel and Edward S. Kozera (Ann Arbor: Wahr, 1953), pp. 7–9.

Like these revolutionaries, we will dwell on the "total" kinds.

Relative deprivation and unilinear revolution: the traditional view on total revolutions

The distinction between "palace," political, and total revolution is hardly new, for it underlies the works of Marx and others who dwelt on something quite different from either a changing of the guard or the form of government.[5] In addition to political revolutions such as the change in France between 1848 and 1851, Marx analyzed and predicted total cultural revolutions. Yet he never put together a consistent theory of total revolutions. At one time he stressed *immizeration* (poverty worsened over a long period of time).[6] Some time later, he abandoned immizeration as explanation and emphasized *increased but unmet expectations,*

See Mao Tse-tung's "Report on an Investigation of the Peasant Movement in Hunan," (February, 1927), in Conrad Brandt, Benjamin Schwartz, and John K. Fairbank, *A Documentary History of Chinese Communism* (Cambridge: Harvard University Press, 1952) pp. 77–89. Leon Trotsky, *The Russian Revolution,* (F. W. Dupee, ed.), (Garden City, N.Y.: Doubleday, 1959). Also see Leon Trotsky, *Revolution Betrayed* (New York: Pioneer Publishers, 1945).
[5] Karl Marx, *The Eighteenth Brumaire of Louis Bonaparte* (New York: International Publishers, 1963).
[6] Karl Marx, *The Communist Manifesto,* in *Capital and Other Writings of Karl Marx,* ed. Max Eastman (New York: Modern Library, 1932), pp. 333–334.

derived largely from earlier material improve-ments.[7] This seeming inconsistency need not

[7] These two theoretical tendencies have been pointed out by James C. Davies in "Toward a Theory of Revolution," *American Sociological Review,* **27** (February, 1962): 5–6. Marx's statement of the the-ory of *heightened expectations,* one cited by Davies, can be found in Karl Marx and Frederick Engels, "Wage, Labour and Capital," in *Selected Works in Two Volumes,* vol. 1 (Moscow: Foreign Language Pub-lishing House, 1955), p. 94:

> A noticeable increase in wages presupposes a rapid growth of productive capital. The rapid growth of productive capital brings about an equally rapid growth of wealth, luxury, social wants, social enjoyments. Thus, although the enjoyments of the workers have risen, the social satisfaction that they give has fallen in comparison with the increased enjoyments of the capitalist, which are inaccessible to the worker, in comparison with the state of development of society in general. Our desires and pleasures spring from society; we measure them, therefore, by society and not the objects which serve for their satisfaction. Because they are of a social nature, they are of a relative nature.

For a discussion of Marx's theory of immizeration, one need look no further than the *Communist Mani-festo, op. cit.,* pp. 333–334:

> The modern laborer . . . instead of rising with the progress of industry, sinks deeper and deeper below the conditions of existence of his own class. He becomes a pauper, and pauperism develops more rapidly than population and wealth. And here it becomes evident that the bourgeoisie is unfit any longer to be the ruling class in society, and to impose its conditions of existence upon society as an over-riding law. It is unfit to rule, because it is incompetent to assure an existence to its slave within his slavery, because it cannot help letting him sink into such a state that it has to feed him, instead of being fed by him. Society can no longer live under this bourgeoisie; in other words, its exis-tence is no longer compatible with society.
>
> The essential condition for the existence, and for the sway of the bourgeois class, is the formation and augmentation of capital; the condition for capi-tal is wage labor. Wage labor rests exclusively on competition between the laborers. The advance of industry, whose involuntary promoter is the bour-geoisie, replaces the isolation of the laborers, due to competition, by their involuntary combination, due to association. The development of modern indus-try, therefore, cuts from under its feet the very foundation on which the bourgeoisie produces and appropriates products. What the bourgeoisie there-fore produces, above all, are its own grave diggers. Its fall and the victory of the proletariat are equally inevitable.

A good theorist always modifies and revises his doctrine in response to new conditions and experi-ences. This should be kept in mind whenever we speak of "contradictions" in the theories of Marx and En-gels. To properly understand these two apparently contradictory notions of revolution, we should exam-ine them in their original setting. If the idea of revolu-

bother us, however, if only because both a theory of worsened poverty and a scheme on relative deprivation may contain kernels of truth—but for different types of revolutions in each case.

Of the two approaches, theories of relative deprivation seem to be the most popular in accounting for total cultural revolutions. The theory of relative deprivation emphasizes the significance of heightened but unmet expecta-tions and simultaneously dwells on the unilin-ear character of total cultural revolutions. A one-path conception and selected illustrations, plus reference to its historical specificity and general limitations, often suffice to explain a revolution. So, for example, certain Marxian theories (such as the one advanced by Alfred Meusel)[8] are essentially both natural and unilin-ear formulations. They view revolutions run-ning a sequential course from gestation through youth and maturity to old age, unless halted at some point by counterrevolution. Many non-

tion is traced through the 50-year accumulation of Marx and Engels' writings, a gradual shift in concep-tion will be discovered. Whereas in the early writings the idea of a sudden, violent insurrection was often stressed, over the years this idea was increasingly de-emphasized in favor of the notion of gradual working-class advance toward the conquest of power. The notion of the "increasing misery" of the proletariat, at least in an absolute sense, was also deemphasized. Although Marx speaks of pauperization in *Capital,* the stress—as George Lichtheim noted—seems to be on relative rather than absolute impoverishment. The im-portant thing is the relation between the theories of Marx and Engels and the changing conditions of the nineteenth century. With the emergence of legal labor movements and workers' parties in the latter part of the century, the concept of revolution was appropri-ately modified. The logic underlying this modification was, of course, later carried to the extreme by the revisionists. For Eduard Bernstein and his collabora-tors, the stabilization of capitalism, the improvement in working conditions, and the growing strength of workers' organizations eliminated the necessity (and possibility) of any kind of revolution. On the preced-ing, see George Lichtheim, *Marxism, An Historical and Critical Study* (New York: Praeger, 1961), pp. 51–62, 122–129, 197; Seymour M. Lipset's review-essay of Lichtheim's study in "The Sociology of Marxism," *Dissent,* **10** (Winter, 1963): 59–70; and Peter Gay, *The Dilemma of Democratic Socialism* (New York: Columbia University Press, 1952), pp. 73–77, 213–238.

[8] Alfred Meusel, "Revolution and Counter-Revolu-tion," in *Encyclopaedia of the Social Sciences,* vol. 13 (New York: Macmillan, 1934), pp. 367–375.

Marxists share this propensity to use the natural historical approach, although qualifications abound in their writings. L. P. Edwards, Crane Brinton, and James C. Davies, among others,[9] pose the problem in terms of one pattern of development, while at the same time each notes that his particular theory has application to a limited number of revolutions.

Revolution and multilinear evolution

Interestingly, few if any of these theorists have observed the implications of multilinear evolutionary theory for developmental conceptions of revolution. We need not make the same mistake, neglecting the views of cultural anthropologists who have both pondered the difficulties associated with social evolution and developed multilinear theories on the evolution of culture. We can note that these writers have used a form of analysis that has implications for the study of revolution. For example, Julian Steward studied many primitive societies and observed the degree to which a particular society's development may correspond to one of several paths of evolutionary progression.[10] In a somewhat different vein, Sahlins and Service have distinguished between general and specific evolution, although implying that the subsequent development of one particular culture may resemble the development of another, with both corresponding to an ideal sequence.[11] The

orientation of these neoevolutionists has made students of revolution aware of the existence of logical alternatives other than those traditionally associated with the unilinear analysis of revolution. Indeed, the form of their analysis has suggested the utility of a multilinear conception of revolution.

The traditional stages of revolution: the property of more than one type of revolution

When we combine this novel idea on revolution, i.e., multilinear form, with the older view of revolutions passing through stages, we can derive a general picture of revolutions moving up their respective staircases, two constructions both similar yet unalike. In each case, the pair of step combinations draws selectively on the following building blocks:

1. Prodromal conditions[12]
2. The coming to power and the rule of the moderates and radicals (power sharing)
3. The accession of the radicals
4. The reign of terror and virtue
5. Thermidor[13]

With two typical paths in mind, we should be able to treat many specific revolutions in terms of their passage through either the *classical* or the *neoclassical* revolution. We can now turn to these two types of revolutions and focus on their prodromal characteristics.

Two types of total cultural revolution: their stage passage and trajectory with a multilinear focus

The *classical* revolution passes through all five stages. It uses all five building blocks. On the other hand, the *neoclassical* stems from unusual prodromal origins, skips the stage of

---

[9] L. P. Edwards, *The Natural History of Revolution* (Chicago: University of Chicago Press, 1922); and Crane Brinton, *op. cit.;* Pitirim Sorokin also developed a natural history scheme of analysis. See his *Sociology of Revolution* (Philadelphia and London: Lippincott, 1925); and *Society, Culture and Personality* (New York: Harper, 1947), pp. 482–495. See James C. Davies, *op. cit.*

[10] Julian H. Steward, *Theory of Culture Change* (Urbana: University of Illinois Press, 1955), pp. 11–30. This concept of multilinear evolution as also adopted by Karl Wittfogel in his account of hydraulic society. See his essay "Developmental Aspects of Hydraulic Societies," in *Irrigation Civilizations: A Comparative Study,* ed. J. Steward (Washington: Pan American Union, Social Science Monographs, 1955), pp. 43–53.

[11] Formal credit for this idea goes to Sahlins, who elaborated it in his chapter in *Evolution and Culture,* eds. Marshall R. Sahlins and Elman D. Service (Ann Arbor: University of Michigan Press, 1960), pp. 12–45. This volume is a good sample of the evolutionist approach developed at the Michigan Department of Anthropology under the aegis of Leslie White.

[12] *Prodromal* conditions are the preliminary conditions of revolution, those which prompt the seizure of state power by revolutionaries.

[13] *Thermidor* refers to the massive reaction against the changes introduced by revolutionaries and the return of many organizational and cultural forms associated with the prerevolutionary regime. This swinging of the pendulum is favored by many who welcome a number of revolutionary changes but tired of the seeming excesses of the revolutionaries. Both of these categories are derived essentially from French revolutionary experience.

TABLE 3   Key Economic Consideration, Outcome, and Type of Revolution

	Outcome	
Key Economic Factor	*Military Success*	*Military Defeat*
Economic improvement plus unmet expectations	Classical revolution	Classical defeat
Economic immizeration and unmet expectations	Neoclassical revolution	Neoclassical defeat

power-sharing, and strives to postpone Thermidor (Table 3 here amplifies Figure 2).

Let us first take up the classical revolution, [14] the type whose outlines are most poignantly analyzed in the writings of Brinton and Davies. Beginning with the preliminary stage of revolution, the classical variety runs a normal course by moving through the four traditional stages (already indicated) and ending with the Thermidorean reaction. At least three things, however, distinguish the *neoclassical* revolution from the classical form.

1. The impetus to the neoclassical revolution derives from (*a*) widespread immizeration associated with worsened conditions suffered on an intergenerational basis as opposed to increased well-being on an intergenerational basis followed by an individual's perception of a glaring discrepancy between the expected and the real—as in the classical revolution and (*b*) psychic deprivation linked with publicized revolutionary descriptions of the inadequate circumstances of the subordinate classes and, less frequently, a sense of psychic deprivation based almost exclusively on a precipitous decline in spending power—as in the case of the classical revolution.

2. Moderates and radicals do not join as near-equals and amalgamate their power groups, thereby sharing command during the Cinderella stage (power-sharing) of revolution. On the contrary, the radicals seize power and refuse to share it with the moderates, although popular slogans may allude to an alliance and thereby rally support from all classes.

3. Thermidor takes place, if at all, long after the end of the reign of terror. Unlike its classical counterpart, the neoclassical revolution is marked by egalitarian party elements recurrently using the state and the party to prevent Thermidor, thereby to embed egalitarian ideals and achievements into the value scheme of the revolutionized society.

Of course, history is littered with both classical and neoclassical revolutions which initially gave every indication of reordering the entire society, only to be defeated militarily because of internal weaknesses due to lack of organization and discipline, or forces of outside intervention. Generally, one or both of these causes can bring a total revolution to a halt.

These distinctions on form, success, and failure should help to clarify our analysis by specifying two types of revolutions and two types of revolutionary defeats: the classical revolution, the neoclassical revolution, the classical defeat, and the neoclassical defeat (See Table 3). This classification, however, tells little about causes and contents, which we will soon consider, dwelling first on prodromal circumstances associated with the coming to power of the revolutionaries within the classical context.

LINKAGE TO SOCIAL MOVEMENTS

Herbert Blumer's classic analysis of general and specific social movements (Section Two) complements our general remarks on total cultural revolutions. Social movements contain the key actors in revolutions. In turn, revolutions pursue a course of development that can be analyzed to emphasize this trajectory rather than the behavior of important participants. But social movements and their stages remain important, and to study them we can learn a great deal from Blumer's work.

[14] This sequence is summarized by Brinton, *op.cit.*, pp. 264–275.

A Reading on Social Movements
Pertinent to Our Understanding of Revolutions

Social Movements

Herbert Blumer

Social movements can be viewed as collective enterprises to establish a new order of life. They have their inception in a condition of unrest, and derive their motive power on the one hand from dissatisfaction with the current form of life, and on the other hand, from wishes and hopes for a new scheme or system of living. The career of a social movement depicts the emergence of a new order of life. In its beginning, a social movement is amorphous, poorly organized, and without form; the collective behavior is on the primitive level that we have already discussed, and the mechanisms of interaction are the elementary, spontaneous mechanisms of which we have spoken. As a social movement develops, it takes on the character of a society. It acquires organization and form, a body of customs and traditions, established leadership, an enduring division of labor, social rules and social values—in short, a culture, a social organization, and a new scheme of life.

Our treatment of social movements will deal with three kinds—general social movements, specific social movements, and expressive social movements.[1]

GENERAL SOCIAL MOVEMENTS

New cultural trends

By general social movements we have in mind movements such as the labor movement, the youth movement, the women's movement, and the peace movement. Their background is constituted by gradual and pervasive changes in the values of people—changes which can be called cultural drifts. Such cultural drifts stand for a general shifting in the ideas of people,

■Taken from Herbert Blumer, "Social Movements," in *Principles of Sociology*, 3rd ed., Alfred Mc Clung Lee (New York: Barnes & Noble) pp. 199–205. Copyright 1939, 1946, 1951, 1955, 1969 by Barnes & Noble, Inc., Reprinted by permission of Harper & Row, Publishers, Inc.

particularly along the lines of the conceptions which people have of themselves, and of their rights and privileges. Over a period of time many people may develop a new view of what they believe they are entitled to—a view largely made up of desires and hopes. It signifies the emergence of a new set of values, which influence people in the way in which they look upon their own lives. Examples of such cultural drifts in our own recent history are the increased value of health, the belief in free education, the extension of the franchise, the emancipation of women, the increasing regard for children, and the increasing prestige of science.

Indefinite images and behavior

The development of the new values which such cultural drifts bring forth involve some interesting psychological changes which provide the motivation for general social movements. They mean, in a general sense, that people have come to form new conceptions of themselves which do not conform to the actual positions which they occupy in their life. They acquire new dispositions and interests and, accordingly, become sensitized in new directions; and, conversely, they come to experience dissatisfaction where before they had none. These new images of themselves, which people begin to develop in response to cultural drifts, are vague and indefinite; and correspondingly, the behavior in response to images is uncertain and without definite aim. It is this feature which provides a cue for the understanding of general social movements.

Characteristics of general social movements

General social movements take the form of groping and unco-ordinated efforts. They have only a general direction, toward which they move in a slow, halting, yet persistent fashion. As movements they are unorganized, with neither established leadership nor recognized membership, and little guidance and control. Such a movement as the women's movement, which has the general and vague aim of the emancipation of women, suggests these features of a general social movement. The women's movement, like all general social movements, operates over a wide range—in the home, in marriage, in education, in industry, in politics, in travel—in each area of which it represents a search for an arrangement which will answer to the new idea of status being formed by women. Such a movement is episodic in its career, with very scattered manifestations of activity. It may show considerable enthusiasm at one point and reluctance and inertia at another; it may experience success in one area, and abortive effort in another. In general, it may be said that its progress is very uneven with setbacks, reverses, and frequent retreading of the same ground. At one time the impetus to the movement may come from people in one place, at another time in another place. On the whole the movement is likely to be carried on by many unknown and obscure people who struggle in different areas without their striving and achievements becoming generally known.

A general social movement usually is characterized by a literature, but the literature is as varied and ill-defined as is the movement itself. It is likely to be an expression of protest, with a general depiction of a kind of utopian existence. As such, it vaguely outlines a philosophy based on new values and self-conceptions. Such a literature is of great importance in spreading a message or view, however imprecise it may be, and so in implanting suggestions, awakening hopes, and arousing dissatisfactions. Similarly, the "leaders" of a general social movement play an important part—not in the sense of exercising direct control over the movement, but in the sense of being pace-makers. Such leaders are likely to be "voices in the wilderness," pioneers without any solid following, and frequently not very clear about their own goals. However, their example helps to develop sensitivities, arouse hopes, and break down resistances. From these traits one can easily realize that the general social movement develops primarily in an informal, inconspicuous, and largely subterranean fashion. Its media of interaction are primarily reading, conversations, talks, discussions, and the perception of examples. Its achievements

and operations are likely to be made primarily in the realm of individual experience rather than by noticeable concerted action of groups. It seems that the general social movement is dominated to a large extent by the mechanisms of mass behavior, such as we have described in our treatment of the mass. Especially in its earlier stages, general social movements are likely to be merely an aggregation of individual lines of action based on individual decisions and selections. As is characteristic of the mass and of mass behavior, general social movements are rather formless in organization and inarticulate in expression.

The basis for specific social movements

Just as cultural drifts provide the background out of which emerge general social movements, so the general social movement constitutes the setting out of which develop specific social movements. Indeed, a specific social movement can be regarded as the crystallization of much of the motivation of dissatisfaction, hope, and desire awakened by the general social movement and the focusing of this motivation on some specific objective. A convenient illustration is the antislavery movement, which was, to a considerable degree, an individual expression of the widespread humanitarian movement of the nineteenth century. With this recognition of the relation between general and specific social movements, we can turn to a consideration of the latter.

SPECIFIC SOCIAL MOVEMENTS

Characteristics

The outstanding instances of this type of movement are reform movements and revolutionary movements. A specific social movement is one which has a well-defined objective or goal which it seeks to reach. In this effort it develops an organization and structure, making it essentially a society. It develops a recognized and accepted leadership and a definite membership characterized by a "we-consciousness." It forms a body of traditions, a guiding set of values, a philosophy, sets of rules, and a general body of expectations. Its members form allegiances and loyalties. Within it there develops a division of labor, particularly in the form of a social structure in which individuals occupy status positions. Thus, individuals develop personalities and conceptions of themselves, representing the individual counterpart of a social structure.

A social movement, of the specific sort, does not come into existence with such a structure and organization already established. Instead, its organization and its culture are developed in the course of its career. It is necessary to view social movements from this temporal and developmental perspective. In the beginning a social movement is loosely organized and characterized by impulsive behavior. It has no clear objective; its behavior and thinking are largely under the dominance of restlessness and collective excitement. As a social movement develops, however, its behavior, which was originally dispersed, tends to become organized, solidified, and persistent. It is possible to delineate stages roughly in the career of a social movement which represent this increasing organization. One scheme of four stages has been suggested by Dawson and Gettys.[2] These are the stages of social unrest, the stage of popular excitement, the stage of formalization, and the stage of institutionalization.

Stages of development

In the first of these four stages people are restless, uneasy, and act in the random fashion that we have considered. They are susceptible to appeals and suggestions that tap their discontent, and hence, in this stage, the agitator is likely to play an important role. The random and erratic behavior is significant in sensitizing people to one another and so makes possible the focusing of their restlessness on certain objects. The stage of popular excitement is marked even more by milling, but it is not quite so random and aimless. More definite notions emerge as to the cause of their condition and as to what should be done in the way of social change. So there is a sharpening of objectives. In this stage the leader is likely to be a prophet or a reformer. In the stage of formalization the movement becomes more clearly organized with rules, policies, tactics, and discipline. Here the leader is likely to be in the nature of a statesman. In the institutional stage, the movement has crystallized into a fixed organization with a definite personnel and structure to carry

into execution the purposes of the movement. Here the leader is likely to be an administrator. In considering the development of the specific social movement, our interest is less in the mechanisms and means through which such a movement is able to grow and become organized. It is convenient to group these mechanisms under five heads: (1) agitation, (2) development of *esprit de corps*, (3) development of morale, (4) the formation of an ideology, and (5) the development of operating tactics.

The role of agitation

Agitation is of primary importance in a social movement. It plays its most significant role in the beginning and early stages of a movement, although it may persist in minor form in the later portions of the life-cycle of the movement. As the term suggests, agitation operates to arouse people and so make them possible recruits for the movement. It is essentially a means of exciting people and of awakening within them new impulses and ideas which make them restless and dissatisfied. Consequently, it acts to loosen the hold on them of their previous attachments, and to break down their previous ways of thinking and acting. For a movement to begin and gain impetus, it is necessary for people to be jarred loose from their customary ways of thinking and believing, and to have aroused within them new impulses and wishes. This is what agitation seeks to do. To be successful, it must first gain the attention of people; second, it must excite them, and arouse feelings and impulses; and third, it must give some direction to these impulses and feelings through ideas, suggestions, criticisms, and promises.

Agitation operates in two kinds of situations. One is a situation marked by abuse, unfair discrimination, and injustice, but a situation wherein people take this mode of life for granted and do not raise questions about it. Thus, while the situation is potentially fraught with suffering and protest, the people are marked by inertia. Their views of their situation incline them to accept it; hence the function of agitation is to lead them to challenge and question their own modes of living. It is in such a situation that agitation may create social unrest where none existed previously. The other situation is one wherein people are already aroused, restless, and discontented, but where they either are too timid to act or else do not know what to do. In this situation the function of agitation is not so much to implant the seeds of unrest, as to intensify, release, and direct the tensions which people already have.

Agitators seem to fall into two types corresponding roughly to these two situations. One type of agitator is an excitable, restless, and aggressive individual. His dynamic and energetic behavior attracts the attention of people to him; and the excitement and restlessness of his behavior tends to infect them. He is likely to act with dramatic gesture and to talk in terms of spectacular imagery. His appearance and behavior foster the contagion of unrest and excitement. This type of agitator is likely to be most successful in the situation where people are already disturbed and unsettled; in such a situation his own excited and energetic activity can easily arouse other people who are sensitized to such behavior and already disposed to excitability.

The second type of agitator is more calm, quiet, and dignified. He stirs people not by what he does, but what he says. He is likely to be a man sparing in his words, but capable of saying very caustic, incisive, and biting things—things which get "under the skin" of people and force them to view things in a new light. This type of agitator is more suited to the first of the social situations discussed—the situation where people endure hardships or discrimination without developing attitudes of resentment. In this situation, his function is to make people aware of their own position and of the inequalities, deficiences, and injustices that seem to mark their lot. He leads them to raise questions about what they have previously taken for granted and to form new wishes, inclinations, and hopes.

The function of agitation, as stated above, is in part to dislodge and stir up people and so liberate them for movement in new directions. More specifically, it operates to change the conceptions which people have of themselves, and the notions which they have of their rights and dues. Such new conceptions involving beliefs that one is justly entitled to privileges from which he is excluded provide the dominant motive force for the social movement. Agitation, as the means of implanting these new conceptions among people, becomes, in this way, of basic importance to the success of a social movement.

A brief remark relative to the tactics of agitation may be made here. It is sufficient to say that the tactics of agitation vary with the situation, the people, and the culture. A procedure which may be highly successful in one situation may turn out to be ludicrous in another situation. This suggests the problem of identifying different types of situations and correlating with each the appropriate form of agitation. Practically no study has been conducted on this problem. Here, one can merely state the truism that the agitator, to be successful, must sense the thoughts, interests, and values of his listeners. . . .

NOTES

1. Attention is called, in passing, to spatial movements, such as nomadic movements, barbaric invasions, crusades, pilgrimages, colonization, and migrations. Such movements may be carried on as societies, as in the case of tribal migrations; as diverse peoples with a common goal, as in the case of the religious crusades of the Middle Ages; or as individuals with similar goals, as in most of the immigration into the United States. Mechanisms of their collective operation will be dealt with in the following discussion of social movements. In themselves, such movements are too complicated and diversified to be dealt with adequately here.

2. C. A. Dawson and W. E. Gettys, *Introduction to Sociology* (Rev. ed.; New York: Ronald Press Co., 1935, chapt. 19).

| Section Three | *Breaking the Eggs and Making the Omelette* |

From Prodromal Conditions to Taking State Power: An Outline

John C. Leggett

THE NECESSARY CAUSES OF CLASSICAL REVOLUTION AND DEFEAT: THE SEIZURE OF POWER

We now examine a general theory of revolution. Admittedly this statement is highly simplified. Later, however, especially in Chapters 5, 6, 8, 12, 13, and 14, we comment at length on the complex phenomena associated with the creation of high levels of consciousness, the evolution of the state immediately before and during the course of revolution, the contradictions within communist revolutionary movements, the force mobilized by counterrevolutionary states such as our own, and finally, the infinite complexity of analyzing and prescribing for grass-roots movements, whether operative in a reformist or revolutionary context. In this section, however, we discuss forces associated with the coming to power of the revolutionaries, bearing in mind that the seeming certitude of the propositional statement fails to indicate the complexity of the reality.

Revolutionary efforts of the *classical* variety acquire the potential for success when a lengthy period of economic and social development of industry plus an increase in laboring-class well-being is followed by conditions which we can label as *preparatory*. These occurrences refer to certain changes in economic substructure and mental framework. Most significant are those considerations which foster the emergence of a deep sense of economic deprivation among the laboring classes.

Preparatory conditions

First, there is an abrupt decline in real income among members of the subordinate class, sharply contrasted with a gradual improvement experienced for several generations prior to the decline in the lower-class standard of living. Second, there are indications that heightened

■This essay was especially prepared for this volume.

but unmet expectations are nevertheless maintained. Both circumstances contribute to, but by no means completely account for, consciousness of class and alienation from legally constituted authority. During this early phase of revolution, militant consciousness and deep alienation mark the minds of growing numbers of workmen, peasants, and intellectuals, who use bloody strikes, land seizures, and polemical tracts, respectively, to express their dissatisfaction.

Although changing circumstances and mentalities may be associated with revolutionary upheavals, these conditions by no means exhaust the sources of expressed discontent. Three other sets of forces previously introduced—facilitating, abdicating, and translating mechanisms—are worthy of our consideration

Facilitating Circumstances

Three *facilitating* considerations seem to be significant. These *continuing* factors prompt alienation, as well as the formation and retention of class consciousness. More precisely, these structural components alert revolutionaries and intensify collective problem-solving and hence consciousness of class and alienation from authority, especially among the disenchanted within the intelligentsia and the subordinate classes:

1. The existence of a subordinate collectivity whose political, economic, and ethnic-racial homogeneity facilitates intensive interaction within an isolated community[1]

2. The presence of impersonal and limited (segmented) sets of relations between supraordinate and subordinate classes which differ considerably from each other in terms of power, wealth, and perhaps ethnic prestige

3. The subsequent proliferation of voluntary associations within the isolated community

These conditions hasten revolution, but they

are by no means a sufficient source of the capturing of state power. Certain additional factors must be considered.

Abdicating Conditions

Two phenomena promote total cultural revolutions: the absence of a parliamentary framework (which might provide a legislative structure for policies formulated by lower-class groups) and the presence of a ruling class largely unwilling to be conciliatory on grievances and hence to make concessions to the lower classes. When parliamentary forces are absent, when as a consequence the aggrieved must create a militant social movement to struggle for the underclasses, and when the ruling classes are bent on oppression rather than compromise, the lower classes will resort to collective force. As they move in this direction, they find a growing number of upper-class persons willing to help. The support of the higher classes, in turn, stems from their personal alienation from the very state power they have wielded. They come to view themselves as the ongoing but illegitimate bearers of state power. To deal with this past, these particular upper-class persons believe it necessary to atone for their prior use of illegitimate authority by aligning with revolutionary groups that specialize successfully in the creation of upper-class guilt and its expiation through services to revolutionaries. Revolutionary organizations thereby press these upperclass persons to act against their own class interests. However, they may be supporting their own personal interests. If the insurgent lower class wins, these former landowners, intellectuals, and associated professionals stand to gain, if only momentarily, recognition and prestige for their sacrifices of property and identity with the underclasses. In fact, the presence and leadership provided by these persons (the *déclassé* contingent) have been in every revolution.

The angry French lower classes gained the support of many alienated landowners, priests, writers, poets, composers, and businessmen when they revolted during the summer of 1789. Hitherto isolated and seemingly with no support outside their own ranks, the revolutionaries found men like the physician Marat and the lawyer Robespierre playing leading, however passing, roles in the revolution.

Translating Mechanisms

Without translating mechanisms, successful revolutions cannot occur. The key mechanism consists of a section of the intelligentsia with a common consciousness. Their radicalism complements their alienation from authority. With this unusual perspective acting as a driving force, this stratum guides six crucial translating mechanisms: (a) a disciplined political organization guided by an appraisal of domestic events rather than by the needs of a foreign power; (b) an abstract utopia (i.e., a general specification of strategies and goals for themselves); (c) a body of prescriptions for utopia, which carefully specify in plain terms the goals, strategies, and tactics of the revolutionary movements; (d) a political and ceremonial backdrop for charismatic leadership; (e) the extension of a revolutionary frame of reference to other regions, classes, status groups, and generations; (f) the creation of communication channels among, and coordination of, pockets of insurrection.[2]

The Chinese revolutionary movement, for example, was not of the classical variety but nonetheless involved the same mechanisms as the classical kind. It steered its own course after 1930 as it cut away from Russian direction. At the same time, it relied heavily on the theoretical writings of Mao, ideas that had to be made real for everyone through plain talk, village mass meetings, and intensive peasant participation in village struggles to redistribute wealth and power. The rallying of people into new cognitive categories of thought, accomplished partly through the staging of top leadership visits, depended heavily at all levels on the creative efforts of the party and its cadre, its most active rank-and-file members. Meanwhile the Chinese soviets' intellectuals proved most adept at using cadre to translate into everyday language for practical-minded peasants Mao Tse-tung's abstract notions on peasant hegemony, people's soviets, the two-stage revolution, and the dictatorship of the proletariat.[3] All the revolutionaries operated within the framework of a disciplined, vanguard party, a phenomenon we discuss in Chapter 6.

When the radical intelligentsia succeed in meshing the six translating mechanisms, these forces take advantage of preparatory, facilitating, and abdicating conditions to generate a typical pattern of struggle during the final phases of the prodromal struggle and into the next revolutionary stage: (*a*) heightened class antagonisms, which take such forms as bloody strikes, street battles, clashing rent strikes—in a word, miniature civil wars; (*b*) further indications of ever greater alienation and desertions of the intellectuals from the established order; (*c*) demonstrations of greater concentration of central governmental power; (*d*) concurrent displays of foolish use of military force, which tend to correlate directly with (*e*) heightened governmental inefficiencies, which tinge class struggle with grim comedy.[4]

Perhaps our best example would be the Russian Revolution, an uprising which occurred in a quasi-agrarian context. During the winter of 1916–1917, Russian workers struck, engaged in battle with czarist police, seized buildings, and supported the overthrow of the Czarist regime by the liberal-left coalition. During this period, many intellectuals withdraw their allegiance, first from the Czarist regime, and then from the Kerensky coalition government.

The end of the prodromal stage and the uneven sharing of power by the moderates and radicals ended predictably with the October, 1917 accession of the radicals. During the spring and summer of 1917, an increasing number of intellectuals went over to the bolsheviks and other opponents of the Russian revolutionary center. These writers, poets, philosophers, and lecturers were appalled by the Kerensky government for its continued involvement in the war and its hesitation to break up large estates owned by the discredited and largely monarchistic landed aristocracy. These symbolic assaults were met by repression, which culminated in the jailing and fierce punishment of many innocent people as well as revolutionaries. Such governmental inability to distinguish friend from foe coincided with the increased inability of the government to keep its troops at the front, its tax collectors in the villages, its peasants on the land, its legislators in support of the war, its currency stabilized, and its factories running. Thus the intensification of repression coincided with the break-up of Russia's infrastructure.

In Russia and elsewhere what happens is clear. All these conditions interact, thereby magnifying their presence within a spiral historical course. The cycle ends with the collapse of the *ancien régime* and the coming to power of the moderates and radicals followed by radicals' seizure of state power.

Several illustrations come to mind. If the analyses of L. P. Edwards, Crane Brinton, and James C. Davies are correct—and apparently they come fairly close to hitting the mark—the French Revolution could be taken as one case history. Perhaps also, the Cuban Revolution (1950–1959) provides illustrative material.

BARRIERS TO CLASSICAL REVOLUTIONARY SUCCESS DURING THE PRODROMAL STAGE

We may remark that the classical defeat lacks one of the preconditions of the successful revolutions. Perhaps the principal deterrents to success are (*a*) the careful, judicious use of military organization by the state, (*b*) the absence of schism within the military, and (*c*) the commitment of revolutionary groups to ill-advised strategies or poorly specified goals. Needless to say, the third consideration often occurs when intelligent leaders make incredible mistakes, as we shall see.

The first and second circumstances are likely to occur when the majority of the dominant class have neither lost their sense of mission nor dismissed political formulas traditionally operating in their favor. In short, they remain committed to their own ideological justifications of the allocation of wealth and power. They do not abdicate. Perhaps an illustration of a classical defeat in which the ruling groups retained their sense of legitimacy, even after military disaster, is the behavior of the upper classes during the German revolution of 1918–1919. The German working class had experienced several generations of increased prosperity, plus a subsequent and sharp decrease in their standard of living at the end of the war, only to fail in revolutionary action. They failed partly because the Junkers, in particular the officers of the German Army, had not lost their sense of esprit de corps.[5]

On the other hand, what happens when large sections of the upper class applaud their own demise, whether as skeptics, nihilists, cynics, rebels, or estranged film buffs? Upper echelons of the army (large sections of which belong to critical sectors of the upper class) then come to share these derisive views of the military class and, hence, of themselves. They perform their duties in ways inimical to the political and economic survival of the dominant class. In other words, these sections become incompetent, and their incompetence erodes their class power.

History has taught us that an upper class cannot lose faith in itself and remain on top, if only because it cannot continue to control its own army. If and when the army goes over to the revolution, then the revolution has for the first time a good chance of winning. For example, by the winter of 1916–1917, large sections of the Russian army favored the elimination of the monarchy and the substitution of a new form, preferably a democratic government. These elements were most active in the Cadet party, although they were found in more reformist groups as well.

The third circumstance conducive to revolutionary failure consists of commitment of the revolutionary organization to strategies specified by outsiders—people removed geographically from the society facing a revolutionary crisis. This commitment to accept the external formula frequently results in poor planning and unfortunate military consequences for the revolutionary forces in question. When intellectuals rely on bad judgments and hence misuse translating mechanisms such as the general strike, the net result can be military disaster. Revolutionary intellectuals generally flounder on matters of judgment when they fail to resolve the contradiction between (a) *the long-term foreign policy interests of a powerful state*, such as Russia between 1919 and 1950, dominant within an international revolutionary movement, and (b) *the objectives of a specific revolutionary movement* (e.g., the Chinese Communist party) to a high degree controlled by the coercive state in question.

The case of Russian foreign policy and the Chinese revolution of 1927 comes to mind. As is well known, Stalin's group, including Chinese intellectuals loyal to his position, resolved the contradiction between (a) the establishment of socialism in one country—Russia (Stalin's *formula*), and (b) a successful Chinese revolution as the turning point in the world revolutionary movement (Trotsky's position) by condemning the latter to oblivion. In this instance, the perceived interests of Russian foreign policy took precedence over the obvious needs of a Chinese Communist movement, and Chinese Communist intellectuals, with a few exceptions, accepted Stalin's decisions. The result was disaster for the Chinese revolution, at least in 1927. The Chinese Communist Party (CCP) followed Stalin's position of coalescing with the leading nationalist revolutionary party in China, namely, the Kuomintang (KMT). The KMT contained a powerful left wing sympathetic to communism. The left KMT also committed itself to work politically and militarily to liberate China. But by the spring of 1927, the right wing element had clearly become ascendant in relation to the KMT's left wing. The right KMT, led by Chiang Kai-shek, moved militarily during the spring of 1927 against the CCP, which had been ordered by Stalin to remain members of a coalition with a partner committed to the elimination of the Communist party. The seeming irrationality of Stalin's position can be partially explained by his fight with Trotsky, who at the time favored a total break with the KMT and the creation of a worker-based revolutionary movement. For Stalin to drop his policy of CCP coalition with the KMT would have been tantamount to admitting the correctness of Trotsky's position. Stalin was not about to admit the "correctness" of his key rival inside the world revolutionary movement, so the CCP remained allied with the Kuomintang through a five-month period of Kuomintang slaughter of the Chinese Party members and sympathizers as well as nonparty militants. Between March and August 1927, the party shrank from approximately 60,000 to 10,000 members. By the time the remnants of the CCP had fled to the hills, Stalin was able to announce the correctness of his position, despite the bloodbath.[6] Stalin was also able to announce the removal of Trotsky from any position of influence within the Russian Communist Party and the Comintern—the official world revolutionary center of Communist parties.

Yet more is necessary for an analysis of the

Chinese and other cases than specification of decisions made by particular political elites: namely, a general theory on the failure and success of translating mechanisms. These matters are considered in the final portions of this book.

THE NEOCLASSICAL REVOLUTION: AN ELABORATION

The neoclassical revolution is marked by extended economic disintegration (one generation or more), personal despair among peasants, and, eventually, the support of broad segments of all classes for the revolution. In this type of collective effort, a greater proportion of revolutionary ideas is infused from without, i.e., delivered from another society or community, generating heightened expectations that do not correspond to the steep and prolonged drop in subordinate-class earnings.[7] In fact, the gulf continues to widen, as the lower classes appear at first to be unable to cope with their problems in an atmosphere of marked anomie. But the revolutionary groups enter, create organization, foster hope, order people's lives, and thereby substitute revolutionary discipline and order in place of collective apathy and community disorganization.

This revolution is usually preceded and accompanied by class antagonisms expressed in such forms as prolonged strikes, boycotts, and correlated activities which initially lock large sections of subordinate classes into continuous conflict with dominant groups. In other ways, too, the prodromal stage of the neoclassical revolution resembles its classical counterpart. There are (a) indications of increased alienation and desertion of the intellectuals from legal authority, (b) demonstrations of greater concentration and centralization of governmental power, (c) signs of increased governmental corruption, (d) inept uses of military force, and (e) growing contrasts in wealth between classes.

Yet there are dissimilarities. Most notable in this regard is the uneven development of city and countryside, as nucleated and relatively advanced industrialization proceeds rapidly against a background of antiquated rural technology. Peasants are expelled from the agrarian regions into modernity because their labor is no longer required in the reorganized farm technol-ogy, and they experience immizerization on an intergenerational basis. In this new and strange setting, they are prepared for political mobilization of a revolutionary variety which—if successful in overthrowing the old regime—will help to drive the intelligentsia and the subordinate flock to shape society, as it skips certain stages of economic development or perhaps combines these stages with others in order to realize revolutionary goals.[8]

Because neoclassical revolutions are also anti-imperialist, and because the subordinated class–racial groups are in fact minorities who have suffered the humiliation and self-abnegations imposed on the colonized by the colonizer, the revolutionary movement dwells on cultural liberation from a massive sense of inferiority. This has been more true of neoclassical revolutions than others. It was more true of the Algerian than the Chinese revolution, for the Algerians, like most colonized peoples and unlike the Chinese, did not bring with them into the colonial era a sense of universal superiority. Yet even in China, where Chinese were barred like dogs from Shanghai's race track graced by the white folk, by the 1930s, many Chinese had come to view China as both technologically and culturally inferior to the white man. In order to divest the Chinese of this sense of inferiority, the Chinese revolutionary movement's nationalism called for the unloading of Western cultural traits, such as widespread drug use. But more to the point, revolutionary killing of the white man, and his native mercenaries, may well have relieved many Chinese of their sense of shame and guilt derived from decades of military defeat, brutish racial discrimination, and generalized cultural derogation. During the liberation of China, killing had a way of expiating guilt and delivering the Chinese sense of dignity back to a people who had lost much during a century of imperialism.

Partly because of the violence that accompanies it, the neoclassical revolution is total. Eventually almost all classes join and subordinate themselves to the radicals in order to reorganize the society from top to bottom, from technology through social structure to culture—including those revolutionary themes expressed through utopia.

Immediately prior to military victory, few if any classes, generations, or status groups stand opposed to the triumphant success of the insurgent group, led and guided almost exclusively by radicals. As you will recall, this cross-group solidarity is uncommon to the *classical* revolution, where loss of morale within the upper classes does not precede their going over *en masse* to the revolution. In the case of the *classical* revolution, upper-class demoralization results in relatively few upper-class members siding with the revolutionary forces and calling for the liquidation of their class. Hence, at a later time, these particles of the past are better able to recover portions of those institutions which were earlier all but obliterated, as when segments of the state apparatus and the church organization reappear.

The classical revolution lacks the total commitment held by very large sections of all classes involved in the neoclassical revolution. Precisely because of this intense zeal, the beginnings of the neoclassical Thermidor either fail repeatedly or reveal themselves in attenuated form. Traditional prostitution, and recurrent debauchery simply do not reappear, even among the elites. The revels and restorations that we associate with the end of the Reign of Terror during the French Revolution have no historic counterparts in the neoclassical revolution, although terror may occur, when, and immediately after, the radicals seize power.[9] Political and religious institutions are permanently dropped or radically altered on a sustained basis, and new forms are introduced to supplant the old. Above all, there is a demand for retention of the new *economic* equality. If and when elements of Thermidor appear, the revolutionary party, or a significant faction within it, will take action to stem this trend and to reverse it, thereby keeping alive the utopian hope of equality.

The neoclassical revolution and class–racial consciousness

In the neoclassical revolution, class–racial consciousness becomes a powerful motivator of workers and peasants alike, especially the uprooted industrial workers[10] and the landless laborers.[11] For them, a sense of class–racial identity minimizes the possibility of their accepting political formulas generated abroad by an imperialist class. This alienation from exported formulas accompanies commitment to the use of the general strike and other forms of direct action in order that traditional inequities might be replaced by the better things outlined in the utopias of revolutionary movements pressing for total cultural revolutions. In turn, the endorsement of the general strike finds expression in class–racial consciousness. It occurs throughout all stages of the revolution but seems to be most evident during the prodromal stage, where racial discrimination and low racial prestige (*a*) exacerbate the economic deprivation of the subordinate class–racial group, and (*b*) intensify class–community isolation from its ultimate and foreign rulers. Both circumstances serve to maximize the subcultural homogeneity of this proletarianized minority. When a subordinate class–racial group faces collective problems, and when this isolated enclave proves to be homogeneous, there follows an intensification of interaction within informal groups and among formal organizations run by these underdogs.

Yet class–racial consciousness will fail to emerge unless some force can overcome a deep sense of hopelessness, a condition associated with immizeration. One antidote is the charismatic leader, a key ingredient in the process of translation. As prophet he must inspire faith under circumstances that work against believing in the possibility of improvement. Moreover, the charismatic leader must link class–racial consciousness to a utopia that is partly his creation, embodying the antithesis of exploitative circumstances. He must build consciousness through the definition of problems in very concrete terms. He must use real dates, names, places, wages, and hours to depict the class–racial enemy and the class–racial goal. But seldom does he get the chance, for the state generally rids society of this type of revolutionary leadership.

The revolutionary leadership must grasp imperially dominated institutions such as the radio and redefine them through revolutionary struggle in order to make them useful for the dissemination of concrete and abstract ideologies. Frantz Fanon's graphic description of how the Algerian revolutionary redefined the radio is a case in point:

> Radio-Alger, the French broadcasting station which has been established in Algeria for

decades, a re-edition or an echo of the
French National Broadcasting System operating from Paris, is essentially the instrument
of colonial society and its values. The great
majority of Europeans in Algeria own receiving sets. Before 1945, 95 per cent of the receivers were in the hands of Europeans. The
Algerians who owned radios belonged mainly to the "developed bourgeoisie," and included a number of Kabyles who had
formerly emigrated and had since returned
to their villages. The sharp economic stratification between the dominant and the dominated societies in large part explains this
state of things. But naturally, as in every
colonial situation, this category of realities
takes on a specific coloration. Thus hundreds of Algerian families whose standard of
living was sufficient to enable them to acquire a radio did not acquire one. Yet there
was no rational decision to refuse this instrument. There was no organized resistance to
this device. No real lines of counter-accul-
turation, such as are described in certain
monographs devoted to underdeveloped regions, have been shown to exist, even after
extensive surveys. It may be pointed out,
nevertheless—and this argument may have
appeared to confirm the conclusions of sociologists—that, pressed with questions as to
the reasons for this reluctance, Algerians
rather frequently give the following answer:
"Traditions of respectability are so important for us and are so hierarchical, that it is
practically impossible for us to listen to radio programs in the family. The sex allusions, or even the clownish situations meant
to make people laugh, which are broadcast
over the radio cause an unendurable strain in
a family listening to these programs."

The ever possible eventuality of laughing
in the presence of the head of the family or
the elder brother, of listening in common to
amorous words or terms of levity, obviously
acts as a deterrent to the distribution of radios in Algerian native society. It is with reference to this first rationalization that we
must understand the habit formed by the official Radio Broadcasting Services in Algeria
of announcing the programs that can be
listened to in common and those in the
course of which the traditional forms of
sociability might be too severely
strained. . . .

It was at the end of 1956 that the real
shift occurred. At this time tracts were distributed announcing the existence of a Voice
of Free Algeria. The broadcasting schedules
and the wavelengths were given. This voice
"that speaks from the *djebels*," not geographically limited, but bringing to all Algeria the great message of the Revolution, at
once acquired an essential value. In less than
twenty days the entire stock of radio sets
was bought up. In the *souks* trade in used receiver sets began. Algerians who had served
their apprenticeship with European radio-
electricians opened small shops. Moreover,
the dealers had to meet new needs. The absence of electrification in immense regions in
Algeria naturally created special problems
for the consumer. For this reason battery-
operated receivers, from 1956 on, were in
great demand on Algerian territory. In a few
weeks several thousand sets were sold to Algerians, who bought them as individuals,
families, groups of houses, *douars, mechtas.*

Since 1956 the purchase of a radio in Algeria has meant, not the adoption of a modern technique for getting news, but the obtaining of access to the only means of entering into communication with the Revolution, of living with it. In the special case of
the portable battery set, an improved form
of the standard receiver operating on current, the specialist in technical changes in
underdeveloped countries might see a sign of
a radical mutation. The Algerian, in fact,
gives the impression of finding short cuts
and of achieving the most modern forms of
news-communication without passing
through the intermediary stages. In reality,
we have seen that this "progress" is to be explained by the absence of electric current in
the Algerian *douars.*

The French authorities did not immediately realize the exceptional importance of
this change in attitude of the Algerian people with regard to the radio. Traditional resistances broke down and one could see in a
douar groups of families in which fathers,
mothers, daughters, elbow to elbow, would
scrutinize the radio dial waiting for the
Voice of Algeria. Suddenly indifferent to the
sterile, archaic modesty and antique social
arrangements devoid of brotherhood, the Algerian family discovered itself to be immune
to the off-color jokes and the libidinous references that the announcer occasionally let
drop.

Almost magically—but we have seen the
rapid and dialectical progression of the new
national requirements—the technical instrument of the radio receiver lost its identity as

an enemy object. The radio set was no longer a part of the occupier's arsenal of cultural oppression. In making of the radio a primary means of resisting the increasingly overwhelming psychological and military pressures of the occupant, Algerian society made an autonomous decision to embrace the new technique and thus tune itself in on the new signaling systems brought into being by the Revolution. . . .[12]

The neoclassical defeat

The neoclassical defeat, when it occurs, is generally a consequence of outside intervention. The hurricane in question sweeps all before it on the home-front. In this regard, the Taiping Rebellion (actually a total cultural revolution) is a singularly good example of what is involved. Only the British armies of Chinese Gordon plus the collaboration of certain domestic groups, themselves a distinct minority, could dissipate this tidal wave, which reportedly enlisted widespread support from many classes and caused the death of approximately 20 million Chinese before it was terminated.[13] Of course, other considerations can operate to halt the revolutionary thrust from below, but their importance is minimal. A thoroughgoing analysis of this phenomenon must be done at a later date.[14]

CONCLUSIONS

Our analyses of revolutions have made frequent references to class and to class consciousness. Both subjects become of great intellectual interest during the earliest stages of total cultural and industrial revolutions. This intellectual concern appeared around the world, wherever industrial capitalism moved to supplant agrarian societies. Most pertinent in this regard were the writings of Karl Marx. Later C. Wright Mills became a leader in the redefinition of class structure as it moved from early through middle to late industrial capitalism.

During this period, class struggle has ebbed and flowed, but whatever the level of class conflict, it has served on the whole as the focus of politics. Hence in the next chapter we turn to the subject of class, class conflict, and class consciousness.

NOTES

1. Industrial conflict has been linked to a similar set of factors. Kerr and Siegel demonstrated that strikes are more likely to occur in industries where working conditions are relatively bad and where the workers "form a relatively homogeneous group which is unusually isolated from the general community and which is capable of cohesion." See Clark Kerr and Abraham Siegel, "The Inter-industry Propensity to Strike—An International Comparison," in *Industrial Conflict*, eds. A. Kornhauser, R. Dubin, and A. Ross (New York: McGraw-Hill, 1954), pp. 189–213.

2. These translating mechanisms have been examined in depth and detail by a number of students of revolution and revolutionaries. Among others, see Harold Lasswell and Dorothy Blumenstock, *Revolutionary Propaganda* (New York: Knopf, 1939); Alfred Meyer, *Leninism* (New York: Praeger, 1962), pp. 19–103; Philip Selznick, *The Organization Weapon: A Study of Bolshevik Strategy and Tactics* (Glencoe, Ill.: The Free Press, 1960); and Ralph H. Turner and Lewis M. Killian, *Collective Behavior* (Englewood Cliffs, N.J.: Prentice-Hall, 1957), chapt. 14–21.

3. For Mao's discussion on peasant hegemony, see his "Report on the Investigation of the Peasant Movement in Human," in Brandt et al., *op. cit.*, pp. 85–89. On soviets, see Mao's "Report to the Second All-China Soviet Conference," *ibid.*, pp. 226–229.

4. The initial pattern of revolutionary struggle has been described by various advocates and analysts of revolution. See, for example, Brinton, op. cit., pp. 70–97; and Leon Trotsky, *The History of the Russian Revolution* (Ann Arbor: University of Michigan Press, 1957), especially chap. 1.

5. For a variety of viewpoints on the German uprising see Evelyn Anderson, *Hammer or Anvil: The Story of the German Working Class Movement* (London: Gollancz, 1945), pp. 39–71; Ruth Fischer, *Stalin and German Communism* (Cambridge: Harvard University Press, 1948), pp. 52–112; Carl Landauer, *European Socialism*, vol. 1 (Berkeley: University of California Press, 1959), pp. 663–689, 809–831; and Kippel S. Pinson, *Modern Germany: Its History and Civilization* (New York: Macmillan, 1954), pp. 350–391.

6. On the revolution of 1927 see Arthur N. Holcombe, *The Chinese Revolution* (Cambridge: Harvard University Press, 1930), pp. 120–296; Harold R. Isaacs, *The Tragedy of the Chinese Revolution* (Stanford: Stanford University Press, 1953), pp. 66–122; and Benjamin I. Schwartz, *Chinese Communism and the Rise of Mao* (Cambridge: Harvard University Press, 1952), pp. 46–108.

7. We attempted to use Guttman scaling when specifying paths followed by revolutions. Our experiment failed. However, one of the interesting generalizations that did come out of our efforts with the Guttman grids is that the general economic conditions of the subordinate class(es) can vary any number of ways, and the expectations (whether externally or internally generated) do not parallel the economic conditions. In the schematization below, economic conditions and expectations are represented by solid and dashed lines, respectively. (See Figure on page 99.)

8. The possibility of a revolution's skipping stages of development was set forth by Leon Trotsky in his "law of combined development." Here he proposed that a long period of capitalist industrial development

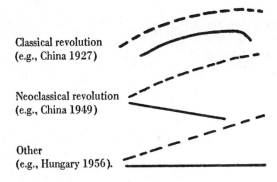

Classical revolution
(e.g., China 1927)

Neoclassical revolution
(e.g., China 1949)

Other
(e.g., Hungary 1956).

(The Hungarian episode suggests a third type of
revolution.)

was not necessary for backward countries such as
Russia. This was possible, he argued, because of the
immediate availability of cultural traits of the more
advanced industrial societies. As the result of cultural
"borrowing," development under a revolutionary regime could thus be telescoped. See the discussion in
Trotsky, *op. cit.*, pp. 3–15. This idea of discontinuous
development has been restated as a more general proposition for cultural evolution by Service in his chapter
"The Law of Cultural Cominance," in Sahlins and
Service (eds.) *op. cit.*, pp. 92–123.

9. Although Brinton spoke of Thermidor in the
Russian Revolution, he admitted that the analogy with
the French Revolution does not hold in certain key
respects. Restoration of the old regime never occurred.
And, after a brief period of moderation during the
New Economic Policy, the excesses of the early years
of the revolution were resumed in even more extreme
form under the totalitarian regime of Stalin. Trotsky's
attitude on the question of Thermidor is less qualified,
at least in his later writings. In *Revolution Betrayed*,
he was quite convinced that the Stalinist bureaucratic
state represented the triumph of the Thermidorean

forces of reaction. However, on this question Trotsky's theoretical acumen suffered because of his polemic intent. Obviously, both Brinton and Trotsky were
correct in their observations of change in content of
the Russian Revolution. However, their analyses became muddled when they attempted to assess these
changes in terms of a somewhat doubtful historical
parallel, some analysts would argue. Yet their views
would seem insightful. Brinton's discussion is in *op.
cit.*, pp. 215-250. Trotsky's various analyses have been
traced in Siegfried Bahn, "Trotsky on Stalin's Russia,"
Survey: Journal of Soviet and East European Studies,
41 (April, 1962): 32-42. Also see Trotsky, *Revolution
Betrayed* (New York: Pioneer Publishers, 1945), pp.
86–115.

10. For a discussion of uprooted industrial workers, see John C. Leggett, "Uprootedness and Working
Class Consciousness," *The American Journal of Sociology*, May, 1963.

11. A number of works have referred to the revolu-
tionary quality of landless peasants. See especially
David Mitrany, *Marx Against the Peasant* (Chapel Hill:
University of North Carolina Press, 1951), pp. 1–145.

12. Frantz Fanon, *Studies in a Dying Colonialism*
(New York: Monthly Review Press, 1965), pp. 69–70,
82 to 84. Copyright 1965 by Monthly Review Press.
Reprinted by permission of Monthly Review.

13. See Morton Brown, *Revolution and Revolu-
tionary Movements in China* (M.A. thesis, University
of California, 1964), pp. 113–129; Chien-nung Li, *The
Political History of China* (New York: Van Nostrand
Reinhold, 1956), pp. 47–95; G. E. Tayler, "The Tai-
ping Rebellion: Its Economic Background and Social
Theory," *The Chinese Social and Political Science
Review*, 16 (January, 1933): 545–615; and Ssu-yü
Teng, *New Light on the History of the Taiping Rebel-
lion* (Cambridge: Harvard University Press).

14. With regard to furthering our analysis of the
various units within the prodromal stage, we found the
common principle of sociological investigation to
hold: "Increased differentiation of categories leads to
decreased utility."

Chapter 5 Class and Class Consciousness in Industrial Societies

Section One   *The Periodicity of Working-Class Consciousness*

MARX'S CONTRIBUTION

What are the sources and political consequences of working-class consciousness? We concern ourselves with the working class, for unless large sections of this population enter politics as highly class conscious, neither widespread revolution nor significant reform will occur. In addressing ourselves to this matter, we must consult the writings of Karl Marx, the nineteenth-century German economist, political scientist, philosopher, and sociologist. Marx was born and raised in Germany but spent much of his later life in Paris and London. As a student of politics, he always linked his observations to his own political participation within European socialist parties—for him there was no artificial separation between scholarly observation and astute political activity.

Marx's views were inseparable from those of his close friend Friedrich Engels. They jointly wrote many articles and books on the rise of the European labor movement and major current events of their time, such as the American Civil War as well as recurrent worldwide depressions. Marx was poor throughout much of his life, and his family suffered accordingly. His biographers tell us of how Marx once burned some of his furniture in order to keep his family from freezing to death during a severe London winter. In those days, there were no university Marxists or philanthropic foundations to sustain the Left's theoreticians.

Marx's principal message was clear: Philosophers have studied history; it is our task to change it. In this spirit we approach his brilliant insights on class and consciousness.

■ This chapter is a summary and extension of my doctoral dissertation, "Working Class Consciousness in Detroit," University of Michigan, 1962. Footnoted documentations appear in the original text—J.C.L.

THE IMPACT OF WORKING RELATIONS AND JOB SEEKING ON WORKING-CLASS VALUES

Crucial in assessing Marx's contribution to the study of working-class consciousness and struggle is an understanding of the difference between the formulations of Marx, who evinced a *historical* interest in the general direction of man's development, and Marx, who considered the *sociological* basis for conflict and consciousness within a community.

When Marx wrote as a historical philosopher, he argued that work relationships involving dominant and subordinate classes were never fixed but always in a state of flux. These work ties were simultaneously characterized by harmony and conflict, with one generally taking precedence over the other for prolonged periods. Applying this overarching view of conflict to capitalist society, Marx characterized the propertied middle and propertyless working classes as involved simultaneously in symbiotic and antagonistic relations. During some historical moments, class relations would be relatively free from bitterness and struggle, as employers and workers cooperated at work and manual laborers accepted the distributive pattern of goods. At this time the class struggle proceeded at a "snail's pace." But during other phases of a society's development—especially during what Marx saw as the final and inevitable period of advanced capitalist technological development and massive unemployment—the bonds between classes would loosen and eventually give way. Relations would then become like those of a marriage about to collapse.

Workers' strikes, company lock-outs, and pitched battles between militia and workmen, scabs and strikers, would climax two earlier phases of economic development: (*a*) a long period of relative prosperity for the community and related peaceful ties between classes, succeeded by (*b*) a short span of economic collapse and consequent questioning of the legitimacy of ruling-class authority. As this pattern was repeated, the resulting class strife would create heightened class awareness among workmen, who would move from qualified but vocal support for their class to outright avowal of socialist equality. Furthermore, once militant goals had become lodged in the minds of workmen, these ideas would constitute an important vehicle of revolutionary change, forces as powerful as the motor itself: the tools, ties, and antagonisms of the workplace which were associated with poverty at home and alienation from self, plant, product, and law. The progressive degradation and mental disengagement of the working class—processes induced largely by capitalism—would press the working class to alter further its perceptions and evaluations of capitalism. Subsequently they would develop a revolutionary level of consciousness capable of contributing to the elimination of capitalism. This class would be transformed from a class *in* itself, one with class form but not awareness, to a class *for* itself, a cohesive body with collective, insurgent spirit.

Selig Perlman was struck by the hiatus between Marx's developmental prediction and the American reality of the 1920s. As a University of Wisconsin labor economist who wrote favorably on American trade unionism during the flapper decade, he observed what he judged to be the bread-and-butter quality of American labor in the early part of this century. Carpenters, plumbers, bricklayers, trainmen, and the like, were less than aggressive in their relations to business interests. Perlman observed that although American workers organized unions and attempted to improve working conditions, wages, and job security, they refused to back tactics such as the general strike. In keeping with this situation, Perlman dismissed the possibility of a general strike in his discussion of American workers' views, but in so doing, he strongly implied that such a strike might well reflect or encourage the formation of consciousness.

Again and unlike Marx, Perlman rejected the assumption that the thoughts of workmen could not be fathomed without reference to property ownership and work relations. He insisted that workmen were "job-oriented," that they were primarily concerned with marketing their labor in a way that would maximize their personal gains. Originally, workers had been forced to market their labor individually on the basis of supply-and-demand considerations. Given a surplus of labor as well as a concentration of power in the hands of business firms and their political allies, workmen's wages were less than adequate. To compound workers' problems, unfair recruitment practices, long work days, and dangerous working conditions forced workmen to defend themselves through the organization of unions. Aiming to elevate wages, shorten work days, establish hiring halls, and improve work rules, unions worked to make their jobs more acceptable to the average workman and to give him greater economic security. These organizational inventions did not appear on the American scene without struggle. Workers fought through unions to press governmental bodies to enact and to enforce laws geared to the improvement of job conditions.

Perlman argued that unions were successful largely because they monopolized the marketing of labor. Thus when employers refused to make concessions to unions, the unions would withdraw the scarce skills of workmen. Given their command over this supply, labor unions could successfully extract economic concessions from businessmen who had no choice but to compromise. On the basis of the success of craft unionists, Perlman inexplicably generalized their victories to the entire blue-collar labor force.

Yet Perlman's efforts to generalize to the entire working class on the basis of craft-union activity failed. As the evidence shows, workmen in the mass industries, even during the 1920s, were not comparable to members of craft and related unions. Industrial workers had lower incomes and status, enjoyed less workplace safety, and commanded less power. They were not part of labor's aristocracy.

Perlman also held that as the conditions of trade unionists improved, the proportion of radical workmen would decrease noticeably. He argued that workmen came to view extremist attitudes as antithetical to working-class interests. In Perlman's analysis, workers reasoned that if revolutionary action were to fail, the defeat would result in the destruction of the material gains made at great cost over the decades. Consequently, even when American workmen were sympathetic to socialism, communism, or syndicalism, they would become increasingly unwilling to support revolutionary action that might jeopardize hard-won gains. In short, given the strategic pragmatism and limited goals of unions, plus their success in collective bargaining, these unions would be incapable of imbuing their members with revolutionary zeal. As a result, Perlman believed, the working class would never rise above a trade-union level of awareness. Strikes would focus on concrete issues, while the struggle for better wages and working conditions would lead to greater equity within the capitalist system. Given their long-term success in resolving bread-and-butter issues, workers would not face material deprivation of the kind that could conceivably move them to fight for the realization of equality through socialism or communism. Perlman published these views during the 1920s, and he believed that events had confirmed his theory.

THE IMPACT OF IMPROVED LIVING STANDARDS ON WORKERS' VIEWS

Marx and Perlman disagreed on the impact of a higher standard of living on the political behavior of workmen. Marx held that the degree of worker consciousness was largely based on economic fluctuations and the kind of social organization that existed at the workplace. He argued that a higher standard of living increased workers' material wants, while at the same time the cyclical character of capitalist economy prevented their demands from being met on a continuous basis. When depression followed prosperity, workers would experience a new standard of living, one that departed drastically from the old consumption levels; clearly the workers' buying power would drop beneath the level of their recent expectations. The result would be a mood of disappointment and disenchantment with normal political procedures which had proved useless in dealing with these problems. Workers would subsequently turn to revolutionary programs to bring about changes in society. However, these ideas would not emerge and remain in a vacuum. Radical ideas would develop among workmen who were simul-

taneously isolated from middle-class contact, accustomed to similar occupational hazards, jammed next to one another at work, and linked together through aggressive unions.

Perlman viewed Marx's analysis as inappropriate. Perlman agreed that the U.S. economy might indeed fail to meet the heightened expectations of American workers. But workmen were patient. More important, they were intimidated by the power of employers to penalize workers by blacklisting or firing. Thus, even though many American workers judged company practices to be unfair, with few exceptions they viewed the capitalist system as essentially tolerable if not improvable. They were inveterate optimists; they believed that they could realize the good things in life by operating within the capitalist system, although on occasion workers engaged in violent strikes and similar insurgent confrontations. However, even during periods of economic malaise, workers were primarily concerned with keeping their jobs or getting back to work. Thus, they were not very apt to give credence to revolutionary formulas. This stress on the essential pliancy of workmen differed considerably from Marx's appraisal.

CLIMATE OF INQUIRY AND DIRECTION OF EVIDENCE: MARX VERSUS PERLMAN

Although Marx and Perlman and their students have discussed approximately the same phenomena, they have drawn statistical support for their respective positions from quite different historical periods. Like social scientists everywhere, they selected data during periods and within communities typified by behavior that was conducive to the substantiation of their theories. Most of the evidence supportive to Marxian analysis was gathered during a period of economic collapse or recession that followed a time of prosperity, whereas Perlman and his supporters have concentrated on data gathered during a long span of good times.

Those influenced by Marxian sociology have successfully researched the propensity of unionized workmen to use the sit-down strike and the picket line to recoup pecuniary losses and to make material gains during periods of economic dislocation or the immediate period thereafter. Thus Alfred W. Jones studied the

Akron sit-down strikes during the mid-1930s and observed a high level of worker consciousness, especially among members of the Congress of Industrial Organizations (CIO). A substantial majority of these rubber workers favored such forms of direct action as the reverse lock-out. A group of Saginaw, Michigan, public utilities workers had devised this tactic to force management out of a power plant which the workmen managed for several weeks before winning a crucial strike. Almost all the striking Akron CIO workers favored such action. By contrast, the notorious "red apples"—workmen who belonged to a company union—were in most cases opposed to it. Thus, much as Marx would have predicted, the unionized workers had acquired a set of views in keeping with their objective conditions.

During the Great Depression the Akron experience was not unique. All across the country workmen acted in ways that were inconsistent with Perlman's thesis. In fact, the dramatic sit-down strikes and violent struggles of Akron rubber workers, San Francisco longshoremen, Chicago steel workers, Detroit auto workers, Minneapolis teamsters, and Schenectady electrical workers contradicted Perlman's blanket assertions on the supine character of American labor. Presumably the passage of fifteen years and a combination of other factors accounted for the difference.

Yet on at least one point Perlman's analysis seemed to be applicable, even during the turbulent 1930s when class struggle was a reality. Jones found that although Akron's unionized rubber workers were radical in a manner quite inconceivable in the 1920s, they still preferred the practical, reform politics of Franklin Delano Roosevelt and the Democratic party to the distant promises and programs of Socialist Norman Thomas and Communist Earl Browder.

For Marxists there were many disappointments. By 1940 it was obvious that the Great Depression had helped to advance aggressive class attitudes and organizations which subsequently and ironically generated a bloc working-class vote commited to a *reform* candidate—one who could better preserve the profit system by making it somewhat socialist-oriented.

In another study, Liston Pope (1929-1931) observed the mill workers of Gastonia, North Carolina. They had suffered wage cuts, orga-

nized a union as a response, and used the strike to rectify their losses. Pope found that the violent conflict between mill owners and textile workers was accompanied by the creation, reinforcement, and persistence of class-conscious attitudes among strikers. Unfortunately, Pope's study only touched on the militant attitudes of the mill workers. It did, however, carefully document the chronology and character of a bloody strike led by outside Communists and supported by local workmen. Leaders and followers alike dedicated themselves to organizing mill unions and eliminating obvious injustices.

Clearly, Marxian theory is helpful in explaining a high level of class consciousness in both Akron and Gastonia *during periods of economic depression.* Not only the poverty of the average person, but the vivid contrasts in wealth, the relative decline in workers' standards of living, and the widening gap between what the worker expected and what the middle class obtained were undoubtedly relevant. Consumption standards and levels were but part of the picture. The social organization of the workplace helped to instill a class point of view. Blue-collar people worked closely together and shared the same backgrounds. Both these conditions fostered communication among workers, the development and extension of close ties within the subgroup, and finally, the formation of labor organizations dedicated to advancing working-class interests.

Marx had made explicit the importance of density of population and the consequent ease of conversation among workmen. Contrasting workmen with farmers, he observed that poverty alone had not moved either French farmers or Indian peasants to develop a militant class perspective. Aware of their position but uncommitted to struggle for their class interests, these agrarians lacked the high population density associated with a factory division of labor. Hence the characteristic work settings were not of the kind that could bring the peasants together informally on a sustained basis to prepare them for class struggle.

Marx's dual concern with the sources and consequences of class consciousness influenced the twentieth-century social scientists. These scientists went on to relate class position and class consciousness to political views during prosperous periods immediately following a great depression. Richard Centers, who studied class opinions sampled from workmen throughout the United States during the mid-1940s, found *(a)* that the majority identified with the working class, and *(b)* that a very large portion of the majority favored New Deal legislation designed to benefit working-class people.

Nonetheless, it is clear that the relation between class identification and political behavior is complex. For example, Mark Abrams surveyed England under historical circumstances similar to those encountered by Centers. But Abrams's observations, unlike those of the University of California sociologist, led him to the conclusion that a sizable minority of workers both identified with the working classes and preferred deferential relations with the upper classes. Far from calling for class struggle and socialism, these workmen voted for the Tories. They viewed themselves as rightfully subordinate within a class system that was essentially legitimate. Yet this lack of class consciousness should not surprise us, since objective positions promoted this mentality. Most of these workers were found in industries, regions, and unions where class conflict was not widely known.

The evidence is mixed but predictable. During periods of economic crisis, workers often exhibit a high incidence of class consciousness. This awareness and commitment helps to explain political affiliation but *not* revolutionary politics. These predispositions remain with most workmen for some time following a depression, even after most have become relatively prosperous and secure. By contrast, Perlman's views have great applicability during periods of prolonged economic prosperity, as during the late 1940s, the early 1950s, and much of the 1960s. Many social scientists examined the American scene at these times and discovered few militant workmen. These sociologists had assumed that if American workers were highly class conscious, they would certainly agree among themselves on the nature of the class order. Surely a class consensus would permeate the working-class community. Conversely, they equated the absence of a class perspective with a low level of class consciousness. The results surprised these investigators. The findings demonstrated time and again that many manual workers were vague or inconsistent when asked to identify their class. They viewed themselves as middle class one moment and working class the next. Perhaps even more disheartening to many social scientists who had hoped for different results, workmen were unable to agree among themselves on the number and structure of classes in their communities. They even failed to use the same criteria for describing or determining their class.

These studies indicated a widespread lack of sophistication on class matters, much as Perlman had maintained. The reading of these results leads one to doubt the pertinence of Marxian theory for understanding the attitudes of most workmen during periods of extended prosperity. Clearly workers had failed to develop a militant mentality capable of withstanding the effects of prosperity.

CONDITIONS LIMITING CONSCIOUSNESS

In keeping with the times, many social scientists during the 1950s abandoned their Marxian assumptions and turned to an examination of why workers in the United States lacked militant class attitudes. One of these observers, Morris Rosenberg, analyzed several important phenomena presumably related to the diminution of working-class consciousness: the structure of large-scale industries, the system of political representation, membership in diverse groups, the contemporary "life style," and the common goals of a society.

Rosenberg maintained that the present organization of the mass industries creates confusion in the minds of workmen concerning who is responsible for problems at the workplace. The formal control net of management and the informal levels of skill specialization within the working class help significantly to promote this confusion. According to Rosenberg, the stockholder and the director wield power in ways unclear to workers. Therefore it is easier for workmen to find fault with the man on the spot—the foreman—than with the owners or executives of the corporation. On the level of aggression, it is easier for manual workers to vent their hostility against the foreman, if only because they tend to think in terms of direct experience. Workmen find it difficult to judge the nonpalpable as reprehensible. Although at times workmen do exercise this judgment, they are never quite sure who, or what, is the guilty party and who should consequently receive blame. When workers do not have precise information on the nature of domination or exploitation, their criticisms become diffuse and hence are a poor source of class consciousness.

An equally important aspect of industrial structure is widespread job differentiation. The full range of hierarchically ordered positions hinders the attainment of class solidarity.

Blue-collar workers range from tool-and-die makers and other skilled workmen to floor sweepers. This job differentiation prompts a collective sense of hierarchy among manual workers. Illustratively, tool-and-die makers often consider themselves to be an elite group, and they demand special contracts and considerations. Those who define themselves as superior insist on receiving considerably more income than less-skilled workmen. This special treatment promotes envy and jealousy and some hostility from below. Hence status ranking plus attendant wage differentials make it difficult for workmen to associate on a sustained basis, within either a labor union or a labor party.

Rosenberg made another observation, one that is often overlooked: The political structure of parliamentary system weakens class solidarity because it operates according to *territorial* representation. The elected are called on to act in behalf of not one but several classes. These classes have conflicting interests, and all demand representation. The system thereby places the politician in a difficult position. He must satisfy the conflicting demands of groups at odds with one another, while simultaneously continuing to rally the support of conflicting collectivities in order to ensure the continuance of his political career. Caught in the middle, the career politician has to compromise the blunt demands of warring parties; consequently, he seldom translates aggressive working class views into legislation. Since these views cannot find a political outlet, they decline, unable to sustain themselves without action and success. A decline in militant views presumably would *not* take place if political representatives were elected along syndicalist—occupational, rather than geographical, lines. For example, were union internationals or occupational categories to elect candidates for state legislatures or Congress, workers would wield direct control, and

programs and consciousness would be less diluted.

Simultaneous membership in groups composed of multiple classes with differing perspectives constitutes a third element working to lessen consciousness. For example, workmen who belong to unions that create and guide their militancy may, at the same time, participate in other groups that promote conservative values. Despite the logical inconsistencies involved, it is possible for workers to admire the views of both groups. In so doing, they may be caught between two definitions of problems and solutions—one proposed by the union, the other perhaps articulated by middle-class organizations such as religious, veterans', and educational groups. Given contradictory appraisals of key issues such as unemployment or automation, workers might very well compromise their views, or perhaps reject any solution, as people often do when faced with cross-pressures. In turn, this rejection might lead to disengagement from all thought and action on class issues. The worker could well become a political drop-out.

"Life style" is the fourth consideration making it difficult for the working class to see themselves as unjustly subordinate and politically insurgent. Contemporary Americans have developed buying tastes that cut across class lines. For example, classes can no longer be differentiated on the basis of the clothes they wear, as was the case fifty, even thirty, years ago. Although changes in dress are partly due to the growth of working-class affluence resulting from a high degree of industrialization, they also reflect the commercialization of taste associated with mass advertising and the mass media.

Finally, when classes in a society share goals, they may reach agreement on ways to achieve common objectives. For example, during World War II all classes agreed that defeating fascism was the first order of business. Workers promised not to strike, and management followed a policy of no lock-outs, no mass firings, and no speed-ups. Under such conditions and admonitions, the idea of harmony is repeatedly encouraged. The notion of class struggle is recurrently rejected and class consciousness diminishes accordingly.

Rosenberg's observations certainly sensitize us to a number of forces inhibiting the development and maintenance of militant class views. But Rosenberg did not present evidence to support his observations. Nor did he examine the origins, variability, and consequences of working-class consciousness. Assuming low levels of class identification and solidarity among American workmen, he simply attempted to account for these phenomena. He did not measure the varying degrees of class consciousness among different types of workers. And yet it is differences among people who otherwise have a lot in common which demand our analytical and research attention when dealing with consciousness.

STATUS POLITICS ONLY?

Another influential current view has bearing on the issue of consciousness. This opinion holds that status politics has replaced class politics. Status politics is an admittedly vague term, but it has come to represent essentially the following position: Economic insecurity is no longer significant in the lives of workers; hence class consciousness and class politics have become irrelevant. Workers now deal with problems of consumption rather than security. As potential purchasers from the windows of glitter, for the residences of clutter, workers focus on competition for prestige derived from consumption of goods—cars with Tiger Paws, homes with Ranch Fences, backyards with Bricked Patios, and weekend hunts for Prized Birds. When a person or group threatens the prestige derived from putting a tiger in their tanks, workers will be predisposed to support the politician or party willing to protect their ongoing acquisitions and status. Hence, status politics.

This point of view has applicability, especially among workers accustomed to a high level of consumption throughout a prolonged period of economic prosperity. For example, after white workers have known twenty years of affluence, they will strive to retain the status derived from home purchase in the proper suburbs. Should an influx of low-status minorities into their neighborhood seem to threaten their possessions or prestige, workmen will vote for the party and/or politician who promises to protect their prestige. Thus efforts to achieve interracial housing may become the basis for one form of status group politics.

STATUS POLITICS AND STATUS-GROUP POLITICS: A DIFFERENCE

Status politics should not, however, be confused with status-*group* politics, the politics of a submerged racial, religious, or ethnic group attempting to release itself from the fetters of discrimination associated with lesser ethnic prestige. Status-group politics is often extremely important, as when black members of the working class acquire class—racial consciousness. They use political expressions fostering internal competition and conflict between the black and white sections of this country's manual labor force.

THE EARLY SOCIALIST CRITICS

A number of writers—most of them Socialists—commented on the problem of status-group politics and status-group conflict around the turn of the last century. They described the forces that militate in favor of the formation of class—racial consciousness and against class solidarity, both in the plant and at the polls. Engels studied the American labor movement as it emerged after the Civil War and discussed the problem of ethnic divisions among workers. For example, he noted how nationality differences had split manual workmen into different language groups, thereby limiting communication among them. When workers can't talk to one another, they have obviously encountered an impediment to the establishment of class solidarity.

Engels did not spell out the implications of his observation for Marxian theory, but they were obvious. Prior to this observation by Engels, Marx had developed a general theory of class consciousness. He had assumed that workers were very much alike. Hence they were able to communicate easily, a necessary precondition for the development of a class consciousness that would permeate the entire working class. Here, of course, Marx was aware of exceptions such as the Irish—English split in England and the black—white division in the United States.

Undoubtedly cognizant of Marx's analyses of the United States, Engels had observed that if American workers were split into different language groups and thus semiisolated from one another, class solidarity would develop only with considerable difficulty. For even though proletarianized ethnic groups were often sparked by class—ethnic consciousness during the 1870s and 1880s when Engels made his observations, Engels recognized that it would be extremely hard for a socialist movement to unite such a fragmented class in political solidarity. How, for example, could a socialist movement bring together the revolutionary commitments of the Irish Molly McGuires of eastern Pennsylvania, the radical black-coal miners of southeastern Ohio, the German radicals of Chicago, and the Italian anarchists of New York and Boston? Their diverse languages and religions made unity all but impossible.

Many European intellectuals took up the ethnic problem, although their focus was different from that of Engels. Whereas he had dwelt on ethnic divisions inside one class, they examined the ethnic quality of interclass conflict. This analytical and political problem was of particular concern to writers who lived in the Austro-Hungarian Empire at the turn of the nineteenth century. The mottled concentrations of ethnic groups had helped to give rise to numerous class—ethnic conflicts within central and southeastern Europe. The Viennese, Ludwig Gumplowicz, for instance, observed how the ethnic makeup of the empire's ruling classes differed markedly from that of subordinate classes. For although the upper class was overwhelmingly German, the peasants and laborers were generally Slavs in Sudetanland, Bohemia, Moravia, Slovakia, Silesia, and many other provinces within the Empire. The most prominent struggles thus involved groups which differed not only in terms of class, but nationality as well. Another Viennese, Joseph Schumpeter, formulated a theory on the rise and fall of "whole classes." He referred to distinct nationalities as constituting entire ruling or subordinate classes swinging in ascent or descent, depending on their material and military fortunes during the historical moment.

As one of the early twentieth-century leaders of the Marxist wing of Austrian Socialism, Otto Bauer had to deal continuously with the problems and conflicts of different ethnic groups working together or against one another inside the Socialist movement. Bauer observed not only that the middle classes were heavily German and the working classes Slavic, but he focused on the way in which class and ethnic stratification shaped class conflict and working-class solidarity. In this sense Bauer made a very important contribution to a Marxism *without* general categories yet able to reflect real ethnic and nationality divisions.

Bauer studied what is today Czechoslovakia and observed how ethnic groups differed in overall occupational position. He used statistical materials and demonstrated a close relation between ethnic group and class position. He also observed when German residents lived in predominantly Czech areas, the Germans were largely entrepreneurs, whereas the Czechs were primarily working-class people who defined themselves as both unfairly treated workers and exploited Czechs. Predictably enough, they viewed their employers both as exploiting property owners and as Germans.

The Germans considered the Slavs to be an inferior group. Hence they were not offended by the critical attitude of Czech workers. Still, the criticisms and ethnic rankings had consequences and differences which often led to strife between German and Czech workers. For example, because Czech workmen had lower status and consequently felt no sense of class affinity with their German counterparts, they often became strikebreakers when German workers shut down a mine, a mill or a factory. In turn, the Germans deprecated the Bohemians, Moravians, and Slovakians and reciprocated by acting as strikebreakers when Czech workmen walked out.

Bauer's remarks have obvious implications for working-class solidarity in the United States. The American black today is the historical counterpart to the Czech, whereas white manual workers are comparable to the German workmen in the Sudetenland, Bohemia, and Moravia prior to World War I. Both in the United States and in the central European settings there were differences in group prestige, skill level, and income; in addition, the isolation factor was present. Like Czechs, blacks have enjoyed less prestige, held proportionately fewer skilled jobs, earned less income, and on occasion acted as strikebreakers. On their side, white workmen have generally discouraged black participation in labor unions. Craft unionists have led in this regard. Discrimination such as this has helped to push blacks to engage in

TABLE 4 Class Structure in Early Industrial Society (Capitalist)*

Class	Occupation	Private Property Ownership	Economic Role Performed	Economic Reward Received
Middle Class (*haute* bourgeoisie)	White-Collar 1. Big business Owners 2. High financiers	Large amounts	Indirect processors: 1. Control investment 2. Manage (in most cases) operation of business	Profit
Lesser Middle Class (*petite* bourgeoisie)	White-Collar 1. Small business owners 2. Small financiers	Small amounts	Indirect processors: 1. Control investment 2. Manage operation of business	Profit
	3. Managers 4. Professionals 5. Clerks	None	Indirect Processors: 1. Coordinate activities at workplace 2. Develop scientific knowledge	Salary or wage
Working Class	Blue-Collar 1. Skilled workers 2. Unskilled workers	None	Direct processors: 1. Extract 2. Process 3. Transport	Wage
	Lumpen proletariat	–	–	–

*This table does not include reference to class structure in rural areas, partly because of the declining significance of this population in industrial society.

status-group politics and bloody job encounters at construction and other job sites. The consequences are obvious. Black and white cannot unite against their common manipulators.

Marx sensed this division, but not its depth.

CLASS:
THE USE AND MODIFICATION OF MARX

In addition to specifying several of the interrelated sources and consequences of class consciousness, Marx stressed the importance of objective measures of class and multiple degrees of class consciousness. But before we examine how Marx saw these measures of class consciousness, we should understand what Marx meant by "class."

Marx generally defined class by using objective criteria: measures of positions occupied rather than specifications of positions sought or preferred by the person observed. Marx's indexes of objective class position were readily

distinguishable from one another and were based on economic and occupational roles (see Table 4).

A member of the *haute* bourgeoisie, for example, was defined as a person who owned private property in large amounts, who indirectly processed raw materials, and in some cases managed their manufacture and distribution. All these activities were done for private profit. The indirect processor of raw materials never directly handled the semifinished and finished goods. These tasks were left to manual workers. The capitalist merely coordinated funds used for investment, raw materials, and manpower. He determined the firm's policies and he guided the work group's division of labor. Included in this class were wealthy manufacturers and financiers.

A second class was the *petite* bourgeoisie, subdivided into (*a*) small-scale owners and investors and (*b*) nonpropertied white-collar workers who coordinated production, distribution, exchange, or who performed related services for the capitalists.

A member of the first group was generally a retailer or farmer who might own property, but who earned his income through business operations. For his efforts he received a profit, which was often meager and frequently doomed to shrink further. In many cases, the small entrepreneur could not simultaneously replace worn-out capital, expand his business, and eke out a profit. Yet, he had to do all three if he was to survive.

Found also within the *petite* bourgeoisie were the white-collar workers who failed to possess private investment property but who indirectly processed goods. These employees provided accounting, legal, architectural, scientific, and other semiprofessional and fully professional services for the large and small owners of capital. For their efforts they generally earned a salary, but on occasion they received a wage.

The working class consisted of those who did not own capital and could not therefore invest funds for profit. Workmen acted as direct processors and performed one of three types of roles: extracting raw materials from nature, as did miners, fishermen, and others in the primary industries; processing unfinished or semifinished goods, as steelmakers and smelter workers in the secondary industries; or transporting either goods or people. Such workers received wages. These wages were equal to only a fraction of the value of what workers produced. In this sense, workers were exploited. But some workers received more than others, irrespective of exploitation but in accord with skill—and hence marketability of their services. Members of the skilled working class are in scarce supply.

Although Marx was well aware of the range of skills within the blue-collar sector, he chose not to comment analytically on the implications of job differentiation to the study of consciousness. He made the distinction between employable workers and the dregs that had sunk permanently to the bottom of the class system. He called this stratum the *lumpen proletariat,* a category of ragged and motley unskilled, generally unemployed and unemployable persons, who were frequently derelict in character and not part of the progressive sections of the working class.

Whatever the merits of this typology for understanding early industrial society, Marx's framework is inadequate for portraying the contemporary scene. It fails to summarize the true outlines of the class structure of today's society. In particular, the growth of a new middle class renders Marx's model obsolete.

The writings of Lewis Corey and C. Wright Mills help us to revise the framework. Crucial in their writing is the distinction among the old middle, new middle, and working classes. Table 5 indicates that the old middle class consists of affluent and marginal elements. The affluent stratum includes big business owners and high financiers who own large investments, process goods as owners, managers, and the like, and receive profit and in some cases, a salary for their efforts. The marginal element operates in a similar way, except that its proportion of total assets is less. Indeed, historically, its overall share has decreased through time.

Since Marx was not a prophet but a social scientist, with little evidential or methodological basis for predicting epochal changes, he did not foresee the growing importance of the new middle class. He was aware of its emergence, but he believed that this group would be small and insignificant in the long run. Corey and Mills, however, have shown that the new middle class, with three important strata—managers, professionals, and white-collar service workers— includes those found in the major growth sectors of the economy. For example, office supervisors, plant directors, store clerks, school teachers, social workers, and computer technicians would fall into this category. Primarily occupied in managerial and service fields, the members of this class sometimes own significant amounts of capital as well. From these investments they derive profits to augment their salaries. The new middle class will soon constitute more than one-half of the entire labor force in advanced industrial societies, including our own.

The main source of income for the modern working class still consists of manual (i.e., blue-collar) labor performed with varying degrees of skill in the extracting of raw materials, the processing of these reworked elements, and their transportation as goods. Although its members on occasion maintain investments, they are meager compared with those enjoyed

TABLE 5   Class Structure in Late Industrial Society (Capitalist)*

Class	Occupation	Private Property	Economic Role Performed	Economic Reward Received
Affluent Old middle class	White-Collar 1. Big Business owners 2. High financiers	Large amounts	Indirect processors: Manage and/or control capital	Profit, and in some cases salary
Marginal	3. Small business owners 4. Small financiers	Small amounts	Indirect Processors: Manage and/or control capital	Profit
New middle class	White-Collar 1. Managers 2. Professionals 3. Clerks 4. Some foremen	1. Large amounts 2. Small amounts 3. None	Indirect processors: 1. Manage business enterprises 2. Perform other indirect functions	Salary, and in some cases profit
Working class	Blue-Collar 1. Some foremen 2. Craftsmen and other skilled workers 3. Factory, mine, and mill workers 4. Other workers (including *lumpen proletariat*)	1. Small amounts 2. None	Direct processors: 1. Extract 2. Process 3. Transport 4. Maintain	Wage, and in some cases profit, and/ or salary

*This table does not make reference to rural classes in late industrial society, largely because of their political, social, and economic insignificance.

by the new and old middle classes. However, despite the absence of significant revenue from investments, most workmen in advanced industrial societies receive incomes considerably greater than is the case in early industrial society. Hence proportionately more workers live well above the line of biological subsistence, no matter how that line is measured. Nonetheless, the working class subsumes a variety of occupational positions, including those lesser paid positions occupied by a recurrently employed *lumpen proletariat*, who are in many ways similar to the poor of early industrial society. Today a smaller proportion of the manual working population is found in this category. In part because of their decline in relative numbers, we have limited our analysis to say little about the very poor. We will emphasize the class views of the remainder.

There are a number of ways of dealing with working-class consciousness. We prefer to define it with respect to the varying degrees to which workers acquire a perspective that emphasizes class terms and calls for the maximization of working-class interests through class struggle—whether at work or in the neighborhood.

This definition is consistent with Marx's, for implicit in Marx's formulations on class is a distinction between "cognitive" emphasis and "evaluative" demand. The cognitive aspect refers to whether workers utilize class terms, identify with their class, and display an awareness of the allocation of wealth within the community or society. The evaluative aspect refers to the extent to which workers think in terms of class struggle in order to achieve *class goals.*

Marx argued that under certain conditions, economic circumstances generate an awareness of membership in a class and the ability to think and verbalize in class terms. For example, he noted how British workmen tended to develop an awareness of the class to which they belonged as a result of what he called "the underground civil war" between the middle and working classes.

But class identification was not the only aspect of working-class consciousness. Perhaps equally important was the ability of the workmen to use class terms spontaneously—to reflect in his language the most important considerations in his life, namely, how he relates to property, work, and wage structures. In *The German Ideology,* Marx argued that if a community contains classes, its inhabitants would learn to use class symbols when circumstances were propitious. As Marx would put it, class symbols reflect real relationships, both present and past. Hence people do not concoct class categories from their imagination; rather, they derive them from their involvements.

Marx touched on yet another facet of working-class consciousness by proposing that in the long run the class struggle would generate not only a common sense of class identity but a high degree of class solidarity and common devotion to class goals. Aware of their class position, workers would agree to act together. When transformed into action, this determination would constitute a reflection of the highest form of consciousness, in which *"the mass unites* and forms itself into a class for itself. The interests which it defends become class interests."

The defense of class interests includes efforts to redistribute the wealth of society. Here Marx favored struggles to minimize inequities within the context of industrial capital. If workmen shared Marx's ideas, they would express a class point of view.

In a study to measure the class consciousness of Detroit workmen, presented in *Class, Race, and Labor,* we employed several criteria derived from Marx's formulation. *Class verbalization* denoted the tendency of working-class individuals to discuss topics in terms of class. *Skepticism* referred to a belief that wealth had been allocated within the community to benefit primarily the middle class. *Militancy* referred to the predisposition to engage in aggressive action to advance the interests of one's class. *Egalitarianism* meant favoring a redistribution of wealth so that each individual within the community

would have the same amount. These four criteria formed the basis of our scale, measuring from low to high degrees of class consciousness.

To measure *class verbalization* we used a battery of eight unstructured questions, each deliberately making no reference to class, so that the answers of each respondent would not be prejudiced. We asked for whom each had voted in the most recent election and why, who was his favorite president and why, and so forth. If a worker used class terms in any of these instances, his comments constituted class verbalization.

Skepticism was weighed through the use of the following question: When business booms in Detroit, who gets the profits? If the respondent answered in terms of categories such as "rich people," "upper class," "big business," or similar references, he was considered class conscious in this regard.

We measured *militancy* by asking the interviewee to project himself into a situation in which workers were about to take action against a landlord and to indicate whether he would join in a series of activities, including picketing. If he answered that he would take part in the demonstration, the study classified him as militant.

Egalitarianism was determined to exist when the worker agreed with the notion that the national wealth should be divided up equally to provide true equality of opportunity.

Linking these various aspects of class consciousness to one another (Table 6), it was possible to type workmen according to the degree to which each had developed a class frame of reference. For example, in the study just mentioned, we found that 75 percent of the workers fell into one of the following five categories: militant egalitarians, militant radicals, skeptics, class verbalizers, and class indifferents. Interestingly, one-fourth of those interviewed maintained a point of view inconsistent with this configuration. Although they were clearly "error types," we were able to categorize them on the basis of a point system suggested by Guttman. Accordingly, from a total of 375 workers, 38 qualified as militant egalitarians, 87 as militant radicals, 114 as skeptics, 98 as class verbalizers, and 38 as class indifferents.

Class consciousness, then, can mean a comprehensive class frame of reference. In the case

TABLE 6 General Classfication of Workmen on Four Aspects of Class Consciousness*

Workers Typed According to Class Perspective	Aspects of Class Consciousness			
	Egalitarianism	Militancy	Skepticism	Class Verbalization
Militant egalitarians	+	+	+	+
Militant radicals	–	+	+	+
Skeptics	–	–	+	+
Class verbalizers	–	–	–	+
Class indifferents	–	–	–	–

*The signs + and – denote class conscious and nonclass conscious, respectively.

of the most militant workers, consciousness refers to:

1. A propensity to use class terms spontaneously
2. A belief in the direct relation between heightened pace of economic activity and flow of wealth to the middle class
3. The commitment to engage in direct action against certain middle-class groups in order to advance working-class interests
4. A predisposition to favor economic equality, if only temporarily, as a collective starting point for a group seeking pecuniary gain and occupational improvement

On the other hand, class consciousness for most workmen generally means considerably less. In the case of the class indifferents, for example, we can observe "false consciousness," the inability—perhaps temporary—to view oneself as a member of a class to which one belongs.

TRANSITIONAL REMARKS

Of the analyses that focus on the conditions under which workers struggle, few surpass Maurice Zeitlin's "Economic Attitudes and the Political Attitudes of Cuban Workers." The outstanding characteristic of this article is Zeitlin's integration of Marx's theory and survey data.

| **Section Two** | *A Reading on Cuban Workers* |

Economic Insecurity and the Political Attitudes of Cuban Workers

Maurice Zeitlin

Analysis of data from interviews with Cuban workers reveals that, among Negroes and whites, those who experienced the most pre-revolutionary unemployment were most likely to support the revolution and, among whites but not among Negroes, to be pro-Communist before the revolution. Those who were securely employed both before and since the revolution were less likely to be revolutionary than those who were employed more regularly since the revolution. Negroes were more likely than whites to support the revolution, even with pre-revolutionary employment status and change in employment status controlled.

Numerous students of working-class politics have noted and studied the relationship between economic insecurity and political radicalism. For example, Karl Marx argued that a major consequence of recurrent unemployment would be the workers' formation of organizations "in order to destroy or to weaken the ruinous effects of this natural law of capitalist production in their class."[1] Karl Kautsky believed that economic insecurity would become so "intolerable for the masses of the population" that they would be "forced to seek a way out of the general misery, . . . [finding] it only in socialism."[2] More recently, some social scientists have interpreted left voting as a conse-

■ From Maurice Zeitlin, *The American Sociological Review*, 31, 1 (February, 1966): 35–51.

Parts of this article appeared in "Political Attitudes of Cuban Workers," a paper delivered at the Annual Meetings of the American Sociological Association, 1963, and in the writer's unpublished doctoral dissertation, *Working Class Politics in Cuba: A Study in Political Sociology*, University of California, Berkeley, 1964. I am indebted to Robert Alford, Seymour Martin Lipset, Gerald Marwell, and Martin Trow for their helpful comments on various drafts of this article; to Frederick Stephan for designing the sample for this study; to the center of International Studies, Princeton University, for a grant which made this study possible; and to its director, Klaus Knorr, for his encouragement.

quence, *inter alia*, of the fact that certain central "needs" are not being met, the "need for security of income" being foremost among them.[3] A good deal of comparative research has found that the workers experiencing the most recurrent unemployment and underemployment are the ones most likely to be discontented with the existing order, to conceive of themselves as its "exploited victims," to be "class conscious," and to support the political left in their country.[4] Particularly apt to our own study is the conclusion by Zawadski and Lazarsfeld in their study of unemployed Polish workers during the depression of the thirties, that "the experiences of unemployment are a preliminary step for the revolutionary mood, but . . . they do not lead by themselves to a readiness for mass action. Metaphorically speaking, these experiences only fertilize the ground for revolution, but do not generate it."[5]

Less than a decade before the Revolutionary Government, headed by Fidel Castro, came to power in Cuba, the International Bank for Reconstruction and Development noted that "the insecurities which result from chronic unemployment and from the instability and seasonal fluctuations of the Cuban economy, continue to keep the worker in a state of anxiety."[6] That the recurrent unemployment and underemployment and the consequent "state of anxiety" of the Cuban workers in pre-revolutionary Cuba later became a significant determinant of their support for the revolution and its leadership is the thesis of this article.

Cuba, prior to the 1959 revolution, was both misdeveloped and underdeveloped. Her economy was subject to the vagaries of export demand for sugar, and this created a "boom and bust" psychology affecting all strata of the population, not merely the working class, and inhibiting general economic growth. Chronic economic stagnation, a fluctuating, perhaps decreasing, *per capita* income,[7] and widespread unemployment and underemployment, both seasonal and structural, characterized the pre-revolutionary economy.

As early as the first decade of this century, Charles Magoon, Provisional Governor of Cuba during the United States occupation, reported that "practically all the sugar cane cutters are unemployed during six months of the year and by August find themselves without money and without means of maintaining themselves and their families."[8] A half century later this situation persisted without substantial change, and an authority of the United States Bureau of Commerce quipped that a Cuban worker might find it "easier to find a new wife than to find a new job."[9]

How correct this remark was, and how strategic an experience in the life of Cuban workers their ability to get work and keep it must have been, can be indicated by the circumstance that in the two years preceding the establishment of the Revolutionary Government, *known* average unemployment and underemployment in the labor force averaged about 20 per cent.[10] This figure for the labor force as a whole *underestimates* the extent of unemployment and underemployment *in the working class alone*. Although there are no industry-by-industry data, we do know that in the major industry of the island, sugar, the vast majority of the workers, including perhaps two-thirds of the mill workers, were unemployed most of the year. In the sugar industry, "most of the workers were employed only during the zafra," which averaged about 100 days a year.[11] The labor force estimates probably are themselves underestimates, then, since *just counting the workers in the sugar industry* (who comprised 23 per cent of the labor force, and about three-quarters of whom worked no more than five months a year) approximately 18 per cent of the labor force was unemployed seven months of the year.[12] Since the volume and value of the sugar crop profoundly affected unemployment not only in sugar but throughout the island's industries, 20 per cent is an absolute minimum estimate of pre-revolutionary average unemployment.

It scarcely seems problematic, therefore, that the severe and recurrent fluctuations of the entire economy, and the consequent widespread unemployment and underemployment in the population, were of major significance in the formation of the workers' political consciousness—especially given the significant influence that revolutionary socialists (first anarcho-syndicalists and then Communists) had always exerted in the Cuban working class.[13]

That Fidel Castro believed unemployment politically significant is clear. For example, in his speech at his trial for leading the abortive attack on Fort Moncada on July 26, 1953, he said that the revolutionaries had based "their chances for success on the social order, because we were assured of the people's support. . . ." Among "the people we count on in our struggle," he said, "are the seven hundred thousand unemployed Cubans, who want to earn their daily bread honorably without having to leave their country in search of sustenance; and the five hundred thousand rural workers who live in miserable *bohios* [huts], work four months of the year and spend the rest of it in hunger, sharing their misery with their children. . . ."[14]

Repeatedly in his speeches since coming to power, Castro has referred to the problem of unemployment, linking it with the meaning and the destiny of the revolution:

> A people which produces below its capacities, and, further, where an appreciable portion of what it produces is carried off by others, is not a people enjoying the economic and social conditions propitious to progress and to resolving its problems. That is why our country suffered that problem of permanent unemployment; . . . that is why there was chronic unemployment in our country extending to several hundred thousand idle citizens; that is why the fields were worked only three or four months a year. That is the reason for the ills of the Republic, which could never have been overcome if the Republic had not adopted forms of social organization and production putting human effort in harmony with the interest of the people in progress and greater production. . . . The issue became one of the revolution having to resolve the unemployment problem and, even more difficult, to resolve it under conditions of economic aggression, embargo on spare parts, raw materials and machinery, and complete suppression of the sugar quota.[15]

That such speeches as these would appeal to the workers, and especially to the ones who had borne the brunt of unemployment and under-employment before the revolution, seems clear. In fact, whatever their own political persuasion, most serious observers of the revolution have argued that this vast reservoir of unemployed and underemployed workers inherited by the Revolutionary Government has been a major source of its popular support, although they were not the initiators of the struggle against the old regime.[16] Once the Revolutionary Government came to power, however, its social base was formed, in the words of Boris Goldenberg, by the "enormous and heterogeneous mass of the economically 'rootless', . . . the unemployed [and] underemployed . . ." throughout the population.[17]

The major hypothesis of the present article, then, is that the revolution's program and policies differentially appealed to the workers in accordance with their relative economic security before the revolution—the greater their pre-revolutionary experience of unemployment, the greater the likelihood of their support for the revolution. The correctness of this hypothesis will be examined following a description of the methods employed to obtain the data for this study.

METHODS

The data for this study are drawn from the writer's interviews with industrial workers in Cuba in the summer of 1962. What was significant about that period as far as this particular study is concerned was that the Revolutionary Government had by then clearly consolidated its power (the Bay of Pigs invasion being a year in the past); the original relatively undifferentiated popular euphoria had by then been long replaced by relatively clear lines of social cleavage generated in response to actions taken by the Revolutionary Government; it was then more than a year since Fidel Castro had declared the revolution to be 'socialist'; and, therefore, a study of the differential appeals of the ideology and social content of the revolution to Cuban workers could be meaningful and valuable.[18]

Our interviews were carried out with a randomly selected sample of 210 industrial workers employed in twenty-one work centers widely scattered throughout the island's six prov-

inces. The writer chose the work centers from a list of all mines, mill, factories and plants functioning in Cuba under the direction of the Ministry of Industries. There were approximately 200,000 industrial workers employed in the industrial work-places under the direction of the Ministry of Industries. Excluded from representation in the sample were the approximately 120,000 industrial workers employed in some 250 industrial work-places under the direction of the Department of Industrialization of the National Institute of Agrarian Reform [INRA]. Thus, sixty-two per cent of Cuba's industrial workers constituted the population from which the sample of workers interviewed for this study was drawn.

The work-places were selected by means of a self-weighting random sample in which the probability of a work-place being chosen was directly proportional to the number of workers employed in it. This sampling method tended to exclude the smaller industrial work-places (known in Cuba as "chinchales") which abounded there.[19]

In each work-place, the ten workers were selected by one of three methods: (*a*) by visiting each department personally and selecting from a list of the jobs in that department (used in fifteen work-places); (*b*) by selecting from a list of all workers employed in the work-place on the shift or shifts during which the interviewing was done (in five work-places); (*c*) by selecting among the homes in the industrial community in which the workers employed in the work-place live (in one work-place).[20]

The advantage of employing method (*a*) for selecting the workers to be interviewed is that the writer was able to see the workers' reactions within the work-places visited—the reactions of the workers chosen to be interviewed as well as of the other workers present at that moment in the various departments. Observation of the general reactions of the workers—of reserve or suspicion, curiosity or friendliness—was an important aspect of this study. Moreover, so as to be certain that the worker selected was, indeed, the worker interviewed, this method of selection was preferable. Perhaps if Cuba had not been the center of controversy and the focus of American hostility during the period in which the study was done, this method would not have been necessary. This precautionary measure was also beneficial to the writer's research since it did provide the opportunity for direct observation of the interaction among the industrial workers themselves and between them and administrative personnel.

The interviews were carried out in Spanish by the writer and his wife, each separately interviewing five workers per work-place. All interviewing was carried out in complete privacy, in a location provided within the workplace, such as a class-room or storage room or office. Each worker interviewed, as well as anyone else concerned, was specifically told before the interviewing, in a variant of the following words, that the writer was

> a correspondent for a liberal objective American news-weekly called *The Nation*, that is published in New York city. We have permission from the Ministry of Industries, your administrator, and the union delegate to interview ten workers here. We have chosen you to be interviewed by selecting at random from a list of the jobs in this department (or all workers in this work-place). That means we do not care to know your name or to be able to identify you personally in any way. These questions are simple and do not require special knowledge. We just want your opinions about some things in your work and in Cuba in general. All your answers are between ourselves and are completely anonymous. We would very much appreciate your permission to interview you.

Every precaution was taken in the interviewing to discover and to prevent dissimulation. Dissimulation, as well as unconscious distortion, must be taken into account in the evaluation of all interview data, in whatever type of study. Internal checks for consistency as well as external checks on reliability must be built into any interview schedule, wherever possible; this was done in our study. The interviews were carried out according to a formal set of questions on a mimeographed interview schedule prepared by the writer. It was quite clear to the worker that he was being formally interviewed in accordance with pre-determined questions, and that notes on his answers were being taken throughout the interview.

Stylized probes were also employed in these interviews to make it especially difficult for the workers interviewed to give answers they did not actually feel to be true. For example, if a worker were asked: "Do you think that your children have the same opportunities, better opportunities, or worse opportunities than others to live comfortably and happily?" and he answered: "All children are equal now," he would then be asked some variant of "How is it possible for all children to be equal? Please explain what you mean." Such probes were freely used throughout the interview.

Because there were obviously some workers who were suspicious or even frightened of the purposes of the interview, every effort was made to establish rapport quickly and to put the respondent at his ease by stressing that the interview was voluntary and completely anonymous, and that the interviews were very important because they would provide the basis for information about working conditions in Cuba to Americans and other non-Cubans throughout the world. Occasionally a respondent would ask that his words not be recorded until the interview had terminated; we complied readily. The interviews ranged in length from forty-five minutes to three-and-a-half hours, averaging about one hour and a quarter, in privacy; a great effort of will would be required in that situation consistently to give answers thought to be suitable to the government and the interviewer. It would require a certain level of dramatic skill to feign enthusiasm or to manifest feelings where these did not exist. Moreover, the refusal rates was very low (eight of 210 respondents, or less than four per cent); in only a few instances did opponents of the regime evidence either hesitancy or fear in speaking their minds freely. Cubans are highly voluble, volatile and loquacious, irrespective of their political views.

The interview schedule was organized in such a way as to begin the interview with questions which were, on the surface, far removed from political questions of any kind—such as length of residence in a particular place, or length of time working in the work-place. The interviews were carried out in accordance with established canons of sociological interviewing, with especial emphasis on anonymity, on the establishment of rapport, and on special probing to ascertain the truthfulness of a response.[21]

In order to get at the workers' attitudes towards the revolution, several questions were asked of them during the interview which are believed to be more or less indicative, taken in concert, of how they viewed the revolution. Of the five chosen for combination into an index of these attitudes, two were 'open-ended' questions to which the variety of responses possible was limited only by the worker's own imagination. The first of these was:

(a) "Speaking in general, what are the things in Cuba that you are most proud of as a Cuban?" One hundred and fifteen workers replied to this question in terms clearly favorable to the revolution. Only such responses as could be regarded as clearly indicating or explicitly stating support of the revolution, such as mention of the revolution itself, of the "socialist government," of specific economic and social reforms of the Revolutionary Government, or of increased work security since the revolution, were counted as 'favorable.' All others, whether more or less 'neutral' responses or 'clearly hostile' ones, were classified as 'not clearly favorable.'

The workers could be especially blunt in their opposition, as was a young worker at a paper milling plant in Cardenas, whose answer was simply, "Of nothing, *chico* ... I don't like Communism," or as a West Indian worker (with two teenage daughters in the militia) at the nationalized Portland Cement plant in Mariel explained (in English): "I stay only because I have two daughters who will not leave—otherwise I'd go away... No one bothers me, I just do not like it. Why? I can't say why. I guess I just prefer the old Cuba...."

In contrast to such clearly hostile remarks were such noncommittal replies as a shoemaker's "Of our movies and our athletes," or a brewery worker's equivocal, "I am a peaceful worker. I have no passionate interest in anything. After my work, I pass my time in my house in Manacas with my little one and my wife," or a cigar-maker's witty but equally noncommittal, "Our women and our cigars."

Occasionally a revolutionary worker would wax poetic, as did a copper miner in Matahambre: "Cuba is a cup of gold to me. It is the only country in the world that is now moving forward...." A sugar worker's simple statement was more typical, however: "I earn good money now. I lack nothing.... All of the workers are with the revolution." A Havana brewery worker said: "I am content with the revolution in general.... For the first time one can do what one wants without fear."

The second of these open-ended questions was (b) "What sort [*clase*] of people govern this country now?"

One hundred and twenty-five workers replied to this question in terms clearly favorable to the revolution.

Given the double meaning in Spanish of the word *clase*, which can mean 'type,' 'sort' or 'kind,' as well as 'class,' the workers could, of course, choose to interpret the question's meaning in a number of ways. As with the preceding question, only replies which could be regarded as clearly favorable to the revolution were counted as such: "the people," "the humble," "hardworking," "good," "sincere," "moral," "honest," "defenders of the poor and humble," "the working class." Responses such as "socialists" or "revolutionaries" which did not clearly commit the worker were not regarded as favorable; neither were such equivocal replies as "Cubans," "Fidel," "Communists," nor replies which were likely meant to be hostile such as "Russians," or "Soviets," or which were undoubtedly meant to be hostile such as "shameless," or "traitors."

"To me," an opponent of the revolution working at the nationalized Texaco oil refinery in Santiago said, "they are completely Communists. All of their accomplishments have been through the work of others—including how they think. I have a sister-in-law and a brother-in-law in prison for speaking against the government—[sentenced to] seven years...." Another worker opposed to the revolution said: "Socialists they say. The kids say Communists. I don't know. Listen, if somebody comes and takes that pen of yours, and you bought it, what are you going to think?"

"Well, I've never been 'political,'" a cigarette-machine operator said. "For me, they are all right." A brewery worker's reply was equally equivocal: "My experience so far is good. I don't worry about such things—neither before the revolution nor now." A skilled electrician in Santiago committed himself only so far as to say that the men in the government are "persons with socialist ideas, who though they have good intentions have committed many serious administrative errors."

"The truth is," a carpenter in a sugar central said, "that *now* those who govern here are Cubans. They are honest and hardworking men." A 67-year-old maintenance man at the Nicaro nickel plant who had been an agricultural worker until recently said: "Look, before I couldn't look a boss in the eye—I looked at my feet. Not now; now we have liberty and walk where we wish, and nothing is prohibited to us. It is a great joy to be alive now. These men [who govern us] are 100 per cent better than before. I have known governments from [Mario Garcia] Menocal [Cuban President, 1913–1921] until Batista left three years ago, and I have never seen any like this government." Equally articulate in his support of the revolution was a twenty-year-old bootmaker in a newly established factory in Guanajay: "*We are the government, we run things. Go to a factory or consolidado anywhere, chico, and see: those who work govern, those who govern work, not like the capitalists who lived without working before the revolution triumphed. Now, the power of the workers and peasants has emerged.*"

The workers were also asked the following two questions with fixed alternatives:

(c) "Do you believe that the country ought to have elections soon?"

Answer	(N)
No	136
Yes	52
No opinion	22

(d) "Do you think the workers have more, the same, or less influence on [en] the government now than before the revolution?"

Answer	(N)
More influence	170
The same	17
Less	16 (includes 8 refusals)
No opinion	7

In addition, this question was included in the index as an 'action criterion':

(e) "Do you belong to the militia?"

Answer	(N)
Yes	110
No	100 (includes 8 refusals)

As is clear, the likelihood that a question would elicit a response clearly favorable to the revolution was directly related to the ease with

which such a response could be given.[22] Favorable responses were distributed as follows:

Question	(N)
e.	110
a.	115
b.	125
c.	136
d.	170

The index of attitude toward the revolution was constructed from answers to all five questions by coding all favorable responses (militia membership included) as +1, and all others as 0 (zero):

	Index	
Points	Definition	(N)
3-5	Favorable (4-5, very favorable, N=100; 3, moderately favorable, N=42)	142
2	Indecisive	24
0-1	Hostile	36
	Total:	202

FINDINGS

Using this index to gauge the differential appeals of the revolution to the workers we interviewed, our expectation that the relative security of their employment *before* the revolution would have a significant bearing on their attitudes toward the revolution *now*, is borne out by our findings, as presented in Table 7.

TABLE 7 Pre-Revolutionary Employment Status and Attitude Toward the Revolution (percent)

Months Worked per Year Before Revolution	Favorable	Indecisive	Hostile	(N)
6 or less	86	9	5	(63)
7–9	74	10	16	(19)
10 plus	62	13	25	(105)

Notes:

1. This and the following tables do not include workers who had not yet entered the labor force before the revolution.

2. Among the workers who were employed 6 months or less and also among those employed 7–9 months before the revolution, 63 percent were "very favorable" to the revolution; among those who worked 10 months or more, only 40 percent were "very favorable."

TABLE 8   Pre-Revolutionary Employment Status and Pre-Revolutionary Attitude Toward the Communists (percent)

Months Worked per Year Before Revolution	Friendly or Supporter	Indifferent[1]	Hostile	(N)
6 or less	35	36	29	(63)
7–9	32	52	16	(19)
10 plus	26	45	29	(105)

[1] Includes three "don't knows."

There is a clear relationship between the average number of months the workers worked during the year before the revolution and the probability of their support for the revolution. The workers with the least pre-revolutionary economic security are the ones who are most likely to support the revolution.

If their relative economic security before the revolution has been of significant consequence for the workers' responses to the revolution, then it should be expected that their pre-revolutionary situation significantly affected their pre-revolutionary political orientations as well. We know, for example, that a major social base of the Communists in the labor movement was among the workers in the sugar industry, i.e., in the industry which was itself most economically unstable and whose workers suffered perhaps the greatest burden of the seasonal unemployment cycle. We should, therefore, expect on both historical and comparative sociological grounds, that the workers who experienced the most unemployment and underemployment before the revolution were the ones who were most likely to support the Communists. (Table 8).

A simple structured question was asked of all the workers in our sample in order to gauge their pre-revolutionary orientation toward the Communists:

"How would you describe your attitude toward the Communists before the revolution: hostile, indifferent, friendly, or supporter?"[23]

Answer	(N)
Hostile	57
Indifferent	83
Friendly	49
Supporter [*partidario*]	10
Don't know	3
Refusal	8

When we compare the workers' pre-revolutionary views of the Communists with their pre-revolutionary security of employment, the evidence indicates that the workers who experienced the most unemployment before the revolution were the ones most likely to be sympathetic to the Communists.[24]

This relationship is strengthened when we view it among only those workers in our sample who were also workers before the revolution. There has been a sizable influx of formerly salaried or self-employed persons, as well as agricultural laborers and peasants, in to the working class since the revolution—and this is reflected in our sample; these non-workers were less likely to support the Communists before the revolution than the workers. When we exclude those who were not workers before the revolution, we find that the gap between the

TABLE 9   Pre-Revolutionary Employment Status and Pre-Revolutionary Attitude Toward the Communists, Among Workers Before the Revolution Only (percent)

Months Worked per Year Before Revolution	Friendly or Supporter	Indifferent	Hostile	(N)
9 or less	40	32	29	(63)
10 plus	27	46	27	(89)

TABLE 10 Pre-Revolutionary Employment Status and Attitude Toward the Revolution, Among Workers Before the Revolution Only (percent)

Months Worker per Year Before Revolution	Favorable	Indecisive	Hostile	(N)
9 or less	87	6	6	(63)
10 plus	62	13	25	(89)

proportions pro-Communist among the pre-revolutionary unemployed and among the employed workers becomes larger (Table 9). There is also a slight strengthening of the relationship between pre-revolutionary employment insecurity and support for the revolution when viewed among only those who were workers before the revolution (Table 10).

To this point we have only referred to the workers' pre-revolutionary economic security, yet there has been a significant change in the economic security of many workers since the establishment of the Revolutionary Government. Among our respondents, for example, more than three quarters (79 per cent) of those who had worked six months or less before the revolution, reported that they were working ten months or more on the average since the revolution, and 19 per cent said they now worked between seven and nine months a year. Thus, 98 per cent of the previously most underemployed workers said they were working more regularly than they had been before the Revolutionary Government came to power. It would seem quite likely that these changes have had consequences for their response to the revolution. In order to test the proposition that the workers whose economic security has been most enhanced since the revolution would be the most likely to support it, we would have to look simultaneously at their pre-revolutionary and present employment status.

The optimum test of the hypothesis concerning the relationship between change in employment status since the revolution and attitude toward it would require relating *decreased* economic security, as well as maintenance of *the same level* of security, to the workers' attitudes. However, as is obvious from inspection of Table 11, not all the necessary types of change in employment status are represented

among the workers in our sample. We can, nevertheless, make some useful inferences concerning the consequences of relative change in economic security on the workers' attitudes by comparing the available groups of workers.

As can be seen from Table 11, our expectation is confirmed that those workers whose economic security is greater than it was in pre-revolutionary years are more likely than other workers to support the revolution—in this case, than those workers who were employed regularly before and have continued to be since the revolution.

RACIAL GROUP MEMBERSHIP

If it is correct, as our evidence seems to indicate, that economic insecurity conduces to revolutionary politics, then it should follow from this that a racial or ethnic group whose position is comparatively less secure economically than that of the racial or ethnic majority should also be more responsive to the revolu-

TABLE 11 The Relationship Between Employment Status Before the Revolution, Employment Status Since the Revolution, and Attitude Toward the Revolution

Months Worked per Year Before Revolution	Percent Favorable		
	Months Worked per Year Since the Revolution		
	10+	7–9	6 or less
10+	62 (101)	(4)	(0)
7–9	78 (18)*	(1)	(0)
6 or less	86 (50)*	82 (11)*	(1)

*Of these 79 workers whose economic security is greater since the revolution, 83 percent support the revolution.

tion than the latter is. From what we know about pre-revolutionary Cuba, it is probably correct to say that Negroes and Mestizos were in general subject to greater economic insecurity than whites. (In our sample, for instance, forty-nine per cent of the Negroes and Mestizos reported that they were employed nine months or less before the revolution, compared to thirty-nine per cent of the white workers.) While Negroes were distributed throughout the occupational structure, they were disproportionately concentrated in the poorest income groups and the most menial jobs—they were, as Lowry Nelson put it, "predominantly the 'hewers of wood and drawers of water'."[25] Apparently, there was also a tendency for Negroes working at the same jobs as whites to receive less pay,[26] although this was primarily true of the workers in the weakest unions and least organized industries. Further, in the urban slums, or *solares*, Negroes predominated; the better rooms were commonly rented only to whites. Insofar as their economic position was particularly insecure, then, it might be expected that Negro workers would be more likely to be revolutionary than white workers.

In fact, some of the most prominent left-wing leaders in Cuba were Negroes; among leaders of the Communist Party, as well as of the non-Communist labor unions, Negroes were well represented. During the revolution of the thirties, *Realengo 18*, the 'soviet' of workers and peasants which withstood the military forces of Batista the longest, right into the early months of 1934, was led by a Negro Communist, Leon Alvarez. Perhaps the most revered labor leader was the martyred Jesus Menendez, the Negro head of the sugar workers' union, who was murdered in 1947 by cohorts of the notorious Eusebio Mujal. Furthermore, Oriente Province, the province with the highest concentration of Negroes in the population—perhaps twice the proportion of other provinces—was the rebel stronghold[27] during the guerrilla struggle against Batista; and Santiago, the province's capital, was the one major city in which the otherwise abortive general strike of April, 1958, was fully supported by the workers, and the entire city shut down.

However, it must also be emphasized that the social status of the Negro in pre-revolutionary Cuba differed markedly from the status of the Negro in the United States. Largely as a result of social processes characteristic of Negro slavery, and of the slaves' emancipation in Cuba—in contrast to slavery in the United States—the barriers to social intercourse between Negroes and whites, well before the revolution, were not as formidable as those in the United States. While these early developments are too complex to explore here,[28] it is important to emphasize that "Jim Crow" laws comparable to those in America have never existed in Cuba, nor were there other legal, political, and social buttresses to Negro exploitation after emancipation from slavery of the type in force in the United States. Compared to the United States, at least, the social history of Cuba involved a relatively high degree of racial integration and inter-marriage, especially in the working class. Nevertheless, racial discrimination was socially and politically enforced to a certain extent. "Before 1959, Negroes were excluded from most of the better hotels, beaches, and places of entertainment patronized by Americans and upper class Cubans."[29] While not a common practice, in some cities the public squares and parks in which Cubans congregate in the evenings had a promenade plaza reserved for whites which was a step higher than the one reserved for Negroes. As the Cuba survey of the Human Relations Areas Files states:

> Opponents of Castro maintain that he invented the racial issue. It is, however, an old problem which has always become more serious in times of political crisis. . . . Many wry Negro proverbs commenting on the relations between Negroes and whites refer unmistakably to home grown attitudes of long standing: "The black fought the war, the white enjoys the peace"; "If you see a black and a white together, either the white man needs the black, or else the black has won a lottery."[30]

That many Negroes recognized their social status as a problem is indicated by the fact that a Negro national federation was organized against racial discrimination.

One further element of importance in the formation of the Negroes' attitudes toward the revolution is the fact that they had a history of experience with broken promises before the revolution and, for that reason, were not likely to take too seriously mere assertions by the

TABLE 12   Racial Group Membership and Pre-Revolutionary Attitude Toward the Communists (percent)

	Friendly or Supporter	Indifferent	Hostile	(N)
Negroes	28	36	36	(50)
Whites	29	45	26	(152)

Revolutionary Government that it would eliminate discrimination. "Before 1959," as the HRAF survey notes,

> various political leaders gained electoral support by promising to uphold Negro rights but subsequently failed to carry out these promises. The legislative initiative gradually fell to the Communists and to the Frente Civico contra la Discrimination Racial, sponsored by the CTC [Confederation of Cuban Workers] and incorporated in Batista's patronage system. Many Negroes resented left wing efforts to capitalize on the issue, and pointed to progress made by the United States in racial matters as a commendable example. Others saw signs of a deliberate imperialist effort to weaken Cuba by depriving it of part of the resources of its population.[31]

Given this complex mix of relative Negro economic insecurity, a rebel tradition, the presence of discriminatory practices despite a relatively high level of social integration, and the probability of disillusionment with political programs, prediction of the differential response to the revolution of Negro and white workers is not without difficulty—although one would probably surmise that Negroes would be more likely than whites to support the revolution. It is particularly interesting, therefore, as Table 12 shows, that, taken as a whole, the Negro workers in our sample were no more likely than white workers to sympathize with *the Communists in pre-revolutionary Cuba*, and

more likely to be hostile to them. We shall take a closer look at this relationship after discussing the differential response of Negro and white workers to the revolution.

Since the revolution, the Revolutionary Government has not only conducted a propaganda campaign in behalf of racial equality, but has also opened all hotels, beaches, and resorts (previously almost entirely privately owned and closed to the public) to all Cubans, regardless of color. "In the larger cities conspicuous desegregation was accomplished although the familiar patterns were to be observed in provincial towns in 1961."[32] Fidel Castro has sprinkled his speeches with allusions to the past exploitation and revolutionary traditions of the Negro, a typical example of which comes from a speech the writer attended at the 26th of July anniversary celebration in 1962 in Santiago:

> In the past when voices were raised in favor of liberation for the slaves, the bourgeoisie would say "impossible, it will ruin the country" and to instill fear, they spoke of the "black terror." Today they speak of the "red terror." In other words, in their fight against liberty they spread fear of the Negro; today they spread fear of socialism and communism.

It seems likely that the social barriers between members of the races were least among workers; consequently, the impact on them of non-discriminatory policies alone should be least, although not necessarily insignificant.

TABLE 13   Racial Group Membership and Attitude Toward the Revolution (percent)

	Favorable*	Indecisive	Hostile	(N)
Negroes	80	8	12	(50)
Whites	67	13	20	(152)

*Among Negro workers the proportion "very favorable" to the revolution is 58 percent; among white workers the proportion "very favorable" is 47 percent.

Most beaches, resorts and hotels were closed to the *poor* of Cuba—white and black alike—and not just to the Negro. Thus, the Negro worker may have felt the impact of *class* more than of *racial* membership. It is unclear whether or not economic policies of the regime have benefitted Negro workers more than white workers. While it is probable that Negroes have felt that their status has improved, the complexity of events since the revolution makes the Negro workers' responses difficult to predict. Our data indicate that the Negro workers in our sample are more likely than their white fellows to support the revolution. (Table 13).

In the preceding discussion both economic and status variables were relevant in predicting the differential appeals of the revolution to Negro and white workers. Perhaps our finding that Negro workers are more likely than white workers to support the revolution indicates only the relatively less secure position of Negro workers as a group before the revolution, i.e., that control for pre-revolutionary employment status would eliminate the Negro-white difference. However, this reasoning is not supported by our evidence. As Table 14 indicates, both among the workers who were recurrently unemployed before the revolution and among those who were regularly employed, Negroes are more likely to support the revolution than whites. The table also shows that the original relationship between pre-revolutionary employment status and attitude toward the revolution holds among both Negro and white workers. The inference is clear that, given the persistence of the differences between Negro and white workers—even with pre-revolutionary economic

TABLE 15 The Relationship Between Racial Group Membership, Change in Employment Status, and Attitude Toward the Revolution

| | Percent Favorable | |
| | Change in Employment Status | |
	Same High Level	Higher
Negroes	71 (21)	90 (21)
Whites	60 (80)	81 (58)

security controlled—the fact of membership in the Negro racial group is in itself significant. Indeed, if we look at the effect on Negro and white workers of change in employment status since the revolution, the results are essentially the same as for pre-revolutionary employment status alone (Table 15). Both among the workers whose employment status is higher and those whose employment status is at the same level since the revolution, Negroes are more likely than whites to favor the revolution. Although employment security is not the only aspect of economic security, it is certainly among the most significant; we might infer that the social status of the Negro racial group accounts for the Negro-white differences.

Although the Negro unemployed are more likely to support the revolution than regularly employed Negro workers, the parallel result does not hold for *pre-revolutionary attitudes toward the Communists* (Table 16). This finding is especially interesting in the light of some recent research to be discussed below. Among

TABLE 14 The Relationship Between Racial Group Membership, Pre-Revolutionary Employment Status, and Attitude Toward the Revolution

| | Percent Favorable | |
| | Months Worked per Year Before Revolution | |
	9 or less	10 plus
Negroes	91 (22)	73 (22)
Whites	80 (60)	59 (83)

TABLE 16 The Relationship Between Racial Group Membership, Pre-Revolutionary Employment Status, and Pre-Revolutionary Attitude Toward the Communists

| | Percent Friendly or Supporter | |
| | Months Worked per Year Before Revolution | |
	9 or less	10 plus
Negroes	27 (22)	32 (22)
Whites	37 (60)	24 (83)

white workers we observe the expected relationship that the workers who experienced the
most pre-revolutionary unemployment were the
most likely to support the Communists. Among
Negro workers, on the other hand, there is no
significant difference between the unemployed
and the regularly employed in their pre-revolutionary attitudes toward the Communists.

INTERPRETATION

There are two fundamental questions about
our findings:

1. Why are the pre-revolutionary unemployed and underemployed workers more likely
than the regularly employed to favor the revolution, and to have had pro-Communist political orientations before the revolution? Indeed,
the general theoretical question of the reasons
for the increased probability of political radicalism among the more economically insecure
workers is at issue.

2. Why are the Negro pre-revolutionary unemployed more likely to support the revolution
than their regularly employed counterparts, despite the fact that they were no more likely to
be pro-Communist before the revolution?

Radical politics and "leftist voting," as Lipset has noted, are "generally interpreted as an
expression of discontent, an indication that
needs are not being met." He suggests, as noted
above, that one such central "need" is "the
need for security of income. This is quite closely related to the desire for higher income as
such; however, the effect of periodic unemployment or a collapse of produce prices, for example, seems to be important in itself."[33] Positing
such a "need" is not, however, a particularly
fruitful formulation, especially as it stands. We
know, for instance, that stable poverty, such as
that of subsistence peasantry, tends to be a
source of political conservatism rather than radicalism, yet their "need" for security of income
is obviously not being met. One crucial factor,
as Lipset himself indicates elsewhere, is whether
or not individuals are exposed by their situation
to possibilities for a life better than their present one.[34] In fact, of course, disemployed
workers have had a better life and lost it.

The question remains, nonetheless, whether
such an interpretation is sufficient to explain

what makes unemployed workers likely to perceive a connection between their private troubles and the economic structure—and in class-
conscious or politically radical terms—rather
than simply to blame themselves and look in-
ward for the source of their troubles. The answer, it is suggested, lies in the very fact of their
observation that their troubles are not private
but rather ones which *simultaneously affect
many of their fellow workers.* Their radical
response, that is, "is especially linked," in Max
Weber's phrase, "to the *transparency* of the
connections between the causes and the consequences" of their situation as unemployed
workers. It is not only the contrast between
their situation and that of employed workers,
which makes them amenable to the appeals of
radical politics, but also (perhaps primarily) the
fact that they can so easily recognize the source
of their problems to be in the "concrete economic order."

> For however different life chances may be,
> [as Weber put it,] this fact in itself, accord-
> ing to all experience, by no means gives birth
> to "class action" ... *The fact of being con-
> ditioned and the results of the class situation
> must be distinctly recognizable. For only
> then the contrast of life chances can be felt
> not as an absolutely given fact to be
> accepted,* but as a resultant from either (1)
> the given distribution of property, or (2) the
> structure of the concrete economic order.[35]

This reasoning, which Weber applied to "the
class situation of the modern proletariat," is
particularly appropriate to the situation of
those who are unemployed and underemployed. Especially in Cuba was the connection
transparent between the "concrete economic
order" and the situation of the unemployed.
For it was precisely from *recurrent disemploy-
ment* that the unemployed suffered. The relationship between the seasonal nature of their
unemployment, and the misdevelopment of the
economy was therefore "distinctly recognizable." It is understandable that they should be
more likely than employed workers to want to
alter radically an economic order which is perceived as the source of their collective troubles
and, therefore, be more amenable to the appeals of Communist political agitation.

This same line of interpretation applies to
our contrasting findings on the Negro unem-

ployed and their political attitudes. Let us compare, first, what John Leggett reported recently concerning his research into sources of class consciousness of Negro and white workers in Detroit. Having found a general relationship between unemployment and class consciousness, he noted that it might be expected that "unemployed Negro workers should be more class conscious than their employed counterparts." His evidence, however, failed "to support this hypothesis. If anything, the Negro unemployed are slightly *less* class conscious than the employed, while the whites are distributed as expected. Clearly, unemployment, considered by itself, is not a source of class consciousness among Negroes."[36] He did find, however, that among *unionized* Negro workers unemployment is related to class consciousness as expected, and that unionized unemployed Negro workers are far more likely than their non-union counterparts to be militantly class conscious. His interpretation of the effects of union membership on Negro workers was, in brief, that the impact of unions is partly to make Negroes more likely "to develop and use a class frame of reference to appraise their circumstances," and "partly because of the behavior of these unions on class and race questions such as unemployment. . . ."[37]

Now, while it is true that class consciousness and left-wing political orientation are not precisely the same, they are certainly similar phenomena, and their determinants have consistently been found to be similar. There is, in fact, a parallel worth speculating about between Leggett's findings and the present ones. Leggett found that "the combination of unemployment and union membership clearly heightens class consciousness." Although on the basis of our data, it was not possible to gauge the effect of union membership on the worker's pre-revolutionary political orientations, we did find, as noted above, that the combination of unemployment and their experience since the revolution apparently heightened the probability of revolutionary political orientations among Negro workers who were unemployed before the revolution. We might speculate, then, that living through the revolution has been an experience for Negro unemployed workers equivalent in significant respects to that of union participation for unemployed Negro workers in Detroit.

The revolution may have had an impact on the Negro unemployed in three relevant ways:

First, since the revolution they have been reached effectively by an ideology which stresses, as Leggett said regarding industrial unions, "a class frame of reference to appraise their circumstances."

Second, the Revolutionary Government's "behavior on class and race questions" has emphasized racial equality both in propaganda and in deed.

Third, to the extent to which revolutionary propaganda and deed have, in fact, altered the social status of the Negro racial group and of the unemployed, the connection between the racial situation and the pre-revolutionary class structure and economic order which the revolution destroyed becomes distinctly recognizable. This process may also be likened to the impact of unionization on unemployed Negroes who may recognize that their unemployment cannot now be 'explained' by (be attributed to) their racial membership alone, but is also a condition affecting members of the working class regardless of race.

This third point may deserve amplification, especially since it relates to our earlier interpretation of the radicalizing effect of unemployment. Class consciousness and political radicalism may not be meaningful responses for unemployed, non-unionized Negroes, because the fact of *being Negroes* is the significant aspect of their lives, to which they probably attribute their situation as unemployed workers. They do not see the interests of organized workers as relevant to their lives because in a significant respect those interests are indeed *not* relevant to them, so long as their *racial group* does not necessarily benefit from the furthering of those interests. *Class* issues become relevant to Negro workers when, as members of the organized working class, *they* benefit as their *class* benefits. A class conscious perspective or radical political orientation can then be meaningful to them.

The same reasoning may apply to the impact of the revolution on unemployed Negroes. Their response to the revolution may have its source in the transparency of the connections between the causes and the consequences of their pre-revolutionary situation and that of unemployed white workers. The connection between the pre-revolutionary racial situation, the pre-revolutionary class structure and economic order, and the new structure of social relations formed since the revolution, may now be recognizable. To Negroes who were unemployed before the revolution, however, the connection between their situation and that of white unemployed workers was not transparent. It is, we may surmise, the revolution which has made the fact of their having been conditioned by the pre-revolutionary economic order, as well as by membership in the Negro racial group, 'distinctly recognizable' to Negro workers who were unemployed before the revolution.

Particularly apt in this connection are the remarks of a Negro worker at the Nicaro nickel refinery in Oriente, when asked what he was most proud of in Cuba. Implicit in his words is the recognition of a connection between the fate of Negroes who were unemployed before the revolution and the pre-revolutionary economic order, yet with emphasis on their racial membership as the significant reason for their situation.

> I am most proud of what the revolution has done for the workers and the *campesinos*—and not only at work. For example, Negroes could not go to a beach or to a good hotel, or be *jefes* in industry, or work on the railroads or in public transportation in Santiago. This was because of their color! They could not go to school or be in political office, or have a good position in the economy either. They would wander in the streets without bread. They went out to look for work and could not get it. But now, no—all of us—we are equal: the white, the Negro, the *Mestizo* . . ."

SUMMARY AND CONCLUSION

Generally, sociological studies of political behavior and of the determinants of 'class consciousness' and political radicalism have been made within (relatively) stable social and political contexts. Consequently, it is difficult on the basis of the findings of such studies, to place much confidence in predictions of political behavior in times of social crisis and especially of revolutionary social change. Therefore, one important aspect of our own findings, from a theoretical point of view, is precisely and paradoxically the fact of how *expectable* they were

on the basis of prior research and theory. From knowledge of a significant fact of their lives before the revolution, namely, their relative economic security, it was possible to predict more or less accurately the workers' differential responses to the ideological and social content of the revolution.

The workers who had experienced the most unemployment during pre-revolutionary years were found to be the ones who were most likely to support the revolution. Pre-revolutionary unemployment was also found to be a significant determinant of pre-revolutionary pro-Communist orientation. Change in employment status since the revolution also proved to be significant; it was found that the workers whose economic security had been enhanced since the revolution were more likely to support it than were the workers who had retained their previously high level of economic security. Negro workers were more likely than whites to support the revolution; this relationship was found to hold even with pre-revolutionary employment status and change in employment status since the revolution controlled. Among Negro and white workers, the original relationships between (a) pre-revolutionary employment status and attitude toward the revolution, and (b) change in employment status and attitude toward the revolution, also were found to hold. In contrast, it was found that while unemployed white workers were more likely to support the Communists before the revolution than their regularly employed counterparts, this was not true among Negroes. In the latter racial group, unemployed workers were no more likely before the revolution than the regularly employed to favor the Communists.

Recurrent unemployment and underemployment led to revolutionary politics among the Cuban workers in part because of their exposure to the possibilities of a better life during periods of regular employment and in part because the connection between their situation and the concrete economic order was so transparent. To the Negro unemployed before the revolution, who very likely saw their racial membership as the prime cause of their situation, a class-conscious or pro-Communist political orientation likely appeared to be meaningless. The revolution apparently made distinctly recognizable the connection between their fate and that of white members of the working class, and the pre-revolutionary economic order. Thus, the combination of their racial membership and of their pre-revolutionary unemployment now reinforced each other, making them more likely than the white pre-revolutionary unemployed to support the revolution.

NOTES

1. Karl Marx, *Capital: A Critique of Political Economy*, New York: Modern Library, 1936, p. 702.
2. Karl Kautsky, "Krisentheorien," *Die Neue Zeit*, 20 (1901-02), p. 140.
3. Seymour Martin Lipset, *Political Man: The Social Bases of Politics*, Garden City, New York: Doubleday, 1959, p. 232. The original article in which this formulation appeared was by Lipset, Paul Lazarsfeld, Allen Barton, and Juan Linz, "The Psychology of Voting: Analysis of Political Behavior," in Gardner Lindzey, ed., *Handbook of Social Psychology, Vol. 2*, Cambridge: Addison-Wesley, 1954, pp. 1124-1175.
4. See Richard Centers, *The Psychology of Social Classes*, Princeton: Princeton University Press, 1949, pp. 177-179; Herbert G. Nicholas, *The British General Election of 1950*, London: Macmillan, 1951, pp. 297-298. Lipset, *op. cit.*, pp. 113-114, 232-237, contains an excellent summary of the literature and findings on the political effects of unemployment. For the earlier literature, see Phillip Eisenberg and Paul Lazarsfeld, "The Psychological Effects of Unemployment," *Psychological Bulletin*, 35 (June, 1938), pp. 358-390. O. Milton Hall, "Attitudes and Unemployment: A Comparison of the Opinions and Attitudes of Employed and Unemployed Men," *Archives of Psychology*, 165 (March, 1954), is a monograph on the effects of unemployment on the attitudes of professional engineers during the depression of the '30's. Also see John C. Leggett, "Economic Insecurity and Working Class Consciousness," *American Sociological Review*, 29 (April, 1964), pp. 226-234, and Richard F. Hamilton, "The Social Bases of French Working Class Politics," unpublished doctoral dissertation, Columbia University, 1963. General economic insecurity in any form—whether because of the fear and presence of unemployment, or being in an economically vulnerable position—apparently conduces to support of radical politics. Thus, Lipset noted in *Agrarian Socialism*, Berkeley and Los Angeles: University of California Press, 1950, pp. 10-18, that: "It was the economically and climatically *vulnerable* wheat belt that formed the backbone of all protest movements from the independent parties of the 1870's down to the contemporary C.C.F. in Canada ... It is highly significant that the first electorally successful Socialist Party in the United States or Canada should have developed in the same Great Plains wheat belt that earlier produced the Greenbackers, the Populists, the Non-Partisans, and other agrarian upheavals." Evidence has also been adduced to show that the general insecurity of small businessmen in a large-scale corporate capitalism re-

sults in their support of *rightwing* 'radicalism'; see Martin Trow, "Small Businessmen, Political Tolerance, and Support for McCarthy," *American Journal of Sociology*, 64 (November, 1958), pp. 270-281.
5. Bohan Zawadski and Paul E. Lazarsfeld, "The Psychological Consequences of Unemployment," *Journal of Social Psychology*, 6 (May, 1935), p. 249.
6. *Report on Cuba*, Baltimore, Md.: Johns Hopkins Press, 1951, p. 359.
7. Real per capita income in 1903-1906 averaged $203; in 1923-26, $212; in 1943-46, $211; and in 1956-58 about $200. Data for first three periods are from Julian Alienes y Urosa, *Caracteristicas fundamentales de la economia cubana*, Havana: Banco Nacional de Cuba, 1950, p. 52. He deflated his income series by means of the old United States wholesale price index, since there was no Cuban index. Money income figures for 1956-58 were adjusted by the writer, using the same set of prices.
8. As cited in Alberto Arredondo, *Cuba: tierra indefensa*, Havana, 1945, p. 176.
9. *Investment in Cuba: Basic Information for United States Businessmen*, Washington, D.C.: U.S. Government Printing Office, 1956, p. 21, fn.
10. The 1953 Cuban census estimated 8.4 per cent of the labor force was unemployed during the year's period of *fullest* employment, namely, at the height of the *zafra* (Oficina Nacional de los Censos Demografico y Electoral, *Censos de poblacion, viviendas y electoral*, Havana: Republica de Cuba, 1953). Systematic data on unemployment and underemployment were not collected in Cuba until 1957. In 1957, 10.8 per cent of the labor force was estimated as unemployed, on the average, during the *zafra*, with a high during the dead season of 15.1 percent. In 1958, the average unemployment in the *zafra* and dead season was an estimated 8.4 per cent and 18 per cent respectively. Annual averages were 12.6 per cent in 1957, and 11.8 per cent in 1958. Estimated *underemployment* averaged 7.6 per cent in 1957, and 7.2 per cent in 1958, making a combined total of known average underemployment and unemployment of 20.2 per cent in 1957, and 19.0 per cent in 1958. These figures are calculated from data in the following: *Anuario de estadisticas del trabajo*, 1959, Geneva: Oficina Internacional de Trabajo, 1959, Table 10, p. 186; Oficina Nacional de los Censos Demografico y Electoral, Departamento de Econometria, "Cantidades y Indices de Empleo y Desempleo," *Empleo y desempleo en la fuerza trabajadora*, Havana: Consejo de Economia, June 3, 1958, mimeographed; *Encuesta sobre empleo, desempleo, y subempleo*, Havana, 1961 (unpublished data made available to the author). A table showing unemployment and underemployment in the Cuban labor force 1957-1958, by month, appears in the author's dissertation, *Working Class Politics in Cuba*, p. 121. "Underemployment" was defined by the Department of Economic Statistics of the Cuban Government to include "persons who work less than thirty hours a week for pay, or 'on their own account' [self-employed] and those who work without pay for a relative." Departamento de Econometria, "Informe Tecnico No. 7," *Empleo y desempleo en la fuerza*

trabajadora, Julio, 1959, Havana: Consejo Nacional de Economia, October 5, 1959, p. 12 mimeographed.

11. *Investment in Cuba*, p. 24. "Only one-third of the millworkers and one-twentieth of the field workers are kept fully employed during the dead season." *Cuba: Economic and Commercial Conditions*, London: Her Majesty's Stationery Office, 1954, p. 39.

12. Cuba Economica y Financiera, *Anuario Azucarea de Cuba, 1954*; Havana, 1954; *Investment in Cuba*, p. 23. If the 1953 census categories, "Craftsmen, foremen, operatives, and kindred workers," "Laborers, except farm" and "Laborers, farm," are taken to constitute the working class, that class numbered 1,111,743 in 1952, or 56.3 per cent of the "economically active population." There were an estimated 474,053 sugar workers; thus they constituted about forty-two per cent of the manual working class, excluding private household workers, service workers, and unclassified occupations, the latter of which totalled about ten per cent of the economically active population. Since most workers in the sugar industry were employed only during the *zafra*, this means that between one-third and two-fifths of the working class in Cuba must have been unemployed and underemployed most of the year before the establishment of the Revolutionary Government.

13. "It must be remembered that nearly all the popular education of working people on how an economic system worked and what might be done to improve it came first from the anarchosyndicalists, and most recently—and most effectively—from the Communists" *Report on Cuba*, p. 366. On the political history of the Cuban working class, see the author's dissertation, *Working Class Politics in Cuba*, Chapters 1 and 2, and the references cited therein.

14. *Pensamiento politico, economico, y social de Fidel Castro*, Havana: Editorial Lex, 1959, p. 38.

15. Speech to the workers' delegates to the Council of Technical Advisers, *El Mundo*, Havana, February 12, 1961.

16. It should be noted, however, that the rebels emphasized that workers were well-represented among them. A youthful unidentified leader of the 26th of July Movement's Labor Front told an interviewer in February, 1958, that he "was eager to dispel the notion . . . that the 26th of July Movement headed by Señor Castro was predominantly a middle class affair. He said that, although Cuban labor leaders were 'on Batista's payroll,' the rank and file sympathized with Senor Castro." (*New York Times*, February 3, 1958, p. 7.) More to the point, Javier Pazos (son of Felipe Pazos, the former head of the Cuban National Bank), who was active in the anti-Batista urban underground, but who is now in exile from Cuba, wrote recently that "of the militants in the action groups, some were students, others were *workers* who were either *unemployed* or sick of a corrupt trade union in league with Batista." *Cambridge Opinion*, No. 32, p. 21, as cited in Robin Blackburn, "Sociology of the Cuban Revolution," *New Left Review*, 21 (October, 1963), p. 80. (Italics mine.)

17. Boris Goldenberg, "El desenvolvimiento de la revolucion cubana," *Cuadernos*, 46 (January-February, 1961), Paris, p. 35. Theodore Draper cites Goldenberg's views with approval in *Castro's Revolution: Myths and Realities*, New York: Frederick Praeger, 1962, p. 53.

18. See the writer's "Labor in Cuba," *The Nation*, 195 (October 20, 1962), pp. 238-241, and "Castro and Cuba's Communists," *Ibid.*, 195 (November 3, 1962), pp. 284-287.

19. In detail, the technique utilized was the following:

a) Using a list of all industrial work-places and the number of workers employed in each, as compiled by the Ministry of Industries, the number of industrial workers was added cumulatively and the sub-totals noted.

b) Twenty-one six-digit random numbers were drawn from a table of random numbers, and twenty-one factories were then selected whose cumulative sub-totals were at least as large as or larger than each of the random numbers.

In each of the work-places a predetermined fixed number of workers (because of time and resources available, ten workers per work-place) was selected at random to be interviewed. In each work-place, the probability that a worker would be selected was inversely proportional to the number of workers employed in it.

The sample consisted, then, of 210 industrial workers selected at random from a population in which each worker had a known equal probability of being selected for the sample. Eight workers refused to be interviewed, and were not replaced by others; this gave a total of 202 actual interviews as the basis of this study. As a check, the refusals were tabulated for the appropriate classification in which the refusals themselves could be construed as significant answers, viz., 'hostile' to the revolution, and in all instances the relationships persisted or were strengthened. We obtained the age, sex, race, average months worked before and since the revolution, and place of work of each 'refusal'.

The above method of sampling may be expressed in the following formula:

$$P = m(s/N) \cdot (k/s) - km/N$$

where

m equals the number of industrial work-places selected to be in the sample.

s equals the number of workers employed in a given work-place for the sample.

k equals the fixed number of workers randomly selected to be interviewed in each work-place.

N equals the total number of workers employed in all work-places from which the sample was drawn.

P equals the probability that a worker in the population would be selected to be interviewed.

The method of sampling was employed to assure the inclusion in the sample of workers actually involved in industrial production using machine power and machine methods of production, rather than handicrafts methods of manufacture. In general, the larger the factory, the more likely that it was actually an industrial center. This was done for the theoretical reason that a major focus of the larger study, of which the findings reported here are a part, was to be the revolution's impact on the workers' estrangement from their work. It was, therefore, particularly neces-sary to interview 'industrial' rather than handicraft workers. It need hardly be pointed out that this meth-od of sampling the working class does not affect the explanatory purposes of our study. "Representative-ness," as Hans Zetterberg points out, "should not be confused with randomization. Randomization can be used to obtain representativeness. However, it is also used as a method of controlling irrelevant factors when testing a working hypothesis." (*On Theory and Verification in Sociology*, New York: Tressler Press, 1954, p. 57).

20. This last method was employed only in the mining town of Matahambre in Pinar del Rio. The selection was not demonstrably random. It was impos-sible to pull men out of the mines during their work. The attempt was made to select names from the list of workers not working during that shift, go to their homes, and interview them there. However, this proved to be impossible because there are no addresses and fewer street names in Matahambre. It was neces-sary, therefore, to go to neighborhoods in the commu-nity in which a high concentration of miners lived, choose a house, and inquire whether or not a miner lived there. If a miner did live there and was home, then, with the miner's consent, he was interviewed. Obviously this is not the most reliable method of assuring a random sample, yet there is no evident bias. The inadequacy here consists in our inability to know what degree of confidence to place in the randomness of the Matahambre sample.

21. The assistance of the Ministry of Industries was enlisted in the realization of this study. The theoreti-cal and historical purposes of this study were ex-plained to the Minister of Industries, Major Ernesto 'Che' Guevara. It was his approval which made this study possible. There were no conditions attached to the writer's work and no restrictions whatsoever placed on his travel or on the kinds of question he might ask. The writer explained the purposes of his research, submitted a copy of the mimeographed inter-view schedule, clarified the purposes (but did not change the wording of a number of questions which appeared to the Minister to be 'loaded', and received permission to enter any mine, mill, factory or plant he wished, and to have workers taken from their work for as long as was necessary for the interviews. The writer was given credentials by the Ministry to identify him to administrators and labor union officials at the work-places visited, and was, after that, left to carry out the research at his own convenience. There was no predetermined schedule of when the writer was to arrive at any work-place, nor, it was evident, had any administrators been informed to expect the writer's visit. On several occasions, administrators or personnel chiefs telephoned to the Ministry of Industries in Havana to check the writer's credentials and his insis-tence that he had permission—which was apparently unbelievable to administrators trying to raise produc-tion levels—to take ten workers from their work for as long as was necessary.

22. Item analysis of the workers' answers to the five questions indicates that the latter form an accept-able Guttman scale, eighty-eight per cent of the work-ers giving answers exactly (67 per cent) or consistently (21 per cent) in conformity with a Guttman model of ideal classification of respondents. The coefficient of reproducibility equals 0.95. See Samuel Stouffer, *et al.*, *Measurement and Prediction*, Princeton: Princeton University Press, 1950, p. 117.

23. It is relevant to note here that, according to this crude measure of their attitude toward the Com-munists before the revolution, twenty-eight per cent of the workers in our sample classified themselves as pre-revolutionary friends or supporters of the Commu-nists; and according to the International Bank for Reconstruction and Development *Report*, written after the Communists had been officially purged from the labor movement, the Communists still had "a strong underground influence in some unions, and some authorities estimate that perhaps 25 per cent of all Cuban workers are secretly sympathetic to them." *Report on Cuba*, p. 365.

24. It may be objected that this relationship be-tween pre-revolutionary unemployment and pro-Communism is an artifact of the circumstance that revolutionary workers are likely to 'recall' a favorable attitude toward the Communists, because of their present support for the revolution. The fact that the proportion favoring the revolution exceeds the propor-tion who favored the Communists before the revolu-tion by more than twice casts doubt on the validity of this objection. Moreover, when we view the relation-ship between pre-revolutionary employment status and pro-Communist attitudes *among revolutionary workers only*, the same relationship holds: 44 per cent of the recurrently unemployed (N=68) supported the Communists before the revolution, compared to 35 per cent of the regularly employed (N=65).

25. Lowry Nelson, *Rural Cuba*, Minneapolis, Min-nesota: University of Minnesota Press, 1950, p. 157 ff. Cf. also Direccion General de Censo, *Censo de 1943*, Havana: Republica de Cuba, 1945; and *Censos de poblacion, vivienda y electoral*, Havana: Republica de Cuba, 1953.

26. Nelson, *op. cit.*, p. 156.

27. *Investment in Cuba*, p. 179. Forty per cent of the population of Oriente was estimated to be Negro or Mestizo, compared to 20 per cent or less in the other five provinces.

28. See Frank Tannenbaum, *Slave and Citizen*, New York: Alfred Knopf, 1948; and Stanley Elkins, *Slavery*, Chicago: University of Chicago Press, 1959.

29. Wyatt MacGaffey and Clifford R. Barnett, *Cuba: Its People, Its Society, Its Culture*, New Haven: Human Relations Area Files Press, 1962, p. 32. Cf. also Nelson, *op. cit.*, pp. 158-159.

30. MacGaffey and Barnett, *op. cit.*, pp. 32-33.

31. *Ibid.*, p. 282.

32. *Ibid.*

33. *Political Man*, p. 232.

34. *Ibid.*, p. 63.

35. Hans Gerth and C. Wright Mills, eds., *From Max Weber: Essays in Sociology*, New York: Oxford

University Press, 1946, p. 184. Except for italicization of "transparency", italics are not in the original.

36. John C. Leggett, "Economic Insecurity and Working Class Consciousness," *American Sociological Review*, 29 (April, 1964), 230.

37. *Ibid.*, pp. 233-234.

Section Three   *Class Consciousness Continued*

Sources and Consequences of Working-Class Consciousness

John C. Leggett

Marx's observations were helpful in specifying more clearly the sources and consequences of working-class consciousness. Needless to say it is not necessary for us to accept his historical predictions as we attempt to cull the sociological wheat from the dialectical chaff.

There is little doubt that both economic insecurity and working-class organizational affiliation are the important sources of working-class consciousness in industrial societies, and class consciousness in turn helps to determine how people act politically.

Economic insecurity takes at least three forms: agrarian–industrial mobility (as in the case of uprooted workers), tenuous occupation position (as among the unemployed), and membership in a marginal racial or ethnic group (as in the case of black manual workers). When one or more of these characteristics is shared by unionized workmen, the net result is an accentuation of class consciousness. Furthermore, regardless of the source, class consciousness becomes significant politically when there is widespread economic insecurity, progressive party organization, a pro-labor candidate available, and a political labor union.

THREE LABOR FORCE CONSIDERATIONS

In an advanced industrial society, persons who are marginal to the labor force will generally seek ways to eliminate their insecurity by creating unions and other organizations. As workers begin to deal with their economic problems, they develop a class frame of reference.

Class consciousness is significant not only in capitalist but in socialist countries as well, for governmental controls and ownership have failed to eliminate job insecurity and consequent worker organization. However, for the purposes of this section we will confine our remarks to capitalist societies.

Industrial societies at all stages of development contain multiple forms of economic insecurity and labor organization. In early industrial societies, where the stress is on the development of primary (extractive) and secondary (manufacturing) industries, mining and factory organizations subject their new labor force to the vicissitudes that we associate with recurrent and sharp digs in the business cycle. In an advanced industrial society, with its tendency to emphasize rapid automation and reorganization of the labor force, business subjects the workers to structural and psychological insecurities. This is done by taking away occupational positions, by minimizing workers' control over pace and kind of work and, in some cases, by severely limiting the economy of an entire region. These conditions may be allayed but not eliminated by business surges associated with expensive wars overseas and miracle production displays in the home country. Still, the upper class prefers to deflate the economy through induced recessions, promises, and continuation of the cycles and, hence, recurrent unemployment.

■ This essay was prepared especially for this volume and is derived from the doctoral dissertation cited on the first page of this chapter.

Whatever the stage of industrialization, we observe that different forms of insecurity generally occur. Indeed they may overlap. Many workers experience a series of economic mishaps, several of them arriving at different points in the same time interval. When we analyze these events as they occur *seriatim*, we obtain a more accurate basis for judging why many workmen become class conscious. For we can observe the impact of the events, and at the same time gauge their interrelatedness (such as the connection between uprootedness and subsequent tenuous job security in an industrial city), as they come to bear on the creation of class consciousness.

If we consider types of marginality that are associated with a society's labor force, the three previously mentioned types appear to be crucial and interconnected: agrarian–industrial mobility, tenuous occupational position, and working-class membership in a marginal racial or ethnic group. Others are also relevant but their determination and elucidation await another analysis.

Agrarian–industrial mobility occurs when people move from a low-prestige class position in an agrarian region to another low-status position in an industrial area. Perhaps we can best understand the importance of agrarian–industrial mobility by showing its connection to agrarian–industrial and industrial (whether early or advanced) societies.

In an agrarian–industrial society, industrial organization plays a relatively unimportant part in the total economy, whereas the labor force derives its livelihood primarily from agricultural pursuits. Yet the society has been touched by industrialization, as evidenced by the beginnings of modern transportation networks, mining, and light industry. Trade has developed between it and industrial societies, as indicated by its dependence on markets in more developed countries. An example is provided by Canada prior to World War I, when the society was overwhelmingly agricultural but nonetheless committed to the development of its lumber, mining, and other primary industries, which in turn were geared to the import needs of England and the United States. Yugoslavia immediately before World War II is another example: British and French firms then played a leading role in developing the mining and railroad industries, but the country as a whole remained overwhelmingly agricultural.

Theoretically, an industrial society exists when the population depends almost entirely on industrial employment for its sustenance, and agriculture supplies only a fraction of the population with its livelihood. Most of the people are located within industrial regions, and the economic and social structures rest on a modern technological base. Obvious examples are the United States and Great Britain today.

In an industrial society, however, there may be areas where industry creates relatively little wealth and where the population maintains agrarian forms of social organization and values. Such an enclave may be called an *agrarian region*. In many ways, the social organization and value system of an agrarian region are like those of an agrarian–industrial society. Our Appalachia is a good illustration; other examples include the Scottish highlands or Quebec's eastern townships.

Agrarian regions should not be confused with rural areas in industrial regions. Industrial regions such as the Midwest may well contain rural areas like the Corn Belt, that is, clusters of agricultural and/or mining communities equipped with modern technological equipment and thoroughly incorporated into the industrial economy. As such, these rural areas differ considerably from agrarian regions, such as Appalachia, which rest on a less developed technology and an economy that is closer to subsistence level.

Movement from agrarian to industrial regions has been a common phenomenon in Europe and elsewhere for the last two centuries. Former peasants have frequently taken positions as industrial workers. Indeed, their movement and resettlement has constituted the human base for the industrialization of many societies. Without the manpower provided by former peasants, industrial societies would have been unable to work mines, construct steel mills, and operate mass industries. When peasants or other inhabitants of an agrarian area move to an industrial region and become part of the working class, the process may be described as *agrarian–industrial mobility*, and those who make this transition may be labeled "the uprooted."

The uprooted have difficulties in adapting

readily to the needs of a modern industrial labor force. Their few salable skills, their lack of formal education, their commitment to agrarian values, indeed, their initial gullibility, make them easy prey for exploitation by employers. When uprooted employees are thus exploited, and when they couple these experiences with similar circumstances that drove them out of agrarian regions, they begin to express class opinions. This tendency finds its fullest expression when workmen move to an industrial town whose working class has effectively confronted employers on matters of pay and production and has consequently created a class frame of reference for the working class as a whole. The uprooted in industrial towns such as Detroit, Toledo, Montreal, and Cleveland should thus express a high degree of class consciousness.

Industrial mobility refers to movement within or between industrial regions, when individuals move from one blue-collar position to another, or in some cases, from mechanized farming to industry. Such individuals may be called "prepared," because they have acquired skills that facilitate their adaptation to an industrial community. Consequently, the prepared should be less class conscious than the uprooted.

Tenuous occupation position refers to workers who are not employed, those who face the immediate probability of becoming unemployed, particularly because of a contraction in the labor force (not because of racial or ethnic discrimination), and those who have little control over the pace and kind of work they do. For example, during a recession, we would find that the unemployed as well as the less skilled are highly class conscious. Or, suppose that workmen face a company policy of speed-up of work (hence a violation of contract). If they protest, they might lose their jobs. Here, economic insecurity stems from the workers' lack of authority to decide how goods are to be produced. Admittedly, control over production is less significant for workmen than unemployment, especially during times of economic recession or its immediate aftermath. Hence, the reader should not be surprised by the unusual emphasis in the literature on unemployment, since many studies have been conducted shortly after the end of a recession.

Another conceptual problem might arise when the reader ponders what we exclude from the rubric "tenuous occupational position." This category fails to include the uprooted, for their problem is not only one of finding and retaining employment when unskilled, but of avoiding and resisting exploitation when employed. For these workers, avoidance of excessive exploitation, however defined, applies not only at a particular point in time but has reference to their entire biography—experienced past, questionable present, and anticipated future. Hence the uprooted worker cannot be defined simply as a person without ready employment or usable skill for a limited span in time.

Working-class membership in a marginal racial (or ethnic) group is another source of class consciousness. A racial group is marginal when the cultural values of an industrial society and/ or a dominant class move employers to engage in racial discrimination against minority *workmen* both at work and elsewhere. Such discrimination contributes to their job insecurity, social isolation, subcultural homogeneity, and intensive interaction within a proletarianized minority subcommunity. All together, these conditions foster organized protest and class (or class-racial) consciousness. Marginal workmen subject to such discrimination become an isolated substratum within the working class, a pocket of beleaguered blue-collar people who belong to the same race. They form a group quite distinct from working-class groups within the dominant racial group (yet quite similar to workers in other racial groups that are collectivities with little prestige, power, and wealth). Marginal workers (such as blacks) may be uprooted or prepared, occupants of tenuous occupational positions or employees who have accumulated high seniority rankings. In this respect, the proletarianized racial enclave is heterogeneous, but it nonetheless acquires unique characteristics, a point worthy of elaboration.

MARGINAL AND MAINSTREAM WORKING CLASS

In order to understand the differing class perspectives of urban American workmen in an advanced industrial community, we must distinguish between the *marginal* and *mainstream* working class, for the marginal working class has many of the characteristics (described by Marx, and Kerr and Siegel) conducive to the formation of class consciousness.

The *marginal* working class refers to a sub-community of workers who belong to a subordinate ethnic or racial group which is unusually proletarianized and highly segregated. Workmen of this type fill many manual roles in heavy industry and face an inordinate amount of economic insecurity. This is evidenced by their large concentration in marginal occupational positions, by their lack of formal education, and finally and most obviously, by their high unemployment rate. The latter factor stems in large part from inadequate training and selective job hiring, which can be traced to racial prejudice and discrimination rooted to some degree in low prestige. In turn, low prestige derives largely from the subordinate group's historic lack of *power*, i.e., the inability to manipulate society's political and economic institutions that allocate *wealth*, *power*, and hence *prestige*. Power is both process and product.

Like the classical Marxian working class, this particular working-class minority—this working-class racial group sharing the same subcultural traditions—is considerably isolated from the remainder of the community in general and from the middle class in particular. Its assimilation being limited, its homogeneity is accentuated. Most of these working-class people share values and norms based on a common place of origin, similar levels of educational achievement, near-identical class backgrounds, and intermarriages and friendships among the group. When they join recreational, religious, and political organizations, they generally remain inside their community. However, some social relationships do cross racial or ethnic boundaries to link members of different groups within labor organizations. For example, industrial labor unions accept marginal group workmen. In fact, a disproportionately large number of them belong to industrial unions. They develop reciprocal, if distrustful, ties with mainstream workmen as they become experienced unionists.

Because of their successful involvement in industrial unions, marginal workmen cannot be characterized as completely isolated or desperately poor. By working-class standards, the majority earn medium and sometimes high in-comes, although almost all are economically insecure, a consideration that accentuates their unrest and militancy.

The term *mainstream* working class denotes a category of workers who are culturally heterogeneous and who belong to a dominant *racial* group. The occupational composition is disproportionately of the white-collar type. Like marginal workmen, they are also situated in an urban, advanced industrial setting. But unlike marginal workmen, they enjoy considerable economic security, in part because they predominate in the more educated and skilled categories of the labor force. These qualifications, plus high racial or ethnic prestige, enhance their relations with middle-class members of their own group and limit ties with members of the marginal working class. In fact, almost all their close relationships occur within their own racial or ethnic group. Familial, peer, and similar relationships often extend across class lines and promote discrimination in the workmen's favor. In this sense, mainstream workmen differ considerably from marginal workers and express relatively less class consciousness.

WORKING-CLASS ORGANIZATION: AN ADDITIONAL CONSIDERATION

Economic insecurity contributes to working-class consciousness. But it is not the only force. Since organizations also help to bring about class consciousness, we must take them into account.

Working-class organizations committed to advancing the economic interests of blue-collar people are of two types. Work groups generally take the form of *unions*. In fact, for the United States, the key work group has been the union—craft or industrial. In addition, there are *neighborhood organizations* which attempt to advance the material interests of the working class. In the United States, this form of organization seems to be of growing significance, especially within the communities formed by residents of particular urban blocks. Both groups are significant because they have the potential to interpret events for workmen in terms of class categories and to involve workers in confrontations or conflicts with business firms, which result in the creation of consciousness.

Unions are the more important of these two

types of organizations, for they have the most bearing on sustenance, an item of considerable interest to workmen when they contemplate maintenance and advancement of their personal and family interests. Because of this vital connection, unions provide the lead on matters conducive to the formation and reinforcement of class opinions. Although unions are significant sources of class consciousness in all stages of all industrial societies, they appear to be most important in communities where they have conducted successful economic and political struggles and have won positive recognition among union people. Cities such as Flint, Akron, and Detroit; Vancouver, Winnipeg, and Sudbury; Liverpool, Birmingham, and London; and Calais, Marseilles, and Lyons are good examples.

THE MULTIFACETED CHARACTER OF WORKING-CLASS CONSCIOUSNESS

Too often we treat class consciousness as a quality either present or absent, much as we would define a person as a Catholic or non-Catholic (using a nominal scale of measurement). Actually, class orientation in the real world is seldom ordered in such terms; rather, it builds step by step (ordinal) as on a continuum. Our conceptual and methodological scheme should reflect this reality if we are to explain and to predict behavior.

Whatever its degree and however great our analytical efforts, class consciousness may combine with racial or ethnic consciousness. Many class conflicts reflect this blending. In some situations, for example, employers are predominantly members of one race, and they discriminate against a marginal segment of the working class. The net result is the creation of considerable class-racial consciousness among working-class people in the marginal racial group.

THE POLITICAL CONSEQUENCES OF WORKING-CLASS CONSCIOUSNESS

Sweeping and summary views are dangerous but necessary if we are to understand where we are. In *early* stages of industrial society, class consciousness is frequently associated with revolutionary social movements. In *advanced* industrial societies and communities, however, class consciousness is seldom linked with calls for total reorganization of society. (The 1968 French insurgence is an exception.) Instead, class consciousness generally finds political expression in reform or labor parties, unless a war paralyzes the economy for a prolonged period of time or threatens to destroy it. In that case, working-class consciousness becomes tied to radical movements committed to seizure of state power and property transformation.

Let us return to the reformist context, the one most common in advanced industrial societies. We have learned from a variety of situations that a high degree of working-class consciousness aids reform politics only when:

1. Large sections of the working class face an economic crisis, and class issues (such as unemployment) loom as significant.

2. A political party presents a program in keeping with working-class interests on relevant issues.

3. A pro-labor candidate supports this party program.

4. A labor union takes advantage of the times and activates workmen, supports the pro-labor party, and embraces the pro-labor politician.

A COMPOSITE VIEW OF CONSCIOUSNESS AND ACTION

At this point we should try to put our observations together. A particular worker would in all likelihood become highly class conscious if he came from an agrarian region, settled in an industrial town, belonged to a marginal racial or ethnic group, joined a labor union, and lived in a neighborhood whose inhabitants were primarily concerned with unemployment and housing. With class consciousness emerging from this background, he would cast a class-conscious vote when the times demanded it, the party solicited it, the candidate sought it, and the union endorsed it. In my 1960 study of Detroit workers I found this to be the case.

Needless to say, under conditions of modern industrial capitalism, blue-collar workers frequently do acquire high levels of consciousness. Because their societies are unable to avoid wars frequently catastrophic to their standard of living, depressions dangerous to their pay envelopes, and employers bent on destroying their unions, their way of life buttresses this level of consciousness. By contrast, it would appear that many white-collar workers have located themselves in occupational positions where not war but cybernation appears to be canceling out their occupations, thereby inducing widespread economic insecurity. Whether this white-collar "salariat," many of them clerical workers and middle-level management people, become radicalized by their experiences is another matter. Their radicalization depends on a number of considerations, a crucial one being the character of the labor unions and political parties in which they are enmeshed. We have learned from historical experience that economic insecurity can drive the middle classes toward what Seymour M. Lipset has correctly referred to as middle-fascism, a totalitarian society oriented toward meeting the economic needs of the middle classes within the context of both private property and severe police control. Should a large section of the middle classes move in this direction, they might well have the support of a minority of working-class people alarmed by the growing militance of America's black proletariat.

A NEW WAY OF VIEWING CONSCIOUSNESS INSIDE THE WORKING CLASS

Our treatment of working-class views does contain certain weaknesses, and perhaps in the future it might be profitable to distinguish among type, level, dimension, degree, and cumulation of consciousness, as indicated in Table 17. As for *type*, we can view consciousness in class, racial, or class–racial terms, depending on the analytic interests of the observer. Of course, the investigator can focus on all three phenomena simultaneously. We should also examine the incidence of low, medium, and high *levels* of consciousness. In our analysis, for example, class verbalization constituted a dimension found at a low level of consciousness, skepticism fell in the middle range, and militancy as well as egalitarianism, respectively, ranked in the higher positions. (Class verbalization constituted a low level because such behavior seems to be easily acquired and retained, at least more so than skepticism, militancy, and egalitarianism, in that order.) These four dimensions of consciousness, however, do not exhaust the logical possibilities. For example, we can substitute the *dimension* of class identification for class verbalization at a low level of consciousness within our larger measure, thereby indicating the flexibility of both concept and measure of working-class consciousness.

Type, level, and dimension constitute three approaches to the subject. In addition, there is the summarizing notion of *degree*. In order to discuss degree of working-class consciousness, we might conceptualize consciousness in terms

TABLE 17   Schematic Presentation of Degree and Dimensions of Working-Class Consciousness

	Degree of Consciousness		
Low *(First Level)*	*Medium-Low* *(Second Level)*	*Medium-High* *(Third Level)*	*High* *(Fourth Level)*
Class verbalization Class identification Other dimensions	Various dimensions including skepticism	Class Militancy Other dimensions	Various dimensions including egalitarianism

One dimension ⟶

Culmination of two dimensions ⟶

Culmination of three dimensions ⟶

Culmination of four dimensions ⟶

of its cumulation of one, two, three, or four (or more) dimensions. For example, we have classified the militant egalitarian as one who has scored positively on class verbalization, skepticism, militancy, and egalitarianism, and hence has expressed a high degree of class consciousness. Each dimension of consciousness, such as class militancy, could also be treated in terms of level, dimension, degree, and cumulation of consciousness, perhaps in a way not too different from the manner in which we have charted the larger measure.

CONCLUSIONS

It must be obvious by now that we reject the view that modern industrial capitalism has eliminated economic insecurity and tranquilized all levels of labor organization so that conditions no longer generate class consciousness and class politics. Specifically, we hold that agrarian–industrial mobility is not confined to early industrialization, although its relative incidence is greatest at this stage. In the same vein, we reject the view that the affluent society, the welfare state, the benevolent corporation, and union leaders have eradicated occupational insecurities. In fact, there is some doubt about the utility of these three categories. Although their importance may swell and dissipate in wavelike fashion, through time they nonetheless give rise to class consciousness, sometimes with racial overtones.

Clearly we disagree with writers like Herbert Marcuse who analyze the American working class as if it were all of one stamp. We view America's blue-collar workers as extremely variegated in terms of both background and consciousness. Black auto workers differ from white craft unionists. Unionized Mexican–American farm workers cannot be placed in the same category as skilled, white, tool-and-die makers. All these subgroups express predictably different levels of working-class consciousness.

We also challenge the view that marginal racial group position creates race consciousness only and fails to produce class consciousness. Similarly, we feel that marginality to the labor force creates more than pockets of concern over obtaining and keeping a job. In maintaining that labor force marginality and labor unions engender class as well as job consciousness, we disagree with Selig Perlman and others who have emphasized job consciousness. At the same time, we part company with those Marxists who point to the presence of class consciousness, while ignoring the significance of the racial factor in accounting for the content and disposition of working-class consciousness. In this regard, the Black Panther party evinces a degree of class and class–racial consciousness far more radical than anything expressed elsewhere in North America. We expect these groups to create the conflict categories and new forms of consciousness during the last third of the twentieth century.

But class analysis is only one approach. There are others, and we must use them when be begin to investigate the state and how it shifts its ideological focus as revolutionary social movements emerge and move successfully toward the seizing of state power and beyond. Not too surprisingly, only a mood of pessimism can permeate this analysis of step-by-step development. But pessimism should not be confused with cynicism, and in the long haul, only an admixture of pessimism and hope can provide the patience necessary to continue the struggle for incremental change through revolutionary action.

6 State, Ideology, Market Society, and the Natural History of Revolution

---

Section One *The Shifting Qualities of the State*

IS THE STATE OVERWHELMING?

The state is never neutral. Along with its beneficiaries, it leans to one side. Especially is this true when the businessman's (or "capitalist") state[1] intervenes to socialize its citizens in market society. In this context, the state works to shape peoples' minds. Before we explore how this is done, it is appropriate to make some preliminary remarks on the nature of the state.

The state is rightly regarded as a socializing institution, the most powerful of disseminating agents. It insists on the prerogative of regulating the flow of information to all its potential taxpayers and future war personnel. Others are also earmarked for concern, but the crucial matter is the way in which state elites investigate, regulate, and, when necessary, punish the nonelites. State elites claim for themselves a monopoly of violence (see Chapter 1). Nor are the political elites without a bias on class, scrutiny, and violent punishment. In a context where land, labor, and goods are produced for profit with minimal amount of state regulation, the businessman's state (more specifically, its leadership) dwells on public schools and scrutinizes texts and teachers of privately run educational institutions.

The state interests itself in the flow of all information. When necessary the state threatens

what it does not own or regulate in the realm of the mass media. In a more paternal way, the state directly communicates to families, private police, churches, and like secondary institutions, it expects obedience, within limits, from these institutions. The state thereby becomes a primary and paternal distributor and censor of information, including accounts of its own nature and the behavior of its officers and functionaries. As a maker of its own design, the state distributes ideology, comprised in good portion, but not entirely, of those ideas which justify and at times obscure the relationships between the state and all other institutions, between the state and all persons in the society, between the propertied who strive to command and staff the upper levels of the state and the propertyless who are taught to obey.

The businessman's state strives to accommodate the demands of an economy geared to the use and exhaustion of human and other resources in order to achieve predictable levels of profit, high levels of corporate longevity (and prestige), and the successful promotion of executive careers. Indeed, the business executive becomes an important owner of investment capital, a person whose prestige, wealth, and knowledge makes him eligible to become a potential occupant of official positions within the state. There he can act to enhance his private career, corporate obligations, personal honor, and private fortunes. The businessman's state, then, is run by propertied directors of organizational power.

In its regulatory actions, the state rejects and often suppresses counterideologies, that is, formulas that question the legitimacy of state control and private property. Above all, the state disallows the serious dissemination of utopian

---

■ I have written another paper, similar to this one and fully-footnoted, that is to appear in Larry Reynolds' *American Society*, to be published by David McKay Co., in 1973.

[1] In this analysis I will be referring primarily to the businessman's state, the state in which the corporate and banking propertied dominate. However, many of my remarks could apply to socialist and other state forms as well. In the last part I discuss revolutionary states of the nonbusinessman's variety.

visions on societal alternatives. For example, the businessman's state prefers to prohibit a positive portrayal of communism in the public school system, for the state's leaders consider a competitive vision to be potentially subversive to its power, which it perpetuates, and to the economic interests, which it serves. The businessman's state looks askance at ideas that might in any way dissolve the ideological glue which supplements the organizational force, for the directors of the state are aware of the integrating function of ideas propounded by the state and other institutions such as religious organizations. Thus, for example, to the degree that people accept the myths of supply and demand and are unaware of the practices of administered pricing, they misperceive a reality defined by state elites as resting on the moral principles of the free market place. To the degree that masses inaccurately perceive but agree with this and related legitimating myths, the state defines these masses as they define themselves—as persons who accept a common moral order. To the degree that people define themselves as loyal to this order, they are less likely to take actions subversive of both state authority and private ownership of the means of production.

Given the signal importance of ideologies for political control, what is their content and how are they received? Here we are concerned both with content of themes and with forms of dissemination used to control populations which the state wishes to inculcate with certain favored ideologies. Previous major formulations on the matter of mental guidance by the state have portrayed a state striving to maintain a monopoly of violence and hence of day-to-day control through the distribution of myths to a readily brainwashed population. *The mass is generally depicted as being passive recipients at the end of a string of institutional disseminators.* From Marx through Mosca, Pareto, and Michels, to Lasswell, this theme recurs. *Paradoxically, the same writers have commented on the conditions under which the subordinate classes break with state ideologies and move toward the creation of revolutionary countersymbolism and revolutionary organizations.* We must concern ourselves with the resolution of this seeming contradiction by approaching the problem in an orderly fashion.

MY ARGUMENT: THE STATE MUST SHIFT GEARS

Concern with the resolution of the contradiction just stated moves me to explore the following thesis, namely, *the ways in which the state formulates its justifications and uses force to maintain political control depend to a high degree on whether state ideologies are in fact being accepted by the mass of people within the subordinate classes.*

Mass acceptance of state myths is to a high degree dependent on whether objective conditions promote a period of political equilibrium or one of revolution. (For discussions of conditions that move states toward, into, and beyond revolution, see Chapters 1, 3, and 4.) During moments of equilibrium, the well-reasoned justification of political pluralism complements a state policy of repressive redirection with a modicum of state violence. During the early periods of revolutionary unrest, however, mass acceptance of state formulas wanes, as masses acquire utopian concern on structural changes. At this time, the state both persists in its commitment to political pluralism and attempts to coopt its critics. Furthermore, the state relies increasingly on shockingly illogical judicial, executive, and administrative actions. In this context, the state uses violence more frequently, and indiscriminately, to punish those deemed beyond the pale of state acceptance.

If the businessman's state fails and the socialist revolution is successful, i.e., if the alternate state becomes the official state, the revolutionary state will momentarily foster the dissemination of formulas consistent with the revolutionary aspirations of the great majority of the masses. Subsequently, the contradictory demands of revolutionary defense negate many of the prior gains associated with the struggle against inequality. Finally, subordinate classes and intellectuals react sharply against the alleged excesses and extremes of revolutionary behavior. Then there exists the slight possibility of rejuvenation of revolution and the achievement of equality through continuous struggle against those forces associated with the new inequality. At this point the state may well pursue a "cultural revolution" and use a modicum of violence to revitalize the revolution.

It is true that masses generally accept the myths (especially those on the inevitability of inequality) presented to them by the state through the institutional network—the mass media, religious institutions, schools, families, prisons, and the like. But not always. Admittedly during moments of equilibrium, the state and ancillary institutions find little opposition to the successful flow of fabricated versions as to how the society is organized, what the societal alternatives are, and how the state can ensure the ideological status quo. By contrast, during protorevolutionary and truly revolutionary periods, ideology runs smack into the continuous and popular opposition of both *counterideology* and *utopian construction.* Counterideology depicts the damned present, while utopia incompletely designs the revolutionary future. Confronted with these increasingly popular expressions from below, the state expresses itself through reaffirmation of its own ideology and the increased use of violence.

The collision between ideology and utopia frequently occurs within the context of a political battlefield. Generally in attempting to analyze the soldiers of struggle, we fall back on the anthropomorphizing of class categories. Many speak of the proletariat standing up, or a coalition of peasants, intellectuals, workers, and progressive bourgeoisie, and so forth. We talk about coalition politics as if whole groups were allied. In fact, we know better, for what we observe over and over again are bits and pieces of classes, status groups, and generations coalescing. This being the case, unrefined class analysis makes little sense. Sections of classes may participate in a struggle, or even lead it, but we should not confuse the part with the whole and go so far as to attribute individual characteristics to an analytic category or a real group.

THE CLUSTERS: MORAL CORE, APOCALYPTIC RADICALS, AMBIVALENT PARTISANS, DELIBERATE RADICALS, AND THE QUIESCENT DUMB

Clusters of political allies draw their membership from various sections of classes, status groups, and generations—the crucial sources of group behavior.

In our time, we can observe again and again that in one corner are the heterogeneous forces of economic conservatism and cultural tradi-

tionalism. These forces are a rag-tag combination drawn from all walks of life, and together they constitute the "moral core." The key carriers of societal folkways and mores, the unconscious purveyors of upper-class beliefs and values, the dreary reciters of eternal verities, they hang like albatrosses around the figurative necks of political movements seeking revolutionary change. Although led by an overwhelming majority of those who monopolize the strategic resources of society, the moral core includes, even as it rests upon, a sizable segment of those whom corporate wealth oppresses. For as numerous writers have indicated, it is normal for many of those who suffer repression—even the double exploitation of class–racial manipulation meted out by the white man in the black colonies—to adapt to circumstances in which the oppressed are without a revolutionary alternative by identifying with their oppressors.

This mental set remains among many of the oppressed as a form of cultural residue, one based on a previous adaptation maintained long after the society has passed from a condition of near-equilibrium to one of revolutionary flux. Political organizations simply have not had time to unwork the mental markings of the past. As such, the residual loyalty of these victims functions to legitimate the moral core's leadership and myths. What better way to make a ruling group respectable than to have an oppressed group testify its loyalty through continued identification and even emulation? After all, the affluent leadership can't be all that bad, since many miserable ones subscribe to it.

Flagrantly opposed to the moral core are the "apocalyptic radicals." Drawn from many classes but especially the *petite* bourgeoisie and the young working classes, these persons bring a total indictment against the corrupt present. They call for the creation of a revolutionary presence on all matters, they see and demand bipolarization now, they fully expect the forces of revolution to triumph soon, they live part of the future within their countercommunities (including both working class and *petit* bourgeois groups), they pen the rough outlines of the new society, thereby justifying the casualties of ongoing and pending armed struggle. The apocalyptic radicals are always visible in societies where a market economy exists—partly because some are publicly adopted and feted by the more cosmopolitan members of the establishment. But they become most obvious when a society moves during the early prodromal period from ready adjustment of various parts to a period of rapid and near-total reorganization. During these moments, their numbers grow as does the din and influence of their revelations. The apocalyptic radicals often become paramount among the rank and file assembled at demonstration sites.

Somewhere between the moral core and the apocalyptic radicals are those who are both ideological and utopian. They are the "segmental partisans"—persons who have compartmentalized their minds to accept (a) portions of justifications of the present (ideology), (b) indictments of the ongoing (counterideology), and (c) formulations on revolutionary alternatives (utopianism). One moment allied with the moral core, segmental partisans consistently admonish those who violate the principles of the past. Yet, the next moment they sarcastically and inconsistently derogate the parameters of the same institutions whose rules and principles they had recently defended. Segmental partisans express contradictory statements, but many of their criticisms run deep. According to segmental partisans—a sizable minority of whom are intellectuals—the state sets boundaries around *institutions,* which behave within prescribed limits to socialize. *They* damn to irrational perdition the very ones whose "autonomous rationality" must be achieved if the moderate goals of the segmental partisans are to be realized.

Sometimes out of despair, the segmental partisans identify with the goals, if not the careening style, of the apocalyptic vanguard. Illustrative would be left-democrats, discussed in Chapter 9.

However confused the segmental partisans may be, it becomes the task of egalitarian movements to eliminate their central inconsistencies and to persuade the ambivalent to accept revolutionary utopias, which the converts can later help design more precisely.

To win the segmental partisans is no routine activity, and from the point of view of many within the radical movement, this task should *not* fall to the apocalyptic radicals, who tend to alienate most people, including each other. Through default, the job generally falls to the

"deliberate radicals," a category in many ways dissimilar to other radicals, especially the apocalyptic variety. Their relative calmness in the art of persuasion complements their insistence on viewing people's political beliefs as falling on a continuum. Indeed, deliberate radicals believe that persons can move up a scale from conservative to radical under the pressure of current events, participatory involvement, critical friendship, and political self-analysis. All those considerations press the deliberate radicals to be flexible but firm when dealing with persons who have internalized chunks of both the mores of the past and the utopian vision of the future. By contrast, apocalyptic radicals are more prone to be frenetic in life style, more apt to view individuals as all good or all bad, certainly more likely to condemn personally those unlike themselves, more predisposed to be impatient, rigid, inflexible, and high-handed.

The deliberate radicals best handle the guidance of the ambivalent partisans through situations in which the ambivalent do as much as they can for a particular cause and where the predictable repression of the state will and anger and press them to do more to solve the particular problem. It is the task of the deliberate radicals to help to interpret certain watershed events as they and the ambivalent partisans pass through crises loaded with potential for radicalization.

But to lead in such a way demands subtlety and perhaps an element of guile, qualities scarcely known among the apocalyptic radicals in search of immediate apocalypse. The deliberate radicals do not accept such a vision of forthcoming events, and above all they reject the related and dichotomous distinctions between the saved and the damned. The deliberate radicals eschew the belief that it is necessary for everyone to choose sides *now* in order to achieve a propertyless, classless, statusless, and stateless society.

Deliberate radicals propound a firm but patient evolutionary view on when and how revolution can take place. They believe that if and when a particular sequence of conditions and processes occurs—and revolutionaries should help to shape and accelerate the processes by widening the base of popular support—then there will in all probability follow a successful revolution. This calculating and activist approach leads many others to view the deliberate radicals as cautious tacticians, if not manipula-tors. This view is correct. They are. They are generally persons with vision and a long-term approach to the problem of relating to people in order to resolve secondary contradictions (i.e., conflicts within one's own camp).

By contrast, the consciousness of the quies-cent dumb is totally different from the perspec-tive of the deliberate radicals. The quiescent dumb seem to be singularly mindless. They act like persons whose cortical areas have been dulled by the litany of all institutions. Their perspectives become antiscientific, especially in the realm of nonwork relations. What charac-terizes these people is unintelligent, nonscientific use of elementary information on the relation between state power and market economy. Their minds appear to be incapacitated, unable to think in terms of how the state and private property systematically control and exploit their very lives. For them their fortunes ride on chance, luck, cosmic dictation, or a combina-tion of these. It is this group which makes a contribution to the old regime, but the worth of the contribution is ordinarily analogous to the significance of giant logs blocking the beach about to be traveled by an assault group.

The quiescent dumb are not part of the moral core, for they carry and practice few of the values of tradition. Quite frequently they believe little or nothing which lies beyond the bounds of their privatized, family-centered lives. Largely unknown to themselves, they are quite frequently cynics or pessimists—people who do not vote and in general do not believe in the pluralistic formulas on political participa-tion. They do not attend church or school, except when necessary. Nor do they subscribe seriously to myths on the life hereafter, not to mention the life before passage. In the United States today, these people seldom apprehend televised materials (although their sets may be turned on for hours every day) or read newspa-pers, books, or magazines. However, when they do, they comprehend information only in a very limited number of areas and only in the most concrete sense.

It's as if they are incapable of learning in areas that vitally affect them. Nor do they share moral-core beliefs on the presumed goodness to be derived from an understanding of public issues. Generally they are out of public life, but they are many. Yet they are sometimes in it, and then they can be significant. During political crises numbers of them can be acti-vated by the defenders of the status quo to leave their political lethargy and to speak and to act on subjects which they only minimally understand. The quiescent dumb derive from all classes, status groups and generations. They are by no means drawn exclusively from the lump-en proletariat and the working poor, some of whose members are both highly informed and committed.

All these types constitute the principal ac-tors who troup about the stage of politics dur-ing moments of equilibrium and revolution alike. But they do not move through time as if all stages were identical. For time includes peri-ods, and if we are to understand history we must at the very least schematize its trajectory. And in our time to do so demands that we make relevant distinctions between the periods of stationary equilibrium and those associated with total cultural revolution:

1. The period of stationary equilibrium, or the preprodromal period
2. The prodromal period itself
3. The coming to power of the radicals
4. The period of encirclement
5. Thermidor—the period of reaction

TRANSITIONAL REMARKS

Before considering the five stages of total cultural revolution, we turn to an important reading, for it should help to give some flesh to the skeleton already presented, as well as to the last section to be considered.

Max Nomad has summarized Waclaw Ma-chajski's turn-of-the-century views on the mis-carriages of revolution fostered by those who pose as revolutionary intellectuals. It's been al-most ten years since I first read this essay, and it's as stimulating now as it was then. The message is clear, although by no means proven. Intellectuals can conceivably abscond with rev-olutionary power and gyp the people in the name of revolution.

Section Two   *A Reading on Revolutionary Outcome*

The Saga of Waclaw Machajski

Max Nomad

New revolutionary theories are hatched daily in the brains of political malcontents and "cranks." In times propitious for their dissemination these new gospels, if backed by a fascinating personality, occasionally find larger or smaller groups of faithful communicants. Particularly is this so when the old, time-honored, standardized parties or movements of protest show no progress in the way of fulfilling their promises. But more often than not these newer theories find a quiet grave in unread books and pamphlets. As historical curiosities, they are mentioned casually in learned conversation, but no longer seriously discussed. Yet the failure of an idea to get recognition during the lifetime of its originator is not always a proof that there was no inherent merit in it. For it might share the fate of certain purely scientific theories which, having lain hopelessly buried among unread "papers," are sometimes discovered and acclaimed after several decades.

The Russian revolutionary movement of the last two generations has likewise had its nonconformists and heretics. They went their own way outside the beaten "legitimate" paths, on the one hand, of the native "Populism" of those intellectuals who championed the cause of the peasants, and, on the other, of the western Marxism of those educated malcontents who saw in the industrial workers the lever for overthrowing tsarism and for Europeanizing Russia. Among those "legitimate" currents might also be mentioned the orthodox, "official" communist-anarchism of Peter Kropotkin, which around the turn of the century viewed the coming Russian Revolution as nothing but a replica of the Great French Revolution.

Those heresies sprang from various sources. Some were the offshoots of the defunct anarchism of Bakunin; another grew out of the Populism of the Social Revolutionaries, and be-

came known as "Maximalism"; and others had their roots in the theories of Karl Marx.

All the advocates of those heresies, although speaking theoretically entirely different languages, had one thing in common: they refused to bow to the generally accepted view as to the character of the coming Russian upheaval. In referring to that impending event, both Marxian Social Democrats and Populist Social Revolutionists had in mind exclusively the bourgeois-democratic revolution. If the Social Democrats sometimes spoke of the "revolution of the proletariat" or the "proletarian revolution," they meant it in a somewhat peculiar sense: the fighters of the revolution were to be "proletarians," but the goal was to be democratic, a term which sounded better than "bourgeois." The native "Populists," although chiefly interested in the peasantry, likewise acknowledged the importance of the manual workers in the approaching upheaval. In a discussion between Plekhanov, the father of Russian Marxism, and Tikhomirov, then still the most important mouthpiece of the terrorist "People's Will," there were coined the notable sentences which, almost in a nutshell, reveal the stand taken by the unsophisticated Populists and their more subtle Marxian rivals. Tikhomirov said, "I admit that the proletariat is very important for the revolution." To which Plekhanov replied, "no, the revolution is very important for the proletariat." That was very sharp. But basically the two opponents were in agreement. Only the later Populist deserter to the camp of the tsarists was more cynical in his readiness to use the workers frankly as a tool for his, the bourgeois revolution; while the later Marxist deserter to the camp of the Russian "bitter-enders" of World War I, more circumspect, meant to say that the bourgeois revolution was of paramount necessity to the workers themselves. The workers might make their choice. . . .

The dissenters went beyond the idea of a mere bourgeois revolution. The unorthodox, i.e., non-Kropotkinian, Anarchists urged a mer-

■ Taken from Max Nomad, *Aspects of Revolt* (New York: Twayne Publishers, Inc., 1959), pp. 96–111, by permission.

ciless terrorist struggle against the bourgeoisie as well as against the government, with the lofty ideal of "Anarchy" as their *immediate* aim, incredible as this may sound. They were the super-romantics of the revolution. The no less heroic, but more reasonable "Maximalists"—the illegitimate sons of the democratic-liberal Social Revolutionary Party—demanded nationalization of industries immediately after the overthrow of the tsarist system. And so did Trotsky, the ex-Menshevik Marxist who went far beyond the Bolsheviks during the Revolution of 1905.

But prior to all of these heresies which sprang up about the time of the first Russian Revolution (1905), there had appeared in the field another champion of dissent—hailing originally from Marx—who was soon to impress his own name upon an entirely new revolutionary theory. His name was Waclaw Machajski (pronounced Vatzlav Makhayski)—now an almost legendary figure. In the circles of the Russian intelligentsia he has chiefly been known as the bad man "Makhayev" who had tried to arouse and to prejudice the manual workers against their educated champions. And even many decades after the movement connnected with his name had disappeared as an organized affair, the term "Makhayevshchina" continued to be used in Russia as a deprecatory designation of all those tendencies or even moods which in one way or another denote a certain antagonism between manual workers and intellectuals.

Waclaw Machajski (1866–1926), a native of Russian Poland, had started his revolutionary career as a Polish nationalist student with a slight socialist tinge. But he was soon to wash off that stain with five years of imprisonment in Warsaw and Moscow and six years of banishment to one of the sub-Arctic corners of northeasternmost Siberia. A few years before his imprisonment he had shaken off the last vestiges of his youthful nationalism and become a revolutionary Marxist. In 1892, impressed by a mass uprising of the workers of Lodz—the Polish Manchester—a group of Polish and Russian revolutionary students in Switzerland issued a manifesto to the workers in revolt. Machajski undertook to smuggle the literature across the border. He was arrested at the start, but the years of his banishment in the frosty wastes were not entirely lost on him and his fellow

exiles. Thanks to the slovenliness which was one of the redeeming features of the pre-totalitarian forms of despotism, Machajski and the rest of the "colony" in Vilyuysk were not bothered by the police when a newcomer brought with him an entire library enabling them to kill their time in the pursuit of revolutionary truth.

Much of that literature—aside from the works of Marx, Rodbertus and other social theorists and economists—dealt with the international socialist movement. After a thorough study of all these works Machajski came in 1898 to the following conclusions:

1. That Socialism, for all its "proletarian" protestations, was the ideology of the rising new middle class of intellectuals, professionals, technicians and white collar workers, and not of the manual workers.

2. That the socialist parties west of Russia, for all the revolutionary verbiage they indulged in on festive occasions, were in fact law-abiding progressive parties advocating political and social reforms, but no longer revolutionary organizations interested in the overthrow of the capitalist system.

3. That the socialist parties working in the underground of tsarist Russia and Russian Poland would follow the example of the western parties as soon as the overthrow of absolutism has enabled them to become legal organizations.

4. That this evolution towards respectability, and away from the idea of an anticapitalist revolution, was due to the fact that the policies of these socialist parties were determined not by their working-class rank and file following, but by the interests of the new middle class of intellectual workers (including self-educated ex-workers) who were ready to make peace with capitalism, provided the latter, through the extension of political liberties and democratic institutions in general, offered them an opportunity of lucrative employment either in the labor movement or in the various cultural, economic and political institutions.

5. That this new middle class of intellectual workers was a rising privileged stratum, fighting for a place in the sun against the old privileged classes, the landed owners and capitalists. Higher education was their specific "capital"—the source of their actual or potential higher in-

comes. Political democracy was the first, and government ownership of industries the next step to their domination. To achieve these objects they needed the support of the manual workers. The confidence of the latter they won by helping them in their early struggles for higher wages and by dangling before them the socialist ideal of equality.

6. That the "classless" society which they promised was meant only as propaganda, as a sort of proletarian religion, but not as an object of struggle for the living generation. The socialism which the socialist parties really aspired to was a hierarchical system under which all industries were owned by the government, the private capitalists having yielded place to office-holders, managers and engineers, whose salaries would be much higher than the wages paid for manual labor and who henceforth would constitute the new and only ruling class, absorbing into their ranks the former capitalists and the self-taught ex-workers.

7. That the introduction of that system was visualized by them as a process of *gradual transition*, precluding any idea of a violent overthrow of the existing system. (Machajski laid down his views at the turn of the century, in the peaceful days of capitalism's upward trend. At that time the rebellious, unemployed or underpaid intellectual or professional of the middle of the last century, was no longer a *mass* phenomenon outside of such politically backward countries as Russia, including Russian Poland, and Spain. That phenomenon was to recur in the wake of World War I when the hordes of unemployed or underpaid professionals and white collar workers began to embrace, *en masse*, the Leninist gospel of *immediate* anti-capitalist world revolution. Hence in 1898 there could be no such organized *revolutionary* anti-capitalist phenomenon as the Communist parties. Syndicalism was still in its infancy, and anarchist-terrorist acts of violence were manifestations of individual protest rather than of a revolutionary mass movement.)

SOCIOLOGICAL INSIGHT
AND REVOLUTIONARY WILL TO POWER

In short, at the turn of the century, that obscure Polish revolutionist had anticipated what was to become a truism a few decades later (1) that the democratic Socialists were at bottom what one might call left-wing New Dealers or liberals, and (2) that in a collectivist State—as exemplified by the U.S.S.R. nearly twenty years after his prediction—the office-holders and managers would constitute the new ruling class.

Most of those ideas were laid down by Machajski in a tiny hectographed volume, published in 1898 illegally in Siberia, which he entitled *The Evolution of Social Democracy* and which was to become Part I of his *Intellectual Worker*.[1]

A detached logician, digesting and accepting Machajski's analysis, would come to the conclusion that the "emancipation of the proletariat" with the "classless society" as its sequel, was a utopian dream. For the socialist movement, with its *uneducated* rank and file and its *educated* leadership of intellectuals, professionals, and self-educated ex-workers, could only result in the establishment of a new class system in which the office-holder and manager took the place of the capitalist.

But not so Machajski. He was a logician, but he was first of all a revolutionist, a conspirator, hoping to father an anti-capitalist world revolution in his own lifetime. So instead of spinning the thread of his thought to its logical conclusion—thus anticipating by twelve years Robert Michels' pessimistic theory of the "iron law of oligarchy"—Machajski actually wrote that the only guarantee against the class-conciliatory opportunism of the socialist parties was "a world organization of the working class, its international conspiracy and concerted action" as the "only way to its rule, to its revolutionary dictatorship, to the organization of the conquest of political power."[2]

The "conquest of political power," allegedly by the "working class," was in contradiction to Machajski's basic sociological thesis about the exploitative, non-equalitarian tendencies animating the owners of higher education with regard to the manual workers who, because of their lack of education, were prevented from exerting any governmental functions. For it implied that those intellectuals and self-educated ex-workers, who were to constitute the bureaucratic setup of a Machajski-controlled revolutionary government, would be exempt from those tendencies. It was as if a philosopher after writing a profound treatise in defense of skepticism or agnosticism were to wind up with the proclamation of his own divinity and infallibility.

Whether it was due to his insight into the inconsistency of that demand *from his own point of view,* or to purely tactical considerations (in order not to repel the Anarchists and Syndicalists whom he hoped to win over to his views)—the fact remains that after his flight from Siberia (1903) Machajski never spoke of a "revolutionary dictatorship" again—although he never *explicitly* repudiated it. In his later writings he maintained the idea of a world-wide "workers' conspiracy"[3]—thus to a certain extent taking up the idea of Bakunin's secret "Alliance" of the late 1860s and early 1870s, and anticipating Lenin's Communist International.

However, he coupled with it no longer the struggle for power, but the *purely economic struggle for higher wages, and jobs for the unemployed,* to be carried on by the method of what the Syndicalists called "direct action." World-wide strikes, he wrote, would "dictate the law"[4] to the privileged classes and their governments. The result of those strikes and of that "dictating" was to be eventually the complete equalization of incomes of manual and intellectual workers.

In his writings reflecting his later phase, as it were, Machajski was not explicit about the changes in the political and economic setup that would occur in the process of those struggles for economic equality. The initiated understood of course that the private employers, being unable to accede to the high wage demands confronting them during the general strike, would simply declare a general lockout, whereupon the government would be forced by the aroused masses to take over the industries and to organize public works for the unemployed. This reticence on the question of nationalization of industries was due to the fact that Machajski was anxious to convey the idea that what the working masses were interested in was higher wages, that is, in a change in the *distribution,* and not merely in a change in the *system of production* which at bottom meant only the enthronement of the office-holders and managers (i.e., the intellectual workers) in place of the capitalist. For a mention of the change in the system of production would confront him with the argument that basically his was merely another tactic for bringing about the nationalization of industries, a goal common to all socialist schools. Moreover, while the various socialist theorists assumed that the nationalization of the means of production would mean the end of the class struggle, Machajski insisted that even after the disappearance of the capitalists the workers would have to keep up their fight until their wages, by bringing down the incomes of their educated masters, have reached the same level as the salaries of the office-holders and technicians.

By deliberately passing over—in his writings—the fact that nationalization of the means of production would be one of the inevitable accompaniments of that bread-and-butter struggle waged on a mass scale, Machajski confused those of his readers who were not smart enough to read that implication between the lines, and gave a pretext to his later Bolshevik critics and detractors to ridicule him by claiming that he "tried to convince the workers that they could reach a standard of wages equal to the profits of the capitalists."[5] A similar gibe was also contained in a footnote to the original Russian edition of Lenin's Works where it was said that the "positive program of the Makhayevtzy could be boiled down to a nebulous demand for an 'equal income' for all while maintaining the class system."[6] That statement about "maintaining the class system" was of course a distortion of Machajski's theory. It is curious, however, that such a gibe should come from the Communists who actually claim that they have *abolished the classes,* while maintaining the crassest inequalities of income.

In further spinning his pipe dream Machajski argued quite logically that equality of incomes would secure *to all an equal opportunity for higher education and thus do away with all class divisions.* The function of government having ceased to be the privilege of an educated *minority,* the State as an instrument of oppression and exploitation would disappear as soon as a new generation had grown up, all of whose members have had the advantage of higher education.[7]

Thus, according to Machajski, a mass movement stimulated and officered by a secret organization—aiming exclusively at the satisfaction of the workers' bread-and-butter demands—

would, by its own momentum, eliminate the chasm between the "knows" and the "know-nots," thus realizing the ideal of a classless, equalitarian society.

That concept implied, of course, what the Marxists call the "withering away of the State"–although Machajski did not use that cliché. However, there is an essential difference: according to the Marxists, the "withering" begins with the elimination of the capitalists to reach its apogee in the "higher phase of communism" with its vague "to-each-according-to-need" Utopia–arrived at, *without any further class struggles,* due to the automatic process of economic development; while, according to Machajski, the process of "withering away" first sets in after not only the capitalists but also the intellectuals had been "expropriated," i.e., after equality of incomes, and hence equal opportunity for the workers' offspring to obtain higher education, had been attained *as a result of an unceasing class struggle of the manual workers and the lower white collar employees against the administrative and managerial bureaucracy of the socialized State.* The end product, as it were, of Machajski's "withering away of the State" thus makes its appearance after all men and women had attained the status of intellectuals or professionals. (The idea that after the elimination of the capitalists those in possession of higher education would constitute the new ruling and exploiting class was expressed as follows by Michael Bakunin more than thirty years before Machajski undertook to build his theory on this concept: "It stands to reason that the one who knows more will dominate the one who knows less. And if there were, to begin with, only this difference in the upbringing and education between two classes, it would in itself produce in a comparatively short time all the other differences, and human society would relapse into its present state; that is, it would split up again into a mass of slaves and a small number of masters, the first working for the latter as they do now in existing society."[8])

THE SAME OLD STORY

There was only one hitch in the entire scheme which, starting out from the bread-and-butter demands of the workers–first against the capitalists and, after their elimination, against

the office-holders and managers–was to lead straight to an egalitarian Utopia. Would the leaders of the international "workers' conspiracy"–educated men, of course, whether college graduates or self-taught ex-workers–content themselves with seeing the masses "dictate the law" to the government? Or would they rather use that opportunity to seize power for themselves, thus establishing that "revoltionary dictatorship" which Machajski had dropped from his propaganda *vocabulary* after his flight from Siberia? In short, couldn't the arguments used by Machajski against the Marxist and other socialist intellectuals be equally used against Machajski and his followers? (The same argument applies, of course, also to Bakunin's idea of the immediate abolition of the State. For, following his own analysis, his own victorious revolution would be immediately confronted by the fact that a "small number of [educated] masters"–including Bakunin's educated followers– would lord it over "the mass of [uneducated] slaves.")

Machajski's active followers–whether intellectuals or self-educated ex-workers–were not out for power, at least *not consciously* so. They accepted the later, quasi-anarchist, version of their teacher's theory, which visualized a sort of "withering away of the State" as a result of revolutionary general strikes for higher wages leading up to the eventual equalization of incomes. They ignored the question of power which, in the process of that struggle might pass from pro-capitalist office-holders to near-socialist and finally socialist politicians–with the followers of Machajski working underground and continually spurring the masses on to higher and higher demands.

Sometimes they would wonder at their own disinterestedness–for it was one of the tenets of their faith that the other radicals and revolutionists were deceiving the masses in the interests of the intelligentsia. So they would ask Machajski what it was that made them act in disregard of their own class interests, as it were. Their teacher's reply was to the effect that what they were after was their "revolutionary career." This they interpreted in the sense that theirs alone would be the *glory* of changing the world and turning a new leaf of history, for theirs was the *only* method of bringing about an anti-bourgeois, working class revolution.

A few years after Machajski's death, which

occurred in 1926, this writer had a conversation with the second in command of that microscopic "workers' conspiracy." On that occasion the teacher's alter ego who alone had enjoyed his full confidence, epitomized the latter's innermost thoughts by the remark that "those get power who offer the masses more than the others do"—the "more" consisting, of course, in the *immediate* satisfaction of the workers' *material* needs, such as jobs for the unemployed and higher wages, rather than the illusion of power offered them by the Communists.

This remark inadvertently took off the group's mask of disinterested championship of the horny-handed underdog. For the purely bread-and-butter, non-political struggle for higher wages and jobs for the manual workers that was to lead straight to an equalitarian social revolution, stood thus revealed as a method of securing *power* for the intellectuals heading the "workers' conspiracy." Now it was clear why Machajski never explicitly repudiated that passage about the "revolutionary dictatorship." It was to serve as a sort of theoretical alibi should a revolutionary situation in which his group played a dominant role give him the opportunity to seize power—the way Lenin was to do it less than two decades later. And he was, no doubt, sure that his followers, for all their professed allergy to power—as long as it was out of reach, that is—would not refuse to participate in it once it was offered them on a silver platter. (It must not be forgotten that during the Spanish Civil War, 1936–1939, the Anarchists, for all their sacred principles anent the negation of the State and rejection of all forms of government, took an active part in the Republican government—from the Cabinet posts down.)

In this connection it may not be amiss to mention Machajski's reply to some of his not overly optimistic followers who asked whether it was not possible to assume that the workers, being uneducated, would continue to be deceived and kept in submission by their educated masters and "liberators" until the end of time. That reply was to the effect that "the means of deception are giving out." Believe it or not, his followers actually took it for an answer—at least for a few years until they grew wiser.

Machajski's ideas about the neo-bourgeois character of the intellectual workers (the "privileged employees of capital,"[9] as he called

them) have gone down in the history of Russian revolutionary movements as an interesting contribution to revolutionary thought. However, his attempt to use his criticism of the socialist intelligentsia and of its neo-bourgeois tendencies as a drawing card for his own ultra-revolutionary organization was a dismal failure.

THE "WORKERS' CONSPIRACY"

After his flight to western Europe in 1903, Machajski stayed chiefly in Switzerland, where he prepared the printed edition of the three parts of his *Intellectual Worker*, his *Bankruptcy of Nineteenth Century Socialism*, and the more popular propaganda pamphlet, *The Bourgeois Revolution and the Cause of the Workers*. All of these writings are in Russian.

No sooner had the last sheet been turned off the press than he shook Geneva's dust from his feet and returned to Russia, where the Revolution of 1905 was already in its defeated stage. With some of his old friends from the Siberian exile, he began his underground activity among the workers and unemployed in St. Petersburg. His followers (called "Makhayevtzy") attacked the tendency of the revolutionary intelligentsia to direct the dissatisfaction of the workers toward the struggle for political democracy. In spite of a very violent counter-activity on the part of the socialists of all denominations the "Makhayevtzy" succeeded at some meetings of the unemployed in putting across their resolutions demanding immediate relief for the unemployed and wide organization of public works. They believed that this campaign, combined with a general struggle for higher wages, by its appeal to the unskilled workers, who were not interested in political slogans, could call forth a real anti-bourgeois mass revolt which would then spread all over the world.

The group of militants, however, was soon broken up by arrests, and late in 1907 Machajski had to flee again. He stayed abroad until the Revolution of 1917, when he returned to Russia.

The name of his group "Workers' Conspiracy," and the identical title of the publication which he issued in 1907, were expressive of the method of organization which he advocated. Even before Lenin had taken his famous stand in favor of a strictly conspirative organization of "professional revolutionists"[10] —for tsarist

Russia alone to be sure—Machajski had come out with the idea of a conspirative organization the world over, whether the countries enjoyed political democracy or not. He believed that the legal form of organization of the various radical parties and movements was an evidence of their law-abiding, peaceful intentions with regard to the existing *status quo*, or at least the first step towards assuming such an attitude.

The attempts made by Machajski and his few followers in St. Petersburg, Odessa, and Warsaw to call forth both a permanent organization and a mass movement inspired by his ideas were dismal failures—except for a short-lived flare-up among the unemployed in St. Petersburg. Any conspiracy that is out to arouse the masses is in need not only of a generalissimo with a theory and a few devoted friends, but also of a large staff of officers recruited from among the educated. But Machajski's attitude towards the intelligentsia, while likely to win him friends among the uneducated horny-handed workers, made his group practically out of bounds as far as revolutionary intellectuals or self-educated workers were concerned. For a selfless idealist in search of an ultra-revolutionary gospel would more likely than not join an anarchist group whose utopian gospel is simplicity itself; while a sophisticated Machiavellian—whether college-bred or self-educated—who would see through Machajski's horny-handed doubletalk and realize that this was only another method of expropriating the capitalists and of establishing the rule of the intelligentsia, would be practical enough to join one of the well-established revolutionary parties of the Marxist or Populist denomination.

The fact is that Lenin accomplished under Marxian slogans and by un-Marxian promises of "peace" and "land" what Machajski had hoped to accomplish by the "syndicalist" tactics of a non-political bread-and-butter struggle under what was later to become known as the Gompersian slogan of "more and always more." The fact is also that outside of Russia Lenin's followers, operating on two different levels at the same time, succeeded in winning the adherence of both the intellectuals and white collar workers on the one hand, and the great mass of manual workers on the other; the former by holding out to them the promise of power, the latter by helping them in their struggle for higher wages. The Communists' frank admission that they were out for power won them an eager staff of educated lower-middle class or ex-horny-handed would-be officers of the coming revolution, while Machajski's outward hostility to the coming rule of the intelligentsia which concealed his real aim that was not different from that of the other anticapitalist intellectuals, left him stranded in the possession of nothing more than a correct sociological theory upon which, however, no successful revolutionary mass movement could be based....

NOTES

1. It appeared under the pen name of A. Volski. A more elaborate edition of the same work, provided with a Preface and a Conclusion, was published in print first in Geneva in 1905 and later in St. Petersburg (during the Revolution of 1905–1906). Volume II, likewise published in Geneva in 1905, was entitled *Scientific Socialism*. It was a rather abstruse criticism of Marx's economic views as expounded in Volume II of *Capital*, in which Machajski saw a defense of the class interests of the intellectual workers as against those of the manual workers. Next to imprisonment, reading that "Second Part," as it was called, was the most harrowing ordeal his followers among the intelligentsia had to endure; for hardly one of them could understand it even after rereading it a dozen times. Volume III stresses the idea that not only the Russian Marxists and Populists (the Social Revolutionaries) but also the Anarchists of Kropotkin's school (the "official" or "orthodox" Anarchists, as it were) viewed the impending Russian Revolution (of 1905) exclusively as a struggle for bourgeois democracy, disregarding the potentialities of its immediate development into a working class revolution.—A few extracts from *The Intellectual Worker* and from Machajski's other writings are available in English in *The Making of Society—An Outline of Sociology*, a symposium edited by V. F. Calverton and published in 1937 by the Modern Library, New York.
2. A. Volski (W. Machajski) *Umstvennii Rabochii* (The Intellectual Worker), Geneva, 1905, Vol. I, p. 30.
3. Preface to Vol. I of *Umstvennii Rabochii*, p. XXIV. Also pp. 61 and 63 of *Rabochii Zagovor* (Workers' Conspiracy) No. 1, September–October, 1907, n. p. [Geneva].
4. The expression used in the Preface to Vol. I of *Umstvennii Rabochii*.
5. E. Yaroslavsky, *History of Anarchism in Russia*, New York, 1937, p. 39.
6. Note 76 to Vol. V, p. 414, of Lenin's Collected Works (in Russian) Moscow, 1925.
7. *Rabochii Zagovor* (The Workers' Conspiracy) No. 1, September–October, 1907, n.p. [Geneva], p. 63.
8. Michel Bakounine, *Oeuvres*, Paris, 1911, Vol. V,

135. See *The Political Philosophy of Bakunin*, ed. by G. P. Maximoff, Glencoe, Ill., 1953, p. 328.

9. *Umstvennii Rabochii* (The Intellectual Worker), Geneva, 1905, Vol. I, Preface, p. VI.

10. At that time a certain romantic glamour was still attached to that term; for the "professional revolutionist" was a heroic and often ascetic bohemian, and not a mercenary adventurer or gangster with an ever-changing political vocabulary dictated by the momentary needs of the government that employs him.

The Stages of Revolution and Their Implications for State Ideology and Counterformulations

John C. Leggett

THE PERIOD OF STATIONARY EQUILIBRIUM

The stage of stationary equilibrium lends itself to analysis, for most people during this period know their slots and act out their roles predictably. Here institutions function much as the structural–functional sociologists tell us they do. Traditions permeate as they radiate from family, church, and school and prove to be consistent with the tenets of the state. At this historical moment, the hierarchical order gives ample indication of timelessness. The upper classes bask in the generally unquestioned brilliance of their own intellectual and material opulence. Contradictions exist, but they are readily ignored at the very moment that their sources remain hidden by lack of either cataclysmic uplifts or detectable microseisms.

Discontent remains largely personalized, seldom articulated behind a mantle of self-congratulation heaped on the upper and middle classes by their scribes. C. Wright Mills observed this phenomenon during the 1950s when he dealt with the art of upper-class self-celebration and the "end of ideology." Almost alone he announced how social-science intellectuals had set aside their radical critiques of the 1930s to posture before the academic foundations and educated publics the themes of collective arrival

■ This essay appears in L. Reynolds' *American Society*.

and pervasive happiness. The conservative formulation was clear. Capitalism had solved its internal problems and would tackle foreign hangups with analyses bereft of Marxism and with programs developed by a *reformed* capitalism. This formulation is presumably dependent both on a subsidized scientism without bias and on a new conservative ethic incorporating the traditional warnings against human presumptuousness.

In these celebrated analyses, mass unemployment had ceased, and people had won democratic political representation. Domestic class strife had ended and what remained to be solved were problems of nonrevolutionary consequence. Put on the agenda were problems of man's alienation from work and self, plus the need to re-create religiosity. Daniel Bell's *The End of Ideology* and his damning article-length review of C. Wright Mills's *The Power Elite* (published in the regular article section by the *American Journal of Sociology*) exemplified the two sides of the ideological coin: (*a*) celebration of private property and its alleged pluralistic political context, and (*b*) damnation of those who would suggest that power was not pluralistic but both concentrated and pyramidal in the context of the institutionalized socialization of a politically inconsequential mass. Mills's counterideological formulations had stung the celebrators, and their cobralike response smacked of the subsidized, vengeful overkill.

Long before Mills's piercing analysis of the power elite (which for many of us was his most influential, however imperfect, work), Marx had noted that the ideology of the ruling class stamps the mentality of all. None can escape.

This conditioned, indeed wholly deterministic, view of man has seemed to be most applicable during intervals of historical lassitude, those moments when trade unions make predictable gains, class struggle barely simmers, class-racial minorities are acquiescent, and the younger generation both slumbers to the purr of success and moves to the demands of career, with its daily, weekly, monthly, and yearly rounds chunked in terms of predictable time intervals fom birth to death. Society seems to assume the symmetrical, cyclical quality of a primitive world described by a British cultural anthropologist (e.g., Radcliffe-Brown).

Here, then, the propertied do not fear the clarion call of revolutionary social movements; rather, through their intellectuals they command a near-monopoly over formulations redounding to the pecuniary and power interests of the upper classes. And this monopoly provides a limited pluralism which cannot escape a conservative mood. For throughout the writings of these particular intellectuals, there's an implicit assumption of hierarchy and order. Terms are defined to express vertical integration among parts along with a mapping commensurate with the pyramidal order of groups in the society. A fairly accurate intellectual outline of the reality does emerge. Yet there is an element of untruth. The unpleasant consequences of private property are generally avoided, and any ugliness in the recent past is characterized as a deficiency resulting from the maniacal efforts of the crazed prophet, the power-bent agitator, or the "true believer." A typological, empirical, and deductive view of the world stands as the best way to comprehend the social order.

Of course, conflict and consciousness exist, even under these conditions, most notably among an upper class whose internal subsections *do* jockey through their political parties for greater state control and intellectual hegemony. There are disputes at the top among the moral core on the questions of what morality is and who its articulators are.

The conservative and progressive subsections of the establishment express their differences and commonalities in a variety of ways, but perhaps most revealing is the way in which they compete. Illustrative would be our newspaper or television media as they give the quintessence of meaning to particular cultural symbols; the way in which the same media overlook certain problems, such as the incidence of aggregate (yearly) unemployment rates, by neglecting to categorize them, hence damning the oppressed by subjecting them to conceptual vagueness (see "Countdown," at the end of Chapter 10). This reluctance to categorize allows the oppressed to wallow in the residual category of things to be dealt with eventually, that is, when the oppressed make trouble. For until these subjects rise and use their own injuries and the deaths of their comrades to publicize their collective case, they are seldom the object of concern and categorization among the elite and their professional dependents. Unless these rebellious acts occur, the moral-core publicists found at the top of the mass media manage to side-step issues, and as a consequence, most people acquire a slim informational base for making judgments. The mass must settle for casual stereotypes of themselves as the basis for understanding events and people at the bottom. An alternative would be a mass-media attack on such problems as understatements of unemployment at all levels: the bureau of labor statistics in question, the newspapers' supine reportage of these official figures, the public gullibility on the use of false figures compiled by the government and reported by the press, television, and radio, as if the given figures were valid estimates.

When the valid, full-fledged formulation does appear, we can observe how the moral core differs among its membership on the creation of countersymbols appropriate to define the problems of the recent past as well as the present. For example, we can note how the moral core disagree on the epistemology best used to intrigue intellectuals already bored by the analytic shabbiness which abounds during these periods. The concerned intellectuals do not agree on how to redefine cognitively the societal landscape—whether in terms of the fairly pleasant abstraction (which portrays a general picture but obfuscates particular social problems) or with respect to particular problems and hence palpable objects (which calls down the uninvited and dissenting exposé).

For the ambivalent partisans wavering at the edge of the moral core, society may well appear to be corrupt, perhaps damnable, if only because of the silence of most intellectuals on social problems. For these dissenters, a substantial readjustment of the society may seem to be in order. Clearly the needs of the poor, the minorities, and the young are being sidestepped by the state and glossed over by the mandarin intellectuals. Meanwhile, ambivalent partisans may feel that the traditional ways of thinking through or around problems reveal a kind of mental arteriosclerosis and show the absence of analytical thinking.

These complaints do not seriously disrupt the ongoing order, but they *do* keep alive criticisms. Clearly, they find their best expressions through plays, poems, and nonacademic journals of limited circulation, distributed among dissenters.

But the value criticisms occur within the frame of cognitive acceptance locked into an hierarchical perspective. The very cognitive categories of thought used by the critics plus the seemingly nonvalued portions of their perspectives, assume a multitiered form. For example, when persons assign themselves and others, through their religions, to the position of lambs led by a sheep herder; when a person nondeliberately stares at a number of cars in a parking lot and absent-mindedly ranks his own vehicle in relation to them; or when an individual sees others of his kind, ranks them preferentially, and jealously places himself in tiered order. At all levels and in every way, intellectuals make invidious, often hostile, comparisons. These symbol specialists thereby semiconsciously emulate the very ones whom they simultaneously reject and honor.

A hierarchical conception of the world finds greatest acceptance among the nondissenting spokesmen on the verities of inequalities. For the moral core, the differential distributions of wealth, power, and prestige are not inequities, since those judged to be genetically unqualified appear to be ineligible for generous public concern on matters of what they fail to get. This ideology is self-righteous. One unqualified should not be ignored entirely by the responsible; those short-changed by genetics are unfortunate and are to be helped paternally, not through a foredoomed redistribution of wealth, but through the timely gift from on high. The ideology generally reeks with prejudice and a phony scientism.

From the point of view of the moral core, *inequities* (*not* the victims) are fortunate results. Inequities recompense as they motivate those whose achieved abilities *merit* differential rewards. These results in turn ensure subsequent and high motivation among those others who are also intellectually endowed.

For the moral core, especially those of conservative background, nothing is more objectionable than the demands for egalitarian freedoms, economic equality, and untempered justice. In their eyes, freedom should mean the right of each class or status group to take full advantage of its peculiar rights, duties, and privileges. For rights are packaged and bundled according to one's station. Those at the top inherit the rights to privilege, and the honors of responsibility, whereas those in the middle and certainly those at the bottom, as a matter of course, have progressively fewer rights, more duties, and harder, less rewarding responsibilities. To the conservative, the weakening of these hierarchical bonds threatens civilization.

And economic equality? From any conservative point of view, it is transparently impossible. It is the intellectual creation of the daft demagogue who would substitute societal chaos and unscrupulous personal aggrandizement for tempered mercy and the free market place. Economic inequality is impossible, for God built inequality into his order when he created man with strength and woman with one less rib—weaker and less able to compete. Complementing this quality of physique is the uneven distribution of naked intelligence. Some were and are inherently dumber, especially women, since they have never had to compete and hence submit their own to the laws of survival of the fittest.

Since the date of pristine creation, these intrinsic inequalities among persons have resulted in the differentiation of the ordinary masses from the gifted eminent, the unrewarded mediocrity from the talented wealthy, the closeted female absurdity from the masculine success. If she has less power, wealth, and status, it is because she has never had the intrinsic, inherited qualities necessary to compete against the man. The conservative views as natural and good that the gifted gentlemen should enjoy leisurely affluence. He also believes that the sifting process involved—the sorting of the talented from the mass—would fail to occur without the threat of economic inequality. Later we will have occasion to discuss how certain deliberate radicals have accepted this position.

Untempered justice? In a polity, all persons can obtain fair and impartial treatment from the government. To the conservatives, justice becomes untempered and hence reprehensible when the personal discretion of the elite (i.e., the judgment and choice of those who are presumably accomplished) is absent from the interpretations of law. In turn, law is nothing more than a firm expression of *mores* derived from centuries of experience sifted by the elite and sanctified by God, supply and demand, or survival of the fittest.

During the period of stationary equilibrium, the conservative opposes the elimination of the right of the upper classes to express punishment through wrath or mercy. Nor do many deny them this right, for the upper-class tautology on legitimate wisdom is generally accepted. When people have intellect, it is because of genetic superiority. When people have intellect, they and they only become qualified to judge others and to temper justice with wisdom. With this genetically based superiority, they rule. Their rule is a sign of this realized superior intellect and, hence, they and they only should temper justice with wisdom.

The mass acceptance of mythical wisdom ebbs noticeably during the beginnings of revolution. It is then that the apocalyptic and the deliberate radicals begin to recruit from the ambivalent partisans and the moral core. Indeed, they start to turn-on a small but growing portion of the quiescent dumb, as radicals put together counterideological formulations and utopian constructions. These in turn force the state to rely less on myth and more on force to maintain political control, and the state begins to lose its legitimacy.

THE PRODROMAL STAGE

On the level of ideas, the hallmark of the early prodromal stage is the growing popularity of counterideologies and utopian theories. Initially, the principal expression of counterideology is dissent, although confrontation later provides a broader basis for an airing of grievances against the system. During the earlier phases of this period, we have the beginnings of deterioration of the myths of the establishment and of the ruling class. State power is questioned but not yet seriously threatened, as it tends increasingly to rule through force. The propensity of the state to use violence to maintain a society marked by great spans of differences in the realms of power, prestige, and wealth now becomes obvious. As conflict increases, the issues and biases voiced by the participants become increasingly clear-cut. In the debates on the issues, the left and its friends win the arguments, but the decisions are made by the state, whose key figures are not only biased but frightened by the rising subversive element. The state backs away from a policy of recurrent tolerance of bizarre and radical ideas. The state elites now associate the growing popularity of cultural and political revolutionary currents with the demise of the legitimacy of the state, its procedures, and its key personnel, namely, themselves. Whereas under conditions of political equilibrium myths could be disseminated and "tempered" justice administered by the courts, university committees, and so on, on behalf of the state. The rules have changed in the prodromal stage. The conservatives begin to panic, and their bad judgment becomes evident in patently wrong or unfair decisions, obvious lies, and the like. Indeed, the state settles more frequently on the use of deliberate physical injury as a way of ensuring political control.

State efforts to solve social problems fail. Parallel to failure in state collective problem-solving, protestors pass in greater numbers from dissent to confrontation; during this passage, they begin to articulate utopian perspectives quite divergent from those of the well-heeled and intellectually well-oiled individuals at the center of the moral core. It is then that ideology comes under full counterideological attack, for along with the appearance of utopian outlines stilettolike diagnoses pierce faltering social institutions. The pyramidal hierarchies within these organizations are correctly portrayed by revolutionaries as inept, corrupt, venal, and hypocritical by *conservative, bureaucratic standards.* An illustration of this occurred shortly before the fall of Chiang Kai-shek's mainland government (1945–1948). Many conservatives and liberal Chinese businessmen, as well as government officials, assailed this regime for the brutality and terror it visited on revolutionaries and nonrevolutionaries alike. As exposé piled on revelation, the institutional hierarchies were shaken. Indeed, the analyses were those of angered and often young ambivalent partisans sensitized to contradictions. The youthful novelists, painters, poets, playwrights, composers, scientists, and social scientists in ever greater numbers moved against institutions depicted as faulty if not deformed. They differed in their motivation—some being driven by alienation from bureaucracy, others by consciousness and class interests, and still more by both or by additional considerations.

At this stage, demonstrations and fierce repressions alternate with moments of quasi-equilibrium. The locus of ultimate power and institutional accommodation becomes even more obvious, as the state transparently attempts to use institutions now filled with internal strife to bring about an end to conflict. This effort requires the use of shootings, gassings and murders of institutional members.

Even state terror sometimes fails to quell civil disobedience and to return secondary institutions to their normal, subordinate position. The chief of state, who depends increasingly on indiscriminate killing, thereby violates his own rules. In cartoons, he often assumes an indecorous posture, with protruding gut, varicose limbs, and a bilious expression.

The issues are now clearer, although there is pronounced vacillation between support for either rebellion or revolution. The debate remains somewhat clouded because the progressive captains of the old core, where and when they can, move to try to solve problems through programs designed to coopt critics.

Yet even when cooptation works, reformers appear to be predoomed to defeat, for their programs fail to alleviate problems. The state is thereby stymied in its efforts to resolve contradictions. Rather, it increases grievances enunciated by the poor, who have been prodded from quiescence and dumbness to activism and consciousness by charismatic leadership. The revolutionary leaders spell out for the oppressed their worsened conditions and outline for those made desperate by their circumstances a remedy—which can only be had by taking action outside a discredited institutional framework. These leaders put into speeches and written prose the masses' deepest beliefs, feelings, hates, and desires.

The net result is the movement of a growing portion of the population from moral-core obsequiousness to open struggle. Indeed, the modern state often fosters international war in an effort to postpone reform and justify repression (a point we will develop in our treatment of the garrison state in a later chapter), at the very moment that it exploits its victims, the poor, who pay for the war through the taxes, inflation, selective service, their lives, and induced unemployment. All wreak havoc with the poor, who come increasingly to support sporadic bombing, lootings, and quasi-insurrections.

What further upsets the leadership of the moral core is the movement of many of the poor from the quiescent dumb and the moral core to the categories of ambivalent partisanship and from there to deliberate and even apocalyptic radicalism. Moving to the left as well are many of those who have been ambivalent partisans for most of their lives. Illustrative would be professional scholars whose experiences radicalize them to the degree that they become systematic, trenchant, and vociferous critics of the state.

The state leadership suffers a loss of legitimacy within an even wider circle of the oppressed and their alienated allies. With the affluence–poverty sequence we find growing consciousness, empathy, and sympathy among young intellectuals who acquire the ability to detect hypocrisy and to react against oppression. Not that all intellectuals tread this path, but enough, certainly, move over to champion the poor in order to become part of a vociferous minority that is capable of becoming an organized and revolutionary majority.

This mutual criticism approaches total castigation on both sides, as first a miniscule and then a noticeably large number within every institution—and at all levels—begin to choose sides and to criticize accordingly. The critics spend a good deal of time correcting conservative misdiagnoses and articulating alternative ideological forms. The radicals take the lead to point out that the system does not suffer from poor leadership and maladministration but rather from built-in faults that will not vanish until the system has been destroyed.

On the level of utopian construction, the apocalyptic radicals appear to be torn between their refusal to sketch the new society and a desire to make clear what the new society is all about. Wishing to avoid the predictable rigidities of theoretical construction, hoping to rely on the oppressed themselves to construct through spontaneous struggle what is soon to be achieved, these particular counterelites flounder until forced by criticism to initiate the intellectual constructions of the future. Still they hesitate to give full delineations, for the process of design would in some ways force them to depict concentrations of power—the very forms, whatever the content, they wish to abolish. This dimly recognized fear is nonetheless sufficient either to halt their efforts to depict utopia or to limit them to a hazy sketch of an ideal society. Rather than turning to the gigantic demands of constructing a grand picture, they express a longing for the demolition of the sagging present and a willingness to leave the reworking of the future to spontaneous activity of the oppressed. In this way would the exploited "electrify" class relations and "shatter" a moribund state.

By contrast, the deliberate radicals begin to portray the future. They emphasize such matters as which classes and class-racial groups will reconstruct a society now torn by struggles just this side of civil war and revolution. What will be the relative strength of the state during the immediate postrevolutionary period as well as in the stages beyond?

To deal with this problem, revolutionaries sometimes call constitutional conventions and carefully draw up statements declared to be alternatives to the present ones which don't work. The radicals pose important questions. How will oppressed minorities organize themselves for the new society? Crucial here is the debate among the radicals on the acceptable form of class-racial pluralism during the transition and beyond. In determining this matter, revolutionaries such as Mao Tse-tung have sometimes gone so far as to adopt a ratio scale of measurement, allocating points to the revolutionary worth of the various classes. What will

be the fate of classes and status groups currently identified with the old regime, and shall they enjoy any rights whatsoever after the radicals take power? What will happen to the old ideologies that have helped to hold the oppressed in bondage? The radicals disagree on whether the new revolutionary institutions will allow detached treatment of castigated ideologies once the revolutionaries have formed a new state. In China, for example, professional party leaders have frequently differed with university academics on the degree to which the state would allow debated scrutiny of all ideas.

What remains largely unspecified is the *pace* of these changes, as well as how they will be effected and at what cost; when will all forms of potential repression disappear; and how will the revolution handle the predictable Thermidorean reaction?

A LATE PRODROMAL CONSIDERATION

Of little interest to revolutionaries absorbed in civil war but of great importance to the revolutionary movement is the question of what will happen after military victory to the people's councils, soviets, radical trade unions, and neighborhood groups, all created during the period of coming to power. Will they continue to be significant after the old state has been beaten, or will the new state abolish the transitional forms and take over their activities? Radicals sidestep this question for fear of even greater division at a time when it is essential to avoid issues that will further exaccerbate differences within the revolutionary movement. Rather, efforts are made to seek issues that will unite. In short, although the deliberate radicals are relatively articulate on utopian construction, they leave much unsaid.

And while people muse over the future, events often move swiftly, for it's entirely possible for a revolutionary vanguard to find itself at the head of a general revolutionary movement running rapidly toward the elimination of the power of the older order without any clear idea of what is to be achieved concretely and how soon the tasks of state reconstruction will be upon them. This lack of intellectual presence disenchants some, but *indiscriminate state oppression* aimed at stemming the tide of revolution generates greater numbers of revolutionaries than even the most apocalyptic cadre can alienate because of intellectual and organizational clumsiness.

THE COMING TO POWER OF THE RADICALS

If and when revolutionaries take power, they must translate utopia into ideology while fighting to maintain the revolution which is at that time being attacked from without as well as from within. During this period of setting up revolutionary institutions and disseminating new ideologies, the radicals define the moment of grasping power as that delicious interval of historical arrival when all the old inequities are to be buried. Obvious celebrants are the manual workers and engineers, themselves operating, however momentarily and imperfectly, their own steel mills, power plants, railroads, farms, banking organization—all come under the *peoples'* hegemony.

Less apparent but still visible are parallel efforts made to destroy the old cognitive structures. Old calendars are dismissed. Alphabets are revised. Downgraded are racist theories which purport to explain the oppression of ethnic and racial minorities. Particular mathematical models are spurned, while others are celebrated. Antiquated terms are either abolished or invested with new meaning. Old forms of address which signified hierarchy are abolished; individuals call each other citizen or comrade. Whole areas of cognitive thought hitherto ignored by the state are given categorization to benefit those who had been oppressed. For example, the reclassification of diseases accompanies new programs against the bacteria, rodents, viruses, and insects slated for elimination.

The state momentarily ceases to be a monopolizer of violence—for it has rivals in the peoples' militias—but rather becomes, however briefly, the near-perfect vehicle of change for the good. The new state is different. This state reflects the expressed aspirations of the former victims by striving to realize an egalitarian society. For the first time, full equality becomes visible at the end of a long road to be traversed and worked by the labor of those devoted to achieving total reconstruction through the eighteen-hour day.

To travel this surface demands the suspen-

sion of static mentality. The new state ideology calls for the succession of a system of thought in which everything is in the process of becoming. The new cognitive categories avoid hard-and-fast definition—including propositional testability—in a world of delectable, dialectical flux. Definitions of reality become malleable as never before in the memories of participants, and people sense a new freedom based on release from the old hierarchical categories. The laws of collective becoming through comradely struggle replace those of frozen stasis through obsequious adaptation. What begins to crystallize is a vision of the radical man—the person who defies as he defines and supplants the bourgeois laws of psychology and sociology. A fresh perspective becomes dominant. Dialectical principles supplant in importance the old natural laws on mind and sociation. The concerns of the applicants of revolutionary theory are narrower than were those of their academic predecessors; thus they are working with propositions that have more specificity (not testability) and, hence, more revolutionary effectiveness when implemented.

THE PERIOD OF ENCIRCLEMENT

The radicals assert their power as the foreign enemies of the revolution continue to use military force and internal espionage to smash the adolescent revolution. At this point, a high incidence of casualties forces the revolutionary leadership to make more explicit *why* the sacrifice must continue.

It is in this context that the deliberate radicals face an awful dilemma. If the revolution is to succeed in breaking encirclement, the dwindling forces of revolution must be coordinated militarily on a dozen fronts by a vanguard party; but to impose coordination is to tighten the reigns of authority, for that is what coordination denotes. Yet to concentrate and centralize authority at the expense of local revolutionary impulse and locally controlled trade unions, soviets, and workers' councils—this means to destroy the vitality of the very revolutionary institutions which people have just learned to use and to misuse in order to control their own lives.

The suppression of these new institutions occurs. With their demise goes the promise of group freedom from future state repression once the peoples' armies have destroyed the encirclement. The suppression is stunning; after all, the vast majority of revolutionary partisans want participatory democracy to last forever.

Yet the demands of revolutionary military success during that historical moment take precedence over the maintenance of revolutionary institutions capable of maintaining a democratic impulse within the revolution. New state power consolidates as it passes whole-hog to the vanguard party and its leadership, who in turn become the leaders of both the Red Army and new moral core.

This sacrifice of people's control later proves to be both tragic and comical when Thermidor descends among those who have survived and led the revolutionary struggle against encirclement. Ironically, the victims of Thermidor are often the very ones who had only recently decided to suffocate the people's institutions—the only groups that might have been able to protect the deposed had these workers' councils, radical trade unions, and peoples' soviets been allowed to survive.

At this pre-Thermidorean juncture, state ideology justifies power concentration but contradicts utopian notions of the necessity to continue decentralization of power within liberated territories. Lost in a wave of rhetoric on postponement is people's control from the bottom up. This defeat angers as it humiliates, depresses, and dehumanizes the few grass-roots militants who have survived the earlier fights against the bourgeois state and its marketing system. In many cases they become further disillusioned when the new state depicts them, of all people, as adventurers and ultraleftists to be placed in the counterrevolutionary category. Until then, this rubric had only included the enemies of revolution lodged within the old moral core, the guts of the *ancien régime*.

What survives during periods of purge is the commitment to build a new society, although now there are no institutions capable of doing so. Efforts are made and celebrated as consistent with the old counterideology and utopian perspective. A brave new attempt is made to impress a skeptical outside world, as many revolutionaries and their foreign apologists discuss the revolution as if no repression had happened. These reconstructions include an effort to build

equality into many relationships. Illustrative are activities to create equality in an army without distinctions in dress but retaining differences in rank; the use of the language of equality at work but within the shells of recently powerful trade unions and workers' councils as well as soviets; the practices of equality in treatment of the two sexes in a political world where top positions of state power are all but devoid of women.

Yet celebrated changes do take place. Not all is fully contradictory. An important subdivision of the period of encirclement is the phase of war communism. Especially in the later moments of this phase, equality becomes the guiding idea and to some degree a living thing for progressive sections of all classes, status groups, and generations. Seemingly unshakable cultural and personality rigidities do fall, as ex-drug addicts become disciplined gun carriers, onetime prostitutes become warriors, former professors become revolutionary staff members, and diligent peasants work as comrades with the former professors. Paradoxically, the new state admonishes conservatives for their lack of revolutionary élan at the very moment when the latest elites resurrect new bureaucratic controls and prepare the way for the acceptance of the classical conservative formulas on why inequality persists.

During the final phase of war communism against foreign encroachment, the distinction between the saved and the damned moves to another level of discussion. What is left-wing? Peoples' lives ride on this definition, as the new state imposes a reign of terror to relieve the society of those who might betray the revolution to foreign enemies and domestic desperados. The new rulers prefer to circumscribe the definition of "left" to include commitment to the maintenance of the new state, and within it, the eventual realization of economic equality through common state ownership and fraternal relations. By contrast, the receding anarchosyndicalists insist on equal access to political decision-making in state government through control of their own organizations.[1] The state should be controlled by the soviets, the workers' councils, and the trade unions. For anarchosyndicalists, these organs should be resurrected and given state power.

In all revolutions the local anarchosyndicalists, whatever their particular designation, argue that unless the people can regain control of their own organizations, they will be unable either to eliminate the remaining economic inequities or to preempt those which would undoubtedly arise in the absence of democratically controlled trade unions, workers' councils, soviets, and neighborhood groups. Without such popular controls, all forms of social stratification would reemerge, and those having the greatest state power through occupation of top decision-making positions would use this power to increase their incomes and embellish their reputations. The indictment is complete. In the absence of grass-roots governance, what would crystallize would be a span of rewards of different form but similar content to that of the old regime. Thus yesterday's left-intellectual leadership would become tomorrow's right wing—a new moral core replete with state power, great wealth, and false honor, plus the unearned reputation of being new and hence potentially progressive. Obviously, those who objectively oppress through unbridled state power win— enough to make cynics of those who had hoped and fought for more.

THERMIDOR

Thermidor is the realization of the anarcho-syndicalist nightmare; it is not a delusion, for the passage of a revolution into the beginnings of Thermidor is unmistakable. Those spent through struggle become ready to examine what is happening around them, for although ennui infects all the survivors, the collective torpor does lend itself to contemplation. They observe the new leaders, captains of the new revolution who try to justify in backhanded fashion the disproportionately large amounts of power, wealth, and prestige which they, as vanguard leaders, have gained for themselves.

Justifications of the new inequities abound. Revolutionary leaders describe the inequities as part of a passing phase and hence of no real interest. Maldistributions of good food, clothing, housing, education, and the like are rationalized as being temporary inconveniences. Among the revolutionary rank and file there is a growing awareness of how the present captains of revolutionary institutions are living. They are now driving new and better vehicles,

sending their children to better schools, speaking a more precise language, treating ordinary citizens with bureaucratic disdain, circumspectly admonishing proletarian minorities for their alleged boorishness, and eating much of the better and scarce food. In addition, they are garnering more of their share of scarce beverages, consuming a larger portion of the scarce and high-quality durable goods, using a disproportionately large share of the high-quality fuels, holidaying at spas used only recently by the leadership of the old regime, earning inordinately large incomes even though the leaders do not create value, and compromising with the old ruling classes and their cultural symbols by reinstituting old religious symbols, calendars, work weeks, personal designations, and even some forms of private property.

In the context of new inequalities now institutionalized, the new moral core generally and eventually fall back on the old structural–functional theories on social stratification. One argument is particularly popular: To the inherently talented go the trained capabilities—and the rewards. In the new society, the state must fulfill certain economic functions if it is to survive. For example, it must cull from the mass the most talented individuals and train them for important positions in the economy. But to select the talented and to train them demands that the state reward both them and their imaginations. How? The state must make known its rewards during training periods for the promising young, so that they will forgo pleasures and give themselves to educational training, in order to maximize personal pleasures once the training is completed and the functionally important jobs are obtained. The intellectuals thereby articulate a theory of the state with overtones of Social Darwinism.

Other responses of the new revolutionary elites to the new inequalities stress revolutionary lag. There are those who accept the new inequities as momentary—distasteful but inevitable. They deliberately rationalize a widening span of rewards by saying that the span will disappear later. They say these things without indicating precisely when the shrinking of the span will begin. Whatever the rationalization, what appears to be full-blown are justifications of social stratification under conditions of state ownership of the means of production and tight state control of ideological dissemination. Suppression of utopian alternatives generally becomes total.

Not content with the demise of equality and the introduction of a new set of privileges, old-time revolutionaries sometimes intervene, but seldom with much effect: Their numbers are few and their actions are irrelevant, since to revitalize revolutionary institutions requires the recruitment of numerous comrades now situated in institutions padded with the fat of limited radical success—the seizure of state power and the enjoyment of its pecuniary rewards.

BEYOND THERMIDOR

On occasion, however, a handful of the revolutionary old guard unite with red youth to attack the members of the middle generation who have faltered and flatulated. When the new alliance occurs and if it receives positive endorsement of the state its members sometimes create a general social movement and invade every institution to smite what they deem to be counterrevolutionary cultural values and activities: Thermidorean commitments and actions which contravene the egalitarian aspirations of the original utopia come under attack.

The red alliance directs liberation struggles in schools, trade unions, government bureaus, collective farms, mines, factories, and universities—wherever people suffer from the reappearance of the old forms cloaked in the new revolutionary jargon. The anti-Thermidorean coalition of the revolution tries to disseminate a simple message through printed leaflets, seized newspapers, chalked blackboards, graffiti, and local bulletin boards, namely: Revitalize and refurbish now through revolution from below.

The attack is aimed against "functional necessity" and the weaknesses of "human nature." On the question of functional necessity, the red alliance revolutionaries argue that the revolution knows no necessities other than the need to rejuvenate itself or to drift until it becomes necessary to destroy the *new* regime. On the level of human nature, a sustained effort is made to indicate the frailties of individual problem-solving when the tracings of the past inequities remain and, simultaneously, the present structures foster elitism.

The cultural revolution in China is illustra-

tive. There, a coalition of new moral-core irregulars—Mao, Chiang Ching (Mao's wife) and Lin Piao among them—united with a large section of youth to revitalize all China. Nowhere has this effort been more obvious and perhaps more successful than in the universities, a favorite bastion and source of elitism in all societies. Recent accounts indicate that there has been a thoroughgoing effort to erase the built-in propensity of the universities to recruit from the favored classes. Rather, the Red Alliance and the rejuvenated state now dispense a university ideology and practice more in keeping with the needs of the lower classes and an egalitarian division of labor. However, one can expect that egalitarian ideologies and practices will come under criticisms from the right wing communists who prefer the return of the traditional bureaucratic rules as the basis for governing universities and other institutions.

But the Chinese success is the exception. Furthermore, there is the distinct possibility that the Chinese state could regress to the predictable pattern of pressing for inequalities. The Chinese state could follow the Russian example and justify the growth of inequities once Mao is gone by citing the need to create an unequal reward structure in order to motivate persons to meet state goals. The state could then move against those revolutionary—egalitarian groups without the institutional base of peoples' councils. The fatal ingredient in the Chinese revolution remains what it has always been: the absence of peoples' continuous control over their own state through their own revolutionary institutions. In the long haul, the vanguard party and Mao's charisma will not be enough.

SPECULATIONS

It is difficult to summarily describe the trajectory of revolution, especially since we observed in Chapter 4 that revolutions can and do follow multiple paths. Rather, we might make an intuitive guess on how a revolution would unfold were it to occur in the United States (although such an event is unlikely to occur within the foreseeable future). However, were the objective conditions present for such a revolution, they would include the privileges of agedness and inflexibility, phenomena which in turn are linked to the abdicating circumstances of revolution. How a second American revolution in the U.S. might develop is of course difficult to guess, but it could conceivably be consistent with our formulations and correspond with the general sequence whose conclusions are as follows:

1. How the businessman's state formulates its rationalization and how the state uses force depend on whether state myths are being accepted by the subordinate classes.

2. During moments of equilibrium, the state emphasizes political pluralism and repressive redirection, while deemphasizing the actual use of state violence; in effect, ideological propaganda plays the key cohesive role.

3. During the prodomal period of revolution, there is at first a slightly discernible but growing decline in the ability of state ideologies to find acceptance among the population. The businessman's state persists, nonetheless, in its praise of the myth of political pluralism; it introduces the technique of massive cooptation of critical rebels, depends less on reasoned argument, and uses violence more frequently if less discriminately. The state engages in this behavior mainly because a large and growing portion of the mass rejects the state's political formulas and engages in rebellious and revolutionary actions.

4. If and when a revolutionary state is created, it will momentarily propagate political formulas consistent with the revolutionary aspirations of the great majority of the turned-on masses, who indeed take action to control the new state through peoples' councils; the state dares not ignore the very ones on whom the state leaders depend for their continued occupancy of state power positions.

5. Under conditions of encirclement and war communism, with their contradictory demands for both (a) military defense of the revolutionary republic through greater concentration of state power and (b) peoples' struggles for the maintenance and extension of a new democratic and decentralized system of workers' councils, autonomous trade unions, and grassroots soviets—many of the egalitarian achievements of the revolution—are lost.

6. During the Thermidorean period, there occurs a slight possibility of rejuvenating the drive for equality—as in the Chinese Cultural Revolution—but the "short-haul" recrudescence of revolutionary egalitarianism may well be followed by the "long-haul" giving (e.g., to the reconstruction of autonomous, authoritarian, bureaucratic elites) unless the people are able to create and direct on a continuous basis their own institutions, and through them, that most powerful of institutions, the revolutionary state.

NOTES

1. Anarchosyndicalists have stood for the abolition of capitalism, the elimination of the state in those geographical areas where revolutionaries have eliminated capitalism, and the creation of workers councils to make key decisions within a highly decentralized economy. Anarchosyndicalists survive to this day, especially in Northern Spain. Anarchosyndicalism was once a powerful political force not only in Spain, but in Italy and to a lesser degree in France, Germany, and eastern and southeastern Europe. In the United States, the anarchosyndicalist was most profoundly expressed inside the Industrial Workers of the World immediately prior to the First World War. Big Bill Haywood was the living embodiment of that movement.

7 Fascism: Left, Right, and Center

Section One   *Fascism and Its Key Varieties*

FASCISM AND DEMOCRACY

The remaining portion of this book deals with industrial societies by dwelling on fascism, communism, and democracy. We will approach all three with the skepticism necessary to make us more critical of modern political systems. Perhaps this perspective will give us the proper balance between curious disdain and utopian optimism so useful for sensitizing us to new parameters worthy of pursuit as our century draws to a close.

Time and again, fascism and not socialism has culminated either in the near-completion of early industrialization or the failure to go far beyond the early capitalist involvement in the development of heavy industry. By the mid-1930s the fascist tendency had crystallized in many countries; in Spain, Hungary, Rumania, Poland, Brazil, Italy, Austria, Japan, and Germany, fascist and quasi-fascist regimes had taken state power. Elsewhere, as in France and Czechoslovakia, Argentina and Cuba, fascist and cryptofascist movements had seriously threatened the left with political eclipse.

Of interest is the technological context of these changes. With the decline in the predominance of extractive industries, such as mining, and the relative growth of heavy industries, which are the essence of the transitional industrial society, fascism became prominent in much of the Western capitalist world. The relative growth of heavy industries coincided with a development of marketing and financial structures that could neither maintain current levels of prosperity under capitalism nor facilitate the introduction of a new society under socialism. It appeared as if once many societies passed beyond the level of early industrial society, they had lost their potential for evolving

new and successful left-wing revolutionary forms at the very times when the old regimes could no longer contend with the problems of governance. To take up the slack as principal problem solvers, fascists entered as clever proponents of solutions to economic malaise as well as pragmatic retainers of many cultural traditions. Why fascism enjoyed such a success is a very complex matter, and these introductory materials can but suggest some of the causes involved. Indeed, our main focus is on another matter: What is fascism, both in its general forms and in its left, right, and center manifestations?

Analyses of fascism have frequently suffered from an inability to separate a general definition of fascism from specific depictions of its main varieties. Some prefer to define fascism as only a manifestation of capitalistic rule, a bourgeois abandonment of democracy in the face of communism. Quite obviously this definition is unacceptable since certain fascist movements have been pronouncedly anticapitalist. *Peronista* fascism is a case in point. Again, aristocrat-led fascism has proved to be most concerned with the salvation and restoration of property owned by throne and altar.

In fascism there is variety. This being the case, if we abandon all generic definitions and opt exclusively for a discussion of kinds of fascism, we would be without an analysis of the fascist kernel, its central meaning. Without it, the subject of fascism would become fragmented if not incomprehensible. Thus in our analysis we attempt to define fascism in a way that takes into account both its generic characteristics and its polycentral tendencies.

Perhaps we can best define fascism *in general* by briefly contrasting it with democracy. Ideally, democracy exists when people control their own lives by electing their own representatives to run their own social institutions, political parties, and pressure groups, each moderate voluntary association and every militant protest collective, so that in *all* these settings *each and every person* has equal access to information, plus an equal right to discuss and debate all issues. Furthermore, each and every person has an equal right both to choose persons for public office and to seek election to these positions. Given these ancillary conditions and processes, democracy includes the right of the elected to succeed, through peaceful processes, those who have lost according to the tally of ballots.

Clearly democracy is more than conformity to parliamentary gymnastics. Indeed, democracy implies the right to revolution in the event that the parliamentary process ceases to reflect the will of the majority.

Democracy connotes people's ownership of all the society's strategic resources. When there is private ownership of public utilities, railroads, banks, land, and industries, the principal owners and managers use their positions to accrue political power for themselves in order to manipulate others in all spheres through the spending of wealth, the monopoly of areas of information necessary to make political decisions, and the accretion of private information. In this sense, the very processes associated with private ownership of the means of production run counter to the conditions which are inextricably part of democracy. For democracy includes not only freedom of speech and assembly, but the realization of a society in which equal access to information gives rational and informed content to what people say when they meet to make political decisions.

Unfortunately, under most circumstances, the majority of people lack this quality, since institutional information is simultaneously *the major* and *a limited* source of knowledge for most persons living in the society defined, hypocritically enough, by their political elites as democratic. These institutions are biased because their upper-class owners and directors slant the information disseminated—by distortion, omission, and exaggeration. At times these persons do so unconsciously. Yet sometimes they act knowingly, and in some cases they deliberately lie. The directors do so to complement their own power, wealth, and prestige. In

the long haul, a society which allows these processes to continue becomes only a caricature of a democracy.

FASCISM IN GENERAL

By contrast, fascism makes few pretenses. Fascism denotes a political system in which the political leader and his party totally, unequivocally, and violently berate democracy and celebrate the state, relying for a political base both on a mass (a cross section of all classes) and on a particular class (such as the bourgeoisie). Both mass and class are cynically manipulated by the political leadership in order to maximize the interests of the leader, his party, and the class on which a dictatorship rests.

Organizationally, fascism is a mass party in the sense that it draws its support from multiple classes, status groups, and generations. Yet fascism is a class party, for it derives its principal support from and showers multiple rewards on a particular class.

Yet the base class does not take the initiative, nor is it allowed to do so, for only the political elite can exercise this power. Fascism requires absolute obedience to the elite in every aspect of life. From the fascist point of view, power is concentrated thus because the great bulk of the population, the mass, is irrational. Because the mass is considered to be incapable of logical thought, their freedoms, whatever they might be, are viewed as tolerable at best and dangerous at worst. For the egalitarian demogogue, if allowed full liberty, can and will play on the mass's intellectual flabbiness. From the fascist perspective, what could be more absurd than to allow freedom of the press, of speech, of assembly, and of organization. To allow freedom from unfair search and seizure to persons biologically incapable of anything more than rambling thought and capricious action *except when* driven along a straight line by the radical demagogue who instills a simplistic logic into his followers is equally absurd. Better to leave matters of political decisions to those elites who have demonstrated their intellectual abilities by seizing and retaining state power in the name of those inherently superior.

All that is expected of the mass is utter conformity to law and order. For those who deviate, there is promised destruction of property and persons.

The blood-letting seizure of state power reveals an essential quality of fascism: the celebration of violence. At the heart of fascist ideology is the notion of physiological impairment of members of the opposition. To seize state power through physical injury and death—indeed, to spill the blood of the enemy on the sacred earth the enemy has desecrated—constitutes a purge both of the enemy and of one's own soul. For the fascist, violence may be legal, illegal, or extralegal. In any event, he is relatively unconcerned about whether it is "legitimate." The term itself can only evoke a fascist smile. The fascist knows full well how the term and the legitimating processes have been abused by hypocritical conservatives, socialists, liberals, communists, as well as by themselves.

From the fascist point of view, violence should be directed by the fascist political elite against domestic traitors and foreign enemies. Violence may be expressed through open warfare, quiet purge, or celebrated assassinations. The forms are many. Whatever the devices, the essence of fascism is its cynical use of violence by a self-appointed political elite in order to obtain, maintain, and extend state power, for the dual purposes of state glorification and elite edification.

Historically, fascism quite frequently emerges during the early phases of transitional industrial societies. More often than not, a fascist regime takes a capitalist form as the society moves from heavy dependence on extractive industries to an economy rooted in heavy manufacturing and service activity. And with this transition go the vicissitudes associated with (a) the accumulation of sizable funds for investment in heavy industry, (b) the associated and brutish absorption of much of what the worker has produced for those who have made this investment, (c) the boom—bust quality of international trade and industrial employment, plus (d) the obvious inability of parliamentary institutions to deal with attendant problems.

Under these conditions, fascism becomes a political form designed to answer the problems of an ailing economy based on the production and distribution of goods and services for predictable profits.

The ailments prove to be social as well as economic. Associated with the boom—bust business cycle is the recurrent and steep decline in the normative integration of populations around institutions to which most individuals have a sense of loyalty: churches, families, schools, and the like. Again, what contributes to the decline of these organizations is their decreased ability, under conditions of recurrent economic slump, to resonate traditional values and beliefs capable of controlling the young. These failures produce anxieties within large sections of the population, especially among the middle-aged and the old.

Accompanying the decline of traditions is the growth of movements that promise new ways of restructuring society. Some movements call for the maintenance of the old social institutions. These movements are frequently fascist or fascistlike. Other movements demand institutional abolition, or drastic reform, plus economic reorganization on a scale that includes the jettisoning of capitalism.

There is a crucial distinction to be made between fascist and communist movements. The various kinds of fascist movements differ significantly among themselves on economic matters, but they have in common the purpose of obtaining the people's loyalties by calling for the retention of their families, churches, and neighborhood organizations (although left-fascism is least bound to the belief in tradition prolongation). By contrast, what appears to be most threatening to many, even the unemployed, is the communist propensity to demand the cultural revolution, at least during the period of seizure of state power. What this involves is the heralded commitment to sweep away, in the long run, all the old traditional forms, class by class, status group by status group, generation by generation. And communists, anarchists, and syndicalists do not mince words when they promise these cultural changes. This is especially true of the apocalyptic radicals.

Under conditions of economic collapse, fascism calls for a change in economy, but with the retention of tradition. For many, fascism offers the best of all possible worlds. However, fascists do not always respect all traditions, notably those of the bourgeoisie. As we intimated, this propensity is especially noticeable among the militant, left-wing fascists, many of whom are anticlerical.

FASCISM: LEFT, RIGHT, AND CENTER

Left-fascism

Fascism takes at least three forms: left, right, and center. Fascism of the left is characterized by a political elite, quite frequently young military officers, attacking the principal holders of land as well as the groups which own the heavy industry, public utilities, mines, and railroads. The intent is to nationalize or in other ways bring these industries under state control in order that the economy can serve the "shirtless ones"—the vast labor pool of unemployed and underemployed who want safe jobs, decent hours, fair pay, health insurance, and their own labor unions. Left-fascists also demand strong curbs on the giant industries since, under conditions that favor the growth of left-fascism, most industries are foreign owned. The workers do not necessarily want parliamentary forms of popularly controlled labor unions. They want results. They do not want to play with electoral procedures—the favorite pastime of some of their enemies. If the left-fascists' political leaders, their parties, and their labor unions can deliver the bread, that is enough. Indeed, to the degree that the political leader can (a) expound a declaration of war against what they perceive to be predatory capital, (b) indicate a program of redistribution of wealth, and (c) move successfully to deliver palpable results, the workers and others will come to accept these leaders as charismatic. And under conditions of left-fascism, to be charismatic is to have popular support for the wielding a great deal of state power.

Like other forms of fascism, left-fascism has certain other qualities which fail to endear it to many antifascist intellectuals. For unlike them, the left-fascists delight in publicizing their techniques of mass manipulation before proceeding to sway their audiences. There is a sense of fascist delight derived from informing the unlettered of their intellectual shortcomings before taking full advantage of these presumed weaknesses to manipulate those who are literate only in a most limited sense. Illustratively, the "quiescent dumb" are easy marks.

By contrast, the bourgeois intellectuals may well manipulate, but they do so with a sense of repugnance or they try to repress recognition of what they are doing. From the fascist point of view, these bourgeoisie engage in forms of self-delusion consistent with their essentially rational conceptions of man. And to the degree that the bourgeoisie apply their conceptions of man to themselves and to others, it appears as if the people have rationally placed in power those who consequently deserve legitimation. With considerably fewer delusions, the left-fascist (like fascists in general) believes that the state rests on myths and violence, not rationality. In keeping with his cynicism, the left-fascist passionately hates those who (a) demand respect for the alleged personal integrity of the individual but (b) also fool the masses through the espousal of self-serving formulas. Fascism derives a portion of its cynicism from this self-righteous liberal "conscience."

Left-fascism draws its principal support from the unemployed and from intellectuals who find communism distasteful because of its extreme antitraditionalism. Nonetheless, as it moves to drive the moneychangers from the temple, left-fascism circumscribes and condemns portions of the sacred. Illustrative was the Argentinian regime of Juan Perón between 1944 and 1955.

Right-fascism

Right-fascists call for the recovery of property by the landed classes. In eastern Europe, for example, the right-fascists have demanded the return of the land to its purported rightful owners: the church and the landed gentry. This economic change would sustain an institutional restoration, a return to the hierarchical estate system. In this perspective, each class-group would have a unique set of duties and privileges. Church, gentry, *haute* bourgeoisie, *petite* bourgeoisie, artisans, professionals, workers, and peasants—each would assume a particular bundle of duties.

At the heart, then, of right-fascism, is resuscitation of the old, resistance to the new, and the desire to regroup the class order, as well as its correlated mores, along traditional lines.

To the right-fascist, nothing is more distasteful than the breakup of the traditional order and its succession by a society that purports to be democratic but in fact turns out to be a mass society, i.e., the society that occurs when political elites can no longer relate to nonelites through organic community ties; rather, they depend on the mass media to bend the mass to believe that *it* is the ultimate holder of power over its governors, when in fact the mass is but a sorry object of elite manipulation. The very ascendance of the myth of popular control indicates to the right-fascist that the estates are in dissolution. When the myth joins a new mobility, the right-fascist finds new confirmations of his fears. When widespread occupational fluidity accompanies a disenchantment with traditional occupational niches, many members of the mass begin to discuss equality. This very subject irks the fascist aristocrat.

While going through these changes, many lesser persons, especially those of peasant origin, make known their doubts and criticisms of traditional morality. Uprooted from time-honored connections associated with agrarianism by the push and pull of the industrial revolution, the ex-peasants move to the cities. When they find, in the urban setting, that their old values, beliefs, and norms no longer work to solve their everyday problems of recurrent unemployment and keeping the family together, they are set adrift. From the right-fascist point of view, former peasants who have moved from a condition of community integration to considerably less become prey to anomie and to the left-wing demagogue.

Under these conditions many aristocratic elites decide that a rapid and ruthless return to the old forms is necessary. The vehicle of return must be powerful: an iron-willed leader, his own political party, a strong-arm police, total repression of leftist revolutionaries, recurrent terror visited on the liberal critics, and a policy of threatened and real violence against selected ethnic minorities. These measures should leave little doubt about where the power lies. Nor should we forget that once right-fascists have taken state power, the question of the poverty of the mass is officially sidestepped by the state, which takes great pride in discounting this matter and pointing toward the salvation of poor souls through a rejuvenated church.

God, state, and family are the celebrated essences of right-fascism. Contemporary Spain and Portugal are cases in point.

Center-fascism

Center-fascism responds to the communist threat to traditional family, state, and god by wooing the large landed interests, threatening giant capital, revamping some working-class organizations and outlawing others, while collaborating with the gentry, accepting the pecuniary support of the bourgeoisie, and improving the financial well-being of the working classes. Center-fascism is most attractive to those of the white-collar salariat who suffer during great depressions from intense competition for paying clients. Center-fascism seeks and finds considerable support among small farmers who earn diminishing incomes but who nonetheless remain loyal to the idea of individual ownership of land. Hence the farmers are personally antagonistic toward communism, with its emphasis on collective ownership of the earth. Center-fascism also gains widespread support from the small businessman.

During the incipient period of center-fascism, this mass movement obtains a significant backing from large numbers of the blue-collar unemployed who favor a ruthless reorganization of the economy, in order that their lives may be spared the personal traumas historically associated with communist reorganization of the capitalist economy, the working class, the workers' churches, and the nation-state.

Center-fascism derives considerable economic support from the bourgeoisie, not only prior to the fascists' coming to power but afterward, for these upper-class individuals view fascism as the only significant wall separating private property from an expropriating communism. Finally, even many of the gentry back center-fascism, for the landed gentry believe that the center-fascists stand as the sole force powerful enough to preserve the neofeudal forms that are threatened by both communism and democracy.

Center-fascism has stood historically for the cynical manipulation by the elite of the middle mass in order to press it to blame ethnic scapegoat minorities for the problems faced by the majority. Indeed, center-fascists delight in persecuting entrepreneurial—ethnic minorities (e.g., via Hitler's concentration camps and gas chambers). As incongruous as this may sound, the historical record is clear. Civilized capitalist societies frequently serve as the arena for blood baths. Not only are the minorities incarcerated and in many cases incinerated, but the behavior of the middle-fascist state allows the majority of nonethnic population to rationalize their indifference by pleading lack of knowledge of the state as ghoul. Since the ethnic minorities—quite frequently gypsies, Jews, Communists, and left-fascists—are forcibly and visibly yanked from the community and outrageously transported to camps, only the autistic can be allowed the luxury of credulity. Being without knowledge of these events would seem most unlikely, for after all, industrial societies are honeycombed with informal nets of communication. In turn, these nets transmit all forms of political gossip with the alacrity of West African drums.

Yet the state is able to create a weak comprehension of hideous events among those who have seen or heard of these brutalities, for the state demands and obtains from the mass nondiscussion of apprehended material. By limiting the connection between ordinary apprehension and conscious comprehension through state-enforced nonarticulation of the culturally distasteful and the personally unbecoming, the political elite is able to carry out murder and foster rationalization for this act without engendering a conscious sense of collective guilt, one which could conceivably work against the elite.

The elite is able to engage in massive physical repression in part because of the subsidence of the humane standards of the many. And these standards have declined in great measure because the moral institutions celebrated in sociological folklore cease to reinforce such moral standards under conditions of fascism, including its agitational prologue. Predictably, this moral collapse is based on survival considerations. Most institutions are in desperate need of restoring the faith of the young in order to perpetuate their organization, yet churches and equivalent organizations are usually without the pecuniary resources and popular prestige to do so. Therefore, these traditional institutions support fascist regimes by deleting or soft-pedaling a humane morality, with the reciprocal understanding that the new state will aid these faltering institutions. Time and again, universities and churches, for example, have expressed gratitude to middle-fascists through priestly, ministerial, professorial, and like professional blessings of a fascist state fully capable of subsidizing the recovery of institutional legitimacy.

With notable exceptions, these social institutions support the center-fascist party by catering to, reinforcing, and at times espousing the propaganda messages carried through the mass media dominated by the political elite. Indeed, such institutions refuse to approach center-fascists analytically for fear of fascist reproach and subsequent repression. Illustratively, there is no place for professional backing of a social science keen to dissect the state under conditions of fascism, whether left, right or center. Social scientists perceive a fascism far less interested in the scientific predictability of its own behavior than in its control of the mass. Presumably, mass control can be best realized through the unity of leadership and myth linked to the application of cynical principles of domination, legitimated by pro-fascist academicians who see fit to adapt to fascism. Illustrative would be those German professors of law and history who failed to emigrate from Germany during the 1930s, retained their posts in German universities, and rationalized the application of Nazi principles to a Europe wrecked by German military invasion. In our time, in the United States, a country whose government is in some ways similar to the middle-fascist type, we can observe the tendency of political leadership to cooperate with intellectuals in order to manipulate a mass around the principles of nationalism and needed war.

By rational standards, the manipulative techniques devised by the fascists are most incredible, for they consist of rational manipulation of subjects who are apparently susceptible to irrational appeals. During periods of massive resistance to the eighteenth-century assumptions on rationality, self-interest, and individual decision-making, critical social scientists leave fascist nations and turn toward propaganda analysis. For it is obvious that fascist political elites rely heavily on their own ability to manipulate the personal predisposition of the mass.

TRANSITIONAL REMARKS

In 1959 Seymour M. Lipset published what is perhaps the most clarifying essay written on fascism. It is a well-documented piece which for some reason has never obtained the recognition it deserves. If only for that reason, we have chosen to include it here.

Fascism–Left, Right, and Center

Seymour M. Lipset

The return of de Gaulle to power in France in 1958 following a military coup d'état was accompanied by dire predictions of the revival of fascism as a major ideological movement, and raised anew the issue of the character of different kinds of extremist movements. Much of the discussion between Marxist and non-Marxist scholars before 1945 was devoted to an analysis of fascism in power and focused on whether the Nazis or other fascist parties were actually strengthening the economic institutions of capitalism or creating a new postcapitalist social order similar to Soviet bureaucratic totalitarianism.

While an analysis of the actual behavior of parties in office is crucial to an understanding of their functional significance, the social base and ideology of any movement must also be analyzed if it is to be truly understood. A study of the social bases of different modern mass movements suggests that each major social stratum has both democratic and extremist political expressions. The extremist movements of the left, right, and center (Communism and Peronism, traditional authoritarianism, and fascism) are based primarily on the working, upper, and middle classes, respectively. The term "fascism" has been applied at one time or another to all of these varieties of extremism, but an analytical examination of the social base and ideology of each reveals their different characters.

The political and sociological analysis of modern society in terms of left, center, and right goes back to the days of the first French Republic when the delegates were seated, according to their political coloration, in a continuous semicircle from the most radical and egalitarian on the left to the most moderate and aristocratic on the right. The identification of

the left with advocacy of social reform and egalitarianism; the right, with aristocracy and conservatism, deepened as politics became defined as the clash between classes. Nineteenth-century conservatives and Marxists alike joined in the assumption that the socioeconomic cleavage is the most basic in modern society. Since democracy has become institutionalized and the conservatives' fears that universal suffrage would mean the end of private property have declined, many people have begun to argue that the analysis of politics in terms of left and right and class conflict oversimplifies and distorts reality. However, the tradition of political discourse, as well as political reality, has forced most scholars to retain these basic concepts, although other dimensions, like religious differences or regional conflicts, account for political behavior which does not follow class lines.[1]

Before 1917 extremist political movements were usually thought of as a rightist phenomenon. Those who would eliminate democracy generally sought to restore monarchy or the rule of the aristocrats. After 1917 politicians and scholars alike began to refer to both left and right extremism, i.e., Communism and fascism. In this view, extremists at either end of the political continuum develop into advocates of dictatorship, while the moderates of the center remain the defenders of democracy. This chapter will attempt to show that this is an error—that extremist ideologies and groups can be classified and analyzed in the same terms as democratic groups, i.e., right, left, and *center*. The three positions resemble their democratic parallels in both the compositions of their social bases and the contents of their appeals. While comparisons of all three positions on the democratic and extremist continuum are of intrinsic interest, this chapter concentrates on the politics of the center, the most neglected type of political extremism, and that form of "left" extremism sometimes called "fascism"—Peronism—as manifested in Argentina and Brazil.

The center position among the democratic tendencies is usually called liberalism. In Europe where it is represented by various parties like the French Radicals, the Dutch and Belgian Liberals, and others, the liberal position means: in economics—a commitment to laissez-faire ideology, a belief in the vitality of small business, and opposition to strong trade-unions; in politics—a demand for minimal government intervention and regulation; in social ideology—support of equal opportunity for achievement, opposition to aristocracy, and opposition to enforced equality of income; in culture—anticlericalism and antitraditionalism.

If we look at the supporters of the three major positions in most democratic countries, we find a fairly logical relationship between ideology and social base. The Socialist left derives its strength from manual workers and the poorer rural strata; the conservative right is backed by the rather well-to-do elements—owners of large industry and farms, the managerial and free professional strata—and those segments of the less privileged groups who have remained involved in traditionalist institutions, particularly the Church. The democratic center is backed by the middle classes, especially small businessmen, white-collar workers, and the anticlerical sections of the professional classes.

The different extremist groups have ideologies which correspond to those of their democratic counterparts. The classic fascist movements have represented the extremism of the center. Fascist ideology, though antiliberal in its glorification of the state, has been similar to liberalism in its opposition to big business, trade unions, and the socialist state. It has also resembled liberalism in its distaste for religion and other forms of traditionalism. And, as we shall see later, the social characteristics of Nazi voters in pre-Hitler Germany and Austria resembled those of the liberals much more than they did those of the conservatives.

The largest group of left extremists are the Communists, who . . . will not concern us much in this chapter. The Communists are clearly revolutionary, opposed to the dominant strata, and based on the lower classes. There is, however, another form of left extremism which, like right extremism, is often classified under the heading of fascism. This form, Peronism, largely found in poorer underdeveloped countries, appeals to the lower strata against the middle and upper classes. It differs from Communism in being nationalistic, and has usually been the creation of nationalist army officers seeking to create a more vital society by destroying the corrupt privileged strata which they believe have kept the masses in poverty, the economy underdeveloped, and the army demoralized and underpaid.

Conservative or rightist extremist movements have arisen at different periods in modern history, ranging from the Horthyites in Hungary, the Christian Social party of Dollfuss in Austria, the Stahlhelm and other nationalists in pre-Hitler Germany, and Salazar in Portugal, to the pre-1958 Gaullist movements and the monarchists in contemporary France and Italy. The right extremists are conservative, not revolutionary. They seek to change political institutions in order to preserve or restore cultural and economic ones, while extremists of the center and left seek to use political means for cultural and social revolution. The ideal of the right extremist is not a totalitarian ruler, but a monarch, or a traditionalist who acts like one. Many such movements—in Spain, Austria, Hungary, Germany, and Italy—have been explicitly monarchist, and de Gaulle returned monarchical rights and privileges to the French presidency. Not surprisingly, the supporters of these movements differ from those of the centrists; they tend to be wealthier, and—more important in terms of mass support—more religious.

"FASCISM" AND THE MIDDLE CLASS

The thesis that fascism is basically a middle-class movement representing a protest against both capitalism *and* socialism, big business *and* big unions, is far from original. Many analysts have suggested it ever since fascism and Nazism first appeared on the scene. Nearly twenty-five years ago, the economist David Saposs stated it well.

> Fascism . . . (is) the extreme expression of middle-classism or populism. . . . The basic ideology of the middle class is populism. . . . Their ideal was an independent small property-owning class consisting of merchants, mechanics, and farmers. This element . . . now designated as middle class, sponsored a system of private property,

profit, and competition on an entirely different basis from that conceived by capitalism. . . . From its very inception it opposed "big business" or what has now become known as capitalism.

Since the war the death knell of liberalism and individualism has been vociferously, albeit justly sounded. But since liberalism and individualism are of middle-class origin, it has been taken for granted that this class has also been eliminated as an effective social force. As a matter of fact, populism is now as formidable a force as it has ever been. And the middle class is more vigorously assertive than ever. . . .[2]

And although some have attributed the lower middle-class support for Nazism to the specific economic difficulties of the 1930s, the political scientist, Harold Lasswell, writing in the depths of the Depression, suggested that middle-class extremism flowed from trends inherent in capitalist industrial society which would continue to affect the middle class even if its economic position improved.

Insofar as Hitlerism is a desperation reaction of the lower middle classes, it continues a movement which began during the closing years of the nineteenth century. Materially speaking, it is not necessary to assume that the small shopkeepers, teachers, preachers, lawyers, doctors, farmers and craftsmen were worse off at the end than they had been in the middle of the century. Psychologically speaking, however, the lower middle class was increasingly overshadowed by the workers and the upper bourgeoisie, whose unions, cartels and parties took the center of the stage. The psychological impoverishment of the lower middle class precipitated emotional insecurities within the personalities of its members, thus fertilizing the ground for the various movements of mass protest through which the middle classes might revenge themselves.[3]

As the relative position of the middle class declined and its resentments against on-going social and economic trends continued, its "liberal" ideology—the support of individual rights against large-scale power—changed from that of a revolutionary class to that of a reactionary class. Once liberal doctrines had supported the *bourgeoisie* in their fight against the remnants of the feudal and monarchical order, and against the limitations demanded by mercantilist rulers and the Church. A liberal ideology opposed to Throne and Altar and favoring a limited state emerged. This ideology was not only revolutionary in political terms; it fulfilled some of the functional requirements for efficient industrialization. As Max Weber pointed out, the development of the capitalist system (which in his analysis coincides with industrialization) necessitated the abolition of artificial internal boundaries, the creation of an open international market, the establishment of law and order, and relative international peace.[4]

But the aspirations and ideology which underlay eighteenth- and nineteenth-century liberalism and populism have a different meaning and serve a different function in the advanced industrial societies of the twentieth century. Resisting large-scale organizations and the growth of state authority challenges some of the fundamental characteristics of our present society, since large industry and a strong and legitimate labor movement are necessary for a stable, modernized social structure, and government regulation and heavy taxes seem an inevitable concomitant. To be against business bureaucracies, trade unions, and state regulation is both unrealistic and to some degree irrational. As Talcott Parsons has put it, the "new negative orientation to certain primary aspects of the maturing modern social order has above all centered in the symbol of 'capitalism.' . . . The reaction against the 'ideology' of the rationalization of society is the principal aspect at least of the ideology of fascism."[5]

While continuing conflict between management and labor is an integral part of large-scale industrialism, the small businessman's desire to retain an important place for himself and his societal values is "reactionary"—not in the Marxist sense of slowing down the wheels of revolution, but from the perspective of the inherent trends of a modern industrial society. Sometimes the efforts of the small business stratum to resist or reverse the process take the form of democratic liberal movements, like the British Liberal party, the French Radicals, or the American Taft Republicans. Such movements have failed to stop the trends which their adherents oppose, and as another sociologist, Martin Trow, recently noted: "The tendencies which small businessmen fear—of concentration and centralization—proceed without interruption in depression, war and prosperity, and irrespective of what party is in power; thus they are *always* disaffected. . . ."[6] It is not surprising, therefore, that under certain conditions small businessmen turn to extremist political movements, either fascism or antiparliamentary populism, which in one way or another express contempt for parliamentary democracy. These movements answer some of the same needs as the more conventional liberal parties; they are an outlet for the stratification strains of the middle class in a mature industrial order. But while liberalism attempts to cope with the problems by legitimate social changes and "reforms" ("reforms" which would, to be sure, reverse the modernization process), fascism and populism propose to solve the problems by taking over the state and running it in a way which will restore the old middle classes' economic security and high standing in society, and at the same time reduce the power and status of big capital and big labor.

The appeal of extremist movements may also be a response by different strata of the population to the social effects of industrialization at different stages of its development. These variations are set in sharp relief by a comparison of the organized threats to the democratic process in societies at various stages of industrialization. As I have already shown, working-class extremism, whether Communist, anarchist, revolutionary socialist, or Peronist, is most commonly found in societies undergoing rapid industrialization, or in those where the process of industrialization did not result in a predominantly industrial society, like the Latin countries of southern Europe. Middle-class extremism occurs in countries characterized by both large-scale capitalism and a powerful labor movement. Right-wing extremism is most common in less developed economies, in which the traditional conservative forces linked to Throne and Altar remain strong. Since some countries, like France, Italy, or Weimar Germany, have possessed strata in all three sets of circumstances, all three types of extremist politics sometimes exist in the same country. Only the well-to-do, highly industrialized and urbanized nations seem immune to the virus, but even in the United States and Canada there is evidence

that the self-employed are somewhat disaffected.

The different political reactions of similar strata at different points in the industrialization process are clearly delineated by a comparison of the politics of certain Latin-American countries with those of Western Europe. The more well-to-do Latin-American countries today resemble Europe in the nineteenth century; they are experiencing industrial growth while their working classes are still relatively unorganized into trade unions and political parties, and reservoirs of traditional conservatism still exist in their rural populations. The growing middle class in these countries, like its nineteenth-century European counterpart, supports a democratic society by attempting to reduce the influence of the anti-capitalist traditionalists and the arbitrary power of the military.[7] To the extent that there is a social base at this stage of economic development for extremist politics, it lies not in the middle classes but in the growing, still unorganized working classes who are suffering from the tensions inherent in rapid industrialization. These workers have provided the primary base of support for the only large-scale "fascist" movements in Latin America—those of Peron in the Argentine and Vargas in Brazil. These movements, like the Communist ones with which they have sometimes been allied, appeal to the "displaced masses" of newly industrializing countries.

The real question to answer is: which strata are most "displaced" in each country? In some, it is the new working class, or the working class which was never integrated in the total society, economically or politically; in others, it is the small businessmen and other relatively independent entrepreneurs (small farm owners, provincial lawyers) who feel oppressed by the growing power and status of unionized workers and by large-scale corporate and governmental bureaucracies. In still others, it is the conservative and traditionalist elements who seek to preserve the old society from the values of socialism and liberalism. Fascist ideology in Italy, for example, arose out of an opportunistic movement which sought at various times to appeal to all three groups, and remained sufficiently amorphous to permit appeals to widely different strata, depending on national variations as to who were most "displaced."[8] Since fascist politicians have been extremely opportunistic in their efforts to secure support, such movements have often encompassed groups with conflicting interests and values, even when they primarily expressed the needs of one stratum. Hitler, a centrist extremist, won backing from conservatives who hoped to use the Nazis against the Marxist left. And conservative extremists like Franco have often been able to retain centrists among their followers without giving them control of the movement.

In the previous chapter on working-class authoritarianism I tried to specify some of the other conditions which dispose different groups and individuals to accept more readily an extremist and demonological view of the world.[9] The thesis presented there suggested that a low level of sophistication and a high degree of insecurity predispose an individual toward an extremist view of politics. Lack of sophistication is largely a product of little education and isolation from varied experiences. On these grounds, the most authoritarian segments of the middle strata should be found among the small entrepreneurs who live in small communities or on farms. These people receive relatively little formal education as compared with those in other middle-class positions; and living in rural areas or small towns usually means isolation from heterogeneous values and groups. By the same token, one would expect more middle-class extremism among the self-employed, whether rural or urban, than among white-collar workers, executives, and professionals.

The following sections bring together available data for different countries which indicate the sharp difference between the social roots of classic fascism and populism and those of right-wing movements.

GERMANY

The classic example of a revolutionary fascist party is, of course, the National Socialist Workers' party led by Adolf Hitler. For Marxian analysts, this party represented the last stage of capitalism, winning power in order to maintain capitalism's tottering institutions. Since the Nazis came to power before the days of public opinion polls, we have to rely on records of the total votes to locate their social base. If classic fascism appeals largely to the same elements as those which back liberalism, then the previous supporters of liberalism should have provided the backing for the Nazis. A look at the gross election statistics for the German Reich between 1928 and 1933 would seem to verify this (Table 18).

Although a table like this conceals changes by individuals which go against the general statistical trend, some reasonable inferences may be made. As the Nazis grew, the liberal bourgeois center parties, based on the less traditionalist elements of German society—primarily small business and white-collar workers—completely collapsed. Between 1928 and 1932 these parties lost almost 80 percent of their vote, and their proportion of the total vote dropped from a quarter to less than 3 percent. The only center party which maintained its proportionate support was the Catholic Center party whose support was reinforced by religious allegiance. The Marxist parties, the Socialists and the Communists, lost about a tenth of their percentage support, although their total vote dropped only slightly. The proportionate support of the conservatives dropped about 40 percent, much less than that of the more liberal middle-class parties.

An inspection of the shifts among the non-Marxist and non-Catholic parties suggests that the Nazis gained most heavily among the liberal middle-class parties, the former bulwarks of the Weimar Republic. Among these parties, the one which lost most heavily was the *Wirtschaftspartei*, which represented primarily small businessmen and artisans.[10] The right-wing nationalist opponent of Weimar, the German National People's party (DNVP), was the only one of the non-Marxist and non-Catholic parties to retain over half of its 1928 proportion of the total vote.

The largest drop-off in the conservative vote lay mainly in the election districts on the eastern border of Germany. The proportion of the vote obtained by the German National People's party declined by 50 percent or more between 1928 and 1932 in ten of the thirty-five election districts in Germany. Seven of these ten were border areas, including every region which fronted on the Polish corridor, and Schleswig-Holstein, fronting on the northern border. Since the party was both the most conservative and the most nationalist pre-Nazi opponent of

TABLE 18   Percentages of Total Vote Received by Various German Parties, 1928–1933, and the Percentage of the 1928 Vote Retained in the Last Free Election 1932*

Party	Percentage of Total Vote					Ratio of 1928 to Second 1932 Election Expressed as Percentage
	1928	1930	1932	1932	1933	
Conservative Party						
DNVP	14.2	7.0	5.9	8.5	8.0	60
Middle-class parties						
DVP (right liberals)	8.7	4.85	1.2	1.8	1.1	21
DDP (left liberals)	4.8	3.45	1.0	.95	.8	20
Wirtschaftspartei						
(small business)	4.5	3.9	0.4	0.3	†	7
Others	9.5	10.1	2.6	2.8	.6	29
Total proportion of middle-class vote maintained:						21
Center (Catholic)	15.4	17.6	16.7	16.2	15.0	105
Workers' parties						
SPD (Socialist)	29.8	24.5	21.6	20.4	18.3	69
KPD (Communist)	10.6	13.1	14.3	16.85	12.3	159
Total proportion of working-class vote maintained:						92
Fascist Party						
NSDAP	2.6	18.3	37.3	33.1	43.9	1277
Total proportion of increase in Fascist party vote:						1277

†The *Wirtschaftspartei* did not run any candidates in the 1933 elections.
*The basic data are presented in Samuel Pratt, *The Social Basis of Nazism and Communism in Urban Germany* (M.A. thesis, Dept. of Sociology, Michigan State University, 1948), pp. 29, 30. The same data are presented and analyzed in Karl D. Bracher, *Die Auflösung der Weimarer Republik* (Stuttgart and Düsseldorf: Ring Verlag, 1954), pp. 86–106. The 1933 election was held after Hitler had been chancellor for more than a month.

the Versailles Treaty, these data suggest that the Nazis most severely weakened the conservatives in those areas where nationalism was their greatest source of strength, while the conservatives retained most of their voters in regions which had not suffered as directly from the annexations imposed by Versailles and in which, it may be argued, the party's basic appeal was more conservative than nationalist. The German-American sociologist Rudolf Heberle has demonstrated in a detailed study of voting patterns in Schleswig-Holstein that the conservatives lost the backing of the small property owners, both urban and rural, whose counterparts in nonborder areas were most commonly liberals, while they retained the backing of the upper-strata conservatives.[11]

Some further indirect evidence that the Nazis did not appeal to the same sources as the traditional German right may be found in the data on the voting of men and women. In the 1920s and 1930s the more conservative or religious a party, the higher, in general, its feminine support. The German National People's party had more female backing than any party except the Catholic Center party. The Nazis, together with the more liberal middle-class parties and Marxist parties, received disproportionate support from men.[12]

More direct evidence for the thesis is given in Herberle's study of Schleswig-Holstein, the state in which the Nazis were strongest. In 1932

[t]he Conservatives were weakest where the Nazis were strongest and the Nazis were relatively weak where the Conservatives were strong. The correlation in 18 predominantly rural election districts between percentages of votes obtained by the NSDAP (Nazis) and by the DNVP (Conservatives) is negative (minus 189). . . . It appears that the Nazis

had in 1932 really succeeded the former liberal parties, like the *Landespartei* and Democratic party, as the preferred party among
the small farmers ... while the landlords and
big farmers were more reluctant to cast their
vote for Hitler.[13]

A more recent analysis by a German political
scientist, Günther Franz, identifying voting
trends in another state in which the Nazis were
very strong—Lower Saxony—reported similar
patterns. Franz concluded:

The majority of the National Socialist voters
came from the bourgeois center parties. The
DNVP (conservatives) had also lost votes,
but in 1932, they held the votes which they
received in 1930, and increased their total
vote in the next two elections. They were
(except for the Catholic Center) the only
bourgeois party, which had not simply collapsed before the NSDAP....[14]

This situation in Schleswig-Holstein and
Lower Saxony also existed in Germany as a
whole. Among the thirty-five electoral districts,
the rank-order correlation of the proportionate
Nazi gain with the liberal parties' loss was greater (.48) than with the conservatives' loss
(.25).[15]

Besides the liberal parties, there was one
other group of German parties, based on the
Mittelstand, whose supporters seem to have
gone over almost en masse to the Nazis—the
so-called "federalist" or regional autonomy
parties.[16] These parties objected either to the
unification of Germany or to the specific annexation of various provinces like Hesse, Lower Saxony, and Schleswig-Holstein to Prussia. In large
measure they gave voice to the objections felt
by the rural and urban middle classes of provincial areas to the increasing bureaucratization of
modern industrial society and sought to turn
the clock back by decentralizing government
authority. At first glance, the decentralist aspirations of the regional autonomy parties and the
glorification of the state inherent in fascism or
Nazism seem to reflect totally dissimilar needs
and sentiments. But in fact both the "state's
rights" ideology of the regionalists and the
Nazis' ideological antagonism to the "big"
forces of industrial society appealed to those
who felt uprooted or challenged. In their economic ideology, the regional parties expressed

sentiments similar to those voiced by the Nazis
before the latter were strong. Thus the *Schles-
wig-Holsteinische Landespartei*, which demanded "regional and cultural autonomy for
Schleswig-Holstein within Germany," wrote in
an early program:

The craftsman (artisan) has to be protected
on the one hand against capitalism, which
crushes him by means of its factories, and on
the other hand against socialism, which aims
at making him a proletarian wage-laborer. At
the same time the merchant has to be protected against capitalism in the form of the
great department stores, and the whole retail
trade against the danger of socialism.[17]

The link between regionalism as an ideology
protesting bigness and centralization, and the
direct expression of the economic self-interest
of the small businessmen may be seen in the
joining of the two largest of the regional parties, the Lower Saxon *Deutsch-Hanoverischen
Partei* and the Bavarian *Bauern und Mittelstandsbund*, into one parliamentary faction
with the *Wirtschaftspartei*, the party which explicitly defined itself as representing the small
entrepreneurs. In the 1924 elections the Bavarian regionalists and the small businessmen's party actually presented a joint electoral ticket.[18]
As Heberle points out about these parties: "The
criticism of Prussian policy ... the demand for
native civil servants, the refusal to accept Berlin
as the general center of culture, were all outlets
for a disposition which had been formed a long
time before the war. ... At bottom the criticism against Prussia was merely an expression
of a general antipathy against the social system
of industrial capitalism. ..."[19]

The appeal of the Nazis to those elements in
German society which resented the power and
culture of the large cities is also reflected in the
Nazis' success in small communities. A detailed
ecological analysis of voting in German cities
with 25,000 or more population, in 1932, indicates that *the larger the city, the smaller the
Nazi vote*. The Nazis secured less of their total
vote in cities over 25,000 in size than did any
of the other five major parties, including the
Catholic Center and the conservative DNVP.[20]
And Berlin, the great metropolis, was the only
predominantly Protestant election district in
which the Nazis received under 25 percent of

the vote in July 1932.[21] These facts sharply challenge the various interpretations of Nazism as the product of the growth of anomie and the general rootlessness of modern urban industrial society.

Examination of the shifts in patterns of German voting between 1928 and 1932 among the non-Marxist and non-Catholic parties indicates, as we have seen, that the Nazis gained disproportionately from the ranks of the center and liberal parties rather than from the conservatives, thus validating one aspect of the thesis that classic fascism appeals to the same strata as liberalism. The second part of the argument, that fascism appeals predominantly to the self-employed among the middle strata, has been supported by three separate ecological studies of German voting between 1928 and 1932. Two American sociologists, Charles Loomis and J. Allen Beegle, correlated the percentage of the Nazi vote in 1932 in communities under 10,000 in population in three states with the percentage of the labor force in specific socioeconomic classes and found that "areas in which the middle classes prevailed (as indicated by the proportion of proprietors in the population and the ratio of proprietors to laborers and salaried employees) gave increasingly larger votes to the Nazis as the economic and social crises settled on Germany."

This high correlation between Nazi vote and proprietorship holds for farm owners as well as owners of small business and industry in Schleswig-Holstein and Hanover, but not in Bavaria, a strongly Catholic area where the Nazis were relatively weak.[22] Heberle's study of Schleswig-Holstein, which analyzed all of the elections under Weimar, concluded that

> The classes particularly susceptible to Nazism were neither the rural nobility and the big farmers nor the rural proletariat, but rather the small farm proprietors, very much the rural equivalent of the lower middle class or petty bourgeoisie (*Kleinbuergertum*) which formed the backbone of the NSDAP in the cities.[23]

The sociologist Samuel Pratt's excellent study of urban voting prior to the Nazi victory related the Nazi vote in July 1932 to the proportion of the population in the "upper middle class," defined as "proprietors of small and

large establishments and executives," and to the proportion in the "lower middle class," composed of "civil servants and white-collar employees." The Nazi vote correlated highly with the proportion in both middle-class groups in different-sized cities and in different areas of the country, but the correlations with the "lower middle class" were not as consistently high and positive as those with the "upper middle." As Pratt put it: "Of the two elements of the middle class, the upper seemed to be the more thoroughly pro-Nazi."[24] The so-called upper class, however, was predominantly composed of small businessmen, so that the correlation reported is largely that of self-employed economic status with Nazi voting.[25] This interpretation is enhanced by Pratt's finding that the Nazi vote also correlated (+.6) with the proportion of business establishments with only one employee—in other words, self-employment. "This would be expected, for plants of one employee are another measure of the proprietorship class which was used in measuring the upper middle class."[26]

The occupational distribution of the membership of the Nazi party in 1933 indicates that it was largely drawn from the various urban middle-class strata, with the self-employed again being the most overrepresented (Table 19). The second most overrepresented category—domestic servants and nonagricultural

TABLE 19 The Ratio of the Percentage of Men in the Nazi Party to the Percentage in the General Population from Various Occupations, 1933*

Occupational Category	1933
Manual workers	68%
White-collar workers	169
Independents[†]	187
Officials (civil servants)	146
Peasants	60
Domestic servants, and nonagricultural family helpers	178

[†]Includes self-employed businessmen, artisans, and free professionals.

*Computed from a table in Hans Gerth, "The Nazi Party: Its Leadership and Composition," in Robert K. Merton et al., eds., *Reader in Bureaucracy* (Glencoe: The Free Press, 1952), p. 106.

family helpers—also bears witness to the party's appeal to small business, since this category is primarily composed of helpers in family-owned small businesses.

The relation of German big business to the Nazis has been a matter of considerable controversy, particularly since various Marxists have attempted to demonstrate that the movement was from the outset "fostered, nourished, maintained and subsidized by the big *bourgeoisie*, by the big landlords, financiers, and industrialists."[27] The most recent studies suggest that the opposite is true. With the exception of a few isolated individuals, German big business gave Nazism little financial support or other encouragement *until* it had risen to the status of a major party. The Nazis did begin to pick up financial backing in 1932, but in large part this backing was a result of many businesses' policy of giving money to all major parties except the Communists in order to be in their good graces. Some German industrialists probably hoped to tame the Nazis by giving them funds. On the whole, however, this group remained loyal to the conservative parties, and many gave no money to the Nazis until after the party won power.[28]

The ideal-typical Nazi voter in 1932 was a middle-class self-employed Protestant who lived either on a farm or in a small community, and who had previously voted for a centrist or regionalist political party strongly opposed to the power and influence of big business and big labor. This does not mean that most Nazi voters did not have other characteristics. Like all parties looking for an electoral majority, the Nazis tried to appeal to some degree to every large group of voters.[29] They clearly had a great deal of success with other middle-class groups, particularly the unemployed.[30] And at the low point of the Great Depression, which affected Germany more than any other industrial nation, discontent with the "system" was widespread throughout the society. However, as a movement, Nazism was most attractive to those with the characteristics summarized above.

A NOTE ON THE GERMAN NONVOTER

Perhaps the most important argument against the thesis that Nazism developed preeminently as a movement of the liberal petty bourgeoisie has been the suggestion that the major source of the first great gain in Nazi strength (between 1928 when they secured 2.6 percent of the vote and 1930 when they captured 18.3 percent of the electorate) was previous nonvoters. Between these two elections, nonvoting dropped sharply from 24.4 percent to 18 percent of the eligible electorate—a fact which has led to the conclusion that the Nazis' great gain came from the traditionally apathetic and from young first voters.[31] The most comprehensive critique of the class analysis has been that of the American sociologist Reinhard Bendix, who suggested a process of growth in which the middle class *followed* the new voters into support of Nazism:

> The importance of the newly eligible voters and of the politically apathetic casts doubt on the conception of fascism as a middle-class movement. This is not to deny that the economic insecurity of middle-class groups was important for the conquest of power as a secondary response. It is to assert rather that the radicalization of the electorate originated among the previous nonparticipants in party politics, who probably came from various social groups, and that the significant support of the totalitarian movement by members of the middle class and of other social groups occurred subsequently in the hope of relief from economic distress and in the desire to gain from backing the victorious movement.[32]

This thesis challenges the class analysis of Nazism and contradicts the generalizations about the growth of new social movements which were presented in the discussion of working-class authoritarianism in the previous chapter. This analysis suggested that the most outcast and apathetic sections of the population can be won to political action by extremist and authoritarian parties only *after* such parties have become major movements, not while they are in their period of early rise. To support a new and small movement requires a relatively complex, long-term view of the political process, which insecure, ignorant, and apathetic persons cannot sustain. This logic should apply to the Nazis as well, and a statistical analysis of the relationship between the decline in nonvoting and the growth of Nazism indicates that in fact it does.

Geiger, Bendix, and others who concluded that the Nazis derived their early backing from traditional nonvoters based this opinion on the overall election figures which showed an enormous increase of Nazi votes simultaneous with the changes in the rates of nonvoting and of the Nazi vote are broken down by districts, we actually find a small *negative* rank order correlation of -.2 between the percent increase in the Nazi vote and the increase in the proportion of the eligible electorate voting. More vividly stated, in only five of the electoral districts where the Nazi gain between 1928 and 1930 exceeded their *average* gain for all of Germany was the increase in the size of the electorate also disproportionately high. In twenty-two of the thirty-five national districts, there is a negative relationship; either the voting gain is low and the Nazi gain is high, or vice versa. The evidence on the decline in nonvoting between 1928 and 1930 thus does not challenge the class analysis of Nazism.[33]

It is true that there are reasons other than a simple inspection of changes in votes which suggest that the Nazis recruited heavily from the apathetic sector of the population. As I pointed out in the preceding chapter, those sections of the population that are normally apathetic tend to have authoritarian attitudes and values.[34] The political interests of the apathetic, however, can be awakened only by a *mass* movement which presents a *simple* extremist view of politics. The Nazis did not fit this category from 1928 to 1930; they did, however, after 1930. Those analysts who concentrated on the Nazis' presumed 1930 gain among the apathetic ignored a growth which, in fact, happened later. The largest single drop in nonvoting in Germany actually occurred in the last election of March 1933, which was held after Hitler took office as head of a coalition government. Nonvoting dropped from 19 percent in 1932 to 11 percent in 1933, a drop of 8 percentage points, while the Nazi vote increased from 33 percent to 43 percent. And if we again correlate the growth in the Nazi vote with the increase in the electorate, we find, precisely as the hypothesis demands, that the two trends show a high positive relationship (.6).

To present the result by district, in twenty-eight out of the thirty-five districts the Nazi vote gain was higher or lower than the national average gain when the increase in the voting electorate was congruently higher or lower than the national average. As a mass authoritarian party whose leader was already chancellor, the Nazi party received additional support (bringing it for the first time above the 40 percent mark) from the ranks of the antipolitical apathetics, thus paralleling the pattern of growth of leftist extremists who also recruit from the most outcast strata as they reach the status of a contender for power. . . .

NOTES

1. In spite of the complexities of French politics, the foremost students of elections in that country find that they must classify parties and alternatives along the left-right dimension. See F. Goguel, *Géographie des élections françaises de 1870 à 1951, Cahiers de la fondation nationale des sciences politiques,* No. 27 (Paris: Librairie Armand Colin, 1951).

2. David J. Saposs, "The Role of the Middle Class in Social Development: Fascism, Populism, Communism, Socialism," in *Economic Essays in Honor of Wesley Clari Mitchell* (New York: Columbia University Press, 1935), pp. 395, 397, 400. An even earlier analysis by André Siegfried, based on a detailed ecological study of voting patterns in part of France from 1871 to 1912, suggested that the petty bourgeoisie who had been considered the classic source of French democratic ideology were becoming the principal recruiting grounds for extremist movements. Siegfried pointed out that though they are

> by nature egalitarian, democratic, and envious . . . they are fearful above all of new economic conditions which threatened to eliminate them, crushed between the aggressive capitalism of the great companies and the increasing rise of the working people. They place great hopes in the Republic, and they do not cease being republican or egalitarian. But they are in that state of discontent, from which the Boulangists marshal their forces, in which reactionary demagogues see the best ground in which to agitate, and in which is born passionate resistance to certain democratic reforms. (André Siegfried, *Tableau politique de la France de l'ouest sous la troisième republique* [Paris: Librairie Armand Colin, 1913], p. 413.)

3. Harold Lasswell, "The Psychology of Hitlerism," *The Political Quarterly,* 4 (1933), p. 374.

4. See also Karl Polanyi, *The Great Transformation* (New York: Farrar and Rinehart, 1944).

5. Talcott Parsons, "Some Sociological Aspects of the Fascist Movement," in his *Essays in Sociological Theory* (Glencoe: The Free Press, 1954), pp. 133–134. Marx himself pointed out that "the small manufacturer, the small merchant, the artisan, the peasant, all fight against the (big) bourgeois, in order to protect their position as a middle class from being destroyed. They are, however, not revolutionary, but conservative. Even more, they are reactionary, they look for a

way to reverse the path of history," quoted in S. S. Nilson, "Wahlsoziologische Probleme des National-sozialismus," *Zeitschrift für die Gesamte Staatswissenschaft*, 110 (1954), p. 295.

6. Martin A. Trow, "Small Businessmen, Political Tolerance, and Support for McCarthy," *American Journal of Sociology*, 64 (1958), pp. 279–280.

7. For an analysis of the political role of the rapidly growing Latin-American middle classes see John J. Johnson, *Political Change in Latin America–The Emergence of the Middle Sectors* (Stanford: Stanford University Press, 1958). The different political propensities of a social group at successive stages of industrialization are indicated by James Bryce's comment in 1912 that "the absence of that class of small landowners which is the soundest and most stable element in the United States and in Switzerland and is equally stable, if less politically trained, in France and parts of Germany, is a grave misfortune for South and Central America." This may have been true in an early period, before the impact of large-scale organization of the farms meant economic competition for small farmers and added them to the rank of the potential supporters of fascism, as the data on Germany and other countries discussed here show. See James Bryce, *South America: Observations and Impressions* (New York: Macmillan, 1912), p. 533.

8. A comparison of the European middle class and the Argentine working class, which argues that each is most "displaced" in its respective environment, is contained in Gino Germani, *Integración política de las masas y la totalitarismo* (Buenos Aires: Colegio Libre de Estudios Superiores, 1956). See also his *Estructura social de la Argentina* (Buenos Aires: Raigal, 1955).

9. See pp. 115–120 of Chap. IV [of Lipset's book].

10. Karl D. Bracher, *Die Auflösung der Weimarer Republik* (Stuttgart and Düsseldorf: Ring Verlag, 1954), p. 94. The parliamentary delegation of this party was almost exclusively composed of businessmen who were active in the interest group associations of small business. See Sigmund Neumann, "Germany: Changing Patterns and Lasting Problems" in S. Neumann, ed., *Modern Political Parties* (Chicago: University of Chicago Press, 1956), p. 364.

11. Rudolf Heberle, *From Democracy to Nazism* (Baton Rouge: Louisiana State University Press, 1945).

12. The most comprehensive set of German election data presenting party vote in different elections by sex may be found in Maurice Duverger, *La Participation des femmes à la vie politique* (Paris: UNESCO, 1955), pp. 56–63; and Gabriele Bremme, *Die politische Rolle der Frau in Deutschland* (Göttingen: Vandenhoeck and Ruprecht, 1956), pp. 74–77, 111, 243–252; see also Heinrich Striefler, *Deutsche Wahlen in Bildern und Zahlen* (Düsseldorf: Wilhelm Hagemann, 1946), pp. 20–22; Günther Franz, *Die politishen Wahlen in Niedersachsen 1867 bis 1949* (Bremen-Horn: Walter Dorn Verlag, 1957), pp. 28–32; Karl D. Bracher, *op. cit.*, p. 476; Herbert Tingsten, *Political Behavior: Studies in Election Statistics* (London: P. S. King & Son, 1937), pp. 37–65.

13. Rudolf Heberle, *op. cit.*, pp. 113, 114, 119 (emphasis supplied).

14. Günther Franz, *op. cit.*, p. 62.

15. The six eastern border districts in which Nazi gain and conservative loss were both high account for the small positive correlation between the two. Without these six districts, the correlation is actually negative.

16. In Schleswig-Holstein, the regionalist *Landespartei* was strong in 1919 and 1921 in the same districts in which the liberal Democratic party secured its greatest vote. These were the same areas which went most heavily Nazi in the 1930s. See R. Heberle, *op. cit.*, pp. 98–100; in Lower Saxony, an examination of the vote suggests that the supporters of the *Welfen*, the Hanoverian regionalists, who were a major party in the state until 1932, went over to the Nazis. Those "middle-class and rural voting districts . . . in which the Welfen secured their largest vote, became the earliest and strongest centers of Nazism." See G. Franz, *op. cit.*, pp. 53–54, also p. 62. In Bavaria, a somewhat comparable party, the *Bayerischer Bauern und Mittelstandsbund*, dropped from 11.1 percent in 1928 to 3.3 percent in 1932. And a study of Bavarian voting patterns suggests that it, like the other regionalist parties, lost its voters predominantly to the Nazis. See Meinrad Hagman, *Der Weg ins Verhängnis, Reichstagswahlergebnisse 1919 bis 1933 besonders aus Bayern* (München; Michael Beckstein Verlag, 1946), pp. 27–28. A sympathetic analysis of the way in which an agrarian regionalist movement paved the way for Nazi electoral victory in Hesse is Eugen Schmahl, *Entwicklung der völkischen Bewegung* (Giessen: Emil Roth Verlag, 1933). This book contains an appendix which analyzes electoral shifts from 1930 to 1932 by a Nazi, Wilhelm Seipel, "Entwicklung der national-sozialistischen Bauern-bewegung in Hessen," pp. 135–167. In the elections for the provincial assembly in 1931, the Hessen Landbund's representation dropped from 14 percent to 3 percent, and the organization shortly thereafter withdrew as a political party, and made an agreement with the Nazis. *Ibid.*, pp. 163–165.

17. Cited in R. Heberle, *op. cit.*, p. 47. The *Hessische Volksbund* expressed similar sentiments in Hesse. *Ibid.*, p. 52.

18. F. A. Hermens, *Demokratie und Wahlrecht* (Paderborn: Verlag Ferdinand Schöningh, 1933), pp. 125–126; and Günther Franz, *op. cit.*, p. 53.

19. R. Heberle, *op. cit.*, p. 49.

20. Samuel A. Pratt, *op. cit.*, pp. 63, 261–266; Heberle also reports that within Schleswig-Holstein, "An analysis of election returns by communities showed a rather strong inverse correlation between the size of the community and the percentage of votes obtained by the NSDAP." R. Heberle, *op. cit.*, p. 89; Bracher, differentiating the 35 large election districts into those which were high or low in voting Nazis, found that the high Nazi districts were more rural than the low ones. This parallels Pratt's findings. See Karl A. Bracher, *op. cit.*, pp. 647–648.

21. All the studies agree that religion affected support of the Nazis *more* than any other factor. The

Nazis were weak in Catholic regions and cities, and secured majorities in many Protestant small communities.

22. Charles P. Loomis and J. Allen Beegle, "The Spread of German Nazism in Rural Areas," *American Sociological Review*, 11 (1946), pp. 729, 730. Catholic affiliation constantly overrides class or other allegiances as a major determinant of party support in practically all election data for Germany, in both the Weimar and Bonn republics. The Nazis' largest support in Bavaria and other Catholic areas came from Protestant enclaves, a fact which makes ecological analysis that does not hold religious affiliation constant relatively useless in such regions.

23. R. Heberle, *op. cit.*, p. 112; Franz also reports that in Lower Saxony, "It was the bourgeois middle-class in the cities, and the farm-owners on the land who supported the NSDAP." Günther Franz, *op. cit.*, p. 62.

24. See Samuel A. Pratt, *op. cit.*, p. 148.

25. Examination of the German census for 1933 reveals that over 90 percent of the "upper middle-class" category used by Pratt is filled by "proprietors," with only a small proportion coming from employed groups.

26. Samuel A. Pratt, *op. cit.*, p. 171.

27. R. Palme Dutt, *Fascism and Social Revolution* (New York: International Publishers, 1932), p. 80.

28. See F. Thyssen, *I Paid Hitler* (New York: Farrar and Rinehart, 1941), p. 102; Walter Gorlitz and Herbert Quint, *Hitler, Eine Biographie* (Stuttgart: Steingrubben Verlag, 1952), pp. 284, 286; Edward Norman Peterson, *Hjalmar Schacht for and against Hitler* (Boston: The Christopher Publishing House, 1954), pp. 112–117; for general discussion and documentation see also August Heinrichsbauer, *Schwerindustrie und Politik* (Essen: Verlag Glückauf, 1948); Arild Halland, *Nazismen i Tyskland* (Bergen: John Griegs Forlag, 1955); and Louis P. Lochner, *Tycoons and Tyrants, German Industry from Hitler to Adenauer* (Chicago: Henry Regnery Co., 1954).

29. An analysis of the sources of the vote for the Social Democratic party in 1930 estimated that 40 percent of the SPD voters were not manual workers, that the party was backed in that year by 25 percent of the white-collar workers, 33 percent of the lower civil servants, and 25 percent of the self-employed in artisan shops and retail business. But the core of the SPD support was employed, skilled manual workers, while the core of the Nazi strength was small owners, both urban and rural. See Hans Neisser, "Sozialstatistischen Analyse des Wahlergebnisses," *Die Arbeit*, 10 (1930), pp. 657–658.

30. Pratt reports a high positive correlation between white-collar unemployment and the Nazi vote in the cities. See S. Pratt, *op. cit.*, Chap. 8.

31. See an early statement of this view in Theodore Geiger, *Die Soziale Schichtung des Deutschen Volkes* (Stuttgart: Enke Verlag, 1932), p. 112; Heinrich Striefler, *op. cit.*, pp. 23–28; Reinhard Bendix, "Social Stratification and Political Power," in R. Bendix and S. M. Lipset, eds., *Class, Status and Power* (Glencoe: The Free Press, 1956), p. 605; Günther Franz, *op. cit.*, pp. 61–62.

32. Reinhard Bendix, *op. cit.*, p. 605. Bendix has since modified his position. See R. Bendix and S. M. Lipset, "On the Social Structure of Western Societies: Some Reflections on Comparative Analysis," *Berkeley Journal of Sociology*, 5 (1959), pp. 1–15.

33. These findings are sustained by the analysis of Loomis and Beegle. They report that in 1932, in the 59 election districts in rural Hanover, the correlation between the proportion of nonvoters and the Nazi percentage of the vote was .43. This correlation also challenges the thesis that the Nazis appealed primarily to the nonvoter. See Charles P. Loomis and J. Allen Beegle, *op. cit.*, p. 733. Both this study and an earlier one by James K. Pollock have been ignored by most of the literature in the field. pollock pointed out that

> In studying another aspect of German electoral behavior, we find little relationship between the size of the vote cast in these elections (1930–33) and the nature of the political result. . . . In these critical years in Germany, many of the urban industrial areas showed a greater electoral interest than did the agricultural areas. At the same time, this increased popular vote in the large cities as a rule was cast against Hitler, while the agricultural areas regularly showed a strong interest in him. (James K. Pollock, "An Areal Study of the German Electorate, 1930–1933," *American Political Science Review*, 38 [1944], pp. 93–94.)

34. See pp. 110–111 [of Lipset's book].

Section Three   *The Consequences of Structural Inconsistencies*

Contradictions Within Fascism
John C. Leggett

FASCIST INTERNAL CONFLICT

Fascism is anything but monolithic, and like members of any political group, fascists face real problems—especially once a group has seized state power. But the problems themselves depend to some degree on the type of fascist group in question. In this section of the chapter, we deal primarily with the principal contradictions within left, right, and center fascist governments.

Left-fascism

In the case of left-fascism, the crucial problem, one which seemingly defies ready solutions, is the conflict between an expropriating fascist state power and an international, nonfascist economic organization committed to the maintenance and extension of private property. Here we are discussing left-fascism as occupant of state power, and not left-fascism as an important unit within a general fascist movement in which power is located ultimately in center groups. In the case of Argentinian fascism, for example, the principal enemy of the Peronista ruling group was not the Soviet Union but the United States, a center of international capitalism committed to the preservation of private ownership of public utilities and public transportation, and minimal mineral exploration. These were the very sectors slated for nationalization by the Peronista government shortly after the Peronista party took power almost three decades ago. As the historical record has made abundantly clear, the U.S. State Department publicly and vociferously opposed these economic policies in general as well as the Perón government in particular.

In the case of left-fascist elements at work within an essentially center-fascist movement, the basic contradiction is the same, but its

■ This essay was prepared especially for this volume.

resolution turns on the ability of the center to use its state power to time the smashing of the left-fascists once state power has been obtained and then to absorb those deemed worthy of amalgamation. Illustrative was the way in which the German National Socialist movement included the left-fascists in the move to take state power but turned immediately toward the violent dissolution of both the left-fascist fraction and its leaders, Gregor and Otto Strasser. The year was 1934, but the decision had been made six years earlier. A lasting coalition had been struck in 1928 between Hitler and the industrialists of the Ruhr and Saar areas. Initially, this upper-class segment stood willing to pay for Hitler's private campaign train. Later—during the early 1930s and as backers of Hitler during the repeated national electoral campaigns—the captains of the coal, steel, chemical, railroad, and machine industries assumed a great part of the extraordinary expenses necessary to outbid a growing communism for the loyalties of the economically insecure. Hitler's surge to power could not have taken place without this financial backing. In effect, the wealthy industrial right-wing helped to propel Hitler into power at the very moment (1933–1934) when the Nazis were in the process of jettisoning the left wing from this center-dominated movement.

By contrast, left-fascism has never been a source of instability within state organization led by right-wing fascists. This has been true because right-fascist leaders and their movements have disallowed flirtation with socialism of any variety and hence have prevented left-fascist entry into a general social movement ultimately controlled by the right. The basis for this repugnance is clear. Right-fascism stands for restoration of stable hierarchy, whereas the left-fascist goal of state appropriation of private capital smacks of an intemperate disruption of a *modus vivendi* that has been negotiated between the right-fascist citadels—throne and altar—and foreign capital.

Center-fascism

Although left-fascism has both domestic and foreign enemies, center-fascism faces deep problems arising largely from domestic opposition. Crucial is its ongoing effort to selectively absorb members of the left-fascist group, whose symbols the center has appropriated, without losing center-fascist appeal to those both alienated from the economic practices of corporate capitalism and mesmerized by the mystical symbols associated with bygone feudal and primitive societies. For the most part, this dual problem can be handled through the creation of jobs for the unemployed and symbols of cultural resuscitation for the mass. These symbols are conveyed, as was frequently the case in Nazi Germany, through colorful ceremonies dedicated to the alleged attributes of an era in which man and community were linked through small-town *gemeinschaft* and hierarchical order.[1] At mass parades, the military both displays feudal–political differentiation and celebrates, through group recitation, the feudal kingdom of origin assigned to each military subunit. Regimental commanders bark group-province-of-origin at parade stance in response to solemn queries from political leaders. Gigantic banners sway above as the orators suggest to marching crowds their diverse, precapitalist origins. Thus through gala ceremony does center-fascism strive to reunite a population only recently divided by class origins and political catastrophes. Antithetical to alienating *gesellschaft* rationalism, the ceremony creates a new tradition by drawing on bits and pieces of the old, now redefined by the mass as sacred *gemeinschaft*, an integrated successor to the fragmented industrial order.

Once center-fascism has consolidated state power, the key contradiction becomes the inability of center fascism to continue to depend on the most rational leaders within the business and the military, people who had already proved their mettle in helping the center-fascists to take power in the first place. Charismatic leadership allows its romantic convictions on irredentism and feudal recrudescence through war to determine for itself a set of chauvinist military beliefs transcending the rational calculations of the best military strategy, given the objective conditions present. This political propensity runs contrary to the judgments of many members of the military elite and many businessmen sympathetic to a regime increasingly alienated from a business community that appears to be moved more by matters of *gesellschaft* judgment than *gemeinschaft* urge. By way of illustration, after the National Socialist party came to power—which would have been impossible without the calculated and combined support of the Rhineland industrialists and the German military elite—Hitler later disregarded many of the key judgments of these advisors on foreign policy. In 1941, for example, Hitler committed the major military error of his life. Going against the recommendations of the army high command and the German business community, and relying on an intuition informed largely by feudal myths, he decided to open a second front against a geographically expansive Russia before the Wehrmacht had finished with that little island, England. Again, Hitler's repeated attacks on the Jews forced many of Germany's most brilliant professional people to leave the country—or go to concentration camps—at the very moment (1937–1938) when the Nazi state was preparing to mobilize, presumably, all intellectual resources to make the pending war a success.

What had happened has become clear. The decisions of a charismatic demagogue were not only infused with romantic irrationality, but they violated the tenets of domestic preparedness for war. If a state hopes to win a war of the scale Hitler had in mind, it cannot (*a*) move to purge itself of a large portion of its most brilliant scientists, bankers, and businessmen, (*b*) allow its political leaders to shelve summarily the most important recommendations of highly competent military and business leaders, and (*c*) invest ultimate state power regarding foreign policy in the hands of a charismatic leader who is at times without the ability to think critically and thereby to martial warfare assumptions rationally.

Right-fascism

The crucial problem to be resolved by right-wing fascism is how to keep one foot in feudalism and the other in modernization—without attaching right-fascism to the very forces that will undo the regime. Right-wing fascism stands for the restoration of a hierarchical order rooted in land ownership and based on the sharing of state power by throne and altar. Here the military is but a sanctified extension of that throne. Were right-fascist groups able to govern a society in isolation, the preservation of that coalition would be possible.

But for better or for worse, right-fascism becomes locked into an imperial, passive role, one generally tied into capitalist relations of the most advanced, sophisticated variety. Illustrative during the 1930s were Rumania (under King Carol), Hungary (under Admiral Horthy), Poland (under Pilsudski), and Yugoslavia (ruled by King Peter)—each of these states was dependent on foreign investment, foreign loans, and other forms of support emanating from the capitalist West in order to facilitate the mining of natural resources for overseas consumption. By contrast, Portugal's fascist regime has connected its resources to regional, indeed, hemispheric military bodies, as part of a Portuguese effort to defend overseas possessions (e.g., Angola and Mozambique) and to launch military attacks against left-wing African governments, such as that of Guinea. Here right fascism plays an active role within an imperial design not of right-fascist creation.

This dependence often becomes vulnerability, for the dominant, nonfascist, capitalist state can for expedient political reasons sacrifice a right-fascist government when it is propitious to do so. As examples, take the Yalta and other World War II agreements signed by Churchill, Roosevelt, and Stalin, which made it impossible for Eastern European fascists to occupy state positions following the war. Today, should the United States opt to drop the Iberian fascists in favor of nonfascist successors, it could do so. And the change of policy would in all probability place fascist regimes at the mercy of popular democratic groups. For example, should the United States decide to withdraw all forms of military assistance from Spain and Portugal, the fascist regimes would be hard pressed to maintain overseas colonies and domestic police terror in the face of probable insurgency from workers and white-collar people, whose very roles and hence numbers have grown as a result of foreign investment.

CONCLUSIONS

In this chapter we have defined fascism in general, as well as the left, right, and center varieties, using a class analysis. Yet this approach has not disallowed the elite–mass categorization discussed in Chapter 6. As you will recall, the differentiation between elite and mass is a political distinction. By contrast, our definition of class is based on the relationship of people to work and property.

We believe that our analysis allows us to say that fascism has occurred most frequently in the countries in which the dominant property form is clear: Persons and firms manipulate land, labor, and goods to produce marketable products for profit. Still, fascism can also occur where ownership of land and exploitation of landed labor still stands as the principal social form, as is so often the case in right-fascist settings.

However we define the fascism and its milieu, it is clear that fascism has served as an alternative to communism. Yet alternatives are not the same as "identities." Although fascism may serve to perform functions that could be handled by communist regimes, the two political forms are quite different. We now address ourselves to a specification of these differences and a detailed statement on the qualities of communism in general as well as communism left, right, and center.

NOTES

1. *Gemeinschaft* has reference to the relations and culture of a community in which (a) the numbers of people interacting with one another is small, (b) the relations among these people are friendly to intimate, (c) the sense of solidarity among people is great, and (d) the population shares a common culture. Illustrative of the *gemeinschaft* community would be a Bavarian village in the sixteenth or seventeenth century. By contrast, *gesellshaft* has reference to a community in which (a) the sheer numbers of people interacting with one another is great, (b) the relations among people are in most instances impersonal and fleeting when friendly, (c) the solidarity among people is weak if not nonexistent due to the extreme competitiveness among persons, classes, status groups and generations, and (d) certain common beliefs, norms, and values may be shared by the population, but the counter-culture of subordinate classes, proletarianized ethnic groups, and alienated generations remains to challenge the common culture.

Chapter 8 Communism: Left, Right, and Center

Section One: *The Goals and Contradictions of Communism*

COMMUNISM IS DIFFERENT

In the earlier chapters we mentioned that egalitarian revolutionary movements in many ways failed to achieve their objectives. Historically, their failures have become most evident during Thermidor—the period of partial pendulum return, the stage of initial, and considerable, restoration of prerevolutionary inequities. Revolutions generally do have their Thermidors, and communist revolutions generally behave accordingly. The return of the aged and jaded has certain sources, however, some consisting of contradictions within the society undergoing revolutionary upheavals. In this chapter we emphasize those contradictions as we dwell on the communist alternative.

Before we proceed to define communism, let us reject certain half-efforts at definition.

There are those who argue that fascism and communism are the same, despite avowed differences, since both are purportedly *totalitarian:* a form of organization which *disallows the operation of associations free from the continuous coordination of the state.* The assumption is clear—only totalitarian states have this quality of state control; by contrast, the principled opposition, the democratic state, allows for full citizen participation through political parties and pressure groups generally unfettered by the state. Perhaps, the matter of *state coordination from above* could best be handled conceptually if we view it in terms of *degree* rather than *dichotomy.* For were we to consider totalitarianism in terms of degree, the empirical problem of measuring state coordination of vol-

■ Much of this chapter is based on E. H. Carr's seven-volume study of the Russian Revolution. See, especially, *The Bolshevik Revolution: 1917–23,* vol. I (London: Penguin Books, 1960).

untary associations could conceivably be solved with fewer epistemological problems and less incredulous viewers than is the case when we hew to "cold war" rhetoric on "totalitarianism." For many onlookers are tired of seeing one yardstick applied to one system and quite another device used to gauge the other. Symbolic trickery abounds. *Concentration camps for the brave* in Russia become *relocation centers for the potentially disloyal* in the United States. *Expressions for freedom* against dictatorial rule in Russia constitute *unwise actions against legitimate authority* in this country.

However, even if we were to reject the totalitarian—free dichotomization as foolish, there is still the widespread belief that both fascism and communism are extremist. In a sense, this belief is valid; both forms *will,* on occasion, violate parliamentary rules and ruthlessly expose parliamentary corruptions. The result is loss of legitimacy; that is, parliaments fail to retain the allegiance of the majority. And to take away the legitimacy of a parliament is bad—the kind of thing too frequently done by communists and fascists. Hence, from the point of view of many who favor the parliamentary system, communism and fascism are simply opposite sides of the same not necessarily desirable coin. So goes the argument.

It is true that both fascist and communist movements have long histories indicative of distrust and rejection of middle-class parliamentary forms. However, the abrasive exposures of such attitudes do not qualify communism and fascism as identical, either in theory or practice, on the vital question of people's control from the bottom up. This distinction will soon become more apparent.

When we define fascism and communism here, let us keep in mind that we are talking about the fascist and communist movements of the last one hundred years. Fascism is *elitist, chauvinist,* and *expansionist.* By contrast, communism neither uniformly adheres to these values nor necessarily behaves in accordance with these principles.

Many communist governments promote antielitism, as in the case of Yugoslavia, where workers' councils are important, although the emergence of a "new class" of party bureaucrats undermines efforts to democratize the country. Mao's thoroughgoing antielitism stood as a principal source of the Chinese Cultural Revolution [see Reading], and this insurgence must rank as one of the foremost egalitarian movements of the century. At the same time, the Chinese Communist party constitutes an elitist institution containing a leadership at best indirectly influenced by noncommunists who are viewed by many party members as objects of manipulation. China contains no grass-roots soviets which could function as assemblies of local and popular decision-making capable of checking the party leadership. Admittedly, during the Great Proletarian Cultural Revolution (1965–1970), the Chinese did establish local units of production control, but these failed to evolve into soviets capable of questioning such party decisions as inviting President Nixon to visit China.

Communist states may also be antichauvinist, in that they do not view their state as intrinsically superior. Again, a good illustration is Yugoslavia, where the state focuses less on its own glorification (e.g., than is the case in the United States or China) and more on the problems stemming from Yugoslavia's ethnic and religious divisions.

The nonexpansionist Communist regimes are legion. They include many of the lesser states, such as those of Eastern Europe, and the principal larger one, China, which is chauvinist but nonexpansionist. Yet China's political leaders are concerned with the fate of the country's traditional outer territories, the areas taken from China during the era of imperialism.[1] But

China is not irreconcilably irredentist. For all the propaganda on Chinese communist military expansion, Communist China has yet to demand and to occupy even a fraction of the areas claimed by Imperial China during the eighteenth century and subsequently taken by others over the last 150 years.

By contrast, the Soviet Union has a long history of foreign territorial aggrandizement through military occupation and subsequent control. The Russian Communists have proceeded to expand, either through the incorporation of foreign territory into the Russian state, or through prolonged Russian military occupation of foreign territory subsequently made autonomous by way of legal instruments which in no way enforce their autonomy.

Clearly then, not all Communist states are without elitism and elitists, chauvinism and chauvinists, expansionism and expansionists. All these phenomena are present in large doses in many Communist countries. But present also are powerful counterforces that have no equivalents in fascist settings. Egalitarianism and egalitarians, internationalism and internationalists, antiexpansionism and antiexpansionists—all assume legitimate places in communist theory and practice.

Taken as a whole, communist practice is mottled. Furthermore, and this point is important, this rich variety produces a multiplicity of complex contradictions between practice and theory. We will have occasion to analyze these antagonisms.

By contrast, when we deal with the distinction between practice and theory as we dissect fascism, our task is relatively simple. Fascists almost invariably practice what they preach. Their cynical philosophy places fewer altruistic demands on them, although fascists must also resolve certain discrepancies between theory and practice, as we observed in the Section Three of Chapter 7.

Precisely because communist theory rejects fascist cynicism and opts for utopian altruism, its definition appears intriguing. On a theoretical and general level, communism's goals[2] are compelling.

---

[1] The military sally into the Himalayan border regions of northern India in 1959 did in fact help the Chinese state to redefine the geographical boundaries of a Chinese nation prior to British incursions into the Tibetan area during the middle and late nineteenth century.

[2] Here I am referring to the goals of communism as a *general* social movement, while admitting that *specific* Communist movements often adopt principles discrepant with these purposes. The general social

1. Public ownership of society's strategic resources and their management by either the people themselves or their representatives.

2. The carefully planned allocation of technology is a way that permits the use, preservation, and extension of man's strategic resources.

3. An interrelation of economic organization and technology that serves to maximize human happiness and to eliminate man's alienation from work, self, and others.

4. The ending of private property, despoliation of the environment, and man's unhappiness, to coincide with the redistribution of income, creating total economic equality in perpetuity.

5. A division of labor such that a person could rotate from job to job according to a weekly, monthly, or yearly round. The people would determine this division, which serves to benefit society and to end alienation.

6. The cessation of the use of currency in the long haul, and hence the departure of a mechanism for facilitating the accumulation of private wealth by the few at the expense of the many.

7. The elimination of supply-and-demand considerations as the key determinants of price for objects produced.

8. The end of prostitution and the realization of sexual equality in the workplace through an integrated division of labor.

9. A division of labor that will both end poverty and guarantee succeeding levels of prosperity for everyone.

10. The creation of lasting peace, through the elimination of economic insecurity, poverty, alienation from work, and exploitation of man; with the disappearance of these evils go the bases for the continuation of class struggles, invidious status distinctions, generational inequities, state repressions, and associated wars.

11. The subsequent withering away of the state, which becomes unnecessary once the class contradictions that foster both civil war at home and warfare abroad have disappeared.

12. The creation of successors to the repressive state, new forms characterized by man's control over his own organizations, be they (a) trade unions maintained during the transitional

movement I have in mind is the one we associate with the last 100, or perhaps 150, years.

period into communism, (b) peoples' political councils organized to obtain and to retain state power during the revolution, as well as (c) workers' councils modeled after the decentralized structures established by workmen and manned by Parisian workers during the Commune (1871). Communist goals, then, *do* include grass-roots control; in this sense, communism and syndicalism[3] are inextricable.

13. The dismantling of all the institutions that have traditionally organized peoples' lives within a hierarchy; organized religion and the traditional family are clearly earmarked by communist principles for early and rapid demise once the revolutionaries have captured state power, for both institutions work against the realization of personal and group potential.

14. The realization of equality in *all* relationships.

These are the noble goals of communism. Altogether, it has stood for government ownership of a society's strategic resources and the people's control of the pace and content of work, all directed toward the creation of economic equality in perpetuity. The presence of representative assemblies directed and controlled by the people, with all the rights of free, unfettered expression, is assumed. What can we say of the practices? The disparities between the nineteenth-century postulations on the beautiful and the twentieth-century realities can best be analyzed by making a distinction between communism, *left, right*, and *center*. For when we consider these three forms, we can confront (a) the range of contradictions *within* each model and (b) the full panoply of antagonistic relations *among* varieties of communism.

THREE TYPES OF COMMUNISM

Briefly, *left-communism* stands for the full realization of communism through a perennial revolution in which left-communists are ascendant. This form of collective insurgence has reference to unrelenting warfare against all in-

[3] Syndicalism has stood for worker's control of the place of work and of the items produced, in a society where the state had ceased to exist and where the workers' control units, representing workers in each industry, actually ran both the work places *and* the nonwork milieu of the entire society.

equality. A perennial revolution is always intense, and at times, much blood is shed. The Chinese Communist revolution has assumed this bloody character over much of the last 50 years, certainly for large chunks of time between 1965 and 1970.

Right-communism views as inevitable the emergence of a communist ruling class which successfully legitimates wide spans of rewards in every conceivable sector. Illustrative of right-communism is the Russian experience during and since the dictatorship of Stalin.

Unlike the left and right varieties, *center*-communism is less a full-blown ideology or a crystallized practice than a *fleeting setting* in which revolutionary groups attempt to resolve the flagrant contradictions within the society, whether moving from left-right communism, or just the opposite.

LEFT-COMMUNISM

If we examine left-communism as a specific social movement in its narrowest sense, we can observe that it calls for (*a*) the near-immediate liberation of mankind from exploitation, and (*b*) the simultaneous creation of equality, freedom, and justice in perpetuity through continuous struggle. In a broader sense, left-communism acts to realize *without compromise* the fourteen points just cited. Not too surprisingly, a disproportionately large number of its supporters are *apocalyptic radicals,* although many left-radicals turn out to be either *deliberate radicals* or an admixture of the two types.

The apocalyptic radicals provide the fury, the fire, and the energy for total goal realization. Yet few goals are met. In the process of attempting to achieve utopia, especially during the early years of the revolution, the left-communists find themselves stymied by a series of virtually uncontrollable cross-tugging forces. We shall refer to these contradictions as (a) the state—movement antagonism, (b) the efficiency—syndicalist contradiction, and (c) the struggle—justice dilemma. In addition, there are lesser contradictions, turning on such questions as public ownership of the means of production.

In examining these contradictions, we rely on the distinctions already made in our discussion of the sociology of revolution, emphasizing the unexpected outcomes that become most apparent during Thermidor.

The state—movement conflict

One of the most obvious contradictions that arises between communist theory and practice, is the *state—movement antagonism.* It appears most sharply immediately after the radicals have taken state power.

Shortly after the revolutionary state emerges, the new *state* officials strive to maximize the political security of the revolutionary state through the creation of amicable relations with foreign, nonrevolutionary states. Hemispheric revolutionary wars are ended. Treaties are signed. Trade ties are resumed. Diplomatic relations are restored. Amenities are observed. Simultaneously, and understandably enough, the left-revolutionary *movement* elsewhere begins to attack *the very nonrevolutionary states which are in the process of negotiating stable diplomatic relations* with the revolutionary state. Thus we see that *goals of traditional interstate relations* are inconsistent with *the subverting activities of the revolutionary movement.*

The revolutionary force calls for the immediate sweeping away of many cultural forms, bureaucratic states, and capitalist economic forms. Illustrative are the recent actions taken by the Chinese state to normalize relations with the counterrevolutionary governments of West Pakistan and Ceylon at the very moment when *movement* left-revolutionaries in these countries, many of them self-styled but nonetheless genuine Maoists, are seeking aid from a Chinese state. However, the state is apparently unwilling to act on the basis of revolutionary commitments held by many movement people living *in* China. The net result has been devastating for the revolutionary movement in South Asia, such as the one in Bangladesh. For with Chinese state support of governments hostile to revolutionaries, the South Asian left-communist peasants and intellectuals are slaughtered whenever they launch an offensive against their respective states. The Chinese state thereby both aids the governments which Communist theory condemns and simultaneously refuses to give military and other forms of aid to Maoist revolutionaries under devastating counterguerrilla attack.

To say the least, this contradiction weakens

the revolutionary left, for only with inconsistency can a state presumed to be revolutionary support the behavior just described. Moreover, contradictory actions by the revolutionary state's diplomatic corps abroad can have serious effects on the work of overseas agents dispatched by the revolutionary home country. Espionage and propaganda efforts can become confused, or they may be neutralized or even hampered by the state–movement antagonism just discussed.

THE SYNDICALIST–EFFICIENCY CONTRADICTION

Within the "revolutionary homeland," the effort to achieve and to maintain economic equality in perpetuity runs smack into the need to recover prerevolutionary levels of production in order to achieve immediately the standard of living of the *ancien régime* for the *lower classes.* If in a flurry to meet these standards the revolutionary state decides to eschew collective moral commitment as the basis for pressing producers to produce, the new regime has no choice but to rely on *individual* wage incentives as the way to maximize economic efficiency and hence high levels of productivity. But individual motivation to promote self-interest through material gain is but part of the old moral order, whose full restoration, presumably to build socialism, does in fact serve to forge a morality in keeping with the restoration of presocialist structural forms.

For the left-communists, the return to individual incentives is a political disaster. How does this return come about? Soon after the seizure of state power, the underlying basis of collective and equal rewards (i.e., worker's councils) declines precipitously. On occasion this happens because of working-class ineptness. Nothing is so successful in discrediting the left-communist policy of allowing workers to determine matters of pace and quality of production as the workers' own technical ineptness and gassy sloganeering under conditions of techno-economic breakdown and the inability of the left to lead a revival of the economy. Products don't get produced. Or when they do, they are of shoddy quality. Under these conditions of economic malaise, the left's influence declines because its ineptness has robbed it of legitimacy within councils of the revolutionary state. Then

the stage is set for the right-moving revolutionary government to fall back on individualized pecuniary motivations—which have survived the period of war communism—to change the economic machine. Motivations of individuals do not wither after several years or decades of socialism; rather they find new forms and become hardened to justify new spans of rewards remarkably similar to those of the old regime.

Unless this contradiction between efficiency and syndicalism is resolved through the creation of equal wage rates rooted in worker's councils the contradiction itself promotes civil war within the revolutionized society. And during this period of intense internecine warfare, there is little room for freedom. (In a positive sense, freedom means group creation of those structures which will permit the full realization of group, and hence individual, potential. In a negative sense, freedom has reference to the absence of those state structures which might throttle group and hence individual creativity, even when such activity would benefit the larger collective with respect to economic efficiency alone.)

Time and again, under conditions of near or actual civil war within a communist society, political leaders prove to be unable to distinguish between fruitful nonantagonistic contradictions (between people found in the same utopian camp) and harmful *antagonistic contradictions* (among those who are either for or against the revolution). The leadership then imposes constraints on discussion and thus freedom is denied.

The struggle–justice contradiction

Under conditions of civil war, the violations of the spirit of both equality and freedom prove consistent with *the Paucity of Justice.* This is a negative phenomenon. Individuals receive unfair treatment from the state as it attacks the individual under conditions of civil war and absence of freedom, for the radical state has discovered that it cannot maintain even rudimentary practices of justice. The revolutionary state has no choice, since those seeking justice include the very ones who would use *just* procedures against the new revolutionary regime by favoring the return of exploitative and repressive forms. Here we should lay our cards on the table, even though our comments may insult certain well-meaning defenders of human rights. The enemies of revolution might take advantage of just procedures in order to create a time interval during which they would subvert everything invented by revolutionaries at such a great expense to the people. Yet, the elimination of just procedures for these counterrevolutionaries, even as a temporary expedient, may lead to the abolition of those egalitarian practices recently obtained at such cost.

LESSER ANTAGONISMS

What to do? In part because of the dilemmas involved, left-communists vacillate and lose their momentum. This loss of surge gives the right-communists the time they need to move for the realization of their alternatives. And right-communism is often able to do so, in good measure because of the prolongation of contradictions faced by a left-communism unable to solve problems. The first ten years of the Russian Revolution offer cases in point (variations on the Russian experience abound) to help us tentatively construct generalizations pertinent to our understanding of contradictions:

1. *On Public Ownership:* The left-communists hold that nationalization of industry is but the "first step." The second major move consists of the reaffirmation and extension of workers' control on matters of pace and content of work. Yet it is workers' control which falters, sometimes because the workers fail in their technical assignments; or because, when they succeed in solving the complex technical tasks, right-communism smashes the workers' control effort in the name of the greater efficiency, or because of the need to encourage an unabrasive relationship with major holders of private capital who have been allowed to remain on a temporary basis for purposes of expediency.

2. *Rational Control of Technology:* Left-communism usually reaches its apogee of influence when declaring the need for the rational, grass-roots control of technology *at the very historical moment* when revolution, civil war, and external intervention have destroyed most of the society's technology and associated material artifacts (e.g., the streets, water pipes, sewers, power stations, and railroads). Left-communists frequently find it impossible to apply their creative ideas about technology on a sustained basis because the period of potential experimentation is marked by the need to spend on urgent repairs the scarce *funds* which, under other circumstances, could have fostered technological innovation and covered the waste associated with collective creativity.

3. *The Interrelation of Economic Organization to Technology:* When much of the traditional labor force is at the military front and the remainder too frequently flounder in their efforts to maintain both workers' control and sufficient urban and rural production to stay alive, conditions are not conducive to *the best possible interrelation between workers' councils and their tools of work.* Thus friendly observers never get a chance to determine the true merit of this interlock. Still, for a short historical interval, workers do manage their own work places. In Russia from 1917 to 1919 and in Spain (most notably Barcelona between the summer of 1936 and the spring of 1937) workers controlled the content and set the pace of work. There was a noticeable decline in alienation from work, an increase in positive conceptions of self, and a surge in the incidence of spontaneous relations with others.

4. *The Elimination of Private Property, Despoliation of the Habitat and Man's Unhappiness, to Coincide with the Creation of Income Equality in Perpetuity:* The left-communists seize private property but are initially unable to restore the old balance of nature, let alone create a new one, precisely because of the ravages of war. By contrast, during civil war, under conditions of massive physical deprivation partly alleviated through egalitarian sharing, the ideal of income equality approaches realization. Sharing through barter becomes widespread because of the worthlessness of the currency.

Ironically enough, at the very moment when the revolution might conceivably begin to focus on the reshaping of environment, the revolutionary political party moves to the right and asks for high levels of production. The new emphasis occurs at the expense of the physical environment and the widespread belief in pecuniary equality. Lost, too, is the idea of motivating workers on the basis of something other than maximization of individual self-interest through production for personal material gain. The result is clear: Skilled workers within an industry begin to earn considerably more money than nonskilled workers.

5. *The Rotational Division of Labor:* This form is precluded by the exigencies of civil war. Because of a sort of revolutionary spin-off, people who might rotate often wind up dead on the battlefield. Whole sections of the division of labor become victims of the vicissitudes of a shifting battlefront. The very continuation of the revolutionary struggle under conditions of high casualty rates becomes dependent on the 24-hour-a-day commitment of persons who are *not* interchangeable. Their casualties are high, as are the pressures mounted by counterrevolution. In Russia, this high level of revolutionary pressure continued almost unabated for nearly *four* years.

6. *The Elimination of Currency:* The all but total devaluation of currency during the civil war is followed by currency resuscitation shortly at the end of the holocaust. Currency resumption coincides with the initiation of payment for services on the basis of a point system attuned to individual motivation. The revolutionary government adopts this dual practice in order to maximize material production by playing on the traditional desire to get ahead through hard work. Much to the chagrin of left-communists, currency resumption helps to create an ideology fully in keeping with the values of non-left-communists as well as overseas counterrevolutionaries.

7. *The Elimination of Supply-and-Demand Considerations as the Key Determinants of Prices for Objects Produced:* To a degree, the left-communists favor and obtain allocations of goods on the basis of fixed prices and communal sharing. But precisely because needed commodities are in short supply while the demand is great, the hiatus between supply and demand fosters the illegal marketing of goods and the predictable forming of two parallel markets: (a) one *egalitarian–legal,* but with few things to sell, (b) the other, *private–illegal,* with a plentitude of goods for those who can afford to pay. This duality remains for a considerable period, i.e., until the right-communists become ascendant, as was the case in the Russian Revolution, and institutionalize the private sector as legal.

8. *Sexual Discrimination:* Left-communists have certainly taken the lead on the abolition of sexual discrimination. They have enjoyed their greatest successes during the period of war communism, the moment of military struggle associated with the radicals coming to power and attempting to retain the reins of the state. Even then, however, women have occupied power positions in numbers out of proportion to their actual strength, both in the general population and in the revolutionary ranks. Relative to right-communists, left-communists are sexually egalitarian. Relative to absolute standards of proportions, left-communists still suffer from the inherent sexism of both capitalism and its offspring, the general revolutionary movement. But even the few left-communist women find their ranks thinned by the normal, attritional forces of revolution and counterrevolution.

Female champions of women's liberation assume primary and secondary leadership positions in the larger liberation group. But precisely because this group often suffers extensive and lasting defeats both before and during the Thermodorean reaction, the women's movement experiences enormous defeats through loss of leadership. Still, during the period of war communism and for a considerable time thereafter, women are in a better position than before the revolution to take full advantage of utopian egalitarian formulations on sex. For example, women can move into a labor force depleted of men who have gone to the front to fight. The state can then justify widespread recruitment of women into all ranks of labor on the basis of both *egalitarian ideology* and *economic need.* Together these reasons are enough to answer traditional critics.

9. *The End of Poverty.* In coming to power, liberation warfare destroys much of the technoeconomic organization of the society. Consequently, a crippled economy faces a grim task of realizing the goals of equality and prosperity. Obviously, the economic sector cannot fully meet these goals. In the place of the elimination of poverty and the creation of prosperity, there develops a practice of sharing scarce provisions under conditions of civil war and foreign encirclement and attack.

Following the period of successful defense of the revolution against domestic and foreign foes, the cameraderie of egalitarianism gives way to a recovery successor. Right-communists introduce sharp wage differentials to create greater productivity aimed, over the long haul, at fostering preconditions for a plentitude that will abolish the need for built-in earning differentials since people will be able to take what they want. Needless to say, this plan never works, for plentitude has no upward limit.

Once the pattern of inequality has been set, only an internal rebellion or revolution can eliminate a gross span of rewards. However, inequality will return even after a successful uprising against right-communism, unless the left-communists pursue a policy of continuous elimination of all indications and sources of inequality that proves impossible.

10. *The Creation of Lasting Peace.* The left-communists fail to achieve a lasting peace in part because the price of revolutionary success consists of recurrently tested revolutionary vigilance. In order to survive, indeed, in order for revolutionary practices to remain, left-communists must fight. They must face up to, and deal successfully with, domestic and foreign enemies. Since this struggle is over control, ownership, and the use of billions of dollars of strategic resources, a seeming revolutionary victor can never be certain of staying in power until his opponents have been vanquished and their resources seized. There is ample structural push for the settlement of differences through bloodshed. Unfortunately for the left-communists, they seldom have sufficient human resources to sustain a prolonged struggle. For military casualties, disease, and an accelerated life-pace nibble away over the years at the small number of first-rate revolutionary cadre, whereas in most instances the new recruits to the left fail to bring with them the revolutionary élan of the older reds. What this shrinkage means for the left-communists and world peace is fairly clear. Because of the decline in strength of left-communism and the ascendance of the right-wing brand, the left-communists face endless defeats. Although they seem to be able to survive their failures, the regressive episodes do, of course, facilitate the continuation of right-communist *repression* and *exploitation,* phenomena whose attenuation, let alone elimination, can only be achieved through recurrent warfare—and hence the absence of a lasting peace.

11. *The Withering Away of the State.* The record is clear. The state does not wither. In fact, in order to fight for survival during the period of war communism, the left has no choice but to strengthen the state. Ironically, the sections of the left itself often advance proposals in favor of concentrating power in fewer political units during the period of war communism. Once power has been concentrated and centralized, these conditions remain. Indeed, both are extended by those who seize on a mood of Thermidorean reaction *against* radicalism in general and *for* efficiency in particular. This technocratic triumph locks the goal of efficiency into the creation of increased state services, structures, personnel and, hence, organizational growth. For many, the *burgeoning* of this bureaucracy becomes in some odd way a measure of the success of the very things bureaucratic personnel were hired to achieve. The means thereby become an end, as professionals redefine the goals of the revolution to coincide with the practice of professional expertise. Insofar as the goal of communism is concerned, the technocrats stress the need to recruit, train, and use professional persons motivated to serve socialism on the basis of their own aggrandizement, i.e., the foreseeable acquisition of personal earnings greater than those rewarded to the seemingly less deserving, or ordinary workers.

What emerges then, is a *socialist* acceptance of a functional perspective on stratification. People are supposedly rewarded on the basis of the relative value of their work tasks, with the right-communist leadership making decisions on this matter. This functional view of social stratification thereby comes to rest on a group of technocrats presumably in the service of the egalitarian goals of the revolution. But their very elitism, on the levels of both ideology and practice, is inconsistent with the egalitarian goals of the revolution. To the degree that the left-communists become aware of these inconsistencies and struggle to eliminate them and convert their perpetrators, to that degree do left-communists stand a chance of containing those powerful forces pressing for the victory of right-wing communists. In Russia, the left-communists lost that fight. In China, the battle continues with Lin Piao one of the casualties.

12. *The Creation of Successors to the Repressive State:* In order that left-communists and the remainder of the people can gain control over their lives, they must fight a revolu-

tion. But *if the reds are to win,* the red military forces must concentrate and centralize all planning on the allocation and use of strategic resources. To the degree that trade unions, workers' councils, and soviet assemblies take scattered and uncoordinated actions that impede the successful implementation of the strategies of the red army and its party leadership, these decisions, even though they represent democratically obtained expressions from below, may upset red military planning. And obviously, the failure of a crucial plan could mean the immediate end of the revolution. Given the propensity of the red military commanders to foresee such potential developments and to plan to coordinate all relevant populations accordingly, we should not be surprised when red militia units move to usurp the power of the trade unions and equivalent grass-roots groups. Once this power is taken away—no matter what good intentions were held by the military (e.g., military expediency demands this undesirable, supposedly short-term suspension)—any basis for subsequent rejuvenation of these bodies may have been annihilated.

13. *The Dismantling of Traditional Social Institutions, Especially the Church and the Family:* During the period of war communism, the left-communists take the lead in attacking both organized religion and the traditional family. Churches are sacked, priests publicly defrocked, church lands are confiscated, religious ideologies are lampooned, and icons are divested of their sacredness as money-fetching attractions; the left-communist atheists pursue a continuous field day. The family suffers a similar but less evident fate.

Parallel to the swamping of the church, the family, too, is "flooded," and norms of family behavior are suspended. To fight the revolutionary war, the state ruthlessly allocates family resources. Of these, the most important is flesh. It wages wars, builds munitions, transports them, and so on, under conditions of forced and extreme geographical shifts of large sections of the total population. Consequently, family groups are separated. Women assume revolutionary roles hitherto assigned only to men. The young lead military units, reversing the traditional seniority-based authority structure. Marriage is often set aside, as free love blossoms and simple separations are agreed to.

The love juice *does* flow among those who are truly about to die.

Both the church and the family as institutions generally survive the throes of war communism, largely because of the political victory of those who favor the creation of socialism in one country. During Thermidor, the revolution's leaders struggle over whether (a) to *extend the revolution and make it world wide, even if this strategy may mean the end of the revolutionary center,* or (b) *to consolidate power at home and attempt to build socialism in one country.*

Generally, when the second alternative wins, its proponents have triumphed on the basis of a nationalist appeal designed to reach all sectors of the population, irrespective of past and present political biases, and including a fragmented and badly battered church. The church accepts a compromise, loyal support to the new communist state, as the basis for its continuation under ultimate control of right-communists. In turn they believe that a church group can be used by the revolutionary party in the short haul, and that in the long run the church will disappear because it can no longer maintain a parasitic relationship with any of the classes previously beholden to the church. What the right-communists fail to realize is that investing the church with a new function can breathe new life into an entity that had seemingly lost its traditional ideology and service relationships. The very resuscitation of the church allows it once more to disseminate prerevolutionary, traditional ideology on such matters as the sacred interconnectedness of church, state, and family. For tactical reasons, right-communists generally prove willing to allow the revival of this function, and others, later on.

And the family? Blessed now by a revived church, the family also becomes an item of revolutionary consolidation in the eyes of practical communists.

The family is viewed correctly and historically by many as a vehicle of retention for every counterrevolutionary idea that can be imagined. Yet the family is useful to reds. The revolutionary state discovers during the Thermidorean period that the family constitutes the only *organization* which can provide continuity in the lives of hundreds of thousands of wandering children. Frequently bereft of parents, shelter, and sustenance, children are sorrowful casualties of revolutionary war. All efforts to restore order into the lives of these orphans by associating them with revolutionary encampments—child-care homes, and the like—fail. The kids refuse to stick to state-sponsored vocational schools, relocation centers, and special nurseries. Often diseased and almost always improperly fed, the children move aimlessly across the landscape. They wander. And families sooner or later adopt them. In effect, the family sustains most of them by providing a continuity in affection if not in material sustenance. Because of the conservatizing influence of the family, this spontaneous adoption is discouraged initially by nearly all communists. Only later do the right-communists accept the institution of the family as a permanent part of the communist state.

Right-communism's acceptance of the family parallels the redefinition of the family as the principal creator and accumulator of personal material gain. The family thereby becomes the vehicle for rejuvenating the very goals of private, unequal gain whose realization goes against the essence of communism, namely, its emphasis on community accumulation and sharing.

Generally, the left loses, and its defeat coincides with the triumph of *right-communism. Its* very essence is elitism, which in turn stands as a negation of egalitarianism. In all areas, including ethnicity and race, there emerges a communist-sponsored hierarchy. What becomes apparent, what crystallizes from the seeming morass of fighting among communists, as well as between them and their enemies, is a series of pecking orders. Revolutionary comradeship gives way to ranked tiers. And their appearance signals the demise of the revolution.

But such may not be the case. For the very failure of the revolution may well help to create the partial basis for another armed insurgence. The term "well" is here used advisedly, for there is nothing automatic about successful revolutionary insurgence. As we observed in Chapters 3 and 4, the winning conditions and processes are many and delicately interwoven.

TRANSITIONAL REMARKS

In this chapter's reading, Wheelwright and McFarlane comment on the overriding problems of incentives and controls within a country containing many communists committed to left-egalitarianism. In that sense, we can not overlook the pertinence of recent China (1970). After this reading, we will return to a major question: social stratification under the conditions of Chinese communism.

Section Two *A Reading on Communist China and the Span of Rewards*

Moral Incentives

E. L. Wheelwright
Bruce McFarlane

The success of most non-material incentives depends on the participant's outlook. Thus, non-material incentives by themselves may not work effectively unless they are accompanied by effective political indoctrination and education. Such propaganda is aimed at heightening personal awareness, putting a particular campaign or drive in proper perspective, and making its technical requisites clear ... They rest on the grounds that greater productivity or product derives mainly from (1) the desire to excel and surpass other individuals and groups—an individual and group competitive motive; and (2) the inclination to do better because of one's strong and close identification with the group—a social or co-operative drive, the opposite of alienation. *. . . .* The manner in which co-operative incentives appear to operate is not inconsistent with what contemporary social psychological theory prescribes for increasing productivity. *The success for operation of certain types of group decision making, criticism, and goal-oriented mass movements is predicated on fundamental psychological needs being met. The individual's need for affection, for a sense of being included in important affairs, and for feeling some control or influence over events which shape his life may be positively carried out through some or all of these co-operative incentives. (Italics added.)*[1]

THE GROWTH OF MORAL INCENTIVES

In the Soviet Union and Eastern Europe it is now taken for granted that the spur of the collectivist interest is insufficient to build a socialist society. Any motivation that does not harness the personal advantage of the individual is dismissed as romanticism. The trend is to seek a shedding of "primitive" socialist ideals, and to realize industrialization through the use of the management techniques and material stimuli associated with the advanced technology originally developed by capitalism.

Such views have never assumed full command among Chinese Communists, despite the operation of joint State-private firms and the New Economic Policy period of 1961-1964. Had not Mao said in the pre-1945 articles, "Serve the People" and "In Memory of Norman Bethune," that an egotistical competitive morality is inferior to working selflessly for the common good? Had not Mao, writing in 1945, said that revolutionaries should "proceed in all

■ Taken from E. L. Wheelwright and Bruce McFarlane, *The Chinese Road to Socialism* (New York: Monthly Review Press, 1970) 143–169. Copyright © 1970 by E. L. Wheelwright and Bruce McFarlane; reprinted by permission of Monthly Review Press.

cases from the interests of the people and not from one's self interest or from the interests of a small group"?[2]

And in 1949, Mao spoke of the danger to the Revolution of the "sugar-coated bullets" of the bourgeoisie—selfishness, bureaucratic arrogance—and urged cadres to "remain modest, prudent and free from arrogance in their style of work," and to "preserve the style of plain living and hard struggle."[3]

In the 1950s the case for moral or ideological incentives was again stressed. A major work, first published in the *People's Daily* on November 29, 1956, pointed out: "Once we have the right system, the main question is whether we can make the right use of it; whether we have the right policies and right methods and style of work. Without this, even under a good system it is still possible for people to commit serious mistakes and to use a good state apparatus to do evil things . . . the task of the communist party and the state is, by relying on the masses and the collective, to make timely re-adjustments in the various links of the economic and political systems."[4]

The publication of Mao Tse-tung's *On the Correct Handling of Contradictions Among the People*, in 1957, marked an even stronger swing toward harnessing moral incentives. In fact, it would be no exaggeration to say that the seeds of the Maoist position in the later Cultural Revolution are to be found in this work, notably in the analysis of the transition period to communism, and in the view that rebellion is justified if it serves the masses. Especially notable was the discussion of problems arising from "contradictions among the interests of the state, the interests of the collective and the interests of the individual, between democracy and centralizing, between the leadership and the led";[5] and the advocacy of a style of economic and political life which involved "stamping out bureaucracy, greatly improving ideological and political education and dealing with all contradictions properly."[6]

Moral incentives had reached their highest postwar peak in 1958 during the Great Leap Forward—a period, incidentally, when Maoism was in full control of the country's affairs. The Water Conservatism Campaign was built on moral rather than material incentives; the idea of sharing things in common, irrespective of the individual's contribution, made progress in the communes. The August 1958 Resolution spoke of the need to promote "the social consciousness and morality of the whole people to a higher degree," to institute universal education and "to break down the differences between workers and peasants"; and later in 1958, shipbuilding workers in Shanghai abolished the systems of bonuses and piecework.[7] All of these became central motifs again during the Cultural Revolution.[8]

Despite the growth of spontaneous market forces and of capitalist farming after 1959, an undercurrent of the Maoist moral incentives policy remained. We referred earlier to the Learn from Lei Feng Movement and the Socialist Education Movement of 1963. In that year the Chinese Communists, in their "Proposal Concerning the General Line of the International Communist Movement," warned that "For decades or even longer periods after socialist industrialisation and agricultural collectivisation, it will be impossible to say that any socialist country will be free from . . . bourgeois hangers-on, parasites, speculators, swindlers, idlers, hooligans and embezzlers of state funds; or to say that a socialist country will no longer need to perform or to be able to relinquish the task

laid down by Lenin of conquering this contagion, this plague, this ulcer that socialism has inherited from capitalism."[9] In 1964 the Learn from Tachai and Taching Campaigns were appeals to moral incentives, and in the same year an official publication criticized Soviet practice for "substituting material incentives for the socialist principle" and for "widening the gap between the incomes of a small minority and those of the peasant workers, peasants and ordinary intellectuals."[10] It went on to ask: "Is our society today thoroughly clean? No it is not. Classes and class struggle remain. We still have speculative activities by old and new bourgeois elements and desperate forays by embezzlers, grafters and degenerates . . . the socialist revolution on the economic front is insufficient by itself and cannot be consolidated. There must be a thorough socialist revolution on the political and ideological fronts."[11]

All of these developments indicate that despite contradiction between the practice of certain segments of the population and some State organs, and the ideology of the Revolution, a key component of that ideology—moral incentives—not only survived but was able to burgeon in the Cultural Revolution launched in 1966. This tremendous emphasis on moral incentives increasingly affected not only management, industrialization, and organization, but the nature of Chinese life itself, especially through Mao's "latest instructions," to which we have referred previously and to which we shall return for a discussion of their *operational* role. Especially important was the part played by the injunction to "fight self," as a central component of the Cultural Revolution which, as Mao said in March 1967, "touches people to their very souls and aims at solving the problem of their world outlook."

Many of these "instructions" of 1967–1968 may seem trite to the outside observer. But their enormous importance is obvious to any visitor, as they appear on virtually every wall, machine, and loom in the country. Moreover, "If this be madness, there is method in it." It is not an idle boast when Peking publications speak of Mao's "great strategic plan." The plain fact is that at each crucial point in the struggles after 1964, he supplied advice to the revolutionaries supporting his line. Following one upon another, these "instructions" constituted a coherent strategy of political attack, political struggle, and political advance. The basis of the whole approach is the view that revolution is not a thing or an institution: it is an experience, an act of will. Mao rejects the view that there is an inevitable historical movement from primitive communism through slavery, feudalism, and capitalism to socialism and communism. On the contrary, he holds that revolution and collectivism are *not* inevitable, that centralist bureaucratic exercises in social engineering can emerge, and that a once socialist country can revert to capitalism. To intervene in these developments, to remove them, it is necessary to establish the idea of revolutionary activity in the sense of audacious human will. As a key article written at the height of the Cultural Revolution put it: "Man's social being determines his thinking. But thinking in turn plays a great active role, or under certain conditions, a decisive role, in the development of the politics and economy of a given society. . . . In what does the old ideology of the exploiting classes lie? It lies essentially in self-interest—the natural soil for the growing of capitalism. This explains why it is necessary to start a great political and ideological revolution. It is a revolution to remould people to their very souls, to revolutionise their thinking. That is why in the course of this revolution we must 'fight self.' "[12]

WHY MORAL INCENTIVES?

From the standpoint of economics, the Maoist emphasis on moral incentives has been justified on a number of counts. Basically Mao denies that the growth of the economy is simply a function of physical investment and technical progress. He claims that there is a missing link in this equation—human motivation; increasingly his strategy has been based on the promotion of the human factor in economic development.

This diagnosis of growth is shared by a number of economists in other countries. Colin Clark, for example, holds that "While investment in capital is undoubtedly necessary for economic growth, it is certainly not the controlling or predominant factor. Economists are not yet in a position to analyse this matter fully; but we can say that the principal factors in economic growth are not physical—natural

resources and invested capital—but human."[13] Earlier "growth models" which assumed that capital is the leading factor in growth are being replaced, even in the West, with the view that organization and skills are to be regarded as an independent parameter which exerts a growing influence on the rate of economic growth.[14]

Another rediscovery of Western economics in recent years is "learning by doing" and its contribution to growth. This is most certainly a proposition that is in the full Maoist tradition, but even this has been embraced by serious Western students of economic development. According to two British economists, "Investment benefits productivity largely because it provides opportunities for learning new methods,"[15] while "Learning theories show economies of scale from learning, quite different from the indivisibilities etc. of traditional economic theory."[16]

All of this has tremendous implications for the *style of* economic management. Earlier industrialization was associated with a system of management which gave managers of enterprises extremely autocratic powers of control. Mao sees this and wants to avoid it. On the level of society as a whole, he considers that Eastern European countries have merely organized socialism as one giant industrial concern, with all power to the technocrats, or (as in Yugoslavia) to an alleged class of bureaucrat-capitalists.

China may be able to profit as a "latecomer" to industrialization by giving more scope to the new *kind* of industrialization—automation and cybernetics—which requires more self-management, and less of the technocratic control implied by the mass-production-line factory; but this remains to be seen. However, if the "new industrial revolution" is introduced into China, people will have been better prepared for it than has ever been the case previously.[17] For as even the Czech Academy of Science has noted: "Everything depends on whether socialism succeeds in working out a system of *civilisation regulators*, of means and rules for adjusting the economic, and also the social, political, psychological and cultural conditions for promoting man's creative abilities and directing his interests to socialism. Modelling economic motivation, moulding the socialist style of life, stimulating democratic initiative, cultivating the collective reason—all these forms of indirect management also imply developing the actual *subject* in society, unfolding and reinforcing the subjectivity of sectors of management that meet the needs of transition to the scientific and technological revolution."[18] It is hard to see Maoist strategists disagreeing with this diagnosis. And there is surely justification for the Maoist emphasis on a high proportion of moral incentives in the amalgam of material-moral stimuli on which any economy depends. For even the Czechs, arch advocates of financial reward and more inequality in income spreads, admit that:

> We have abolished capitalist property and thereby paralysed the former driving force of the economic self-movement. This negation, however, has not by itself created any higher stimuli and forms of movement of the economic development, it has not brought into being a particular socialist system with a universal spirit of enterprise. The negation has merely transferred the direction of the whole economy to the centre which under these conditions had to succumb to bureaucratisation and subjectivism. Outside the centre this has led to a lack of interest and irresponsibility.[19]

In terms of the motivation of economic behavior, this is the crux of the matter, for self-interest and material gain *are* the driving force of the capitalist system. The same motivations cannot continue to be the driving force of a socialist system; they must be replaced by others. If they are not, a basic contradiction results, caused by the continued coexistence of motivation based on individual material advancement, operating within the framework of a collectivist ethos and institutions. In such a contradiction something must eventually give way—either the motivation of individual material advancement, or the collectivist ethos and institutions. The Czechs are here pointing out that no attempt has been made in their case to resolve this contradiction; the expedient adopted has been a bureaucratic direction from the top downward. Thus, socialism has become bureaucratized, inefficient, and inhuman—hence the lack of response and effort, and the development of dissident groups whose opposition takes the form of opposing both bureaucracy and socialism, which become equated.

In an attempt to get out of the morass, emphasis is placed on a return to the material incentives and individual interest and advancement of the previous social order. In the last analysis, Mao's argument boils down to this: one cannot have a stable socialist society operating with the motivations of a capitalist society; if the motivations are not changed sooner or later there will be a reversion to a form of capitalism, for the old values of the old society will reassert themselves, helped by influences from outside on both the élite and dissident groups.

Maoists then may be said to have challenged not only the *morality*, but also the economics and the psychology of monetary incentives as a motor driving the economy. From the *sociological* point of view, Maoist strategy also makes a good deal of sense, premised as it is on similar fears that have been expressed by anthropologists and sociologists about the consequences, in economically backward countries, of the emergence of a great gulf between senior élite groups of specialists and political leaders, and the mass of peasants. Many of the old assumptions of anthropology are being challenged by the "new" anthropology,[20] for instance, the explanation of economic backwardness in terms of values and psychological characteristics of the native population; the assumption that it is desirable to avoid rapid, disruptive changes;[21] and the assumption that the main process by which economic development occurs is diffusion from an industrial center.[22] Nor is Mao the only revolutionary thinker to have challenged the orthodox view that the historical jump from presocialist to socialist forms comes about only by an increase in social wealth as a result of the "rationalization" process imposed on laborers by industry; or to note that this "rational" method of developing society conflicts with the self-realization of the individual.[23]

The Maoist approach, like that of many sociologists, is to discover why the masses have lost the power to direct their own lives in society. Why, even in collectivist societies, is it possible for man to be separated from his product, as a result of the centralized political and bureaucratic control of production engendered by a technological society, in which life is regulated by machines? Mao uses moral incentives as an essentially practical way of getting people to take a more active part in deciding how their material creations are to be used, and how to arrange their social lives without subordinating the mass to the élite. Hence the continued emphasis on the line of "from the masses—to the masses" as the normal style of political work of all in positions of authority.

Sociologists also increasingly realize that "The ability of forms of life to adapt to a great variety of conditions, frequently under the greatest handicaps, in order to survive, grow and function, suggests a mode of creativity." [24] This means that "Moral problems may have potentially, at least, a practical or technological solution . . . moral rules develop where there are no clearly defined technological patterns of instrumental activity, where the usual rules of living break down, or where individuals and societies are left on their own to structure actions deemed proper." [25] Mao has had to build on the fractured society left by the Chinese Civil War; it is no wonder then, that he has analyzed the "nonantagonistic" contradictions between people, and between people and State, in the transition period to the socialist society he wishes to see emerge in China. If he permits the continuance of some older Chinese moral values, it may be because he realizes, as some sociologists do, that "To ignore the existing structure of value facts is to operate in a vacuum, and to do so would be to make decision illusory and unrealistic." [26] Thus he both recognizes the continuing influence of older moral incentives and the need to give them a new direction. As a recent Maoist article put it: "Confucius died more than 2000 years ago. But his thinking still stubbornly spreads to corrupt people's minds and influence public opinion in society . . . the proletariat must vigorously create revolutionary public opinion, launch a large scale ideological revolution in which hundreds of millions of people take part." [27]

The direction of change Mao seeks, then, is to promote moral incentives within the framework of Marxism-Leninism as he interprets it. These incentives are the utopian ones of Marxism-Leninism, which are being used to break down older values and reorient them. Thus, for example, the reference above to Confucian thought corrupting people's minds and influencing public opinion in society relates to the fact that the Confucian system was based on

respect for and obedience to authority of the rulers, whether in the form of the head of the extended family, the emperor, or the officials or organs of the State. This has had a profound influence on the thinking of the Chinese people about the role of the State. As Hegel pointed out: "The morality of the State is not of the ethical kind in which one's own conviction bears sway; this latter is rather the peculiarity of the modern time, while the true Antique morality is based on the principle of abiding by one's duty to the State at large." [28] Related to this is the Chinese tradition that any group which isolates itself from the State and takes its own path is considered a conspiracy and is suppressed. For that reason the progressive minority cannot risk an experiment in the hope that others will follow if it is successful. The minority favoring a renewed system must seize power and impose its will on the majority by force. [29]

To combat this problem, Mao has often said that "the minority is sometimes right" and "it is right to rebel." This call to revolt issued to youth in the Cultural Revolution is, as Han Suyin points out, totally against the tradition of Confucian China, but Confucius was also repudiated in a previous period of cultural and political ferment, between 1890 and 1919. [30] This also explains Mao's apparent willingness to permit the shattering of the old Party apparatus during the Cultural Revolution, as well as the great stress he places on the new education system, under which contact between people—especially between intellectuals and peasants—should replace contact between people and State organs. On State organs, Mao said in April 1968 that "The most fundamental principle in the reform of state organs is that they must keep in contact with the masses." In 1968 the big campaign began to send youth and intellectuals to the countryside, and a series of Mao's latest "instructions" were issued to this effect, while at the same time other "directives" enjoined the working class to visit the schools. [31] This reduces people's *vertical* dependence on State and Party, and increases their *dependence* on each other in developing ideology and moral incentives.

This strategy may be seen from a number of different viewpoints. Some will see merely Mao's yearning for a return to the spirit and methods of the prewar period in the "red" base at Yenan. Others will see it as a way of bringing into national life the creative experience of the masses, and not merely the empiricism of planners and top officials. The Chinese are fond of quoting Lenin's point that "Practical experience is ten times more valuable than a conceited Communist who is ready at any time of the day or night to write theses. Less intellectualist and bureaucratic conceit, more study of what our practical experience reveals is what science can give us."[32] Mao rephrased this when he said in 1968 that "We communists seek not official posts, but revolution," just as in 1967 he said that "People do different types of work at various posts, but no matter how high-ranking an official anyone is, he should be like an ordinary worker among the people. It is absolutely impermissible for him to put on airs."

Assuming that such moral exhortations are intended to take on an operational character, the role of *consciousness* is understandable. It helps to show people that there is a "correct" solution to problems where practical experience is combined with correct theory. This also reflects the firmly held Chinese Communist belief that, in the Soviet Union, consciousness is not trusted—that individual, selfish material incentives have already replaced the "correct" policy of exchanging ideas and experiences in the collective. They believe there has been a soviet counterrevolution in economic administration, and the restoration of a bureaucratic manipulation of the economy through selfishness campaigns. The Chinese operational principle of "fight self, fight self-interest" provides the counterstrategy to the rising of a similar development in China. Hence the stress on the need to use moral incentives, not only to handle the contradictions that inevitably arise between the economic base and the superstructure, but also to release the "mind-forged manacles" which otherwise would retard the rapid expansion of the forces of production. What Maoists claim for their Great Proletarian Cultural Revolution is, essentially, that they have been able to overcome, by a principled combination of unity and struggle, the tendencies gravitating toward capitalism and/or bureaucratic management and control.

A final motivation for the moral factor stress is to show the relevance of socialist morality to other economically poor countries, to underline the practical possibilities of socialism here and now for Asia, Africa, and Latin America. As Gurley puts it:

> The Maoists have pulled the peasant from the muck of ignorance and poverty. Listen to us, the Maoists whisper,—"first enrich the people and you will enrich yourself." But the peasant with an eye on his private plot also has an ear for the song of the "revisionists": "first enrich yourself and you will then enrich the people." In which appeal, I wonder, lies the greater hope for the world's poor?[33]

The Maoist view, then, is that the role of consciousness, even in underdeveloped countries, permits individuals to leap across whole historical epochs of thought, even if not consistently, and to adopt, on the whole, the morality of communism. Such individuals in the revolutionary movements within the "third world" in fact constitute a "mass" which form enclaves within colonial and postcolonial societies. This line of thought also aims to break the hegemony of Soviet ideology over underdeveloped countries. From the Maoist viewpoint the Chinese Revolution broke more than a material structure of power; it also broke an intellectual stranglehold, which had impeded many revolutionaries and socialists from achieving a correct appraisal of the balance of social forces in their own countries, and led them to misdirect their political and organizational tactics. Mao Tsetung consolidated creative Marxism by basing the Chinese Revolution on new assumptions. No longer could theorists of revolution in the West or the Soviet Union claim theoretical and practical preeminence.

FEATURES OF MORAL INCENTIVES

As shown in the previous chapter, Chinese economic strategy has sought a mixture of economic decentralization and ideological unity, the latter being exercised by the use of the "little red book" of quotations, the "three constantly read articles," Mao's poetry, and his "latest instructions." The centralizing force in this has been the Cultural Revolution Group around Mao, and the revolutionary committees which are under his strong influence.

Before ideological unity, however, there was ideological struggle. We have already emphasized the role played by Mao's work, *On the Correct Handling of Contradictions Among the People,* of 1957, as the most cogent analysis of the need for ideological struggle. Later, after 1965, Liu Shao-chi was opposed by the Maoists with the allegation that his theories and policies did not fit in with the "fight self" approach and a collectivist way of life. Putting it more crudely, the ideological fundamentalists supporting Chairman Mao Tse-tung, who were prepared to sacrifice specialization and large scale market efficiency for the ideal of building a selfless nation, were opposed by hard-headed technocrats who had their supporters not only in the State organs, but within the Party itself.

Specifically, the criticism made of those aspects of Liu Shao-chi's approach which tended to block the "fight self" strategy were as follows:

1. His "seventy points" charter for industry excluded workers' control and the hegemony of "politics in command," by putting material incentives first, or "bonuses in command," so that industrialization would be achieved purely through running the economy by economic methods.

2. In agriculture, his *"san zi yi bao"* policy had released the forces of kulakism and capitalism.

3. In the agricultural brigades he put work points in command instead of voluntary public service.

4. Like Bukharin, he argued that class struggle in China would die away as socialism in China won more victories.

5. He denied that "political work is the lifeblood of economic work," as taught by Mao.

6. He upheld the maintenance of Party discipline and unity as an absolute principle, in opposition to the Maoist view that "the minority is often right."

A second feature of the drive for moral incentives, and one which follows from the criticisms of Liu Shao-chi, is the rejection of the notion that in each country, at every point of time, there is a "correct" amalgam of material and moral incentives. Rather, under the system of socialist social property, the responsibility of working communities and collectives is to participate in both the labor process and decision making, in a way that is both positive and unified. People must have the right to self-management and the obligations stemming from it. One of these is the need for a "unified State plan"—the unity of a new right and a duty which ensures against economic and other relationships turning into a conflict of rights, and therefore also ensures against socialist society becoming a competitive commercialized market and small-holder community of the old type, which would be even more irresponsible as a result of being freed from the check put on it by the risk faced by the owner of private capital.

Many commentators have seen the "personality cult" as a main feature of moral incentives. Certainly there is a tremendous emphasis on Mao's contribution. The Peasant Revolts of 1921, 1925, and 1927, as well as many other activities, are attributed to him personally. The idea behind this seems to be somewhat as follows. The will to struggle already exists. Mao Tse-tung's thought can concentrate that will. But in order to concentrate it, there must exist an instrument, as well as people who analyze society, analyze reality, who see the road taken by the economy, the forces that direct the economy, and at the same time the masses' state of spirit, capacity, resolution, and combative will. Analysis, experiment, the drawing of conclusions, the organization of programs cannot be done without an instrument—of such a character that it is linked to the life of the masses. Such an instrument, say the Maoists, is Marxism and, in particular, Marxism in the current epoch as set out by Mao Tse-tung.

Here we come up against the problem of "charismatic bureaucracy" and its role. As Seligman notes:

> The great man influences society only when society is ready for him. If society is not ready for him, he is called, not a great man, but a visionary or a failure. He is great because he visualizes more truly than anyone else the fundamental tendencies of the community in which his lot is cast, and because he expresses more successfully than others the real spirit of the age. . . .
> History is full of examples where nations, like individuals, have acted unselfishly and

have followed the generous promptings of the higher life. . . .

The content of the conception of morality is a social product; amid the complex social influences that are operated to produce it, the economic factors have been of chief significance . . . pure ethical or religious idealism has made itself felt only within the limitations of existing economic conditions.

Unless the social conditions, however, are ripe for change, the demands of the ethical reform will be fruitless.[34]

The "charismatic bureaucrat" is both a product of his times and an agent of change. But also, as Weber noted,[35] charisma tends to transform itself ("routinize itself," as Weber said) in order to serve as a durable base for a political order. The usual way this occurs is for charisma to attach itself to the office and not to the person, or for an hereditary line to develop. In either case, the charismatic bureaucracy is replaced by a legal-rational one.

Mao Tse-tung has attempted to counter this in two ways (apart from developing moral incentives which promote his own ideology). In the first place, by his big character poster entitled "Bombard the Headquarters," and his campaign against Liu Shao-chi, he has robbed the "office" of President of its charisma. Second, he has handled the Cultural Revolution in such a way that no personal struggle for succession will follow his death. The aim is to give the succession to a party interested in serving rather than ruling the people; authority has been given to the broad masses, not to the administration.

Nor can Mao's regime be regarded as a legal-rational bureaucracy in Marx's sense: "Bureaucracy is a circle no one can leave. Its hierarchy is a hierarchy of information. The top entrusts the lower circles with an insight into details, while the lower circles entrust the top with an insight into what is universal, and thus they both deceive each other."[36] No account of Chinese government or Party conduct resembles this picture.

ASSESSMENTS

A number of Western economists and sociologists reject the view that moral incentives can play a predominant role in a modern economy, pointing to the emergence of black markets and incentive-lags during periods of war, or arguing that people in underdeveloped countries are actually interested in the idea of maximum gains.[37] To a large extent this reflects the methodology of looking at Asian societies through the prism of a Western economic theory designed for a completely different institutional setting. . . . Surely it is a more commonsense view to say that a country like China sets up the institutions to achieve its own goals; that the functions capitalists perform in the West are absent; and that various new ways of managing the economy are being tried.

The other main source of doubt about the genuineness of the use of moral incentives emanates from the Soviet Union. Soviet theoreticians assess the Cultural Revolution in terms of Chinese tradition,[38] and little else. Their idea is that Mao has simply become the focus of age-old chiliastic religious fervor, based on the hope that a leader will appear to "raise his fist in the name of harmony and justice"—and that this has been the psychological background of countless Chinese uprisings. Maoism is not even explained as "petty-bourgeois" socialism of the peasant type, and is openly attacked as bringing less peasant democracy than did Sun Yat-sen.[39]

However, Marxism itself has always contained two elements. One of these is its appeal to the "jacquerie" [a French term for rising of the peasantry, especially in 1357–1358, in France] its romanticism and appeal to communal living, revolution, and brotherhood. This aspect of Marxism has always had a big impact on people living in predominantly precapitalist forms of society (Russia in 1917, China, Cuba). The second element is the emphasis on raising the level of productive forces through industrialization. The first of these two elements has been very strong at various times; certainly it is not an insignificant strand of Marxist-Leninist thought. One does not, therefore, need to explain the Cultural Revolution in terms of "Chinese tradition"; it is in the mainstream of Marxism itself.

There are two difficulties in analyzing the role of the moral factor, however. We have to distinguish what Maoists are trying to achieve by this method, and what they have actually implemented. This requires a close study of individual plants and institutions. . . . The second difficulty concerns the basis on which the myriads of moral incentives are constructed. To work effectively these incentives must provide a totality of experience, and people will have to come to "Maoist" conclusions for themselves, from their own existence. Moral incentives need to function as a technique for promoting creative effort. It is not a question, then, of teaching the people the Maoist ideology, but of the Chinese people learning a certain *way* of reasoning things out, and a way of fitting in their activities with society's goals.

NOTES

1. Charles Hoffman in *An Economic Profile of Mainland China* (New York: Praeger, 1968), pp. 488, 491.

2. Mao Tse-tung, "On Coalition Government," *Selected Works* (Peking: Foreign Languages Press, 1961), Vol. III, p. 315.

3. Mao Tse-tung, "Report to the Second Plenary Session of the 7th Central Committee of the C.P.C." March 5, 1949; reprinted in *Peking Review*, November 29, 1968.

4. *More on the Historical Experiences of the Dictatorship of the Proletariat* (Peking: 1957), p. 17.

5. Mao Tse-tung, *On the Correct Handling of Contradictions Among the People* (Peking: Foreign Languages Press, 1967), pp. 3-12.

6. *Ibid.*, pp. 45-46.

7. Reported in *Chieh Fang Ji Pai* (Shanghai), October 19, 1958; see SCMP, No. 1947.

8. Even the use of big character posters to air individual viewpoints and make suggestions and criticisms in factories, villages, and shops was not invented during the Cultural Revolution—but was part of the "mass line" in 1958 and 1959, and was described in M. Shapiro, "China's First Ten Years," *Marxism Today*, October 1959.

9. *A Proposal Concerning the General Use of the International Communist Movement*, March 30, 1963 (Peking: 1963), p. 37.

10. *On Khrushchev's Phoney Communism and Its Historical Lessons for the World*, July 14, 1964 (Peking: 1964), p. 27.

11. *Ibid.*, pp. 63-64.

12. "Fight Self, Repudiate Revisionism Is the Fundamental Principle of the Great Proletarian Cultural Revolution," *People's Daily*, October 6, 1967; reprinted in *Long Live Victory of the Great Cultural Revolution* (Peking: 1968), pp. 41-48.

13. Colin Clark, *Growthmanship: A Study in the Mythology of Investment* (London: Barrie and Rockliff, 1961), p. 13.

14. R. M. Solow, "Technical Change and the Aggregate Production Function," *Review of Economics and Statistics*, August 1957.

15. R. T. Hahn and R. C. O. Matthews, "The Theory of Economic Growth," *Survey of Economic Theory* (London: Royal Economic Society, 1967), p. 69.

16. *Ibid.*, p. 67.

17. This view is disputed by economists and sociologists in Eastern Europe and the Soviet Union. The Czechs argue that the "human factor" becomes crucial only "above a certain level of civilization." See Richta *et al.*, *Civilisation at the Crossroads: Report of the Czechoslovak Academy of Sciences* (Sydney: 1968), p. 15 n. A Russian writer holds that communes "possess only primitive means of production. Simple reproduction proceeds laboriously, labour productivity is extremely low, and economic activity and the entire life of the community bears the stamp of seclusion. . . . History has not given us an example of communal forms of ownership, which are a survival of the clan system, being able to engender a socialist society." V. Afanasyev, *Scientific Communism* (Moscow: 1967), p. 174. This last is a rather obvious thrust at the Chinese communes and the Chinese "road" to socialism.

18. Richta *et al.*, *Civilization at the Crossroads*, p. 203.

19. R. Richta, "Models of Socialism," *Rude Pravo*, July 11, 1968.

20. K. Gough, "Anthropology—Child of Imperialism," *Monthly Review*, April 1968, p. 20.

21. Claude Levi-Strauss, *Structural Anthropology* (New York: Basic Books, 1963), Ch. 16.

22. *Ibid.*, pp. 330-333.

23. H. Marcuse, *Soviet Marxism: A Critical Analysis* (New York: Columbia University Press, 1961), p. 20.

24. Paul Kurtz, *Decision and the Condition of Man* (Seattle: University of Washington Press, 1965), p. 56.

25. *Ibid.*, p. 260.

26. *Ibid.*, p. 244.

27. Hsieh Sheng-wen, "Great Struggle in a Great Era," *Peking Review*, March 28, 1969.

28. G. W. F. Hegel, *Philosophy of History*, J. Sibree, trans. (New York: Wiley Book Company, 1944), p. 41.

29. L. Kyuzayhyon, *The Chinese Crisis, Causes and Character* (Moscow: 1967), p. 26.

30. Han Suyin, *China in the Year 2001* (New York: Basic Books, 1967), pp. 27, 165.

31. See the Appendix [of Wheelwright and McFarlane's book] for "latest instructions" on the need for the educated to visit the countryside and the working class to visit the schools. By March 1969, 25 million people or 15 percent of the urban population had visited the countryside for ideological exchanges (*Australian Financial Review*, April 2, 1969). Incidentally, such appeals to educated youth to visit the Chinese masses, and to struggle to find ideas which would enable China to survive, were pursued by Mao's foremost Marxist forerunner, Li Ta-chao, in a series of articles in *New Youth*, in 1917-1920. Impressed by the Populist Movement in late nineteenth-century Russia, Li Ta-chao urged young intellectuals to go out and awaken the laboring classes, claiming that the peasantry would be the base of revolution in China.

32. V. I. Lenin, "The Single Plan," *Pravda*, February 22, 1921; see *Selected Works* (New York: International Publishers, 1935–1938), Vol. II.

33. John G. Gurley, "The Economic Development

of Communist China" (Stanford University, mimeographed).

34. E. R. A. Seligman, *The Economic Interpretation of History* (New York: Columbia University Press, 1902), pp. 31, 97, 126.

35. Max Weber, *The Theory of Social and Economic Organization*, T. Parsons, ed. (New York: Oxford, 1947), p. 328 ff. In fact Weber did not attempt to prove that newer or more recent eruptions of charisma will always be increasingly institutionalized along legal-rational lines. He merely assumed this to be true because it was the historical trend.

36. Karl Marx, "Critique of Hegel's Philosophy of the State," 1843, *Writings of the Young Marx on Philosophy and Society*, L. D. Easton and K. H. Guddat, eds. (Garden City, New York: Doubleday, 1967), pp. 185-186.

37. Harry G. Johnson, *Money, Trade and Economic Growth* (Cambridge: Harvard University Press, 1966), p. 157.

38. Kyuzayhyon, *The Chinese Crisis*, pp. 17-24.

39. *Ibid.*, p. 24.

Section Three   *New Bottle, Old Content?*

Is Social Stratification Inevitable Under Conditions of Communism?

John C. Leggett

There are those who would argue that the very developmental sequence of revolution both creates new inequalities and removes any possibility of their elimination. Please note: A basic distinction is made between the creation of inequalities and their long-term retention. We will argue that although the sociology of revolution is characterized by a step-by-step movement away from the old inequalities through a period of egalitarianism into a new social stratification system, there nonetheless exists the possibility of revolution from below against the new social stratification system. But then, such a rejuvenation may be both unwise and unnecessary.

There are those who argue that for any society to survive it must perform certain functions, generally the following: (*a*) the production of goods and services for the community, (*b*) the distribution and exchange of the things produced, (*c*) the social and political control of those involved in the production and distribution of resources, and (*d*) the physical reproduction of persons to staff the division of labor, fill the instructional slots, and guide the state.

■ This essay was prepared especially for this volume.

To fill important societal positions, the society must be organized to motivate persons to want to fill the more important roles in the system.

Every system contains a division of labor, which can be analyzed in terms of roles. Roles differ in terms of the amount of skills invested in their performance—clearly some require more skills than others. When roles demand high skill levels, we judge them to be functionally more important than those requiring fewer skills, since the replacement of the skilled individuals by others who are also skilled is more difficult than replacing the unskilled by similar others. The replacement of the skilled is most difficult, since the skilled are in relatively scarce supply because of the unequal distribution of talent.

But even when the intrinsically bright ones are present, they do not automatically acquire occupational vocations. The relatively bright must be induced by the system to defer gratifications and to opt for a period of training during which they will learn the dexterity, finesse, and flexibility involved in the jobs they are being prepared for. The society can accomplish this if it offers these talented persons foreseeable and very positive rewards, including predictable earnings and such ancillary prerequisites as pleasure in performing work tasks.

Once the society has successfully originated a system of education and differentiated rewards, all social institutions tend to legitimate this tiered reward system. And for good reason. Without a system of social stratification, society would be unable to generate and maintain a division of labor. People can anticipate this alternative, and to forego predictable chaos, they must create and legitimate a span of rewards that is absolutely adaptive for everyone.

It will be remembered that this argument applies not only to capitalist countries but to socialist ones as well. In 1920–1921, the Russian Bolsheviks realized that the four basic functions already mentioned were not being realized on a day-to-day basis. Goods were not being produced in sufficient quantity, distributed to persons in need, and allocated with the predictability necessary. The whole economic network was in fact a shambles. Indeed, Russia's population may well have been failing to reproduce itself. After four years of revolution, civil war, and struggle with foreign invaders, the Soviet Union had become an economic mess. To deal with this problem, the Russian Communist leadership did forsake the use of moral incentives and did opt for work–income differentiation to motivate people at their jobs. Especially did the more lucrative rewards go to the technicians and the skilled blue-collar workers. These rewards were positively sanctioned by an efficiency-minded Communist party bent on restoring the prerevolutionary standard of living and later elevating the standard to make it commensurate with the promise of mass prosperity without exploitation.

Once this differential reward system was endorsed by the Party, the state, and others, the new span of rewards stuck. Its sticking negated the goals of Communist egalitarianism, but the contradiction by itself was not sufficient to result in a successful revolution against the new system of stratification.

In China, as in Russia, many of the same contradictions were present, and vexing, and by the early 1960s the Chinese conditions created pressure for a revolution against an increasingly corrupt party organization. In 1965 the great Chinese Cultural Revolution began. Once the insurgence had gotten under way, a minority of the CCP leadership legitimated it. Their endorsement was crucial, especially the affirmative nod of the charismatic leader Mao Tsetung, in moving people toward revolution over the following basic question: How shall communism reward those who maintain it? Should there be differential rewards linked to personal (or familial) interest, with the hope that motivated persons will over the long haul improve the well-being of the collective? Or should the system provide a lump reward to a collective, which will then share the wealth so as to improve the well-being of everyone?

The Chinese chose the second alternative, and we might benefit from E. L. Wheelwright and Bruce McFarlane's analysis of how China has moved along this second path (1970):

1. *The Chinese Communists (Maoists) admit that China must both develop and maintain certain productive, distributive, exchange, and control facilities.* The Chinese add, however, that technology and economic organization are insufficient bases for building a communist society. More important than economic growth and a rational economic organization are the motives of those who use the technology and man the economic structure. People must be powered by the internal urge to improve communism. And they must be propelled to act whenever possible.

2. *The Chinese would certainly agree that in order for these facilities to operate, there must be a division of labor which specifies roles.* Yet the Chinese would qualify this proposition by noting that the role structure should be flexible. Indeed, it should be dissolved and replaced whenever this structure ceases to serve the needs of the people. For example, during the Chinese Cultural Revolution, the division of labor in whole regions came to a halt, disintegrated, and gave way to forms in many ways different from their predecessors. The Maoists thereby demonstrated that from their point of view there is nothing sacrosanct about an ongoing economic organization.

3. *The Chinese would also probably admit that some roles are more important than others, in the sense that relatively more skills are associated with these positions.* The Chinese acknowledge the extreme importance of positions

demanding extensive backgrounds in physics and mathematics. And the Chinese have recently begun to upgrade their universities, placing a very heavy emphasis on instruction in these two subjects for students who will eventually return to mines, farms, factories, and the like.

4. *Yet the Chinese would hesitate to assume that society finds it difficult to replace skilled workers because of some presumed lack of people bright enough to learn the necessary skills.* Only recently the Chinese reopened their universities, which had been closed for several years. When the Chinese did reopen the campus gates, mostly peasants and workers walked through them. In determining the new enrollment, the Communist leadership deliberately overrepresented the peasants and workers, who were to feast on an intellectual diet of mathematics, physics, other hard sciences, and the perennial political education.

From the Chinese point of view, when people have the correct political motivation, their drive to learn accelerates to the point where masses of people of lower-class background can gain expertise in the most difficult of subjects. The Chinese do not pin low IQ scores on their poor, consequently condemning them to educational–occupational limbo.

5. *On the contrary, the Chinese hold that what is generally lacking in the capitalist world is the necessary group support to motivate populations whose overall span of intrinsic ability is limited but whose past socialization experiences vary tremendously in terms of preparing people to learn and to act.* Chinese Communists reject the view that earth is blessed with supermen whose intelligence far exceeds that of the others, namely, the dullards. From their point of view, the span of intrinsic intelligence is rather narrow; what happens in most societies, however, is that a small minority comes to command a monopoly of strategic resources. In turn, these resources give to these relatively few the educational experiences that place the lesser uneducated mass at a great disadvantage in all areas, including the sharpening of the intellect.

6. *Group support can take the form of group effort to press a person politically to acquire the occupational skills necessary to serve the community and through it—the individual.* Political indoctrination heavily emphasizes the need to curb the individual self. "Fight

self," say the Maoists. Unlike most Western Communists, the Chinese Maoists press to develop the interests of the collective—be it the farm, the shop, the office, or the mine. From Mao's point of view, as the collective prospers, so does the individual: His well-being flows from the welfare of the collective, and not vice versa.

7. *Group support often takes the form of learning while doing.* The work collective teaches the necessary skills as the individual learns his job. On-the-job training saves the state considerable funds. No longer must it rely so heavily on expensive educational academies.

It would appear that universities stress the teaching of primary skills—the symbols and logic of science—whereas the work sites place a heavy emphasis on secondary skills—the complex routines and ordinary tasks of the workplace.

8. *Group support also takes the form of collective downgrading of the individual's moving to increase his own material gain within a widening span of rewards.* The Chinese Communist party, most certainly its Maoist wing, has striven to minimize the span of pecuniary rewards among individuals. Unlike the Russians, the Chinese do not press the individual to maximize his own personal income in the hope that his individual efforts will in the long haul enrich both himself and the collective. As a result, the overall span of pecuniary rewards in China gives little indication of approaching the substantial income differentials common to Russia.

9. *In place of competition between individuals, whole groups are urged to compete with one another.* Whole teams and work places are urged to compete on the level of production, and the Chinese state rewards them with money and with honor. Work places, for example, are used as sites for collective rewarding ceremonies, and there is ample publicity on the radio and in the newspapers. Group honor is important in the Chinese situation. In fact, group prestige complements political ideology as the Chinese left-party personnel proceed to play down the value of money as a prize.

10. *The group will then maximize its own productivity, and the results will be shared equally, although small wage differentials may separate the most from the least productive.* The varieties of payment are many. Still there is

an underlying principle involved on payment for labor rendered. The work group computes its profit at the end of a time interval and distributes most of its earnings in this manner (once, of course, funds have been set aside for taxes, welfare, and old-age assistance).

A small portion of the collective's monies is allocated to producers differentially in order to reward, however slightly, those with the greatest productivity. Yet the amount is not great. Nor does this system of minimal differential rewards obtain under all circumstances. In some instances, there have been no special pecuniary rewards for highly productive individuals. These instances tend to become more pronounced during struggle stages of the Chinese Revolution. Such was the case throughout much of China during the Great Leap Forward (1957–1961). However, during China's New Economic Policy (NEP) period (1961–1964), the number of such positions declined precipitously while the overall span of rewards for all Chinese workers widened. Then during the Cultural Revolution (1965–1970), the Red Guard and others pressed for and won the return of a more egalitarian system of rewards. Today there are some indications that the Chinese reward system is reassuming a NEP-like character. Yet the overall egalitarian, collective emphasis remains.

11. *The Chinese Communists emphasize group moral incentives at the expense of individual gains, for they believe that only collective motives are consistent with a collective society.* On this matter Mao is most clear, as indicated in our final point.

12. *If communists attempt to unite individual incentives, and hence personal aggrandizement, with collective achievement, the latter will not long survive; for individual incentives would foster an ethos of personal gain that could well become the ethic of counterrevolution. The ethic would find full support among the old bourgeoisie, plus the new state capitalists.* These forces would unite behind the new ideology to turn back the clock from communism to capitalism. From Mao's point of view, there is nothing inevitable about the completion of all the evolutionary stages by a communist society. On the contrary, a communist society can slide into becoming a capitalist form. In this sense Mao is not an ironclad determinist committed to a particular predestination for

China. Everything depends on what people do. What people do depends to a high degree on personal motivation. And mentality depends on *political education*, which remains central to the Chinese Communist system. But the questions remain: Who is to elect and control the educators? How is this to be done? And is education enough?

It would appear to be inevitable for communist-controlled systems to evolve wide spans of institutionalized rewards on the levels of wealth, prestige, and power. That being the case, is *political education* sufficient to motivate people periodically to rejuvenate egalitarian communist forces in order to stem the trend toward traditional, socially stratified systems and to return a communist system to its originally specified track? Quite obviously, political education by itself does not do the job. Such education must be locked into decadinal total cultural revolutions within the communist system if it is to hew to the egalitarian path. But who will be able to launch these cultural revolutions every decade without the charismatic leadership of communist heroes who earned their revolutionary medallions and legitimacy during a period of war communism increasingly distant from the decadinally red intervals that left-communists have in mind? Could a cultural revolution have occurred in China during the 1960s without Lin Piao and Mao? Many doubt it. Can such a cultural revolution erupt again in 1980, 1990, or 2000? Lin Piao is dead, apparently a victim of a "right-turn" inside the Party. Soon Mao will have passed. Given the loss of revolutionary leadership, which force, if any, can emerge to check what would appear to be an inevitable trend toward the creation of wide spans of rewards under conditions of right-wing communism? The party can not be expected to take such leadership. Indeed, its predictable periodic corruptions make it the main target rather than initiator of cultural revolution from below.

CONCLUSIONS

How historical forces answer these questions in the distant future remains uncertain. At present it might be wise to emphasize what we have observed, while keeping a speculative eye on the future. Communism takes many forms. The crucial distinction, however, is between left- and right-communism. The differences become most glaring during revolution itself. And generally the right-communists succeed in imposing their model on the new society. The seeming exception is China, where left-communists have only recently triumphed. However, their victory may be shortlived. For unless left-communist goals and procedures are institutionalized through forms that go beyond temporary "three-in-one committees" (discussed by Wheelwright and McFarlane), a party oligarchy will in all likelihood reemerge, thereby necessitating either compliance to its dictates or revolution against its elitism. Will cyclical rejuvenation be possible after the death of the left-revolutionary grandfathers? Time and events will test this question, but in the absence of democratic control from below through elected political assemblies, however understandable and pardonable this omission might be, China may well follow the Russian path.

Chapter 9 Left-Wing Democracy: Its Ideology and Criticism

Section One   *The Fight Against Big Capital*

DEMOCRACY: LEFT, RIGHT, AND CENTER

Left-democracy differs considerably from its right-wing counterpart. When people demand equality and view its achievement as possible through the parliamentary process, they place themselves in a camp far removed from those where elites insist on obedience to parliamentary procedures as the goal as well as the means of democracy. In the middle is the center-democratic position. Essentially social democratic, the center stands for the use of parliamentary processes to alleviate social problems stemming from a capitalist structure viewed as amenable to slow but continuous alteration.

To define democracy—left, right, and center—with more precision, we will concern ourselves with the ideology, structure, and the criticisms of all three forms. However, this chapter dwells primarily on left-democratic phenomena.

LEFT-DEMOCRACY

The ideology of left-democracy reflects its class, status, and generational bases. Historically, the most numerous supporters of left-democracy have been:

1. *The small farmers,* locked into a one-crop economy dependent on a world market price structure over which they have had little control.

2. *The marginal working class,* trapped also by economic vicissitudes such as cyclical unemployment.

3. *The intellectuals and students,* blessed with a plentitude of knowledge on the workings of the system but with little power to rectify structural problems.

Wheat farmers, black industrial workers, minority farmers, alienated ministers, rebellious priests, wild poets, intense junior faculty, and finally, as well as most significantly in the United States today, the cyclically volatile students—all are committed to achieving either considerably greater equity for the downtrodden or the systematic introduction of equality into all aspects of human relations. In this regard, the most popular bromide has been "equality of opportunity," a vague self-contradictory formula whose very denotation of equality implies an inequality of origin. However, many left-democrats would press for economic, political, and social equality in perpetuity. Indeed, an occasional left-democrat goes so far as to favor grass-roots socialism, all the way from a left-agrarian populism to urban industrial democracy. In both instances the people would run their own co-ops, neighborhood councils, and city halls. Unlike social democrats and right-democrats, the left-democrats find little room for coordination from above. Hence left-democrats reject city managers, urban planners, and other elites *unless* the ordinary folk can instruct the managers continuously on how to carry out their tasks. Left-democrats believe: Let the people do it themselves.

Left-democratic *declarations* (and *not* my opinion) can be summarized as follows:

1. *Ultimately it is only through socialism or highly abridged capitalism that democracy can be made meaningful.* So long as powerful interests own the society's strategic resources, these interests will use their financial power to undermine the proper functioning of parliamentary procedures. They will cease to reflect any popular mandates for change. Given corporate obstruction of the parliamentary process, the people can and must regulate these vested interests. In the long haul, however, the people will

learn the pragmatic utility of a just but stern appropriation of monopoly capital—the giant corporations, bent on excessive profits, consumer overcharges, and legislative manipulations, which withstand governmental efforts to break them up into smaller units that are less capable of collusion. This state takeover of the monopolies is absolutely essential if the people are to achieve justice through parliamentary means.

2. *Agrarian socialism includes the nationalization of all corporate and banking resources.* Slated for nationalization would be heavy and light industries, public utilities, transportation, banking, and urban agglomerations of land. Set aside for private ownership would be considerable *land* in small and medium-size acreages, belonging to landholders engaged in farming; *small retail outlets* owned by those who have suffered long from the practices of monopolies and oligopolies; *private homes* owned by the persons who would continue to define their homes as their castles; *many producer and consumer cooperatives* established by the people themselves in such areas as artisan production, food retail, educational television and radio; the *mass media,* retained in large part by private persons to allow the people to continue to exercise their rights to justly criticize one another, as well as the state; and the *people's churches,* maintained separate from a state whose secularism could conceivably undermine an institution of mixed utility.

3. *Nationalization is but one step—it must be followed by people's control over production and distribution.* Let the people run every sphere. Wherever they may be, let the people govern. More specifically, let the people elect as they coordinate the managers of factories, mines, offices, retail outlets, recreation groups. Unless the people can participate in their own ongoing democratization, they will remain in a state of complete alienation. When folks become so alienated, the very condition encourages the formation of an organizational oligarchy. *It* constitutes the very antithesis of democracy.

For every Tennessee Valley Authority, let there be a people's council to guide it. For every organic food distribution center, let the folk elect their own representatives. For every university coffee house, let the employees set and enforce policy.

4. *Left-democratic theory assumes that, if and when the state nationalizes industries selectively and the people control them appropriately, the people will have taken a giant step toward control of their own political destinies.* The ideology consists of the following stipulations. Too long have powerful corporations and banks used their financial and related political powers *to prevent* the achievement of justice, *to distort* the natural functions of the legislature, *to undermine* the executive powers of the President, and *to bend* the judicial branches of government. By nationalizing these vested interests, establishing popular control, but allowing for the retention of a private sector, the popular state will create the preconditions for the meaningful operation of parliamentary forms.

5. *If and when the people do nationalize industries selectively, there will nonetheless re-emerge an oligarchy in many ways as reprehensible as those only recently replaced, unless the people can directly control their own institutions.* As odious as private capitalism is *state capitalism,* which has reference to a society in which the state nationalizes industries, concentrates decision-making on economic matters in the hands of the few, and deliberately denies significant decision-making power to the many. It distributes wealth and prestige to favor political leaders, markets goods on a profitable basis for the state-owned firms, and indeed treats labor as if it were a commodity. Current Communist Russia would be illustrative. In this sense, state capitalism is as bad as its predecessor. State capitalism in fact, proves to be synonomous with right-communism. And as such it is vulnerable to criticisms emanating from both the left-communist and left-democratic camps.

6. *On the penalty of losing: If and when the left fails to nationalize basic industries and capitalism remains, the corporate concentrators of private wealth and coercive strength will proceed to use their economic power to strangle even harder what remains of the parliamentary process through both gross and subtle purchases of politicians, parties, administrators, judges, and sundry others.* A heavy left-democratic defeat leaves a vacuum that invites a new formula justifying inequalities. The formula—pluralism—takes many forms, but foremost is the idea of people exerting an equal influence over political elites through the formation and use of pressure groups. In fact, the empirical world is different.

What passes for pluralistic lobbying of all concerned interests is in fact a lopsided purchasing of political figures always in need of campaign funds for the coming reelection, parties in need of recurrent financial replenishment, administrators in need of staff and favorable decisions on governmental and private appropriations, judges in need of career promotions, and so forth. After a serious left-democratic defeat, capital exacerbates those tendencies, creates new lacerations, and further demeans the parliamentary process.

7. *When the wealthy continue to control the parliamentary processes after a telling defeat of left-democrats, the great mass of people cannot solve their economic problems.* In the United States the major left-democratic battle was fought and lost between 1912 and 1918; a lesser effort occurred between 1930 and 1938. It, too, failed. Since that time the upper classes have governed with little threat from below. These upper classes continue to control the Congress, the chief executive and the judiciary.

Today many Americans have found that they cannot solve the country's major economic and overseas problems while working through the federal political processes controlled by the upper classes—unless their interests and those of the upper classes happen to coincide, which seldom happens. Hence, long-standing and deep grievances have generally accumulated—except when a benevolent and enlightened sector of the upper class sees fit to intervene in order to lessen the burden of blue-collar workers.

8. *When people cannot solve their problems through the parliamentary process, they have the right to revolution.* Ever since Samuel Adams, Thomas Paine, and Thomas Jefferson, left-democrats have held that if and when people cannot rely on the parliamentary process to solve their problems, they have the right to revolution. More recently, William O. Douglas has laid this right on the line:

George III was the symbol against which our Founders made a revolution now considered bright and glorious. George III had not crossed the seas to fasten a foreign yoke on us. George III and his dynasty had established and nurtured us and all that he did was by no means oppressive. But a vast restructuring of laws and institutions was necessary if the people were to be content.

That restructuring was not forthcoming and there was revolution.

We must realize that today's Establishment is the new George III. Whether it will continue to adhere to his tactics we do not know. If it does, the redress, honored in tradition, is also revolution.[1]

Needless to say, this left-democratic opinion fails to find acceptance among contemporary right-democrats.

9. *The revolution directs its energies for the people and against those giant corporations and corrupt politicians who perpetuate both domestic exploitation of politically undefended workers and overseas wars that encourage the oppression of colonized people.* Should this revolution occur, it must direct its attention to deep domestic problems and overseas immoralities. Currently, such persistent domestic problems as poverty and environmental destruction demand immediate attention.

Overseas, our imperialist efforts must halt. U.S. military forces must no longer strive to protect areas traditionally used by American corporations as (a) sources of cheap raw materials, unskilled labor, and inexpensive goods, (b) purchasers of overpriced U.S. goods, (c) sites of U.S. investment, (d) stockyards for the accumulation of military hardware and the billeting of cannon-fodder, plus (e) battle areas established and maintained overseas by U.S. military forces to prevent insurgent revolutionary forces from taking state power. The United States must change its ways and encourage the withdrawal of its corporations from dependence on imperial roles at that moment when the progressive state instructs the U.S. military to withdraw from foreign battlefields.

The most urgent problems remain the domestic ones, although obviously the foreign and the home-front areas are intertwined.

10. *The domestic exploitation includes every kind of private and public chicanery that one can imagine.* With the elimination of imperialism the United States will have sufficient funds to deal with problems already thoroughly studied.

Indeed, the left-democrats lead in research concerned with corruption. Their exposés fill not only the lesser journals but the major news-

[1] William O. Douglass, *Points of Rebellion* (New York: Vintage Books, 1970), p. 95.

papers and popular bookshelves as well. Illustrative would be the current work of Ralph Nader.

Despite their energetic exposés, left-democrats remain caught within a contradiction. The ambivalence of the left-democratic movement can be captured in the following propensities: (a) to engage in parliamentary politics even though the movement has already defined these politics as useless for gaining peoples' power because of the intrinsic corruption of the parliamentary process, and (b) to back those revolutionaries who have opted against parliamentary forms and for urban guerilla warfare. Here the left-democrats philosophically straddle two quite different alternatives. In the meantime, they become principally involved in parliamentary politics. And on occasion they win a victory. Its occurrence, however infrequent, nonetheless vindicates their "choice." But the choice has little structural impact. Left-democratic drift into the morass of recurrent campaigns and predictable defeats is marked by a decadinal victory of little practical consequence.

LEFT-DEMOCRATS AS POTENTIAL FASCISTS: THE NATURE OF THE ACCUSATION

In the last two decades a number of intellectuals have condemned left-democrats as authoritarian, antidemocratic and even antisemitic. Especially have these criticisms been directed against the agrarian populists of America's Great Plains—the agrarian radicals of Oklahoma, Kansas, Nebraska, South Dakota, North Dakota, and by implication, the prairie provinces of Canada. The charge of the critics is clear: the populists once did (and continue to) display a disrespect for elected authority by insisting on their right to recall duly elected representatives judged to be faulty, their power to initiate legislation viewed as necessary, and finally, the right to use the referendum to undo legislation passed by "responsible" political leaders. Furthermore, this mass of culpable farmers and equally dislikable allies have on occasion used derogatory stereotypes to blacken certain respectable members of the community engaged in functionally important roles associated with grain storage, grain sale, farm implement manufacture, farm equipment purchase, railroad transportation, agricultural credit, and the public utilities. Perhaps even more disgusting was

the way in which populist demagogues played on public gullibility in order to sway the ordinary folk to believe that political improprieties were somehow linked to the manipulative propensities of corporate wealth.

So much for the criticisms of the past and ongoing populists. What has been their historical residue?

A more current condemnation of the populists has taken the form of blaming them for the advent of McCarthyism: the purge of American intellectuals from university and government positions, which ran between 1950 and 1956. The anti-McCarthy indictment holds that the key supporters of Senator Joseph McCarthy came from the geographical areas in which populism and rural progressivism had once flourished. Indeed, it was alleged, these two forms had prepared the way for McCarthyism by creating an intolerance of ambiguity, a rejection of the foreign, a repugnance against the complex, and a dislike of the sophisticated Easterner. All these attitudes comprised a syndrome which Joe McCarthy manipulated in order to get himself elected to Congress, where he could terrorize Eastern intellectuals of more gentle temperament and reformist persuasion. From Richard Hofstadter through Daniel Bell and many of their contemporaries, we find this indictment of America's foremost contributors to the left-democratic tradition.

But the historical record indicates that Hofstadter was wrong. For one thing, there has been little effort on the part of Hofstadter and like-minded essayists to clarify all the epistemological ambiguities associated with being "politically authoritarian." But even if we accept the term as a basis for carrying on discussion, we can only comment that there has been no sound basis for accusing the agrarian democrats of serious antisemitism or profoundly antidemocratic inclinations. None of America's strong antisemitic movements flourished in geographical zones with populist traditions. Rather, antisemitism, especially in its more virulent forms, such as those which thrived during the 1930s, has been principally a metropolitan phenomenon, popular among classes and status groups without populist commitments. Here we are talking about big-city "brown shirts," uniformed and violent imitators of the German Nazi phenomenon. It was Eastern and Midwestern, but especially urban, German, Protestant, lower-middle and upper-working class. These antisemites were concentrated in cities such as New York, Detroit, and Chicago. Bitter antisemitism has also surfaced in some small towns, as in the case of the notorious Black Legion during the 1930s. But then, not everyone in those small towns falls within the populist tradition. Many residents did not, and perhaps many of these were the vicious antisemites. We do not know. Only time and research will tell us. Until then essays can not demonstrate whether the populist tradition was at fault.

The antidemocratic charges leveled against the populists have been grossly unfair, although it is true that grain farmers have frequently shown a disrespect for political leaders who were obviously acting in collusion with corporate interests. In this sense the populist democrats did view political authorities as potentially crooked. And they attempted to create mechanisms whereby each and every adult would have an electoral way of exerting his or her influence to correct these situations. These agrarians created the "recall," the "initative," and the "referendum" to try to exact from legislatures machinery that would shape an economy consistent with the right to engage in the unrestricted expression of political ideas. It will be observed that this effort was not one of undoing civil liberties, but rather one of creating liberties that would merge with altered social conditions to allow for the full attainment of justice, freedom, and equality.

True, the interests of corporate wealth would be violated by such political efforts. During the process of appropriation, as well as the events leading to it, the agrarian democrats might use cartoons, speeches, and other forms of propaganda to stereotype the ones deemed worthy of such depictions. Granted also was the presence of orators, a small minority of them were antisemitic. But they articulated the grievances of farmers who were overcharged for the storage of their grains, cheated on the price of grain sold, unduly burdened by the costs paid for commodities shipped to markets, charged too much for the farm implements purchased from the farm machinery oligopoly, and squeezed periodically in the vice of fixed farm prices and declining grain prices, while being ignored by traditional politicians only

superficially concerned with wheat farmers' grievances, ruled against by state and federal judges committed to a laissez-faire ideology shared by the same individuals who dominated an economy and polity that obviously did not work to the advantage of the one-crop agrarians. Given the battles waged by agrarian democrats (especially one-crop wheat farmers) *against* oligarchical authorities and *for* the democratic right to carry on that struggle through a more direct, representative parliamentary system, it would be surprising indeed to discover that these agrarians had left a legacy which might predispose their sons to favor the repression of civil liberties.

For the record, when we examine the arguments and evidence alleging that populists were predecessors to McCarthyism, we are struck by the absence of such a correlation. Mike Rogin's study has provided us with this refutational material.[2] Not the Great Plains agrarians but certain cold-war intellectuals have created this correlation. And they have done so, not on the basis of statistical materials, but largely out of their own imaginations.

THE CURRENT PERTINENCE OF THE POPULIST INDICTMENT

Until recently it was popular to debate whether the United States has been ruled by a "power elite" or "governed through a plurality of contending pressure groups." Prominent in these discussions have been C. Wright Mills, Robert Dahl, David Riesman, and William Kornhauser. Perhaps these arguments are somewhat dated. In any event, we consider them more thoroughly in Chapter 10. By the year 1972, sufficient empirical material had been gathered to indicate the degree to which wealthy families in the United States have used their economic power, whether as family units or corporate entities, to bend the parliamentary processes and move them to work for these families. At times this bending creates a caricature of government—for example, when Congress creates a federal agency to regulate a private industry whose executives subsequently and informally pick as agency heads the very persons the agency is supposed to regulate.

[2] Michael P. Rogin, *The Intellectuals and McCarthy: The Radical Spector* (Cambridge, M.I.T. Press, 1967).

G. William Domhoff compiled an impressive amount of documentation on these and related matters, and we spend considerable time discussing his materials.[3] He has taken up the following items:

1. The control of the corporate economy.
2. The shaping of American foreign policy.
3. The control of the federal government.
4. The military, the CIA, and the FBI.
5. The control of state and local governments.

Unfortunately, we can summarize only part of these materials. We examine the first two matters in considerable detail, as we attempt to investigate the fallacious quality of the indictment against the populist charges.

THE CONTROL OF CORPORATE ECONOMY

Domhoff demonstrated the existence within the United States of an interlocking directorate which in fact runs the national corporate economy. Only several thousand families are involved. Their Social Register listings, familial wealthy, private school affiliations, club membership ties, corporate directorships, and top managerial positions *plus their high levels of overall agreement despite the presence of ideological differences* strongly registers this group as a nationwide upper class *acting for itself.* Nor are Domhoff's findings unique. They are consistent with the materials gathered by Floyd Hunter as well as W. Lloyd Warner and James Abegglin.[4]

In carrying out these activities, the American upper class depends heavily on the profession of law, and many upper-middle-class attorneys aspire to the upper class. Lawyers and law firms service the upper classes in a multiplicity of ways—as consultative specialists on corporate law, as representatives before judges prone to issue antilabor injunctions, or as legislative specialists committed to the promotion of special interests through the precise framing of law.

And they are found in many institutions, including foundations, foreign policy associations, and universities. These are but a fraction of their services.

THE SHAPING OF THE AMERICAN POLITY

Certain institutions enjoy a strong and constant influence on the shape of U.S. politics. *Shape* should not be confused with *control,* which is too strong a designation. But as Domhoff indicated, the establishment exercises a powerful directional influence on institutions in the United States.

I. *A Summary of Domhoff's Analysis*[5]
Domhoff analyzed the following institutions; here we merely list a portion of the totality:

A. *Tax-Exempt Charity Foundations*—such as the Ford Foundation and the Rockefeller Foundation; groups which provide funds for a great variety of cultural, intellectual, and educational activities.
B. *Special Associations Aimed at Shaping Public Opinion on Special Issues.* Pertinent here is the Council on Foreign Relations (CFR) and the Foreign Policy Association (FPA). Both emphasize foreign affairs. Domestic issues receive careful scrutiny and singularly incisive recommendations through the Business Advisory Council (BAC), the Committee for Economic Development (CED), the National Advertising Council (NAC), and the National Association of Manufacturers (NAM).
C. *The University,* especially the elite institutions which train most of the country's leading lawyers, academicians, and physicians. These schools provide high-quality expertise for those to be trained as well as for those already trained but in need of ongoing advice.
D. *The Mass Media,* themselves important in the spread of information and the related creation of opinion.

II. *An Elaboration of Domhoff's Analysis*
We can now examine more carefully each of these points.

---

[3] G. William Domhoff, *Who Rules America?* (Englewood Cliffs, N.J.: Prentice-Hall, 1967).

[4] Floyd Hunter, *Community Power Structure* (Chapel Hill: University of North Carolina Press, 1953); W. Lloyd Warner and James C. Abegglen, *Big Business Leaders in America* (New York: Atheneum, 1963).

[5] Domhoff, *op. cit.,* pp. 63–83. Copyrighted material, reprinted by permission of Prentice-Hall, Inc., Englewood Cliffs, N.J.

A. *The Foundations*

Domhoff focused on the thirteen largest foundations in the United States. His condensed summary on their control structure defies further abstraction:

Our data should be presented on a foundation-by-foundation basis, but to avoid tediousness we will restrict ourselves to several examples after making the following generalizations. Twelve of the top 13 foundations are controlled by members of the power elite, with two-thirds of their trustees coming from the upper class (51 percent) of major corporations (16 percent). The only exception is the Kellogg Foundation, which is controlled by local interests in central Michigan. The one-third of the trustees who are neither members of the upper class nor corporate executives are professional persons, most of them college presidents or college professors. Just over half of all trustees attended Harvard, Yale, or Princeton; 22 earned Phi Beta Kappa keys; 20 are in the Links Club of New York; and eight are on the board of the RAND Corporation, the Air Force "think factory" supported primarily by government contracts. There is a considerable interlock among the Ford, Rockefeller, Carnegie, Sloan, and Commonwealth foundations, and this group has weaker ties to the Duke Endowment and the Danforth Foundation. No generalizations can be made about the ideological commitments of the foundations. Some support liberal and educational interests and ideological struggles which we have seen to be present within the upper class. In the following paragraphs we will go into more detail on six of the foundations: Ford, Rockefeller, Carnegie, Lilly, Pew, and Danforth.[6]

The Ford Foundation has been impressive. It is by far the biggest foundation. We can observe that between its inception during the early 1950s and approximately 1967 it has spent more than $80 million on educational television. This figure grows by $6 million a year. Indeed, the chief creation of the Ford Foundation has been National Educational Television (NET), a network of 90 independent stations.

NET offers late-afternoon and evening cultural and informative programs, as well as material for children. Nor is this programming reactionary. As Domhoff indicated, NET provides one of the many lines of communication between the more progressive sections of the upper-class and the upper-middle-class intelligentsia.

Consistent with this channel of idea dissemination and the liberality of the packaged opinions are other projects heavily supported by the Ford Foundation:

1. The Ford Foundation gave a $15-million grant to the Fund for the Republic, a group which opposed McCarthyism (after it had already been responsible for considerable devastation).

2. The Ford Foundation was instrumental in establishing the liberal-oriented Center for the Study of Democratic Institutions in Santa Barbara, California.

3. The Ford Foundation largely subsidized Harvard's Russian Research Center, a group whose undisguised interest in the cold war is favored by certain sections of the U.S. government.

Turning to another Ford benefaction in the educational realm, the foundation has taken over the financing of Harvard's Russian Research Center from the Carnegie Foundation. It gave $131,000 of the center's budget for 1965, with the remaining $9,000 coming from Carnegie funds. With a staff of 57 scholars drawn from the many colleges and universities in the Boston area, this center provides consultants to the State Department and the CIA, as well as lecturers to the Army War College, the Foreign Service Institute, and the Council on Foreign Relations.[7]

Consistent with the Ford Foundation all-embracing concern is the breadth of upper-class backgrounds common to the Ford Foundation's Trustees (1967).

TRUSTEES OF THE FORD FOUNDATION[8]

Upper-Class Trustees

Stephen Bechtel is head of the little-known, but very large, Bechtel Construction Corporation of Oak-

[6] *Ibid.,* p. 65, reprinted by permission of the publisher.

[7] *Ibid.,* p. 66, reprinted by permission of the publisher.

[8] *Ibid.,* pp. 66–68, reprinted by permission of the publisher.

land, California. Mr. Bechtel is also a director of Morgan Guaranty Trust, Southern Pacific, Continental Can, Bechtel-McCone Corporation, and Stanford University, among others.

Eugene Black is a Southern-born aristocrat who is a long-time employee of the Rockefeller interests. He is a director of Chase Manhattan, IT&T, *The New York Times,* Cummins Engine, the Brookings Institution, and Johns Hopkins University, among others.

John Cowles (Exeter, Harvard) of Minneapolis is co-owner of the family publishing empire, which includes *Look* Magazine and newspapers in Minneapolis and Des Moines. He is also a trustee for the Carnegie Endowment for International Peace, and a director of the First National Bank of Minneapolis and the Equitable Life Insurance Company of Iowa.

Donald K. David is a Harvard Business School professor and dean who sits on several corporate boards.

Benson Ford (Hotchkiss, Princeton) is a director of the National Safety Council and chairman of the Board of the Traffic Safety Committee. He is a vice-president at Ford Motor Company.

Henry Ford II (Hotchkiss, Yale) is a director for General Electric, General Foods, and Philco.. He runs the Ford Motor Company.

Roy E. Larsen (SR,* NY) is chairman of the executive committee of Time, Inc.

John J. McCloy (SR, NY) is a director of many corporations. As a former chairman of the board at Chase Manhattan he is a key interlock between the Ford Foundation and the Rockefeller empire. Mr. McCloy is chairman of the Ford Foundation trustees.

Joseph Irwin Miller, the head of Cummins Engine Company, is a director of AT&T and many other corporations.

Bethuel Webster (SR, NY) is a corporation lawyer who was a consultant for John J. McCloy when McCloy was High Commissioner of Germany.

Charles E. Wyzanski, Jr. (Exeter, Harvard), is a Jewish member of the upper class. Judge Wyzanski is married to another member of the Jewish aristocracy, Gisela Warburg, who came to this country to escape the Nazi persecution.

Others

Mark F. Ethridge is the editor of the *Louisville Courier-Journal,* which is owned by Barry Bingham, who sits on the board of the Rockefeller Foundation....

Laurence Gould is president of Carleton College.

Julius Stratton is president of MIT.

*"SR" designates membership in the local community's *Social Register,* a reputed indication of membership in the upper class.

Henry T. Heald was president of Ford Foundation at the time of this study. He was the president of Illinois Institute of Technology (1940–1952) and NYU (1952–1956) before joining the Ford Foundation. His training was as an engineer. He is a director of AT&T, U.S. Steel, Equitable Life, and Lever Brothers.

The Rockefeller and Carnegie foundations are structured along almost identical lines. The activities of the Rockefeller Foundation, the oldest and most famous if not the largest of the foundations, include studies of tropical diseases, subsidies to the Population Research Center at Harvard, and a Russian research center at Columbia as well as numerous other subsidies of universities. The Trustees of the Rockefeller Foundation (1967) can be classified according to whether they are (*a*) upper-class members, (*b*) representatives from upper-class businesses, and (*c*) others.

TRUSTEES OF THE ROCKEFELLER FOUNDATION[9]

Upper-Class Members

Barry Bingham (Middlesex School, Harvard) is the publisher of the *Louisville Courier-Journal* and the *Louisville Times,* and an heir to a Standard Oil fortune. He is an Episcopalian, a Democrat, and like many upper-class Southerners, a listee in the Washington *Social Register.*

Lloyd D. Brace (SR, Boston) is a Boston banker who sits on many corporate boards.

Arthur Amory Houghton, Jr. (SR, NY), is president of Corning Glass and a director of New York Life Insurance and U.S. Steel, among others.

John R. Kimberly (Phillips Andover, MIT) inherited the Kimberly-Clark Company of Wisconsin, which was originally a paper-making firm. He sits on the boards of Northwestern Mutual Life, First National City Bank of New York, Corning Glass, Lawrence College, and the Episcopalian Church Foundation, as well as being president and chairman of the family firm.

Lord Frank of Headington is an English lord.

John D. Rockefeller III (SR, NY) is the Rockefeller brother who specializes in cultural matters. As chairman of the foundation he has a firm grip on its activities. Other trustees come and go—he does not. He is president of the Japanese Society, the Asia Society, and the Council on Economic and Cultural

[9] *Ibid.,* pp. 68–69, reprinted by permission of the publisher.

Affairs. He is chairman of the National Council of the United Negro College Fund.

Thomas J. Watson, Jr. (SR, NY), is head of IBM and a director of Bankers Trust, Time, Inc., Cal Tech, and Brown University.

William B. Wood Jr. (SR, Baltimore), is vice-president of Johns Hopkins.

Representatives from Upper-Class Businesses

Frank M. Stanton is a retired investment banker who was a vice-president of the Rockefeller-associated First Boston Corporation from 1934 to 1955. He has been a First Boston Corporation director since 1940. He is not related to the Frank Stanton who is president of CBS and chairman of the Center for Advanced Study in the Behavioral Sciences.

George D. Woods is chairman of the board at First Boston Corporation, which is the biggest under-writer of utilities in the world.

Others

Ralph Bunche (AB, UCLA; Ph.D., Harvard) is one of the nation's most prominent Negro citizens. A professor before he became a United Nations official, he won the Nobel Peace Prize in 1950.

Lowell T. Coggeshall, formerly a research physician with the foundation, is a dean at the Rockefeller-founded University of Chicago and a director of Commonwealth Edison of Chicago.

John S. Dickey is president of Dartmouth.

Lee A. DuBridge is president of Cal Tech.

Robert F. Goheen is president of Princeton.

Clifford M. Hardin is president of the University of Nebraska.

J. George Harrar, a former professor, is an expert on plant pathology who is the foundation's director for agriculture as well as its president.

Theodore Hesburgh is president of Notre Dame.

Clark Kerr was president of the University of California.

Of the Carnegie Corporation's fourteen trustees, twelve are members of the upper class. Several of the foremost members are: Frederick Eaton, who sits on the Commonwealth Fund as well as on several corporate boards; C. D. Jackson, of Time, Inc.; Devereaux Josephs, a member of the Sloan Foundation board as well as a multitude of corporate boards; Margaret Carnegie Miller; and Charles A. Thomas, president of Monsanto Chemical Company.

B. *The Associations*

The associations are intimately connected with the country's corporate elite, and they include the following:

1. The Council on Foreign Relations. Founded in 1921, CFR began during the late 1920s to receive considerable financial support from the Rockefeller and Carnegie foundations. Members of the Council were heavily involved in U.S. State Department affairs during World War II. Who are its members? How is it financed? What are its activities?

The membership is restricted to 700 resident members—citizens whose residences or places of business are within 50 miles of the New York city hall—and 700 nonresident members. As Smoot points out, most members occupy important positions in business, finance, communications, and education. Our study of a sample of 210 resident members of the CFR shows that 82 were listed in the *Social Register,* which is 39 percent upper-class membership by this one criterion alone. However, even more significant is our study of the 51 men who have been directors since the council's inception. Ten of the 51 are currently trustees of one of the foundations studied in the previous section. Of the 22 recently or currently directors, 14 are in the *Social Register.* Among the better-known upper-class directors, past and present, are Paul Cravath, Norman Davis, Arthur H. Dean, Allen Dulles, Lewis Douglas, Averell Harriman, Devereux Josephs, Walter Lippmann, Adlai Stevenson, Myron Taylor, Paul Warburg, and Owen D. Young. Perhaps it is enough to say that John J. McCloy and David Rockefeller have been high officers in the association in recent years.[10]

The financing of the CFR indicates the extent of horizontal interlock which connects upper-class institutions. Of the CFR's income in a recent year, $231,700 came from foundation grants, whereas $112,000 emanated from "corporate service," which in turn entails a minimum fee of $1,000. The CFR also receives $210,300 from the publication of the highly influential journal, *Foreign Afffairs.* The Council penetrates the normal political activities of our country's more plush panel rooms and auditoriums. The CFR presents speakers and seminars to those who subscribe to its Corporation ser-

[10] *Ibid.,* p. 72, reprinted by permission of the publisher.

vice and to the Committees on Foreign Relations which the CFR has created in 30 cities.

The local committees are composed of 40 to 80 people who are generally the community leaders. They are professors, public-relations executives, lawyers, and corporate vice presidents, as well as several top members of the American business aristocracy residing in a particular city.

It will be remembered that this association derives much of its income from foundations. It will also be recalled who governs the foundations. Keep in mind, for example, that in 1967, 12 of the 14 trustees of the Carnegie Foundation enjoyed an upper-class standing. Hence they were in a position to relate to upper-class folk on the local CFR committees. This being the case, there can be little doubt that the "local committees" constitute key links between the national upper class, its local members, the upper middle class in general, and the powerful foundations.

In order to emphasize control at the top, Domhoff pointed to the documentation on the relation between the major foundations and the CFR in 1961:

For example, 10 of the 14 trustees of the Carnegie Corporation were members of the CFR in 1961. The overlap of the CFR with other major foundations is as follows: 10 of the Ford Foundation's 15 trustees are also members of the CFR; 12 of the 20 from the Rockefeller Foundation; 18 of the 26 from the Carnegie Endowment for International Peace; 15 of the 26 from the Carnegie Foundation for the Advancement of Teaching; 12 of the 16 from the Sloan Foundation; 6 of the 10 from the Commonwealth Fund; 13 of the 20 from the Twentieth Century Fund; and 7 of the 18 from the Fund for the Republic.[11]

2. The Foreign Policy Association, the Committee for Economic Development, the Business Advisory Council, the National Advertising Council, and the National Association of Manufacturers are involved in the same kind of horizontal interlock. It finds yet another extension in university governance.

C. *The Universities*

Domhoff showed that control of the country's leading universities by members of the American business aristocracy is more direct, certainly more visible, than with any other institution controlled by the upper class. Still, the upper classes do not mold opinions within universities. Faculty can promote considerable diversity, since the system of tenure protects all but the most wild of faculty outlaws. So Domhoff contended—the Leggett—Roach paper argues differently at the end of this chapter.

Nevertheless, upper-class control does exist. Most important is the occupancy of boards of directors positions by this class. Illustrative is the Board of Trustees of Columbia University (see Table 20.) The upper classes also have a habit of granting private financial support to universities. Family endowments, personal gifts, foundation grants, and corporate gifts extend the powerful base of upper-class influence.

Corporate control of the direction taken by universities should not be ignored. Members of the business aristocracy have stressed technical and practical training as opposed to traditional and classical education:

Thus, Joseph Wharton gave the University of Pennsylvania $600,000 to found the Wharton School of Business and Finance, and George Eastman gave $20 million to MIT between 1912 and 1920. According to Curti and Nash, the role of the Carnegie foundations and Rockefeller's General Education Board cannot be overestimated in understanding the structure of American higher education. The relationship between the corporate rich and academia is best exemplified by a school such as the University of Rochester. Most of the university's board is made up of officers of such Rochester-based corporations as Eastman Kodak, Xerox, and Taylor Instrument. The chairman of the board, who is also the president of Xerox, explained the relationship as follows:

To put it as crassly as possible, it's a matter of sheer self-interest—dollars and cents. Xerox will live or die by technology.[12]

---

[11] *Ibid.*, p. 73, reprinted by permission of the publisher.

[12] *Ibid.*, p. 78, reprinted by permission of the publisher.

TABLE 20 The Ruling Elite of Columbia University (The Top 22: 1968)

	Mass Media Corporations[1]	International Corporations[2]	National Corporations[3]	Defense Research Nexus[4]	Real Estate and Finance[5]
1. Walter N. Thayer (Trustee)	Whitney Communications Corp. (Pr*)	John Hay Whitney Charitable Trust (1958)^X (Tr)	National Dairy Products (Di)		Bankers Trust Co. (Di)
2. Arthur B. Krim (Trustee)	United Artists (Pr) Phillips, Nizer, Benjamin, Krim & Ballon (Pa)	African–American Institute^X (Di)	New School for Social Research (Di) Field Foundation (Tr)		
3. William A. M. Burden (Trustee)	Columbia Broadcasting System (Di)	American Metal Climax (Di) Fairfield Foundation (Di)^X Atlantic Council (Di)^X	Allied Chemical (Di)	Lockheed Aircraft (Di) Institute for Defense Analysis (CB)	Manufacturer's Hanover Trust (Di) William A.M. Durden & Co. (Pa)
4. John R. Dunning (Dean, School of Engineering)			National Urban League (Ad) Nuclear Energy Corp. (Di) Vitro Corp. (Di) National Science Foundation (Ad)	Defense Department (Ad) U.S. Army (Ad) Atomic Energy Office, U.S. Navy (Di) Oak Ridge Institute of Nuclear Studies (Di) City Investing Corporation (Di) Riverside Research Institute (Tr)	
5. Lawrence A. Wien (Trustee)	Educational Broadcasting Corporation (Tr)	Institute of International Education (Tr)^X	Consolidated Edison (Di) Jonathan Logan (Di)		Wien, Lane & Klein (Pa)
6. Grayson L. Kirk (Trustee)		Socony–Mobil Oil (Di) Asia Foundation^X (Di) Institute of International Education^X (Tr)	Consolidated Edison (Di) IBM (Di)	Institute for Defense Analysis (Tr)	Morningside Heights, Inc. (Pr) Greenwich Savings Bank (Tr) Dividend Shares (Di) Nation-Wide Securities (Di)

Table 20 (Continued)

	Mass Media Corporations[1]	International Corporations[2]	National Corporations[3]	Defense Research Nexus[4]	Real Estate and Finance[5]
7. Adrian M. Massie (Trustee)					Uris Building Corporation (Di)
					Greenwich Savings Bank (Tr)
					U.S. Life Insurance (Di)
					Investment Management Co. (Di)
					Pacific Insurance (Di)
					Trust Comm., Chemical Bank N.Y. Trust (Me)
8. Samuel R. Walker (Trustee)					William C. Walker & Sons Inc. (CB)
					City Investing Co. 1948–1967 (Di)
					Equitable Life Assurance (Di)
9. Harold F. McGuire (Trustee)		Shell Oil (Di)			Wickes, Riddell, Bloomer, Jacobi & McGuire (Pa)
					Seaboard Surety (Di)
10. Frank S. Hogan (Trustee)					District Attorney of New York County since 1941
11. Percy Uris (Trustee)					Uris Buildings Corporation (CB)
12. William S. Paley (Trustee)	Columbia Broadcasting System (CB)				
13. Arthur Hays Sulzberger (Trustee)	New York Times (CB)	Rockefeller Foundation (Tr)			
		Woodrow Wilson Foundation (Di)			
		American–Korean Foundation (Di)			

216

Table 20 (Continued)

	Mass Media Corporations[1]	International Corporations[2]	National Corporations[3]	Defense Research Nexus[4]	Real Estate and Finance[5]
20. William E. Peterson (Trustee)					Irving Trust Co. (Pr)
21. Benjamin J. Buttenwieser (Trustee)			Benrus Watch Co. (Di)		Uris Building Corporation (Ad)
			Revlon (Di)		Kuhn, Loeb & Co. (Pa)
			Chock Full O'Nuts (Di)		Tishman Realty & Construction (Di)
					Title Guarantee Co. (Di)
22. William C. Warren (Dean, School of Law)	ABC Vending (Di)				Central Savings Bank (Tr)
					Guardian Life Insurance (Di)

*LEGEND: (Di) - Director
(Ad) - Advisor
(Pr) - President
(Pa) - Partner
(CB) - Chairman of the Board

xOrganizations marked with this sign (x) secretly received funds from the CIA.

[1] Mass Media Corporations: Eight of the Top 22 are leading figures in major communications firms. Particularly heavy is CBS's representation (Paley, Burden, Brown). The prestigious New York Times is represented by their Board Chairman. The Whitney communications empire of television, radio, and publishing owned the now defunct New York World-Journal-Tribune. Krim's law firm is counsel for important communications companies. This concentration of interests is reflected in Columbia's large and expanding School of Journalism which produces skilled labor for the media industry. The School also houses the industry's American Press Institute. Columbia avails itself of these connections to manufacture a favorable public image.

[2] International Corporations: Administering the Empire. Seven Columbia rulers have primary ties to either U.S. corporations or non-profit organizations with an international domain. Kirk, McGuire, and Kappel are on the boards of oil companies dependent on foreign reserves for their survival. These and other corporations (such as Burden's American Metal Climax with mining interests in Africa) require skilled managers to oversee the corporate fiefdoms carved out by U.S. economic interests. Columbia's School of International Affairs is underwritten by these same corporations and in turn serves as a finishing school for the managers. The School is headed by State Department consultant and ex-U.N. administrator Cordier, who is noted for his role in the execution of the Congolese nationalist Patrice Lumumba. The Regional Institutes of the School perform research and intelligence that reinforce anti-nationalist ideology. Covert financing by the CIA has been uncovered in one institute project on Eastern Europe.

Six of the seven trustees engaged in overseas activity are prominent functionaries in seemingly apolitical organizations secretly funded by the CIA. For instance, Burden was a founder and is a director of the Farfield Foundation, used by the CIA to pass over one million dollars to intellectual projects run by the Congress for Cultural Freedom. Kirk has played a crucial role in the CIA-founded and -funded Asia Foundation, which encouraged "cultural interaction" through publications, exchange programs and research.

(Continued on following page)

218

(Continued from preceding page)

[3] National Corporations: Administering the Home Country. Five of the Top 22 have primary relationships with leading national corporations and several of the others have secondary interests. Corporations such as Consolidated Edison (represented by Trustees Kirk, Wien and Luce) gain private advantage through their ties to Columbia. The University manipulates land-holdings for and rents property from Con Ed. In addition to direct gain, national corporations benefit from the University's production of highly skilled labor, especially by the professional schools (Law, Business, Engineering and Applied Science). The Watson computer lab is operated by Columbia and IBM (of which Kirk is a Director). Teachers College and the School of Social Work manufacture the professionals to organize the national and local infrastructure to service corporate needs.

[4] The Defense-Research Nexus: The Top 22 include five representatives of the military-industrial complex. Burden's Lockheed Aircraft and Moore's General Dynamics together receive 10% ($3.6 billion) of all U.S. military contracts. Their existence is dependent upon production of the aircraft presently used in Vietnam. As Chairman of the Board of the Institute for Defense Analyses (IDA), Burden directs $15 million worth of Pentagon-financed war research. IDA, specializing in evaluations of advanced weaponry and counterinsurgency technology, serves as a major idea factory for the Department of Defense. Sponsored by twelve major universities (including Columbia), IDA is shielded from attack by its academic facade. President Kirk adds to IDA's academic lustre by serving on its Board of Trustees. Columbia's officials also provide an academic cover for the Riverside Research Institute (formerly the Electronics Research Lab of Columbia University), whose secret military work is coordinated by IDA. RRI trustee Dunning, a Defense Dept. consultant and expert on atomic weapons, is a director of three private corporations dependent on military contracts. For example, Dunning's City Investing Corp. is a major subcontractor of Burden's Lockheed Aircraft and manufactures spray defoliant systems for chemical warfare.

[5] Real Estate and Finance: Of the Top 22, at least fifteen have primary interlocking relationships with New York City's major real estate and finance companies. With over 60% of its $245 million endowment in real estate Columbia is one of the largest property holders in New York City. Most disturbing is the association of four Columbia rulers (Uris, Massie, Buttenwieser and Brown) with the real estate and construction empire of Uris Building Corporation. Uris himself conveniently serves as President Kirk's advisor on University construction and expansion, a position well-suited for the promotion of his company. The proposed "Piers Project" between 125th and 135th streets adjacent to Hudson River will be constructed by Uris's firm. Trustee Hogan, doubling as District Attorney, can overlook any conflicts of interest. Tishman Realty and Construction is represented by Trustee Buttenwieser, and Trustee Wien is famous for his billion dollars speculation in property.

The lifeblood of real estate is the capital of banks, insurance companies and investment concerns which underwrite mortgages and loans. Columbia's real estate men are intimately connected with the largest banking and insurance firms. Dean Brown is an advisor to Chemical Bank New York Trust Co.; Trustee Massie is a director of Chemical Bank, sits with Kirk on the Board of Greenwich Savings Bank, and is a director of two major insurance companies; Buttenwieser is a partner in the investment concern of Kuhn, Loeb; Burden is a director of Manufacturer's Hanover Trust; Temple is a director of First National City Bank and Atlantic Mutual Insurance. The Rockefeller Brothers, who rent the land under Rockefeller Center from Columbia, have two of their financial concerns (Chase Manhattan Bank and Metropolitan Life Insurance) represented at Columbia by Kappel.

■ This information is based on a chart in "Who Rules Columbia" prepared by the North American Congress on Latin America (NACLA), New York.

Sometime ago, Hubert Beck published a study entitled *Men Who Control Our Universities,* providing the kind of detailed information necessary to help determine whether members of the upper class control the nation's leading universities. Again, Domhoff's terse summary will suffice:

Beck studied 727 trustees from 30 major universities, 14 private and 16 public. Among the universities were such prestigious Eastern schools as Harvard, Yale, Princeton, Columbia, Johns Hopkins, and Cornell, as well as such highly regarded public institutions of the Midwest and West as Ohio State, Illinois, and the University of California. At the time of the study, 1934–1935, the 30 schools, which comprised the United States universities in the elite Association of American Universities, made up only 2.2 percent of the total number of institutions of higher education. However, they had 20 percent of the undergraduate students, 24 percent of the faculty, 47 percent of the graduate students in professional schools, 50 percent of the graduate students in the arts and sciences, and 77 percent of the awarded doctoral degrees. Needless to add, they also possessed a corner on talent. Nearly one-half of the college graduates in the *Who's Who* for 1929 had attended one of these institutions. In 1936, 50 graduates of Yale alone were college or university presidents.

As was the case for corporate directors and Wall Street lawyers, just about one-third of the trustees were in the *Social Register.* This percentage is especially impressive when it is added that the Southern-based University of North Carolina had 104 (!) trustees, and that most of the others not listed in the *Social Register* came from state universities which have no *Social Register* cities nearby. As might be expected, the trustees listed in the *Social Register* were much more likely to be at private institutions, and it goes without saying that Harvard, Yale, Princeton, and Columbia are controlled by members of the upper class. Beck developed other interesting information on the trustees of the elite universities which shows that they are members of the power elite. Nearly half of the top 200 industrial corporations and the top 200 financial corporations were represented on the 30 boards. One hundred seventy-five men from 194 of these top 400 companies held 1321 positions as corporate directors, an average of seven to eight per trustee. This average is very similar to those found in our studies of corporate directors. Other findings by Beck include the fact that lawyers and judges made up 25 percent of the total group of trustees, while bankers and manufacturers each contributed 15 percent of the total. Some 45 percent of the trustees were listed in Poor's *Register of Corporations, Directors, and Executives.* The trustees held 54 directorships in 29 major foundations; 24 trustees were on J. P. Morgan's 1929 "preferred list" to receive "new issue securities at less than their market value"; and 12 were on mining magnate James W. Gerard's (SR, NY) list of "52 men who run America." Seven of the trustees were on two boards in the top 30.

There is only one possible objection to Beck's little-known but definitive study: It is based upon the years 1934–1935. While these years are within the time span with which we are concerned, it might be claimed that changes have taken place over the past 30 years. There is no reason to believe that the dominance of the elite universities by members of the power elite has diminished, however. A study of 100 men from the 12 foundations showed that one-third of them also served as university trustees or university presidents. There were six interlocks with Duke University, three with Yale, two with Princeton, two with Amherst, two with Dartmouth, two with Cornell, and one each with such elite schools as Harvard, Smith, Stanford, Cal Tech, and Vanderbilt. As another example of this continuing interlock, there were 60 interlocks with universities among the top 20 industrials studied in Chapter 2.[13]

D. *The Mass Media* help to shape and fill our consciousness. Yet it is difficult to gauge the impact of newspapers, magazines, television, and radio, except to say that they decide the limits within which discussion occurs. Perhaps the most persuasive influ-

---

[13] *Ibid.,* pp. 78–79, reprinted by permission of the publisher.

ence is indirect—that is corporate advertising:

Newspapers and magazines, for example, are highly mechanized business operations which are run on a profit-making basis, and only a small part of their income is from reader support. When advertising is important, the threat of its discontinuance can often have effects upon editorial policy. However, what is even more important is that the dependency on advertising keeps the subscription price of the magazine or newspaper very low and thus makes it impossible for publications to exist which must depend in their infancy on reader support. The problem, in short, is getting a newspaper or magazine started in the first place. The role of advertising in keeping subscription prices low has precluded the entrance of new periodicals into the field. Thus, when a new magazine begins, it is dependent upon large financial backers, as was the case when sociologist Daniel Bell and publishing executive Irving Kristol founded *The Public Interest* in 1965. According to *Time* magazine, they relied "on backing from Wall Street, and other friends. . . ."[14]

Then of course there are the newspaper chains. The most famous is the Hearst Empire. Not as powerful as it once was, it is nonetheless impressive: twelve newspapers, fourteen magazines, three television stations, six radio stations, a news service, a photo service, a feature syndicate, and Avon paperbacks. The Hearst chain is but the best known and largest of chain newspapers.

Domhoff's summary remarks can be paraphrased as follows:
1. The majority of the instruments of the mass media are owned or directly controlled by members of the national upper class.
2. Yet a crazy-quilt kind of pluralism survives. There are plenty of locally owned newspapers, hundreds of independent and at times far-out radio and TV stations, plus numerous little magazines for every race, religious creed, and political denomination.

3. But by controlling *major* opinion-molding institutions in the country, upper-class persons play a very important part in shaping the outer boundaries within which debates and discussions occur.
4. Still, as Domhoff put it:

Such factors as diversity within the upper class, the American libertarian tradition, the non-upper-class backgrounds of most reporters and scholars, and the myriad of locally or religiously controlled colleges, newspapers, and magazines keep this upper-class domination of major opinion-molding institutions from being translated into complete and monolithic control of American opinion.[15]

TRANSITIONAL REMARKS

One reaction to upper class controls has been agrarian socialism. Let us examine the social and political structure of North America's earliest experiment in agrarian socialism, one with clear-cut origins going back to the populist movement: the socialist government elected to office during World War II in the Canadian wheat province of Saskatchewan. We will observe the heavy emphasis placed by the ordinary citizens on popular participation at all levels of government. Indeed, the absence of authoritarianism, by any definition, is striking.

Although this socialist provincial government did pioneer work in various forms of social legislation, it did not, it could not, establish by itself a fully socialist government based on state ownership of a means of production directed by the people. Still, the government's behavior was a far-cry from the Joe McCarthy antics that would be expected of it if the Hofstadter thesis were correct.

More to the point is the wielding by the upper-class of controls to further their own interests, including their participation in university decision-making, a topic explored in the Leggett—Roach paper on antiwar demonstrations and upper-class repression at the University of Connecticut.

[14] *Ibid.,* p. 81, reprinted by permission of the publisher.

[15] *Ibid.,* p. 83, reprinted by permission of the publisher.

Social Structure and Political Activity

Seymour M. Lipset

Various observers of the North American scene have called attention to the problems of mass passivity and political apathy in our culture. Myrdal has pointed out that the masses in America "are accustomed to being static and receptive. They are not daring, but long for security. They do not know how to cooperate and how to pool risks and sacrifices for a common goal. They do not meet much. They do not organize. They do not speak for themselves; they are the listeners in America. They seldom elect representatives from their own midst to Congress, to state legislatures or to city councils. They rather support friendly leaders from the upper strata, particularly lawyers."[1]

Myrdal's description is accurate for most parts of the United States and Canada. It does not, however, give a picture of Saskatchewan political activity. The Saskatchewan Cooperative Commonwealth Federation [CCF—a socialist political party now in power in the province of Saskatchewan. It won 75 percent of the provincial legislative seats in a June, 1971 election] has succeeded in involving more people in direct political activity than any other party in American or Canadian history, with the possible exception of certain similar farmers' parties.[2] In 1945 the party had a dues-paying membership of 31,858, or approximately 4 percent of the total population and 8 percent of the 1944 electorate. CCF membership in the province has reached the equivalent of a national dues-paying membership of about 500,000 in Canada and 6,000,000 in the United States. One can hardly speak here of mass passivity. An examination of the factors related to the attainment of so large a membership should throw light on some of the reasons for political apathy in other areas of the continent.

■ Taken from Seymour M. Lipset, *Agrarian Socialism*, rev. ed. (Berkeley: University of California Press, 1971), pp. 199–219. Published by the University of California Press; reprinted by permission of The Regents of the University of California.

The most important single factor differentiating the Saskatchewan social scene from other regions is the high degree of individual participation in community organizations in rural districts. There are from 40,000 to 60,000 different elective rural posts that must be filled by the 125,000 farmers. There is, then, approximately one position available for every two or three farmers. Table 21 indicates the nature of these posts.

The large number of positions in rural Saskatchewan does not mean that one out of every two or three farmers is a community official, for many rural leaders are active in a number of organizations. In most communities the same people are on the rural municipal councils, the boards of directors of local cooperative stores, and the executive of the United Farmers of Canada (Saskatchewan Section). A rough estimate, drawn from many interviews and more than 800 questionnaires filled out by Saskatchewan rural leaders, indicates, however, that at least 15 percent of the farmers hold community posts to which they have been elected by their neighbors. This proportion of formal community leaders to total population is much larger than has been attained in any urban area. It is probably also greater than that found in other rural areas, for Saskatchewan has the largest cooperative movement on the continent and more local governmental units than any other American rural state.[3]

This situation is a result of an almost unique combination of factors that have created the formal structural conditions for widespread individual participation in community affairs. The farmers have been faced, in the forty years since the province was created, with a series of major social and economic challenges requiring the establishment of a large number of community institutions to meet them. Pioneering on the unsettled prairie in the two decades before the First World War, farmers had to establish local rural governments, hospitals, schools, and a telephone system. They were faced with the

TABLE 21 Elective Positions, Rural Saskatchewan

Position	No. of Local Groups	No. of Officials in Each	Total
Municipal council	304	7	2,128
School-board member	5,184	3	15,552
Hospital-board official	79	6	474
Telephone-board director	1,127	5	5,635
Wheat Pool and other marketing cooperatives	1,257	10	12,570
Cooperative store	519	8	4,152
Community hall	203	5	1,015
Miscellaneous cooperatives	48	5	240
United Farmers, etc.*	—	—	—
Lodge*	—	—	—
Church group*	—	—	—
Political party*	—	—	—
Minimum total			41,766

*Figures not available.

hazards of a one-crop wheat economy that was subject to extreme fluctuations in income because of variability in grain prices and climatic conditions. Their position as isolated individual producers and consumers at the end of the distribution system left them exposed to monopolistic exploitation by the railroads, the grain companies, and the retailers. Through the formation of cooperatives and political pressure groups, Saskatchewan farmers sought to improve their competitive position in the fluctuating price economy and to reduce the cost of the articles they bought. All these community and economic associations had to be organized by a handful of people.

The area of effective community action in the wheat economy of Saskatchewan is necessarily limited by distance. Wheat farms are large, and wheat regions are consequently sparsely settled. The rural municipalities, the local governmental units, contain less than 400 families, and each municipality (about eighteen square miles in area) contains a number of distinct communities. There are about 1,500 railroad stops, over 1,100 rural telephone companies, and more than 5,000 local school districts in Saskatchewan.[4]

The sheer need for extensive community organization would not necessarily result in widespread participation in community affairs by farmers. In many rural areas on this continent,

the community institutions serving farmers are controlled by members of urban business and professional groups of the neighboring towns. County government positions and consolidated school-district posts are open to non-farmers in many agricultural districts. Within the rural areas of the Southern States or in parts of California, where significant social and economic cleavage exists within the rural community, the wealthier and upper-class farmers are the formal community leaders, and the bulk of the poorer farmers are politically apathetic.

Rural Saskatchewan, however, is socially a "one-class" community. Differences in income and status do exist within individual rural communities, but they are not large enough to bring about the emergence of distinct social classes. The wheat farmers have more in common with each other economically and socially than with any other group. The organized community life of the agrarian population is conducted independently of the activities of neighboring towns and cities. Very little intermingling takes place between the cliques of the town and those of the countryside.[5] Almost all the formal community positions must be held by farmers. Neither the rural municipal councils nor the rural school boards are legally open to town lawyers or other members of the urban middle class. The cooperatives are almost completely rural organizations.

Under these conditions, any farmer who has executive ability is forced to accept community responsibility. A large portion of the population has become accustomed to playing an active role in different organizations. Rural leaders must conduct meetings, write reports, make speeches, and recruit members. One informant described the effect on his father of being in a leading position:

My father was elected vice-president of the S.G.G.A. local early in the 'twenties. He hadn't wanted the job, but he was a leading farmer in the district and had been a member for a long time, so some of the other officials prevailed on him to take the post.

Shortly after he was elected, the local sponsored a meeting by a Progressive M.P. The chairman of the lodge took sick and my father was told that he would have to preside over the meeting. He tried to get out of it, for he had never made a speech in his life. He couldn't, however, and had to preside. For days before the meeting he stopped all work and went around the house reciting a five-minute speech which he had memorized. The family almost went crazy listening to it.

On the day of the meeting, he delivered the speech and afterward was complimented on his ability by the M.P. After that he lost his fear. He would chair meetings and gradually began to make speeches for the organization. By the time the CCF was organized he had no fear in facing a meeting of hundreds and speaking for hours. Before he died he must have delivered hundreds of speeches at CCF meetings, cooperative meetings, and other farmers' gatherings.

As officials in cooperative and governmental units, local farm leaders study and make decisions on the policies of larger organizations and governments. The members of school boards, hospital boards, and rural municipal councils become acquainted with the problems of taxation and administration, and with the policies of provincial and federal governments. The leaders in farmers' cooperatives and educational organizations must act on the policies of governments that affect them. The 11,000 or more Wheat Pool committee men are kept up to date by the Pool's educational department on all national and international aspects of the wheat problem. They learn at once of government decisions that may affect their economic position. The Pool has sixteen field men who visit the committees periodically to keep them informed of problems of the cooperative movement.[6]

This structure of grass-roots participation provides direct channels of communication between the mass of farmers and their leaders. The Saskatchewan rural community is highly receptive to outside pressures and can be quickly mobilized by its leaders. A striking example of this mobilization took place in 1941–42. Wheat prices were fixed by the Canadian federal government at 70 cents a bushel in 1941. The Wheat Pool had demanded a higher price, but the government refused because the Nazi conquest of Europe had closed many Canadian markets. Crop conditions were bad and the farmers who had anticipated a period of war prosperity began to fear that 1941 would be another depression year for them, though the prices of goods they bought were rising. Wheat Pool committees passed resolutions demanding that the provincial organization take action to gain a higher price and crop insurance. The Pool leaders organized meetings throughout the province to discuss the problem. "Farmers by the thousands flocked to these meetings, leaving their threshing machine standing idle in many instances, in order to raise their voices in the interests of a better deal in agriculture."[7]

The Wheat Pool officials, who are relatively conservative, desired to limit the farmers' protest to resolutions and to personal pressure on members of Parliament. This, however, did not satisfy the farmers of Saskatchewan. A grass-roots demand for action swept the province. One militant old farmer described what happened at one Pool meeting.

When in 1941 things got intolerable and we resorted to mass meetings I was at the one in Swift Current. I was never at a meeting where the audience was so hostile to the platform. You could feel it like a chill through the church and there were noted men on it too.

A little old fellow got up and moved that we send two men from each sub-district to Ottawa and demand dollar wheat. There was a loud guffaw, but he soon got a seconder and it carried unanimously. The point I want to make is this: it was right from the grass roots, there were no paid officials on this, though there was one on the platform. The idea went through the Province like a prairie fire. Forty thousand dollars were collected in spite of the determined opposition of the Liberal machine. Four hundred men were sent to Ottawa; preachers, sinners and lawyers. Twenty cents more per bushel was eventually secured.[8]

The "March on Ottawa" is but one of a number of movements which the dirt farmers began and carried through against the opposition of the bureaucracy of farmers' organizations and of the government.[9] Though the forces making for bureaucratic control of the farmers' movement exist in Saskatchewan as they do elsewhere, the structural conditions for rank-and-file participation and for resistance to such control are stronger there than in most other areas. There are comparatively few paid positions in the farmers' cooperative and educational movements. The secondary leaders of all the farm groups are working farmers who are just as much affected by economic pressures and general currents of opinion as are the rank and file. Unless these leaders express the feelings of their neighbors, who have chosen them, they will be replaced by others who do. The extent of direct participation means that the farmers' movement must always be receptive to the needs of the members. Further, it results in heightened awareness by the farmers of large-scale political and economic events.

This widespread activity makes for rapid political changes. Its effects can be seen in the influence of the "March on Ottawa" movement on the growth of the CCF. In 1941 the CCF was the only party to support fully the demands of the organized farmers. The federal Liberal government refused to meet some of them. This fact was known to the rural leaders and, through them, the knowledge spread to most of the farmers of the province. Between August 31, 1941, and July 31, 1942, the period of the agitation resulting in the "March on Ottawa," CCF membership rose from 4,460 to 9,813.[10] This increase is highly significant, for it occurred between elections at a time when there was no prospect of another election and party membership normally could be expected to decline.

In the past the social organization of the economy—the fact that almost all the farmers were wheat farmers and therefore had common interests and problems—meant that "solutions" to problems in one area were rapidly accepted in others. Each rural community in Saskatchewan is a replica of every other. An example of rural flexibility in adopting a common solution to a community problem can be seen in the rapid spread of the municipal doctor scheme, which began in the early 'twenties. Saskatchewan farmers have always found it difficult to secure adequate medical care at a reasonable cost. There was often a rapid turnover in physicians and it was difficult to get good ones. In 1921 the rural municipality of Sarnia decided to hire a doctor on salary, so that farmers could be assured of medical services and the physician would be guaranteed his salary.[11] This plan proved successful, and gradually spread until, by 1944, in spite of opposition from the organized medical profession, one-third of the rural municipalities of Saskatchewan had doctors on salary. Once it had proved itself in a few areas, the system was accepted and advertised throughout the province by the organized farmers' movement. The United Farmers of Canada (Saskatchewan Section) spread circulars and other propaganda materials, such as the following:

> At present we are committed to pooling our wheat and other farm products. The municipal doctor scheme is in reality a pooling of our doctor bills. Or we might look on it as an insurance against unduly high doctor bills in any one year—an equalization scheme. . . .
>
> In no case where the municipal doctor scheme has been tried has there been any complaint from either ratepayers or doctors. In ——— Municipality during eight years under this scheme their death rate is much below the average for the province and they have had no maternal deaths during this time. . . .
>
> For additional information before voting on this important question, attend a meeting to be held in the Orange Hall on Friday, December 7, at 3 p.m. sharp. The meeting will be addressed by Mr. ____ of the Research Department of the United Farmers of Canada. Mr. ____ and Mr. ____, Secretary-Treasurer and Reeve, respectively, of the Municipality.[12]

The rapid acceptance of new ideas and movements in Saskatchewan can be attributed mainly to the high degree of organization. The small rural communities are forced to adjust to changing economic and social situations. Interest in political and economic matters is continually being stimulated. Farmers derive most of their ideas and knowledge of larger problems and policies from well-informed neighbors who hold community posts.

The Wheat Pool, the cooperatives, the agrarian Progressive Party of the 1920s, and the CCF were all built rapidly through this structure of organized farmer opinion. The role of the social structure of the western wheat belt in facilitating the rise of new movements has never been sufficiently appreciated by historians and sociologists. To the economic and cultural factors usually associated with the development of these movements should be added the variable of social structure. Repeated challenges and crises forced the western farmers to create many more community institutions (especially cooperatives and economic pressure groups) than are necessary in a more stable area. These groups in turn provided a structural basis for immediate action in critical situations.

Though it was a new radical party, the CCF did not have to build up an organization from scratch. It was organized from the start by the local "class" and community leaders of rural Saskatchewan. The fact that the province was so well organized on an occupational basis enabled the new party to obtain the support of the politically conscious community leaders. By the early 1940s, CCF committees, composed in the main of the same people who were the officials of the other rural organizations, were operating in almost every district in the province. It was this "machine" that brought the CCF to power.

Today the CCF has become the political voice of the organized agrarian community. The organized farmers are brought into direct contact with "their" government by active participation in a class political party that controls the state.

The basic unit of political organization in rural Saskatchewan is the poll, the smallest voting district. Each provincial constituency is divided into from one hundred to two hundred polls. The CCF has attempted to build up in each district a working committee of two or three people who will take charge of CCF edu-

cational work among the one hundred to two hundred voters in the poll. Above the local organizations is the constituency. A CCF constituency has a committee of twelve to twenty-five members and an executive committee of seven to twelve members. The committees are elected at annual conventions, which are attended by three delegates from each poll. The leading body of the entire party is the Provincial Council, which has representatives from each constituency and meets several times a year. The provincial party organization supervises the work of each constituency body. Between Council meetings, the party is governed by an executive body of nine. This provincial organization is controlled by the annual provincial convention. Each constituency convention elects ten delegates to the provincial convention. The convention elects top party officers and determines policy.[13]

If the formal pattern of the CCF party organization were actually followed, about 24,000 people would be active party members, either as members of poll committees or as delegates to the party conventions and committees. Actually, this optimum figure is never reached, for many districts have no active poll committees. In recent years the average attendance at the fifty annual CCF constituency conventions has been about 100 delegates, 5,000 people in all. Many more electors, however, are active in the local organizations than attend as convention delegates. One could safely estimate that between 10,000 and 15,000 people take part in the actual operation of the party.

Between elections, this activity does not include much formal party work. Poll committees usually meet once or twice a year to discuss the work of the local and larger party bodies. They arrange public meetings for party leaders and enroll new members. In some areas, committees meet regularly to discuss party policy and to analyze books and outlines suggested by the provincial office. The constituency committees, which have about 1,000 members, have much greater responsibilities and consequently meet from six to twelve times a year. These committees are the grass-roots bodies which influence the work of the CCF members of the legislature and the provincial party.

The fact that the majority of CCF members and officials are not continuously active in party work does not mean that they are not acting politically in other community roles. Most of the active CCF members have administrative tasks in rural organizations. They are members of local cooperative store boards, Wheat Pool committees, and U.F.C. executive bodies, and do not differentiate between their activities in these organizations and in the CCF. One informant expressed this feeling clearly.

> It's really all one movement that we have here. We are building socialism through the Wheat Pool, through our co-op store, through our U.F.C. local, as well as through the CCF. They are all part of one movement, the "people's movement." Sometimes one organization or fight is more important than the other, but we need them all. The fact that our poll committee doesn't meet except before conventions doesn't mean the CCF'ers here don't care about the party. We feel that we are building the CCF when we build our co-op store, and we are building cooperation and destroying the profit system when we build the CCF.

At first glance the relationship between the CCF and other rural community organizations appears similar to the pattern of party–society relations advocated by the Communist Party. Communists want to be the vanguard of the working class, the class leaders. To accomplish this, they attempt to permeate working-class organizations and become their officials. In the Soviet Union, Communists are placed in key positions in trade unions, cooperatives, and local governments. In democratic countries they use the tactics of "boring from within" to achieve positions of leadership.[14]

In Saskatchewan, however, the "vanguard," the leaders of the farming community, started the CCF. As a result, CCF activity and community activity are closely interrelated. This situation is not a result of any planned action, but is, rather, a consequence of the tight organization of the farming community on an occupational basis. The CCF is the class party, the farmers' party, and thus controls the farmers' organizations. Many leaders of the CCF and of rural organizations are not aware of this close interrelationship. The party makes no direct efforts to influence other institutions and has no explicit policy for its members to follow in them. There are no CCF caucuses in the cooper-

atives or other rural groups. In practice, however, most of the secondary leaders are CCF members and therefore support the policy of the party and the CCF government. The leaders are, in fact, continually engaged in political activity.

The relationship between the CCF and rural community organizations is a two-way affair. CCF leaders in their capacity as local government officials and cooperative leaders know the needs of the community and the effect of government policies on the rural community. They use the party organization as a direct channel of communication to the legislature and the cabinet. A stream of resolutions moves constantly from local and constituency committees to the Provincial Council and the government.

Since the election of 1944, interest in CCF conventions and governing committees has grown greatly. Through participation in this organization at least 10,000 people are led to feel that they are taking a direct part in the establishment of government policy. The vitality of grass-roots participation in rural Saskatchewan leads to vigorous criticism of the activities of the government and the party. The active members in the CCF are mainly experienced local leaders, who represent the grass-roots, not the summits, of the rural community. The CCF differs from many European socialist parties and the non-socialist parties in the United States and Canada in that its secondary leaders are unpaid and receive little additional status from their party position. The party officials had status in the community before they became CCF leaders, and therefore are relatively independent of top control. This pattern of grass-roots democracy runs through all the farmers' movements in Saskatchewan, and the CCF is only continuing it. In order to perpetuate interest and loyalty to the party, CCF leaders are almost forced to encourage criticism and suggestions from the rank and file. Many CCF leaders, from Premier Douglas down, reiterate that they are only the servants of the majority of the party. Theoretically, the party leadership and the government must accept any policy adopted by the provincial convention.

Many members of the CCF now conceive of government as a tool to be manipulated by the people. They come to constituency conventions fully prepared to let the government know their opinions. The resolutions adopted at conventions reveal the operation of this conception of direct democracy:

> That the Government investigate and pass legislation which will stop completely the overloading and crowding of live stock in stock cars, trucks or any other vehicle.
> That a stop be made to the shipping of live stock unfit for human consumption to packing houses or stock yards. The only exception being stock clearly designated for purposes other than human consumption.[15]
> Whereas the Department of Health is prepared to go to considerable work and expense to have all citizens tested for T.B. to have the disease controlled and
> Whereas after the test has been taken and even if your family shows no signs of the disease they may go home and drink milk from a diseased cow
> Therefore be it resolved that the Government make an extensive test of all cattle as soon as possible regardless of whether the present veterinary profession have time to do it all or not.[16]
> That we the delegates of Saltcoats Convention, especially the women members, desire the Government to investigate the possibility of the Woolen Mill handling woven materials, as blankets from this class of goods fulfill many useful purposes on the farm.[17]

The lack of inhibitions in criticizing government policy can be seen in a number of resolutions.

> Be it resolved that we consider the five CCF Cabinet Ministers who talked and voted against the resolution to exempt single men up to $1,200 and married men up to $2,500 on the Federal Income Tax, were badly out of line, ... especially Mr. Fines, who actually implied that he would tax the lower paid classes exactly as the Capitalist King Government is doing.[18]
> Whereas the existence of natural gas and oil in commercial quantities in the Province of Saskatchewan has been proven conclusively;
> And whereas the CCF as a Socialist Party believes in and advocates the public ownership of the natural resources of this Province for the benefit of the people of Saskatchewan;
> And whereas a resolution was passed at the 1945 Provincial Convention urging the Government of Saskatchewan to undertake the development and distribution of natural gas and oil in this Province;
> And whereas natural gas and oil in the Province of Saskatchewan continues to be extensively exploited by private persons and concerns;
> Therefore be it resolved that the Government of Saskatchewan be called upon to show cause why the exploitation of these resources has been allowed to fall into private hands.
> And be it further resolved that the Government of Saskatchewan be immediately called upon to place these resources under social ownership, control and operation for the immense benefit of the people of Saskatchewan.[19]

Free forums, such as the constituency conventions provide, strengthen the CCF in innumerable ways. The top leaders can never depart far from the thinking of the rank and file without being made aware of it. The conventions serve, also, to preserve the vitality and support of the party. In interviews many CCF members stressed this existence of direct democracy through the party.

> Well, what did you think of that speech? I really made B. (a Cabinet minister) squirm. Don't misunderstand it though. I think B. is doing a good job, but like all men, he makes mistakes and he has to be told about them. That's the wonderful thing about this party. The members really run it. No one in this room would have the least hesitation about telling anyone from Coldwell or Douglass down that he is wrong if he thinks so. Can you see any Liberal supporter doing that to old Gardiner? Why, did you know the Liberals haven't had a convention since 1933?[20]

To what degree can the formal structure and appearance of grass-roots democracy in the CCF be said to be real? Do the people really govern? One cabinet minister, in discussing the role of conventions, said:

> They are today the most important part of the CCF organization. I think we are doing good work and that the majority of the people approve our policies. However this will not keep us in power. A lot of good governments have been defeated and lost power. Our people will not actively support and work for the CCF once their feeling of "Get the Rascals out" is over. . . .
> The one thing that maintains our active

support is the feeling that the people run the government, that we are only their servants. The conventions reinforce that feeling every year. It is therefore important that we never refuse to carry out anything demanded at the Provincial Convention unless we have a darn good explanation. Our supporters will put up with mistakes or with inefficiency, but they won't stand for dictation. The one thing that can kill the CCF is the idea that we are another party like the Liberals and Conservatives, that the government is composed of another group of politicians and "hellers" who come around every four years for votes.

Cabinet ministers and party leaders appear to act on these principles. *This does not mean that they do not make policy.* In fact, almost all important provincial policies are set by the cabinet and the members of the legislature. At provincial conventions the final form of resolutions, suggesting changes in policy, is usually determined by top leaders. This control, however, is exercised by men who combine superior oratorical ability, status, and information. When the leaders oppose a resolution they are able to control the overwhelming majority of delegates.

In the 1946 convention a resolution proposing government ownership of gas and oil appeared to be favored by the majority of the delegates, for it had been a traditional demand of the farmers' movement and of the CCF. Two cabinet ministers armed with statistical data were able to convince the convention that the oil and gas fields were not yet proved commercial fields and that the cost of developing them as a risk investment was beyond the financial ability of the province.

On certain issues, however, government and party leaders have been voted down and accepted their defeat. The 1946 provincial convention adopted two resolutions recommending changes in government policy that had previously been rejected by the cabinet and the CCF legislative caucus: one supported the right of married women to work for the government, and the other urged the forty-four-hour week for labor with no reduction in pay. At the following session of the legislature both proposals of the convention were adopted.

There has been, however, one major issue in which the government has not completely followed convention instructions. The 1945 and 1946 conventions urged the government to fill all policy-making positions in the civil service with persons who support CCF ideals. The cabinet at first refused, but gradually has been making concessions to the pressure from the conventions.

Direct democracy in the CCF and other Saskatchewan farm organizations is limited by the extent of the knowledge, experience, and interests of the secondary leaders. CCF conventions fail to pass resolutions on a multitude of important problems because the delegates lack opinions about, or knowledge of, these problems. The conventions rarely bother with the details of a government health scheme, the methods of operation of government industry, the problems of debt refunding or repayment, priorities in economic planning, or provincial proposals to Dominion—provincial conferences, though these administrative details may be more important than the broad over-all policies with which the resolutions deal. Other important issues neglected by the conventions are foreign policy and other aspects of national affairs that do not affect agriculture. The overwhelming majority of resolutions reflect the day-to-day economic and social concerns of farmers and workers: farm regulations, provincial tax legislation, roads, liquor laws, and social services.[21]

The extensive grass-roots discussion of governmental problems is not new in the history of the province. Long before the CCF was formed, the Saskatchewan Grain Growers' Association met in annual district and provincial conventions to adopt policies to be urged on governments. The annual meeting of the S.G.G.A. was known as the "Farmers' Parliament" and was well attended. The Liberal Party, which then controlled the province, paid close attention to the actions of these conventions and wherever possible implemented the recommendations of the S.G.G.A. In order to maintain the support of the organized farmers, it offered cabinet posts to Grain Growers' officials.[22] The provincial Liberals lost their hold on the farmers' movement when the Progressives were formed in 1920, because the federal Liberal Party would not meet many of the agrarian demands.

The fact that extensive participation in the Saskatchewan CCF is not a result of the growth of a new political movement or of some characteristic inherent in the CCF becomes clear if the organization is compared with the party else-where in Canada where it has been successful. Of those voting for the CCF in Saskatchewan, 15 percent were party members. The British Columbia CCF, which is largely an urban working-class movement, won 39 percent of the total vote in the 1946 provincial election, but less than 5 percent of its supporters are mem-bers of the party. In one Vancouver constitu-ency that has elected socialist or CCF candi-dates since 1930, party leaders do not know who their supporters are, and only a handful of them are in the party.[23] In Toronto the CCF received 133,443 votes in 1945, but has never enlisted more than 3.8 percent of this figure in the movement. Actually, the Toronto CCF has considerably less than 1,000 active members. The growth of the CCF movement in Toronto and Vancouver has not been the result of, nor has it resulted in, an increase in direct political participation by the masses. The party in these cities resembles the traditional North American parties, with little direct contact between the organization and the major part of the elector-ate.

If one notes the differences between the community structure of Saskatchewan and that of cities such as Toronto and Vancouver, the relationship between structure and the extent of political activity becomes clear. The 600,000 rural residents of Saskatchewan elect 2,100 members of municipal councils and 15,000 members of school boards. Large cities, how-ever, have an insignificant number of commu-nity positions compared to their total popula-tion. The 800,000 citizens of Toronto elect only 24 members of a council and 18 members of the school board.

In most North American cities the majority of political and community posts are held by members of the middle and upper classes.[24] The city councils are filled with lawyers and other business or professional people. Many community organizations such as hospital boards, Y.M.C.A. boards, and community chests are dominated by members of the upper classes. This again is in striking contrast to rural Saskatchewan, where farmers must fill these posts themselves.

Trade unionism is the major institutional exception in urban life in which workers are given an opportunity to hold office and take responsibility. The ratio of officials to total union membership, however, is often very low. There are many union locals with thousands of members and two to twenty officials. In Sas-katchewan the ratio of members to officials in the cooperatives and educational organizations ranges from five to one to twenty to one. The Saskatchewan Wheat Pool, the largest farm or-ganization, has a total membership of 60,000 to 70,000. About 11,000 farmers are elected members of Wheat Pool committees in their localities. One out of every six members of this organization, which most closely approximates a trade-union in rural Saskatchewan, is a local official who meets regularly with others from six to twelve times a year to discuss and act on local, provincial, and national matters. Local members usually attend meetings twice a year. The average local Pool organization has about sixty members.

The cooperative movement is extremely weak in the urban areas of Canada and the United States. In contrast with Europe, cooper-atives in America have not succeeded in inter-esting many workers. The cooperatives, there-fore, do not serve as a basis for training leaders and creating channels of communication be-tween workers and larger institutions. The few urban cooperatives that do exist tend to be led by members of the middle class. The break-down or absence of real neighborhoods in ur-ban centers has also served to prevent the for-mation of a local corps of leaders. The political machine has provided the only effective urban leadership group, and it could hardly be ex-pected to be a vehicle for new ideas and for social change. Outside the factory, the urban working class is dispersed. There are few chan-nels for genuine intra-class communication.

The building of a new mass political organi-zation is, therefore, much more difficult in a city than in a rural community or small town. It is almost impossible to locate the informal leaders of the lower classes. The people are not accustomed to making political decisions. In the anonymity of city living, organized person-to-person political contact is difficult.

It it is true that popular interest and partici-pation in political activity are facilitated by the wheat economy of Saskatchewan, one should expect similar patterns of behavior in compara-ble areas. Saskatchewan's neighbors permit such comparisons. The state of North Dakota, economically and geographically, is almost a replica of Saskatchewan. It is sparsely settled, has a one-crop wheat economy, and is rural for the most part. The environmental and economic challenges which forced the farmers of Saskatchewan to establish many different organizational structures were similar in North Dakota. This state should therefore be expected to have a high degree of political activity.

The historical facts tend to confirm this expectation. In that state the Non-Partisan League secured its greatest strength and membership. At its height, in 1920, it had 50,000 members, which was 7.7 percent of the total population. The League won more than 1,000,000 votes in various states and had 300,000 members, but in no other state was the ratio of its membership to population or to its electoral support so high as in North Dakota.[25] Today the Farmers' Union, which is politically the most active of the major farmers' organizations, is strongest in North Dakota.

> The Farmers' Union is by far the biggest single force in the state, and its North Dakota unit is probably the strongest farmers' organization in the whole country on a state level. . . . Of the 57,000 farmers in North Dakota, more than 30,000 are members, which must be something of a record for saturation in any movement.[26]
>
> Fifteen hundred local groups of the National Farmers' Union (of North Dakota) meet with staff organizers once or twice a month for discussions on local, national and world problems. . . . Each year with wives and children over sixteen voting in addition to the farmers themselves, the locals elect their officers and their delegates to the state convention where the next year's program is planned.[27]

In Canada, Saskatchewan's neighbor on the west, Alberta, is somewhat similar in economic and social structure. It too has widespread community participation through local governments and cooperatives. Politically, also, Alberta tends to resemble Saskatchewan. The last thirty years have seen the growth of three large social movements: the Progressives and the United Farmers of Alberta in the 'twenties, the Social Credit Party in the last decade, and a growing CCF movement today. Alberta farmers, like those of

Saskatchewan and North Dakota, are quick to react politically when a threat to their society or economy arises.

Manitoba, Saskatchewan's eastern neighbor, however, has had much less community and political activity. Its cooperative movement is considerably weaker than those of the other provinces. There has not been a significant farmers' political movement in Manitoba since the early 'twenties. It is the only one of the three Prairie Provinces that does not have a farmers' educational and political pressure organization such as the U.F.C. (Saskatchewan Section) or the United Farmers of Alberta. The differences between Manitoba and the rest of the Prairie Provinces help to confirm our hypothesis as to the causes of political apathy.

Manitoba has been less exposed to the vagaries of weather and price fluctuations than the rest of the northern prairie region. Only a small part of Manitoba is in the drought belt. The province is no longer a one-crop wheat region. Many of its rural residents practice mixed farming and have a large immediate market in Winnipeg. This tends to reduce economic hazards. The economic need for a large cooperative movement is not so great.

A second reason for the smaller degree of political participation is the strength of urban influence in rural Manitoba. The inhabited portion of Manitoba is a much smaller area than that of either Alberta or Saskatchewan. Much of the rural part of the province is close to the large city of Winnipeg. The important community and provincial institutions are concentrated in the one city that is accessible to most farmers. The need for duplicating the community services that exist in urban areas is not so great in rural Manitoba as it is in Saskatchewan and, consequently, local activity is weak. The Manitoba Wheat Pool has only two districts as compared with Saskatchewan's sixteen.

Manitoba is the oldest of the Prairie Provinces. Its pioneer days are almost a generation behind those of Saskatchewan. The striving to create and maintain basic community institutions ended long ago. Other things being equal, older organizations tend to enlist less participation and interest than new ones. It is significant that during the period between the 1890s and the early twentieth century, when economic and ecological conditions in Manitoba approximated those of Saskatchewan and Alberta to-day, the Manitoba agrarian political movement was strong. In the 'nineties the wheat farmers organized a strong third party. The Manitoba Grain Growers' Association and later the United Farmers of Manitoba were large and powerful pressure groups which made and un-made governments and built the first large co-operative movement in western Canada.

A Saskatchewan informant who took part in a recent CCF election campaign in Manitoba indicated clearly the effect on political life of the lack of community participation.

> I was in Manitoba at the last Federal election in Russell, the home of Hon. J. A. Glen, and was able to see the CCF in operation. Many of the conditions were akin to Saskatche-wan, but the ground work was missing. No trained speakers were at hand. Many were poorly equipped to conduct a meeting. No experience had been gained like Saskatche-wan's Wheat Pool Delegates and field men had gained in meeting the exacting demands of the farmers under contract to the Pool. If Glen had been running in a Saskatchewan riding he wouldn't have lasted as long as a snowball in hell.
>
> They have no system of carrying on co-operative education in Manitoba like in Sas-katchewan. The farmers just aren't used to attending meetings and discussing their prob-lems.

Myrdal has described the relationship be-tween political apathy and the lack of commu-nity organization in America.

> In local politics, America has, on the whole, not spread political responsibility upon countless citizens' boards, as have, for exam-ple, the Northern European countries (including England), thereby widening politi-cal participation and making politics more anonymous and less dependent on outstand-ing leadership. Much more, not only of broad policy making, but also of detailed decisions are, in America, centralized in the offices of salaried functionaries. *Political participation of the ordinary citizen in America is pretty much restricted to the intermittently recurring elections. Politics is not organized to be a daily concern and responsibility of the common citizen.* The relative paucity of trade unions, coopera-tives, and other civic interest organizations tends to accentuate this abstention on the part of the common citizens from sharing in the government of their communities as a normal routine of life. In this essential sense American politics is centralized.[28]

A description of the Saskatchewan scene is the inverse of Myrdal's description of the Amer-ican scene. The tendency in local politics has been to spread political responsibility among countless citizens' boards; this has brought about wider political participation and has made politics more anonymous and less depen-dent on outstanding leadership. *Political partici-pation of the ordinary citizen in Saskatchewan is not restricted to the intermittently recurring elections. Politics is organized to be a daily concern and responsibility of the common citi-zen.* The relatively large number of farmers' organizations, cooperatives, and other civic-interest organizations encourages common citi-zens to share in the government of their com-munities as a normal routine of life. In this essential sense, Saskatchewan politics is decen-tralized.

Widespread community participation and political interest have developed in Saskatche-wan in response to the environmental and eco-nomic problems involved in creating a stable community. No one factor—the small units of government, the vulnerable one-crop economy, the "one-class" society, the sparse settlement of the area, the continual economic and climatic hazards—developed because of an interest in maintaining an active grass-roots democracy or a concern for politics. The combination of all these factors, however, has made for a healthy and active democracy. Unplanned structural conditions have facilitated rapid popular re-sponse to economic and social challenges and the acceptance of new methods and ideas.[29]

The Saskatchewan pattern, while offering confirmation of the "small democracy" theo-ries, provides no panacea for those who would plan society so as to create the basis for popular community activity. Early in the nineteenth century Thomas Jefferson advocated "general political organization on the basis of small units, small enough so that all its members could have direct communication with one an-other and take care of all community af-fairs."[30] This and similar proposals have been ignored, for small communities were not func-tional in the development of a great industrial nation. In the nineteenth century, anyone who objected to the growth of large cities was called a "reactionary" or a "utopian" trying to block the march of civilization.

The small agrarian community in Saskatchewan has been preserved only because this pattern was functional in the wheat economy. The grain companies, the cooperatives, the political parties, and the farmers, all would have preferred larger communities and more centralization. They would laugh at the rational democrat's argument for their type of living and their type of economy. To the people of the West, decentralization has meant poor community services and little access to many material and cultural values. They welcomed the automobile and better roads, which are resulting in the breakdown of the smaller communities and the growth of large towns and cities. It remains true, however, that the smaller the community and organizational unit, and the less economically and socially stratified the society, the better are the possibilities for grass-roots political activity. Saskatchewan demonstrates that widespread and continuous political interest is not incompatible with efficient, large-scale organization.

NOTES

1. Gunnar Myrdal, *An American Dilemma* (New York, Harper and Brothers, 1944), p. 714.

2. Nathan Fine, *Labor and Farmer Parties in the United States* (Rand School of Social Science, New York, 1928); John D. Hicks, *The Populist Revolt* (University of Minnesota Press, 1931), p. 80; Paul Fossum, *The Agrarian Movement in North Dakota* (Baltimore, Johns Hopkins Press, 1925), pp. 85–86.

3. The cooperative organizations of the province have 477,000 members, though there are only 125,000 farmers. See Saskatchewan *News*, March 22, 1948, p. 3; also Department of Municipal Affairs, *Report* (Regina, 1948).

4. G. E. Britnell, *The Wheat Economy* (University of Toronto Press, 1939), p. 188.

5. Jean Burnet, "Town–Country Relations and the Problem of Rural Leadership," *Canadian Journal of Economics and Political Science*, August, 1947, pp. 395–419.

6. Hugh Boyd, *New Breaking* (Toronto, J. M. Dent and Sons, Ltd., 1938); Saskatchewan Cooperative Producers, Ltd., *Annual Report* (Regina), 1924–47.

7. Saskatchewan Cooperative Producers, Ltd., *The Wheat Pool and Its Accomplishments to 1946* (Regina, 1946), p. 12.

8. George Robson, "Letter to Editor," *Western Producer*, January 30, 1943, p. 2.

9. In the past, many agrarian protest movements succeeded despite the initial opposition of the top officials of the organized farmers. The Grain Growers' Grain Company was organized in spite of the fact that the heads of the Saskatchewan Grain Growers' Association opposed it. After the First World War, independent political action was forced on the leaders of the S.G.G.A. The Wheat Pool succeeded despite the early reluctance of the officals of the S.G.G.A. and the Saskatchewan Cooperative Elevator Company. The 100 percent pool plan was adopted in 1929 and 1930, though the leaders of the U.F.C. and the Wheat Pool were opposed to it.

10. Records of Saskatchewan CCF.

11. C. Rufus Rorem, *The Municipal Doctor Scheme in Rural Saskatchewan* (Chicago; University of Chicago Press, 1931).

12. *Ibid.*, pp. 83–84.

13. CCF (Saskatchewan Section), *Handbook* (Regina, 1946).

14. Commission of the Central Committee of the Communist Party of the Soviet Union, *History of the Communist Party of the Soviet Union* (New York, International Publishers, 1939), pp. 46–49.

15. CCF (Saskatchewan Section), *Provincial Convention Delegates' Handbook* (Regina, 1945), p. 33.

16. *Ibid.*

17. *Ibid.*, 1946, p. 51.

18. *Ibid.*, p. 45.

19. *Ibid.*, p. 51. It should be noted that the last two resolutions were passed at constituency conventions at which cabinet ministers were present.

20. The Saskatchewan Liberal Party held a convention in 1947.

21. CCF Convention, *Handbook*, 1945, 1946, 1947.

22. Hopkins Moorhouse, *Deep Furrows* (Toronto, George J. McLeod, Ltd., 1918), pp. 230-33, 265.

23. From interviews with CCF leaders.

24. Myrdal, *op. cit.*, p. 714.

25. S. Roy Weaver, *The Non-Partisan League in North Dakota* (Canadian Reconstruction Association, Toronto, 1921), p. 13.

26. John Gunther, *Inside U.S.A.* (New York, Harper and Brothers, 1947), p. 242.

27. Henry Wallace, "Report on the Farmers," *New Republic*, June 30, 1947, p. 12.

28. Myrdal, *op. cit.*, p. 717. (Italics in original.)

29. Similar results were found in an unpublished study of a small, self-contained housing community in an industrial area. Craftown, a community of 2,500, was found to be much more active politically than neighboring urban areas. The community, like rural Saskatchewan, was a small, relatively homogeneous town, with four-fifths of its population industrial workers. Similarly, it faced a series of problems that demanded organized action. Because of the lack of public services, the working-class citizenry had to start volunteer police and fire departments and a cooperative store. These associations provided opportunities for learning collaborative techniques and leadership skills which were also put to use in political action.

Joined in an interlocking complex, these factors of the manageable size of the local community, a new and flexible social structure, a continuing flow of problems visibly common to the group and a nucleus of men and women equipped through experience with skills of collaboration all contributed to the building of an actively participating citizenry. (Robert K. Merton and Patricia Salter, An Interim

Report: *The Lavenburg–Columbia Research on Human Relations in the Planned Community. The First Year's Work—1945–1946* [New York, 1946]. Mimeographed.)

30. John Dewey, *Freedom and Culture* (New York, G. P. Putnam's Sons, 1939), p. 159.

Section Three   *University Governors Mobilize*

UConn Story: Rhetoric and Repression

John C. Leggett
Janet Roach

THE MYTH

In the United States the university has generally been a mixture of democratic myth and power politics. Yet until recently this contradiction remained unexposed. It took the Movement to reveal the realities of university government—its centralization and concentration of power at the top.

We propose to review the experience of four members of the UConn faculty in 1968–1969 in the context of these power relationships juxtaposed to the democratic myth. We contend that their experiences can more adequately be understood when one highlights the importance within the university of a ranked elite—a board of trustees, administrative leadership, and their faculty helpers—mainly older, senior, and trustworthy. We would like to point out that UConn is not unique. It typifies our decade's hypocrisy and repression. Aware of their probable extension and intensification in the next decade, we plan to fight back. Hence, we shall conclude with recommendations on strategy for university radicals based on the UConn experience.

Recent events throughout the country have elicited numerous statements from administrators, faculty, and students which reveal their deep, extensive commitment to what we call the democratic myth. Indeed, the statements

made in public and private universities, large and small colleges, and from the three levels within all these institutions are virtually interchangeable. What is the picture of the university so widely shared—the picture that has, in many instances, obscured perception of blatant exercises of power?

This myth can be summarized in a few paragraphs. The university is devoted to the search for truth through dispassionate scholarship. The faculty is free to investigate and discuss any ideas which facilitate the search for truth, constrained only by scholarly standards, individual conscience, and the obligation to protect the rights of others. Because of the university's noble purpose, its members have a special immunity from the criticisms and sanctions of everyday life. This immunity is called academic freedom.

In a public university the Board of Trustees insulates the faculty from the hasty judgments of the legislature and the electorate. Along with the chief administrative officers the Board interprets the institution's needs to the legislature, assuring a continuous flow of adequate funds. The Board comprises a devoted group of public-spirited citizens who, if not representative of the entire citizenry, represent all "responsible" interests in the larger community.

Such matters as the hiring of faculty and decisions about contract renewal, salary increases, and the granting of tenure, etc., are decided by the faculty and passed to the Board

* Taken from John C. Leggett and Janet Roach, "The UC Story," *New Politics*, Vol. VII, No. 3, Summer 1968. (Printed, June, 1969.)

by the Administration for its automatic approval. This assures that only the twin criteria of teaching and research are applied in such decisions in accord with the necessities of academic freedom.

From time to time differences arise in the academic community. These disputes are settled through free and open discussion under the prevailing rule of reason. Representative bodies offer everyone within the community an adequate means of expressing disagreement and offer all an adequate means of securing change through democratic procedures. Thus reason, free and open discussion, and democratic procedures combine to assure academic freedom and justice. They are regarded as the key mechanisms in the governing of the university.

This base makes the university a fragile structure—particularly vulnerable in the face of power (as opposed to reason). Indeed, the institution cannot survive confrontation politics and the exercise of power, which are viewed as infringing upon individual rights. The university is apart from the rest of the world, governed internally and guided by a noble purpose rather than by the changing objectives of the outside world. Seen in the context of society as a whole it is a neutral institution.

This picture has been constructed from statements by board members, administrators, faculty, and students at UConn and elsewhere in reaction to demands by radical faculty and students. We sometimes feel that the Board members and administrators are merely using the rhetoric of the faculty to "cool" them into acquiescing to repressive measures. Be that as it may, there has been widespread resort to the myth in dealing with campus dissent.

Now let us test the myth against the actual experience of dissenters, the nature of administrative reaction to them and, most importantly, the exercise of power.

THE REALITY

At the University of Connecticut, the President, Homer Babbidge, simultaneously occupies positions of authority within the State's economy and the Board of Trustees of the University of Connecticut, the highest policy-making body for the school. As President, he is the State's highest paid civil servant. His salary is higher than Governor John Dempsey's. Babbidge guides one of the two key centers of research (the other is Yale) for the major enterprises in the state, its banking, defense, and insurance corporations. As coordinator of university talent in training, he also locks into the very firms which depend upon the university's resources. He is a member of the board of directors of the following organizations: Hartford National Bank, Kaman Aircraft, Holt, Rinehart and Winston, Connecticut Indemnity Company, and the Gannett Foundation, publisher of the *Hartford Times.*

As a Yale graduate in history and a holder of key positions in not only the economy but in education (including, for example, the New England Board of Higher Education, the Connecticut Commission to Aid Higher Education, and President Nixon's Advisory Commission on International Education and Cultural Affairs), he is an across-the-board policy maker for the State and hence a member of its governing class. G. William Domhoff, the author of *Who Rules America,* would recognize him as having national potential.

At the UConn Board of Trustees level, the President associates with persons drawn from the same class. Some of them are John J. Budds (Chairman of the University of Connecticut Board of Trustees and member of the Board of Travelers Insurance Corporation); William Benton (Chairman and Publisher of the Encyclopedia Britannica, Trustee of the University of Chicago as well as Brandeis University and the University of Bridgeport; founder, past president and past Chairman of the Board of Benton and Bowles Advertising Agency; former U.S. Senator from Connecticut (1949–53), appointed by former Governor Chester Bowles); Alfred C. Fuller (Chairman of the Fuller Brush Company; regent of the University of Hartford, member of the Board of Trustees of the Hart College of Music); Guy B. Holt (Vice-President of the Connecticut Bank and Trust Company and former Connecticut State Treasurer); Joseph R. McCormick (President of Hartford Electric Light Company); Ellie C. Maxcy (Director of United Aircraft Corporation, Veeder Industries, Inc., Southern New England Telephone Company and the Union New Haven Trust Company); and Mrs. Barbara Bailey (wife of John Bailey, the Chairman of the State Dem-

ocratic Committee and Chairman of the Democratic National Committee).

ELITE RECIPROCITY

This incomplete list suggests that the upper
classes are in a position to act to promote their
mutual interests at the university level. The
choices of these barons is not by chance, since
all of them, with the exception of a handful
elected by the alumni and a few who serve *ex
officio,* are appointed by the Governor—a Democrat and very close associate of Bailey and
Babbidge. The top is small and tight.

When Homer Babbidge sits down for lunch
or brunch with his Board of Trustees to map
university policy, he chats and eats with a fair
representation of the state's corporate and political elite. When Babbidge sips coffee with the
Board of Directors of the Hartford National
Bank and Trust Company, he undoubtedly
talks to the amiable Bernard Flaxman (Director
of the Hartford National Bank and Trust Company, Trustee of the Mechanics Savings Bank,
Chairman of the Finance Committee, a director
of the Hartford Insurance Group as well as
director of the Hartford Fire Insurance Co.).
With these kinds of friends, Babbidge automatically becomes a member of the informal
fraternity at the top, one whose recreational
activities would bring together men of power
such as Flaxman and Carl A. Gerstacker, a
director of the Hartford Fire Insurance Co.,
director of Dow Corning as well as the Chemical Bank and Trust Company, member of the
international advisory committee of the Chase
Manhattan Bank, and Chairman of the Board as
well as director of Dow Chemical Corporation,
the very group we so successfully prevented
from recruiting on the UConn campus during
the Fall of 1968.

Given the chumminess and ecological clus-
tering of Connecticut's governing classes in the
West ends of Hartford and New Haven, we
would not be surprised to observe Babbidge,
Flaxman, and Gerstacker teeing-up at the club
on a warm, sunny Sunday morning. For if nothing else, the upper classes do recreate together.
We are not privy to their conversations, but we
suspect that on occasion they discuss the student—faculty question.

Whatever they say, they seem to be able to
arrive at a consensus on items such as corporate
recruiting on campus and university research
for private corporations and military cousins.
The military does immense favors for the state's
booming war industries, including its university.
In 1966–67, 76 percent of all of the University
of Connecticut's Research Foundation funds
came directly from the U.S. Government; 25
percent of all UConn's Research Foundation
funds is expended on research projects for the
U.S. Army, Air Force, and Navy. These projects
include research on metal fatigue and human
detection systems. In addition, through its endowment funds, the university has investments
in Chase Manhattan Bank, Eastman Kodak, and
the Pacific Gas and Electric Company. These
corporations have investments in apartheid
South Africa.

Since the mutual service principle character-
izes the elites, beyond and within UConn, we
find that the school's Board of Trustees and its
President define corporate recruitment on campus as a "central function of the university."
Corporate recruiters can post themselves on
campus at university expense and interview our
student graduates. The mutual servicing principle is also a self-serving principle, since the
school's ranked elite—its board of trustees, administration, and senior faculty—and the state's
corporate leaders are not mutually exclusive.
Decision makers in the economy maintain ultimate control of the ranked elite—the university's governing class.

DOW SHALL NOT DEMONSTRATE

Given the class interests of the Babbidges,
the Bentons, and the Flaxmans, we were not
surprised when the Board responded in October
of 1967 to anti-Dow Chemical demonstrations
over recruitment by ruling in favor of Mr. Gerstacker. Thenceforth, the Board ruled, any
member of the university who participates in
anti-recruitment activities will be subjected "to
the most severe of institutional penalties."
They had job termination in mind.

On October 30, 1968, several hundred
UConn faculty and students protested against
the presence of a Dow Chemical recruiter. A
demonstration occurred, a faculty—student—
administration debate took place inside the recruiting room, heated and measured words were

exchanged—but there was bodily injury to no one. Ten faculty members and approximately 75 students simply went inside the recruiting room and encouraged the Dow Corporation interviewer to leave the campus. He did. A "central function" of the university had been impaired.

That evening President Babbidge issued a televised statement. Its opening paragraph made clear what he had in mind, indicating that the faculty participants had made themselves subject "to the most severe of institutional penalties." He called upon a Standing Faculty Committee of Three (old and loyal members of the Faculty Senate) to appoint a Committee of Five to investigate the incident.

The President thereby acted contrary to a 1964 National AAUP resolution which called on administrations to conduct an informal investigation of controversial events before setting up formal proceedings against faculty members. The President ignored the AAUP resolution, since the AAUP is a feeble company union, especially on the Storrs campus. It can be counted upon either to legitimate ranked elite punishment or to issue feeble protests. To cite but one illustration, when Babbidge wanted some respectable legitimation of planned axing of several faculty at the Board's January 15 meeting, he invited the Northeastern Region of the AAUP to send an observer. Without contacting the involved faculty, the Regional Office appointed a member of the faculty at Columbia University to attend the hearings. He cancelled his plan to apply the Seal of Good Housekeeping after the faculty accused sent him a heated public telegram telling him to stay away from UConn and to take the Brooklyn Bridge to Ocean Hill-Brownsville where he might be able to do some good. The local chapter's only public reaction to the events of the Fall was to circulate a newsletter implying that obstruction of recruitment interfered with freedom to learn and academic freedom.

BLOODY TUESDAY

A series of demonstrations against on-campus recruitment followed the Dow incident. These sustained efforts, coupled with dissatisfaction with Administration's harsh reaction to the ambiguous Dow situation, led a growing number of moderate faculty and students to demand a moratorium on employment interviewing and clarification of the differences between peaceful demonstration and obstruction. The former request was steadily resisted. Indeed, early in December when the University's three deliberative bodies of faculty and students considered recommending a moratorium, Babbidge was to take the unusual step of appearing before them to throw the prestige of his office on the side of continued interviews.

On November 25, an interviewer from the Olin–Mathieson Co. left the campus after a guerilla theater presentation spilled over into the room where he was interviewing. November 26 he returned.

Overnight the Administration had developed a set of guidelines for demonstrators. In part they read:

> Any person who enters this building without authorization, or who trespasses on its porch or stairs shall be subject to civil and institutional penalties, including the possibility of arrest and prosecution. Activities obstructing ingress and egress of authorized persons to this building shall similarly constitute violations of University policy and civil law.

Interviews were moved to a frame house slightly away from the center of campus.

At 10:00 A.M. the first of an estimated 200 demonstrators began to assemble. Six University security police were on the porch facing the street, Provost Gant, several other administrative officials, and additional members of University security were inside. Two miles away 75–100 State Police awaited a call to the campus. Unknown to the demonstrators was the fact that a number of faculty who were present outside had been summoned to Breakfast with Babbidge. They were there at his request to help "control the demonstration."

About 10:15 Jack Roach walked up the steps of the building. He pointed out that he had transgressed the newly promulgated guidelines and asked to be arrested. His request was refused. He then attempted to hurdle the railing and was pushed from the porch to the ground. He calmed the crowd by telling them he had slipped and was not hurt.

As the number of demonstrators grew, the sidewalk filled with people. Part of the group moved onto the steps where they stood joking with the crowd. At no time was an effort made to clear the steps or the sidewalk in accord with the guidelines. Leggett left around 10:40 to teach his class.

Around 11:00 an interviewee tried to gain entrance to the building through the front door. Unable to get up the crowded stairs, he attempted to leap onto the porch· The Security Officers moved toward him, and some of the demonstrators on the steps moved onto the porch.

Blackjacks and nightsticks were used to repel them. They were swung hard at the heads and bodies of the demonstrators. When the porch was cleared, the Security Officers retreated into the building. A hail of missiles—rocks, sticks, and fireworks—was thrown at the building, breaking a number of windows.

During the melee the riot act was read from an upstairs window. Most demonstrators claim that a defective bullhorn made it unintelligible. Word came that the State Police had arrived on the campus. Roach and Brover left for an off-campus restaurant.

Provost Gant's official account of these events differs from the preceding one in several important respects. It compresses the time which elapsed between Roach's attempts to be arrested and the outburst of violence. In the interval a jovial atmosphere prevailed for some time, but Gant's account implies that Roach's actions stirred the crowd to violence. He also states that the student assault on the building preceded arming the Security Officers. His account mentions that a Security Officer was hit by a heavy object. According to a number of observers, the "heavy object" was a nightstick wielded by a fellow officer.

After the arrival of the State Police, Dean of Students Robert Hewes, now known appropriately as the "Finger Dean," moved about the area pointing out persons who were promptly arrested. By noon 8 students, a former University psychiatrist, the minister assigned to the Campus Christian Foundation, and two faculty members were in custody. Roach had returned to surrender himself for arrest after receiving an erroneous report that there was a warrant out for him. He was pointed out by Dean Hewes and arrested for failure to disperse on reading of the riot act. Colfax was standing across the

road behind a fence. The minister had arrived on the scene after the riot act was read. Both he and Colfax were ,also charged with failure to disperse.

Four or 5 students sought treatment of head injuries at the University Infirmary where they were greeted by the healers as "long-haired s.o.b's." Several others bore traces of their encounter with the oak billy clubs for some time. Roach required medical care for an injury to his hand received while he was trying to pull a demonstrator from the grip of a stick-wielding officer.

In the weeks to come as the movies and still pictures were reviewed and the reports of the Faculty Superspies and State Police plainclothesmen came in, 18 more students and 4 more faculty members were arrested. Among the faculty members were Leggett and Charles Brover. The Faculty Four and the core of the SDS [Students for a Democratic Society] face from 2 to 5 charges each. These range from interference with a proclamation, failure to disperse, injury to private (sic) property, possession of fireworks, illegal discharge of fireworks, and conspiracy, to resisting arrest. The last offense was an act of non-cooperation, not active resistance. Even now it is difficult to determine who is charged with what as charges were added and changed.

On December 6, the Committee of Five which was already investigating the activities of the Faculty Four at the Dow demonstration received for its action a report of the Four's alleged obstruction of the Olin—Mathieson interviews. The Provost forwarded no such report to the Committee on the other two faculty who were arrested. The administration responded to inquiries about this omission with, "That is a police matter."

The same week about a dozen of the students who were arrested were notified that their activities at the Olin-Mathieson demonstration would be investigated by the Student Conduct Committee. They had been the most vocal participants in the Dow demonstration, SDS meetings, and guerilla theater performances. Hearings have not yet been held, pending the outcome of the criminal charges against them.

Olin—Mathieson completed their scheduled interviews on November 26. The corporate elite's interests were served at the cost of some bloody heads, 32 arrests, and the presence of State Police who remained on the campus until the Christmas recess.

FACULTY GUTLESSNESS AND REPRESSION

Time and again during the Fall–Winter controversy, the accused faculty members found that the right to a fair investigation depended upon the decisions of a wise President formally or informally locked into the very firms against which they were protesting. The President could not have gotten by with his shenanigans so easily if it had not been for his obsequious senior faculty. It took the Committee of Three some time to persuade the necessary number of persons to join the Committee of Five, but lesser members of the ranked elite finally agreed to serve. Some of those who declined did so on the grounds that the Committee's "investigation" would only legitimate a decision which had already been made, but their argument did not affect those who finally agreed to serve.

For reasons never made clear by either the Committee or the university administration, only four of the ten faculty participants in the Dow incident were singled out for formal investigation. The four happened to be the ones most vocal at the demonstration. During the month of December, at the direction of President Babbidge, Provost Gant forwarded charges arbitrarily extending the Committee of Five's purview to include not only the Dow demonstration but the activities in the Olin–Mathieson demonstrations of November 25 and/or November 26 of Professors Brover (English Department) and Colfax, Leggett, and Roach (Sociology). This extension was accepted without question by the Committee of Five.

Throughout November and much of December, the Committee of Five held closed hearings despite the protests of the Faculty Four. They and their attorney demanded open hearings (denied, allegedly to "protect" the accused), the presence of witnesses, and the use of cross examination—the ordinary items associated with trial by jury. Because the Committee preferred Star Chamber proceedings to "sunshine justice," the Faculty Four refused to take part in the investigation.

On December 23, the Committee of Five formally recommended to the Board that Leggett be made the object of "the most severe of institutional penalties" for his participation in the first Olin–Mathieson demonstration and that Roach's penalty for his participation in the second Olin–Mathieson demonstration be somewhat less severe. The Committee spent almost no time considering either Colfax or Brover. Nor did the Committee recommend sanctions against the two, even though all four faculty had worked together as a unit throughout the Fall period. There is a plausible explanation, however, one which does not appear in the Committee's ten page recommendation and the 350 page transcript of committee proceedings. Both documents neglected to mention that one month prior to issuance of the Committee's recommendations the English Department had moved to give Brover a terminal contract, while the ranked elite would be able to get rid of Colfax in March, when he was to be considered for tenure. Colfax was subsequently considered and dumped by the ranked elite. Brover is going in 1970.

On January 25, the Board of Trustees met and decided that Leggett's one-year contract would not be renewed. He and the other three were put on probation, a penalty nowhere defined by the administration. But the implication was clear: stay in line or face immediate dismissal. The Board of Trustees had received and used a Christmas gift, but not before they had reworked it.

The Board had ignored the recommendations of the Committee of Five while acting in the shadow of the committee's legitimacy. The Committee had argued that Leggett should be canned for his participation in the first Olin–Mathieson demonstration (one involving guerilla theatre) but that no action should be taken against him because of his participation in the Dow Chemical demonstration or in the second Olin–Mathieson affair (the one involving 30 arrests and five student injuries, most of them scalp splits, requiring temporary hospitalization). However, the Board ruled that Leggett was to leave the school because of his participation in both Olin–Mathieson demonstrations and the Dow Chemical confrontation. All remaining faculty members, not just Roach, as recommended by the Committee, were punished for their participation in these demonstrations. The Board's failure to consult with the Committee of Five when it did not agree with the Committee's recommendations was a departure from the rules of academic due process. Yet the departure seems to have escaped serious consideration. It failed to disturb the senior faculty, who had by this time adjusted to the power if not the temper of the times.

FACULTY STANCE—LIMP

Subsequently, through a mailed ballot, the faculty of the College of Arts and Sciences voted 202–81 that corporate recruitment is not a central function of the university. Yet they deferred to the inherent prerogatives of the Board by refusing to set up a procedure to implement this statement of principle. They even voted to refuse to meet with the Board to discuss the problems posed by their previous vote. We expected this cowardice from a faculty heavily loaded with senior members who are tied into private and government research which is responsible for professorial comfort and continued research activities.

In keeping with their career and professional interests, the majority of faculty indicated time and again that any faculty efforts to prevent recruitment were in violation of a presumed right of persons to interview for jobs. We have never heard of such a right—either in law or in principle. Yet most faculty placed this "right" on the same level as the right of a Vietnamese child to avoid napalm and hence the right to live in a world where protestors can prevent U.S. corporations from using student graduates in manufacturing endeavors designed to foster an imperialism which indiscriminately swathes whole villages with burning liquid jelly. The majority of faculty could not bring themselves to believe that perhaps there is, at the very least, a scale of right—with some being patently more important than others.

Myopic vision characterized yet another situation, one in which the State of Connecticut at the request of the University Provost demanded and obtained a most extraordinary, temporary injunction against Professor Roach. The university administration went to a State Superior Court judge in early February and obtained an ·injunction which forbids Professor Roach to do a number of things, including the telling of

falsehoods. Violation of this court order would result in Professor Roach being immediately fined $1,000 and subject to at least 90 days in jail. Roach is enjoined from "any act which might impair or prevent the accomplishment of any lawful activity, process or function of the University of Connecticut, *including the disruption of placement interviews. ...*" He is not prohibited from "making public comments or stating opinions . . . carrying signs on University premises stating certain facts and opinions if . . . *such statements and comments are not untrue, malicious, or calculated to incite or encourage others to do or participate in unlawful acts.*" (Emphasis ours.) The President subsequently referred to the use of this injunction and other legal actions as the "counterstrokes" largely responsible for campus quiescence during the spring semester.

The local ACLU people, mainly UConn faculty, went along with the university-sought injunction, largely because its leaders are the senior faculty who wholly support Babbidge, a person whom they define as a leader clearly superior to an old guard president only recently replaced at UConn; Babbidge had proved successful in obtaining salary increases and other benefits for the faculty. These senior people are still in his bag, despite Connecticut Civil Liberties Union opposition to their acquiescence, his tactics, and ACLU anger. The national and state organizations are taking the Roach injunction directly to the U.S. Supreme Court. The national office's reaction is clear. Its spokesman said:

> Injunctions are being used right and left to halt protests, but this one is the worst I've seen. It's a flagrant violation of the First Amendment protecting free speech.
>
> One would not have thought that a court through the injunction power could validly make departure from the truth, except under oath, a criminal offense.

Despite its questionable constitutionality, the injunction proved to be an effective "counterstroke."

The campus repression that spring took crass as well as respectable forms. The chairman of the two-man Department of Journalism did a pro-Babbidge piece for the *New York Times* Sunday Magazine section. The *Times* printed the article on February 23, even though the "Faculty Four" had protested to the *Times* on

December 26 that they knew of Professor Hill's preparation of the forthcoming article as well as his opinions and interests. They asked the editor not to publish the piece, for in view of a number of considerations, publication of the article would constitute not reportage but a political act. It was pointed out that:

1. Mr. Hill was wearing "two hats"—journalist and, as Head of the Journalism Department, administrator. Further, as Head, the future of his department was partially dependent on the goodwill of higher administrative officers than himself.

2. Members of Mr. Hill's classes had been assigned the task of interviewing faculty about some of their more "colorful" colleagues. The "Four" questioned the ethics and reliability of using these interviews.

3. The letter pointed out Mr. Hill's absence either as a spectator or participant from most of the fall events which he would presumably discuss and questioned the accuracy of any reports he might write.

4. It was noted that Mr. Hill had already publicly expressed hostility to the New Left at UConn and his admiration for the university's administration.

5. Further, it was spelled out how Mr. Hill's handling of his office of advisor to the student newspaper had made him *persona non grata* to SDS members and supporters. It was suggested that this would prevent his access to a number of persons who had been centrally involved in protest activities.

6. Finally, the Four argued that his expressed pleasure in the fact that SDS has "broadened discussion" of the issues revealed lack of sensitivity to administrative incompetence, beatings and arrests of protestors, and the constitutional implications of reading the riot act to a peaceful assembly of persons.

For these reasons the Faculty Four questioned "Mr. Hill's ability to comprehend the nature of the issues involved, much less to provide a fair account of what has occurred here over the last six weeks."

THE BLACKBALL AND QUADRUPLE JEOPARDY

The *New York Times* article packed a wallop across the country. In spring, when the Faculty Four went job hunting, they stumbled across a pattern. Wherever they sought employment, the lesser ranked elite used the article as "evidence" against the four faculty to stop them from obtaining new appointments. Their conversations revealed their positions: The *New York Times* does not lie; therefore it cannot lie. Hence you are either irresponsible madmen or left-wing fascists out to destroy all that is sacred and good, like the "fabric" of the university. Rich schools, poor schools, private ones and public ones, West Coast and East Coast, with very few exceptions, the reaction was the same—these guys are guilty. The passive Sunday morning reader passed a sloppy and self-righteous judgment—then meted out the penalties. Subsequent replies to the Hill article attempted to correct the errors, but they had no effect. The UConn Four were blackballed.

To make matters even worse, they have found themselves held in quadruple jeopardy. First, they face a total of 13 charges on breach of peace and other misdemeanors. None of the charges have been dropped. Second, the Board of Trustees and others within the ranked elite have imposed penalties of academic "probation," termination of contract, and denial of tenure. Third, they are being blackballed from their profession. Fourth, the State's Superior Court granted the injunction against one of them. In February it was rumored that the university had prepared three additional temporary injunctions to be used against the remaining faculty should they continue to protest against recruitment.

Wilder yet, the quadruple jeopardy has applied even though in some instances the Four are being punished for actions they could never have committed. Leggett, for example, was charged with failure to disperse after the alleged reading of the riot act at 11:05 on Tuesday, November 26 when the policemen and students clashed. In fact, at that time, and for 15 minutes before and 90 minutes after the time when the act was purportedly read, he was lecturing his political sociology course. Many of the other charges against faculty and students are of the same order. Of course, they may be able to appeal pending convictions and win in the federal courts after thousands of dollars are spent and a federal judge throws out the convictions. In the meantime, the damage to the Movement is done. In the meantime, the Faculty Four will have to live with the firings and blackball.

. . . Within the university, senior faculty have used their positions to successfully urge and support administration's efforts to fire the UConn Four. In at least two instances, their efforts contributed to the overturning of democratically arrived-at recommendations of their own departments when these specifications did not suit their own interests. The Sociology Department had voted in favor of tenure for Colfax and contract renewal for Leggett.

WHAT MUST BE DONE

On the positive side, radicals can organize to deal with this kind of repression. Already, radical caucuses have been formed within the national and regional associations of sociology, anthropology, political science, linguistics, and others. They were originally geared to the Vietnam War and U.S. racism, but they are now turning to the related question of reorganizing the various disciplines to create a new set of values. Hopefully, action on the basis of these values will transform the multiversities and our corrupt professions.

Some activities which radicals and progressives whose base is the university might undertake and perspectives they might adopt come readily to mind:

1. Most concretely, we must deal with the problems of our colleagues who have lost, or are in process of losing their jobs because of their political activities. Their actual number and identities are unknown. For this reason we suggest immediate listing of those who have been excluded from the academic establishment. Such a list would help us to locate those who need financial support if they are to remain radicals. It would also serve as a focus for efforts to reemploy them.

2. Within our departments, we must attempt to block lower ranks of the elite, the faculty helpers, when they assist administration in purging dissenters. Strategies must be created to stop those who obstruct and oppose future appointments and prevent promotion, tenure, and pay increases for those who lean to the left. One tactic in this fight might be their immediate, public exposure including, whenever possible, publication of letters and other documents involved. This would make it more difficult for

them to maintain the democratic myth as reality.

3. At the national level of our various disciplines the leading professional journal should be pluralized immediately. For example, the pages and sections of the *American Sociological Review* might be divided among blacks, white radicals, moderates, and conservatives. The latter have dulled what should be centers of controversial, exciting opinion, and variety in scholarship. Perhaps left-wing helium would counter right-wing tedium.

4. Despite formation of radical caucuses, the university left remains internally fragmented and lacks reciprocal ties with the outside world. We are isolated from minorities, the middle class, and the working class—groups whose help we need. Efforts to broaden our base need not be seen as entirely self-serving. Such efforts offer us the opportunity of placing our specialized knowledge at the disposal of groups other than the ruling elites which our disciplines have served so long. For example, a *Berkeley Barb* for the working class, a humorous paper, put together by faculty and students could tell the groups we wish to reach what is going on inside and beyond the Halls of Ivy and Red Brick. It could counter the day-to-day distortions which provide false consciousness for the many. While exposing to them how the university's power structure commits it to researching the shameful, teaching the pedestrian, firing the recalcitrants, and killing their kids, such a paper could clearly describe the part the power structure plays in their lives. The growth of oligopolies in the retail food industry, administered high price policies of the chain stores, and the relation of this new bigness to inflation everywhere can be interpreted to the working class.

5. Participation in umbrella organizations such as the Peace and Freedom Party (and in Canada the New Democratic Party) can assist us not only in striking up alliances with other segments of society but also in politicizing faculty and students. The Left needs a party. Elites can be counted upon to become increasingly repressive. Unless the Left becomes better organized than it is, it will not succeed or survive.

6. Finally, as we ally ourselves with segments of society outside the universities, let's

stop talking about academic freedom. At best it meant possession of rights denied to the masses. In recent years, commitment to the ideal combined with a belief that it is a reality have cloaked actual practices which would be unthinkable in even the most corrupt court of law. Closed hearings held in the guise of protecting the faculty; investigative committees manipulated by administrations which bring charges, prosecute them, select the evidence, and impose the penalties masquerading as academic "due process" protecting the faculty from the outside world; the deliberations and recommendations of representative bodies twisted to justify decisions ultimately made by the elite—all this has fostered the illusion of academic freedom. Point to the "duly selected committee," the elected "governing" bodies, the protection afforded to the accused, ignore the presence of dictation and repression, and you have academic freedom. Faculty who have less protection of their freedoms than the ordinary citizen who is protected by his union, state laws, and the Bill of Rights have been conned into believing they enjoy extra privilege.

Faculty members are free to engage in endless discussion and debate of any issue as long as they never ACT in opposition to the ruling elite. The elite urges that the "channels of communication be kept open," and it listens, listens, listens. It is willing to talk "anytime, anyplace" with dissenters. Then it acts in accord with its own interests. As long as faculty pursues *academic* freedom, defined in terms of free, open discussion of ideas and academic due process, the elite control the situation. Let us pursue Freedom instead. We want it. Let's get it.

CONCLUSIONS

Left-democratic is grass roots. The ideology of left-democrats is clear: The people should run government, either to modify capitalism severely enough to make the situation livable or to disengage capitalism totally and create concurrently a socialist successor. The successor should be without government oligarchs. The successor should be run by peoples' co-ops, grass-roots unions, local assemblies, and the like. To be left-democratic is to place a profound faith in the ability of the people to govern themselves to build the good society.

Not so right-democratic. This tendency, this camp, dismisses the mass as incompetent to govern. Right democratic places its faith in a political elite. Admittedly they will deign to compete for popular acceptance. Still this tory form of governance believes that the essence of democracy consists of popular abiding by rules which may or may not lead to the elimination of imperialism and domestic inequities. The emphasis is procedural. The tory line is clear: Keep the mass in tow. That is the message. And part of that symbolic manipulation includes hoodwinking the mass into believing that they do in fact govern through the mysterious politics of pressure groups.

Chapter 10

The Right-Democratic Alternative

WHERE IT IS

What is right-democratic? Do its contentions about itself square with evidence on its performance?

As we indicated in Chapter 9, right-democratic ideology places heavy emphasis on the need for adult conformity to electoral procedural matters associated with parliamentary processes. Both the electoral and the parliamentary activities are buttressed by a host of legal mechanisms designed to sheathe the entire political system. More specifically, right-democratic ideology and practice stress the importance of electoral politics. This ideology dramatizes as it praises the relevance of worthy political elites competing with one another for the support of an electorate. Presumably the electors participate both in the choice of their political leaders and in the organization of their citizens' pressure groups—once they have selected those to run the state.

Let us be more precise about how right-democratic ideology defines the workings of the electoral process:

1. *Worthy political elites compete periodically at the polls in order to garner the affection and votes of the multitude.* Joseph A. Schumpeter undoubtedly stands as the foremost spokesman on right-democratic theory. A Catholic, born in Austria in the last half of the nineteenth century, Schumpeter was a well-known Christian-Democrat, political activist, cabinet minister, and antifascist. During the 1930s he emigrated to the United States, where he taught at Columbia University. Recognized for the brilliance of his lectures and books on political as well as economic theory, Schumpeter articulated his right-democratic revision of classical democratic theory in *Capitalism, Socialism, and Democracy.*[1]

In this volume Schumpeter rejected classical democratic theory, principally on the grounds that there is no common will on which people can act, since people cannot agree on the goals of a political system. Furthermore, even if everyone could agree on common ends, the ordinary person lacks the rationality to act on them consistently. It will be observed that Schumpeter attacked the key assumptions of English utilitarianism and not those of American populism—the populist movement did not assume that there exists a common good for all; rather, it insisted on the distinction between the people and the malefactors of wealth, since the goals of each were quite different.

In place of commitment to classical theory, Schumpeter argued for a different, more "realistic" definition of democracy: "The democratic method is that institutional arrangement for arriving at political decisions in which individuals acquire the power to decide by means of a competitive struggle for the people's vote."[2] In this chapter's readings, we will observe how Schumpeter attempted to justify this inversion of control from the bottom up.

Later in *Capitalism, Socialism, and Democracy* he discussed the implications of his analysis by noting that, according to this view:

> democracy does not mean and cannot mean that the people actually rule in any sense of the terms "people" and "rule." Democracy means only that people have the opportunity of accepting or refusing the men who are to rule them. But since they might decide this also in entirely undemocratic ways, we

---

[1] Joseph A. Schumpeter, *Capitalism, Socialism and Democracy* (New York: Harper, 1950).
[2] *Ibid.*, p. 269.

have had to narrow our definition by adding a further criterion identifying the democratic method, viz., free competition among would-be leaders for the vote of the electorate.[3]

For this elitist form of democracy to succeed, certain preconditions must be met: "The first condition is that the human material of politics—the people who man the party machines, are elected to serve in parliament, rise to cabinet office—should be of sufficiently high quality."[4]

In the same context, Schumpeter argued that the only guarantee for the presence of such qualified persons:

> is in the existence of a social stratum, itself a product of a severely selective process, that takes to politics as a matter of course. If such a stratum be neither too exclusive nor too easily accessible for the outsider and if it be strong enough to assimilate most of the elements it currently absorbs, it not only will present for the political career products of stocks that have successfully passed many tests in other fields—served, as it were, an apprenticeship in private affairs—but it will also increase their fitness by endowing them with traditions that embody experience, with a professional code and with a common fund of views.[5]

Schumpeter's statements on democracy required revision, as indicated by the works of such eminent political sociologists as Morris Janowitz.

2. *For a democratic election to take place, competing political candidates and their followers must abide by the rules of peaceable exchange of political ideas which are meaningfully deliberated by a participating electorate both concerned with electoral outcome and blessed with self-confidence under conditions that minimize the manipulative potentiality of the mass media.*

Morris Janowitz and Dwaine Marvick have indicated[6] their intellectual dependence on Schumpeter (as well as Harold Lasswell) in their definition of what constitutes democratic elections. From their point of view, a democratic election (a) demands competition between two (or more) opposing candidates; (b) requires efforts to maintain traditional voting blocs, seek independent voters, and recruit converts from the opposition; and (c) presses both parties to participate vigorously in an effort to win the election. But no matter who wins, both parties will do their best to enhance the likelihood of their winning subsequent elections.

Still, the meeting of these prerequisites is not enough for a democratic election to occur, for a politician can obtain a popular mandate through manipulation of unqualified voters rather than through the support of participating, self-confident citizens.

Janowitz and Marvick set forth four conditions that must be met if the results of a competition are to represent the voters' wishes (i.e., the consent of the electors.)[7]

First, there must be a high level of citizen participation among all social groups. Voting constitutes a form of participation. It indicates a propensity to play the game and to accept the outcome of the election according to the rules. But a high turnout by itself is by no means a sufficient indication of election through consent.

The second criterion has a social-psychological quality. Whether the politics of consent has occurred depends on how much of the citizen participation is based on attitudes of political self-confidence and a sense of self-interest in the outcome of the election. Crucial in this regard is how the voter feels about the impact of the election's outcome on his self-interest. If the belief that there is a relation between electoral outcome and self-interest is widespread, then a primary quality of politics of consent prevails. Related to sense of outcome is presence of self-confidence. Does the voter feel that he can affect public policy through his vote? If so, he fulfills a prerequisite for participation in democratic politics.

Third, if the politics of consent is operative, then competition must stimulate effective de-

[3] *Ibid.* pp. 284–285. Reprinted by permission of Harper & Row, Publishers.
[4] *Ibid.,* p. 290. Reprinted by permission of Harper & Row, Publishers.
[5] *Ibid.,* p. 291. Reprinted by permission of Harper & Row, Publishers.
[6] Morris Janowitz and Dwaine Marvick, *Competitive Pressure and Democratic Consent* (Ann Arbor: Bureau of Government, Institute of Public Administration, University of Michigan, 1956), pp. 1–10.
[7] *Ibid.,* pp. 4–10.

liberation on the issues (and the candidates) to create a meaningful basis for voting decisions. Here the voter is simply called on to weigh the merits of the most important issues raised by the competing parties and to arrive at a "net judgment" on which party and/or candidate presents the better case for him.

The fourth and final point is straightforward and deals with the propensity of politicians to command portions of the mass media in order to manipulate voting publics. For the politics of consent to function appropriately, both sides must be able to make wide use of mass communications and to mobilize extensive pressure by means of the party canvass and primary-group relations. At the same time, the bulk of the voters must be able to retain freedom of choice in indicating political consent. Needless to say, institutional and legal controls must act as safeguards. But more is involved. The voters' predispositions must act as a safeguard against manipulation. Most important in this regard would be the climate of opinion common to primary groups such as the voter's family and his associates at work. They will tend to mediate the mass media, and ideally their collective opinions should help to safeguard the person from manipulation.

Here Janowitz and Marvick assume that when people are concerned with the outcome of an election and when they express high degrees of self-confidence, the mass media can do little to manipulate them. These authors also assume that voting is a measure of self-interest, whereas self-confidence is generally derived from primary relations, such as those associated with the family. In their study of the 1952 presidential election, the two writers discerned that television exposure is greatest among those who have high interest and self-confidence and lowest among those with the least interest and self-confidence. That being the case, apparently we have little to worry about insofar as the manipulative propensities of the mass media are concerned, for the media's greatest manipulative potential occurs among those who seldom watch television.

Janowitz and Marvick's revision of Schumpeter lacks at least one quality. It does not take into account the importance of pressure groups and their use of the mass media. Perhaps the foremost exponent of this subject is David Riesman, whose formulations we attempt to distill

in our discussion of the third major point in the right-democratic definition of the workings of the electoral process.

3. *Contrary to the opinions shared by the left within the United States, there exist two conditions favorable to the proper functioning of democracy: (a) plurally organized, status groups and generations, drawn from all classes, and equally able to use the lobby technique to secure the passage or defeat of legislation; and (b) the genuine possibility that those who are yet unorganized will become organized.* The result is clear. No one group can entertain a commanding power relationship over any other group on matters of power over government. In fact, one group can quite readily veto the efforts of others, so that fair compromise becomes the order of the day. In short, political power begets a countervailing force that results in the veto of the bad law, the reversal of the brazen court order, or the overturning of the harsh administrative ruling.

David Riesman, Nathan Glazer, and Reuel Denney[8] have held that, although in the late nineteenth century there did exist a business ruling class in the United States, today the mass of people are found in groups which have the power to prevent events that might be inimical to their interests. The only exception consists of those unorganized and sometimes disorganized persons who have not yet invented their veto groups. But they will soon.

The vetoing goes on all the time at all political levels, so Riesman *et al.* allege, with the result that an amorphous power structure has been created. So much has this become the case that it is difficult to distinguish the rulers from the ruled, the good guys from the bad guys, the farm workers from the growers, the hospital workers from the administrators, and the auto workers from the auto magnates. Because of their similarities, no one group can make a singularly impressive moral case nowadays. Hence, it is difficult to take sides in alleged struggles. Partially because of the absence of moral certainties and associated bipolarizations, the political system works. Indeed, it deserves our loyal participation.

For Riesman and others, political elites are

[8] David Riesman, Nathan Glazer, and Reuel Denney, *The Lonely Crowd* (Garden City, N.Y.: Doubleday-Anchor, 1956).

somewhat less obvious than they appear in the formulations of Schumpeter and Janowitz. Still they are there, and their guidance qualities enable a legitimate system to work, even for the downtrodden.

4. *Political elites and masses recognize both (a) the legitimacy of governmental legal authority and associated parliamentary procedures, and (b) the illegitimacy of the mass demonstration; the consequence is clear: political change through either violent means or nonviolent but violence-provoking techniques becomes unacceptable, even among the poor.*

Indeed, right-democratic theorists classify both insurrectionary behavior and police-irritating demonstrations, in the context of availability of parliamentary forms, as nonpolitical. These acts deserve the designation "nonpolitical" because they circumvent (a) the use of personal appeal to the executive, (b) the legal submission of the argumentative brief, (c) the workings of parliamentary bodies, and (d) reliance on pressure groups, the only forms of political expression allowable under the democratic system. And to define acts as nonpolitical is to suggest that they are unrelated to successful problem-solving. To make this propositional association is to judge such demonstration to be unacceptable and its instigators, perhaps, to be mentally unbalanced, for only the neurotic would rebel against such an obviously worthwhile system. And to make this aspersion is to discredit the instigators.

Crucial to this conservative position is the sanctity of the law. For example, during the initial moments of the Berkeley Free Speech Movement (October 1, 1964), there occurred an episode involving university students who tried to prevent a police car from leaving campus with an arrested student by surrounding the vehicle. A number of faculty had already addressed those assembled when Seymour M. Lipset spoke to the throng and charged that the students were acting "like the Ku Klux Klan." Southern segregationists also believed in breaking the law when they rejected it, instead of obeying decisions adopted in a democracy. Lipset had assumed that the university is a democracy and had thus earned student acceptance of its regulations.[9]

Pluralists such as Riesman and Lipset would admit that problems do occur within a democracy. But differences on problem resolution are to be handled peaceably by a contending plurality of heterogeneous groups. This approach should minimize the display of passion, despite contending group interests, in order to use and to maintain the parliamentary process, which is vulnerable to extremist pressures.

Even the poor should peaceably hold hat in hand—indefinitely, if need be—for the important thing is the preservation of the parliamentary forms. Nor should the poor give up, because even they can act successfully through the parliamentary system. As Arnold Rose has indicated,[10] it is true that rich people can use their money to obtain special political opportunities through the use of lobbyists, advertisements, and campaign contributions. Yet these three channels are by no means closed to poor people:

A volunteer campaign worker for a congressman will have more influence on him than most lobbyists, and as much influence on him as a campaign contribution equivalent to the voluntary labour, roughly speaking. The fact that the political party in most states is an open, if not entirely democratic, voluntary association, and the fact that it is the single most important influence on most elected officials, also gives the non-wealthy citizen access to political power often greater than that of the wealthy, but not politically active, citizen.[11]

Indeed, all that the poor need do is give one dollar a year to garner control of wayward politicians in need of the campaign dollar:

Even a nominal financial contribution from a majority of the citizens—say $1.00 a year—would pay most of the cost of running all the political campaigns. (It has been estimated that $175,000,000 was spent in all of the 1960 campaigns—national, state, county, and municipal. It is not likely that this amount would be spent in non-presidential election years. . . .) An increase in the number of volunteer workers would reduce the money costs of campaigning. If there were these two forms of increased participation,

[9] Hal Draper, *Berkeley: New Student Revolt* (New York: Grove, 1965), p. 47.

[10] Arnold Rose, *The Power Structure* (New York: Oxford University Press, 1967), pp. 491–492.

[11] *Ibid.,* p. 491. Reprinted by permission of Oxford University Press.

there would then be no obligation on the elected officeholders to return political favors for large campaign contributions. Even if this sum of money should not quite suffice to pay all campaign costs, the citizens who had made a small contribution would not be likely to tolerate the buying of political favors with large contributions. Simple public awareness of the large costs of campaigning would produce enough pressure to achieve the democrat's dream of getting a significant amount of free publicity for political campaigns. These developments, along with more effective controls on certain types of campaign expenditures, would eliminate the pressure on public officeholders to be inequitable in their public actions.[12]

Yet as Rose later noted, politicians have ways of circumventing the laws they have to govern their own campaign expenditures. The modal technique is to make the agencies and powers designed to enforce the law somewhat vague. Another device is to create campaign committees to support candidates, with the assumption that they can gather and spend as much as they wish, irrespective of regulations on expenditures for candidates. Of course, even if some of the present loopholes were closed, others could be opened.

Rose admitted that all this may move the poor to wonder about their dollar-a-year contribution.

THE LEFT-DEMOCRATIC CRITICISM

Left-democrats fail to share the perspective summarized above. Briefly, their criticisms of right-democratic declarations are as follows:

1. *On worthy elites competing periodically at the polls in order to garner the votes of the mass.* What remains unclear in Schumpeter's formulation is his definition of merit. What is its content? He seems to stress professionalization. But clearly that is not enough, for professionalization could mean not only the acquisition of skills but crookedness, narrowness, selfishness, and like sins associated by some with such professions as medicine. The left-democratic criticism would argue that profes-

sionalization does not provide the key for understanding or controlling political elites.

More important is the power of the upper classes to decide which professionals will run for positions such as the presidency of the United States. Indeed, many presidential candidates are themselves millionaires and members of the upper class. These top politicians make themselves available, much as would a debutante, and they in turn sometimes find millionaires who will adopt them. Of course there are exceptions. Eugene McCarthy was an example. But even he depended heavily on millionaire support. Illustrative was the way Eugene McCarthy obtained campaign contributions from not only the ordinary citizen but the wealthy as well:

> The McCarthy campaign had at least five contributors who gave $100,000 or more. On the record, the largest contributor was Stewart R. Mott, philanthropist and son of a pioneer in the automobile industry, one of the founders of General Motors. After spending $100,000 trying to persuade Rockefeller to run, . . Mott turned to McCarthy and contributed and spent, by his own calculations, approximately $210,000 on McCarthy's campaign. One gift of $100,000 was publicly and dramatically announced at the August 15 [1968] M-Day rally at Madison Square Garden. Mott also became coordinator for special gifts and helped to raise substantial amounts in addition to his own contributions. Mott also gave $43,700 to other Democrats and $11,000 to various miscellaneous committees, for a total of $364,700 in political contributions in 1968.
>
> Mr. and Mrs. Jack J. Dreyfus, Jr., are listed as $100,000-plus contributors, although some accounts say they gave as much as $500,000 and are considered by some to be the single largest contributors to the McCarthy campaign. Dreyfus was a senior partner of the Wall Street firm of Dreyfus and Co., and a business associate of Howard Stein, McCarthy's finance chairman. . . .[13]

Wealth would appear to be relevant in determining outcome on not only the chief executive but the judicial levels as well. G. William Domhoff argued and demonstrated that in

---

[12] *Ibid.,* p. 478. Reprinted by permission of Oxford University Press.

[13] Herbert E. Alexander, *Financing the 1968 Election* (Lexington, Mass.: Heath, 1971), p. 50.

America the upper classes dominate the executive level of government, and through it, the judiciary. Here the connections are clear, for the President has discretionary appointment power to the judiciary. By contrast, when we consider the legislative level of government, the controls are less clear-cut. Nonetheless, they are telling.[14]

The upper classes control the chief executive position through their intervention, which is by no means unified, at the level of the presidential nominations. In order for a man to become a serious contender for the presidency, he must initially have the support of persons willing to pump hundreds of thousands of dollars into a campaign designed to build his image and to attract funds as well as public support. Illustratively, Eugene McCarthy needed and obtained a million dollars to initiate his campaign for the presidency.[15] The normal procedure for a candidate is to find a millionaire campaign manager, who in turn seeks to obtain a number of wealthy persons who agree to support the candidate. If the campaign manager succeeds, he then surfaces his candidate as a person with sufficient resources to make himself a serious contender.

There is a reciprocal side to upper-class control of the chief executive's position, and although merit may be pertinent, its relevance seems to remain obscured by the significance of the ability to give. Once a candidate has won the presidential office, he appoints to important positions a number of upper-class campaign contributors, in proportions which go well beyond their relative population size. These upper-class appointments heavily favor key overseas diplomatic posts. However, not all such overseas positions are filled on the basis of size of campaign contribution. Appointments are sometimes based on seniority in the diplomatic service, merit, and like criteria based on presumed skill in pertinent interpersonal relations. Still, Nixon's 1968–1969 appointments to overseas slots and the size of the appointees' contributions (which far exceed Rose's recommendation) to the 1968 campaign are of more than passing interest (see Table 22).

By contrast, the amount of an individual's contribution to the successful presidential campaign appears to be a much less significant factor in obtaining appointments to powerful executive posts at home. Here the most important variable seems to be the past effective loyalty of the powerful to the successful chief *or* the presumed fairness or neutrality of the selected (provided, of course, that the person is established in an upper-class position). Domestic upper-class appointments tend to include the major secretaryships—State, Treasury, and Defense. Upper-class appointments to a slightly lesser degree predominate in the Department of Commerce, and, of all places, in the Department of Labor, which should be staffed by representatives of organized labor in a society that is organized along pluralistic lines. Domhoff has observed that this class-biased appointment pattern for cabinet posts applies to both Republicans and Democrats.

In the cases of key cabinet posts, it appears that the criteria of "merit," whatever they might be, are confined to assessments of upper-class folk, and for good reason, since the upper classes are the ones who back the contenders in the race for the presidency. And to the victor goes the power to make appointments of the winning candidate's judiciary friends and colleagues. This does not mean that there is consensus at the top of the class structure on which meritorious figures should assume executive posts. On the contrary, the appointments tend to reflect the class—ethnic—religious backgrounds of the victorious managers and donators. For example, upper-class, white, Anglo-Saxon Protestant Republicans, occupying heavy industrial positions, have predominated in the selection and support of their party's presidential candidates. In turn, on leaving the winners' circle, the Hoovers, Eisenhowers, and Nixons have favored them when making key executive appointments. Jews, Catholics, blacks, and Chicanos receive short shrift. By contrast, the Democratic party hopefuls have looked to businessmen representing lighter industries, retail enterprises, and real estate. Unlike the homogeneous array of Republican upper-class contributors (the Rockefellers, the Mellons, the Pews, the Du Ponts, *et al.*), the key Democratic con-

---

[14] G. William Domhoff, *Who Rules America?* (Englewood Cliffs, N.J.: Prentice-Hall, 1967), pp. 84–96, 103–107, 111–114. Reprinted by permission of the publisher.

[15] Alexander, op. cit., p. 37.

TABLE 22 Contributions Among Selected Nixon Appointees, 1968–1969

Name	Appointment	Contributions (in dollars)
Annenberg, Walter H. Wynnewood, Pennsylvania	Ambassador to Great Britain	2,500 Rep.
DeRoulet, Vincent New York, New York	Ambassador to Jamaica	44,500 Rep.
Dudley, Guilford, Jr. Nashville, Tennessee	Ambassador to Denmark	51,000 Rep.
Gould, Kingdon Laurel, Maryland Washington, D.C.	Ambassador to Luxembourg	22,000 Rep.
Humes, John P. New York, New York	Ambassador to Austria	43,000 Rep.
Marshall, Anthony D. New York, New York	Ambassador to Malagasy Republic	25,000 Rep.
Melady, Thomas Patrick New York, New York	Ambassador to Republic of Burundi	500 Rep.
Middendorf, J. William, II New York, New York	Ambassador to Kingdom of the Netherlands	15,500 Rep.
Moore, John D. J. New York, New York	Ambassador to Ireland	1,000 Rep. 500 Dem.
Pritzlaff, John D., Jr. Phoenix, Arizona Scottsdale, Arizona	Ambassador to Malta	23,000 Rep.
Replogle, Luther I. Oak Park, Illinois	Ambassador to Iceland	6,500 Rep.
Rush, Kenneth New York, New York	Ambassador to Federal Republic of Germany	1,000 Rep.
Schmidt, Adolph W. Pittsburgh, Pennsylvania	Ambassador to Canada	500 Rep.
Symington, J. Fife Lutherville, Maryland	Ambassador to Trinidad and Tobago	5,000 Rep. 500 Misc.

Data from: Herbert E. Alexander, *Financing the 1968 Election* (Lexington, Mass.: Heath, 1971), pp. 353-354.

tributors constitute a mixed bag. Many are old-line aristocrats of Northeastern Protestant background, such as the Harrimans and the Roosevelts. Some are rich southerners, such as Senator James Eastland, the Mississippi-delta multi-millionaire. Not a few are Catholic, like the Kennedy family. Of the wealthy, upper-class contributors to the Democratic party cause, a disproportionately large number are Jewish, like Mr. and Mrs. Jack Dreyfus, Jr., already mentioned as key backers of Eugene McCarthy.

There is truly ethnic pluralism among the millionaire supporters of the Democratic party. Of course, this upper-class breed of pluralism does not make the Democratic party the "party of the common man," as commonly held belief would suggest. Although plenty of working-class people vote Democratic, especially during economic recessions, these working-class people have little, if anything, to say about the selection of presidential candidates or the form of legislation to be passed in its behalf.

In this sense, Schumpeter's assumption—that democracy works through political elites going to the ordinary man rather than having the man in the street make the original as well as the final selection of the candidates—is not unreasonable. Schumpeter's theoretical opinions would be consistent with the data of both Domhoff and Alexander. What remains highly questionable is the subject of merit, especially on such matters as the selection of judicial elites.

Once nominated and elected to office, the President becomes a crucial figure in selecting members of the federal judiciary. What is less clear are the President's criteria for selection, although we can observe the numerous devices through which the upper classes can and do exert their influence. First, the President selects his appointees from a list drawn up by party leaders on the state level. Many of the state leaders themselves belong to the upper class as does the President. But more is involved, and here we encounter the invidious control exercised by a judiciary both sensitive to its class expectations and limited by its reactionary attitude to moderate ideology. For the judiciary itself has the power to screen and to delete potentially controversial appointments:

Working through an 11-member committee of lawyers, the [American Bar Association]

has won for itself the privilege of evaluating at a very early stage in the search for candidates, the merits of each person seriously considered by the Attorney-General for nomination to the federal bench. While the Committee's actual influence has varied with the Administration in power, it has had, at a minimum, considerable success in deterring the nomination of judges it deems unqualified. . . . (During the Eisenhower Administration), Attorney-General Rogers was under instructions not to recommend a nomination over the objections of the Committee except in unusual circumstances. . . . During the first two years of the Kennedy Administration, 158 adverse reports were made, of which eight were disregarded by the Attorney-General.[16]

Domhoff went on to point out:

Members of this committee are selected by the president of the American Bar Association with the advice of the incumbent committee chairman. In the case of Bernard Segal, chairman of the committee from 1956 through 1962, the power to advise the bar president was in effect power to appoint. A graduate of the University of Pennsylvania, Segal is a member of one of Philadelphia's most eminent upper-class law firms, Schnader, Harrison, Segal, and Lewis. He is a Jewish member of the power elite. Who are the other members of the committee? To answer this question Joel Grossman studied a sample of 51 men which included all those who had served from 1946 to 1962. He found that they tended to come from large law firms, to have distinguished careers within the ABA, and to live in cities with populations over 100,000. James Moore supplemented Grossman's study by compiling more detailed information on 28 of the men who served between 1953 and 1963. Eight of these 28 men—29 percent—were members of the upper class. Three more were from large (power elite) law firms, four others had attended Harvard Law School, and five others were corporation directors. The rest came from elite law schools in their region, such as the University of Virginia and the University of Michigan. Except for those who lived in states where we have little information on the upper class, most of the non-upper-class committee members were in

[16] Domhoff, op. cit., p. 109. Reprinted by permission.

socially elite clubs. [One of the requirements of the committee is that it have at least one member from each federal court circuit, so there are necessarily members from all parts of the country—Domhoff's note.]

Who are the men finally chosen as judges? In terms of the lower federal judiciary, they are men politically acceptable to local and state politicians, who usually recommended them to Washington friends in the first place, and politically and professionally acceptable to the judiciary committee of the ABA. A study by Moore of 25 judges from six of the 11 circuit courts and the U.S. Court of Customs and Patents revealed that three were members of the upper class and that 20 had attended Ivy League schools. Thirteen of the 25 judges were from Harvard and Yale alone. Twenty had been invited into one or more of the socially elite clubs listed in the 12 city editions of the *Social Register*. Since Moore chose his districts with the hope of maximizing the number of upper-class judges, it was necessary for us to look also at a circuit that would minimize that possibility. The fifth circuit, which encompasses the Deep South and Texas, had two judges who could be considered members of the upper class and four who could not. It can be concluded that most of the judges of the lower federal judiciary are not members of the upper class, but that they have rather substantial professional and political credentials that are carefully checked beforehand by a legal arm of the power elite, the Committee of the Federal Judiciary.

Turning to the Supreme Court, the situation is not different in terms of socioeconomic status, training, and political connections. John Schmidhauser, in *The Supreme Court,* reported on his study of the 92 Supreme Court justices between 1789 and 1959. He found that the justices came

> from socially advantaged families. . . . In the earlier history of the Court, he very likely was born in the aristocratic gentry class, although later he tended to come from the professionalized upper-middle class. . . . It seems reasonable to assume that very few sons of families outside the upper, or upper-middle, social and economic classes have been able to acquire the particular type of education and the subsequent professional, and especially political, associations which appear to be

unwritten prerequisites for appointment to the nation's highest tribunal.[17]

Although the power to select the President and the members of the judiciary helps the upper classes to secure their political position and thereby reinforce their economic well-being, they remain unsatisfied with their considerable strength. The upper classes reinforce their ability to influence and to coerce through congressional initiation and a *de facto* veto based on their control of committee chairmanships in the two houses of Congress. Here not merit but longevity in office determines who will become chairman. Seniority, committee chairmanships, and upper-class positions appear to be highly interconnected. First, as Domhoff has demonstrated, a disproportionately large number of these chairmen are members of the upper class themselves. Second, there is the power exerted by lobbies created, subsidized, and directed through committee chairman, both upper and upper-middle class. Studies show that these particular lobbies are most effective when their intent is to block legislation rather than to create it; still, the power to initiate is by no means absent. Third, the U.S. business aristocracy attempts to get its way through shaping of public opinion, which is led to express itself through blanket protests to Congressmen. Large sums of money are spent to create "grass-roots campaigns" which strongly suggest to voters and politicians alike that the public is storming for or against a particular proposal. Another device cited and documented by Domhoff is the use of the mass media, almost all of which are owned by the upper classes, to narrow the limits of debate over a particular issue and, perhaps, to forge one or several acceptable opinions.

The upper classes exert their influence through the President's inner circle of advisors as well as through the diplomatic corps. But perhaps the greatest mockery of both popular control *and* merit appointments stems from upper-class staffing and influence of the very agencies designed to regulate industries owned by these particular upper-class persons. Of these 33 agencies, certain ones stand out: the Federal Trade Commission (FTC), the Federal Communications Commission (FCC), the Interstate

[17] *Ibid.,* pp. 109–111. Reprinted by permission.

Commerce Commission (ICC), the Securities and Exchange Commission (SEC), and the Federal Power Commission (FPC). Domhoff documented the discrepancy between original intent and subsequent practice:

> The constituent groups—the industries of the American business aristocracy that the agencies supposedly regulate—control the regulatory agencies in several ways. First, through committees and associations of specific industries, the industries give advice to the agencies. Second, they are able to control key appointments to the agencies by providing as candidates for the positions corporation executives, corporation lawyers, and various other salaried specialists. Most importantly, the industries can appeal to the President to block appointments that are not acceptable to them. Indeed, appointive power is the only power which the Executive branch legally holds over the regulatory agencies, which are not responsible to it. However, the importance of this appointive power can be seen in certain of President Eisenhower's appointments, which were explained by economist Seymour Harris:

>> Former congressman Albert M. Cole had voted against most public housing measures, so he was made head of the Housing and Home Finance Agency.

>> John B. Hollister was an outspoken isolationist, so he was the perfect choice to guide the International Cooperation Association.

>> The Chairman of the Federal Power Commission, Jerome F. Kuykendall, who was supposed to represent the public against the public utilities, had represented gas utilities in cases before the United States Public Service Commission.

Since no government report or academic study yet published contradicts our claim that those who are supposedly being regulated dominate the regulatory agencies, it is not necessary to go into laborious detail on any one agency. The reader is referred to Henry Kariel's *The Decline of American Pluralism*, Bernard Nossiter's *The Mythmakers*, and Grant McConnell's *Private Power and American Democracy* for relevant examples and detailed bibliography. A quote from one of the sources on regulatory agencies will suffice. It is from Judge Lee Loevinger, who was head of the Antitrust Division of the

Department of Justice at the time of the drug hearings in the early 1960s:

> Unfortunately, the history of every regulatory agency in the government is that it comes to represent the industry or groups it's supposed to control. All of these agencies were fine when they were first set up, but before long they became infiltrated by the regulatees and are now more or less run by and for them. It's not a question of venality, either. More, the agency people consort with this or that representative of some special-interest group, and finally they all come to think alike. Every company that's concerned about government control and is big enough to manage it hires a man—or maybe four or five men—at anywhere from thirty to seventy thousand dollars a year to find out what we're up to. And, by God, they find out! They wine and dine the agency people and get to be great friends with them. Like a lot of people without much money, some bureaucrats are impressed by being around big shots and by the big life. Sooner or later, all of these agencies end up with constituents. And they represent them damned well, too.[18]

Apparently many leading political figures have "passed many tests in other fields—served, as it were, an apprenticeship in private affairs" and thereby qualified in Schumpeter's terms for higher political office. Whose interests they serve other than their own, however, is a matter to be determined. It would seem that decisions reached by key congressional committees, judges, and the chief executive branch itself have over the decades benefited the upper-class persons who control the span of political nomination.

2. *On the meaningful deliberation of political issues by a participating electorate both concerned with electoral outcome and blessed with self-confidence under conditions that minimize the manipulative potentiality of the mass media.* Here the critics would argue that Janowitz and Marvick missed the point. Democracy means, at the very least, that all sectors of the citizenry have equal access on matters of influencing government and that such equal influ-

[18] Ibid., pp. 107–108. Reprinted by permission.

ence does not occur when the mass media are both owned by millionaire moderates (and conservatives) and directed to the maximization of their material interests at the expense of those less fortunate. The upper classes own most of the mass media, which are organized by the upper classes to earn profit. As Domhoff and many others have indicated, the TV programming, radio programs, and newspaper coverage are geared to this activity rather than to activities which might consistently and thoroughly expose the conditions and dilemmas faced by subordinate classes found within the capitalist system. Were the merchandizing of information on poverty profitable, television, radio, and newspapers might conceivably stress the bleak circumstances of the coal miners, the day-to-day anomie of many ghetto residents, the meager incomes of the Great Basin poor, and the cognitive poverty of many Americans intellectually overwhelmed by events around them. Furthermore, even when people are filled with self-confidence and committed to getting things done through the parliamentary process, they find that the mass media can manipulate electoral outcomes through the power to limit the discussion of certain issues, to overstress the insignificant, to disregard salient issues, to exaggerate the consequences of a progressive or radical proposal, to dwell on the extraneous nuances of politicians' personality characteristics—and to do all this with little likelihood of encountering public challenge and so being forced to terminate electoral *schmaltz*. The people must have their own media—perhaps noncentrally owned TV stations, magazines, newspapers, and radio—in order that challenging views might be expressed by their sponsors. In the meantime, the progressives and radicals remain hamstrung electorally.

What radical democrats most resent is the power of the TV oligopolies to set the limits within which national debates take place. How does limitation work? Here is one illustration: Popular, left-democratic candidates must use television to carry their messages on the need for progressive taxation of excess corporate profits, selective government ownership of utilities and industries, and enforcement of government laws on monopolistic and oligopolistic practices. Yet to use television to carry their arguments requires vast sums of money for candidates. These sums, millions of dollars in the case of presidential candidates, must be obtained primarily from private sources. The working class lacks that kind of money for political contributors. The middle classes will donate part of it, but not enough. It is the upper classes who must give the lion's share. But why should they donate money to a left-democratic presidential candidate who threatens to increase the taxes of their corporations, nationalize some of *their* industries (utilities, for example, as part of regional development such as TVA) and break-up some of their profitable monopolistic practices? They won't give unless and until the left-democrat moves over towards the political center and thereby abandons his left-democratic point of view. The abandonment of that point of view constitutes a narrowing of limits of debate. Hence, the left-democratic position fails to find persistent and extensive expression through mass-media debate. Janowitz himself has recognized general limits of the mass media in his discussion of the public-relations efforts of the military.[19] If the mass-media owners can define the limits of debate, they can use this power to maximize the potentiality for effectiveness of a chosen pressure group. Here wealth is pertinent, as we shall see.

3. *On the possibility of all classes, status groups, and generations organizing pressure groups lobbying for issues, passing legislation, and vetoing the reprehensible.* The left's criticism of the Riesman position is quite clear. One's ability to organize and sustain powerful lobbying groups and associated media is a direct function of the amount of wealth that can be mobilized, whereas amount of wealth available is directly related to class position. There are exceptions, such as organized labor; but the key decisions on lobby spending for labor are made by oligarchs who often have salaries, life styles, and attitudes barely distinguishable from many sections of the upper classes. The poor get left out. They have neither the economic resources, the organizational basis, nor the trained talent to lobby for change or to use the legal system. Lobbyists cost money. Cajoling key congressional chairmen through payment for expensive

[19] Morris Janowitz, *The Professional Soldier* (New York: Free Press, 1960), pp. 401–402.

outings, courting the important members of state legislatures through banquets, wining and dining powerful members of city councils, making large contributions to the elections of any of these politicians—all this pressure grouping requires a large and continuous supply of funds channeled through on-going sophisticated organizations. The poor and the ordinary can't afford it. As a result, lobbying remains largely the political province of the economically powerful persons and groups. The upper classes may veto each other, or on occasion a section of the upper class may set aside a benevolent moment for the lower classes, as in the case of the Kennedy family support of the United Farm Workers in California, but such interludes are rare. Furthermore, once the upper classes have decided to intervene on the side of the poor, they decide where, how, and when the intervention will take place, how long the help will continue, and under what circumstances the behavior of the poor will result in the termination of upper-class support. Discretion to take away accompanies the power to give.

On the ethical side, as you will recall, Riesman *et al.* argued that it is hard to take sides politically because of the ongoing veto power of all groups and the claimed amorphous quality of power relations. To the left-democrat, the lines of power become clear during crises (i.e., during moments when the poor strike at extant power relations in the economy). Illustrative would be an effort on the part of farm workers in a California valley to organize a union. Under those circumstances, a working alliance is revealed between state politicians, appointed judges, elected sheriffs, subsidized Congressmen, elected mayors, chosen city council members, and local growers—all within the net of local privilege lodged within an even larger combination of powerful groups and individuals on the regional and national levels. The would-be organizers confront those who wield the power to issue an antilabor injunction, enforce the law, break the law, write the law, and avoid the law in order to continue to suppress the insurgent lower classes. The lower classes are committed to the use of the strike, the boycott, the rent-stoppage, the massive demonstrations, and the hard-nosed picket line. And this power is used to jail labor leaders, to do violence to labor organizers, and to intimidate the others.

This pattern has occurred most blatantly in California, Texas, Arizona, New Mexico, Colorado, and other areas where proletarianized ethnic groups (e.g., Chicano and other minorities) are subject to ongoing control by the growers. One's ethical sympathy is extended to these groups because they seek greater equity, and justice—by the standards of the French Revolution.

Needless to say, the members of many groups who laud Social Darwinism and repressive toryism will dismiss the ethical claims of the poor. These groups can be found not only in off-campus areas but in the ivy halls. A minority of university intellectuals have been known to speak of conditions characterized by physical suffering and political powerlessness in abstract terms that conceal a cold and often sanguinary reality. This includes swinging clubs, damp jails, moldy food, and unusually long prison sentences, as well as a high infant mortality rate and a protein-starved segment of the population. To speak of the oppressed uniformly and continuously organizing effective veto groups and significant dollar-a-year clubs is absurd, as we have learned from the extraordinary but episodic political battles of the 1960s and 1970s.

4. *On political elites and masses recognizing and abiding by the legitimacy of legal authority and associated parliamentary procedures.* Left-democrats hold that governments must win and retain legitimacy by making democracy work for all, especially the oppressed. If and when parliamentary bodies become bound to the interests of "the few," then "the many" have the right to revolution or lesser rebellions.

From a left-democratic perspective, there is nothing sacrosanct about a government or a system. Either it does the job or it can expect to be succeeded. Indications of succession as a possibility can be seen when people circumvent moribund parliamentary bodies and take to the streets to demonstrate and to take other forms of direct action (which generally result in the police or a military body initiating the use of violence to discourage the choice of the demonstration as a political technique). Under these circumstances, the charge that the protestors should use legislative or pressure group channels makes little sense from a left democratic point of view, since in many cases those protesting have already tried these avenues of redress and found them to be jammed. Furthermore, to argue that crowds induce violence through peaceful however vociferous demonstrations by provoking an easily irked police is pointless. Police are supposed to be trained professionals who can deal with the shouts, the yells and the hoots without inflicting bodily injury on the demonstrators. Again, to argue that these cat-calls and shouts constitute *violent* acts is incorrect, since the definition of violence clearly excludes the voice and includes blood-letting and bone crushing. Left-democrats are loathe to allow conservatives to indulge in the self-serving extension of definition.

Of interest here is the tendency of the left-democrats and the left-radicals to coalesce during prodromal or prodromal-like conditions in order to deal on a day-to-day basis with the minions of power and wealth. The right-democrats form an alliance with power and wealth to maintain the parliamentary system and private property. These extremely unstable alliances are likely to fall apart under many circumstances. For example, during a presidential campaign the left-democrats generally support a presidential candidate of moderate to moderate-left persuasion, thereby eschewing the politics of direct action favored by many left-radicals. Also, during presidential campaigns the right-democrats, especially the intellectuals, generally support a political candidate of right-moderate persuasion in a protracted electoral game which drains the body politic of most of its critical energies.

TRANSITIONAL REMARKS

As we indicated earlier, Joseph A. Schumpeter stands as the foremost theorist of right-democratic persuasion. His clearly formulated arguments lend themselves to easy summary, as indicated in our earlier analysis. Yet one can take issue with his assumptions, as we have in this chapter, especially after acquaintance with empirical materials of the kind presented by Herbert E. Alexander in his study of the 1968 election. We have included portions of this sound study in Section Two of this chapter.

Following the Alexander reading, we present an essay on the U.S. Bureau of Labor Statistics. Curiously, many professional academicians entertain the view that professionals can maintain their autonomy on critical matters when employed within state organizations which are highly influenced by upper-class business interests, schooled in the techniques of skewing the original purposes of federal government bureaus. We will learn otherwise.

| **Section Two** | *A Reading on Presidential Elections* |

The 1968 Election

Herbert E. Alexander

INTRODUCTION

The voting and financing patterns of the 1968 Presidential election were in sharp contrast: In voting it was one of the closest elections in history; in financing the Republicans

■ Taken from Herbert E. Alexander, *Financing the 1968 Election* (Lexington, Mass: Heath, 1971), pp. 1–11, 30, by permission.

outspent the Democrats by more than two to one. Unlike 1964, when a Republican financial advantage clearly did not affect President Johnson's reelection campaign, the Democrats in 1968 were seriously handicapped by their relative lack of funds. Overall, politics in 1968 set new records for expenditures, with the Presidential contests leading the increases.

Rising costs have been a feature of the

TABLE 23   Summary of Political Spending at the National Level, 1968 General Election (in millions)

Committees	Gross Disbursements[a]	Lateral Transfers[b]	Total Campaign Costs	Transfers Out[c]	Direct Expenditures[d]
37 Republican	$28.9	$ .1	$28.8	$ 3.4	$25.4
93 Democratic	19.2[e]	6.0	13.2	1.6	11.6
37 Labor	7.1	1.0	6.1	4.2	1.9
3 Wallace	7.2	—[f]	7.2	0	7.2
52 Miscellaneous	4.3	.2	4.1	2.1	2.0
222 Total	$66.7	$7.3	$59.4	$11.3	$48.1

[a]Data derived from reports filed with the Clerk of the U.S. House of Representatives.

[b]Transfers between the Committees included in the table.

[c]Transfers to Senatorial, Congressional and other candidates, and to state and local committees.

[d]Including debts, if any.

[e]Includes $2.8 million (received from contributions and loans) spent by state and local nonreporting committees for obligations incurred by the DNC; called constructive disbursements in financial report of DNC treasurer Robert Short.

[f]$25,000.

American political system, especially since the mid-1950s, and the rate of increase has been accelerating. In 1952, the first Presidential election year for which total political costs were calculated, it was estimated that $140 million was spent on elective and party politics at all levels of government.[1] Total political costs rose to $155 million in 1956, $175 million in 1960, and $200 million in 1964.[2] This represents a 43 percent increase in 12 years. For 1968, the total estimated political costs were $300 million—an extraordinary 50 percent increase in four years.

Only a portion of all political expenditures are covered by federal and state reporting laws, and politicians are usually reluctant about divulging campaign fund information, so that precise data on all spending cannot be ascertained. However, the data which are available and the political conditions in 1968 support the estimate of a very significant increase in costs since 1964. Some of these data and conditions were: The expenditures (total costs) of national level political committees (detailed in Table 23) increased 71 percent; political broadcasting costs reported by the Federal Communications Com-

mission increased 70 percent; there were costly Presidential prenomination contests in both parties, unlike 1960 or 1964 when the competition for nomination was mainly in one party; the ante was raised in both parties by the candidacies of Robert F. Kennedy and Nelson A. Rockefeller, both millionaires, for Presidential nomination; there was protest activity both within and outside the two major parties—in the McCarthy campaign, the Wallace campaign, the New Party efforts, as well as the Black Panthers, Yippies, and others; there were special efforts to gain control of state legislatures in order to control reapportionment after the 1970 census; there was a general price rise of about 12 percent since 1964. There were no known reductions in political expenditures that would offset the increases.

The national-level committees which are covered under Federal reporting laws include the major party national committees as well as labor and some Congressional and other committees which operate in more than one state on behalf of one or more Federal candidates in the general election. The number of such committees has been rising along with expenditures;

there were 70 in 1960, 107 in 1964, and 222 in 1968. Table 23 details the expenditures of these committees.

The $59.4 million in total campaign costs of these committees compares with $34.8 million spent in 1964. Republican committee expenditures increased 68 percent from 1964, while combined Democratic and labor spending[3] increased 23 percent. Table 24 shows the relation of Republican and Democratic (and Wallace) committee spending for the last four Presidential election years. (The percentages are based on direct expenditures, as in the last column in Table 23, excluding miscellaneous committee spending.) Excluding spending by Wallace committees, the ratio of major party spending in 1968 was 65 percent for the Republicans and 35 percent on behalf of the Democrats (30 percent by Democratic committees and 5 percent by labor committees). Thus, the Republican financial dominance, customary in recent years, continued.

The costs of campaigning for the Presidency in 1968 were the largest component of the year's political bill, and the 1968 Presidential selection process was the most expensive in American history. The Presidential bill of $100 million (of which more than 90 percent can be accounted for fairly accurately) was an increase of 67 percent over the 1964 costs of $60 million, a significantly larger increase than even the 50 percent estimated increase for total political costs.

The Presidential bill for $100 million, which is one-third of the total political expenditures in 1968, included: $37 million for national-level costs for Democrats and Republicans in the general election; $25 million in the Democratic prenomination period; more than $20 million in the Republican prenomination period; $9 million for George Wallace's American Independent Party, beginning in 1967. These known costs total $91 million. State and local spending on behalf of Presidential candidates in both the pre- and postnomination periods would make up a large part of the difference. In addition, one must count in party and delegate expenses related to the national nominating conventions, and spending by activists giving parties, travelling, and telephoning paid out-of-pocket directly by the individuals concerned.

Data on the expenditures of national-level committees primarily concerned with the Presidential general election are available from 1912. The figures in Table 25 exclude spending by labor and miscellaneous committees, which generally do not benefit the Presidential candidates. Although there were some unusual years, the rise in expenditures was gradual from 1912 to 1952. Since 1956, the rise has been even more rapid than the big increases in overall political costs, with 1968 again occupying a unique position.

Calculations of the cost-per-vote for the Presidency since 1912 show a variable pattern for more than 40 years, and then a steady rise

TABLE 24   Ratios of National-Level Direct Spending, 1956, 1960, 1964, 1968 (in percentages)

	1956[a]	1960	1964	1968
Republican Committees	59	49	63	55
Total on behalf of Democrats	41	51	37	29
Democratic Committees:	37	47	34	25
Labor Committees:	4	4	3	4
Wallace Committees	—	—	—	16
Total	100	100	100	100

[a]Derived from Heard, *Costs,* p. 20, and *1956 General Election Campaigns,* Report to the Senate Committee on Rules and Administration, Subcommittee on Privileges and Elections, 85th Congress, 1 Session (1957), Exhibit 4, p. 41. 1956 deficits are listed by this Report as bills unpaid as of Nov. 30, 1956. Heard's figures for Republican and Democrats are for full calendar year 1956, but labor figures are for Jan. 1–Nov. 30, 1956. Heard's ratio for 1956 has been revised to include deficits.

TABLE 25 Direct Campaign Expenditures by National-Level Presidential and Party Committees, General Elections 1912-1968[a] (in millions)

1912	$ 2.9[b]	1932	$ 5.1	1952	$11.6
1916	4.7	1936	14.1	1956	12.9
1920	6.9	1940	6.2	1960	19.9
1924	5.4[b]	1944	5.0	1964	24.8
1928	11.6	1948	6.2[b]	1968	44.2[b]

[a]Data for 1912-1944 include transfers to states. Total for 1948 includes only the expenditures for the national party committees. For 1952-1968, data do not include transfers to states, but do include all national-level committees.

[b]Totals include significant minor party spending.
Source: Citizens' Research Foundation.

since the mid-1950s, culminating in an enormous leap for 1968.[4] From 1912 to 1956, the cost-per-vote ranged from a little more than 10 cents (in the wartime election of 1944) to around 31 cents (in the intense 1928 and 1936 elections); but after each rise, there was an almost comparable drop so that in 1912 the cost-per-vote was just over 19 cents and in 1956 it was just under 21 cents. By 1960, the cost-per-vote had risen to almost 29 cents and in 1964 it set a record at more than 35 cents. But for 1968, the record was shattered as the cost-per-vote jumped to 60 cents.

The 60-cent figure for 1968 includes Wallace spending beginning in February—which would normally be the prenomination period. But the American Independent Party had no convention, so no distinction can be made between primary and general election costs. If the Wallace votes and national-level expenditures are excluded from the calculation, the 1968 cost-per-vote was still a record high of close to 51 cents.

There are two sets of reasons for the extraordinary cost of the 1968 Presidential campaigns: one set is unique to the year; the other includes factors which must be considered continuing components of Presidential campaigns, likely to contribute to high costs in future years.

In the second category are the scientific and technological advances which have contributed to increased campaign costs in the 1960s, particularly in the areas of travel, polling, computers, and broadcasting. The ability to have

more and wider contact with the electorate via jet plane first entranced Richard Nixon in his 1960 campaign, and has since become a standard and major expense in the Presidential campaigns. Extensive private polling was first used by John F. Kennedy in that same year, and its use, importance, and cost are increasing as the candidates, the poll-takers, and the techniques have become more sophisticated. The use of computers in planning campaigns and simulating elections is at an early stage, but can be expected to grow.

The cost of political broadcasting is the most measurable of these technological factors. Television is much more expensive than radio, and its use and cost are continually increasing. Charges for political broadcasts in the general election for network television, which covers almost exclusively the Presidential contest, were $2.9 million in both 1956 and 1960, rose to $3.8 million in 1964, and then jumped to $7.4 million in 1968.[5] The total broadcast expenditures (radio and television, network and station) for the 1968 Presidential and Vice-Presidential prenomination and general election contests were $28.5 million, 2.2 times greater than the comparable 1964 expenditures.[6]

The one intangible component of the rising costs is the role of the President. For many reasons—including the increased role of the United States in the world during the last decades, the power potential which the President holds, a growing view of the President as the initiator as well as executor of the nation's policies, and the direct impact of federal policy on more people—the Presidency is more important today than previously, and therefore the stakes for achieving it are greater.

The major unique causes of the high Presidential costs in 1968 were the prenomination contests in both parties; the candidacy of a millionaire in each major party; protest activity both within and outside the major parties; and the Nixon-Humphrey contest, in which neither was an incumbent, and both were challenged by the Wallace candidacy.

In most Presidential years, the candidate of one party is fairly certain of winning nomination and there is little major opposition. In 1964, this was true for the Democrats, who had an incumbent President; in 1960, the Republicans had the Vice-President, who was heir apparent; and in 1956, the Republicans had an enormously popular President. Not since 1952 had there been real uncertainty and major contests in both parties for the Presidential nomination as there were in 1968, and for more than 20 years before 1952, the Presidential nomination in one (or both) of the parties was not seriously contested. For all these reasons, the costs of the 1968 Presidential campaigns reached the record-breaking total of $100 million; and some of the stated reasons suggest that costs of future Presidential campaigns cannot be expected to return to their pre-1968 level.

THE PRENOMINATION CAMPAIGNS

Costs

The Presidential prenomination campaigns of 1968 bore little resemblance to time past. In the Democratic and Republican parties combined, about $45 million was spent before Richard Nixon and Hubert Humphrey won the nominations, with the Democrats spending $5 million more than the Republicans. By comparison, the much-publicized clash between Hubert Humphrey and John Kennedy in 1960 seems, in retrospect, as if it took place in another era: the two candidates combined were reported to have spent only a little more than $1 million.[7] Both Humphrey and Nixon were candidates in both 1960 and 1968: In 1960, about $500,000 was spent in Nixon's prenomination campaign and about $250,000 on Humphrey's shorter one; in 1968, more than $10 million was spent on Nixon's nomination campaign and $4 million for Humphrey's—increases of twenty times from eight years earlier. Even the famous Eisenhower-Taft contest of 1952, costing at least $5 million,[8] and the bitter Goldwater-Rockefeller confrontation in 1964, which cost an estimated $10 million,[9] can hardly be compared to the $20 and $25 million spent by prenomination candidates in the Republican and Democratic parties, respectively, in 1968.

In most Presidential campaign years, there is competition in only one party for the nomination: the "in" party will nominate either the incumbent or his accepted successor. But in 1968, there were intense struggles in both parties. In addition, there were more than two

major candidates in each party; there was an intensely felt issue (Vietnam) which brought many new people and much new money into the political process; and there were unusually wealthy candidates in both parties. Each of these factors acted to spur higher campaign spending, and they combined to create the most expensive prenomination process in American politics. There was more Democratic than Republican competition in the period of the primaries, particularly when Robert Kennedy was one of the contestants. In the Republican primaries, Nixon was without serious opposition from before the New Hampshire primary, when Romney withdrew, until Oregon, where Reagan was entered although not an announced candidate; competition heightened when Rockefeller finally entered. In the interim period, of course, Nixon had to spend to make a good showing and prove he could be a winner—much as he did in 1960—but this time at much greater expense and with a greater accumulation of liabilities. Humphrey, in 1968, was in Nixon's 1960 spot, an incumbent Vice-President with whatever advantages or disadvantages that meant. Nixon's 1968 drive was a long one, whereas Humphrey was able to run only after President Johnson withdrew. Although neither contested primaries, Humphrey's costs were lower than Rockefeller's; Humphrey was an incumbent with strong factional party support, whereas Rockefeller was a challenger. On the Democratic side, both McCarthy and Kennedy were challengers. And challengers, especially wealthy ones, often spend more.

The involvement of both a Rockefeller and a Kennedy in a single year did much to raise the ante for all the other candidates.[10] It is not only the actual spending of wealthy candidates which spurs spending by others; the possibility or threat of their spending also acts as a spur to higher spending. One of the ironies of this situation is that when a Rockefeller or a Kennedy is running, his fund raising if often handicapped by the feeling of many that the candidate can afford to spend his own money; then if he does spend substantially from his own resources, he is criticized for it.

Since Federal disclosure laws do not cover prenomination campaigns, most information which is available has been provided voluntarily by candidates or contributors. As might be expected, campaigners are usually more willing to disclose expenditures—how much they spent and on what—than the sources of their funds, particularly from large contributors. However, even the admittedly incomplete information available reveals bigger contributors, on the record, then at any time since the 1920s.

Sources of funds

The largest known contribution was from a Rockefeller family member who gave more than $1.5 million to one committee (and might have given more which was not recorded). There are believed to have been at least three $500,000 contributors in the prenomination period: one each to the Nixon, McCarthy, and Kennedy campaigns. One contributor gave and spent a total of $300,000 in 1968, divided between Rockefeller (before he became an announced candidate) and McCarthy. There were also two, possibly three, $200,000 contributors to Romney's campaign, while McCarthy is believed to have had one $300,000 contributor and at least three other contributors of $100,000 or more. The Kennedy and Rockefeller campaigns also had $100,000 contributors outside the immediate families, and several dozen persons are known to have given between $500,000 and $100,000 to these and other campaigns. These contributions were for the most part not publicly reported, although there was more openness about giving, and more publicity given to who gave how much, than at any other time. The press seemed more aware in 1968; there were several luncheons or dinners widely reported at which very large sums were pledged, and in the McCarthy campaign, there were open rallies at which large pledges were publicly announced. More will be noted about individual large contributors to individual candidates in the sections below.

The combination of Kennedy, McCarthy, Johnson, Humphrey, Romney, and Rockefeller brought more left-of-center or moderate money onto the political scene than at any time in American history. Conventional belief has it that, apart from candidate family money, the liberals in American politics are relatively financially starved. Generally, Republicans, conservatives, and centrists have found their funding came easier; this seemed natural if one followed the simplistic notions that political money came mainly in large sums, that only the well-healed could afford to give in large sums, and that the wealthier elements tended to be more conservative and tended to give liberally to conservative candidates.

Prior to 1968, the Goldwater campaign of 1964 was one of the two most expensive prenomination campaigns on record (the other was Rockfeller's 1964 campaign, mostly family-financed); Goldwater was unique, however, in having 300,000 contributors in the preconvention period. That unprecedented achievement in financial participation did attract some ultraconservatives previously outside the two-party political process, but in general it proved that hundreds of thousands of nonwealthy Americans would contribute to a political candidate.

If 1964 demonstrated that a conservative candidate could attract very large sums of money from thousands of small givers, 1968 demonstrated that with the proper mix of issues, events, and men, liberal candidates could also raise large sums of money from many relatively small contributors. No liberal Democrat had ever raised so much from so many—not John F. Kennedy nor Adlai E. Stevenson nor Estes Kefauver. Although the Kennedy, McCarthy, and Humphrey prenomination campaigns in 1968 all left deficits, in terms of money actually raised, it was clear that political affluence and financial involvement in America had reached the liberals. (The Rockefeller and Romney campaigns left no deficits because the debts were paid by family and friends.)

The McCarthy mix of a few very large contributors and many small contributors may have been unique, but if it did nothing else it dispelled the notion that only Republicans or conservatives could find major, non-family financing. And with several moderate and liberal candidates in the 1968 Presidential race, the combined fund-raising record of center and left-of-center candidates was indeed impressive and unprecedented.

On the other side, of course, the two conservative candidates in 1968 (Nixon and Reagan) did very well in their fund raising. And outside the nominal two-party system, George Wallace did extraordinarily well in fund raising throughout 1968; he attracted an estimated 750,000 contributors, many of whom gave one dollar in order to sign petitions to get Wallace's American Independent Party on the ballot.

Cost overstatements

Descriptions of the financing of the 1968 prenomination campaigns require two explanations, one general and one relating to the Democrats. When travel costs for a campaign are given, there may be a considerable inflation of the actual cost. When finance managers say, for example, that travel cost $1 million, the statement may be true but does not take into account the fact that perhaps as much as half of the total is reimbursed by media travellers—newspaper, magazine, radio, and television reporters—who are charged for transportation by the campaign. The bulk of this reimbursed transportation is for riding in the candidate's plane (or another plane provided by the campaign), but some ground transportation may also be charged, such as press buses. When the candidate and staff fly with enough reporters, substantial portions of cost can be recouped, as figures relating to Nixon's general election campaign will show.

For the Democrats, the final disposition of the deficits from the McCarthy, Kennedy, and Humphrey campaigns will affect the spending totals. When campaign totals are given they represent committed costs, not actual cash expenditures. If outstanding bills are settled for less than their full amount—as has been done with at least some of the debts from the Kennedy, McCarthy, and Humphrey campaigns—the total real cost of the campaign will obviously be less. For example, the Kennedy campaign left a debt of $3.5 million, but efforts were made to settle accounts at an average of about 33 cents on the dollar. If all outstanding Kennedy campaign debts were settled at that rate, the total real cost of the campaign would be about 25 percent less than the listed, committed cost. After the November general election, the Democratic National Committee (DNC) assumed $1 million in debts from each of the Humphrey and Kennedy prenomination campaigns, and a very small amount from the McGovern campaign. These debts will presumably eventually be handled in conjunction with the more than $6 million in other debts of the DNC, which is discussed in detail below.

The Republicans

The Republican contenders spent more than $20 million in the nomination competition, with Nixon's winning campaign accounting for more than half the total. Rockefeller, without entering any primaries, spent more than $8 million; Romney spent $1.5 million in his aborted campaign; about $750,000 was spent on Reagan's behalf; and Harold Stassen's campaign cost $90,000. While most of this money was spent in 1968, some expenditures and much of the planning dated back to 1966–1967.

In some cases, Presidential hopefuls may begin working toward their goal as early as the preceding convention or election, as John F. Kennedy did after 1956 and Barry Goldwater after 1960, and some may truly be last-minute candidates, as Adlai Stevenson was in 1952 or Robert Kennedy was in 1968, but the usual beginning of Presidential speculation and organization is after the midterm Congressional elections. After the 1966 elections, three prominent Republicans were the subjects of Presidential speculation, and, in fact, were then beginning their campaigns. Two of them, Governors Romney of Michigan and Reagan of California, had just won impressive electoral victories, and the third, Richard Nixon, had been a tireless and effective campaigner on behalf of many Republican candidates across the country. Each of these three Presidential candidates held his first strategy meeting soon after the November elections, and the shape of their campaigns began to form.[11]

The Democrats

The six Democratic contenders incurred costs of $25 million in their quests for the Presidential nomination, but the deficits and debt settlements noted above probably make the total actually spent about $21 million. McCarthy's effort was the longest and the most expensive, lasting nine months and costing about $11 million. Kennedy's 11-week whirlwind campaign, which included seven primary contests, cost $9 million. The combined campaigns of Johnson, Humphrey, and their Indiana and California stand-ins (Branigan and Lynch) cost close to $5 million, with Humphrey's effort accounting for more than 80 percent of that total. McGovern's brief campaign and Maddox's even briefer one cost, respectively, $74,000 and $50,000. Unlike the Republican campaigns, virtually all the Democratic spending occurred in 1968.

NOTES

1. Alexander Heard, *The Costs of Democracy* (Chapel Hill: The University of North Carolina Press, 1960), pp. 7-8. This volume contains most data comparisons prior to 1960 used in this book.

2. Herbert E. Alexander, *Financing the 1964 Election* (Princeton: Citizens' Research Foundation, 1966), p. 13, hereinafter cited Alexander, *1964*. This volume contains most data comparisons for 1964 and 1960, and certain earlier years, used in this book; but also see Alexander, *Financing the 1960 Election* (Princeton: Citizens' Research Foundation, 1962), hereinafter cited as Alexander, *1960*.

3. Labor is combined with Democratic spending on the assumption that most labor money goes to support Democrats.

4. In these calculations, the total vote for each Presidential election is taken from: for 1912 and 1916, Louise Overacker, *Money in Elections* (New York: The Macmillan Company, 1932), p. 80; for 1920-1964, Richard M. Scammon, ed., *America at the Polls* (Pittsburgh: Governmental Affairs Institute, 1965), pp. 1-23; for 1968, Theodore H. White, *The Making of the President 1968* (New York: Atheneum Publishers, 1969), Appendix A. Labor and miscellaneous expenditures are not included in these calculations.

5. *Survey of Political Broadcasting, Primary and General Election Campaigns of 1968* (Washington: Federal Communications Commission, August, 1969), Table 3. Publication hereinafter cited as FCC, *Survey* 1964 and FCC, *Survey 1960*.

6. FCC, *Survey 1968*, pp. 1-2.

7. Alexander, *1960*, pp. 16-19.

8. Heard, *Costs*, pp. 334-5.

9. Alexander, *1964*, pp. 17-18, 23-24.

10. For an interesting brief discussion of the comparative wealth of the Kennedy and Rockefeller families, see Lewis Chester, Godfrey Hodgson, and Bruce Page, *An American Melodrama: The Presidential Campaigns of 1968* (New York: The Viking Press, 1969), pp. 214-5.

11. See White, *Making*, pp. 35, 38-40, 50-52.

Section Three   *An Understanding of Blue-Collar Deprivation and Its Consequences*

Countdown

John C. Leggett
Claudette Cervinka

SYSTEMATIC UNDERSTATEMENT

This paper constitutes a preliminary attempt to develop a systematic review of one aspect of the actual conditions that prevail in the American working class. One of these conditions includes the systematic undercounting of their unemployed. How are the unemployed underestimated in this country? How in particular are proletarianized racial minorities undercounted by the U.S. Bureau of Labor Statistics? Al-

■ This essay was originally prepared to appear in James Henslin and Larry Reynolds's forthcoming book (to be published by Holbrook Press) on contradictions within class structure in the United States.

though we are not labor economists, but rather social scientists with relatively limited backgrounds on the analysis of official labor statistics, we feel it nonetheless necessary to comment on both their sophistication and bias precisely because of the hesitance of many economists to analyze and to publicize what is basically a violation of a working class right to fair statistical treatment by its own government. There is a deeper political issue involved as well, and this paper will comment on this unseemly contradiction. Publicly, the executives of the welfare state pose as helpers of the down-and-out. Privately, this state has maneuvered to minimize, through the use of invalid statistical measures, the very condition of its working class citizens, in order that the state may slight the very ones it purports to help.

The U.S. Department of Labor's Bureau of Labor Statistics (BLS) conveys a fairly straightforward message: The welfare state takes care of its own. Despite the discrepancy between this assertion and the reality, the Department of Labor and its political leadership, the President of the United States, can deceive the many on the true incidence of unemployment because of the paucity of persons in structural positions to discover the invalid quality of the Department of Labor's statistics. Few nonprofessional persons have either the leisure or the group affiliations to create the sustained curiosity necessary to wade through the labyrinth of official statistical obfuscation in order to piece together the immensity of the falsification involved. By way of illustration, when on September 21st of [1971] the *New York Times*, on its front page, stated in a leading caption "State's Joblessness 5.7% in August, Off From 6%," and followed with the statement, "The unemployment rate in New York State was 5.7% in August as against 6.1% in July, according to figures released yesterday by the State Department of Labor,"[1] who could catch the subtle *New York Times* qualifier built into that statement, one which sets aside the question of *New York Times* responsibility for assessing the validity of their figures. Objectively, what the *Times* did was to present a figure which grossly understates the number of people who would like to have a just job and who would take a job, were the welfare state to function as its ideologists have contended. We are told: Only 5.7% are unemployed. What does this figure in fact disguise? What is the true figure and what do estimations of its size suggest about the nature of our country's economic system? We can begin to answer some of these questions.

BLS UNEMPLOYMENT STATISTICS AS PARTICULAR IDEOLOGY: THE ASSERTION

But when dealing with federal governmental statistics, we must keep in mind that we are not dealing with "hard statistical facts" but rather statistical generalizations and underlying assumptions which belong more in the realm of particular ideology. As you will recall, in *Ideology and Utopia*[2] Karl Mannheim made the distinction between particular and total ideology. In the case of *particular* ideology, Mannheim referred to the ways in which a group can deliberately falsify a reality through the conscious application of formulas, half-truths, innuendos, and plain lies. For example, one group can use distorted or warped statements to paint a damning or glowing picture at the expense of certain groups in the community. By contrast, in the case of *total* ideology, Mannheim has referred to the way in which objectively false portraits of reality pervade human relations so as to mar the perspectives of people, none of whom have consciously or maliciously forged this distortion of reality. In this sense, total ideology most clearly resembles many definitions of culture.[3]

With this distinction in mind and the BLS procedures and tabulations before us, we can only conclude that we are discussing an instance of particular ideology—for, as we will demonstrate, the BLS has clearly gone out of its way to minimize the true unemployment situation within an analytical framework that deliberately understates the seriousness of the unemployment problem and thereby paints a more glowing picture than our capitalist system deserves.

BLS STATISTICS AS PARTICULAR IDEOLOGY: AN INSTANCE

A most crass instance of statistical obfuscation occurred in January, 1971, when the U.S. Department of Labor changed certain of its counting procedures. Harry Brill, a sociologist at the University of Massachusetts and a skilled interpretor of labor statistics, noticed the change and sensitized a number of us to what was going on when he editorialized on the pages of *The Nation* as follows:

President Nixon recently told the press and the public that the actual unemployment rate averaged lower in 1970 than during the recession years of the 1960's. He is, unfortunately, mistaken. Actually, the current estimate of unemployment would read higher had the Department of Labor not changed its counting procedures. Until 1967, the Department in its monthly survey counted as

TABLE 26 Employment Status of 14–15-Year Olds by Sex and Color, September 1971 (in thousands)

	Total			White			Negro and Other Races		
	Both Sexes	Male	Female	Both Sexes	Male	Female	Both Sexes	Male	Female
Noninstitution population	8,147	4,127	4,019	6,987	3,552	3,436	1,159	576	384
Civilian labor force	1,338	782	555	1,249	731	518	88	51	37
Employed	1,223	717	505	1,168	682	486	54	35	19
Agriculture	159	136	23	150	131	19	10	5	5
Nonagricultural industries	1,063	581	482	1,019	551	468	45	30	14
Unemployed	115	65	50	81	49	32	34	16	18
Not in labor force	6,809	3,345	3,464	5,738	2,821	2,917	1,071	524	547
Keeping house	28	6	21	15	4	11	13	2	11
Going to school	6,675	3,288	3,387	5,627	2,778	2,848	1,048	510	538
Unable to work	8	3	5	7	3	4	2	–	2
All other reasons	98	48	51	90	35	55	9	–[1]	–[1]

[1] Detail not shown owing to inconsistencies resulting from the small number of sample cases.
Taken from: Employment and Earnings, **18**, No. 4 (October, 1971), p. 43.

unemployed all those who volunteered that they were too discouraged to look for work. According to its own study, the rate, then would have been 50 per cent higher if it had solicited the reasons for not actively seeking work. Despite these findings, the Department of Labor decided to assume that any-one not actively looking for work must therefore not be interested in working. So now even those who volunteer their despair—and more are despairing—are no longer regarded as unemployed.

The Department counted as unemployed until those who were actively seeking a job within the last sixty . . . [1967] days. This too was drastically changed—to four weeks. Altogether dropped from the calculations of the unemployment rate . . . [in 1967] were the youngest members of the labor force, ages 14 and 15. Since their chances of being out of work are extremely high, excluding them from the labor force count further reduces the official rate of unemployment. . . . tallied as unemployed [prior to 1967] were workers who had jobs, but for various reasons were not working and were looking for work. For example, workers laid off because of weather conditions, such as those in the construction trades, fall into this category. Those belonging to this group are now counted as employed even though they are not receiving pay and are actively in pursuit of work.[4]

Deleted, then, from the officially un-employed are people who failed to seek work in the last month even after they had earlier sought work in vain and later given up. Dropped from the unemployed are the fourteen and fifteen year olds who seek employment. Gone from the roles of the unemployed are job holders who may seek another job because in-clement weather and like hazards have moved them into a category of temporarily laid-off. But in effect they are unemployed during the winter months, or whatever the span might be. Still they are counted as employed.

Most curious is the deletion of the 14–15 year-olds. Officially they are no longer in the labor force. In fact, and strangely enough, they are still counted by the Bureau of Labor Statistics. (See Table 26). One's curiosity on this matter is whetted by what the findings indicate:

1. There are proportionately more blacks than whites unemployed (especially among women). Indeed the ratio is 6–1 rather than the generally accepted figure of 2–1 for blacks and whites (for all of the black and white labor force participants).

2. Less obvious, however, is the extremely *low* incidence of official unemployment among 14–15 year old whites. So low is this figure for whites that it compares favorably with data on

all whites during the same period, i.e., September, 1971. Among white 14–15 year-olds, there are fewer than 7 percent unemployed. In the case of the entire white labor force, the unemployment figure is approximately two-thirds this percentage.

What the data suggest is that dropping out of school to go to work has quite different consequences for blacks and for whites. In the case of blacks, dropping out of school quite often means becoming either unemployed or a nonparticipant in the labor force. In the case of whites, dropping out of school seldom means dropping out of the labor force, or becoming an employed seeker of work, although the acquisition of a job may mean employment in a low paying occupation. By contrast, blacks frequently fail to obtain even these low status positions. What Table 26 suggests is that racial discrimination is severely operative among young dropouts. In a broad sense, dropping out of school is not the problem. Race apparently is. It would appear that we lose a great deal of insight on the operation of our economy when we delete the 14- and 15-year-olds.

The dropping of these kinds of persons accompanied an unadjusted comparison. As you will recall, the Bureau of Labor Statistics did draw a comparison between the unemployed of the early 1970s with those of the early sixties without telling us how if at all the BLS had removed the recently deleted categories from the earlier estimates so as to allow for a fair comparison. No such statistical control was applied; unadjusted comparisons were made. The BLS is comparing oranges without peelings (1971) against oranges with peelings (1961) while forgetting to inform the general public how the comparison has been made. Rather than comparing adjusted figures, the BLS supplies added but separate figures on dropped groups so that if the researcher wishes, he can compute an adjusted figure.[5] Needless to say, the BLS does not add to our general knowledge of working-class unemployment by suggesting such techniques.

There is no professional excuse for (1) the juggled criteria on unemployed, (2) the unqualified statements on the trend comparisons, and finally, (3) the elementary error of comparing two noncomparable quantities.

BEING A MEMBER OF THE LABOR FORCE, THE UNEMPLOYED, AND THE EMPLOYED

Before we can go any further in our analysis we must acquaint ourselves with the way in which the BLS does in fact gauge three things: (1) being a member of the labor force, (2) being unemployed, and finally, (3) being employed.

First, who is in and who is out of the labor force?

Persons under 16 years of age are excluded from our count of the labor force, as are all inmates of institutions, regardless of age. All other members of the civilian noninstitutional population are eligible for the labor force by our definitions. Therefore, persons age 16 and over who have no job and are not looking for one are counted as "not in the labor force." For many who do not participate in the labor force, going to school is the reason. Family responsibilities keep others out of the labor force. Still others suffer a physical or mental disability which makes them unable to participate in normal labor force activities.

Most of these situations are quite clear: Bob Jones reports that he is attending college; Barbara Green feels that her two young children need her care; or Stephen Smith would like to work, but his doctor told him that he must not because he recently suffered a heart attack. All three of these people are not in the labor force and are classified accordingly, in their respective categories: "in school," "keeping house," and "unable to work."

There is a fourth group of persons who are not in the labor force. They are classified "other," which includes everyone who did not give any of the above reasons for nonparticipation in the labor force. Such persons may be retired and feel that they have made their contribution to the economy throughout the course of their lives, they may want to work only at certain times of the year, or they may believe that no employment is available for workers with their experience or training.[6]

The illustrations are less than wholly inclusive. The category of labor force excludes, for example, hundreds of thousands of prison inmates who labor in our prisons and asylums. The Attica events [of 1971] have brought their labor and their conditions to the forefront of our consciences but not into our statistical columns where they belong. In addition the labor force category also excludes millions who are tired of looking for work and have subsequently disappeared from the ranks of the unemployed. They get shoved into the limbo of beyond the labor force.

Let us now turn to those whom the BLS has in fact counted (in its monthly survey of 50,000 Americans) as *unemployed*. By 1967, the definition of unemployed had become what it is today:

> Persons are unemployed if they have looked for work in the past 4 weeks, are currently available for work, and, of course, do not have a job at the same time. Looking for work may consist of any of the following specific activities:
> Registering at a public or private employment office;
> Meeting with prospective employers;
> Checking with friends or relatives;
> Placing or answering advertisements;
> Writing letters of application; or
> Being on a union or professional register.

There are two groups of people who do not have to meet the test of having engaged in a specific jobseeking activity to be counted as unemployed. They are: (a) persons waiting to start a new job within 30 days, and (b) workers waiting to be recalled from layoff. In all cases, the individual must be currently available for work.[7]

Finally, who are the employed?

There is a wide range of job arrangements possible in the American economy, and not all of them fit neatly into a given category. For example, people are considered employed if they did any work at all for pay or profit during the survey week. This includes all part-time and temporary work as well as regular full-time year-round employment. *Persons are also counted as employed if they have a job at which they did not work during the survey week because they were:*
   On vacation;
   Ill;
   Involved in an industrial dispute;
   Prevented from working by bad weather; or
   Taking time off for various personal reasons.
These persons are counted among the employed and tabulated separately as "with a

job but not at work," because they have a specific job to which they will return.[8] [Italics added.]

Let us contemplate this specification. Missing from the unemployed, but counted among the employed, are people who work ten, twenty, or thirty hours a week. In fact, all forms of part-time help count as employed. But that ain't all. Finding their way into the employed category are short and long-term strikers,[9] the short and long-term ill (non-institutionalized), plus the two week as well as two month vacationers. To be employed, then, is not the same as to be engaged at work. Stop and think about that one. The distinction between (a) non-work-employment and (b) work employment is a subtle one that many of us miss even though these millions of the non-working employed fail to earn incomes, as is often the case during a strike, an illness or a vacation. Perhaps I should mention that the category non-working employed suggests the official category of working unemployed—those wretched chiselers on the unemployment rolls who do in fact work but cheat a government duty-bound to assess their awful numbers.

What people sometimes overlook, however, is how both (a) the narrow base for computing who is unemployed and (b) the extraordinarily broad criteria for determing who is beyond the labor force—serve to inflate the relative importance of the *employed* in the computation of statistics on unemployment. How does this triangular relationship among numerator, denominator, and outcome work? Since many of the objectively unemployed have been secreted by the BLS into the limbo of "not in labor force," where they cannot serve as a sizable portion of what would otherwise be a fairly large numerator in the overall statistical figure on percentage unemployed, and since the not-in-labor-force category fails to include the strikers, the ill, and the vacationers, and futhermore, since these three categories count as employed, the officially unemployed stand as whittled gnats in statistical ratio to the padded employed. In effect, we have an unduly puny numerator peering down at a bloated denominator. What we have is a Kafkaesque situation where a sudden and numerous increase in strikers[10] (hospital patients and/or vacationers) would inadvertently contribute to the immediate minimization of the official figure on unemployment, even under circumstances of slight increase in the number of those officially counted as unemployed. Think about that one, especially in communities such as Detroit.

THE AGGREGATE UNEMPLOYMENT RATE

Perhaps more puzzling than the "mistaken ratio" of the employed to the unemployed would be the periodicity of the count. Even if we were to assume that monthly reports, corrected for their underestimation, would be useful, we could nonetheless use what would appear to be a more demonstrative measure of unemployment, one in fact computed by the BLS but inadequately publicized by it. From the point of view of at least some unemployed, far more important than a monthly rate is the *aggregate unemployment rate*. This BLS rate refers to the number of people who are *unemployed over a period of one year*. Harry Brill makes clear why he thinks this yearly rate is more important:

> If on the average, four million people are jobless each month, that does not necessarily mean that the individuals who are counted as unemployed in one month are the same who are counted as unemployed a month later. Turnover among the unemployed occurs, and thus the total percentage, or number, of those who have been unemployed during each year must exceed the average monthly count.
>
> This is not news to the Department of Labor. According to the testimony delivered by Secretary of Labor Wirtz before the Senate Committee on Employment and Man Power, "approximately fourteen million men and women were unemployed at some time during the year of 1962." Fourteen million individuals are roughly twenty per cent of the total "labor force"! Therefore, the total annual rate (twenty per cent) is 3.77 times the average monthly rate (5.3 per cent) of that year. To that must be added millions of unemployed persons who are not counted by the Department of Labor; and the figure soars to represent eighteen or twenty million individuals.[11]

In other words, average monthly gross figures of four million would contrast with a yearly

number of approximately 14 million persons, perhaps unemployed for an average duration of time that is rather considerable. Often times the average length of time is between eight and ten weeks.[12] The figure of 14 million unemployed for such an average length of time does strongly suggest that something may well be organically wrong with such an economy even if one were to discount later those people between jobs, i.e., the frictionally unemployed. In fact, short-term unemployed could be subtracted from an aggregate unemployment rate to give us a better however incomplete picture of the objectively unemployed without detracting from the critical portrait of structural unemployment in the United States.

THE CONTRIVED CONSEQUENCES

The BLS has come under considerable criticism because of its slanting of unemployment news. Perhaps in part because of these external criticisms, the BLS has experimented with measures which have in fact more clearly indicated the true number of people without work but with the desire to work should a job become available. In 1964, during the rosy days of Johnson's administration, the Department of Labor published figures which indicated that total monthly unemployment might be considerably higher than the 4.5 million specified in the official figures. The experimental–statistical measure on unemployment did in fact include those not in the official labor force. Specifically, the "unemployed" for the first time included (1) those who had worked part-time but wanted full-time jobs as well as (2) those who had given up the search for work, plus (3) all the others found beyond the pale of labor force participation e.g., those who had never searched for work. The BLS appeared to be on its way to evolving a measure of work force, one with a more realistic and humane definition than "labor force." The impact of the additional categories was clear:

> The figures show that among white men aged 45 to 54 with four years of education or less, 221 of every 1000 are not working. Of these, 84 are listed as unemployed and 137 as "not in the labor force."
>
> Among those with college degrees, the corresponding figure shrinks to 39 who are

not working, including ten unemployed and 29 not in the labor force.[13]

Curiously enough, this more representative measure was dropped by the BLS soon after its innovation. In this sense, the BLS erased its justifiable innovation on work force measurement and opted for continuation of the traditional labor force categorization.

Some groups have suffered more than others from the consequences of undercount. Who they are is not too difficult to guess. Blacks and women are cases in point. Many of their objectively unemployed fail to get counted. Hence, their cases and their community's case fail to get the publicity warranted by their circumstances:

> What's more, experts say, the Administration view overlooks what has been happening to the black labor force. As of November, it has shrunk somewhat despite population growth and the return of more black veterans from Vietnam. In the 16 to 19 age group, for instance, the black male force slumped 12% to 396,000 for the 12 months ended last November; the percentage of eligible blacks in this group working or seeking work dropped to 40.5% from 48.4% a year earlier. (Meantime, the white male teen-age work force was swelling, in both size and participation rate.)
>
> But while fewer black teen-age males were working or seeking work, the group's jobless rate was holding at 21% to 25% of the total work force.
>
> "Some people become so depressed they simply drop out of the labor force," explains Dale Hiestand, associate professor of business at Columbia University's graduate school of business. "But when they do, they aren't counted as unemployed—even though they really are."[14]

Pondering this material, three points come to mind:

1. As of November, 1971, the black labor force was shrinking despite black population growth and the return of black veterans from Vietnam. What this trend indicates is a decrease in the black labor force and an increase in the number of potential black workers. Today, a curious and widening gap may well haunt the black community.

2. In the case of black late-teenagers found within the labor force, their absolute number dropped by one-eighth over a period of one year. This shrinkage occurred within an overall statistical category that was undoubtedly larger in November, 1970, than a year earlier.

3. In this 16 to 19 age category, the percentage of blacks working or seeking work dropped to approximately 40 percent of their overall number. That figure is somewhat shocking, for apparently the employed is considerably less than the 40 percent labor force total, since the group's official *un*employment percentage was approximately one-fifth of the 40 percent figure. In other words, around one-third of the young blacks were employed; hopefully all of the employed had jobs. But then many of the employed could have been strikers, patients, and vacationers. Unfortunately we do not know what these numbers of "employed" might be, although the BLS (or some other governmental bureaus) may perhaps have the data if not the processed tabulations. We do have data on strikers by industry and by community, and in the case of Detroit where many of the strikers are indeed black members of industrial unions, we would not be surprised to discover thousands of blacks, counted as employed over the average year, have been in fact strikers for one or more strike periods during the one year interval.

Strikers aside, we do know that the official number of black unemployed has increased sharply in the last several years as the economy has slid into a recession. Paul Flaim and Paul Schwab's article[15] documents this point, and we present their data (Table 27) on "employment status by color, age, and sex, 1969 and 1970."

What our preceding analysis on blacks suggests is that (a) young blacks found beyond the labor force plus (b) young blacks found in the officially unemployed category; these two groups, together, constitute an overall figure several times greater than the officially employed. Let's not forget, also, that the 16–19 year-old employed subsumes part-time employed blacks, including high school students working part-time. Of course, many black high school students do not have work. They are clearly not in the labor force. Nor will many of them join it soon after their graduation because

TABLE 27   Race, Employment Status, Sex, and Age: 1969–1970 (in thousands)

Employment Status, Sex, and Age	Total		White		Negro and Other Races	
	1970	*1969*	*1970*	*1969*	*1970*	*1969*
Both sexes, 16–19 years						
Civilian labor force	7,246	6,970	6,439	6,168	807	801
Employment	6,141	6,117	5,568	5,508	573	609
Unemployment	1,105	853	871	660	235	193
Unemployment rate	15.3	12.2	13.5	10.7	29.1	24.0

Taken from: Paul O. Flaim and Paul M. Schwab, "Changes in Employment and Unemployment in 1970," *Monthly Labor Review,* **94** (February, 1971), p. 3.

of the paucity of jobs for blacks with high school degrees.

These figures on persons with and without work should be computed, published, and publicized to indicate the seriousness of the black case. Put in yet another way, when we consider the beyond-the-labor-force category, let us not forget that their numbers are as immense as the *Wall Street Journal* article indicates and by no means near or equal to the official unemployment incidence.

BLACK UNEMPLOYMENT AND SPANISH-SPEAKING PEOPLE

Not known to many is the way in which black unemployment can be made to appear less serious than it is by the BLS simply counting the Spanish-speaking unemployed as white unemployed even when many Spanish-speaking unemployed define themselves, and are defined as, non-white. What are the consequences of this inexplicable inclusion? Although ludicrous, this elimination of a Spanish-speaking statistic and its inclusion in the white category has detrimental consequences not only for Chicanos and Puerto Ricans—who don't even have their own separate rates of unemployment—but for blacks who must compare their case with unreal figures on white unemployment. By padding the white rate with Spanish-speaking incidence of officially unemployed, the overall ratio of white-to-nonwhite unemployment is lessened. Indeed, should there be an inordinately great increase in Spanish-speaking unemployed, their increase would so inflate the official number of white unemployed—in certain regions of the United States—that the result would startle even the most callous of social scientists. The climbing rate of so-called white unemployed would in fact diminish the percentage gap between white and nonwhite unemployed. Optimistic interpreters could then conceivably argue that the figures strongly suggest that progress is being made in American race relations, for the traditional 2-to-1, black-to-white unemployment differential would be decreasing. Nor is this possibility an impossibility in places such as sourthern California where the rate of Spanish-speaking unemployed plus voluminous but normal increases in their incidence would seem to be often greater than comparable statistics for the black population.

Again, another statistical uncertainty with very certain results for blacks, this one certainly of lesser significance than the Spanish-speaking case because of the relative paucity of numbers involved, occurs when the BLS takes people of Asiatic background, at least one group of which (the Japanese-Americans) has an extremely low level of unemployment, and lumps them with blacks inside the nonwhite category. In the case of Japanese-Americans, for example, their loading into the nonwhite category lowers the incidence of unemployment for nonwhites, a category generally perceived as essentially black. And in places such as the Bay Area and Hawaii, where there are numerous Japanese-Americans, their addition would certainly obscure the true incidence of unemployment among blacks.

WOMEN: GROWTH IN THEIR NUMBER OF EMPLOYED AND UNEMPLOYED

During the last several years, women have posted a net gain in the labor force participation. This has also meant an increase in their employment. As Flaim and Schwab put it:

> Given the uneven pattern of employment changes by industry, it is not surprising that some labor force groups experienced greater difficulties than others. Adult men, for example, saw their employment growth halted by the sharp job cut-backs in the goods-producing sector. Adult women, on the other hand, being concentrated largely in the less affected service sector, managed to post a relatively sizable employment gain despite the economic slowdown.[16]

But the same article points to increased unemployment among women as a whole, even though some categories of women did post an increase:

> Traditionally employed in the service-producing industries (which were not severely affected by the recent slowdown) women 20 years and over managed to post an employment gain of about 550,000 in 1970. But even this advance—largely in part-time employment—was considerably below the average job gains achieved by women in recent years. The result was a 350,000 increase in female unemployment and a rise in their jobless rate from 3.7 to 4.8 percent. On balance, however, the year-to-year increase in unemployment among women, although substantial, was relatively less sharp than among males.[17]

This "on balance" view of women having a less serious increase in unemployment may well be accounted for by the real possibility of many women losing their jobs and then dropping out of the labor force by sliding back into the roles of housewives. Once back in the housewife roles, many do not search for regular jobs and hence do not count as unemployed. Their failure to qualify for the unemployed category would have as a consequence a dampening effect on the growth of female unemployment rates.

THE STRUCTURAL CONSEQUENCES OF STATISTICAL PECULIARITIES

We would like now to comment on some of the structural consequences of these statistical peculiarities before making certain interpretive and concluding remarks. In private correspondence with the authors, Harry Brill has commented on the consequences of systematic underestimation of unemployment for people in general, and for black people (as well as women) in particular. And here we paraphrase his key comments: since the BLS systematically understates the employment problem, their doing so focuses the issue on the victim and not on the questionable structure.

The human consequences of this focus should not be overlooked. When shuffling back and forth between the comforting *New York Times* figures of 5 and 6 percent we can afford to be somewhat blasé about the unemployed and to dwell on a relative handful of unfortunate individuals as we accept these official statistics. In the ordinary community, to see and to feel sorry for those unfortunate five or six persons out of one hundred is one thing. Little concern, guilt, or critical structural analysis seems warranted. It is quite another matter, however, when we make valid and private revisions on unemployment estimates that relegate not five or six but twenty or twenty-five out of one hundred to the category of out of work. Furthermore, we have reason to believe that many of these 25 out of 100 would in all probability go to work immediately, were just-paying jobs available. This very thing did happen during World War II. War contracts created millions of just-paying jobs. Federal FEPC opened many of them to all. The jobs were subsequently filled by industrious persons, many of whom today would be termed hard-core unemployed, totally and irretrievably beyond the labor force. Indeed, once the Second World War was over, many of the war workers became hard-core unemployed once again because of the cyclical character of the economy and the presence of effective racial discrimination. In this sense their labor force participation became a poor measure of their work force potential.

The political consequences of invalid measures are less clear but perhaps of equal structural significance. Were BLS statistics to focus on the accordion-like quality of the U.S. job market and to use, as well as to publicize, valid labor force measures of the aggregate unemployed as the official and most significant unemployment rate, we would undoubtedly be astounded by the size of the yearly rates in question.

No doubt powerful persons within our federal government are aware of potential relationships between such an annual governmental announcement and the further delegitimation of our capitalist order. With this sensitivity spurring many of these elites on to questionable statistical heights, these powerful persons have acted both to minimize the official incidence of the unemployed and to maximize the presumed occurence of *other* statistical deviants. Let us cite a case in point. Statistics on "crime in the streets" seldom get understated by government bureaus. In fact, some studies indicate that these figures—such as those on black sniping at police in our cities—get overstated officially and picked up locally (as well as reciprocally) by local right-wing groups geared to launch "support your local police" campaigns. By contrast, the unemployed are not involved in such a relationship with any government bureau.

WHY BLS BIAS?

Why does the BLS do the poor the way it does? Why do our unemployed, and the overwhelming majority are blue collar, get such sorry treatment from their government's BLS? In some instances, BLS behavior can be momentarily rationalized if not completely justified. In the case of Japanese-Americans, for example, *perhaps* certain leaders of the Japanese-American community have pressured the BLS to make its true incidence of unemployment unknown to the general population for fear of white reprisals against their property or person, as was the case during World War II. Publicized estimates on Japanese landholdings (and fishing fleets) on the West Coast undoubtedly helped to pave the way for the detainment of Japanese in camps and the seizure of Japanese-owned land (and fishing fleets) soon after the Second World War began. We say "perhaps" because we do not know whether Japanese-American leaders gave applied such pressure on the BLS, or whether the BLS, out of paternal concern for Japanese-American group welfare, acted to hide these people's true condition within the larger group of black Americans.

In the case of Chicanos and Puerto Ricans and other Spanish-speaking peoples in the United States, there is no evidence to our knowledge that the leading Chicano militants prefer to be defined as a part of the white population. Just the opposite. However, this is the contemporary preference of labor leaders and/or militants such as Chavez and Gonzales as well as Tijerina. Today's ethnic surge in the Chicano community does not speak for the very recent past when a more mild Mexican-American leadership sought the assimilation of their group and perhaps their statistical extinction as well. Further, these moderate gentlemen may well have made known their preference(s) to the BLS, and the BLS may have acted accordingly. If that kind of pressure has been exerted, and if the BLS did in fact go the assimilation route accordingly, it would perhaps be a little unfair at this point to demand of the BLS that it now turn half-circle while anticipating ten years from now another 180-degree shift, this one back to the point of assimilation–categorization. But these possibilities, past, present, and future, remain just that—speculation which can only be tested on the basis of historical research.

Despite these cautions on change and its potential sources, certain definite affirmative statements can be made: Spanish-speaking unemployed deserve a separate category so that they can demand and get the separate help they deserve. Blacks also need this categorization. As we have observed, the BLS has treated not only Spanish-speaking people but blacks so as to deprive them of the right to say convincingly: "Hey man, half of us are out of work! The government says so! And the government should work with us to do something about it!"

Perhaps the upper classes are responsible for undercount and misassignment even if we don't label them racists, a designation which many of them do in fact deserve. Perhaps blacks and others are in part chance victims of a general effort on the part of the upper classes to understate unemployment for everyone (and misassign unemployment for many) and hence for every ethnic group, blacks included. G. William Domhoff has observed[18] that the U.S. contains families who have considerable wealth, class consciousness, and manipulative ability. These families include breadwinners who relate to one another as an interlocking directorate. They preside as key decision-makers within boards of directors, trustees, and governors of almost every major corporation, bank, and ancillary institution in the United States. We are not saying that they all agree on every matter, including the presentation of statistical materials on unemployment. As policy makers of these organizations, these directors by no means create a consensus on all subjects. On the contrary, these people—plus their professional subordinates—set policies which enhance their own interests. The directors either occupy positions of power in the U.S. government, or they exert immense amounts of economic and political strength from its immediate periphery in order to shape state policy. And these directors are always sensitive to country-wide, state, and local unemployment. The reasons are many, but some appear more important than others. From the point of view of many upper-class persons, growing unemployment adversely affects upper-class interests, in part because the upper classes believe that its misinterpretation can further worsen the nature of an economy going into, coming out of, avoiding, or caught within the very middle of, an economic slump. If, for example, publicized statistical figures frighten potential consumers and thereby hasten the further decline of an economy, as many upper-class persons have argued, then these announced statistics are having an adverse effect from the point of view of these same upper-class persons. In this kind of situation, and from the point of view of a sizable proportion of the upper classes, upper-class persons do face a responsibility to revise fact-gathering techniques in order to arrive at overall unemployment figures which will minimize the psychic insecurities of potential spenders, people whose very purchasing power is necessary both to revive an economy and to keep it going. Once moving at a proper clip, whatever the sources of the recovery, the economy allows these directors to obtain corporate enhancement, related personal prestige, and heightened family earnings. And as usual, we have to ask the question—at whose expense?

SUMMARY AND RECOMMENDATION

For trained economists and statisticians, many with doctorates, to continue to impose invalid statistics on the people of the United States constitutes not fraud, not outrage, but

predictable service on the part of professionals who owe their jobs and their careers to the politicians found in the executive branches of the federal government. In turn, most politicians of this calibre have developed a reciprocal set of ties with upper-class persons on the assumption that what is good for private corporations on matters of statistics must be good for the state on matters of its longevity. We do not agree.

Our task is to bring to light the presence and conditions of the foregotten unemployed so that we can unite with them and others in order to transform this country. As a beginning in this direction, we can strive to develop a typology of those whom the BLS refuses to count as unemployed. Fortunately, work has already gone forward in this direction. Harry Chester, Research Associate for the International union offices of the UAW, has developed a most useful 4-part typology on workers now counted as "nonparticipants" in the labor force:

1. The discouraged workers. (This group is counted by BLS, but classified as "persons not in the labor force".) These are workers who, even though they desired work, were not engaged in job-seeking activities within the past four weeks because they thought that jobs in their line of work were not available or because they thought that employers would refuse to hire them due to their age or their race or simply because they had been job hunting prior to the most recent four-week period and had given up in despair. According to BLS this group of discouraged workers amounted to 807,000 in the first quarter 1971 and to 685,000 in the second quarter 1971.
Actually the number of discouraged workers is probably much larger. Various studies in depth have shown that because of the pressure of public opinion workers are reluctant to admit that they have stopped looking for work because they can't find a job. Many pretend instead that they stopped seeking work because they are disabled or are chronically sick.
2. The nonpersons. Checks on the population census have shown that government surveys are unable to enumerate persons who are without a fixed residence. (Persons who sleep in condemned buildings, on park benches, at railroad stations, etc.) This group of persons is not represented in the BLS la-

bor force sample and we don't know any-thing about this group except that it is very clear that the group's unemployment rate is much higher than the national average.

3. *Unemployed workers who are tempo-rarily sick.* In order to be counted as un-employed a person must be available for work in the survey week. Consequently un-employed workers who, in the survey week, are temporarily sick are counted as persons not in the labor force even though they need a job and even though except for this tem-porary sickness they would have been seek-ing work and would have been available for work.

In addition to causing a serious undercount of unemployment this rule also causes the following anomaly: A worker with a job who is temporarily sick is considered a mem-ber of the labor force. But an unemployed worker who is temporarily sick is classified as a person not in the labor force.

4. *Workers enrolled in government train-ing programs.* The enrollees of government training programs are classified either as "employed" even though they don't have a regular job or they are classified as persons not in the labor force even though they need a job and engage in a job-seeking activity by getting themselves trained for a job.

Prior to 1965 this group was classified as "unemployed." The magazine "Human Re-sources" (Fall 1969) which first raised this point estimated that this reclassification has the effect of reducing the overall unemploy-ment rate by 0.4 percentage points.[19]

Can we expect professional BLS statisticians to move to include these people in the category of unemployed? Current events would suggest the possibilities are indeed slim. Unfortunately, professionals employed by the BLS are appar-ently not in a position to do much about that kind of thing. Even so, their mild efforts to be objective in their monthly press briefings and written reports have been curtailed by a Nixon administration bent on allowing his own imme-diate political emissaries, and they only, the right to handle important tasks involved in the releasing of statistics on unemployment.[20]

Yet there are several things *we* can do be-sides develop useful typologies. First, some of us could develop weighing techniques which would allow us to publish revised statistical figures on aggregate unemployment within the labor force. Admittedly because of cost con-siderations we must apparently rely on figures ultimately based upon BLS statistics. But this reliance does include certain brighter aspects, such as our use of BLS estimates on the conse-quences of systematic undercounting of the un-employed. Second, we might be able to develop a more precise estimate of aggregate un-employed through our own creation and use of a stratified, list random sample over a sufficient length of time within a particular community. Admittedly, our use of one community does have its limits, but our findings might be of sufficient importance to spur the BLS to follow in our footsteps. This spurring process would include our publication of valid measures and significant findings. Both items would contrast vividly with government figures. Today they are both without professional credibility for social science *and* positive utility for working-class people. In fact, the BLS figures now do the working-class people a disservice by understat-ing the overall unemployment condition of the working class. What we need are valid measures of unemployment, the kinds of scientific statis-tics which will allow us to build a sound case for those millions of Americans who would work, were jobs available.

Finally, we must encourage strikers to de-nounce publicly a Bureau of Labor Statistics which insists on counting them as employed when in fact they are on strike, without work, without pay, without unemployment compen-sation, and in some cases, without jobs! People must be encouraged to control *their* counters *and their* computers! Democratize the statis-tics! Liberate the statisticians!

CHAPTER CONCLUSION

Clearly the alternative proposed by the right-democrats differs from that of the left-democrats of the George McGovern stripe. The right-democrats place their faith in elites, thus making assumptions that populist democrats would find hard to accept. Despite their differences, however, both types belong in the democratic camp, although we can observe that the right-democrats in particular have a propensity to express their democratic commitments in a most bi-zarre way: They support overseas imperialism as well as domestic neocolonialism, topics we will consider in Chapters 12 to 14. But before doing so, let us consider the center-democratic alternative.

NOTES

1. See "States Joblessness 5.7% in August, Off from 6.1%", *The New York Times*, September 21, p. 1.

2. Karl Mannheim, *Ideology and Utopia* (London: Routledge and Kegan Paul, 1953), pp. 49–53.

3. Mannheim dealt primarily with the cognitive categories unconsciously accepted by the group. By contrast, he did on occasion analyze valuations as well; and when he did, his definitions of "utopias" did resemble those associated from counter-culture, a term in turn derived from the circumscribed definition of culture. The circumscribed definition of culture denotes the beliefs, values, and norms common to a society. By contrast, the all-encompassing specification, one for example accepted by the Leslie White school of anthropology, would include "everything" but habitat. By everything is meant not only the idea but the organizational and technological systems as well.

4. Harry Brill, "Unemployment: Official and Real," *The Nation*, 212 (January 25, 1971), p. 100.

5. We were able to obtain this information on unadjusted comparisons plus the option of do-it-yourself adjusted comparisons from Miss Kohlnieser of the New York office of the Bureau of Labor Statistics.

6. "How the Government Measures Unemployment," Bureau of Labor Statistics Report Number 312 (June, 1967), pp. 7–8. The now-used definition of participation in the labor force is more narrow than it was prior to 1967, when groups such as 14- and 15-year-olds were included. Briefly put, the labor force consists of the employed and the unemployed persistently seeking work. The BLS has evolved certain standard techniques for obtaining information on these groups:

> Statistics on the employment status of the population, the personal, occupational, and other characteristics of the employed, the unemployed, and persons not in the labor force, and related data are compiled for the BLS by the Bureau of the Census in its Current Population Survey (CPS). A detailed description of this survey appears in *"Concepts and Methods Used in Manpower Statistics from the Current Population Survey"* (BLS Report 313). This report is available from BLS on request.
>
> These monthly surveys of the population are conducted with a scientifically selected sample designed to represent the civilian noninstitutional population 16 years and over. Respondents are interviewed to obtain information about the employment status of each member of the household 16 years of age and over. The inquiry relates to activity or status during the calendar week, Sunday through Saturday, which includes the 12th of the month. This is known as the survey week. Actual field interviewing is conducted in the following week.
>
> Inmates of institutions and persons under 16 years of age are not covered in the regular monthly enumerations and are excluded from the population and labor force statistics shown in this report. Data on members of the Armed Forces, who are included as part of the categories "total noninstitutional population" and "total labor force," are obtained from the Department of Defense.
>
> Each month, 50,000 occupied units are designated for interview. About 2,250 of these households are visited but interviews are not obtained because the occupants are not found at home after repeated calls or are unavailable for other reasons. This represents a noninterview rate for the survey of about 4.5 percent. In addition to the 50,000 occupied units, there are 8,500 sample units in an average month which are visited but found to be vacant or otherwise not to be enumerated. Part of the sample is changed each month. The rotation plan provides for three-fourths of the sample to be common from one month to the next, and one-half to be common with the same month a year ago.

See "Labor Force Data," *Employment and Earnings*, 18, No. 3 (September 1971). U.S. Department of Labor, Bureau of Labor Statistics.

7. *Ibid.*, p. 5. Also see *Employment and Earnings, op. cit.*, p. 140.

8. *Ibid.*, p. 4. Also see *Employment and Earnings, op. cit.*, p. 140.

9. In communities such as Detroit, this matter of counting the unemployed strikers as employed involves not a few people. In metropolitan Detroit for example, in 1964, there were 95 work stoppages involving 114,000 workers who were idle a total of 2,060,000 work days. Were the BLS to count these workers as unemployed or nonparticipants in the labor force, the overall incidence of unemployment would undoubtedly increase significantly. See U.S. Department of Labor, Bureau of Labor Statistics, *Analysis of Work Stoppages*, Bulletin No. 1460, October 1965, p. 17.

10. Since 1967, the technique used to count the unemployed has been one of including those who have sought work in the last twenty-eight days. Excluded from this category, however, are people who have sought work in the last twenty-eight days but not been available to take a job in the week prior to the interview because they were attending school. For a more precise idea on the fact gathering questions used to gather materials, see Office of Statistical Policy, Bureau of the Budget, *Household Survey Manual* (Washington: Office of Statistical Policy, 1969), pp. 13–17.

11. Harry Brill, "Can We Train Away the Unemployed?" *The Feedback*, III (November–December, 1965), pp. 5–12.

12. Paul O. Flaim and Paul M. Schwab have observed that:

> Most of the persons who became unemployed in 1970 managed to find work after a relatively short period of job hunting. Thus, the average duration of unemployment increases only moderately during the year. At an 8.8 week average, it was only 1 week higher than in 1969, but well below the levels that, in earlier years, had been associated with unemployment rates of the magnitude reached in 1970. Nevertheless, a gradually higher proportion of the unemployed (about one-fifth at year's end) had been jobless for at least 15 weeks, while a limited number apparently had left the labor force.

See their "Changes in Employment and Unemployment in 1970," *Monthly Labor Review*, 94 (February 1971), p. 13.

13. "The 'Hidden' Jobless Figures," *The San Francisco Chronicle*, March 11, 1964, p. 14.

14. " 'Discouraged' Blacks Leave the Labor Force, Distorting Jobless Rate," *The Wall Street Journal*, January 8, 1971, p. 1.

15. Flaim and Schwab, *op. cit.*, p. 18. As we indicated earlier, the conditions facing the younger blacks, and here again we consider only the civilian noninstitutional population of 14- and 15-year-olds, are even more dire. In September 1971 of those who were black members of the labor force, fifty-four thousand were employed and thirty-four thousand were unemployed. The incidence of unemployment was particularly high among female blacks. Comparable figures for white were considerably lower. Less than *seven* percent of that section of the labor force was unemployed. See U.S. Department of Labor, Bureau of Labor Statistics, *Employment and Earnings*, 18 (October 1971), p. 43.

16. *Ibid.*, p. 16.

17. *Ibid.*, p. 18.

18. G. William Domhoff, *Who Rules America?* (Englewood Cliffs, N.J.: Prentice-Hall, 1967), pp. 1–27, 138–156.

19. Private correspondence with Harry Chester, Research Associate, UAW (Solidarity House, Detroit, Michigan), in a letter written by him and dated September 28, 1971.

20. "Reporting on Economy," *The New York Times* (March 23, 1971), p. 62. *The Times* most recently indicated the degree to which the Nixon administration and top BLS administrators are bringing pressure to bear on the BLS professional. In an editorial entitled "Politicizing the B.L.S.?", *The Times* states:

> Two ranking economists are reportedly planning to leave the bureau on the eve of a reorganization that would considerably reduce their areas of authority. Administration spokesmen insist that the shakeup, part of a general overhaul of Federal statistical services announced last July, has nothing to do with politics. The initial list of new appointees rushed out by the White House yesterday had done a little (*sic*) to dispel reports of political maneuvering in connection with B.L.S. restaffing.

See "Politicizing the B.L.S.?" *The New York Times*, September 30, 1971, p. 46.

Three thoroughgoing reports reprinted in the Congressional Record indicate that more is involved than press briefings. A thoroughgoing reorganization of the Bureau of Labor Statistics plus a purge of key BLS officials is in the process of occurring, with business-oriented officials supplanting career officials in key posts dealing with statistical analysis. See especially Alexander Uhl's "Statistical Hanky-Panky? Nixon Administration Orders Drastic Reorganization of Economic Reporting," *Congressional Record–Senate*, 117, No. 1/57, pp. S16718–S16719. Also pertinent is Duane Emme's "Moore on the Spot–Proxmire Probe Sheds New Light on Shakeup Among BLS Personnel," *Ibid.*, pp. S16719–S16720. Also pertinent are Hubert Humphrey's remarks on the demotion of Mr. Goldstein, formerly a leading member of the BLS, *Ibid.*, p. S16722.

11 Center-Democratic: Its Strengths and Weaknesses

CENTER-DEMOCRATIC: ITS BASE AND CONTENT

At the level of the upper classes, center-democratic articulates the judgments of corporate liberals and wealthy sections of ethnic—religious minorities. There are exceptions. Many center-democrats stem from old-line families which have broken with genteel conservatism in order to salvage a badly sagging order. Whatever their background, center-democrats have preferred John Lindsay, John Kennedy, Robert Kennedy, Eugene McCarthy, and others of center-democratic persuasion. When we examine the industrial and financial backgrounds of center-democrats, we discover that many derive much of their incomes from light industries, the new speculations in real estate, and high finance; they also aid in the management of such enterprises. Not a few belong to the Democratic party.

What is center-democratic? How does it differ from its right and left counterparts? Previously we indicated that center-democratic—whether a party, movement, or government—is committed to the amelioration of social problems faced by the less fortunate. But this is an incomplete description of a political tendency led by the more progressive sections of the upper classes. Under modern circumstances, center-democrats represent an effort to join moderate bureaucratic organizations wedded to mild social change to domestic grass-roots social movements with considerably more in mind. These movements aim for the immediate elimination of problems of unemployment, disease, bad housing, poor health, irresponsible police, and associated concerns common to lower-class life. These adverse material conditions are derived in large part from upper-class decision-making expressed through political elites who view private corporate welfare as synonymous with the well-being of the nation-state, even at the expense of the poor and the near-poor. Thus sections of the upper class may be allied with the poor against other sections of the upper class and the political power structure. Illustrative would be the coming together of the political and economic power wielded by Robert Kennedy and the California farm workers' movement led by Cesar Chavez against corporate landed and banking wealth of California's Central Valley.

LEFT- AND CENTER-DEMOCRATIC: A COMPARISON

Left-democratic has little faith in the bureaucratic world of politics, believing that he who links democratic aspirations to bureaucratic organizations must inevitably produce an oligarchy in many ways as noxious as the one used by the establishment and the power structure for purposes of repression. Hence, unlike center-democratic groups, left-democrats shy away from continued reliance on large-scale party organizations, governmental departments, bureaus, and traditional unions. On occasion left-democrats contradict themselves by initially helping to create struggle organizations quite obviously hell-bent to become bureaucratic. In this sense, left-democrats react anxiously to center-democratic efforts to consolidate social movement gains by offering help to fledgling unions and welfare rights groups. Put it this way. Left-democrats supported Robert Kennedy's effort to help the California farm workers. But left-democrats are nonetheless leery of potentially adverse organizational consequences. These include the possible adaptation

of an increasingly successful and hence bureaucratic grass-roots group into the sterile politics
practiced by existing unions and political parties. The adaptation could only accelerate the
formation of the authoritarian qualities that
characterize bureaucratization.

RIGHT- AND CENTER-DEMOCRATIC:
A COMPARISON

Center- and *right*-democratic differ considerably in their relation to grass-roots movements.
Whereas center-democrats generally hail the
emergence of progressive social movements,
work with them, and frequently forego efforts
to absorb them—often viewing civil rights movements, student protests, and insurgent labor
organizations as essentially positive and vital to
the periodic revitalization of the political system—the *right*-democrats condemn as they
eschew grass-roots movements. Right-democrats
view insurgent grass-roots groups as potential
precursors to a fascist overthrow of the parliamentary system. Hence, wherever they can, the
right-democrats attempt to steer protest activities into institutionalized channels, and as soon
as possible. Ever since the turbulent 1920s and
1930s when millions were involved in fascist
and communist movements, there has existed a
politically significant category of right-
democrats wary of nonparliamentary politics,
especially those involving mass movements.
These right-democrats either ignore or condemn
a mass movement. They seldom join it. During
the 1960s, for example, these upper-class persons and associated intellectuals avoided participating in the civil rights movement, generally
condemning both black militants and their
white allies, and hewing very closely to a legal-
istic and cautious strategy advocated by the
NAACP. When white civil rights activists went
into the antiwar movement, militant antiwar
protests were greeted with similar criticism by
right-democrats such as Daniel Bell, Lewis
Feuer, Nathan Glazer, Sidney Hook, Irving
Kristol, Morris Janowitz, and Seymour M. Lipset.

In general, right-democrats differ from center-democrats in yet another way. Although
both recognize the "necessity" of organizing
society bureaucratically in order to install semiautonomous elites in positions of formal politi-

cal power both in party and government, these
two tendencies differ profoundly on matters of
how best to relate to the military high command. Center-democrats have observed and on
occasion exposed the propensity of military
elites and their civilian partners to engage in
covert design of foreign policy decisions in order to accomplish ends that might be very un-
popular were they made public. Illustrative
were the joint publisher and editorial–staff
decisions on the part of *The New York Times*
to publish the so-called Pentagon Papers in
1971, and the parallel agreement of the same
parties to label the Kennedy—Johnson—Bundy—
McNamara—Westmoreland decision on Vietnam
as "clandestine."[1] By contrast, the right-
democrats will generally support the decision of
military civilian elites to deny the public information on matters of foreign policy decision-
making. The accompanying rationalization is
straightforward: To oppose publicly the right
of the military and civilian elites to be secretive
on matters of foreign policy plans and to expose the military civilian elites when they do
prevaricate is to invite ridicule and hence to
weaken their legitimacy. Illustrative would be
Nixon's and Agnew's criticisms of *The New
York Times* for its publication of the Pentagon
Papers.

Clearly, then, these differences among cen-
ter- and right-democrats indicate real disputes
among corporations, government officials, politicians and associated persons on how best to
relate to domestic social movements and military elites. Their mutual recriminations have

---

[1] In the Introduction to *The Pentagon Papers* (New
York: Bantam, 1971), Neil Sheehan observed:

Clandestine warfare, as this collection of *New York
Times* articles on the Pentagon papers will illustrate, naturally has an important effect on public
events. Covert operations also occasionally violate
treaties and contradict open policy pronouncements. No matter what vintage, therefore, documents related to clandestine war are, in the bureaucratic phrase, 'excluded from downgrading' under
the classification regulations, in order to avoid embarrassing the Executive Branch and the men responsible. (p. xii)

In the same book's Forward, Hedrick Smith noted:

The Pentagon account notes that at times the highest Administration officials not only kept information about their real intentions from the press
and Congress but also kept secret from the government bureaucracy the real motives for their written
recommendations or actions. (p. xxiv)

erupted most recently over the disclosures of the Pentagon Papers, the China recognition overtures, governmental and the devaluation of U.S. currency. These controversies do not mean that right-democrats stand as a confirmed bloc on all issues. Nor is each right-democrat consistent over time. Still, the most important demarcation point is between right and center, especially when it comes to upper-class decision-making on world issues of the kind just mentioned. Right-democrats depict the Communist and insurgent world as proto- or ongoing totalitarian (and the capitalist world as essentially free and democratic, and hence worthy of our protection). Center-democrats, however, generally believe that the best approach to overseas revolutionary movements is to attempt to destroy them through counterinsurgency (i.e., counterrevolutionary) activity *but*, if that strategy fails, to deemphasize the totalitarian label and stress reconciliation between the Communist and capitalist worlds through summit conferences, investment aid, trade agreements, mutual diplomatic recognition, and like devices. These mechanisms are geared to the cooptation of the overseas revolutionary leadership and the integration of such movements into parliamentary politics and international agreements, where revolutionary ideology and left-revolutionary remnants can be more readily managed by oligarchical rulers two or three steps removed from a helpful U.S. political leadership dedicated to the rewarding of right-communists. Once again, we can observe the propensity of center-democrats to work with an insurgent movement in order to defang but not to alienate it.

A NEEDED QUALIFICATION

Here as elsewhere we are not contrasting all-or-nothing qualities but rather speculating on presumed differences between center- and right-democrats in our analysis of political propensities. For example, it may be that many right-democrats favor a bundle of policies virtually indistinguishable from those of center-democrats during a particular phase of development. In the long haul, however, people will generally frequent one camp or the other.

Although center- and right-democrats differ considerably on matters of ideology, both have come to rely on bureaucratic organizations in order to mobilize and to sustain human energies in a disciplined way. Discipline has been necessary to create predictable behavior coordinated by the few around their goals, which are generally publicized as everyone's goals. In capitalist society, these have most frequently taken one of two forms: (*a*) private bureaucratic organizations' dedication either to profit-making or to socializing the young in a manner consistent with these purposes, (*b*) state articulation of policies and programs designed to comfort corporate organizations and their associates. Thus the state need not be governed by the upper class, although often its governors do come from this group. What *is* essential is that the state rule to complement upper-class interests. (See Alan Stone's review-article on Ralph Miliband's *The State in Capitalist Society* in Section Two of this chapter.) To do so has demanded increased rationalization within vertically structured large-scale organizations. Viewed historically, the vertical, authoritarian structures were baldly apparent in almost every case until World War II, when there appeared a number of organizations whose lines of authority were obfuscated by human relations techniques. Human relations techniques are forms of human manipulation based on organizational use of persuasion rather than coercion. Built into manipulation through persuasion is the effort to create affectional, near-intimate ties between the manipulator and the manipulated. Illustrative would be a police neighborhood unit in New York City attempting to manipulate neighborhood residents into cooperating with the police by (*a*) holding informal get-togethers where the police convey a new image of themselves as the people's protectors and at the same time attempt to develop with the residents a first name, chummy relationship, and (*b*) abandoning the use of police cars where it makes sense for police pairs to walk a beat and so enable the policemen to get to know people on a first-name basis.

THE CENTER PREFERS THE PROFESSIONAL BUREAUCRATIC TO THE STIFF AND STODGY

In Max Weber's time (i.e., sixty to seventy years ago), the relational contours of an organization that was called bureaucratic resembled those of a rational, military organization such as the German army, civil service, or university.[2] Nor were the German illustrations unique. The emerging pattern was becoming near-universal, as the small business firm gave way to corporate and governmental organizations. People lodged themselves in large-scale organizations within hierarchies of roles, and the accompanying duties were clearly delineated and sanctioned within organizational subunits having narrowly defined functions. Persons were recruited, promoted, and deposed on the basis of merit. Merit was decided on the basis of personal achievement—grades, degrees, and job performance. Gone were the days of nepotism and informal affectional ties as the basis for obtaining jobs and relating to others at the workplace. Formal relations linked role occupants and departments within a visibly vertical structure—most notably among white-collared salaried employees.

Center-democrats have led in the creation of a new style-bureaucracy—referred to by some as "professional bureaucratic.[3] This model is most popular among those who have worked to create and/or to sustain the human relations school of thought within industrial sociology and large-scale organization.[4] The thought model's creation, it might be added, both accompanied and reflected ongoing organizational changes, as the human relations school attempted to redefine the authority structure of large-scale groups such as academic research centers, factory organizations, and university groups. Essentially, the professional bureaucratic organization has united as it has partitioned the *rational, role-specific subunits,* associated with Max Weber, from the *hang-loose, human relations bureaus,* made popular more recently within a larger organization which comes to rely on *both* forms, depending on the task in question. Where the task is predictable,

the organization mobilizes its "rational, role-specific" components. Where the task is generally unpredictable, "the human relations unit(s)" is given the job.[5]

Those of center-democratic persuasion have gravitated toward this modified Weberian model of bureaucracy because they have learned that the prudent and selective application of human relations techniques gives organizational elites greater manipulative control not only over their own expensively acquired personnel but over those whose attachment to the organization is external: most notably, *unpredictable* "clients," "movements," "publics," "students," and like bodies to which the bureaucratic organizations in question must now relate.

Professional bureaucracy has quite frequently created a pliant, positive, reasonable, democratic (and hence acceptable) "self-image" among potentially hostile clients and even among many of its own members because its leadership works to obscure its truly hierarchical (and hence objectionable) character. Critics have commented that while the ugly authoritarianism may disappear, the vertical structure remains. Still, despite these criticisms, professional bureaucratic leaders continue to engineer this collective perception, in part by promoting fraternal relations among those in contiguous and near-proximate positions as well as those located at quite different levels of the overall, organizational pecking order. Note: The professional bureaucratic organization is in fact organized along hierarchical lines, most visibly in those departments which deal with predictable events (e.g., a university office in charge of recording grades). In the case of a registrar's office, the predictable flow of grades demands precise role behavior in relation to "clients," whose behavior is equally predictable. But in many university bureaus such is not the case, especially in those subunits where the tasks are unpredictable yet significant and require professional expertise. For example, consider the problems of the public relations bureau of a State university. University lobbyists working with and through a public relations group must relate positively to State legislative committee chairmen in charge of drawing up budgets for the university in question. Here we can some-

---

[2] Max Weber, "Bureaucracy," in H. H. Gerth and C. Wright Mills, *Max Weber, Essays in Sociology* (New York: Oxford University Press, 1953), pp. 196–264.

[3] See Eugene Litwak, "Models of Bureaucracy which Permit Conflict," *American Journal of Sociology,* 47 (January, 1961), pp. 177–184.

[4] For an excellent, comparative analysis on the origins of the human relations school, see Reinhard Bendix "The American Experience," in his *Work and Authority in Industry* (New York: Wiley, 1956), pp. 254–340, especially pp. 287–340.

[5] See Litwak, *op. cit.*

times observe a subpart of a professional bureaucratic organization employing human relations techniques such as glossy press releases, casual telephone conversations, cocktail parties, luncheon gatherings, golf games, fishing expeditions, and perhaps even mountain climbs to resolve differences between a university and its legislative parent. Of course, the use of human relations techniques by no means guarantees success; but clearly professionals are out on their own, attempting to solve difficult tasks on the basis of schooled ingenuity and not hopelessly useless role specifications. Presumably the less restricted professional will have greater success.

The presence of a "hang-loose" quality, however, should not be confused with the absence of intraorganizational criticisms. Within a professional bureaucratic organization, the chiefs promote criticisms and self-criticisms (relaxed, however harsh) at all levels, much as they engender a sense of community and chumminess among people found at all levels of the group. This sense of community aids organizational allies who depend on well-versed professionals who can be recruited and retained only by drawing heavily on the organization's human and financial resources. Indeed, as we noted, a deliberate effort is made *not* to force brainy professionals to act within a particular role. Rather, people and organizational subunits are given their tasks and are expected to do them on the basis of their professional expertise. Merit remains relevant, although it may be difficult to ascertain individual achievement (since team performance in good measure determines organizational success for persons caught up in informal relations that work against mutual evaluation in terms of objective criteria). Still, the professional bureaucratic approach has proved to be *relatively* successful when dealing with tough problems that have cropped up in community institutions.

PROFESSIONAL BUREAUCRACY, THE CENTER, AND THE GRASS ROOTS

Professional bureaucracy constitutes an intrinsic part of the center-democratic approach to grass-roots social movements on the left. During the 1960s, especially during the Kennedy–Johnson era, it was not unusual in the United States for representatives of the federal bureaucracy to approach civil rights and peace activists to enlist their support in projects sponsored by federal departments and bureaus. These units of government were professionalized to the degree that they allowed their "outside" people considerable flexibility when negotiating with movement people on the recruitment of those who could help to create antipoverty programs and legal services for the organized poor. Left-democrats were often given the bureaucratic task of meeting movement "contacts" at university coffee houses and like places to convince radicals of the necessity of merging "novel" federal governmental programs and social movement efforts in order to translate recent leftist victories into significant alterations of ongoing institutions. When center-democrats and radicals established federally sponsored groups like CRLA (the controversial California Rural Legal Assistance program), the new collectivities took on a professional bureaucratic quality—with its admixture of discipline and casualness. For the new service groups had no choice but to invest considerable discretionary authority in the hands of hip but professionally astute organizers, lawyers, and other professionals. These agencies had to work with groups of poor people who often did not trust middleclass professionals when they offered free services.

Another failure became obvious as well: that of the traditional organizations common to elementary and secondary schools in our larger cities. Old-line school principals were no match for the grass-roots people and their new demands.

What was true of schools was also true of overburdened, outdated yet socially involved law offices. They found it difficult to deal with the complex legal needs of individual as well as organized welfare clients, for example. Hence, center-democrats moved to create and sustain groups like CRLA. In this case, the coming together of incipient protest groups and streamlined legal aid programs often proved effective in overcoming short-run obstacles such as injunction-prone judges.

Needless to say, many *right*-democrats often recognized the combination of organizational flexibility and activist professional technique frequently led to minimal success for both the federal agencies of change and the poor peoples' movements, while the successes of their opponents were quite limited. Despite the small advantages won, however these right-democrats tried to break up this coalition. Illustrative has been the action taken by Governor Reagan of California against CRLA in 1972. It has been successful (1971) in winning court cases on issues hitherto never contested—such as the rights of welfare clients and home ownership prerogatives. These struggles have seldom dented the power of corporate wealth, however, despite the cleverness of the poor plaintiffs' counsels. But because in the past such victories were few and far between, their increased winning incidence has caused alarm among those who view poor peoples' initial success as portending a dire future should the poor be allowed continuous and sprightly legal counsel. Hence, these particular right-democrats often move to eliminate professional bureaucratic organizations. In turn, their staff sometimes abandons their federal salaries and their counterelitist roles and go so far as to join striking farm workers or tenants' groups. In these few cases, federal organizers have truly joined the people.

CENTER-DEMOCRATIC AND ITS PROBLEMS

Still, center-democrats are hampered by serious contradictions. In the capitalist West, the most persistent problem is the simultaneous commitment of center-democratic organization to the preservation of *both* private property and human justice. Overseas, center-democrats pursue essentially counterrevolutionary policies, despite hypocritical statements on winning the hearts and minds of "the people," not a few of whom have failed to survive center-democratic-sponsored napalm and massacre. (See Eqbal Ahmad's "The Theory and Fallacies of Counterinsurgency or Why We Were Sure to Lose in Vietnam," in Section Two of Chapter 12.) Domestically, the best illustration of persistent inconsistency is the behavior of the "multiversity." (See Section Three of this chapter—a research-essay on the 1964 University of California Sproul Hall Sit-In.)

Outwardly dedicated to the objective pursuit of knowledge but privately bound to the service of the state, and through it, large private corporations, the multiversity has occasionally failed to use human relations techniques or has used them unsuccessfully. An example is the recurrent tendency of multiversities to fall back on the inflexible "rules" orientation of a traditional bureaucracy when marshalling violent sanctions to deal with students whose anger stems from the abuses of racial minorities, student rights, the unfair treatment of agricultural farm workers by agro-corporate wealth, and, increasingly over the years, the substitution of faculty—administration—student committee work for the realignment of power inside the university. This enduring problem can be phrased in yet another way. Given the "merger" of what Clark Kerr called the "military-industrial complex" and the "university"—we are not surprised to find that university authorities act against protesting students and in behalf of economic and political elites who, at second remove, determine the policy of a multiversity administration through the occupancy of, and immediate access to, governing board positions. In this merger, military and business operations are conducted on a continuous basis on a university campus. Military training programs plus research activities become a permanent part of the university's operations. Business groups, such as agricultural firms, establish research institutes specifically committed to the use of campus facilities, faculty and funds to carry out academic research and teaching geared to the expressed needs of the major growers and banks involved in agricultural production and distribution activities.[6] A multiversity elite could conceivably create and use organizational structures to attempt to manipulate students through human relations techniques, although students are in many instances alienated by the mere existence of the elite's techniques and their technicians. Even so, the human relations approach appears to be more popular and successful today than it was when university chancellors believed that tamed quiescence could be commanded from students through a short, "reasonable" pitch bellowed through a bullhorn, as at Berkeley's Sproul Hall in 1964. More recently, for example, university administrators have cooperated with others to enlist

---

[6] Clark Kerr has expressed this opinion admirably in *The Uses of the University* (New York: Harper & Row, 1963), pp. 85-126, especially p. 124.

student radicals in transparent "ecology projects"—such as the systematic collection of cans and bottles in communities where corporations continue to dump millions of gallons of untreated sewages in regional waterways with little university protest. Everything but the sewage gets "cooled-out."

As a rational service unit, professional bureaucracies may nonetheless decide to forgo the use of glib manipulation and to act violently against radicals and their companions when the protestors turn militantly to actions of consequence. That an organizational elite should behave thus is consistent, for after all, rationality and violence are certainly not mutually exclusive in the twentieth century. Indeed, they work well together when persons attempt to achieve certain collective ends. Near-perfect in their command of rational people with high levels of professional expertise, and committed to manipulation of phrases, programs, and memoranda in preference to police, tear gas, and bullets, professional bureaucratic organizations may nonetheless supplement manipulation of symbols with destruction through bloodletting.

The U.S. military today exudes a patina of streamlined violence. Morris Janowitz has demonstrated how the new military has (*a*) abandoned traditional organization and behavior, (*b*) opted for a civilian-like division of labor, (*c*) moved against the traditions of racism within its own organizations, (*d*) used human relations techniques to recruit and to maintain its own expensive and hard-to-retain military personnel, and (*e*) learned to manipulate civilian masses and political elites.[7]

For all its sophistication, however, this professional group still makes war, sometimes commits atrocities, as in Vietnam, and thereby increases the solidarity of those who have both escaped victimization and kept their loyalties to the revolutionary movement.

On the homefront, many of the professionally organized police departments in our larger cities also make war, of a sort. They frequently do so when dealing with militant minority group members, sometimes with the police defining militants' headquarters as "free fire

[7]Morris Janowitz, *The Professional Soldier* (New York: Free Press, 1960), pp. 3–17.

zones." A case in point is the alleged massacre by the Chicago Police Department of Black Panthers Fred Hampton and Mark Clark. Similar episodes have occurred in Los Angeles and Jersey City. There, as elsewhere, police use of violence results not in the ready manipulation and subsequent submission of the oppressed, or the easy coalition of the reform bureaucrats and the grass roots, but the creation of significant personal distrust among the survivors.

These violent acts often increase in-group solidarity among the decimated ranks, although under certain circumstances oppression works: The translating mechanisms of a specific social movement are smashed and there remain few persons available to declare their solidarity to one another. Indeed, many become demoralized. Still, there are many exceptions. In the case of the University of California (Berkeley, 1964), where the student protestors survived a series of substantial blows, the University administration used police violence against "go-limp" protestors. The administration thereby revealed an ability to use the tactic of violent repression. The violence that attended the punishment created a broad student solidarity based on a shocked awareness of how far a university was prepared to go in order to smash the center of a regional civil rights movement. The students had openly challenged some of the most powerful financial, auto, newspaper, and hotel interests on the West Coast, and they had publicly scoffed at the requests of the Democratic Governor (Pat Brown) to drop the tactics and issues involved and to return to normal student ways.

It was during the middle and late 1960s that the clash between student movements and university authorities revealed to many the degree to which the state, including its universities, must rely on violence to subdue persons with grievances widely recognized as genuine. For example, the crucial turn in the white student movement occurred in 1964, when a nonviolent student group in Berkeley attempted *to use on-campus facilities to mount off-campus demonstrations that might eventuate in mass arrests.* The students had successfully used the university as an embarkation platform throughout the spring and summer of 1964 before the University authorities intervened. However, in August, 1964, the acting chancellor not only outlawed this practice but withdrew the student right to solicit funds for political parties and signatures for political petitions on campus. The University also denied students the right to use University property for holding mass meetings, which were then devoted almost exclusively to agitation for the civil rights of blacks. Admittedly these well-attended meetings during the spring and summer of 1964 were sometimes followed by massive picketings and sit-ins of the kind that irritated the establishments of Berkeley,[8] San Francisco,[9] and Oakland.[10] Given this unprecedented onslaught against the establishment, University authorities by the summer of 1964 responded by cooperating with economically and politically powerful elements not only in the Bay Area but in the State Capitol as they tried to stifle the center of civil rights movement in the Bay Area: the Berkeley students. Ironically, the result of University-initiated action was a revolutionlike conflict: protracted struggle, considerable student and faculty bombast, sit-ins, several police riots, dozens of student suspensions, plus several deaths among the protestors, as the student movement gradually broadened its membership and its goals during the middle and later 1960s. Hippies with militant predispositions joined a movement which left behind single-issue campaigns and moved to indict what a growing number of students judged to be an odious imperial system.

[8] In one instance CORE picketed (*simultaneously*) *185* downtown Berkeley business establishments for bigoted hiring policies.

[9] In San Francisco, (*a*) an estimated 1200 protestors sat-in at the Sheraton-Palace Hotel before approximately 750 were arrested, (*b*) thousands participated in massive sit-ins in the showrooms and sales lots within the city's car-retail district, (*c*) hundreds demonstrated against the Bank of America, and (*d*) hundreds of interracial demonstrators openly joined the anti-Goldwater forces at the 1964 national G.O.P. convention.

[10] The same spring, civil rights activists had confronted both ex-Senator Knowland's nearly all-white *Oakland Tribune* and the owners of the Jack London Square restaurant complex.

Throughout this period, center-democrats at Berkeley and elsewhere often found it difficult to manage their professional bureaucracies. Student protest proved too much, although clearly university administrators and faculty advisors were learning a great deal from the various bouts. (For a recent analysis of one Berkeley Free Speech Movement episode, see Max Heirich's reading in Section Two of this chapter.)

What was lost in the conflict, among other things, was a positive conservative attribute: the possibility of viewing episodes passing through a natural cycle. In Section Three, in our account of the arrest process experienced by students, we have attempted to advance certain hypotheses on this natural history. We have more to say about students in our next chapter, for as a driving challenge to traditional upper-class domination during the 1960s, they deserve our extended attention.

TRANSITIONAL REMARKS

Perhaps the best recent analysis of state power is Ralph Miliband's *The State in Capitalist Society.* By the same token, the best review of the book was Alan Stone's "How Capitalism Rules," a review we are about to consider.

Focusing on a smaller facet of state power, we obtain in our final reading a more detailed glimpse of one well-known multiversity, the Berkeley campus of the University of California. Finally, in Section Three, we present an analysis of the flow and the incidence and form of violence inflicted on the Berkeley students by the arresting police. This empirical effort lends some substance to our otherwise very general analyses by revealing how center-democrats used a professional bureaucracy to dispense violence in order to atomize student opposition. This essay thereby counters the view that professional bureaucracies always set aside violence and rely on symbols alone when quelling dissent.

How Capitalism Rules
Alan Stone

While Marxist attempts to describe the economy of the modern capitalist system have grown increasingly sophisticated, until the publication of Ralph Miliband's *The State in Capitalist Society*,[1] conceptions of the political system in capitalist society have not advanced since the early and incomplete formulations of Marx and Lenin. Yet, no one can possibly accept as an adequate explanation of the state's role under capitalism Lenin's assertion in *State and Revolution* that the capitalist state is simply the "organ of oppression of one class by another." The capitalist state, indeed, engages in an enormous number of activities, from granting shipping subsidies to banning cigarette commercials on television and radio, most of which have no readily perceivable connection with the "oppression of one class by another." Nor can the classical Marxist formulation even explain what has become a central preoccupation of political decision-makers in capitalist society—the use of fiscal and monetary policies to manage the economy.

Prior attempts to remedy the transparent defects of the classical Marxist theory of the capitalist state are equally unsatisfactory. For example, Anna Rochester's *Rulers of America* and Victor Perlo's *Empire of High Finance* developed detailed descriptions of the interlocking relationships between industrial and financial executives and entrepreneurs, which purport to show that certain financial ("Wall Street") interest groups run American government. Yet this conspiracy theory is transparently wrong: The very complexity of American government and the large number of people who make or participate in the making of important decisions militate against acceptance of such a "conspiracy" theory.

▪ Taken from Alan Stone, "Modern Capitalism and the State," *Monthly Review*, Vol. 23, No. 1, May 1971, pp. 31–36. Copyright © by Monthly Review, Inc.; reprinted by permission of Monthly Review Press.

Partially as a result of these deficient formulations, Marxism has not been treated seriously as a theory of political power in capitalist society, a subject of great contention in American political sociology between the followers of C. Wright Mills, who argue that a triumvirate of political, military, and business elites rules capitalist society, and the predominating pluralists who assert that a multitude of groups vie for power, with the state acting as an impartial umpire, sometimes rewarding one group, sometimes another. With the publication of Miliband's important and impressive work, Marxism is at last effectively coping with the central problem of political sociology.

Miliband's central thesis is that, while the capitalist class does not govern, it effectively rules. The capitalist class rules because in a capitalist society the well-being of corporations and financial institutions is—and, indeed, must be—perceived as the equivalent of the national interest. President Eisenhower's first Secretary of Defense, Charles Wilson, was simply stating a political truism when he proclaimed that "what is good for General Motors is good for the country." The critical place of giant business firms in the economy, coupled with the fact that public officials cannot permit economic disruption, compels public officials to equate the public good with the economic well-being of corporations. The government cannot afford to institute policies which jeopardize business confidence and well-being, and the state, accordingly, must pursue fiscal, monetary, and other policies which promote the probability of business prosperity and produce a state of confidence which encourages new investment. In a word, there is such perceived mutuality of interest between the political executive and the key executives of the large corporations that the latter's veto power is virtually tantamount to the exercise of political power in the areas of business concern.

Short of changing the economic system, the

government in capitalist society must, therefore, serve capitalist interests in several respects.
Negatively, the state protects capitalism by re-
pressing anticapitalists by such direct methods
as the outlawry of anticapitalist parties, or the
harassment of such parties, or electoral manipulation to prevent left-wing parties from being
on the ballot, or the use of repressive trials to
quell left-wing dissenters and, more importantly, to frighten away other prospective dissenters. "Governments, in other words, are
deeply concerned . . . that the 'democratic
process' should operate within a framework in
which left-wing dissent plays as weak a role as
possible" (p. 83). That all of the foregoing
methods have at various times been employed
in America is scarcely open to question.

The structure of bureaucracy also operates
to maintain the status quo, and hence, capitalism. Bureaucrats are specialists at sitting still
and not effecting change, and their ideological
conservatism is not due to chance. Loyalty
oaths and recruiting and advancement procedures for upper-level civil servants assure a
"spectrum of thought of which strong conservatism forms one extreme and weak 'reform-
ism' the other" (pp. 120–124). Further, government and business form cozy relationships
which are due to the links between business
sectors and the bureaucracies which are supposed to regulate them. Outside aspirations of
civil servants and interchanging personnel are
the principal facets of this relationship. Businessmen increasingly find their way into the
state system, and civil servants increasingly find
their way into corporate life (pp. 124–127).
Finally, if a maverick manages to filter through
the recruitment process and loyalty oaths and
avoid the symbiotic relationship between business and government, "there remains the vast
weight of pressure which organized business is
able to apply upon recalcitrant or hostile officials" (p. 128). Thus, the capitalistic ambience
within which the civil service operates tends to
produce a procapitalist bias within the bureaucracy.

But why have there been few serious challenges to capitalist domination of the political
structure in the advanced capitalist countries?
Miliband argues that socialization processes
have been far more effective means of preventing such challenges than oppression. And he
finds that the capitalist class dominates virtually all the socializing institutions in our society.

First, of course, capitalists own the organs of
mass communication and shape expression accordingly; socialist viewpoints are almost entirely excluded from them (pp. 219–238).
Again, capitalist advertising tends to associate
not only products but the entire free-enterprise
system with socially approved values and norms
and, indeed, with happiness (pp. 216–218).
Against these resources, anticapitalist forces are
relatively helpless and their views are portrayed
in the capitalist sources of communication as
"irrelevant eccentricities, which serious and reasonable people may dismiss as of no consequence" (p. 238). Scoffing and ridicule are
often far more effective ways of throttling anti-
capitalist thought than outright suppression.

Next, Miliband charges that the educational
system, from the lower grades to graduate
schools, inculcates capitalist values in its students and confirms the class destiny and status
of most students. At the lowest school levels,
lower-class students are given educations inferior to middle- and upper-class children. "And
the very fact that some working-class children
are able to surmount these handicaps serves to
foster the notion that those who do not are
themselves, because of their own unfitness, the
architects of their own lowly fate, and that
their situation is of their own making" (p. 241).
Again, witchhunts, loyalty oaths, and the attendant apparatus of fear deter recruitment of
teachers with remotely controversial or "ec-
centric" points of view and deter the teaching
of such views (p. 245).

Universities, which are heavily dependent
upon state and business financing, cannot afford to permit social science teaching which
affronts capitalism. (A few "eccentrics" are,
however, permitted to show that there is freedom of expression.) Further, academics are increasingly employed as consultants by business
and government, and such academics thereby
have developed a community of interest with
businessmen and government policies (p. 250).
Next, Miliband observes that most schools are
geared to supplying personnel for business
needs: business schools and law schools are
among the more conspicuous examples of this
process. Not only are such students taught management skills, but also "the ideology, values

and purpose of capitalist enterprise" (p. 253). This is done not through a conspiracy, but because most teachers are themselves the products of this consensus in favor of capitalism (pp. 250–259). But even when teachers attack the status quo at universities, the economic and social system is not called into question; rather, the emphasis is on how to solve such problems within the system's framework and not on socialist alternatives. Such safe controversy deflects "attention from the greatest of all 'problems,' namely that here is a social order governed by the search for private profit" (p. 261).

Miliband has convincingly shown why the state is ruled by capitalism, even if it is not governed by capitalists. He convincingly shows that the governmental and nongovernmental institutions within modern capitalistic societies strongly favor the preservation of that system.

It is in no way intended to detract from Miliband's substantial achievement to observe that while his analysis clearly shows what policies are effectively *excluded* from consideration by those who govern in capitalist society, he does not seek to show us why specific policy alternatives are, in fact, followed. Why, for example, has America followed certain Cold War policies in foreign policy rather than others? Why are certain policies followed which are detrimental to certain firms or industries (e.g., the termination of cigarette advertising on radio and television)? What are the real purposes and effects of regulatory legislation and administration? In a word, Miliband's ground-breaking analysis must be expanded so that a political-economic theory is able to explain and categorize all the various policy outputs of the state under modern capitalism.

It is beyond the scope of a review of this kind to do more than make a few pertinent suggestions, but there have been many case studies which very ably explain certain categories of policies. For example, historian Gabriel Kolko has shown that much Progressive Era legislation was enacted because important economic interests sought to "utilize the power of the federal government to solve internal economic problems which could not otherwise be solved by voluntary or non-political means."[2] Again, political scientist Theodore Lowi has developed a classificatory scheme for policies by which one can predict with reasonable accuracy the kinds of groups which are contesting policy alternatives: when, for example, does one firm battle another or one industry battle another, and when is most of the capitalist class unified on proposed policy?

A key future task is the integration of the findings of these and other studies with Miliband's splendid analysis so that we may, finally, be able to explain adequately the state's conduct under modern capitalism.

NOTES

1. New York: Basic Books, 1970.
2. *Railroads and Regulation* (Princeton, N.J.: Princeton University Press, 1965), p. 239. See also Kolko's *The Triumph of Conservatism* (New York: Free Press, 1963).

The Conflict Deepens: Round Two

Max Heirich

THE SHOWDOWN

Over the Thanksgiving recess, to the complete surprise of the Free Speech Movement leadership and indeed of the campus at large, disciplinary letters were sent to four students

■ Taken from Max Heirich, *The Beginning: Berkeley, 1964* (New York: Columbia University Press, 1968), pp. 193–206. Reprinted by permission.

for violations of university regulations during the demonstrations of October 1 and 2. Most observers had assumed this period was covered in the ad hoc faculty committee's report. Vigilers a few days before had not heard the directive from the Regents, ordering administrators to draw up disciplinary charges for events occurring after September 30. But this action had, in fact, been ordered.

During the week after the Regents meeting, therefore, Edward Strong and Thomas Cunningham's staff went to work, documenting charges against students who had been involved in the pack-in and the police melee on the afternoon of October 1. They considered only cases where there was clear, documentary evidence of violations. On Saturday, November 28, Strong sent out letters of citation to Brian Turner, Jackie Goldberg, Art Goldberg, and Mario Savio.

The letters charged the FSM leaders with entrapping a university police car and an arrested person:

> On October 1 and 2, 1964, you led and encouraged numerous demonstrators in keeping a University police car and an arrested person therein entrapped on the Berkeley campus for a period of approximately 32 hours, which arrested person the police were then endeavoring to transport to police headquarters for processing.

In addition, Savio's letter charged him with leading demonstrators into Sproul Hall for a pack-in that blocked doorways and passageways:

> ... disrupting the functions of that office and forcing personnel to leave through a window and across a roof. ...
> You led and encouraged demonstrators forcefully and violently to resist the efforts of the University police and the Berkeley city police in their attempts pursuant to orders, to close the main doors of Sproul Hall on the Berkeley campus. On October 1, 1964, you bit Berkeley city police officer Phillip E. Mower on the left thigh, breaking the skin and causing bruises, while resisting Officer Mower's attempts to close the main doors of Sproul Hall.

Art Goldberg's letter had this charge:

> You threatened Sgt. Robert Ludden of the University police by stating to him, in substance, that if police reinforcements attempted to remove the prisoner from your control and that of the demonstrators, he, Sgt. Ludden, and other police officers stationed at the entrapped police car, would be violently attacked by you and other demonstrators.

The letters ordered Savio and Goldberg to attend a hearing by the Faculty Committee on Student Conduct: "You may be represented by counsel at the hearing. The recommendation of the Faculty Committee on Student Conduct will be advisory to me."[1]

Dean Katherine Towle considered the action most unwise and voiced her strong disapproval before the letters were sent out. She was overruled, however, on the grounds that the Regents had ordered disciplinary action for events occurring after September 30.[2]

Word of the letters spread quickly. The FSM Steering Committee reconvened as soon as possible, holding an emergency meeting Sunday at 4:00 P.M. Bettina Aptheker since has stated her reaction, which was shared by many others on the Steering Committee:

> I knew that was it. That's what we were waiting for—for the final atrocity. ...
> I was sick and tired of hanky-pankying around with their negotiations, and not knowing what they were going to do. ... Kerr was a great maneuverer. He was much smarter than we were, in terms of that. The thing he didn't have was support. But we did. I was much more comfortable in mass action than in any of these kinds of negotiations.[3]

At 8:30 P.M. on Sunday the Steering Committee issued a statement:

> The Administration sees the free speech protest as a simple problem of disobedience and refuses to recognize the legitimacy of the students' needs. ... By again arbitrarily singling out students for punishment, the Administration avoids facing the real issues.
> Its action violates the spirit of the Heyman Committee report and can only be seen as an attempt to provoke another October 2. We demand that these new charges be dropped.[4]

When reached by the *Daily Californian*, Chancellor Strong would not confirm that disciplinary letters had or had not been sent: "Out of concern for the students, no matter what the occasion, the Chancellor's office makes no announcement of students being called up for disciplinary action."[4]

Members of the Steering Committee were sure they knew why the university had acted. They were convinced that the November 23 sit-in had persuaded the administration that the

FSM was weak and demoralized and that now it could get away with such action.[3]

The FSM battle plan was simple: its members would issue an ultimatum, demanding that the university withdraw charges against Savio, Turner, and the two Goldbergs. If the administration refused, as they expected it would, they would begin a sit-in in Sproul Hall on Wednesday, December 2. They would remain in the building overnight, hoping to be arrested. They were sure that a large number of arrests would lead to a general student strike, which the graduate students in the FSM had been encouraging. If the administration ignored the sit-in, they would call a strike for Friday, anyway, hoping to have engendered enough sympathy in the meantime to get a large response.[3]

On Monday, November 30, Chancellor Strong rejected demands that the charges be dropped:

The Heyman Committee limited itself to charges of misconduct up to and including September 30, and declined to consider charges of violations after that date. . . . These further charges have been referred to the Faculty Committee on Student Conduct for hearing. . . .
. . . In threatening to engage in direct action if the charges are not dropped, those who make such threats demand a decision based not on facts but on intimidation. The charges, properly, will be subjected to the test of evidence.[5]

The Graduate Coordinating Committee of the FSM announced a meeting on December 1 "to plan for a T.A. [teaching assistant—that is, a graduate student who assists in the teaching of courses] strike." Rumors spread over the campus not only that four FSM leaders had been cited, but also that eight organizations affiliated with FSM were facing disciplinary action. Administration spokesmen refused to comment on the charge.[5]

The next day, December 1, a letter from President Kerr, dated November 30, appeared in the *Daily Californian:*

Relying on the *Daily Californian* as a medium of information is like relying on smoke signals. You can gain an impression that something is being said, but you can never be quite sure what. My current concern is

the continued unwillingness of the Editors to quote what I actually said in an item which has been discussed within the University community from time to time, with the *Daily Californian* being the chief carrier of misquotations.

Now I realize that misquotations may be more interesting than quotations and the *Daily Californian* succeeds in being interesting. With the hope that it might also be accurate, I am turning to the Icebox[6] as a last resort, hoping it may be open also to the cause of accuracy as it is to so many other and sometimes quite contrary causes.

Herewith are two actual quotations which are a lot less interesting than the misquotations:

1. At a press conference held in conjunction with a speech before Town Hall in Los Angeles on October 6 and in response to a reporter's question, I said:
"Experienced on-the-spot observers estimated that the hard core group of demonstrators—those who continued as part of the demonstrations through the night of October 1—contained at times as much as 40 per cent off-campus elements. And, within that off-campus group, there were persons identified as being sympathetic with the Communist Party and Communist causes."
2. On October 2 at a press conference in San Francisco following a meeting of the American Council on Education, I said:
"I am sorry to say that some elements active in the demonstrations have been impressed with the tactics of Fidel Castro and Mao Tse-tung. There are very few of these, but there are some."

The *Daily Californian* answered President Kerr's letter with the following statement:

Early in the Bancroft-Telegraph "free speech" dispute President Kerr was quoted as saying that 49 per cent of the student demonstrators were Mao-Marxists.
The *Daily Californian* never ran that so-called quotation at any time because we understood it was not accurate.
We believe that we acted for the "cause of accuracy."[7]

There was no mention in Kerr's letter of the current dispute. It was printed the day that the FSM Steering Committee made a formal ultimatum to the administration, backed up by an announcement from the Graduate Coordinating Committee that teaching assistants would strike on Friday, December 4, "if conditions warrant."

The FSM ultimatum was printed as a handbill and circulated. It said, in part:

A SPECTRE IS HAUNTING THE UNIVERSITY OF CALIFORNIA–THE SPECTRE OF STUDENT RESISTANCE TO ARBITRARY ADMINISTRATIVE POWER.

The Board of Regents has used Chancellor Strong to attack leaders of the Free Speech Movement:

Chancellor Strong has summoned Arthur Goldberg, Mario Savio, and Jackie Goldberg before his Faculty Committee on Student Conduct. These three students have been singled out—from among thousands—for their participation in the demonstrations of October 1st and 2nd.

The Administration has also initiated disciplinary action against these student organizations: Campus CORE, Young Socialist Alliance, Slate, Women for Peace, W.E.B. Du Bois Club, University Friends of SNCC.

WE DEMAND THE FOLLOWING ACTION BE TAKEN BY WEDNESDAY NOON:

That disciplinary procedures against Arthur Goldberg, Mario Savio, Jackie Goldberg, and the student political organizations be halted. That the Administration guarantee there will be no further disciplining of students or organizations for political activity that occurs before a final settlement is reached.

That freedom of political activity be protected by revision of present University policy so that:

—Only the courts regulate the content of political expression.

—Faculty, students, and Administration jointly determine and enforce all regulations governing the form of political expression.

—All regulations which unnecessarily restrict political activity be repealed.

Two missing ingredients for collective response had now been added, one by action of the administration, the other by action of the Free Speech Movement. First, the disciplinary action and the refusal to comment on rumors of further discipline against political organizations provided compelling "evidence" that the

claims of the FSM about the meaning of the November Regents meeting and the intentions of the university administration were well founded. Second, the FSM ultimatum,[8] with its twenty-four-hour deadline, provided a time limit that sharpened the fuzzier deadline implied in the administrative letters requiring students to report for a disciplinary hearing.

That evening the ASUC [Associated Students of the University of California] Senate passed a "demonstration resolution":

(1) . . . the FSM no longer has the extension of on-campus political rights as its goal, and . . . its present plans for civil disobedience are directed solely toward meaningless harassment of the University.

(2) . . . the ASUC Senate encourages all responsible students to avoid the scheduled sit-in December 2nd. . . .

(3) . . . the ASUC Senate . . . encourages department chairmen . . . to make preparations to accommodate students . . . [if] any teaching assistants neglect their classes.

(4) . . . the ASUC Senate encourages all students to continue to attend their classes . . .

(5) . . . the ASUC Senate shall fully investigate the manner in which the administration has pursued prosecution of students involved in demonstrations throughout this semester.[9]

Clark Kerr was out of town when the FSM ultimatum was delivered to his office. After telephone calls and staff conversations it was decided that no response would be made to the ultimatum.

Noon on December 2, 1964, was the deadline the FSM had set for a reply to its ultimatum. By 12 o'clock a very large crowd—perhaps four or five thousand people—had assembled in Sproul Hall Plaza to see what would happen. Joan Baez had returned to lead singing for the rally and sit-in.

The ASUC had set up loudspeakers in the Student Union Plaza, one level below and just to the west of Sproul Plaza, and was conducting its own rally. In contrast, it was poorly attended.[10]

The FSM rally of December 2 had a quality different from any which had preceded it.[11] Speakers were far more excited; their voices were strident and harsh. There was an urgency in striking contrast to the pace of FSM rallies in the past. Previously some speakers may have been militant, and speaking styles varied widely, but there had been an element of rational discourse, of charm of expression, in most of the rallies. On December 2 this was gone. The tone, the rhythms, the tense, searing timbre of voices were similar to those heard during an altar call in a major religious revival campaign. The crowd felt the tension. The speakers made it clear that in their view anyone who did not enter Sproul Hall was deserting his fellow students, leaving them to the mercies of the police and an untrustworthy administration. A number of people turned to their neighbors, talking loudly, breaking the spell.

Early in the rally Charles Powell, ASUC president, had appeared in fraternity garb (bleeding madras sport shirt), to ask the students not to sit-in. Mario Savio called him a traitor and a fink.

There is little need to present the order of speakers or their messages, for the definition of crisis had been set earlier, along with the action that would be needed to resolve it. All that was required at this rally was a reminder, along with pressure to act in response to the crisis.

Savio gave a speech that day which became a classic, one frequently referred to on the campus thereafter. He said, in part:

> We have an autocracy which runs this university. It's managed. We were told the following: "If President Kerr actually tried to get something more liberal out of the Regents . . . why didn't he make some public statement to that effect?" And the answer we received from a well-meaning liberal was the following: he said, "Would you ever imagine the manager of a firm making a statement publicly in opposition to his Board of Directors?" That's the answer.
> I ask you to consider: if this is a firm, and if the Board of Regents are the Board of Directors, and if President Kerr in fact is the manager, then . . . the faculty are a bunch of employees and we're the raw material. But we're a bunch of raw material that don't mean . . . to be made into any product, don't mean to end up being bought by some clients of the university. . . . We're human beings.
> And that brings me to the second mode of civil disobedience. There is a time when

the operation of the machine becomes so odious, makes you so sick at heart, that you can't take part; you can't even passively take part, and you've got to put your bodies upon the gears and upon the wheels, upon the levers, upon all the apparatus and you've got to make it stop. And you've got to indicate to the people who run it, to the people who own it, that unless you're free, the machines will be prevented from working at all.

Joan Baez told the demonstrators:

> . . . The only thing that occurs to me, seeing all you people there—I don't know how many of you intend to come inside with us—but that is that you muster up as much love as you possibly can, and as little hatred and as little violence, and as little "angries" as you can—although I know it's been exasperating. The more love you can feel, the more chance there is for it to be a success.

As Joan Baez sang, "We Shall Overcome," demonstrators began filing up the Sproul Hall steps and into the building. They came in groups, a steady stream, somewhere between a thousand and fifteen hundred people.

As the crowd poured in, Joan Baez sang, "Oh, Freedom." Then Dustin Miller, in a hoarse but rhythmic, almost sing-song voice, defended "what have been called Marxist tactics." He urged a mass sit-in, saying that the more people participated, the less danger there would be of reprisal.

The pressure built up. Mario Savio called the people inside the building persons "committed to the cause of free speech. Those sympathizers outside are less committed." He urged them to man a sympathy picket line if they were afraid to go inside, and to cooperate with the student strike when it came. Jack Weinberg hoarsely urged all present "to defend freedom of speech by going inside."

Savio said, "Some of our best faculty were forced to leave in the 1950 loyalty oath controversy. Some of our best students may be expelled now." (There was scattered laughter in the crowd.)

Bettina Aptheker came out to announce that there were 1500 demonstrators in the building. "There is now no danger of reprisal," she said and called on more students to join them.

People continued to enter (and some to leave) Sproul Hall all through the afternoon.

The building was officially closed down and staff members were sent home.

Here are two students' explanations of why they entered Sproul Hall. The first was written by a mathematics major, a sophomore in his third semester on the Berkeley campus. He had joined the vigil of September 30 but did not sit down around the car.[12]

My attention was attracted by the mass demonstrations that took place from September on. I became active once I decided that the Regents were very wrong in their decisions. The student protests were a natural result of the Regents' actions. . . . I decided to participate in the December strike and sit-in (before arrests) because I was convinced that the students were right. It took me that long to decide that they were. . . . The Regents wouldn't listen. The normal channels were tried in vain by other students. I don't know the details. . . .

No one encouraged me, personally, to act. . . . Mario was eloquent. I found the moral arguments most persuasive. I was also persuaded by Jefferson and de Toqueville.[13]

A freshman girl, planning to major in art and living in a college dormitory, had followed earlier FSM activities sympathetically but had not become involved until she joined the December sit-in.[14] She writes:

The situation influenced me. It seemed the only way. I joined when I came to the self-realization that I had not acted on what I believed in, in the past. I had not acted on a principle I believed in. It was a major crisis for me. I was aware, generally, of what other people around me thought. I wouldn't have been there, otherwise.[13]

Inside Sproul Hall, a myriad of activities went on through the afternoon and evening. The FSM had announced that they would conduct a Free University inside Sproul Hall. Each floor of the building was devoted to a different kind of activity so that people could locate themselves by preference for how they would spend their time. There was a study hall, a discussion area, a sleep area, and square dancing and movie areas. Laurel and Hardy movies were shown. (Rumors spread around the community that the banned Genet film had been shown.) A Jewish Chanukah service, attended by about four hundred demonstrators, was conducted on the first floor. Joan Baez sang and led folk singing. A Peace Corps trainer conducted a Spanish class in one area of the building, a sociology faculty member discussed the theory of conflict in relation to Clark Kerr's handling of the Free Speech issue, a Quaker addressed a class on civil disobedience. Spirits were high.[15]

At 7 o'clock the doors to Sproul Hall were locked. Anyone who wanted to leave was allowed to, but no one was permitted to enter. A number of students gained admittance, however, by means of a rope tied to the second-floor balcony, and baskets of food were brought in by the same method. Many students had left before the doors were locked. Others continued to leave to go to evening classes or on other errands. Some apparently were convinced that the sit-in would last indefinitely without action by the university and settled down for a long stay. Others became uneasy when the doors were locked and decided it was time to get out.

That night the university Young Republicans formally withdrew from the FSM. Warren Coats, their president, said, "What the FSM is asking, in effect, is that the administration cease to be an administration.[16]

Inside Sproul Hall, the sit-in continued. At 11 P.M. Joan Baez decided that nothing was going to happen that night, and left. Unknown to the students, it was at that precise hour that things began to happen in earnest.

Earlier in the evening Clark Kerr had called an emergency meeting of key members of the Board of Regents. Beginning at 7:30 P.M., he met with Edward Carter, the chairman of the Board of Regents; and Donald McLaughlin and Theodore Meyer, the chairmen of the Regents' two principal committees, Finance and Educational Policy, at the Hilton Inn near the San Francisco Airport.[17]

President Kerr brought these Regents up to the minute on developments in the controversy and proposed a simple procedure. The building would be sealed off so that no one else could get in. Lights and water would be left on, and any person who wished to leave would be allowed to do so with impunity, simply by identifying himself. Identification would be asked in order to provide a basis for dealing with what were believed to be a large number of non-students in the building. Then, at 10 o'clock the next morning the entire matter would be reviewed again with the Governor. (Governor Brown was attending a banquet in Los Angeles, and Kerr had been unable to reach him.) The plan covered that night only and did not extend past 10:00 A.M. the next day.

The Regents at the meeting indicated that the situation was a matter for administrative, rather than Regents', decision. The meeting ended about 9:15 P.M.

Vice-President Earl Bolton, who had gone with Kerr to the airport, kept in touch by phone with Vice-Chancellor O. W. Campbell and Police Chief Frank Woodward on the Berkeley campus. The campus officers were aware that the meeting was taking place.

After the meeting ended, Earl Bolton drove Clark Kerr to the president's home in El Cerrito. As they reached the house, the call that Kerr had been trying to make to the Governor came through. After talking with Governor Brown, Kerr came out to tell Bolton the Governor agreed with the plan. Bolton then went to Dwinelle Hall to talk with Chancellor Strong and inform him of these developments.

At about 11:05 P.M. a call came through the Dwinelle switchboard for Bolton from President Kerr. The Governor had called Kerr back to say he had changed his mind. As Bolton remembers the conversation, Kerr said that the Governor felt it was necessary to ask the law enforcement officers in Alameda County to clear the building, in order to keep peace in the state. Brown ordered the State Highway Patrol to implement the plan.

Although Governor Brown ordered the building cleared, he did not order the arrest of the students. When the local law enforcement officers planned their strategy, however, they decided the only practical way to implement the order was to arrest the demonstrators for trespassing.

The arrests began at 3:05 A.M. on December 3, after Chancellor Strong had gone from floor to floor with a bull horn, saying,

May I have your attention. I am Dr. Edward Strong, Chancellor of the Berkeley campus. I have an announcement.

This assemblage has developed to such a point that the purpose and work of the University has been materially impaired. It is clear that there have been acts of disobedi-

ence and illegality which cannot be tolerated in a responsible educational center and would not be tolerated anywhere in our society.

The University has shown great restraint and patience in exercising its legitimate authority in order to allow every opportunity for expressing differing points of view. The University always stands ready to engage in the established and accepted procedures for resolving differences of opinion.

I request that each of you cease your participation in this unlawful assembly.

I urge you, both individually and collectively, to leave this area. I request that you immediately disperse. Failure to disperse will result in disciplinary action by the University.

Please go.[17]

Outside the building approximately 635 policemen had been assembling for nearly an hour. They were members of the Alameda County Sheriffs Department, Oakland Police Department, Berkeley Police Department, University Police Department, and California Highway Patrol.

Inside the building students had been aware that arrests were imminent. The FSM Steering Committee wanted the entire campus to see the arrests. Therefore members advised students to go limp; if each person had to be carried out, the job could not be finished before other students would be returning to the campus. They were sure that these other students would strike when they saw police carrying the demonstrators off the campus.

The Steering Committee decided that Steve Weisman should leave to coordinate the graduate teaching assistants in striking the next day. Although the campus police had announced earlier that anyone could leave the building simply by identifying himself at the door, the Steering Committee was not at all sure that this blanket permission would extend to leaders of the sit-in. Consequently they lowered Weisman from a second-story window by means of a rope.

Meanwhile a number of students were trying to decide what to do. One student, who left just before people on his floor were due to be arrested, described to me how he walked up and down the halls, trying to make up his mind. He would go down the stairs to the front door, see someone he knew, become ashamed, and go back up the stairs. Finally caution overcame his sense of shame, and he left. Another student called home to tell his parents that the police were about to start arrests; he was having trouble deciding what to do. When his parents ordered him to leave the building, his mind was made up: he returned to his seat on the floor and was arrested. Although a number of people did leave as the arrests took place, 773 persons stayed and were booked.

The first person arrested was the civil rights attorney, Robert Truhaft. All arrested persons were given the choice of walking or being carried. If they went limp, they were charged with resisting arrest. Truhaft said this was the first time civil rights demonstrators had been charged with resisting arrest for going limp.

There was a small scuffle when the police tried to confiscate the FSM's public address system, which had been set up in the second-floor lobby; otherwise the arrest procedure was relatively efficient. The police cleared the fourth floor first, and then moved to the third. They interrupted their efforts there to begin removing students from the second floor after people from the first and the third floors began piling together on the second floor. Apparently many who had been on the third floor hoped to avoid being carried down an extra flight of stairs. On the other hand, some originally on the first floor wanted the arrests to take longer. The police seemed to consider this movement to the second floor to be a "jam-in."

Most of the people who were arrested early in the procedure report that they were handled carefully and fairly gently by the police. As the morning wore on, however, treatment apparently became rougher. Altogether it took the police twelve hours to clear the building. That weekend several students on the second floor told me that as the police got tired they began to be less careful how they carried people down the long marble staircase. Some students reported having their heads bounced on the steps; others said that their hair was pulled, their arms were twisted, and the like. There were many charges of "police brutality" by the students, many of whom had previously never been arrested or faced handling by the police.

The students were taken to the university police station in the basement of Sproul Hall

and booked. They were then put in paddy-wagon buses belonging to Alameda County, for transportation to various jails and eventually to the Santa Rita Prison Farm operated by the county. For many of the middle-class university students, being treated as a criminal came as a severe shock. They knew that they were going to jail for a cause they believed in, but they were not prepared for the impersonal discipline they received.

When the students were released from jail, widespread tales of brutal treatment at police hands circulated on the campus. Lawyers representing the students urged them to report all injuries. The Berkeley chapter of the American Civil Liberties Union began working with the lawyers and the arrested students, trying to document cases of police brutality. No charges were ever brought in court, however, in spite of many hours of poring over pictures of the arrest and obtaining sworn testimony from various students. Therefore, although the police were probably quite rough toward the end of the period of duty (and some officers may have been less than courteous to students as their backs grew weary and their tempers short), it is unlikely that "brutality" in the normal *police* understanding of this term occurred often, if at all. To the students and their friends, however, such technicalities were unimportant. They were shocked at the treatment that "moral witnesses" had received from those who considered them to be "criminals." Reaction across the campus was severe.

NOTES

1. Excerpts from these letters, as quoted in the *California Monthly*, February, 1965, p. 58.

2. Reported to me separately in interviews with Katherine Towle and with Arleigh Williams.

3. Tape-recorded interview with Bettina Aptheker, Friday, July 2, 1965.

4. Quoted in the *California Monthly*, February, 1965, p. 59.

5. *California Monthly*, February, 1965, p. 59.

6. "The Icebox" is the *Daily Californian*'s letters-to-the-editor column.

7. *Daily Californian*, Tuesday, December 1, 1964, p. 8.

8. Quoted in the *California Monthly*, February, 1965, p. 59.

9. *California Monthly*, February, 1965, pp. 59–60.

10. When I arrived about 12:40 P.M., there were

seven students dressed in coats and ties. I assumed they were to be speakers.

11. The account that follows is based on my notes made at the time, on written accounts in the *California Monthly*, February, 1965, pp. 60–64, and on a KPFA tape, recorded on December 2, 1964.

12. This student went into Sproul Hall but left before he was arrested.

13. From essays written by members of the Free Student Union in May, 1965.

14. This student remained in the building to be arrested.

15. The account of events inside Sproul Hall dur-

ing December 2 and 3 is based on news accounts in the *California Monthly*, February, 1965, and on KPFA tapes made at the time.

16. In rally speeches, Savio had been saying that the university administration should "sweep the sidewalks" and that *policy* should be made by students and faculty.

17. The account that follows is based on summaries in the *California Monthly* chronology, February, 1965, pp. 61–62, notes made from KPFA tapes of the arrest, and interviews made on December 3, 4, and 5, 1964, with arrested students.

Section Three   *An Instance of Violent Oppression of Nonviolent Protestors*

The Natural History of An Institutional Arrest and the Lessons of the Sproul Hall Sit-In

John C. Leggett
Gunilla Napier
Joyce Bailey

THE INSTITUTIONAL SETTING AND THE MASS ARREST

When the state uses mass arrests and bodily force within institutional settings to disband mass demonstrators committed to nonviolence and civil disobedience, how do law enforcers break up these gatherings? For example, how might they disassemble a sit-in located inside a university building? This problem has seldom gained the attention of research scientists, largely because of the difficulties involved in gathering statistical information. However, the civil rights movement and its free speech ancillaries have created local opportunities for investigating the problem of how an arm of the state dispatches an organized collectivity both (*a*) flaunting its rejection of law and (*b*) publicizing this group's prior loyalty to abstract ideals. In the last 10 years, SNCC (Student Nonviolent Coordinating Committee), SCLC (Southern Christian Leadership Conference), CORE (Con-

■ This essay was originally prepared to be read before the 1966 meetings of the American Sociological Association.

gress on Racial Equality), and to a lesser degree, the NAACP (National Association for the Advancement of Colored People), have launched many campaigns, and not a few have resulted in direct confrontations with the police. Other groups have borrowed the sit-in and like techniques. On occasion, demonstrators have met police inside buildings owned by universities, social agencies, and the like. In these settings, the officers of the law have often used force and coerced dissenters in order to break up protests. The character of some of these institutional arrests[1] has prompted moral indignation in certain quarters. However, this reaction often misses a point fascinating to social science: How do law enforcers use techniques of force within institutional settings as the officers move from point of initial encounter through local booking and vehicle transport to public prison.

Perhaps traditional theorists and current observers can help us solve this problem. Sorel celebrated violence and viewed its use against the state as an alternative to palliatives proffered by social democracy.[2] By contrast, Max Nomad has discussed rebel use of violence and

inveighed against its use,[3] whereas Oppenheimer and Lakey have suggested how to defend oneself against violence used by legal authorities to dissolve demonstrations.[4] On a
more analytical level, Mosca, Pareto, Michels,
and Lasswell[5] have commented on the adaptive
functions of police use of violence. These writers have led us to believe that injury-inflicting,
state-sanctioned violence can be expected when
a civilian group no longer recognizes the legitimacy of state authority. For them, nonrecogni-
tion becomes obvious when these populations
organize themselves to flout the law in a manner judged by many to be disrespectful. When a
group acts in this manner, the state often uses
violence to lessen if not to fracture the *esprit de
corps* of the dissenters. Admittedly, the state
will use violence against domestic populations
only as a last resort. When the state must repeatedly rely on violence in order to crack
group cohesion and insurgence, state officials
believe that they are endangered—and rightly
so, for they must contend with a population no
longer mesmerized by political formulas. These
insights we have derived from the classical elite
theorists.

Although these formulations give us the big
picture, they fail to indicate the manner of
state use of violence. The classical formulations
do not note which repressive techniques are
most popular among enforcers of the law and
how these techniques of control may vary according to where the arrestees are located in the
arrest process. However, this oversight need not
deter us, for we can begin to construct what
may be a general developmental pattern—an
arrest flow appropriate for an institutional setting—and to observe the degree to which one
episode corresponds with the general formulation. Of course, there are undoubtedly many
general ways in which the police can conduct a
mass arrest of the kind to be discussed; we will
dwell on but one of them, however, partially
because we have empirical information on just
one such event.

The state plus its police favor certain techniques over others when law enforcers move
from the initial through transitional to final
stages of a mass arrest designed to end peaceful
disobedience within institutional settings. Although the police may go through an initial
"hesitation period" before launching their attack, they generally prefer the roughest techniques during first contacts with organized
opposition. After the police break up such a gathering, individual protest becomes paramount,
and the police favor techniques involving considerable finesse and minimal pain, for these are
quite enough to handle individual protest. This
transition, which occurs during the mass arrest
process, accompanies yet another tendency.
Use of any kind of force wanes as the arrested
move from organized opposition through individual protest to settled arrestee. The state
thereby pulverizes organized civil disobedience,
throttles individual action, and escorts pacified
person.

THE FREE SPEECH MOVEMENT, SPROUL HALL, AND THE USE OF FORCE

The celebrated Sproul Hall Sit-In prompted
an institutional arrest. Perhaps the sit-inners
rejected legal authority in both a public and
self-righteous manner, as some judges have suggested. Indeed, from a conservative legal point
of view, students had violated University rules
and pronouncements on the use of University
buildings.

But more important, the State of California
contained many powerful people beyond the
University. Of these, some perceived the sit-in
as a flagrant violation of law and order. Students had collectively expressed their contempt
for both. Certainly the Governor of California
reacted this way, and he called out the police to
squelch those who behaved as if they no longer
viewed authority of the state as legitimate.
Hundreds of police moved in on the student
demonstrators camped inside the University's
central administration building, but they did
not use violence immediately to quell the demonstration:

Most of the people who were arrested early
in the procedure report that they were handled carefully and fairly gently by the police. As the morning wore on, however,
treatment apparently became rougher. Altogether it took the police twelve hours to
clear the building. That weekend several students on the second floor told me that as the
police got tired they began to be less careful
how they carried people down the long marble staircase. Some students reported having

their heads bounced on the steps; others said that their hair was pulled, their arms were twisted, and the like. There were many charges of 'police brutality' by the students, many of whom had previously never been arrested or faced handling by the police.[6]

The police booked slightly fewer than 800 persons, and almost all were students and their relatives. In order to find out what happened to the arrestees, we tried to interview them all We put together a 52-page interview schedule, and gathered information on 701 of the 77? arrested.[7]

When the police conducted the arrests, they forcefully handled 148 interviewees, at least according to our calculations. These figures may underestimate the incidence of force, for we interviewed only 90 percent of the arrestees.

During the interview, many students recalled the less than subtle techniques used by some of the officers when they arrested and guided the arrestees:

When police went to get Weissman, I was standing at the balcony window. I was pummeled to the floor from behind and jumped on. (Male)

When the police wedge came up about 10 A.M. to get the PA system, one officer even kicked me in the head with his foot. (Female)

They arrested me on the fourth floor. I went limp. They dragged me to the elevator; they then dragged me to the office. I walked to the cage (for the booking). After insulting inquiries, I refused to walk to the paddy wagon. I was then roughly dragged to the paddy wagon. (Female)

When I was pulled from the elevator, my arm was twisted behind me, so I slumped over and I was kneed in the stomach. (Female)

The hand of my left arm was grabbed as they tried to drag me in an awkward manner. When I didn't get up, I was kicked in the stomach. (Female)

I was kicked several times in the elevator. My arms were twisted en route to the wagon from Sproul. I was dragged by the hair by Policewoman No. 372 in the basement of Sproul Hall. (Female)

The zipper of an officer's jacket ripped my face. He pulled my hair, grabbed me around the neck, dragged me by the collar, and bounced me painfully down every step. (Male)

I was hit by the feet of several officers as they climbed over me when going to get Jack Weinberg and when they returned carrying him. I was hit by a club when the police attempted to get Steve Weissman. A Policeman was swinging his club and he hit me on the head. (Female)

One of the policewomen twisted my wrist. I wasn't seriously hurt. There was simply no reason for her to do so. (Female)

I was choked until I passed out. I had been roughed up upstairs and when we had gotten to the basement I was choked. On the bus I was forced to crawl down the aisle by the driver. This I don't remember. I was still "out." (Male)

In the basement I was kicked twice and put in a double hammerlock by two Oakland officers. (Male)

I was sitting cross-legged and a policeman put his foot between my legs and kept pressing it. I asked the cop next to him to tell him to cut it out—which he then did. (Female)

An attempt was made by an Oakland cop to trip me. I was forcefully pushed down the hall even as I was quite willing to go without prompting. (Male)

While being dragged down the stairs, the police purposely threw me against the bannister. (Male)

While sitting down I was thrown into the wall. The cops wanted to arrest someone behind me first. (Male)

While on the third floor by the elevator [evidently while sitting by the elevator waiting for it to return] I was in the way because I was pushed by a cop's foot. While being dragged from the elevator to the fingerprinter and photographer, my arms and hands were twisted, my throat and jaw were gouged, and I was kneed in the back of my head. (Male)

My arms were twisted and I was dragged by my hair some distance. (Male)

I went limp at the foot of the stairs. I was lifted by four police, while the fifth supplied the motive power by pulling my hair. In the basement gauntlet I was slapped, and one cop hit me with his club. (Male)

When they dragged me out at about 6 A.M., they twisted my wrist to get me to walk. (Male)

My crotch was squeezed, face gouged and hit. My right arm was twisted. They carried me roughly by all fours. They bounced me on the spine (not rump). One officer put his knee on my chest as he applied his full weight. (Male)

In the elevator, my arm was twisted behind me and my thumbs bent back. I sustained a sprained wrist. (Male)

I was subjected to the rough slapping of my person while being booked in Sproul. (Male)

After I had gone limp at the time of the arrest, I was put in the elevator where the police forcefully stood me up. My picture was taken and I was shoved to the floor and stepped on purposefully by the police. I was also shoved when loaded into the bus that went to Santa Rita prison. (Male)

At the time of the attack on the substitute microphone at the top of the front stairs to the second floor, the police tried to get through, struck my face, and threw me down the stairs. (Male)

They handled me roughly. I reached my arms up so that my sweater wouldn't be ripped, but I was pulled directly by the sweater. It was ripped open. (Male)

In the elevator a cop kneed me in the groin. In the basement I was kicked five times by cops on my head and body. (Male)

At 2:30 P.M., before being arrested, I was thrown on my head on the floor. Shortly after the arrest, I was dragged downstairs. My arms and elbows were twisted. I was struck in the scrotum with a billy club and dragged over an iron railing. (Male)

The cops grabbed me under the shoulders and dragged me down the hall past lines of jeering cops. I have a beard, so I was careful so I wouldn't get bopped. (Male)

Around 2 P.M., on December third, on the third floor of Sproul, before being arrested, we were pushed into a corner. Those that didn't move fast enough were thrown. (Male)

THE FINDINGS

Perhaps more significant than individual tales of woe was how the stories partially confirmed our expectations. First, although police acts of violence against the Sproul Hall student collective did not begin simultaneously with the first arrests, once the police swung into action, violent acts *against students* occurred most frequently during the near-initial stages of contact with the police and then declined, however unevenly, until the final stage of transfer, when physical and forceful contact between police and arrestees proved to be almost nonexistent (see Table 28). We had expected something like this pattern to occur, for personal use of force should diminish as the arrested group passes from collective dissidence through individual protest to personal docility. However, we were somewhat surprised by the sharp increase in forceful actions at the stage of booking, and we will comment on this unexpected turn of events when we analyze the booking operation.

Second, our information only partly supported our beliefs on type and flow of force used in the arrests. In order to explain what we mean by this assertion, let us examine each stage and illustrate our point. For the purposes of analysis, it might be useful to make a distinction between six stages in the arrest process:

1. Pre-transfer, non-face-to-face encounter
2. Pre-transfer, face-to-face encounter
3. Primary transfer
4. Institutional booking
5. Secondary transfer
6. Tertiary transfer

STAGES OF THE ARREST FOR THE INDIVIDUAL

Pre-transfer, non-face-to-face encounter

In this situation, the potential arrestee does not expect physical contact with the police and is not prepared for it. The person does not see the officer before being contacted by his arm and/or leg. Consequently, considerable surprise and some shock generally accompanies such acts, as when an officer walks up to a sitting student and pushes him gently (or otherwise) on the back of the neck, without in any way indicating to the person beforehand that such contact is about to occur. In Sproul Hall, we had originally expected the officers to use a disproportionately large number of rough techniques at this point in the arrests. However, such was not the case. Fifty percent of the

TABLE 28 Type, Place, Incidence and Flow of Force in Sproul Hall Arrests for Individual Students

	Place of Treatment[a]						
Type of Police Treatment[b]	No. 1, Pre-Transfer, Non-Face-to-Face Encounter	No. 2, Pre-Transfer, Face-to-Face Encounter	No. 3, Primary Transfer	No. 4, Institutional Booking	No. 5, Secondary Transfer	No. 6, Tertiary Transfer	Total
Mild							
Hand and arm							
Mild Hand[c]	(4) 50%	(27) 32%	(35) 60%	(38) 48%	(13) 70%	(0)	(117)
Elbows	(1)	(8)	(6)	(3)	(1)	(0)	(19)
Rough							
Hand and Arm							
Fists	(0)	(2)	(0)	(5)	(0)	(0)	(7)
Billy Clubs	(1) 20%	(5) 17%	(1) 16%	(3) 22%	(1) 15%	(0) –	(11)
Other Hand[d]	(1)	(11)	(10)	(11)	(2)	(1)	(36)
	50%	68%	40%	52%	30%		
Knees and feet							
Knees	(0) 30%	(22) 51%	(6) 24%	(13) 30%	(1) 15%	(0)	(42)
Feet	(3)	(33)	(10)	(13)	(2)	(0)	(61)
Total	(10) 100%	(108) 100%	(68) 100%	(86) 100%	(20) 100%	(1) –	(293)

aPlace of treatment can refer to more than one for any respondent.

bType of treatment can refer to more than one for any respondent.

cBody pushed, arm twisted, person dumped.

dHair pulled, throat choked, groin lifted, clothes ripped, wrist handcuffed and dragged, and similar treatment,

encounters were mild, involving only the standard use of hands and elbows. Perhaps the officers favored a norm of not using the limbs in rough fashion unless an active encounter was involved. Such contact would mean face-to-face confrontation between organized police and linked demonstrators. Under these circumstances, the resistance would be definitely collective, deliberate, fisible, and hence quite deplorable (if not insolent) from the point of view of the police and the state. Under these conditions, the rules of confrontation may be quite different (i.e., they may allow the use of heavy force).

Pre-transfer, face-to-face encounter

Here we have deliberate and initial confrontation between arresting officers and resisting dissidents. In Sproul Hall, for example, when the police rushed to grab a bull-horn located on the second floor of the building, several hundred students locked arms and remained where they were, placing their bodies in the path of the police. Consequently our findings do not come as a surprise. As Table 28 indicates, 68 percent of the 108 encounters were rough, and not a few of the episodes involved police use of their feet. Also favored was rough hand treatment, although there was slightly less hair-pulling, throat choking, groin lifting, clothes ripping, and assorted acts along these lines. However, it is clear that the more mild forms of handling arrestees occurred relatively less often, for only 32 percent of the encounters consisted of mild body pushing, wrist twisting, and torso dropping.

Primary transfer

In this situation, the police transfer arrestees from place of initial encounter to point where the booking process begins. Two potential moves are involved, and an arrestee might confront bodily force at one stage or at both. For example, if one step were the transfer of arrestees to a terminal point, such as an elevator or a stair well, the other transfer would be the movement of the person to a point where the booking could begin. Such a relocation might include a trip down an elevator or stairs to the point designated for the booking process.

The police generally used standard techniques to lead the arrestees from Sproul Hall.

Some methods were painful but not out of the ordinary. On the other hand, the police sometimes used novel holds, such as the scrotum tug. One arrestee was picked up by three officers and carried face down before he was thrown against a wall adjacent to an elevator. Here's what happened. One policeman raised the student's left arm. Another officer elevated his right one, and a third policeman lifted the young man by his reproductive sac. All three then carried him down the hall, face down, through the crowd of students, cameramen, and the like, and then threw him against the wall, there to await further passage. A local television station taped the event and showed this remarkable lift to an eager Bay Area audience. To many laymen, what the lift lacked in finesse it gained in novelty, even by Berkeley standards.

However, what is more important than the bizarre quality of some of the holds was the overall decline in crude treatment, as police turned increasingly toward milder forms of guidance and away from rough techniques, especially the use of the feet and knees. Indeed, police preference for the rough use of hands remained relatively constant during the first four stages of the arrest. When police began to minimize their use of rough force, they preferred to downgrade the use of feet. Perhaps feet and knees become relatively unnecessary after the police have dissolved collective signs of militant solidarity, as when they break the arm locks between sitting students who are reluctant to make way for the police.

Institutional booking

In the booking setting, the police fingerprint, photograph, and in general carry out preliminary procedures associated with an institutional arrest. In a sense, the police itemize cargo in passage when conducting an institutional arrest. After the police gathered up the Sproul Hall sit-inners, the officers simply and conveniently took them to the University jail located in the basement of Sproul Hall. When performing this operation, the police used a great deal of rough treatment immediately prior to photographing and finger-printing arrestees. The behavior of the police thereby went counter to our study's expectations, for we had anticipated considerably less rough handling at this point in the arrest flow.

Why the police used such a relatively high number of rough techniques is difficult to explain. Fifty-two percent of the encounters were marked by the abrupt use of force. This was a higher percentage than for all but the initial stage of organized confrontation. Why had the officers behaved this way? Perhaps some of the arrestees had evinced a posture of rebelliousness and thereby beckoned a wallop or a knee. (This way would be consistent with our expectations, had the students given some indication of collective dissent.) What might have promoted protest? Perhaps the students recommenced talking to one another at the booking depot when they viewed the technical hardware of an arrest—for it was then that they saw for the first time the consequences of an arrest—a finger-printed police record, one that would follow them throughout their lives. At that moment, student apprehension may have changed to open dislike for the police, had the police officers, for example, denied the students what they believed to be their legal rights—such as the right to make two free phone calls or the right to call an attorney. Once again we may guess about this matter and speculate on the consequences of student concern. Perhaps students initiated heated discussions and coalesced into temporary dyads or triads to complain about the arrest in general or the booking procedure in particular. Had they done so, the police might have viewed such students as belligerents and treated them according to the time-honored tradition of the police.

Obviously, these remarks are quite tentative. Although the explanation may seem to be acceptable, we have not processed our data to discover the extent to which this plausible explanation did in fact constitute a recurrent event.

Secondary transfer

Next the arrestees moved from the point of booking to the place of vehicular transportation. The Sproul Hall arrestees passed from the basement of Sproul Hall to buses provided by the police. Here, there was a noticeable tapering off in both the incidence of forced handling and rough techniques utilized. Only twenty forceful encounters occurred, and 70 percent of these consisted of the milder forms of personal handling.

Tertiary transfer

The final stage is the shipping of the arrestees to the prison. In the case of the Sproul Hall dissidents, most went ultimately to the county jail. The trip was almost without incident, for there was only one instance of police use of personal force. The quiet character of this stage contrasts vividly with the earliest stages. During the final transfer, the arrestees ceased to display resistance. The crowd had been quelled.

QUALIFICATIONS

Of course, one might argue that police behavior stemmed from sadistic impulses and not from the state need to fracture the organized resistance and to pacify the rebel person. However, had sadism been the moving force, then the more rollicking forms of personal coercion would have been more evenly distributed throughout the arrest process. Certainly there would have been more than one such encounter during the final stage, for the bus-ride would have placed sadistic police in a position where they would have been free from the observations of television cameras and other neutral if not hostile observers. However, no acts of sadism took place. Of course, we are not saying that sadism was absent. But the presence or absence of this psychic phenomenon does not explain the patterned character of type and incidence of the forceful encounters.

However, even if we discount the significance of sadism and comparable psychological arguments, we might wonder whether the arrestees told the truth. Perhaps a crack-pot minority had simply invented a series of falsifications. This argument would be hard to reject, except for one thing. Bay Area television viewers witnessed dozens of the incidents reported to me (J.C.L.) by the arrestees. Television tapes, which recorded much of the arrest flow, clearly validated the stories told afterward by the arrestees. Not only the tapes shown to the Bay Area audiences but those not released to the public revealed the pattern of the arrest. In addition to the television tapes, newspaper reporters and other observers witnessed the spectacle and departed from the scene with very similar impressions.[8] Hence, we have little reason to doubt the veracity of the reports given to us by the arrestees, although we would be the first to admit the possibility of the existence of a (normal) low number of liars. In this sense, our research would suffer from the same difficulties characterizing studies concerned with voting behavior and similar topics that deal with questions over which public sentiment is aroused.

However, even if we discount the impact of lying, we might still be concerned with how the arrest process was documented; for it took approximately twelve hours, and perhaps the character of the entire arrest process changed through time as the arrestees flowed from point of initial confrontation to bus and prison. Indeed, such changes did take place, especially within the earlier stages of the arrest flow. During the first several hours of the arrest, the process went quite smoothly, and relatively few instances of force were reported during this period, partly because students did not present collective barriers to police carrying out their assignments. However, when the police attempted to seize a bull-horn used by students to announce the progress of the arrests, the students placed their bodies around the prized item, locked arms with one another, and thereby created a sea of interlaced bodies. In dealing with the problem by walking through and over the students, the police used an amount of force deemed necessary. At this point, the confrontation was total. After this resistance had been broken, there were similar confrontations elsewhere inside Sproul Hall during the arrests, but nothing so testy as this particular episode. It would seem, then, that the arrest process may change, but during a crisis period, the pattern assumes a form depicted earlier in the first part of this paper.

Perhaps we should not overlook another counterargument, one that stresses police perception and values. Some would say that how a police officer relates to arrestee depends on how he defines the situation. If the officer believes that bodily force is necessary, he will act accordingly, and his actions will stem from his frame of reference. This argument makes some sense, provided we realize that his frame of reference includes his job superiors and that these bosses set rules (i.e., specify limits, within which the police should act). Police officials (and/or their political bosses) make clear what

is tolerable. They can tightly control the behavior of the ordinary police officer, or they can allow him considerable discretion, all depending on how the chiefs define a situation.

We're sure that many of you have encountered police when they were not allowed to act simply on the basis of their own attitudes toward demonstrators. These officers had to conform to departmental advice that closely restricted their behavior. Let us be more specific. On occasion we have observed police officers smacking their clubs against their black leather gloves rather than belting the soft vulnerable skulls of civil rights demonstrators. A short time later, perhaps a week or so, the same potential clubees have sometimes encountered the same police in nearly identical circumstances and have found the police more than willing to use their clubs to bop skulls.

And what is the position of authority on this matter? In the first setting, it seems clear that the orders do not allow for violence, no matter how the demonstrators related to the police. By contrast, in the second situation, police chiefs and leading politicians frequently not only justify but advocate such action. They thereby legitimate the prudent use of pulverization.

In short, the police officer does not operate in a vacuum but moves in a power-structured world. In this sense, he is no different from the rest of us.[9]

"Of course," some would counter, "we obviously live in a power-structured world, but we live in a causal world as well, and your natural history fails to specify those considerations associated with the creation of the first and succeeding stages of development. For example, what are the general sources of the pre-transfer, face-to-face encounter, one in which the students frequently express solidarity with one another? Perhaps students express such *esprit de corps* only after their leaders have carefully laid the ground rules for informal resistance."

Another possibility might occur to such a critic. Perhaps the students reject the suggestion of formal leaders (i.e., offer no resistance) and follow the directions of informal leaders (i.e., lock arms). In any event, the significance of leadership—its presence, militance, and directions—may pave the way for the passage of the group through this stage to the outer limits of primary transfer, where other determinants come into operation. Certainly this kind of causal analysis should not be confused with our descriptive specification.

At least one more qualification seems to be in order. Only the rare institution can maintain the luxury of having its own jail and police force, and in this sense, the multiversity is quite fortunate. Many colleges, for example, cannot afford such embellishments. Hence, we hold that only a limited number of institutional mass arrests will correspond neatly with our statement on a six-stage developmental pattern. In many cases, police must and will bypass the institutional booking procedure and send the arrestees directly to the city or county prison.

CONCLUDING REMARKS

We have analyzed how police can proceed to carry out a mass arrest within an institutional setting. We have focused on the incidence and form of police force used within an arrest flow for each individual. We did not analyze the sequence of the arrest for the Sproul Hall collective, although it, too, may have passed through a development with similar stages:

1. Lull
2. Sanguinary encounter
3. Decline in forceful treatment

In our study, we found that as the frequency of force declines, the form of forceful contact also changes, as policemen minimize the use of the rougher types of personal handling and come to prefer milder techniques. We are not saying that this developmental sequence need occur in all institutional arrests, but we do suggest that it may be appropriate for institutions which have their own jails. However, even in these settings, there may be more than one general form. Only time, more mass arrests, and future research can clarify this point.

Above all, we have not considered why students cohere and collectively struggle against the police. Why students should behave this way is an important question, for they have become the Wobblies of the late twentieth century and have challenged other institutions in addition to the university. Students have sparked the civil rights and peace movements and have sallied forth on foot, in cars, and airplanes against government offices, conserva-tive banks, traditionalist hotels, newspaper offices, army bases, car dealers, and so forth. Whatever the occasion, student militance appears to be relevant, for it is undoubtedly related to the behavior of the police. Why should students be so militant and cohesive, even when they face certain dangers?

When trying to answer this question, perhaps we can suggest an analogy worth pursuing extensively at some future date. Clark Kerr and Abraham Siegel have written an interesting paper on why some workmen become highly class conscious.[10] These authors have observed that workmen, when they face multiple economic problems and also share common subcultural characteristics within the confines of an isolated working-class community, become highly cohesive, express a high degree of working-class consciousness, develop militant unions, and engage in strikes that sometimes take on the character of class warfare. Kerr and Siegel have in mind workers in longshore, mining, fishing, lumbering, and like industries.

Elsewhere, Kerr has suggested that there is an analogy between these workmen and student subgroups in the multiversity.[11] Students entering a large university face multiple problems, although many of these have more to do with the size and impersonality of the institution than the monetary sacrifices involved. Yet students' views are not all alike when they deal with their problems. How students define their problems undoubtedly has a good deal to do with where they attach themselves. University students generally differentiate and form three subcommunities, each being relatively homogeneous and isolated: the fraternity–sorority subcommunity, the independents, and the folknik–politicos. All three are subject to the vicissitudes associated with poor teaching, sloppy class scheduling, and like problems common to the multiversity. However, the folknik–politicos seem to be the most irritated by the multiversity because of the school's recurrent political harassment, stemming from the desire to confine student political activities to the campus and thereby to limit protests against the military–industrial complex. For the multiversity's deep attachments to the military and the business communities become inflamed when students "sally forth with impunity" into the community and annoy these new partners of the multiversity.[12] When the multiversity attempts to limit off-campus student political activity, the folknik–politicos mount a drive against the policies and practices of the multiversity administration and call for support of their civil liberties. Generally what follows is a promise of university crackdown supplemented by outside offers of aid during a predictable crisis. A fight occurs, often culminating in a sit-in. The students lose on the arrest but later appeal to, or threaten to use, the courts and win back some if not all of the rights associated with American citizenry. Struggle continues, however, as students involve themselves in other off-campus actions resulting in mass arrests and university crackdowns, student protests, and police repression. The embattled students soon come to resemble the scarred Wobblies, as they develop class consciousness and political ideology.

The emergence of students as a politicized class strongly suggests that mass struggles are not over, and we can expect similar mass arrests and sit-ins during the stormy years ahead, as the multiversity, the state, and the police join hands to repress militant student movements aligned with civil rights and peace groups. The coming period offers us considerable research material, the kinds of data so useful when reformulating and testing our notions on the natural history of an arrest.

FINAL COMMENTS

Our analysis of center-democratic has taken us into the inevitable: a look at the conflict between university administrators and students. This conflict is by no means simple to analyze, and we have dwelt on but one small facet of the problem. In order to widen the scope of what is involved, we would now like to turn to the garrison state hypothesis and to an analysis of the weakness of the student movement as these developments became apparent after a decade of near-exhausting struggle.

NOTES

1. An institutional arrest is simply an arrest that occurs on the property of an institution, whether public or private. The arrest may or may not involve large numbers, but generally large-scale arrests are the pattern. We have in mind the taking into custody of large numbers of people who had conducted a massive demonstration on the property of a university, a gov-ernment, or a private firm, although these categories by no means exhaust the possibilities.

2. George Sorel, *Reflections on Violence* (Glencoe: Free Press, 1950).

3. See Max Nomad, *Aspects of Revolt* (New York: Collier, 1963).

4. Martin Oppenheimer and George Lakey, *A Manual for Direct Action* (Chicago: Quadrangle, 1965), pp. 100–115.

5. See Gaetano Mosca, *The Ruling Class* (New York and London: McGraw-Hill, 1939); Vilfredo Pareto, *Mind and Society* (New York, 1935).

6. Max Heirich, *The Beginning* (New York, Columbia University Press, 1970), p. 205.

7. This is no place to review the literature on the Sproul Hall Sit-ins. However, certain references should not be overlooked. See Hal Draper's *The New Student Revolt* (New York: Evergreen, 1965); Seymour M. Lipset and Paul Seabury, "The Lesson of Berkeley," *The Reporter*, XXXII (January 28, 1965); Gene Marine, "No Fair! The Students Strike at California," *The Nation*, 199 (December 21, 1964); James Petras, "Berkeley and the New Conservative Backlash," *New Left Review*, XXXI (May–June, 1965).

8. A listener-supported Berkeley radio station, KPFA, taped the entire arrest. A KPFA reporter obtained information from many arrestees on police use of force while the arrests were going on. The remarks made by the students confirm our materials. KGO-TV (Channel 7), San Francisco, showed a great deal of material on police use of rough force. Perhaps of more interest was a systematic study done by Caroline Estes and Larry Duga for the American Civil Liberties Union. The report, entitled "ACLU Northern California Berkeley–Albany Chapter Report on Events at Sproul Hall on December 3rd, 1964," scrutinized arrestee reports on what happened to them inside Sproul Hall and further confirmed our observations. The report was based on tabulated materials derived from a careful analysis of statistical data. For reasons not entirely clear, the East Bay American Civil Liberties Union decided not to approve or release the report.

9. Police departments carefully prepared police officers for the Sproul Hall arrests. Charles E. Moore has described the preparation made for the arrests in his "Anarchy On The Campus," in *The Police and the Changing Community—Selected Readings*, edited by Nelson A. Watson, Project Supervisor, Research and Development, International Association of Chiefs of Police. According to the editor, Addison H. Fording, Chief of Police, Berkeley, California, invited Moore to Berkeley in January, 1965, to review and research the aspects of civil disobedience disorders at the University of California. Mr. Moore, Director of Public Relations, International Association of Chiefs of Police, Washington, D.C., complied.

Mr. Moore commented in his subsequent report on how after the earlier October sit-in, the University never advised law enforcement representatives on how they planned to take care of any future sit-in demonstration(s). Nonetheless, the local and concerned police departments proceeded to make their own plans.

10. See Clark Kerr and Abraham Siegel, "The In-

terindustry Propensity to Strike—An International Comparison," in Arthur Kornhauser, Robert Dubin, and Arthur M. Ross, *Industrial Conflict* (New York: McGraw-Hill, 1954), pp. 189–212.

11. In 1963, Kerr observed:

If the alumni are concerned, the undergraduate students are restless. Recent changes in the American university have done them little good—lower teaching loads for the faculty, the choice of faculty members based on research accomplishments rather than instructional capacity, the fragmentation of knowledge into endless subdivisions. There is an incipient revolt of undergraduate students against the faculty; the revolt that used to be against the faculty *in absentia*. The students find themselves under a blanket of impersonal rules for admissions, for scholarships, for examinations, for degrees. It is interesting to watch how a faculty intent on few rules for itself can fashion such a plethora of them for the students. The students also want to be treated as distinct individuals.

If the faculty looks on itself as a guild, the undergraduate students are coming to look upon themselves more as a "class"; some may even feel like a "lumpen proletariat." Lack of faculty concern for teaching, endless rules and requirements, and impersonality are the inciting causes. A few of the "non-conformists" have another kind of revolt in mind. They seek, instead, to turn the university, on the Latin American or Japanese models, into a fortress from which they can sally forth with impunity to make their attacks on society.

If the federal grants for research brought a major revolution, then the resultant student sense of neglect may bring a minor counterrevolt, although the target of the revolt is a most elusive one.

Clark Kerr, *The Uses of the University* (Cambridge: Harvard University Press, 1963), pp. 103–104.

12. Kerr has commented on the quality of this partnership, but one wonders if Kerr has a love affair in mind:

... David Riesman has spoken of the leading American universities as "directionless ... as far as major innovations are concerned"; they have run out of foreign models to imitate; they have lost their "ferment." The fact is that they are not directionless; they have been moving in clear directions and with considerable speed; there has been no "stalemate." But these directions have not been set as much by the university's visions of its destiny as by the external environment, including the federal government, the foundations, the surrounding and sometimes engulfing industry.

The university has been embraced and led down the garden path by its environmental suitors; it has been so attractive and so accommodating; who could resist it and why would it, in turn, want to resist?

Ibid., p. 122.

We wonder if Kerr is talking about a school such as the University of California or a pick-up area such as the San Francisco Tenderloin. But he settles all doubt on this matter in the very last part of his book. He definitely is talking about the university and how it has become part of something quite bigger and more powerful than itself: "Intellect has also become an instrument of national purpose, a component part of the 'military industrial complex.' " *Ibid.*, p. 124.

Chapter 12 Counterinsurgency and Social Class in the American Community

---

Section One   *Upper-class Directorship*

INSURGENCY AND IMPERIALISM: THE INTERLOCK

What is the relationship between counterinsurgency overseas and social class in the American community? The concept of interlock is the key to our attempt to arrive at an initial working formulation on this relationship: specifically, upper-class organizational ties between its corporations and the executive level of the federal government. The formulation refers to the propensity of upper-class persons to dominate on matters of overseas affairs and domestic municipal governance. In the case of overseas policy, the matter is fairly straightforward. When discussing local community politics, however, the relationships are more subtle.

More precisely, in order to understand our particular conception of interlock in this country, we must observe the two-winged quality of political influence and domination executed by the upper classes both at home and abroad. This does not mean that those who govern domestically and overseas do in fact rule—in the sense of determining all that can and cannot happen. Indeed, we must make certain distinctions on matters of power if we are to comprehend what is involved. Power takes at least eight forms:

Power to coerce
Power to assert
Power to initiate
Power to assent
Power to withhold
Power to veto
Power to solidify
Power to influence (which subsumes the power to persuade)[1]

[1] Power to coerce has reference to A forcing B to act in ways deemed appropriate by A. Power to assert

Naturally, all these discrete forms are related. They seldom occur separately in the real community. They tend to be tied to one another in many instances, and their use over time is most frequently expressed in upper-class circles—but not always. And here we part with many elite and class theorists. For under some circumstances the people themselves can and do exert their strength in many power areas. Illustrative would be people's power wielded during the surge of massive grass-roots reform movements. (e.g., agrarian populists in the early 1890s). Again, during the final phases of prodromal revolutionary periods, the people seize the time—and the place—much to the dismay of large sections of both the upper classes and many, but by no means all, state officials. But corporate and banking directors normally function as principal stockholders and managers in ways that combine these powers within cliques of upper-class persons; together they foster the due maximization of upper-class political power—all varieties—through a host of organizational forms such as educational foundations and political associations locked directly into the formal political power structure of the cen-

occurs when A states a series of propositions to an audience with the possibility that the statement will have a generalized impact. Power to initiate is present when A takes action which he hopes will lead to *organizational* changes. Power to assent refers to the right to approve a proposal and thereby help to determine its outcome. Power to withhold has reference to A not giving assent and thereby helping to suspend the final decision on a proposal. Power to veto refers to A summarily rejecting and thereby defeating a particular proposal. Power to solidify has reference to A taking action which increases the solidarity of people in his camp. Power to influence is the power to help shape an outcome through the device of suggestion. Power to influence sometimes takes an argumentative form of suggestion.

tral government. Be it on matters of foreign or domestic policy, this pattern is pronounced.

INTERLOCK AND POLICY

In the case of the United States, the interlocks on matters of foreign policy are fairly straightforward. Let us outline their substance:

1. *As G. William Domhoff and others have indicated, the upper class is more than a useful analytical category: Its families share a common sense of who they are.* An upper class exists and consists of self-sustaining families substantially supported by dividends. In maintaining themselves, these families perpetuate their class, for these families are relationally and ideologically bound to one another. They also share a common consciousness, and as part of that consciousness, a common understanding of who they are. Hence they record and rank one another within community social registers and use these registers to reconfirm continuously their solidarity through such devices as the consultation of registers for gatherings, vacations, marriages, economic appointments, political opportunities, and the education of the young.

In this sense, the upper classes can use their wealth to solidify their own ranks. The power to solidify in turn rests in part on their ability to influence recruitment of persons into their associations through persuasion and other modes of suggestion that have the effect of keeping certain people *out* and allowing others *in*. Racial, ethnic, and class criteria are used. People are screened, accepted, and rejected. These discrete upper-class persons may on occasion find it ill-advised to use publicly such criteria for fear of being accused of poorly timed racism or undue snobbery. In these cases, they use their power to assent to token acceptance of minorities. Or, if the upper-class persons decide that the timing of nonacceptance is okay, they use their power to assert publicly that they retain the right to pick and to choose as they see fit. If neither acceptance, assertion, nor a blackballing veto seems to be in order, the upper classes can simply prolong admission decisions on Jews, blacks, and others through the power to withhold. To cite but one well-known instance of upper-class prejudice, we can note the habit of Philadelphia's upper class of banning Jews from joining essentially Protestant, upper-class clubs and political associations, frequenting resort spas, and marrying into upper-class families.[2] Of course, if minorities get too assertive, mounting a heavy civil rights demonstration, for example, the management can always call the cops. Never underestimate the ability of the upper classes to coerce.

2. *These upper-class families plant their members in key directorships and, in some cases, in top managerial positions within firms that upper-class families control through investment.* However, this practice does not preclude the use of upper-middle-class professionals, in many cases intent on their becoming members of the upper class. Indeed, upper-class members depend on the services and the loyalty of such individuals to run their organizations and to become new members of the upper class themselves. The upwardly mobile executive can only benefit from devices such as the stock option, a form of reward which can be used to lure brilliant talent and to enrich it:

> The stock option, a tax-avoidance factor of tremendous importance to corporate executives, was introduced in the 1950 Revenue Act, and it has become a major means of compensating members of the economic elite. By 1957, 77 percent of the largest manufacturing corporations had set up option plans. Under the terms of the Act, an option on a company's stock is offered to an executive at no less than 85 percent (in practice, it is generally 95 percent) of the current market value. The executive must wait at least eighteen months before he exercises the option—if he chooses to exercise it. If the market price rises, as it almost invariably does in an inflationary economy, the executive buys the stock at its original low price; then, if he waits six months to sell, he pays only the capital-gains tax on the profit. If the stock's price falls 20 percent or more below the option price, the option price can again be reduced to 95 percent of the average market price for the twelve months preceding the new change.
>
> "In the past five years," *U.S. News & World Report* observed in 1955, "these options have produced a whole new crop of millionaires." One aircraft company gave

[2] E. Digby Baltzell, *Protestant Establishment: Aristocracy and Caste in America* (New York: Random House, 1964).

thirteen executives an option on 30,000 shares in 1951; in 1955, they realized a 370 percent profit. A rubber company granted a vice-president an option on 10,000 shares worth $213,800 in 1951; in 1955, they were worth $547,000. In 1957, Frank Pace, Jr., and John J. Hopkins exercised their options to buy General Dynamics stock then valued at $1,125,000 and $1,220,000, respectively; their option price was about one-third the market value at the time of the stock sale. In January, 1956, Donald W. Douglas, Sr., of Douglas Aircraft, exercised an option for 15,000 shares at $16.50 each at a time when the market price had risen to $86—a profit of more than $1 million. During 1956, when executives at Pittsburgh Plate Glass purchased 40,000 company shares at an option price of $41, the market price ranged from $74 to $96. Beginning in 1951, U.S. Steel granted its executives stock options with a face value of $49 million; on August 8, 1957, the stocks were worth $133 million on the market.[3]

In a sense, the upper classes can use the stock option as a device to bring about organizational changes by recruiting executives known for their approval of an alternative organizational format. The announced recruitment may be accompanied by publicized comments on the extraordinary size of the stock options, thereby suggesting to regular employees the need for *them* to change. This power to influence may also parallel a decision to withhold promotion for regular employees who had believed, until the recruitment announcement, that they were in line for promotion. The upper classes may thereby use their power to post decisions on career lines within the organization and, in doing so, avoid the sometimes nasty business of using their power to veto unwanted promotions.

3. *Upper-class families use their wealth, their prestige, their directorship positions, their managerial slots, and the expertise of their professionals to garner directorship positions within many institutions, including universities.* Membership on university boards of directors, regents, and trustees allows upper-class persons to deliberately promote the creation of exper-

tise in keeping with the vital interests of their class, their property, their corporate positions, their careers, and their professionals. (See Chapter 9.) Noam Chomsky has been most explicit on this matter in his analysis of professional service of upper-class interests on matters of foreign policy.[4]

Crucial here are such matters as the power to assert a proposal on university reorganization and the power to initiate through financial allocation with respect to the formation of special institutes, departments, etc., with predictable and positive consequences for the upper classes. Not all proposals need come from the upper classes, however, for this elite can assent to both plans and suggestions coming from administrative, faculty, or student groups. If the proposals seem to be unworthy, the directors can withhold approval or veto the recommendations from below. On the other hand, the directors of the university can approve proposals that please them, with the hope that a long-term consequence of a favorable act will be the increased solidarity of their university and their class.

4. *The interlock between the upper classes and the universities finds fondest expression through the mediating influence of major foundations whose boards of directors consist almost entirely of members of the upper class.* These foundations set limits within which many forms of large-scale research can take place. By setting the breadth of the research interval, the foundations help to determine which subjects both faculty and students will study. Here the upper classes take advantage of the powers to assert, initiate, assent, withhold, and veto, and seekers of academic grants take heed, especially when they use their personal radar to discover which projects the foundations will fund. In a sense, foundations exert the power to influence without engaging in persuasion.

5. *Upper-class families feign fiduciary neutrality in their roles as honorific guides of foundations whose leadership uses prestigious foundation slots as springboards into guidance positions in less visible political associations.* Here we encounter the power to assert, as when the university president, the foundation representative, and the dutiful faculty, use public

[3] Gabriel Kolko, *Wealth and Power in America* (New York: Praeger, 1962), pp. 41–42, reprinted by permission of the publisher.

[4] Noam Chomsky, *American Power and the New Mandarins* (New York: Pantheon, 1969), pp. 57–68.

gatherings as means to announce good works at the very moment university presidents, foundation leaders, and selected faculty, slip into political associations where their decisions are more difficult to justify. Yet justification can occur, in part because of the ideological solidarity of the ranks achieved through the recruitment of persons who generally agree on political premises.

6. *Despite broad similarities among the viewpoints of foreign policy association members, these individuals nonetheless carefully debate the full range of problems and upper-class positions on proper alternative courses of action.*[5]

Since the upper classes occupy critical positions in these associations, they reserve for themselves the right to specify an agenda. Here the power to assent (and to veto) can be used to deal with members who generally understand that these powers exist and who behave accordingly. Yet the debate may assume a truly theatrical quality, perhaps culminating not in a decision but at a blank wall—namely, the leadership exerts its power to withhold, should those at the top of the association disapprove of decision(s) within their group. If need be, the executives of the group may even reserve for themselves the power to veto, perhaps also using the power to assert a counterposition through either a general meeting or a televised appeal. They can thereby use the power to influence in order to help coerce the rank and file to drop their former proposal and to devise recommendations to which the leadership can assent.

7. *Once the foreign policy associations have taken their positions, these are made explicit and forceful to the President of the United States, who is reached through numerous conduits.* These include briefings, well-written reports, articles published in intellectually impressive journals, as well as partisan and prolonged involvement as policy initiators and implementors.[6] Clearly, plentiful economic resources

back the power to influence through persuasion, or the power to initiate, as when the Council on Foreign Relations proposed the basic elements of the Marshall Plan and NATO—two organizational innovations designed to halt the spread of Communism to Western and Southern Europe following World War II.

8. *The recommendations join others which are jointly considered by the chief executive within a context of genuine upper-class concern expressed through the foreign policy associations in question.* These recommendations come from many sources. Yet few can claim to be as soundly researched, dutifully scientific, indeed, technically neutral, as those emanating from upper-class foreign policy associations. Chomsky has aptly portrayed the overall tenor of recommendations derived from these dens of presumed ideological abstinence:

> Perhaps the most interesting aspect of scholarly work such as this is the way in which behavioral-science rhetoric is used to lend a vague aura of respectability. One might construct some such chain of associations as this. Science, as everyone knows, is responsible, moderate, unsentimental, and otherwise good. Behavioral science tells us that we can be concerned only with behavior and control of behavior. Therefore we *should* be concerned only with behavior and control of behavior; and it is responsible, moderate, unsentimental, and otherwise good to control behavior by appropriately applied reward and punishment. Concern for loyalties and attitudes is emotional and unscientific. As rational men, believers in the scientific ethic, we should be concerned with manipulating behavior in a desirable direction, and not be deluded by mystical notions of freedom, individual needs, or popular will.[7]

Presumably, propositional validity becomes obtainable through antiseptic formulation.

9. *The President then acts on these proposals, often adopting sizable portions of the materials, for the Chief Executive has treated state interests as consistent with those of the propertied and their recommendations.* Most useful, for example, are the recommendations made by such persons as William Bundy, who

---

[5] *The New York Times, The Pentagon Papers* (New York: Bantam, 1971), especially pp. 158–306.

[6] G. William Domhoff, *Who Rules America?* (Englewood Cliffs, N.J.: Prentice-Hall, 1967), pp. 71–74. John Franklin Campbell, *The Death Rattle of the Eastern Establishment, New York* 4 (September 20, 1971), pp. 47–51. G. William Domhoff, "Who Made American Foreign Policy, 1945–1963?," in David Horowitz, *Corporations and The Cold War* (New York: Monthly Review Press, 1969), pp. 25–69.

[7] Chomsky, op. cit., pp. 57–68.

has helped to write at least one fulfilled scenario on how U.S. policy in Vietnam should unfold.[8] In some cases, however, it is admittedly difficult to locate so precisely the true source of foreign policy recommendations. But the decisions, once set, take on a normative character subscribed to by various sections of the upper class. These tacit agreements sometimes conflict with the presumably immodest demands proferred by the Third World countries through the United Nations. These demands include the idea that U.S. businesses should relax to some degree their near-maximal control of trade and investment policies in Third World countries.[9] Here, as Horowitz demonstrated, is the most blatantly explicit evidence of U.S. and British policies on economy (which were formerly open instances of imperial *coercion*) regarding crucial matters of international trade and Third World internal investment.

On these crucial matters the President undoubtedly supports a propensity for his United Nations Ambassador to veto any resolutions both emanating from the Third World nations and aiming toward greater control over U.S. investments in the Latin American, African, and Asian countries which have traditionally served as locales of private U.S. investment and areas of advantageous trade. As Horowitz pointed out, the United States in particular has been active in stymieing the economic independence of the third world countries. One example is the way it consistently voted against general propositions advanced by third world countries before the United Nations Conference on Trade and Development during the early 1960s (see Table 29). In this country, veto use implies the power to coerce Third World countries to accept ongoing imperial relations unless and until they wish to confront the U.S. state and big business interests and to pay the consequences (as has been the case in Cuba and Chile, where the assertiveness of these countries on matters of nationalization has resulted in

their being denied useful foreign markets and aid). Indeed, Congress has supported the President by passing legislation that bars foreign aid, including monies for hospitals, highways, and irrigation projects, to countries which have expropriated U.S. private investments, even under circumstances most clearly suggesting that prior U.S. injustices had led to the nationalization.

10. *The decision to favor a propertied point of view generally reflects a propensity to endorse an imperial perspective on chastisement—* namely, the extended support of sanctions against overseas countries which attempt to deal with colonial contradictions by tampering with normal routines on U.S. investment, trade, military defense, resource appropriation, and the like. General decisions on these matters are customarily designed for developed countries by corporation executives, banking directors, foreign office officials, intelligence agency officers, and military elites located in the decision-making nerve centers of capitalist countries.

Of course, not all goes well on the level of economic investment and political control. There are at least three contradictions in question, and here we paraphrase Andre Gunder Frank[10] on their precise nature:

a. *The contradiction of expropriation –appropriation of economic surplus,* in which the American firms expropriate a considerable portion of the value of what the overseas workmen have produced and then appropriate this value for themselves in the form of funds available for profits and investments. This exploitation increases both working-class consciousness and profit margins, thereby setting the stage for insurgence from below and counterrevolutionary repression from above.

Counterinsurgency from above entails the power of the President to use counterinsurgency organizations such as the Central Intelligence Agency (created by President Truman in the late 1940s). The CIA represents an effort to develop an intelligence group capable of dealing successfully, on the levels of information gathering and covert direct action, with both expanding Commu-

---

[8] See ch. 5, "The Covert War and Tonkin Gulf: February—August, 1964," in *The Pentagon Papers,* op. cit., pp. 234—306.
[9] See Irving L. Horowitz, "The United Nations and the Third World: East—West Conflict in Focus," in *Three Worlds of Development* (New York: Oxford University Press, 1966), pp. 164—192.

[10] André Gunder Frank, *Capitalism and Underdevelopment in Latin America* (New York: Monthly Review Press, 1967), pp. 6—14.

TABLE 29 General Propositions of the United Nations Conference on Trade and Development

Propositions[a]	Asian Bloc	Latin America	African Bloc	United Kingdom	United States	Soviet Union	Eastern Europe	Western Europe	Vote Explanation[b]	Composite Vote Yea +	Nay –	Abstention 0
(G.P. *I*) Economic relations between countries shall be based on respect for the principle of sovereign equality of states, self-determination, and non-interference in internal affairs.	+	+	+	0	–	+	+	+	Australia, Ireland, & New Zealand voted Yea. Portugal abstained.	113	1	2
(G.P. *II*) There shall be no discrimination on the basis of differences in socio-economic systems. Adoption of trading methods shall be consistent with this principle.	+	+	+	0	–	+	+	+	Germany & Canada Against. S. Africa, Spain, Monaco, Sweden, Switzerland, Netherlands, Norway abstained.	96	3	16
(G.P. *III*) Every country has the right to trade with others, and freely to dispose of its natural resources in the interest of the economic development of its own people.	+	+	+	–	–	+	+	+	Germany abstained. Nicaragua, Peru, and Japan abstained.	94	4	18
(G.P. *IV*) All countries will pursue internal and external economic policies designed to accelerate economic growth throughout the world, at a rate which would narrow the gap between developed and developing nations.	+	+	+	–	–	+	+	+	Belgium, Finland, France, Italy, Holy See, Japan, Luxembourg, Monaco, Peru, Netherlands, Nicaragua, S. Africa, Switzerland abstained.	98	1	17
(G.P. *V*) Economic policies should be directed towards attaining an international division of labor in harmony with needs for diversification of developing economies.	+	+	+	0	0	+	+	+	As in vote explanation for G.P. *IV*, plus Canada and Spain abstained.	97	0	19
(G.P. *VI*) All countries should cooperate in creating conditions of international trade conducive to the achievement of the rapid increase in the export earnings of developing countries.	+	+	+	+	–	+	+	+	Taiwan (China) abstained.	114	1	1

TABLE 29 (Continued)

Propositions[a]	Asian Bloc	Latin America	African Bloc	United Kingdom	United States	Soviet Union	Eastern Europe	Western Europe	Vote Explanation[b]	Composite Vote Yea +	Nay −	Abstention 0
(G.P. VII) Developed countries shall progressively eliminate barriers that hinder trade and consumption of products from developing countries, and take steps to create new export markets for developing countries.	+	+	+	−	−	+	+	+	Denmark and Switzerland Against.	87	8	19
(G.P. VIII) Developed countries should grant concessions to developing nations without extracting similar concessions in return. Special preferential arrangements presently in effect should be regarded as transitional.	+	+	+	−	−	+	+	0	Austria, Iceland, Sweden, Switzerland, Against. Brazil, Rwanda, Uganda, Venezuela abstained.	78	11	23
(G.P. IX) Developed countries participating in regional economic groupings should ensure that their economic integration does not cause injury to or adversely affect expansion of imports from developing countries.	+	+	+	+	+	+	+	0	Austria, Finland, Sweden. Switzerland did not abstain.	106	0	10
(G.P. X) All forms of economic cooperation should result in an expansion of intra-regional and extra-regional trade and encourage their growth and diversification with due regard to special features of each nation.	+	+	+	+	+	+	+	+	Japan abstained.	115	0	1
(G.P. XI) Developed countries should increase net flow of international financial, technical, economic assistance to aid export earnings of underdeveloped countries. No political or military conditions.	+	+	+	−	−	+	+	0	Australia, F.R. Germany, Against.	92	5	19
(G.P. XII) Resources released as outcome of agreement on disarmament should be allocated to economic developing by the fully developed countries.	+	+	+	0	−	0	0	0		83	1	30
(G.P. XIII) (land-locked countries)	+	+	+	+	+	+	+	+		108	0	0

312

Proposal	Votes	Comments	For	Against	Abstain
(G.P. *XIV*) Complete decolonization as in U.N. Declaration of granting independence & liquidation of all forms of colonialism is necessary for economic development and exercise of sovereign rights over natural resources.	+ + + − 0 + + 0	Australia Against	90	2	22
(G.P. *XV*) Different levels of development to be recognized in individual developing countries and special attention to least developed to insure equitable opportunity.	+ + + + + + +	Albania, Brazil, Canada, Iceland, Jamaica, Syria, Liechtenstein, Japan, Spain abstained.	101	0	12
(S.P. *1*) Developed countries should cooperate with developing countries in setting targets for expansion of trade of the latter and in periodically reviewing measures taken for their achievement.	+ + + 0 − + + +	Canada Against	99	2	15
(S.P. *2*) Developing countries should modernize agriculturally and industrially. Developed countries should supplement these efforts through financing, training programs and expanding imports of processed and manufactured goods from developing countries.	+ + + + + + +		116	0	0
(S.P. *3*) No action.					
(S.P. *4*) Developing countries have the right to protect their infant industries.	+ + + + 0 + + +		115	0	1
(S.P. *5*) Domestic support for primary commodities in developed countries shall not preclude a fair proportion of the domestic consumption being supplied by developing countries.	+ + ? 0 + + +	Australia, Austria, Belgium, F. R. Germany, Finland, France, San Marino, Greece, Holy See, Iceland abstained.	91	0	25
(S.P. *6*) Developed countries should help developing countries promote new uses for products whose use has been reduced by synthetic innovations, by research, etc.	+ + + + + + +		116	0	0
(S.P. *7*) Whenever international measures taken are to stabilize primary product prices in relation to manufactured goods, equitable arrangements should be made in terms of facilitating the implementation of economic development plans.	+ + + − − 0 0 0	Australia, Austria, Canada, Denmark, F.R. Germany, Iceland, Japan, Norway, S. Africa, Switzerland, Liechtenstein, Against.	85	13	18

TABLE 29 (*Continued*)

Propositions[a]	Asian Bloc	Latin America	African Bloc	United Kingdom	United States	Soviet Union	Eastern Europe	Western Europe	Vote Explanation[b]	Composite Vote Yea +	Composite Vote Nay −	Composite Vote Abstention 0
(S.P. 8) In the disposal of agricultural surpluses, developed countries should undertake to apply internationally agreed upon criteria of surplus disposal so as not to affect adversely export prospects of developing countries heavily dependent on the export narrow range of primary products. Criteria should also govern the disposal of all primary product surpluses and stockpiles.	+	+	+	0	−	+	+	+	Denmark, France, Iceland, Monaco, Sweden, S. Africa abstained.	106	1	9
(S.P. 9) Countries shall refrain from all forms of dumping.	+	+	+	0	0	+	+	+	Norway, S. Africa, Sweden abstained.	107	0	9
(S.P. 10) Scientific and technological achievements should be made accessible under favourable conditions to all developing countries and their application to the trade and development needs of those countries should be encouraged by an expansion of bilateral and multilateral programmes of technical assistance.	+	+	+	+	+	+	+	+		116	0	0
(S.P. 11) All countries should support an expansion of multilateral economic assistance to developing countries especially within the framework of the U.N. as well as bilateral assistance.	+	+	+	0	0	+	+	0	Japan, S. Africa abstained.	93	0	23

(S.P. 12) All countries should cooperate in devising measures to help developing countries build up transport for their economic development, to ensure the unhindered use of such facilities and to promote tourism in these countries in order to increase their earnings and reduce their expenditure on invisible trade.

+	+	+	1	1	1	+	+	+	0	Canada, Japan, Ireland abstained.	92	7	17

(S.P. 13) Mutually beneficial bilateral and multilateral trade and payments arrangements between developing countries constitute an essential element in the expansion and diversification of international trade.

+	+	+	+	0	+	+	+	+	Australia, Canada, Japan, Liechtenstein abstained.	111	0	5

[a](G.P.) stands for General Propositions; (S.P.) stands for Special Propositions.
[b]When a given nation does not vote with its given bloc, it will appear in the vote explanation column.

Taken from Irving L. Horowitz, *Three Worlds of Development: The Theory and Practice of International Stratification.* Copyright © 1966 by Irving L. Horowitz. Reprinted by permission of Oxford University Press, Inc., New York.

nism and threatening nationalism. Once created, the CIA has pursued proposals on such as how to deal with an Iranian prime minister who had moved to nationalize private oil cartel holdings which had thrived on excess profits (Mossadegh, deposed, Iran, 1953); a liberal prime minister who had attempted to expropriate land owned by U.S. plantation interests but not used by them (Arbenz, deposed, Guatemala, 1954), and of course, a premier who had maintained an anti-Communist government but who had outlived his usefulness in the eyes of the American President (Diem, assassinated, South Vietnam, 1963)[11] . These three exam-

[11] For material on the Iranian case, see Richard J. Barnet, *Intervention and Revolution* (New York: World, 1968), pp. 226–229; Walter LaFeber, *America and The Cold War, 1945–1971* (New York: Wiley, 1972) pp. 155–156; Ronald Radosh and Murray N. Rothbard, eds., *A New History of Leviathan* (New York: Dutton, 1972) pp. 251–252; Joyce and Gabriel Kolko, *The Limits of Power* (New York: Harper & Row, 1972), p. 419; David Wise and Thomas B. Ross, *The Invisible Government* (New York: Random House, 1964), pp. 110–114.

In the case of the Arbenz overthrow in Guatemala, the following sources are useful: David Green, "The Cold War Comes to Latin America", in Barton J. Bernstein, ed., *Politics and Policies of the Truman Administration* (Chicago: Quadrangle Books, 1970), pp. 187–188; LaFeber, op. cit., pp. 158–160; the Kolkos, op. cit., p. 701; Wise and Ross, op. cit., 165–183.

If we examine documentation on the assassination of the South Vietnamese Premier, Ngo Dinh Diem, the most compelling document is one emanating from the Pentagon itself. As Hedrick Smith writes in *The Pentagon Papers:*

> The Pentagon's secret study of the Vietnam war discloses that President Kennedy knew and approved of plans for the military coup d'état that overthrew President Ngo Dinh Diem in 1963.
>
> "Our complicity in his overthrow heightened our responsibilities and our commitment" in Vietnam, the study finds.
>
> In August and October of 1963, the narrative recounts, the United States gave its support to a cabal of army generals bent on removing the controversial leader, whose rise to power Mr. Kennedy had backed in speeches in the middle nineteenfifties and who had been the anchor of American policy in Vietnam for nine years.
>
> The coup, one of the most dramatic episodes in the history of the American involvement in Vietnam, was a watershed. As the Pentagon study observes, it was a time when Washington—with the Diem regime gone—could have reconsidered its entire commitment to South Vietnam and decided to disengage.
>
> At least two Administration officials advocated

disengagement but, according to the Pentagon study, it "was never seriously considered a policy alternative because of the assumption that an independent, non-Communist SVN was too important a strategic interest to abandon."

> The effect, according to this account, was that the United States, discovering after the coup that the war against the Vietcong had been going much worse than officials previously thought, felt compelled to do more—rather than less—for Saigon. By supporting the anti-Diem coup, the analyst asserts, "the U.S. inadvertently deepened its involvement. The inadvertence is the key factor."
>
> According to the Pentagon account of the 1963 events in Saigon, Washington did not originate the anti-Diem coup, nor did American forces intervene in any way, even to try to prevent the assassinations of Mr. Diem and his brother Ngo Dinh Nhu, who, as the chief Diem political adviser, had accumulated immense power. Popular discontent with the Diem regime focused on Mr. Nhu and his wife.
>
> But for weeks—and with the White House informed every step of the way—the American mission in Saigon maintained secret contacts with the plotting generals through one of the Central Intelligence Agency's most experienced and versatile operatives, an Indochina veteran, Lieut. Col. Lucien Conein. He first landed in Vietnam in 1944 by parachute for the Office of Strategic Services, the wartime forerunner of the C.I.A.
>
> So trusted by the Vietnamese generals was Colonel Conein that he was in their midst at Vietnamese General Staff headquarters as they launched the coup. Indeed, on Oct. 25, a week earlier, in a cable to McGeorge Bundy, the President's special assistant for national security, Ambassador Lodge had occasion to describe Colonel Conein of the C.I.A.—referring to the agency, in code terminology, as C.A.S.—as the indispensable man:
>
> "C.A.S. has been punctilious in carrying out my instructions. I have personally approved each meeting between General Don [one of three main plotters] and Conein who has carried out my orders in each instance explicitly. . . .
>
> "Conein, as you know, is a friend of some 18 years' standing with General Don, and General Don has expressed extreme reluctance to deal with anyone else. I do not believe the involvement of another American in close contact with the generals would be productive.". . .
>
> So closely did the C.I.A. work with the generals, official documents reveal, that it provided them with vital intelligence about the arms and encampments of pro-Diem military forces after Mr. Lodge had authorized C.I.A. participation in tactical planning of the coup.
>
> So intimately tied to the conspiracy did the Ambassador himself become that he offered refuge to the families of the generals if their plot failed— and he obtained Washington's approval. Near the end, he also sent a message to Washington seeking authority to put up the money for bribes to win over officers still loyal to President Diem. . . .
>
> (Reprinted by permission from Neil Sheehan and E. W. Kenworthy, *The Pentagon Papers* [New York © 1971 by The New York Times Company. Reprinted by permission.], pp. 158-159.)

Also pertinent are Barnet's analysis, op. cit., pp. 212–214; and Wise and Ross, op. cit., pp. 155–164. For a critical analysis of faculty involvement in work-

ples are simply illustrative. Of course when dealing with CIA proposals of this magnitude, the President has wielded the power to assent . . . or to withhold assent. He also retains the power to veto. On the whole, his variety of powers adds up to the perceived and actual power to coerce any overseas government which moves to appropriate U.S. holdings.

b. *The contradiction of metropolis– satellite polarization,* in which the crucial process is the imminent centralization of the capitalist system, such that a disproportionately large amount of resources flows to the metropolises of the capitalist world at the expense of drained satellite areas. Perhaps these dependent zones should be more appropriately thought of as hinterlands, often rural, poor, and growing poorer. The process fosters revolution in the countryside by making more vivid the contrasts between the metropolis of glitter and the hinterland of wretched.

To foster revolution is one thing. For the revolution to take place is something else. For the revolution to become a success, the translating arm of revolution must be maintained. (See Chapters 3 and 4.) And this maintenance is by no means simple in the face of U.S. police and military power. We will discuss these matters in Chapter 13.

c. *The contradiction of continuity in change,* in which the capitalist system expands and develops over the centuries, and yet remains continuously dedicated to the mobilization of land and labor for the production of profitable commodities within a system that moves from early mercantile to advanced monopolistic–capitalist forms of the kind which exist today. In effect, much remains the same, as a great deal changes. For example, the exploitation of tin miners and peasants in Bolivia continues in altering forms, which are subsumed in the purview of a flexible and changing capitalism. Despite capitalist alterations, however, the constant "exploitation" sometimes combines with other elements to create revolutionary movements.

11. *If and when the President of the United States supports imperial policies to deal with the maintenance of the foregoing contradictions, he sometimes finds it necessary to do so by spending a lot of money to maintain overseas armies committed to counterrevolutionary activities.* The "if and when" qualifier should not fool us into believing that the President can set a policy of failing to support U.S. investments overseas. There has never been such a President, since built into the role of President are ongoing specifications on how the Chief Executive must relate to his own Departments of State and Defense, the Congress, the intelligence agencies, and top advisors in order to promote the economic interests of the upper classes. Indeed, the members of this class head the key governmental groups which surround the President, bringing with them a general ideology—and hence a set of mutually understood formulas—which permeate all discussions.

In this sense, upper-class clichés—counterinsurgency, free world, governmental legitimacy, logistical demands, body count—premeate all assumptions made within a logic that goes unquestioned. Thus key people are coerced to act in particular ways when they make their assertions, initiations, assents, vetoes, and persuasions. Here the President can simply nod his head affirmatively at their compliance with a given style of thought. If and when certain underlings rebel, he can influence them to backtrack; or if that tactic fails, he can veto major promotions or coerce people to leave. Junior and dissenting overseas members of the State Department, as well as heads of the Bureau of Labor Statistics, have recently felt the sting of these sanctions. The President can thereby exact the acceptance of imperial expenditures judged by some to be misappropriations in sup-

ing with the CIA in South Vietnam and the consequent creation of a police apparatus complicitly involved in the 1963 murder, see Irving L. Horowitz "Social Scientists Must Beware the Corruption of CIA Involvement," in Young Hum Kim, ed., *The Central Intelligence Agency* (Lexington, Mass.: Heath, 1968), pp. 64-74.

Perhaps the best known CIA intervention is the Bay of Pigs fiasco, in which the CIA led and organized efforts to invade Cuba in the spring of 1961. For pertinent materials, see Green, op. cit., p. 178; LaFeber, op. cit., pp. 222–224; Wise and Ross, pp. 8-90, 184–203, 328–347. Another instance was CIA participation in the 1965 U.S. overthrow of the government of the Dominican Republic in May, 1965. See Barnet, op. cit., pp. 153–180.

port of unjustifiable wars. The decisions to escalate and to further fund the Vietnam war during the mid-1960s were not received with unanimous enthusiasm by all major voices in the government. Nonetheless, most critics got in line on both the predictable human costs and the Congressional appropriations necessary. They did so largely because of the President's discretionary use of his previously enumerated powers.

12. *In turn, the allocation of funds to imperial adventures—especially their escalation, as was the case for the United States for the Vietnam war during the mid-1960s—makes less readily available funds that might be used to rebuild communities at home in order to solve problems of economic organization, political participation, and social disintegration.* More specifically, we still lack sufficient funds to attempt to deal with the problems of decline in employment, increases in environmental pollution, and inadequacy of mass transportation and police protection.

Yet the President can obfuscate the responsibility for failure to fight poverty effectively by feigning concern through his powers (*a*) to initiate programs portrayed as substantively productive (but on later analysis shown to be predictably defective), and (*b*) to assent to cabinet suggestions which are limited in their positive consequences for the lower class but which are packaged—through the use of the cabinet's power to assert—as if a dramatic initiation of governmental reorganization and a fresh policy marked a new era of Judeo-Christian uplift. Illustrative is the publicity accompanying purportedly new programs for welfare recipients, a great deal of which consist of trumpeted announcements regarding the same old can of beans.

The exercise of the various powers cited previously reveals (*a*) the existence of the power to mask the real consequences of decisions, and (*b*) the consequences of one power decision on another. For example, we know that once the armed forces have reached a size that permits them to carry on a full-scale counterrevolutionary war, as in Vietnam, the subsequent withdrawal of troops from that theatre is followed by only a slight decrease in military expenditures (because of the necessity of maintaining a military organization in readiness for another such major altercation). It is estimated,

for example, that should U.S. troops withdraw altogether from the Indo-Chinese war, the amount saved would be considerably less than 10 percent of the overall Department of Defense budget. Thus we see the government's need for the power of persuasion—regarding the continued necessity for large military budgets. Whether a withdrawal from Indo-China would have a similar effect on the CIA's costs can not be ascertained, since the amount and sources of this agency's budget are unknown except among the few at the very top of the executive branch of the federal government. And they ain't telling. And they need not tell, as long as they are empowered to withhold any decision on whether the government should divulge the size, sources, and consequences of CIA funding. Furthermore, nobody but the President has the *de facto* power to make the CIA directly and publicly responsible to the President on the sources and expenditures of its funds.

Given the overseas expenditures, what remains obviously absent is the availability of information and funds for the rebuilding of major American cities and the lives of people in them. For tax money is scarce, and once funds have been allocated to military adventures, little remains for domestic reorganization, especially in nonconstabulary activities. Quite the contrary, domestic tax money flows in increasingly larger amounts into police control of geographical areas where domestic insurrection might occur. Apparently, there is no desire to win the hearts and minds of our black and brown proletarianized ethnics. Rather, the decision to win on the basis of police control and coercion seems to have been made. This decision seems to flow from, or to accidentally parallel, the U.S. policy on Vietnam. In the work cited earlier, Chomsky quoted Morton H. Halperin, a social scientist at the Harvard Center for International Affairs:

> The events in Vietnam also illustrate the fact that most people tend to be motivated, not by abstract appeals, but rather by their perception of the course of action that is most likely to lead to their own personal security and to the satisfaction of their economic, social and psychological desires. Thus, for example, large-scale American bombing in South Vietnam may have antagonized a number of people; but at the same time it demonstrated to these people that

the Vietcong could not guarantee their security as it had been able to do before the bombing and that the belief in an imminent victory for the Vietcong might turn out to be dangerously false.[12]

Chomsky continued:

In short, along with confiscation of chickens, razing of houses, or destruction of villages, we can make effective use of 100 pounds of explosives per person, 12 tons per square mile, as in Vietnam, as a technique for controlling behavior, relying on the principle, now once again confirmed by experiment, that satisfaction of desires is a more important motivation in human behavior than abstract appeals to try to control the behavior of a rat by winning its loyalty rather than by the proper scheduling of reinforcement.[13]

In the United States, funds are spent to train local police, state patrol, national guard, and regular army, and increasingly the training features guerilla warfare theory and practice (derived in good measure from experience in Vietnam, but adjusted to suit dealings with domestic insurgents). These expenditures represent an effort to deal with potential dissidents on the level of perceived personal security rather than loyalty to authority, commitment to change, or enhancement of financial success. A power-initiated choice has been made in favor of police club, helmet, tear gas, mace, helicopter and above all, special organizational training to deal with persons who have cyclically demonstrated a predisposition to riot.

13. *The priority decisions for overseas expenditures and domestic counterinsurgency have created considerable unrest and perpetuated many gross inequities.* This problem has contributed to recent and costly outbursts among many of our poor, with the result that some upper class sometimes involve themselves on a sustained basis in remedial efforts, even though there is little or no public money to solve local problems. By way of illustration, the major auto corporations in Detroit avoided the problem of how to provide jobs and income for Detroit's unemployed blacks until a major insurrection occurred in 1967. At that point, the auto companies, in particular the Ford Motor Company, intervened to attempt to create several thousands of permanent and full-time jobs for a fraction of the permanently unemployed blacks located in the community. Ford was able to put approximately 6000 blacks to work after the company had spent a relatively large sum to train and to hire them. However, once the racial crisis had subsided, and the business cycle had dipped, the upper-class concern ebbed, and the newly employed in most instances lost their new jobs.

The Ford Motor Company had reacted to the class—racial destruction of an estimated $175 million dollars worth of private property in Detroit by asserting before the American public in general and Detroit blacks in particular that the company would initiate a massive, novel, job-creating program for black people who had been traditionally defined as hopelessly unemployed. In this sense, Ford hoped to solidify support from the various classes, status groups, and generations for a new kind of "responsible" business leadership. Later, when most of those trained became unemployed because of job cutbacks, Ford could use both its power *not* to initiate a new program *and* its power *to* withhold assent of job and/or income proposals emanating from the black caucuses of the United Automobile Workers. Needless to say, without Ford's endorsement, these union proposals had little consequence.

14. *Rather than act locally, the many upper-class persons have preferred to establish a domestic economic policy for all local communities by working through national pressure groups such as the Committee on Economic Development* (CED) (see Figure 3). These organizations foster direct connections with the federal government and foreign policy associations. In fact, many upper-class persons can and do claim joint membership as policy formulators on both the CED and the CFR, as Domhoff has pointed out.[14] Here the power to initiate proper appointments rests with the trusted officers of the associations in question.

15. *Still, there is ample room for upper-class persons aligned with local and relatively small corporations to exert various forms of power*

---

[12] Chomsky, op. cit., pp. 55–56.
[13] Loc. cit.

[14] See Domhoff, "Who Made American Foreign Policy, 1945–1963?," op. cit., pp. 36–41.

FIGURE 3   Interlock: Class and Foreign as well as Domestic Policy.

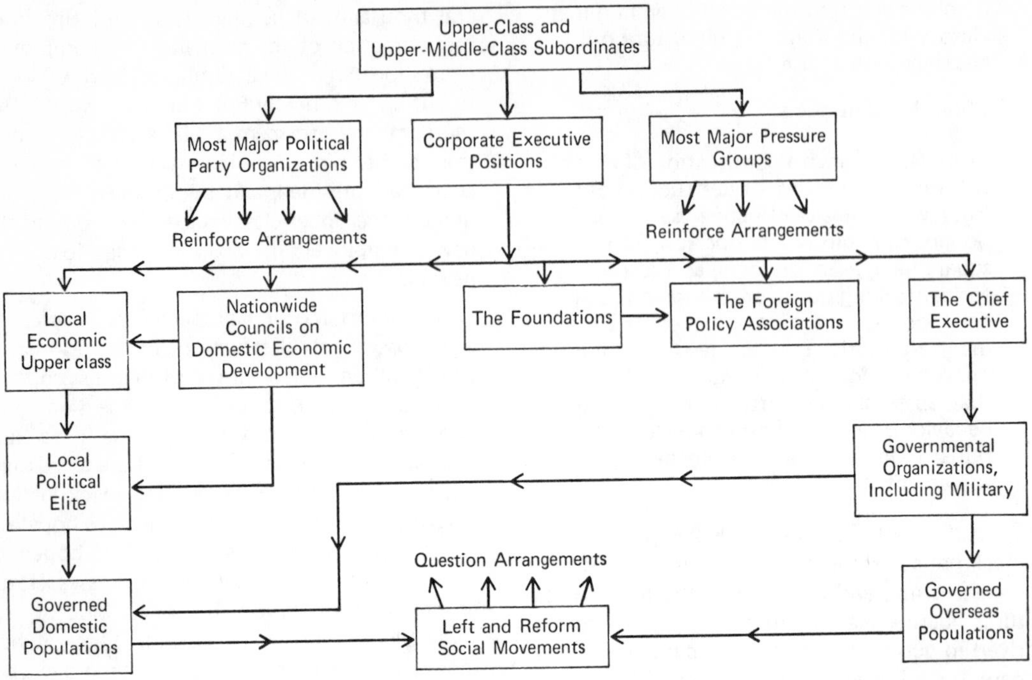

on the local level through sustained concern on everyday matters of city plumbing, schools, police, welfare, and hospitals and other medical services. (See the Mills reading in Section Two of this chapter on the traditional schisms and reciprocities between national and local upper class.) Indeed, as Robert A. Dahl has indicated,[15] these upper-class persons do work closely with a variety of local professional cliques on numerous issues, so that for every concrete issue there surfaces a new constellation of middle-class professionals and old-family upper-class persons. In these coalitions the middle-class professionals tend to dominate on matters of service and to discharge their political responsibilities without the participation of the working class.

But this seeming middle-class domination proves to be chimerical. The upper classes can assent to middle-class proposals without fear of losing their potential power to coerce. This power remains intact at the same time that professionals can use influence to bend upper-

[15] See Robert A. Dahl, *Who Governs?* (New Haven: Yale University Press, 1961), especially pp. 115–163.

class persons to act as benevolent Tories and to allow, indeed subsidize, the people's efforts to exercise greater control over schools and neighborhoods through the creation of block clubs and neighborhood associations which sometimes evolve into militant direct action groups committed to total participatory democracy. Needless to say, this militancy sometimes invites the termination of elite-directed subsidy. What becomes clear, time and again, is the ultimate power of the upper classes to influence, to veto, or to withhold consent on all matters, including appropriations geared to programs with consequences that would appear to be of questionable desirability to them. Therein lies the flexibility of the center-democratic bourgeois aristocrats. On examination, their powers assume mammoth proportions, perhaps best understood as lying on a scale quite distinct from that of ordinary blue-collar workers.

16. *However, even though the working class is seldom involved in the solution of political problems, this need not always be the case.* In New Haven, for example, where Dahl had earlier observed that the working classes were excluded from political decision-making on com-

munity projects, the Black Panther party may well have exerted some influence for a short period in such realms as welfare policy and poverty programs. In cities such as New Haven, Detroit, and St. Louis, Black Panther power might well have been momentarily significant. Social research will have to decide this issue.[16] In the meantime, we must depend largely on journalistic, qualitative data, which now point to the occasional willingness of the upper classes to compromise on issues posed by the Black Panthers and their equivalents at that historical moment when the community's police, sometimes working with Federal authorities, have moved to dissolve *that* black organization.[17] In this sense, a grass-roots group momentarily wielded the power to assert legitimate programs

---

[16] See William B. Helmreich, *The Black Crusaders: A Case Study of a Black Militant Organization* (New York: Harper & Row, 1973). This study of the St. Louis Black Panthers is by far the best examination ever made of a black militant organization.

[17] Perhaps the best study to date of persecution of black activist groups is William Helmreich's *The Black Crusaders,* op. cit.

We have relevant data on the Black Panthers as well. The most telling is the Seattle case, which was reported by the *New York Times* and covered by Seattle radio station KIRO. The *Times* reported as follows (Feb. 9, 1970, p. 70):

Mayor Wesley C. Uhlman has said that he turned down a Federal proposal for a raid on Black Panther headquarters in Seattle because he did not want to popularize the Panthers' cause. He also said that such raids smacked of gestapo-type tactics.

Mayor Uhlman, who has been in office only two months, said a Federal law enforcement agency asked for city participation in an "information gathering" raid on Panther headquarters a month ago. The raid did not take place.

In an interview, the Mayor criticized the tactics of some other cities in raids on Panthers and said "a great many people are having second thoughts about midnight Gestapo-type raids."

The police raided Panther headquarters in Chicago on Dec. 4, killing two Panther leaders. A coroner's jury ruled the deaths justifiable homicide.

A Los Angeles police raid on Panther headquarters resulted in the wounding of three policemen and two Panthers. The police seized arms and ammunition in both cities.

The Seattle Administration is under considerable public pressure because of 18 unsolved terrorist bombings in Seattle in the last seven months.

"The easy-answer thinkers say we can eliminate the bombings by eliminating the Panthers," Mayor Uhlman said. "We've been taking a lot of pressure to act precipitously, but we're going to withstand the pressure and do it the right way." The police have not publicly connected the Panthers in any way with the bombings.

The Mayor would not comment on the progress of the investigation. The latest bombing, early yesterday, damaged the home of a state Senator.

Mayor Uhlman would not say which Federal agency requested the joint raid, but The Seattle Post-Intelligencer reported that it had learned that it was the Alcohol, Tobacco, and Firearms Tax Unit of the Internal Revenue Service. Local spokesmen for the unit, which searches out illegal firearms, refused comment.

In Washington, a Treasury Department spokesman said that the unit was enforcing the gun registration laws and was not conducting any campaign against the Panthers as such.

The Seattle headquarters of the Black Panther party would not comment on the Mayor's remarks. (© 1970 by The New York Times Company. Reprinted by permission.)

In a companion article on the same date, the *Times* added:

Mayor Uhlman disclosed the Federal raid proposal in a talk to the University District Community Relations Committee last week. The committee is trying to improve communication between the police and University of Washington students and "street people" who inhabit the business district adjacent to the university's campus.

The Seattle Black Panther headquarters is in an old, two-story dwelling in the central part of the city where most of Seattle's 40,000 black citizens live. The police described the second floor as well fortified against attack.

The Seattle police conducted a raid in the summer of 1968, when the Black Panther headquarters was in another part of the city. The search warrant authorized the police to recover two typewriters that, police said, had been stolen from the Seattle Legal Aid Bureau. The Panthers convinced a judge that the typewriters had been given to them, and two Panthers who had been arrested in the raid were acquitted.

In further coverage the next day, this time from Washington, D.C., the *Times* reported (p. 30):

The Internal Revenue Service confirmed today that its agents wanted to raid a Black Panther headquarters in Seattle last month but changed its plans at the request of the city's police.

The I.R.S. Commissioner, Randolph W. Thrower, in effect confirmed what Seattle Mayor Wesley C. Uhlman said last week. Without naming the agency, Mayor Uhlman said that a Federal law enforcement agency had asked his administration to help in a raid on Panther headquarters. The Mayor said that he had replied that he did not want to make martyrs of the Black Panthers.

Mr. Thrower denied Mayor Uhlman's statement that the raid was for the purpose of gathering information.

"Contrary to news reports," Mr. Thrower said, "the I.R.S. at no time planned either an 'information gathering' raid or nighttime service of the warrant."

His statement said that I.R.S. investigators received evidence early in January "indicating probable cause of criminal violations of the federal gun laws by certain persons in Seattle who were believed to be members of the Black Panthers." (© 1970 by The New York Times Company. Reprinted by permission.)

and to initiate actions which, when combined with the Panthers' militance, gave them the power to persuade.

In an even broader sense, we can observe that although the American working classes have generally failed to mount sustained and successful attacks against the upper classes on matters of power, wealth, and prestige, these blue-collar workers have on occasion solidified and expressed relatively high levels of class consciousness in efforts to organize and to maintain industrial unions and like associations. Illustrative would be the relatively successful behavior of millions of factory workers in the 1930s and tens of thousands of farm workers during the late 1960s and early 1970s. These men and women have been able to obtain economic and political concessions from the state by working closely with middle- and upper-class persons committed to center- and left-democratic politics. Most important has been the power of blue-collar people to come together and to initiate major organizational innovations such as the Congress of Industrial Organizations (1936) and the Agricultural Farm Workers Organizing Committee (1966).

17. *Apparently, the upper classes do not determine everything that happens in the community.* In many cases, the upper classes may be virtually indifferent to certain events which transpire locally, as when, for example, a moderate racial voluntary association evolves a job-creation program of little consequence. Under these conditions, the local upper classes, especially the national corporate set, engage in approbation, a kind of power to assent. In turn, assenting implies the presence of political pluralism. In fact, assent here signifies no more than the acceptance of the politically innocuous.

Clearly, then, conspiracy to control everything is not involved. The upper classes cannot and would not want to be able to manipulate and coerce everything at will along preconceived lines. Even where their interests are involved, especially if they are center- or left-democrats, they must and will compromise with reality, especially if working-class people are in motion and professionals show signs of disaffection from upper-class norms and beliefs. Illustrative would be the mid- and late-1960s, when black worker insurrections moved many

professionals and hence corporations to involve themselves in programs that contradicted previous corporate policies, not to mention those of politicians with whom the corporations had in the past made alliance. Compromise was the order of the day. During the late 1960s the upper-class desires to minimize recurrent revolt and to maximize loyalty to the beliefs of private property and the state moved large sections of the upper class to be conciliatory. The hope for compromise with the rebelling wretched proved to be both primary and ascendant for a considerable length of time, i.e., until the blacks ceased to burn down whole sections of cities.

COUNTERINSURGENCY

Thoughtful on matters of domestic policy, many upper-class persons have also expressed considerable ingenuity when dealing with the task of undoing insurgent movements overseas. Let us be more precise on matters of overseas counterinsurgency, while holding in abeyance any discussion of possible parallel domestic policy. Actually, the term "counterinsurgency" can be analyzed on two levels:

1. The level of the upper classes, who view counterinsurgency as efforts on the part of their government to put down uprisings of insurgent masses unjustifiably manipulated by certain counterelites against overseas governments deemed to be essentially legitimate

2. The level of revolutionaries, who view counterinsurgency as efforts to engage in activity designed to smash the translating mechanisms of revolutions.

In the second sense, a counterinsurgency equals counterrevolutionary destruction of revolutionary charismatic leaders, political parties, military forces, concrete and abstract ideologies, and like forms associated with the organizational core of revolution. In place of revolution, the upper-class left- and center-democrats offer the ineffective palliatives of foreign aid.[18]

Domestically, counterinsurgency has taken a similar form. Reconstruction of metropolitan areas has in effect been abandoned. Rather, we

[18] Pierre Jalée, *The Pillage of the Third World* (New York: Monthly Review Press, 1968,) pp. 56–84, 97–115.

see the harassment, exile, and destruction of many revolutionary leaders as well as the elimination of several revolutionary political parties. Indeed, popular and tolerable access to revolutionary political material becomes limited to a relative handful of university intellectuals whose publicized freedom serves only to legitimate a political system which in fact effectively denies the bookish ones a mass political base. Remember that the upper classes fill most boards of governors positions and use their power to assent in favor of free expression only when it is in their interests not to veto free expression. Lest we forget, there are moments when the upper-class members employ the reserved right to initiate a purge of left-faculty through, for example, the powers to veto tenured appointments and to demand dismissal hearings. After all, some faculty, by supporting antiwar and other questionable activities, fail to adjust to upper-class norms. Worse yet, some social scientists on occasion neglect to pursue a behavioral science in keeping with the best interests of the university and the state. In this sense, these scientists fail to give science its proper direction and the university its proper due, at least in the eyes of its governors.

As we have seen, counterinsurgency assumes a scientific quality, as most social scientists collaborate with other professionals and attuned upper-class persons to use behavioral science to plot the best strategies for smashing revolutionary movements. Illustrative would be the ways in which American social scientists operate from a university base to advise and to do research for political elites.[19] Here there is a writing, lecturing, and mutual consulting relationship between the mandarin intellectuals and the professional state policy formulators, both of whom have positive and relatively secure ties with various sections of the upper class. This does not mean that all is sweetness and harmony. There is plenty of discord at the top and near the top, for clearly no one camp is omniscient, as numerous failures indicate. Were establishment camps without such histories, all total cultural revolutions in our time would have failed. But revolutionary successes have occurred, as in China and perhaps Vietnam, and

[19] Clark Kerr, *The Uses of the University* (New York: Harper Torchbooks, 1963), especially pp. 46–126.

they continue to create headaches for advisors to state on matters of how best to influence on matters of foreign policy.

Counterinsurgency has real consequences for real people, whatever the level of abstraction of the general formulations might be. French Indo-China is a case in point, as Ahmad has indicated (see his reading in Section Two of this chapter). Adverse consequences include death, wounds, and tortures among all classes of the native population undergoing revolution from within and counterrevolution from without. Very obvious, however, is the frequency with which death and pain find their victims among lower-class persons, who are most visible in the countryside where free-fire zones, troop movements, bombing missions, and occasional massacres decimate or even annihilate civilian populations unprotected from automatic rifles, artillery shellings, phosphorus bombs, and napalm innundations. Can we underestimate this power to coerce among and against the survivors of decimation?

Counterinsurgency does have consequences, but they are in part obscured not only by the apparent neutrality of the language of reporting of these deaths but by the thought model used to depict the victims of shot and shell, as Ahmad indicates. For counterinsurgency as practiced by this country includes presidential power to assent to the use of a language that reduces persons to symbols readily manipulated within a formal logic. When dealing with the victims, there is a propensity to substitute a high level of analytic generality for a gut-level of concrete atrocity within a terse deductive frame, thus obscuring to many the real world of screams and smells—the odor of released bowels mingled with blood which accompanies the military contingency of village massacre.

It is sometimes argued that all this need not happen, as if behavior were not determined by group demand, but rather by innocent, however mistaken, free will, and hence by a bad choice among available options. Overlooked in this antisociological perspective are the distinctions between left-, right-, and center-democratic, for the distinction presses us to observe the ideological and structural considerations that move center-democrats to compromise with insurgent guerrilla armies and revolutionary governments only after these governments have proved their mettle in battle and their people have experienced their decimation through war.

We can make successful predictions because people have known group associations and linked folkways, mores, and the like, not to mention certain styles of logic and class credos, as well as class and status-group interests. These structural and experiential forces press people to act within narrow limits. In effect, the idea of "choice of anything possible"—such as the upper-class abandonment of all its imperial interests and activities—runs counter to the historical practice of people (especially upper-class persons, with their long traditions of class consciousness) to choose along predictable lines within limits specified by antecedent and concomitant associations. That would be one clearcut instance of determinism. And determinism, after all, is the basis for a social science geared to quantification. From a positivist point of view, the free-will option is gossip with neither scientific foundation nor plausible explanation.

Difficult to explain, perhaps, is the behavior of the groups in America which have movingly opposed the U.S. government on the vital issues of the 1960s. Most significant in this regard are the students. Daring one moment, they disappear the next, only to surface later. Perhaps this behavior stems *in part* from very serious structural and ideological contradictions within a waning student movement. Perhaps efforts to resolve these systemic disharmonies have left little time or energy for the maintenance of high levels of participation among student leadership and the rank and file. In any event, in Section Three of this chapter we consider contradictions that emerged during the late 1960s. These issues, moreover, must be resolved before the Movement can regroup to deal with the reformulation of issues during the 1970s.

CONCLUSIONS AND TRANSITIONAL REMARKS

Admittedly we have not focused on the mechanisms of decision-making within the groups which have rendered important decisions on matters of overseas and domestic politics. Still, as we observed, *The New York Times's Pentagon Papers* substantiate our position that the upper classes make decisions in a manner consistent with their objective interests, although many of these persons have sufficient sense to know when a strategic withdrawal in the face of defeat is the best alternative. *The New York Times*'s decision to publish the Pentagon Papers illustrates the middle-democratic flexibility on how to pull back from a losing fight by damning publicly those who persist in hawkish postures, thus removing support from their prior legitimacy.

It is rumored that in addition to the detailed analyses of clique decisions on Vietnam there exist similar official documentaries on other world crises, such as the 1954 CIA takeover in Guatemala, the 1965 crisis in the Dominican Republic, and approximately ten other situations involving heavy U.S. military intervention since 1945.

Were we to have access to information like that contained in the Pentagon Papers, we would be better able to sharpen the propositions advanced in this chapter. These statements, sometimes phrased as if they were time- and data-tested propositions, nonetheless receive some support from the readings to be considered. In "The Theory and Fallacies of Counterinsurgency," Ahmad has placed in focus the role of the right- and center-democrats on matters of counterinsurgency overseas. But we should not view these overseas matters as if they were completely unrelated to what happens in this country. Money appropriated for overseas counterrevolutionary activities, after all, cannot find its way into antipoverty programs at home. And we must all live with the consequences of this overseas expenditure and home-town negligence.

To understand the home town, we cannot overlook the classic on the subject, C. Wright Mills's essay on "local society." Actually, his essay, for all its imperfections, gives a general picture of local power. His portrait sensitizes us to parameters of empirical evidence. A brilliant man, Mills. American political sociology, and certainly G. William Domhoff, is indebted to his political genius. Next to Mills, the political sociologists of our time pale in significance.

The Theory and Fallacies of Counterinsurgency

Eqbal Ahmad

To write on counterinsurgency one must first explain what the so-called insurgencies really are. In the United States that may be difficult because for the most part the social scientists who write on revolutionary warfare have been proponents of counterinsurgency. As a result, the biases of incumbents are built into the structure, images and language of contemporary Western, especially American, literature on the subject. We have come to accept ideologically contrived concepts and words as objective descriptions.

One could take innumerable examples—terrorism, subversion, pacification, urbanization, protective reaction, defensive interdiction, etc.—and expose the realities behind these words and phrases. The term counterinsurgency is itself an excellent example. Like all coinages in this area, it is value-laden and misleading. In fact, counterinsurgency is not at all directed against insurgency, which Webster defines as "a revolt against a government, not reaching the proportions of an organized revolution; and not recognized as belligerency." The truth is, the Congress and the country would be in uproar if the government were to claim that U.S. counterinsurgency capabilities could conceivably be available to its clients for putting down "revolts not reaching the proportions of an organized revolution." The truth is the opposite: Counterinsurgency is a multifaceted assault against organized revolutions. The euphemism is not used by accident, nor from ignorance. It serves to conceal the reality of a foreign policy dedicated to combating revolutions abroad; it helps to relegate revolutionaries to the status of outlaws. The reduction of a revolution to mere insurgency is also an implicit denial of its legitimacy. In this article, counterinsurgency and counterrevolution are used interchangeably.

Analytically, counterinsurgency may be discussed in terms of two primary models—the

■ Taken from *The Nation*, August 2, 1971, pp. 70–85; reprinted by permission.

conventional-establishment and the liberal-reformist; and two ancillary models—the punitive-militarist and the technological-attritive. I term these latter ancillary because they develop after the fact—from actual involvement in counterrevolution, and from interplay between the conventional and liberal institutions and individuals so involved. The models, though identifiable in terms of the intensity and scope of their application at given times, and in terms of the agencies and individuals favoring them, are operationally integrated in the field. I outline them here:

Although monolithic in its goal of suppressing revolutions, the theory and practice of counterinsurgency reflects the pluralism of the Western societies to which most of its practitioners and all of its theoreticians belong. A pluralistic, bargaining political culture induces an institutionalized compulsion to compromise. Within a defined boundary, there can be something for everyone. Hence, the actual strategy and tactics of counterinsurgency reflect compromise, no one blueprint being applied in its original, unadulterated form. This give-and-take contributes to a most fateful phenomenon of counterrevolutionary involvement: groups and individuals continue to feel that their particular prescriptions were never administered in full dosage and at the right intervals. They show a tendency toward self-justification, a craving to continue with and improve their formulas for success. Severe critics of specific "blunders" and "miscalculations," they still persist in seeing "light at the end of the tunnel." I shall return to this in discussing the Doctrine of Permanent Counterinsurgency.

SET BATTLES; "LIBERAL" DOCTRINE

We might view the conventional-establishment approach as constituting the common denominator of the assumptions and objectives shared by all incumbents; viz., an *a priori* hostility toward revolution, the view that its origins are conspiratorial, a managerial attitude toward it as a problem, and a technocratic-military approach to its solution. In strategy and tactics, this approach prefers conventional ground and air operations, requiring large deployments of troops, search-and-destroy missions (also called "mop-up operations"), the tactics of "encirclement" and "attrition"—which involve, on the one hand, large military fortifications (bases, enclaves) connected by "mobile" battalions (in Vietnam, helicopter-borne troops and air cavalry); and, on the other hand, massive displacement of civilian population and the creation of free-fire zones. The conventionalists also evince deep longings for set battles, and would multiply the occasions by forcing, surprising or luring the guerrillas into conventional showdowns. The results of these pressures are bombings (e.g., North Vietnam) or invasion of enemy "sanctuaries" across the frontiers of conflict (e.g., Cambodia) and the tactic of offering an occasional bait in the hope of luring the enemy to a concentrated attack (e.g., Dienbienphu, Khe Sanh).

If the conventional-establishment attitudes constitute the lowest common denominator of counterrevolution, the liberal-reformists are the chief exponents of its doctrine, and the most sophisticated programmers of its practice. They provide the core of the policies specifically associated with counterinsurgency: the creation of counter-guerrilla guerrillas (Special Forces); the stress on irregular tactics, on the one-ness of civilian and military roles; the insistence on maximum use of mercenaries, psychological warfare, counter-terror, and above all pacification. The term "liberal-reformist" reflects the expressed goals as well as the political background of individuals involved in defining and practicing this form of counterrevolution. Its rhetoric is reformist and liberal: "freedom," "progress," "development," "democracy," "reforms," "participation" and "self-determination" are its favorite working words. For the most part, its theorists, of whom a majority come from France and the United States, have been men of impeccable liberal credentials.

In France, the liberal-reformists included such eminent liberal politicians as Jacques Soustelle and Robert Lacoste. In the army its exponents were reputedly the most progressive commanders, those who had fought in the Re-

sistance against Nazi occupation or with the Free French Army. Humiliated by defeat in Indochina, they determined to practice *pacification* in Algeria. There, again frustrated by failures, these soldier-reformers increasingly meddled in politics. They helped destroy the Fourth Republic, rebelled against the Fifth, became accomplices of the European Ultras whom they had once openly detested and from whom they had been promising to deliver the Algerians, founded the fascistic OAS and ended by mercilessly massacring the natives whose freedom they had been claiming to protect.

In the United States, many of Kennedy's New Frontier men, and well-known university professors of liberal reputation at prestigious campuses, are prominent liberal-reformists. Research and development on counterinsurgency expanded dramatically during the Kennedy administration. As a sign of his special interest, Mr. Kennedy ordered that the Special Forces wear green berets, a symbol of elitism that had been resisted by the Joint Chiefs of Staff. Hanson Baldwin, military analyst for *The New York Times*, complained that counterinsurgency "has become a fetish with the President, and of course all the military schools are reflecting this White House concern." Even the Chaplains' Corps developed a counterinsurgency program.

The punitive-militarist style is a product of the liberal-reformist doctrine of counterinsurgency; but it invariably acquires a life of its own. It entails irregular tactics, small-unit deployments, efficiently and relentlessly executed reprisals against civilians suspected of aiding guerrillas, the systematic use of torture, the murder of prisoners, and the institution of total control over the population. In theory, pacification demands that the friendly or neutral population be treated with kindness and consideration. In practice, it is impossible to distinguish between friendly and hostile villagers: the men are seldom around; the women are always sad and solicitous; the children, sullen or noisy. Strangers and afraid, soldiers in an alien environment strewn with booby traps can do no else than perceive the civilians as hostile and meet their ordered or understood quota of body counts. They make few pretenses about winning hearts and minds, although in deference to the principles of pacification candies are sometimes distributed, music is played, and food and first aid are provided to survivors—especially after a hard strike.

In Algeria this form of warfare was known as "*style-para,*" in reference to the paratroopers of General Massu whose exploits included "winning" the hair-raising Battle of Algiers. In Vietnam it is practiced more generally; although it appears to be especially popular with the U.S. Special Forces and the mercenaries recruited by them, the Koreans and the ARVN ranger battalions. The main virtue of this style is that, unlike the massive "mop-ups" and impersonal bombings of conventional operations, it produces somewhat personalized massacres, like that of My Lai, which give the victims no less than the killers a sense at least of human contact; it also generates some public understanding of the war crimes which counterrevolutionary interventions often entail.

WAR BY PROXY

An increasing reliance on technological-attritive methods signals the shift of counter-revolutionary foreign intervention in a genocidal direction. When a war to crush a revolution has been definitively lost—i.e., when the moral isolation and illegitimacy of the client regime become total and irreversible; when even a prolonged and massive foreign intervention fails to break the "enemy's" will to resist, while producing widespread anti-war sentiment at home; when draftees become restive and resistant; when the protracted war is seen to be bad for business and begins to contribute to the compounded distress of inflation and recession, then a great power caught in counterrevolutionary operations has but two choices: it can negotiate withdrawal, as de Gaulle did in Algeria, or it can continue the war, and subsequently a quasi-permanent occupation of the belligerent country, at a price acceptable to the people at home, but costly to the "insurgents" abroad. It is the latter choice that President Nixon has made with his policy of Vietnamization. A "semantic hoax," as Sen. Harold E. Hughes described it, Vietnamization is a euphemism for further mechanization of the war. It is also, as Senator George McGovern has stated, a manipulation to "tranquilize the conscience of America while our government wages war by proxy. . . ."

Sir Robert Thompson, a trusted adviser of Mr. Nixon and renowned expert on counterinsurgency, whose optimistic evaluation of Vietnamization was cited in the President's policy statement as proof of its success, describes it as a "long haul, low cost" strategy. It is worth noting a few of the considerations that went into its making. First, Sir Robert warns in *No Exit from Vietnam* of the impact made in a democratic society "by the coffins coming home, and by higher taxes." Second, he estimates that it "will certainly take ten to fifteen years" to achieve the desired goal—a politically stable, non-Communist, independent state of South Vietnam. Hence, he advises that, in order to maintain public acceptance of a protracted involvement, one must show some progress: "As soon as progress is visible, even though success may still be many years away, time ceases to be such an important factor. There will be few indeed who are not then prepared to take the extra time required for victory." Third, Sir Robert thinks that "there is nothing new about the horror and tragedy of the Vietnam war except that it has been exposed to the camera and brought into the sitting room." He notes that "running insurgency sores in some Latin American countries . . . have made very little impact outside the area of conflict."

Making the war domestically acceptable, then, means turning it into a "forgotten war" (Laos is a model), demoting it to the back pages of newspapers, keeping it at a maximum distance from TV cameras. It means stimulating illusions of progress, whatever the reality. Above all, it demands lowering the monetary costs and the American casualties. The former requires a reduction of the expensive American manpower; the latter dictates avoidance of active fighting by U.S. ground forces. Both measures help maintain the illusion of progress and keep the public quiet.

At the same time, if victory is ever to be grasped, the war must remain very expensive for the enemy. His strength must be sapped, his political "infrastructure" destroyed, his morale undermined, his resources and base depleted. It should be underscored that the latter is identified by Sir Robert as being "not outside the country" nor "jungles and swamps" but the "populated areas" "under insurgent control" and even those "areas still ostensibly under government control." He recommends a return to the techniques of counterinsurgency which he successfully practiced in Malaya and which he has been prescribing as an adviser on Vietnam for more than a decade—in the conviction, of course, that they have never been fully implemented. These include: inducing the Saigon regime to act lawfully, but without preventing it from passing emergency laws; improving civil and military administration; defining the obligations of the central government and the villages; selecting priority areas for pacification; mounting fix-and-destroy operations in the areas outside the selected "ring." Finally: "Offensive operations into contested and enemy held areas will still be necessary, for which reason the securely held areas should be limited to allow for an adequate reserve of forces for such operations."

Obviously, if the goal of defeating the NLF while minimizing American costs and casualties is to be attained, the Saigon government must progressively take over the task of governing and fighting. If the Saigon regime does not or cannot do so, then the United States, unwilling to negotiate withdrawal, has only one choice: maximum replacement of men with machines, for "cost-effective" offensive operations in the areas Sir Robert defines as enemy base. Later on in this article, I shall return to the irrelevance of Sir Robert's and others' administrative prescriptions for a country that has been fighting a long and bitter war of national liberation, and where no amount of managerial manipulation by a foreign power can equip its native "elite" with even a semblance of legitimacy. Especially it cannot do so when that elite carries the stigma of treachery, having actively collaborated with colonial France and now sanctioning the systematic destruction, by the succeeding foreign power, or the people and country it claims to govern. Hence, notwithstanding the counterinsurgents' recommendations, and their deep faith in the power of borrowed, bureaucratic, "cost-effective" "innovations," the Saigon government could not take over the war even in "ten to fifteen years," as Sir Robert surmised in his most optimistic year of the war in Vietnam. A brief look at the facts compels a very somber estimate of the prospects for Vietnamization.

A NATION OF REFUGEES

As a consequence of the massive American military presence and the bomb-induced "urbanization" (in Laos, the "strategic movement of people"), the Saigon regime is now in a worse predicament than ever, although a "residual" American force might keep the government in power indefinitely. A third of South Vietnam's people are estimated to be refugees (so are 25 percent of Laotians, and more than a million Cambodians), almost entirely because of the "air support" provided by the United States. The Senate Judiciary Subcommittee on Refugees, headed by Sen. Edward Kennedy [see "Indochina: A Slaughter of Innocents" by Sen. Edward M. Kennedy, *The Nation*, June 28, 1971], has shown how the pacification agencies and the Saigon government collaborate to "solve" the refugee problem by "reclassifying the refugees out of existence."

I mention the refugees rather than the dead because this "urbanized" mass, though classified out of existence, is still a reality; it makes the cities as hopeless for the incumbent regime as are the rural areas. Students, workers and Buddhists have recently risked severe repression to raise their voices in opposition. Informed sources in Paris tell me that Saigon's shrewdest politicians are quietly currying favor with the Provisional Revolutionary Government (PRG); some courageous conservatives like Deputy Ngo Con Duc openly favor a provisional, coalition government of reconciliation.

In 1970 inflation rose by 50 percent in Vietnam. According to *The New York Times* (July 27, 1970) ARVN's rate of desertion was "up nearly 50 percent during the summer months of 1970," despite what officials termed the "morale building effects of recent operations in Cambodia." In Cambodia itself two paratrooper battalions of the expeditionary force "were operating with only 65 percent of their manpower—the rest having deserted." General Do Cao Tri, Commander of the III Corps area which includes Saigon, and leader of the Cambodian expedition, is reported to have been less conservative with his estimates. General Tri was killed last March commanding the ill-fated Laotian invasion. He told newsmen in Dalat that 75 percent of his soldiers desert; of those remaining less than half wish to fight, and for every ARVN soldier killed in battle, nine desert.

Meanwhile, *The New York Times* (October 19, 1970) disclosed a top-secret CIA report to the effect that, in response to Vietnamization, the NLF had infiltrated some 30,000 spies, reaching the highest levels of the Saigon government and including its secret services; that the "VC infrastructure" remained impenetrable, and that both conditions depended upon the complicity of the majority of the government's civilian and defense employees. The "disclosure" may have been meant to prepare the public for more repression and purges by the Thieu-Ky regime, but its significance is clear: its foreign trustees know that the regime, isolated from the people, is also hollow and eroding from within. Even Sir Robert is reported to have returned gloomy from his recent "mission to Macedonia," as he unblushingly calls Vietnam, fancying his relationship to Mr. Nixon as being the modern equivalent of the expert-advisers to Roman emperors.

Such being the realities of Vietnamization, a U.S. government intent on winning can only mechanize the war. GIs are being replaced by airplanes, electronic devices, helicopter-gunships, long-range artillery, a variety of anti-personnel weapons, massive defoliation, crop destruction, and depopulation. The details of these daily crimes and the amount of damage they do is not and may never be completely known, especially since the U.S. Government remains the primary source of information. As *The New York Times* has commented editorially, "The headlines gradually faded, but the air-war did not." Nor did the chemical war, nor helicopter hunting, nor the gruesome anti-personnel weapons which maim indiscriminately and leave so many disabled to be cared for.

If the population is to the guerrillas what water is to fish, the ultimate weapon of a degenerate but powerful counterinsurgency is to drain the water. Mr. Johnson embarked on that course, and Mr. Nixon is continuing it more skillfully, and perhaps more consciously, than did his predecessor. The policy may not be genocidal in intent; its goal appears to be attrition. And depending on how technically the word genocide is defined, it may not be so in effect if it succeeds, as I believe it will not, in yielding to the United States the beaten and sunk remainder of a once proud and brave people—a sort of 20th-century Indian reservation in the heart of Asia.

In counterinsurgency, then, democratic "pluralism" is experienced by the targetted population in its corrupt, morally inverted form. In the field the different styles blend. The guerrillas and the masses suffer all four: they are swept and bombed conventional style; punished and tortured para-style; quartered and controlled pacification style; and finally, face the prospects of a "long-haul, lowcost" technological extermination. In the lexicon of counterrevolutionaries these wars are "limited" only in their consequences for the intervening power. For the people and country under assault, they are total.

THE BLUNDERS OF BIAS

The attitudes and assumptions shared by all believers in counterinsurgency may be summarized as follows:

Revolutionary warfare is seen as a threat. In *To Move a Nation*, Roger Hilsman recalls that, "from the beginning of his administration, the President [Kennedy] was convinced that the *techniques* of 'revolutionary warfare' constituted a special kind of threat. . . ." In an address to the National War College, Vice President Humphrey spoke of this "bold, new form of aggression which could rank with the discovery of gunpowder" as constituting "the major challenge to our security." If guerrilla warfare is viewed as the latest enemy weapon, Vietnam is its testing ground. "If guerrilla techniques succeed in Vietnam," wrote James Reston in *The New York Times*, "nobody in Washington dare assume that the same techniques will not be applied in all Communist rimlands from Korea to Iran." It is this view of revolutionary warfare as a menacing technique, a weapon lethal to the interests of the United States, that has led counterrevolutionary scholars like W. W. Rostow to portray the invasion of Vietnam as a war to end wars. He told a University of Leeds audience that:

> . . . if we have the common will to hold together and get on with the job—the struggle in Vietnam might be the last great confrontation of the postwar era. . . . If the Cuban missile crisis was the Gettysburg of the cold war, Vietnam could be the Wilderness for, indeed, the cold war has been a kind of global civil conflict. Vietnam could be made the closing of one chapter in modern history and the opening of another.

The negative bias prevents an understanding of the unprecedented popularity of armed revolutions in the Third World today, and the capacity of some to expand and sustain their struggle against incredibly heavy odds. Their purpose being counterrevolutionary, the theorists and practitioners of counterinsurgency cannot grasp or will not acknowledge the illegitimacy of incumbents, the finality of broken political and social links, and the forging of new ones. A recognition of the revolutionary process, its causes, creative thrust, inherent justice, and the legitimacy that can be attained by a revolutionary movement would cost the counterinsurgent his *raison d'être*. Understandably, he concentrates on studying and imitating the "techniques" and "tactics" of revolutionary warfare, while never comprehending the essence, the inner logic, of revolutions. I. F. Stone has accurately described a peculiarity of the literature on counterinsurgency in *In Time of Torment:*

> In reading the military literature on guerrilla warfare now so fashionable at the Pentagon, one feels that these writers are like men watching a dance from outside through heavy plate glass windows. They see the motions but they can't hear the music. They put the mechanical gestures down on paper with pedantic fidelity. But what rarely comes through to them are the injured racial feelings, the misery, the rankling slights, the hatred, the devotion, the inspiration and the desperation. So they do not really understand what leads men to abandon wife, children, home, career, friends; to take to the bush and live gun in hand like a hunted animal; to challenge overwhelming military odds rather than acquiesce any longer in humiliation, injustice or poverty. . . .

SIMPLIFICATION BY TECHNIQUE

There is a theory that views revolutionary warfare as being the product of conspiracy which should be handled primarily as a technical problem; i.e., a problem of plotting and subversion on the one hand and of intelligence and suppression on the other. As the chief conspiratorial group, the "Communists" are alleged to be the most likely initiators and beneficiaries of such revolutions. As was evident from the earlier quotations on the threat of guerrillas, "technique" is a key word in coun-

terinsurgency. "We have a long way to go," Defense Secretary McNamara told a Congressional committee in 1963, "in devising and implementing effective counter-measures against the Communist techniques. But this is a challenge we must meet if we are to defeat the Communists in this kind of war. It is quite possible that in the decade of the 1960s the decisive struggle will take place in this area."

Given the preoccupation with technique, conduct of counterinsurgency is viewed as largely an exercise in the strategy and tactics of pacification and combat—that is, in managerial and military experimentations which come to be viewed as two facets of "one war." The military advantages of guerrillas—mobility, freedom from logistical tethers, good intelligence, surprise, etc.—are studied, and countermeasures are developed. Irregular and covered terrain is considered a primary condition for guerrilla warfare, as is the complicity of a coerced population. Therefore, counterinsurgent troops are trained in jungle warfare, and are taught to WHAM (Win Hearts And Minds).

The desire for technical experience has given U.S. officials their only credible, though infrequently expressed, justification for invading Vietnam. In 1963, Gen. Maxwell Taylor explained to a Congressional committee:

> Here we have a going laboratory where we see subversive insurgency, the Ho Chi Minh doctrine, being applied in all its forms. This has been a challenge not just for the armed services, but for several of the agencies of government, as many of them are involved in one way or another in South Vietnam. On the military side, however, we have recognized the importance of the area as a laboratory. We have teams out there looking at the equipment requirements of this kind of guerrilla warfare. We have rotated senior officers through there, spending several weeks just to talk to people and get the feeling of the operation, so even though not regularly assigned to Vietnam, they are carrying their experience back to their own organizations.

Six years and at least 4 million casualties later, General Westmoreland said that Vietnam had in fact been a valuable laboratory for testing new weapons and techniques; that the "lessons" and "devices" coming out of there are "revolutionizing" the techniques of warfare;

that having inflicted in Vietnam "over two-thirds of enemy casualties," long-range artillery and the air force have proved their capacity to "rain destruction anywhere on the battlefield within minutes . . . whether friendly troops are present or not"; that with new electronic devices the enemy can be mechanically located, tracked and targetted; and that technology will achieve a "tremendous economy of manpower." The General is technically accurate; he may even be right in believing that "no more than ten years" separate us from the "automated battlefield." If that is so, U.S. withdrawal may yet meet Sir Robert's timetable.

However, the trouble with the tracking, targetting, and locating devices is that they are even less capable of distinguishing between civilians and combatants than are the GIs; they cannot even distinguish between human beings and animals. Such, for example, is the defect of that most recent device for counterinsurgency—the "people sniffer." Some purists of pacification disapprove of such weapons, but by so doing they only accuse themselves of inconsistency, for these devices are the logical product of the interaction between counterinsurgency and technology. When a technologically superior country commits itself to developing techniques against a people's war, it must end by producing and using weapons of mass murder.

ORDERS FROM MOSCOW

The conspiratorial theory provides justification for counterinsurgency and foreign intervention. The French theorists were notorious for ascribing all "insurgencies" to communism. In their view Algeria's FLN was a puppet alternately of Moscow, Peking, and Cairo; today their American colleagues view the NLF as a puppet of North Vietnam and/or China. Even Sir Robert Thompson, the shrewdest and by popular acclaim the most cogent exponent of counterinsurgency, begins his first book, *Defeating Communist Insurgency*, with a discussion of communism which, he says, "was no real threat to *the security of the colonial governments or the well-being of the peoples of Southeast Asia*" until after World War II (italics added). Sir Robert is not unique in coupling the security of the foreign presence with the welfare of the natives; his French and American

counterparts do the same. Nor is the habit of viewing anti-colonial and radical nationalist movements as facets, or at least dupes, of the international conspiracy uncommon, even among certified "anti-colonialist" American liberals. The association of communism with guerrilla warfare and radical nationalism helps justify U.S. involvement in counterrevolutionary operations ranging from Ethiopia to Uruguay.

The conspiratorial theory of revolution also permits distorted interpretations of the revolutionary process. For example, Sir Robert Thompson believes that the place and time of insurgency depends on "orders from Moscow." He notes that in liberated areas insurgents are "careful to reduce taxes on land and crops well below the government level, or even to remit them for a period." "This," he asserts, "they can afford to do, having no overheads, and still not lack for money." The absence of overheads is not explained; and his suggestion that the Malayan Races Liberation Army, and the NLF (Vietnam) are financially better off than their British and American opponents would be hilarious if it were not so cruel.

A logical component of the conspiratorial theory is the belief, held with particular tenacity by counterrevolutionary army officers, that any revolutionary movement is inspired, directed, and controlled from abroad. The sanctuary from which guerrillas can smuggle supplies and where they train their troops is considered the primary factor to their success. W. W. Rostow, Special Assistant to President Kennedy, stated in a widely acclaimed speech of 1961 that "We are determined to help destroy this international disease, that is, guerrilla war designed, initiated, supplied, and led from outside an independent nation." Indeed so strong was the belief in the external origins of guerrillas that Washington promoted plans for "offensive use of guerrillas" against undesirable regimes. Their performance in the Bay of Pigs, and inside North Vietnam does not appear to have discouraged the enthusiasts. The *Times* of London (April 20, 1968) reported that (*a*) the South Vietnamese agents were trained by the CIA in Special Forces camps; (*b*) 95 percent casualties were admitted in 1963 ("a complete fiasco"); and (*c*) these operations became a conduit for opium trade.

It is hard to comment briefly on such simplification of a complex problem. An active sanctuary can be very important, especially in cases where a great power intervenes with its full might. However, it is not essential to success. In Cuba, Yugoslavia, and China the revolutionaries did not have active sanctuaries. In Burma, and to a lesser extent in Greece, sanctuaries proved of limited value. Neither the extremely effective Morice line in Algeria, nor the Lattre line around the Red River Delta, nor the armored Ping-Han Japanese railroad in North China had much effect on the outcome of these wars. Politically and militarily, revolutionary guerrillas tend to make a fetish of self-reliance, and can go on fighting indefinitely even if infiltration from across the border stops. There is overwhelming evidence that, before massive U.S. escalation of the war necessitated Northern aid, the NLF was entirely self-sufficient in South Vietnam; the bulk of its arms was captured or bought from Saigon. John Mecklen, a former U.S. senior diplomat in Saigon, put it succinctly when he stated (*Mission in Torment*) that the interdiction of Northern supplies to South Vietnam would weaken the Vietcong "probably not much more than the efficiency of the Pentagon would be reduced if the air-conditioning were shut off."

On the other hand, pressure by the incumbent or occupying army for conventional attack on an external sanctuary is a good indicator that the war has been lost on the home ground. When they engage in revolutionary warfare, professional armies trained for conventional combat follow a vicious logic of escalation which derives from acute frustration over a foe so elusive as to put in question, not only their effectiveness but the very validity of their training and organization. Moreover, the morale of professional soldiers cannot be maintained if they know they are fighting against a popular revolution. Hence, the compulsion to believe that behind the popular behavior lies the terror of an army trained, equipped, and directed by a foreign power, and the wish to draw the enemy into open battles. (Military officers often attest that they subject civilians to artillery fire and air raids in the hope that, deprived of civilian cover, the guerrillas will be forced to come out and fight a major engagement.)

Since reprisals against the population fail to produce the desired result, carrying the war to some other sovereign nation becomes the only road to a conventional showdown. In Algeria, it led the French to participate in the invasion of Suez, then to a single bombing raid of the Tunisian border town of Sakiet Sidi Youssef, which produced considerable international protest, including that of John F. Kennedy. Had the French Government succumbed to the urgings of its army, France would have been the first power to violate the international practice of respecting the rights of sanctuary—a principle that was observed in Korea, Greece, Cyprus and Malaya. We can guess what the United States might do if the Vietnamese were to bomb its sanctuaries in Thailand or the Pacific Ocean. But what position will it take, as the major world power, when Portugal, Rhodesia and South Africa follow its example and invade the African "sanctuaries" of their opponents? When practiced by a superpower, counterinsurgency involves the progressive breaking of the few rules that help keep potentially conflagrating conflicts within national boundaries.

WHO BUILDS; WHO DESTROYS

The revolutionary movement is believed to enjoy considerable advantage because, in the words of W. W. Rostow, "its task is merely to destroy, while the government must build and protect what it is building." Whether seriously held or consciously contrived, the view contradicts the findings of those who have studied and observed these movements. Given the inevitable, and generally vast, disparity of military strength between the guerrillas and the government, the success of a revolutionary movement depends on covert and sustained support from a substantial portion of the population. Revolutionary warfare does not occur from simple discontent of the sort that produces riots and demonstrations but from a sense of desperation and a determination to end injustices, foreign occupation, and humiliation. It demands patience under prolonged suffering, and a resolute conspiracy of silence and militancy. A people can summon up such strength only if it feels morally alienated from its formal rulers, when the latter's title to authority is actively rejected by the masses.

Once a revolutionary movement enters the guerrilla phase, its central objective is to confirm and perpetuate the moral isolation of the discredited regime by creating "parallel hierarchies." The major task of the movement, then, is not to outfight but to out-legitimize and out-administer the government. It must establish a measure of land reform, reduce rents, equalize wages, build an administrative structure to collect taxes, provide some education and social welfare, and maintain a modicum of economic activity. A revolutionary guerrilla movement which did not have these constructive concerns and structures to fulfill its obligations to the populace would degenerate into banditry. Even while clandestine, the parallel government must prove its efficacy, and maintain a measure of accountability to the population. These are not easy tasks, nor destructive undertakings. It would be a rare revolutionary war in which the government's destruction of civilian population and property did not surpass, by a wide margin, the guerrillas' selective terror and sabotage.

The liberal-reformist theorists of pacification have gained a certain comprehension of the interdependence of political, military and psychological factors in revolutionary warfare. While still holding that guerrilla wars result from conspiracy and are waged by remote control, they see that the cooperation, or at least the neutrality, of a passive population is essential to their success. They recognize that politics plays the dominant role in such conflicts, and that, for revolutionaries, civilians are and remain the primary subject of attention. They admit the central importance of "ideology" and a "cause" around which the masses can be mobilized, and allow that acute grievances stimulate popular support for revolutionaries.

Having understood that much, these theorists draw heavily on what they construe to be the revolutionary model. They search for a counter-ideology to compete with the revolutionary one. Strategic hamlets are the intended equals of popular base areas. Psychological warfare counters revolutionary political work. Pacification teams duplicate the revolutionary cadres. Re-education centers seek to reverse the guerrillas' commitment.

REMEMBERING THE REDSKIN

The limited insight into the revolutionary process is dissipated by the colonial antecedents of counterinsurgency, its bureaucratic bias, and continued focus on coercion as a means of obtaining popular support. Since classical liberalism provides little justification for counter-revolutionary involvements abroad, pacification theorists seek it in related Western traditions. This invariably entails a revival of the colonial and conservative ethos of the nation. The French, much like their American colleagues, emphasize that "pacification" is part of the Western tradition, that conventional warfare gained ascendancy only during the two World Wars, and that it is again being superseded by "limited," unconventional conflicts. In their search for Western models and cultural continuity, the French theorists invoked the heyday of colonialism. They frequently cited the colonizers of North Africa—General Bugeaud, Marshals Lyautey and Gallieni. They extolled the doctrine of these men on the identity of civilian and military authority, the role of *officier-administrateur* and *officier-educateur*; they emulated their methods.

In the United States the experience with the Indians and other colonial exploits provide the source of inspiration. "It is ironic that we Americans have to learn this military lesson again in the twentieth century, . . . " wrote Roger Hilsman. After reminding his audience of American experiences in irregular warfare, in "Indian fighting," he recalls the colonization of the Philippines:

> We Americans have also forgotten that it was we who fought one of the most successful counter-guerrilla campaigns in history—in the Philippines back at the turn of the century. We learned some fundamental military lessons then, and it is time we remembered them. . . .

Mr. Hilsman then recites some gory details, and draws some "fundamental lessons" from the defeat of the "extremists" and "bands of religious fanatics" who were vile enough to resist foreign occupation. The lessons include: (*a*) Maximum use of native mercenaries, as demonstrated by the "fabulous exploits" of the "famed Philippine constabulary." (*b*) Leadership role for Americans—"over each group [of native recruits] we put a trained American officer—a bold and determined leader." (*c*) Adoption of the "Indian fighting" tactic of surprise and night-time attacks—"the solution is to adopt the same weapons to fight him." Mr. Hilsman does not mention that the "successful"

Philippine campaign was, in the words of Bernard Fall, " ... the bloodiest colonial war (in proportion to population) ever fought by a white power in Asia; it cost the lives of 300,000 Filipinos."

Despite a rhetoric that stresses the primacy of politics and calls peaceful revolution the goal, the liberal-reformists treat counterinsurgency essentially as an administrative problem, subject to managerial and technical solutions. Even Sir Robert Thompson, who shows keen understanding of some aspects of revolutionary warfare, sees the problem from a fundamentally bureaucratic viewpoint. "The bias of this book," he says in the introduction of his highly acclaimed *Defeating Communist Insurgency*, "is heavily weighted on the administrative and other aspects of an insurgency." He offers a detailed and technically impeccable critique of the weaknesses of counterinsurgency in Vietnam—cabinet-style government is lacking, the country is divided into too many provinces, hamlets are too small to be viable administrative units, the army has become larger than the police, security forces are fragmented, strategic hamlets are carelessly administered.

Sir Robert's criticism is correct but irrelevant, for no amount of bureaucratic wisdom could win the war in Vietnam. A relevant analysis would consider the actual or potential legitimacy of the local as well as national authority represented by the Saigon regime, and would appraise honestly the causes and character of the linkages between the revolutionary movement and the Vietnamese masses. But the colonial and bureaucratic mentality that wages counterinsurgency precludes such objectivity.

"UNDERSTANDING" THE "PROBLEM"

As noted earlier, revolutionary warfare demands the development of new styles and institutions before power can be attained. In order to elicit, under conditions of extreme stress, full and voluntary participation by the people, the revolutionary leaders and cadres must form organic ties with them. Revolutionary style and institutions are most successful when they are qualitatively different from the existing ones and, at the same time, appeal to the deepest and most natural yearnings of the masses. In revolutions, therefore, life begins to manifest

itself in forms that are incomprehensible to bureaucrats and social engineers. Wolin and Schaar's analysis (in "Berkeley: The Battle of People's Park," *New York Review of Books*, June 19, 1969) of the "educational bureaucracy" applies admirably to the counterinsurgency experts: "The bureaucratic search for 'understanding' does not begin in wonder, but in the reduction of the world to the ordinary and manageable. In order to deal with the world in the cognitive mode, the world must first be approached as an exercise in 'problem-solving.' " Finding the solution implies devising the right techniques; hence "reality is parsed into an ensemble of discrete though related parts, and each part is assigned to the expert specially assigned to deal with that part."

Examples of the "reduction of the world to the ordinary and manageable" abound in the literature of counterrevolution. One will suffice here: Prof. Ithiel de Sola Pool rules out as "not acceptable" "the inclusion of the Vietcong in a coalition government or even the persistence of the Vietcong as a legal organization in South Vietnam." That yields him a problem: "the Vietcong is too strong to be simply beaten or suppressed." Whereupon cognitive dissonance theory suggests the solution: "discontented leadership" has "the potential for making a total break when the going gets too rough." The latter having been achieved by American firepower, the Vietcong will need "a political rationalization for changing sides." Pacification must address itself to this task. The Vietcong "image of reality" and "naive ideology," which regards the Saigon government as consisting of America's puppets and the peasants' exploiters, must be replaced by a more realistic view. Toward this end reforms should be introduced; and the Vietcong cadres who will then desert should be given the opportunity to serve the government.

Prof. de Sola Pool is no novice in political analysis; he is chairman of the Political Science Department at M.I.T. Nor is he a stranger to Vietnam; over the years he has been conducting research there for the Pentagon. Yet, that is how he understands the dedication and motivation of the men who have successfully resisted, for more than two bloody decades, the fully employed might of one great power and one superpower. In counterrevolution, political analysis bows to the pathology of bureaucratic perception.

Similarly, while the counterrevolutionaries display deep interest in revolutionary programs and organization, they see these as being opportunistically and instrumentally motivated. For example, land reform by revolutionaries is thought to be an instrument for establishing control in the countryside, not as the positive outcome of the complex interaction between the revolutionary movement and the masses, nor as the result of strongly held convictions. "In many cases," writes Douglas Pike, the U.S. Government's most renowned expert on Vietnam, of the NLF land reform, "this amounted to a virtual bribe; the rural Vietnamese was offered the thing he wanted above all else: Land." He does not say in his book, *Vietcong*, why Saigon and the United States have been unwilling or unable to offer a similar "bribe," nor what happens to the peasant's land when the government regains control of a village.

HOW THE THREAD WAS LOST

It is natural that their own opportunism and preoccupation with stability and control should lead these theorists at first to qualify, then to distort, and finally to abandon their central, and only positive theme—that revolutionary warfare has its basis in acute grievances, and that the achievement of social, economic, and political progress will reduce the chances of its outbreak and/or success.

The qualification begins with the argument that, although "modernization" is essential in the "long run," social and economic inequities and injustices pose no real threat to stability until they are exploited by conspirators. The essential requirements of stability are, therefore, efficient administration ("that 'steel frame' in which India takes such just pride ... " says Hilsman); and policing of the population. Hence, reforms are seen only as useful auxiliaries to "pacification." Hilsman concludes: "To summarize my feeling on popularity [of government], reform, and modernization: (*1*) they are important ingredients but are not the determinants of events; (*2*) their role must be measured more in terms of their contribution to physical security than we generally realize." As the dialectic of pacification ap-

proaches its denouement, a counterrevolutionary "revisionism" emerges from these qualifications that is totalitarian in precept, genocidal in effect. It postulates that the population's behavior, not its attitude, the revolutionary infrastructure's destruction, not the establishment of a government's popularity, are the operative factors in defeating "insurgency."

The distortion develops, among other reasons, from a continuing conviction that "coercion" and "terror" are the bases of the guerrillas' mass support. At their best, counterinsurgency experts display obvious contradiction between their rhetoric and their perception of reality. Sir Robert states that the "Communists are normally careful, however, not to murder a popular person before he has been discredited ... are careful not to undertake general terror against the population as a whole. ... Terror is more effective when selective. This allows the Communist behavior toward the people as a whole to be good and strict discipline is used to enforce it." Yet he describes it as a "policy of wholesale murder ... designed to keep the local population completely cowed."

Similarly CIA specialist Douglas Pike presents considerable evidence that except in the rarest instance, the NLF's use of sabotage and assassination is sociologically selective, politically judicious, and psychologically liberating. Yet his conclusions stand out in glaring opposition to his facts. One is struck by the schizophrenic quality of his study. Such distorted appraisals provide justification for the government's "counter-terror," which begins with "selective" reprisals only to escalate into massive and indiscriminate violence.

The fact is, however, that a highly committed but covert civilian support cannot be obtained at gun point. Only degenerate or defeated guerrillas are known to have risked the loss of mass support by terrorizing civilians. In order to be effective, terror must be regarded by the people at large as an extragovernmental effort to dispense justice long overdue; and it must have the effect of freeing oppressed communities from the constraints of coercive, illegitimate authority.

Given their low opinion of the masses, incumbents belatedly discover that their "counter-terror" produces results quite opposite from those expected or desired. This realization increases their frustration and feeling of moral isolation. Instead of being a corrective, this late and hazy perception of reality only augments their desperation and brings incredible acts of inversion. For example, the bombing and burning of villages are often justified on the ground that the affected villagers will blame the Vietcong for "exposing" them to government reprisals; it is believed that the enemy thus loses popular support.

Since they are interested only in operational payoffs, the counterinsurgents' investigation into revolutionary theory and practice tends to be selective, superficial and systems-oriented. For example, the military writings of Mao Tse-tung are reproduced and cited out of their political context; their specific, local character is ignored, and Mao is presented as a system-builder, rather than the leader of a historical revolution. "Systems" orientation as well as the conspiratorial view produce a bias in favor of seeking similarities among revolutions. Hence, the theorists often overlook the fact that, despite many similarities with the Chinese, the Vietnamese, Algerians, and Cubans fought very different wars, and owed little to Mao's "doctrine." At the same time, these same theorists rarely acknowledge that the similarities among those revolutions result more from common conditions (e.g., foreign occupation) than from a common doctrine of source of conspiracy.

The counterrevolutionists are ultimately concerned with order more than participation, with control more than the consent of the governed, with stability more than change. As a result, their prescriptions combine a considerable technical expertise with an oblique if not altogether distorted view of the needs and demands of the people. Their indebtedness to what they construe to be the insurgent model is unmistakable; but their understanding of it remains crooked. The "reflection in the mirror is sharp," wrote Peter Paret of the French counterrevolutionary doctrine in Algeria, "while the thing reflected remains shadowy." And so we return to Stone's classic description of these men, "watching a dance from outside through heavy plate glass windows. They see the motions but they can't hear the music. . . ."

Incumbents are by definition incapable of seriously seeking the removal of the causes upon which a successful revolution may be based.

France, America, and their local collaborators could not credibly claim national liberation to be their goals in Algeria and Vietnam. Algerian *colons* and Vietnamese landlords, who formed the backbone of incumbency, could not be serious about instituting meaningful land reforms. Lacking a genuine revolutionary, even reformist, commitment, unable or unwilling to acknowledge the real aspirations of the people, the counterrevolutionists miss the crux of the matter. Hence, they progressively give up on winning the hearts, and concentrate instead on conquering the minds ("it's the minds that matter," says Sir Robert), and destroying the bodies. It is a nemesis of the liberal-reformist approach that it breeds among its believers contempt for the very liberal values and democratic institutions which they claim to represent.

IMPORTED IDEOLOGY

Contemporary revolutions have been occurring in the non-Western world, but to a man the counterinsurgency theorists are Westerners. More than their native clients they need ideological and moral arguments to justify their intervention. Hence the counterinsurgent ideology seldom develops in response to local needs; it is mechanically manufactured or imported, and characteristically lacks not only native roots but even the necessary adaptations to local culture and values. In his famous *Foreign Affairs* article (October 1964), Gen. Edward G. Lansdale, the high priest of counterinsurgency in America, stated that the "Communists have let loose a revolutionary idea in Vietnam and that it will not die by being ignored, bombed or smothered by us." The answer, says the General, is to "oppose the Communist idea with a better idea. . . ." And to do so "on the ground itself," he proposes that the United States take two steps to establish a "political base":

First . . . state political goals founded on principles cherished by free men, which the Vietnamese share . . . ; Second . . . start the Vietnamese moving realistically toward those political goals. In essence, this is revolutionary warfare, the spirit of the British Magna Carta, the French "Liberté, égalité, fraternité" and our own Declaration of Independence.

The ideology of the Vietnamese "revolution" then is to be British, French or American.

General Lansdale devotes the bulk of his article to advocating further American intervention in native affairs in order to endow the Vietnamese with the "will to be free." The "thesis" of his article is that, due to the extent of our involvement, and because everything depends on that motivation, Americans cannot escape responsibility [of "finding the motivation for conducting successful counterinsurgency effort"]. The "great lesson" of Malaya and the Philippines is that "there must be a heartfelt *cause* to which the legitimate government is pledged, a cause which makes stronger appeal to the people than the Communist cause. . . ." Given the "correct" use of the "right" cause, the anti-Communist fight becomes a pro-people fight.

Search for an ideology led the French theorists to propound national-Socialist and Catholic-authoritarian ideologies which they thought would appeal to Algerian Muslims and which, strangely enough, invoked the revolutionary spirit of 1789. (The American theorists refer to those of 1776.) General Lansdale is moved to propose (*1*) a direct American involvement in Vietnamese politics in order to supply it with an ideology; and (*2*) a rewriting of Vietnam's recent history in order to produce a "heartfelt cause." He assumes that the natives lack the spirit to produce "a dynamic political answer with which to meet and overcome foreign ideas introduced by the Communists." Like all counterinsurgent theorists, he fails to examine the components of his local adversary's ideology and organization; if he did, he might be less certain that Vietnamese culture wants dynamism. Instead, he believes that "lacking such a dynamic answer," Vietnam should not be left to its own political resources. Hence, the "concept that the United States should give advice and counsel on waging revolutionary warfare . . . involves exporting American political principles. . . ." He argues that Americans have the added responsibility to implement the exported principles, and cities occupied Japan and West Germany as successful examples of American-sponsored political development. And, of course, the colonial example is the most pertinent: "We tutored the Philippine people and encouraged them in self-government in the same brotherly spirit which elsewhere could make all the difference in struggles between freedom and communism."

Lansdale's views deserve attention because they represent the collective thinking of liberal America's foremost scholars, and because they still form the basis for policy. (In addition to its occupation of Vietnam, the United States maintains counterinsurgency programs and commitments in some twenty underdeveloped countries.) The colonialist character of the approach, the damages it is doing to the disadvantaged, the validity of analogies with postwar Germany and Japan, and the correctness of considering the Philippines a success, have been discussed elsewhere. It should be noted, however, that though foreign attempts to foster political development are doomed to fail, they often result in Western military interventions and the enlargement of local conflicts. Improved techniques and professionalism are not the chief ingredients of political and social development. It requires a vision of society, the choice of values and goals, and these are not exportable goods or skills to be packaged as part of a foreign aid program. Furthermore, no foreign power can endow a native government with legitimacy, nor with the will and capacity to open channels for peaceful change. On the contrary, such identification erodes a regime's legitimacy.

MYTH AS POLICY

Diem is a case in point. It is fashionable now to deplore him, who had once been billed as a democratic alternative to Ho Chi Minh, for his many failings. Yet few liberals have acknowledged that it was morbid optimism on their part to expect an absentee aristocrat, propped by American dollars and guns, to substitute for the heroic leaders and cadres who had devoted a lifetime to the independence of their country, and to defeat a movement whose organic ties with the peasants were cemented by a bitter struggle for social justice no less than national liberation.

Given the historical situation, Diem had little choice; his only possible weapons were a power apparatus to regiment the population, all but support of the Catholic minority and the privileged, and widespread terror. These were not the aberrations of a program but the program itself. The fundamental responsibility for the totalitarian and corrupt character of successive Saigon regimes does not lie with poor Diem, or the degenerate generals who once collaborated with colonial France and are now sanctioning the systematic destruction of a people they claim to govern. It rests with those who created Diem, and still sustain in authority men who can be regarded by their countrymen only as traitors.

Myths play an important role in politics, but the men involved in counterinsurgency possess a special capacity for myth making. It has been widely noted that, despite its rhetoric of winning the hearts and minds of the people through progress and participation, counterinsurgency often culminates in massive official crimes against the population. One reason is that counterinsurgency's myths are totally contrived and, lacking a basis in popular perceptions, fail to elicit a favorable response. The French counterinsurgency propagandists spoke of Bugeaud and Lyautey as the liberators of North Africa, and invoked French history and heroes to promote Algerian loyalty to France. General Lansdale typifies the counterinsurgent version of Vietnam's contemporary history which, whatever its value in boosting GI morale, can only insult Vietnamese sensibilities.

"The great cause in Vietnam which last united the overwhelming majority of Vietnamese . . . was independence," reports the General, and proceeds to expropriate the *nationalist cause*. On just one page he makes the following assertions: (*1*) "Nearly all" the Vietnamese leaders on the American side fought to win independence by revolutionary means; (*2*) the tragedy of Vietnam's revolutionary war of independence was that its "Benedict Arnold was successful"; (*3*) Ho helped by other Russian and Chinese agents (Giap, Truong Chinh, Pham Van Dong) "secretly changed the goals of the struggle"; (*4*) in 1954 the Vietminh was widely hated by the Vietnamese people; (*5*) "the national revolution was reborn in South Vietnam when Ngo Dinh Diem placed the fate of the nation in the people's hands in 1955" and was elected President almost "unanimously"; (*6*) soon after this popular election, the Communists, fearful of losing the plebiscite the Geneva Accords required, obtained its annulment.

Lansdale's academic colleagues express much the same view—less precisely and more pompously. Their writings belong in the lowest category of colonial historiography. It is a measure of their capacity for self-deception that after more than a decade of counterinsurgency, these analysts and policy makers still hope that given the protracted, and increasingly air-oriented protective shield of American military power, the Saigon generals (all of whom fought with the French puppet army against Indochina's independence), landlords, and other war profiteers will produce a viable government in Vietnam. One wonders how a program whose architects and administrators have so little respect for the history, intelligence, wisdom and patriotic feelings of the Vietnamese people could expect, much less deserve, to "win their hearts and minds."

There are innumerable examples of what "going deep into every local revolutionary problem and helping solve them" in "brotherly spirit" and in accordance with the "revolutionary spirits of 1776" has come to mean in Vietnam. William Nighswonger, a senior pacification official in Vietnam during 1962–64, cites an AID report (March 1965), comparing the "new life hamlets" with the "Vietcong villages," stated that the latter were well-organized, clean, economically self-supporting, and had active self-defense systems. New canals were being dug, pineapples were under cultivation, cottage industry flourished, and there was even a relocation program for younger families. The report added that "Vietcong strength in the countryside has made a 'quantum leap' from its position of early 1962," i.e., after the USOM and National Police had unsuccessfully experimented in the area with "population and resources control methods." But it welcomed a compensating factor: "The counterinsurgent military capability was revolutionized by substantial American troop inputs" which, of course, permitted new "experiments" with "material and human resources control" to be carried on. These were necessary because, "Given the enormous numbers of South Vietnamese citizens presently allied with the Vietcong (for whatever reasons), the recovery of these peasants for the national cause must be made one of the central tasks of the pacification enterprise." Counterinsurgency possesses an unremitting logic of escalation.

A previous AID study (February 1965) had mentioned some difficulties in the pacification program—government forces "stealing, robbing, raping . . . in rural areas." An example is cited of an ARVN officer who killed a draft dodger, "took his heart and liver out and had them cooked," after which "the heart and liver were eaten by a number of soldiers." Nighswonger considers such conduct as counterproductive, in view of the contrasting Communist behavior. The "success of pacification requires," he perceptively points out, "that there be survivors to be pacified," and given the "sheer magnitude of American, Korean, Australian and indigenous Vietnamese forces" it is sometimes difficult to insure this minimum condition.

By 1970 a third of the Vietnamese fell into the "recovered" category. The experts saw in their plight an opportunity, and even progress. In a statement to the Senate Refugee Subcommittee (September 30, 1965), Roger Hilsman said: "The refugees, in my judgment, are the key to such a program [winning an honorable peace]. In the first place, they are a substantial number of the people of Vietnam, the people whose allegiance must be won, and because their plight is so visible they will be a test case, a symbol of whether the government does indeed care." He conceded that the allies "working with the refugees start out with a strike against them" because "it was not Vietcong terrorism" but "American and Vietnamese bombing and shelling" that "drove the refugees from their ancestral homes to the cities and towns." This, however, is no reason for the United States to end its occupation; in fact, it increases American responsibility to go on—"all this means that even greater effort must be made to win over these people, precisely because of their initial resentment." Helping the refugees, however, is not the goal but a useful means of winning the war. Mr. Hilsman added: "But beyond winning the allegiance of the refugees, it seems to me that they offer a positive opportunity for furthering an effective counterinsurgency program."

Mr. Hilsman said in his testimony that such a program had yet to be tried in South Vietnam, "although there have been one or two false starts," adding that "Ambassador Lodge, however, is determined to persuade both the Vietnamese and the Americans concerned to make the effort." Mr. Hilsman, like General Lansdale,

who under Ambassador Lodge headed the Senior Liaison Office in Saigon during the worst years of escalation, judged the bombing of North Vietnam to be a tactical mistake. But neither man will probably ever acknowledge that the decisions to bomb the North, and to tear the South to bits by saturation bombing and "substantial American troop inputs" were the direct results of the failure of counterinsurgency, which had been tried for a decade.

ANY PRICE FOR VICTORY

Counterinsurgency experts believe in what one may call the "doctrine of permanent counterinsurgency." No price—not the distortion of their professed values by the acceptance of totalitarian practices and institutions, not the destruction of a culture, not the dispossession and displacement of a people—is ultimately too high for these men who play with the lives and future of the masses in the manner of obsessed gamblers intent on a final win. They tend to explain away their failures by pointing to specific flaws which only underscore the need for "greater effort"—paucity of trained personnel, sabotage by politicians or conventional generals, the failure of public will at home to sustain a protracted struggle.

The doctrine of permanent counterinsurgency presupposes a refusal to acknowledge the absence or loss of governmental legitimacy. Mao Tse-tung told Edgar Snow that he had read Gen. Maxwell Taylor's *The Uncertain Trumpet*, and some of the U.S. anti-guerrilla manuals which sought to apply Mao's ideas in reverse. Their weakness, Mao said, is that they ignore "the decisive political fact that . . . governments cut off from the masses could not win against wars of liberation."

I. F. Stone commented in February 1965: "The failure to grasp Mao's point in South Vietnam does not arise from any special stupidity. The trouble is that the situation there has degenerated to the point where any government which was not cut off from the masses would respond to their war weariness. It would open negotiations with the rebels and ask our troops to leave." Fear of precisely that development led the very men who had helped install Diem to sanction his overthrow and murder; it was also the cause of the brutal suppression of the Buddhists in 1966, and of the continuing repression of neutralists, and the refusal to accept a coalition government as part of a negotiated settlement.

If Roger Hilsman, friend and adviser to the Kennedys, considers the refugees an opportunity, Prof. Samuel P. Huntington, chairman of the Department of Government at Harvard, and adviser to Presidential aspirant Hubert Humphrey, regards them as an accomplishment. He believes that, by bombing the peasants out of their villages and homes, America accelerated the process of urbanization which has introduced "momentous changes in Vietnamese society during the past five years." He explained (*Boston Globe*, February 17, 1968): "So long as the overwhelming mass of the people lived in the countryside, the Vietcong would win the war by winning control of those people—and they came very close to doing so in both 1961 and 1964. But the American-sponsored urban revolution undercut the Vietcong rural revolution."

Similar claims were made by the French experts for the estimated 3 million displaced Algerians. The main difference between France and the United States is that in France, soldiers, not professors, dominated this field. Moral distortion and intellectual degeneration are inherent in the theory and practice of counterinsurgency. One of his colleagues may have been too harsh in judging Professor Huntington, but metaphorically he summed up the fate of the majority in this field when he said publicly that "Sam has simply lost the ability to distinguish between urbanization and genocide."

FROM "HEARTS AND MINDS" TO "LAW AND ORDER"

I noted earlier that the dialectic of counterinsurgency leads these theorists to qualify, distort, and finally forsake their liberal-reformist pretenses. I have discussed the qualifications, and given some examples of the distortions, which include Professor Huntington's euphoria on the urbanization process. As their experiments in counterinsurgency fail, despite the laboratory conditions permitted by the strategic hamlets, re-education camps, refugee population, and the protection of mighty armed forces, they progressively abandon their only positive theme—the need for "winning the hearts and minds." Failure augments their sense of isolation from and hostility toward the mass. Since their attitudes and politics are concerned primarily with establishing order and stability, they begin to jettison their reformist and liberal pretenses when these fail to bring operational payoffs, and seek justifications for massive destruction, repressive measures and new avenues to victory. Lately, the American experts have been providing a rich harvest of "revisionist" literature on counterinsurgency. These form the bases and provide the rationale for the strategy of attrition which was adopted by Johnson following the Tet offensive of 1968 and which, under Nixon, came to be described as Vietnamization.

Recent interest in elaborating and supplying empirical content to the "theory of relative deprivation" is a case in point. It postulates, to the accompaniment of much jargon and a depressing excess of statistics, what students of politics have observed since the advent of industrialism—that the "mobile" social classes, the people who are aware of social and economic gaps, the hopeful rather than the abject poor, are most inclined to agitate for change. When applied to specific situations by the counterinsurgent scholars, this perfectly viable theory produces novel conclusions. Thus a well-known "statistical analysis of factors affecting government control" in Vietnam "reveals" a positive correlation between "inequality of land tenure" and the "extent of government control." It concludes that the "provinces where few peasants own their own land, the distribution of land-holdings is unequal, and land redistribution has not been carried out" are "precisely the areas of greatest security. The observed relationship is between greater inequality and greater control—not the reverse." The author of this RAND study (Edward J. Mitchell: "Insurgency and Inequality: A Statistical Analysis of South Vietnam") believes that the "behavioural explanation" for this phenomenon lies "in the relative docility of poorer peasants and the firm authority of landlords in the 'more' feudal areas." Mr. Mitchell has used questionable methods and assumptions to reach this conclusion. It is typical of counterrevolutionary analysts that one disregards even the obvious explanation for the correlation between landlordism and government control: landlords have influence in the Saigon government and have troops sent to protect their lands. "Secure areas" after all are secure only in that they are occupied by government or U.S. troops.

Given a preoccupation against revolutions and for stability, such insights can only cool the liberals' enthusiasm for reforms and augment their emphasis on law and order. In an important policy statement issued by the Freedom House Public Affairs Institute, the "moderate segment of the academic community" (which included some of the most prestigious and liberal American scholars on Asia) emphasized that "Indeed many types of reform increase instability, however desirable and essential they may be in long-range terms. For people under siege there is no substitute for security." And Prof. Ithiel de Sola Pool has this to say: "In the Congo, in Vietnam, in the Dominican Republic, it is clear that order depended on somehow compelling newly mobilized strata to return to a measure of passivity and defeatism from which they have recently been aroused by the process of modernization."

In another revisionist essay (Chapter 3 of *United States Policy and the Third World*) Charles Wolf of the RAND Corporation questions the "core of currently accepted doctrine about insurgency," which admits the "central role of popular support" to its success and which holds that "socio-economic improvement programs, especially in rural areas, are essential for an effective counter-insurgency effort." Belief in popular support and reforms, Wolf says, "has an undeniable appeal to those grounded in Western ideologies and values. It strikes a particularly responsive cord in the Populist symbols and sentiments of American tradition, but it may be stronger on symbolism and sentiment than on realism." Whereupon he produces a formula suited to the needs of the natives:

> *Given the characteristics of transitional societies in less developed countries,* an effective insurgency and guerrilla activity can grow and gather momentum among a population that is passive or even hostile to the movement. [Italics are his.] The growth of the Vietcong and of the Pathet Lao probably occurred despite the opposition of a large majority of the people in both Vietnam and Laos. . . . *By the same token, successful counterinsurgency programs can be con-*

> *ducted among a rural populace that is passive or even hostile, rather than loyal, to the government.* [My italics.]

What an insurgent movement requires for successful and expanding operations is not popular support, in the sense of attitudes of identification and allegiance, but rather a supply of certain inputs (e.g., food, recruits, information) at reasonable cost, interpreting "cost" to include expenditure of coercion as well as of money. These costs may be "reasonable" without popular sympathy for the insurgents, *and, conversely, the costs may be considerably augmented without any increase in allegiance to the government . . . resource flows may be interdicted, or made more costly to the insurgency without any increase in the popular support for the government.* [My italics.]

The ground is thus prepared for Wolf to introduce an "alternative approach" which postulates that the "main concern of counterinsurgency efforts should be to influence the behavior of the population rather than their loyalties and attitudes." It is not possible even to outline the numerous proposals which emerge from Wolf's application of "input-output" theory to this formulation. Many of them are already part of the American strategy in Vietnam. He argues that "socio-economic improvement programs" may have "no effect or a perverse effect, on the cost and availability of inputs that the insurgents require for their operations." His equation is that if people are well off, so shall be the guerrillas: "The supply of what the insurgents need from the villages may expand and its cost may decline, *notwithstanding increased popular support for the government.*" [His emphasis.] From this it follows first that "the policies that would increase rural income by raising of food prices, or projects that would increase productivity through the distribution of fertilizers or livestocks may be of negative values during an insurgency." (This may partly explain why the United States spends only about $400 million annually on economic aid to Vietnam, the major portion of this aid enriching the living standards and Swiss accounts of its South Vietnamese allies.) Secondly, the government must interdict the guerrillas' supplies. The most common methods blocking the insurgents' "inputs" are crop defoliation, buffalo killing, and the destruction of rural products.

Wolf believes that it is all right to inflict massive penalties on the population, but that these should not be random, lest it become "impossible for the populace to infer anything about the relationship between the harsh conduct of the government forces and their own behavior." After citing some examples ("confiscating of chickens, razing of houses or destruction of villages") of reprisals that have "a place in the counterinsurgency efforts," Wolf reaffirms that "*Whatever* harshness is meted out by government forces [must be] unambiguously recognizable as deliberately imposed because of behavior by the population that contributes to the insurgent movement." Thus it is not surprising that, in contrast to the economic, American military "aid" to Vietnam has been costing, since 1965, an average of about $30 billion a year. The Vietnamese people have been its sole recipients.

THE BRUTALITY OF DEFEAT

Since unascertainable amounts of time elapse between the preparation of a proposal and its publication, it is often difficult to say whether analysis only justifies policy or assists also in its formulation. In any case, this new approach which, by Wolf's "admission" differs from the old "only" in "degree," is obviously congenial to the brutal and destructive character which American counterinsurgency acquire in Vietnam when its political defeat had become apparently irreversible.

Prof. Morton H. Halperin, former White House aide and now a Brookings Institution Fellow, provides in *Contemporary Military Strategy* "empirical" proof of the validity of the "behavior not attitude" formula. The United States, he says, "with its vastly superior logistics capability, its heavier fire-power, and its ability to use air power, has been able to prevent large-scale Vietcong victories, regardless of the loyalties of the people." He reports that "American bombing in South Vietnam may have antagonized a number of people; but at the same time it demonstrated to these people that the Vietcong could not guarantee their security as it had been able to do before the bombing. . . ." This proves that "people tend to be motivated, not by abstract appeals, but rather by their perception of the course of action

that is most likely to lead to their own personal security. . . ."

But bombs do not break social and political links. Massive reprisals fail to elicit the desired behavior from the people. They do, however, open fresh opportunities for managing and manipulating the beleaguered population. As Wolf puts it, the government must impose "restrictions that limit the availability of resources that the insurgency can draw from the rural areas." Concentration camps, strategic hamlets, and "urbanization" are the most common instruments for imposing such control. Sir Robert Thompson judiciously lists some others—preventive detention, identity cards, family photographs, snap checks, inventories of belongings and visitors, and travel restrictions.

The specific recommendations of Wolf's "alternative approach" are also the stock items of counterinsurgency—a system of rewards to "motivate" the killing of guerrillas, severe punishments for cooperation with them, an "incentive system" to encourage defection and intelligence, including a "price" scale on NLF cadres and leaders. His proposal to "buy up" rural supplies in return not for money, which insurgents may use, but for such consumers' products as cannot be of use to guerrillas, is a variant on the older policy of collective confiscations and grain burning. More than ever before, pacification now stands for massive reprisals and regimentation of the population.

That preoccupation with success as well as with management and manipulation lead the experts on counterinsurgency to embrace totalitarian precepts and Fascist practices is most evident in the theory and practice of psychological warfare. Peter Paret has pointed out that the French theorists drew from the Pavlovians the belief that people can be conditioned to think and act in specific ways; Gustav Le Bon taught them lessons on the manipulation of groups and crowds; Eugen Hadamovsky, the Nazi theorist, gave guidance in the use of symbols, slogans, demonstration, and violence in forging a mass "will."

Techniques of brainwashing were perfected and widely practiced in the re-education camps where prisoners were divided into hard, soft and curable categories. Paret adds that "To be useful, their theories not only had to explain how to manipulate a mass and re-educate an individual, but also had to insure that the influence exerted was more than temporary." It proved impossible to prevent a brainwashed Muslim from backsliding into nationalism once he had been released from his re-education camp.

Again, the only answer was to seek an increasingly controlled social environment. Col. Roger Trinquier, a leading French theorist, told a journalist in Algeria; "What we have to do is to organize the population from top to bottom. I don't care if you call me a Fascist; but we must have a docile population, every gesture of which shall be subject to our control."

In both Algeria and Vietnam the inner logic and destructive nature of counterinsurgency were fully exposed to the world, stripped of the liberal, reformist pretenses of its practitioners. Yet there might be a fateful difference. Algeria marked the end of France's involvement in counterinsurgency; its exponents ended up in prison or oblivion. Vietnam appears to have been a testing ground and training area rather than the terminal point for American counterrevolution. Its practitioners attend conferences and join public forums to discuss the "lessons" of Vietnam. The American military is known to count among the benefits the unusual opportunity to develop and test new weapons for "irregular" warfare. A new generation of officers and men has gained combat experience in guerrilla warfare in unfamiliar terrain. Lessons learned in Vietnam have led to improved techniques of pacification in the client states of Asia and Latin America.

Developments in Indonesia, Thailand, Guatemala, above all in Laos and Cambodia, indicate that the "lessons" of Vietnam have reinforced the most barbaric and destructive components of counterinsurgency. It is now likely to be practiced in its latest, revised form, which stresses totalitarian controls over the population, massive displacement and dispossession of the peasants, and rapid and ruthless reprisals with maximum reliance on technology—bombings, napalm and defoliation—rather than troops. At a conference on Violence and Social Change, organized by the Adlai Stevenson Institute in the summer of 1969, Robert W. Komer, former Deputy Ambassador in charge of the American Pacification Program in Saigon, explained that Vietnam had proved the inefficacy

of "gradual" escalation which permitted the "guerrillas" to make "adjustments" and withstand allied pressure. Hence, the "lesson" was to escalate ruthlessly and rapidly; "snow them under," he said.

It is a measure of the helplessness of humanity rather than of freedom in America that, in my concern for the survival of the Indochinese people and culture, I must share public forums with men who, in the opinion of qualified persons, including Gen. Telford Taylor, are at least deserving of trial as criminals of war.

COUNTERINSURGENCY COMES HOME

A full discussion of the ways in which the practice of counterinsurgency erodes the democratic processes and institutions of metropolitan countries is beyond the scope of this paper. The fall of the Fourth Republic, the French army officers' involvement in the clandestine OAS, and their open rebellion in 1962 are examples for Americans to ponder. The pursuit of counterrevolutionary foreign policy undermines a democracy in many ways. It enhances executive as well as secret service power, over which parliamentary institutions can exercise little or no control, and whose activities public organs (press, political parties, etc.) are normally unable to report and censure. The expanded role of the CIA, and of the armed forces' special branches are examples. As their activities and influence increase, such agencies not only circumvent representative institutions but even begin to infiltrate and corrupt civilian life. The CIA's clandestine use of the National Students Association and of several universities is a case in point.

In order to overcome the checks of parliamentary institutions and public opinion, a government involved in counterinsurgency seeks ways to reduce its accountability to elected bodies, and to manipulate public opinion. Expansion of the secret services is only one of many devices. Another favorite tactic is to employ puppet armies and experts to subvert foreign governments and fight wars by proxy. E. L. Katzenbach stated the proposition in the anthology by T. N. Greene which received the approbation of President Kennedy:

> We need not only troops which can strike on the peripheries of the free world, but also

troops which can be sent not merely to fight but also to maintain order. *We need not only useful troops but usable troops—that is to say, troops which are politically expendable,* the kind of troops who can do the job as it is needed without too great a political outcry in a nation like our own which so abhors war. . . ." [Italics added.]

The desire for "usable troops" led the French to rely heavily not only on special units of enlisted men (e.g., the parachutists) and on African regiments but also, and increasingly, on the mercenary Foreign Legion units, composed largely of Germans. As for the Americans, in addition to providing armaments, training and "advisers" to counterrevolutionary clients, they raise secret private armies. The Cuban exiles who invaded Cuba, the murder squads who have been terrorizing the Guatemalan peasants, the *Khmer Serei* who spearheaded the move to overthrow Sihanouk and invade Cambodia, and Vung Pao's clandestine army in Laos are examples. In their Special Warfare units, they have also been recruiting Central and Eastern European exiles. Of them I. F. Stone wrote in 1961:

> They seem to come chiefly from right-wing elements. I was told that there were many former Chetniks among them; these were the Royal Yugoslav partisans under Mihailovitch, who collaborated during certain periods with the Nazis. The anonymous memorandum in the *Army Navy Air Force Journal* [April 8, 1961] ends by saying, 'the two names . . . who are most mentionable in this field are Colonel Ed. Lansdale, OSO, and Slavko N. Bjelajac, Special Warfare.' When I reached Mr. Bjelajac by phone at the Pentagon, he admitted he had served with the Yugoslav partisan forces under Mihailovitch.

Failure to defeat revolutionaries in protracted war alienates participants in counterinsurgency against the democratic values and institutions of their own country. The war is eventually seen as being lost at home rather than in the field; domestic dissent and divisions contrast with the enviable solidarity and dedication of the enemy; and democratic institutions increasingly appear unworkable in revolutionary settings. The "powerlessness" of the "democratic ideology" was the common complaint among the supporters of counterinsurgency in France. In America too it is becoming a familiar theme, in scholarly analyses no less than political pronouncements.

Disaffection from the existing system occurs also among the opponents of counterrevolutionary war, since their protests produce no result, and new elections, while producing new promises, fail to yield a new policy. The divisions and disillusionments that follow involvement in counterrevolution ultimately reduce the legitimacy of existing institutions, inspire opposition to or contempt for them, and weaken the will to resist their corruption.

Above all, involvement in counterinsurgency politicizes the military and encourages its intrusion into civilian life. In France it produced at first deep extra-constitutional involvement of the military in the political affairs of the country, and finally a rebellion. In the United States public disclosures have now been made of massive military surveillance of civilians. Training and participation in counterinsurgency necessarily involve a recognition of the identity and interrelatedness of civilian and military tasks and authority. It is not realistic to expect that military men who are trained also to traffic in politics will remain apolitical concerning problems at home. A double standard of the army's role abroad and at home becomes especially difficult to maintain when the war is seen as being lost at home. The determination to equip the natives with the "will to fight" emerges eventually in the metropolitan country. The crusade abroad may find expressions at home when the society is viewed as needing moral or political regeneration.

Counterrevolutionary chickens, therefore, have a tendency to return home to roost. Whether the "homecoming" is complete or partial depends on the strains and stresses of involvements abroad, and a government's ability to extricate from the war in good time. The Fourth Republic survived the first Indochinese war but collapsed during the Algerian. It is impossible to tell how many more Vietnams the American Republic can sustain. There is, however, considerable evidence that the forces of law and order, including the Army and several local police departments, are applying the theories of pacification and counter-guerrilla warfare to problems at home. In recent years the Army and Marine Corps have been engaged in research (and presumably training) in "urban-guerrilla warfare." In 1968 a Directorate of Civil Disturbances was established in the Office of Secretary of the Army, and the Pentagon now houses a Situation Room for domestic disturbances.

Less easy to identify, but more pervasive. are the effects that involvement in counterinsurgency abroad have on attitudes toward and styles of dealing with political problems at home. The treatment, in recent years, of dissenters in America is probably not unrelated to the war in Vietnam. Official violence against demonstrators in Chicago during the Democratic Party Convention is one example. Somewhat later, during the demonstrations for a People's Park in Berkeley, helicopters sprayed the CS variety of gas that is widely used in Vietnam but outlawed by the Geneva Conventions. The commander is reported to have regretted the "discomfort and inconvenience to innocent bystanders," adding that "it is an inescapable by-product of combating terrorists, anarchists, and hard-core militants on the streets and on the campus." Many of the 800 persons arrested reported that they were beaten and tortured,

and a district court judge issued restraining orders against such practices in the Santa Rita jail. Alameda County's Sheriff Madigan explained that "We have a bunch of young deputies back from Vietnam who tend to treat prisoners like Vietcong."

The years of Vietnamization have witnessed an acceleration of this trend. The police murder of Fred Hampton and his companion, the killings at Kent State, Jackson and Orangeburg, the offhanded use of conspiracy laws and grand juries against political dissenters indicate an extension of the repressive arm of executive authority. The expansion, admitted and justified by the Attorney General, in the use of unauthorized wire-tapping and electronic surveillance, growing evidence that authorities use agents not only to inform on dissenters but also to provoke them into violence. the justifications offered by Mr. Nixon for the arrest without warrant of some 7,000 demonstrators in Washington, are all indicative of the erosion of civil liberties in the United States. One can only hope that these and other similar incidents do not constitute a preview of things to come.

Local Society

C. Wright Mills

In every town and small city of America an upper set of families stands above the middle classes and towers over the underlying population of clerks and wage workers. The members of this set possess more than do others of whatever there is locally to possess; they hold the keys to local decision; their names and faces are often printed in the local paper; in fact, they own the newspaper as well as the radio station; they also own the three important local plants and most of the commercial properties along the main street; they direct the banks. Mingling closely with one another, they are quite conscious of the fact that they belong to the leading class of the leading families.

All their sons and daughters go to college,

often after private schools; then they marry one another, or other boys and girls from similar families in similar towns. After they are well married, they come to possess, to occupy, to decide. The son of one of these old families, to his father's chagrin and his grandfather's fury, is now an executive in the local branch of a national corporation. The leading family doctor has two sons, one of whom now takes up the practice; the other—who is soon to marry the daughter of the second largest factory—will probably be the next district attorney. So it has traditionally been, and so it is today in the small towns of America.

Class consciousness is not equally characteristic of all levels of American society: It is most apparent in the upper class. Among the underlying population everywhere in America there is much confusion and blurring of the lines of demarcation, of the status value of clothing and

■ Taken from *The Power Elite* by C. Wright Mills (New York: Oxford University Press, 1956), pp. 30–46. Copyright © 1956 by Oxford University Press, Inc. Reprinted by permission.

houses, of the ways of money-making and of money-spending. The people of the lower and middle classes are of course differentiated by the values, things, and experiences to which differing amounts of income lead, but often they are aware neither of these values nor of their class bases.

Those of the upper strata, on the other hand, if only because they are fewer in number, are able with much more ease to know more about one another, to maintain among themselves a common tradition, and thus to be conscious of their own kind. They have the money and the time required to uphold their common standards. A propertied class, they are also a more or less distinct set of people who, mingling with one another, form compact circles with common claims to recognition as the leading families of their cities.

1

Examining the small city, both the novelist and the sociologist have felt most clearly the drama of the old and the new upper classes. The struggle for status which they have observed going on in these towns may be seen on a historic scale in the modern course of the whole of Western Society; for centuries the parvenues and snobs of new upper classes have stood in tension with the "old guard." There are, of course, regional variations but across the country the small-town rich are surprisingly standardized. In these cities today, two types of upper classes prevail, one composed of rentier and socially older families, the other of newer families which, economically and socially, are of a more entrepreneurial type. Members of these two top classes understand the several distinctions between them, although each has its own particular view of them.[1]

It should not be supposed that the old upper class is necessarily 'higher' than the new, or that the new is simply a *nouveau riche.* struggling to drape new-won wealth in the prestige garments worn so easily by the old. The new upper class has a style of life of its own, and although its members—especially the women—borrow considerably from the old upper-class style, they also—especially the men—debunk that style in the name of their own values and aspirations. In many ways, these two supper sets compete for

prestige and their competition involves some mutual deflation of claims for merit.

The old upper-class person feels that his prestige originates in time itself. "Somewhere in the past," he seems to say, "my Original Ancestor rose up to become the Founder Of This Local Family Line and now His Blood flows in my veins. I am what My Family has been, and My Family has always been among the very best people." In New England and in the South, more families than in other regions are acutely conscious of family lines and old residence, and more resistant to the social ascendancy of the newly rich and the newly arrived. There is perhaps a stronger and more embracing sense of family, which, especially in the South, comes to include long-faithful servants as well as grandchildren. The sense of kinship may be extended even to those who, although not related by marriage or blood, are considered as "cousins" or "aunts" because they "grew up with mother." Old upper-class families thus tend to form an endogenous cousinhood, whose clan piety and sense of kinship lead to a reverence for the past and often to a cultivated interest in the history of the region in which the clan has for so long played such an honorable role.

To speak of "old families" is of course to speak of "wealthy old families," but in the status world of the old upper class, ready money and property are simply assumed—and then played down: "Of course, you have to have enough of this world's goods to stand the cost of keeping up, of entertaining and for church donations . . . but social standing is more than money." The men and women of the old upper class generally consider money in a negative way—as something in which the new upper-class people are too closely interested. "I'm sorry to say that our larger industrialists are increasingly money-conscious," they say, and in saying it, they have in mind the older generation of industrialists who are now retired, generally on real-estate holdings; these rich men and their women folk, the old upper class believes, were and are more interested in "community and social" qualifications than in mere money.

One major theme in old upper-class discussions of smaller business people is that they made a great deal of money during the late war, but that socially they aren't to be allowed to count. Another theme concerns the less respectable ways in which the money of the newly moneyed people has been earned. They mention pin-ball concessionaires, tavern keepers, and people in the trucking lines. And, having patronized them, they are quite aware of the wartime black markets.

The continuance of the old-family line as the basis of prestige is challenged by the ripsnorting style as well as the money of the new upper classes, which World War II expanded and enriched, and made socially bold. Their style, the old upper classes feel, is replacing the older, quieter one. Underlying this status tension, there is often a tendency of decline in the economic basis of many old upper-class families, which, in many towns, is mainly real estate. Yet the old upper class still generally has its firm hold on local financial institutions: in the market centers of Georgia and Nebraska, the trading and manufacturing towns of Vermont and California—the old upper-class banker is usually the lord of his community's domain, lending prestige to the businessmen with whom he associates, naming The Church by merely belonging to it. Thus embodying salvation, social standing, and financial soundness, he is accepted by others at his own shrewd and able valuation.

In the South the tension between old and new upper classes is often more dramatic than in other regions, for here old families have been based on land ownership and the agricultural economy. The synthesis of new wealth with older status, which of course has been under way since the Civil War, has been accelerated since the slump and World War II. The old southern aristocracy, in fictional image and in researched fact, is indeed often in a sorry state of decline. If it does not join the rising class based on industry and trade, it will surely die out, for when given sufficient time if status does not remain wealthy it crumbles into ignored eccentricity. Without sufficient money, quiet dignity and a self-satisfied withdrawal comes to seem mere decay and even decadence.

The emphasis upon family descent, coupled with withdrawal, tends to enhance the status of older people, especially of those older women who become dowager judges of the conduct of the young. Such a situation is not conducive to the marriage of old upper-class daughters to sons of a new but up-and-coming class of

wealth. Yet the industrialization of the smaller cities steadily breaks up old status formations and leads to new ones: the rise of the enriched industrialist and tradesman inevitably leads to the decline of the land-owning aristocracy. In the South, as well as elsewhere, the larger requirements of capital for agricultural endeavor on sufficient scale, as well as favorable taxation and subsidy for "farmers," lead to new upper-class formations on the land as in the city.

The new and the old upper classes thus stand in the smaller cities eyeing one another with considerable tension, with some disdain, and with begrudging admiration. The upper-class man sees the old as having a prestige which he would like to have, but also as an old fogy blocking important business and political traffic and as a provincial, bound to the local set-up, without the vision to get up and go. The old upper-class man, in turn, eyes the new and thinks of him as too money-conscious, as having made money and as grabbing for more, but as not having acquired the social background or the style of cultured life befitting his financial rank, and as not really being interested in the civic life of the city, except in so far as he might use it for personal and alien ends.

When they come up against the prestige of the old upper class on business and on civic and political issues, the new upper-class men often translate that prestige into "old age," which is associated in their minds with the quiet, "old-fashioned" manner, the slower civic tempo, and the dragging political views of the old upper class. They feel that the old upper-class people do not *use* their prestige to make money in the manner of the new upper class. They do not understand old prestige as something to be enjoyed; they see it in its political and economic relevance: when they do not have it, it is something standing in their way.[2]

2

That the social and economic split of the upper classes is also a political split is not yet fully apparent in all localities, but it is a fact that has tended to become national since World War II.

Local upper classes—new and old, seen and unseen, active and passive—make up the social backbone of the Republican party. Members of the old upper class, however, do not seem as strident or as active politically in the postwar scene as do many of the new. Perhaps it is because they do not feel able, as Allison Davis and others have suggested of the old southern upper classes, "to lessen the social distance between themselves and the voters." Of course, everywhere their social position "is clearly recognized by the officials. They are free from many of the minor legal restrictions, are almost never arrested for drunkenness or for minor traffic violations, are seldom called for jury duty, and usually receive any favors they request."[3] They are, it is true, very much concerned with tax rates and property assessments, but these concerns, being fully shared by the new upper classes, are well served without the personal intervention of the old.

The new upper class often practices those noisy political emotions and status frustrations which, on a national scale and in extreme form, have been so readily observable in The Investigators. The key to these political emotions, in the Congress as in the local society, lies in the status psychology of the *nouveau riche*. Such newly enriched classes—ranging from Texas multimillionaires to petty Illinois war profiteers who have since consolidated their holdings—feel that they are somehow held down by the status pretensions of older wealth and older families. The suddenly $30,000-a-year insurance salesmen who drive the 260 hp cars and guiltily buy vulgar diamond rings for their wives; the suddenly $60,000-a-year businessmen who put in 50-foot swimming pools and do not know how to act toward their new servants—they feel that they have achieved something and yet are not thought to be good enough to possess it fully. There are men in Texas today whose names are strictly local, but who have more money than many nationally prominent families of the East. But *they* are not often nationally prominent, and even when they are, it is not in just the same way.

Such feelings exist, on a smaller scale, in virtually every smaller city and town. They are not always articulated, and certainly they have not become the bases of any real political movement. But they lie back of the wide and deep gratification at beholding men of established prestige "told off," observing the general reprimanded by the upstart, hearing the par-

venu familiarly, even insultingly, call the old wealthy by their first names in public controversy.

The political aim of the petty right formed among the new upper classes of the small cities is the destruction of the legislative achievements of the New and Fair Deals. Moreover, the rise of labor unions in many of these cities during the war. with more labor leaders clamoring to be on local civic boards; the increased security of the wage workers who during the war cashed larger weekly checks in stores and banks and crowded the sidewalks on Saturday; the big new automobiles of the small people—all these class changes of the last two decades psychologically threaten the new upper class by reducing their own feelings of significance, their own sense of a fit order of prestige.

The old upper classes are also made less socially secure by such goings on in the street, in the stores, and in the bank; but after all, they reason: "These people do not really touch us. All they have is money." The newly rich, however, being less socially firm than the old, do feel themselves to be of lesser worth as they see others also rise in the economic worlds of the small cities.

Local society is a structure of power as well as a hierarchy of status; at its top there is a set of cliques or "crowds" whose members judge and decide the important community issues, as well as many larger issues of state and nation in which 'the community' is involved.[4] Usually, although by no means always, these cliques are composed of old upper-class people: they include the larger businessmen and those who control the banks who usually also have connections with the major real-estate holders. Informally organized, these cliques are often each centered in the several economic functions: there is an industrial, a retailing. a banking clique. The cliques overlap, and there are usually some men who, moving from one to another, coordinate viewpoints and decisions. There are also the lawyers and administrators of the solid rentier families, who, by the power of proxy and by the many contacts between old and new wealth they embody, tie together and focus in decision the power of money, of credit, of organization.

Immediately below such cliques are the hustlers, largely of new upper-class status, who carry out the decisions and programs of the top—sometimes anticipating them and always trying to do so. Here are the "operations" men —the vice-presidents of the banks, successful small businessmen, the ranking public officials, contractors, and executives of local industries. This number-two level shades off into the third-string men—the heads of civic agencies, organization officials, the pettier civic leaders, newspaper men, and, finally, into the fourth order of the power hierarchy—the rank and file of the professional and business strata, the ministers, the leading teachers, social workers, personnel directors.

On almost any given topic of interest or decision, some top clique, or even some one key man, becomes strategic to the decision at hand and to the informal coordination of its support among the important cliques. Now it is the man who is the clique's liaison with the state governor; now it is the bankers' clique; now it is the man who is well liked by the rank and file of both Rotary Club and Chamber of Commerce, both Community Chest and Bar Association.

Power does not reside in these middle-level organizations; key decisions are not made by their membership. Top men belong to them, but are only infrequently active in them. As associations, they help put into effect the policy-line worked out by the higher circles of power; they are training grounds in which younger hustlers of the top prove themselves; and sometimes, especially in the smaller cities, they are recruiting grounds for new members of the top.

"We would not go to the associations, as you call them—that is, not right away," one powerful man of a sizable city in the mid-South told Professor Floyd Hunter.

A lot of these associations, if you mean by associations the Chamber of Commerce or the Community Council, sit around and discuss "goals" and "ideals." I don't know what a lot of those things mean. I'll be frank with you, I do not get onto a lot of those committees. A lot of the others in town do, but I don't. . . . Charles Homer is the biggest man in our crowd. . . . When he gets an idea, others will get the idea . . . recently he got the idea that Regional City should be the national headquarters for an International

Trade Council. He called in some of us [the inner crowd], and he talked briefly about his idea. He did not talk much. We do not engage in loose talk about the "ideals" of the situation and all that other stuff. We get right down to the problem, that is, how to get this Council. We all think it is a good idea right around the circle. There are six of us in the meeting. . . . All of us are assigned tasks to carry out. Moster is to draw up the papers of incorporation. He is the lawyer. I have a group of friends that I will carry along. Everyone else has a group of friends he will do the same with. These fellows are what you might call followers.

We decide we need to raise $65,000 to put this thing over. We could raise that amount within our own crowd, but eventually this thing is going to be a community proposition, so we decide to bring the other crowds in on the deal. We decide to have a meeting at the Grandview Club with select members of other crowds. . . . When we meet at the Club at dinner with the other crowds, Mr. Homer makes a brief talk; again, he does not need to talk long. He ends his talk by saying he believes in his proposition enough that he is willing to put $10,000 of his own money into it for the first year. He sits down. You can see some of the other crowds getting their heads together, and the Growers Bank crowd, not to be outdone, offers a like amount plus a guarantee that they will go long with the project for three years. Others throw in $5,000 to $10,000 until—I'd say within thirty or forty minutes—we have pledges of the money we need. In three hours the whole thing is settled, including the time for eating!

There is one detail I left out, and it is an important one. We went into that meeting with a board of directors picked. The constitution was all written, and the man who was to head the council as executive was named . . . a third-string man, a fellow who will take advice. . . . The public doesn't know anything about the project until it reaches the stage I've been talking about. After the matter is financially sound, then we go to the newspapers and say there is a proposal for consideration. Of course, it is not news to a lot of people by then, but the Chamber committees and other civic organizations are brought in on the idea. They all think it's a good idea. They help to get the Council located and established. That's about all there is to it.[5]

3

The status drama of the old and the new upper class; the class structure that underpins that drama; the power system of the higher cliques—these now form the rather standard, if somewhat intricate, pattern of the upper levels of local society. But we could not understand that pattern or what is happening to it, were we to forget that all these cities are very much part of a national system of status and power and wealth. Despite the loyal rhetoric practiced by many Congressional spokesmen, no local society is in truth a sovereign locality. During the past century, local society has become part of a national economy; its status and power hierarchies have come to be subordinate parts of the larger hierarchies of the nation. Even as early as the decades after the Civil War, persons of local eminence were becoming—merely local.[6] Men whose sphere of active decision and public acclaim was regional and national in scope were rising into view. Today, to remain merely local is to fail; it is to be overshadowed by the wealth, the power, and the status of nationally important men. To succeed is to leave local society behind—although certification by it may be needed in order to be selected for national cliques.

All truly old ways in America are, of course, rural. Yet the value of rural origin and of rural residences is sometimes ambiguous. On the one hand, there is the tradition of the town against the hayseed, of the big city against the small-town hick, and in many smaller cities, some prestige is achieved by those who, unlike the lower, working classes, have been in the city for all of one generation. On the other hand, men who have achieved eminence often boast of the solidity of their rural origin; which may be due to the Jeffersonian ethos which holds rural virtues to be higher than the ways of the city, or to the desire to show how very far one has come.

If, in public life, the farm is often a good place to have come from, in social life, it is always a good place to own and to visit. Both small-city and big-city upper classes now quite typically own and visit their "places in the country." In part, all this, which even in the Middle West began as far back as the eighteen-nineties, is a way by which the merely rich attempt to anchor themselves in what is old and esteemed, of proving with cash and loving care and some-times with inconvenience. their reverence for the past. So in the South there is the exactly restored Old Plantation Mansion, in Texas and California the huge cattle spread or the manicured fruit ranch, in Iowa the model farm with its purebred stock and magnificent barns. There is also the motive of buying the farm as an investment and as a tax evasion, as well as, of course, the pleasure of such a seasonable residence and hobby.

For the small town and the surrounding countryside, these facts mean that local status arrangements can no longer be strictly local. Small town and countryside are already pretty well consolidated, for wealthy farmers, especially upon retiring, often move into the small city, and wealthy urban families have bought much country land. In one middle-western community, Mr. Hollingshead has reported, some twenty-five families of pioneer ancestry have accumulated more than sixty per cent of the surrounding one hundred sixty square miles of rich agricultural land.[7] Such concentration has been strengthened by marriages between rural and urban upper-class families. Locally, any "rural aristocracy" that may prevail is already centered in at least the small city; rural upper classes and the local society of smaller cities are in close contact, often in fact, belonging to the same higher cousinhood.

In addition to the farms owned by city families and the town-centered activities and residences of rural families, there is the increased seasonal change of residence among both rural and small-town upper classes. The women and children of the rural upper classes go to "the lake" for the summer period, and the men for long week ends, even as New York families do the same in the winters in Florida. The democratization of the seasonable vacation to coast, mountain, or island now extends to local upper classes of small cities and rural district, where thirty years ago it was more confined to metropolitan upper classes.

The connections of small town with countryside, and the centering of the status worlds of both upon the larger city, are most dramatically revealed when into the country surrounding a small town there moves a set of gentlemen farmers. These seasonal residents are involved in the conduct and values of the larger cities in which they live; they know nothing and often care less for local claims to eminence. With their country estates, they come to occupy the top rung of what used to be called the farm ladder, although they know little or nothing of the lower rungs of that ladder. In one middle-western township studied by Evon Vogt, such urban groups own half the land.[8] They do not seek connections with local society and often do not even welcome its advances, but they are passing on these country estates to their children and now even to their grandchildren.

The members of local society, rural and urban, can attempt to follow one of two courses: they can withdraw and try to debunk the immoral ways of the newcomers, or they can attempt to join them, in which case they too will come to focus their social ways of life upon the metropolitan area. But whichever course they elect, they soon come to know, often with bitterness, that the new upper class as well as the local upper-middle classes, among whom they once cashed in their claims for status, are watching them with close attention and sometimes with amusement. What was once a little principality, a seemingly self-sufficient world of status, is becoming an occasionally used satellite of the big-city upper class.

What has been happening in and to local society is its consolidation with the surrounding rural area, and its gradual incorporation in a national system of power and status. Muncie, Indiana, is now much closer to Indianapolis and Chicago than it was fifty years ago; and the upper classes of Muncie travel farther and travel more frequently than do the local middle and lower classes. There are few small towns today whose upper classes, both new and old, are not likely to visit a near-by large city at least every month or so. Such travel is now a standard operation of the business, educational, and social life of the small-city rich. They have more friends at a distance and more frequent relations with them. The world of the local upper-class person is simply larger than it was in 1900 and larger than the worlds of the middle and lower classes today.

It is to the metropolitan upper classes that the local society of the smaller cities looks; its newer members with open admiration, its older, with less open admiration. What good is it to show a horse or a dog in a small city of 100,000 population, even if you could, when you know that *The* Show will be in New York next fall? More seriously, what prestige is there in a

$50,000 local deal, however financially convenient, when you know that in Chicago, only 175 miles away, men are turning over $500,000? The very broadening of their status area makes the small-town woman and man unsatisfied to make big splashes in such little ponds, makes them yearn for the lakes of big-city prestige, if not for truly national repute. Accordingly, to the extent that local society maintains its position, even locally, it comes to mingle with and to identify itself with a more metropolitan crowd and to talk more easily of eastern schools and New York night clubs.

There is one point of difference between the old and the new upper classes in the smaller cities that is of great concern to the old, for it causes the new to be a less ready and less reliable cash-in area for the status claims of the old. The old upper class, after all, is old only in relation to the new and hence needs the new in order to feel that all is right in its little world of status. But the new, as well as many of the old, know well that this local society is now only local.

The men and women of the old upper class understand their station to be well within their own city. They may go to Florida or California in the winter, but they go always as visitors, not as explorers of new ways or as makers of new business contacts. They feel their place to be in their own city and they tend to think of this city as containing all the principles necessary for ranking all people everywhere. The new upper class, on the other hand, tends to esteem local people in terms of the number and types of contacts they have with places and people outside the city—which the true old upper-class person often excludes as "outsiders." Moreover, many articulate members of the middle and lower classes look up to the new upper class because of such "outside" contacts which, in a decisive way, are the very opposite of "old family residence." Old family residence is a criterion that is community-centered; outside contacts center in the big city or even in the national scene.[9]

4

Today "outside contacts" often center in one very specific and galling reminder of national status and power which exists right in the local city: During the last thirty years, and especially with the business expansions of World War II, the national corporation has come into many of these small cities. Its arrival has upset the old economic status balances within the local upper classes; for, with its local branch, there have come the executives from the big city, who tend to dwarf and to ignore local society.[10]

Prestige is, of course, achieved by "getting in with" and imitating those who possess power as well as prestige. Nowadays such social standing as the local upper classes, in particular the new upper classes, may secure, is increasingly obtained through association with the leading officials of the great absentee-owned corporations, through following their style of living. through moving to their suburbs outside the city's limits, attending their social functions. Since the status world of the corporation group does not characteristically center in the local city, local society tends to drift away from civic prestige, looking upon it as "local stuff."

In the eyes of the new upper class, the old social leaders of the city come gradually to be displaced by the corporation group. The local upper classes struggle to be invited to the affairs of the new leaders, and even to marry their children into their circles. One of the most obvious symptoms of the drift is the definite movement of the local upper-class families into the exclusive suburbs built largely by the corpo ration managers. The new upper class tends tc imitate and to mingle with the corporation group; the "bright young men" of all educated classes tend to leave the small city and to make their careers within the corporate world. The local world of the old upper class is simply bypassed.

Such developments are often more important to women than to men. Women are frequently more active in social and civic matters—particularly in those relating to education, health, and charities—if for no other reason than that they have more time for them. They center their social life in the local cities because "it is the thing to do," and it is the thing to do only if those with top prestige do it. Local women, however, gain little or no social standing among the corporate elite by participating in local affairs, since the executives' wives, corporation- and city-centered, do not concern themselves with local society, nor even with

such important local matters as education; for they send their own children to private schools or, on lower executive levels, to their own public schools in their own suburbs, distinct and separate from the city's. A typical local woman could work herself to the bone on civic matters and never be noticed or accepted by the executives' wives. But if it became known that by some chance she happened to be well acquainted with a metropolitan celebrity, she might well be "in."

Local women often participate in local and civic affairs in order to help their husband's business, but the terms of the executive's success lie within his national corporation. The corporate officials have very few business dealings with strictly local businessmen. They deal with distant individuals of other corporations who buy the plant's products or sell it materials and parts. Even when the executive does undertake some deal with a local businessman, no social contact is required—unless it is part of the corporation's "good-will" policy. So it is quite unnecessary for the executive's wife to participate in local society: the power of the corporation's name will readily provide him with all the contacts in the smaller city that he will ever require.

5

Perhaps there was a time—before the Civil War—when local societies composed the only society there was in America. It is still true, of course, that every small city is a local hierarchy of status and that at the top of each there is still a local elite of power and wealth and esteem. But one cannot now study the upper groups in even a great number of smaller communities and then—as many American sociologists are prone to do—generalize the results to the nation, as the American System.[11] Some members of the higher circles of the nation do live in small towns—although that is not usual. Moreover, where they happen to maintain a house means little; their area of operation is nation-wide. The upper social classes of all the small towns of America cannot merely be added up to form a national upper class; their power cliques cannot merely be added up to form the national power elite. In each locality there *is* an upper set of families, and in each, with certain regional variations, they are quite similar. But the national structure of classes is not a mere enumeration of equally important local units. The class and status and power systems of local societies are not equally weighted; they are not autonomous. Like the economic and political systems of the nation, the prestige and the power systems are no longer made up of decentralized little hierarchies, each having only thin and distant connections, if any at all, with the others. The kinds of relations that exist between the countryside and the town, the town and the big city, and between the various big cities, form a structure that is now national in scope. Moreover, certain forces, which by their very nature are not rooted in any one town or city, now modify, by direct as well as indirect lines of control, the local hierarchies of status and power and wealth that prevail in each of them.

It is to the cities of the Social Register and the celebrity, to the seats of the corporate power, to the national centers of political and military decision, that local society now looks—even though some of its older members will not always admit that these cities and corporations and powers exist socially. The strivings of the new upper class and the example of the managerial elite of the national corporation cause local societies everywhere to become satellites of status and class and power systems that extend beyond their local horizon. What town in New England is socially comparable with Boston? What local industry is economically comparable with General Motors? What local political chief with the political directorate of the nation?

NOTES

1. Much of this chapter is based upon my own observations and interviews in some dozen middle-sized cities in the Northeast, the Middle-West, and the South. . . . I have also used field notes made during the course of an intensive study of a city of 60,000 in Illinois during the summer of 1945. Unless otherwise noted, all quotations in this chapter are from my own research. . . .

2. The woman of the new upper class has a somewhat different image: she often sees the prestige of the old upper class as something "cultural" to appreciate. She often attempts to give to the old status an "educational" meaning: this is especially true among those younger women of the station-wagon set whose husbands are professional men and who are themselves from a "good college." Having education themselves, and the time and money with which to organize cultural community affairs, the new upper-class women have more respect for the "cultural" component of the old upper-class style than do their men. In thus acknowledging the social superiority of the older class, new upper-class women stress those of its themes which are available to them also. But such women form today the most reliable cash-in area for the status claims of the old upper classes in the small towns. Toward the middle classes, in general, such women snobbishly assert: "They might be interested in cultural things but they would not have the opportunities or background or education. They could take advantage of the lecture series, but they don't have the background for heading it."

3. See Allison Davis, *et al*, op. cit. p. 497.

4. I have drawn in this section from various parts of Floyd Hunter's first-hand study, *Community Power Structure* (Chapel Hill: University of North Carolina Press, 1953).

5. Cf. ibid. pp. 172-4.

6. See Richard Hofstadter, *The Age of Reform* (New York: Knopf 1955), pp. 46 ff.

7. See Hollingshead, op. cit. p. 59. On farm ownership in a southern county, see Allison Davis, op. cit. p. 276.

8. On urban ownership of farm land in a Middle-Western county, see Evon Vogt, op. cit.

9. More aggressive than the old, the new upper-class criterion for the really top people is not only that they are rich but that they are "going places" and have connections with others who are "going places" in an even bigger way than they. In one typical small city, the heroes of the new upper class were described to me as

> Boys with a lot of dynamite. . . . They're in there together going places and doing everything that's good for [the city]. They operate nationally, see, and that's very important in their outlook. They're not very active in strictly local affairs, but they are active men. They have active investments all over, not money just lying around doing nothing.

Stories of old families that have fallen and of active new families that have risen illustrate to the new upper class the "workings of democracy" and the possibility of "anybody with the energy and brains" getting ahead. Such stories serve to justify their own position and style, and enable them to draw upon the national flow of official myths concerning the inevitable success of those who know how to work smartly. The old upper classes do not tell such stories, at least not to strangers, for among them prestige is a positive thing in itself, somehow inherent in their way of life. and indeed, their very being. But to the new upper-class man, prestige seems something that he himself does not truly possess, but could very well use in his business and social advancement; he tends to see the social position of the old upper class as an instrument for the "selling" of a project or the making of more money.

> You can't get anything done in this town without them [the old upper class]. The handles on those names are very important. . . . Look, if you and I

go out on a project in this town, or any other town we've got to have names with handles. Investors, proprietors, and so on, they just hold back until we do that. Otherwise if we had the finest project in the world, it would be born dead.

10. Compare, on the small city and the national

corporation, Mills and Ulmer, 'Small Business and Civic Welfare,' op. cit.

11. For an example of the confusion of small town with nation to the point of caricature see W. Lloyd Warner, *American Life: Dream and Reality* (Chicago: University of Chicago Press, 1953).

Section Three   *An Opposition and Its Internal Difficulties*

Contradictions Within the New Left

John C. Leggett

THE REGULARITIES

As Clark Kerr has indicated,[1] many forces press students to become radicals. Yet a number of contradictions within the university student movement serve to minimize extensive radicalization of the student body. What are these conflicts? Briefly, they are problems associated with the strategies of action, the commitments to equality, and the demands of career. Qualifications for comment on these matters are relevant. My own extensive and intensive participation within and at the periphery of New Left groups between 1960 and 1970, not to mention my very real careerist commitments, has given me ample bases for such comment.[2]

STRATEGIES OF ACTION

Theoretical formalism worsened by crisis irrationality

When leftist students map their strategies, they necessarily encounter the problem of *theoretical formalism worsened by crisis irrationality*. In order to deal with a complex reality and to be able to move from the general to the specific, radical strategists are obliged to express their formulations on a high level of abstraction, and they must do so with logical

■ Paper presented at Case Western University and at the Edwardsville campus of Southern Illinois University in January, 1970. Also read in revised form before the 1972 American Sociological Association Meetings.

thoroughness. They and a critical rank and file must use a language which allows for both generality and distinctions. The language must also use the cognitive categories of struggle for radical students have been objectively involved in conflicts with university administrators, corporate elites, and military organizations. Radicals with this background generally incorporate the categories of conflict associated with anarchosyndicalist—Marxism as well as existentialism. Historically, these have been the languages of radical forces and individual choices, respectively. This vocabulary then serves as political ammunition expressed through heated argument in which the radicals debate one another, their peripheral friends, or their enemies. Although heated, the argument is not intrinsically irrational: We can always separate affect from validity, although the enemies of the student left have often been hesitant to do so. Charges of left irrationality are generally misplaced.

Not just heated formalism but the occasional rhetoric alienates many of the left-leaning students who are often drawn to the left because it and it alone appears to offer ideas and programs for solving such concrete problems as war, racism, imperialism, and associated forms of human degradation. Yet sympathetic students are often repelled by what they judge to be the rhetoric of the movement. Indeed, in the heat of battle, left vocabulary frequently loses its substantive references, conceptual clarity, and logical neatness. To the moderate-left, embroiled *non sequiturs* often serve as poor substitutes for the brilliant arguments the left can usually present. What remains is the repulsive and now illogical cant. How does one explain this recurrent intellectual failure?

Because left-students are in the forefront of conflict with the minions of state bureaucracy (see "The Natural History of an Institutional Arrest and the Lessons of the Sproul Hall Sit-In," Section Three of Chapter 11), corporate wealth, and military personnel, and in part because left-students are very frequently bright and sensitive people, they become extremely aware of the grotesqueness of the establishment, the ruling class, and the conditions they sponsor. Left-students generally understand quite well how the system works both to exploit persons and to repress problem-solvers—the students included. This consciousness of exploitation and control energizes a left whose incapacity to alter repression angers its members to the point where they develop, as a group, low threshholds of tolerance and hence less than adequate ways to communicate properly. This drawback becomes most apparent when new left leadership must continuously restate to their potential supporters what has become patently obvious at those historical moments when there is precious little time for repeated expression. During campus confrontations, for example, both time and patience are at a premium. At those times, radical consciousness and political impotence—this vicious combination which compels and stymies simultaneously—frequently drives radicals to repel their own political periphery at the very moment it is most needed.

Initiate but not sustain

Given the inability to attract and to organize a disciplined political group with a broad student base, the student radicals find themselves *unable to initiate and sustain major offensives, but able to lead broadly based student reactions against gross atrocities*—such as the invasion of Cambodia and the killings at Kent State. They lack the power to initiate and to sustain because both activities require an organizational apparatus. Yet no organizational apparatus of significant import can emerge because it would contradict the liberal—anarchist ethics of personal freedom. What *can* occur, under these conditions, is the spontaneous veto of a morally outrageous policy. In effect, what remains for radical and left-democratic leadership is the power to guide a massive and temporary reaction. We may refer to this contradiction as *reaction politics.*

Reaction politics can be observed when the power to check, to veto, is not followed by a surge to organize and grow so that the movement gains a position that enables it to time its blows for maximum effectiveness. Unfortunately for the student left, what follows the adrenaline of immediate and total involvement of the many is the slumber of the multitude, until another atrocity is committed. Between atrocities and protests, careers are pursued, tattered loyalties repaired, institutions are refurbished, and minimal concessions to troublemakers are made. Many students are dimly aware of this hopeless cycle, but seldom do they have the time to think it through or to contemplate its political implications. But in a vague way, they are aware of the consequences of reaction politics, and their limited awareness dampens their feelings toward the student left. In turn, the student left fumbles along and eventually adopts another strategy.

Issue hopping

In part because of the inability to initiate and to sustain much more than reaction politics and in part because of the prompting of the mass media, the student left settles for a strategy of *issue hopping*. Because the student left is not part of a disciplined political body with a semimilitary chain of command, the left-students are not bound by an organization that could choose an issue and stick with it to a (successful or otherwise) conclusion. Rather, we can note the periodic jumping from issue to issue, long before the matter initially under consideration can be solved to the benefit of the left. One moment the left rallies to the defense of left-faculty who are being purged . . . but before the question is settled, they move on to organize a strike to support an ethnic studies program . . . before the ethnic studies program is safe from faculty and administration emasculation, the left-students begin to mount an offensive for greater student power in university departments . . . a few months later they are off into the community in an effort to build alliances with the working class . . . or the minorities . . . or slum tenants . . . followed by a march on the nation's capitol to stop the war in Vietnam. Issue hopping seems to be endless. It may even by cyclical.

Hop, hop, hop, and seldom are issues fully illuminated, let alone won! What often emerges after an altercation with a university administration is a compromise that fails to meet the original purpose underlying student action, as the deans, provosts, and presidents package a stylized program for safe-keeping. The net result is a great deal of energy input but very little structural reorganization along radical lines. What continues is the spread of U.S. military involvement throughout this country, the establishment of ethnic studies programs bereft of the original radical impulse, plus the cooptation of many former protestors by establishment political parties, governmental job programs, and university employers.

Issue hopping is as American as violence and apple pie. We are taught to consume a bit of the unknown and to drop it once we've tasted it. Having tried something, we lose interest in it. We are a nation of consumers. We dig new thrills—cars, clothes, drugs, hair styles, music, alcohol—just so it's new, fun, and exciting. We extend this consumerism to our politics. And the net result is waste. Perhaps what the left needs most are issues with built-in obsolescence. After one of them had been frittered around with, it could disintegrate. But since the problems in question are enduring, let's forget about issues with built-in obsolescence.

Reformist changes
through revolutionaries' activities

Mapping includes the ability to judge the output of radicalism and, when it appears to be little more than reform, to ask whether the radicals should make the efforts and the sacrifices: What is involved is the *contradiction of reformist changes through revolutionaries' activities.*

Pushing for qualitative change, the student radicals in the United States must apparently settle for incremental reform. That's what happened in the 1960s. After years of heated campus conflict, a modicum of change has occurred in relations with the subordinate races and the poor. These alterations, ironically enough, have

made the system more tolerable. More than that, the greatest number of concessions have been made to the wrong people, not to the proletarian minorities and the overseas oppressed, but to their champions, the students. After the smoke of campus battle has cleared and the Dow Chemical recruiter has fled, what the radicals have generally achieved is a noticeable elimination of university abuses: the creation of special courses or programs, the extension of scholarship programs, the *de facto* abolition of university regulations serving to inhibit student sexual activity, the placing of one or several students on a university board of regents, the abolition of grades and the substitution of a pass-or-fail system, the establishment (or improvement) of teacher evaluation programs, the creation of student representation on departmental committees, the establishment of ethnic studies programs (without departmental autonomy), and the extension of campus recreation programs to include pubs. The concession seems endless. Nonetheless, the university chain of command remains intact.

This dilemma is clear: The more successfully the left-students struggle over concrete issues—and the radicals have no choice but to fight on abuses that are palpable—the less odious the system becomes, and the more likely will it prove to be acceptable to most students. In any event, if the radicals go too far and refuse to accept reform through compromise, they appear unreasonable. Or, in the absence of that damning depiction, they are made to appear as persons who deliberately exploit concrete issues to further their own narrow ends.

An analogy from the 1930s comes to mind. In their heyday, the American Communists moved into industrial unions and did an excellent job of improving factory, dock, and mine conditions—so much so, that their and other brands of radicalism became unacceptable when presented at the polls. Yet as trade unionists, they and their skills remained quite acceptable to many rank-and-file workers until the Cold War began (1947–1948). Indeed, as piecemeal reformers they did such a fine job of organizing and maintaining industrial unions that radicalism as well as radicals later became dispensable once the dirty work had been done. After the early battles were over, more moderate men could later afford to unload the left with the aid of a red-baiting onslaught led by Joe McCarthy. However, McCarthy's fears were misplaced. Retrospectively, it would seem that Communist radicals were great ameliorators, noteworthy perpetuators of capitalism, no matter what their thunderous rhetoric might have portended.

Adventurism

Mapping also involves the problems of *adventurism*. Adventurism refers to radical groups taking militant, hazardous action without a mass base. Can adventurism be avoided? Generally depicted as a consequence of excessive ego-centrism, in fact adventurism has a genuine organizational basis.

In sophisticated leftist circles, the cardinal rule is, Don't be an adventurist. But unless left-students embark on an adventurous course to *initiate* struggle in a community, their movement will attract few supporters. Generally speaking, unless the left uses power tactics such as guerrilla theatre, they will fail to lift the center-left students from their traditional torpor. To be successful, the tactics must not only excite the imaginations of the center-left but go beyond the experiences of the enemy. In effect, these tactics must be "far-out," surprising, hopefully amusing, and perhaps obstructive—in order to obtain publicity necessary for a victory of little consequence except to celebrate the end of torpor and the beginning of a new solidarity. The victory and its celebration can then depict the left as tactically successful. The net effect can only be the further attraction of the center- and left-democrats to the left-wing winner.

But the very moment students use adventurous devices, the mass media parade students as both "freaks without proper respect" and "destroyers beyond the moral order." The slander finds its audiences. Most working-class and minority people, many of whom suffer abuses on a regular basis and hence would seem to qualify as the natural allies of the student radicals, passively accept the hostile pulp and film images presented by established groups. Worse yet, the subordinate strata view the subsequent state repression of the left as natural, perhaps good. Over and over again, left-students have not only embarked on spectacular campus and community campaigns *without a mass base* but

have carried this potential base of hostile spectators on their backs!

Hence to map a course of creative involvement and to act in relation to this charted course often results in the objectively correct criticism of adventurism. But what are the alternatives in a society where institutions have directed persons to avoid what the left properly deems to be the moral obligation of all students to act to stop overwhelming immorality? The overseas napalmings, the slaughterous invasions, the village burnings, the bombings of innocent civilians, all occur without deep public concern, unless and until radical students depart on an adventurous course. The comfortable, middle-aged men of moderate bent and balanced pen should never forget that the left-students have become the conscience of the cautious, phlegmatic ones simultaneously enmeshed in bureaucratic routine, humanist jargon, careerist involvements, *and* political sobriety.

Participatory democracy

How can the student left discuss their many problems without identifying themselves and their weaknesses to their enemies? Until recently, the student left favored participatory democracy. Many still do. Yet the *contradictions inherent in participatory democracy* are numerous. Worse yet, its retention would seem fatally necessary.

If center-left students are to become involved in politics on a continuous basis, they must be able to participate fully in meetings which result in everyone's having had at least some influence on political decisions. Discussions and decisions should involve the right of each one to speak and to act spontaneously. This antiparliamentary form allows for the widest breadth of membership participation and inclusion.

Yet widespread, spontaneous student participation in group meetings tempts informers to infiltrate the group. In turn, the informers report strategic and tactical information to the police and the university administrators, who use this "intelligence information" to beat the students in political conflicts. Time and again agents of the police and the university have successfully penetrated a movement. In one case, a bit of California opera buffa, a local left group's photographer took excellent photos at student demonstrations, slept with leading left-wing activists, and obtained considerable intelligence information, which he turned over to the police, along with dozens of damaging photos. As an informer, he may have had many employers, perhaps as many bosses as loves. Who knows?

What to do? For the student movement to tighten up decision-making by concentrating its authority in the hands of the few, would be to lay the groundwork for the isolation of the leadership and the demoralization of the rank and file. Because of the pervasiveness of the hang-loose ethic, when radical student leaders centralize authority and demand self-discipline and radicalized regularity, the subculturally determined reaction of the rank and file is to criticize the leadership as authoritarian and to withdraw from participation. A leadership so rejected becomes isolated and readily coopted, for it, too, can be demoralized by shrinking ranks. Faced with this sell-out, followers become apathetic in their politics and caustic in their personal criticisms of the former leadership. The basis thereby exists for mutual castigation under conditions of left-dissolution.

Tighten up . . . and shut it down

Under these abject conditions, the call of the left-student for centralism can be heard by many of his peers, although most reject it. However, the rejection does not eliminate the dilemma on centralism: Either tighten up or shut it down; but if the radicals do tighten up, their action itself *will* shut it down—people will *leave.*

Left folklore abounds with tales, generally true, of infiltrators. Such objectively real circumstances as the presence of infiltrators, plus the actual threats of state imprisonment of observed radicals, press people to reorganize their politics along the lines of democratic centralism. But the activities of this kind of organization alienate many leftists, who see in the group many of the uglier attributes of the society they are trying to remake. Centralization of decision-making, officiousness in interpersonal affairs, the hierarchical chain of command, the invidious status distinctions among the membership, the haughtiness of the political superiors, the egoism of the leadership, the unquestioning

obedience of orders on pain of penalties, and other negative qualities, either fail to attract students or repel those already recruited.

Many students want and seek their freedom from repressive political and economic authorities now. And the vanguard party—whether Maoist, or Trotskyist, or "other"—does not offer them that freedom. Only a decentralized, loosely organized political group allows for unfettered personal expression. But this organizational form also includes political sloppiness, and to be sloppy is to lose to one's enemies.

THE COMMITMENTS TO EQUALITY

Ranking among egalitarians

Ironically, what little organization left-students display contradicts the general commitments to equality common to both the left-democrats and left-radicals. What occurs is the *contradiction of ranking among egalitarians.* For a radical movement to recruit those predisposed to join, the movement must exude egalitarianism, a taste of the utopian future. In order to be successful in recruiting from a periphery with futuristic propensities, the movement cannot express a ranked quality, a pecking-order relationship that students find so unacceptable in the worlds of the tier-ordered university and the status-flawed community. Ranking repels those young persons seeking equality and justice.

Yet even when radical organizations deliberately avoid a formal, hierarchical chain of command in their groups, they create a *de facto* hierarchy in decision-making. Illustrative was the traditional SDS, with its ideological deemphasis on organization. In this case, hierarchy not only existed but found reinforcement through various rewards, which were many and sometimes obvious, as left-student leaders can readily testify. For example, one crucial step was the sifting-selection of lieutenants recruited personally by the campus commander-in-chief. Rewards included personal invitations to caucuses, parties, and dinners. As critical as being invited was being overlooked. Negative sanctions also included public deprecations.

For better or for worse, tiered power and correlated reward structures have contributed to the pigeon-holing of persons to the accompaniment of sanctioning systems. In turn, the very ranking processes and the tiered orders have contravened the principle of equality and thereby alienated many of those seeking equality now.

In-group—out-group

The ranking occurs not only within the ranks of specific radical organizations but between it and its periphery, so that what emerges is an *indivious in-group—out-group distinction between high-status radicals and low-status periphery*. This distinction all but seals the radicals to themselves as they engage in pathetic efforts to recruit those already defined by them as unworthy of left-wing prestige. Many persons peripheral to the left have occasionally noticed the personality counterparts of this in-group phenomena: elitism, arrogance, narrowness, intolerance, sectarianism, and outright conceit. Unfortunately, these depictions become generalized to stereotypy rather than directed to particular types of leadership within the movement. Be that as it may, these personal qualities *do* exist and have added to the in-group propensity to alienate those many students who are also turned off by the corporate establishment, the governing class, and university-ranked elites.

THE DEMANDS OF CAREER: HAVING YOUR LEFTISM AND EATING TOO

When left-democratic students become alienated from left-radicals, left-democrats take on a sensitivity to certain contradictions on group solidarity within the radical camp itself. When one is sensitized, it becomes obvious that one cannot be a long-term radical and a bureaucratic trainee at the same time without appearing to be a phony: Being caught in this contradiction may be called the desire to *have your leftism and eating too*.

Apparently oblivious to this contradiction, many radicals attempt to follow egalitarian and elitist paths simultaneously, if only momentarily. A number of leftists, for example, are divided between militant commitments and career objectives.

On the one hand, the radical camp demands that its own people be fully committed to the realization of revolutionary change and to sacrifice accordingly. On the other hand, because radical students are involved in career training, and because their brightness predicts professional and institutional success—at the cost of withdrawal from radical activities that could conceivably demand heavy sacrifice—many leftist students eventually succumb to professional coaxing (and coaching), bend before parental and peer pressures, and drop their radicalism altogether, sometimes to become voyeurs of the actions of feminists, black militants, and Third World guerrillas.

Preceding this drop-out, the center- and left-democrats clearly see the sketchy involvement of left-radicals who are obviously moving up career ladders. Their immediate annual rounds belie their long-term commitments. The semester cycle leads the left-periphery to wonder whether the leftist student is an analog to "nigger" or "flake." Typically, fall political activities are followed by final exams, and the Movement momentarily dies. Spring semester follows a similar course. When summer vacation arrives, students are off to the resorts, the beaches, the visits, the summer jobs—and the left-campus movement languishes as administrators move to plug academic loopholes and to chastise politically suspect faculty. What becomes obvious to many is the predictable unevenness, the cyclical come-and-go of the left-students as they play directly into the hands of the university administration. Unlike students, the university staff and employees function more or less continuously, fifty-two weeks of the year.

During the lulls, the university administration punishes the Movement, not necessarily the left-student leaders, although they can expect the full range of penalties from warnings to blacklistings. Repeatedly put to the wall are left-wing faculty as well, while academic administrators and senior faculty interpret academic freedom to mean the right of administrators to determine that the leftist faculty and students have fewer rights than those found beyond the pale of the university.

However, if the radical student does make it through graduate school, school administrators will generally give the young leftist one or several chances to prove himself to be a responsible academic—responsible to them, the bosses. Most ex-student radicals opt for the responsible alternative, and the former student thereby loses his political virginity. All this is obvious to many of the nonradical students.

CONCLUSIONS

The foregoing contradictions, and many more, make it impossible to create an ongoing, politically significant, student left. Contradictions thereby undercut objective conditions and radicalizing processes. Were the situation otherwise, the circumstances cited by Kerr and others would yield continuous campus ferment.

We have neglected one significant contradiction. The movement abounds with faculty spokesmen who earn as much annually as ten or fifteen student leftists considered simultaneously. Indeed, some faculty not only draw sizable salaries but earn additional amounts posing as left-firebrand speakers. In fact, they are coddled by a university honorarium at times one-third to one-half of the yearly income of comrades on the speaker's platform. Radical student leaders have on occasion done nearly as well. Thus some movement people accumulate more loot than others. And in booty there is wonder about duty.

Yet in all this committed effort, and growing skepticism, what seems to be lacking among the egalitarians is a sharing of the consequences of commitment. The key consequence of commitment certainly should include a guaranteed minimum yearly income in a movement so diversified in specialities, so punished by authority, and hence differentiated by income. Many New Left people have been active in various struggles. They are now without jobs or blacklisted. One would think the egalitarians would divide their incomes equally. But they do not share. Those who are better rewarded accrue for themselves, or in some cases for their families. The family does not share. It accumulates.

After several years of experiencing the contradiction of *wide span of monetary rewards within the movement*, many of its members become cynical. Many also wonder about the grim necessity of taking risks that redound to the obvious benefit of the few. Many wonder whether those who live *for* the movement should continue to create financial well-being for those who live *off* the movement. But seldom do these skeptics go beyond doubt and withdrawal to recommend what would seem natural among egalitarians, namely, the sharing of individuals' yearly, personal catches.

But students do not need to face this concern, for their positions are not permanent. They graduate soon after the acquisition of consciousness. In turn, graduation plunges the person into new roles and to totally different problems. Thus, unlike the blacks in this country, the American student does not experience contradictions as permanent problems but rather as temporary irritants.

In desperation, some students have turned to terrorism in order to prepare people psychologically for ideological transformation. This strategy has failed to increase militant consciousness. If anything, terrorism has created within the nonterrorist left the belief that the terrorist activities have given the state an excuse to smash the entire left and its left-center periphery. Some feel that the terrorists may be deliberately setting up the entire student left for concentration camps in the hope that massive incarceration will radicalize the left, its sympathizers, and the entire generation of young workers. Given this assessment, not a few of the nonterrorist left and its periphery can anticipate jail cells. And they have decided to withdraw from any political activities which go beyond mild dissent, for fear that if they do march, demonstrate, or confront, they may be associated with terrorists by the state and arrested during a subsequent round-up of radicals. Left-terrorism thereby serves to split the progressive youth and to press them to pull back from radical political activities under objectively real circumstances of hopelessness.

NOTES

1. Clark Kerr, *The Uses of The University* (New York: Harper Torchbooks, 1966), especially ch. 3, "The Future of the City of Intellect," pp. 85–126.

2. It is with considerable hesitation that I list the following activities. Yet I should indicate the participatory basis for my analysis.

1. *Ann Arbor, Winter–Spring, 1960:* University of Michigan campus organizer of mass student–townspeople picketing against retail stores which practiced racially discriminatory hiring and/or service practices.

2. *Detroit, Spring 1961:* (a) Participant in picketing at national headquarters of national chain store because of its Southern service practices; (b) participant in mass demonstration against the Bay of Pigs invasion.

3. *San Francisco, October, 1962:* Participant in massive demonstration on the Russian–Cuban–U.S. missile crisis.

4. *Berkeley and Sacramento, Spring and Fall, 1963:* (a) *Spring:* CORE-sponsored sit-ins within the

State capitol building in favor of the Rumford Bill on minority housing rights; (b) *Fall:* CORE-sponsored, massive picketings for equal employment practices among downtown Berkeley merchants.

5. *Phoenix, Arizona, Spring, 1964:* Coorganizer (along with CORE West Coast Regional Organizer) of massive sit-ins at State Capitol building in pressing for an equal public accommodations law.

6. *San Francisco and Oakland, Spring, 1964:* Participant in mass demonstrations against San Francisco hotels and Oakland restaurants engaging in racially discriminatory hiring practices.

7. *Berkeley, Fall of 1964 and Winter of 1965:* Participant in Berkeley Free Speech Movement.

8. *Berkeley, Delano, Oakland, and San Francisco, 1965–1966:* (a) *Berkeley:* Organizer of funds and food for Delano grape strikers; (b) *Delano:* Participant in flying picket operations in Delano; (c) *Oakland:* Recurrent coorganizer of successful pickets against loading of "hot" grapes in Oakland; (d) *San Francisco:* Successful participant in illegal picketing (later in effect declared lawful by court) which stymied efforts of the Di Giorgio Corporation (a Standard Oil of California subsidiary) to use a court order (to prevent picketing from San Francisco docks) in an attempt to ship scab-picked grapes. Arrested in San Francisco. Case later dismissed by a municipal court after a federal court had dismissed the original court order.

9. *Berkeley, Spring 1966:* Faculty participant in University of California campus antiwar demonstrations against liberal establishment's efforts to escalate the war in Vietnam. Given academic warning by President Heyns for distribution of antiwar literature.

10. *Vancouver, British Columbia, January–February, 1967:* Publicly protested through Socialist member of Provincial Parliament against Royal Canadian Mounted Police interrogation of student(s) on political content of lectures made by three Simon Fraser University professors, including T. B. Bottomore, then Chairman of the Political Science, Sociology, and Anthropology (P.S.A.) Department, and Dean of the School of Arts.

11. *Vancouver, Spring and Summer, 1967:* Faculty supporter of students (and faculty) being purged for either participating in off-campus demonstrations or on-campus liberties defense work.

12. *Vancouver, Summer, 1968:* Faculty participant in democratization of P.S.A. Department and Simon Fraser University.

13. *Storrs, Connecticut, Fall, Winter, and Spring, (1968–1969):* Participant in antiwar demonstrations at the University of Connecticut. Arrested for participation in antiwar demonstrations against Olin-Mathieson Corporation, a leading U.S. manufacturer of ammunition used in Vietnam. Court later dismissed case.

14. *Vancouver, Fall, 1969:* Participant in Simon Fraser University faculty–student strike against the university administration strategy to release activist, liberal and radical faculty from P.S.A. Department.

15. *Vancouver, 1969–1973:* Actively involved in defense of purged P.S.A. faculty at Simon Fraser University.

Chapter 13 The Permanent Wartime State

DENIAL AND PROBLEM SPECIFICATION

We must reject the myths of people's supremacy and great-man advocacy on matters of foreign policy which together constitute points of ideological confusion for many of us. We can instead consider a more challenging conception: the garrison state.

First let us deal with the myth of people's supremacy. It is argued that American citizens register their views on foreign policy through parliamentary bodies and an elected chief executive. In fact, until quite recently, many social scientists have been able to avoid documentation on U.S. foreign policy, although they have piously asserted that "the people" forge goals and recommended strategies through pressured politicians and bloc-voting minorities. Seemingly these politicians have been compelled to heed and to comply with the wishes of the groups having the greatest numbers and hence the greatest electoral power. Foreign policy has merely registered as it has reflected an aroused public opinion.

However, as we indicated in Chapter 12, revelations such as those produced by the Vietnam war have demystified this pluralistic formula on popular control. Nor was the Vietnam war unique during the 1950s and 1960s; associated evidence on Cuba, Guatemala, the Dominican Republic, Iran, the Congo, and Thailand points in the same direction. These materials have revealed the degree to which federal executive political elites generally derive from the upper class, selectively ignore public opinion, and covertly determine foreign policy, with the intent of developing programs in ways consistent with the traditional interests of the upper classes on matters of overseas trade, investment, and politics.

Having determined objectives and specified strategies, this upper-class political coterie, often no more than ten or fifteen people, has time and again succeeded in manipulating voting publics to give the illusion of a public consent. Later the myth of public consent has been redefined by economic and political elites through the mass media and academic scholars to create the illusion of popular, prior determination of a general will, respected by a listening group of political representatives who are duty-bound as receptive inkblotters to pursue wars to their logical and consensual conclusion. Only when later events, e.g., the Pentagon Papers, have disclosed the accompanying elitist chicanery do we discover how selected members of the upper class created and used various mechanisms to falsify both the content and steps of the sequences involved.

Perhaps as difficult to accept is the view that a "great man" determines foreign policy; hence not wealth but intrinsic brightness or some similar measure of greatness is involved when *he* sets foreign policy. Whether the foreign policy formulator is in fact "great" is difficult to determine unless we wish to assume that by making foreign policy the bright one has demonstrated his greatness. But this is circular reasoning, and it fails to establish independent criteria for assessing, first, greatness, second, the forging of foreign policy, and third, the empirical relationship between greatness and the setting of foreign policy. In other words, one of the lamentable attributes of tautological reasoning is the analyst's tendency to simply assume conclusions that he should demonstrate through evidence. It could equally well be asserted that muddling people determine foreign policy, that what has occurred is (*a*) the ascendance of mediocrity into positions of power and (*b*) the use of power by the intellectually unqualified to try to maximize their class interests through foolish declarations and improper actions on foreign policy. It is entirely possible that a combination of relatively bright and mediocre people jointly set foreign policy as part of bureaucratic routine. We suspect that this may well be the case. In any event, whether the great-man-as-architect, the triumph-of-mediocre-man, or some other eclectic synthesis stands as most correct misses the important point: Who benefits materially from the politics involved? That kind of evidence would seem to be more appropriate.

What needs to be determined is not only the *amount* of wealth garnered by our upper classes from their overseas investments but the *degree* to which our country's upper classes have worked to maximize these returns by turning much of the world into militarized zones of challenged insurgencies and police controls.[1] In this regard we need not look far to assess the consequences of upper-class reorganization of the military police both at home and abroad. But raw information is not enough, if we are to gauge the historical sweep as well as the actual numbers involved. We need a general framework as well. When we assess the relation between the upper classes and the military, let us consider one particular model, for it will suggest to us parameters that might otherwise be overlooked. We refer to "the garrison state," a construct perhaps most appropriately understood as a modern society in which the military elite are paramount.[2] With this slight but work-

able frame in mind, we pose the following question:

When our upper classes promote counterinsurgency overseas, how do the same upper classes thereby engender the formations of garrison states both at home and abroad? Here we focus on upper classes, universities, the military, and above all, the militarized police. With these axes cited as pertinent, let us tentatively consider our country as perhaps resembling a garrison state.

THE QUALITIES OF THE GARRISON STATE AND THE PERMANENT WARTIME STATE AS PROXIMATION

It is useful to keep certain facts in mind when considering expository and argumentative materials on the garrison state:

As of September 1, 1969, the United States had some 1.2 million servicemen stationed abroad (out of a total armed strength of 3.5 million men), in more than 30 countries and overseas possessions, and aboard the Atlantic and Pacific Fleets. In addition to uniformed personnel, there are some 26,000 U.S. civilians, 350,000 dependents and 255,000 foreign nationals attached to U.S. overseas installations.

The U.S. presently maintains some 2,270 military installations abroad (not including bases in South Vietnam and Laos, which number in the hundreds), of which 340 are designated "major" bases. "Major" installations are defined by the Pentagon as bases "which are large in number of acres occupied or personnel accommodated, or which represent a high acquisition cost to the United States Government, or which are used in support of a principal U.S. military activity or mission." Major bases include large air bases, ship yards and fleet facilities, principal headquarters and command complexes, large communications facilities and troop training and housing compounds. "Minor" installations include navigational aids, small communications facilities, and small administrative buildings supporting incidental activities. Military missions and military assistance advisory groups (MAAGS) are also included in this category.[3]

U.S. military bases protect trading areas, investment sites, capital investments, and friendly

---

[1] Most relevant are the following four documents: "AID Police Programs for Latin America—1971–72," *NACLA* (North American Congress on Latin America) *Newsletter*, 5, (July—August, 1971); NACLA, *The University—Military—Police Complex: A Directory and Related Documents;* 1970; NACLA, *U.S. Military and Police Operations in the Third World* (New York: NACLA, 1970); NARMIC (National Action/Research on the Military—Industrial Complex), *They're Bringing It All Back. . . . Police on the Homefront* (Philadelphia: NARMIC, 1971).

[2] Here the most pertinent document is Harold Lasswell's "The Garrison State," *American Journal of Sociology,* XLVI (January, 1941) pp. 431–444. The most up-to-date modification of the garrison state model has been expressed by Marc Pilisuk and Thomas Hayden "Is There a Military—Industrial Complex Which Prevents Peace?: Consensus and Countervailing Power in Pluralistic Systems," *The Journal of Social Issues,* XXI (July, 1965), pp. 67–117.

[3] See *U.S. Military and Police Operations in the Third World,* op. cit., p. 2.

governments. This occurs under the direction of the federal executive who leads a country in which upper-class powers to initiate and to coerce are maximal. At the same time U.S. upper-class-directed business firms generally exude an international quality, for members of upper classes all over the world jointly command positions of decision-making and places of key investment in these firms. In turn, these overseas upper-classes seek and find protection from the states from which they derive, and through which they wield, a variety of powers. By the same token, it would be unwise to exaggerate this cosmopolitan arrangement and to overlook powerful banks and corporations, which take on definite national colorations. Some corporations are predominantly controlled by the citizens of one country. Their directors and technicians derive from a particular society served by a nation-state. It reciprocally serves as it regulates corporate leaders, who in turn serve on state regulating and policy-making bodies. Thus reciprocity is ensured under conditions of merger of class and state personnel.[4]

In this sense, we can view many American-based manufacturing, mining, and petrochemical multi-national corporations as being essentially part of a U.S. imperialism protected over the decades by an increasingly powerful executive branch of this country's *central government* locked into a U.S. *upper-class directorate.* This directorate and its corporations have invested heavily in overseas operations since the 1880s. However, since World War II, U.S. imperialism has been especially active not only on the level of economic investment, but it has begun programs of massive political intervention as well.[5]

These global activities have helped to create in our country a state closely resembling a *permanent wartime state.*[6] Ideal typically, it is in many ways similar to the garrison state, except for one crucial attribute. In the permanent wartime state, the military lack the power to coerce compliance from civilian political elites. Yet, from a military point of view, coercion does not seem to be necessary, since the military use other forms of power to obtain most of what they want from the civilian sector. This is possible in part because many civilian state leaders generally adopt and maintain over the decades military beliefs, norms, values, and cognitive categories when assessing and acting in the realms of overseas and domestic politics, thereby helping to accentuate a particular tendency. In general, the historical trend is one of accentuation of both military exercise of power and militarization of thought categories used by civilians located in key political offices. Accentuation is important, for the permanent wartime state, although civilian controlled, evolves over time to acquire an increasingly larger number of attributes of the garrison state. Once acquired, these attributes gradually become full-blown traits, seemingly awaiting their horizontal integration through a military coup d'état, although admittedly, there may be no reason for one to occur.

In the garrison state formulation advanced by Harold Lasswell,[7] the military occupy decision-making slots as heads of state. Of course, this occupancy is not normal by democratic standards, not even right-democratic standards, for in the garrison state model the military hold the principal power to coerce. Yet there is a similarity between garrison state and right-democratic political supremacy, for in both forms power is concentrated and centralized. In the garrison state framework, the power to coerce is centralized in the sense that fewer governmental bodies perform more functions than previously. For example, the federal executive level of government might gradually and increasingly assume activities hitherto monopolized by state and local governments. Coercive power is concentrated as well. State organiza-

---

[4] Most pertinent is Harry Magdoff's *The Age of Imperialism* (New York: Monthly Review, 1969), especially pp. 173–208; David Heilbroner's "The Multi-national Corporation," *The New York Review of Books,* February 11, 1971, pp. 20–26.

[5] William Appleman Williams, "The Large Corporation and American Foreign Policy," in David Horowitz, *Corporations and the Cold War* (New York: Monthly Review, 1969), pp. 71–104.

[6] I have derived this designation "permanent wartime state" in part from the writings of T. V. Vance, author of numerous articles during the early 1950s on the development of a permanent wartime economy inside the United States. His pathfinding pieces appeared in *The New International* (New York: Independent Socialist League, circa 1949–1952).

[7] See Harold Lasswell, op. cit.

tions wield considerably more and heavier sanctions, both negative and positive.

Examining only these two power dimensions, we can observe that the U.S. state today would be a case in point. The executive branch of the central government distributes both monetary rewards and restrictive penalties in a manner and to a degree far out of proportion to what was the case forty and certainly eighty years ago. By the same token, the federal judiciary has become an object of deliberate manipulation by the Chief Executive through his power to make appointments to the Supreme Court. In the same vein, the federal legislature, Congress, has become largely a part-time debating society with little more than the power to veto, temporarily, pieces of legislation whose content, even in the short run, can nonetheless find its way into law through deft Presidential management of Congressional bills, executive orders, and other forms of Presidential discretion.[8]

In the garrison state model, with power both centralized and concentrated, military officers stand as primarily interested in the carrying on of successful overseas warfare. This fighting occurs on a more or less continuous basis, with small-scale wars interspersing and at times accompanying major altercations.

In the modern world, these wars have generally pitted revolutionary movements against U.S. military and police forces, although with increasing frequency Third World mercenary leaders have received military training and arms from the United States and have attempted to quell revolutionary movements, largely by using their own police and troops. (See the reading, "AID Police Programs for Latin America, 1971–72," in Section Two.)

The recent record has been fairly clear-cut, especially since World War II: direct confrontation between U.S. military units and major revolutionary movements as in Vietnam, or U.S. participation in relatively limited antiguerrilla actions, as in Uruguay. Illustratively, we can cite some of the major/minor conflicts or crises

[8] For a recent and highly readable overview of the subject, see Tristram Coffin, "On Power as a Disease: The American Presidency," *The Nation*, Vol. 213, December 20, 1971, pp. 649–653.

where U.S. naval units have been deployed to deal with foreign but localized crises:

Turkey (4/46): USSR–Iran hostilities and USSR–Turkey diplomatic tensions; Naval unit deployed as affirmation of U.S. intentions to shore up Turks against Soviet imperialism.

Trieste (7/46): Trieste ownership dispute; U.S. and British Naval units dispatched to scene with open warfare imminent. Commenced Adriatic Patrol which lasted until Trieste issue resolved in 1954.

Greece (9/46): Political crisis. Naval Units visit requested by U.S. Ambassador.

Indochina War (11/46–7/54): Naval units employed in evacuation, assistance, alert status.

Israel (6/48–4/49): Naval units assigned UN mediator for the Palestine Truce Evacuated UN team eventually in July.

Greek Civil War (46–49): presence and alert.

Korea (50–53): Combat operations.

Tachens Crisis (7/54-2/55): Evacuation of civilians/military personnel; alert and operations.

Vietnam Guerilla War (9/55–Present): Presence, assistance, combat operations.

Red Sea (2/56): Naval units patrols established in view of developing Suez Crisis.

Jordan Tension (7/56): Alert.

Pre-Suez Tension (7/56): Alert.

Suez War (10–11/56): Alert, evacuation, provided presence.

Jordan Crisis (4/57): External conspiracy charged with intent to subvert Jordan. Naval units dispatched.

Kinmen Island (7/57): Communist shelling. Naval units dispatched to defend Taiwan.

Haiti Disorders (6/57): Alert, surface patrols.

Syria Crisis (8–12/57): Alert, provided presence.

Lebanon Civil War (5/58): Support operations.

Jordan/Iraq Unrest (8–12/58): Alert, surveillance, surface patrol.

Cuba Civil War (12/56–12/58): Alert, evacuation, provided presence.

Quemoy–Matsu Crisis (9–10/58): Evacuation, combat operations.

Panama Invasion (4/59): Provided presence.

Berlin Crisis (5/9/59): Alert, provided presence.

Nationalist China–Communist China Crisis (7/59): Provided presence.

Panama Demonstrations (8 and 11/59): Alert.

Laos Civil War (12/60–5/61): Alert, provided presence.

Congo Civil War (7/60–8/63): Alert, evacuation.

Caribbean Tension (4–12/60): Alert, air and surface patrols.

Guatemala–Nicaragua (11/60): Alert, air and surface patrols.

Bay of Pigs Crisis (5/61): Alert.

Zanzibar Riots (6/61): Alert.

Berlin Crisis (9/61–5/62): Alert, provided presence.

Dominican Republic (11–12/61): Alert, air and surface patrols.

Guantánamo Tension (1 and 7/62): Alert, provided presence.

Guatemala (3/62): Alert, provided presence.

Thailand (5/62): Alert, provided presence.

Quemoy–Matsu Crisis (6/62): Provided presence.

Cuban Missile Crisis (10–11/62): Provided presence and intervention.

Yemen Revolts (2–4/63): Alert, provided presence, surface patrols.

Laos Tension (4/63): Alert, provided presence.

Jordan Crisis (4/63): Alert, provided presence, surface patrols

Caribbean Tensions (1963): Alert, air and surface patrols.

Vietnam Civil Disorders (8–9 and 10/63): Alert, air and surface patrols.

Dominican Republic (9/63): Alert.

South Vietnam Crisis (11/63): Following death of President Diem. Provided presence.

Indonesia–Malaysia (12/63): Alert, provided presence.

Panama (1–4/64): Alert, provided presence and evacuation.

Guantánamo Tensions (4–7/64): Provided presence, surface patrols.

Panama (5/64): Provided presence.

Dominican Republic (6 and 7/64): Air and surface patrols.

Tonkin Gulf (8/64): Combat operations.

Dominican Republic (4/65): Intervention and combat operations.

Arab–Israeli War (6/67): Alert, provided presence, covered evacuation of U.S. citizens.

Pueblo Capture (1–4/68): Redeployment of forces; maintained presence in area to take actions as directed.

EC-121 Loss (4/69): Redeployed forces; maintained presence to take actions as directed.

■ Reprinted from *U.S. Military and Police Operations in the Third World*, p. 3, with the permission of the North American Conference on Latin America (NACLA), P.O. Box 57, Cathedral Station, New York, N.Y., 10025, and P.O. Box 226, Berkeley, Calif. 94701.

In maintaining a garrison state presence, both overseas and at home, military forces have altered themselves to give a civilian character to their very content. For example, the armed forces must create a parallelism between themselves and the civilian occupational structure.

In the United States there is no such control, although we can observe the "narrowing skill differential between military and civilian elites":

> The new tasks of the military require that the professional officer develop more and more of the skills and orientations common to civilian administrators and civilian leaders. The narrowing difference in skill between military and civilian society is an outgrowth of the increasing concentration of technical specialists in the military. The men who perform such technical tasks have direct civilian equivalents: engineers, machine maintenance specialists, health service experts, logistic and personnel technicians. In fact, the concentration of personnel with "purely" military occupational specialties has fallen from 93.2 percent in the Civil War to 28.8 percent in the post-Korean Army, and to even lower percentages in the Navy and Air Force.
>
> More relevant to the social and political behavior of the military elite is the required transformation in the skills of the military commander. This hypothesis implies that in order to accomplish his duties, the military commander must become more interested and more skilled in techniques of organization, in the management of morale and negotiation. This if forced on him by the requirements of maintaining initiative in combat units, as well as the necessity of coordinating the ever-increasing number of technical specialists.[9]

The American military have not only changed their occupational structure, they simultaneously have increased their power to influence political and business elites. In many cases, military officers have used military power to present within staged conferences self-initiated proposals on the best strategies for reckoning with world revolutionary movements. Here as elsewhere, the military have employed human relations techniques both to streamline their internal structures and to manipulate civilians predisposed to accept military proposals.[10]

But it is mainly in the realm of managing

[9] Reprinted with the permission of the Macmillan Company from *The Professional Soldier* by Morris Janowitz, pp. 9–10. Copyright © 1960 by The Free Press of Glencoe.

[10] Ibid., pp. 8–9, 12–15.

university intellectuals, both in the garrison state model and in the observable actions of the United States, that the military use behavioral science theory and research to obtain the maximal amount of intellectual productivity:

Studies of the attitudes of professional research personnel indicate that *organizational* incentives (such as opportunity for advancement into management) and *material* incentives (higher salaries) are not closely related to technological productivity. In contrast, *professional* incentives (e.g., allowing the individual a high degree of freedom and flexibility in choosing his own work assignments in terms of what he feels will be professionally challenging) are likely to be associated with higher levels of both professional and organizational productivity among scientists and engineers. In one survey of work attitudes, research professionals indicated that they were highly motivated by the opportunity to contribute to scientific knowledge, and by association with other professionals of recognized ability, and were poorly motivated by membership in a company producing reputable goods and essential services. It is not hard to deduce from this data that universities provide the environment most likely to assure high technological productivity. In confirmation of this view, Dr. Frederick Seitz, past President of the National Academy of Sciences, told a Senate committee in 1963 that:

... a certain fraction of the best minds find the type of freedom and flexibility peculiar to the university best suited for their work. In addition, the presence of many inquiring young minds in the formative period, particularly the research students, adds a particular freshness and vitality to research. I do not mean to say that excellent work is not done elsewhere. ... What is important is that any program which does not take maximum advantage of the capability of the university will not advance in the most effective way possible.

This analysis has prompted the Defense Department to establish military research centers at selected universities, to enlist the help of university administrators in the creation of independent research organizations (as in the case of the Institute for Defense Analyses), and to offer financial incentives to universities which agree to adopt an existing facility (as witnessed in the University of Rochester's agreement to administer the Center for Naval Analyses). Where direct university participation has not proven feasible, the Pentagon has found it expedient to create a network of para-universities—independent research organizations which boast a campus-like environment and adhere to the many rituals of academic life (the most famous example of this kind of institution is the RAND Corporation). The network of non-profit research organizations ... should be viewed, then, as an extension of the university world and not as a unique phenomenon.[11]

In order to make this military–civilian link more successful (see "The Military Research Network—America's Fourth Armed Service" in Section Two of this chapter), both in the garrison state formulation and the U.S. practice, the military believes that it is necessary (*a*) to eliminate traditional sources of internal division within the military, and (*b*) to minimize conflict between the military and the civilian sectors. In order to remove relational sources of internal military division, thereby promoting a sense of solidarity within the military, it is incumbent upon military officers to see that racism is eliminated inside the armed forces and elsewhere. Such efforts have met with a modicum of success in this country, although the failures would seem to outweigh the persistent efforts of some officers to produce an integrated armed service.[12]

Even when the garrison state has overcome problems of racism, its government cannot manipulate civilian populations unless the state does away with economic insecurity. With this foresight, the garrison state leadership opts for the elimination of mass unemployment and job insecurity for the employed. Poverty is largely abolished. Mass unemployment disappears. A small number of poverty-stricken unemployed remain, but their numbers are highly concentrated in proletarian ethnic groups, scapegoated by the state as incorrigible derelicts whose very poverty simply signifies to military publicists

[11] Reprinted from *The University–Military–Police Complex,* op. cit., p. 3, with the permission of the North American Congress on Latin America (NACLA), P.O. Box 57, Cathedral Station, New York, N.Y. 10025 and P.O. Box 226, Berkeley, Calif. 94701.
[12] Janowitz, op. cit., pp. 10–11.

the intrinsic inability of certain minorities to be anything but poor.[13]

Such is not the case here in the U.S., although local governments may scapegoat blacks and equivalent others, especially in rural areas.[13] In large cities, however, the minority groups wield sufficient political power of the sort associated with a permanent wartime state. In this model, although minorities do not have the power to coerce, they can summon, if only temporarily, great strength on local issues. Efforts by blacks to wield power in the United States stem in part from their conditions and their consciousness. Indeed, within larger cities there exist conditions, states of consciousness, and contradictions on the levels of both class and status. Not just a small number of proletarianized ethnic groups but many such persons, plus a sizable proportion of the entire working and new middle classes, become unemployed on a long-term basis. Mass unemployment being the case, most pronouncedly during economic recessions, personal and family incomes are by no means ensured.

Income is but one of the problems. Throughout a variety of class—racial strata, low-cost housing is administered with traditional capitalist forms of exploitation: (a) excessive landlord profiteering from renters, and (b) inordinately high interest rates for home purchasers, especially working-class people. The income of an American Family today is by no means guaranteed in an economy still characterized by cyclical recessions, uneven but ever-upward inflations, and predictably high profit margins. The importance of U.S. inflation cannot be underestimated. Even when largely secure, family incomes have less spending impact than they might otherwise have, in large part because of high levels of profit exacted from consumers by corporations and associated professionals through administered prices. In this country and in the model of the permanent wartime state, declining real spending power creates problems for upwardly mobile families who can no longer afford to put their children through a university training.

Especially do these considerations of infla-

tion and college graduate unemployment weigh heavily on those who have made the greatest sacrifices from family incomes: working-class blacks, Puerto Ricans, Chicanos, Appalachian mountaineers, and native Americans. For them, objective insecurities and blockages are in part responsible for not only *recurrent* periods of intensive class—racial warfare as during the mid- and late 1960s but *continuous* conflict between these working-class minorities and the better-off sections of the communities' populations: New York, Los Angeles, Chicago, Philadelphia, Detroit, San Francisco, Cleveland, St. Louis, Pittsburg, Boston, Baltimore, Milwaukee, Atlanta, and Newark come to mind. On a day-to-day, month-to-month, year-to-year basis, our upper classes have learned to observe the consequences of "two cities." The upper classes, whether in suburban developments or central-city high-rise areas, can envisage for themselves, burglaries, muggings, and killings, linked to efforts on the part of the poor to get more wealth for themselves.[14]

In part because the American poor require coercive containment, from the point of view of many members of our upper classes, and in part because our universities are fonts of wisdom on these matters, certain upper-class persons have gone to the universities in order to obtain the information and skills deemed necessary. But all this does not make the country a garrison state.

In the garrison state, *all* institutions, including universities and their cousins, the service-oriented think-tanks, come under the coercive control of the military. At all levels of all institutions, the military wield every variety of power. Certainly such a situation does not obtain here today. Nonetheless, here the civilianized military character of a permanent wartime state cannot be overworked. The "civilian" component works with military elites, especially during moments of domestic insurrection. Surely the best example would be our universities. In our time we can observe the degree to which American universities have invited military penetration, while the military has created and subsidized near-universities in order to obtain

---

[13] For a discussion of the importance of packed proximity within black, northern, industrial subcommunities, see John C. Leggett, *Class, Race and Labor* (New York: Oxford University Press, 1968), ch. 4.

[14] Most recently, these events have extended to the suburbs themselves, where whites had hoped they would be able to obtain the necessary insulation from the dank inner city.

resources for containing potential insurgents at home and abroad. The universities have not only carried on research for the military but have established police training programs in order to determine how best to stop revolutionary insurgencies before they become uprisings with widespread support and long-term consequences. (See reading, "U.S. Police Assistance Programs in Latin America," by Mike Klare, in Section Two.)

In carrying on these operations, near-universities such as the RAND Corporation and university institutes such as the Institute for Defense Analyses (IDA) have been established. The result has been to hasten the formation of garrison states overseas and islands of police control at home. These overseas monuments to police thoroughness, such as the Brazilian and Greek right-fascist regimes, are designed to prevent the triumph of left-communism in their respective countries. Let us spend some time on the organizational interconnections at play. When we observe the role of the U.S. state in this planning and implementation, we note that there is a peculiar alignment of upper-class interests, upper-class actions, potential and real professorial earnings, military concern, and university, as well as near-university, hospitality. This constellation has been most readily accepted among university intellectuals engaged in research to promote counterinsurgency activity.

A PECULIAR CONCATENATION

The juncture of upper-class directorship, armed services invitation, and counterguerrilla warfare occurs within the RAND Corporation.[15] During World War II, the Air Force organized a unique research group. Its chief intention was to perpetuate the partnership between military men and university scientists that had been established during the war emergency. In the words of the founder, General Henry H. Arnold, the RAND Corporation would "get the best brains and turn them loose on problems of the future."[16] With high-flying expectations on Red aggressiveness and "free world" defense, RAND's initiators provided a

campuslike environment and informal working conditions, i.e., an atmosphere most congenial for the recruitment of academic scientists who might spurn direct employment by the Department of Defense.

The Douglas Aircraft Corporation initially administered the RAND group. However, in 1948, the RAND Corporation became "an independent nonprofit corporation with financial help from the Ford Foundation."[17] The RAND staff now includes 1100 persons. Of these, 600 are research professionals (1971).

The organization's basic Air Force contract, Project RAND, brings to the organization approximately two-thirds of its $22-million-dollar budget. Over the years, "Typical projects under the Air Force contract include studies of rocket propulsion systems, orbiting space stations, and inter-continental ballistic missiles. Much of this work incorporates the system's analysis and cost-effectiveness methodologies developed by RAND scientists."[18]

More recently, the corporation has turned to the nitty-gritty of antiguerrilla research. RAND has obtained contracts from such branches of the military as the Advanced Research Projects Agency (ARPA) and the Office of the Assistant Secretary of Defense for International Security Affairs (OASD/ISA):

> These contracts have resulted in interdisciplinary studies of problems in the areas of nation building, the function of foreign aid, and counter-guerrilla warfare. Recent RAND reports for OASD/ISA include: "Viet Cong Motivation and Morale," "Support Systems for Guerrilla and Limited Warfare," and "Politics and Economic Growth in India."[19]

This interlock with the Department of Defense allows the Department to channel information back to federal groups such as the Agency of International Development and its offshoot, the Office of Public Safety (both parts of the State Department). We will consider this contingency shortly.

In keeping with our expectations on the class quality of counterinsurgency measures, we can observe that the RAND Corporation fails to draw from a cross section of the community.

[15] See NACLA, *The University—Military—Police Complex, op. cit.,* pp. 28–29.
[16] Ibid., p. 28.

[17] *Loc. cit.*
[18] *Loc. cit.*
[19] Ibid. Reprinted with the permission of NACLA.

However, its Board of Trustees (1967) and leading members *do* speak for quite a mixture of leading business firms, universities, and law offices:

The RAND Corporation's origin, purpose, function, trustees, and leading members support a sizable staff committed to developing theory applicable to counterinsurgency use by this country's military and police, as well as overseas equivalents. In this sense, the RAND Corporation does not stand alone.

Along with RAND, we should note the operations of comparable research organizations,

---

[20] Ibid., pp. 28–29. Reprinted with the permission of NACLA.

most notably the IDA. It is most definitely a university-type institution interlaced among traditional universities. Stanford University, M.I.T., Tulane, and Case (now Case-Western Reserve), as well as the California Institute of Technology together founded IDA in 1956 as a nonprofit corporation. These universities constituted the members of the new corporation, and elected IDA trustees. Later, the universities of Michigan, California, Illinois, and Chicago, plus Princeton, Columbia, and Penn State joined the founding group. However, this consortium was dissolved in 1968, following Columbia student demonstrations against, among other things, IDA's presence on that campus. Individual IDA chapters continue to exist.

The origins, function, and use of IDA indicate its direct application to the elimination of ongoing or embryonic translating mechanisms in revolutionary movements:

> IDA's initial function was to provide scientific and technical support to the Weapons Systems Evaluation Group (WSEG) of the Department of Defense. Because of its ability to mobilize the scientific resources of its member universities, IDA has been able to greatly expand its activities, and the Institute now holds contracts with the Advanced Research Projects Agency (ARPA), National Security Agency, and—most recently—the Department of Justice. IDA's total receipts from Defense Department contracts in fiscal 1967 amounted to $15.8 million.
>
> IDA's research for WSEG and ARPA consists principally of studies on the effectiveness of proposed weapons systems, particularly ballistic missile systems. Since the onset of the Vietnam war, however, IDA has emphasized research on counterinsurgency and unconventional warfare. This work has included studies of the utilization of chemical and biological warfare and tactical nuclear weapons in counterinsurgency.
>
> Within the past two years, IDA has been commissioned by the Federal government to employ its capabilities in the areas of systems analyses and operations research in the development of new systems for the suppression of urban disorders in the United States. Under a $498,000 contract with the President's Commission on Law Enforcement and the Administration of Justice, IDA prepared a task force report on the application of science and technology to crime control. The

IDA report recommended the application of military counterinsurgency systems to domestic police operations, and particularly to antiriot operations.[21]

The upper-class representation (1967), indeed its interlock with eminent university administrators and law firms, is clear:

[21] Ibid., p. 26. Reprinted with the permission of NACLA.
[22] Ibid., pp. 26–27. Reprinted with the permission of NACLA.

As early as 1965, the IDA Corporation expressed a deep interest in overseas and domestic counterinsurgency alike. This interuniversity consortium articulated an acute concern over the presumed paucity of Justice Department funds available to deal with local insurgent groups. In many ways its recommendation laid the groundwork for the Omnibus Crime Control and Safe Streets Act of 1968. It was especially aimed at countering black revolutionary groups of the kind that had emerged in black ghettos across the country. (See reading, " 'R & D' for the Homefront War" in Section Two.)

Both the RAND Corporation and the IDA parallel normal university institutes, and the country is sprinkled liberally with such organizations. The University of Michigan Institute of Science and Research is a case in point. With this enterprise in mind, the North American Congress on Latin America (NACLA) has again tersely summarized a theory and research adventure which has ultimate consequences for revolutionary peasants *and* the upper-class Board of Regents of the University of Michigan:

UNIVERSITY OF MICHIGAN
INSTITUTE OF SCIENCE AND TECHNOLOGY

Michigan's Institute of Science and Technology, organized in 1959, is a composite of several university scientific facilities, the most important of which is the Willow Run Laboratory (WRL) located in Ypsilanti, Mich. The Institute has a combined staff of some 650 scientists and technicians, and operates on an annual budget of about $14 million. WRL, which works closely with the Advanced Research Projects Agency (ARPA) of the Department of Defense, receives some $11 million annually from defense contracts.

In addition to WRL, the Institute comprises the Cooley Electronics Laboratory and three Department of Defense Information Analysis Centers—the Ballistic Missile Radiation Analysis Center (BAMIRAC), the VELA Seismic Information and Analysis Center (VESIAC), and the Infrared Information and Analysis Center. These units are responsible for collecting, analyzing and disseminating information on ballistic missile re-entry phenomena, seismic detection of underground nuclear explosions (Project VELA-UNIFORM), and infrared technology, respectively.

Michigan's expertise in these areas and related fields is applied to classified research on counterguerrilla surveillance systems, avionics (the design of aircraft fire-control and navigation systems), electronic countermeasures (for jamming enemy radar and listening devices) and ballistic missile defense. Recent projects include studies of the projected Strat-X missile—an advanced intercontinental ballistic missile (ICBM) under development by the Army—and operation of a $4.3 million infrared observatory atop Mount Haleakala on Maui Island, Hawaii. The observatory, financed by ARPA, will be used to track ICBMs and military satellites.

Michigan has been active in America's Southeast Asian war effort since the early 1960s. In 1961, for instance, Michigan scientists were engaged in research to "analyze the coast and landing beach physiography affecting military operations in Southeast Asia." Later ARPA sent a team of WRL scientists to Thailand to study the effect of tropical conditions on guerrilla surveillance devices. In 1967 WRL received a $1 million ARPA contract to develop a "Joint Thai—U.S. Aerial Reconnaissance Laboratory."

The flying lab will use infrared detection equipment to pinpoint enemy guerrillas at night.[23]

As NACLA has indicated, this institute is not the only one that is active on the Michigan campus. Like many major schools, the University of Michigan has contained a variety of research efforts ultimately geared to counteract dissident movements sometimes portrayed as criminal activities (see box).

The RAND Corporation, the IDA, and the university institutes can make direct recommendations to one or more of the armed services under the Department of Defense. More recently, however, many recommendations have gone directly to the police sector: to the Office of Public Safety (OPS—a division of the U.S. Agency of International Development [AID]):

The OPS and the Inter-American Police Academy (IPA—later changed to the International Police Academy) were both estab-

[23] Ibid., pp. 19–20. Reprinted with the permission of NACLA.

NI-027 $50,714   From 6/30/69 to 6/30/70
Grantee: University of Michigan, Ann Arbor
Title: Methodological Studies of Crime Classification
Abstract: The accurate assessment of the volume of crime and of particular kinds of crime is the objective of this study. It is expected to evaluate the factors that affect the classification of major index crimes and to develop ways of estimating base populations for victim statistics.

NI-034 $13,280   From 6/30/69 to 3/15/70
Grantee: University of Michigan, Ann Arbor
Title: Interdisciplinary Seminar in Criminal Justice
          Administration and Corrections
Abstract: An interdisciplinary seminar will be established by the University of Michigan Law School to discuss research needs in the area of crime and delinquency. Its objective is the germination of better research ideas.

NI-040 $59,130   From 7/1/69 to 6/30/70
Grantee: Institute for Social Research, The Regents of the University of Michigan, Ann Arbor
Title: Alternative Responses to School Crisis
Abstract: It is a goal of this project to work with three schools to try out several models of alternative and more creative response to crisis and disruption. It is also a goal of this project to develop and demonstrate programs to create new links between protesting student groups, educational leaders and police officials. Representatives of law enforcement systems need to understand better the particular issues and potentials in student-school crises, and the ways they may be most helpful to students and educators. The latter groups need a better understanding of the potential role of law enforcement systems, and the implications of school unrest for local police and judiciary agencies.

■ Reprinted from: *The University—Military—Police Complex: A Directory and Related Cocuments,* p. 76, with the permission of the North American Congress on Latin America (NACLA).

lished by President Kennedy in 1962. The OPS program trains ranking officers of Third World police forces at the IPA and other U.S. institutions, sends advisors to foreign countries to train rank and file policemen, and provides equipment, such as radios, mobile units, weapons, ammunition and computers, to local police forces.[24]

On another front in Latin America, the AID has sponsored research on population growth and birth control with the intent of fostering family-planning programs that will curtail population growth in Third World countries. For AID, population limitation means the elimination of population pressures of the kind associated with widespread lower-class unrest which has helped to contribute to immizeration and hence to the preconditions and the subsequent victories of revolutionary movements such as the Chinese. Thus the agency must develop population policies on family size limitation which are consistent with the type of military operations favored by the CIA. In this sense, AID attempts to minimize preparatory conditions of revolution as the CIA works to destroy the translating mechanisms of revolution and to prop corrupt political regimes that might otherwise abdicate from leadership after a relatively short period of intense civil war. Again, AID policies complement CIA activities, and for good reason, especially in countries such as Laos and Cambodia, since both government agencies have merged under the aegis of the CIA. The perspective of the intellectuals in charge of this merger seems clear. Population size limitation should help to make possible more thorough state political control, since left-wing groups would be deprived of the unrest associated with overpopulation misery.

The AID commitment to non-communist alternatives, including the Brazilian fascist variety, appears most evident in its funding of the Office of Public Safety. The purpose underlying AID's involvement has been succinctly stated.

> Why does the U.S. involve itself in the internal situations of these countries, to the extent of forming and developing the local police forces? Private U.S. interests have over $12 billion invested in Latin America. Protection of corporate investments, expansion and profit require a stable climate. Existing governments in Latin America are increasingly threatened by revolutionary movements, and the stability desired by U.S. investors is being shattered. In addition, Washington must reduce the possibility of the rise to power of groups not firmly aligned with the United States.
>
> Urban areas in Latin America are growing rapidly, while conditions continue to deteriorate (unemployment, housing and food shortages, etc.). Increasingly, guerrillas in countries such as Argentina, Brazil and Uruguay, are launching attacks against their governments from urban centers. Police forces have proved incapable of responding effectively to these threats, and are in need of assistance. Since it is in the interests of the United States to do so, Washington provides this assistance in the form of extensive training and equipment.[25]

The Office of Public Safety stresses control over insurgency through the local police. This approach has been endorsed by upper class persons, most notably one of the leaders of U.S. corporations, foundations, foreign relations associations, universities, and a major political party—Nelson A. Rockefeller.

ROCKEFELLER'S RECOMMENDATION TO NIXON ON POLICE AID

> In addition, there is not in the United States a full appreciation of the important role played by the police. There is a tendency in the United States to equate the police in the other American republics with political action and repression, rather than with security. There have, unfortunately, been many such instances of the use of police. Yet well-motivated, well-trained police when present in local communities, enforce the laws, protect the citizenry from terror, and discourage criminal elements. At the present time, however, police forces of many countries have not been strengthened as population and great urban growth have taken place. Consequently they have become increasingly less capable of providing either the essential psychological support or the internal security that is their major function. . . .
>
> The United States should respond to requests for assistance of the police and security forces of the hemisphere nations by pro-

---

[24] NACLA, "AID Police Programs for Latin America 1971–72", *op. cit.,* p. 1.

[25] Ibid., p. 2.

viding them with the essential tools to do their job.

Accordingly, the United States should meet reasonable requests from other hemisphere governments for trucks, jeeps, helicopters and like equipment to provide mobility and logistical support for these forces; for radios, and other command control equipment for proper communications among the forces; and for small arms for security forces.[26]

To facilitate the training of overseas police within their native countries and in the United States, the Office of Public Safety has established a number of police programs. In the case of Brazil, the exact nature of OPS activity has been clearly specified by AID itself (see Table 30).

But this funding for overseas police training is by no means the only counterinsurgency activity in question. Within the United States the burgeoning of programs for training U.S. police as professional counterinsurgents can be observed. All this has been done through the use of relatively minimal funds and near-guaranteed loyalty to the state. Whether overseas or at home, however, a country's armed services are a less efficient weapon against insurgency. They are more costly, less professional, and under certain conditions definitely disloyal to the state—or even loyal to the movement they are supposed to suppress. In order to develop the police side of oppression, federal funds have been pumped into a university—police complex that is both sizable and efficient. Presented in capsule form on page 375 is the basic information on this new political manifestation.

Training for repression

By Lee Webb

American universities have traditionally acknowledged their "obligation to society" by training military officers in time of war; now, as the homefront war begins to monopolize the attention of the government authorities, universities are being encouraged to provide training for police officers. Over 750 colleges

[26] *Ibid.,* p. 11. This excerpt from "Quality of Life in the Americas," reprinted by AID indicates the report's recommendations to President Nixon from Governor Rockefeller following his fact-finding trip to Latin America in 1969, pp. 51, 54. Reprinted with the permission of NACLA.

currently offer courses in "police science"—a fivefold increase since 1960.

According to the International Association of Chiefs of Police, 257 colleges now offer associate degrees in law enforcement, and 44 offer bachelor's degress; the comparable figures for 1960 were 40 and 15, respectively. This massive increase is a consequence of the Omnibus Crime Control and Safe Streets Act of 1968, which authorized the Law Enforcement Assistance Administration (LEAA) to finance the education of policemen, corrections officers, court personnel, and others working in the "criminal justice system."

These police training programs are mirror images of the Pentagon's ROTC programs. Both police and military officials believe that the sophisticated systems and weapons being introduced require manpower with more than a high school education. Supported with grants from LEAA, police departments are attempting to utilize the new military systems developed for use in Vietnam. New "command and control" systems, communications equipment, "night vision devices," and computerized intelligence systems can only be operated by skilled and trained personnel.

A college education is now being viewed by top police officials as yet another weapon for controlling insurgent groups within the population. Quinn Tamm, Executive Director of the International Association of Chiefs of Police, once said that "a man who goes into our streets in hopes of regulating, directing or controlling human behavior must be armed with more than a gun and the ability to perform mechanical movements in response to a situation. Such men as these engage in the difficult, complex and important business of human behavior. Their intellectual armament—so long restricted—must be no less than their physical prowess." (Quoted in the report of the President's Commission on Law Enforcement and the Administration of Justice.)

Over 65,000 police are being trained at 720 colleges and universities thanks to the largesse of the U.S. Department of Justice. Through LEAA's Office of Academic Assistance, the Department provides loans to students preparing for careers with the police, courts or prison system, and makes grants to "in-service" personnel taking specialized courses or attending night school. Pre-service students can receive up to $1,800 a year in loans, and in-service students up to $300 per semester in grant aid.

Police officials and university administrators counter student and faculty hostility to police training programs by explaining that such programs will "professionalize" and "humanize" the police. Professionalization of the police means exactly what it does in the Army: a fascination with technique and modern equipment, a de-politization of the department, and a readiness to carry out any orders from above. Profes-

TABLE 30 AID Project Data for Brazil

PROJECT TITLE	ACTIVITY	FUNDS
Public Safety	Public Safety	Economic

PROJECT NUMBER	PRIOR REFERENCE	INITIAL OBLIGATION	SCHEDULED FINAL OBLIGATION
512-11-710-070	P. 26, FY-1971 LA P.D.B.	FY: 1959	FY: 1972

Project Target and Course of Action: To improve the capability of the Brazilian federal and state civil security forces to maintain law and order, and security against subversion by supporting development of Federal Police Department capacity to provide training and technical support internally and for state police departments nationwide. USAID efforts are primarily directed toward training to effect improvement in police organization, management and operations. Project emphasis is on the concept of police service to the public.

Progress to Date: Through December 1970, the Public Safety project in Brazil has assisted in training locally over 100,000 federal and state police personnel. Additionally, approximately 600 persons received training in the U.S. Major project accomplishments include: construction, equipping and development of curriculum, staff and faculty for the National Police Academy, National Telecommunications Center and National Institutes of Criminalistics & Identification. All are functioning effectively in support of police departments throughout the country. Also, the project has supported a substantial increase in police telecommunications with the construction and installation of base and mobile facilities and equipment which provide for communication from every state to Brasilia as well as limited intra- and inter-state communications. Substantial increases in police mobility have been achieved, primarily through Brazilian funding

for Brazilian manufactured vehicles. Self-help contributions to the program by Brazilian police agencies total more than $25 million for construction, supplies and equipment, and related costs.

FY 1972 Program: Change in program direction, started in FY 1969, will continue: emphasis will be on strengthening the Federal Police Department and efforts to further develop national police institutions, particularly the National Police Academy and Telecommunications Center. Further emphasis will be given to the implementation of Federal Police Department Mobile Training Teams, one of the principal means for providing field assistance to various states.

U.S. Technicians: Four U.S. direct-hire Public Safety Advisors will work with the Federal Police Department from July 1 to December 21, 1971, and three U.S. Advisors from December 31, 1971 to June 1972.

Participants: Short-term training for 35 Brazilian police officers and officials mainly at the International Police Academy, Washington, D.C.

Commodities: No commodities are programed for FY 1972.

Other costs: International Travel.

U.S. DOLLAR COSTS (in thousands)

	Obligations	Expenditures	Unliquidated
Through 6/30/70	7,898	7,557	341
Estimated FY 71	370	561	
Estimated through 6/30/71	8,268	8,118	150
		Future Year Estimated Obligations	Total Cost
Proposed FY 72	174		8,442

OBLIGATIONS

Cost Components	Estimated FY 1971			Proposed FY 1972		
	Direct AID	Contract	Total	Direct AID	Contract	Total
U.S. Technicians	225		225	100		100
Participants	100		100	70		70
Commodities	40		40			
Other Costs	5		5	4		4
Total Obligations	370		370	174		174

Reprinted from: "AID Police Programs for Latin America—1971–72," *NACLA Newsletter,* Vol. 5, July–August, 1971, p. 18, with the permission of the North American Congress on Latin America (NACLA), P.O. Box 57. Cathedral Station, New York, N.Y. 10025; P.O. Box 226, Berkeley, Calif. 94701.

sionalization will not liberalize the police—but rather will make it a more powerful and versatile instrument in the hands of the Nixon–Agnew Administration.

■ Reprinted from *The University—Military—Police Complex: A Directory and Related Documents,* p. 63, with the permission of the North American Congress on Latin America (NACLA), P.O. Box 57, Cathedral Station, New York, N.Y. 10025, P.O. Box 226, Berkeley, Calif. 94701.

Most impressive is the NACLA statistic that more than 65,000 police are being trained at 720 American colleges and universities. Drawn from various parts of the nonsocialist world, including the United States, these police are being trained with little popular knowledge, let alone requests that the training be administered.

In none of these training programs are ordinary folk consulted except through the desultory processes associated with periodic elections where the issue of police militarization is seldom discussed. Yet we sometimes suffer from rationalizations proffered by our upper classes. The police programs and the suppression of revolutionary movements are justified by those who govern in terms of our and their "nation's interests." The phrase obscures the real winners in this war preparation and university reorganization. It is the relatively small number of people who monopolize the country's strategic resources who stand to benefit from the suppression of revolutionary lower classes.

In all fairness to American upper classes, it should be pointed out that, given their ownership and control of this country's 500 largest corporations and their international holdings, they can hardly be expected to act otherwise. It is to their interests to smash what they cannot tame overseas, for the overseas insurgent could conceivably seize U.S. corporate assets, as occurred in China.

To carry on counter-insurgent activity, the U.S. upper classes have at their disposal resources which include:

1. Their family wealth
2. Their corporate directorships
3. Their corporate managerial control
4. Their control of the two major political parties
5. The foundations
6. The foreign policy associations
7. The universities
8. Important federal departments, including Defense, State, and Justice
9. Their control over the directorate of a federal agency which specializes in counterrevolution, namely the Central Intelligence Agency[27]
10. Their influence with an agency which specializes in police elimination of revolutionary groups: the Office of Public Safety of the U.S. Agency of International Development
11. Appointive discretion over the federal judicial structure
12. Ownership and directorship of the mass media
13. Auxiliary support from allied governments

It is amazing that any revolutionary movement can stand up before such power. Only internal contradictions within the American upper class, and hence their division into right-, left-, and center-democrats, prevents upper-class members coming together to create a monolithic power capable of smashing all revolutionary movements at their inception. These contradictions consist primarily of long-term antagonisms rooted in religious and ethnic status differences, associated pecking orders, and predictable discriminatory actions. All contribute to ongoing conflicts amongst Protestants, Catholics, and Jews, not to mention ethnic antagonisms *within* our upper class. Needless to say, it is in the interest of radicals to promote these tribal differences among those at the top in order to forestall the creation of a consensual monolith.

Despite differences among the wealthy on how best to suppress, techniques learned overseas have been applied in the United States since the mid-1960s. All these adaptations demand our attention if we are to gauge the degree to which the country has become a permanent wartime state. Mike Klare has analyzed at length these new domestic controls (see "Bringing It Back: Planning for the City," in Section Two). Vince Pinto has discussed

[27] See G. William Domhoff, *Who Rules America?,* pp. 127–129, for a detailed breakdown of the affiliations of the men who run the CIA.

some of the major weapons: smoke, sound, and other nonlethal weapons; guns, dumdum bullets, barbed tape, and armored cars (see his "Weapons for the Homefront" in Section Two). The data presented leave us with only one conclusion: Whatever the principal source of integration within this country, it does not consist of consensual agreement among its citizens. To a very large degree, law-abiding behavior in the United States is attributable to the visible presence of military hardware and associated personnel.

Yet to blame part or all of America's upper classes for what the country has become is unfair. Our country does have a history. Slavery permeated its beginning. And slavery seemed natural, for this country's upper-class members derived disproportionately from northern Ireland, where its tradition of Irish and English exploitation and suppression of the Irish Catholic "racial" minority found apt transfer to, and function within, a polity in need of a religious ideology to justify the exploitation of enslaved blacks. This religious—racist ideology permeated all institutions, and to this day it survives. Giv-

en the religious background of many of this country's upper-class families, it has become relatively easy for them to justify the current actions taken against nonwhite people such as peasant Brazillians and Vietnamese. Cecilia Karch has analyzed this Irish Protestant inheritance in Section Three of this chapter.

Keeping in mind the last several chapters, including their readings, we can schematically summarize our views through Figure 4, which suggests the following tentative propositions for critical concern:

1. Upper-class members belong to foundations whose upper-class members set policy as directors of foreign policy associations in direct relation to the President and his cabinet and through them the Department of State and hence the AID, a counterrevolutionary group which subsumes the Office of Public Safety, a highly specialized portion of the state, committed to quelling both domestic and foreign revolutionaries.

2. Upper-class members are policy-makers for the CIA, which often sets policy, when

FIGURE 4 Schematization, Amplified in Text, of the Support of and Concern for the Office of Public Safety on the Part of the Upper Classes

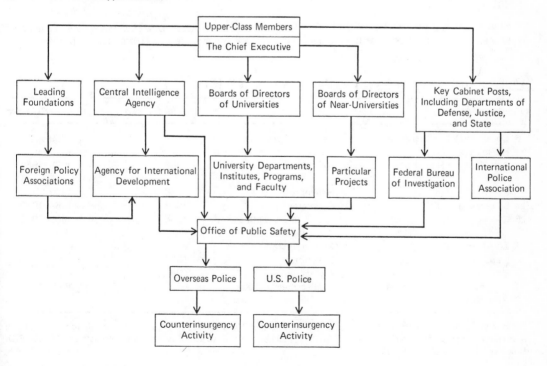

other sections of the federal executive fail to do so, for the AID, one of whose principal subsections is the OPS, which institutes new programs designed to train U.S. policemen on matters of counterinsurgency for overseas and homefront duty.

3. Upper-class members sit on boards of directors or universities and near-universities, as well as university institutes, which in turn preside over university departments, programs, and professors locked into research and training programs set up as contract work for the CIA, the AID, and the OPS, not to mention *direct* work for U.S. and overseas police.

4. Upper-class members help to select Secretaries of Defense who relate to military officers who, in theory and practice, complement the upper classes' desire to *provide supplementary aid* when necessary to the cited state groups committed to counterrevolution. At the same time, and as is well known, the military *on its own* will attack revolutionaries with full force whenever necessary, as in Detroit and Vietnam. The 101st and the 82nd Airborne Divisions have acted to suppress revolutionaries in *both areas.*

CONCLUSIONS

Because U.S. upper-class families and their state seem incapable of passage from a capitalist to a Socialist form, and because this limited potential leads the U.S. to smother militarily those movements which persist in pursuing a left-Communist alternative these families and their state have helped to create a permanent wartime state. However, the United States is not a garrison state, for the military does not have the power to coerce civilian political authority. But the country does resemble a permanent wartime state. In this sense, the military have cooperated with large sections of the upper class to rework major institutions such as the university to deal with overseas and domestic revolutionary movements in ways consistent with upper-class interests. To the degree that these processes have gone forward, the United States appears to be developing many attributes whose full realization is reminiscent of Harold Lasswell's model.

Overseas, we have on occasion helped to foster states which have acutely resembled the garrison state construct. Not only police training programs but military arms have served in these ventures. In the case of Brazil, for example, a country which tortures political prisoners, the United States has done its best to stabilize reactionary control.[28] Such U.S. state action deserves from us more than sociological

[28] See NACLA, *U.S. Military Operations and Police Operations in the Third Word,* op. cit., pp. 10-11.

TABLE 31   U.S. Arms Transfers to the Third World 1968–1969 (Brazil only)

Number of Items	Description	Date Ordered	Date Delivered
5 Lockheed C-130 E Hercules	Transfer aircraft	1968	1969
11 Hughes 500	Helicopter	–	–
7 Bell 206A Jet Ranger	Helicopter	1968	1968–1969
6 Bell UH-1D Iroquois	Helicopter	1968	1969
4 Sikorsky SH-3D	Helicopter	1968	1969–1970
25 Cessna T-37C	Trainer/ground attack Aircraft	1968	1969–1970
5 Lockheed T-33	Trainer aircraft	–	–
– Fairchild Hiller FH-1100	Helicopter	1968	–
15 McD-D A-4F Skyhawk	Fighter aircraft	(1969)	–
1 Destroyer, "Fletcher" class	Displacement: 2100 t.	–	1968
2 Gunboats	–	–	–

Reprinted from: U.S. Police and Military Operations in the Third World, p. 17, with the permission of the North American Congress on Latin America (NACLA), P.O. Box 57, Cathedral Station, New York, N.Y. 10025, P.O. Box 226, Berkeley, Calif. 94701.

generality as we bring this portion of the chapter to an end; and Table 31 supplies hard statistics.

TRANSITIONAL REMARKS

The North American Congress on Latin America (NACLA) has provided ample research materials and hence evidence for the propositions advanced, and it is worthwhile to present their basic research and to scrutinize the selections presented in Section Two. The National Research/Action on the Military—Industrial Complex (NARMIC) have done their homework. We can certainly profit from their carefully documented observations, although we may have certain misgivings about their conclusions.

Imperial policies are generally racist. These policies also enjoy considerable support, not only among those who stand to profit directly and enormously but among those who have little to gain except in terms of psychological rewards. Clearly a large section of the working classes here and abroad have supported imperial policies. Most appear to be mainstream workmen. Their behavior stems in part from their occupancy of higher status positions within the working class as well as their organizational attachments to groups notoriously racist in character. In any event, suave upper-class persons who set our foreign policies could not do so without working class persons who have often used religious categories to justify imperial policies. With upper-class dependence on widespread mainstream working-class support for imperial policies in mind, we can follow the readings of Section Two with the excellent essay by Cecilia Karch on the Ku Klux Klan and the Orange Order (Section Three). Both groups use religious or quasireligious motivations to justify class—racial exploitation.

| Section Two: | *Readings on International Police Control* |

Aid Police Programs for Latin America 1971-72

Written and published by the North American Congress on Latin America (NACLA)

The U.S. is fast becoming the world's policeman in the most precise sense of the word. This status has been achieved not only by placing our own men in the front lines of combat, as in Indochina, but by taking it upon ourselves to develop, train, equip and indoctrinate the police forces of countries throughout the underdeveloped world. U.S. police assistance to Latin America has contributed to the development of police states. Local forces have received extensive training not only in routine police matters,

■ Reprinted from *NACLA Newsletter*, 5, No. 4 (July—August 1971), pp. 1–5, with the permission of the North American Congress on Latin America (NACLA), P.O. Box 57, Cathedral Station, New York, N.Y., and P.O. Box 226, Berkeley, Calif. 94701.

but in paramilitary and counterinsurgency techniques to deal with the threat of internal subversion.

This assistance has been handled by the Office of Public Safety (OPS), a division of the U.S. Agency of International Development (AID). The OPS and the Inter-American Police Academy (IPA—later changed to the International Police Academy) were both established by President Kennedy in 1962. The OPS program trains ranking officers of Third World police forces at the IPA and other U.S. institutions, sends advisors to foreign countries to train rank-and-file policemen, and provides equipment, such as radios, mobile units, weapons, ammunition and computers, to local police forces.

The following document is a country-by-country description of the OPS request to Congress for Latin America for fiscal year 1972. In order to understand the realities behind the sterile, sanitized language of the document, however, it is necessary to discuss the underlying reasons for the existence of such a program.

Why does the U.S. involve itself in the internal situations of these countries, to the extent of forming and developing the local police forces? Private U.S. interests have over $12 billion invested in Latin America. Protection of corporate investments, expansion and profit require a stable climate. Existing governments in Latin America are increasingly threatened by revolutionary movements and the stability desired by U.S. investors is being shattered. In addition, Washington must reduce the possibility of the rise to power of groups not firmly aligned with the United States.

Urban areas in Latin America are growing rapidly, while conditions continue to deteriorate (unemployment, housing and food shortages, etc.). Increasingly, guerrillas in countries such as Argentina, Brazil and Uruguay, are launching attacks against their governments from urban centers. Police forces have proved incapable of responding effectively to these threats, and are in need of assistance. Since it is in the interests of the United States to do so, Washington provides this assistance in the form of extensive training and equipment.

In justifying the program to Congress, OPS officials have come up with a series of arguments about why the police should receive aid. Basically, the local police are seen as the first line of defense against subversion, and with proper training should be able to deal with an internal disorder before it grows into a full-scale guerrilla movement or mass insurrection. Police are interspersed among the population, which brings them close to the unrest and facilitates intelligence work. They can move quickly to the scene of a crime, and because they carry out the normal functions of police work, it is presumed that they will have gained legitimacy among the population. For this reason they are more acceptable than the military for maintaining law and order. In addition, the military tends to overreact to such situations, thus polarizing the population and radicalizing many.

Police forces are cheaper to maintain than armies because they do not require expensive hardware such as tanks and planes.[1]

One reason for backing police forces never mentioned by OPS officials is that, in general, police are a highly trained and indoctrinated professional force, whereas the rank and file of the armed forces are filled with relatively untrained and unmotivated draftees—peasants, Indians and other exploited groups.

At the core of all these arguments is the hope that an effective police force can reduce the need for massive military intervention, thus avoiding future Vietnams. At the 1965 graduation exercises of the IPA, General Maxwell Taylor stated this explicitly:

> The outstanding lesson [of Vietnam] is that we should never let another Vietnam-type situation arise again. We were too late in recognizing the extent of the subversive threat. We appreciate now that every young, emerging country must be constantly on the alert, watching for those symptoms which, if allowed to develop unrestrained, may eventually grow into a disastrous situation such as that in South Vietnam. We have learned the need for a strong police force and strong police intelligence organization to assist in identifying early the symptoms of an incipient subversive situation.[2]

OPS itself has the power to respond to crises. If an insurrection breaks out, OPS can fly in emergency aid within hours to cope with the situation. If an underground movement exists, OPS can organize special training courses in infiltration, fingerprinting and other intelligence work. Working hand-in-hand with the State Department and the CIA, OPS can anticipate as well as respond to crises. In Guatemala for example, a fleet of paddy wagons was shipped to local police shortly before the Arana government declared martial law in November, 1970.

Thousands of officers are being trained not in the routine police functions of crime prevention, but in counterinsurgency techniques and ideology. As of January, 1970, 3500 officers of commissioned status had graduated from the IPA.[3] A majority of them to date have come from Latin America, but increasingly they are from Africa, Asia and the Middle East. The instructors at IPA come from the ranks of the

FBI, CIA and other U.S. law enforcement agencies. For example, Michael McCann, the director of the Academy, worked with the FBI before assuming his present position. Instruction at IPA involves courses in police management, operations and internal security. . . .

Over 2000 officers have received related training at other institutions, such as courses in penology and correctional institutions at Southern Illinois University; documents investigation (forgery, counterfeiting, tracing) through the Post Office Department[4] and a series of briefings and war games at the John F. Kennedy Special Warfare Center at Fort Bragg, on the relation between the police and the military in counterinsurgency operations.[5] General Taylor explained another lesson that has been learned in Vietnam:

> We also recognize the importance of the police force in its relations to the armed forces of its own country. In South Vietnam the military effort never stands alone. It blends with the paramilitary and the police function and these in combination blend with the economic social programs.[6]

In addition to training received in the United States, Latin American police officers are trained on-the-spot by ninety U.S. public safety advisors.[7] Many of these advisors come from the FBI and CIA. Six OPS advisors in the Dominican Republic in 1967 were later discovered to be CIA agents.[8] Dan Mitrione, who had been chief of police in Richmond, Indiana, and had received instruction at the FBI Academy, was the director of the public safety mission in Uruguay. Mitrione, who was an expert on the Tupamaros, was kidnapped and later executed by the Tupamaros when the Uruguayan government refused to release political prisoners in exchange. Mitrione had also been an advisor to the police in Brazil before going to Uruguay. Obviously OPS advisors have hazardous duty. In the admiring words of *Kiwanis Magazine:*

> While giving assistance to police from the Bolivian jungles to Iran's snowy mountains, Public Safety advisors have been threatened, ambushed, shot and bombed. During the course of the conflict in South Vietnam, six have died.[9]

A major focus of OPS training is the creation of nationally coordinated police forces under unified command which can deal with problems anywhere in the country more effectively than scattered local forces. For this reason, aid and equipment have been supplied in the key areas of communication (computers, radios), mobility (cars, helicopters), intelligence gathering (infiltration and interrogation) and ID systems and roadblocks that monitor the movement of people and goods. The assistance in developing communications is not limited to national boundaries; cooperation among many Latin American countries is encouraged, especially along borders.

A less overt, but nevertheless key element of police aid is psychological warfare. Many tactics and uses of equipment by the police are designed to subdue the population and to intimidate not only existing, but also potential opposition movements. Large numbers of patrol cars, a cop on every corner, visible machine guns, riot gases, helicopters, checkpoints, all create fear and hopelessness in the minds of the victims of technology. This sense of hopelessness is perhaps best described in a passage by psychologist Frantz Fanon who studied the Algerian resistance to the French, in *The Wretched of the Earth:*

> In the innermost recesses of their brains, the settlers' tanks and airplanes occupy a huge place. When they are told "action must be taken" they see bombs raining down on them, armored cars coming at them on every path, machine gunning and police action . . . and they sit quiet, they are beaten from the start.[10]

Many of the OPS country summaries [compiled by NACLA] refer to "improving records and identification facilities" and establishing communications centers. Put bluntly, this really means developing a nationwide data bank and ID system which is at the fingertips of every police officer, thus enabling a more efficient control of the population. For example, a national ID system has already been highly developed in South Vietnam, initially through U.S. assistance to the police force. Every South Vietnamese fifteen years or older must register with the government and carry an ID card. Anyone without a card is considered a Viet Cong suspect and subject to arrest. The police and military authorities now have a full set of fingerprints, information on political beliefs, biographical data and photographs for nearly 12,000,000 people in South Vietnam.[11] With the help of this kind of a system and an elaborate network of roadblocks and checkpoints, government police detained over 153,000 people in 1970 alone.[12] Similar ID systems are being implemented in varying degrees in Latin America, as well as the United States.

The OPS budget request to Congress for 1971–72 is $26 million. About two thirds of this total is earmarked for Southeast Asia. Compared to the overall AID and military assistance budgets of $3.44 billion, this is a relatively small amount. However, OPS grants are complementary and necessary to economic development grants. Both kinds of "aid" are aimed at stabilizing capitalist penetration of Latin America. In addition, by placing the money in strategic areas of police work, such as communications, intelligence and mobility, a great deal of leverage is achieved with a small amount of money. For example, in describing to Congress the 1966 OPS plan for police assistance to the Dominican Republic, AID noted: "The FY (fiscal year)–67 DG (direct grant) assistance proposed . . . of approximately $720,000 is but 4.7% of the police budget. *For U.S. objectives it provides the necessary leverage*" (emphasis added–NACLA).[13]

> OPS exerts global influence vastly disproportionate to its small size. For example, by helping other countries set up their own police academies and by organizing field training teams, U.S. Public Safety advisors in 1968 reached 110,000 policemen in thirty-one countries.[14]

There have been many criticisms of the OPS program, especially where aid has been given to brutal dictatorships. Senator Frank Church, who conducted secret hearings on repression in Brazil in May, 1971, summed up his findings as follows:

> . . . the U.S. aid programs to Brazilian military and police agencies . . . serve mainly to identify the U.S. with a repressive government. The hearings revealed an altogether too close identification of the U.S. with the current Brazilian government, and they raise a serious question about the wisdom of assistance to the Brazilian police and military.[15]

In addition, the current regimes in Guatemala and the Dominican Republic, two large U.S. AID clients, have been condemned by the Organization of American States as violators of human rights.[16]

David Bell, a former director of AID, insists that Public Safety assistance is not given to support dictatorships. "It is obviously not our purpose or intent to assist a head of state who is repressive. On the other hand, we are working in a lot of countries where the governments are controlled by people who have shortcomings."[17] (meaning "We don't discriminate, some of our friends happen to be torturers.")

In justifying continued OPS aid to such regimes, Bell explained, ". . . the police are a strongly anti-communist force right now. For that reason it is a very important force to us."[18]

Because police in Latin America have a tradition of brutality and repression, OPS places a strong emphasis on the building of "humane," efficient police forces. Officials understand that it is important to minimize the violence to prevent the polarization of the population and to avoid creating martyrs.

However, there are contradictions between the ideology of OPS and the practice of Latin American police forces, which have long been used as instruments of official repression. The people harbor suspicion and resentment of the police because of the widespread use of brutality and torture and the elimination of any political opposition.

In addition, the police are often the base for quasi-clandestine right-wing terrorist groups (which operate, in reality, with unofficial government approval), such as "Mano Blanca" and "Ojo por Ojo" in Guatemala, "La Banda" in the Dominican Republic and the "Death Squad" in Brazil. . . . Off-duty policemen and other right-wing terrorists do the dirty work so the hands of the legitimate police can appear clean. The terrorist groups keep the population frightened and intimidated. In the long run, however, they build support for the left, even among one-time "moderates" or "apolitical" people, thus invalidating all that the OPS officials claim has been achieved.

A further contradiction for OPS is its perception of all subversive activity as caused by small sectors of the population that can be isolated and wiped out. In reality, these movements reflect the growing popular determination to end oppression and to establish governments that are responsive to the needs of the people. Thus, the programs are doomed to failure in the end, because the underlying premise of OPS, and in fact of all counterinsurgency efforts, is based on miscalculations of the people's will to resist.

NOTES

1. The data for this paragraph and much of the background for this chapter are from a chapter on police aid in a book on counterinsurgency by Michael Klare, to be published by Alfred Knopf in 1972.

2. Address by Maxwell D. Taylor, Graduation Exercise, International Police Academy, Washington, D.C., Dec. 17, 1965. (U.S. Agency for International Development press release, same date.)

3. U.S. Department of State, Agency for International Development, Office of Public Safety, *Program Guide–Public Safety Training* (Washington, D.C., 1968).

4. *Ibid.*

5. "The IPA Faculty," *IPA Review* (January 1967), p. 11. The *IPA Review* is published by the U.S. Department of State, Agency for International Development, Office of Public Safety.

6. Taylor, *op. cit.*

7. U.S. Department of State, AID, Statistics and Reports Division, Operations Report, Data as of June 30, 1968.

8. See *NACLA Newsletter* Volume IV, No. 7.

9. Peter T. Chew, "America's Global Peace Officers," *The Kiwanis Magazine* (April 1969), p. 23.

10. Frantz Fanon, *The Wretched of the Earth*, Grove Press (New York), 1961, p. 63.

11. U.S. Department of State, AID OPS, *The Role of Public Safety in Support of the National Police of Vietnam* (Washington, D.C., 1969), pp. 8–9.

12. Tad Szulc, "U.S. Plans to Increase AID to Foreign Police to Help Fight Subversion," *The New York Times*, June 14, 1971.

13. For full document see *NACLA Newsletter*, April 1971, p. 26.

14. Chew, *op. cit.*, p. 24.

15. Dan Griffin, "Senator Church Assails U.S. Aid to Brazil Police," *The Washington Post*, July 25, 1971.

16. "U.S. to End Police Aid to Brazil," *The Washington Post*, July 15, 1971.

17. U.S. Senate, Committee on Appropriations, Foreign Assistance Appropriation, 1965. Hearings, 89th Congress, second Session (Washington, D.C., U.S. Government Printing Office, 1964), p. 82.

18. *Ibid.*, p. 75.

The Military Research Network –America's Fourth Armed Service

Michael Klare

Our colleges and universities must be regarded as bastions of our defense, as essential to the preservation of our country and our way of life as supersonic bombers, nuclear-powered submarines, and intercontinental ballistic missiles.
    —John A. Hannah, when President of Michigan State University, at a Parents' Convocation in 1961.

The Military Unification Plan of 1947, drafted by Clark Clifford during his service as special counsel to President Truman, fixed the present composition of the U.S. Military Establishment. The Plan recognized three military services—Army, Navy, and Air Force—which were made subordinate to the centralized command structure of the Department of Defense. A *fourth* armed service—as crucial to the national defense as the first three—was not given

■ Reprinted from *The University–Military–Police Complex: A Directory and Related Documents* (New York: North American Congress of Latin America, 1970) pp. 2–12, with the permission of NACLA.

formal recognition under the Plan. This service is the nexus of university laboratories and research institutes which constitute the military research network, Without the support of this Fourth Service, the United States would not have produced the atomic bomb, would not have developed missile guidance systems, and would not have been prepared for the challenge of Vietnam.

Until the present century, new weapons were developed by hit-or-miss experimentation, or through continuous refinement of existing devices. It is only in the past three decades that instrumentalities of warfare have emerged from organized scientific investigations, in which the talents of many researchers are pooled in the quest for novel military systems. The Manhattan Project of World War II was the prototype for all such efforts—at its peak thousands of scientists were engaged in various subtasks of the project, many without being aware of the final objective of their work. In order to mount other large-scale research projects, the War Department found it necessary at the onset of the war to establish a network of mammoth laboratories devoted to intensive research on advanced weapons systems. Since the only reservoir of trained scientific manpower available for such work was the university community, it was inevitable that the nation's institutions of higher education be mobilized for the establishment of a military research service. Speaking of this wartime effort, Gerard Piel of *Scientific American* wrote in 1965 that during World War II,

> The universities transformed themselves into vast weapons development laboratories. Theoretical physicists became engineers, and engineers forced solutions at the frontiers of knowledge. MIT and Harvard undertook to create the strategy and tactics as well as the instruments of radar and counter-radar; from Johns Hopkins came the proximity fuse that brought the conventional high-explosive artillery shell to its peak of lethality, and Columbia, Chicago, and California joined in the successful engineering and manufacture of the most fateful weapon of all. The universities and the scientists then dealt with the military not as contractors, but as privateers bringing along their own novel weapons.[1]

During the course of the war, a number of university laboratories developed into sizable institutions, employing thousands of scientists and technicians. (Many of the research centers described below, including MIT's Instrumentation Lab, Penn's Ordnance Research Lab, and California's Los Alamos Lab, can trace their origins to this period.) The wartime mobilization of university resources was organized by the National Defense Research Committee (NDRC), the first body of academic scientists to have an important policy function in the administration of military research. Headed by Dr. Vannevar Bush of the Carnegie Institution, the NDRC was expanded into the Office of

Scientific Research and Development, which coordinated the country's overall scientific effort throughout the war and supervised the initial development of the atomic bomb project.

The World War II military research laboratories had been organized on the premise of expediency, and had not been intended to outlast the war. As victory approached, however, the military services and some of the universities sought to prevent the dissolution of these installations. With the dawn of the Cold War, a new era of university–government cooperation commenced, as the Pentagon found itself with the task of "containing communism" on a front that stretched from Berlin to Seoul. In succeeding years, the former imperial powers of Europe were separated from their colonies in Africa and Asia, and the U.S. theater of operations was expanded as we moved in to protect the new states from the threat of "internal disequilibrium"—i.e., from movements for national liberation. These enormous tasks required an unprecedented "peacetime" expansion of the U.S. military establishment, and the upgrading of its ability to engage in unconventional and counterinsurgent warfare. As a result, the Pentagon found it prudent to maintain, and ultimately to expand, the military research network.

THE INSTITUTIONALIZATION OF RESEARCH

The outstanding characteristic of university warfare laboratories—the concentration of scientific personnel under conditions of relative autonomy (and freedom from ordinary teaching responsibilities)—make them particularly attractive to the Pentagon as performers of military research work. University research centers have grown in importance in direct proportion to the increasing value placed on this country's "technical intellectual resources"—the scientists and engineers whose intellectual efforts lie at the root of all technological advancement. The increased value placed upon these human resources can be detected, according to the Stanford Research Institute (SRI), in the concern "expressed by many countries over the loss of their engineers and scientists through the 'brain drain,'" and in "the efforts of aerospace companies to sell their technical intellectual capability rather than their technology."[2]

Since there is limited supply of this highly marketable commodity, the motivations, incentives and working conditions which determine the employment patterns of the technical workforce are matters of great concern to Pentagon research administrators—who naturally seek to employ the best minds available on any given project. Studies of the attitudes of professional research personnel indicate that *organizational* incentives (such as opportunity for advancement into management) and *material* incentives (higher salaries) are not closely related to technological productivity. In contrast, *professional* incentives (e.g., allowing the individual a high degree of freedom and flexibility in choosing his own work assignments in terms of what he feels will be professionally challenging) are "likely to be associated with higher levels of both professional and organizational productivity among scientists and engineers."[3] In one survey of work attitudes, research professionals indicated that they were highly motivated by the "opportunity to contribute to scientific knowledge," and by "association with other professionals of recognized ability," and were poorly motivated by "membership in a company producing reputable goods and essential services."[4] It is not hard to deduce from this data that universities provide the environment most likely to assure high technological productivity. In confirmation of this view, Dr. Frederick Seitz, past President of the National Academy of Sciences, told a Senate committee in 1963 that:

> ... a certain fraction of the best minds find the type of freedom and flexibility peculiar to the university best suited for their work. In addition, the presence of many inquiring young minds in the formative period, particularly the research students, adds a particular freshness and vitality to research. I do not mean to say that excellent work is not done elsewhere. ... What is important is that any program which does not take maximum advantage of the capability of the university will not advance in the most effective way possible.[5]

This analysis has prompted the Defense Department to establish military research centers at selected universities, to enlist the help of university administrators in the creation of independent research organizations (as in the case of the Institute for Defense Analyses), and to offer financial incentives to universities which agree to adopt an existing facility (as witnessed in the University of Rochester's agreement to administer the Center for Naval Analyses). Where direct university participation has not proven feasible, the Pentagon has found it expedient to create a network of para-universities—independent research organizations which boast a "campus-like environment" and adhere to the many rituals of academic life (the most famous example of this kind of institution is the RAND Corporation). The network of non-profit research organizations ... should be viewed, then, as an extension of the university world and not as a unique phenomenon.

In its postwar effort to reconstitute the military research network, the Pentagon was able to count on the enthusiastic cooperation of many university scientists and administrators. The causes of such cooperation are not hard to determine; for the first time in American history, scientists and academicians had come to enjoy positions of considerable prestige and influence in Washington. Experiments that would have been prohibitively expensive before the war now enjoyed abundant government financing. Moreover, the establishment of large research organizations had freed many professors from the restraints of conventional academic procedure and permitted them to pursue laboratory studies without being accountable to their colleagues in tradition-minded university departments. For some scientists—more interested in the application of their research to the "real world" of industry and national security than to the advancement of higher education—this development was most welcome. In a Senate speech on "The War and Its Effects," Sen. J. William Fulbright commented that,

> Disappointing though it is, the adherence of the professors [to the military-industrial complex] is not greatly surprising. No less than businessmen, workers, and politicians, professors like money and influence. Having traditionally been deprived of both, they have welcomed the contracts and consultantships offered by the Military Establishment.[6]

The Cold War also provided a new impetus on the part of the universities to engage in defense work. Participation in military research not only provided the reward of being part of the "stirring events of the time," but also, in the feverish days of Cold War hysteria, constituted a demonstration of one's loyalty. Thus even in 1967, when a special faculty committee was established to examine Princeton's ties with the Institute for Defense Analyses (IDA), some professors argued that affiliation with IDA "symbolizes a choice by the University to integrate itself into the life of the nation . . . and to acknowledge its obligations to the defense of the society of which it is a part."[7]

For this combination of reasons, scores of semiautonomous military research organizations were established by American universities in the postwar period. Some of these installations have come to enjoy a special relationship with the government as "Federal Contract Research Centers" (FCRC's), also known as Federally Funded Research and Development Centers (FFRDC's). These institutions receive at least 70 percent of their income from Federal agencies, and work "under the direct monitorship of the Government." According to National Science Foundation nomenclature, FFRDC's are "organizational units associated with universities and colleges whose creation and operation are not primarily related to the main function of the administering universities and colleges."[8] FFRDC's receive a substantial portion of the Federal research-and-development (R&D) funds available to the university community: in fiscal 1967, university-administered FFRDC's received $907.5 million from the government, compared with the $1,324.1 million awarded directly to the universities for R&D activities.[9]

Even when not recognized as FFRDC's, campus research centers can be found on most university campuses.[10] Most of these institutions engage in research on military and space "hardware"—the mechanical equipment needed to outfit an army or launch a space vehicle. Increasingly, however, such organizations are devoting their energies to the development of "software" systems—the mathematical and analytical models used in systems analysis, operations research, and related methodologies. University research centers have played an important role in the development of military software systems, and many of the organizations described in this directory—particularly the para-universities like RAND and IDA—have become noted for this kind of work. University social scientists, foreign area specialists, and educational researchers also found it profitable to establish autonomous research centers when the R&D budgets of non-military Federal agencies exploded in the 1960s. The development of foreign affairs research centers is documented in [a] State Department document. . . . Gerard Piel discussed the growing proliferation of university-based software research institutes in a 1965 talk to the American Philosophical Society as follows:

> The new science of "human engineering" at the "man–machine interface" has brought psychology into the circle of disciplines favored by the project contract/grant. Regional research institutes, organized at the primary initiative of the Department of State and the great private foundations to illuminate hitherto dark regions on the world map, have brought sociology and anthropology into the ambience of the Department of Defense. Lately, even the humanists, who had previously been confirmed to such servile chores as consulting on official histories of the last war, have found more positive assignments in "area and language training for military personnel and studies of certain strategic peoples." With funds abounding for projects in every field of learning, the university campus has come to harbor a new kind of condottieri, mercenaries of science and scholarship hooded with doctorates and ready for hire on studies done to contract specification.[11]

WAR RESEARCH IS GOOD BUSINESS

As Cold War defense appropriations soared, ambitious researchers—many of them associated with the Defense Department as consultants—were able to secure substantial research contracts from the government. Most of these contracts went to the autonomous research organizations like Michigan's Willow Run Laboratory and the Cornell Aeronautical Lab which could meet the Pentagon's strict security requirements. Today, some of these organizations enjoy the budget and facilities of a large university. The University of California, for instance, operates the Lawrence Radiation Laboratory and the Los Alamos Scientific Lab—installations which have a combined staff of 11,850 scientists, technicians, and support personnel, and an annual operating budget, in 1968, of $288 million (an amount that exceeds the higher education budget of most states). Many of the scientists associated with these institutions have been able to further augment their income by setting up defense-oriented "spin-off" companies which market the products developed in university laboratories.

In fact, as one penetrates further and further into the military research network, the more the distinction between academic and non-academic functions disappears. The trustee or administrator of a university research institute is more than likely the executive of a spin-off company located in the nearby industrial park, and at the same time a consultant to the Pentagon bureau which monitors contracts in his field of research. The independent "think-tanks" like RAND and IDA often act as middlemen in these consortia. Through such a system, the government can buy top scientific talent while by-passing low civil service salaries and avoiding accountability to Congress. Defense industry corporations, whose executives often dominate the boards of trustees of the research institutes and think-tanks, gain access to classified information and have the opportunity to "evaluate objectively" the projects they are trying to sell to the government. The universities, in return for their participation in the consortia, receive large research contracts and lucrative consulting fees for their professors. Examples of this arrangement can be found in most university communities, and are especially prevalent at the large research-oriented campuses like MIT, Stanford, and Johns Hopkins.

The spirit of cooperation that unites the components of America's military research networks is not surprising when one discovers that more often than not the universities themselves are governed by men representing the corporations that stand to profit most from the university's research activities. An investigation of the board of trustees of almost any college or university will uncover at least one or two entrepreneurs associated with a major defense contractor—and in some cases the number will be considerably higher. Using Columbia University

as an example, we find a total of five trustees who occupy positions of authority in the defense industry. Columbia trustees include William A. M. Burden and Maurice T. Moore, directors, respectively, of the Lockheed Aircraft Corporation and General Dynamics—the first and third largest Defense contractors in fiscal 1969. Burden is also President of the Institute for Defense Analyses, whose ties with Columbia helped sparked the 1968 student uprisings at that university.[12]

The Massachusetts Institute of Technology has become so thoroughly linked to the Department of Defense that no fundamental changes can take place at the Institute without altering its corporate entity. MIT has, in fact, become fixed in the popular imagination as the very paradigm of university–military collaboration. This image is nurtured by the Institute itself: in 1966 MIT spokesman Edward B. Hanify told Cambridge residents at a public hearing that:

> MIT is in the front rank of the forces of Science dedicated to the essential research which the Government of the United States considers indispensable to the National Defense. It is a scientific arsenal of democracy. From its halls and laboratories come the knowledge and technique, the brain power and the resources which contribute to our national survival in an era where the laboratories and technicians of our enemies work sleeplessly to outdistance us in the race to harness the latent secrets of nature as tools of their supremacy.[13]

All of the phenomena associated with the military research network are most pronounced here: of the top 75 Defense contractors in fiscal 1968, officers from 19 are represented on the MIT Corporation (the governing body of the Institute); if multiple directorships and memberships are taken into account, there are a total of 41 "crossovers" between MIT and these companies.

The extraordinary concentration of scientific and engineering talent at MIT—the "technical intellectual resources" described above—has inspired the formation of hundreds of research-oriented "spin-off" companies in the greater Boston area. (So many of these firms have located along Route 128, the circumferential highway that connects Boston's suburbs, that this phenomenon has come to be known as the

"Route 128 Complex.") In order to understand the dynamics of the spin-off phenomenon, the National Aeronautics and Space Administration commissioned MIT's Sloan School of Management to conduct an investigation of the Route 128 Complex.[14] The Sloan project has identified a total of over 160 new companies formed by people who had been full-time employees of MIT. Some of these firms, like the ITEK Corporation and Teledyne, Inc., have become giant enterprises with thousands of employees and annual sales in the hundreds of millions of dollars. Also included among the spin-offs are a number of military research organizations that continue to maintain close ties with the Institute; of these, the foremost is the MITRE Corporation, set up by MIT in 1958 to take over work being done by the Institute's Lincoln Laboratory on the SAGE air-defense system. [15] (MITRE's Chairman is the same as that of the MIT Corporation: James Killian.)

The pattern of university–military–industrial cooperation evident at MIT can be detected at many other large universities, although naturally on a smaller scale. Thus an investigation of Columbia University, sparked by demonstrations against the university's affiliation with the Institute for Defense Analyses, revealed that the Director of Columbia's Electronic Research Laboratory (ERL), Lawrence O'Neill, had served, simultaneously, as (a) a professor and associate dean of the Columbia School of Engineering; (b) head of ERL; (c) a consultant to the Department of Defense and IDA; and (d) an owner of the Federal Scientific Corporation, an R&D firm set up to market research performed at ERL.[16]

THE WAR PROFESSORS

America's Fourth Armed Service, the military research network, is not represented on the Cabinet with its own Secretary; this Service, nevertheless, has its representatives at the highest levels of policy formation. In the past quarter-century the U.S. government has created a network of scientific advisory panels with the aim of opening up new lines of communication between the Pentagon and the R&D community. These panels, composed of some of the nation's outstanding scientists and engineers,

provide the Defense Department with instantaneous access to the university scientific community when help or advice is needed on the development of new weapons systems.

A recent survey by *Armed Forces Journal* determined that there are some 105 defense R&D advisory boards and committees, of which the senior boards are: the Defense Science Board (DSB), Air Force Scientific Advisory Board (SAB), Army Scientific Advisory Panel (ASAP), and the Naval Research Advisory Committee (NRAC), Another 132 advisory boards are associated with other government departments. The whole scientific advisory complex is supervised by the President's Science Advisor, Dr. Lee A. DuBridge. As head of the President's Science Advisory Committee and of the Office of Science and Technology (part of the Executive Office of the President), Dr. DuBridge is in fact the Cabinet representative of the Fourth Armed Service.[17]

University scientists, according to a Stanford Research Institute report, supply a majority of the members of these panels. . . . Actually, most of the panelists have multiple associations with university, industry, and non-profit organizations. Because these men are active in both the scientific and military communities, the advisory panels constitute the "infrastructure" of the military research network. Thus the Pentagon describes the function of the DSB as follows: "Through its membership of distinguished men representing industry, government and the academic world, the Defense Science Board serves as the connecting link between the Office of the Director of Defense Research and Engineering and the scientific and technical community of the United States."[18]

The Defense Science Board was established in 1956 "to advise the Secretary of Defense, through the Director of Defense Research and Engineering (DDR&E), on scientific and technical matters of interest to the Department of Defense." The Board was created in response to a recommendation of the Commission on Organization of the Executive Branch of the Government (Hoover Commission) that a committee be appointed to "canvass periodically the needs and opportunities presented by new scientific knowledge for radically new weapons systems."[19] The DSB consists of 28 members, eight of whom serve ex-officio as representatives of government R&D agencies or of the other military advisory panels.

The President's Science Advisory Committee (PSAC) originated as the Science Advisory Committee of the Office of Defense Mobilization. The PSAC was reconstituted as a presidential agency on Nov. 22, 1957, a few days after the Soviet Union launched its second satellite. *The New York Times* reported in 1968 that during the Eisenhower Administration, "the committee spent 90 percent of its time on secret military matters, chiefly missiles, space, and the first step toward a nuclear test ban." [20] Civilian work was given somewhat more emphasis under Presidents Kennedy and Johnson, but the Nixon administration has chosen to re-emphasize military concerns.

The oldest and largest of the Service panels, the Air Force Scientific Advisory Board (AFSAB), was established in 1944 to assist the Army Air Force, and reorganized in 1946 to "advise the Chief of Staff, U.S. Air Force, on all scientific/technical matters relevant to the mission of the Air Force." [21] The AFSAB is composed of some 75 members, who serve on one of nine sub-panels on such subjects as Nuclear Warfare, Aerospace Vehicles, and Missile Guidance and Control. The Naval Research Advisory Committee (NRAC) and Army Scientific Advisory Panel (ASAP) were founded in 1946 and 1951, respectively, and perform the same duties for the research chiefs of their respective services. [22]

One non-governmental advisory group has come to occupy a particularly influential position in the military research network: the Jason Division of the Institute for Defense Analyses. Jason was established in 1958 with the encouragement of the Pentagon's Advanced Research Projects Agency (ARPA), which continues to provide financial support. The group consists of some 40 "outstanding university scientists who devote as much of their available time as possible to studies in the vanguard of the scientific aspects of defense problems." [23] In the first years of its existence, Jason members reportedly concentrated on "theoretical analyses of ballistic missile defense and exoatmospheric detonations." In 1964, however, "a new excursion was made. Increased Government attention to such problems as counterinsurgency, insurrection and infiltration led to the suggestion that

Jason members might be able to provide fresh insights into problems that are not entirely in the realm of physical science." [24] As part of this "excursion," Jason in 1967 held a secret conference on Thailand with the intent of mobilizing university social scientists for U.S. counterinsurgency operations in that country. [25]

The basic function of the scientific advisory committees is set forth in Department of Defense (DoD) Directive 5030.13 of April 20, 1962, "Regulations for the Formulation and Use of Advisory Committees." According to the Directive, advisory committees are formed "to provide a means of obtaining advice, views, and recommendations of benefit to the operation of the Government from industrialists, businessmen, scientists, engineers, educators, and other public and private citizens whose experience and talents would not other wise be available to DoD." [26] Specifically, the advisory panels provide essential services to the government by: Informing the Pentagon of new scientific discoveries applicable to weapons development; Finding the scientists best able to accomplish a specified research task; recruiting talented graduate students for careers in military research work; and providing a reservoir of scientific manpower available for work on crash military projects.

Activities of these panels are not normally publicized by the Defense Department or the participants themselves; nevertheless, it is sometimes possible to detect their influence. When former Defense Secretary Robert S. McNamara initiated a crash program to build an electronic anti-infiltration barrier across the Demilitarized Zone of Vietnam, he persuaded members of the DSB and the PSAC to head the effort. [27] The thorny problems of chemical and biological warfare (CBW) have been the subject of several studies by the advisory panels: Nobel laureate Dr. J. D. Watson told reporters from the *Washington Post* that he had served on a special CBW subcommittee of the PSAC from 1961 to 1964; members of the ASAP attended a meeting on CBW strategies at the Army's Edgewood, Md., Arsenal on Feb. 16–18, 1969. [28] The Vietnam war and its effects on military doctrine has not surprisingly been the subject of many research projects undertaken by the panels. Thus the 1967 Annual Report of IDA notes that "Jason continued work on technical problems of counterinsurgency warfare and systems studies with relevance to Viet-Nam."[29] These problems evidently had not been solved by the end of the 1960's, for in February 1970, Presidential Advisor Henry Kissinger met with officers of the PSAC to ask for help "in ferreting out problems and new approaches" to the Vietnam war effort."[30]

RESEARCH VS. EDUCATION: THE CONFLICT IN PRIORITIES

In the summer of 1965, a subcommittee of the House Committee on Government Operations held a series of hearings on "Conflicts Between the Federal Research Programs and the Nation's Goals for Higher Education." The committee subsequently issued a report to the Congress in which it was argued that, "While both research and higher education share the common goals of extending scholarship and developing the intellectual resources of the Nation, *the immediate interests of one are not necessarily those of the other.*"[31] [Emphasis added.] Federal research programs, the committee explained, are designed to advance the nation's technological capabilities—particularly in the areas of defense, atomic energy, and space—while our goals for higher education call for the maximization of opportunities for all Americans—regardless of race, nationality, or income—to obtain a college education. On the basis of the testimony and reports it examined, the committee concluded that, "Our Federal research programs, on the one hand, and the Nation's goals for higher education, on the other, are in increasing conflict."[32]

The first conflict, according to the committee, "is in the present use of scarce manpower." We return, therefore, to the question of the utilization of America's technical intellectual resources:

> Scientists and engineers are indispensable to research and development. They are also indispensable as teachers in the expanding higher education system. Since their numbers cannot be greatly increased over the short run, too much diversion into the one means deprivation of the other." A second conflict arises between the present use of manpower resources and the need for invest-

ment in future manpower resources: "research demands *performance* now. . . . [whereas] education by its nature demands *investment* now in training young people so that the Nation can have the benefits of performance later.[33]

In its report, the House committee indicated that Federal expenditures on R&D grew at the rate of 20 percent per year in the period 1950–65, and concluded that "any demand on the economy, public or private, of the size of Federal spending for research and development [amounting to $16 billion in 1965] is also a demand for manpower on a large scale."[34] Using National Science Foundation (NSF) figures, the committee estimated that two-thirds of all scientists and engineers engaged in R&D work were employed on Federally funded projects. Since almost 90 percent of all Federal R&D funds are contributed by either the Department of Defense ($7.3 billion in fiscal 1965), the National Aeronautics and Space Administration ($5.4 billion), or the Atomic Energy Commission ($1.5 billion), it is safe to assume that a majority of these scientists and engineers were committed to defense-related work. This diversion of scientific manpower to military work has meant that an inadequate number of qualified scientists are available for college teaching positions (particularly at the smaller colleges). Since the scientists engaged in defense R&D tend to become specialists in narrow fields of particular interest to the military, this diversion of manpower has also meant that when defense R&D spending is curtailed (as it was in 1969–1970), these scientists often lack the broad background that would enable them to switch into teaching work or non-military research.

The committee found the same kind of skewed priorities *inside* the universities:

> Federal competition for scientific manpower has not stopped at the gates of colleges and universities. Of the $16 billion in Federal Government obligations for research and development in fiscal 1965, about $1.1 billion was farmed out directly to colleges and universities, and an additional $700 million to research centers and laboratories operated by them. [The equivalent figures for fiscal 1968 are: $1.4 billion for R&D at universities, and $945 million for R&D at university-

operated laboratories.] With these funds, constituting about 70 percent of all research funds received each year by educational institutions, and perhaps 15 percent of the Nation's total annual expenditures on higher education, the Federal Government reaches within the higher education system to claim a substantial share of the working time of college and university faculties, and a very high share of the time of science faculties.[35]

The consequences of this phenomenon are as obvious to the committee as they are to most other observers of university education:

> Colleges and universities have responded to Federal demands for research by channelling an increasing number of professional employees into research work, by reducing teaching time of research-performing faculty, and by offering such reductions as inducements to attract new faculty.[36]

The resulting downgrading of undergraduate education—manifest in huge lecture classes and the use of poorly qualified teaching personnel—has become a fact of life at every large university.

Federal research programs—concentrated as they are in the physical sciences—have created a deepening split between science and nonscience departments within the university. The government's priorities are eloquently expressed in the distribution of R&D funds: in fiscal years 1963, 1964, and 1965, the physical sciences received 68 to 69 percent of all Federal support of basic research; the life sciences, 26 to 28 percent; the social sciences, about 2 percent; and all other fields, less than 0.5 percent.[37] (The comparable figures for fiscal 1967 are: physical, environmental, and engineering sciences, 60 percent; life sciences, 30 percent; social sciences, 3 percent; all other fields, 3.5 percent.[38]) The abundance of Federal funds for research in the physical sciences has naturally created vast imbalances within the university. Grants for summer research, consulting fees, and other extracurricular research work give a monetary advantage to the scientist. Following the 1969 student disorders at Harvard University, the campus newpaper published a "Report on the Future of the University," which contained the following warning:

> A chasm is developing between science and

non-science that is splitting many universities apart. Scientists have a high turnover rate; they participate less in university-wide decision-making. Their commitment is more to their research and whoever provides them with money to do that research than to whatever university they happen to be doing the research in. Data shows that the more research a faculty member does, the less time—by far—he spends on administrative duties. Scientists are becoming less and less members of the academic community.[39]

While this statement represents the biases of the non-scientist, it is a good indicator of the divisions that have occurred within the university community as a result of Federal programs.

The most conspicuous result of the conflicts between Federal research programs and the nation's goals for higher education is unquestionably the concentration of Federal funding in a small circle of what Clark Kerr calls "Federal grant universities." These favored schools receive up to 85 percent of their income from Federal research funds, and up to 100 percent of their research budget from this source. The number of such institutions is not large. Using fiscal year 1967 figures, we find that the top 100 recipients of Federal obligations for higher education received 69 percent ($2,278 million) of all such funds, and 88 percent ($1,166 million) of all Federal R&D funds. Fifteen universities alone captured 38 percent ($507.9 million) of all R&D funds available directly to universities; these same fifteen schools received 49 percent ($447.4 million) of Federal funds going to university-administered Federally Funded Research and Development Centers (FFRDC's). If one subtracts the funds going to FFRDC's administered by university consortia (e.g., the Argonne Universities Association, Oak Ridge Associated Universities), one discovers that these fifteen universities share 47 percent ($955.3 million) of all Federal R&D funds going to universities and university-based FFRDC's, while another 2,100 universities must compete for the remaining 53 percent of Federal R&D funds.[40]

This pattern of concentration is even more pronounced in the distribution of defense/space/atomic energy R&D funds. In fiscal 1967, the Department of Defense awarded $264.1 million in R&D funds to universities, the National Aeronautics and Space Administration awarded $109 million, and the Atomic Energy Commission $89.7 million (these figures exclude awards to FFRDC's). The top 100 recipients of Federal R&D expenditures received 89 percent of DoD funds, 94 percent of NASA funds, and 92 percent of AEC funds, while the top 15 universities received 52 percent, 39 percent, and 51 percent, respectively, of these funds. DoD/NASA/AEC awards to university-administered FFRDC's are overwhelmingly concentrated in a few hands: five schools (CalTech, Stanford, California, Johns Hopkins, and MIT) administer 74 percent ($647.9 million) of all such funds going to the FFRDC's. These same five schools share 25 percent ($116.4 million) of DoD/NASA/AEC R&D funds going directly to the universities; their combined income from these agencies, then, is $764.3 million, or 57 percent of $1.3 billion annual outlay for military, space, and atomic energy research at the universities.[41]

The favored status of the Federal grant universities, which can in most cases be traced back to World War II, has become a self-perpetuating phenomenon. The objective of federally funded research, according to the House committee, "is the most research at the least costs." Since the government is most likely to entrust its R&D funds to scientists with considerable research experience, "the objective of buying research to the exclusion of other considerations will lead inexorably to the concentration of Federal research funds at the major universities." This system works as follows:

> If proposals are judged on the basis of the previous research experience of investigators, scientists affiliated with major institutions will tend to be selected. Because of their lighter loads, they will have had greater opportunities to engage in research. Moreover, they will have had a more compelling experience record for, as senior investigators, they will have had previous grants accepted; or, as younger investigators, they will have had opportunities to work on projects headed by luminaries in the field.[42]

This principle operates even with non-military research programs: in fiscal 1967, for instance, the top 100 university recipients of Federal R&D obligations received 88 percent of all National Science Foundation research funds and

the same percentage of Health, Education, and Welfare Department funds.[43] As in the case of military research expenditures, a handful of big universities capture the lion's share of NSF funds—despite the fact that this agency is specifically charged to assist science education on a national scale.

The concentration of Federal R&D funds at a relatively small number of universities has created severe inequalities in the distribution of scientific resources in the nation's higher education system:

> The pattern of concentration of research funds has meant a similar concentration of research opportunities and incentives for scientists and engineers. Favored universities have been able to attract and keep the best scientists and graduate students. Institutions not so favored have lost many of their ablest professors, and are unable to compete on equal terms for replacements. *Thus, the Federal research programs have not only made already strong institutions stronger. They have done so partly at the expense of the weak.*[44] [Emphasis added.]

The ability of top universities to attract the best scientists has in fact created a "brain drain" from poorer institutions—four-year colleges, junior and community colleges—and from certain sections of the country—Appalachia, the Deep South, the Plains and Mountain states. A 1965 survey of the top 25 recipients of R&D funds from key government agencies indicated that all were Ph.D.-granting institutions or advanced institutes of technology. With a few exceptions, all of these schools are located in the Northeast, Middle-Atlantic, Great Lakes, or Pacific Coast areas. Six states (Massachusetts, New York, Pennsylvania, Illinois, Michigan, and California) received 43 percent of all Federal funds going to universities and colleges in fiscal 1967, and Federal R&D expenditures at schools in these states were even more concentrated.[45]

PROJECT THEMIS

Since many communities—not without justification—believe that research-oriented universities serve as magnets for advanced-technology industries seeking new locations, inequalities in the distribution of Federal R&D funds have frequently provoked criticism in the Congress.

In 1966 and 1967, the Subcommittee on Government Research of the Senate Government Operations Committee held a series of hearings on the "Equitable Distribution of R&D Funds by Government Agencies," which were designed to allow witnesses from the "so-called have-not universities" in the "have-not areas" to testify on the effects of government R&D spending.[46]

The resulting testimony did not entirely fall on deaf ears: The Department of Defense, which relies upon the cooperation of key Southern Congressmen for its mammoth appropriations, in 1967 instituted Project THEMIS, "A Program to Strengthen the Nation's Academic Institutions." The project's ostensible goals were formidable:

> Through Project THEMIS, the Department of Defense intends to meet part of its long-term research needs, strengthen more of the nation's universities, increase the number of institutions performing research of high quality and achieve a wider geographic distribution of research funds, and thus enhance the United States' academic capability in science and technology.[47]

Under the project, universities "not at present heavily involved in DoD-supported programs" would be awarded 50 percent of the costs of new research programs. Any project selected for funding by the Pentagon would have to demonstrate its relevance to the "Defense mission"; prospective applicants for such funds were warned that "THEMIS is not an 'institutional development program,' but rather a Department of Defense research program. There will be detailed annual technical reviews of the progress made by each THEMIS project. There is no guarantee of funding beyond the initial 3-year commitment." It was made abundantly clear that the Pentagon's motive in developing THEMIS was to expand the sources of technical intellectual resources that it could draw upon in future weapons programs:

> [THEMIS-funded] programs should develop the potential of groups and individuals, including young faculty members, for research of high quality leading to results of significant value to Defense agencies and departments.
>
> It is anticipated that, as a THEMIS research activity gains a higher degree of competence, it will become increasingly active in the regular research programs of the DoD and other agencies.[48]

It is questionable if THEMIS has had much effect on the present uneven distribution of Federal R&D funds. Only universities with doctoral programs in the sciences and engineering were eligible for THEMIS grants, and an examination of THEMIS funding ... discloses many awards to universities which already enjoy substantial Federal support. Moreover, in 1970 the THEMIS program was reduced from $20 million to $12 million annually as a result of R&D cutbacks imposed by Congress.

WAR MOBILIZATION AND THE UNIVERSITIES— AN ASSESSMENT OF THE CONSEQUENCES

At this point in our narrative, it is appropriate to draw some conclusions of the effects of university—military collaboration in the postwar era. The data presented above suggests that American colleges and universities have become divided into two camps—with the big R&D performers on one side, and those with few R&D contracts on the other. As we have seen, the large research-oriented universities are able to maintain their favored status by "bleeding off" the intellectual resources of less-favored schools. This process tends to perpetuate the underdeveloped condition of the "have-not" schools, which consist of women's colleges, black colleges, four-year liberal arts colleges, state and municipal schools attended by working class and lower-middle class youth, agricultural schools, and other non-Ph.D.-granting institutions. These lack adequate equipment and facilities, are unable to attract outstanding faculty members (particularly in the sciences), and cannot offer opportunities for faculty and students to engage in advanced research projects. These schools cannot, in sum, provide their students with a first-rate education.[49]

The big R&D-oriented universities are, of course, strong where the have-not schools are weak—they can boast ultramodern facilities, star-studded faculties, multiple research opportunities. But by becoming dependent upon Federal research contracts for their operating expenses, these schools have lost any claim they might once have enjoyed to be called "independent centers of knowledge." As we have seen, the patterns of cooperation between university R&D performers and Federal R&D consumers tends to become self-sustaining. This phenomenon is admirably summarized in this passage from the *Harvard Crimson's* 1969 "Report on the Future of the University:"

> The government, to a large degree, has created its own need for itself among the universities. It is not merely a case of the universities needing money and the government providing it; the government has built up large-scale scientific research as an almost totally new function for universities, a function that only the federal government can finance. . . .
>
> As the sale of the research product became more and more profitable to universities (especially after Sputnik in 1957), the universities began to reorient their resources—and their own concept of their function—to be able to provide the produce more easily. The universities developed a deep dependence on the government, which caused them to anticipate what the government wanted from them and brought them to believe the government's interests were the same as their own.[50]

It is quite clear that by orienting its activities so as to anticipate the research needs of the government, the universities have by default neglected those areas of inquiry that might embarrass the government or threaten its prerogatives. This fact has been noted by many critics of the government–university relationship, including Sen. J. William Fulbright, who, in a major Senate speech on "The War and its Effects," commented:

> The universities might have formed an effective counterweight to the military–industrial complex by strengthening their emphasis on the traditional values of our democracy, but many of our leading universities have instead joined the monolith, adding greatly to its power and influence.[51]

Federal R&D funds do make some contribution to higher education, Fulbright conceded, but they do so at a price:

> That price is the surrender of independence, the neglect of teaching, and the distortion of scholarship. A university which has become accustomed to the inflow of government funds is likely to emphasize activities which will attract those funds. These, unfortunately, do not include teaching undergraduates and the kind of scholarship which, though it may contribute to the sum of human knowledge and to man's understanding of himself, is not salable to the Defense Department or the CIA.[52]

Fulbright concluded that the current wave of student unrest is due not to inferior education but to "the student's discovery of corruption in the one place . . . which might have been supposed to be immune from the corruptions of our age." While one may not agree with the Senator that the universities are "the last citadels of moral and intellectual integrity" in this country, we can hardly question his assertion that they are "lending themselves to ulterior and expedient ends," i.e., have 'sold out' to the Military Establishment.

MILITARY RESEARCH AND THE CAMPUS REVOLT

For the past two years, student opposition to university-conducted military research has been a major issue on campuses all over the country. Efforts by student radicals to "move beyond protest" in the struggle against U.S. intervention in Vietnam led to campaigns against local manifestations of the "War Machine"—ROTC, Armed Forces recruiters, Dow Chemical Company representatives, and military research projects. As campuses became mobilized behind concrete demands—"ROTC Off The Campus," "No More War Research"—symbolic protests and vigils gave way to mass civil disobedience and ultimately to violence. Opposition to Columbia University's membership in the Institute for Defense Analyses culminated in a strike which effectively paralyzed the school for two months. The Columbia action, which occurred in April and May of 1968, was followed a year later by a "spring offensive" against military research that led to sit-ins, strikes, and in some cases, violent confrontations with police, at many of the large research universities. Finally, the Cambodian invasion of April–May 1970 precipitated a nationwide wave of protests against war research and military ROTC training. These successive campaigns have produced a number of conspicuous realignments in the military research network.

Sever prominent research centers have lost their university affiliation (American University's Center for Research in Social Systems, George Washington's Human Resources Research Office, MIT's Instrumentation Laboratory, and the Stanford Research Institute), and several others have been compelled to restrict their military research activities.

Because of the controversy which now surrounds the subject of university-military collaboration, it would be worthwhile to conclude this essay with a discussion of some of the questions which have arisen in the past few years as a result of the student revolt. Among the most frequently asked questions are; (1) Is university research *really* important to the Pentagon? (2) Granting that *secret* research is "bad," why object to *unclassified* military research? (3) Has the campus revolt had any effect whatsoever on the functioning of the War Machine? Provisional answers to these questions appear below.

1. Is university research important to the Pentagon?

This question has been answered in the affirmative by the Pentagon itself on many occasions. When some conservative Congressmen recently proposed in budget hearings that the Pentagon terminate research contracts at universities which cancel classified contracts, the Director of Defense Research and Engineering, Dr. John S. Foster, Jr., replied that "I do not think that this would help us. We need their help. I am disappointed that we cannot get as much as they could give us, but I am grateful for that which they are willing to do."[53]

Over and over, the advocates of university participation in the Pentagon's research programs have argued that the advancement of weapons technology requires access to the intellectual resources of the academic community. Perhaps the strongest argument for university participation in military research was made by Lt. Gen. Austin W. Betts, the Army's Chief of Research and Development, who stated:

Only our enemies could justify a position that says we should not have adequate military strength. To have an adequate military posture, we must apply the most advanced technology to our weapons and equipment. To stay abreast of advances in technology,

the military must be intimately involved in the support of research. *The citadels of research are the universities. It would be a national disaster if they could not make an appropriate contribution to our national strength.*[54] [Emphasis added.]

At this point, it is appropriate to emphasize that this university-Pentagon partnership was not created exclusively by and for the military; on the contrary, it is clear that many members of the university community actively sought out and cultivated such ties. In a revealing talk on Defense Department support of academic research, Dr. Foster indicated that "we receive far more proposals [for such research] than we can fund. In fact, every year—including this year [1969]—we receive requests for funds six to eight times greater than our budget for the R&D considered appropriate for academic effort."[55]

2. Why object to classified research?

In the past two years, several prominent universities, including Penn and Columbia, have adopted regulations barring the performance of classified research on their campuses. When some activists proposed a ban on *all* Pentagon contracts, most administrators and senior faculty members sought to distinguish between secret research, which was "bad," and unclassified research, which could not be banned without infringing upon an investigator's right to "pursue knowledge wherever it may lie." This argument holds that the major objection to secret research is its restriction on the publication of any findings which result from a given research project; what's at stake here, then, is a concern with "academic freedom"—and not with the uses to which American military technology is ultimately put. Since classified research in fact, constitutes only four percent of all Pentagon-financed studies performed by universities[56] (excluding research performed by the Federally Funded Research and Development Centers), the question of the *uses* of knowledge, rather than of its publishability, is the paramount one facing the university community.

The function of the military establishment is to wage war; constitutional and Congressional restraints prohibit the Pentagon from engaging in any activities which do not contribute to the national defense. Since most unclassified research projects call for basic research with no apparent relationship to military problems, defenders of such projects usually imply that the Defense Department is performing a "public service" by financing research that would not otherwise receive support. But the Pentagon eschews such an interpretation of its role; thus General Betts wrote in 1968 that:

> Generally, it has been our experience that those in universities who work under contract to the Army on basic research are sincerely and positively dedicated to one goal, that is, the pursuit of knowledge. They should understand, and most of them fully recognize the fact, *that the knowledge may and probably will be used to strengthen our military posture.*[57] [Emphasis added.]

The ultimate military utilization of any research effort may not be immediately apparent—but Pentagon sponsorship implies that someone in the Department of Defense believes that it will be useful to the military in some fashion. "The university laboratories," Dr. Foster explained, are "involved in basic research designed to deepen our scientific insights into fundamental problems that impede progress in key areas of defense technology."[58]

In 1967, a campaign against chemical and biological warfare research at the University of Pennsylvania led to the demand that Penn refuse classified research projects. When questioned about this episode at a Congressional hearing, Dr. Foster argued that no sanction be taken against the university if it adopted such a stand; to defend his position, Foster produced a list of 41 unclassified research projects being conducted by Penn that he maintained fulfilled the Pentagon's need for research "into fundamental problems that impede progress in key areas of defense technology."[59] The nation's highest military research official concluded:

> Most of the value of university research work is in the unclassified area. I do not want to minimize in any way the classified work that is performed by these institutions. Nevertheless, *I believe the most important part is the basic unclassified work performed by the universities.*[60] [Emphasis added.]

If our opposition to military research stems from an abhorence of U.S. foreign and military policies (with their implied goal of an expanding U.S. world empire), we cannot perpetuate the artificial distinction between classified and unclassified research.

3. Has the campus revolt had any effect on the war machine?

It has been argued here that the most important military function of the university is the production, and concentration in useful form, of what has been called "technical intellectual resources." A Stanford Research Institute study summarized this function as follows:

> The university is a major performer of defense R&D; a supplier of advisers and consultants to defense R&D agencies; a producer of the technical professional workforce that is the prime production factor in the many government, non-profit, industrial, and academic laboratories that produce defense R&D; and a provider of continuing, updating education to the defense R&D workforce.[61]

Any evaluation of the movement against war research would have to conclude that the only *measurable* results achieved by the campus revolt have been confined to the *first* role identified by SRI, i.e., the production of defense R&D directly by the universities. Some universities have placed bans on secret research or otherwise objectionable projects (e.g., work on chemical and biological warfare), and some research institutes have been severed from their parent university. No limitations, however, have been placed on any of the other defense R&D roles performed by the university. It is questionable, moreover, whether any of the actions taken by the university have had any effect on the day-to-day functioning of the Fourth Armed Service: non-university research organizations have been found to assume responsibility for projects abandoned by the universities, and institutes that have lost their university sponsorship are fully capable of continuing work on their own. Thus even the institutional measures adopted by the universities to divest themselves of defense R&D work will not substantially alter the composition of the military research network: the cohesion of this network, after all, depends not so much on formal arrangements as on its ability to funnel information to the Pentagon and money back to the research performers—a process which goes on unabated.

If any results have been achieved at all by the campus protest movement, they would have to be manifest in the most fundamental area of all: the attitudes and loyalties of the people who comprise the nation's technical intellectual resources. If America's outstanding scientists and engineers are persuaded to abandon military work, the Fourth Armed Service would be seriously impeded from carrying out its responsibilities. And if young scientists and graduate students eschew a career in those fields which are closely tied to "defense technologies," the impediment will be of a lasting nature.

In a guest article in *The New York Times*, Dr. Foster clearly revealed that the Pentagon is concerned by the growing alienation of young scientists from military research work. This phenomenon received national attention on March 4, 1969, when thousands of scientists participated in a one-day research strike to "protest the misuse of technology and the complicity of the scientific and technological community with the growing power and influence of the military-industrial complex." On the positive side, the strike was called to encourage scientists to seek "means for turning research applications away from the present overemphasis on military technology towards the solution of pressing environmental and social problems." Participants in the March 4th strike at MIT heard an impassioned plea from Harvard biologist George Wald for nothing more than "a reasonable chance to live, to work out our destiny in peace and decency." Wald, a Nobel laureate, told an appreciative audience that while "our government has become preoccupied with death, with the business of killing and being killed," the business of scientists "is with life, not death."[62] Recognizing that these arguments constitute a dangerous challenge to the morale and discipline of the troops under his command, Foster felt compelled to respond on a moral plane to the anti-military campaign:

> Today the spirit and vigor [which created this country] often appear in the form of youth "revolution"—a tenacious and sometimes violent insistence on "relevance," . . . an unrelenting protest against affronts to the quality of life.
>
> The theme of these young people is

> valid—our talents and our physical resources should be directed primarily toward enhancing the quality of life. . . . Unhappily, one compelling attribute of the current era, the end of which is not in sight, is the fact and prospect of war. Security from external threat to our nation is a prerequisite, therefore, to the improvement of the quality of life. . . .[63]

Lurking in the background, then, are the faded imperatives of the Cold War; from this perspective, "Research in areas of interest to defense is not in itself immoral. But to deny others the right to pursue defense research and to find alternatives for the common defense is, in my judgment, immoral."[64]

There is of course no way to determine who is being most persuasive in this struggle for the loyalties of young scientists. Nevertheless, there is some indication that the Pentagon will not, as in the past, be able to choose at random among the brightest minds in the nation when lining up staff for important research projects. Disenchantment with the military orientation of the "Science Establishment" was clearly visible at 1969 and 1970 meetings of the American Physical Society and the American Association for the Advancement of Science, where activists shattered the normally placid atmosphere of the proceedings to challenge those who unquestioningly accepted the present utilization of scientific resources. ("Our job as scientists," one protestor shouted, "is to see that science resources benefit the people.") At MIT, the Science Action Coordinating Committee, sponsor of the March 4th research strike, has succeeded in winning a pledge from the Institute's administration to seek non-military financing for MIT's defense-oriented Special Laboratories. More portentous, perhaps, are recent press accounts of young scientists who have quit defense research to work on environmental problems—or who quit science altogether to become full-time political activists.

The Pentagon is well aware that it can shift university research projects to "less competent but more 'cooperative'" private research organizations. To do so, Dr. Foster argues, would be "a great disservice to the nation." In final confirmation of the analysis that has been presented here, Dr. Foster argued that:

> It would be an even graver disservice to the

nation to bar defense-related research from all campuses, as advocated by some. National security requires nothing less than the best research talent offered.

The Federal Government must be free to enlist those talents wherever they are found—and they flourish particularly in the university community.[65]

NOTES

1. U.S. House of Representatives, Committee on Government Operations, *Conflicts Between the Federal Research Programs and the Nation's Goals for Higher Education.* Responses from the Academic and Other Interested Communities to an Inquiry by the Research and Technical Programs Subcommittee, 89th Congress, 1st Ses., (Washington, D.C.: U.S. Government Printing Office, 1965), p. 362. (Hereinafter cited as *Responses.*)

2. Albert Shapero, Kendall D. Moll, Robert A. Hemmes, and Richard P. Howell, *The Role of the University in Defense R&D* (Menlo Park, Calif.: Stanford Research Institute, 1966), p. 10. (Hereinafter cited as *Role of the University.*)

3. *Ibid.*, p. 14.

4. *Ibid.*

5. See U.S. Senate, Committee on Aeronautics and Space Science, *Scientists' Testimony on Space Goals, 88th Cong. 1st Ses., 1963.* Cited in *Role of the University*, p. 13.

6. *Congressional Record—Senate* (Dec. 13, 1967), p. S18485.

7. Princeton University, *Report of the Majority of the Special Committee to Examine Princeton's Relationship to the Institute for Defense Analyses*, p. 13.

8. National Science Foundation, *Federal Support to Universities and Colleges, Fiscal Year 1967* (Washington, D.C.: National Science Foundation, 1969), p. 45. (Hereinafter cited as *Federal Support FY67.*)

9. *Ibid.*, pp. 36–7.

10. Most campus research centers are identified in A. M. Palmer and A. T. Kruzas, Eds., *Research Centers Directory*, 2nd Ed. (Detroit: Gale Research Co. 1966). Foreign affairs research centers are identified in *University Centers of Foreign Affairs Research* (Washington, D.C.: U.S. Department of State, 1968).

11. *Responses*, p. 369.

12. For a thorough discussion of Columbia power structure, see *Who Rules Columbia?* (New York: North American Congress on Latin America, 1968).

13. As reported in the Boston *Herald-Traveler* (Feb. 21, 1966).

14. While the spin-off phenomenon is most conspicuous at MIT, it can be detected at many other large research-oriented universities. The Stanford Research Institute has identified 16 spin-offs from Stanford University in the Palo Alto area; another 16 spin-offs have been traced to the University of Michigan, and six to the University of Minnesota. See *Role of the University*, pp. 96–102.

15. For carefully documented discussions of the "Route 128 Phenomenon," see E. B. Roberts and H. A. Wainer, "New Enterprises on Route 128," *Science Journal* (Dec., 1968), 78–83; and "MIT and Military Capitalism," Science Action Coordinating Committee *Newsletter* (Sept. 17, 1969).

16. For a description of the "Columbia University Defense Establishment," see *Who Rules Columbia?*

17. Brooke Nihart, "Science Advisory Boards: Bargain or Boondoggle?," *Armed Forces Journal* (March 7, 1970), 18–24.

18. Office of the Director of Defense Research and Engineering, *Organization and Purpose of the Defense Science Board* (April 1, 1968).

19. *Ibid.*

20. *The New York Times* (Feb. 20, 1968).

21. *Role of the University*, Table A-1.

22. *Ibid.*

23. Institute for Defense Analyses, *Annual Report* (1964).

24. Institute for Defense Analyses, *Annual Report* (1966).

25. As disclosed in the *Student Mobilizer* (April 2, 1970), published by the Student Mobilization Committee to End the War in Vietnam.

26. As cited in Nihart, "Science Advisory Boards," p. 19.

27. *Washington Post* (Oct. 25, 1968).

28. *Army Research and Development Newsmagazine* (April, 1968).

29. Institute for Defense Analyses, *Annual Report* (1967).

30. *Armed Forces Journal* (Feb. 14, 1970).

31. U.S. House of Representatives, Committee on Government Operations, *Conflicts Between the Federal Research Programs and the Nation's Goals for Higher Education.* Report, 89th Cong., 1st Ses. (Washington, D.C.: U.S. Government Printing Office, 1965), p. 1. (Hereinafter cited as *Conflicts.*) This report should not be confused with the collection of *Responses*, which has the same title (see note 1).

32. *Ibid.*

33. *Ibid.*, pp. 1–2.

34. *Ibid.*, p. 15.

35. *Ibid.*, p. 17.

36. *Ibid.*, pp. 17–18.

37. *Ibid.*, p. 55.

38. National Science Foundation, *Federal Funds for Research, Development, and Other Scientific Activities, Fiscal Years 1967, 1968, and 1969* (Washington, D.C., 1968).

39. James K. Glassman, "A Report on the Future of the University," *Harvard Crimson* (May 7, 1969).

40. *Federal Support FY67*, pp. 24–5, 31–3, 36–7.

41. *Ibid.*, pp. 31–3.

42. *Conflicts*, pp. 43–4.

43. *Federal Support FY67*, pp. 31–3.

44. *Conflicts*, p. 31.

45. *Federal Support FY67*, pp. 17–18.

46. U.S. Senate, Committee on Government Operations, Subcommittee on Government Research, *Equitable Distribution of R&D Funds by Government Agencies.* Hearings, 90th Cong., 1st Ses., May 10, 11,

17 and 18, 1967 (Washington, D.C.: U.S. Government Printing Office, 1967).

47. Office of the Director of Defense Research and Engineering, *Project THEMIS* (Washington, D.C., Nov., 1967), p. iii.

48. *Ibid.*, pp. 1–7.

49. One should not conclude from this assessment that "have-not" schools do not make any contribution to the War Machine. In fact, many of these schools— particularly state and municipal colleges—are major suppliers of Army officers through the ROTC program. Other schools provide trained manpower for local defense industries. The division of American colleges into two camps is not the result only of disproportionate support for one side but rather represents a conscious need for a hierarchy of services which include the training function of have-not schools.

50. Glassman, "Report on the Future of the University."

51. *Congressional Record—Senate* (Dec. 13, 1967), p. S18485.

52. *Ibid.*

53. U.S. House of Representatives, Committee on Appropriations, Subcommittee, *Department of De-*

fense Appropriations for 1968. Hearings, 90th Cong., 1st Ses., Part 3, p. 90. (Hereinafter cited as *Appropriations 1968.*)

54. Lt. Gen. Austin W. Betts, address to the Armed Forces Communications-Electronics Association, as published in *Army Research and Development Newsmagazine* (Nov., 1968).

55. John S. Foster, Jr., address to the American Nuclear Society, as published in *Army Research and Development Newsmagazine* (Aug.-Sept., 1969).

56. *Ibid.*

57. Betts, in *Army Research and Development Newsmagazine* (Nov., 1968).

58. *Appropriations 1968*, p. 25.

59. *Ibid.*, pp. 90–91.

60. *Ibid.*, p. 93.

61. *The Role of the University*, pp. 3–4.

62. As reported in the *Boston Globe* (March 8, 1969).

63. John S. Foster, Jr., "Defense Role of U.S. Colleges," *The New York Times* (Jan. 12, 1970).

64. *Ibid.*

65. *Ibid.*

U.S. Police Assistance Programs in Latin America

Michael Klare

The by now familiar panacea for domestic ills, "law and order," has long been described as the principal aim of U.S. policy in the Third World. Clearly, an attractive climate for capital investment cannot develop in an atmosphere of disorder and instability. In the rapidly urbanizing nations of the Third World, however, civil disorders have become a common phenomenon as landless peasants stream to the cities in search of economic and cultural opportunities. Since most of these countries cannot satisfy the aspirations of these new city-dwellers under present economic and social systems, built-up tensions are increasingly giving way to attacks on the status quo.

Since the late 1950s, a preeminent concern of American policymakers has been the preservation of social stability in Third World countries deemed favorable to U.S. trade and invest-

■ Reprinted from *U.S. Military and Police Operations in the Third World* (New York: North American Congress on Latin America, 1970), pp. 9–11, with the permission of NACLA.

ment. U.S. military planning has been shaped by the need to provide, on a moment's notice, trained counterinsurgency troops that can be flown to the aid of friendly regimes threatened by popular insurrection. The Military Assistance Program has been used to upgrade the capabilities of indigenous forces to counter the same kind of threat. Finally, on the premise that the police constitute a "first line of defense against subversion," the foreign assistance program has been utilized to provide Latin American police forces with equipment and training.

The task of providing assistance to Latin police forces is the responsibility of the Office of Public Safety (OPS) of the U.S. Agency for International Development (AID). During hearings on the Foreign Assistance Appropriations for 1965, former AID Administrator David Bell described the function of OPS as follows:

Maintenance of law and order including internal security is one of the fundamental responsibilities of government. . . .

Successful discharge of this responsibility is imperative if a nation is to establish and maintain the environment of stability and security so essential to economic, social, and political progress. . . .

Plainly, the United States has very great interests in the creation and maintenance of an atmosphere of law and order under humane, civil concepts and control. . . . When there is a need, technical assistance to the police of developing nations to meet their responsibilities promotes and protects these U.S. interests.[1]

The Public Safety program is not large in comparison to the military aid program—but its supporters offer some impressive arguments to underscore its importance. They argue, for instance, that the police—being interspersed among the civil population—are more effective than the military in controlling low-scale insurgency. According to Administrator Bell,

The police are a most sensitive point of contact between government and people, close to the focal points of unrest, and more acceptable than the army as keepers of order over long periods of time. The police are frequently better trained and equipped than the military to deal with minor forms of violence, conspiracy and subversion.[2]

Police forces are also cheaper to maintain than military forces, since they do not require expensive "hardware" like planes and tanks.

On the basis of these arguments, Bob Kennedy and John F. Kennedy were persuaded in 1962 to expand the small police assistance program that had been functioning since 1954, and to centralize U.S. police programs in the Office of Public Safety. A State Department memorandum, issued in November 1962, declared that AID "vests the Office of Public Safety with primary responsibility and authority for public safety programs and gives that Office a series of powers and responsibilities which will enable it to act rapidly, vigorously, and effectively . . . powers greater than any other technical office or division of AID."[3] (These special powers are discussed further below.) Bob Kennedy was also instrumental in the establishment of the Inter-American Police Academy in the Panama Canal Zone (the Academy was later moved to Washington, D.C. and renamed the International Police Academy).

Under the Public Safety program, the U.S. aids Latin police forces by: (1) providing "in-country" training for rank-and-file policemen; (2) providing training in the U.S., Puerto Rico, and the Canal Zone for senior police officers and specialists; and (3) supplying communications equipment, patrol cars, jeeps, anti-riot gases, and related equipment. Approximately 2,000 Latin police officers have received training at the International Police Academy, and some 90 "Public Safety Advisors" (mainly ex-FBI agents and former municipal police officers) are now stationed in Latin America to conduct in-country training programs. Total OPS expenditures in Latin America are indicated in Table 32; a breakdown of OPS programs . . . is provided as an appendix.

In providing such assistance, OPS notes that most countries possess a unified "civil security service" which, "in addition to regular police include paramilitary units within civil police organizations and paramilitary forces such as gendarmeries, constabularies, and civil guards which perform police functions and have as their primary mission maintaining internal security."[4] The AID program is designed to encompass all of these functions; according to OPS,

Individual Public Safety programs, while varying from country to country, are focused in general on developing within the civil security forces a balance of (1) a capability for regular police operations, with (2) an investigative capability for detecting and identifying criminal and/or subversive individuals and organizations and neutralizing their activities, and with (3) a capability for controlling militant activities ranging from demonstrations, disorders, or riots through small-scale guerilla operations.[5]

As noted in the State Department memo cited above, OPS possesses unique powers not granted to other AID bureaus. These powers enable OPS to "act rapidly, vigorously, and effectively" in aiding Latin regimes threatened by popular uprisings. "In order to deal with the dynamics of internal security situations," Mr. Bell explained, "the public safety program has developed and utilized methods to deliver to threatened countries, in a matter of days, urgently needed assistance including equipment, training, and technical advice."[6] When a crisis develops in a Latin capital, OPS officials often stay up "night after night" in their Washington,

TABLE 32 AID Public Safety Program Expenditures in Latin America, 1956–1970
(amounts in thousands of dollars)
(FY = Fiscal Year)

Country:	Program Initiated FY	Expenditures Through 6/30/69	Estimated Expenditures in FY 1970	Estimated Expenditures Through 6/30/70	FY 1971 Request
Bolivia	1956	1,900	118	2,018	143
Brazil	1959	6,830	732	7 562	456
Chile	1963	1,571	90	1,661	71
Colombia	1963	4,350	217	4,567	240
Costa Rica	1963	985	240	1,225	200
Dominican Rep.	1962	2,583	470	3,053	423
Ecuador	1962	3,290	186	3,476	134
El Salvador	1961	1,825	87	1,912	86
Guyana	1966	711	311	1,022	232
Honduras	1960	1,074	167	1,241	165
Jamaica	1967	272	172	444	70
Panama	1959	3,059	383	3,442	135
Peru	1962	3,528	114	3,642	0
Uruguay	1962	869	230	1,099	200
Venezuela	1963	2,318	285	2,603	210
Totals:		35,165	3,802	38,967	2,765

Source: U.S. Agency for International Development, Program and Project Data Presentations to the Congress for Fiscal Year 1971. (Does not include data for countries where OPS program terminated prior to FY 1970.)

D.C. office to insure that needed supplies—including radios and tear-gas—reach the beleaguered police of the friendly regime.

Several instances of such rapid action by OPS can be identified. In 1962, when the government of Venezuela (then headed by President Romulo Betancourt) came under heavy pressure from guerrillas of the Armed Forces of National Liberation (FALN), John F. Kennedy launched a crash program to upgrade the Caracas police. According to Peter T. Chew, a journalist sympathetic to OPS,

In May 1962 John "Jake" Longan, a slow-talking, fast-thinking Oklahoman, flew secretly to Caracas and set up an advisory group. . . .
Longan's men worked with city policemen, teaching such fundamentals as how to approach a suspicious car on foot and how to still a sniper in a building without harming residents. They persuaded Venezuelan police to favor the old-fashioned shotgun and showed how shotguns, firing buckshot and gas grenades, could be effectively used against terrorists. . . . They also demonstrated how to bounce birdshot off the pavement for effective non-lethal riot control.[7]

A year later, when OPS was satisfied with the performance of the Caracas police, "Longan and some of his advisers quietly slipped away from Venezuela."

OPS advisers were also brought into the Dominican Republic after the 1965 insurrection. Thousands of Dominican police received training in riot-control techniques from an American team that included several former members of the Los Angeles Police Department.

AID officials state flatly that OPS assistance is "not given to support dictatorships." Yet there are exceptions to this rule: Administrator Bell told a Senate Committee that in one country,

Despite the limitations of the present government, it is considered desirable and proper to continue to assist in the improvement of the efficiency of the civilian police force to counteract the small amount of Communist-led terrorism and to make sure the police can confront and stop any larger effort. . . .[8]

On the basis of this statement, it is possible to conclude that Mr. Bell is talking about Brazil, a country which continues to receive a substantial OPS subsidy (see Appendix), despite well-documented reports of the torture of political prisoners by Brazilian police. In justifying continued OPS aid to such regimes, Bell explained that ". . . the police are a strongly anti-Communist force right now. For that reason it is a very important force to us."[9] In the twilight world of Cold War hysteria inhabited by these men, a "small amount of Communist-led terrorism" is sufficient reason to subsidize the repressive instruments of a totalitarian regime.

OPS officials are fully aware that in many Latin countries the police are regarded with suspicion and resentment by the population because of their brutal behavior. Since provocative police behavior frequently inspires anti-government campaigns, an important aspect of the Public Safety program are efforts to encourage "the development of responsible and humane police administration and judicial procedures." Students at the various OPS schools are advised to "stay out of politics" (i.e., to support whatever regime happens to be in power), and are trained in the techniques of "non-lethal crowd control" (i.e., the massive use of riot gases). The main objective of this approach, according to OPS Director Byron Engle, is to prevent situations in which "an oppressive police force drives a deep wedge between the people and their government."[10] Anti-riot measures are successful, from this perspective, when "no martyrs are created."

Despite the many contradictions between OPS ideology and the practices of Latin police forces, Administrator Bell concluded his Senate statement with the observation that

> Public safety forces have done and can do much to prevent conspiracy and the development of disruptive situations, and to insure an environment of law and order which supports the orderly social, economic, and political development of emerging nations.[11]

NOTES

1. U.S. Senate, Committee on Appropriations, *Foreign Assistance Appropriations, 1965*, Hearings (Washington, D.C.: U.S. Government Printing Office, 1964), p. 72. (Hereinafter cited as *Foreign Assistance Hearings 1965*.)
2. *Ibid.*, pp. 72–73.
3. Cited by Holmes Alexander in undated article inserted in *Foreign Assistance Hearings 1965*, p. 76.
4. "A.I.D. Assistance to Civil Security Forces," OPS press release dated Feb. 11, 1970.
5. *Ibid.*
6. *Foreign Assistance Hearings 1965*, p. 74.
7. Peter T. Chew, "America's Global Peace Officers," *The Kiwanis Magazine* (April, 1969), p. 24.
8. *Foreign Assistance Hearings 1965*, p. 75.
9. *Ibid.*
10. *The Los Angeles Times* (Feb. 10, 1963).
11. *Foreign Assistance Hearings 1965*, p. 75.

APPENDIX: AID PUBLIC SAFETY PROGRAMS IN SELECTED LATIN AMERICAN COUNTRIES, 1970

(Note: the following project description is drawn verbatim from the A.I.D. *Program and Project Data Presentations to the Congress for Fiscal Year 1971*.)

Brazil
Project Target and Course of Action: To improve the capability of the Brazilian federal and state civil security forces to maintain law and order, and security against subversion, by supporting development of Federal Police Department capacity to provide training and technical support internally and for state police departments nationwide. Project emphasis is on the concept of police service to the public.
Progress to date: Through December 1969, the Public Safety project in Brazil has assisted in training locally over 100,000 federal and state police personnel. Additionally, 523 persons received training in the U.S. Major project accomplishments include: construction, equipping and development of curriculum, staff and faculty for the National Police Academy, National Telecommunications Center, and National Institutes of Criminalistics and Identification. All are functioning effectively in support of police departments throughout the country. Also, the project has supported a substantial increase in police telecommunications with the construction and installation of base and mobile facilities and equipment which provide for communication from every state to Brasilia as well as limited intra- and inter-state communications. Substantial increases in police mobility have been achieved, primarily through funding for Brazilian manufactured vehicles.
FY 1971 Program: Emphasis will be on strengthening the Federal Police Department and efforts to further develop national police institutions, particularly the National Police Academy and Telecommunications Center which are in their first year of operation. Expansion of the telecommunications network and of vehicular mobility will be supported with added stress on development of internal capability for improved maintenance and repair.
U.S. Technicians: Thirteen U.S. direct-hire Public Safety officers will work with Brazilian federal and state police throughout FY 1971.
Participants: Short-term training for 80 Brazilian police officers and officials mainly at the International Police Academy, Washington, D.C.

"R&D" for the Homefront War
- The Science of Repression

Written and published by NACLA

By 1965, the United States could boast a sophisticated counterinsurgency apparatus in Southeast Asia—and then the Watts ghetto of Los Angeles exploded, revealing the total inadequacy of our homefront counterinsurgency forces, the local police, in coping with major urban disorders. A researcher for the Defense Research Corporation (DRC), John L. Sorenson, wrote in 1965,

> Investigations by DRC of the state of the field in 1964 indicate that the United States is inadequately prepared to counter urban insurgency [UI]. The preventative or responsive measures available to national and local policy-makers are few. . . . While basic tactics are available to handle routine riots and occasional terrorism, the broader concept of a whole program of counterinsurgency is hardly even discussed among police here or abroad. The military often is called in to control a situation which has exceeded the capacity of the regular police, but they too lack a doctrine, training, or materials to do more than simply quell mass action. An alarming operational and doctrinal vacuum pervades our own and other democratic countries in the face of the UI threat.[1]

In order to fill this "operational and doctrinal vacuum," the government hurriedly began a program of research designed to upgrade our ability to control urban violence. Not surprisingly, Washington called in its battle-tested experts on Third World counterinsurgency to plan the new attack on domestic instability. To launch this campaign, the Institute for Defense Analyses (IDA), a university-sponsored military think-tank, was asked to prepare a "Task Force Report" on Science and Technology for the President's Commission of Law Enforcement and the Administration of Justice.

In its report to the Commission, IDA noted that,

■ Reprinted from *The University—Military—Police Complex: A Directory and Related Documents* (New York: North American Congress of Latin America, 1970), pp. 72, with the permission of NACLA.

The Defense Department spends about $7 billion a year on research and development, about 13 percent of its regular budget. In contrast, as recently as 1965, the Justice Department was the only Cabinet department with no share of the roughly $15 billion Federal Research and Development budget. The research and development budget in other criminal justice organizations is negligible.[2]

This situation should be changed, IDA argues, since

> The experience of science in the military . . . suggests that a fruitful collaboration can be established between criminal justice officials on one hand and engineers, physicists, economists, and social and behavioral scientists on the other. In military research organizations these different professions, working with military officers in interdisciplinary teams, have attacked defense problems in new ways and have provided insights that were new even to those with long military experience. Similar developments appear possible in criminal justice.[3]

Using military research organizations as a model, IDA proposed that the Federal government establish a research institute devoted to law enforcement research: "Probably the most important single mechanism for bringing the resources of science and technology to bear on the problems of crime would be the establishment of a major prestigious science and technology research program within a research institute."[4] This proposal was adopted by the President's Commission and subsequently incorporated into legislation.

The Omnibus Crime Control and Safe Streets Act of 1968 (Public Law 90-351) creates a National Institute of Law Enforcement and Criminal Justice as the research arm of the Law Enforcement Assistance Administration (LEAA). The Act authorizes the Institute to conduct research studies with its own staff, and

> To make grants to, or enter into contracts with, public agencies, institutions of higher

education, or private organizations to conduct research, demonstrations, or special projects pertaining to . . . the development of new or improved approaches, techniques, systems, equipment, and devices to improve and strengthen law enforcement.

In order to establish guidelines for such projects, LEAA commissioned IDA to prepare "A National Program of Research, Development, Test, and Evaluation on Law Enforcement and Criminal Justice."

Using the IDA proposal as a model, the Institute subsequently awarded several million dollars' worth of contracts to universities and other non-profit institutions. Many of these projects call for the application of social science research in determining how the anger and frustration of youth and minority peoples can be channeled into "constructive," non-violent activities. Other projects are designed to modernize police communications, intelligence, and "command-and-control" systems. A list of these projects, reproduced from the First Annual Report of the Law Enforcement Assistance Administration, appears below.

NOTES

1. John L. Sorenson, *Urban Insurgency Cases* (Santa Barbara, Calif.: Defense Research Corp., 1965), pp. 6–7.
2. Institute for Defense Analyses, *Task Force Report: Science and Technology* (Washington, D.C.: Government Printing Office, 1967), pp. 2–3.
3. *Ibid.*, p. 2.
4. *Ibid.*, p. 82.

Bringing It Back: Planning for the City
by Michael Klare

Counterinsurgency research has been accorded the status of a science only within the past few decades; its purpose, however, is centuries old. Historically its role has been to maintain dominion over a colonial population with a limited allocation of the military strength of the home country. The duration and breadth of any empire is ultimately determined by the ability of its armies to maintain order in colonial territories without overtaxing the manpower and financial resources of the homeland.

The occupation army of an imperial power is always outnumbered by the indigenous population of a colony; in order to maintain hegemony, therefore, it must maintain a supremacy in armament and organization that outweighs its numerical inferiority. When a nationalist movement has secured the active support of the population, in sufficient numbers to offset the technological advantage of occupying forces, colonialism is doomed.

Since the end of World War II, the United States has assembled the largest empire in the history of mankind. (The term "empire" as commonly used today means American cultural, political, and economic hegemony over other countries.) For the most part, it has tried to exercise its influence over the internal affairs of its "allies" and satellites through economic and political sanctions. The security of this empire has been threatened, however, by the periodic outbreak of national liberation movements. Vietnam has shown the U.S. that the price of empire can be very costly indeed, that Che Guevara was probably right in proposing that the American Empire could be destroyed by the simultaneous creation of "two, three . . . many Vietnams."

The U.S. government has responded to the danger posed by national liberation movements by accelerating its preparations for counterinsurgency operations in "remote areas." Our scientific and technical resources have been mobilized for research aimed at improving the "kill effectiveness" of our expeditionary forces. American universities have undertaken the task of collecting and evaluating intelligence on the revolutionary process in underdeveloped areas.[1] Through the Military Assistance Program, the Defense Department has trained the armed forces of friendly nations for counterguerrilla

■ Taken from *They're Bringing It All Back . . . Police on the Homefront* [Philadelphia: National Action/Research on the Military–Industrial Complex (NARMIC), 1971] pp. 66–72. Reprinted with the permission of the author.

operations, and provides them with specially trained cadres from the Special Forces schools in the U.S. and the Panama Canal Zone.

Sophisticated research on counterinsurgency is one of the many innovations of the "McNamara Revolution" in national security policy. Soon after taking office in 1961, McNamara established "Project Agile"—a multi-million dollar program in counterinsurgency research—under the auspices of the Pentagon's Advanced Research Projects Agency (ARPA). Using the systems-analysis approach of the military think-tanks, Pentagon scientists provided the U.S. with a greatly enhanced capability to engage in counterguerrilla warfare in remote and relatively inaccessible areas.

In order to be successful in counterinsurgency operations, "remote" or domestic, the guardians of an empire must possess:

—a close-knit and highly disciplined organization which can compensate for the psychological effects of being surrounded by a hostile (and usually ethnically different) population; a comprehensive intelligence network which can penetrate insurgent organizations and identify their leadership; detailed knowledge of the physical and social characteristics of the territories being patrolled; superior mobility and communications, so that small units can outmaneuver large numbers of opponents; weapons whose superiority in firepower is directly proportional to the numerical superiority of opposing forces; the promise of help from the home country, in the form of supporting troops from a "strategic reserve" which can be brought in quickly when the local forces lose control of a situation.

Since the onset of the Vietnam war, America's think-tank intellectuals have been devoting increasing amounts of time to the development of techniques and devices to improve U.S. capabilities in these areas. Lightweight radios have been designed which can penetrate heavy jungle cover; new armored personnel carriers can travel through swamps or rice paddies; helicopter tactics have been advanced immeasurably; infrared surveillance techniques provide new data on enemy troop movements at night; special computers assign letter grades (A to E) on the "reliability" of every hamlet in South Vietnam. Research on counterinsurgency is continuing at special Pentagon laboratories in the U.S. and Thailand to prepare for the "Vietnams of the future."

WATTS, 1965

America woke up to discover that its domestic colony, the urban ghetto, was no longer secure and that the local garrison troops had been overwhelmed. Vietnam had come home.

Like any colony, Watts had been patrolled by a small occupation army, recruited from the white society outside and compliant blacks. When Watts rebelled, these forces were overrun, and regular troops had to be brought in. When this was repeated in Newark, Detroit, and Chicago, it became clear that such domestic operations were going to strain America's manpower commitments abroad. Our domestic occupation forces would therefore have to be equipped with an advanced counterinsurgency capability in order to ease the burden of the overall strategic requirements of the empire. Every succeeding development in police technology is a manifestation of this requirement.

From a military point of view, counterinsurgency in U.S. ghettos poses the same problems as counterinsurgency in any hostile environment in which the occupation forces are outnumbered by potential insurgents; consequently, domestic operations must conform to the six principles cited above. Specifically, the anti-ghetto forces must be able to: move in disciplined formations in order to control the movements of rioters and hostile crowds, even when being severely taunted and provoked; infiltrate militant black organizations and identify their leaders for quick arrest when trouble begins; seal off entire sections of the ghetto in accordance with predetermined contingency plans, in order to contain rioting; maintain effective communications between anti-riot forces (i.e., municipal police, state police, National Guard, etc.), while blocking insurgent communications; spot, encircle, and eliminate snipers and fire-bombers without suffering casualties; bring in National Guard and Army units which have been trained in anti-ghetto operations, and whose officers are familiar with the terrain and social characteristics of the conflict area.

Beginning in 1965, the Federal Government initiated a substantial research program in order to determine U.S. capabilities in the areas defined above. The officials involved were appalled to discover the primitive nature of standard police tactics during riot situations. Whereas throughout the Third World the U.S. has equipped local armies with a sophisticated capability for counterinsurgency operations, America's own garrison troops, the police, had been allowed to languish in nineteenth-century conditions. The weapons of domestic riot-control—billy-club, teargas, and shotgun—hadn't undergone any technological innovations in fifty years, nor had any new tactics been developed for their use. Furthermore, no money was being spent on *new* weapons and anti-riot techniques. It was clear that the Federal Government would have to assume responsibility for this critical problem.

Not surprisingly, the government turned to its Vietnam-tested consultants when it undertook a major program of research on urban counterinsurgency. The Office of Public Safety of the State Department's Agency for International Development (AID) was already training police officials from the underdeveloped areas at the International Police Academy in Washington, D.C.; now this expertise would be used to develop training programs for domestic law enforcement officials. Selected universities would be asked to furnish strategies for a new pacification program in the home country.

Beginning in 1965, Project Agile—the Pentagon's principal counterinsurgency research program—was redirected to include studies of "urban disequilibrium." Using a cross-cultural approach that linked ghetto riots in the U.S. to urban rebellions in Latin America, Agile contractors sought to delineate the essential characteristics of urban insurgency and to suggest a workable strategy for urban counterinsurgency. As part of this effort, the Defense Research Corporation (DRC) of Santa Barbara, Calif., prepared a series of "Urban Insurgency Studies" which comprised "an inventory of urban insurgent and counterinsurgent techniques, tactics and doctrines."[2]

The Pentagon hurriedly appropriated additional funds for further research in this area. The Research Analysis Corporation (RAC) drew up a technical paper entitled "A Summary Report of Research Requirements for Sensing and Averting Critical Insurgent Actions in an Urban Environment." In this classified report "the special problems of insurgency in an urban setting are defined, and suggested tactics, techniques and hardware for counterinsurgent forces are examined."[3] In yet another program of "Urban Insurgency Studies," the Simulmatics Corporation of New York City conducted "an analysis of communications, coordination and requirements during the Watts Riots."[4] The Center for Research in Social Systems (CRESS), then at American University in Washington, D.C., contributed a "Selected Bibliography of Crowd and Riot Behavior in Civil Disturbances," and a handbook entitled "Combating Subversively Manipulated Civil Disturbances." The author of the handbook, Adrian H. Jones, described his report as follows: "A systematic study of the patterns of development of civil disturbances and the tactics of the subversive manipulators is made to identify countermeasures for controlling the subversive manipulation of civil disturbances."[5]

In 1966 the Institute for Defense Analyses (IDA), whose work on counterinsurgency has been discussed elsewhere,[6] was commissioned by the President's Commission on Law Enforcement and the Administration of Justice to organize a task force on Science and Technology in crime control. Members of the task force's Science Advisory Committee included Adam Yarmolinsky, a Harvard Law professor and former aide to Defense Secretary McNamara, and Dr. Robert L. Sproull, Vice President and Provost of the University of Rochester and currently chairman of the Defense Science Board. From IDA's own staff came Joseph Coates, an expert on chemical warfare.[7]

Emphasizing the advantages of a systems-analysis approach to police operations, the task force concluded:

> The experience of science in the military . . . suggests that a fruitful collaboration can be established between criminal justice officials on one hand and engineers, physicists, economists, and social and behavioral scientists on the other. In military research organizations these different professions, working with military officers in interdisciplinary teams, have attacked defense problems in new ways and have provided insights that were new even to those with long military experience. Similar developments appear possible in criminal justice.[8]

The bulk of the IDA report is devoted to suggestions for how modern communications and data-processing systems can be applied to the problems of domestic counterinsurgency, in order to increase the efficiency of local police agencies. Noting that most law enforcement agencies in the U.S. lacked the means for any kind of systematic research on anti-riot techniques, IDA later urged that the Federal Government establish a centralized crime research organization modeled on the Pentagon's Advanced Research Projects Agency. IDA subsequently received a $152,000 contract from the Justice Department to design a "National Program of Research, Development, Test and Evaluation on Law Enforcement and Criminal Justice."

Many of IDA's recommendations were incorporated into the Omnibus Safe Streets and Crime Control Act of 1968, which was passed by the Congress in the wake of the nationwide rioting which followed the assassination of Martin Luther King, Jr.[9]

A report on anti-riot operations prepared by Cyrus R. Vance[10] known as the "Detroit Book" is reported to have influenced government strategy during the April 1968 round of ghetto disturbances. A censored version of the secret report was subsequently made available to the press, a summary of which appeared in the *New York Times* for April 14, 1968. A principal feature of the Vance report is the recommendation that riot areas be inundated with police, National Guardsmen, and if necessary Army troops at the earliest outbreak of violence. Gunfire would be kept to a minimum, but the liberal use of tear gas encouraged. An early curfew, stringently enforced, was another key recommendation.

CONTROLLED RESPONSE

Both the IDA task force findings and Vance's report reflect a new pattern in urban counterinsurgency doctrine which will be familiar to those who have read Herman Kahn's manifestos or who have studied the air war against North Vietnam. Like the Air Force doctrine of "instrumental escalation," counterinsurgency strategy in the ghetto now encompasses a graduated series of phased escalations, whereby the government seeks to achieve its desired objective—the restoration of stability—through the minimum use of force. Thus whereas in Newark and Detroit excessive police violence at the early stages of the rioting provoked increased community resistance, the new strategy would conserve heavy firepower for later phases of an uprising in the hope that less violent tactics would achieve quicker results.

The principle of "controlled response" to urban disorders was introduced by William W. Herrmann[11] of the System Development Corporation at the Second National Symposium on Law Enforcement Science and Technology. In a paper entitled "Riot Prevention and Control: Operations Research Response," Herrmann explained:

> Insufficient, or inadequate, levels of response—whether offensive or defensive—are quite likely to result in the dissipation of resources with no significant effect other than a possible further weakening of the government's position. Overresponse, on the other hand, although it may accomplish a given tactical objective such as the neutralization of a specific individual, group of individuals, or "target," may do so at the expense of some other strategic objective. For example, overly aggressive tactics may effectively neutralize a given threat, but do so at the expense of more people becoming disaffected from the government and its aims and more closely allied with the dissident forces or causes.

This view is entirely in accord with the flexible response strategy advocated by former Defense Secretary McNamara for dealing with insurgencies in the Third World. In fact, U.S. government officials regularly apply McNamara's analysis to the domestic crisis. In 1967 the Treasury Department's Director of Law Enforcement Coordination, Arnold Sagalyn, remarked that,

> Our obsolescent, 19th Century police weapons are . . . posing a danger to the peace and welfare of our urban communities. . . . For the police officer's basic weapon, his gun, lacks the *flexible response capability* needed to deal with the specific type of problem involved. The inability of the police officer to control the degree and deadliness of this physical force in proportion to the nature and quality of the threat has put

him—indeed the entire community—in a critical dilemma.[12]

NOTES

1. Mike Klare, "Universities in Vietnam," *Viet Report* (January, 1968), pp. 12–14; see also, *The University-Military-Police Complex,* 1970, available for $1.25 from NACLA, P. O. Box 57, Cathedral Station, New York, N.Y. and P.O. Box 226, Berkeley, California, and Mike Klare, "The Military Research Network," *The Nation,* October 12, 1970.

2. John L. Sorenson, *Urban Insurgency Cases* (Santa Barbara, California: Defense Research Corporation, 1965).

3. John M. Breit, Dorothy K. Clark, John H. Glover, and Bradish J. Smith, *A Summary Report of Research Requirements for Sensing and Averting Critical Insurgent Actions in an Urban Environment* (McLean, Va.: Research Analysis Corp., 1966), abstract.

4. Ithiel de Sola Pool, David J. Yates, Aprodicio Laquain, Richard Blum, and Michael Weatlake, *Report on Urban Insurgency Studies* (New York: Simulmatics Corp., 1966), abstract.

5. Adrian H. Jones, *Combating Subversively Manipulated Civil Disturbances* (Washington, D.C.: American University, Center for Research in Social Systems, 1966), abstract.

6. Cathy McAffee, "IDA: The Academic Conscripts," *Viet Report* (January, 1968), pp. 8–11.

7. *Joseph Coates* subsequently prepared two special studies on police operations for IDA: "Non-Lethal Weapons for Domestic Law Enforcement Officers" (a paper presented at the First National Symposium on Law Enforcement Science and Technology 1967), and "The Police Function in Stability Operations" (IDA report no. TN-547, May 1968).

In the earlier paper, Coates argues that "chemical agents could provide the police with new graduated and controlled levels of force, and an opportunity to give more responses proportional to the needs of the situation. They also offer opportunities to deal with situations which hitherto have not been satisfactorily dealt with, such as . . . the apprehension of the fleeing youth or the immobilization of a number of people at the same time." A much condensed version of this paper appeared in the *New York Times Magazine* for Sept. 17, 1967 under the heading, "Wanted: Weapons That Do Not Kill."

8. The Institute for Defense Analyses, *Task Force Report: Science and Technology* (Washington, D.C.: U.S. Government Printing Office, 1967), p. 2.

9. The Omnibus Act superseded an earlier law, the Law Enforcement Assistance Act of 1965, which was signed into law by President Johnson on September 22, 1965 (shortly after the Watts riots). A complete list of projects supported by this law appears in *Grants and Contracts Awarded Under the Law Enforcement Assistance Act of 1965, Fiscal Years 1966–1968* (Washington, D.C.: Office of Law Enforcement Assistance of the U.S. Department of Justice, 1968).

10. *Cyrus R. Vance* is one of the most conspicuous figures in the Federal Government's efforts to upgrade national strategies for the containment of ghetto rebellions. A former Deputy Secretary of Defense and principal aide to Robert S. McNamara, Vance served as McNamara's representative in Detroit during the disorders of 1967, and later as an assistant to President Johnson during the riots in Washington, D.C., which followed the assassination of Dr. Martin Luther King, Jr.

It was on Vance's orders that the Army's computerized data of information on civilian "troublemakers" was started. He wrote: "I cannot overemphasize the importance of such information, particularly when the Federal team has to make a determination as to whether the situation is beyond the control of local and State law enforcement agencies. . . . I believe it would be useful to assemble and analyze such data for Detroit, Newark, Milwaukee, Watts, et cetera." Quoted in U.S. House of Representatives, Committee on Appropriations, *Department of Defense Appropriations for 1971,* part 3, Hearings, 91st Congress, Second Session (Washington, D.C.: U.S. Government Printing Office, 1970) p. 156.

11. *William W. Herrmann* was one of the few professionals in the Los Angeles Police Department who had received his Bachelor's, Master's, and Doctor's degrees (in 1952, 1956, and 1960, respectively). His last assignment was Officer in Charge, Advanced Systems Development as well as patrol, investigative, intelligence and special civil disturbance control units. After he left the Police Department in 1967, he continued the same kind of work in Thailand as an advisor to the Thai National Police Department. In 1968 he transferred to South Vietnam and was awarded a Certificate of Appreciation for his service in support of counterinsurgency efforts. This information from his "Curriculum Vitae" distributed at the Third National Symposium on Law Enforcement Science and Technology, April 1970.

12. Treasury Department press release, March 9, 1967, entitled "Remarks by Arnold Sagalyn . . . Before the National Symposium on Law Enforcement Science and Technology. . . ." (emphasis added).

Weapons for the Homefront
By NARMIC/Vince Pinto

The convergence of two related combat technologies—one developed for the jungles and hamlets of the Third World continents, the other for the ghettos and campuses—is taking place rapidly. Both abroad and at home the U.S. Government sees active or potentially active insurgent populations. Nowhere is there a front line of combat; engagements are episodic, occurring at unpredictable times and places. No large-scale troop and equipment movements telegraph intentions to the other side. While the preponderance of force is on one side, as is the manpower and technology, this very advantage is a drawback compared with the self-reliance and flexibility of the insurgent. Conventional forms of warfare a generation or two old have become obsolete.

Of course, there are also many important dissimilarities between Vietnam and an urban or campus trouble spot in the United States. Though the two struggles are not identical, it should not be surprising to find the same weapons and techniques developed for combat in Vietnam used to quell domestic struggles for liberation. Gas, helicopters, infrared detection, tanks, armored vehicles, barbed wire and hand grenades have been used both in Vietnam and the United States.

But domestic counterinsurgency weapons and methods have lagged behind those developed for international applications. Up until recently the standard arsenal for the patrolman was the sidearm and nightstick. Occasionally a labor strike was met with riot guns and gas bombs. Today's rapid expansion in the variety of the police arsenal illustrates the rapid expansion of domestic counterinsurgency planning. Today's police can employ a number of different gas dispensing devices, from shotguns to helicopters; carry individual two-way radios; fire machine guns on the practice range and high-powered rifles from moving aircraft; wear helmets and body armor; carry MACE in their

belts; engage in mock confrontations; as well as use computers to sort out large quantities of information in seconds. Recently, for instance, the Pentagon announced plans to provide $20 million worth of riot control equipment to the National Guard—including face shields, batons, protective vests, shotguns, floodlights, public address systems, radios and tear gas.[1]

The hardware for a beefed-up police network is avidly supplied by a cabal of equipment manufacturers. Naturally the strongest supporters of law and order, some of these companies provide think-tank contingency plans, or work closely with organizations like the Institute for Defense Analyses. Papers delivered at an Annual Symposium on Law Enforcement Science and Technology in Chicago's Statler Hilton Hotel show the interest of military aerospace and electronics companies in police work. RCA representatives delivered a paper titled "Night Surveillance Systems for Law Enforcement." The company is working on a number of surveillance units for the Defense Department, as well as making components for the SAM missile system. Jet Propulsion Laboratory contributed "Evaluation of Helicopter Patrols." The man from Motorola spoke about "New Concepts of Portable Radio Communication." Motorola makes miniature circuits for a 2.75-inch antipersonnel rocket fuse ordered by the military. The Stanford Research Institute looked to the future with "Application of Aerospace Technology to Law Enforcement Problems."

Police expenditures on tear gas and other "non-lethal" weapons have skyrocketed in the past few years. The *Washington Post* reported January 13, 1969, that domestic law enforcement agencies spent $22 million for anti-riot weapons in 1968, compared to $1 million in 1967. The major U.S. suppliers of riot-control gases are the Lake Erie Corp. (a subsidiary of the Smith and Wesson Company, which in turn is a subsidiary of the Bangor Punta Corp.) and Federal Laboratories, Inc. (a subsidiary of the Breeze Corp.). The Federal Government has also been purchasing large quantities of such weapons. In January 1969, the Army purchased $10 million worth of CS anti-riot gas from the

■ Taken from *They're Bringing It All Back ... Police on the Homefront* [Philadelphia: National Action/Research on the Military–Industrial Complex (NARMIC), 1971], pp. 74–89. Reprinted with the permission of the author.

Thiokol Chemical Corp., and another $1 million worth of CS grenades from Federal Laboratories.

Police often consider gases to be valuable not only against mass demonstrations but also against an unruly individual in the station house; one squirt of chemical MACE in the face is enough to incapacitate. The writer of one "riot control" textbook feels,

> This development is the first significant breakthrough in individual police weapons since the advent of the hand gun. Currently, over 4,000 law enforcement departments are making increasing use of chemical MACE to control individual violence and civil disturbances, usually without the necessity of resorting to other means of force such as the gun or nightstick.[2]

A shell filled with liquid CS gas and fired from an ordinary shotgun can penetrate the barricade of a sniper. A tear gas fixture which screws into an ordinary light bulb socket can be tripped by photo-electric cell or other alarm device and is normally used to protect bank vaults and restricted areas.

It is easy to defend the use of chemical weapons as humane simply by comparing them to weapons whose effects are designed to be lethal. Moreover, even though there are no clear-cut guidelines, the public generally believes lethal weapons occupy the last position on an escalating-degree-of-force scale. When guns are used by the police, many believe the "peacekeepers" had no other recourse. For chemical weapons there is not even this vague and weak restriction. Even the victims of a gas attack on a non-violent sit-in may be uncertain that the police had used excessive force in halting the action. Political censure caused by the indiscriminate rain of bullets—such as Jackson and Kent State—can be avoided by the smooth tactical use of gas. On August 13, 1968, the Attorney General of the United States spelled it out:

> Although they are not universally adaptable to all police uses, nonlethal chemical agents represent the best immediate alternative to the use of deadly force—or no force at all. They are now proven to be the most effective, safest, and most humane method of mob control. Used with caution when the

need arises, they will reduce death, physical injury, and property loss to a minimum.[3]

The Federal Government advocated use of gas after the Newark and Detroit riots, according to Colonel Rex Applegate, a pioneer in the field of riot control. He says, "Emphasis on the non-lethal chemical weaponry aspects of individual command and riot control is expected to be extremely heavy in the years ahead."[4]

The most commonly encountered gas in U.S. demonstrations is designated CN. Mild in effect, it was used to train soldiers in World War I to wear their masks correctly.

CS gas is more violent and is named for Corson and Stoughton, two scientists who concocted it in 1928. Its effects are stronger and last longer; according to Applegate, "...CS is normally recommended for use in the escalating-degree-of-force scale after the milder CN has failed, and/or just prior to the use of firearms."[5] The morality of shooting gassed people is not mentioned.

DM gas causes vomiting and severe distress, and unlike the other two mentioned, normally requires medical attention. DM will poison water and open food in the area around which it has been released. Because it takes a few minutes to work, it is usually mixed with CS to insure an immediate effect.

All these gases and chemical irritants come packaged in a variety of ways and can be delivered and disseminated in different ways.

The SKITTER by Brunswick Corp., and JET SPIN by Lake Erie Chemical, are both gas grenades that jump and wiggle so that they can't be thrown back. The TRIPLE CHASER by Federal Laboratories breaks into three smoke-trailing sections, each taking off on an unpredictable path, spewing gas and smoke.

The gas grenade disperses its material either by burning, which presents a fire hazard, or by exploding and creating a shrapnel hazard and serious injury if it explodes in the hand. The third method, pressurized release, is slower but safer and is disadvantageous to the police since it can be thrown back easily.

Gases come in visible or invisible form. Invisible gas can not be photographed by the press nor easily avoided by those gassed. For Colonel Applegate, this is a decided advantage: "The psychological panic-producing effect of invisible gas on rioters is relatively much more pronounced. This is one reason dust, micro-fine particles of CS and CN agents are more tactically flexible and generally used."

Even though deaths from the mild CN gas have been reported in medical journals[6] the riot control manual just quoted assures its readers,

> The world reputation and successful use of CN-type tear gas as a nonlethal riot-control agent is well established. During the past four decades, under normal street and field conditions, it has been proven a reliable, nontoxic chemical agent during thousands of incidents involving people of all age groups and physical condition.

Reliance on chemical weapons will be "extremely heavy in the near future," as Applegate stated.

Some rapid changes in gas grenade technology were made in 1963 at the request of the Agency for International Development (AID). Since AID has been the largest single purchaser of tear gas weapons in the last five years, its request for a new model was not taken lightly.

The Agency's Office of Public Safety sent a memo to U.S. manufacturers of gas weapons describing the kind of grenade they wanted. In about thirty "under-developed" countries around the world AID was, and still is, helping to train civil police forces in riot and insurgent control, and the grenade's specifications were based on real tactical experience. The AAI Corporation of Baltimore came up with the desired model, a blast-type hand- or rifle-launched 3" X 6" weapon encased in color-coded DuPont DELRIN plastic. Advantageous because it eliminated the need for a special 37mm gas gun, and storable in a temperature range from 0° to 120°, it was designated MPG (Multi-Purpose Grenade). AAI Corporation guarantees the weapon for six years.

In addition to chemical irritants such as CN, CS, and MACE, domestic police forces have used or experimented with and stocked a number of other civil disturbance weapons.

SMOKE

Smoke is a very ancient weapon, used in warfare at least as early as the Crusades. Both offensive and defensive, it can be used to create confusion and cover troop movements. Today the employment of smoke to control civil insurrections has a new twist. In *Riot Control Materiel and Techniques* Applegate states:

> Colored smoke concentrations produce greater initial psychological and panic effect than white smoke. Certain colors have a more dramatic impact than others. Caucasians are said to have a greater repugnance to brilliant green smoke, which is associated with disagreeable personal experiences such as seasickness, bile and vomit. Negroids (*sic.*) and Latins are declared to be most adversely affected by brilliant red.

He goes on to say,

> Rioters confronted with strong concentrations of colored smoke feel, instinctively, that they are being marked, or stained, and thus they lose anonymity. Colored particles of volatilized dye in the smoke cloud adhere to persons, objects and clothing, etc., and produce in the presence of moisture and perspiration, indelible stain. Such stains will be especially noticeable on neckbands, collars, and shirt cuffs. These stains are often of assistance to the police in later identifying mob participants.[7]

These smoke munitions are manufactured by the same companies that make chemical irritants.

SOUND

Sound as a weapon is even more ancient, according to the Biblical account of the battle of Jericho. Our modern version, called the CURDLER, is for use not against fortification, but against people. The CURDLER (also called SUPERSOUND and PEOPLE REPELLER) is usually used as an ordinary speech amplifier by police or firemen on a rescue mission, but it can deliver 350 watts of modulated shrieks and screams when needed. The noise produced is rated at 120db at 30 feet, like being next to a jet engine at take-off. Ordinary speech projected over this weapon can be understood *two and one-half miles away*. Apart from causing its victims to drop what they have to cover their ears, its weird effect produces disorientation and nausea. Usually the CURDLER is mounted on an armored personnel carrier or helicopter, although its manufacturer, Applied Electro Mechanics of Alexandria, Va., also makes a portable version. Purchasers include New York City police and fire departments, E.I. DuPont Company, Allegheny Airlines, the Navy, Air Force, Coast Guard and Marines of the United States, and the police of Madrid.

OTHER "NON-LETHAL" WEAPONS

Tear gas, smoke, and noise will soon be joined by several new products in the crowd-control armory. "RioTrol" (also known as the "instant banana peel") is a by-product of the petroleum industry that has potential for use in the ghetto. Heretofore, the powdery white polyethylene oxide was used as lubricant for oil-drilling equipment. When 2 kilograms of the substance are spread over 600 square feet of sidewalk and watered down, the area becomes more slippery than ice. According to a sales brochure, police officers, equipped with special boots and gloves, would be able "to go amongst writhing bodies and remove riot ringleaders." One danger to unpadded victims—what about concussions from the resulting falls? The product, which sells for $5.95 a pound, is manufactured by the Western Co. of Richardson, Texas.

Another proposed tactic for the control of hostile crowds is the use of dense foam to immobilize and confuse rioters. The origin of this material is the foam sprayed on airfields to cushion the touchdown of damaged aircraft. The use of this product for control of crowds presents certain already-demonstrated dangers, however—recently a salesman for the Defensor Protective Equipment Corp. of Media, Pennsylvania (manufacturer of the "Defensor" High Volume Foam Generator) was asphyxiated when he slipped and fell into the foam during a demonstration of its potential riot-control applications.

A proposed incapacitating agent which is still in the experimental stage is the long-barreled tranquilizer gun using drugged darts. The device was developed by Dr. William C. Conner, a psychiatrist at Emory University Hospital in Atlanta. Dr. Conner has been experimenting with darts that are ordinarily used to subdue wild animals for capture or tagging. In the tests, a pistol-shaped gun uses a carbon dioxide cartridge to propel the darts, which are composed of a needle three-fourths of an inch long attached to a cylindrical projectile syringe containing sleep-inducing drugs. The missile, which has a range of about 30 feet, injects automatically on impact. The device used in the test was manufactured by the Palmer Chemical and Equipment Co. of Douglasville, Ga., which manufactures tranquilizer guns for use against animals.

Hypodermic darts of the type tested in Atlanta could be used to disable fleeing rioters and looters when it is deemed undesirable to fell them by gunfire. The problem with such drugs, however, is that each individual reacts differently to them. A dose which would knock out a 200-pound man could endanger the life of someone weighing half as much. The darts might also strike the eyes or other vulnerable points, and thus cause permanent damage.

GUNS

Despite all the talk about non-lethal weapons, every urban police force has an abundant supply of lethal anti-riot weapons, i.e., guns. The Philadelphia police force carries its armories around on wheels to be handy in case of trouble—each of the mobile armories, known as Stakeout cars, carries the following armament:

2 M-70 Winchester rifles, 30/06 cal., with BalVarscope, sling, case, and 200 rounds ammunition;

2 M-12 Winchester shotguns, 12 gauge with case and 100 rounds .00 buck ammunition;

1 Thompson submachine gun, .45 cal., with 500 rounds ammunition;

1 M-1 carbine, .30 cal., with 200 rounds ammunition.

This list of guns is hardly exceptional. In Detroit, for instance, the police have purchased 500 new carbines, 300 shotguns and 150,000 rounds of ammunition.

The standard anti-riot gun is the 12-gauge shotgun, because of its wide field of fire. The .00 buck charge is a favorite shell, because the nine ball-bearings in the load umbrella out in broad fanning patterns. With a charge like that, a policeman can just point the gun and fire—and be sure of hitting one or more people. Among new shotguns, the favorite is High Standard's Model 10, a semi-automatic, five-shot weapon, with lightweight plastic stock and a searchlight on top. Anything the light covers will be in the shot pattern, so aiming at night is an easy matter. The Model 10 uses a 12-gauge, 12-pellet high-velocity magnum load. Police departments favor the gun because it can be fired with one hand like a pistol.

Like other categories of anti-riot weaponry, new guns are now being developed for use in urban counterinsurgency. Most prominent among the gunsmiths working on this problem is Edward Stoner, inventor of the Army's new M-16 rifle. Stoner has developed a new high-velocity assault rifle that can penetrate a brick wall. The Stoner gun, made by the Cadillac Gage Company, is being purchased in substantial quantities by police agencies for use as an anti-sniper gun. According to the rifle's manufacturer, "the *proper* way to shoot a sniper is through the wall." With the addition of various interchangeable parts, the Stoner rifle can be converted into a carbine, submachine gun or medium machine gun.

DUMDUM BULLETS

Dumdum bullets are soft lead rounds with a hollow, slotted nose. Since 1899 they have been outlawed for use in international warfare because of the terrible wounds they cause. When the bullet strikes the flesh it flattens out to twice its size, virtually causing a small explosion in the body. The wound is almost always fatal. In 1909 the United States Congress adopted the Hague Conference Declaration against their use between warring countries.

Despite the fact that the use of dumdum bullets is a war crime, they are standard ordnance in almost half the police departments in the United States, among them the sheriffs of Los Angeles County and police in Kansas City, Miami, St. Louis, Tucson and Nashville. The U.S. Treasury Department, the Secret Service, the Bureau of Narcotics and the White House police are some of the Federal purchasers.

At least two large companies make the bullet, Super-Vel Cartridge Corp. of Shelbyville, Indiana and Remington Small Arms Company in Bridgeport, Connecticut (Remington is controlled by DuPont).

Smaller manufacturers of the bullet are Norma Projetilfabrik, a Swedish company with offices in South Lansing, New York; the Dutch Speer Ammunition Company in Lewiston, Idaho; and Winchester-Western, a division of Olin-Mathieson.[8]

BARBED TAPE

Once the police have rounded up rioters and other law-breakers, their problems are not over. The mass arrests which usually follow the outbreak of ghetto disturbances place tremendous logistical and manpower demands on the anti-riot forces at a time when they need all available resources for continued operations in the ghetto. Thus the police must devise procedures for the detention under guard of thousands of prisoners with the minimum outlay of manpower.

One solution to the problem of guarding prisoners was recently devised by the U.S. Army Mobility Equipment Research and Development Center at Fort Belvoir, Va. The Army's contribution is the "instant obstacle"—barbed tape. A substitute for conventional barbed wire, this tape is thin, razor-sharp stainless steel, 64% lighter and more compact than barbed wire. One 40-pound package of the tape forms a barbed-wire fence 75 feet long and 2-1/2 feet high; the tape can be rolled out from the back of a jeep in a matter of minutes. The instant barbed wire has several applications to anti-riot operations in addition to the detainment of prisoners. If enough of it were available, an entire ghetto could be cut off from the rest of the city to halt the spread of violence to the "white" part of town, and to prevent the inflow of weapons and other supplies. In addition, the tape could be used to protect police stations and other targets of mob activity *inside* the conflict area.

ARMORED CARS

A number of U.S. firms have begun producing smaller heavily armored wheeled or tracked vehicles for use in city streets. Cadillac Gage Company, Detroit, makes a wheeled model called the COMMANDO. Accommodating 12 men, it travels 60 mph on the highway, 4 knots on the water. Vertical gun ports allow firing hand guns even at high targets. The armor will protect against any small arms fire, and is angled to deflect bullets. Twelve COMMANDOS were in operation during the Detroit riot in 1967.

Bauer Ordnance Company of Warren, Michigan produces a wheeled vehicle built on a Chevrolet truck chassis which looks very similar to a

Brinks armored car. It weighs two tons and is equipped with a 360° turret for mounting a machine gun, riot gun, gas dispenser or water cannon.

Fiercest of all is a ten-ton track tank from B&H Enterprises, Leesburg, Fla. Slow but powerful, the model R2 can push down masonry walls. In addition to a crew of 3 it can carry 15 other men. Standard equipment includes "built-in Molotov cocktail protection." Tanks for tear gas are provided. An optional item is the CURDLER.

Some cities, under civilian pressure, have cancelled plans to buy tanks. But the press has reported at least two actual field uses, in raids on the Black Panther Party in New Orleans.[9] (The tank was purchased for the Louisiana police by the Justice Department's Law Enforcement Assistance Administration for $16,464.)[10]

In the competition for police appropriations, the armored car may ultimately lose out to a more versatile transport, the helicopter. The Chicago Police Department recently allocated $168,000 for three helicopters that will be used for an "anti-burglar patrol" as well as for mobile observation posts during riots. In the eyes of police officials, the helicopter has an outstanding attraction in that it can be used to spot snipers and keep them pinned down until apprehended by ground forces.

THE ROLE OF THE FEDERAL GOVERNMENT

The Law Enforcement Assistance Administration of the Justice Department is concerned with all aspects of police work. In addition to dispensing research and training grants to universities and think-tanks, LEAA is also engaged in establishing weapon and equipment standards and tests. Such standardization will aid what LEAA calls "the police officer as consumer" and will be beneficial to industry. At present, the word is going out about the possibilities for profit. As was explained in *The Police Chief*, "LEAA, both through state grants and Institute funding, is fostering the recognition of police by industry as a specific market."[11]

LEAA's first report pointed out, "There is no central source at present to research and test product capabilities and set up minimum and optimum standards for police and other use." Such a source would "help overcome the fragmentation problem that besets industry in its dealings with law enforcement agencies," improve the effectiveness and lower the costs of standardized equipment.[12]

Accordingly, LEAA's National Institute of Law Enforcement and Criminal Justice has contracted with the National Bureau of Standards to plan (and eventually to establish and operate) a new Users Standards Laboratory for police equipment from fingerprint kits to prison door locks. As the second LEAA report describes it:

> The new laboratory will serve as the cornerstone of a "consumer testing service" for the nation's criminal justice agencies. It will: (1) define performance standards for equipment; (2) develop uniform procedures for measuring equipment quality; (3) inspect and certify commercial testing laboratories; and (4) develop standard design specifications so that equipment from different manufacturers can be used together easily and economically.... Quality standards will be proposed to industry for voluntary acceptance and compliance.[13]

Additionally, the Institute is supporting the development of a Police Weapons System Program by the International Association of Chiefs of Police. Its purpose is to (a) evaluate current policies and practices in the acquisition and use of offensive and defensive weapons, (b) survey current weapons systems research and development, (c) establish a central source of police weapons data. The IACP is to study "firearms, chemical weapons, batons, explosives and protective equipment ... nonlethal chemical weapons will receive special emphasis."[14]

LEAA's job was summed up dramatically by Dr. Alfred Blumstein[15]:

> Think of where military technology would be if each battalion commander were responsible for his own research and development. A national agency was needed to represent the combined interests of police departments across the nation. The creation of the Law Enforcement Assistance Administration, and especially its research and development arm, the National Institute of Law Enforcement and Criminal Justice, was an important step in that direction.[16]

In its present form LEAA looks like a baby Department of Defense, beginning to engage in the same pattern of activity practiced by its bigger brother. It is creating the framework around which a national police force can easily be built, and an important part of that framework will be the growing police-industrial complex.

SOME MANUFACTURERS OF WEAPONS AND ORDNANCE

The companies listed in Table 33 were selected on the basis of amount of information available at the time of publication, including: their connections with defense work, sales volume, ownership (when known), and the "brand name" of their products.

These companies make all types of firearms, ammunition, gases, and other devices commonly considered weapons. Not listed are the makers of the considerable array of detection, surveillance, control, and data processing equipment which extends the long arm of the law thousands of times.

Whether or not the following companies actively recruit on the college campus is difficult

TABLE 33   Selected Manufacturers of Weapons and Ordnance for Domestic Police Forces

Company	Police Weapons and Ordnance	Some Recent Department of Defense Contracts
AAI Corp. (Aircraft Armaments Inc.) P.O. Box 6767 Baltimore, Md. 21204 (Plant at Cockysville, Md.) Phone (301)666-1400	Tear gas generators Smoke generators Smoke grenades Tear gas grenades FERRET Barricade Penetrating Cartridge filled with liquid CS gas	Prime contractor for SPIW (Special Purpose Individual Weapons) Torpedo countermeasure evaluation Development of prototype arms rack for M-16 rifle
Ed Agramonte Inc. 41 Riverdale Ave. Yonkers, N.Y. 10701 Phone (914)965-3600	Ammunition Firearms Gas masks Smoke grenades Tear gas grenades Machine guns Rifles Shotguns Armored vests	
Alcan Company 3640 Seminary Rd. Alton, Illinois 62002 Phone (618)462-0001	Ammunition	
Applied Electro Mechanics 2350 Duke St. Alexandria, Va. 22314	Super Sound (CURDLER or PEOPLE REPELLER—350 watts of shrieks and shrills; 120 dB at 30 ft.)	
Bell Helicopter (Textron Company) P.O. Box 482 Fort Worth, Texas 76101 Phone (817)280-2011	Helicopters	Several AWS contracts (Aircraft Weaponization Systems), including XM58 production, a fire control device for helicopters, and MK8, a sight-reflex fire control

TABLE 33   Selected Manufacturers of Weapons and Ordnance for Domestic Police Forces (continued)

Company	Police Weapons and Ordnance	Some Recent Department of Defense Contracts
B&H Enterprises P.O. Box 709 Leesburg, Fla. 32748 Phone (904)787-1340	Armored vehicles (R2 model Multi-Purpose Armored Police Vehicle—10 tons weight)	
Brunswick Corp. (Technical Products Division) 69 W. Washington St. Chicago, Ill. 60602 Phone (312)341-7000	Ammunition Smoke grenades Tear gas grenades SKITTER gas grenades	AWS (Aircraft Weaponization System) contract for production of XM200, a 2.75in. rocket launcher for helicopters SUU-7C/Z, a $2 million Air Force contract for 4,200 units of a smoke and fragmentation bomb dispenser
Colt Industries (Firearms Div.) 150 Huyshope Ave. Hartford, Conn. 06102 Phone (203)278-8550	Firearms Tear gas grenades Machine guns Rifles Shotguns	Development and production of the M-16 rifle. As of 4/30/69 Colt had delivered to the Armed Forces 1,196,495 units and was under contract for over half a million more. Contract calls for a production rate of 40,000 per month.
E.I. Du Pont de Nemours & Co. Wilmington, Del.	Chemical munitions	Wide variety of explosives Developed concept for new Micro-Gravel high explosive anti-personnel mine. Total defense awards for fiscal 1969, $211,965,000
Fairchild Hiller Germantown, Md. 20762 Phone (301)948-9600	Helicopters Aircraft	Development of the AR-15 rifle, used as the prototype for the M-16 rifle Semi-automatic rocket and flare launchers Total defense awards for fiscal 1969, $148,586,000
Federal Laboratories, Inc.* P.O. Box 305 Saltsburg, Pa. 15681	Ammunition Firearms Gas masks Tear gas generators Smoke generators Tear gas grenades Smoke grenades Machine guns	Largest maker of "irritant" gases

TABLE 33 Selected Manufacturers of Weapons and Ordnance for Domestic Police Forces (continued)

Company	Police Weapons and Ordnance	Some Recent Department of Defense Contracts
	Rifles Shotguns Armored vests SPEDEHEAT M7A1 Gas Grenade TRIPLE CHASER Gas Grenade	
General Ordnance and Equipment Corp.** P.O. Box 11211 Freeport Road Pittsburgh, Pa. 15328 Phone (412)782-2161	Tear gas generators Smoke generators Chemical MACE PEPPER FOG Gas Generator	
Hughes Tool Co. (Aircraft Div.) Centinela and Teale Sts. Culver City, Calif. 90230	Aircraft	Production of various weapons and fire control systems for helicopters under the AWS program (Aircraft Weaponization Systems) A laser-beam range finder Total defense awards for fiscal 1969, $439,016,000
Lake Erie Chemical Co.** Foreman Road Rock Creek, Ohio 44084 Phone (216) 563-3681	Gas masks Smoke grenades NEW SPIN Gas Grenade MIGHTY MIDGET Gas Grenade JUMPER-REPEATER Gas Grenade TRU FLITE Barricade-Penetrating Gas Shell	
Lyncoach & Truck Co. 3200 Chestnut Street Oneonta, New York 13820 Phone (607)432-2900	Armored vehicles	Tactical and support vehicles
Maze Chemical & Mfg. Co. 1628 S. Hanley Rd. St. Louis, Mo. 63144 Phone (314)647-5648	Tear gas generators Smoke generators	
O.F. Mossberg & Sons 7 Grasso Avenue North Haven, Conn. 06473 Phone (203)288-6491	Firearms Rifles Revolvers	
Penguin Industries P.O. Box 97 Parkesburg, Pa. 19365 Phone (215)384-6000	Ammunition Gas masks Smoke grenades Tear gas grenades BASEBALL blast-type gas grenade	

TABLE 33 Selected Manufacturers of Weapons and Ordnance for Domestic Police Forces (continued)

Company	Police Weapons and Ordnance	Some Recent Department of Defense Contracts
Smith & Wesson** P.O. Box 520 Springfield, Mass. 01101 Phone (413)736-0323	Firearms Gas masks Tear gas generators Smoke generators Tear gas grenades Smoke grenades Rifles	
Super-Vel Cartridge Corporation P.O. Box 40 Shelbyville, Ind. 46176 Phone (317)398-7262	Ammunition, including dumdum bullets	
Winchester-Western (Olin-Mathieson Chemical Corp.) New Haven, Conn. 06504 Phone (203)777-7911	Ammunition Firearms Rifles	New Haven plant: product improvement tests on M-16 rifle LaPorte, Ind. plant: VRFWS (Vehicle Rapid Fire Weapon System) to "provide highly mobile gun system to defeat Soviet armor threat of the 1970's." Olin makes the ammunition. Total defense awards for fiscal 1969 to Olin-Mathieson, $354,359,000

*Subsidiary of the Breeze Corp. in New Jersey; very little is known about this company.
**Part of the Smith & Wesson "Law Enforcement Group" owned by the Bangor Punta conglomerate.

to establish at this time. Certainly DuPont does, but smaller companies may employ agencies, and a sharp eye is needed to detect such activity. Any information uncovered should be reported to the Law Enforcement Research Center at Goddard for future publication.

NOTES

1. Dana Adams Schmidt, "Laird Authorizes More Guard Arms and Riot Drilling," *New York Times,* November 11, 1970, p. 1.
2. Col. Rex Applegate, *Riot Control Materiel and Techniques* (Harrisburg, Pa.: Stackpole Books, 1969), p. 196.
3. *Ibid.,* p. 128.
4. *Ibid.,* p. 129.
5. *Ibid.,* p. 132.
6. *Journal of Forensic Sciences,* vol. 9, no. 3, July 1964.
7. Applegate, pp. 188–9.

8. Robert Wells, "Vietnamization on Main Street," *The Nation,* July 20, 1970, pp. 38–41.
9. *New York Times,* September 16, 1970, and *Philadelphia Bulletin,* November 11, 1970.
10. Joseph C. Goulden, "The Cops Hit the Jackpot," *The Nation,* November 23, 1970, p. 521.
11. Walter Key, "A Report from the National Institute," *The Police Chief,* November 1969, p. 15.
12. *First Annual Report of the Law Enforcement Assistance Administration* (Washington, D.C.: U.S. Department of Justice, 1969), p. 27.
13. *Second Annual Report of the Law Enforcement Assistance Administration* (Washington, D.C.: U.S. Department of Justice, 1970), p. 91.
14. *Ibid.,* p. 210.
15. Dr. Blumstein was the Institute for Defense Analyses' director of the Science and Technology report to the President's Commission on Law Enforcement and Administration of Justice. He left IDA to become director of the Urban Systems Institute at Carnegie-Mellon University.
16. Dr. Alfred Blumstein, "Science and Technology for Law Enforcement," *The Police Chief,* December 1969, p. 61.

SHORT BIBLIOGRAPHY ON POLICE WEAPONS

Applegate, Rex (Col.), *Riot Control Materiel and Techniques.* Harrisburg: Stackpole Books, 1969.

Department of the Army. *Civil Disturbances and Disasters.* Army Field Manual 19-15. Washington: Government Printing Office, March 1968.

Hersch, Seymour. "Your Friendly Mace," *New York Review of Books,* March 27, 1969.

International Association of Chiefs of Police (IACP). *The Police Chief* (monthly magazine). (Note: Each October issue contains a comprehensive list of firms from which police purchase all types of supplies.)

Klare, Mike. "The Intelligent Agitator's Guide to Domestic Counterinsurgency," *Viet-Report,* Summer 1968.

Law Enforcement Assistance Administration (LEAA). *First and Second Annual Reports.* Washington, D.C.: U.S. Dept. of Justice 1969 and 1970.

Professional Standards Division, International Association of Chiefs of Police. "Guidelines for Civil Disorder Mobilization and Planning (September 1968)." IACP, 1319 18th Street, N.W., Washington, D.C. 20036.

U.S. Department of Justice, Federal Bureau of Investigation. *Prevention and Control of Mobs and Riots.* Washington, D.C.: U.S. Government Printing Office.

Webb, Lee. "Repression as a Growth Industry," *The Guardian,* December 27, 1969.

Wills, Gary. *The Second Civil War.* New York: Signet, 1968.

A fairly comprehensive list of companies from which police regularly purchase all types of supplies can be found in the October 1969 issue of *The Police Chief.*

Section Three *A Partial Source of Colonialism and Counterinsurgency*

Anglo-Saxon Ethnocentrism: Its Roots and Consequences in Northern Ireland and the Southern United States

By Cecilia A. Karch

TERMINOLOGY

Throughout this essay I avoid using the term *caste* and instead use *class-racial categories* to describe the socioeconomic statuses operating in both the Southern United States and Northern Ireland. Both societies are a product of one capitalist class system. Double exploitation has been operative here. Blacks and Irish Catholics have been kept in a subordinate position by the ethos of capitalism, the doctrines of racial prejudice, the practices of low wage return for high labor output, and the discrimination of employers on the matters of hiring, promoting, and dismissing. For many centuries the English chose to categorize the Irish as a separate race and many academic treatises were written to buttress a doctrine on Irish racial inferiority

■ This essay was prepared especially for this volume.

and their correlated lower caste position. Similar doctrines were penned by the English on blacks. However, in my opinion the term *caste* only serves to confuse the issue. Unlike the Hindu system with its long-term condition of near-impermeable boundaries separating occupational categories of caste and subculture, a far greater amount of upward job mobility and cultural assimilation of majority group culture has occurred among southern U.S. blacks and the Northern Irish. Yet the mobility is limited by barriers. The white upper classes of both societies integrate Anglo-Saxon racial and ethnic biases into the class-racial structures to heighten competitive antagonisms among the lower classes of both the dominant and subordinate racial groups. In both the southern United States and Northern Ireland, the bulk of the subordinate racial group can be found in the lower and middle classes; indeed, the Blacks and Irish Catholic have been overwhelmingly lower class. By contrast, the upper-class blacks and Irish Catholic have been few in number. Consequently, when the term upper-class black and/or Irish is used in this paper, it is used only to demonstrate that there are class divisions within race—ethnic groups. It should be made clear that these upperclass minorities have constituted only a fraction of the entire upper class and, furthermore, have wielded little or no political power.

NORTHERN IRELAND AND THE UNITED STATES

This essay demonstrates the linkages of ethnicity and race to problems of class between Northern Ireland and the American South. This is an attempt to examine one angle of the problem of social stratification that has not been scrutinized. As such, it is meant to imply that the problems of racial and class stratification in these areas demonstrate economic and political similarities derived from a planter class and a colonial system that has left both sections ripe for antagonisms both of a class and racial ethnic nature. Both sections were colonized by a similar group of people who established an agricultural system of race—ethnic stratification. The system necessitated the development of a set of myths and mores that served to bolster the practical realities of life. In both sections, despite the passage of time, these supremacy myths act as an impediment to viable socioeconomic change. Despite the disadvantages suffered by a majority of the dominant group, the continued existence of the value system which buttresses competition between these groups in a class system inhibits alignments with the subordinate group in attempts at reformation.

We begin the analogy by tracing the similar development of economic and social relationships in both sections. The planter class of the South, which W. E. B. DuBois has stipulated comprised 7 percent of the population and owned 75 percent of the land, was Anglo-Saxon in background, being descendants of either English or Scotch-Irish settlers. They were for the most part of humble origin, although members of the English upper class settled in the Tidewater region of Virginia and Maryland. The plantation system arose out of the English venture of colonialism, which had already estab-

lished a planter class of the same ethnicity in Ireland. By the time of the plantation system in the southern colonies, the English had effectively conquered the Gaelic natives of Ulster and then moved en masse to reservations on the rocky coast of Ireland. The exceptions consisted of those who, out of necessity, were kept on as chattels to till the soil. The Plantation of Ulster had brought in that group of Scotch-Irish who form the basis of ethnic conflict in Northern Ireland today.

Under James I, the Gaelic lords were scattered. The king then granted charters to Scottish noblemen commissioning them to colonize Ulster. The Scotch-Irish nobles arrived with their poorer tenants. Unlike the Irish, the Scots were settled in communities and forever changed the social order in Northern Ireland. The Gaelic Irish, however, were not to be pacified. Warfare similar to that on the frontier of America was waged between the conquerors and the natives.

SCOTTISH PROTESTANTISM AND COLONIAL VENTURES

The Lowland Scots had just recently embraced Protestantism under the banner of John Knox and were vehemently anti-Catholic. Hilaire Belloc has noted that although the Catholic Church throughout Europe in the sixteenth century was inundated with abuses, it was at its very worst in Scotland. There, it was not unusual to witness illiterate priests, often under the influence of alcohol, stumble through the Latin phrases of the mass. Furthermore, the Church worked in conjunction with the noblemen to overtax the poor Scottish peasants.[1]

In light of all the debauchery and oppression, there arose a mass movement which eagerly accepted a grim brand of Calvinism. Since the political allegiances of the time were based on religion, the Scottish peasants who left for Ireland, seeking better soil and fairer weather, brought with them a hatred of Catholic Ireland. This hatred was transferred into religious ethnic conflicts as the Scots fought to retain their holdings taken from the Catholic indigenous population. The Irish wars were considered by the English and Scottish soldiers to be the worst of fates. To be sent to fight the Irish was viewed as tantamount to the death sentence.

It must be borne in mind that this was

England's first colonial venture, and that the descendants of those who both settled Ulster and those who fought the Irish wars were the soldiers and colonials of America. It is H. Mumford Jones's contention that the difficulties that the English encountered when dealing with the Irish were the main reason for the late entry of the English into the colonial race.[2] The reports of the ferocity of the native Americans struck a familiar note to English and Scotch-Irish ears. At that historical moment, when attempts at pacification had failed miserably so close at hand, why venture to play the same game far across the ocean where it was certainly far more difficult to retreat to the safety of English soil? The repression meted out to the Irish by the English and Scotch-Irish was undoubtedly partially responsible for the English cruelty and viciousness toward the American Indian and to the black slaves.

Colonization and constant warfare with the Irish had instilled in the Scotch-Irish settlers not only a hatred of Catholicism and of the Irish, but a feeling of superiority in culture as well. This ethnocentrism accompanied the Scotch-Irish when they left the Emerald Isle to seek a less strife-ridden settlement in America.

The Scotch-Irish were by far the most numerous of the early immigrants to America. Their names have been made immortal by the Daughters of the American Revolution for their viciousness in fighting the Indian and for carving out the lands that were to become the first thirteen states of the United States of America. That twelve U.S. presidents have Scotch-Irish backgrounds has instilled pride in their descendants in Northern Ireland today, in much the same way that the status of John F. Kennedy does in the Republic.

In the South it was the same ethnic groups of English and Scotch-Irish settlers who formed the basis of the planter class and of the lower orders. Southerners are fond of pointing out the homogeneous nature of their society. Anglo-Saxon ethnocentrism, which spiraled under the heyday of English imperialism and formed the basis for nativism in this country (100 percent Americanism being the slogan of the Ku Klux Klan and other such movements), has its roots in the origins of these settlers. One of the frequent explanations given in the development of the North—South conflict has been the theory that the South as a region was alienated from the North by its ties with England. Culturally and economically, the plantation South remained linked to the English imperialist venture. Thus the planters in the South differed little from the English planters in the West Indies (with all the racial biases implied) or from that later group of English planters in India and Africa.

U.S. SOUTH AND NORTHERN IRELAND: LANDLORD OPPRESSION

Thus the "peculiar institution" of the South differed little from other systems of colonial exploitation in operation at the time in the rest of the world. Whereas in the South the planter class comprised 7 percent of the population, the large landholders in the North of Ireland comprised 1 percent of the population. Many landlords in Ireland were English absentee landlords whose estates were managed by Scotch-Irish. As might be expected, the Protestant yeomanry of Ulster were better off than their Catholic counterparts in the rest of Ireland. The most prevalent form of cultivation was huge estates run by Protestant managers with Catholic peasants tilling the soil.

A doubly captive class structure was in operation both in Ireland and in the South. In Ireland the planter class consisted of English landlords who were either of royal blood or were upwardly mobile entrepreneurs. This latter group was to become dominant in the Victorian era of industrial expansion through the mechanism of patronage. Absentee landlordism was especially prevalent in this class. The colonizers were further stratified into a rising middle class of Dissenter merchants (i.e., Presbyterian, not Church of England) and the lower classes of Protestant yeomanry and peasants. The Protestant peasantry were able to squeeze tenant-right reforms from the upper class at a much earlier date than their Catholic counterparts. A tiny minority of Catholics managed to maintain their upper-class status through co-optation. Others, formerly belonging to the upper class, retained at least a middle-class status by entering into capitalistic activities. Both the Dissenters and Catholics suffered discrimination based on religion. Like the Jews, they turned to trade activities when the professional doors were closed. This small middle class formed the leadership cadre of the libertarian United Irish-men, the Irish revolutionary response to the ideas of the American and French revolutions. Beneath the upper crust was the mass of the population, the Irish Catholic peasantry, chattel property of the English landowners.

NORTHERN IRELAND
AND ETHNIC DISTINCTIONS

Since there were few Protestant peasants in the south of Ireland, it was in Northern Ireland that the distinctions based on ethnicity were most evident. The majority of Protestant peas-antry kept the religion of their fathers, a strict Calvinistic, fundamentalist form of religion, similar to that of the Bible Belt of the southern United States. The Catholics of Ireland, like the blacks of America, had few rights. They were forbidden to speak their language, to practice their religion, or to acquire an education that would permit them to rise in social status through the professions. What was created by this system of apartheid was a large illiterate peasant mass, beasts of burden to be used to exploit their own land for the benefit of Moth-er England. The Catholic peasantry of Ireland were little better off than the blacks in the South, nor much different in status from them. The only technical difference was that they were native to the soil of Ireland and did not need to be part of a slave trade. No price was paid for their labor. They were as much a part of the land to exploit as the humus in the soil. In fact after Cromwell's rape of Ireland, many Catholics were sent as slaves to the West Indies to work on the plantations there. Vestiges of their forced resettlement can especially be seen in Montserrat, where the natives speak with an Irish brogue. The blacks of the West Indies did not know what to make of the Irish, since the English overlords treated their Irish slaves more cruelly than they did the blacks.[3]

THE SOUTHERN U.S. SIMILARITY

In the southern United States a similar class-racial system prevailed. The white peasant eked out a living on the poorest soil. He suffered from disease and malnutrition and neither bene-fited from nor produced anything in quantity for the system in operation. These "po'

whites," as they have disparagingly been la-beled, differed in economic and social status. Pushed out of the areas most suitable for single-crop production, many yeoman farmers lived in respectable "poverty" and were able to feed themselves if not produce much for market. Within this class were some who could afford a slave who worked with the farmer in the fields. Another group of whites, slightly better off, lived and earned a living in the small towns as merchants and craftsmen. From this class of *petit* bourgeois came many of the overseers on plantations. The lowest group of whites were the "clayeaters," or "mean whites," as they were called. Reduced to extreme levels of pov-erty, many were perhaps seen eating dirt to glean from it certain minerals and other sub-stances in an attempt to counteract the diseases that plagued their bodies.[4]

Depending on the region, these people lived mainly by hunting and fishing and scratching what subsistance they could from the soil. The lowest orders of whites were illiterate and non-churchgoers. After the Civil War these people formed the mass of sharecroppers and tenant farmers. As the Industrial Revolution pene-trated the South (with the establishment of cotton mills by northern and a few southern capitalists from the upper orders), these people, in the main, formed the backbone of the south-ern proletariat. Inducements were also made to the mountain men and to small independent farmers, who were suffering from low agricultur-al prices, to move to the mill towns, forsake the land and become cogs in the wheels of southern capitalism. It is this class that sparked the vehe-ment drive to keep blacks out of industry.

Before the Civil War the skilled artisans of the South were black slaves hired out to capital-ists in the larger cities. After the war, the whites soon reversed the roles. Unable to sustain them-selves before the war because of competition from black slave labor, they were opposed to competing for jobs with blacks for wages. Thus, until recently, whites formed the backbone of the skilled proletariat in the South.

Reconstruction and the Industrial Revolu-tion reinforced the stratified social relations in the South. The promise of 40 acres and a mule never came to fruition. Both the black and the white rural populaces remained subordinate to the Bourbon planters, who were able to reinstate their claims after the Civil War. The bulk of the farming population in the South today are exploited by the landed "gentry," and the people have no access to the authorities for infringements on agreements or other abuses. Black landowners in the South form a minute stratum of the population. Victor Perlo has demonstrated that often black farmers and black landless laborers are more economically disadvantaged than their white equivalents, although both suffer from landlord exploitation, whether under the sharecropper or factory–farm system. Child labor laws and other labor measures such as a 40-hour week, or safety regulations, are often unknown to the farm proletariat of the South. They are solely dependent on the patronage of the planters.

As in Ireland, the frequency of absentee landlordism is high. Tenants rent their acreage either for cash or crops with no security of tenure. Legally binding written agreements are rare, and class–racial sanctions prevent a black tenant from filing suit against a white planter.[5] Law enforcement in rural areas until very recently was a prerogative of class. Planters are expected to reprimand their tenants. Local law enforcement is an upper-lower and lower-middle class profession. The upper classes control the governmental apparatus and are above the law for most infractions. They have therefore left local law enforcement in the hands of lower class whites. A similar practice is in operation in Northern Ireland, where the Protestant paramilitary B Specials were allowed to vent their frustration on lower-class Catholics. The vigilante system of law enforcement is a common phenomenon in both geographical sections.

The rise of the cities in the South has called for a modification of traditional economic and social roles. Distinctions were drawn in the labor force between black and white blue-collar jobs. By and large the most menial tasks are still "nigger" jobs, and the more skilled labor is a white prerogative. The taboo on social relations between upper- and middle-class whites and blacks effectively operated to exclude the latter from white-collar employment, whereas assigning the majority of unskilled labor positions to blacks effectively cut into the number of job opportunities available to lower-class whites. "Before the Depression the existence of "negro

jobs" sanctioned by the caste dogma of the division of labor, provided a basis of subsistance for the colored society and actually worked to the economic disadvantage of the white people in lower occupational groups."[6]

With the introduction of federal relief during the Depression, whites began to undercut blacks in the unskilled occupations. However, divisions were maintained by further stratifying job positions. When that became impossible, whites were given responsibility over their black coworkers. The entrance of blacks into the skilled blue-collar professions through black-owned enterprises has done much to modify class–racial occupational relationships, further weakening the lower-class white's status position in a society based on white supremacy. Black society in the Southern cities *is* class divisible. There are black lawyers, doctors, and other professionals as well as a long-established black middle class of entrepreneurs. Although an upper-class black still suffers the impediments of racial discrimination in certain social situations, it can be said that through his interactions with white professionals found within the upper-middle class, the lot of an upper-class black is manifestly better than that of a lower-class white. The economic status of upper-class blacks has modified the class racial structure to the extent that except for the most intimate personal relationships, the racial barriers are virtually redefined in order to accommodate the separate status of the individuals.

THE GENERAL LESSON

The insidious function of a socioeconomic system based on upper-class–racial supremacy is

FIGURE 5 Class and Race Barriers

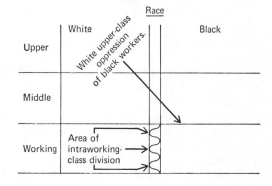

to cloak the class divisions manifestly apparent in most capitalist societies. White upper-class racial groups have utilized this decoy tactic to further consolidate their own positions. The class-racial distinctions are so tightly drawn that crystal-clear class alignments and the formation of a solid working-class movement are almost impossible. As such, the supremacy value system in the South has served as a method of unimpeded double exploitation for the subordinate group (see Figure 5).

THE IRISH CASE

We now turn to Northern Ireland and examine another society in the process of "modernization" which exhibits a similar lack of working-class solidarity. The class-racial distinctions nurtured so successfully by the avowedly Anglo-Saxon ethnic group that reigns supreme in the South are equally apparent in the north of Ireland.

The mechanism by which the traditional society of Northern Ireland was transformed into a modern mixed economy with strong class cleavages was the same mechanism utilized by the dominant class in the South—textile mills. The Northern Irish and English mill system no doubt was the model on which the American system was built. As in the South the mills drew heavily from the marginal farming class of Northern Ireland. Long raped by England for her agricultural commodities, Irish land during the nineteenth century was increasingly turned into pasture, forcing the peasants to turn to other means of employment. The port city of Belfast soon became the center of textile activity.

The years of improper utilization of the land brought on the Famine, and the present working-class demarcations in the city of Belfast were formed after this era. Both groups lived in mill houses built by the Presbyterian capitalists to lodge them, and their descendants continue to occupy these very houses. Housing in Northern Ireland is drawn along ethnic-religious and class lines in much the same way as it is in the South. Both working classes live around the mills and places of work in the decaying central city. The upper classes of both groups have evacuated to the suburbs.

The Catholics and the Protestants form two homogeneous blocs leading out in different directions from the city. Protestant and Catholic middle classes generally do not mix in neighborhoods, but rather have equal housing in separate suburbs. Within the economic system, Protestants and Catholics do not mix on the job except in the new factories established by primarily English and American multinational corporations. Even there, the traditional patterns are often followed so as to avoid conflict. (Protestants on the whole are mainstream working-class, skilled laborers, whereas Catholics are marginal and unskilled.) The economic market, partly as a result of civil strife, continues on a downward spiral. Northern Ireland, the Minister of Development recently stated (1971), was nearly bankrupt after two years of violence. Many industries, no matter what the inducement, are either closing their subsidiaries in Northern Ireland or refusing to come at all. One of the most pressing economic problems for the state of Northern Ireland has been her de facto provincial status, which has led to a considerable drain of commodities and taxes going to Britain. The Exchequer of Great Britain yearly must "donate" £one hundred million to keep the place operating at all. Industries are offered tax write-offs and factories are built to specification in the hopes of persuading industrialists to come to Northern Ireland. But the fact of the matter is that the factories are foreign-owned, and the moment the market falls, the subsidiary company in Northern Ireland is closed.

Outwardly, it appears that in Northern Ireland, as in the American South, "race" issues are at the root of the problem. However, discrimination in Northern Ireland, although based to a certain extent on "ethnic" animosity, is in the main due to economic duress which in turn exacerbates "ethnic" tensions. Both Northern Ireland and the American South have been fair pickings for highly industrialized capitalist societies. The leadership of both communities has maintained itself through a single-party apparatus based on supremacy. By dividing the lower orders (which was a deliberate policy in Northern Ireland at the turn of the century when the proletariat was organizing), the establishment is able to maintain its position through the numerical superiority of Protestants over a sizable Catholic minority. For both in the South and in

Northern Ireland, the black and Catholic minorities, respectively, form a considerable portion of the populace. The fear of cheap labor and the competition for scarce jobs have prompted the poorer Protestant Anglo-Saxon population of both areas to respond violently in order to prevent what they perceive as both a loss of status and of economic position. Their position is tenuous to say the least. The cultural values of the dominant Anglo-Saxon ethnic group of both communities support a similar response. The contention of the writer is that the common heritage of both groups has led to similar responses to the perceived threats to their status.

James McEvoy of the Sociology Department of University of California, Davis, has stated in his book, *Radicals or Conservatives*, that the Goldwater and Wallace movements in American society share "an intense nationalism, patriotism and a high degree of expressive and ritualistic "Americanism"—all forms of socially integrative behavior described by Katz, Kelman, and Flacks as examples of symbolic integration."[7] According to McEvoy the origins of the intense nationalism of these groups

> is found in the fact that they identify their life styles and locations in the prestige order with a mythical (although partially historically based) concept of the state. Thus, while the contemporary state has been a prime agent in the disruption of the prestige order of American Society, these groups evolve in their defense a concept of the State based on a reactionary view of history and harken back to the time when the state represented the values they hold dear and positively sanctioned the norms they admire. The function of this invocation is obvious. It is an effort to bolster declining prestige by creating a direct identification of the affected group with the most powerful formal political structure in the Society—the state.[8]

This reaction may be prevalent in most societies, but in the Anglo-Saxon-dominated societies it has taken on particular attributes. It is to these we now turn.

THE BESIEGED MENTALITY

Both Northern Ireland and the South suffer from a "besieged" mentality, viewing themselves as an embattled minority within a hostile nation. In Northern Ireland the threat of Home Rule and the Easter Rebellion (1916), led to the division of Great Britain and Northern Ireland into three sections. Ireland was split North and South, while Northern Ireland's relationship with Great Britain remains one of a misunderstood poorer province. American Civil War, with memories of Reconstruction, gave birth to and maintained a "Lost Cause" mentality, a regional inferiority complex with defensive psychological manifestations. Both the South and Northern Ireland, before their respective wars, had fought to maintain their distinctive institutions, and both remained highly sensitive on the subject. After the civil war in Ireland and with the introduction of the state of Northern Ireland, a one-party totalitarian organization based on Anglo-Saxon supremacy was inaugurated. Each section retains the myths in order to bolster the political setups: The Protestants of the North had their battle cry of "No Surrender" to the forces of popery. (On July 1, 1690, the Protestant King William of Orange defeated Catholic James II at the Battle of the Boyne, thus ensuring that Protestant hegemony would prevail against the ravages of popery.) The U.S. South retains the romance and chivalry of a cultured nation hacked to pieces by a greedy North.

Surrounded on all sides by a hostile Catholic nation and within their province by fellow Catholic "citizens" who comprise one-third of the population, the Protestants of Ulster have used the one-party system of government to disenfranchise that third of the populace. In the Irish North, through the medium of business and property qualifications, Catholics were prevented from exercising voting rights. "One man, one vote" was a crucial issue in Northern Ireland. Local government is of the utmost importance in the politics of Northern Ireland. For through the maneuverings of gerrymandering and franchise disqualifications, Protestants have managed to retain their supremacy even in Catholic strongholds of the country. In this sense, even where Catholics could vote, the effect of their ballots has been minimal. In somewhat the same sense, southern Negroes were officially disenfranchised either through statute or through the device of the poll tax and literacy test.

LAW AND RIGHTS

Law enforcement in both regions is a prerogative of the dominant group, blacks and Catholics having little access to the law for redress. In Northern Ireland the paramilitary B Specials exerted the overwhelming repressive apparatus of the Protestants when Catholics began to get "uppity" in much the same manner as did the lynchings and actions of the state troopers in the South.

One effect of voting qualifications in both sections was to disfranchise large numbers of poor whites and poor Protestants. In both sections the machinery of government has long been the special prerogative of an elite, whether the Bourbons of the South—or their ancestral inspiration, the Anglo-Irish aristocracy with their private desmesnes in Northern Ireland. Both societies can be categorized as modernizing, although until recently they were treated as static and traditional by establishment developmental theorists. Until the 1970 general election, the one-party oligarchy of Northern Ireland was able to circumvent all potential grievances from turning into party realignments by drumming up the issue of the border and Protestant supremacy at every election. Each prior election thus had been a plebiscite for Protestant supremacy. But with the impetus toward "modernization and development," and the rise of a strong middle class in both sections, contention for power has emerged as significant. The professional and middle classes of both sections are seeking control of the reins of government. With the dawn of the civil rights struggles in both sections, the lower orders as well, so long neglected and nonparticipatory due to the predominance of the "race" issue, are rebelling and demanding a share of the pie. Both George Wallace and Ian Paisley speak the language and air the grievances of certain sections of the lower classes.

THE ETHNIC COMPLETION
OF CLASS STRUGGLE

It has been indicated that the similarities of property relations and social stratification in the two communities are striking. The reasons are clear. Under the circumstances of the ethnic-race stratification described, the oppression meted out by the dominant groups on party politics is always similar. The class struggle in both communities is classic, and both societies could be termed modernizing societies in turmoil, coupled with racial overtones that often distort the basic struggle. Furthermore, the two communities are similar in that the upper-class participants in the struggle are of the same ethnic composition. Their historical economic situation is the product of one and the same venture by the Anglo-Saxon civilization to attempt to gain control of the markets of the world for their personal consumption. Because of the vast landmass of America, it took longer for the former colonies to reach the sophistication that the mother country possessed in the eighteenth century. Nevertheless, the values of the mother country which aided in internal development also affected foreign policy at a later date.

Since the American South received little ethnic input from varying cultures, the values of the Anglo-Saxon were allowed to fertilize and become hybridized in American soil. In the most important particulars, therefore, the culture remained intact. It is these values and cultural traits that we now consider for an explanation of the manner in which the turn of events in both Ireland and the southern United States has been shaped and formed to varying degrees by their dominance, and by England's imperialist ventures and the Scotch-Irish embroilment and identification with this process.

VALUES AND CULTURE TRAITS

Religion has always been a very serious business to the people of the South. Their Scotch-Irish ancestors brought with them a fear of God, belief in the literal word of the Bible, an overriding concern with morality and the sins of the flesh, and a deep hatred of Catholicism. Both the South and Northern Ireland share the cultural trait of evangelicalism, and a fundamentalist outlook that colors every facet of life. The Calvinistic notion of the elect permeates both communities, thereby adding to the myth of the Children of God surrounded on all sides by evildoers. Both sections suffer from conformity complexes within their ranks. Outsiders are suspect, and any tampering with the status quo is tantamount to damnation. In 1904 the Methodist Bishop Warren A. Candler of Georgia, in his *Great Revivals and the Great Republic,* declared the Anglo-Saxon to be divinely appointed for the advancement of evangelical religion in the world. A Baptist minister had declared that other regions had lost

> whatever there is of advantage in this unmixed Anglo-Saxon blood. Romanism had flooded their cities, and invaded and dispoiled the old patriotism and the old culture and political ideas. The hope of the world is America, the hope of America is evangelical religion of the most orthodox type, the hope of the American church is the Southern Evangelical churches.[9]

Anglo-Saxon ethnocentrism and evangelicalism were linked in a distinctive Southern ideology that differed little from the ideology of Protestant Ulster, its roots. Both Northern Ireland and the South have much higher Church membership and attendance rate in their respective sections than in their respective nations as a whole. Southern Ireland, the Republic, is always viewed by outsiders as a strongly religious country. Indeed it is. But Church influence and membership in Northern Ireland is higher (67 percent membership) in comparison with the rest of the British Isles.

This pervasive influence of the Protestant churches within the dominant strata has meant that the values of the religious community are also the moral values of the body politic. In a world of increasing secularism, both Northern Ireland and the American South have viewed themselves as bastions of Christianity pitted against the forces of secular communism and perverted liberalism. Drinking regulations and recreation on Sundays are legislated against in both sections—an example of the influence of the dominant group, despite the proclivities of the rest of the population. People's Democracy, the student-led civil rights movement, has just recently been successful (1970) in putting forward a bill to open the swimming pools on Sunday for Catholic children in Northern Ireland.

When the social gospel of Protestantism, pressing for similar reforms, entered the South in the 1920s, it ran head-long into a gathering momentum of Fundamentalism. By virtue of their importance in all walks of life, the various Southern churches naturally assumed class distinctions as well. Denominations and sects are as class-aligned as the people who sit in the pews. Church membership in the Presbyterian and Lutheran churches is drawn mainly from the upper and upper-middle classes. Their parishes are primarily urban and their ministers and congregations highly literate. Sermons often deal with theological abstractions rather than with the "nitty-gritty" of life. According to Liston Pope, in the 1930s, Presbyterian and Lutheran ministers who were required to do missionary work in the wilds of the mill villages and rural areas had little rapport with these congregations, and attendance dropped off. The class and educational gaps were too wide to permit mutual understanding. By far the most popular religion in the mill villages, where the congregation often had little more than a grammar school education, were the newer Fundamental sects, such as Church of God and Free-Will Baptists. In a survey Pope took in 1939, which by current accounts is valid today, he found that out of eleven Church of God ministers, eight had received a level of education of grammar school or less, and three had finished high school. Of the Presbyterian ministers, however, all fourteen had a college degree in theology.[10] The Baptist and Methodist churches have been declining in numbers among the poorer classes as the denominations become more "establishment" oriented.

Northern Ireland exhibits similar distinctions. Although the majority of the populace is either Church of Ireland or Presbyterian, depending on the area, one or the other is very definitely the dominant order. For example, Belfast is a Presbyterian city founded by wealthy Presbyterian merchants. The lower classes are predominantly Church of Ireland because when they were brought in from the rural areas to work the mills, they retained the religious affiliation of their aristocratic landlords. However, a goodly number of the lower classes are Presbyterians, the descendants of the Scottish peasants who came with the Plantation of Ulster. But increasingly among the working class, especially the lowest level of the working class, the inroads of Paisleyism and other forms of evangelicalism have made great strides. Belfast is called the Bible Belt of Ireland. There, Dr. Donald Soper, a proponent of Protestant unity with Rome, was stoned by a Paisleyite mob after he had referred to Belfast as "a city of religious nightclubs." Within these run-down mission halls "star-studded attractions" such as the ex-priests reveal the evil master-plannings of the "communist" Catholic Church.

Like the South in the 1920s and again in the 1960s, rising unemployment, general economic decline, and a burden of guilt on unwilling shoulders, instills in the minds of these confused and unhappy people the spirit of a crusade to preserve the values demeaned by society at large. They have been ignored in the political spectrum and are aware of their declining prestige as a marginal group. The predominant force of religion in their lives can reach a fever pitch in chaotic and uncertain times. Revivals in the South are a throwback to the "salvation" of the elect practiced in the mission halls of Northern Ireland.

The forgotten and unimportant people of both sections are the poor whites and the poor rural and small-town Protestants of Northern Ireland. They are an important tool in the maintenance of the supremacy of the dominant class, a tool to be pitted against the subordinate, using the dialogue of race/ethnicity in order to undermine class consciousness. Living marginally as they do, not quite middle class, some *petit* bourgeois (most very poor, yet one step higher in status from their neighbor of the pariah "caste") they can be whipped to a frenzy if they are told that their status positions and prestige are in jeopardy.

CONSERVATIVE IDEOLOGY, THE KKK, AND THE ORANGE ORDER

Perhaps the clearest manner in which to present the continuing influence of the conservative ideology of this stratum of Anglo-Saxons is to portray the two most blatant examples of folk movements which epitomize the cultural traits and ideology of this group: the KKK and the Orange Order. I choose to label the Orange Order the granddaddy of the KKK because of the similarity of rituals, the secrecy of the organization, the religious overtones, and the inherent "supremacy" attitudes.

Back in the eighteenth century, when the plight of the agricultural tenants, Protestant and Catholic, was insufferable, the Orange Order was founded as an agricultural secret society to wage war on the rack-renting landlords. However, it quickly became a means, under the cloak of secrecy, for burning out Catholic tenants. A fraternal order endowed with ritual and mystery, the Orange Order allowed its members to turn the night sky red on missions of destruction. Warfare between the two sections was rampant. In 1798 the upper echelons sensed the utility of the Orange Order and used the group as a peasant militia to stamp out a revolt. For a time the wealthiest and most aristocratic of patrons showered their favors on the Order. The English Parliament, however, eternally on guard against the potential strength of their colonial allies, very quickly felt compelled to disband the Order at the end of the eighteenth century. From that time until the late nineteenth century, the Orange Order deteriorated into a fraternal drinking club in the rural areas. Yet the Order was a means of fostering solidarity among the Protestants. The Orange Hall meetings provided a place where members could remind themselves, in the face of continuously bad agricultural years, that they were at least a step higher than their Catholic counterparts. It is "said" that

An Orangeman who was asked how long his order had been in existence answered off-hand that Orangeism could be traced back to the Garden of Eden. This was a thoroughly accurate statement. He meant simply to convey that all the essentials of a perfect nature and of an exalted religion were to be found associated in the primal day of our race. Our relationship to the Father of our spirits was renewed, and while we maintained that relationship by faith and obedience no one could take away our inheritance. That was Protestantism, that was Orangeism. Popery however obscured the truth, and while affecting to lead man right plunged him into a moral quagmire, into a wilderness of error and superstition. Against Popery's usurpation of the office of our redeemer, Orangeism which is organized Protestantism, is the only effective weapon, and so we reach the conclusion that the triumph of Bethlehem depends in the long run on Belfast.[11]

Orangeism in its modern form, which came into being after the collapse of the Penal Laws (Ireland's version of the Jim Crow laws), represented an attempt by the poorer class of Protestants to achieve by mob violence what their ancestors had achieved by the more decorous method of legislative enactment. Following Catholic emancipation, the poorer orders attempted to maintain their status in society by violence and fear if necessary, just as the formation of the KKK in 1865 had followed the emancipation of the slaves in the South. With virtual control over lands and tenancy, however, the aristocracy no longer needed the Protestant rabble to keep the Catholics in their place. In fact, the aristocracy preferred and generally obtained Catholic tenants, who expected less and raised no questions about rights and privileges.

At the turn of the century, with the advent of the Catholic party in Parliament and the cries for Home Rule, the Orange Order was again revived. Once more, positions of control were dominated by the upper classes, who feared loss of ascendancy if Parliament were to return to Dublin. The Orange Order formed the grass-roots basis of the Unionist party, the totalitarian apparatus manipulating Northern Ireland today. Although most members of the upper classes profess disdain for the Order, they have found it expedient to belong, and no one rises in the Unionist party hierarchy who is not in the Order. On July Twelfth the poor Protestant can hold his head up high as he participates in the parades that are organized throughout Northern Ireland. For on the Twelfth, marching with the Prime Minister and other notables, the Orangeman tells himself that he is a better man than his Catholic counterpart, peeking behind closed shutters at the marchers in their bowler hats and sashes. Today the marches are protected by the British Army. Yet, the Order, like the Klan, has been under considerable attack and suffered much abuse from liberal British journalists covering the action in Northern Ireland. As such among the lower classes, the Orange Order has again become an organizational plebiscite of their solidarity in the face of opposition on all sides:

> *The dark eleventh hour draws on and sees us sold.*
> *To every foreign foe we fought against of old.*

This little ditty was published in Paisley's *Protestant Telegraph* at a time when fear was running high that the annual Twelfth processions were to be cancelled for fear of violence:

> Orangemen all over the North are under attack. Tremendous and far-reaching attempts are being made to force a cancellation of the Twelfth processions . . . why should the Northern politicians, Communists and a motley crew of liberals and progressives all seek an end to the Orange parades? It's really very obvious. It has been recognized for some time that the Unionist government is largely an irrelevance. It is the Protestant Cause, and the Orange Order which stands for that cause, that binds Ulster together.[12]

These statements were made under the headline "The Final Betrayal." The same paper has called Harold Wilson a "Red" and has labeled the Pope a supporter of subversive Communist activities in the North of Ireland. In Belfast, you often hear little children say that the Pope is planning to build a castle in Ireland once the Catholics take over. According to one anti-Catholic book, mass Protestant repatriation back to England is the design of the Vatican plotters.

In all the literature, the same current of thought is driven home. The Ulstermen are the last bastion of the great Anglo-Saxon Protestant traditions. England has become demoralized and decadent. It is they, the Orangemen, who must take up the banner and save Christianity from the pagans. Every Orange Lodge has a chaplain to lead the faithful in prayers, and every Twelfth of July the platforms in "The Field" are filled with ministers exhorting the faithful to remain steadfast in the face of all the odds.

Because of the disturbances, Orangemen are increasingly critical of the upper-class Unionist party. As a result, Orangemen are running their own candidates on reactionary platforms. They are calling, of course, for stringent measures on the issue of law and order.

The leader of the Protestant *petit* bourgeois, unemployed youth, and marginal working class, is (1971) Ian Kyle Paisley, a breakaway gospel tabernacle minister who holds a degree from that bulwark of Fundamentalism—Bob Jones University in South Carolina, U.S.A. Ronald Cooke, an exponent of Paisleyism in the United States, has stated in his polemic "The Thunder of Papal Propaganda" that:

> To any thinking person the Roman Catholic

Church is a far greater threat to our freedom than Communism. . . . God has stamped Paisley's ministry with his own approval. The world may rage and pagan popery may lie blatantly, and weak-kneed evangelical papers like *Christianity Today* may crawl along with the rest, but God blesses Paisley's ministry and all Hell cannot deny that such is the case. The Free Presbyterian Church is enjoying a meteoric rise and each church emphasizes sound doctrine, soul-winning missionary outreach and separation from apostasy and compromise. A man of God does not need the propaganda and power which Rome enjoys in the World today, one with God is a majority, Paisley like Luther before him, has trust in Almighty God . . . the forces of evil, no matter how firmly arrayed they might be, are doomed to defeat.[13]

Bob Jones University is well known as the vanguard of racism and white supremacy. Its radio station and newspapers waft forth biblical quotations supporting white supremacy and the subordinate position of "the Negro." As one might guess, Bob Jones University is blatantly anti-Catholic and anti-Red. Those so portrayed generally include anyone to the left of George Wallace. The founder of the university, Bob Jones, Sr., was a "big-wig" in the KKK back in the 1920s. When he perceived a cultural drift toward legitimation of racial views through college endorsement, he invested his money in the university he billed "the world's most unusual." Jones was the most popular evangelist of his time. By the age of forty he had converted a million people:

> When he hit town things happened. People didn't just march down to the mourner's bench for an evening's catharsis and then forget it. The fear of God hung over the community long after the Reverend Jones had departed. When he preached in Dothan, Alabama, the people decided to close the brewery, although it was the chief industry. Fifty years later it is still closed.[14]

Jones is an example of the militant Fundamental fervor that flooded the South after World War I. The disappointments of the war, the nativism that it had aroused, the return of Negro soldiers from the front, "uppity" after their freedom abroad, falling agricultural prices, and the return to the dull, listless life of the small

towns—all were responsible for the rise of the KKK in the 1920s.

The Klan was revived by an Alabaman, William Joseph Simmons, who in the darkness of Thanksgiving night 1915, climbed Stone Mountain with a group of friends in white robes. They gathered beside a flag-draped altar with a Bible open to Romans 12. There, "Bathed in the sacred glow of the fiery cross, the invisible empire was called from its slumber of a half a century to take up a new task."[15] The Klan was resuscitated. The newly founded Klan struggled for five years to make converts. But with the nationwide showing of D. W. Griffith's *Birth of a Nation*, heralded by President Wilson as "the pageant that finally told how history should have been written," 100 percent Americanism began to rear its head—hand-in-hand with Klan revival. Simmons had declared: America is no melting pot. It is a garbage can . . . my friends, your government can be changed between the rising and the setting of one sun . . . when hordes of aliens walk to the ballot box and their votes outnumber yours, then the alien horde has got you by the throat.[16]

The South was industrializing. Poor whites were moving to the cities to take up factory jobs. The typical poor white was uprooted and confused. And here was the Negro returning from the war and the immigrants in the North competing with his labor. To the uprooted, the Klan mollified the poor white's sense of confusion and defeat by dubbing him a Knight of the Invisible Empire. To the small shopkeeper and artisan the Klan, with its economic boycott, became a powerful tool in his competition with Jews and Catholics. Like Paisleyism and fascism in general, the KKK was chiefly a phenomenon of the small towns and growing cities, not rural areas:

> The Klan was a means of giving them an instrument with which they could affect their community and become important. The robes, the flaming crosses, the spooky processionals, the kneeling recruits, the occult liturgies, all tapped a deep urge toward mystery and brought drama into the dreary routine of a 1,000 communities.[17]

Wilbur Cash has observed:

> Here in ghostly rides thru the moonlit, aro-

matic evening to whip a negro or a prostitute or some poor white given to violate the 7th commandment . . . to tar and feather a labor organizer or a schoolmaster who had talked his new ideas too much—in slow, swaying noonday parades where every Negro was gone from the streets, and the Jews, Catholics and aliens had their houses and shops shuttered—here was surcease for the personal frustrations and itches of the Klansman of course. But the old coveted, splendid sense of being an heroic blade, a crusader sweeping up mystical slopes for White supremacy, religion, and morality, and all that had made up the faith of the Fathers: of being the direct heir to continuous line of the confederate soldiers at Gettysburg, and of those old Klansmen who had once driven out the carpetbagger and tamed the scalawag; of participating in ritualistic assertion of the South's continuing identity, its will to remain unchanged and defy the ways of the Yankee and the world in favor of that one which had so long been its own.[18]

The Klan in the 1920s was a move against modernization and secularism. In fact, one cannot differentiate between the rise of fundamentalism and the Klan—both were products of the same mentality. The Klan waged war against all immoralists, against Catholics, Jews, and all non-Anglo-Saxons. The "True American" movement was popular in the South during the rise of the Klan; it witnessed one of its proponents, Governor Sidney J. Cats, stand firm against the imminent transfer of the Holy See to Florida. Florida, it would appear, is not so far from Belfast. The True Americans in Birmingham were successful in ousting Catholics from county and municipal jobs.

Both the Orange Order and the Klan, with their ritual and secrecy, were largely derived from the panoply of that other "great" institution, the Masonic Order. Fraternal orders appear to be culturally aligned to the Anglo-Saxon psyche. Like the Orange Order, the Klan had powerful connections with the churches. Charles Alexander in his treatise on the Klan in Texas, *Crusade for Conformity*, has noted that the Klan often took to marching unannounced into Sunday services in order to present the minister with a donation.

The Klan courted the Protestant ministers by making them exempt from payment of initiation fees and dues, by posing as the defender of the conservative moral code, by warring on bootleggers, by contributing money to impoverished preachers and their churches and by urging members of the order to attend church regularly and contribute freely. If Klansmen were to be 100 percent Christians, they had to go to Church every Sunday. Give your support and encouragement to your ministers; send your children to Sunday school.[19]

Like the Orange Order, the KKK entered into politics. In the early 1920s the Klan was in complete control of the cities of Atlanta, Birmingham, Houson, Dallas, Fort Worth, Tulsa, and Little Rock. Thousands of officeholders owed their places to the Klan, and more reached the House and Senate thanks to Klan-delivered votes. Total membership reached a peak of 3 million in 1923; according to another source, 8 million had joined the Klan by 1925.

The Klan's influence in politics faded after 1925. Unlike the Orange Order, the Klan never developed a specific political program, nor did it have a dynamic leadership. After scandals involving the two main organizers of the movement—Clarke and Mrs. Tyler (found carousing in bed together) and the imprisonment of the Grand Wizard for murder and rape—the Klan disintegrated quickly. But the social ideology behind the Klan never faded. It is said that in small towns in rural areas, sheriffs often wear hoods at night when prowling for disobedient blacks. Lynchings, tar and featherings, burnings, all were numerous and inglorious in the 1920s. In the South, the rise of the black civil rights movement witnessed a revival of violence and the reemergence of the Klan. A similar development arose in Northern Ireland with the advent of Catholic civil rights. Paisley's henchmen, militant Orangemen, embarked on an equally violent crusade with disastrous results for the statelet of Northern Ireland.

As we have noted, in the South as in Northern Ireland, politics is controlled by the upper classes to the extent that partisan politics in the current U.S. definition has always been unknown. In fact, black voting registration in Dixie was a mere 5 percent in 1940. By 1950 it had climbed to 20 percent and by 1960 up to 28 percent. Registration reached 44 percent for the 1964 presidential election. However, in many areas registration hovered nearer the earlier figures.[20] Although voting participation has risen considerably among the white population in subsequent elections, often the only participation in the body politic by these poor Protestants is in the area of local law enforcement. In both sections the police and local magistrates are drawn from the lower classes. What this has meant with regard to justice and attempts to achieve civil rights, is violence and bloodshed. In the South today, as in Ulster, the upper classes have organized themselves into "respectable" racist bodies, be they White Citizens' Councils or the upper- and middle-class manipulation of the Orange Order and the recent Vanguard Movement. In both sections these respected bodies and personages, making speeches about law and order, stir the passions of the crowd with attacks on all who oppose their principles—the doctrine of white Anglo-Saxon supremacy. Like the Orange Order, the Citizens' Councils have succeeded where the Klan failed as an institution, and few politicians in the South can be elected without their endorsement.

THE SUBORDINATE MENTALITY

The system that operates in Northern Ireland and the South has served to bolster a subordinate mentality among the discriminated groups in both sections. This phenomenon has been labeled "projection" or "seriality" by many theorists:

> Projection is one of the most common consequences of repression. When an individual attributes to another individual or group those traits and motives which actually threaten his own peace of mind, and when, by so doing, the individual manages to reduce or rationalize away some of his own feelings of guilt, anxiety, or envy, as the case may be, that process is called projection. This psychodynamic process may be found at work in the collective as well as individual behavior, and it is especially prevalent where inter-group, inter-ethnic, and international relations are concerned. Some of the most thoroughly documented examples of projection may be found in case studies of anti-semitism conducted by psychoanalysts and clinical psychologists.[21]

More specifically,

In the South this attitude has produced the Negro "shuffle" while in Northern Ireland, and in all of Ireland prior to independence, the "stage Irishman" was made famous in the English dance halls and plays. It is interesting to note, that during the heyday of English Anglo-Saxon ethnocentrism parallels were frequently drawn between the "childish" Irish and the Negro race. Both the Blacks and the Irish had to be protected from their own inferiorities by a paternalistic Anglo-Saxon race. Both the Blacks and the Irish used this protection and developed it into a self-preservation mechanism. It has become a means whereby one can mask one's own feelings by projecting the stereotype believed by the upper class to be one's own identity.[22]

This mode of psychic operation is passing with the increased militancy of both orders, black and Catholic Irish. The young militants castigate the middle-class and upper-class members of their group for their cooptation by the establishment. The Churches in both sections have served to bolster the doubly-exploitative system by their "pie-in-the-sky" attitude. As well, the history of the established Churches in both sections has been one of close collaboration with the authorities. At times the Churches have not only sanctioned the authorities but also have gone so far as to help suppress movements for freedom.

The complete subordination of both Irish Catholics and Southern blacks over the passage of time has instilled a defeatist attitude in the minds of the most oppressed. In the South attempts at increasing the voting prerogative of the black are still thwarted by black fear, ignorance, and cynicism—especially after Martin Luther King's defeats. Acceptance of a militant stance by Catholics in Northern Ireland has met with similar difficulties. Raising the level of consciousness of both groups is an uphill task for militants in both sections.

FINAL REMARKS

In conclusion then, the class–racial structure found in the American South shares many similarities with a social structure operating in Northern Ireland. This paper has attempted to demonstrate that these similarities are not merely coincidental. They are the product of ethnocentrism and like economic exploitive systems. The Anglo-Saxon culture that gives the South its distinctive institutions is derived from the parent culture developed in the nine counties of Ulster. The mentality that produced the Anglo-Saxon value system put into operation a class–ethnic system to bolster the dominant economic position of the upper classes.

The cleavages instituted by this exploitative system are bearing fruit in both quarters. Class consciousness continues to be thwarted by the supremacy values of the dominant class–racial group. Few inroads have been made in uniting the lower classes of both "races." In fact, the opposite effect predominates. The insecurity of status (both position and prestige) in the face of subordinate group militance has driven the lower classes of the dominant group to right-wing ideology. The upper orders continue to rule the roost. Principles of "divide and rule" still govern class relationships in Northern Ireland and in the southern United States, and will no doubt continue to do so for some time.

CONCLUSIONS

In emphasizing power wielded from above we have neglected to consider how people have and can organize at the grass roots to implement social change. We have also neglected to specify in depth problems around which people do organize. In the next chapter we deal with this problem by emphasizing organizing from the bottom up on questions such as housing.

NOTES

1. James G. Leyburn, *The Scotch-Irish* (Chapel Hill: University of North Carolina Press, 1962), p. 51.
2. Howard Mumford Jones, "The Colonial Idea in England," in *Three American Empires* (New York: Harper, 1967), p. 37.
3. Gary N. Jessen, dissertation in progress, *Black Community Life in the British West Indies*, University of California, Davis, Calif.
4. A. N. J. Den Hollander, "The Tradition of 'Poor Whites,' " in W. T. Couch (Ed.), *Culture in the South* (Chapel Hill, University of North Carolina Press, 1934), pp. 412–413.
5. Victor Perlo, *The Negro in Southern Agriculture* (New York, International Publishers), 1953, p. 79.
6. Allison Davis and Burleigh Gardner, *Deep South* (Chicago: University of Chicago Press), 1941, pp. 425–426.
7. James McEvoy, *Radicals or Conservatives? The Contemporary American Right* (Chicago: Rand McNally, 1971), p. 155.
8. *Ibid.*, p. 155.

9. George Brown Tindall, *The Emergence of the New South*, Vol. X, *History of the South*, (Baton Rouge: Louisiana State University Press, 1967), p. 196.
10. Liston Pope, *Mill Hands and Preachers*, Yale Studies in Religious Education (New Haven, Yale University Press, 1942), p. 108.
11. James Winder Good, *Ulster and Ireland* (Dublin and London: Maunsel, 1919), p. 156.
12. *Protestant Telegraph*, July 11, 1970, p. 1.
13. Ronald Cooke, *The Thunder of Papal Propaganda* (Pasadena, Calif., 1969), pp. 13–15.
14. Robert Sherrill, *Gothic Politics in the Deep South* (New York, Grossman, 1968), p. 218.
15. Tindall, *op. cit.*, p. 187. (from testimony by W. J. Simmons, Hearings before the Committee on Rules, the Ku Klux Klan, House of Representatives, 67 Congress, 1 Session, 1921.)
16. *Ibid.*, p. 190.
17. *Ibid.*, p. 191.
18. Wilbur Cash, *The Mind of the South* (New York: Knopf, 1941), p. 337.
19. Charles C. Alexander, *Crusade for Conformity: The Ku Klux Klan in Texas 1920–1930*, Texas Gulf Coast Historical Association Publication Series VI, Houston, 1962, p. 102.
20. Sherrill, *op. cit.*, p. 306.
21. L. P. Curtis, Jr., *Anglo-Saxons and Celts*, Bridgeport, Conference on British Studies, University of Bridgeport, Connecticut, 1968, p. 6.
22. Celia Karch, M.A. thesis [University of California (Davis)], *Northern Ireland: The Development of a Pre-Revolutionary Society*, December, 1971.

BIBLIOGRAPHY

Cash, Wilbur. *The Mind of The South*, New York: Knopf, 1941.

Cooke, Ronald. *Thunder of Papal Propaganda*, Pasadena, Calif., 1967.

Curtis, L. P., Jr. *Anglo-Saxons and Celts*, Bridgeport, Conference on British Studies, University of Bridgeport, Connecticut, 1968.

Couch, W. T. (Ed.). *Culture in the South*, Chapel Hill: The University of North Carolina Press, 1934.

Davis, Allison; and Gardner Burleigh. *Deep South*, Chicago: University of Chicago Press, 1941.

Good, J. W. *Ulster and Ireland*, Dublin & London: Maunsel, 1919.

Higham, John. *Strangers in the Land*, New Brunswick, N. J.: Rutgers University Press, 1955.

Jackson, Kenneth. *The Ku Klux Klan in the City 1915–1930*, New York: Oxford University Press, 1967.

Jones, Howard Mumford. "The Colonial Idea in England," in *Three American Empires*, New York: Harper, 1967.

McEvoy, James. *Radicals or Conservatives?*, Chicago: Rand McNally, 1971.

Pope, Liston. *Mill Hands and Preachers*, Yale Studies in Religious Education, Vol. XV, New Haven, Yale University Press, 1942.

Protestant Telegraph, Ravenhill Rd., Belfast, Northern Ireland, 1971.

Sherrill, Robert. *Gothic Politics in the Deep South*, New York: Grossman, 1968.

Tannebaum, Frank. *Darker Phases of the South*, New York, Putnam, 1924.

Tindall, George Brown. *The Emergence of the New South, 1913–1945*, Vol. X, *History of the South* Baton Rouge: Louisiana State University Press, 1967.

Wakefield, Dan. *Revolt in the South*, New York, Grove, 1960.

Chapter 14 From the Bottom Up

Section One	*Context and Technique*

ORGANIZING AGAINST LARGE-SCALE ORGANIZATIONS

Political potential of the oppressed. How can it be realized? More specifically in the years ahead how can incipient grass-roots groups best organize the alienated on the neighborhood and residential-district levels against large-scale organizations? It is our task to diagnose, at this level, the nature of bureaucratic opposition and allies, to suggest grass-roots strategies, and to comment on the difficulties of implementation. In so doing, we will rely on the experiences of twenty years.

One of the problems encountered in organizing at the grass roots involves the overwhelming sense of hopelessness common to the alienated. Those beset by multiple problems time and again assume that it is impossible to alter the structures around them. At first glance, this assumption does seem to be correct. Witness the multiple failures in the 1960s of block and neighborhood associations ·to survive, let alone restructure communities.

With these failures in mind, we will add to our analysis the need for the role of a vanguard party and a militant union on matters of organizing grass-roots persons judged to be almost universally lacking in a sense of their own ability to create and to use various forms of power.

Despite this assumption of widespread sense of hopelessness, however, we do not view these blue-collar people as without class, racial, and class—racial consciousness. Paradoxically, there are many who simultaneously believe that the situation is hopeless but also hold that they would take part in direct action, should the proper occasion arise. And when a high degree

■ I am indebted to Eugene Litwak for this chapter's major ideas.

of class or class—racial consciousness exists among the ambivalent, even they sometimes act. The question is when.

It is our judgment that how vanguard parties, neighborhood organizations, and militant industrial unions relate to these persons will largely determine whether grass-roots people will eventually become activated and organized. Of course any popular involvement occurs in a milieu replete with large-scale organizations, which also have goals, strategies, enemies, and allies. Hence we treat grass-roots groups as they surface in a world where bureaucratic friends and opponents have become all too visible.

The traditional literature on large-scale organizations discusses them in terms of form, not content. The skeleton rather than the blood and guts of large-scale organization too frequently receives our attention. It is as if large-scale organizations in our country were without pro-capitalist bias, when in fact most of them support capitalism in various ways. We have tried to make this point in previous chapters, especially 9 through 13. We have commented on private business corporations and how they relate reciprocally to the state. But we have said little about large-scale organizations, both private and state. We must now compensate for this neglect, for we need to understand both content *and shape* if we are to be able to confront large-scale groups in order to extract concessions from them during the present period. In dealing with problems faced by grass-roots, action-oriented neighborhood groups, we focus on both bureaucratic content and form.

When seeking this synthesis, we can observe that our upper classes depend heavily on most of the large-scale organizations typical of advanced industrial societies of capitalist bent: many trade unions, business organizations, and state and local governments come to mind. To-gether they constitute the institutionalized ba-sis for socialization and control, each organiza-tion being guided by principled partisans from both the establishment and its service person-nel. Both groups have been analyzed by writers such as G. William Domhoff. Although Dom-hoff's analysis is certainly instructive, he ne-glected the forms of authority structure com-mon to large-scale organizations. We need not do so, especially when dwelling on domestic cyclical combat between ghetto populations and business organizations.

THE STRUGGLE PERSISTS

It is sometimes said that this battle no longer exists, since the U.S. business establishment has sought and found a racial enlightenment which no longer tolerates discrimination in hiring practices. True, a fraction of the business com-munity no longer discriminates; but we must not confuse the smidgeon with the totality. Again, some would argue that what has oc-curred has been a shift from class–racial strug-gle between proletarian minorities and upper-class WASPs to internecine warfare involving racial minorities and working-class whites. Cer-tainly such a struggle goes on within blue-collar ranks, and its continuous character deepens tra-ditional cleavages among various sectors of the working class. However, the intensification of such a conflict over a decade or more does not preclude class–racial struggle between marginal working-class and high-status upper-class groups. Both forms of struggle—within the working class and between it and the owners of strategic resources—can and do occur, and both must be taken into account by those working to eliminate traditional forms of oppression.

And the conflict between classes can be mounted by coalitions of working-class minori-ties working with progressives from various class strata within the white population. This coalition, however, need not confine its activi-ties to formal party and pressure group politics, as some writers have suggested. For there are times when people feel that they must bypass formal parties and pressure groups and take to the streets in order to have an impact during crises. Illustrative have been mass actions asso-ciated with tenants' strikes and tenement take-

overs in the Bronx and Manhattan. In some cases tenement dwellers took the lead and ob-tained considerable support for their activities from the Young Lords (a militant Puerto Rican youth group) and like organizations, as the alliance confronted both landlords and police. The issues have included the right to occupy and run buildings condemned for urban renewal but not yet razed for that purpose.

When dealing with matters of large-scale or-ganizations, whether realty firms, police organi-zations, school administrations, or like groups, we might find it worthwhile to take the tradi-tional formulations concerned with bureau-cratic leadership and stand them on their heads, thereby allowing us to help people traditionally defined as subjects to become manipulative actors in the class–racial struggle. For indeed, tenants have on occasion initiated and sustained attacks on landlords and city officials. They have taken the puck to the other end of the ice. In this sense, we can define large-scale organiza-tions as targets, the units to be manipulated. If we take this analytical course, we will find many of the ideas advanced by Max Weber,[1] as well as the more current notions of writers such as Eugene Litwak,[2] to be of great use.

The following skeletal analysis is replete with ideal-typical distinctions designed to be helpful in mapping political territory and strat-egy. Needless to say, no revolutionary formulas come to mind. Just incremental possibilities seem to be in order, especially at present, when the mood among the oppressed appears to be so similar to Thermidor.

THE INCEPTION OF BLOCK CLUBS

Since the early 1930s, grass-roots organiza-tions have emerged and become important in American big-city politics. The grass-roots neigh-borhood groups have been of two general types: middle class (based on white-collar membership and concerned with social reform) and working class (based on blue-collar people who are con-

[1] See Max Weber, "Bureaucracy," in H. H. Gerth and C. Wright Mills, Eds., *From Max Weber: Essays in Sociology* (New York: Oxford University Press, 1946), pp. 196–266.
[2] Eugene Litwak, "Models of Bureaucracy Which Permit Conflict," *American Journal of Sociology,* Vol. 67, September, 1961, pp. 177–184.

cerned with both social control and social change). It is to be observed that in both class situations middle- and working-class intellectuals have played important roles. These political and quasi-political persons and organizations have been extremely active in American cities including New York, St. Louis, Detroit, Chicago, and San Francisco. In New York, both types of clubs have flourished. In St. Louis, the Teamsters Union worked during the mid-1960's to establish blue-collar groups. In Chicago, neighborhood improvement associations and neighborhood youth organizations, especially those given initial impetus and guidance by Saul Alinsky (see the Alinsky reading in Section Two) have formed. In San Francisco, the Hunter's Point and Fillmore districts have experienced considerable organization. In Detroit, hundreds of block clubs have been established—at times with city support—inside and on the periphery of the city's various black ghettos. It is in Detroit that block clubs have done well both in terms of numbers and longevity and where I did considerable research on the subject matter (described in the Leggett reading in Section Two). Our model of neighborhoods is based largely on the Detroit experience. Yet Detroit is but part of a larger, worldwide setting that must be kept in mind, as we speculate on the generality of the Detroit generalizations.

A number of writers have commented on the domestic costs of imperialism. They have observed that imperialism cannot wage costly adventures abroad and simultaneously afford social democracy at home. One of the two must be neglected, and since the end of World War II that neglect has been most obvious in black ghettos, where a string of palliatives has characterized the relations of concerned reformers to the oppressed ghetto residents. These "war on poverty" bromides have failed to solve complex problems such as housing. But the ameliorative efforts fostered the growth of organizations with the potential of supporting the rebirth of neighborhoods.

Neighborhood councils and block clubs, then, were initially the creation of subelite reformers, largely reformist city politicians, planners, social workers, and social scientists. The reason was clear. Central city officials and their subelite subordinates have faced many problems over the last two decades; two of these

have been "urban blight" and crime. These problems have occurred partly because many individuals in the central cities do not or cannot police their own blocks and neighborhoods as well as residential districts. (Here *a block* is a zone characterized by social relations between contiguous families found within an area enclosed by several streets; *a neighborhood* can be defined as a zone containing clusters of contiguous blocks linked together by their informal representatives; *a residential district* is a zone consisting of many contiguous neighborhoods having a common history and set of interests.)

From the point of view of many reformers, the problems of neighborhood deterioration and heightened crime, and their corollary—the flight of the well-heeled residents to the suburbs, continue to be of signal importance. This is partly because city officials, even when they have a cogent program and a modest resource base, cannot reach the families located in many neighborhoods, especially the slums. Few if any organizations provide liaison between public officials and blacks located in working-class districts. That is, from the point of view of liberal technocracy, in most towns there has been a lack of voluntary associations that could make a connection between city officials, administrators, and planners and the citizens in working-class neighborhoods largely composed of racial minorities.

What this perspective overlooks, of course, is that although the city elite may be able to relate to people through clubs, there is no guarantee that the local organizations will remain subservient to the demands and expectations of the bureaucracy. Once established, such groups may develop and retain, for however short a time, sufficient autonomy to bring them to the point of attacking their creators. Thus a benevolent city officialdom may spawn its own potential critics. In the chapter's readings we learn how and when these block clubs may become politically independent and critical and how, perhaps, they be linked to insurgent urban movements.

With these matters in mind, let us return to the question posed earlier: How can incipient grass-roots groups best struggle on the neighborhood and residential district levels against large-scale organizations. Clearly, we assume that nothing will happen unless the people are organized at the grass roots around their everyday problems. But block clubs by themselves will not change a great deal of what's wrong with any given ghetto. Left to themselves, block clubs can become and remain simple service organizations to be used as the city elites see fit. There must be a political component—as we learned in Detroit. This component should comprise counterelite committees, not necessarily formalized. Its key members should consist of militants, including the radical working-class intellectuals who live in the neighborhoods and belong to the block clubs. They must take a lively part in all the activities and work to mobilize the clubs for political purposes whenever and wherever necessary.

The counterelite committee can suitably be organized along the lines of democratic centralism, as recommended by two people with a long history of intensive participations in Detroit's block-club movement (see the Boggs reading in Section Two). For, as these authors put it, unless local radicals organize themselves as a disciplined vanguard unit, nothing will change. Recurrent spontaneous uprisings of ghetto residents will be unable to alter structures.

MECHANISMS OF PERSUASION AND LEADERSHIP

Despite the apparent pitfalls, if such a counterelite committee were established, it could relate to block clubs and their periphery through a wide variety of mechanisms of persuasion in order to apply pressure on state and private bureaucratic organizations, including businesses, business unions, and governments.

In turn, the counterelite group could be part of a larger vanguard party organization with sufficient resources to link block clubs and neighborhood associations to militant industrial unions (see Figure 6). Such a linkage could make possible, though certainly never guarantee, militant union services to grass-roots groups in need of union lawyers, advice, loans, boycott cooperation, and other forms of aid. This relationship would of course be a delicate one, for the counterelite committee activity might be perceived by the rank and file as misappropriation of union funds and other resources. However, there might be a great deal to gain by telling the truth about the use of the funds. Let the organizers convince the rank and file of the necessity of helping others. Rank-and-file unionists should be taught the need to aid those who are down and out by union standards. In this sense, such union activity could help to build a sense of *esprit de corps* within the working class and diminish that unhealthy attitude, so typical of craft unions in spirit and so ugly in content; namely, me first and others later—if ever.

These complex relationships between disciplined political party, union rank and file, and local clubs involve other hazards as well, and we discuss many of them at the end of this chapter. Suffice it to say that if the relationship is simply a one-way affair, i.e., if communications

FIGURE 6   Vanguard Party and its Direct and Transitive Relations to Block-Club Members.

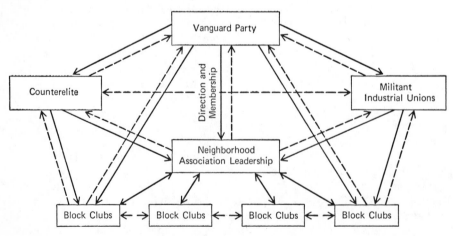

flow from the vanguard party to those below, the net result might be the quick transformation of a fresh, young, vanguard party into a middle-aged crank political sect. Hence the information should always flow in two ways—from the people, to the people. This rule should always be kept in mind when the counterelite makes choices on the following mechanisms of persuasion:

1. Rallies
2. Direct pressure
3. Direct action
4. The bloc vote
5. Bypass the subelite
6. The front group
7. The boycott
8. The common messenger

1. *Rallies* are simply mass meetings. Ideally they generate enthusiasm, solidarity, and funds. They are also useful for publicity and group recruitment purposes. Often this device has its greatest impact when the counterelite group can associate the name of a celebrity with a common cause and publicize the issue through the mass media. As a technique, however, the rally has certain weaknesses, as we shall see.

2. *Direct pressure* takes the form of several delegates from one or more of the local organizations directly confronting political and other authorities during decision-making meetings and then demanding permission for the delegates to present their positions before the gathering. Often this tactic is referred to as "confronting," a device often accompanied by acrimonious exchanges between authorities representing block clubs and ancillary groups such as left-wing political associations (imagine a Board of Education meeting packed by such delegates).

3. *Direct action* occurs when social mechanisms designed to cushion relations between social structures are ignored by groups using collective force as a means of bringing the operations of target groups to a halt. Direct action differs from direct pressure in that direct pressure emphasizes changing the character of the discussion rather than disrupting all activities. Direct action is organized to halt normal, ongoing activities. Direct action can assume a variety of forms, including sit-ins and lie-ins. Direct action may or may not involve the breaking of

the law (civil disobedience) or instant physical injury (violence). To repeat, direct action occurs, by definition, when the struggle for organizational control and reward allocation takes place outside the normal political processes, and militant actors halt ongoing activities. For example, under most circumstances, voting is not a form of direct action, but picketing landlords or engaging in a sit-down strike would be so considered if the intent were to bring an operation to a halt.

4. *The bloc vote* may be used to elect politicians friendly to the group's point of view, or at least to oust the greater of the evils. The technique consists of efforts to mobilize familial and gang groups within a block (or neighborhood or residential district) behind a person or party in an election.

5. *Bypassing the subelite* takes place when the grass-roots leadership seeks to convince an eminent political authority located one or more organizational levels above the group or person from whom the dissidents are attempting to exact a particular decision. The technique is marked by efforts to obtain an elite judgment which is both positive and binding on those in secondary power-wielding positions. If such persuasion of a top figure is followed by a favorable decision, the neighborhood leadership can celebrate its victory, perhaps through a rally, and thereby enhance the prestige of both the association and the counterelite groups.

6. *The front group* consists of an association established by the counterelite group to draw together rank-and-file members and block-club friends within a formal collectivity led by hardcore organizers who are directly responsible to both their own vanguard organizations and the front group's rank-and-file located within their particular constituencies—be they block clubs or some other grass roots collectivity. Of course, the degree to which any group is centrally controlled, or decentrally democratized, varies. Irrespective of this consideration, the front group has one important characteristic: whether the group is to be sacked or allowed to remain is determined ultimately by the hardcore political organizers, hopefully with the interests of the grass-roots collectivity in mind. Quite frequently, however, this tough choice does not exist, for the front-group itself often withers on the vine to the lament of organizers

committed to its continuation. While alive, however, the front group should exude the scent of independence.

7. *The boycott* occurs when a collectivity withholds, wholly or in part, business or some other form of intercourse with another group. An example would be the successful grape boycott mounted during the mid- and late 1960s by the Delano strikers.

8. *The common messenger* refers to a conveyor of a printed message—generally in leaflet form—between two persons. For example, when a child brings home his report card, both parents and school authorities are articulated through the child.

One final word. The counterelite group can direct the use of one or more of the foregoing mechanisms either at one point in time or in series.

Given these mechanisms, what circumstances foster the emergence of a population capable of grasping and then using these means to fashion change?

THE EMERGENCE OF A MILITANT GRASS-ROOTS MOVEMENT

When we ask where a militant grass-roots movement is likely to appear, no ready answers appear, as we have observed earlier. Still, three conditions seem to be associated with the emergence of a left-democratic movement with political potential:

1. *Positive material conditions,* which create consciousness, in that they link the life chances of the person's key primary groups such as the family to the operation of social institutions and economic organizations in the community.

2. *A concrete ideology,* which delineates the real world of enemies and alternatives.

3. *Opinion leaders,* who help to create class, racial, or class–racial consciousness and to translate inchoate solutions into concrete answers of a programmatic sort.

Essentially, if the analyst assumes that the cited three conditions are important, he faces three questions:

1. What conditions heighten consciousness of the relation between economic, political, and social institutions on the one hand and primary-group life chances on the other?

2. Does the concrete ideology in question clearly specify a realistic organizational solution for the group that has become fully class-conscious?

3. Is there a militant local opinion leader present to translate rational anger into effective response?

Concrete ideology and militant opinion leaders, by themselves, will not cause a grass-roots group to emerge. In addition, consciousness is necessary. Of course, local leadership can maximize consciousness through interpretive activities, but consciousness would appear to be based on five interrelated circumstances:

1. *Basic inequalities* in the distribution of wealth, power, and status, stemming in great part from the character of property relationships and the operation of bureaucratic organizations

2. *The spatial concentration* of a subordinate population both culturally homogeneous and socially isolated in areas bordering on more affluent neighborhoods, thus presenting vivid contrasts in the outward symbols of wealth, power, and status

3. *A growth in various forms of economic insecurity,* which is paralleled by an increase in formal education for the group as a whole

4. *Group discussion of problems within the context of primary groups* articulated to one another and isolated from everyone else except through secondary ties. This isolation includes remote ties with holders of corporate private property, either within or beyond the neighborhood.

5. *Minimal problems of social control faced by these primary groups.* Here we assume that when a group faces multiple problems of thievery, drug control, and alcoholism, for example, groups such as block clubs and industrial union locals will focus largely on problems of social control, thereby neglecting the forces exterior to the block or neighborhood that create problems. In this context, persons often ignore the consequences of the operations of propertied organizations and ancillary institutions. Individual tend to personalize their own problems in accounting for a neighborhood's behavior—for example, by referring to their neighborhood as

queer or to its members as odd. When a group focuses largely and continuously on immediate problems of social control, this group has few remaining resources and little time to arrive at class-conscious interpretations on the social sources of its problems.

Again a combination of the foregoing circumstances maximizes the formation of consciousness.

Let us now bring together some of the considerations already discussed, as indicated in Table 34. In the case of the first alternative (*A* in Table 34), we can observe a population with the potentiality of making a major contribution to the emergence of a militant grass-roots group. The level of consciousness among the rank and file is high, and the local opinion leaders are militant in terms of consciousness and action. These opinion leaders initiate the discussions of local and other issues with their neighbors. They convince individuals not only on the basis of credibility of the argument presented but through the use of primary ties with their listeners and informers. In each instance, the opinion leader is Mr. Sensitivity

Man, the person who senses as he articulates ideas in ways that allow him to activate people and to reinforce and change attitudes. The opinion leader can sometimes "con" nonmilitant persons on the basis of affection, although there are limits to his manipulative effectiveness. Thus people sometimes act contrary to their narrow self-interests, as they see them, *when* they are bound in friendly relations with an opinion leader, e.g., a precinct captain, a ward heeler—or a block-club president. Indeed, the opinion leader can sometimes use affection as the basis to turn nonmilitant people out for a political rally, march, picnic, or demonstration.

In Situation *B,* the opinion leaders can be both divisive and decisive. In a setting where the community at large may be moving toward potential involvement in struggle, the antimilitants may attempt to convince friends, even militant opinion leaders, not to support the emergence of grass-roots groups such as tenants'-rights associations. Unfortunately for the radicals, the opinion leaders can wield influence sufficient to create severe ambivalence among those who both respect the opinon leader's views *yet* side with the idea of people moving

TABLE 34 Likelihood of Emergence of Grass-Roots Movement Based on Block Clubs According to Various Combinations of Constants and Variables

Constants: *Block clubs, militant counter-elite groups, mechanisms of persuasion, and clear ideological solutions*

Variables: *Militant or antimilitant opinion leaders*

Level of Consciousness Among Rank-and-File	Situation	
	Militant Opinion Leaders	Antimilitant Opinion Leaders
High	*A*— Population capable of high degree of emergent activity	*B*— Population will be ambivalent
Medium	*C*— Population capable of medium degree of emergent activity	*D*— Population capable of limited emergent activity
Low	*E*— Population capable of low degree of emergent activity	*F*— Nothing happening

against the target in question. Admittedly, in this context, militant persons might consciously consider and set aside the opinion leader's wishes, but not without considerable ambivalence.

MILITANT UNIONS CAN HELP

Rather than discuss the four other situations of Table 34, it might be wise at this point to stress the importance of militant unions in the emergence of such grass-roots groups. Militant unions furnish a milieu in which direct action and like techniques can be viewed as normal by grass-roots people. Militant industrial unions can also make available persons trained to create and direct their own associations against those with propertied and political power. Militant unions such as the UAW thirty years ago and Local 1199 (of the New York–Central New Jersey hospital workers union) of today can provide class-conscious opinion leaders. Money, legal services, joint undertakings, and helpful advice can be organized by union leadership plus the rank and file. Again, when working-class people successfully create and maintain a union local, they help to undercut the generalized, alienated feeling that blue-collar people cannot beat the propertied and/or city hall. A militant union can also deliver, if only for a limited time, the full-time organizers who are crucial in carrying a grass-roots group from the level of emergence, through sustained existence, to mobilization against targets. However, before a militant union can have this input, it must itself be organized politically from within by a vanguard political party concerned with the lower elective levels of the union local. There, the vanguard party people can more readily relate to the rank and file with an ideology consistent with a class-conscious perspective. In this context, elected persons, such as union chief stewards, must teach blue-collar people to see the world of the opponent not only as a carrier of exploitation but as an oppressor *whose effectiveness varies in part because of its structural composition.* That being the case, it is necessary to know how to recognize the variety of bureaucratic structures. And this requires a typology on large-scale organizations.

THE CHARACTER OF BUREAUCRATIC OPPOSITIONS AND ALLIES

The character of bureaucratic organization can be delineated by radicals in terms of structure, goals, and behavior.

TABLE 35   Aspects and Types of Bureaucratic Organizations

Aspects of Organization	Type of Bureaucratic Organization		
	Rationalistic	Human Relations	Professional
Hierarchy or colleague	Hierarchy	Colleague	Both
Role specified or diffuse	Specified	Diffuse	Both
Functions Specified or diffuse	Specified	Diffuse	Both
Merit or nonmerit	Merit	Merit	Merit
Formal or informal	Formal	Informal	Both

On the level of structure, a useful distinction can be made between three types of bureaucratic organizations: rationalistic, humanistic, and professional (see Table 35 and Chapter 10).

The rationalistic bureaucracy is *identical* with the Weberian model (see note 1). Briefly, it is a large-scale organization marked by (*a*) formal and hierarchical relationships, (*b*) highly specified roles and departmental functions and procedures, and (*c*) selection, promotion, and dismissal of personnel on the basis of achievement. It is gauged in terms of measured success.

This organization is most effective in predictable situations requiring knowledge in traditional areas. Thus a rationalistic police organization would perhaps be most effective in white working-class neighborhoods marked by a relatively low incidence of crime and a high degree of traditional allegiance to the maintenance of controls over all ethnic group members on the question of minimization of violent crime inside the neighborhood. This maintenance is based primarily on a traditional respect for law and order and a willingness to cooperate with the police, who derive their strength from an ethnic-religious–based tendency to obey.

On the other hand, when dealing with non-uniform and unpredictable events—such as the arrival of a new and volatile working-class ethnic group in a neighborhood—a rationalistic police organization would be least effective, for the police would act rigidly when dealing with the new population. Because of this woodenness, the many police departments in large cities such as New York have created human relations departments at the local levels. These human relations subunits in many ways resemble the human relations model of bureaucracy.

Unlike the rationalistic form, the *human relations* bureaucracy occurs most frequently where all levels of personnel must cope with unpredictable events and where the staff should use manipulative skills. Although this bureaucracy does contain a hierarchy, many relations are nominally egalitarian, informal, and affective, especially among persons on the same or contiguous levels. Interdepartmental relations are easy-going; nonetheless, and along with the rationalistic bureaucracy, this organization also selects and promotes people on the basis of merit.

Most survey research centers are excellent illustrations of the human relations prototype. The emphasis here is on purpose realization (not procedural regulation), task accomplishment (not conformity), and investment of skills in professional persons (not specification of tasks in assigned roles). Clearly the human relations bureaucracy performs best in areas characterized by a high degree of unpredictability, for the flexibility of the organization allows full use of skilled personnel. Illustrative would be the ability of survey research organizations to adjust rapidly and successfully to subgroup and individual opposition among those being interviewed, or the propensity of the same kind of organization to slide sharply up and down in terms of size of internal organization, depending on the current funding of an often unpredictable payroll.

The *professional bureaucracy* stands as a synthesis of the rationalistic and human relations types, uniting them in one organizational framework. Thus when certain departments require traditional knowledge areas and deal with uniform events, they lean toward the creation of highly structured and formalized relations, as in the processing of an arrested person. At the same time, other departments within the same organization depend heavily on social skills for dealing with the unpredictable and the unmanageable, e.g., the police removal of tenant squatters or rent-strikers. Hence these sub-divisions hew to the human relations model. Another illustration comes to mind. Many universities are organized along professional bureaucratic lines, having a rationalistic registrar's office. But by contrast, the dean's office is orga-

TABLE 36 Goals and Behavior of Bureaucratic Organizations

Behavior	Goals	
	Favors Change	*Does Not Favor Change*
Tries to bring about social change	All-weather liberal organization	Timid conservative organization
Does not try to bring about social change	Fair-weather liberal organization	Consistent conservative organization

nized to allow maximum flexibility on such questions as university hiring of minorities and women.

But specification of structure, as in Table 35, is not enough. In addition, we must sketch briefly the goals and behavior of bureaucratic organizations. Drawing from a simple distinction made by many sociologists (see Table 36), we can type bureaucratic organizations as:

1. All-weather liberal organizations
2. Fair-weather liberal groups
3. Timid conservative organizations
4. Consistent conservative organizations

THE AVOIDANCE OF ERRORS

When dealing with bureaucratic organizations, whether they are friends or allies, the grass-roots group must strive to avoid certain errors, and as we have already suggested, this may require the political acumen of people who have had labor union and left-political experiences. Briefly, these errors are: absorption through coalition, and loss through compromise of essentials.

In the case of "absorption" through coalition, the counterelite group inadvertently allows the bureaucratic organization to capture the framework of friendly alliance,—that is, to take over the grass-roots group through the manipulation of a united front. This capture can be accomplished in a variety of ways, including the following:

1. *Coalition and formal absorption.* Here the bureaucratic group amalgamates the entire grass-roots group as an organic part of a larger, formal, public, legally constituted structure, as when an independent block club becomes part of a city's department of city planning.

2. *Coalition and gradual assimilation.* This process occurs initially through united front cooptation of the protest group's leaders, then later through enlistment of the rank and file. For example, block club officers might become paid civil administrators of a poverty program, and this would lead to ordinary members receiving lesser amounts of largesse, such as part-time antipoverty jobs. Here the ranks are gradually absorbed into the larger public organizations.

3. *Coalition and seizure of power* is a case of the "friendly" bureaucracy simply, dramati-

cally, and quickly seizing the reins within the grass-roots group by a means such as supporting one local faction against another. In this instance the bureaucracy may allow the grass-roots association to survive nominally, although in fact the bureaucracy calls the shots through a leadership it controls.

The second major way a grass-roots organization can lose is through *compromise of essentials.* Here the group simply dumps its goals as the price of continued organizational maintenance. This accommodation can often be brought about by a large-scale organization by simply threatening to withdraw from the grass-roots group the funds on which the local group had become dependent. For example, if a tenants'-rights organization allowed itself to become dependent on a salary source originating in government bureaus, the government could threaten to eliminate this source when the subsidized grass-roots group acted counter to the perceived interests of the salary-dispensing group, which time and again proves to be a professional bureaucratic organization with a fair-weather liberal inclination.

But why should bureaucratic allies of liberal persuasion undercut a grass-roots organization? What is to be gained? Briefly, monopoly of services.

A militant block-club group and its allies can expect decided opposition from bureaucratic allies, partly because a bureaucratic organization irrespective of ideology values the importance of working through the formal machinery provided either by it or by other bureaucratic organizations. Since bureaucratic organizations like to pursue normal procedures in solving problems, they devalue direct action and resort to techniques subscribed to by militant counterelite groups. This, of course, is because bureaucrats view the efforts of grass-roots movements as providing courses of action alternative to those rendered by bureaucratic organizations in general, and liberal organizations in particular. These alternatives include such measures as the initiation of a Black Panther (or block club or church group) breakfast program, as well as the maintenance of the program once it has been started.

Bureaucratic organizations devalue militant organizations dispensing services in the community, for the militant groups such as the Panthers thereby invade the traditional task-territory of the welfare organizations and suggest not only the utility of a radical alternative but the dispensability of the traditional welfare, bureaucratic organization. It is conceivable, for example, that should the Black Panther Party today continue to pursue its currently adopted and moderate strategy, city governments such as those of Berkeley and even San Francisco might prefer to channel funds and benefits through the Panther welfare programs rather than traditional government agencies. The next step is clear. Under these circumstances, the state could lessen its funding for the traditional bureaucratic organization in the same way that it absorbed the grass roots group through coalition devices or created a new agency headed and staffed by eager liberals. And of course, a concurrent diminution of funds or personnel for the traditional bureaucratic service group could only weaken its coercive power and overall status. Hence the traditional agency always keeps its grass roots covered by falling back on the formulas of amalgamation and assimilation wherever possible.

THE INTRINSIC QUALITIES OF MECHANISMS OF PERSUASION

Along with the foregoing general considerations on possible strategic errors, the intrinsic qualities of mechanisms of persuasion must be kept in mind when dealing with bureaucratic organizations, liberal and conservative alike. For unless the counterelite can assess its mechanisms of persuasion, the group may fail in its efforts to make correct prescriptions and implementations.

The intrinsic qualities associated with mechanisms of persuasion can be specified in terms of the following criteria:

1. Personal initiative
2. Focus
3. Intensity
4. Scope

1. *Personal initiative* denotes the amount of a person-to-person contact between *the initiator* of contact and *the person* who received the message. Here we have in mind a one-to-one relationship. In this setting, the initiator of contact must seek out the person who is to receive the message. We can treat all eight mechanisms

of persuasion (rallies, direct action, etc.) as high, medium, or low. For example, direct pressure is a mechanism with a high degree of personal initiative. By contrast, a rally is a mechanism with a low degree, for little if any person-to-person contact is initiated by the rally's speakers.

2. *Focus* refers to the degree to which a mechanism lends itself to a logical, knowledgable, precise statement of a problem. A mechanism high in this attribute is "bypass the sub-elite," for the argument can go forward and lead to an exchange which can refine positions. At the other extreme is the bloc vote, where people move collectively on the basis of multiple and long-term predispositions based on general arguments which are difficult to refine once they have been crystallized for electoral purposes. Indeed, the hoopla of electoral campaigns may do more to confuse the issues as originally defined than to clarify them. The boycott is a mechanism in the middle. Here rational discussion and mass appeal operate simultaneously, allowing for some refinement as the prolonged effort proceeds.

3. *Intensity* has reference to the amount of affect typical of the mechanism. The rally and direct action are high in this regard. By contrast, the common messenger carries less affective sting, for the contact is not direct; the mechanism does not involve immediate interpersonal relations, whether in a crowd or a small setting.

Where rational cognition can readily supplement interpersonal affect, the double-binding phenomenon can be powerful, as in direct pressure. In this instance, an informed and angry throng could confront formal state or corporate authority through mass-supported counterelites. By contrast, a transitive relationship (one where person A acts as intermediary between B and C) invites a more dispassionate appraisal. An example of this kind of relationship would be the common-messenger type of situation in which a police officer specially trained in human relations was used to serve eviction notices on tenants when a landlord himself would be hesitant to approach tenants, let alone act to evict them.

4. *Scope* refers to the number of people contacted, the bulk of humanity reached by a message. Mechanisms high in scope are the boy-

TABLE 37 Mechanisms of Persuasion and Criteria for Their Evaluation: The Stage of Emergence

	Mechanisms of Persuasion							
Criteria for Evaluation	*Rallies*	*Direct Pressure*	*Direct Action (Sit-in)*	*The Bloc Vote*	*Bypass the Subelite*	*The Front Group*	*The Boycott*	*The Common Messenger*
Personal initiative	Low	High	Medium	Medium	High	High	Low	Low
Focus	Medium	High	Low	Medium-low	High	Medium-high	Medium	Medium
Intensity	High	Medium	High	Medium-high	Low	Medium-high	Medium	Low
Scope	High	Low	High	High	Low	Medium	High	High

cott, the rally, the bloc vote. The common messenger falls half-way between, whereas direct pressure and bypassing the subelite are low.

When we apply these four criteria of assessment to the eight mechanisms of persuasion, a tentative and admittedly intuitive cross classification of all mechanisms with our four criteria emerges (Table 37).

SUMMARY AND TRANSITIONAL REMARKS

We have presented some of our basic categories on organizing from the grass roots. Before proceeding with an extension of this argument, we would like to make available several readings which should give the reader a better idea of what is involved. Presented first in Section Two is the material by the late Saul Alinsky, representing one of his last efforts to organize at the local level. Second, there is a selection from my own study of workers in Detroit. There follow a current news story about neighborhood welfare-rights organizations and an assessment of the devastating milieu within which they must operate. Finally, there is Grace and James Boggs's prescription for black organization.

Readings on the Grass Roots

Tactics
Saul Alinsky

We will either find a way or make one.
—Hannibal

Tactics means doing what you can with what you have. Tactics are those consciously deliberate acts by which human beings live with each other and deal with the world around them. In the world of give and take, tactics is the art of how to take and how to give. Here our concern is with the tactic of taking; how the Have-Nots can take power away from the Haves.

For an elementary illustration of tactics, take parts of your face as the point of reference; your eyes, your ears, and your nose. First the eyes; if you have organized a vast, mass-based people's organization, you can parade it visibly before the enemy and openly show your power. Second the ears; if your organization is small in numbers, then do what Gideon did: conceal the members in the dark but raise a din and clamor that will make the listener believe that your organization numbers many more than it does. Third, the nose; if your organization is too tiny even for noise, stink up the place.

Always remember the first rule of power tactics:

Power is not only what you have but what the enemy thinks you have.[1]

The second rule is: *Never go outside the experience of your people.* When an action or tactic is outside the experience of the people, the result is confusion, fear, and retreat. It also means a collapse of communication. . . .

The third rule is: *Wherever possible go outside of the experience of the enemy.* Here you want to cause confusion, fear, and retreat.

General William T. Sherman, whose name still causes a frenzied reaction throughout the South, provided a classic example of going outside the enemy's experience. Until Sherman,

military tactics and strategies were based on standard patterns. All armies had fronts, rears, flanks, lines of communication, and lines of supply. Military campaigns were aimed at such standard objectives as rolling up the flanks of the enemy army or cutting the lines of supply or lines of communication, or moving around to attack from the rear. When Sherman cut loose on his famous March to the Sea, he had no front or rear lines of supplies or any other lines. He was on the loose and living on the land. The South, confronted with this new form of military invasion, reacted with confusion, panic, terror, and collapse. Sherman swept on to inevitable victory. It was the same tactic that, years later in the early days of World War II, the Nazi Panzer tank divisions emulated in their far-flung sweeps into enemy territory, as did our own General Patton with the American Third Armored Division.

The fourth rule is: *Make the enemy live up to their own book of rules.* You can kill them with this, for they can no more obey their own rules than the Christian church can live up to Christianity.

The fourth rule carries within it the fifth rule: *Ridicule is man's most potent weapon.* It is almost impossible to counterattack ridicule. Also it infuriates the opposition, who then react to your advantage.

The sixth rule is: *A good tactic is one that your people enjoy.*[2] If your people are not having a ball doing it, there is something very wrong with the tactic.

The seventh rule: *A tactic that drags on too long becomes a drag.* Man can sustain militant interest in any issue for only a limited time, after which it becomes a ritualistic commitment, like going to church on Sunday mornings. New issues and crises are always developing, and one's reaction becomes, "Well, my heart bleeds for those people and I'm all for the

■ Taken from Saul Alinsky, *Rules for Radicals* (New York: Vintage Books, 1971), pp. 126–145. Copyright © 1971 by Saul Alinsky. Reprinted by permission of Random House, Inc.

boycott, but after all there are other important things in life"—and there it goes.

The eighth rule: *Keep the pressure on*, with different tactics and actions, and utilize all events of the period for your purpose.

The ninth rule: *The threat is usually more terrifying than the thing itself.*

The tenth rule: *The major premise for tactics is the development of operations that will maintain a constant pressure upon the opposition.* It is the unceasing pressure that results in the reactions from the opposition that are essential for the success of the campaign. It should be remembered not only that the action is in the reaction but that action is itself the consequence of reaction and of reaction to the reaction, ad infinitum. The pressure produces the reaction, and constant pressure sustains action.

The eleventh rule is: *If you push a negative hard and deep enough it will break through into its counterside;* this is based on the principle that every positive has its negative. We have already seen the conversion of the negative into the positive, in Mahatma Gandhi's development of the tactic of passive resistance.

One corporation we organized against responded to the continuous application of pressure by burglarizing my home, and then using the keys taken in the burglary to burglarize the offices of the Industrial Areas Foundation where I work. The panic in this corporation was clear from the nature of the burglaries, for nothing was taken in either burglary to make it seem that the thieves were interested in ordinary loot—they took only the records that applied to the corporation. Even the most amateurish burglar would have had more sense than to do what the private detective agency hired by the corporation did. The police departments in California and Chicago agreed that "the corporation might just as well have left its fingerprints all over the place."

In a fight almost anything goes. It almost reaches the point where you stop to apologize if a chance blow lands *above* the belt. When a corporation bungles like the one that burglarized my home and office, my visible public reaction is shock, horror, and moral outrage. In this case, we let it be known that sooner or later it would be confronted with this crime as well as with a whole series of other derelictions,

before a United States Senate Subcommittee Investigation. Once sworn in, with congressional immunity, we would make these actions public. This threat, plus the fact that an attempt on my life had been made in Southern California, had the corporation on a spot where it would be publicly suspect in the event of assassination. At one point I found myself in a thirty-room motel in which every other room was occupied by their security men. This became another devil in the closet to haunt this corporation and to keep the pressure on.

The twelfth rule: *The price of a successful attack is a constructive alternative.* You cannot risk being trapped by the enemy in his sudden agreement with your demand and saying "You're right—we don't know what to do about this issue. Now you tell us."

The thirteenth rule: *Pick the target, freeze it, personalize it, and polarize it.*

In conflict tactics there are certain rules that the organizer should always regard as universalities. One is that the opposition must be singled out as the target and "frozen." By this I mean that in a complex, interrelated, urban society, it becomes increasingly difficult to single out who is to blame for any particular evil. There is a constant, and somewhat legitimate, passing of the buck. In these times of urbanization, complex metropolitan governments, the complexities of major interlocked corporations, and the interlocking of political life between cities and counties and metropolitan authorities, the problem that threatens to loom more and more is that of identifying the enemy. Obviously there is no point to tactics unless one has a target upon which to center the attacks. One big problem is a constant shifting of responsibility from one jurisdiction to another—individuals and bureaus one after another disclaim responsibility for particular conditions, attributing the authority for any change to some other force. In a corporation one gets the situation where the president of the corporation says that he does not have the responsibility, it is up to the board of trustees or the board of directors, the board of directors can shift it over to the stockholders, etc., etc. And the same thing goes, for example, on the Board of Education appointments in the city of Chicago, where an extra-legal committee is empowered to make selections of nominees for the board and the mayor then uses his legal powers to select names from that list. When the mayor is attacked for not having any blacks on the list, he shifts the responsibility over to the committee, pointing out that he has to select those names from a list submitted by the committee, and if the list is all white, then he has no responsibility. The committee can shift the responsibility back by pointing out that it is the mayor who has the authority to select the names, and so it goes in a comic (if it were not so tragic) routine of "who's on first" or "under which shell is the pea hidden?"

The same evasion of responsibility is to be found in all areas of life and other areas of City Hall Urban Renewal departments, who say the responsibility is over here, and somebody else says the responsibility is over there, the city says it is a state responsibility, and the state says it is a federal responsibility and the federal government passes it back to the local community, and on ad infinitum.

It should be borne in mind that the target is always trying to shift responsibility to get out of being the target. There is a constant squirming and moving and strategy—purposeful, and malicious at times, other times just for straight self-survival—on the part of the designated target. The forces for change must keep this in mind and pin that target down securely. If an organization permits responsibility to be diffused and distributed in a number of areas, attack becomes impossible.

I remember specifically that when the Woodlawn Organization started the campaign against public school segregation, both the superintendent of schools and the chairman of the Board of Education vehemently denied any racist segregationist practices in the Chicago Public School System. They took the position that they did not even have any racial-identification data in their files, so they did not know which of their students were black and which were white. As for the fact that we had all-white schools and all-black schools, well, that's just the way it was.

If we had been confronted with a politically sophisticated school superintendent he could have very well replied, "Look, when I came to Chicago the city school system was following, as it is now, a neighborhood school policy. Chicago's neighborhoods are segregated. There are white neighborhoods and black neighborhoods and therefore you have white schools and black schools. Why attack me? Why not attack the segregated neighborhoods and change them?" He would have had a valid point, of sorts; I still shiver when I think of this possibility; but the segregated neighborhoods would have passed the buck to someone else and so it would have gone into a dog-chasing-his-tail pattern—and it would have been a fifteen-year job to try to break down the segregated residential pattern of Chicago. We did not have the power to start that kind of a conflict. One of the criteria in picking your target is the target's vulnerability—where do you have the power to start? Furthermore, any target can always say, "Why do you center on me when there are others to blame as well?" When you "freeze the target," you disregard these arguments and, for the moment, all the others to blame.

Then, as you zero in and freeze your target and carry out your attack, all of the "others" come out of the woodwork very soon. They become visible by their support of the target.

The other important point in the choosing of a target is that it must be a personification, not something general and abstract such as a community's segregated practices or a major corporation or City Hall. It is not possible to develop the necessary hostility against, say, City Hall, which after all is a concrete, physical, inanimate structure, or against a corporation, which has no soul or identity, or a public school administration, which again is an inanimate system.

John L. Lewis, the leader of the radical C.I.O. labor organization in the 1930s, was fully aware of this, and as a consequence the C.I.O. never attacked General Motors, they always attacked its president, Alfred "Icewater-In-His-Veins" Sloan; they never attacked the Republic Steel Corporation but always its president, "Bloodied Hands" Tom Girdler, and so with us when we attacked the then-superintendent of the Chicago public school system, Benjamin Willis. Let nothing get you off your target.

With this focus comes a polarization. As we have indicated before, all issues must be polarized if action is to follow. The classic statement on polarization comes from Christ: "He that is not with me is against me" (Luke 11:23). He allowed no middle ground to the money-changers in the Temple. One acts decisively only in the conviction that all the angels are on one side and all the devils on the other. A leader may struggle toward a decision and weigh the merits and demerits of a situation which is 52 percent positive and 48 percent negative, but once the decision is reached he must assume that his cause is 100 percent positive and the opposition 100 percent negative. He can't toss forever in limbo, and avoid decision. He can't weigh arguments or reflect endlessly—he must decide and act. Otherwise there are Hamlet's words:

And thus the native hue of resolution
Is sicklied o'er with the pale cast of thought,
And enterprises of great pith and moment
With this regard their currents turn awry,
And lose the name of action.

Many liberals, during our attack on the then-school superintendent, were pointing out that after all he wasn't a 100 percent devil, he was a regular churchgoer, he was a good family man, and he was generous in his contributions to charity. Can you imagine in the arena of conflict charging that so-and-so is a racist bastard and then diluting the impact of the attack with qualifying remarks such as "He is a good churchgoing man, generous to charity, and a good husband"? This becomes political idiocy.

An excellent illustration of the importance of polarization here was cited by Ruth McKenney in *Industrial Valley*, her classical study of the beginning of organization of the rubber workers in Akron, Ohio:

[John L.] Lewis faced the mountaineer workers of Akron calmly. He had taken the trouble to prepare himself with exact information about the rubber industry and The Goodyear Tire and Rubber Company. He made no vague, general speech, the kind the rubberworkers were used to hearing from Green [then president of the A.F. of L.]. Lewis named names and quoted figures. His audience was startled and pleased when he called Cliff Slusser by name, described him, and finally denounced him. The A.F. of L. leaders who used to come into Akron in the old days were generally doing well if they remembered who Paul Litchfield was.

The Lewis speech was a battle cry, a challenge. He started off by recalling the vast profits the rubber companies had always made, even during the deepest days of the Depression. He mentioned the Goodyear labor policy, and quoted Mr. Litchfield's pious opinions about the partnership of labor and capital.

"What," he said in his deep, passionate voice, "have Goodyear workers gotten out of the growth of the company?" His audience squirmed in its seats, listening with almost painful fervor.

"Partnership!" he sneered. "Well, labor and capital may be partners in theory, *but they are enemies in fact.*"

... The rubberworkers listened to this with surprise and great excitement. William Green used to tell them about the partnership of labor and capital nearly as eloquently as Paul Litchfield. Here was a man who put into words—what eloquent and educated and even elegant words—facts they knew to be true from their own experience. Here was a man who said things that made real sense to a guy who worked on a tire machine at Goodyear.

"Organize!" Lewis shouted, and his voice echoed from the beams of the armory. "Organize!" he said, pounding the speaking pulpit until it jumped. "Organize! Go to Goodyear and tell them you want some of those stock dividends. Say, So we're supposed to be partners, are we? Well, we're not. *We're enemies.*"

• *The real action is in the enemy's reaction.*
• *The enemy properly goaded and guided in his reaction will be your major strength.*
• *Tactics, like organization, like life, require that you move with the action.*

The scene is Rochester, New York, the home of Eastman Kodak—or rather Eastman Kodak, the home of Rochester, New York. Rochester is literally dominated by this industrial giant. For anyone to fight or publicly challenge Kodak is in itself completely outside of Rochester's experience. Even to this day this company does not have a labor union. Its attitudes toward the general public make paternalistic feudalism look like participatory democracy.

Rochester prides itself on being one of America's cultural crown jewels; it has its libraries, school system, university, museums, and its well-known symphony.... We were coming in on the invitation of the black ghetto to organize them (they literally organized to invite us in). The city was in a state of hysteria and fear at the very mention of my name. Whatever I did was news. Even my old friend and tutor, John L. Lewis, called me and affectionately growled, "I resent the fact that you are more hated in Rochester than I was." This was the setting.

One of the first times I arrived at the airport I was surrounded by reporters from the media. The first question was what I thought about Rochester as a city and I replied, "It is a huge southern plantation transplanted north." To the question why was I "meddling" in the black ghetto after "everything" that Eastman Kodak had done for the blacks (there had been a bloody riot, National Guard, etc., the previous summer), I looked blank and replied, "Maybe I am innocent and uninformed of what has been happening here, but as far as I know the only thing Eastman Kodak has done on the race issue in America has been to introduce color film." The reaction was shock, anger, and resentment from Kodak. They were not being attacked or insulted—they were being laughed at, and this was insufferable. It was the first dart tossed at the big bull. Soon Eastman would become so angry that it would make the kind of charges that finally led to its own downfall.

The next question was about my response to a bitter personal denunciation of me from W. Allen Wallis, the president of the University of Rochester and a present director of Eastman Kodak. He had been the head of the Department of Business Administration, formerly, at the University of Chicago. He was at the university when it was locked in bitter warfare with the black organization in Woodlawn. "Wallis?" I replied. "Which one are you talking about—Wallace of Alabama, or Wallis of Rochester—but I guess there isn't any difference, so what was your question?" This reply (1) introduced an element of ridicule and (2) it ended any further attacks from the president of the University of Rochester, who began to suspect that he was going to be shafted with razors, and that an encounter with me or with my associates was not going to be an academic dialogue.

It should be remembered that you can threaten the enemy and get away with it. You can insult and annoy him, but the one thing that is unforgivable and that is certain to get him to react is to laugh at him. This causes an irrational anger.

I hesitate to spell out specific applications of these tactics. I remember an unfortunate experience with my *Reveille for Radicals*, in which I collected accounts of particular actions and tactics employed in organizing a number of communities. For some time after the book was published I got reports that would-be organizers were using this book as a manual, and whenever they were confronted with a puzzling situation they would retreat into some vestibule or alley and thumb through to find the answer! There can be no prescriptions for particular situations because the same situation rarely recurs, any more than history repeats itself. People, pressures, and patterns of power are variables, and a particular combination exists only in a particular time—even then the variables are constantly in a state of flux. Tactics must be understood as specific applications of the rules and principles that I have listed above. It is the *principles* that the organizer must carry with him in battle. To these he applies his imagination, and he relates them tactically to specific situations.

For example, I have emphasized and reemphasized that tactics means you do what you can with what you've got, and that power in the main has always gravitated towards those who have money and those whom people follow. The resources of the Have-Nots are (1) no money and (2) lots of people. All right, let's start from there. People can show their power by voting. What else? Now a melange of ideas begins to appear. Use the power of the law by making the establishment obey its own rules. Go outside the experience of the enemy, stay inside the experience of your people. Emphasize tactics that your people will enjoy. The threat is usually more terrifying than the tactic itself. Once all these rules and principles are festering in your imagination they grow into a synthesis.

I suggested that we might buy one hundred seats for one of Rochester's symphony concerts. We would select a concert in which the music was relatively quiet. The hundred blacks who would be given the tickets would first be treated to a three-hour pre-concert dinner in the community, in which they would be fed nothing but baked beans, and lots of them;

then the people would go to the symphony hall—with obvious consequences. Imagine the scene when the action began! The concert would be over before the first movement! (If this be a Freudian slip—so be it!)

Let's examine this tactic in terms of the concepts mentioned above.

First, the disturbance would be utterly outside the experience of the establishment, which was expecting the usual stuff of mass meetings, street demonstrations, confrontations and parades. Not in their wildest fears would they expect an attack on their prize cultural jewel, their famed symphony orchestra. Second, all of the action would ridicule and make a farce of the law for there is no law, and there probably never will be, banning natural physical functions. Here you would have a combination not only of noise but also of odor, what you might call natural stink bombs. Regular stink bombs are illegal and cause for immediate arrest, but there would be absolutely nothing here that the Police Department or the ushers or any other servants of the establishment could do about it. The law would be completely paralyzed.

People would recount what had happened in the symphony hall and the reaction of the listener would be to crack up in laughter. It would make the Rochester Symphony and the establishment look utterly ridiculous. There would be no way for the authorities to cope with any future attacks of a similar character. What could they do? Demand that people not eat baked beans before coming to a concert? Ban anyone from succumbing to natural urges during the concert? Announce to the world that concerts must not be interrupted by farting? Such talk would destroy the future of the symphony season. Imagine the tension at the opening of any concert! Imagine the feeling of the conductor as he raised his baton!

With this would come certain fall-outs. On the following morning, the matrons, to whom the symphony season is one of the major social functions, would confront their husbands (both executives and junior executives) at the breakfast table and say, "John, we are not going to have our symphony season ruined by *those people!* I don't know what they want but whatever it is, something has got to be done and this kind of thing has to be stopped!"

Lastly, we have the universal rule that while one goes outside the experience of the enemy in order to induce confusion and fear, one must not do the same with one's own people, because you do not want them to be confused and fearful. Now, let us examine this rule with reference to the symphony tactic. To start with, the tactic is within the experience of the local people; it also satisfies another rule—that the people must enjoy the tactics. Here we have an ambivalent situation. The reaction of the blacks in the ghetto—their laughter when the tactic was proposed—made it clear that the tactic, at least in fantasy, was within their experience. It connected with their hatred of Whitey. The one thing that all oppressed people want to do to their oppressors is shit on them. Here was an approximate way to do this. However, we were also aware that when they found themselves actually in the symphony hall, probably for the first time in their lives, they would find themselves seated amid a mass of whites, many of them in formal dress. The situation would be so much *out of their experience* that they might congeal and revert back to their previous role. The very idea of doing what they had come to do would be so embarrassing, so mortifying, that they would do almost anything to avoid carrying through the plan. But we also knew that the baked beans would compel them physically to go through with the tactic regardless of how they felt.

I must emphasize that tactics like this are not just cute; any organizer knows, as a particular tactic grows out of the rules and principles of revolution, that he must always analyze the merit of the tactic and determine its strengths and weaknesses in terms of these same rules.

Imagine the scene in the U.S. Courtroom in Chicago's recent conspiracy trial of the seven if the defendants and counsel had anally trumpeted their contempt for Judge Hoffman and the system. What could Judge Hoffman, the bailiffs, or anyone else, do? Would the judge have found them in contempt for farting? Here was a tactic for which there was no legal precedent. The press reaction would have stunk up the judge for the rest of time.

Another tactic involving the bodily functions developed in Chicago during the days of the Johnson-Goldwater campaign. Commitments that were made by the authorities to the Woodlawn ghetto organization were not being met by the city. The political threat that had originally compelled these commitments was no longer operative. The community organization had no alternative but to support Johnson, and therefore the Democratic administration felt the political threat had evaporated. It must be remembered here that not only is pressure essential to compel the establishment to make its initial concession, but the pressure must be maintained to make the establishment deliver. The second factor seemed to be lost to the Woodlawn Organization.

Since the organization was blocked in the political arena, new tactics and a new arena had to be devised.

O'Hare Airport became the target. To begin with, O'Hare is the world's busiest airport. Think for a moment of the common experience of jet travelers. Your stewardess brings you your lunch or dinner. After eating, most people want to go to the lavatory. However, this is often inconvenient because your tray and those of your seat partners are loaded down with dishes. So you wait until the stewardess has removed the trays. By that time those who are seated closest to the lavatory have got up and the "occupied" sign is on. So you wait. And in these days of jet travel the seat belt sign is soon flashed, as the airplane starts its landing approach. You decide to wait until after landing and use the facilities in the terminal. This is obvious to anyone who watches the unloading of passengers at various gates in any airport—many of the passengers are making a beeline for the men's or the ladies' room.

With this in mind, the tactic becomes obvious—we tie up the lavatories. In the restrooms you drop a dime, enter, push the lock on the door—and you can stay there all day. Therefore the occupation of the sit-down toilets presents no problem. It would take just a relatively few people to walk into these cubicles, armed with books and newspapers, lock the doors, and tie up all the facilities. What are the police going to do? Break in and demand evidence of legitimate occupancy? Therefore, the ladies' restrooms could be occupied completely; the only problem in the men's lavatories would be the stand-up urinals. This, too, could be taken care of, by having groups busy themselves around the airport and then move in on the stand-up urinals to line up four or five deep

whenever a flight arrived. An intelligence study was launched to learn how many sit-down toilets for both men and women, as well as stand-up urinals, there were in the entire O'Hare Airport complex and how many men and women would be necessary for the nation's first "shit-in."

The consequences of this kind of action would be catastrophic in many ways. People would be desperate for a place to relieve themselves. One can see children yelling at their parents, "Mommy, I've got to go," and desperate mothers surrendering, "All right—well, do it. Do it right here." O'Hare would soon become a shambles. The whole scene would become unbelievable and the laughter and ridicule would be nationwide. It would probably get a front page story in the London *Times*. It would be a source of great mortification and embarrassment to the city administration. It might even create the kind of emergency in which planes would have to be held up while passengers got back aboard to use the plane's toilet facilities.

The threat of this tactic was leaked (again there may be a Freudian slip here, and again, so what?) back to the administration, and within forty-eight hours the Woodlawn Organization found itself in conference with the authorities who said that they were certainly going to live up to their commitments and they could never understand where anyone got the idea that a promise made by Chicago's City Hall would not be observed. At no point, then or since, has there ever been any open mention of the threat of the O'Hare tactic. Very few of the members of the Woodlawn Organization knew how close they were to writing history.

With the universal principle that the right things are always done for the wrong reasons and the tactical rule that negatives become positives, we can understand the following examples.

In its early history the organized black ghetto in the Woodlawn neighborhood in Chicago engaged in conflict with the slum landlords. It never picketed the local slum tenements or the landlord's office. It selected its blackest blacks and bused them out to the lily-white suburb of the slum landlord's residence. Their picket signs, which said, "Did you know that Jones, your neighbor, is a slum landlord?" were completely irrelevant; the point was that the pickets knew Jones would be inundated with phone calls from his neighbors.

JONES: *Before you say a word let me tell you that those signs are a bunch of lies!*

NEIGHBOR: *Look, Jones, I don't give a damn what you do for a living. All we know is that you get those goddam niggers out of here or you get out!*

Jones came out and signed.

The pressure that gave us our positive power was the negative of racism in a white society. We exploited it for our own purposes.

Let us take one of the negative stereotypes that so many whites have of blacks: that blacks like to sit around eating watermelon. Suppose that 3,000 blacks suddenly descended into the downtown sections of any city, each armed with and munching a huge piece of watermelon. This spectacle would be so far outside the experience of the whites that they would be unnerved and disorganized. In alarm over what the blacks were up to, the establishment would probably react to the advantage of the blacks. Furthermore, the whites would recognize at last

the absurdity of their stereotype of black habits. Whites would squirm in embarrassment, knowing that they were being ridiculed. That would be the end of the black watermelon stereotype. I think that this tactic would bring the administration to contact black leadership and ask what their demands were even if no demands had been made. Here again is a case of doing what you can with what you've got. . . .

NOTES

1. Power has always derived from two main sources, money and people. Lacking money, the Have-Nots must build power from their own flesh and blood. A mass movement expresses itself with mass tactics. Against the finesse and sophistication of the status quo, the Have-Nots have always had to club their way. In early Renaissance Italy the playing cards showed swords for the nobility (the word *spade* is a corruption of the Italian word for sword), chalices (which became hearts) for the clergy, diamonds for the merchants, and clubs as the symbol of the peasants.

2. Alinsky takes the iconoclast's pleasure in kicking the biggest behinds in town and the sport is not untempting. . . ." —William F. Buckley, Jr., *Chicago Daily News*, October 19, 1966.

From the Bottom Up

John C. Leggett

We have already demonstrated that within the Negro community, many workmen express extremely high degrees of consciousness, which they translate into political choice. We have attempted to account for Negro class consciousness by emphasizing the impact of job discrimination, uprootedness, and union membership on workers who are able to discuss their common problems at the workplace and in their neighborhoods. But how does grass-roots leadership organize workers into a politically active community? To answer this question, the author became a participant observer in the Detroit block-club movement.

Contrary to the opinion that the city, especially the working-class section, is marked by

■ Taken from John C. Leggett, *Class, Race, and Labor: Working-Class Consciousness* (New York: Oxford University Press, 1968), pp. 130–143. Copyright © 1968, by Oxford University Press. Reprinted by permission.

"the relative absence of intimate personal acquaintanceship, the segmentalization of human relations which are largely anonymous, superficial and transitory, . . . " we believe that collective problem-solving on the neighborhood level is not impossible. Moreover, many Negro working-class districts have the potential for creating enough solidarity to foster political militancy. This is particularly true of neighborhoods that support neighborhood organizations, contain many union members, consist largely of uprooted workmen, and face an economic crisis.

For our model of neighborhood organizations we will use the Detroit block-club movement. This movement originated in the mid-1950s and concerned itself with problems widespread within the Negro ghetto: rats, urban renewal, unemployment, bank foreclosures on home mortgages, negligent landlords, inadequate recreational facilities, segregated schools, poor police protection, and the like. Detroit block clubs began as an answer to the problem of how to prevent central city neighborhoods from becoming slums.

As is well known, urban blight has been a problem in large American cities since World War II. In part, it spreads when many families who live in near-slum areas do not know how to maintain and upgrade their own blocks and neighborhoods. The problem of developing and upholding standards of house maintenance was difficult when city officials and working-class families could not communicate with each other. Prior to the mid-1950s, most large cities had few ties between city officials, administrators, and planners on the one hand, and citizens in slum neighborhoods on the other. Thus, planners could not coordinate their actions with those who sought help or with those who would be receptive to suggestions on neighborhood upkeep.

In response to this lack of communication, a section of Detroit's city planning commission revised its traditional policy on neighborhood preservation and, in the mid-1950s, established local organizations built around the block and neighborhood. Twelve members of the commission set up a special subunit to organize the grass-roots block clubs. They contacted neighborhood leaders who had some interest in social problems and who were active in church groups, P.T.A.'s, labor unions, and settlement houses. In many cases, individuals approached the team of city planners first, in the hope that the latter would help organize their block. Once the initial contacts were made, the city planning commission staff and organizers attempted to establish homogeneous groups on the block level by recruiting home buyers and home owners. Most of the home owners had moved to run-down neighborhoods after World War II and had invested their wartime savings in a down payment on older, single-family houses. The block-club organizers assumed that these potential home owners would be more motivated to upgrade and preserve the character of the neighborhood than those who rented. In addition, the home owners' common backgrounds allowed them to communicate readily with one another. (Generally southern-born Negroes, they were almost all factory workers and union members, with the overwhelming majority belonging to the C.I.O.) The social scientists and social workers who initiated the block-club movement encouraged housing maintenance and worked to promote close friendships within the community.

UPGRADING, RECREATION, AND PROTECTION

Although block clubs dealt with social problems in general, they emphasized neighborhood conservation and home improvement. Anyone living on a block where a club existed could join it, providing he paid his dues. Meetings attracted from 5 to 90 percent of the inhabitants of the block, with the clubs generally enjoying their largest turnout during their early period of organization. Attendance later tapered off until the active membership included not more than 10 to 20 percent of those living on the block.

The block clubs' conservation activities were extended to the schools to involve parents in efforts designed to promote the interests of their children. Block clubs and elementary schools sometimes jointly sponsored a "clean-up day," on which the entire neighborhood turned out to clean up alleys, streets, and lawns. On one occasion, the local elementary school, including the principal, assistant principal, and band, cooperated with parents in nearby block clubs to clean alleys inside the school district. School representatives took pictures of the alleys before, during, and after the collective assault on garbage cans, old debris, and the like, and the activity was symbolized by the theme of a "war on rats," a graphic way of attacking the removal of alley litter. On D-Day in this gray neighborhood, the school band led a "company" of children armed with swords made of painted cardboard.

The local school had helped to arouse the youngsters' interest in the campaign. In art and English classes, teachers encouraged pupils to express their concern through drawings and poetry. The children responded by portraying a variety of scenes, most of which contained pictures of rats. The "rat theme" made students, parents, schools, and block clubs participants in community reform.

Block clubs did other things to promote intimacy among families living in the same area.

They often sponsored parties, which were informal gatherings. Friends met to play cards, dance, or engage in similar types of recreation with the proceeds going to the block club or perhaps to a member with a medical bill. There were also outdoor parties, generally held within the confines of a blocked-off street. These all-day affairs were almost wholly child-centered: there were picnics on the pavement, and youngsters competed in bag races, fifty-yard dashes, and other events organized by their parents. Free soda pop, popcorn, and ice cream purchased by the block club contributed to the carnival mood. Such entertainments attracted as many as fifty to one hundred children and their parents, thereby giving block-club organizers the opportunity to get acquainted with parents reluctant to attend block-club meetings. Children thus became the basis for the extension of club membership.

Once organized and solidified by recreation activities, block clubs expanded their services and enhanced local prestige by sponsoring paint-up, fix-up, and weed-up campaigns. A person with skill in carpentry might contribute his services to help other families in his block club. Those families reciprocated by performing such tasks as house-painting, seed-planting, and the like. Sometimes the specific form of this reciprocity would be discussed and stipulated at meetings of the block club. Tactics were also reviewed: which houses were in need of repair, the choice of paints, and the division of labor for projects. The results were visible improvements in the neighborhood and greater cohesion among families, who could take pride in their collective achievements.

Block clubs learned to deal successfully with legal authorities and city departments, and in this way obtained many benefits to the community. For example, some block clubs sponsored baseball teams which they financed through parties. Block-club officers persuaded recreation and other city officials to allow the block club to convert vacant lots into baseball diamonds. The police and city officials found that a policy of cooperation was rewarding, and block clubs often worked with precinct police officers to protect neighborhoods from local and outside criminals.

In some cases, the clubs supplemented the efforts of protective authority; during a crime wave, for example, one club provided a protection service for those who had to walk in the neighborhood at night. The club provided escorts and asked families to leave their porch lights on. Seventy-five percent of the households cooperated even though only one-fifth of the adults in the area were active in the block club.

Prevention of crime occasioned yet other types of collective action, such as the neighborhood meetings with police officials cosponsored by block clubs. Unfortunately, these gatherings did not attract those whose behavior block-club members found most reprehensible, namely, criminals and delinquents. Nonetheless, the meetings did help to strengthen ties within the clubs and between clubs and the police, especially those in charge of the precinct.

Although these efforts were successful in integrating a sizable number of families into block clubs, too frequently the meetings bypassed an important category: older white people, who were reluctant to take an active part, often because of poor health or racial attitudes. In order to obtain their verbal support, if not their participation, block-club members sometimes offered to shovel snow from their sidewalks or helped older persons with minor repair work around the house. These efforts had some effect, at least from the point of view of the block club, for these outsiders did subsequently participate in some campaigns. Still, it was difficult to obtain the continued involvement of older people.

Young couples also tended to remain inactive, but even here block clubs on occasion evolved techniques for integration, such as offering baby-sitting services. Of course, block clubs did not deliberately set out to manipulate people through any of these devices. Rather, they experimented with different solutions and when one worked, the clubs accepted it. The block clubs depended upon the process of collective problem-solving.

UPGRADING AND POLITICS

The movement was eventually forced to become political in order to protect and extend its interest in neighborhood welfare. Questions of zoning, urban renewal, police protection, school boundary gerrymandering, and the like were of vital interest to the block-club families, and over half the clubs became politically involved in at least one of these issues. Certain clubs, particularly on Detroit's west side, became very active politically. When municipal organizations erected barriers to the achievement of their goals of neighborhood conservation, the block clubs sought to change these policies. Representatives were sent to speak before local groups to put pressure on the municipal government. At election time, almost all the clubs became active—some sponsored meetings for candidates; often the clubs arrived at an informal or explicit decision to support a particular candidate.

Many city politicians reacted negatively to what they considered annoying block-club demands. These politicians finally abolished that section of the planning commission that had organized and maintained the clubs. The city had created a problem-solving agent which it could not control. In fact, the block clubs sometimes opposed the proposals of the city planning commission. Moreover, because they fought pressure groups such as organized real estate interests, which traditionally worked closely with the planning commission, the city council, and powerful economic interests, the clubs invited opposition. Yet, to the amazement of many, hundreds of block clubs continued to flourish without the support of the city planning commission.

Dependence of clubs on the neighborhood council

Aid from neighborhood councils helped the clubs survive. The neighborhood council generally consisted of (1) elected delegates representing between 25 and 40 block clubs in the neighborhood and (2) a number of others acting on behalf of prominent voluntary associations in the area. Like block clubs, each council met monthly to discuss its problems and those of the particular clubs.

The neighborhood councils duplicated many service functions of the block clubs: they sponsored parties, dances, and the like. In addition, they gave advice to block clubs on a variety of topics: how to obtain a stop sign for a street intersection; how to complain about poor garbage collection; how to obtain surplus government paint; how to plant grass seed; how best to uproot weeds. To instruct block-club delegates on some of these matters, some neighborhood councils called upon leaders of home-

improvement groups in the upper middle-class white suburbs.

Ties with the middle class assumed other forms as well. Neighborhood councils cooperated with police precincts, church groups, political organizations, and leaders of labor unions. Yet they were not always asking for advice; sometimes they made political demands on these groups. The councils sent delegates to meetings of the Detroit Common Council, where they confronted and debated with representatives of city agencies, real estate interests, and other groups. The councils became involved in local elections, and supported candidates for mayor, city council, governor, and Congress, although their endorsement was more often covert rather than explicit. Although they expressed a wide range of political interests, councils were most effective in swinging political support to candidates for municipal office. During the 1961 campaign, the councils, along with other Negro groups (including the Trade Union Leadership Council, church organizations, the NAACP, the Cotillion Club, and the Negro press), worked successfully to unseat a mayor and a police commissioner opposed by Negroes because of alleged toleration of police brutality. In this mayoralty race, neighborhood councils helped a young reform candidate by marshaling the support of Negroes, who constituted 30 percent of Detroit's electorate. In the election of the Common Council, also conducted on the basis of a city-wide vote, a former member of the city planning commission and the original organizer of the block clubs had the least number of votes among the nine elected. However, he was among the top three in precincts well organized by block clubs.

Neighborhood councils became politically involved in still other ways. For example, some west side neighborhood councils donated time and funds to carry on legal suits against a Detroit school board, which, they claimed, gerrymandered school districts along racial lines. The councils also instigated and supported boycotts against firms that discriminated against Negroes.

Neighborhood and district councils

Neighborhood councils sometimes elected delegates to a residential district council, whose membership consisted also of representatives of social agencies and settlement houses, school teachers, and police officers. These nondelegates on the whole steered the group in a way that promoted better relations with schools, social agencies, unions, and churches. They acted as a moderating influence on what otherwise might have been an organizational center and central clearing house for militant groups.

At one meeting of the district council, for example, rank and file delegates passed a resolution condemning Chrysler Corporation for working men overtime while many former auto workers who had been laid off remained unemployed. Several of the nondelegate officers were given the responsibility of forwarding this complaint to the Chrysler Corporation and the U.A.W. The officers maintained, however, that such a resolution was improper, and that it would upset relations with industry. Unknown to the delegates, they chose not to forward the complaint. Again, more moderate nondelegates held meetings and workshops on matters such as automation and unemployment, but they generally restricted the range of key participants to exclude militants such as the Reverend Albert Cleague, a black nationalist and a leading member of the Detroit executive board of the NAACP.

District council leaders could not punish neighborhood councils and block clubs through such measures as personal expulsion or charter suspension. Because district councils could not levy serious sanctions, individual block clubs and neighborhood councils enjoyed considerable autonomy, which allowed them to be as radical or militant as they wished. In this respect, the structure of the block-club movement was far different from labor unions, which have concentrated and centralized power at the top of their organization.

BLOCK CLUBS AND THE CREATION OF RADICAL VIEWS

The views of Negro block-club members on collective action can be understood more clearly when they are related to the industrial and agricultural changes that have been taking place in America since the end of the Second World War. Rapid mechanization of agriculture in the South displaced large numbers of rural workers. Industrial positions in the North provided many with a standard of living markedly superior to

their former one. However, the 1958 recession threatened this new-found prosperity. Widespread unemployment and economic insecurity made many of Detroit's Negro unemployed consider the probable consequences of economic depression.... [I]n many instances, these conditions engendered the creation of political militancy.

What may occur is a spontaneous endorsement of grass-roots action—even when it leads to class or class-racial warfare. We have already noted that under certain conditions economic insecurity breeds hostility toward the economic order, and leads to antagonism among political groups and commitment to political radicalism. All these attitudes appeared in a study we conducted in two predominantly Negro neighborhoods in Detroit during the summer of 1958.

While economic insecurity cannot, of course, be equated with a readiness to engage in violent behavior, an important precondition for the initiation of violence may well be the development, within a group, of a definition of the conditions under which violence becomes a probable or expected outcome of economic crisis.

Block club, economic insecurity, and radicalism

Our study, conducted in May and July of 1958, was based upon interviews of heads of households. The initial aim was to explore the problem by covering a single neighborhood in which there was considerable indigenous political activity and militant leadership within the block club. Soon after, we decided to repeat the study in a neighborhood matched, as far as possible, on all variables except block-club organization and political activity. Although this research site was not wholly free of political organization, it did provide a contrast to the political activity of the first neighborhood.

The west side area we chose coincided with the boundaries of a block club which had recently added the functions of a political pressure group to its principal concerns of cleaning up the area and sponsoring recreational and other social activities. This club had joined with others in Detroit in an attempt to persuade the governor to declare a moratorium on home mortgage payments for the unemployed. Three militant leftists residing in the neighborhood were active in the block-club movement, both in the local and city-wide groups.

The east side neighborhood had no such club. Although its meetings were decidedly political, they were poorly attended, having, at the most, twenty-five people. The west side group, on the other hand, organized one political action meeting which attracted an audience of three to four hundred.

In many ways, however, the two neighborhoods were similar. Almost all residents were home owners or home buyers. In addition, between 75 and 85 percent of the respondents in both areas were Negroes. The vast majority of these were born in the South and worked in blue-collar, unionized occupations, mainly in the automobile industry. From 50 to 60 percent of the Negroes interviewed in both settings were unemployed or working part-time; and many of the remainder feared unemployment. In all, we interviewed 92 from both neighborhoods.

In our 1960 study, 120 of the sample were Negroes residing in neighborhoods very similar to those studied in 1958. We used comparative information from the more recent study conducted during a period of heightened economic activity to contrast workers' views on the economic order under different economic conditions.

We asked all workers the following question: If a bad depression were to happen, what do you think would happen in this country? When workers anticipated violence, their replies were classified according to the form the violence was expected to take—either collective (revolution, rioting, civil war, and so on), or individual (killing, robbing, stealing, crime waves, etc.). Previous research suggested that predictions of violence would be frequent in both neighborhoods, since the two areas (1958 studies) had suffered extensive unemployment. It also seemed probable that expectations of *collective* violence would be more prevalent in the neighborhood that was highly organized and largely guided by militants. In addition, we assumed that unemployed Negroes would take more extreme views than comparable whites, since the frequency and consequences of unemployment were more striking among the former than the latter. In the 1960 study, it was hypothesized

that these radical views would be more widely shared among Negroes interviewed in 1958 than in 1960, when unemployment had declined.

The incidence of political militancy

In general, the information gathered supported these predictions. A large percentage of those interviewed in both neighborhoods in 1958 felt that some form of violence would take place if and when a serious depression occurred. Sixty-three percent of the Negroes in the west side neighborhood and 58 percent on the east side expected violence. Even more significant, perhaps, is the breakdown. On the west side, 35 percent predicted collective violence and 28 percent mentioned individual forms. A not unexpected reversal of attitudes was found among east side respondents: only 22 percent foresaw collective violence, while 36 percent expected individual action. In the 1958 sample, the Negro unemployed (almost all of whom were unionized) proved to be singularly concerned with violence. On the west side, 71 percent of the unemployed as opposed to 53 percent of the employed expected violence to occur. The east side Negroes concurred in this opinion, although the percentage differences were not as great.

In general, Negroes tended to expect violence more than did whites, although a comparison of the 1958 and 1960 samples showed that for the 1960 recovery period, both Negro and white workmen were less inclined to expect unrest.

Many of the replies to our question were remarkably strident. More importantly, when workmen expected collective and violent action, they showed a tendency to overlook—but not to dismiss—the relevance of the central government during such crises. Perhaps some assumed that a serious economic depression could not occur if the government were careful, but that in the event this did happen, the people should attempt to settle their problems through collective action. Such action might precipitate federal help designed to relieve the lower classes of their economic problems. Whatever their assumptions, the replies often remained inchoate and the radical ideas uncrystallized. Nonetheless, we found that of those who foresaw the possibility of collective violence, a disproportionately large number also favored government ownership of all industries. In all, their replies blend militancy with doubt about government ability. Why such views should develop is a complex question not easily answered. Yet we have tried to give a partial explanation.

In a city where the lives of many working-class people, particularly Negroes, are seriously affected by industrial unions, the successful creation of block clubs may derive largely from organizational experiences and successes with unions. In this chapter we have shown that when Negro workers join block-club organizations to solve neighborhood problems, many develop a collective and radical outlook. In thus far demonstrating the connection between block clubs and political militancy, and the positive effects of the clubs in solving some of the working man's problems, we have said little about the negative aspects of block clubs, particularly as they relate to a multiracial working class.

Perhaps the most important weakness of the block clubs is their one-sidedness. Since Negroes are ghettoized within certain residential districts, and since neighborhood councils and block clubs are organized on a spatial basis, the clubs may promote class–racial consciousness among Negroes, but they cannot produce a similar frame of reference within white working-class groups beyond the ghetto and the block clubs. The block clubs thus contribute to the furtherance of consciousness in only one sector of the working class.

"Property protection associations" organized on a neighborhood basis may appear in white neighborhoods, but they bring about racial strife among blue-collar workmen found in the community. These racial antagonisms inside the blue-collar world make difficult but do not prevent the formation of organizations that bring black and white workmen together to focus on their common difficulties.

Two Groups Ignite Welfare Explosion

Austin Scott

The welfare explosion of the past six years might never have happened had not two different movements joined forces and begun to work together.

One started five years ago as an idea among a handful of welfare recipients, and grew into the National Welfare Rights Organization. Today NWRO claims more than 700 chapters and 125,000 members, all of them on welfare.

The other movement was an offshoot of the federal government's War on Poverty. This is the Neighborhood Legal Service program, established to provide legal aid for the poor, and funded by the U.S. Office of Economic Opportunity. Young activist lawyers eager to challenge the Establishment flocked to the program, and the federal government soon found itself paying the freight for lawsuits against itself and the states.

■ Taken from *The Home News*, New Brunswick, N.J., January 12, 1972. Reprinted by permission of the Associated Press. Austin Scott is a writer for the Associated Press.

Working together, NWRO and Legal Services attacked the welfare system in the streets and courts. The growing statistics of the welfare crisis are evidence enough of their success in opening the rolls to thousands. After a brief downturn, the figures are heading upward again: $10 billion spent in the last year on 14.3 million recipients, twice the people and three times the expenditures of 1960.

NWRO's members have "marched, sat-in, waited-in, laid-in, kicked-in, lobbied, litigated and politicked in their five-year quest for adequate income, dignity, justice, and an opportunity to participate in making policy decisions that affect their lives," said Dr. George Wiley, the organization's first and only executive director.

The NWRO members, most of them welfare mothers with little formal education, have done more than demonstrate. Making themselves experts on the complexities of welfare regulations, which vary from state to state, they have actively recruited and assisted others in applying for and getting welfare assistance.

Litigation has been in the hands of the Legal Services lawyers. Clint Bamberger, the program's first director and now dean of Washington's Catholic University Law School, recalled in an interview:

Our role was something more than just to see that a person who could not afford a lawyer had a lawyer. A (poverty) lawyer's role was to use the system of laws and administrative agencies and the courts and the Constitution to improve the condition of people who were in poverty.

Despite its militance, NWRO has attracted almost no national criticism.

Legal Services is another matter. Its activities have made it the most controversial of all the antipoverty programs. As a result, the administration is attempting to get passage of a bill to set up an independent corporation to run the program.

Opposition to the program was summed up by William Mallory, city manager of Belle Glade, Fla., where Legal Services has hauled the city into court 40 times. "We don't feel Legal Services is even attempting to represent the poor," said Mallory. "They're more interested in promoting social reform."

As the relief rolls soared, NWRO stepped up efforts to spread its message that if poor people organized they could get a better deal from a welfare system that, it charged, "degraded, harassed and humiliated the poor."

"We found that welfare recipients' biggest problem was welfare," said Wiley. "Not enough money."

Writing in the *Black Law Journal*, Wiley argued that public welfare is designed to "insure that no one who is able to work will seek welfare as an alternative . . . no matter how menial or low paying the job."

In an interview, HEW Undersecretary John Veneman said the system was having exactly the opposite effect.

"The whole system is posing a challenge to the wage structure of the country," said Veneman. "Seven and one-half million people are working for less than the minimum wage. It's (welfare) a fundamental challenge to low-wage, marginal employment. It creates an alternative, seriously undermining these jobs."

Welfare recipients tend to see such changes as the new law requiring most persons on relief to sign up for jobs or training as means of forcing them to seek marginal jobs. "I'm not going to take no meaningless job," said Ethel Briscoe, a Washington welfare mother. "But that's what they want us to do, to go back to work cooking and being maids."

NWRO's most publicized victories were won with a tactic first employed in New York City. Armed with mimeographed checklists of items to which they were eligible, but had not received, including special furniture and clothing grants, recipients besieged welfare offices demanding delivery.

Until then, said Nancy Gooding, an early welfare activist in Brooklyn, "You had to scuffle to buy a table if you needed it. I don't know what you were supposed to eat off of. The caseworkers never told you you were entitled to it."

Welfare recipients found out about the special grants, she said, after caseworkers went on strike against the city, and some of them tipped off the NWRO.

The demonstrations resulted frequently in broken glass, overturned furniture, tear gas and arrests. They also produced the special furniture and clothing grants, averaging $300 to $400 per family. Five months into the 1968 campaign, New York City's Department of Social Services said it could not estimate the total number of additional grants.

"We're so busy filling out the forms, we haven't had time to add it up," said one official.

The New York demonstrations later would be duplicated with nearly equal successes in cities from Washington to Las Vegas, and there is talk within NWRO of reviving them again this spring to fight benefit cuts being imposed by 26 states.

As government officials, hard pressed for cash, sought ways to cut costs, sometimes by issuing new and complex regulations, sometimes by purging the rolls as Alabama did in November when it cut off aid to 33,000 people, Legal Services lawyers moved in.

Using class-action suits, where a decision in one case was binding in all similar incidents, the antipoverty lawyers often succeeded in opening the rolls even more. Ruling on suits filed by Legal Services, the U.S. Supreme Court knocked out the "man in the house" rule, which states had used to cut off families whenever caseworkers found a man in the house.

It ruled unconstitutional the one-year residency requirement which states and counties had used to keep newly arrived migrants from getting benefits.

It threw away the "unsuitable home" rule, a regulation used to cut off benefits from thousands on the grounds that mothers were not properly caring for their children.

The effect of the legal services' blitz, said Bamberger, was to show "that people on welfare had rights that they weren't receiving and that they could make claims for them."

There was ample precedent for NWRO's street actions. During the Depression, thousands of the homeless and the unemployed stormed welfare centers for food, money and housing. There was virtually no precedent for the legal campaign.

"Federal public assistance programs were set up in 1932," said attorney Henry Freidman, director of the OEO-funded Center for Welfare Policy and Law at Columbia University. "Illinois challenged residency in 1941. Other than that, there was not a single challenge to the program until Legal Services was set up in 1964."

While Legal Services faces a challenge in Congress, the National Welfare Rights Organization is threatened from within by a simmering dispute over its tactics.

Welfare officials, stopped by demonstrations and court orders from cutting costs by new regulations, are changing state laws so grants may be cut back legally.

A 10 percent cut by New York City this past summer marked the first time the city had paid below its own definition of minimum need. Some states are contemplating much sharper cuts than that.

NWRO members argue that welfare families cannot live on the amounts of money contemplated, but they agree there is no sure way to stop the cuts.

The problem has set off a debate over which way NWRO should move to increase its membership, and thus its influence. Two main schools of thought have emerged.

One, advanced primarily by the women who make up the bulk of the membership and hold most of the policy-making positions, argues for greatly increased organizing efforts among welfare mothers.

The other, advocated by a group of veteran community organizers, wants to broaden the base of the NWRO to include unemployed workers, Vietnam veterans who can't find jobs, and low-paid workers who earn less than they could get on welfare.

Abandonment of Federal Housing Blights Inner City

John Herbers

Chicago—the square, brick apartment buildings called Woodlawn Gardens stand like military pillboxes along both sides of Cottage Grove Avenue, survivors of a strange process of burning and abandonment that has ravaged block after block of adjacent housing.

But now even this almost new $9-million project, the pride of one of the nation's best-

■ Taken from *The New York Times*, January 13, 1972. © 1972 by The New York Times Company. Reprinted by permission.

known community groups, the Woodlawn Organization, is in jeopardy as a systematic, piece-by-piece destruction of vast areas of inner-city Chicago goes forward.

Like hundreds of other federally subsidized and guaranteed housing projects in inner-city neighborhoods, Woodlawn Gardens has run into trouble and is in default of its mortgage payments, a victim of the dynamics of the disposal of old residential areas of the core city.

Without any stated policy for doing so, the United States is disposing of great chunks of its central city housing, which in another culture would have been made to last for many generations more.

Abandonment is occurring on a large scale in New York, Philadelphia, Baltimore, Detroit and St. Louis and to a lesser but increasing degree in other cities. Dr. George Sternlieb of Rutgers University conducted a study of the subject for the House Banking and Currency Committee and concluded that "the phenomenon has a life force of its own."

"Good housing and substantial shells which are much needed are being swept away by abandonment," he said.

As the process has taken place, much of the housing that has been rehabilitated, built or guaranteed by the Federal Government in recent years as an effort to renew the cities is endangered, raising the likelihood of large-scale Federal losses and the emergence of a new crisis in urban areas.

Many of the federally sponsored rehabilitation projects completed in the late nineteen-sixties have already fallen to the process of abandonment and destruction, and in the last few months the new construction has shown signs of going the same way.

What has happened in the Woodlawn area provides a dramatic example of what is involved in cities across the country.

TRANSFORMATION TO SLUM

Woodlawn is an area of about one square mile immediately south of the University of Chicago in the South Side of the city. Once a comfortable, middle-class neighborhood with three- and four-story, walk-up apartment buildings of 15 or 20 units, and private homes, it became a slum after World War II, a "port of entry" for thousands of black rural poor from the South.

In 1960, Saul D. Alinsky organized a strong community movement under the Woodlawn Organization, which was recognized nationally as a pioneering effort in community action. One of the organization's accomplishments was the accumulation of land for Woodlawn Gardens.

The 504 units were begun six years ago under a program in which the Federal Government guaranteed 100 percent of the mortgage and paid part of the interest. The boxlike build-

ings are three-story walk-ups spread for three blocks to assure low density.

Woodlawn never had a riot, but in 1967 the process of fires and abandonment began. It was preceded by crime, vandalism and overcrowding in some of the older buildings. The owner would be sued by the city for failure to meet code requirements. Rather than invest more money in the neighborhood he would simply abandon the building. Then the fires would come mysteriously in the night and the next morning the building would be only a charred shell.

The fires reached a peak last summer, the main season for burning. Many of the lots have been cleared and stand vacant, but for block after block there are burned-out buildings standing starkly against the winter sky, interspersed with those still in use. Some are simply abandoned with all windows broken.

In the four-year period of the fires, the population has declined from about 65,000 to about 35,000. Those who left are both the burned-out poor and residents who were terrified by the violent change going on around them.

"What effect has it had on the neighborhood?" said Leon Finney, director of the Woodlawn Organization. "They are demoralized."

No one seems to know who sets the fires. The stench of kerosene and other evidence of arson are everywhere after a fire, the residents said, and several persons have died in the flames. In a number of cases the apartments were still occupied when the fire began.

NO ONE CAUGHT

The authorities have not pin-pointed the blame and Mr. Finney said: "We must have had over 20 large fires and not one person has been caught. Why is this?"

There are many suspicions. *The Chicago Daily News* last summer quoted an unnamed real estate agency as saying: "If you can't make money on a building you can sure as hell collect insurance on it by burning it down. It is known that if you want a fire to occur you can have it arranged."

Perhaps. But more and more the process is accepted as part of the business of phasing out central city housing. No one wants the buildings, burned or unburned, after they have been ruined by the ravages of social distress.

The effects have not been all bad. Mr. Finney said that most of those who have moved away were the burned-out poor. Thus there is less concentration of poverty, the schools are less crowded and even the Blackstone Rangers, one of the most publicized South Side street gangs, are gone.

But many expect the process of burning and abandonment to continue. The vacant land is still worth little now. Eventually it goes back to the city or Federal Government and is put up for sale. Speculators are buying it, knowing that some day when large blocks of it are available it will be valuable.

The cycle of vandalism and despair that brought the old apartments to the burning stage has reached Woodlawn Gardens. The project is having to pay large management fees and repair charges to keep it up to the standards of decency. It is having to pay rising costs as well as its share of the burden of dismantling the central city, in the form of steadily rising taxes.

"The taxes last year rose 35 percent," Mr. Finney said. "This year they are expected to go up more than 50 percent." Cities across the country have had to levy higher taxes as their tax base has declined.

Woodlawn Gardens has mostly the kind of tenants who cannot afford further rent rises, Mr. Finney said. They range from welfare families to those with four or more children earning $11,000.

"CARRIED" BY GOVERNMENT

The Federal Government is "carrying" Woodlawn Gardens in the sense of postponing mortgage payments rather than foreclosing. There is the chance that under these circumstances the project may survive, but the fire and abandonment process is endangering other neighborhoods and other federally guaranteed property.

For the burned-out poor are not leaving the city. They're moving to other marginal neighborhoods—chiefly on the South Shore, the next stop down from Woodlawn—where the process of abandonment and decay is starting all over again, perhaps under a different form.

One of these neighborhoods is on the West Side, where the streets have Polish names and where a two-year-old apartment project called Kedvale Square more recently went into default of its mortgage payments.

Kedvale Square, in the Lawndale neighborhood, is a 116-unit, $2-million federally subsidized project on a five-acre plot. It is surrounded by a factory, transit tracks and row housing that looks less substantial than that in Woodlawn.

The project was completed three years ago by the Community Renewal Society, a long-established organization that helps poor migrants to the city. The society has sponsored about $19-million in new and rehabilitated housing, most of which is in default of mortgage payments.

As a result, the society has stopped building and is struggling to keep afloat that housing for which it holds a moral obligation. Reuben A. Sheares 2d, who heads the society's community development section, and other authorities interviewed here said that they did not expect the thousands of units of subsidized housing built in the central city in recent years ever to meet the mortgage obligations.

A more pressing question is whether the housing can survive even with the Government acting as generous landlord.

MAJOR REPAIRS NEEDED

Kedvale Square was built by a private builder for the society and won an award for distinguished design from the American Institute of Architects.

But now the project is having to make major repairs, not only because of the high incidence of vandalism but also because of poor construction, a problem with most of the new subsidized housing, caused by a complexity of factors ranging from unrealistic Government restrictions to abuse by private interests involved.

In an analysis of the problems, the sponsors informed the Federal Housing Administration that "low quality materials were used which now require replacement, such as doors and locks." Also cited were "inadequate roof drainage and complete absence of yard drainage in courtyards."

The sponsors informed the Government that steps were being taken to put the project on a

paying basis—admission of less destructive tenants, for example—but in the end they concluded: "No promise of future payment can be
made."

The Role of the Vanguard Party

James Boggs

Grace Boggs

All over the world this spring, wherever
Marxist-Leninist parties have come to power,
there will be mammoth celebrations of the hun-
dredth anniversary of Lenin's birth. Where
Marxist-Leninist parties are still striving to win
power, often struggling with each other over
how to achieve it, celebrations will also take
place. There will even be celebrations by parties
that call themselves Marxist-Leninist but have
never even conceived of themselves taking power. Liberals also will take advantage of the occasion to try to discredit Lenin, exposing what
they call the "bureaucratic tendencies" inherent in his concept of the vanguard party and
trying to make him responsible for everything
that has taken place in Soviet Russia since his
death. Whatever one's political complexion, everyone is compelled to recognize that what
Lenin thought and did has fundamentally altered the course of the world in which we live.

Today many people talk about Marxism-
Leninism without any understanding of the historical development of Marxist thought which
Lenin represents, much less of the historical
developments in revolutionary politics that
have taken place in other parts of the world
since Lenin.

Marx, writing in nineteenth-century Western
Europe where the rapidly advancing industrial
revolution was creating a powerful capitalist
class and a burgeoning working class, developed
a scientific, i.e., historical and dialectical, method for analyzing the conflict of social forces
developing inside capitalist production, projecting the working class—disciplined, united, and
organized by the process of production itself—
as the social force to overthrow capitalism and

institute a new mode of socialized production.
Lenin, tackling the problems of backward Tsarist Russia a generation later, utilized Marx's
method to analyze the development of Russian
capitalism, to anticipate the class struggle inseparable from this development, and to project
the socialist revolution as the only solution. But
when the Russian working class began its economic struggles, Lenin did not wait upon its
"inevitable" revolt to bring about the socialist
revolution. Instead, practically single-handedly,
he assumed the awesome responsibility of
building the kind of tightly disciplined organization which would be able to take state power
at the head of the Russian working class and all
the other oppressed and discontented strata of
Russian society. Without this party which it
took Lenin seventeen years of unpublicized,
protracted struggle to build, the power which
lay in the streets in 1917 Russia might have
ended up in the same kind of hands which
picked it up in 1968 France. What few people
realize is that until 1917 Lenin rarely addressed
himself to a mass audience, either in writing or
speaking, or appeared on the public platform.
Instead, he concentrated his extraordinary abilities and energies on the task which he had
concluded was decisive to the success of the
Russian Revolution: the building of an apparatus of dedicated, disciplined revolutionists to
lead the masses in the struggle for power.

For the revolutionary movements developing
today in every country, the great contribution
of Lenin was the clarity with which he put
forward and acted upon his fundamental convictions regarding the vanguard party: (1) that
the purpose of a revolutionary party is to take
absolute power in order to revolutionize the
economic and social system as the only way of
resolving fundamental popular grievances; (2)
that it is absolutely essential to build a revolutionary vanguard party if you are serious about

■ Taken from James Boggs and Grace Boggs, "The
Role of the Vanguard Party," *Monthly Review*, April,
1970, pp. 9–24. Copyright © 1970 by Monthly Review, Inc.; reprinted by permission of Monthly Review
Press.

taking power and not just playing with the phrase; and (3) that a revolutionary party can only be built by (*a*) unceasing ideological struggle, (*b*) strict discipline, (*c*) organized activity of every member, and (*d*) merciless self-criticism.

In the United States, as the black movement struggles to define its goals and the means to achieve them, the question of what constitutes a black revolutionary party is going to become increasingly the center of discussion and controversy. In order for this discussion and controversy to be meaningful, the black movement will have to make a serious study of the concept of the vanguard party as developed and practiced by its originator. To believe that the black revolutionary movement can evade such a study because Lenin was white and European would be just as ridiculous as for an African freedom fighter to refuse to fly an airplane because the Wright brothers were white Americans. Blacks don't refuse to drive Cadillacs because they are made by General Motors or to watch television because Philco (Ford) manufactures TV sets. Whatever has been achieved in human history, whether technological or political, blacks have a right to inherit. The very high development of the theory and practice of the vanguard party as originated by Lenin in Russia, and subsequently developed by Mao and Ho in Asia and Amilcar Cabral in Africa, belongs to all the oppressed people of the world, providing those who seek to end the domination of man by man with guidelines which they ignore at their peril. It must be borne in mind at the same time that these guidelines can be applied only in relation to the specific conditions of a particular country and only by an organization that has developed out of indigenous forces and is not totally dependent upon external or foreign aid for its existence.[1]

Fifty years ago the Old Left tried to adapt Lenin's view of the vanguard party to party-building in the United States. However, they were responding more to revolutionary momentum in Russia and Europe than to conditions in the United States. It was therefore impossible for them really to understand Lenin's concept of the vanguard party which had been developed to resolve the specific historical contradiction recognized by Lenin in the Russia of 1900, namely, the narrow or superficial scope of revolutionary work by Russian militants in comparison with the breadth of the spontaneous movement of Russian workers. The dilemma of white radicals in this country has been and still is the exact opposite, namely, their own intensive theoretical and organizational activity compared with the narrow scope of the spontaneous movement in the American working class which, nevertheless, in their theory remains the chief social force for the American revolution. Only for a brief period during the thirties was this not the case. But by that time the Marxist parties in this country had oriented their politics so completely around what was happening in Soviet Russia that they had not developed any perspective or program for taking power in the United States. Having occupied themselves for so long in proving a theory rather than programing for revolution, they were unprepared for anything more than militant trade-union leadership when the industrial workers erupted in the thirties.

Today black revolutionaries are confronted with a contradiction very similar to that faced by Lenin when he first began to lay the foundations of the vanguard party. Ever since 1964 the black masses in every Northern city have been either in, or on the verge of, spontaneous eruption. Every year millions of black people, and particularly black youth, are made "ready for anything" by the worsening conditions in every black community, the obvious inability of white power to cope with the critical social problems of an advancing technology, the mushrooming of white counterrevolutionary groupings, and the growing division among whites and within the ruling class as to which course to pursue to overcome the crisis. As in Lenin's day (and in his words) the movement has already produced "enormous numbers of people . . . who desire to protest, who are ready to render all the assistance they can in the fight against absolutism. . . . At the same time we have no people, because we have no leaders . . . no talented organizers capable of organizing extensive and at the same time uniform and harmonious work that would give employment to all forces. . . ." (*What Is To Be Done?*) The scope of spontaneous activity among the black masses has been growing far beyond the capacity of the black movement to provide revolutionary political leadership.

For the black movement and the black community the necessity for rapid development of a party able to give revolutionary leadership to the masses is not an abstract question. It is a matter of the utmost urgency. Every day thousands of blacks are made "ready for anything," often by a "routine" incident of police, foreman, school-principal, or social-worker brutality. Periodically a major "incident," such as the murder of Martin Luther King or Fred Hampton, transforms millions of blacks into potential revolutionaries. Just because a vanguard party with a revolutionary perspective, program, and trained cadres is not at hand to give direction to these rebels does not mean that they disappear from the historical stage. Rather they find other outlets for their rebellious energies. They drift from one Black Nationalist grouping or Black Power street gang to another, going "wherever the action is," or engage in different forms of hustling or banditry which as often as not are directed against other members of the black community. The result in the black community is a sense of unending crisis, chaos, and desperation from top to bottom. The situation in Northern cities is thus beginning to resemble more and more that of the Chinese countryside before the Communist Party and the Red Army under Mao were able to develop the revolutionary perspective, the cadres, and the program to politicize and incorporate the unemployed or underemployed youth who were pillaging the peasants in independent gangs or as part of the numerous warlord armies.

Before the black movement can summon up the profound theoretical and practical energies to create a vanguard party, it must first destroy—root and branch—the illusion that the spontaneous eruptions of the black masses are sufficient to achieve revolutionary change. Not until this illusion has been completely eliminated can black would-be revolutionaries apply themselves to the task of building a vanguard party with the urgency and energy that are required. Only then will they be ready to face up to the awesome responsibility which Lenin faced, of building that structure without which there can be no successful revolution. To destroy every remnant of this illusion in himself and those around him was the task Lenin set himself in *What Is To Be Done?*

It is only since the Watts rebellion in 1965 that the black movement and black leaders have begun to rely upon the spontaneous eruption of the masses. Prior to 1965, when the action was chiefly in the South, black militants recognized the need for organization as the only means for initiating mass action and as the necessary condition for survival in a society where open dictatorship and violence by whites left no room for democratic illusions. (Organization in the South in that period did not, of course, take the form of building a revolutionary party, since the aim of the movement was not Black Power but integration.)

In the last five years, however, side by side with the talk of Black Power, black leaders have acted as if all they had to do in order to advance the revolution is to act as spokesmen for the "brothers on the street." This is due, first of all, to the speed with which the brothers on the city streets have exploded, as if in a chain reaction, from city to city, giving the movement the assurance that "something is always going to happen." Secondly, the pride, aggressiveness, and unity which these eruptions have unleashed in all segments of the black community have created a sense of increasing excitement and momentum. And, finally, the skill with which a threatened white power structure has manipulated TV exposure of black militants and black salesmen for the American Way of Life (commercials), funding of community projects ("reparations"), highly visible and highly paid jobs for black careerists, and a steady stream of black publications, has created the widespread illusion that the actual and/or threatened spontaneous eruptions of the black masses are bringing Black Power closer.

Meanwhile, in fact, overall conditions in the black community have been deteriorating, while at the same time the spontaneous activities of the black street masses and the much publicized but futile reform efforts of the white power structure have aroused the "white backlash," which is only another name for the fascist counterrevolution.

There is little point in complaining about the skillful use of the Almighty American Dollar to coopt Black Power or the rise of the fascist counterrevolution. In confusing, undermining, and mobilizing to repress the black movement, white power is only doing what its self-interest dictates. If the fault lies anywhere, it is with the black movement for failing to arm the black community theoretically and politically against the predictable strategy and tactics of the enemy and to make clear that fascism cannot be stopped short of a total revolution dedicated to ending man's domination of man and his fear of those whom he dominates.

To do this, the black movement must recognize and keep pointing out the limits of what can be achieved by the black masses, for the same reason that Lenin insisted on the limits of what could be achieved by the spontaneous eruptions of Russian workers. The spontaneity of the workers does not take them beyond the level of the immediate, palpable, concrete interests of the everyday economic struggle, as Lenin kept pointing out. In a similar vein, black revolutionists must realize that the spontaneous eruptions of the black masses do not take them beyond the demand that white power alleviate their accumulated grievances, no matter how angry or explosive the masses are or how much Black Power talk and symbolism accompany their actions. Reliance upon spontaneity is, therefore, a form of liberalism because, in effect, it increases the illusion that the issues and grievances of the masses can be resolved without taking power away from those in power.

A revolutionary party becomes historically necessary and justified when the contradictions and antagonisms of a particular society have created a mass social force whose felt needs cannot be satisfied by reform but only by a revolution which takes power away from those in power. In addition to mobilizing this mass social force around its own grievances, the revolutionary party must then be ready to fulfill two additional tasks: (1) it must be able to project the vision of a new society which will solve these grievances by destroying the system that has created the domination of man over man, thus making life more human for everybody; and (2) it must have developed cadres of leaders with whom the masses can identify, and programs of struggle that will take the masses stage by stage to ever higher levels of political struggle, political consciousness, and actual control of facets (or bases) of power. Thus the revolutionary vanguard party serves the function of escalating the vision and leading the masses from a sense of grievance or unsatisfied *wants* to an awareness of social *needs*, or what

is necessary to remedy their grievances. By escalating the struggles of the masses, it raises their consciousness beyond the point of blaming the enemy for their plight and/or depending on him to alleviate it, to the point of depending upon their own efforts and their own power and responsibility to effect real change. At this stage, when the masses are already in motion, any party or organization which simply keeps them in a high state of agitation, confrontation, or mobilization, is not a revolutionary party, no matter what it claims. A revolutionary vanguard party cannot limit itself to the demands of the masses; it begins to make demands upon the masses themselves to exert greater power and greater responsibility.

"The greater the spontaneous uprising of the masses, the more widespread the movement becomes, so much the more rapidly grows the demand for greater consciousness in the theoretical, political, and organizational work" of the revolutionary leadership, Lenin insisted. At this point militancy without ideology becomes as dangerous as theory without practice. Lenin accused those who passively adapted themselves to the level of the masses instead of raising the masses to a higher political and social level. He called them "opportunists," professing to lead the masses when in fact they were only taking advantage of the masses' spontaneous activity to speak for the masses. To the counter-accusation that he was setting up a centralized apparatus to control the mass movement, he replied that a tight organization is necessary not only to combat the opportunists and moderates but to safeguard the movement against the premature actions undertaken by those who mistake the beginning of a struggle for its end.

The polemical style of Lenin's politics has turned off black revolutionaries because their chief acquaintance with it is in the form which it has assumed in the American Marxist groupings, of debates and discussion about what should be done in other countries, or in relation to the black movement to which white radicals cannot in any case give leadership. It is only when you recognize that Lenin's opponents represented real tendencies and real dangers to a spreading mass movement needing revolutionary direction that you can understand why he waged such a merciless ideological struggle against opportunists, liberals, and anarchists.

In the United States black militants have shirked the responsibility for this kind of ideological struggle, partly because of the deep hunger for unity which exists in all sections of the black movement, and partly because of the general political backwardness of this country which makes it much easier to deal with one's political opponents by character assassination and physical force than by political criticism and ideological struggle. The fact is that, ever since the emergence of the Black Power stage in 1966, serious political differences over the meaning of Black Power have been inevitable. Because these differences have not been clarified politically, they have tended to appear personal, and the movement has declined accordingly. Tendencies which could easily have developed a practical working relationship with one another in action have tried to live together within the same political organization until the political differences have festered into bitter antagonisms. What the black movement has not understood is that the clarification of political differences through ideological struggle by no means implies that there should be disunity in action, particularly on questions of defense against the common enemy or in the struggle for community control of various institutions inside the black community, objectives on which all tendencies in the black movement are agreed. The creation or encouragement of a United Front or Fronts to implement this unity in action and the development of the proper relations between the revolutionary party and the United Front are critical to the success of any revolution. But the first step in creating correct relations is a clear distinction between the purposes and organization of the vanguard party and the purposes and organization of the United Front.[2]

"We must first divide and then unite," Lenin kept saying. "Better fewer but better." A revolutionary party cannot be built on the quicksand of ideological confusion. Obviously there are a lot of people in the black movement whose political positions are dead wrong, and someone has to have the courage to say it, even if it busts wide open the façade of unity. A political split, like a divorce, is often healthier than trying to live together in the same house when you have fundamental differences. Blacks don't all think alike just because they are black

any more than Africans or Chinese or Vietnamese do. There are political differences inside the black movement representing different socioeconomic layers inside the black community. It is better to start the vanguard party from scratch with the serious few who are committed to the perspective of making the revolution that is necessary to meet the needs of the deepest layers of the black community than with many assorted persons who are all going in different directions and who are therefore bound to split at the moment of crisis, just when the need is for maximum organizational strength and unity. This does not mean that those who cannot or will not accept the ideology and discipline of the vanguard party cannot play a role in the movement or in concrete struggles for liberation that will culminate in the taking of power. But their place is in the various organizations of mass struggle, not in the vanguard party.

At the present time, among those who have been active in the movement over the past few years, there are quite a few people who are considering the formation of a black revolutionary party. Many of them believe that their past record of dedicated struggle in the movement is sufficient qualification for membership or leadership in a revolutionary party. They do not understand that with the emergence of Black Power the black movement left behind it the old stage of reform and integration and entered on a new stage of revolutionary struggle. As long as the black movement and black people were seeking primarily to reform or integrate into the system, what was required from black leadership was relatively simple. It was the outspoken, relentless condemnation of racism, in all its forms, arousing the black masses to a heightened sense of indignation and grievance against the society. This is something that black leaders have always done well and which the Black Power spokesmen of the past period have done superbly. However, ever since the movement changed direction, from being essentially an attempt to reform the system to a revolutionary struggle for power, what has been required from black leadership has been much more difficult because it is something for which blacks have had little previous training. Revolutionary struggle for power requires less rhetoric and more calculation. It requires a different kind of organization with a different, more scientific ideology; different, more disciplined, and committed members who are so convinced of the need for Black Revolutionary Power that the concept could be erased from their minds only by death itself; different, more strategically developed programs for escalating struggles; different, more carefully worked out structures to implement these programs; and different, less flamboyant leadership.

When Lenin first began to build the party in the early 1900s, intellectuals like Martov who had been active and outspoken wanted to be members, but they did not want to break with their past ideas, practices, and associates, and accept the discipline of a party branch or unit. This refusal to break with the politics of the past was the issue around which the split took place at the 1903 Congress of the Russian Party, between the Bolsheviks who stood for a tightly disciplined organization and the Mensheviks who wanted a loose structure which would leave members free to speak, write, and move about as they had been doing. The same question is bound to arise in the organization of any black revolutionary party today. It has already surfaced in a number of black organizations, usually during or after a crisis when the opportunities to take the center of the public stage are most numerous and most difficult to resist. This is not because of the lack of sincerity or dedication of any one individual but because the transition to a new stage of political struggle usually requires new people who can meet the new tasks and/or old experienced people who can make a serious self-criticism of their previous political habits and transform their political personalities to meet the new needs. This kind of self-evaluation and transformation is not easy for most people to make. As the objective situation becomes more revolutionary, an increasing number of militants begin to feel the need of an organization to help them make the many decisions that now become pressing. How to respond to the growing demands from the masses for leadership or to the provocations and opportunities proffered by the enemy to render one useless; what to do, what not to do, how to organize one's time and energies most effectively—all these become decisions beyond the capacity of a single individual to make. On the other hand, these same individuals can find the discipline of the party constraining or "bureaucratic" unless they are continually internalizing through criticism and self-criticism the urgent necessity for a highly organized, disciplined structure as the key to black liberation at this stage.

Recent revolutionary history in Asia, Africa, and Latin America has demonstrated that the most effective revolutionists are those who insist upon this kind of self-criticism and transformation as a normal procedure inside the organization, because they understand that the political energy generated thereby can itself become a force for rapid political development. On the other hand, where nationalist leaders have not insisted upon building self-criticism into the operations of the political organization, political weaknesses have become entrenched, and the masses and the new elite have become more vulnerable to neocolonialist subversion.

Black people are not only powerless, which is the condition of any oppressed people; they are also undeveloped, because of the national character of their oppression which is similar to that of a colonial people. It is no accident that the concept of rapid political development through self-criticism, originated by Lenin in backward Russia, has achieved its highest development in colonial, i.e., systematically exploited and systematically undeveloped countries like Vietnam, China, Cuba, and Guinea-Bissau. To build the party that is necessary to take power and revolutionize society, the members of the party themselves must undergo rapid political development into new people. The only means available to them to achieve this is also the best means, i.e., the method of constant struggle, constant criticism and constant transformation, utilizing the energy created by the dynamic of error to advance the political maturity of the organization, getting rid of every vestige of liberalism, opportunism, sectarianism, adventurism, egoism, and every tendency toward "militarism" or the separation of military from political struggle. The ideological struggle against other political tendencies and against remnants of these tendencies in every member removes political education from the sphere of abstract generalizations about other revolutions which come so easily to intellectual revolutionaries. It compels the revolutionary organization to develop its own revolutionary concepts from its concrete experiences and practices in party-building, internally and in relation to the masses and other organizations.

In this article we have tried to point out some of the important lessons in building a revolutionary party that the black movement in the United States can learn from Lenin. But everything that Lenin said and did cannot be applied automatically and mechanically to the American Revolution. Black revolutionaries must analyze for themselves the specific situation in the United States in this, the last third of the twentieth century. They must determine for themselves the critical contradiction in this country, which is at one and the same time the technologically most advanced and politically most backward country in the world. From this determination they must project the fundamental goal of a revolution in this country: to create a society of politically conscious, socially responsible individuals able to use technology for the purpose of liberating and developing humanity. They must arrive at their own appraisal of the revolutionary social forces available to achieve this revolutionary humanist objective and of the interrelation between these revolutionary social forces and other social forces in the country. They must make their own appraisal of the present stage of struggle and the programs necessary to advance the struggle towards the projected objective. (See James Boggs, *Racism and the Class Struggle*, Monthly Review Press, 1970; also *Manifesto for a Black Revolutionary Party*, Pacesetters Publishing House, P.O. Box 3281, Philadelphia 19121.)

Scientific, i.e., dialectical and historical, method requires the systematic examination of the specific conditions, contradictions, and antagonisms in one's own country and one's own time; the projection of fundamental solutions to these contradictions; and programs of struggle to achieve these solutions. It is only because he understood this, which is the essence of the scientific method, that Lenin was able not only to build the party which led the Russian masses to victory over Tsarism, but also to make the analysis of imperialism and of the colonial struggle (neither of which had matured in the time of Marx), and from this analysis to recognize the revolutionary character of the nationalist movements in Ireland, Asia, Africa, and among black people in the United States.

Most old radicals thinking about Lenin in the United States today are still thinking of what he did in Russia and the concepts he evolved to achieve the Russian Revolution. In that sense they have become dogmatists, not recognizing that Lenin was building a party for his time, to change intolerable conditions in his country, based on the analysis of the specific conditions in that country. Lenin is not relevant to us unless we have done the same for this country and for our time. Similarly they do not recognize that Marx was writing at a specific stage in Western history and that, if he were living today, he would have advanced his theory far beyond what he wrote in the middle of the nineteenth century, for the simple reason that society itself has advanced to another historical stage.

The Russian Revolution, like every successful revolution since then, took place in a country where the working class was a small fraction of the population. Lenin would have been the first to recognize that a revolution not led by the working class could take place because he recognized that the rising colonial world was composed primarily of oppressed peoples who were not proletarians but who were nevertheless compelled because of their dual oppression by native and foreign rulers to overthrow their oppressors and institute a new economic, social, and political order. The one thing which Lenin was firm about, regardless of the conditions varying from country to country, was the need for a vanguard party whose members recognize the necessary difference between themselves and the revolutionary masses in terms of a firm ideology, programmatic commitment, and discipline, before they go to the masses to interact with them and give them leadership. If this distinction is blurred, what comes into being is not a revolutionary vanguard party but a mass party, however small in actual size, which incorporates into its membership those who should in fact be its followers and supporters. Such a party cannot lead the masses; it can only tailgate or follow after them.

For revolutionists all over the world, the

study of Lenin is relevant, *not* from the standpoint of his analysis of the Russian working class as the main social force for the Russian Revolution, but for his concept of building a revolutionary vanguard party on the basis of that section of the population of a given country which is both the most oppressed and the chief revolutionary social force. If the working class constitutes the chief revolutionary social force in a particular country, the revolutionary party must be built on it. If the chief revolutionary social force is the peasantry, as in China, then base the party on the peasantry. If it is the black masses, as in the United States, then build the revolutionary party on the basis of the black revolutionary social forces.

NOTES

1. In the last period because of the understandable concentration on black pride and black consciousness, there has been a tendency among black would-be revolutionaries to refuse to have anything to do with anything or anyone that was not all-black. The result in some cases has been ludicrous, e.g., black militants unable to discuss theoretical and political questions among themselves because the only language they have in common is English, or black history teachers glorifying African rulers of the past who were no less abusive of their subjects than white tyrants of the same epoch.

As Black Nationalism undergoes the necessary transition into Black Revolutionary Nationalism, what is and what is not historically relevant to black people will have to be redefined. Black revolutionary historians cannot limit themselves to studies that inspire black people with pride and consciousness. They must also give the black movement that sense of historical continuity with a revolutionary past which every revolutionary movement needs in order to develop a sound basis for its present theory and practice. In the very difficult period ahead, every source of theoretical and political strength must be mined. The richest source, apart from the ongoing struggle of the masses, is

undoubtedly what has been attempted by other revolutionists in this and other countries. Thus black revolutionary historians must provide the movement with critical studies in two main arenas:

First, with regard to black liberation leaders of the past (from Toussaint L'Ouverture, Denmark Vesey, Nat Turner, Frederick Douglass, Marcus Garvey, W. E. B. DuBois, to Martin Luther King, Malcolm X, Stokely Carmichael, Rap Brown, and Huey Newton), what each achieved, what each was unable to achieve, and how much this falling short of the goal of black liberation was due to objective conditions of the time and how much to subjective factors, i.e., inadequate revolutionary theory and practice. In this respect the black movement in the United States has an incalculable advantage over white radical groupings because it has this tremendous wealth of historical experiences to draw upon and evaluate. By contrast, white "revolutionaries" throughout American history from the Founding Fathers to the present, with the sole exception of the Abolitionists, have always defined the American problem in terms of white–white relations, dealing with white–black oppression, if at all, only as an afterthought.

Second, with regard to revolutionary movements and the theory and practice of revolutionary leaders of the whole world, and particularly those of that part known as the Third World. Until the black revolutionary movement is ready to take seriously the scientific approach to revolution developed by Marx, Lenin, Ho, and Giap, it will still be depending upon mystical or external guidance to achieve the power which can only be achieved by the most rigorous scientific appraisal of social forces. Mao, Ho, and Cabral did not reject the necessity for a scientific approach to revolution because the founders of this approach were white. They used the method of Marx and Lenin, being careful at the same time to distinguish between the specific conditions of their own countries and those of Europe and Russia.

2. To learn more about the theory and practice of building the United Fronts which, in the course of protracted *popular* struggles over concrete issues and the control of social institutions, develop into dual-power structures or parallel hierarchies, we have to look, not to Lenin and the revolution in Russia, but to the revolutions which combine national and social struggle, e.g., in China, Vietnam, and Guinea-Bissau.

"The Doing"
John C. Leggett

THE APPLICATION OF MECHANISMS OF PERSUASION TO A VARIETY OF SITUATIONS

Now we can apply mechanisms of persuasion identified in Section One to a variety of situations.

Considering Table 38, Situation 1, where we try to bring together various elements, let us suppose that the problem is generally one of activating a large number of people who are predisposed to support a given cause and who live in a neighborhood where conditions foster the formation of consciousness among a majority. In this and other situations, we must avoid the unnecessary use of resources. Don't waste the goodies. We try not to use mechanisms involving a high degree of personal initiative, since there is no need to apply precious organizational resources to convince people who are already convinced. In this situation, we should use mechanisms that are intrinsically low in cost, high in scope and, ideally, productive in output. Rallies, the front group, and the com-

■ This essay was prepared especially for this volume.

mon messenger should do the trick in a setting where people are predisposed to become involved.

In situation 2, it is desired to activate in a block-club type of organization a small number of people who share a low degree of consciousness. The people live in a neighborhood where, although conditions favor consciousness and there are numerous militant opinion leaders, only a minority has yet attained consciousness, owing to the conditions.

In this situation, there should be no hesitation about using resources. Spend, but do so wisely; use expert professional organizers through such mechanisms as the front group. The front group might bring together professional opinion leaders and persons with a low degree of consciousness, making it possible for the professional organizer to press the ordinary member through the opinion leader. How? Through the establishment and continuance of primary ties. Where? Certainly in front groups such as tea clubs and tenants' associations. In addition, the organizer can participate as an

TABLE 38   Essential Mechanisms of Persuasion Recommended for Block Clubs and Militant Counterelites Under Various Circumstances in the Context of the Neighborhood

Preparatory Conditions*:	A—Conditions Maximize Consciousness		B—Conditions Maximize Consciousness		C—Conditions Minimize Consciousness		D—Conditions Minimize Consciousness	
Type of Opinion Leader:	Militant		Nonmilitant		Militant		Nonmilitant	
Situation— Consciousness†:	1—High	2—Low	3—High	4—Low	5—High	6—Low	7—High	8—Low
	Rallies The front group The common messenger	The front group	The front group Bypass the subelite Direct pressure	Ignore?	The front group Rallies Direct action The bloc vote	The front group	The front group Bypass the subelite Direct pressure	Ignore?

*Conditions A–D refer to the lettered conditions in Table 34.

†"Consciousness" here indicates the degree of consciousness of family members.

observer at demonstrations, and he can involve others, including opinion leaders and members of the rank and file. The latter should become susceptible to mobilization *after* they have witnessed public displays of camaraderie between their opinion leaders and the radical organizers. In this situation, the rank and file associate the class frame of reference entertained by the radical organizers with their own positive opinion reference—the militant opinion leaders. Thus demonstrations can heighten consciousness and make the participants eligible for even greater involvement at subsequent rallies.

In situation 3 it is absolutely necessary to isolate and to undercut the authority of an opinion leader who lacks consciousness and, presumably, conversion potential. It would be wise to remove old leadership and to train new opinion leaders. Until the replacement occurs, the organizers must contend with a set of opinion leaders who may use their affective attachments and associated arguments to create ambivalence toward, withdrawal from, or opposition to, the grass-roots movement.

An attack against this kind of conservative leadership should use a mechanism high in personal initiative. The front group might be the ideal device, for it represents a combination of the professional organizer and the ideology to which potential activists are attracted. Again, direct pressure, and bypassing the subelite, might be useful at this stage of activation, for once within the front group, militant rank and file can participate in actions that will solidify their ties with a growing grass-roots movement precisely because the action may involve state oppression. These processes in turn teach the militant rank and file to identify their interests with those of the incipient grass-roots movement.

The above-mentioned mechanisms of persuasion might also have a latent function; namely, to place the hard-core organizers among the rank and file as both elements confront conservative opinion leaders. To allow rank and file to be alone with these opinion leaders—persons often gifted in swaying opinions on the basis of buddy-buddy ties rather than actions in keeping with the working-class interests—might be unwise. The counterelite can carry on part of this isolation operation by using mechanisms high in personal initiative to answer questions as they

arise from those suffering stress due to purge of the esteemed opinion leader.

Clearly, the ideal grass-roots movement contains many of the attributes of a well-oiled machine, perhaps even a professional bureaucratic organization—for hierarchy is present, however beclouded it might be by the utopian rhetoric of the movement. Still, as Roberto Michels once put it, those who strive for democracy must establish organization; and wherever organization emerges there follows hierarchy, and many of the conditions that had originally set people in motion against inequality.

Apparently, the only corrective is a counterelite group capable of meeting periodically and discussing this deformation of egalitarian ideals. Long-term remedies would also seem to be in order. Local groups in the United States, and not just those in the Communist world, thoroughly need a cultural revolution every ten years. Otherwise the counterelite can become just one more oppressor.

The need for a counterelite and hence a division of labor is most obvious in situation 4 of Table 38, where families with a low degree of consciousness live in a neighborhood in which conditions tend to generate consciousness although, ironically, neither the people nor the opinion leader are militant.

This situation is almost a lost cause, and perhaps the movement strategists should ignore this category of individuals unless someone in the vanguard group has already dealt effectively with this setting. The nonmilitants in situation 4 may well become a group opposed to the grass-roots movement, and if this occurs, the problem is no longer one of activation but one of neutralization—taking a course of action that will paralyze the dissidents. If the population is organized, then perhaps the best tactic would be one of infiltration of the group and redirection of its goals.

In the fifth situation, we want to activate a small number of people who are already predisposed to support our cause; however, conditions in their neighborhood fail to support the development of consciousness, notwithstanding the presence of a militant opinion leader.

What to do? Let us assume that where a number of like individuals constitute a minority, it is best to bring them together so that they can support one another for purposes of self-defence and realization of radical aims. Both can be accomplished when countering the opinions of a less organized majority and when attempting to convert those who are neutral but who might accept activation.

How might this minority of verbal militants be brought together? The front group could serve to create liaison between professional organizers, opinion leaders, and local militants. After these ties have been created, the organizers should try to solidify them through joint participation in activities which are medium to high in intensity: rallies, direct action, and the bloc vote.

What not to do? Don't use the common messenger, for it is low on generation of affect and cohesion.

In situation 6, we can observe a condition identical to the fifth variation, except that the level of consciousness of family members is low. To be low in consciousness does not generally mean opposition to a highly class or class-racially conscious point of view. Hence the procedure is to press persons to sympathize with neighbors who are highly conscious. In this setting, it would seem to be necessary to use a mechanism high in personal initiative, since the counterelite group must spend considerable time removing false conceptions of reality as well as educating the persons to a view with open eyes the real operations of private property and brainwashing institutions.

The mechanism should be medium in focus, since a certain amount of rational disputation will be necessary. Ideally, the mechanism should be high in intensity, since the persuading group must overcome traditional affect as well as argument. Finally, the mechanism can be medium in scope, since relatively few people are involved. The mechanism that qualifies in this regard, once again, is the front group. Its members should include persons from the counterelite group, representatives of the neighborhood and residential district councils, and the local opinion leaders as well. Along with helpful union people, these individuals can set up and use the front group in order to relate on an affective basis, through the opinion leaders, to that sizable number of misinformed people who belong to the existing block clubs. In this situation, mechanisms low on personal initiative and intensity should be avoided.

In situation 7, the conditions minimize consciousness, the opinion leaders are nonmilitant, and the people who are highly conscious constitute a minority. Here, it might be possible to bring the highly conscious ones into the movement through a mechanism that is medium or high in personal initiative, medium or high in focus (to clarify issues and to reinforce perspectives), medium or high in intensity (to create and to reinforce solidarity on a relational basis), and low or medium in scope (since so few are involved). Relevant mechanisms are: the front group, bypassing the subelite, and direct pressure. Obviously mechanisms low in personal initiative would be of no use.

Situation 8 is hopeless.

In the fruitful situations so far discussed, what if it is impossible to establish a front group? It then becomes necessary to rely on organizers who do not have this group cover but who are nonetheless facile when dealing with the local population, the neighborhood councils, and the opinion leaders. And to have trained and militant organizers requires dependence on *vanguard party organizations and militant industrial unions.* The first can seek out and train the personnel. The second can provide the necessary experience. Of course, government agencies may be willing to supply "change agents," but these persons quite frequently misdefine the nature of oppression and instill points of view that are at variance with an exploitative and oppressive reality. The change agents are generally wrong in their diagnoses of what oppresses people: It's not that the working classes suffer from "cultural deprivation," "high taxation," "high unemployment" and the like—or if such phenomena do exist, they are effects of belonging to the working class. The problem specifications fail to clearly identify the root sources of working-class adversity, namely, *corporate* exploitation of people and corporate political control of citizens.

What is happening is clear. To varying degrees, working-class lives are made miserable by corporations which administer prices and lead the country into war-inducing imperial relations, as the same corporations use parlimentary processes to achieve their narrow ends. Change-agent definitions avoid this question of upper-class control and confuse grass-roots persons who are otherwise capable of coming together and acting collectively as well as successfully when rank-and-file leadership defines the exact nature of class and institutional oppression.

ACTION, CONTRADICTIONS, ENERGY AVAILABLE, AND ERRORS

What happens when the people unite successfully? Generally, they can act, but in doing so they discover antagonisms in their own camp, and the many serious potential consequences of internal bickerings should not be underestimated. Yet we would be foolish to confuse these internecine disputes with those hostile relations which take place when enemies mix and friends help. To clarify this matter, let us make a distinction between two types of contradictions: inimical and antagonistic. An inimical contradiction is a condition of opposed forces, ranging from interpersonal feistiness to open warfare, *within one's own group*. Such contradictions are to be resolved, wherever possible, on the basis of discussion. By contrast, antagonistic contradictions drive forces in conflicting directions as grass-roots groups relate to enemies and/or to allies. In these instances, the contradictions must sometimes be resolved through force. Of course, it is crucial to be able to recognize the conditions under which the inimical antagonism passes over to become an antagonistic contradiction *within* what had

been the camp of progressive struggle before fission.

In light of these problems, let us consider a typical situation, one in which the block clubs, led by the militant counterelite group, decide to mobilize their members in a fight against a landlord or an employer. Here the inimical contradictions may well result in numerous factional fights and protracted despondencies among the rank and file; moreover, there will be little energy left for careful thought on the connection between diagnosis of the situation, the prescription for this setting, and the implementation of the strategy.

There are seven types of errors that can derive in part from inimical contradictions within the grass-roots organization (see Table 39). In the case of the type-1 error, there is correct diagnosis of the situation and correct selection of tactics, but these elements are incorrectly applied. In some instances, especially where an individual's group is torn by recurrent and deep controversy, he simply cannot effectively use his resources, despite prior correct appraisal of the situation and subsequent recommendations.

A type-2 error consists of correct diagnosis of the situation and incorrect selection of tactics, but proper application of the incorrect weapons. We might best label this combination the Movement Monster.

The type-3 error, the "New-Left Malady," is correct diagnosis of the objective situation, wrong selection of tactics, and imperfect application of the tactics selected.

TABLE 39   Types of Errors in Diagnosis, Prescription, and Implementation

Type of Error	Diagnosis	Prescription	Implementation
Type 1	+	+	−
Type 2	+	−	+
Type 3	+	−	−
Type 4	−	+	+
Type 5	−	−	+
Type 6	−	−	−
Type 7	−	+	−

In type-4 errors, which might be called the Liberal Delight, there occurs incorrect diagnosis of the objective situation, correct selection of tactics (given the initial but incorrect assumption), and perfect application of the devices *chosen*! Disaster.

The fifth situation consists of the wrong diagnosis and the wrong tactics—perfectly applied. Situation 6 is a total loser, and error type 7 is somewhat more complicated but equally lacking in promise.

We could spend a lot of time discussing how inimical contradictions promote tactical errors on mobilization; clearly, however, one of the greatest contradictions is the division between theory and evidence. Here the counterelite decision-makers impute to their theoretical assumptions a validity that could only exist if empirical evidence could be mobilized to substantiate the assumptions themselves. The original diagnosis, made without evidence, is often a fond projection of wishes: There is a disregard of the need to connect general thought to empirical regularities.

With this misgiving in mind, let us consider Table 40. In situation 1, bearing in mind the potential errors and contradictions, we encounter a problem more typical of the 1930s than of the 1970s. It is one of mobilizing a sizable militant group against a wooden, consistently conservative bureaucratic organization which is not equipped to deal with nonuniform events. Under these circumstances, the only approach that would *not* be appropriate is the utilization of a large number of professional organizers; use anything but mechanisms high in personal initiative. In fact, the militant organizations can create and recruit potential leadership as a result of these struggles and send the recruits elsewhere for training before they are committed to organizational struggles. This supplementation of human resources must be continuous, since social movements burn out professional organizers. For whenever a person must dexterously and continuously confront the state, the state inadvertently brings to the fore his personal anxieties, guilt, and fears associated with attacking authority. The reasons for burnout are evident. First, the professional has a chance to observe what happens to those who continuously and conspicuously move against the state. Second, fear of career losses if not personal injury becomes reinforced by the admonitions of peers and relatives, equally aware

TABLE 40   Types of Bureaucratic Opposition Encountered by Neighborhood Councils and Militant Counterelite Groups in Various Situations

Preparatory Conditions[†]:	Situations in Which a Type[*] of Bureaucratic Opposition Is Encountered							
	A—Conditions Maximize Consciousness		B—Conditions Maximize Consciousness		C—Conditions Minimize Consciousness		D—Conditions Minimize Consciousness	
Type of Opinion Leader:	Militant		Nonmilitant		Militant		Nonmilitant	
Degree of Consciousness of Family Members:	High	Low	High	Low	High	Low	High	Low
Rationalistic, Consistent Conservative Bureaucratic Opposition	1	3	5	7	9	11	13	15
Professional Fair-weather Liberal Bureaucratic Opposition	2	4	6	8	10	12	14	16

*There are at least a dozen types of bureaucratic opposition, including, in addition to the two above: (*a*) rationalistic, fair-weather liberal; (*b*) human relations, fair-weather liberal; (*c*) human relations, consistent conservative; (*d*) professional consistent conservative.

†Conditions A—D refer to the lettered conditions in Table 34.

of dire consequences. The consequent and peculiar concatenation of personal fears, anxieties, and observations, as well as family pressures and state sanctions, further raises the individual's level of anxiety. The resulting and exhausting mental crises debilitate the organizer both physically and mentally. In this situation, the successful organizer generally prefers the quiescent alternative of cooptation to the choice of continuous struggle. Even when stamina remains, the state can incarcerate and in other ways bring to an end the forays of the organizer. Hence there is always the need to recruit new blood from struggle situations to replace predictable casualties.

In situation 2 (Table 40) the problem centers on how to mobilize a militant group against a nonrigid bureaucratic organization which is equipped with special departments designed to deal with such militant organizations. Unlike the rational bureaucratic outfit, the professional fair-weather liberals are equipped to take the attack to the enemy. For example, it can send its staff members into neighborhoods to head off trouble. Under these circumstances, the problem is basically one of determining how a grass-roots organization can move flexibly and intelligently at all times. What is potentially the most destructive error in this situation? An intuitive answer would be type 4: For example, the grass-roots group misdiagnosed the structure of the opposing group as "bureaucratic" and hence "inflexible" but then moved rationally and consistently to select an appropriate technique and to carry it out. If the enemy had been misdiagnosed no skilled grass-roots organizers would be present to defend the grass-roots groups at the very moment when the bureaucratic professionals were using human relations skills to soften the impact of the grass-roots mobilization and perhaps to turn a carefully planned episode into a farce. In other words, a professional bureaucratic group could serve their opponents both coffee and jobs, and thereby take the steam out of the insurgency. Under these circumstances, one mechanism of persuasion in particular is necessary: the front group, with its store of left-professional experts in positions to relate continuously to key personnel. Equally high in focus is the mechanism of expertise. The other mechanisms would be useful, but they should be prescribed and used

only in conjunction with the professional expert.

Jumping to situation 6, we encounter the following problem: The conditions maximize a high degree of consciousness, and the families are in fact quite class conscious; yet the leadership is non-militant. Here, of course, we are not referring to all the families but to many of those in this setting.

When dealing with a professional bureaucratic organization and opinion leaders of this sort, we should use very-high-focus mechanisms. The front group would be ideal.

In this context, one error that might readily occur would be the type-1 variety (correct diagnosis; proper mechanism selection; imperfect application). Why? Even if the first two hurdles were overcome, the opinion leader would undoubtedly oppose any mobilization by either disrupting the activities of the front group. Alternatively, if the conservative opinion leader were neutralized, his inexperienced successor might misapply the tactics associated with the mechanisms in question.

In situation 9 we are dealing with a minority of rank and file, i.e., considerably less than half of the area's population. Minorities in such situations tend to lack cohesiveness, especially when scattered spatially, as they usually are. Hence the organizers should act to create and to reinforce ties between them.

Which mechanisms should be used and why? Let us assume that when we first attempt to mobilize a militant rank and file as well as opinion leaders in a setting where both are undoubtedly a minority—and the opposition is a rationalistic, class-conscious organization—it may be useful to use mechanisms that are medium in personal initiative, medium in focus, high in intensity, and low in scope. The *personal initiative* mechanism need only be medium because the opinion leader and the rank and file are already with us, whereas the bureaucratic opposition is less than adequately equipped to upset the mobilization effort. The bureaucratic opposition lacks the personal hitting power of a professional bureaucratic outfit. In a setting like this, large numbers of professional experts associated with the front group are unnecessary. The mechanism of persuasion need only be medium in *focus*, for the population is already knowledgeable. The mechanism

TABLE 41 Relation of Types of Bureaucratic Allies, Types of Bureaucratic Opposition, and Other Variables in Situations Encountered by Neighborhood Councils and Militant Counterelite Groups

Type of Bureaucratic Allies	Type of Bureaucratic Opposition	Preparatory Conditions*:	Situations in Which Bureaucratic Opposition of Allies Is Encountered							
			A—Conditions Maximize Consciousness		B—Conditions Maximize Consciousness		C—Conditions Minimize Consciousness		D—Conditions Minimize Consciousness	
		Type of Opinion Leader:	Militant		Nonmilitant		Militant		Nonmilitant	
		Degree of Consciousness of Family Members:	High	Low	High	Low	High	Low	High	Low
Professional All-Weather Liberal	Rationalistic Consistent Conservative		1	7	13	19	25	31	37	43
	Human Relations Fair-Weather Liberal		2	8	14	20	26	32	38	44
	Professional Fair-Weather Liberal		3	9	15	(21)	27	33	(39)	45
Professional Fair-Weather Liberal	Rationalistic Consistent Conservative		4	10	16	(22)	28	34	40	46
	Human Relations Fair-Weather Liberal		5	11	17	23	29	35	41	47
	Professional Fair-Weather Liberal		6	12	18	24	30	36	42	48

*Conditions A–D referred to the lettered conditions in Table 34.

should be high in *intensity* in order to develop affective ties between families objectively a minority and often isolated from one another. Finally, the mechanism can be low in *scope*, since few families are involved.

What kinds of mechanisms should we use? In the beginning, direct action and the boycott would seem to be most appropriate. Later we might want to use the front group to solidify ties.

Perhaps the most likely error is the type-4 variety, where an incorrect diagnosis is followed with a correct prescription and implementation. Initially we can assume that the entire population within the block—or neighborhood—is low in consciousness because of the material conditions of the area and because there are outward indications of lack of consciousness.

Other types of situations come to mind, but rather than consider alternatives, let us add another problem: the nature of the bureaucratic ally and the problems it presents. When dealing with bureaucratic allies, at least two types of errors can crop up:

1. The error of absorption—the loss of control of one's own organization to the bureaucratic ally
2. The error of compromise—the unnecessary watering down of programs.

Case A: Putting It Together

When we add these additional considerations to those already discussed, we can focus on situation 3, specified in Table 41, for it is one which has constituted a recurrent stumbling block for grass-roots groups.

We have in mind a black working-class neighborhood in a city such as Detroit. The majority of working adults are unionized industrial workers, and there is a sprinkling of middle-class professionals. (School teachers and social workers seem to prevail in this neighborhood's small minority of white-collar people.) Most of the men work in the auto plants. The immediate problem they face is a common one: Community real estate interests are urban-renewing a black, lower-lower-class slum lo-

■ I am indebted to several of my former Berkeley students for portions of this example.

cated several miles from the black neighborhood we are considering. Even more predictably, the real estate interests involved are attempting to relocate many of those being driven from their homes by urban renewal by depositing them in the well-organized, decidedly working-class district we have cited. To take the first step in this lucrative transplant, a real estate firm has successfully lobbied to rezone an area allowing the conversion of single-family dwelling units into multiple-family dwelling units to be crowded into by tenants in flight from the nearby renewed area. The arrival of these poor black people can only be perceived by the black working class—most of whom are industrial unionists—as the beginning of school deterioration and neighborhood lawlessness.

To make the neighborhood change even more unpalatable to black labor unionists, the police have allowed organized prostitution to enter the neighborhood, and along with this vice, hard-drug traffic as well. Early in the morning it is not unusual to observe bedraggled customers leaving the neighborhood whorehouse. Calls of protest to the police fail to elicit a crackdown on what is becoming a raucous bawdy nuisance in an area where people have worked hard through their neighborhood clubs to create more for themselves and their children.

To deal with the problem, the neighborhood association looks for allies and selects a target. The ally selected consists of a black voluntary association committed to incremental change and stressing the importance of improvement in black education (to be made possible largely through the donations of white liberals). Some of the white liberals in turn belong to the professional fair-weather liberal target: the network of real estate firms and associated banks. Many top executives of these firms openly donate large sums to quasi-philanthropic groups committed to Negro uplift through education. Less publicly, however, they exploit not only black tenement dwellers on welfare but black working-class people driven from neighborhood to neighborhood in search of an equanimity made elusive by white real estate entrepreneurs who have become rich by manipulating land and dwelling units.

In this context, grass-roots group decides to

use a variety of mechanisms of persuasion to force the most vulnerable real estate firm to cease (a) their involvement in urban-renewal projects which, in effect, rob the lower-lower-class poor; and (b) their efforts to turn the organized, black working-class neighborhood into another slum to be groomed for this destiny by the target firm, related businesses, and the city's police, not to mention the complying civil servant technicians associated with the urban renewal project.

In this solid working-class neighborhood, the mobilization problem would not warrant the heavy allocation of scarce resources to the organizing of grass-roots folk. The people are ready. Indeed, many had participated in an urban insurrection which several years ago destroyed an estimated $175 million worth of the city's private property. The main problem is figuring out what to expect from the professional fair-weather liberal friend. Although the leaders are black the political coloration could become predictably Oreo: black on the outside and white on the inside when Whitey applies financial pressure.

In this situation, it is absolutely necessary to have experienced political people operating from the framework of a vanguard party in order to diagnose the maneuvers of the liberal ally, to prescribe tactics, and to lead in their use. A Black Panther party or its rational-revolutionary equivalent comes to mind. It would be the task of these militants to serve the people, to coordinate them, and to listen to them. And the pitfalls are many, for what is involved is a three-way relationship between one's own cluster and those of the enemy, and the ally as well.

Should the counterelite lead even a mild attack on the offending real estate group, the two professional bureaucracies—including one's ally—might become so involved in the bartering of good will that the specific issues would become generalized and solutions watered down in order to accommodate both groups, the enemy and the ally. Here, an overriding commitment of both sides to gentlemanly techniques is most probable. Needless to say, this type of cooperation would not necessarily serve the partisan interests of the grass-roots militants, who are out to stop real estate ruination of

their neighborhood. Under these circumstances, there is a danger that the bureaucracies, characterized as they are by social skills and expertise, might form an *entente cordiale*, recruit from both the leadership and the ranks of the militant organizing group, and thereby eliminate the militant voluntary association's power through the process of absorption.

To deal with this possibility of loss of membership, the militant voluntary association must wage an all-out campaign to test and prove numerical strength, thus increasing the prestige of the group, so that the members will remain loyal. However, given the nature of the alliance, the choice of the tactics might require considerable delicacy. In an alliance with a professional, consistently liberal organization, the important thing to keep in mind is that these people prefer needling to knifing an opponent. Hence, the militants' breadth of tactics is necessarily limited. Given this circumstance, the bureaucratic allies might serve, at best, to generate enthusiasm and to attract adherents to the cause through the use of inoffensive techniques. Rallies could be planned for publicity, not notoriety, in order to draw the community's attention to the issues. For a show of strength, front groups could be convinced to endorse the goals of the militant voluntary association. Unremitting direct pressure could be brought to bear to overwhelm the opposition with a fusillade of words. Here the professional ally would be particularly helpful, for he could suggest techniques and pull the wires necessary to obtain decisions through influence. Once the ally becomes committed, his very commitment paves the way for his subsequent support of bloc political votes and related solutions, such as a boycott on economic issues. Of course, all action anticipated within situation 3 (Table 41) suggests collusion rather than collision—to a point. At a certain juncture in the struggle, the militant counterelite group may decide to unload the liberal ally or to attempt to take him with the group as it leads the rank and file in a more militant course of action.

Situations other than the one we have been discussing could be diagnosed and acted on in a manner suggested by our previous analyses. Illustrative are the following two situations: Cases B and C.

Case B: Outline for Grass-Roots-Level Community Organization

I believe that the most opportune time for the formation of a grass-roots-level organization would be after an incident. From the instant one gets the notion to organize, I do not envision having to wait too long for a controversial incident to occur if one is dealing with a community where the minority groups do not have control over their destinies and are not a part of the political-economic structure. The first time I saw the people getting ripped off I would move to put my plan of action in effect. For instance, let us deal with the educational structure in a given community. We know from the beginning that minority students are not being given the opportunity to participate to the fullest extent in the workings and benefits of their school. We are cognizant that many schools work on a track system that relegates a lot of students, mostly minority, to second- and third-track status. They are able to receive high grades but are still forced to remain in a course level and academic programs that do not prepare them for college.

When people know they are getting a raw deal, they are apt to react to that which has been perpetrated against them; this is especially true of young people. This is where I come in. Someone will have to work with the parents and lend a bit of organizational strategy to their emotional efforts to aid their children. Let us take a situation where some black students have been suspended. My first act would be to get the students along with their parents together to discuss a course of action.

I would circulate flyers throughout the black community, informing the people what was coming down on them. I would tell them the date and place of the meeting. Everyone would assume, hopefully, that the rest of the concerned citizens will attend, which will prompt them to come to the meeting. Before the arranged time for the general meeting to come off, I would contact individual leaders with whom I have already established rapport. It will be like the coming together of the brain trust. This would serve to prevent a dogmatic type of

• This essay was written by Esther Hardy Jennings, a student enrolled at Livingston College.

atmosphere where one person, namely myself, is spear-heading all the activities.

This caucus group that I have called together will make up a rough draft of a list of demands to be made by the students, as well as an agenda. This would serve to provide some leadership for the group and to limit the dialogue from endless suggestions of what the group wants to do.

We will arrange for the mass meeting as soon as possible in order that we catch the people in an emotional state. We cannot afford to let apathy set in. The same day as the incident would be the best time, I surmise. At the meeting, I will appeal to the pride of the group. I will throw emotional questions to them like, "The man is not satisfied with just kicking us in our ass. Now he is doing a job on our kids. Are we going to stand for it?" Hopefully, they will shout back in the negative, which will actually be positive to my way of thinking.

At this general meeting we will decide to demand or request, depending on the size of the attendance, that the Board of Education meet with the black community to hear our grievances.

The Board will most likely prefer to meet with only those parents whose children were directly involved. They would have us at the disadvantage if we had a one-to-one confrontation. However, we will try to get all the people that we possibly can to come to the meeting with the Board of Education. We just don't tell the Board what our plans are.

I will contact and invite any members of the local press whom the brain trust feels are sympathetic to our cause to attend the meeting of the parents and the Board. There is hardly such a thing as fair press coverage of minority groups. Newsmen are sworn to uphold the position of the power structure. Often they are not even allowed to print things as they see them. The editor reserves the right to censor and withhold the facts. It would be advantageous to get newsmen present who will give us a decent account of what takes place at the meeting, even though I do not expect a news release slanted toward us and against the school board.

I will make sure that the students themselves appear at the meeting with the school board. The Board will probably flip. They are known to be reluctant to address themselves to students, especially in front of the parents. Students also have a way of becoming more bold when they know that they have the support of their parents.

We will present our list of demands, all of which we do not expect to get. On first glance, the board will most likely overwhelmingly reject our demands, as they do not like to be put in a position of yielding to so-called pressure groups. We have left ourselves room for bargaining. If we place great emphasis on what we do not expect to get, the Board will probably concede to us what we really want.

If our demands are not met, we will do either one of two things: boycott the school, if the people are in favor, or stage a sit-in or takeover.

In the event that the students and their parents want to stage a boycott of classes, the school board stands to lose some of their state aid as they will not have the required amount of students present for a given time.

Freedom Schools can be set up in the local black church. I assume that some of the black professional staff will place themselves at our disposal for the purpose of instructing the Freedom School.

While the boycott is in progress, I will continue to bombard the black community with leaflets informing them of our progress.

If the people prefer to stage a takeover, fine. In any event, we still present our list of demands. There is an added possibility that the students involved in the sit-in will have to confront the fuzz. I cannot foresee the school administration being able to handle the situation without the assistance of the police.

There is one sure thing that working-class black people will fight over—*their kids.* Since I have already anticipated a clash between the students, parents, administration, and fuzz, I will of course encourage law suits against anyone who so much as puts his hands on a kid. We will also contact the State Commissioner of Education in Trenton.

At this point of the struggle, it may be to our advantage to make contact with a labor union group and seek out their assistance. They may be helpful in terms of strategies that we may not have thought of, providing our group access to their legal staff, and even funding. Hopefully, some members of our grass-roots group may be involved with such a union or know someone on the inside who will be able to identify with our efforts and make the link between our struggle and theirs.

By this time, I will know every person in the community that I can count on in the future. I will know who has leadership ability and who can get the work done. I will be aware of those that can offer only criticism and excuses. These individuals will go on my "white" list. I will steer away from them in the future. Those individuals, groups, and organizations that can hurt me will also not go undetected. It is folly not to know who the enemy is, or to underestimate his power.

My next course of action will be to implement a listing of the target-area community, block by block, with notes on their involvement in the struggle for liberation, or their lack of it. I will select block leaders, one for each street in the ghetto.

I am sure that the Board will try to bring order back into the school system at any cost. Schools try to avoid unfavorable publicity whenever it is possible for them to do so without losing face. After a few window-breaking episodes, they will probably agree to bargain with us in good faith. They will most likely call upon what they consider to be moderates, and if I have any luck at all, I will be included.

The Board will agree to some of our more acceptable demands in return for our help in restoring calmness to the school. We will inform the Board that the people will not listen to us unless we can promise them amnesty. We will hold out until we get it. I cannot afford to allow the people to lose in their first unified effort to fight back at their enemies. We will get what we sought.

The next plan of action will be a victory celebration. It will be the first of many.

I will work for the creation of a physical structure for the use of the black community. I will call upon all people of good will to contribute toward its funding. I will contact the Town Council for money in the way of a bribe. I will tell them that the youth demand a place where they can meet for studying and social life. Otherwise they will be out on the streets. Everyone knows what happens when the restless youth are out on the streets—trouble. I will get the money.

There is no black community without its share of construction contractors. I will call upon them to contribute their skills for their own young people. This center will grow until it is able to provide a variety of services for the entire community.

I will purchase all that I can from the black community for the needs of the center. The center will contain a black library and a kitchen. The people will be able to hold all their meetings there, free of charge.

The center will include the following:

Day care
Steel-drum band
Chess matches
Debating team
Swim club
Drum-and-bugle corps
Judo instruction
Dance lessons
Sewing lessons
Tutoring
Black theatre
Films
Afro-American history instruction
Antidrug program
Baby-sitting swap
Sports and games
An African language course
Any other activities that the
    ghetto community wants

My total objective is to establish an intellectual nucleus. When the people are in trouble, I want them to turn to their center. By the same token, when the center is in need, it will turn to the people. If the people need a lawyer, I want them to come to their center. If they need an apartment, the center will act as a clearing house.

I hope to receive a permanent source of funding from the local, state, and or national government. I surmise that civic groups and white liberals can also serve as a means of carrying on some of the programs of the center. I hope that in the near future we will be able to use some of the money that the black community pays in taxes to generate more funds. For instance, we may work it so that the black community, in the form of a co-op, will be able to supply some of the needs of the schools and hospitals. The school children have to have

milk. Why then should we not own and manage a dairy? The hospitals need linen service. We can do the laundry. These are some things that the town finds contracts for. They are generating more wealth by using the taxpayers' money, but all the returns go to the white community. We want a piece of the action. We can form a ground crew to take care of city landscaping. We demand that some of the wealth be generated back into the black community also.

ALL POWER TO THE PEOPLE!

We now have a base in the people's center. We will use our influence to bring economic power to the black community.

The same time that we are involved in all the other activities that I have just run down to you, we will work to put certain men and women in organizations that have political power, such as the Board of Education and the mayor's seat. I, personally, will not serve in such a capacity as I will use my skills to keep the black community organized around issues. My presence will also lend an air of stability to the group as members come and go. The center, with the help of the brain trust, will always have someone groomed to take over a position when the time is right. We will see that our friends and white liberal allies are seated on every policy-making board in the town. They will give us a constant feedback as to what is going on and coming down in our town.

We will not rest until every black man and woman in our town is registered to vote, even if we have to set up a registration day at our own center, go and get the people in our own cars, baby-sit with their children until they have registered, and deposit them back at their own doorsteps. We will instruct the people on the correct way to write in a candidate's name on a ballot, and we will get them jobs working at the polls. The two major political parties pay on the average of $30 a day for people to work at the polls on election day. Our people will get some of that action from now on. We will tell the people that it is not wrong to take a five dollar bill, or whatever, in return for a promise of voting a certain ticket, as long as you take the money and vote any way you damn well please. Some people think that they can tell if you actually voted the way you said you would, but we will hip them to the facts of it.

When in the future we tell the people that they will have to address themselves to this question or that, they will know that we can be trusted and that we cannot steer them wrong, because our destiny is all tied up in theirs. I cannot be free until you are, my brother. We will work together to remove that which oppresses us. Together we cannot fail.

Case C: CATS # 5

TIME: NOW
PLACE: Urban America—third-class city—approximately 100,000 population with a commission form of government.
WHO: CATS # 5—*Citizen's Action To Save 5th Street*

BACKGROUND—POLITICAL

This city has had the experience of going through Republican, Democratic, and Socialist governments on the local level, with the distinguished record of never electing the same mayor twice in succession. It has an active Democratic party which is continually scrapping internally during primary elections for city council and school board seats, with maybe five to ten people running for two or three positions. The city itself carries a Democratic majority but has elected, on occasion, Republican mayors, city councilmen, and school board members. The county offices, by and large, are held by Republicans because of the suburban and rural vote which is largely Republican.

The Republican party is held intact, with their internal fights being kept secret, if there are any at all. Usually, there are really no significant primary fights; consequently, resources can be saved for general elections. As is the case in most areas, business and the two newspapers (owned by the same person), support the Republican party. The Democratic party generally has labor support with labor candidates running for public office and sometimes winning. Altogether, the Democratic party can be considered

---

• This essay was written by Ruth Mathews, another Livingston student, who has proposed an approach to the problems somewhat different from the one specified by Esther Hardy Jennings. Mathews's approach is equally imaginative.

more progressive than the Republican party in that it has initiated and supported social reforms, not without reform pressure though.

Social

Approximately one-sixth of the city is either black or Puerto Rican, and the majority of these men and women are not registered. They are confined to primarily the southern part of the city, with neighborhood scatterings just north of the main drag. Politically, they have tried to affect, by voting, certain issues and elections—even running black candidates—without success. The only prestige positions they hold are appointed ones with subdivisions of the local government.

The schools are integrated, in that most of the minority ethnic groups also live south of Main Street. For example, the Polish, the Greeks, and the Italians all have gravitated to an area common to their respective ethnic groups. For the most part, the children attend the same elementary and junior high schools. There is only one public high school. There are, however, a few Catholic schools offering alternatives.

There is one liberal arts college within the city limits, no community college, and one state college approximately 25 miles away. Recently, there has been an organization of militant blacks who, according to the newspapers, have disrupted all traditional learning processes within the public schools. There also has been much talk that this group has been trained by outside influences for this very purpose.

This city has a fine labor tradition. At one time it was a two-industry-controlled city—the railroad and the hosiery industry—but both of these have definitely deteriorated. Neither the railroad nor the textile industry took well to labor organizing campaigns, and violent eruptions took place in which people were killed, state police beaten, and a great amount of property damage incurred. Also, the largest textile industry held out until just a few years ago when the Steelworkers Union organized them. Since then, most of the labor unions have quieted down, with just a few militant steelworkers' locals bucking the majority. For the most part, labor has integrated itself with local government as decision-makers, especially through the Democratic party.

Religion

Both Catholic and Protestant churches are in evidence. Most ethnic groups have their own churches, with two Jewish temples, maybe three black churches, and one Greek church. Church attendance, like everywhere else, is pretty well confined to the older people and the very young.

Industry

Industry now is considerably diversified, with the greater amount being union organized. The home-building industry is not organized, because the unions have confined their organizing to larger contractors who only do big jobs. There are three banks with many branches. The utilities and Western Electric Company hire the most people, all organized, and these employers have been condemned for their discriminatory hiring policies.

Overall character of the city

It is basically conservative in nature, with a few splinter reform organizations here and there. They have put pressure on the bureaucracies for much-needed reforms. Public opinion is pretty much shaped by the newspaper, which is conservative. Very few organizations or candidates for public office have won, once condemned by the newspaper. In all, life is peaceful and that's the way they like it.

Problem

South 5th Street is a wide street that runs about three blocks from Main Street. It happens to be the last remaining section of town that contains old, well-built, large, stone structures. Most of these structures have been made into apartments, landlord-occupied and well maintained overall. They are both black and white owned and occupied. Reasonable rents are charged, for the most part, attracting people who want to live close to center city. For example, many older people reside in this area in order to have easy access to buses, shopping, and the train terminal. The neighborhood contains a few corner grocers, a cleaning establishment, two hairdressers, a hardware store, two churches (Catholic and black Baptist), the Social Security office, and a library. Recently, the city installed new lights on both sides of the street, thereby making it as safe to walk as streets in any other neighborhood.

But all of this is threatened. What has happened is that the newspaper has run, in two of its issues, an urban renewal plan. It is under the auspices of the Redevelopment Authority. Its purpose is to tear down all these buildings on South 5th Street back to their nearest half-street, build a shopping mall (to be an extension of the one planned for the main street), which will, supposedly, attract business back into the city. While I was shopping at one of the grocery stores, two other residents approached me to see if we could take any kind of action to prevent this plan from going into effect. Since I was the defeated Democratic committeewoman of that area, they verbalized an attempt to organize the residents outside any political party and felt that I could guide them in some way. The grocer also was quite upset and said he would do anything he could to help.

My first job now is to do my homework and do it well. Initially, I must contact the planning commission and find out what stage the plan is in. Other information I must also obtain before I can begin to evaluate how much time the organization would have before actual demolition takes place would include:

1. Was the plan approved by City Council?
2. If so, were the plans subsequently sent to H.U.D. [Housing and Urban Development] for their final approval for funding.
3. Will there be public hearings regarding the plan—if so, when and where?
4. How much money are we talking about—federal, state, and local?
5. Does the Redevelopment Authority have in its hands any kind of commitment from the federal government on the preliminary drawing of the plan?
6. Who are the consultant, the developer, and the architect?

Knowing the type of bureaucracy I'm up against, I recognize the real problem will be to pinpoint responsibility. But first, I must find out just how sensitive and conscious the residents of the area are to this problem. I acquire a voters' registration list of the area, a City Directory, and a telephone street list. I will make up a card file comparing all three lists in order to get every resident in the area. On each 3 × 5 card, I will place the following information: male member of the household, job, member of a union, if so what union; spouse (if any), her job, her union; whether they rent or own the house; when they voted last; do they vote in primaries or just general elections; children (dependent or working); telephone number; and any other family members. I will also evaluate these cards as to who has been significantly active in other political or social issues, so that they can be contacted first.

Realizing that this means door-to-door canvassing, I contact the other two residents who had been to see me initially, and we split up the cards and decide to try and meet all the people listed personally. On these visits, we will try to elicit other kinds of information such as their church associations, their general feelings of retaining the area, their primary-group ties in the block or neighborhood, and in total making a judgment, in our own minds, on the degree of commitment we could expect. Also, as we go around, we seek out new names that would not have appeared on any of the lists we had used.

We all agree that on visiting neighborhood residents it is our job to hear them out and at all cost refrain from even trying, at this particular time, to change their minds. Risking potential consciousness by coming on strong is something we can't afford. It is of the utmost importance to know where we stand before we begin. I explain to my assistants that timing their visit is most important.

1. You never interrupt anyone during mealtime—any time between 5 and 6:30 P.M.

2. You never visit after 9:30 P.M.

3. When visiting, try to speak to both man and wife, and if at all possible to other members of the family as well.

4. If they are busy, either try to make your visit brief or pick another time mutually acceptable.

Above all, you listen—they talk.

While this action is going on, I do some further research. I get information regarding elected city council members' official department assignments, including the mayor's. In addition, through offices in City Hall, I find out who is "top apple" in those particular offices.

In many cases, it is not necessarily the official head but the political head who carries the ball. I make it my business to find out what positions in these particular departments are appointed, who appoints them, and when, if at all, these appointments expire. In general, I need to know who has advantage of the most patronage appointments.

The same kind of information must be acquired on the Redevelopment level. The Authority members are appointed by the Mayor with the approval of City Council, and they in turn hire the Executive Director, who, in most cases, is the political choice of the power in charge. Appointments to the authority are usually staggered to deter any one political party packing the Authority, so I need to know whose terms are soon expiring and who is set for the time being. I also find out that staff members of the Authority go through much the same process. In this case, usually the Executive Director, through political pressure, refers a person along with his qualifications to the authority for their approval. It is important then, that I have in my possession information of the authority members, including their political persuasion and what they do for a living. Authority members who are not paid serve as private citizens overseeing the affairs of the Redevelopment business. In essence, they are our representatives—in reality they, in most cases, are the rubber stamps of the Executive Director's policies and decisions. Sometimes, there is friction and it's my job to find out what and where it is.

Knowing of some issues of conflict, I take to the library to read past issues of the newspaper. I must find out if there are any conflicts between Authority members themselves, between Authority members and staff, between Authority members and the Mayor, between the Mayor and the staff, between the Mayor and City Council, between City Council and the staff or the Authority. In general, how much accord exists over urban renewal and how much conflict exists? What is important? Were there any differences? Who came out on top most often, and who, if anybody, is the agitator?

Once armed with this information, plus our visits, we have acquired a wealth of information on the area. We can now begin to make concrete plans.

1. We decide to have primary group meetings in homes before an all-out mass meeting is called. Out of these first meetings, we will come up with a committee who will act as our core or counterelite committee. Our core now establishes a front group which we name CATS #5 (Citizen's Action To Save 5th Street).

2. The core represents the most concerned and socially conscious citizens in the area. They also have connections with both churches in the area, the volunteer fire company that services the area, plus other volunteer associations, some of which include ethnic-based clubs.

3. The core will now begin to visit their respective organizations either as a group or in pairs, seeking help and cooperation in the form of money, people, or services.

4. The core also has contacted two militant members of two strong steelworkers' local unions who live in the area. These two union members will now begin to make the necessary arrangements within their unions.

The next step cannot be taken until these contacts are made and results are correlated. While these meetings are progressing, I go to the Historical Society and talk with the Director, who is only too willing and able to go into much detail about the history of South 5th Street. He provides me with all the information and pictures I need to assure the citizenry that this area is the "last stronghold of solid tradition" and, once gone, can never be replaced. The Director also assured me, although timidly, but nevertheless assured me, that he will personally, at his next board meeting, speak on the matter, or will allow us to send a representative to speak on it. I make a mental note of when the meeting of his board will take place and have a representative there.

My next excursion takes me to the Director of the Senior Citizens' Association—funded by the United Fund. I relate to her the number of people over 65 who will be affected and uprooted because of this new urban-renewal plan and who, probably, will have to be placed or relocated into public housing where there is already a two-year waiting period for admittance. Since I have in my possession their names, I can speak personally of them and their problems. I explain to her just how many cases there are of people whose life savings are sunk in homes which they are maintaining to the best of their ability, thereby retaining self-dignity. She, too, was sympathetic, and invited a member of our organization to speak at the next board meeting. She also offered her own services, including a meeting room which holds about 250 people.

My next venture was to the liberal arts college in the city. I spoke with the Political Science Department head, who had been active in past reform movements. I asked whether there were any students available who could research urban-renewal programs in other areas similar to ours. Specifically, we needed to know some answers to several nitty-gritty answers—for example, how long did it take before there was a taxpaying structure erected on demolished land? Was the inner city improved or degraded because of the length of time involved? How many court cases were involved over land acquisition? What happened to the uprooted minority groups—were they relocated? If so, where? He was quite cooperative. In fact, he too assured me of his personal support in addition to soliciting support from other faculty members. I impressed upon him the need for this kind of information as soon as possible.

The next stop was at the county court house, where I went over the tax base of the area, making a list of evaluations and taxes paid to both the city and country at the present time. Even with the two churches and the library, which are tax exempt, the area was a repository of a large amount of tax revenue.

After all contacts are made, the core committee, the chairman of the front group and myself have a meeting to evaluate where we stand and plan our strategy. It adds up to the following;

1. This particular urban-renewal plan was conceived by the Redevelopment Executive Director and the city planner. Preliminary forms were filed with H.U.D. with the approval of the Authority. The planning commission had supposedly gone over the Master Plan of the city, found no problems, and approved the plan. It was now up to City Council to give their approval in order for them to continue. The plan would be submitted the H.U.D. in steps.

2. A consultant had been hired for $50,000, but the Authority needed City Council's ap-

proval to begin to pay him from city funds. The federal government would not allow money for consultant fees until the plan was finally approved. Then the city would get credit toward the portion for the consultant fees they had paid.

3. The consultant and the developer had been in a "kickback" scandal in another state involving Authority members. Hiring a consultant was supposed to be on the basis of a competitive bid—it was not done. The consultant had also performed a "windshield" survey, without contacting the planning commission nor looking at the Master Plan himself.

4. Two Democratic councilmen were up for reelection this year and were therefore vulnerable.

5. Our figures from canvassing the neighborhood indicated approximately 90 percent support. More obvious support came from homeowners, but also there was extremely strong feeling from the small businesses.

6. The contact to other associations brought some further support.

a. The steelworkers' union would supply us with printing materials and a mimeograph machine. They also said they could offer us any other materials we might need that could be charged to office expense like stamps, envelopes, or posters.

b. The Teamster's Union had been contacted, and they offered use of their hall plus auto service to transport any of our members.

c. The churches offered their facilities for baby-sitting. People volunteered to baby-sit, or do other volunteer work from the church.

d. The volunteer fire company came up with a donation of $25.00 plus people would volunteer upon contact.

7. The core had set up a telephone chain with three people in each block responsible for contacting 10 families, keeping them informed about meetings and so on.

8. Our students researched two other urban renewal plans in cities similar to ours. There findings included,

a. It took approximately 12 years before the cities began to make any tax money from reconstruction.

b. They took pictures of these areas that had been leveled and, in most cases, they either looked like they had been recently bombed or they had been made into parking lots.

c. They supplied us with relocating figures that simply boggled your mind. Usually minorities were not relocated because of the lack of public housing and, in fact, they could not even trace their whereabouts. The same held true for the elderly and poor.

d. Another interesting point was that the litigations over land acquisition were, for the most part, initiated by private citizens who had not received a fair valuation. Business almost never was involved.

Our strategy

1. Hold a mass meeting, inviting those residents bordering the planned "urban-rip-down" and use this meeting as the "kick-off."

2. Invite the press by personal contact. (There is always one reporter who covers Redevelopment business—we make sure he gets a personal invitation.)

3. The meeting will be short, informative, and emotional. It will be used strictly to show that there is an organization and its ready to move.

a. The chairmen of the front group will run the meeting, with only two others speaking. Each speaker will be known as an area resident.

b. The businesses in the area have donated cold-cuts and beer.

c. A neighborhood resident who is a photography buff will blow up pictures of the area including those of the other urban renewal areas the students took. It will be like a before, now, and future look, using the historical society's pictures, ones we took, and those of the students. They will decorate the meeting hall.

4. At the meeting we will pose such questions as the consultant, his fee, his survey, and his hiring. When will a public hearing be held and was there any zoning variance given in order to accommodate this mall.

We find that access to the Senior's Citizens' hall has been denied us by the Director under orders from the United Fund. This forces us to use the Teamster's hall which is further away, which means shuttling people back and forth. The meeting, however, is held—good attendance, good press coverage, and some community reaction.

After the meeting the core begins to put the pressure on.

1. We put out a mailing to the businessmen north of Main Street going into great detail about how the city intends to entice business back to center city but has never helped them. We show how this mall will provide for 15 to 20 new stores, and that all these will simply lease from the Redevelopment Authority while they (the north-side businessmen) have had to go it alone. Now, not only that, but the competition will be greatly increased, with them getting the shaft.

2. We contact a housing authority employee and make a deal to get hold of the waiting list for public housing. We mail a letter to each person on that list telling them the bare facts: that if this urban plan goes through it will force the Redevelopment Authority to use their relocation right in relocating the South 5th St. people first. We take great pains in explaining how a two-year wait will now probably be a four-year wait for them.

3. We contact our militant black group, and they deliver to blocks in the city leaflets containing pictures of the black, Puerto Rican, and poor white families with captions underneath the pictures, "What Will Happen to These People When the Government Takes Their Homes." This trick will move the white middle class who sit safely in their segregated neighborhood to wonder.

After this, we decide to wait a few days and get some feedback on community reaction. This is rather easy in that the community, being naturally conservative, will react soon and hard. First reaction comes when the press begins to interview Authority members personally for their reaction, and that reaction is garbled. Next, there is a talk show on the radio from 5 to 7 P.M. nightly, and that reaction is hot and heavy. Citizens, businessmen, along with certain groups are getting upset. We plant a few phone calls ourselves just to "fan the fire." Finally, the break comes when a councilman calls the radio station to make a statement. He says he will not vote for this issue when it comes up and that he personally is going to investigate what has been going on. Of course, it is politically to his advantage to make this stand because he is one of the two that is up for reelection. He can lose nothing—only gain.

It is now time to go to an open meeting of the City Council with specifics. The press is always there and we make our stand intelligently and support it with facts. We comply with all the rules, in that you must seek and get approval 24 hours in advance from the Mayor's office to address a council meeting. Copies are made of all our facts, our demands, and our pictures for each councilman and the Mayor. We also see that the newspaper gets a copy of our speech plus the other material, so that we are not misquoted. Our facts are:

1. The amount of tax revenue that will be lost from land acquisition to reconstruction.

2. The shift of possible school attendance to other schools already overloaded.

3. The study of the other urban-renewal areas showing the disastrous affects, including a higher crime rate.

4. A list of all the people who will have to be relocated into public housing, putting a further burden on the housing shortage.

5. We demand a study be made regarding the master plan and the consultant's part in the planning.

6. Last, we ask that the councilmen vote the plan down today.

THEY DO—WE WON.

This organization situation I used was over a very relevant issue to those involved in it. I also recognize that, once this issue is resolved, keeping the organization viable is an altogether different job. However, the potential is there and it should be noted that it could be now shifted into a larger structure to fight city-wide or even county-wide problems. My doubts regarding this shift come because I feel that any organization must not only face issues close to its members and relating directly to them, but the group must have a feeling of winning. When any situation looks hopeless, people drop out.

● ● ●

INTRINSIC WEAKNESSES COMMON TO NEIGHBORHOOD GROUPS

We have so far failed to make reference to the many weaknesses intrinsic to neighborhood groups. These shortcomings are obviously important, since they constitute a major source of grass-roots failure to ameliorate to a significant degree the people's lot. For the record, let us recite some of these problems and then comment on how the vanguard party and the militant industrial union local can help to solve them.

First, let us consider a check list of internal contradictions that can exist within block club and neighborhood associations:

1. To build a solid, stable leadership and mass base requires permanency of membership. Yet neighborhood residents are highly mobile. Indeed, mobility from the organized neighborhood may well be highest among the leadership, for their proven brightness suggests ability to increase their family incomes and hence their eligibility to move into circumstances more pleasant than the neighborhoods that constitute the struggle areas.

2. To build and maintain a solid neighborhood group requires concentration on issues that have the potential for deeply involving people (e.g., schools). Yet if the neighborhood associations dwell on the education problem, for example, they discover a double-binding dilemma. Given present conditions of state and corporate control of education, it is almost impossible to modify school systems significantly. That being the case, local groups generally lose in their struggles. If and when grass-roots collectives are able to mount a sustained and militant offensive, the best they can generally do is to wring minor concessions from those with power. These concessions in turn are portrayed by counterelites as victories—signs of people's power. These alleged victories are, of course, no such things, as the masses soon discover, and this insight reinforces a sense of powerlessness among many of the rank and file, including the militants.

3. To be successful in defeating organizations which are national or international in scope, a comparable peoples' organization is needed. What the people need is a new International. Such is the goal, but the reality is gloomy. The people are fragmented. Seldom do they create effective organizations, even on a city-wide basis.

4. In order to defeat landlords, employers, and educators in local struggles, hundreds if not thousands of militants must be amassed to confront those who command police violence, not to mention the men in uniform themselves. Generally these militants are in short supply. Nor do the available militants possess the sophistication necessary to confront modern military techniques used by counterrevolutionary constabulary.

5. Obviously, to link local organizations to a vanguard party and militant unions requires the presence of such parties and unions. But today, left-wing people seldom create a vanguard party, and when they do, sectarian arrogance, intellectual authoritarianism, and/or unforgiveable self-righteousness combine to make the party repulsive to sensible populists located at the grass roots and inside unions. Many of these unions certainly have the potential for radicalization, as indicated by the large number of militants among the membership. But the militants will not travel in a radical direction until the left finally creates a vanguard party with humility, sympathy, and understanding.

This list is by no means complete, for there are other problems as well. Altogether, their solution rests on the left's ability to create a new vanguard party having the following qualities:

1. The party must recruit only those persons willing to work on a nearly full-time basis to realize the goals of left-egalitarianism.

2. When people join, they must be able to participate in the selection and change of leadership, strategy, and programs. This means that there must be full debate of issues and democratic participation based on one man, one vote.

3. Once the leadership has been selected, the strategies agreed on, and the program hammered together, the rank and file should act in a disciplined way to realize the specific objectives of the group.

4. The leadership must act as a central committee fully empowered to select tactics between meetings of the organization.

5. The leadership should also have the

power to initiate strategic changes if these seem to be warranted and where necessary to initiate expulsion proceedings. However, the leadership must be held accountable for its actions by full membership meetings.

These are some of the essential qualities. There are others as well. But rather than making them explicit, it might be worthwhile to speculate on how a vanguard party could aid grass-roots associations solve some of the problems mentioned earlier:

1. A vanguard party could attempt to recruit neighborhood leaders, forge primary ties among them, and establish communal living arrangements for those who want them within the neighborhoods. The party's leaders could also teach the rank and file to reject the values that equate personal pecuniary success with movement into middle-class neighborhoods and hence out of neighborhoods where their leadership is so important.

2. The vanguard party must explain to people that although they need to focus on the basic issues, they should have few illusions about their ability to make substantial changes within the system, precisely because of the way in which the system's upper classes make choices on the allocation of scarce resources—in favor of overseas imperial wars and against major appropriations for non-upper-class needs.

3. The vanguard party must begin to combat the ideology of "doing your own thing," as well as the alienated mood of predetermined failure, by establishing national and state-wide organizations. If they come together, the next step would be the creation of a nationwide confederation of local grass-roots groups, militant political parties, and spirited union locals.

4. Vanguard parties can begin to build militant groups comparable to the flying squadrons of the 1930s and 1940s. Their militance, however, must be accompanied by sophistication in dealing effectively with the new weaponry of domestic counterinsurgency. Here the vanguard organization could provide appropriate schools and training. All this could and should be done while making clear the vanguard party's opposition to violence unless initiated by representatives of the state. In that instance, it should be made clear that people have the right, stemming from the American Revolution, to act in the name of justice to defend themselves against their violent oppressors, for the right to collective self-defense is as American as apple pie.

5. The vanguard party must continuously fight the spirit of elitism. For example, criticism and self-criticism sessions, absolute freedom of expression at all levels within the party, as well as in peripheral organizations are absolutely necessary if we are to avoid the counterproductive egoism of yesterday's left-wingers.

To serve the people requires that we be humble yet resolute, flexible yet disciplined, dedicated yet self-critical, radical yet pluralistic.

CONCLUSIONS

Needless to say, the foregoing recipes for incremental change apply only to situations having a high degree of evolutionary potential. Many central cities during the 1960s come to mind. Suggested strategies and possibilities do not apply to neighborhoods and residential districts that have been flattened by recent failures. Today we can observe these defeated zones throughout the United States. Even though no revolution occurred, they might be characterized as products of Thermidor. The moods of fatigue and despair are often present, and it will take some time to recover enough to take advantage of the privilege of newness. But the beaten have a way of coming back—in Chicago, Detroit, New York, San Francisco, St. Louis, and Philadelphia. The people will triumph if they will pull together. And admittedly more is involved than ahistorical recipes of the kind advanced in this chapter. Still, our making explicit particular assumptions may help the movement to gather its thoughts on matters of strategy.

We have advanced a skeletal statement on organizing from the bottom up. Admittedly we have emphasized form. But we have done so in order to present in a few pages the decisive consideration: the need for workers who fully realize the many difficulties involved to interlock grass-roots activities, vanguard party action, and militant union activity.

Admittedly the grass-roots approach has several weaknesses—most notably the absence of any provisions for intercommunity and interregional coordination. On the other hand, a genuine vanguard party, if present, could perform this service and partially remedy the problem. But even if this contingency worked, the grass-roots efforts might suffer from the high turnover in neighborhood membership, including its foremost activists. This turnover seems to be higher in a local neighborhood than in a factory. Factory workers, too, have another asset over members of a neighborhood organization—when workers go on strike,

*there are immediate, immense, and palpable conse-
quences for management and stockholders. Neighborhood groups lack this degree of power, although boycotts and rent strikes can have considerable effect.*

*During the 1970s we will have occasions to deal
with these problems as we perfect persuading techniques, invent others, and alter our portion of the
globe.*

Chapter 15 Propositional Conclusions and Women's Liberation

Section One   *The Politics of Uneven Development*

THE POLITICS OF UNEVEN DEVELOPMENT

How can we summarize our main points and extend them to cover strategic materials so far neglected in our presentation? Perhaps the best approach is to state in propositional form observations deemed to be of signal importance. Subsequently we will link the final proposition to a discussion of women's liberation.

Let us advance the following fifteen propositions and subsidiary elucidating materials:

1. *If we assume that it is useful to analyze society in terms of substructure and superstructure; if we take a general evolutionary view that distinguishes between primitive, agrarian, and industrial societies; and if we dwell on the ways in which the various parts of society generate external as well as internal antagonisms, then we have included within our skeletal schema the necessary parts for focusing on subordinate classes, status groups, and generations locked into recurrent challenges with superordinate classes, status groups, and generations, and state organizations.* What we reject, then, are positions holding that one can analyze politics solely in terms of elites and mass,[1] or in terms of the impact of a monocausal force such as man's tools and their techniques of use (technology).[2] Mass society theorists overlook the frequency with which political elites must deal with organized, subordinate collectivities which are often in opposition to these political elites. In many situations people at the grass roots are organized, especially during crises, in ways not at all acceptable to political elites. Hence we have

[1] See, for example, William Kornhauser, *The Politics of Mass Society* (Glencoe: Free Press, 1959).
[2] See John Kenneth Galbraith, *The New Industrial State* (New York: Signet, 1967).

indications that political elites do not or cannot manipulate all collectivities at will. Certainly the people at the base of society are not a mass of undifferentiated, unorganized persons ready to be manipulated by elites or by their state. This is not to say that political elites, acting as representatives for themselves or upper classes, are without resources to limit information for the ordinary person and to manipulate opinion, especially in crises. In the long haul, however, clusters of classes, status groups, and generations do get organized and do act in ways often at variance with the interests and attitudes of political elites. And the underdogs are able to do so with some success because the upper classes are themselves divided into left, right, and center on the question of how best to relate to grass-roots protest groups.

Our approach, then, emphasizes the ideological coloration of actors in helping to determine a great deal of activity, including that of man's tools and their techniques of use. Technology is not a first-order cause of human behavior; it never exists apart from economic and political organizations. And the directors of both the economic organizations and the state make decisions on matters of technology: what and how, where to put it, where not to put it, where to destroy it, when and where to forbid its introduction, and why its pace of alteration should be accelerated or toned down. In our country and in our time, directors of large-scale organizations amass and dispose of fixed capital associated with technological innovation. Admittedly, competitive market forces press decision-makers to favor certain technological innovations in keeping with greater economic efficiency. But market forces on competition are not the same as decisions on technology; directors must experience and bring to bear varying degrees of sophistication, and hence consciousness, when rendering decisions on how best to introduce new technological items into the workplace. Given the availability of the same technological inventions, the uses to which they are put will vary. Once items of technology are introduced as machines and other fixed capital goods of course, they have an impact as second-order causal phenomena on what a division of labor can do. But that is another matter, one not in the same category as arguing for the primacy of technology.

2. *When we dwell on challenge-protest among primitive peoples against the intensive incursion of colonialism, we can observe the ways in which the Law of Evolutionary Potential helps to explain the differential responses of bands, tribes, and chiefdoms to colonialism.* The Law of Evolutionary Potential, as you will recall, runs as follows:

> The more specialized and adapted a form in a given evolutionary stage, the smaller is its potential for passing to the next stage. Another way of putting it which is more succinct . . . is: Specific evolutionary progress is inversely related to general evolutionary potential.[3]

The absence of centralized and concentrated authority on the tribal level preempts cooptation of the entire protest leadership, promotes geographical as well as political autonomy, and invites spontaneous as well as variegated protests not readily mapped and hence not readily controlled by colonial authority. That being the case, we were not surprised to discover that cargo cults flourished at the tribal level of organization but languished or failed to emerge on the chiefdom level both in Melanesia and beyond in zones such as Polynesia.

3. *If we dwell on the collective response of agrarian peoples to the imperialism of an incipient industrial capitalism, and if we distinguish between feudal and hydraulic societies, we can observe (a) the absence of a relatively powerful state organization under feudalism, which allows a bourgeois democratic revolution, and (b) the presence of a relatively powerful state organization under hydraulic agrarianism, which in-*

hibits the emergence and retention of right-, left-, and center-democratic governments but which, in the long haul, promotes total cultural revolution. We have neglected the distinction between democratic revolutions, such as those in Great Britain and the United States, and colonial revolutions, such as those in China and Vietnam. Rather, we have stressed the *classical* and *neoclassical,* if only because many democratic revolutions have proven to be less moving than either the prototypical French and Chinese—real forms that have exemplified these two ideal types of revolution discussed. So instead of using the historical categories of democratic and colonial, we have developed ideal models with the intent of suggesting that we analyze their proximates, stage by stage and step by step.

4. *When agrarian–hydraulic society sustains decades of intensive contact with imperial–industrial countries, its very inability to modify its relatively advanced and encrusted state economic forms in order to minimize imperial incursions becomes an important precondition for total cultural revolution.* The unpreparedness for structural and ideological change, the organization of the state around the punishment of the harbingers of change, plus the failure to stop the growth of imperial economic and political advances—these three considerations together make revolution the only long-term alternative realizable *when* the preconditions of revolution are present.

5. *As important as state repression and inflexibility under conditions of disintegration of hydraulic society and introduction of its industrial–capitalist (or socialist) successor, is the presence of class and class–racial consciousness, mental phenomena studied most carefully, ironically enough, where its forms prove somewhat less strident, namely, in industrial communities found in advanced industrial societies where the Law of Evolutionary Potential does indeed apply.* We have been able to observe, perhaps at needlessly great length, the forms, the content, and the incidence of class consciousness within the cyclical business cycle which are common to advanced industrial capitalism. Struck as we are by its ebb and flow, hence, its periodicity, we reject formulations having reference to its linear decline, we observe its more recent class–racial forms, and we note its infinite variations

[3] Marshall D. Sahlins and Elman R. Service, *Evolution and Culture* (Ann Arbor: University of Michigan Press, 1960), p. 97.

among revolutionary peasants and workers in insurgent China and Vietnam. Certainly we have not allowed the massive false consciousness typical of many American workmen during long periods of prosperity to blind us to its incidence both in our own country and in colonial settings.[4]

6. *When we observe the relationships among market societies, the state, and total cultural revolutions, we can once again note a pattern consistent with the Law of Evolutionary Potential: As the state meanders from stability on to becoming a jaded Thermodorean enterprise—indeed, as it traverses the natural stages of revolution itself—persons who originally lacked knowledgeable political commitment can use their blank-slate potential to develop a keen political sensitivity. This mental state is reflected in high levels of class and class—racial consciousness at the very moment when many persons, initially most conscious, become political scoundrels whose political cynicism is antithetical to the facets of consciousness committed to action.* It is a classic case of unevenness of the kind Trotsky observed.[5] And like Trotsky, apparently we must live with unevenness; for ironically, the ones most talented as structure-shattering revolutionaries one moment often become the most practical, efficient state bureaucrats during that period when growing numbers within the new revolutionary society call for the return of order and stability, albeit within a new structure.

7. *Any successful revolutionary movement that allows its more staunch captains and lieutenants to use it inappropriately in the name of egalitarian revolutions adds credence to that part of the fascist formula which views elitism, and hence the rejection of equality, as historically necessary under all conditions.* Yet fascism by no means rejects revolutionary change. We have noted its left-Peronista formula. But the general fascist prescription insists on the messianic role of a nationalist, perhaps a class nationalist, elite which relates in charismatic

style to a class-differentiated mass seeking liberation. The fascist elite generally favors diverse forms of one or more classes over others, and on the basis of a fascist movement's choice, we can categorize it as left, right, or center.

8. *The fascist argument becomes most credible when the specific evolution of right-communist forms are clearly discrepant with the initial ideals of communist egalitarianism.* Right-communism catches our attention if only because its hierarchical form runs directly counter to its egalitarian rhetoric. A small political elite masquerades as a representative vanguard within a formula that parades this political elite as the spokesman for a working class and peasantry who in fact lack a syndicalist representational basis for giving the formula more than the content of a charade. Nor are there any guarantees that left-communist regimes will speak for the oppressed when the people do not have the power to initiate challenges and to veto state policies. Illustratively, the Chinese people were preempted from the March, 1971, Chinese state decision to lend the West Bengal military government millions of dollars at the very moment this military dictatorship had initiated the political oppression of a popular government and the genocidal murder of countless residents of what is now Bangladesh.[6]

9. *The fascist argument seems to be doubly relevant when we observe the ideals and practices of right-democratic politicians, an approach that removes the mass of citizens from the power to initiate significant changes from below.* Certain democratic theorists discount mass popular participation in the initiation of changes within their own government. They prefer an alternative style according to which democracy consists of political elites who initiate political innovations and maintain ongoing structures, excluding a mass whose involvement is but periodic and more or less uninformed. When, furthermore, such theorists view mass participation as essentially fixed, inbred, and unchanging rather than as a deliberate outcome of upper-class creation of false consciousness, the right-democrats' position can be distinguished from the fascist formula only on matters of parliamentary form. The content, with

---

[4] For a review of materials on the periodicity and global quality of class consciousness, see John C. Leggett, *Class, Race, and Labor* (New York: Oxford University Press, 1971), p. 8–17.

[5] Leon Trotsky, *History of the Russian Revolution* (Ann Arbor: University of Michigan Press, 1957), pp. 3–15.

[6] Were Chinese soviets to exist, the Chinese people would be able to participate directly on such a proposal.

respect to the matter of participation, is the same. The mass—the working class and vast bulk of middle-class persons—are condemned out of hand as cloddish recipients of change.

10. *The center-democratic response represents an effort to use grass-roots domestic movements and coopt overseas revolutionary groups—all within flexible limits.* The center-democrats stand privately as elitists but publicly as paternal egalitarians. Privately skeptical about the ability of those other than the few to govern, they openly celebrate the power of the poor to initiate change as if their periodic forays into politics were the common achieved or soon-to-be achieved practices of democracy. Illustrative have been the efforts of many center-democrats to attach themselves to grass-roots movements such as the United Farm Workers Organizing Committee led by Cesar Chavez.

11. *While the right- and center-democratic strategies lead to the elimination of parliamentary governments as a means through which subordinate classes and status groups can solve elementary problems, left-democrats tend to argue in favor of the right of citizens to use political revolution to abolish a moribund state and economy.* Perhaps the most forgotten point in the democratic formula has been stressed by left-democrats. Under certain conditions—namely, when the machinery of the democratic state can no longer serve to solve people's problems—subordinate populations have the right to revolution. Left-democrats such as Supreme Court Justice William O. Douglas have generalized this perspective to include any intolerable regime, regardless of whether it is even nominally democratic.

12. *Left-democratic sympathies extend to world revolutionary movements whose activity invites state repression from imperial countries whose soaring counterrevolutionary expenses abroad prohibit significant structural reforms at home and thereby lead to the creation of cyclical and pocketed insurrections among working-class members of class—racial groups suffering from the double exploitation of racism and wage labor.* We have learned from overseas massacres and domestic failures that it is impossible to prohibit total cultural revolutions abroad and build social democracy at home. Indeed, the failures at home have created cyclical do-

mestic protests in many ways parallel to overseas revolutionary movements. Not too surprisingly, the use of specially trained police to smash foreign revolutionary movements before they can assume the dimensions of a threat has aided the U.S. state on how to limit radical protest at home.

13. *When right- and center-democrats suppress the groups which have and use the greatest potentiality for revolution, both at home and abroad, these democrats are promoting a type of elitism, a type of middle-fascism, which we associate with both the garrison state and the permanent wartime state.* Middle-fascism stands for maximizing the interests of the middle classes, protecting while fostering the well-being of the upper classes, and finally, splitting the working class into various sectors with some receiving more favor than others. Middle-fascism also stands for the *elimination* of parliamentary forms, and in this sense it closely resembles the garrison state.

14. *The permanent wartime state is inadequate, by definition, for meeting the popularly defined needs of groups having the evolutionary potential to create and to use neighborhood and factory organizations to build limited social democracy.* Absence of funds and organizations for minimal domestic changes on housing, employment, welfare, and medicine keep alive militant commitments desirous of realizing change by way of organization from the bottom up. Although limited by forces of control of every conceivable variety, these organizational efforts nonetheless persist because of the many and deep problems which wartime state parliaments cannot handle.

15. *In all the foregoing situations, women have frequently taken revolutionary roles; yet seldom have they shared equally with men the full fruits of revolution.* In every total cultural revolution, women have played important roles at all levels. The Thermidor period, however, has time and again been associated with the rolling back of the clock on women's rights.

WOMEN AND THE TAKING OF STATE POWER

Let us speculate on the reasons for the backward state of women's rights. I hesitate to discuss this matter partly because I am not especially well acquainted with the literature on women's rights. Still, failure to comment would constitute an inexcusable oversight in a book on politics.

Women have been overridden after revolutionary seizure of power in part because they have never occupied enough positions of power within the revolutionary party to allow them to retain victories won during earlier stages of revolution. Women have failed to obtain their equal share of revolutionary state positions precisely because they did not occupy *one half or more* of the top positions within the revolutionary party at the time *it* seized state power and wedded its leadership to top positions within the new revolutionary state. A revolutionary state might be new in dedication, but its actions would be traditional on a number of matters, including the retention of many male personnel and associated sexual biases on recruitment. Had women shared and used revolutionary state power to initiate *immediately* new rules and practices giving women parity on holding of state power positions, these powerful women might have been able to spur the state to maintain female parity indefinitely.

This analysis suggests the necessity for women to garner positions of power within revolutionary movements during the early prodromal period. Once lodged in positions of power within a movement, they can stake out claims and rights for women, educate men to end their chauvinism, and penalize male recalcitrants found within and beyond the movement. Women can make clear to male revolutionaries that unless women obtain sexual equality *now,* they will create such a vacuum within the revolutionary movement that its objectives will not be achieved. In this sense, women's liberation as immediate goal preempts the pie-in-the-sky promises of economic transformation, egalitarian citizenry, and racial equality.

Today the Movement[7] has fumbled and stumbled in part because it is racked from within by conflicts between male and female on whether the sexist canons of capitalism should be allowed to survive and to pervade a movement presumably committed to qualitative change at all levels. These practices are allowed

[7] The general movement for change in the United States, including women's liberation, antiwar, civil rights, black power, student, gay liberation, Chicano liberation, and like groups.

to remain even though the history of revolutions has taught us that unless revolutionary members struggle against male chauvinism during the early stages of revolution—from the prodromal period through the Reign of Terror—the state will subsequently use its resources during the Thermidorean and post-Thermidorean period to return women to their traditional occupational roles. (See the Salaff and Merkle reading.)

To carry on militant action, women must make the kinds of assessments specified in Chapter 14, adding to the importance of race, class, and class—racial consciousness the dimensions of women's identity and militance. Indeed, we might view feminist consciousness as taking forms similar to those discussed in Chapters 5 and 14. From a different perspective, we might suggest that the highest level of class consciousness could consist of a blending of class and sexual consciousness. For until such an amalgamation is reached: *(a)* many persons will remain attached to a cultural traditionalism that is characterized by low levels of class consciousness and high levels of political conservatism, and *(b)* upper-class groups will be able to continue to separate women from men by stressing the need for women to maintain cultural traditions that are at variance with women's liberation and militant class ties but in keeping with political conservatism.

Most American women occupy traditional slots. In the United States, while women are enmeshed in domestic sexual roles, they reinforce the most abyssmal traditionalism of block and neighborhood unless local neighborhood organizations enlist them to carry on economic (and, in the process, sexual) struggles against the landlord as the profiteer, the employer as the exploiter, and the man as the user. If women become involved locally and continuously in grass-roots struggles of the kind suggested in Chapter 14—as indeed many already have, in rent, strikes, tenement takeovers, agricultural workers' strikes, and battles for welfare rights, child care legal aid, and so on—they might then move into leadership slots in reformist movements having a high degree of revolutionary potential

Should they come to occupy a parity portion of power positions at the head of housing, workplace, welfare rights, child care, legal aid, unemployed, environmental, and like groups, women could demand maximal change yet obtain minimal reform, and thereby demonstrate *in the long haul* the inability of the state to carry on both significant social reform at home and sustained counterrevolutionary activity overseas. For feminist activists, the real danger remains the state oppression of those female persons and their organizations through the use of techniques discussed in Chapter 14.

Absorption and cooptation are the principal enemies of all movements, including the women. Those who resist absorption and cooptation will find sufficient grist for their agitational mills:

1. There are 13 million husbandless women working in this country, and many seek and obtain work throughout most of their adult lives, not just prior to a marriage.

2. Six million of these women head households containing a total of 20 million persons, which, as Carol Shaw Bell, a professor of economics at Wellesley College has pointed out, depend *solely* on a women for support of the household, and this dependence is continuous while their incomes are often discontinuous and paltry relative to those of men.

3. Rates of unemployment for all adult women are significantly higher than for adult men.

4. Unemployment for women who *alone* support their families runs almost twice as high as unemployment among married men—and almost half of all unemployed married men enjoy the familial, financial support of working wives.

5. Unemployment for women strikes a female labor force which consists overwhelmingly of full time workers. Meanwhile, official Bureau of Labor statistics on unemployment seriously understate the percent of unemployed women.

6. Half of the unemployment for women (as of January, 1972) stemmed from the employer decisions to lay off women, and not, as the stereotype suggests, from a "voluntary" decision on the part of women to leave their jobs.

7. Nor can we assume that the wages of women are of incidental significance to family welfare, for in 1970, 8 million wives earned between $4000 and $7000, and two-thirds of these women were married to men who earned less than $10,000.[8]

How women fight on these issues is their business. Once the strategy and the tactics are set, however, they can and should demand the aid of class- and class-racially conscious men to carry on this struggle. All parties to these fights may find something of value in the heritage of Alinsky, Luxemburg and others who fought to make this world egalitarian. Equality is the message.

FINAL COMMENTS

Is the women's movement really necessary? Or, is imperialism really necessary? When we juxtapose these questions, we realize how ludicrous they are, for both the women's movement and imperialism spring from sources that dictate their continuation.

It seems fitting to end this volume with an excellent article by two women scholars on the sources of women's repression, and liberation as seen in the historical context of Russia and China.

[8] "Economist Scores Jobless Figures," *The New York Times,* March 11, 1972, p. 32.

Women in Revolution: The Lessons of the Soviet Union and China

Janet Weitzner Salaff
Judith Merkle

(This paper was not written as the work of two area specialists who happen to be women. It is an effort by women who happen to have access to relevant data to answer questions of interest to women. We felt that only the co-operative effort of women could remove the male bias in the materials of the area specialists and give a picture of the problems of women in revolution which would reflect women's own interests in the cultural and historical questions involved. Much of the work on this paper was joint work. Specific credit should go to Janet Weitzner Salaff who prepared the materials on China, to Judith Merkle who prepared the materials on Russia, and to Ann Swidler who, as editor, helped to clarify and unify the paper.)

Rather than simply changing the political system, twentieth-century revolutions have tried to transform the structure of society itself. Unless there are concomitant social and economic changes, the political goals of the revolution are inevitably subverted. The Russian and Chinese revolutions have attempted to mobilize new groups into the political system and to break down old forms of power and authority in society as a whole. In both of these societies, women and efforts to change the position of women have been central to the process of revolutionary transformation.

The destruction of the political power of the old regimes in China and Russia required an attack on the inherited forms of authority in the family, community, educational system, and government. While the destruction of traditional social organizations freed both men and women, women and young people benefited more. Women had been particularly oppressed under the feudal legal and economic restrictions

■ Taken from *Berkeley Journal of Sociology*, Summer, 1970, pp. 166–191. Reprinted by permission of the University of California, Berkeley.

of the old system, and one key to the revolutionary political transformation of Russia and China was the change in authority relationships which kept women in bondage. In their traditional positions, women were repositories of old social values; the institutions which most oppressed women, the clan and the family, were the elementary units of traditional authority in the society as a whole.

The status of women was also changed by their involvement in the process of revolution itself. Mobilizing support for revolutionary change meant involving formerly disadvantaged groups in political action, while social disruption during the revolutionary period enabled people more easily to escape from fixed social roles. In the period of revolutionary transformation, women were called upon to perform new tasks, and women revolutionaries occasionally found that, in their role as revolutionaries, they could participate on an equal footing with men. During the height of revolutionary change Russian women attained a temporary freedom, even notoriety. This also seems true of the position of young Cuban women in the first postrevolutionary decade.[1] A capsule history of the revolutionary role of women in the Soviet Union and China, however, tells us that even during the most democratic period of rapid change women played limited roles in the revolution.

The participation of women in the Russian and Chinese revolutions took several forms. As revolutionary fighters and political actors they participated as individuals, as stars and heroines, leaving the collective power of women unchanged. Alternatively, women were placed in the rear where they were brought into economic production more fully than ever before but were left out of the structure of power which grew up during the revolutionary struggle. Although the economic position of women improved relative to prerevolutionary times, women remained largely in traditional types of work and did not gain control over the means of coercion which were responsible for the revolution.

After the first stage of revolutionary mobilization and the seizure of power, can we expect continued advancement in the position of women? In Russia and China, the first stage of revolutionary victory was followed by a period of concentration chiefly on the economic goal of increasing production. In the conflict between efficiency and liberation, liberation had second priority. Women were brought more fully into economic production and the legal barriers to the advancement of women were removed during this stage. Although individually talented women could rise to new positions, in general the goal of liberating women was redefined in terms of the legal and economic accomplishments of the revolution. Women were given equal salaries for equal jobs, equal rights to property, and equal rights to control the means of production. But the oppression of women was culturally, politically, and economically institutionalized: The traditional image of women, the subordination of women in the family, and the economic and political inequality of women were not eliminated by the revolution.

An examination of the fate of Russian and Chinese women may alert us to the obstacles to liberation even in revolutionary societies; and the experiences of women in the Russian and Chinese revolutions may teach us something about the forms of revolutionary participation most likely to improve the position of women.

RUSSIAN WOMEN: STAGES OF EMANCIPATION

Contemporary materials on the situation of women in the Soviet Union create the illusion that women's liberation in Russia is a direct product of the Socialist Revolution and that it has progressed steadily since October of 1917. Yet the contemporary situation of women in Russia cannot really be examined in isolation. The history of women's changing roles in pre- and post-revolutionary Russia makes it clear that liberation, for women, has progressed in waves of alternating freedom and repression, and that the groundwork for the changes fol-lowing the October Revolution was laid over a century before. More than a hundred years of struggle, publicity, and the development of both women's consciousness and men's acceptance of such development preceded the radical changes of October. While October qualitatively changed the terms of women's struggle, it did not end the waves of repressive reaction to women's attempts to gain freedom, for many of the basic social conditions remained the same.

Possibilities for the liberation of women were limited by the general social and economic constraints that restricted the liberty of all citizens. When a class or category is unfree, the women of that category are also unfree; thus the maintenance of an authoritarian state or the existence of deprived classes sets absolute limits to the progress that women as a whole can make. The century of preparation for women's emancipation was confined to one class, and this fact determined the dynamics of postrevolutionary liberation. The successes of Soviet women's liberation depended to a large extent on this period of preparation, and yet to the extent that these early changes had been limited to a narrow class, the movement failed to achieve real equality for women.

RUSSIAN WOMEN BEFORE THE REVOLUTION

Three hundred years ago, the women of Russia were the most oppressed in Europe. The oppressive social legacy of the Mongols had been added to the common ideology of medieval Europe; no cult of Mariolatry softened the male orientation of the Byzantine Christianity of the "Third Rome"; women were not simply maintained in the legal status of children—they were chattels, pure and simple. The "Domostroi," a sixteenth century book of household rules, supported the absolute power of the extended patriarchal family, a power modeled on the fierce and often brutal control of the Tsar, the "Little Father," over his people. The women of all classes, illiterate and superstitious, went in fear of their husbands' outbursts of temper; and the day that a maiden gave up her relative freedom to go and live with strangers, having been wed at the bidding of others, was traditionally sad and frightening:

> *Don't expect, my dear sister*
> *That your father-in-law will wake you up gently*

That your mother-in-law will give orders nicely.
They will howl at you like wild beasts,
And they will hiss at you like snakes.[2]

The lot of upper class women, was, if anything, worse than that of the peasant women because they were even more isolated. The comparatively greater resources of such families meant that, in "the Tartar fashion," women could be kept absolutely segregated from men in a special portion of the house, and their ignorance of anything in the outer world preserved. The husband's horsewhip, which he used in the "training" of his wife, was customarily hung at the head of the bed.[3]

Even after Western influence began to change the role of women among the nobility, much of the traditional authoritarianism of the Russian family remained. As late as the nineteenth century, lithographs of "barbaric Russia" depicted the public punishment of noble women by flogging. Other observers leave the impression that much of the primordial brutality of Russian marital relations was unchanged.[4] The truth of the matter was that in an unfree society women could not be free either; the state properly considered that the despotism of men over women, as that of the nobility over the serfs, was an important support of the despotism of the state over all male citizens. Russia was constructed like a vast pyramid, based upon the Table of Ranks, in which the continuous labor of the men of the upper classes for an absolute state was made possible economically by the "binding" of those classes lower on the scale to the servants of the state in their turn. How could women hope to escape the fate of the nation in general?

In this picture of the relationship of Russian women to the society, government, and economy, we can discern the basic factors which shaped the consciousness of women in the nineteenth century and which continued to restrict their real emancipation even under the socialist regime that followed. In the first place, Russia, to compete and survive militarily in the constant wars of the West, was under the harshest economic constraints. Long before Stalin, the need to *"dognat' i peregnat' "* (catch up and overtake) was paramount. If the backward economy could not produce sufficient resources, then the only apparent solution was for the government to establish absolute control over the society in order to free the few available resources by force. While the overriding need for economic resources dictated the preservation of the autocratic power relationships within society and of the dictatorial power of the state over society, technology could not develop without Western education; but Western education was inherently disruptive of these power relationships. Theories of political and social freedom penetrated Russia along with theories of mathematics and weapons design, setting up powerfully contradictory forces in Russian society which have not worked themselves out even yet.

Prior to the nineteenth century, only an occasional wealthy woman attained any degree of freedom: The liberation of women *as a category*, rather than as individuals, dates from the development of a Westernized, intellectual class of men who idealized their own search for liberty from a traditional autocratic state. By the reign of Alexander I, this new *intelligentsia*, heavily influenced by European postrevolutionary thought, was deeply involved with the new forms of humanism: constitutional reforms, bettering the lot of the serfs, and the new idea of romantic love. "To love—but whom?" asked Lermontov in anguish. "In love there must be equality in physical and in moral feeling."[5] The idealization of Love in place of Duty created a demand for women with social consciences to be companions of the young idealists. But while men were educated, the women of the same class (not to mention those of other classes) were as ignorant as ever.

> "Sometimes, one wants some sort of shelter . . . the desire takes you . . . to exchange a few words with some one. Well—would you believe it—you can't," remarks a character of Ouspensky. "No development at all—and in their heads, insanity, pure and simple."[6]

Although the only solution to the search for Love was to find an intelligent woman and educate her, the conservative forces of the *status quo* considered the traditional home necessary for preservation of society. And to keep women in the home, they were denied any education except French, a little music, and embroidery.[7] Women who wanted a real education were forced to flee abroad so that they could return to Russia as members of the *intelligentsia*, and thereby try to advance the cause of social justice.[8] As the numbers of emancipated women increased, the image of the emancipated woman, a disheveled figure with masculine habits, who endlessly smoked Russian *papirosy* and frequently cut her hair short, entered Russian literature.

As education seeped down to the middle classes, so did the "Love Problem,"[9] with the result that the increasingly radical *intelligentsia* had a number of emancipated women, considered by the men of this category to be their equals in every way. But conservative society did not approve of "emancipated women," and such women were subject to considerable harassment and repression. One woman was arrested after the Tsar saw her on the street in mannish clothes and was forced to sign a statement that she would let her hair grow.[10] Love without marriage was greeted with moral outrage by conservative society. Some educated women found loopholes that permitted them to enter government employment, but they were fired *en masse* when discovered by the Tsar. Like the men of the radical *intelligentsia*, women could find employment only in the rudimentary private economy as writers and teachers and therefore moved into increasingly radical activity.[11]

After the defeat in the Crimea under Alexander II, an attempt was made to "get Russian society going again" by liberalizing it according to the reforms long espoused by the *intelligentsia*. The serfs were freed, limited local government was established, and an experimental attempt was made to provide professional education for women in the form of a series of medical lectures. The experiment was a brilliant success. Not only did women doctors win medals for their military service, but women entered such fields as mathematics and achieved world-wide reputations.[12] While the women of the peasantry or of the ordinary merchant class were less emancipated than their European counterparts, the intellectual women of Russia were far more advanced than women in the West. They went everywhere without escorts or fear of the consequences, while young ladies in France went to lectures at the University accompanied by their mamas and young Americans found their reputations "ruined" if they visited a man's room unchaperoned. But when a young woman, Sophia Pirovskaya, was found among the assassins of Alexander II, the subsequent reactionary regime drew the appropriate conclusions. They tried to choke off not only political activity and liberal education in general, but also women's education in particular.

WOMEN IN RUSSIA'S REVOLUTION: FEBRUARY AND OCTOBER, 1917

As the ignorant, pious, fashionable woman became the conservative ideal, the emancipation of women emerged more clearly as a plank in the revolutionary platform. Women were prominent in all of the socialist movements in Russia, beginning with agrarian reformers and ending with the Bolsheviks. Women participated in the "going to the people" movement, in agitation, and in every form of political terrorism. They shared exile and prison with their husbands and earned horrifying sentences of their own as political assassins. The result was that by the time of the First World War, there were enough trained and centrally located women in the *intelligentsia that the question of women's rights could be considered one of the paramount issues of the revolution.* The strategic location of fully conscious feminists in the revolutionary circles is one of the central explanations for the Bolsheviks' concern with women's rights, as well as for the major differences between the Bolsheviks and the bourgeois Provisional Government on this subject.

Before the revolution, both the bourgeois democrats and the socialists were interested in The Woman Question (as it was called), but from different points of view. The wealthy, liberal women of the bourgeois faction had developed a sort of reformist consciousness: they wished to uplift the uneducated women of the lower classes. The first political organization for women, the "Union for the Equality of Women's Rights," came into being after the 1905 revolution, attained a certain success in all classes, and presented a 12-point program to the Duma. The second women's organization, "The Feminine Progressive Party," had monarchist tendencies.[13] The women among the Social Democrats, however, had the more lasting effect, for they gave shape to vague Marxist generalizations about changes in family structure and impressed *specific plans of action and their rationale* upon the party leaders. As a result the Bolsheviks developed an ideology which saw the liberation of women as an integral part of the revolution, so important that it was a measure of the success or failure of the revolution itself. Many of Lenin's specific writings about women on the eve of the revolution were inspired by the work and thought of his wife, Krupskaya, her friend, Inez Armand, and Alexandra Kollontai, an ardent women's rightist in the Party.[14] Although he favored the destruction of the bourgeois family, Lenin did not approve of militant feminism when it implied sexual liberation. He found sexual freedom *per se* distasteful, and he thought that the substitution of sex for class struggle could undermine the revolution. Kollontai actually engineered the coalition between orthodox Marxism and feminism, pointing out that the concept of women as property was a specific feature of capitalism, and claiming liberty of education, profession, and sexual relationships for the women of the new era.

The social upheaval caused by the war also created opportunities for women even as it brought about the revolution itself. The terrible losses in manpower put a premium on the labor of women. As in the West, women organized Red Cross services and relief services and replaced laborers missing from the production lines. Unlike their Western counterparts, however, Russian women managed to serve in the military under combat conditions. Dashing "aristos," bourgeois women who romanticized warfare, as well as plain peasant women defending their homes and families, served in combat.

One example of military participation by women during the period of revolutionary upheaval, the Women's Battalion, became the sensation of the Western press. Created by the beleaguered Provisional Government, the Women's Battalion fought in two battles: In the last Russian offensive of the War against Germany six women were killed and thirty wounded, and in the defense of the Winter Palace against the Communists, the Provisional Government troops were defeated and the Women's Battalion surrendered without a loss. [15] Its failure is often seen as an example of the inability of women to unite or to fight together successfully. Louise Bryant, who interviewed the "girl-soldiers" before and after their last

battle, concluded that the battalion failed because of "segregation." Women had been successful in battle when integrated with the regular troops, and Russian women had often fought alongside their men. The battalion had developed major internal crises, and its commander, an "aristo," had cried that she would never have anything to do with *women* again, after being beaten up by the dissident members of her command.[16] The reports of the Red Guards that the surrendered women had huddled in a back room to have hysterics[17] confirmed the picture.

Yet the women's own stories create a somewhat different impression. Apparently, the government had undertaken to form the group, attracting a few "aristo" women soldiers for commanders and then advertising in the villages for heroic women to replace the exhausted men at the front. The poor village girls and city seamstresses that answered the call were bitterly disillusioned to find that there was not enough equipment to outfit them, that they were to be stationed in the capital, and that the principal reason for organizing them was not for real duty, but "to shame the men." Louise Bryant discovered that there were not boots or overcoats for them, and she found some wearing dancing slippers and frivolous "French waists" with their men's trousers. The result was a bitter split between the outfitted aristo commanders who continued to support the Provisional Government when it tried to eliminate the Bolsheviks and the plain lower-middle-class girls, who wanted to go over to the Bolsheviks.[18] Under these conditions, their defense of the Winter Palace could only end in failure. The Women's Battalion was an effort to exploit women for publicity's sake, rather than an organization growing out of the concerns of women themselves. This group of women, organized by men for symbolic value, is testimony to the ease with which men can manipulate women for their own ends. Had the Women's Battalion, or any other group of women organized for combat, been an autonomous effort by women fighting for women's rights, they would doubtless have been forcibly disbanded.

The most dramatic military participation in the events of October was not that of individual women with revolutionary or even emancipated histories, but that of the poor women of Petrograd who stormed out to defend the Red Revolution alongside boys of ten and men armed only with shovels. These women must indeed have been poor, for they were visibly deformed by overwork and malnutrition and were without weapons or even adequate clothes. "Women ran straight into the fire without any weapons at all. It was terrifying to see them. . . . The Cossacks seemed to be superstitious about it. They began to retreat."[19]

The victorious left had pledged to better the lot of just such women as these. They pledged to let them participate in production under equal conditions with men, and with equal pay; to teach them to read and bring them into contact with the culture of the broader world; to free them from the necessity of continual childbearing, household chores, and the medieval aspects of marital subjugation. What, then, was the first response of the men who made the revolution?

In 1918, the Workers' Soviet of Vladimir made a proclamation which, in the words of the scandalized American press, "nationalized women." Declaring that the bourgeoisie's monopoly on the means of production gave them the best looking women of the nation, the Soviet announced that henceforward every woman over the age of 18 would become the property of the state, being required to register at a central bureau of free love. Men and women both had the right to choose a partner at a rate up to one per month. However, "in the interests of the state," men of 19–50 could choose any registered woman without her consent. The offspring of these unions were to be the property of the state.[20] This masculine-oriented version of the "free love" theories of Kollontai was soon squelched on orders from the center, but it indicated the obstacles to genuine emancipation of women prevailing in the population at large.

The same sort of reservations about women's equality could be sensed at the highest levels of the government as well, even during the early days of the revolution. When the Bolsheviks assumed power, a handful of women were installed in leading government posts. While this represented a vast increase in representation over the Tsarist government, some of these posts had already been held by women under the Provisional Government. The difference in the Bolshevik incumbents was one of consciousness—do-good Lady Bountifuls like the Countess Panina were replaced by real Marxist feminists, such as Mme. Kollontai. Yet it surprised Western feminist observers that a party with the avowed goal of equalizing the position of women, and which possessed such great resources of active, ideologically sincere, and talented women, put such a small percentage of women in positions of actual power. Two of the women in the government, Angelica Balabanova and Maria Spirodonova (a revolutionary heroine who had assassinated the governor of Tambov at the age of 19), made excuses in terms of the scarcity of women with the proper training and stable temperament.[21] Yet this was an era when untrained workmen and peasants were taking over many of the important tasks of the nation. The subsequent history of women in Russia was to show that the socialist revolution itself did not eliminate the structure of male supremacy.

AFTER THE REVOLUTION: THE DESTRUCTION OF VICTORIOUS FEMINISM

In understanding the responses of the Bolsheviks to women's emancipation, it is important to remember that the leaders of the Party were irrevocably committed to a program of industrial development which required the imposition of social and economic control from the top. After the revolution, it became clear that the emphasis on economic development ran counter to many of the demands of the very same poor and oppressed groups which had swept the Bolsheviks into power. The crushing of the Kronstadt revolt in 1921 was symbolic of this separation of the new Communist state from its "spontaneous" revolutionary origins and its decision to impose the "people's" program of economic development on the people.

Yet Russian society was not immediately prepared for the strains of rapid industrialization. Revolution, civil war, and the resulting famine caused incredible suffering, population losses, and economic setbacks. A decision was thus made to retreat from "war communism" and enable the society to repair itself under the comparative liberalism of the NEP (New Economic Plan). The Party retained control of the "commanding heights," drew up the first five-year plan, and waited for the revolutionary forces to play themselves out during the 1920s. The "spontaneous" interest groups that had arisen—trade unions, women's groups, and even "rich" peasants (kulaks) and private traders (NEP-men)—could not be allowed to gain sufficient power to interfere with the Party's development policy. When these groups threatened to become too powerful, they were systematically crushed in order to make way for the rapid industrialization campaign. This process did not originate with Stalin, but it bears his name because he brought it to completion in the 1930s, and because many of the most bizarre excesses of the policy can be attributed to the aberrations of his personality.

The conflicting pressures of "spontaneity" (popular social demands), the need to preserve Party power, and the requirements of industrial development were the postrevolutionary version of the age-old social, political, and economic forces which had always determined the fate of Russian women. Looking at these three forces in relation to feminism, one can see how the defeat of women's emancipation was engineered.

To begin with, the "spontaneous" demands of the oppressed classes were everywhere for self-determination and, what is more, for realization of this aim by grass-roots organization of the concerned groups. Trade unions demanded control of industry; workers, peasants, and soldiers demanded control of the government and economy through a system of Councils (Soviets) of those directly concerned with each function. The women of the radical *intelligentsia*, who were also a suppressed group drawn into political action by the revolution, made a series of demands best expressed by Alexandra Kollontai. Mme. Kollontai, a general's daughter, an emancipated woman who raised her child alone, was the first Bolshevik Minister of War Relief as well as the first (and last) Russian woman ambassador. She was the foremost exponent of the development of a new type of male-female relationship to replace the forms of bourgeois possession characterized as "marriage." In her famous "glass of water" statement she claimed that sex is a natural appetite, like thirst, and should be just as easily satisfiable. She advocated easy abortions and

divorce on grounds that women should have control over their own bodies. Most characteristically Marxist was her insistence that women could only attain freedom through equal participation in production. This participation, however, had to be backed by adequate maternity leave, child-care arrangements and mass-household services. Otherwise, she argued, their participation in production would simply perpetuate the age-old double burden of poor women who had given birth among the machines and returned home after work to endless household chores.

For a time, an alliance was formed between the interests of women and the political self-interest of the Bolsheviks. The Marxist "feminists" impressed upon the Bolshevik leaders, especially Lenin, the regressive effects that failure to liberate women would have on the revolution itself, and hence on Bolshevik power. The majority of Russian women were still illiterate and socially oppressed to a degree unheard of in the West. By educating and indoctrinating women, the Bolsheviks could attack the traditional Russian family and the conservative way of life it perpetuated. To emancipate women would require the destruction of the conservative power relations which held them, and through them much of Russian society, in place. The masses of illiterate women preserved the oral culture, rich in myth, superstition, and the legendary legitimations of royalist authority. Orthodox religion, a powerful force for conservatism, was preserved in this "women's subculture" even after it had lost its hold upon Westernized men. The Bolsheviks had to reach into the home to weaken the grip of the "women's subculture" by breaking paternal and marital authority, by educating women, and by bringing them into the male world of production.

The feminists of the Party were allowed to establish the organizational means for attacking the traditional family. A series of laws was passed between 1917 and 1921, culminating in the Statute on the Family, probably drafted by Kollontai.[22] Women were granted equal rights in work; marriages could be made by registering at a civil bureau (Z.A.G.S.); a wife could keep her maiden name; divorce could be obtained by notification; abortions were made legal; and the legal distinction between legitimate and illegitimate children was abolished. L. Lilina, the wife of Zinoniev, advocated the nationalization of children. Campaigns for literacy and special education were carried out by the *Zhenotdely* (Women's Bureau).[23]

Reinforced by the puritanism of the Party leaders and the traditionalism of working-class men, the exigencies of industrialization abruptly stifled the women's drive for self-determination. When such expenses of liberation as the cost of replacement of women's services and the competition of women for favored jobs became visible, the men in control hastened to put women back into their traditional place "for the good of society as a whole." The reaction to the women's reforms came very quickly. In the first place, male factory workers objected to the employment of women in any but their traditional capacities. But in addition to psychological resistance to women's legal equality, there were economic considerations. In the ruined economy, most of the work laws (leave, limitations on hours, childcare) were simply not practical. Resources were lacking to provide enough state-operated services such as nurseries and laundries for the women who needed them. Finally, the dislocations of the war had already caused such serious problems as the wild children who roamed at will living on petty thievery—without the additional disruptions which would be caused by liberating women from the traditional family. When all this was added to Lenin's own moralistic opposition to sexual freedom (he denounced the "glass of water" theory, saying it was driving Communist youth mad), the result was inevitable.

In 1923, a Party resolution was passed against the "feminist" deviationism of the *Zhenotdely:* They were accused of turning people away from the class struggle under the pretext of cultural uplift. The Party was turning against the equality of women in substance, and not merely for ideological or moralistic reasons; this retrogressive policy is indicated by a Party resolution of the following year which censured the *Zhenotdely* for excessive complaint about the material conditions oppressing women. By 1926, Lenin's view that "feminism" was anti-Marxist, converting the class struggle to a sex struggle, finally triumphed. The old family code was rescinded, and a new, conservative code

promulgated in its place. Women were left with the "right" to work, but with social conditions which made it clear that the cheap labor of women in the home and the factory was necessary to free resources for the development of socialist society.

The Stalin years replaced "feminism" with a lasting version of emancipation which was not economically or politically costly. This was the "star system," or the elevation of female models, in place of the equalization of salaries and opportunities for advancement. A few highly publicized individuals are elevated to the highest positions in Russian society, and legal barriers to the advancement of women are removed, while the social conditions of women's oppression are not challenged. A recent example of the "star system" in operation is the Soviet choice of the world's first female astronaut. Indeed, such tokenism masks the failure to achieve real emancipation of women. The "star system" combined with Soviet claims about equality of women, at least begins to change the cultural image of women, which is more than the United States has attempted.

More common in the Soviet Union is the pattern of professional "takeover," resembling that in the United States, although the specific professions differ. When women move into a profession which men abandon, it eventually becomes a "women's job," at which point its prestige, power, and financial rewards decline. In the Soviet Union, more women work and more professions are open to women than in the United States. Taking the often-cited case of medicine, we find that the proportion of Soviet doctors who are women is very high (about seventy-five percent), but the profession of general practitioner in the Soviet Union is neither well paid nor high status.[24] The general practitioners have attained the status of a skilled trade, in contrast to the highly educated medical researchers, of whom a higher proportion are men. Similarly, when we look at the diplomatic corps or the politburo, we find no women. In the military, although there are many stories of female heroines and there was even a women's bomber regiment in World War II,[25] we find a pattern of discriminatory ranks and duties closely resembling the United States military. In short, women are kept well away from the instruments of power.

The industrialization begun under Stalin required a reversal of the liberation which the revolution had begun. The legal structure of the family (e.g., divorce laws) was reimposed, and women were pulled into the labor force without adequate child care or other support. At the same time, the power of individual women and of women's organizations was broken by the anti-feminist campaign and by massive propaganda which urged women to return to traditional patterns of accommodation.

The revolution vastly improved the lot of many Russian women, increasing literacy, education, and legal rights. Most Soviet women work out of choice as well as necessity, and child care is available. But these accomplishments fall far short of the hopes of the women revolutionaries or the early promises of the revolution itself. Despite the favorable ideological stance of the Bolsheviks toward women's emancipation, women did not win the power to enforce their interests when these interests conflicted with economic goals, political expediency, or cultural bias. It is clear that without such power revolution alone will not liberate women.

CHINESE WOMEN AND THE REVOLUTION

The twentieth century in China is marked by a radical change in the political and social position of women. Where some talented women raised under special circumstances occasionally participated in political life, their participation in politics later came to signify the broad organization of hitherto quiescent classes of women. However, the transition was neither easy nor complete. During and after the Chinese revolution, many educated, talented women could take advantage of their new equality before the law and move rapidly, as far as their talents would take them, into newly created and expanded positions in government, politics and industry. But the mass of women still found their roles structured in accordance with traditional categories of sex, age, and class. Despite major changes in the position of women in China, the revolution has not yet eradicated political, cultural and economic barriers to the equality of women.

POLITICAL PARTICIPATION BEFORE THE REVOLUTION

In traditional China women were denied participation in any political institutions of the community. Leadership in the lineage and village institutions was reserved for men, since such positions were arranged with the civil bureaucracy and local leadership had to negotiate with it. Chinese women lacked legal rights in family councils and in the disposal of property. Kept in this position of powerlessness and dependency, Chinese women were bound by the kinship structure. Political action mystified them, and concerted group action to achieve social goals was unthinkable. In fact, their only source of power was the manipulation of kinsmen.

As individuals, however, upper class Chinese women had traditionally been less confined than women in many other premodern societies. Wealthy fathers had their daughters tutored at home, and, where the families were non-Confucian or non-Han, wealthy parents allowed their daughters considerable freedom to develop their talents. Those daughters of "boxers" who belonged to Taoist cults and often served as guards even received training in the martial arts. Aboriginal generals trained their daughters in soldiery along with their sons. Such women entered the quasi-political arena as rebels or social bandits. For instance, during the early stages of the midnineteenth-century T'aip'ing Rebellion, men and women were organized into separate combat units[26] with their own officers. The separation of sexes was for religious reasons, since cultic brothers and sisters were expected to abstain from sexual relations and to maintain singleminded devotion to warfare. Although most of the T'aip'ing women's brigades did work considered appropriate to their sex, such as the weaving brigades, some women did engage in combat. Contrary to Chinese practice and unlike the Han women, they fought because they had undergone martial training at home. The religious crusading spirit may also have encouraged sexual egalitarianism during the early years of the rebellion. After the T'aip'ings took Nanking, women were taken out of combat and placed in secluded quarters of their own to do "more fitting" work than warfare.

EARLY TWENTIETH-CENTURY CHANGES IN CHINA

The twentieth century saw the introduction of modern educational and political institutions as well as contact with the Western ideology of sexual equality. The structure and goals of women's political participation changed accordingly. The first upsurge of the feminist movement occurred as part of the social upheaval of the revolutionary period. An early effect of the political changes in this period was that individual women and groups of women, particularly from the upper class, could participate in new realms of activity, even though the general position of women remained unchanged. The introduction of modern schooling enabled women to become teachers, and militant women teachers were able to mobilize their new constituency of women students for political action. The schools radicalized students by age-grading pupils and isolating them from their communities, and women were turned toward feminist goals by learning ideas about freedom to love, reading translations of Western romantic literature, and discussing Western suffragettes.

The first woman martyr of the Revolutionary Period, Ch'iu Chin, provides an example of the political goals and the style of female participation on the eve of the 1911 Revolution.[27] Typical of many upper-class women of the time, Ch'iu Chin was the daughter of a wealthy literati who had her tutored in classical education. Unhappy in an arranged marriage to a man of lesser talent, she fled from her husband and two children to assume a position as headmistress in a Chekiang modern women's middle-school and teacher in a boy's school. Ch'iu Chin trained her students in military tactics, until enough parents and girls resisted the training to bring it to an end. Like other militant women, she was influenced by the acts of Russian anarchists and the political spirit of anti-dynastic revolutionary sentiment in Chekiang. Her goal was to organize her pupils to stage an uprising and end the Ch'ing dynasty. She was a feminist and started the first feminist newspaper. She also attempted to introduce the issue of sex role differentiation into her lifestyle. Wearing Western man's clothes, she rode into town astride a horse, provoking a riot

which her students had to quell. Ch'iu Chin's attempt to assassinate the Governor and create armed insurrection in the schools failed, and she died a martyr's death defending the movement. As the first woman to die for the revolution she had wanted to prove herself equal in martyrdom itself.

Although many were uprooted by the political chaos of the early Republican period and some fought bravely for both feminist and revolutionary goals, the mass of women were not brought into the anti-dynastic struggle. Other women followed Ch'iu Chin's example, including her own students who formed a short-lived paramilitary brigade to fight in the 1911 revolution to avenge their teacher's death, as well as the militant woman teacher Sophia Chang, who took her name from Sophia Pirovskaya, one of the assassins of Tsar Alexander II. During the 1911 revolution, many women joined the women's brigades of the decentralized revolutionary armies, although the women's army was disbanded after the inauguration of the Republic by decree of the Provisional Government in Nanking. The Government found the military wing of the women's rights movement too threatening. Thereafter they resisted the formation of military brigades of women and deflected them toward the Red Cross.

Through the May 4th Movement, 1919, the women's movement organized around such bourgeois demands as the right to marry freely, vote, be elected to office, own property, and be educated. This was later known as the "five proposal movement." Some women's rights organizations petitioned the Provisional Parliament in 1912 and asked that the Constitution grant equal rights to both sexes, but they were ignored. In protest, on May 19, a number of young women stormed Parliament, broke its windows and injured its guards. This was an unprecedented event in China, and the women's movement was almost suspended because of it. Another upsurge of the women's movement in the latter stages of the May 4th movement gained momentum from women students actively interested in political affairs. Although some of their demands were granted in the Constitution under Sun Yat-sen's insistence, most were promised but not realized. As a commentator of the period noted: "the women's militia movement was quelled by this legal grant of equality in the constitution as ice melting in the spring sun. . . . Like a waterfall flowing to the plain, the women's movement flowed into eddies and whirlpools and never rose in a wave again."[28]

After 1922, the women's movement split into moderate and revolutionary wings. The one (The Women's Suffrage Association) demanded constitutional equality for women; the other (The Women's Rights League) in addition called for women to join the revolution, to overthrow the feudal warlords, and to struggle for a democratic society.

CHANGES IN WOMEN'S LIBERATION UNDER THE COMMUNISTS

Communist revolutionaries heralded the revolution of women's rights as part of the destruction of the old social order. Revolution meant the restructuring of fixed social relationships—class, political status, and the power of the clan head and the lineage system in the community. For this reason, the revolution promised to give highest priority to women's liberation. Women were to be freed as a means of attacking the extended family and destroying the power of the clan head, the *paterfamilias*.

In fact, while some women were trained as political cadres, and women's labor power was liberated, the Communist Revolution stopped far short of altering the social status of all women. The Chinese Communist leadership regarded women's oppression as a special issue which could, however, be solved in the larger context of the revolution. In his *Report on an Investigation into the Peasant Movement of Hunan*, 1927, Mao Tse-tung wrote that women were specially oppressed. One of the goals of the peasant movement was "overthrowing the clan authority of the elders and ancestral temples, the religious authority of the city gods and local deities, and the masculine authority of the husbands." He continues, clearly implying that the oppression of Chinese women is greater than that of men,

As to women, apart from being dominated by these three systems, they are further dominated by men. These four types of authority—political authority, clan authority, religious authority, and the authority of the husband—represent the ideology and institution of feudalism and patriarchy; they are the four bonds that have bound the Chinese people, particularly the peasants.

As the Communists consolidated their power, they followed this analysis by promulgating reforms in the marriage law and land reform law. These laws reinforced each other: The marriage law freed women from the authority of the family by granting their economic and civil rights of inheritance and property in case of divorce, while the land reform law attacked the political power of the lineage system (which took male supremacy for granted) and granted important economic rights to women. At least in a legal sense, these laws did help to liberate women from the four bonds of political, clan, religious, and male authority.

The Codes of the Kiangsi Soviet Period, 1931, included the first Marriage Law which, in conjunction with land reform, was designed to free the women for political action. The first goal was to "activate the emotions of the young women and consolidate their revolutionary determination."

The most important object of the women's movement is to mobilize the broad masses of toiling women to join the revolution. Only the land reform, only the Soviet Government, can liquidate the feudal forces and liberate the women.

The second goal was the liberation of women to participate in production. These two goals, essentially designed to double at one stroke the political and economic power of the movement, were fundamentally contradictory. The political liberation of women turned out to be economically costly. Women were needed in the fields of the villages in the Border Region to maintain production, freeing the men to fight in the People's Liberation Army (PLA). These women were organized into brigades for productive labor, to outfit the 5 million PLA troops. Women in the north were inexperienced in agricultural labor, and great efforts were made to bring them out of the "small home" to do collective work for the revolution. Edgar Snow translates an illustrative instruction regarding mobilization for production in the border region. Women were brought directly into production, especially where the male population had declined as a result of enlistments in the Red Army. The instruction reads:

> To mobilize women, boys, and men to participate in spring planting and cultivation, each according to his ability, to carry on either a principal or an auxiliary task in the labor process of production. For example, "large feet" [women with unbound feet] and young women should be mobilized to organize production-teaching crops, with tasks varying from land-clearance up to the main tasks of agricultural production itself. Small feet, young boys, and old men must be mobilized to help in weed-pulling, collecting dung, and for other auxiliary tasks.[29]

Bringing women into production was one step in giving them meaningful social tasks and control over their lives. However, as the above instruction indicates, sex-typed division of labor remained, even when women were used in production. Women were relegated to the ranks of old men and children while the men went off to wage war.

The myth of political participation of women as fighters in the Chinese revolution is not entirely groundless. Some heroic women did participate as fighters, but more important was the ideological emphasis which the Chinese Communists placed on the participation of women in the revolution and the extraordinary appeal of this idea. The image of women as revolutionary fighters has a firm place both in Chinese propaganda and in the chronicles of revolutionary history. However, only about fifty (out of over fifty thousand) of those who went on the Long March from the Kiangsi Soviet to the Northern Border Region were women. Often women were trained as guerrilla fighters in those villages where there were skirmishes and where the men were absent. For instance, Li Fa-ku of Kiangsi joined the Party at 14 years of age. She participated in the Long March, in warfare with the Nationalist Army, and rose through the political ranks in Yenan. During 1934-37 she served as a guerrilla. Her story, with that of other fighters, including a few women, was reprinted in *The Red Flag Waves* (Hung-chi'i p'iao-p'iao), a 16-volume collection of memoirs written in Peking in 1957 as a tribute to the revolutionaries.[30] But most women remained in the rear, producing for the revolution, not fighting for it. Try as they might, women in the PLA were not allowed at the front, except in the communications or public health corps or running supplies. K'uo Ch'ün-ch'ing disguised herself as a man and rose rapidly in PLA ranks; she was awarded the highest award the army could give her, that of "distinguished serviceman." When she was wounded and her sex was discovered in the military hospital, she replied to questioning that the reason she had hidden her sex was so that she might remain in the army. However, she was quickly removed to a more appropriate post in the public health section of the army with other women. Even though women were allowed to participate in the PLA, they still performed sex-stereotyped tasks. More importantly, they were not allowed to do the actual fighting, and they never gained control of the means of coercion.

Thus, during the thirty-eight year series of wars and revolutionary struggles that separated the collapse of the Dynasty and the final victory of the Communists, women were freed from a heritage of years of oppression. In the areas where the Communists held power, women were granted political and economic rights. Implementation of land reform (or rent reduction), the marriage law, and the initial organization of women into the Women's Association cleared the way for an attack on the private forms of sexual oppression. But legal changes were not always enforced, and formal changes in the rights of women did not attack the private structures of authority and the informal prejudices which kept women in their places. The further effort to liberate women would have required costly political struggles which would have slowed down economic production. The tension between production and liberation was to block further efforts to emancipate women during the revolutionary period, and the same tensions would recur even in the struggles of the Communist period.

WOMEN'S LIBERATION IN COMMUNIST SOCIETY

After the success of the revolution, the Communist leadership faced the problem of whether women were a specially oppressed group in the new society, or whether their oppression could be ended by improving the economic condition of the entire population. Their treatment of women underwent several changes, depending on the political policies of the moment. In the beginning, the Communists genuinely hoped to change the structure of women's roles, and did so by implementing the Marriage Law and bringing women into the Women's Association, a mass organization empowered to treat the special problems of women. The structure, customs, and rules of the village made the emancipation of women from their traditional family and community roles very difficult. The Marriage Law was implemented in mass movements lasting roughly from 1950 to 1953. The purpose of the law was to establish Communist power by destroying the power of the corporate lineage resting on the patrilineal family structure that denied women legal rights. The Marriage Law granted to women their rights to property, inheritance, marriage without regard for family alliances, divorce, and custody of children.

The means of implementing the Marriage Law changed as the resistance to it increased in the villages. In the first year or so, the law was implemented in a period of revolutionary terror. Women were to be completely liberated from the bonds of the "feudal family"—by divorce if necessary. All marriages arranged by the parents were subject to dissolution, and these, of course, included the majority of village marriages. The Marriage Law was commonly known as the "divorce law." This period of the law created tremendous resistance in the villages. The cadres empowered to implement the law refused to take it seriously, and the opposition to this law by the village men was compounded by the difficulties of organizing women into collectives. Further, the economic implications of this law were potentially very disruptive. After divorce, women were allowed to withdraw from the family all of their own property, which was damaging to the village economy, and, if carried far enough, could have driven the poor peasant supporters of the revolution to destitution. The first stage of revolutionary terror was soon halted, and a more moderate tactic to implement the law followed in late 1952. In place of efforts to destroy the family structure, mediation for family problems was encouraged and violent struggle against family members was discouraged.

We will describe the process of implementation of the Marriage Law in one village in late 1952, as it was reported in the press. Even though implementation was comparatively moderate by this time, the reform clearly brought some benefits to women, particularly by emphasizing the political organization of women to attack family problems. Given the need to preserve the family structure and to maintain the majority of existing relationships, alternative means of reforming the family were considered. The Communists developed a unique approach to political change through the tactic known as "small groups." This tactic was designed to unify the women of individual households and isolated families into a social movement. Like other "directed" movements, the campaign had an ideological component, "that set of ideas which specifies discontents, prescribes solutions, and justifies changes." The ideology helped to channel existing discontent and generated collective energy by unifying individual experiences into a "paradigm of experience." In other words, the movement to implement the Marriage Law used ideology to turn private grievances into public issues; family structure itself became a political issue. Mobilization through the movement was also a means of organizing women and developing leadership for use in local organizations.

One source[31] begins by noting the resistance to the movement encountered among the leadership:

> After the Fukien People's Court began revolutionary reconstruction in October, 1952, an experimental point in Min Ch'ing County was organized to implement the Marriage Law. The work team under the direction of the CCP committee of Min Ch'ing spread knowledge of the Marriage Law and accelerated an early completion of the fall harvest within twenty days.

The cadres expressed concern over possible harm to production. The defensive tone of the article suggests that the leadership realized how the cadres used the excuse of production to oppose a movement they really did not support. The cadres feared the escalation of a special movement which threatened their masculine authority in the family and community.

To meet these objections, the work team first studied with the county level committee. . . . They then convened an enlarged meeting of the cadres of six districts and repeatedly explained both the basic spirit of the Marriage Law and even wrote a report on the connection of the Marriage Law work with the work of gathering the harvest. Such study finally "broke through" the cadres' thinking and overcame their deepest concerns that implementation of the marriage work was contradictory to harvest work.

Once initial reluctance by the leadership was overcome, the campaigns were apparently relatively efficient in organizing women to participate. Mass action was used to accomplish what the cadres alone could not. The new work-form of mutual aid teams and elementary cooperatives had organized the villagers into groups whose composition differed from the kinship associations. Meetings of special interest groups of women, the youth, and the elderly provided support for villagers to initiate discussion of family problems.

> Sixteen work groups were organized, comprised of county, district and village cadres. Expanded cadre meetings discussed the thorough implementation of the Marriage Law in the villages. Finally, the cadres and activists convened an old people's meeting, a women's meeting, youth meeting, and meeting of the peasants' association in the village. The work group participated in harvest work while they propagandized the Marriage Law and activated the masses. The peasants discussed the Marriage Law in their work groups during rest periods at least twice. . . .

The report continues to describe how the dynamics of the movement reformed family relationships.

> Once the masses were mobilized we began to evaluate concrete family conditions, a good way to clarify the implications of the Marriage Law. We spoke of five kinds of families—model households, ordinary households, households with marital discord, acutely inharmonious households, and those in which there was mistreatment of a criminal nature. We evaluated these families according to the spirit of the Marriage Law. In every village we convened a movement to evaluate the masses' own families. After evaluation we held a village meeting and organized "speak bitterness," developed the struggle further, and thoroughly aroused the

masses' activism against the feudal marriage system.

(Because the leadership preferred to mediate all difficulties rather than to send families to the divorce court, only 5 percent of the marriages were declared unreconcilable.)

> We praised the model husbands and wives and model households, and then called meetings to democratize the inharmonious households. Then the work groups held mediation committee meetings, and the Women's Association set up a temporary court to handle each article of the Marriage Law. Many activist elements appeared in the course of the movement, and all were brought into the leadership structure of mediation and the Women's Association.

The mobilization crystallized the already hostile sentiment of women toward the feudal family system, and aroused women's anger through the group discussions and "speak bitterness" meetings. The work groups assisted family members in resolving interpersonal tensions at a more harmonious level. Women were organized, and many emerged to assume leadership in the new associations.

The movement to implement the Marriage Law was a political movement, which fundamentally changed the position of women in the village community and the family. But this movement ended with the onset of the first Five-Year Plan of 1953–57. Political mobilization and struggle in the village and family were economically counterproductive. For the next decade the struggle to improve women's condition was absorbed by the struggle of the Chinese people to improve productive conditions. Many national political goals were subordinated to the overriding national policy of meeting new quotas. It was now claimed that women were "liberated," or as the Chinese said, women had "turned over" (*fanshen*). It was true that women were liberated in two new senses. First, the discriminatory laws favoring men over women in wages and family matters were ended. Second, individually talented women were allowed to rise in the political and economic hierarchies as far as their training and talents would take them. Higher status women in fact complained bitterly that there was job discrimination, but on the basis of political connections, rather than sex. During the "Let

100 Flowers Bloom" period of 1957, individual women registered their complaints of political discrimination in job assignment, and leaders in the Women's Association complained that wives of cadres were given preference in administrative positions.[32] The freeing of women to climb individually did not alter the fact that the status of women was not truly equal to that of men.

From the onset of the first Five-Year Plan to the Cultural Revolution, bringing women into production was the dominant policy of the Communist regime, although implementation varied according to the rate of economic growth and the priorities on various sectors of the economy. Crèches were few, jobs in industry fewer, and it was not always easy to find working capital. In the Great Leap Forward, roughly 1958–59, a social movement of intense normative pressure propelled women into the labor force to work in small-scale handicraft enterprises. But the emphasis on production within the accepted framework of the sexual division of labor served to shield from criticism the special authority structures that exploited women. Following the economic disaster of the Great Leap Forward and the ensuing three years of bad harvests, energy was directed toward restoring past production levels, not establishing new ones. When jobs were few, there was a reassertion of traditional structures, and women were encouraged to go back into the home. Women were discouraged from becoming politically organized during the period of recovery, 1961 to 1964. While some media were concerned with the women problem and stressed several aspects of it during this period, they all neglected the reality of persistent male supremacy in the home and local community. The propaganda of the period, as seen especially in short stories and literature, emphasized respect for the aged, the reassertion of the importance of kinship obligations, and awe toward the authority of the paterfamilias.[33] The unique importance of women in reproduction and household economy was emphasized in *China's Women*, journal of the Women's Association. The drive to raise agricultural production in this period dampened the drive to alter the collective image of women.

Beginning in mid-1966 the Cultural Revolution again renewed concern that the tight fami-

ly authority structure, the hierarchical relations of social deference, and obligations between the generations and sexes hindered political participation. This problem had not been dealt with for over a decade, but the political exigencies of the new struggle over political and economic policies demanded an overall line on increased political participation. The revolutionary upsurge extended to all areas of power and authority relations: It dictated that women unite politically to attack the rigid authority structure of the bureaucracies with which they had contact—the urban residential administration in particular.

Although women had been out of the political arena as a faction for so long that they had neither developed new leadership nor prepared themselves for political discussion in the home, two themes were operative in the struggle to activate women during this phase of the Cultural Revolution. One was that women must be politically mobilized; the other that women must be encouraged to participate in economic production for the public good. The economic policies emerging from the Cultural Revolution required total involvement of women.

The journal of the Women's Association came under attack for its previous policies. In its last issue before it ceased publication (August, 1966), *China's Women* issued a self-criticism of its previous six years of underplaying the political role of women:

> Tung Pien [the editor], the black gang element, under the pretext of helping women cadres and women staff and workers handle the "contradictions between family duty and children and revolutionary work," massively proselytized such bourgeois and revisionist fallacies as "women live for revolution as well as for husband and children"; "to have a warm small family is happiness itself"; to bear and nuture children is women's "natural duty"; there must be "common feelings and interests" in selecting lovers (spouses). These absurd views were intended to create ideological confusion so that women cadres and women staff and workers would be intoxicated with the small heaven of motherhood, bearing children, and managing family affairs, and sink into the quagmire of the bourgeois "theory of human nature," forgetting class struggle and disregarding revolution. This is an echo of the

reactionary themes advocated by modern revisionism, such as "feminine tenderness," "mother love," and "human sentiments."...

The black gang element Tung Pien overtly distorted the policy of the party by turning on the green light for the demons and snakes and by introducing in undisguised form such extremely reactionary and feudalistic conceptions as respecting men but denigrating women and demanding obedience at the three levels (obedience to father, son, and husband) to spread massive doses of poison in her publications. Under the pretext of presenting opposite views in discussions, she published without any criticism, such reactionary articles as "For Women to Engage in Enterprises is Like Flying Kites Under the Bed," "Women Live for the Purpose of Raising Children," "Women Should Do More Family Duties," thus openly attacking and insulting all the women of new China....[34]

The article condemns the fact that women's role in political struggle was overlooked and points out that they are a major labor resource. Political struggle serves a double goal: organized collectives outside the home not only raise the level of women's political activity, they liberate women for production as well. The implication is that political liberation encourages rather than conflicts with economic production.

The Cultural Revolution stresses women's political liberation as part of an overall attempt to shake up the entrenched power structure. Requiring the political participation of all groups, the Cultural Revolution also encourages women to participate in political activity. Women are encouraged to engage in propaganda study, small group political work, and criticism of their families. For example, women can use Mao's work to criticize domineering family members, such as parents, in-laws, or husbands; and they are to persist until they have reformed the exploitation and prejudice which they experience in the home. Articles in the press include the following statements which encourage the women to criticize family members in study sessions.

> Over thousands of years our family relations have been that son obeys what his father says and wife obeys what her husband says. Now we must rebel against this idea.... We should make a complete change in this.... It should no longer be a matter of who is

supposed to speak and who is supposed to obey in a family, but a matter of whose words are in line with Mao Tse-tung's thoughts. . . .

Significantly, articles emphasizing women's participation came to the fore in the Cultural Revolution at a time when a concerted attempt was being made to break down the rigid political structure and the social structures reinforcing it. This timing indicates a recognition of the link between women's liberation and revolutionary change: the fact that women neither generally participated in political action *as women* nor questioned the authority of the household head and male political leadership was seen as jeopardizing the goals of the political struggle.

The course of the Chinese revolution suggests that the cause of women's emancipation is advanced when broad popular revolutionary participation is the policy. During phases when economic goals are stressed, political activities are subordinated to production and, in consequence, women's emancipation is minimized. While the same relationship between economic priorities and women's liberation has held true in the Soviet Union as well, only China during the Cultural Revolution has been prepared to sacrifice any measure of economic efficiency in order to maintain the impetus of revolutionary political participation. The current period of participation, because it includes the encouragement of women to participate by way of female collectives in political organization, also seems to be a period in which problems of male supremacy are attacked. However, whether Chinese women could retain their level of participation if it collided with a new national policy which would restore economic needs to the highest priority is still unclear.

CONCLUSION

The crumbling of the old regime creates a potential for women's liberation which cannot exist in prerevolutionary society. To the degree that women are oppressed by the same structures of authority that also keep men in their place and maintain the traditional government (such as lineage systems or village hierarchies), revolutions that attack these forms of social authority will tend to liberate women. Likewise, when the conditions which oppress women can be attributed to exploitive traditional economic structures, then revolutionary efforts to change the economic system will also liberate women. Thus, in the Russian and Chinese cases, the revolution, as it broke apart the old order, freed women, primarily by removing the legal restrictions which bound them to the family and kept them from participating in production.

But women's oppression is not simply a result of general social and economic oppression; it is, in addition, a *special* form of oppression resulting from the unique conditions which affect women alone of all social groups. The oppression of women inheres in the most intimate, private areas of life, pervades cultural tradition and historical experience, and profoundly benefits, both economically and psychologically, those whom women serve. Thus, it is in the interest of the revolution to liberate women to the extent that this liberation helps to destroy the traditional social structures which support the old regime. But this process will stop short of the additional effort required to liberate women from their special oppression. The costs are too great.

One of the major reasons that the postrevolutionary regimes in Russia and China have not been willing or able to make the effort required to liberate women fully is that both societies have suffered from pressing economic scarcities. In both cases, attempts to change the position of women were eventually blocked when they become too costly in terms of either direct economic costs such as child care and household services or political resistance and disruption resulting from attempts to change the family or to bring women equally into production. It may be that women have a better chance for liberation in revolutions occurring in advanced industrial societies rather than in revolutions which set traditional societies on the path of modernization.

In Russia and China, two special forces worked for women's emancipation: the feminists themselves and the revolutionary ideology which they only in part had influenced. The feminists, a small group of very competent and militant women, fought primarily for the liberation of women within the context of a new and free society. The revolutionary ideology insisted that the liberation of women was a necessary part of the revolutionary transformation creating that new society. The conflict of these forces with the political and economic exigencies of the revolutionary regimes led to a most curious synthesis: The liberation of women remained a central ideological premise in both revolutions even when attacks on basic oppression of women in the family and their inequality in economic and political life were lessened. Simultaneously, a "star system" with the double advantages of co-opting the minority of active talented women and providing propaganda support for the ideology of women's liberation came to absorb the energy of the feminists' drive for the emancipation of all women. Despite the crucial symbolic role played by feminist revolutionaries and the importance of the ideology of women's liberation even now, the outcome has been clearly a system in which individual women are elevated as symbols of the fulfillment of revolutionary promises rather than a substantial commitment to end the oppression of women *as a category*. This postrevolutionary synthesis appears to result from the fact that women were not organized as a class during the revolutionary period. A militant minority, primarily from privileged bourgeois or aristocratic backgrounds, pressed the demands of women in general, but women were not united in their pursuit of equality during the revolutionary period. Because women did not form a definite power bloc, neither the revolutionary feminists nor the ideological commitment to women's emancipation were powerful enough to maintain the impetus for change when the costs became high.

The inevitable conclusion produced by study of these two major social revolutions is that, given the many obstacles to liberation and the conflicting demands of different oppressed groups during the revolutionary period, women must win and hold power itself during this flexible transition phase. *Legal or even substantive changes in women's position cannot replace the necessary ability to enforce their interests even in the face of rival interests and demands.* In particular, women in Russia and China, despite their heavy contribution to the revolution, never gained control of the means of *coercion*—armed force—which would have guaranteed their power. In addition, they did not develop mass political power or political leverage through the control of key positions in the economy, party or state apparatus. Without a power base, the demands of women were met only when their liberation was beneficial to the political and economic interests of the revolutionary regime.

NOTES

1. Chris Carnavano, "On Cuban Women," *Leviathan*, II:1 (May, 1970), pp. 39–42.

2. An old Russian wedding song quoted in Henrietta Yurchenko, "Introduction," in Rubin and Stillman (eds.), *A Russian Song Book* (New York: Random House, 1962), p. x.

3. L. Tikhomirov, *Russia, Political and Social*, Vol. II (London: Swan Sonnenschein and Company, 1892), Chap. II, "The Woman Question."

4. Sergei Akaskov, *The Family Chronicle* (New York: E. P. Dutton & Co., 1961).

5. Tikhomirov, *op. cit.*

6. *Ibid.*

7. A. S. Rappoport, *Home Life in Russia* (London: G. P. Putnam's Sons, 1906), Chap. XVII, "The Education of Women," notes that this pattern of learning was first encouraged by Catherine the Great. Its rationale was: French for the unity of the family; piano for the pleasure of the husband; and knitting and embroidery for surprises (*sic*).

8. *Ibid.*

9. Tikhomirov, *op. cit.*

10. *Ibid.*

11. *Ibid.*

12. *Ibid.*; Hélène Zamoyska, "La Femme Soviétique," in P. Grimal (ed.), *L'Histoire Mondiale de la Femme* (Paris: Nouvelle Librairie de France), Vol. III, p. 387; Rappoport, *op. cit.*, Chap. XVIII, "Literary Women."

13. Zamoyska, *op. cit.*,

14. *Ibid.*, p. 390; Louise Bryant, *Six Months in Red Russia* (New York: George H. Doran, Co., 1918), Chap. X.

15. *Ibid.*, Chap. XXI.

16. *Ibid.*, p. 397.

17. John Reed, *Ten Days That Shook the World* (New York: International Publishers, 1967), p. 105.

18. Bryant, *loc. cit.*

19. *Ibid.*, p. 178.

20. Zamoyska, *op. cit.*, p. 390.

21. Bryant, *op. cit.*, p. 169.

22. Zamoyska, *op. cit.*, p. 395.

23. *Ibid.*, p. 393.

24. William M. Mandel, "Soviet Women and their Self-Image," unpublished paper delivered at the Far Western Slavic Conference, University of Southern California, May, 1970.

25. *Novyi Mir*, Nos. 5 and 8 (1969), cited in *ibid.*, note 48.

26. William James Hail, *Tsêng Kuo-fan and the Taiping Rebellion* (New York: Paragon Book Reprint Corp., 1964), pp. 125–140, 285–286.

27. Mary Backus Rankin, "The Revolutionary Movement in Chekiang: A Study in the Tenacity of Tradition," in Mary Clabaugh Wright (ed.), *China in Revolution* (New Haven: Yale, 1968), pp. 319–365.

28. Ch'en Tung-yüan, *Chung-kuo fu-nü sheng-kuo shih* (History of the Life of Chinese Women) (Shanghai: Chung-kuo wen-hua shih ts'ung shu, 1937), pp. 358–360.

29. Edgar Snow, *Red Star Over China* (New York: Grove Press, 1961), pp. 232–243.

30. Summaries of these memoirs are in Robert Rinden and Roxane Witke, *The Red Flag Waves: A Guide to the Hung-ch'i p'iao-p'iao Collection* (Berkeley: University of California Center for Chinese Studies China Research Monograph, No. 3, 1968).

31. *Fukien Jih Pao*, January 9, 1953.

32. Roderick MacFarquhar, *The Hundred Flowers Campaign and the Chinese Intellectuals* (New York: Praeger, 1960), pp. 229–230.

33. Ai li Chin, "Family Relations in Modern Chinese Fiction," in Maurice Freedman (ed.), *Family and Kinship in Chinese Society* (Stanford: Stanford University Press, 1970), pp. 87–120.

34. *Chung-kuo Fu-nü* (China's Women), 1966, No. 8.

Bibliography

The bibliography indicates works that are pertinent for this book, but the list is by no means exhaustive. At the same time, an effort has been made to avoid listing the references in the bibliography of Gerhard Lenski's classical *Power and Privilege*.

Aberle, David F. *The Peyote Religion Among the Navaho*, Viking Fund, New York: 1966.

Adamic, Louis. *Dynamite, the Story of Class Violence in America*, Chelsea House, New York: 1958.

Alexander, Herbert E. *Financing the 1968 Election*, Heath, Lexington: 1971.

Alinsky, Saul D. *Reveille for Radicals*, Random House, New York: 1969.

Alinsky, Saul. *Rules for Radicals*, Random House, New York: 1971.

Allen, Robert L. *Black Awakening in Capitalist America*, Doubleday, Garden City, N.Y.: 1969.

Anderson, Martin. *The Federal Bulldozer*, M.I.T. Press, Cambridge: 1964.

Arendt, Hannah. *On Revolution*, Viking, New York: 1963.

Baltzell, E. Digby. *An American Business Aristocracy*, Collier, New York: 1962.

Baltzell, E. Digby. *Philadelphia Gentlemen*, Free Press, New York: 1958.

Baltzell, E. Digby. *The Protestant Establishment*, Vintage, New York: 1966.

Banfield, Edward C. *The Moral Basis of a Backward Society*, Free Press, New York: 1958.

Baran, Paul A., and Sweezy, Paul M. *Monopoly Capital*, Monthly Review, New York: 1966.

Beckford, George L. *Persistent Poverty*, Oxford University Press, New York: 1972.

Beer, M. *The General History of Socialism and Social Struggles*, Vols. I and II, Russell & Russell, New York: 1957.

Bell, Daniel. *The End of Ideology*, Free Press, Glencoe: 1968.

Bell, Inge Powell. *CORE and the Strategy of Nonviolence*, Random House, New York: 1968.

Bendix, Reinhard. *State and Society*, Little, Brown, Boston: 1968.

Bendix, Reinhard, and Lipset, Seymour. *Class, Status and Power*, Free Press, Glencoe: 1957.

Bennis, Warren G., Benne, Kenneth D., and Chin, Robert. *The Planning of Change*, Holt, New York: 1961.

Bergeron, Léandre. *The History of Quebec: A Patriot's Handbook*, New Canada Publications, Toronto: 1971.

Bernstein, Barton J. *Towards A New Past: Dissenting Essays In American History*, Random House, New York: 1968.

Béteille, André. *Social Inequality*, Penguin, Baltimore: 1969.

Birnbaum, Norman. *The Crisis of Industrial Society*, Oxford University Press, New York: 1969.

Birnbaum, Norman. *Toward a Critical Sociology*, Oxford University Press, New York: 1971.

Blauner, Robert. *Alienation and Freedom*, University of Chicago Press, Chicago: 1964.

Blumer, Herbert. "Collective Behavior," in Alfred McC. Lee (ed.) *Principles of Sociology*, Barnes & Noble, New York: 1955.

Bottomore, T. B. *Classes in Modern Society*, Pantheon, New York: 1966.

Bottomore, T. B. *Elites and Society*, Basic Books, New York: 1964.

Bottomore, T. B., and Rubel, Maximilien. *Karl Marx*, Watts, London: 1956.

Boyer, Richard O., and Morais, Herbert M. *Labor's Untold Story*, Cameron, New York: 1971.

Brinton, Crane. *A Decade of Revolution*, Harper, New York: 1934.

Brinton, Crane. *The Anatomy of Revolution*, Vintage, New York: 1952.

Broderick, Francis L., and Meier, August. *Negro Protest Thought in the Twentieth Century*, Bobbs-Merrill, Indianapolis: 1965.

Brooks, Thomas R. *Toil and Trouble*, Dell, New York: 1964.

Bukharin, Nikolai. *Historical Materialism*, Russell & Russell, New York: 1965.

Burridge, Kenelm. *Mambu*, Harper, New York: 1960.

Cammett, John M. *Antonio Gramsci and the Origins of Italian Communism*, Stanford University Press, Stanford: 1967.

Caplovitz, David. *The Poor Pay More*, Free Press, New York: 1963.

Carr, E. H. *Socialism in One Country*, Vols. I and II, Pelican Books, Great Britain: 1970.

Carr, E. H. *The Bolshevik Revolution*, Vols. I, II, III. Pelican Books, Great Britain: 1969.

Carr, E. H. *The Interregnum*, Pelican Books, Great Britain: 1969.

Chomsky, Noam. *American Power and the New Mandarins*, Random House, New York: 1969.

Chow, Tse-tung. *The May Fourth Movement*, Stanford University Press, Stanford: 1967.

Clark, Kenneth B. *Dark Ghetto*, Harper, New York: 1967.

Cleaver, Eldridge. *Soul on Ice*, McGraw-Hill, New York: 1968.

Cockcroft, James D, Frank, André Gunder, and Johnson, Dale L. *Dependence and Underdevelopment*, Doubleday, Garden City, N.Y.: 1972.

Cohn, Norman. *The Pursuit of the Millennium*, Harper, New York: 1961.

Cole, G. D. H. *A Short History of the British Working Class Movement*, Allen & Unwin, London: 1930.

Conot, Robert. *Rivers of Blood, Years of Darkness*, Bantam, New York: 1967.

Cook, Terrence E., and Morgan, Patrick M. *Participatory Democracy*, Harper, New York: 1971.

Cornforth, Maurice. *The Open Philosophy and the Open Society*, International Publishers, New York: 1968.

Dahl, Robert A. *Who Governs?* Yale University Press, New Haven: 1963.

Dahrendorf, Ralf. *Class and Class Conflict in Industrial Society*, Stanford University Press, Stanford: 1959.

Demerath, N. J., III. *Social Class in American Protestantism*, Rand McNally, Chicago: 1965.

Diamond, Stanley. *Culture in History*, Columbia University Press, New York: 1960.

Djilas, Milovan. *The New Class*, Praeger, New York: 1961.

Dole, Gertrude E., and Carneiro, Robert L. *Essays in the Science of Culture*, T. Y. Crowell, New York: 1960.

Domhoff, G. William. *The Higher Circles*, Random House, New York: 1970.

Domhoff, G. William. *Who Rules America?* Prentice-Hall, Englewood Cliffs, N.J.: 1967.

Draper, Hal. *Berkeley: The New Student Revolt*, Grove, New York: 1965.

DuBois, W. E. Burghardt. *Black Reconstruction in America*, Russell & Russell, New York: 1962.

Edwards, Lyford P. *The Natural History of Revolution*, Russell & Russell, New York: 1965.

Edwards, Richard C., Reich, Michael, and Weisskopf, Thomas E. *The Capitalist System*, Prentice-Hall, Englewood Cliffs, N.J.: 1972.

Eldersveld, Samuel J. *Political Parties: A Behavioral Analysis*, Rand McNally, Chicago: 1964.

Engels, Friedrich. *Anti-Dühring*, Foreign Languages Publishing House, Moscow: 1962.

Engels, Friedrich. *The Conditions of the Working Class in England*, Macmillan, New York: 1958.

Engels, Friedrich. *The Origin of the Family, Private Property, and the State*, International Publishers, New York: 1942.

Engels, Friedrich. *The Role of Force in History*, International Publishers, New York: 1968.

Fan, K. H. *The Chinese Cultural Revolution: Selected Documents*, Grove, New York: 1968.

Fanon, Frantz. *Black Skins, White Masks*, Grove, New York: 1967.

Fanon, Frantz. *Studies in a Dying Colonialism*, Monthly Review, New York: 1965.

Fanon, Frantz. *The Wretched of the Earth*, Grove, New York: 1968.

Fischer, Ruth. *Stalin and German Communism: A Study in the Origins of the State Party*, Harvard University Press, Cambridge: 1948.

Frank, André Gunder. *Capitalism and Underdevelopment in Latin America*, Monthly Review, New York: 1967.

Fucho, Estelle. *Picket at the Gates*, Free Press, New York: 1966.

Galbraith, John Kenneth. *The New Industrial State*, New American Library, New York: 1968.

Gamson, William A. *Power and Discontent*, Dorsey, Homewood, Ill.: 1968.

Ganshof, F. L. *Feudalism*, Harper, New York, 1961.

Gerth, Hans, and Mills, C. Wright. *Character and Social Structure*, Harcourt, New York: 1953.

Gerth, Hans, and Mills, C. Wright. *From Max Weber: Essays in Sociology*, Oxford University Press, New York: 1953.

Goffman, Erving. *Asylums*, Doubleday, Garden City, N.Y.: 1961.

Gordon, Milton M. *Social Class in American Society*, Duke University Press, Durham, N.C.: 1958.

Gouldner, Alvin W. *The Coming Crisis of Western Sociology*, Basic Books, New York: 1970.

Gouldner, Alvin W. *Studies in Leadership*, Russell & Russell, New York: 1965.

Graham, Hugh David, and Gurr, Ted Robert. *The History of Violence in America*, The New York Times, New York: 1969.

Grant, Joanne. *Black Protest: History, Documents, and Analyses, 1619 to the Present*, Fawcett, Greenwich, Conn.: 1968.

Greenwood, Ernest. *Experimental Sociology: A Study in Method*, King's Crown, New York, 1945.

Guevara, Ernesto. *Episodes of the Revolutionary War*, International Publishers, New York: 1968.

Hagart, Richard. *The Uses of Literacy*, Oxford University Press, New York: 1970.

Harris, Marvin. *The Rise of Anthropological Theory*, T. Y. Crowell, New York: 1968.

Heilbroner, Robert L. *The Worldly Philosophers*, Simon & Schuster, New York: 1953.

Heirich, Max. *The Beginning: Berkeley, 1964*, Columbia University Press, New York: 1970.

Herberle, Rudolf. *Social Movements: An Introduction to Political Sociology*, Appleton, New York: 1951.

Hill, Christopher. *Reformation to Industrial Revolution: The Making of Modern English Society*, Vol. I, 1530–1780, Pantheon, New York: 1967.

Hinton, William. *Fanshen: A Documentary of Revolution in a Chinese Village*, Monthly Review, New York: 1967.

Hobsbawm, E. J. *Industry and Empire*, Pantheon, New York: 1968.

Hobsbawm, E. J. *Primitive Rebels*, Manchester University Press, Manchester: 1959.

Hobsbawm, E. J. *The Age of Revolution*, World Publishing, New York: 1962.

Hook, Sidney. *From Hegel to Marx, Studies in the Intellectual Development of Karl Marx*, Humanities, New York: 1950.

Horowitz, David (Ed.). *Corporations and the Cold War*, Monthly Review, New York: 1969.

Horowitz, David. *Empire and Revolution*, Vintage, New York: 1969.

Horowitz, David (Ed.). *Marx and Modern Economics*, Monthly Review, New York: 1968.

Horowitz, Irving L. *Foundations of Political Sociology*, Harper, New York: 1972.

Horowtiz, Irving L. (Ed.). *The New Sociology: Essays in Social Science and Social Theory in Honor of C. Wright Mills*, Oxford University Press, New York: 1964.

Horowitz, Irving L. (Ed.). *The Rise and Fall of Project Camelot: Studies in the Relationship Between Social Science and Practical Politics*, M.I.T. Press, Cambridge: 1967.

Horowitz, Irving L. *Three Worlds of Development: The Theory and Practice of International Stratification*, Oxford University Press, New York: 1966.

Hunter, Floyd. *Community Power Structure*, University of North Carolina Press, Chapel Hill: 1953.

Hunter, Floyd. *Top Leadership, U.S.A.*, University of North Carolina Press, Chapel Hill: 1959.

Hunter, Guy. *Industrialization and Race Relations*, Oxford University Press, New York: 1965.

Huntington, Samuel P. (Ed.). *Changing Patterns of Military Politics*, Free Press, New York: 1962.

Huntington, Samuel P. *Political Order in Changing Societies*, Yale University Press, New Haven: 1968.

Isaacs, Harold R. *The Tragedy of the Chinese Revolution*, Stanford University Press, Stanford: 1951.

Jacobs, Paul. *Prelude to Riot: A View of Urban America from the Bottom*, Vintage, New York: 1968.

Jacobs, Paul, and Landau, Saul. *The New Radicals: A Report with Documents*, Vintage, New York: 1966.

Jacobson, Julius (Ed.). *The Negro and the American Labor Movement*, Anchor, Garden City, N.Y.: 1968.

Janowitz, Morris. *The Professional Soldier: A Social and Political Portrait*, Free Press, New York: 1960.

Janowitz, Morris, and Marvick, Dwaine. *Competitive Pressure and Democratic Consent: An Interpretation of the 1952 Presidential Election*, Bureau of Government, Institute of Public Administration, University of Michigan, Ann Arbor: 1956.

Jones, Alfred. *Life, Liberty, and Property: A Story of Conflict and a Measurement of Conflicting Rights*, Octagon, New York: 1964.

Joseph, Alvin M., Jr. *Red Power*, McGraw-Hill, New York: 1971.

Josephson. Matthew. *The Politicos, 1865–1896*, Harcourt, New York: 1938.

Josephson, Matthew. *The Robber Barons: The Great American Capitalists, 1861–1901*, Harcourt, New York: 1962.

Kaplan, Morton A. *The Revolution in World Politics*, Wiley, New York: 1962.

Kendall, Walter. *The Revolutionary Movement in Britain 1900–21: The Origins of British Communism*, Weidenfeld and Nicolson, London: 1969.

Kerr, Clark. *The Uses of the University*, Harper, New York: 1963.

Killian, Lewis M., *The Impossible Revolution?*, Random House, New York: 1968.

Kirscht, John P., and Dillehay, Ronald C. *Dimensions of Authoritarianism: A Review of Research and Theory*, University of Kentucky Press, Lexington: 1967.

Kornbluh, Joyce L. (Ed.). *Rebel Voices, An I.W.W.*

Anthology, The University of Michigan Press, Ann Arbor: 1964.

Kornhauser, Arthur, Dubin, Robert, and Ross, Arthur M. *Industrial Conflict*, McGraw-Hill, New York: 1954.

Kornhauser, William, *The Politics of Mass Society*, Free Press, Glencoe, Ill.: 1959.

Krader, Lawrence, *Formation of the State*, Prentice-Hall, Englewood Cliffs, N.J.: 1968.

Lanternari, Vittorio. *The Religions of the Oppressed, A Study of Modern Messianic Cults*, Knopf, New York: 1963.

Lasswell, Harold. "The Garrison State," *American Journal of Sociology*, Vol. XLVI, January, 1941, pp. 431–444.

Lasswell, Harold D. *The Political Writings of Harold D. Lasswell*, Free Press, Glencoe, Ill.: 1951.

Lasswell, Harold, and Blumenstock, Dorothy. *World Revolutionary Propaganda*, University of Chicago Press, Chicago: 1941.

Lasswell, Harold D., and Kaplan, Abraham. *Power and Society: A Framework for Political Inquiry*, Yale University Press, New Haven: 1950.

Lazarsfeld, Paul F., and Rosenberg, Morris (Eds.). *The Language of Social Research: A Reader in the Methodology of Social Research*, Free Press, Glencoe, Ill.: 1955.

Lefebvre, Henri. *The Explosion: Marxism and the French Revolution*, Modern Reader Paperbacks, New York: 1969.

Leggett, John C. *Class, Race, and Labor, Working-Class Consciousness in Detroit*, Oxford University Press, New York: 1968.

Lenin, Vladimir, I. "What Is To Be Done," *Selected Works*, Vol. 2, International Publishers, New York: 1943.

Lenski, Gerhard E. *Power and Privilege: A Theory of Social Stratification*, McGraw-Hill, New York: 1966.

Lin Piao, *Report to the Ninth National Congress of the Communist Party of China*, Foreign Languages Press, Peking: 1969.

Lindenfeld, Frank (Ed.). *Reader in Political Sociology*, Funk & Wagnalls, New York: 1968.

Lipset, Seymour M. *Agrarian Socialism*, Doubleday, Garden City, N.Y.: 1968.

Lipset, Seymour M. *Political Man*, Doubleday, Garden City, N.Y.: 1963.

Lithwick, N. H., and Paquet, Gilles (Eds.). *Urban Studies: A Canadian Perspective*. Methuen, Toronto: 1968.

Lukács, Georg. *History and Class Consciousness, Studies in Marxist Dialectics*, M.I.T. Press, Cambridge: 1971.

Lundberg, Ferdinand, *The Rich and The Super-Rich*, Bantam, New York: 1968.

Lutz, William, and Brent, Harry (Eds.). *On Revolution*, Winthrop, Cambridge: 1971.

Luxemburg, Rosa. *The Accumulation of Capital*, New York: Monthly Review, 1964.

Magdoff, Harry. *The Age of Imperialism, The Economics of U.S. Foreign Policy*, Monthly Review, New York: 1969.

Malcolm X. *The Autobiography of Malcolm X*, Grove, New York: 1966.

Malcolm X. *Malcolm X Speaks*, Grove, New York: 1965.

Mandel, Ernest. *Marxist Economic Theory*, Vols. I and II, Monthly Review Press, New York: 1968.

Mankoff, Milton. *The Poverty of Progress*, Holt, New York: 1972.

Mannheim, Karl. *Essays on the Sociology of Culture*, Routledge & Kegan Paul, London: 1967.

Mannheim, Karl. *Essays on the Sociology of Knowledge*, Routledge & Kegan Paul, London: 1964.

Mannheim, Karl. *Essays on Sociology and Social Psychology*, Routledge & Kegan Paul, London: 1966.

Mannheim, Karl. *Freedom, Power and Democratic Planning*, Routledge & Kegan Paul, London: 1965.

Mannheim, Karl. *Ideology and Utopia*, Harvest, New York: 1936.

Mannheim, Karl, and Stewart, W. A. C. *An Introduction to the Sociology of Education*, Humanities, New York: 1964.

Mao, Tse-tung. *Mao Tse-tung: An Anthology of His Writings*, Anne Fremantle, Ed., New American Library, New York: 1962.

Mao, Tse-tung. *On the Correct Handling of Contradictions Among the People*, Foreign Languages Press, Peking: 1964.

Marcuse, Herbert. *Reason and Revolution: Hegel and the Rise of Social Theory*, Humanities, New York: 1954.

Marine, Gene. *The Black Panthers*, New American Library, New York: 1969.

Martinet, Gilles. *Marxism of Our Time: Or The Contradictions of Socialism*, Monthly Review, New York: 1964.

Marx, Karl. *Capital, A Critique of Political Economy*, Modern Library, New York: 1906.

Marx, Karl. *The 18th Brumaire of Louis Bonaparte*, International Publishers, New York: 1963.

Marx, Karl. *Letters to Americans, 1848–1895*, International Publishers, New York: 1953.

Marx, Karl. *The Civil War in the United States*, Citadel, New York: 1961.

Marx, Karl. *The Communist Manifesto*, Appleton, New York: 1955.

Marx, Karl. *The German Ideology*, International Publishers, New York: 1947.

Marx, Karl. *The Grundrisse*, Harper, New York: 1971.

Marx, Karl, and Engels, Friederich. *On Colonialism*, Progress, Moscow: 1965.

Masannat, George S., and Madron, Thomas William. *The Political Arena: Introductory Readings in Political Science*, Scribner's, New York: 1969.

Meier, August, and Rudwick, Elliot M. *From Plantation to Ghetto: An Interpretative History of American Negroes*, American Century Series, Hill & Wang, New York: 1968.

Meisel, James H. *The Myth of the Ruling Class: Gaetano Mosca and the "Elite,"* University of Michigan Press, Ann Arbor: 1958.

Michels, Robert. *Political Parties: A Sociological Study of the Oligarchical Tendencies of Modern Democracy*, Free Press, Glencoe, Ill.: 1949.

Merton, Robert K. *Social Theory and Social Structure*, Free Press, Glencoe, Ill.: 1957.

Meyer, Alfred G. *Marxism: The Unity of Theory and Practice*, Harvard University Press, Cambridge: 1954.

Miliband, Ralph. *The State in Capitalist Society*, Basic Books, New York: 1970.

Miller, Hermann P. *Rich Man, Poor Man*, T. Y. Crowell, New York: 1971.

Mills, C. Wright. *Images of Man*, Braziller, New York: 1960.

Mills, C. Wright. *Power, Politics and People*, Ballantine, New York: 1963.

Mills, C. Wright. *The Causes of World War Three*, Simon & Schuster, New York: 1958.

Mills, C. Wright. *The Marxists*, Dell, New York: 1962.

Mills, C. Wright. *The New Men of Power: America's Labor Leaders*, Harcourt, New York: 1948.

Mills, C. Wright. *The Power Elite*, Oxford University Press, New York: 1961.

Mills, C. Wright. *The Sociological Imagination*, Grove, New York: 1959.

Mills, C. Wright. *White Collar*, Oxford University Press, New York: 1951.

Moore, Barrington, Jr. *Social Origins of Dictatorship and Democracy*, Beacon, Boston: 1966.

Morel, E. D. *The Black Man's Burden*, Modern Reader Paperbacks, New York: 1969.

Mosca, Gaetano, *The Ruling Class*, McGraw-Hill, New York: 1939.

Mott, Paul E. *The Organization of Society*, Prentice-Hall, Englewood Cliffs, N.J.: 1965.

Myrdal, Gunnar. *Beyond the Welfare State*, Bantam, New York: 1960.

Myrdal, Jan. *Report from a Chinese Village*, New American Library, New York: 1965.

Nettl, J. P. *Rosa Luxemburg*, Vols. I and II, Oxford University Press, London: 1966.

Nomad, Max, *Aspects of Revolt*, Bookman, New York: 1959.

North American Congress on Latin America (NACLA), *The University–Military–Police Complex: A Directory and Related Documents*, NACLA, New York: 1970.

National Action/Research on the Military–Industrial Complex (NARMIC), *They're Bringing It All Back . . . Police on the Homefront*, NARMIC, Philadelphia: 1971.

O'Connor, Harvey. *World Crisis in Oil*, Monthly Review, New York: 1962.

Oglesby, Carl (Ed.). *The New Left Reader*, Grove, New York: 1969.

Oliver, Douglas L. *The Pacific Islands*, Doubleday, Garden City, N.Y.: 1961.

Orwell, George. *Homage to Catalonia*, Harcourt, New York: 1952.

Perrucci, Robert, and Marc Pilisuk, *The Triple Revolution Emerging*, Little, Brown, Boston: 1971.

Popper, Karl R. *The Poverty of Historicism*, Beacon, Boston. 1957.

Porter, John. *The Vertical Mosaic*, University of Toronto Press, Toronto: 1967.

Preis, Art. *Labor's Giant Step*, Pioneer, New York: 1964.

Phillips, Paul. *No Power Greater*, B.C. Federation of Labour, Vancouver: 1967.

Polanyi, Karl. *The Great Transformation*, Beacon, Boston: 1957.

Pope, Liston. *Millhands and Preachers: A Study of Gastonia*, Yale University Press, New Haven: 1942.

Rabow, Jerome (Ed.). *Sociology Students and Society*, Goodyear, Pacific Palisades, Calif.: 1972.

Radosh, Ronald. *American Labor and United States Foreign Policy*, Random House, New York: 1969.

Rainwater, Lee, and Yancey, William L. *The Moynihan Report and the Politics of Controversy*, M.I.T. Press, Cambridge: 1967.

Renshaw, Patrick. *The Wobblies*, Doubleday, Garden City, N.Y.: 1968.

Ridgeway, James. *The Closed Corporation, American Universities in Crisis*, Ballantine, New York: 1968.

Rogin, Michael P. *The Intellectuals and McCarthy: The Radical Specter*, M.I.T. Press, Cambridge: 1967.

Rose, Peter I. (Ed.). *Slavery and Its Aftermath*, Atherton, New York: 1970.

Rose, Arnold M. *The Power Structure: Political Process in American Society*, Oxford University Press, New York: 1970.

Roszak, Theodore (Ed.). *The Dissenting Academy*, Pantheon, New York: 1968.

Roszak, Theodore. *The Making of a Counter Culture*, Doubleday, Garden City, N.Y.: 1969.

Ryan, William. *Blaming the Victim*, Random House, New York: 1971.

Sahlins, Marshall D. *Social Stratification in Polynesia*, University of Washington Press, Seattle: 1958.

Sahlins, Marshall D. *Tribesmen*, Prentice-Hall, Englewood Cliffs, N.J.: 1968.

Sahlins, Marshall D., and Service, Elman R. *Evolution and Culture*, University of Michigan Press, Ann Arbor: 1960.

Schumpeter, Joseph A. *Capitalism, Socialism and Democracy*, Harper, New York: 1947.

Schumpeter, Joseph A. *Social Classes and Imperialism: Two Essays*, Meridian, New York: 1955.

Schurmann, Franz. *Ideology and Organization in Communist China*, University of California Press, Berkeley and Los Angeles: 1968.

Schurmann, Franz, and Schell, Orville. *Imperial China: The Decline of the Last Dynasty and the Origins of Modern China: The 18th and 19th Centuries; Republican China: Nationalism, War, and the Rise of Communism, 1911–1949; Communist China: Revolutionary Reconstruction and International Confrontation: 1949 to the Present*, Random House, New York: 1967.

Selznick, Philip. *The Organizational Weapon: A Study of Bolshevik Strategy and Tactics*, Free Press, Glencoe, Ill.: 1960.

Service, Elman R. *Primitive Social Organization*, University of Michigan Press, Ann Arbor: 1965.

Sheehan, Neil. *The Pentagon Papers*, Bantam, New York: 1971.

Sheppard, Harold L. (Ed.). *Poverty and Wealth in America*, Quadrangle, Chicago: 1970.

Skolnick, Jerome H. *The Politics of Protest*, Ballantine, New York: 1969.

Sturmthal, Adolf. *Workers Councils: A Study of Workplace Organization on Both Sides of the Iron Curtain*, Harvard University Press, Cambridge: 1964.

Szwed, John F., and Whitten, Norman E., Jr. (Eds.). *Afro-American Anthropology*, Free Press, New York: 1970.

Teng, Ssy-yü, and Fairbank, John K. *China's Response To The West*, Harvard University Press, Cambridge: 1954.

Thompson, E. P. *The Making of the English Working Class*, Pantheon, New York: 1963.

Tonnies, Ferdinand. *Community and Society*, Harper, New York: 1957.

Trotsky, Leon. *The History of the Russian Revolution*, University of Michigan Press, Ann Arbor: 1967.

Tucker, Robert C. *The Marx–Engels Reader*, Norton, New York: 1963.

Weinstein, James. *The Decline of Socialism in America: 1912–1925*, Monthly Review, New York: 1967.

Wheelwright, E. L. and McFarlane, Bruce. *The Chinese Road to Socialism*, Monthly Review, New York: 1970.

White, Leslie A. *The Evolution of Culture*, McGraw-Hill, New York: 1959.

Willhelm, Sidney M. *Who Needs the Negro?*, Doubleday, Garden City, N.Y.: 1971.

Wilson, Edmund. *To the Finland Station: A Study in the Writing and Acting of History*, Doubleday, Garden City, New York: 1953.

Wilson, James Q. (Ed.). *Urban Renewal*, M.I.T. Press, Cambridge: 1967.

Wittfogel, Karl A. *Oriental Despotism: A Comparative Study of Total Power*, Yale University Press, New Haven: 1957.

Wolf, Eric R. *Peasant Wars of the Twentieth Century*, Harper, New York: 1968.

Worsley, Peter. *The Trumpet Shall Sound*, MacGibbon & Kee, London: 1968.

Zeitlin, Irving M. *Ideology and the Development of Sociological Theory*, Prentice-Hall, Englewood Cliffs, N.J.: 1968.

Zeitlin, Maurice (Ed.). *American Society, Inc.*, Markham, Chicago: 1970.

Zeitlin, Maurice. *Revolutionary Politics and the Cuban Working Class*, Harper, New York: 1967.

Index of Names

Index of Subjects

73 74 75 76 77 9 8 7 6 5 4 3 2 1